P9-BJQ-384

TODAY'S PROFESSIONAL PARALEGAL

DEVELOPING PARALEGAL SKILLS

Paralegal Today

THE LEGAL TEAM AT WORK

FOURTH EDITION

DELMAR CENGAGE Learning

Options.

Over 300 products in every area of the law: textbooks, online courses, CD-ROMs, reference books, companion websites, and more – helping you succeed in the classroom and on the job.

Support.

We offer unparalleled, practical support: robust instructor and student supplements to ensure the best learning experience, custom publishing to meet your unique needs, and other benefits such as Delmar Cengage Learning's Student Achievement Award. And our sales representatives are always ready to provide you with dependable service.

Feedback.

As always, we want to hear from you! Your feedback is our best resource for improving the quality of our products. Contact your sales representative or write us at the address below if you have any comments about our materials or if you have a product proposal.

Accounting and Financials for the Law Office • Administrative Law • Alternative Dispute Resolution • Bankruptcy Business Organizations/Corporations • Careers and Employment • Civil Litigation and Procedure • CLA Exam Preparation • Computer Applications in the Law Office • Constitutional Law • Contract Law • Court Reporting Criminal Law and Procedure • Document Preparation • Elder Law • Employment Law • Environmental Law • Ethics Evidence Law • Family Law • Health Care Law • Immigration Law • Intellectual Property • Internships Interviewing and Investigation • Introduction to Law • Introduction to Paralegalism • Juvenile Law • Law Office Management • Law Office Procedures • Legal Nurse Consulting • Legal Research, Writing, and Analysis • Legal Terminology • Legal Transcription • Media and Entertainment Law • Medical Malpractice Law Product Liability • Real Estate Law • Reference Materials • Social Security • Sports Law • Torts and Personal Injury Law • Wills, Trusts, and Estate Administration • Workers' Compensation Law

---

DELMAR CENGAGE Learning
5 Maxwell Drive
Clifton Park, New York 12065-2919

For additional information, find us online at:
www.delmar.cengage.com

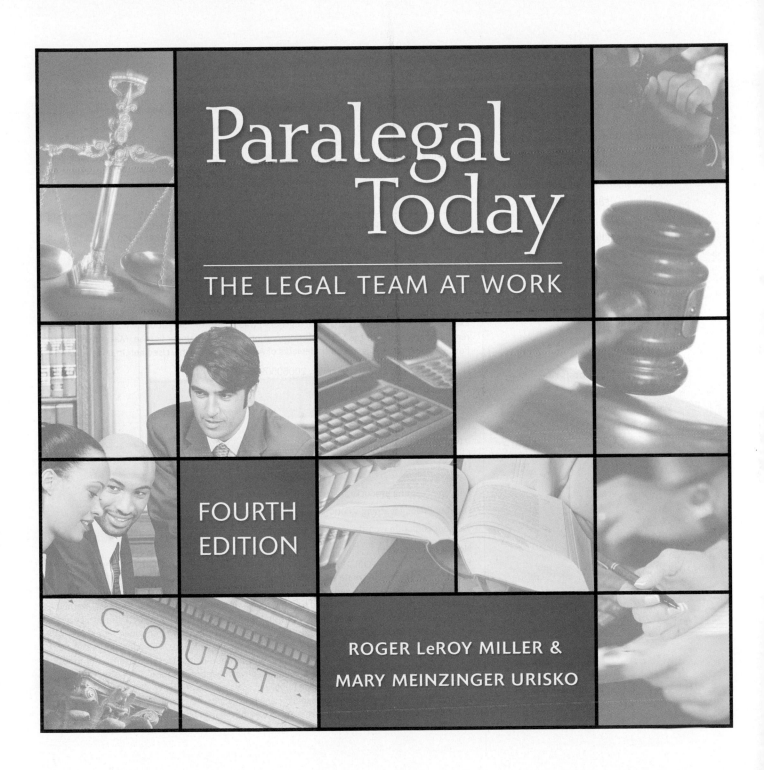

Paralegal Today

THE LEGAL TEAM AT WORK

FOURTH EDITION

ROGER LeROY MILLER &
MARY MEINZINGER URISKO

DELMAR
CENGAGE Learning

Australia • Brazil • Japan • Korea • Mexico • Singapore • Spain • United Kingdom • United States

PARALEGAL TODAY
The Legal Team at Work
Fourth Edition
Roger LeRoy Miller and
Mary Meinzinger Urisko

Vice President: **Dawn Gerrain**

Acquisitions Editor: **Shelley Esposito**

Senior Product Manager:
Melissa Riveglia

Editorial Assistant: **Melissa Zaza**

Director of Production:
Wendy A. Troeger

Senior Content Project Manager:
Betty L. Dickson

Technology Project Manager:
Sandy Charette

Art Director: **Joy Kocsis**

Director of Marketing:
Wendy Mapstone

Marketing Manager: **Gerard McAvey**

Text and Cover Design: **essence of 7**

© 2007, 2004, 2000 Delmar Cengage Learning

ALL RIGHTS RESERVED. No part of this work covered by the copyright herein may be reproduced, transmitted, stored or used in any form or by any means graphic, electronic, or mechanical, including but not limited to photocopying, recording, scanning, digitizing, taping, Web distribution, information networks, or information storage and retrieval systems, except as permitted under Section 107 or 108 of the 1976 United States Copyright Act, without the prior written permission of the publisher.

For product information and technology assistance, contact us at
Professional & Career Group Customer Support, 1-800-648-7450

For permission to use material from this text or product, submit all requests
online at **www.cengage.com/permissions**
Further permissions questions can be emailed to
permissionrequest@cengage.com

ExamView® and ExamView Pro® are registered trademarks of FSCreations, Inc. Windows is a registered trademark of the Microsoft Corporation used herein under license. Macintosh and Power Macintosh are registered trademarks of Apple Computer, Inc. Used herein under license.

Library of Congress Control Number: 2006050905

ISBN-13: 978-1-4180-5011-5

ISBN-10: 1-4180-5011-3

Delmar Cengage Learning
5 Maxwell Drive
Clifton Park, NY 12065-2919
USA

Cengage Learning products are represented in Canada by Nelson Education, Ltd.

For your lifelong learning solutions, visit **delmar.cengage.com**

Visit our corporate website at **www.cengage.com**

Notice to the Reader

Publisher does not warrant or guarantee any of the products described herein or perform any independent analysis in connection with any of the product information contained herein. Publisher does not assume, and expressly disclaims, any obligation to obtain and include information other than that provided to it by the manufacturer. The reader is expressly warned to consider and adopt all safety precautions that might be indicated by the activities described herein and to avoid all potential hazards. By following the instructions contained herein, the reader willingly assumes all risks in connection with such instructions. The publisher makes no representations or warranties of any kind, including but not limited to, the warranties of fitness for particular purpose or merchantability, nor are any such representations implied with respect to the material set forth herein, and the publisher takes no responsibility with respect to such material. The publisher shall not be liable for any special, consequential, or exemplary damages resulting, in whole or part, from the readers' use of, or reliance upon, this material.

Printed in China
3 4 5 10 09 08

DEDICATION

To Sylvain Blanquart,
Your singing, composing, and
playing skills keep getting
better and better. Just don't
forget your old friends when
you become a star.

R. L. M.

To Anne and Mike,
For all you do
this book's for you.
With love and gratitude,

M.M.U.

CONTENTS IN BRIEF

APPENDICES

CONTENTS

PART

2

INTRODUCTION TO LAW 147

PART

 LEGAL PROCEDURES AND PARALEGAL SKILLS 449

APPENDICES

PREFACE

One of the fastest-growing occupations in America today is that of the paralegal, or legal assistant. It seems fitting, then, that you and your students should have a textbook that reflects the excitement surrounding paralegal studies today. *Paralegal Today: The Legal Team at Work*, Fourth Edition, we believe, imparts this excitement to your students. They will find paralegal studies accessible and interesting. This book is up to date, colorful, and visually attractive, which encourages learning. We are certain that you and your students will find this text extremely effective.

Paralegal Today, Fourth Edition, makes the paralegal field come alive for the student. We use real-world examples, present numerous boxed-in features, and support the text with the most extensive supplements package ever offered for an introductory paralegal textbook. *Paralegal Today*, Fourth Edition, draws on the expertise of publishers that have had a long history of encouraging excellence in legal education.

All of the basic areas of paralegal studies are covered in this edition of *Paralegal Today*. These areas include careers, ethics and professional responsibility, pretrial preparation, trial procedures, criminal law, legal interviewing and investigation, legal research and analysis, computer-assisted legal research, and legal writing. For the Fourth Edition, we have added more in-depth coverage of substantive law, including bankruptcy, contracts, intellectual property, torts, product liability, real property, estates, business organizations, negotiable instruments, and family law. In addition, there are a number of key features, which we describe in this preface.

A PRACTICAL, REALISTIC APPROACH

There sometimes exists an enormous gulf between classroom learning and on-the-job realities. We have tried to bridge this gulf in *Paralegal Today*, Fourth Edition, by offering a text full of practical advice and "hands-on" activities.

Exercises at the end of each chapter provide opportunities for your students to apply the concepts and skills discussed in the chapter. Many of the book's other key features, which you will read about shortly, were designed specifically to give students a glimpse of the types of situations and demands that they may encounter on the job as professional paralegals. A special introduction to the student, which appears just before Chapter 1, contains practical advice and tips on how to master the legal concepts and procedures presented in this text—advice and tips that your students can also apply later, on the job.

Paralegal Today, Fourth Edition, also realistically portrays paralegal working environments and on-the-job challenges. Each chapter, for example, describes realistic situations in which a paralegal's ethical obligations are challenged. These situations give students a better understanding of how seemingly abstract ethical rules affect the day-to-day tasks performed by attorneys and paralegals in the legal workplace.

TECHNOLOGY

We have attempted to make sure that *Paralegal Today*, Fourth Edition, is the most modern and up-to-date text available in today's marketplace. To that end, we have included in the Fourth Edition a number of features and materials indicating how the latest developments in technology are affecting the law, the legal workplace, and paralegal tasks. Among other things, these features and materials will help your students learn how to take advantage of technology, including the Internet, to enhance their efficiency and productivity as paralegals.

A Chapter on Computer-Assisted Legal Research

An entire chapter on computer-assisted legal research (Chapter 18) shows students how they can do legal research and investigation using CD-ROMs, the legal databases provided by Westlaw® and Lexis®, and online information available at various Web sites.

A Feature Focusing on Technology

The *Technology and Today's Paralegal* feature, which appears in each chapter, has been retained for the Fourth Edition of *Paralegal Today*. These features, most of which have been either replaced or updated, focus on how technology is affecting a specific aspect of paralegal work or on how paralegals can use technology to their benefit. For example, in Chapter 2 (Career

From Chapter 13 . . .

Technology and Today's Paralegal

WHO BEARS THE COSTS OF ELECTRONIC DISCOVERY?

Traditionally, the party responding to a discovery request has had to pay the expenses involved in obtaining the requested materials. If compliance would be too burdensome or too costly, however, the judge could either limit the scope of the request or shift some or all of the costs to the requesting party. How do these traditional rules governing discovery apply to requests for electronic evidence?

WHY COURTS MIGHT SHIFT THE COSTS OF ELECTRONIC DISCOVERY

Electronic discovery has dramatically increased the costs associated with complying with discovery requests. It is no longer simply a matter of photocopying paper documents. Now the responding party may need to hire computer forensics experts to make "image" copies of desktop, laptop, and server hard drives, as well as removable storage media (including CD-ROMs, DVDs, and flash drives), back-up tapes, voice mail, cell phones, and any other form of digitally stored data.

In cases involving multiple parties or large corporations with many offices and employees, the electronic discovery process can easily run into hundreds of thousands—if not millions—of dollars. In one case, for example, concert promoters alleged that thirty separate defendant companies had engaged in discriminatory practices. The federal district court hearing the case found that the complete restoration of the back-up tapes of just one of those defendants would cost $9.75 million. Acquiring 200,000 e-mail messages from another defendant would cost between $43,000 and $84,000, with an additional $247,000 required to pay an attorney to review the retrieved documents. Restoring the 523 back-up tapes of a third defendant would cost $395,000 plus $120,000 for the attorney to review them. The judge hearing the case decided that the plaintiffs and defendants would share in these discovery costs.[a]

WHAT FACTORS DO COURTS CONSIDER IN DECIDING WHETHER TO SHIFT COSTS?

Increasingly, the courts are shifting part of the costs of obtaining electronic discovery to the party requesting it (which is usually the plaintiff). At what point, however, should this cost-shifting occur? In *Zubulake v. UBS Warburg LLC,*[b] the court identified a three-step analysis for deciding disputes over discovery costs. First, if the data are kept in an accessible format, the usual rules of discovery apply: the responding party should pay the costs of producing the data. A court should consider cost-shifting only when electronic data are in a relatively inaccessible form, such as in back-up tapes or deleted files.

Second, the court should determine what data may be found on the inaccessible media and whether a sampling of the data might be sufficient. Requiring the responding party to restore and produce documents from a small sample of the requested medium is a sensible approach in most cases. Third, the court should consider a series of other factors, including, for example, the availability of the information from other sources, the total cost of producing the information compared with the amount in controversy, and each party's ability to pay these costs.

TECHNOLOGY TIP

Paralegals should keep in mind not only the high costs of some electronic discovery requests but also the possibility that the court may shift some of these costs to the party requesting discovery. Suppose, for example, that you are assisting a corporate defendant in a product liability lawsuit brought by a plaintiff who was seriously harmed by one of the defendant's products. If the plaintiff requests extensive electronic evidence during discovery, the defendant corporation may be required to pay a significant portion of the costs of the discovery.

a. *Rowe Entertainment, Inc. v. William Morris Agency,* 2002 WL 975713 (S.D.N.Y. 2003).
b. 2003 WL 21087884 (S.D.N.Y. 2003).

Opportunities), the feature looks at the career opportunities available for tech-savvy paralegals. Titles of other *Technology and Today's Paralegal* features include the following:

- The Legal Issues Regarding Online Scams and Spam (Chapter 7).
- Online Resources Concerning Insurance Claims (Chapter 9).
- Environmental Compliance (Chapter 12).
- Who Bears the Costs of Electronic Discovery? (Chapter 13).
- Technology and the Sixth Amendment (Chapter 16).
- Be Prepared for the Unexpected (Chapter 18).

Margin Web Sites

Most chapters include several features titled *On the Web* in the margins. These features offer Web sites that students can access for further information on the topic being discussed in the text.

From Chapter 1 . . .

Chapter-Ending Internet Exercises

To help your students navigate the Web and find various types of information online, we have included at the end of each chapter one or more Internet exercises in a section titled *Using Internet Resources*. Each exercise directs the student to a specific Web site and asks a series of questions about the materials available at that site.

From Chapter 8 . . .

 USING INTERNET RESOURCES

1. Go to an article in the FindLaw for Legal Professionals Library, which is located at **http://library.findlaw.com/1999/Jan/1/241463.html**.

   a. Scroll down to the heading "Consideration," and read the summary provided. How many examples are given? Then read the next section titled, "Typical Contract Provisions." How many different types of clauses are discussed? Write down the types of clauses identified.

   b. Go to FindLaw's main site on contracts, at **http://www.findlaw.com/01topics/07contracts**. Then click on "FindLaw Corporate Counsel Center—Sample Business Contracts." There, you can access contracts listed by industry, by type, or by company name, or you can browse through the most recent contracts added to the site. Using any of the methods available, select a contract to view. Note the name of the contract and its general purpose. Does the contract use all of the clauses you noted in part a of this question (typical contract provisions)? Does it use any? If so, which of the typical clauses are used?

2. Go to the Web site of the U.S. Patent and Trademark Office (USPTO) at **http://www.uspto.gov**. This site offers a wealth of information concerning applying for patents and registering trademarks. You can also search existing patents and trademarks, get copies of records, and check the status of applications (among other things).

   a. Click on "FAQ" on the top menu. Browse through the questions and answers for a few minutes, and then answer the following questions:

   (1) What are the two categories of patents that are available? Briefly describe them.

   (2) On average, how long does it take for a patent application to be processed?

   (3) How long does it take to register a trademark?

   (4) Can you download the forms to apply for a patent or register a trademark?

   (5) Can you apply for a patent electronically?

   (6) Can you apply for trademark protection electronically?

   b. Although paralegals may fill out trademark registration documents, only paralegals who are authorized as "agents" by the USPTO can complete patent applications. You can find information about becoming a patent agent at the USPTO's Enrollment and Discipline Web site, located at **http://www.uspto.gov/web/offices/dcom/gcounsel/oed.htm**. Go to that page and review the links under "Exam Resources." What is generally required to become an agent? Must the applicant meet certain minimum educational requirements? Take a test? Pay a fee? Write a one-page summary of your findings. Conclude by stating whether you might be interested in becoming a patent agent in the future.

3. For additional resources, visit our Web site at **http://www.paralegal.delmar.cengage.com**.

PARALEGAL ONLINE RESOURCE CENTER

The Delmar, Cengage Learning Paralegal Web site, at **http://www.paralegal.delmar. cengage.com**, continues to offer numerous resources for paralegal professionals, instructors, and students. At this site, you and your students will find many links to legal and paralegal information sites. The site also hosts a page dedicated to *Paralegal Today*, Fourth Edition, where you and your students can find text updates, hot links, and other resources.

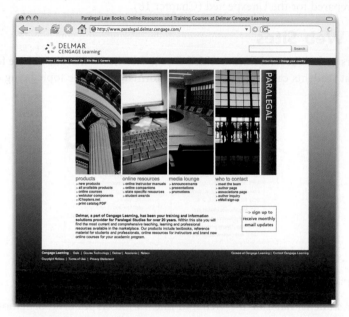

THE ORGANIZATION OF THIS TEXTBOOK

As every paralegal instructor knows, ideally materials should be presented in such a way that students can build their skills and knowledge bases block by block. This is difficult because, no matter where you begin, you will need to refer to some information that has not yet been presented to the student. For example, if you try to explain what paralegals do on the first or second day of class, you will necessarily have to mention terms that may be unfamiliar to the students, such as *litigation* or *substantive law* or *procedural law*. In writing this text, the authors have attempted, whenever possible, to organize the topics covered in such a way that the student is never mystified by terms and concepts not yet discussed.

Content Presentation

We realize that no one way of organizing the coverage of topics in a paralegal text will be suitable for all instructors, but we have attempted to accommodate your needs as much as possible by organizing the text into three basic parts. Part 1 (Chapters 1–4) focuses primarily on the paralegal profession—its origins and development, the wide array of paralegal careers, the threshold ethical responsibilities of the profession, and the requirements and procedures that students can expect to encounter in the legal workplace.

Part 2 (Chapters 5–12), after a discussion of the sources of law and the American court system, focuses on substantive law. We have expanded the number of topics covered for the Fourth Edition of *Paralegal Today*. The areas of law now treated in this part of the text include torts, product liability, consumer law, contracts, intellectual property, insurance, real property, estates, family law, business organizations, negotiable instruments, employment, bankruptcy, and environmental law. Additionally, for the Fourth Edition we have added to the chapters covering substantive law many numbered, highlighted examples to provide real-world illustrations of the legal concepts being discussed.

Part 3 (Chapters 13–19) looks in detail at legal procedures and paralegal skills. The student learns about the basic procedural requirements in civil and criminal litigation, as well as the skills involved in conducting interviews and investigations, legal research and analysis, and legal writing.

A Flexible Arrangement

It is our hope that this organization of the materials will allow the greatest flexibility for instructors. Although to a certain extent each chapter in the text builds on information contained in previous chapters, the chapters and parts can also be used independently. In other words, instructors who wish to alter the presentation of topics to fit their course outlines, or who wish to use selected chapters or parts only, will find it relatively easy to do so.

KEY FEATURES

In addition to the *Technology and Today's Paralegal* features, which we have already discussed, every chapter in this text has the following features. Each feature is set apart and used both to instruct and to pique the interest of your paralegal students.

Developing Paralegal Skills

The *Developing Paralegal Skills* boxed-in features present hypothetical examples of paralegals at work to help your students develop crucial paralegal skills. The features include checklists and practical tips. Some examples are the following:

- Finding Government Information Online (Chapter 2).
- Estate Planning (Chapter 10).
- Assisting with a Workers' Compensation Claim (Chapter 11).

From Chapter 1 . . .

Developing Paralegal Skills

PROOFREADING LEGAL DOCUMENTS

Geena Northrop, a paralegal, works for a solo practitioner (a one-attorney law firm). Among her other duties, she handles a significant part of the legal writing for the attorney who owns the firm. Geena has learned that when creating a legal document, writing the document is only half the job. The rest is proofreading—and not just once. She has learned the hard way that one proofreading is simply not enough to catch every error or typo that may be in the document. Now she has adopted the motto of one of the instructors in her paralegal program, "Proof, proof, and proof again!"

Today, she has set aside some time to proofread carefully a last will and testament that she created yesterday for one of the firm's clients. Geena prints out a copy of the document for proofreading purposes, because she has learned that it is difficult to proofread a document on a computer screen. Moreover, style and formatting problems are often not as evident on even a high-resolution screen as they are on hard copy. Her first step in proofreading the document is to make sure that the document reflects all of the relevant information from her notes. Geena reviews her notes point by point from the client interview and from her later discussion with the attorney about the will and checks the document. All looks well in this respect, so she proceeds to her second step in proofreading: checking style and format. Are all of the headings in the correct size and font? Is the spacing between headings consistent? Are all of the paragraphs properly indented? She finds a couple of problems and marks her hard copy to make the appropriate changes. She then reads through the document word for word to ensure that there are no grammatical problems, spelling errors, or typos. Finally, she revises the document on her computer, prints it out, and takes it to the attorney for his review.

CHECKLIST FOR PROOFREADING LEGAL DOCUMENTS

- When you create a legal document, do not assume that one proofreading will be sufficient to catch all problems or errors that the document may contain.
- Read through the document again to make sure that the style and formatting elements are consistent throughout.
- Print out the document, and go through the contents line by line to make sure that it includes all required or relevant information.
- Finally, read through the document word for word to ensure that it is free of grammatical errors, misspelled words, and typos.

- Checking the Accident Scene (Chapter 14).
- PowerPoint Presentations (Chapter 15).

Ethics Watch!

Every chapter presents a number of *Ethics Watch!* features. These features typically take a student into a hypothetical situation that clearly presents an ethical problem. When possible, students are told what they should and should not do in the particular situations being discussed. Some examples are the following:

- The Importance of Being Honest (Chapter 2).
- Clarifying Instructions (Chapter 9).
- Client Information and the Duty of Competence (Chapter 10).
- Using Secondary Sources (Chapter 17).

From Chapter 6 . . .

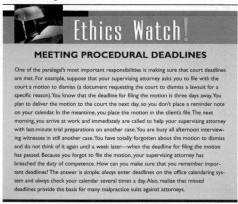

Ethics Watch!

MEETING PROCEDURAL DEADLINES

One of the paralegal's most important responsibilities is making sure that court deadlines are met. For example, suppose that your supervising attorney asks you to file with the court a motion to dismiss (a document requesting the court to dismiss a lawsuit for a specific reason). You know that the deadline for filing the motion is three days away. You plan to deliver the motion to the court the next day, so you don't place a reminder note on your calendar. In the meantime, you place the motion in the client's file. The next morning, you arrive at work and immediately are called to help your supervising attorney with last-minute trial preparations on another case. You are busy all afternoon interviewing witnesses in still another case. You have totally forgotten about the motion to dismiss and do not think of it again until a week later—when the deadline for filing the motion has passed. Because you forgot to file the motion, your supervising attorney has breached the duty of competence. How can you make sure that you remember important deadlines? The answer is simple: always enter deadlines on the office calendaring system and always check your calendar several times a day. Also, realize that missed deadlines provide the basis for many malpractice suits against attorneys.

Paralegal Profiles

Every chapter includes a profile of a paralegal who is currently working in a specific area of law. These profiles open with a short biography of the paralegal and then present the paralegal's own answers to questions asked by the interviewer. The paralegal tells of his or her

From Chapter 9 . . .

Kirtrena S. Deen　　PARALEGAL **profile**

INSURANCE PARALEGAL

Kirtrena S. Deen received her bachelor of arts degree in legal administration from the University of West Florida in Pensacola, Florida, in 1996. On graduation, she worked at a large law firm as a legal assistant for approximately a year and a half in the area of personal-injury and employment law. She then accepted a position as a claims representative for a national automobile insurance company.

In September 1998, Deen received her Florida Department of Insurance Adjusters license. Additionally, she serves on the University of West Florida Legal Administration Program Advisory Board as a paralegal representative in the corporate/public sector.

What do you like best about your work?

"I enjoy the responsibility and exposure of investigating, evaluating, and negotiating a variety of automobile claims as opposed to adjusting only specific types of automobile claims. Some examples of the claims I am assigned to adjust include property, bodily injury, arson, theft, vandalism, and weather-related claims. I also enjoy the investigative process of meeting the parties involved, securing recorded statements, conducting scene investigations, and canvassing for witnesses."

What is the greatest challenge that you face in your area of work?

"Once a claim has been reported, the claims representative must investigate to establish coverage, finalize legal liability, and inspect the reported damage. Once the claim has been thoroughly investigated,

it must be evaluated to determine a fair settlement and negotiated accordingly. Therefore, the greatest challenge of adjusting claims is completing the investigation, evaluation, and negotiation process promptly and fairly while complying with the terms of the insurance policy and governing statutory laws."

What advice do you have for would-be paralegals in your area of work?

"My advice is to possess strong interpersonal skills, as well as superior writing and oral communication skills. Due to the variety of claims assigned, claims representatives in my area daily communicate and negotiate with insureds, claimants, and other claims representatives, as well as attorneys, regarding the settlement of claims. Additionally, regular meetings and communication with paint and body shop managers is needed regarding the assessment of automobile damage. Thus, the ability to communicate effectively with all kinds of people is a great asset to possess in my area of work."

"[T]he ability to communicate effectively with all kinds of people is a great asset to possess in my area of work."

What are some tips for success as a paralegal in your area of work?

"Know the terms and conditions of the insurance policy and regularly refer to the policy to substantiate them. The insurance policy is the contract between the insurance company and the insured to which they must adhere. Know the statutory laws governing claims handling in your area and keep abreast of changes. Be detail oriented and analytical in the investigation process. Feel passionate about your work. Passion for your work will enable you to go that extra mile to handle claims promptly and fairly."

greatest challenges on the job, gives suggestions about what he or she thinks students should concentrate on when studying to become paralegals, and offers tips for being a successful paralegal in his or her line of work. This feature gives your students insights into various legal specialties and the diversity of paralegal working environments.

Featured Guest Articles

Each chapter features a contributed article written by an educator or an expert in the field. These articles offer your students practical tips on some aspect of paralegal work relating to the topic covered in the chapter. Some examples are the following:

- "The Interrelationship of the Various Areas of Law," by S. Whittington Brown, an attorney with the Arkansas Department of Human Services (Chapter 5).

- "Is There a Place for Paralegals in the Field of Medical Malpractice?" by Beth Walston-Dunham, a paralegal educator and writer whose most recent publication is *Medical Malpractice Law and Litigation,* published in 2005 by Thomson Delmar Learning (Chapter 7).

- "Protecting the Real Estate Purchaser: The Due Diligence Team," by Daniel F. Hinkel, vice president and corporate counsel for ING Investment Management, LLC, in Atlanta, Georgia (Chapter 9).

- "Ethical Considerations for the Corporate Paralegal—Whom Do You Represent?" by John E. Moye, a founding partner in a Colorado law firm that acts as general counsel for corporate clients on a regional, national, and international basis (Chapter 11).

- "Tips for Making Legal Writing Easier," by William Putman, an attorney who has specialized in paralegal education for many years and who has published a number of texts on legal analysis and writing (Chapter 19).

From Chapter 6 . . .

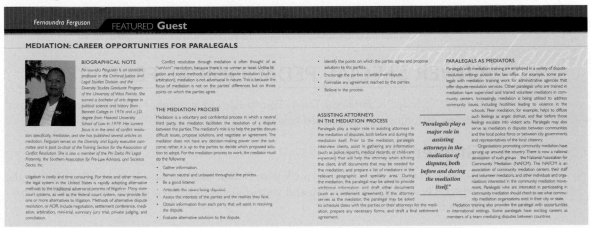

Today's Professional Paralegal

Near the end of every chapter we have included a special feature entitled *Today's Professional Paralegal*. This important feature exposes your students to situations that they are likely to encounter on the job and offers guidance on how certain types of problems can be resolved. Some examples are the following:

- A View from the Inside: Assisting a Civil Litigation Paralegal (Chapter 2).
- Confidentiality Agreements (Chapter 8).

- Handling and Avoiding Malpractice Claims (Chapter 9).
- Meeting with the Personal Representative (Chapter 10).
- Preparing the Internal Memorandum (Chapter 19).

From Chapter 15 . . .

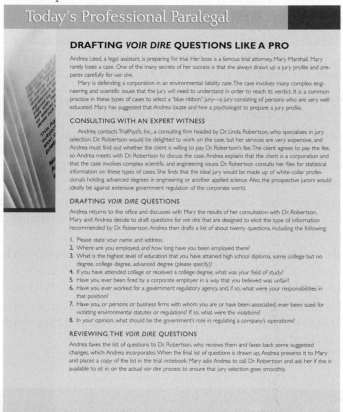

OTHER SPECIAL PEDAGOGICAL FEATURES

We have included in *Paralegal Today*, Fourth Edition, a number of additional pedagogical features, including those discussed below.

Chapter Outlines

On every chapter-opening page, a *Chapter Outline* lists the first-level headings within the chapter. These outlines allow you and your students to tell at a glance what topics are covered in the chapters.

Chapter Objectives

In every chapter, just following the *Chapter Outline*, we list five or six chapter objectives. Your students will know immediately what is expected of them as they read each chapter.

Margin Web Sites

As already mentioned, *On the Web* features appear in the page margins throughout the text. These features direct students to specific Web sites for further information on the topics being discussed. Note that Web sites are sometimes deleted and URLs are frequently changed as sites are redesigned. If you or your students encounter difficulties accessing one of the margin Web sites, refer to the instructions that appear in the Introduction to the Student, following this preface.

Vocabulary and Margin Definitions

Legal terminology is often a major challenge for beginning paralegal students. We have used an important pedagogical device—margin definitions—to help your students understand legal terms. Whenever an important term is introduced, it appears in colored type and is defined. In addition, the term is listed and defined in the margin of the page, alongside the paragraph in which the term appears (see the examples on the right).

At the end of each chapter, all terms that have appeared in colored type within the chapter are listed in alphabetical order in a section called *Key Terms and Concepts*. Your students can briefly examine this list to make sure that they understand all of the important terms introduced in the chapter. If they do not understand a term completely, they can return to the chapter materials and review the term. For easy reference and review, each term in this list is followed by the number of the page on which the term appeared in colored type and was defined.

All terms in colored type are again listed and defined in the *Glossary* at the end of the text. Spanish equivalents to many important legal terms in English are provided in a separate glossary—see Appendix K.

estate administration
The process in which a decedent's personal representative settles the affairs of the decedent's estate (collects assets, pays debts and taxes, and distributes the remaining assets to heirs); the process is usually overseen by a probate court.

joint tenancy
The joint ownership of property by two or more co-owners in which each co-owner owns an undivided portion of the property. On the death of one of the joint tenants, his or her interest automatically passes to the surviving joint tenant or tenants.

Chapter Summaries

We have included a graphic chapter summary at the conclusion of each chapter in the Fourth Edition. These summaries illustrate the important concepts from the chapter and show how the concepts are related to one another. The major topics discussed in the chapter appear in the left-hand column of the summary, with a synopsis of the concepts discussed under each topic listed in the right-hand column. This visually appealing format facilitates the student's review of the chapter contents.

From Chapter 6 . . .

chapter summary	The Court System and Alternative Dispute Resolution
Basic Judicial Requirements	
	1. *Jurisdiction*—Before a court can hear a case, it must have jurisdiction over the person against whom the suit is brought (*in personam* jurisdiction) or the property involved in the suit (*in rem* jurisdiction), as well as jurisdiction over the subject matter.
	a. Limited versus general jurisdiction—Limited jurisdiction exists when a court is limited to a specific subject matter, such as probate or divorce. General jurisdiction exists when a court can hear any kind of case.
	b. Original versus appellate jurisdiction—Courts that have authority to hear a case for the first time (trial courts) have original jurisdiction. Courts of appeals, or reviewing courts, have appellate jurisdiction; generally, these courts do not have original jurisdiction.

Exhibits and Forms

When appropriate, we present exhibits illustrating important forms or concepts relating to paralegal work. Many exhibits are filled in with hypothetical data. Exhibits and forms in *Paralegal Today*, Fourth Edition, include those listed below:

- A Sample Client Bill (Chapter 4).
- The Articles of the U.S. Constitution (Chapter 5).

- A Typical Case Flowchart (Chapter 13).
- Examples of Boolean Searches (Chapter 18).

CHAPTER-ENDING MATERIALS FOR REVIEW AND STUDY

Every chapter contains numerous chapter-ending pedagogical materials. These materials are designed to provide a wide variety of assignments for your students. The chapter-ending pedagogy begins with the *Key Terms and Concepts*, followed by the chapter summaries, which we have already mentioned. Next are the materials described below.

Questions for Review

In every chapter are a number of relatively straightforward questions for review. These questions are designed to test the student's knowledge of the basic concepts discussed in the chapter.

Ethical Questions

Because of the importance of ethical issues in paralegal training, we have also included two or more ethical questions at the end of each chapter. Each question presents a hypothetical situation, which is followed by one or two questions about what the paralegal should do to solve the dilemma.

Practice Questions and Assignments

The hands-on approach to learning paralegal skills is emphasized in the practice questions and assignments. There are several of these questions and assignments at the end of each chapter. A particular situation is presented, and the student is asked to actually carry out an assignment.

Questions for Critical Analysis

Every chapter has several questions for critical analysis. These questions are designed to elicit critical evaluation and discussion of issues relating to the topics covered in the chapter.

Projects

There are two or more projects at the end of every chapter. These are specific work tasks that your students can carry out. Often, these projects involve obtaining information from sources that paralegals may deal with on the job, such as a library, a court, a prosecutor's office, or a police department.

Using Internet Resources

As already mentioned, concluding the chapter-ending materials in each chapter is a section titled *Using Internet Resources*. The Internet exercises presented in these sections are designed to familiarize students with useful Web sites and with the extensive array of resources available online.

APPENDICES

To make this text a reference source for your students, we have included the appendices listed below.

A	NALA's Code of Ethics and Professional Responsibility
B	NALA's Model Standards and Guidelines for Utilization of Legal Assistants
C	NFPA's Model Code of Ethics and Professional Responsibility and Guidelines for Enforcement
D	NALS Code of Ethics
E	Paralegal Ethics and Regulation: How to Find State-Specific Information
F	Paralegal Associations
G	Information on NALA's CLA/CP Program
H	Information on NFPA's PACE Examination
I	Information on NALS Certification
J	The Constitution of the United States
K	Spanish Equivalents for Important Legal Terms in English

FOR USERS OF THE THIRD EDITION

Those of you who have used the Third Edition of *Paralegal Today* will probably want to know some of the major changes that have been made for the Fourth Edition. Generally, all of the elements in the Fourth Edition—including the text, exhibits, features, and end-of-chapter pedagogy—have been rewritten, revised, or updated as necessary to reflect new laws, procedures, and technological developments. We think that we have improved the text greatly, thanks in part to the many suggestions that we have received from users of previous editions as well as from other paralegal educators and legal professionals.

Organizational Changes and Expanded Coverage

In order to incorporate additional topics into the chapters on substantive law, we have reorganized and streamlined the presentation of the topics in Part 2, resulting in changed chapter titles and an additional chapter. We have added to this part of the text coverage of the following areas:

- **Insurance law**—A section on insurance law (in Chapter 9) examines the purpose of insurance, typical provisions in an insurance contract, the concepts of indemnification and subrogation, and examples of paralegal tasks in this area of the law.

- **Negotiable instruments**—Chapter 11 (Laws Affecting Business) now includes a thorough discussion of negotiable instruments. This new section explains the law governing negotiable instruments, how checks and other instruments are transferred from one party to another, the law governing check acceptance and deposits, and the various methods of transferring funds electronically through the use of debit cards and other devices.

- **Bankruptcy law**—We have added a detailed section (in Chapter 12) covering bankruptcy law. This new section includes the latest changes to bankruptcy law as set forth in the Bankruptcy Reform Act of 2005.

New Features and Other Changes

Most of the *Featured Guest* articles and more than half of the *Paralegal Profile* features are new to this edition. We have also rewritten or significantly revised a number of the *Technology and Today's Paralegal, Today's Professional Paralegal, Developing Paralegal Skills,* and *Ethics Watch!* features. Other additions and changes for the Fourth Edition include the following:

- **Updated ethical rules**—The rules of ethical conduct for attorneys and other legal professionals have been updated as necessary.

- **New highlighted, numbered examples**—As mentioned earlier, throughout the chapters in Part 2 of this text (Chapters 5–12, covering substantive law), we have added highlighted and numbered examples. These examples illustrate how the concepts being discussed apply to real-world situations, thus making it easier for the student to understand the basic legal rules and principles.

- **New photos**—Each chapter now includes a photo of a paralegal at work in a specific job environment.

- **New exhibits**—We have added a number of new exhibits for this edition, including exhibits illustrating insurance classifications (Chapter 9), insurance provisions and clauses (Chapter 9), various types of negotiable instruments and indorsements (Chapter 11), a subpoena (Chapter 16), and sample results of a Boolean search (Chapter 18).

- **New and updated appendices**—The appendices now include the NALS Code of Ethics (Appendix D), NALS state chapters (Appendix F), and information on NALS certification (Appendix I). The remaining appendices have been updated as necessary.

Significantly Revised Chapters

Beside the changes already mentioned, we have made many other changes to the text for the Fourth Edition. We summarize here the most significant changes to the chapters that have been made for this edition.

- **Chapter 1** (Today's Professional Paralegal)—This chapter has been updated to include recent trends and developments in educational programs and certification designations, paralegal compensation, and the use of technology in the law office. A new section discusses the NALS and AAPI certifications, and more detail concerning California's CLE requirement has been added.

- **Chapter 2** (Career Opportunities)—The chapter has been revised extensively to reflect the results of the latest surveys showing trends in paralegal specialization and compensation. The chapter also includes a discussion of the Department of Labor's 2004 FairPay rule concerning overtime wages.

- **Chapter 3** (Ethics and Professional Responsibility)—Much of this chapter has been rewritten to include changes in the ABA's Model Rules of Professional Conduct and Model Guidelines for the Utilization of Legal Assistant Services. Additionally, the sections discussing attorney-client confidentiality and conflicts of interest have been revised to clarify the meaning and application of the rules.

- **Chapter 4** (The Inner Workings of the Law Office)—The discussion of paralegal billing rates has been updated, and the sections discussing billing and timekeeping procedures have been rewritten as necessary to focus more on computer-based billing systems.

- **Chapter 5** (Sources of American Law)—The section on statutory law has been expanded and now includes subsections on the federal government's constitutional authority to enact laws, the expansion of national powers under the commerce clause, federal and state lawmaking processes, and conflicts between federal and state laws. The discussion of constitutional law has been strengthened by a new exhibit setting forth the articles of the Constitution and by a *Featured Guest* article focusing on the relationship between constitutional law and other areas of law. The section discussing administrative law has been expanded to include some of the materials that were presented in Chapter 11 of the Third Edition.

- **Chapter 7** (Tort Law, Product Liability, and Consumer Law)—The section on consumer law, which was included in Chapter 11 in the Third Edition, now appears in this chapter. Separate sections now describe the paralegal's duties relating to both intentional torts and negligence. A section on the Fair and Accurate Credit Transaction Act of 2003 has been added to the section discussing consumer law.

- **Chapter 8** (Contracts and Intellectual Property)—The contracts section in this chapter now includes discussions of unconscionable contracts and clauses, adhesion contracts, and punitive damages. The intellectual property section has been updated to reflect current developments in this area of the law.

- **Chapter 9** (Insurance Law and Real Property)—In the Third Edition, real property was combined in Chapter 9 with estates and family law. For the Fourth Edition, we have added a new section on insurance law to this chapter, as noted previously. Estates and family law are now covered in Chapter 10.

- **Chapter 11** (Laws Affecting Business)—For the Fourth Edition, we have added a section on negotiable instruments to this chapter, as noted earlier. The chapter has also been revised to include a discussion of the Sarbanes-Oxley Act of 2002 and the provisions of the Uniform Partnership Act that are applicable in the majority of states today.

- **Chapter 12** (Bankruptcy and Environmental Law)—As already noted, we have added coverage of bankruptcy law, based on the 2005 Bankruptcy Reform Act, for the Fourth Edition. Environmental law, which appeared in Chapter 11 in the Third Edition, now appears in this chapter.

- **Chapter 13** (Civil Litigation—Before the Trial)—This chapter has been revised to reflect current practices with respect to electronic filing and electronic discovery.

- **Chapter 17** (Legal Research and Analysis)—This chapter has been rewritten and reorganized as necessary to streamline the discussion of primary and secondary research sources and to make the material more accessible to the student reader. The section discussing the West key-number system has been expanded to clarify how this system can assist the legal researcher, and the sample court case has been replaced with a more recent court opinion.

- **Chapter 18** (Computer-Assisted Legal Research)—Because of the many changes in technology and online research that have developed since the last edition of *Paralegal Today,* this chapter required extensive rewriting and revision. The chapter now discusses currently used search engines and search operators and includes a section discussing Boolean logic and showing, in an exhibit, examples of Boolean search results. The chapter also presents updated URLs for a wide array of Web databases that can be used for factual and legal research. In addition, the chapter has been reorganized to make the discussion proceed more logically from the basics of Internet research to more sophisticated research using services such as Westlaw and Lexis.

SUPPLEMENTAL TEACHING/ LEARNING MATERIALS

Paralegal Today, Fourth Edition, is accompanied by what is arguably the largest number of teaching and learning supplements available for any text of its kind. We understand that instructors face a difficult task in finding the time necessary to teach the materials that they wish to cover during each term. In conjunction with a number of our colleagues, we have developed supplementary teaching materials that we believe are the best obtainable today. Each component of the supplements package is described below.

Instructor's Manual

Written by the authors of the text, the *Instructor's Manual* contains the following:

- A sample course syllabus.
- Chapter/lecture outlines.
- Teaching suggestions.
- Answers to text exercises and questions.
- Transparency masters, handouts, and PowerPoint presentations available online.

Online Companion™

- **Study Guide**—At **http://www.paralegal.delmar.cengage.com**, students can review chapter overviews and chapter objectives to reinforce chapter learning goals. This resource also contains extensive outlines for each chapter that will help students organize information and show how the concepts in the text relate to each other. In addition, students will discover study tips and practical advice that will help ease the way through studying, test taking, writing essays, and more.

- **Online Quizzing**—Also at **http://www.paralegal.delmar.cengage.com**, student interactive online quizzing is available. With the click of a mouse, students can access this study alternative and become better prepared for classroom exams. Interactive online quizzing provides students with a chance to answer review questions directly relating to the text for each chapter. Each answer presents students with instant feedback and clarifies the rationale for correct and incorrect choices. This self-assessment tool can be accessed at school or at home, giving students more flexibility and opportunity to study.

- **The Bankruptcy Reform Act of 2005**—Prepared by text co-author Roger Miller, a guide to the bankruptcy reform legislation of 2005 is available online.

Computerized Test Bank

The Test Bank is available in a computerized format on CD-ROM. The platforms supported include Windows™ 98, ME, 2000, XP or a more recent version and Macintosh® system 8.5 or a more recent version, including OS X in Classic mode.

- Multiple methods of question selection.
- Multiple outputs—that is, print, ASCII, RTF.
- Graphic support (black and white).
- Random questioning output.
- Special character support.

Webtutor™

An accompanying Webtutor™ on Web CT and Blackboard platforms facilitates active engagement with the course content. The Webtutor encourages review of lecture material, expands the depth of course content, and promotes self-directed learning. The Webtutor will provide *immediate feedback* from quizzes, and its contemporary format will appeal to today's student.

Citation-At-A-Glance

This handy reference card provides a quick, portable reference to the basic rules of citation for the most commonly cited legal sources, including judicial opinions, statutes, and secondary sources, such as legal encyclopedias and legal periodicals. *Citation-At-A-Glance* uses the rules set forth in *The Bluebook: A Uniform System of Citation*. A free copy of this valuable supplement is included with every student text.

Delmar Cengage Learning's Paralegal Studies Web Site

Come visit our Web site at **http://www.paralegal.delmar.cengage.com**, where you will find valuable information specific to this book and other Delmar, Cengage Learning Paralegal texts.

Westlaw

West's online computerized legal research system offers students hands-on experience with a system commonly used in law offices. Qualified adopters can receive ten free hours of Westlaw. Westlaw can be accessed with Macintosh and IBM PCs and compatibles.

Please note that Internet resources are of a time-sensitive nature and URL addresses may often change or be deleted. Contact us at

delmar.paralegal@cengage.com

ACKNOWLEDGMENTS FOR PREVIOUS EDITIONS

Numerous careful and conscientious individuals have helped us in this undertaking from the beginning. We continue to be indebted to those whose contributions helped to make previous editions of *Paralegal Today* a valuable teaching/learning text. We particularly thank the following paralegal educators for their insightful criticisms and comments:

Laura Barnard
Lakeland Community College, OH

Lia Barone
Norwalk Community College, CT

Chelsea Campbell
Lehman College, NY

Linda S. Cioffredi
Woodbury College, VT

Jeptha Clemens
Northwest Mississippi Community
  College, MS

Arlene A. Cleveland
Pellissippi State Technical Community
  College, TN

Lynne D. Dahlborg
Suffolk University, MA

Kevin R. Derr
Pennsylvania College of
Technology, PA

Bob Diotalevi
Florida Gulf Coast University, FL

Donna Hamblin Donathan
Marshall University Community
College, OH

Dora Dye
City College of San Francisco, CA

Wendy B. Edson
Hilbert College, NY

Leslie Sturdivant Ennis
Samford University, AL

Pamela Faller
College of the Sequoias, CA

Gary Glascom
Cedar Crest College, PA

Dolores Grissom
Samford University, AL

Paul D. Guymon
William Rainey Harper College, IL

Sharon Halford
Community College of Aurora, CO

Linda Wilke Heil
Central Community College, NE

Jean A. Hellman
Loyola University, Chicago, IL

Melinda Hess
College of Saint Mary, NE

Louise Hoover
Rockford Business College, IL

Marlene L. Hoover
El Camino College, CA

Susan J. Howery
Yavapai College, AZ

Jill Jasperson
Utah Valley State College, UT

Melissa M. Jones
Samford University, AL

Deborah Winfrey Keene
Lansing Community College, MI

Jennifer Allen Labosky
Davidson County Community
College, NC

Dora J. Lew
California State University, Hayward, CA

Mary Hatfield Lowe
Westark Community College, AZ

Gerald A. Loy
Broome Community College, NY

Linda Mort
Kellogg Community College, MI

Constance Ford Mungle
Oklahoma City University, OK

H. Margaret Nickerson
William Woods College, MO

Martha G. Nielson
University of California, San Diego, CA

Elizabeth L. Nobis
Lansing Community College, MI

Joy D. O'Donnell
Pima Community College, AZ

Anthony Piazza
David N. Myers College, OH

Francis D. Polk
Ocean County College, NJ

Ruth-Ellen Post
Rivier College, NH

Elizabeth Raulerson
Indian River Community College, FL

Kathleen Mercer Reed
University of Toledo, OH

Lynn Retzak
Lakeshore Technical Institute, WI

Evelyn L. Riyhani
University of California, Irvine, CA

Melanie A. P. Rowand
California State University,
Hayward, CA

Vitonio F. San Juan
University of La Verne, CA

Susan F. Schulz
Southern Career Institute, FL

John G. Thomas III
North Hampton County Community
   College, PA

Loretta Thornhill
Hagerstown Community College, MD

Julia Tryk
Cuyahoga Community College, OH

ACKNOWLEDGMENTS FOR THE FOURTH EDITION

During the preparation of the Fourth Edition of *Paralegal Today*, several professionals offered us penetrating criticisms, comments, and suggestions for improving the text. While we haven't been able to comply with every request, the reviewers listed below will see that many of their suggestions have been taken to heart.

Laura Barnard
Lakeland Community College, OH

Carol Brady
Milwaukee Area Technical College, WI

Rhonda Brashears
Certified Paralegal, TX

Debra Brown
Coastline Community College, CA

We also are grateful to the following paralegal educators, our featured guests in *Paralegal Today*, Fourth Edition, for enhancing the quality of our book with their tips and illuminating insights into paralegal practice:

Sally Bisson
College of St. Mary, Omaha, NE

Deborah E. Bouchoux
Georgetown University, Washington, DC

S. Whittington Brown
Attorney, Arkansas Department
   of Human Services

Daniel G. Cantone
Private Law Practice/Syracuse
   University, NY

Wendy B. Edson
Hilbert College, NY

Chere B. Estrin
Estrin Professional Careers, Studio City, CA

Fernaundra Ferguson
University of West Florida

Nancy R. Gallo
Sussex County Community College, NJ

Daniel F. Hinkel
Vice President and Corporate Counsel,
   ING Investment Management, LLC,
   Atlanta, GA

John Moye
Corporate Counsel, Moye White, LLP,
   Denver, CO

Lisa L. Newcity
Roger Williams University, RI

P. David Palmiere
Oakland University, MI

William Putman
Paralegal Educator/Author

Brent Roper
Private Law Practice/Author

Ken Rosenblum
Ivy Tech Community College, IN

Sidney K. Swinson
Attorney, Gable & Gotwals, Tulsa, OK

Beth Walston-Dunham
Paralegal Educator/Author

Pamela Poole Weber
Seminole Community College, FL

E. J. Yera
U.S. Attorney's Office, Miami, FL

Additionally, we extend our gratitude to those on-the-job paralegals who agreed to appear in the *Paralegal Profiles* of *Paralegal Today*, Fourth Edition.

In preparing *Paralegal Today,* Fourth Edition, we were also the beneficiaries of the expertise brought to the project by the editorial and production staff of the Delmar, Cengage Learning Paralegal program. Our editor, Shelley Esposito, successfully guided the project through each phase and put together a supplements package that is without parallel in the teaching and learning of paralegal skills. Melissa Riveglia, our senior product manager, was also incredibly helpful in putting together the teaching/learning package. We also wish to thank Betty Dickson, senior content project manager, and Joan Conlon for their assistance throughout the production process. Additionally, we wish to thank Gerard McAvey, our marketing manager, and Joy Kocsis, our art director, for their valuable contributions to the project.

A number of other individuals contributed significantly to the quality of *Paralegal Today,* Fourth Edition. We wish to thank Katherine M. Silsbee and Lavina Leed Miller for their assistance in creating what we believe is the best introductory paralegal text on the market today. We also thank Vickie Reierson and Roxie Lee for their help in coordinating the authors' work on this edition of *Paralegal Today,* and Suzanne Jasin for her efforts on the project. We were fortunate to have had the copyediting skills of Beverly Peavler, and we are grateful to Pat Lewis, Suzie DeFazio, and Martha Ghent, whose proofreading skills will not go unnoticed. Finally, we are indebted to the staff at Parkwood Composition, our compositor, whose ability to generate the pages for this text quickly and accurately made it possible for us to meet our ambitious printing schedule.

We know that we are not perfect. If you or your students have suggestions on how we can improve this book, write to us. That way, we can make *Paralegal Today* an even better book in the future. We promise to answer every single letter that we receive.

Roger LeRoy Miller
Mary Meinzinger Urisko

INTRODUCTION TO THE STUDENT

The law sometimes is considered a difficult subject because it uses a specialized vocabulary and requires substantial time and effort to learn. Those who work with and teach law believe that the subject matter is exciting and definitely worth your efforts. Everything in *Paralegal Today: The Legal Team at Work,* Fourth Edition, has been written for the precise purpose of helping you learn the most important aspects of law and legal procedures.

Learning is a lifelong process. Your learning of legal concepts and procedures will not end when you finish your paralegal studies. On the contrary, the end of your paralegal studies marks the beginning of your learning process in regard to law and legal procedures. Just as valuable to you as the knowledge base you can acquire from mastering the legal concepts and terms in *Paralegal Today,* Fourth Edition, is a knowledge of *how to learn* those legal concepts and terms. The focus in this introduction, therefore, is on developing learning skills that you can apply to any subject matter and at any time throughout your career.

The suggestions and study tips offered in this introduction can help you "learn how to learn" law and procedures and maximize your chances of success as a paralegal student. They can also help you build lifelong learning habits that you can use in other classes and throughout your career as a paralegal.

MASTERING YOUR TEXT

A mistake students commonly make is assuming that the best way to understand the content of written material is to read and reread that material. True, if you have read through a chapter ten times, you have probably acquired a knowledge of its contents, but think of the time you have spent in the process. What you want to strive for is to use your time *effectively*. We offer here some suggestions on how to study the chapters of *Paralegal Today* most effectively.

Read One Section at a Time

A piano student once said to her teacher, "This piece is so complicated. How can I possibly learn it?" The teacher responded, "It's simple: measure by measure." That advice can be applied to any challenging task. As a paralegal student, you are faced with the job of learning complicated legal concepts and procedures. By dividing your work up into manageable units, you will find that, before long, you have achieved your goal. Each chapter in *Paralegal Today,* Fourth Edition, is divided into several major sections. By concentrating on sections, rather than chapters, you will find it easier to master the chapter's contents.

Assume, for example, that you have been assigned to read Chapter 11 of *Paralegal Today,* Fourth Edition. That chapter covers basic concepts and principles involving agency law, negotiable instruments (such as checks), business organizational forms, and employment law. Mastering each of these topics requires you to learn a number of different legal concepts and terms. You will find it easier to master all of these topics if you concentrate on just one topic at a time. For example, you might begin with the section on agency law and focus only on that section.

Once you have read through a section, do not stop there. Go back through the section again and organize the material in your mind. Outlining the section is one way to mentally organize what you have read.

Make an Outline

An outline is simply a method for organizing information. The reason an outline can be helpful is that it illustrates visually how concepts relate to each other. Outlining can be done as part of your reading of each section, but your outline will be more accurate (and more helpful later on) if you have already read through a section and have a general understanding of the topics covered in that section.

The Benefits of Outlining

Although you may not believe that you need to outline, our experience has been that the act of *physically* creating an outline for a chapter helps most students to greatly improve their ability to retain and master the material being studied. Even if you make an outline that is no more than the headings in the text, you will be studying more efficiently than you otherwise would be.

Outlining is also a paralegal skill. As a paralegal, you will need to present legal concepts and fact patterns in an outline format. For example, paralegals frequently create legal memoranda to summarize their research results. The legal memorandum is usually presented in an outline format, which indicates how the topics covered in the memo relate to one another logically or sequentially. There is no better time to master the skill of outlining than the present, while you are a student. You can learn this skill by outlining sections and chapters of *Paralegal Today*.

Identify the Main Concepts in Each Section

In outlining a chapter, you can use the outline at the beginning of the chapter as a starting point. The chapter-opening outlines include the headings of the major sections within the chapter. Use these headings as a guide when creating a more thorough and detailed outline. Be careful, though. To make an effective outline, you have to be selective. Outlines that contain all the information in the text are not very useful. Your objective in outlining is to identify main concepts and to arrange more detailed concepts under those main concepts. Therefore, in outlining, your first goal is to *identify the main concepts in each section*. Often the headings within your textbook and in the chapter-opening outlines are sufficient as identifiers of the major concepts. You may decide, however, that you want to phrase an identifier in a way that is more meaningful to you.

Outline Format

Your outline should consist of several levels written in a standard outline format. The most important concepts are assigned uppercase Roman numerals; the second most important, capital letters; the third most important, numbers; the fourth most important, lowercase letters; and the fifth most important, lowercase roman numerals. The number of levels you use in an outline varies, of course, with the complexity of the subject matter. In some outlines, or portions of outlines, you may need to use only two levels. In others, you may need five or more levels.

As an example of how to use numerals and letters in an outline, we present below a partial outline of the contracts section in Chapter 8 of *Paralegal Today,* Fourth Edition.

FUNDAMENTAL LEGAL CONCEPTS: CONTRACTS

I.   Definition of a contract: A contract is any agreement (based on a promise or an exchange of promises) that can be enforced in court. A promise is an assurance that one will or will not do something in the future.

II. Requirements to form a valid contract

    A.   Agreement—Agreement is divided into two events: an offer and an acceptance. One party must offer to enter into a legal agreement, and another party must accept the terms of the offer.

        1.   The offer—Three elements are necessary:

            a.   The offeror (the party making the offer) must have the intent to be bound by the offer.

            b.   The terms of the offer must be reasonably certain or definite (note that some terms may be left open in sales contracts).

            c.   The offer must be communicated to the offeree (the party to whom the offer is made).

        2.   Termination of the offer—The offeror can normally revoke (take back) an offer at any time prior to acceptance.

            a.   Both a rejection of the offer and the making of a counteroffer (by the offeree) terminate the original offer.

        3.   Acceptance—Acceptance by the offeree results in a legally binding contract (provided that all of the other requirements of a valid contract are met).

            a.   The terms of the offer must be accepted exactly as stated by the offeror (the mirror image rule).

            b.   Acceptance must be timely—within the time period designated by the offeror or within a reasonable time.

            c.   Under the mailbox rule, acceptance becomes valid the moment it is deposited in the mail (even if it is never received by the offeror).

    B.   Consideration . . .

Consider Marking Your Text

From kindergarten through high school, you typically did not own your own textbooks. They were made available by the school system. You were told not to mark in them. Now that you own your own text for a course, you can greatly improve your learning by marking your text. There is a trade-off here. The more you mark up your textbook, the less you will receive from the bookstore when you sell it back at the end of the semester. The benefit is a better understanding of the subject matter, and the cost is the reduction in the price you receive for the resale of the text. Additionally, if you want a text that you can mark with your own notations, you will have to buy a new one or a used one that has no markings. Both carry a higher price tag than a used textbook with markings.

The Benefits of Marking

Marking is helpful because it enables you to become an *active* participant in the mastery of the material. Researchers have shown that the physical act of marking, just like the physical act of outlining, helps you better retain the material. The better the material is organized in your mind, the more you will remember. There are two types of readers—passive and active. The active reader outlines and/or marks. Active readers typically do better on exams. Perhaps one of the reasons that active readers retain more is because the physical act of outlining and/or marking requires greater concentration. It is through greater concentration that more is remembered.

Different Ways of Marking

The most commonly used form of marking is to underline important points. The second most commonly used method is to use a felt-tipped highlighter or marker, in yellow or some other transparent color. Marking also includes circling, numbering, using arrows, making brief notes, and any other method that allows you to locate things when you go back to skim the pages in your textbook prior to an exam—or when creating your outline, if you mark your text first and then outline it.

Points to Remember When Marking

Here are two important points to remember when marking your text:

1. *Read the entire section before you begin marking.* You cannot mark a section until you know what is important, and you cannot know what is important until you read the whole section.

2. *Do not mark too extensively.* You should mark your text selectively. If you fill up each page with arrows, asterisks, circles, and underlines, marking will be of little use. When you go back to review the material, you will not be able to find what was important. The key is *selective* activity. Mark each page in a way that allows you to see the most important points at a glance.

Memory Devices

During the course of your study of *Paralegal Today,* Fourth Edition, you will encounter numerous legal terms that will most likely be new to you. Your challenge will be to remember these terms and incorporate them into your own "working" vocabulary. You will also need to remember legal concepts and principles. We look here at some techniques for learning and retaining legal terms and concepts.

Flash Cards

Using flash cards is a remarkably effective method of learning new terms or concepts. Through sheer repetition, or drilling, flash cards force you to recall certain ideas and repeat them. Although published flash cards are available in many bookstores, you should try to create your own by writing terms or concepts on index cards. Write the key term or concept on one side and the definition, process, or description on the other side.

There are several advantages to creating your own flash cards. First, the exercise of writing the information will help you insert the term into your permanent memory. Second, you do not need flash cards for terms that you already know or that you will not need to know for your particular course. Third, you can phrase the answer in a meaningful way, with unique cues that are designed just for your purposes. This personalizes the flash card, making the information easier to remember. Finally, you can modify the definition, if need be, so that it matches more closely the particular definition preferred by your instructor.

It is helpful to create your flash cards consistently and routinely at a given point in the learning process. One good moment is when you are reading or outlining your text. Make a flash card for each term in colored type and write the margin definition on the flash card.

Take your flash cards with you everywhere. Review them at lunch, while you wait in line, or when you ride on the bus. When a flash card contains a term that is difficult to pronounce, say the term aloud, if possible, as often as you can. When you have a term memorized, set that card aside but save it as an exam-review device for later in the term. Prepare new cards as you cover new terms or concepts in class.

Mnemonics

One method that students commonly employ to remember legal concepts and principles is the use of mnemonic (pronounced "nee-*mahn*-ick") devices. Mnemonic devices are merely aids to memory. A mnemonic device can be a word, a formula, or a rhyme. As an aid to remembering the elements of a cause of action in negligence (see Chapter 7), for example, you might use the mnemonic ABCD, in which the letters represent the following concepts:

A represents "A duty of care."
B represents "Breach of the duty of care."
C represents "Causation (the breach must cause an injury)."
D represents "Damage (injury or harm)."

Similarly, to remember the basic activities that paralegals may not legally undertake (see Chapter 3), you might use the mnemonic FACt, in which the letters represent the following concepts:

F represents "fees"—paralegals may not set legal fees.
A represents "advice"—paralegals may not give legal advice.
Ct represents "court"—paralegals, with some exceptions, may not represent clients in court.

Whenever you want to memorize various components of a legal doctrine or concept, consider devising a mnemonic. Mnemonics need not make sense in themselves. The point is, if they help you remember something, then use them. Any association you can make with a difficult term to help you pronounce it, spell it, or define it more easily is a useful learning tool.

Identify What You Do Not Understand

One of the most important things you can do prior to class is clarify in your mind which terms, concepts, or procedures you *do not* understand. You can do this when marking your text by placing check marks or question marks by material that you find difficult to comprehend. Similarly, you can include queries in your outline. For example, in the sample partial outline of contracts presented earlier in this introduction, you might add a query following the subsection on acceptance that reads, "What is considered to be a 'reasonable time'"?

Once you have outlined and marked your text, go back to any problem areas that you have encountered and *think about them*. You will find that it is very exciting to figure out difficult material on your own. If you still do not understand a concept thoroughly, make a note to follow up on this topic later in the classroom. Perhaps the instructor's lecture will clarify the issue. If not, make a point of asking for clarification.

As a paralegal, you may be frequently asked to undertake preliminary investigations of legal claims. Identifying what facts are *not known* is the starting point for any investigation and focuses investigatory efforts. As a student, you might think about class time as an opportunity to "investigate" further the subject matter of your course. Identifying before class what you do not know about a topic allows you to focus your "investigative" efforts, particularly your listening efforts, during class and to maximize classroom opportunities for learning.

LEARNING IN THE CLASSROOM

The classroom is the heart of your learning experience as a paralegal student. Each instructor develops an overall plan for a course that includes many elements, which are integrated, or brought together, during class sessions. A major element in your instructor's course plan will be, of course, the material presented in your textbook, *Paralegal Today,* Fourth Edition. As discussed in the preceding section, reading your textbook assignments thoroughly before class is one way to enhance your chances of truly mastering the subject matter of the course. Equally important to this goal, though, are listening carefully to your instructor and taking good notes.

Be an Active Listener

The ability to listen actively is a learned skill and one that will benefit you throughout your career as a paralegal. When your supervising attorney gives instructions, for example, it is crucial that you understand those instructions clearly. If you do not, you will need to ask the attorney to further clarify the instructions until you know exactly what your assignment is. Similarly, when you are interviewing clients or witnesses, you will need to be constantly interacting, mentally, with the information the client or witness is giving you so that you can follow up, immediately if necessary, on that information with further questions or actions.

As a paralegal student, you can practice listening skills in the classroom that you will need to exercise later on the job. The more immediate benefit of listening actively is, of course, a better chance of obtaining an excellent course grade.

In a nutshell, active listening as a student requires you to do the following:

1. *Listen attentively.* For anything to be communicated verbally by one person to another, the listener has to pay attention. Otherwise, no communication will take place. If you find your attention wandering in the classroom, make a conscious effort to become alert and focus on what is being said.

2. *Mentally interact with what is being said.* Active listening involves mentally "acting" on the information being conveyed by the speaker (your instructor). For example, if your instructor is discussing the elements required for a cause of action in negligence, you do not want simply to write down, word for word, what the instructor is saying. Rather, you first make sure that you *understand* the meaning of what is being said. This requires you to think about what is being said in the context of what else you know about the topic. Does the information make sense within that context? Does what you are hearing raise further questions in your mind? If so, make a note of them.

3. *Ask for clarification.* If you do not understand what the instructor is saying or if something is confusing, ask for clarification. How you do this will depend to some extent on the size of your class and the degree of classroom formality. In some classes, you might feel comfortable raising your hand and questioning the instructor at that point during the lecture or discussion. In other classes, you might make a note to talk to the instructor about the topic after class or later, during the instructor's office hours.

Take Good Notes

The ability to take good notes is another skill that will help you excel both in your paralegal studies and on the job as a paralegal. Ideally, you will understand clearly everything that is being said in the classroom, and note taking will simply consist of jotting down, in your own words, brief phrases and sentences to remind you of what was stated. Often, however, you may not understand fully what the instructor is talking about, or the class period may be half over before it becomes clear to you where your instructor is going with a certain idea or topic. In the meantime, should you take notes?

The best answer to this question is, of course, "Ask for clarification." But in some situations, interrupting a lecturer may be awkward or perceived as discourteous. In these circumstances, the wiser choice might be to take notes. Write down, to the extent possible, what the instructor is saying, including brief summaries of any examples the instructor is presenting. Later, when you have more knowledge of the subject, what the instructor said during that period may fall into place. If not, find an opportunity to ask for clarification.

Two other suggestions for taking good notes and making effective use of them are the following: (1) develop and use a shorthand system and (2) review and summarize your notes as soon as possible after class.

Develop and Use a Shorthand System

There may be times during a lecture when you want to take extensive notes. For example, your instructor may be discussing a hypothetical scenario to illustrate a legal concept. Because you know that hypothetical examples are very useful in understanding (and later reviewing) legal concepts, you want to include a description of the hypothetical example in your notes. Using abbreviations and symbols can help you include more information in your notes in less time.

In taking notes of a hypothetical example, consider using a single letter to represent each person or entity involved in the example. This eliminates the need to write and rewrite the names as they are used. For example, if a hypothetical involves three business firms, you could designate each firm by a letter: *A* could stand for Abel Electronics, *B* for Brentwood Manufacturing, and *C* for Crandall Industries.

Certain symbols and abbreviations, including those listed below, are fairly widely used as a kind of "shorthand" by legal professionals and others to designate certain concepts, parties, or procedures:

Δ or **D**	defendant
π or **P**	plaintiff
≈	similar to
≠	not equal to, not the same as
[	therefore
a/k/a	also known as
atty	attorney
b/c or **b/cz**	because
b/p	burden of proof
cert	*certiorari*
dely	delivery
dep	deposition
disc	discovery
JML	judgment as a matter of law
JNOV	judgment *non obstante veredicto* (notwithstanding the verdict)
JOP	judgment on the pleadings
juris or **jx**	jurisdiction
K	contract
mtg	mortgage
n/a	not applicable
neg	negligence
PL	paralegal
Q	as a consequence, consequently

re	regarding
§ or sec	section
s/b	should be
S/F	Statute of Frauds
S/L	statute of limitations

You will want to expand on this short list by creating and using other symbols or abbreviations. Once you develop a workable shorthand system, routinely use it in the classroom and then carry it over to your job. Most firms or corporations you will work for will also commonly use symbols and abbreviations, which you can add to your shorthand system later. It may also be helpful to become familiar with proofing symbols, which are listed under "proofreading" in the dictionary.

Review and Revise Your Notes after Each Class

An excellent habit to form is reviewing and revising your class notes as soon as possible after the class period ends. Often, at the moment you write certain notes, you are not sure of how they fit in the overall design of the lecture. After class, however, you usually have a better perspective and know how the "pieces of the puzzle" fit together. Reviewing and summarizing your notes while the topic is still fresh in your mind—at the end of each day, for example— gives you the opportunity to reorganize them in a logical manner.

Consider typing up your notes using any available computer. That way, when you want to review them, you will be able to read them quickly. Using a basic outline format when typing your notes (or rewriting them, if you didn't have a computer available when needed) will be particularly helpful later. You can understand at a glance the logical relationships between the various statements made in class.

Although reviewing and summarizing your notes each day or at other frequent intervals may seem overly time consuming, in the long run it pays off. First, as with outlining and marking a text, reviewing your notes after class allows you to learn actively—you can think about what was covered during the class period, place various concepts in perspective, and decide what you do or do not understand after you complete your review. Second, you have probably already learned that memory is fickle. Even though we think we will not forget something we learned, in fact we often do. When preparing for an exam, for example, you will want to remember what the instructor said in class about a particular topic. But, if you are like most people, your memory of that day and that class period may be rather fuzzy several weeks later. If you have taken good notes and summarized them legibly and logically, you will be able to review the topic quickly and effectively.

Networking in the Classroom

Several times in *Paralegal Today*, Fourth Edition, the authors, the featured guests, and the paralegals profiled mention the importance of networking. The best time to begin networking is in the classroom. Consciously make an effort to get to know your instructor. Let him or her come to know you and your interests. Later, when looking for a job, you may want to ask that instructor for a reference.

Similarly, make an effort to become acquainted with other students in your class. Compared with students who are taking other college courses, such as math and history, those of you in paralegal studies are more likely to be working in the same geographic area and may eventually belong to the same paralegal associations. Establishing connections with your classmates now may lead to networking possibilities later on the job; this offers many benefits for paralegals. One good way to establish long-term relationships with other students is by forming a study group.

Forming and Organizing a Study Group

Many paralegal students join together in study groups to exchange ideas, to share the task of outlining subjects, to prepare for examinations, and to lend support to each other generally. If you want to start a study group, a good way to find potential members is to observe your classmates and decide which students participate actively and frequently in class. Then approach those individuals with your idea of forming a study group. The number of participants in a study group can vary. Ordinarily, three to five members are sufficient for a good discussion. Including more than six members may defeat the goal of having each member actively participate, to the greatest extent possible, in group discussions.

Some paralegal students form study groups that meet on an "as needed" basis. For example, any member can call a meeting when there is an upcoming exam or difficult subject matter to be learned. Other students establish ongoing study groups that meet throughout the year (and sometimes for the entire paralegal program). The group works as a team and as such is an excellent preparatory device for working as part of a legal team in a law firm. Study groups can also continue on after course work is completed to prepare for certification exams. These groups also provide a great way to build relationships with other future paralegals with whom you may want to network later on the job.

Meeting Times and Places

It is helpful to set up a regular meeting time and hold that time sacred. The members must be committed to the meeting times and to completing their assignments, or the group will not serve its purpose. Study groups can meet anywhere. You might meet in a classroom, another school room, a member's home, a park, or a restaurant. Many paralegal schools and colleges have multipurpose rooms or study areas available to students who wish to meet in small groups. Some rooms are equipped with easels or drawing boards, which facilitate discussions. Audiovisual equipment may also be available for the group's use, such as a television with a DVD player for viewing recorded lectures. The group should select a meeting place that has limited distractions and sufficient space to accommodate each member's opened books, notes, and other materials.

Work Allocation

Teamwork is very important in the paralegal profession. Study groups can help you learn to function as a member of a team by distributing the workload among the group. Tasks (such as outlining chapters) should be allocated among the group members. It is important to define clearly who will be doing what work. It may be a good idea at the close of each meeting to have each member state out loud what tasks he or she will be responsible for completing prior to the next meeting. Whatever work one member does, he or she should make copies to distribute to the other members at the meeting.

Evaluating Your Group

You should realize from the outset that your study group will be of little help if you are doing most of the work. You need to make sure that everyone who joins the group is as committed to learning the material as you are and that you make this concern known to the others. The teamwork approach is only effective if everybody does his or her share. Teamwork involves trust and reliance. If you cannot trust one of the members to form an accurate outline of a topic, you will not be able to rely on that outline. You will end up doing the work yourself, just as a precaution. Therefore, be very selective about whom you invite to join the group. If you join an already existing group, leave it if it turns out to be a waste of your time.

ORGANIZING YOUR WORK PRODUCT

A part of the learning experience takes place through special homework assignments, research projects, and possibly study-group meetings. For example, if you are studying pretrial litigation procedures, you will read about these procedures in Chapter 13 of *Paralegal Today,* Fourth Edition. Your instructor will also likely devote class time to a discussion of these procedures. Additionally, you may be asked to create a sample complaint or to check your state's rules governing the filing of complaints in state courts. You also might have notes on a study-group discussion of these procedures.

How can you best organize all the materials generated during the coverage of a given topic? Here are a few suggestions that you might find useful. If you follow these suggestions, you will find that reviewing the information before exams is relatively easy—most of the work will already have been done.

Consider Using a Three-Ring Binder

An excellent way to integrate what you have learned is by using a three-ring binder and divider sheets with tabs for the different topics you cover. As you begin studying *Paralegal Today,* Fourth Edition, for example, consider having a different section in your binder for each chapter. Within that section, you can place your chapter outline (formed while reading the text), notes taken in the classroom or during other reading assignments, samples of projects you have done relating to topics in that chapter, and so on.

Integrate Your Notes into One Document, If Possible

If you have used a computer to key in your chapter outlines and class notes, consider incorporating everything you have learned about a topic into one document—a master, detailed outline of the topic. You can do this relatively easily by using the "cut and paste" feature of word-processing programs. The result will be a comprehensive outline of a particular topic that will make reviewing the topic prior to an exam (and perhaps later, on the job) a simple matter.

THE BENEFITS OF USING A COMPUTER

Many of the paralegals profiled in *Paralegal Today,* Fourth Edition, mention the importance of computer skills. If you do not already have a personal computer, consider acquiring one, if possible. Alternatively, see if you can arrange with someone else to use his or her personal computer on a routine basis. If your school or college has computers available in the library or some other place for student use, you might use one of those computers. Find out when there is usually a computer available—such as early in the morning—and use the computer routinely at this time.

Using a computer provides many benefits. First, you can practice your keyboarding and word-processing skills (essential paralegal skills) simultaneously as you take notes or work on research or other class projects. Second, if you have a computer available, you can type up and better organize your notes. Such time is well spent because it not only increases your knowledge of the topics but also makes it easy to review what you have learned prior to exams.

Finally, a key benefit of using a computer is the quality of any work product or homework assignment that you submit to your instructor. The editing and formatting features of word-processing programs allow you to correct misspelled words, reorganize your presentation, and generally revise your document with little effort. The spell-checker and grammar-checker features help you avoid glaring errors. The formatting features allow you to present your document in an attractive format. You can change margins and use different fonts (such as italics or boldface) to emphasize certain words or phrases.

As a paralegal, you will be using a computer and a word-processing program to generate your work. You will also be expected to know how to use computers to create quality work products. The more you can learn about computers and word processing as a student, the easier it will be for you to perform your job as a paralegal.

GOING ONLINE

Another benefit of using a computer is, of course, the ability to go online—that is, connect to the Internet—and access the vast resources available on that worldwide computer network. In Chapter 18 of *Paralegal Today,* Fourth Edition, you will learn how the Internet can be used by legal professionals to obtain information on a variety of topics. Most colleges and universities offer free Internet access to their students. If you do not have a personal computer, check with your library to see if you can go online using one of the computers the library makes available to students.

You can obtain information online about most of the topics covered in this text. To help you learn how to find and evaluate specific online information, every chapter in this book ends with one or more Internet exercises in a section titled *Using Internet Resources.* Additionally, we have provided Internet addresses for numerous Web sites in the margins of the pages. If you go to these Web sites, you will find additional information about the topic being discussed in the text. In the *Technology and Today's Paralegal* features throughout this text, we have provided other Web sites when appropriate, and Chapter 18 ("Computer-Assisted Legal Research") contains numerous references to specific Web sites that offer useful information for paralegals and other legal professionals.

Realize that Internet sites tend to come and go, and there is no guarantee that a site referred to in this text will be there by the time this book is in print. We have tried, though, to include sites that so far have proved to be fairly stable. If you do have difficulty reaching a site (that is, if your destination is "Not Found" or has "No DNS Entry"), do not immediately assume that the site does not exist. First, recheck the Web site address (uniform resource locator, or URL) shown in your browser. Remember you have to type the URL exactly as written: uppercase and lowercase are sometimes important. If it appears that the URL has been keyed in correctly, then try the following technique: delete all of the information to the right of the forward slash that is farthest to the right, and press "Enter."

For example, suppose that you have tried unsuccessfully to access the University of Washington's Internet Legal Resources at the following Web site: **http://lib.law.washington. edu/research/research.html**. First, check the URL as you keyed it in to make sure it is correct. Then delete the final "research.html" from the URL, and press "Enter." If you still have problems, delete "research," which is now the term farthest to the right. Eventually, you will get back to the home page and can attempt to locate the information you are looking for from there. If the home page is no longer functioning, you can try using the search function on your browser (enter "University of Washington Internet Legal Resources") to determine if the site still exists.

PREPARING FOR EXAMS

Being prepared for exams is crucial to doing well as a paralegal student. If you have followed the study tips and suggestions given in the preceding pages of this introduction, you will have little problem preparing for an exam. You will have at your fingertips detailed outlines of the topics covered, a marked textbook that allows you to review major concepts quickly and easily, and class notes. If you have integrated your outlines and class notes in one comprehensive, detailed outline, you will have an even easier task when it comes time to prepare for an examination.

In addition to mastering the material in *Paralegal Today,* Fourth Edition, and in the classroom, if you want to do well on an exam you should develop an exam-taking strategy. For example, prior to any exam, you should find answers to the following questions:

- What type of exam are you going to take—essay, objective, or both?
- What reading materials and lectures will be covered on the exam?
- What materials should you bring to the exam? Will you need paper to write on, or will paper be provided?
- Will you be allowed to refer to your text or notes during the exam (as in an open-book exam)?
- Will the exam be computerized? If so, you will probably need to bring several number 2 pencils to the exam.
- How much time will be allowed for the exam?

The more you can find out in advance about an exam, the better you can prepare for it. For example, suppose you learn that there will be an essay question on the exam. One way to prepare for the question is to practice writing timed essays. In other words, find out in advance how much time you will have for each essay question—say, fifteen minutes—and then practice writing an answer to a sample essay question during a fifteen-minute time period. This is the only way you will develop the skills needed to pace yourself for an essay exam. Because most essay exams are "closed book," do your timed essay practice without using the book.

Usually, you can anticipate certain essay exam questions. You do this by going over the major concept headings in your lecture notes and in your text. Search for the themes that tie the materials together, and then think about questions that your instructor might ask you. You might even list possible essay questions as a review device. Then write a short outline for each of the questions that will most likely be asked. Some instructors give their students a list of questions from which the essay questions on the exam will be drawn. This gives you an opportunity to prepare answers for each of the questions in advance. Even though you cannot take your sample essays to class and copy them there, you will have organized the material in your mind.

TAKING EXAMS

While taking exams, you can employ several strategies to improve your grade, including those discussed below.

Following Instructions

Students are often in such a hurry to start an exam that they take little time to read the instructions. The instructions can be critical, however. In a multiple-choice exam, for example, if there is no indication that there is a penalty for guessing, then you should never leave a question unanswered. Even if there are only a few minutes remaining at the end of the exam, you should guess at the answers for those questions about which you are uncertain.

You also need to make sure that you are following the specific procedures required for the exam. Some exams require that you use a number 2 lead pencil to fill in the dots on a machine-graded answer sheet. Other exams require underlining or circling. In short, read the instructions carefully.

Finally, check to make sure that you have all the pages of the examination. If you are uncertain, ask the instructor or the exam proctor. It is hard to justify not having done your exam correctly because you failed to answer all of the questions. Simply stating that you did not have them will pose a problem for both you and your instructor. Do not take a chance. Double-check to make sure.

Use Exam Time Effectively

Examinations are often timed. Timed examinations require that a question or cluster of questions be answered within a specified period of time. If you must complete thirty multiple-choice questions in one hour, then you have two minutes to work on each question. If you finish fifteen of those questions in one minute instead of two, then you will have banked fifteen minutes that can be spent elsewhere on the examination or used to double-check your answers.

Consider the following example. Assume that you have ninety minutes for the entire exam—thirty minutes to answer the multiple-choice questions, fifteen minutes to answer the true-false questions, and forty-five minutes to answer a long essay question. If you can shave ten minutes off the time it takes to answer the multiple-choice section and five minutes off the time it takes to answer the true-false questions, you will have fifteen additional minutes to complete the long essay question.

Taking Objective Examinations

The most important point to discover initially with any objective test is whether there is a penalty for guessing. If there is none, you have nothing to lose by guessing. In contrast, if a point or portion of a point will be subtracted for each incorrect answer, then you probably should not answer any question purely through guesswork.

Students usually commit one of two errors when they read objective-exam questions: (1) they read things into the questions that do not exist, or (2) they skip over certain words or phrases.

Most test questions include key words such as:

- all
- always
- never
- only

If you miss these key words, you will be missing the "trick" part of the question. Also, you must look for questions that are only *partly* correct, particularly if you are answering true-false questions.

Never answer a multiple-choice question without reading all of the alternatives. More than one of them may appear at first glance to be correct. If several answers seem correct, make sure you select the one that seems the *most* correct.

Whenever the answer to an objective question is not obvious, start with the process of elimination. Throw out the answers that are clearly incorrect. Even when there is a penalty for guessing, if you can throw out several obviously incorrect answers, you may wish to guess by choosing among the remaining ones because your probability of choosing the correct answer is relatively high. Typically, the easiest way to eliminate incorrect answers is to look for those that are meaningless, illogical, or inconsistent. Often, test authors put in choices that make perfect sense and are indeed true but are not the answer to the question you are to answer.

Writing Essay Exams

As with objective exams, you need to read the directions to the essay questions carefully. It is best to write out a brief outline *before* you start answering the question. The outline should present your conclusion in one or two sentences, then your supporting argument. You should take care not to include in your essay information that is irrelevant, even if you think it is interesting. It is important to stay on the subject. We can tell you from firsthand experience that no instructor likes to read answers to unasked questions.

Finally, write as legibly as possible. Instructors will find it easier to be favorably inclined toward your essay if they do not have to reread it several times to decipher the handwriting.

THE PARALEGAL PROFESSION

TODAY'S PROFESSIONAL PARALEGAL

1

CHAPTER OUTLINE

AFTER COMPLETING THIS CHAPTER, YOU WILL KNOW:

► What a paralegal is.

► What kinds of tasks paralegals perform.

► The names of some of the professional associations of paralegals.

► What kinds of education and training are available to paralegals.

► Whether paralegals must be certified or licensed.

► Some skills and attributes of the professional paralegal.

INTRODUCTION

If you are considering a career as a paralegal, be prepared to be part of an exciting and growing profession. In an effort to cut the cost of legal services to clients, law firms are giving more and more responsibilities to paralegals. The opportunities for paralegals who want to work outside of law firms (in corporations or government agencies, for example) are also expanding dramatically. Despite a short recession in 2001–2002, the paralegal profession has continued to grow in recent years. At the same time, the average paralegal salary has increased. In fact, according to one survey, paralegals in 2005 enjoyed one of the largest increases in over ten years (11.2 percent) and were earning an average salary of $51,078. This survey also showed that nearly three out of four paralegals feel they are paid fairly.[1]

How do you know if you want to become part of this dynamic profession? The first step in finding out if this is the right career for you is to become familiar with what a paralegal is, what kinds of work paralegals do, and what education and skills are needed. These are the topics we cover in this first chapter. In Chapter 2, you will learn about where paralegals work, how much they earn, and how they got their jobs. As you read through each of the chapters in this book, remember that this is only an introduction to the profession and the starting point of your education. You should supplement what you learn in the classroom by talking and networking with paralegals who work in various professional environments. After all, in today's competitive job market, whom you know can sometimes be as important as what you know in getting the job you desire.

WHAT IS A PARALEGAL?

For years, the issue of how, exactly, the term *paralegal* should be defined has been debated. This debate probably stems from the fact that paralegals perform such a wide variety of duties that it is difficult to come up with a "one-size-fits-all" definition. Adding to the problem is the use of two different labels—*paralegal* and *legal assistant*—to describe essentially the same job or person. These different labels often confuse the public and have fueled debates within the profession as well.

In this book, we use the terms *paralegal* and *legal assistant* interchangeably, as is often done in the legal community. Although some individuals or groups may prefer one label to another, such disagreement does not mean that the labels describe different job duties. Indeed, some persons who are trained professional paralegals may be called something else entirely at their workplace, such as *legal technician* or *legal research specialist*.

After years of disagreement, two of the major organizations involved have finally reached a consensus on the definition of paralegal. The **American Bar Association (ABA)**, which is a national association for attorneys, and the **National Association of Legal Assistants (NALA)**, which is the largest national organization of paralegals, now jointly agree to the following definition:

> A **legal assistant** or **paralegal** is a person qualified by education, training, or work experience who is employed or retained by a lawyer, law office, corporation, governmental agency or other entity who performs specifically delegated substantive legal work, for which a lawyer is responsible.

The **National Federation of Paralegal Associations (NFPA)**, which is the second largest paralegal association, prefers the term *paralegal* to *legal assistant*.[2] Members of NFPA were concerned by the fact that many attorneys refer to their secretaries as legal assistants and wanted to distinguish the role of paralegals as professionals.

Regardless of what they are called, paralegals or legal assistants today perform many functions that traditionally were performed by attorneys. The paralegal's work falls somewhere between that of an attorney and that of a legal secretary. As the definition above indicates,

American Bar Association (ABA)
A voluntary national association of attorneys. The ABA plays an active role in developing educational and ethical standards for attorneys and in pursuing improvements in the administration of justice.

National Association of Legal Assistants (NALA)
One of the two largest national paralegal associations in the United States; formed in 1975. NALA is actively involved in paralegal professional development.

paralegal or legal assistant
A person qualified by education, training, or work experience who is employed or retained by a lawyer, law office, corporation, governmental agency, or other entity who performs specifically delegated substantive legal work, for which a lawyer is responsible.

National Federation of Paralegal Associations (NFPA)
One of the two largest national paralegal associations in the United States; formed in 1974. NFPA is actively involved in paralegal professional development.

On the Web

For more information on the definitions of *paralegal* and *legal assistant* given by the ABA, NALA, NFPA, and AAfPE (American Association for Paralegal Education), go to the following Web sites:

ABA: **http://www.abanet.org**
NALA: **http://www.nala.org**
NFPA: **http://www.paralegals.org**
AAfPE: **http://www.aafpe.org**

paralegals perform substantive legal work that they are trained to perform through education, experience, or (usually) both.

WHAT DO PARALEGALS DO?

Paralegals assist attorneys in many different ways. The following list is just a sampling of some of the tasks that legal assistants typically perform in a traditional setting—the law office. Keep in mind, though, that today's paralegals work in many nontraditional settings, including corporations, government agencies, courts, insurance companies, real estate firms, and virtually any other entity that uses legal services. Throughout this book, you will read about the specific tasks that paralegals perform in different settings.

A Sampling of Paralegal Tasks

Typically, legal assistants perform the following tasks:

- *Conduct client interviews and maintain general contact with clients*—provided that the client is aware of the status and function of the legal assistant and the legal assistant does not give legal advice.

- *Locate and interview witnesses*—to gather relevant facts and information about a lawsuit, for example.

- *Conduct legal investigations*—to obtain, organize, and evaluate information from a variety of sources, such as police reports, medical records, photographs, court documents, experts' reports, technical manuals, product specifications, and other statistical data.

- *Calendar and track important deadlines*—such as the date by which a certain document must be filed with the court or the date by which the attorney must respond to a settlement offer.

- *Organize and maintain client files*—to keep the multitudes of documents in each client's file readily accessible.

- *Conduct legal research*—to identify, analyze, and summarize the appropriate laws, court decisions, or regulations that apply to a client's case.

- *Draft legal documents*—such as legal correspondence, interoffice memoranda, documents to be filed with the court, contracts, wills, and mortgages.

- *Summarize witness testimony*—such as when depositions (sworn testimony) are taken of individuals out of court or when the parties have given written statements.

- *Coordinate litigation proceedings*—communicate with opposing counsel, court personnel, and other government officials; prepare all necessary documents for trial; and schedule witnesses.

- *Attend legal proceedings*—such as trials, depositions, real estate closings, executions of wills, and court or administrative hearings—with an attorney.

- *Use computers and technology*—to perform many of the above tasks.

Paralegals' Duties Vary

The specific tasks that paralegals perform vary dramatically depending on the size of the office, the kind of law that the firm practices, and the amount of experience or expertise the paralegal has. If you work in a one-attorney office, for example, you may also perform certain secretarial functions. Your tasks might range from conducting legal research and investigating the facts to photocopying documents, keying data into the computer, and answering the

Ethics Watch!

PARALEGAL EXPERTISE AND LEGAL ADVICE

Paralegals often become very knowledgeable in a specific area of the law. If you specialize in environmental law, for example, you will become very knowledgeable about environmental claims. In working with a client on a matter involving an environmental agency, you might therefore be tempted to advise the client on which type of action would be most favorable to him or her. Never do so. As will be discussed in detail in Chapter 3, only attorneys may give legal advice, and paralegals who give legal advice risk penalties for the unauthorized practice of law. Whatever legal advice is given to the client either must come directly from the attorney or, if from you, must reflect exactly (or nearly exactly) what the attorney said with no modification on your part. After consulting with your supervising attorney, for example, you can say to the client that Mr. X (the attorney) "advises that you do all that you can to settle the claim as soon as possible."

telephone while the secretary is out to lunch. If you work in a larger law firm, you usually have more support staff (secretaries, file clerks, and others) to whom you can delegate tasks. Your work may also be more specialized, and you may only work on certain types of cases. If you work in a law firm's real estate department, for example, you may deal only with legal matters relating to that area of law. (For a discussion of tasks that a paralegal might perform at a personal-injury law firm, see this chapter's *Featured Guest* feature on pages 6 and 7.)

Although paralegal duties vary, drafting legal documents, handling client relations, and conducting legal research are the tasks that paralegals report spending the most time performing.[3]

Paralegals and Technology

As technology advances, the role of many legal assistants is expanding, and they are increasingly becoming the technology experts at law firms. Because lawyers are busy with the practice of law and paralegals are often in the best position to know the firm's needs, many paralegals today take a leading role in reviewing and recommending new specialized legal software programs and online databases. In one survey conducted by *Legal Assistant Today*, 54.3 percent of paralegals polled said that they were part of the technology decision-making process.[4]

Computer use and technical knowledge have thus become invaluable to today's paralegal. Paralegals use new computer software packages for internal case management to organize client files, manage calendars, share research, record reference materials, and track the number of hours billed to clients. Attorneys and paralegals use time and billing software to manage expenses, generate bills, calculate accounts receivable, and produce financial reports. Legal databases available on the Internet or on CD-ROMs allow paralegals to perform sophisticated legal research without leaving their desks. When cases that involve many documents must be prepared for trial, litigation support software can help retrieve, categorize, and index the various materials for presentation. These technologies will be discussed in the appropriate chapters throughout this book. The point here is that technology is one of the foremost

On the Web

The Web site for the ABA's Standing Committee on Paralegals is **http://www.abanet.org/ legalservices/paralegals**. (*Note.* No Web address ever ends in a comma, period, or semicolon. Consequently, you should ignore such punctuation when it appears at the end of Web addresses cited in this book.)

THE PARALEGAL AT WORK

BIOGRAPHICAL NOTE

Sally Brown Bisson, J.D., received her bachelor of arts degree in communication and English from the University of Nebraska at Omaha in 1978 and her law degree from the University of Nebraska College of Law in 1981. She worked for a regional banking corporation and numerous nonprofit organizations before becoming a paralegal instructor in 1992. She is currently an associate professor and director of the ABA-approved paralegal studies program at the College of Saint Mary in Omaha, Nebraska, where she teaches family law, litigation, and real estate law and directs the internship program. She is also the campus pre-law adviser. In addition to her teaching responsibilities, she serves as a reviewer for several legal publishers and has been a presenter at local, state, and national paralegal conferences.

Imagine that you have just graduated from a paralegal program and are starting work at your first job at the Morris and Buckley law firm. It is a personal-injury law firm that represents plaintiffs and employs seven attorneys and two paralegals. Your supervising attorney, Melanie Buckley, will be meeting with a new client, Barbara Kaiser, and has asked you to sit in on the interview.

THE FACTS

Barbara Kaiser was employed by a local plant and garden nursery when she was injured in a car accident on April 4, 2007. On the day of the accident, she was not scheduled to work, and a severe thunderstorm occurred. The greenhouse at the nursery was damaged by the storm. Another employee called Kaiser and told her that the greenhouse was flooding and its roof was damaged. Kaiser told the employee that she would help by purchasing new roofing material and a pump to remove the water.

Kaiser drove her own car as she left the house to purchase the necessary supplies. She lost control of her vehicle near a stoplight and collided with a utility company truck that was speeding on its way to repair a power outage. Kaiser was trapped in her car and sustained serious injuries, including broken bones and a back injury. She spent several weeks in the hospital recovering from the accident.

Kaiser has been unable to work and has lost her job. It has been five months since the accident. She applied for workers' compensation benefits from the state, but they were denied because the state determined she was not working when the accident occurred. The utility company's insurance company has paid her hospital expenses but has refused to pay for continuing therapy for her back pain. Kaiser wants the law firm to advise her as to whether she can sue her former employer, the state, and/or the utility company to obtain compensation for her injuries.

THE PARALEGAL'S ROLE—CASE MANAGEMENT

One of the first things you will do is open a case file for Barbara Kaiser. Many law firms use litigation support software for this function so that the file will be easily accessible. You will need to enter contact information for the client, her employer, the driver of the utility truck,

areas of expanding paralegal responsibility, and those entering the profession should realize that technological skills will greatly enhance their marketability.

PARALEGAL EDUCATION

The first paralegals were competent legal secretaries who learned from on-the-job training how to perform more complex legal tasks given to them by the attorneys for whom they worked. No formal paralegal education programs existed until the late 1960s, when the demand for lower-cost legal services increased. Once attorneys realized that using paralegals was extremely cost-effective and benefited both the client and the firm (as you will read in the utility company, and the insurance companies that are involved in the case. You will also need to keep track of the time you spend on the case and include a description of the activities you perform for accurate billing.

Client Relations, Legal Research, and Investigation.
Paralegals generally have a great deal of contact with clients, keeping them informed about the status of their cases and answering questions. You will be expected to provide appropriate updates to the client but must be careful to ensure you are not providing legal advice. If legal advice is requested, check with your supervising attorney and then share the response with the client.

Attorney Buckley may ask you to help evaluate the viability of Kaiser's claim. You may be asked to research applicable statutes and case law and prepare a summary of your findings in a written memorandum. Your investigation of her claim could also include interviewing witnesses, obtaining copies of police and hospital records, and visiting the accident scene to take photographs. You may also be asked to verify the exact weather conditions that existed at the time of the accident. All of the information you gather during this phase of the case must be documented and included in the client's file.

Initiating the Lawsuit and Trial Preparation.
Once the attorney has determined that there is a basis for the client's claims, you may be asked to prepare the document that initiates a lawsuit, called a *complaint*. The complaint will be taken to the courthouse and then delivered or mailed to the defendants. The filing of the complaint

> *"Paralegals ... are an important part of the litigation team."*

triggers a variety of due dates in the litigation process, so it is essential that you accurately record the applicable dates in the case management system.

The next step in the litigation process is called *discovery*. During this time, the parties to the lawsuit obtain as much information as possible from each other and from outside sources to prove their case. You may be asked to draft various discovery documents and respond to requests from the defendants.

Before scheduling a trial date, attorney Buckley may try to reach an agreement with the defendant to have the defendant compensate Buckley's client without a trial. This process, called a *settlement*, is encouraged by judges to avoid unnecessary trials. You may be asked to prepare a settlement brochure that outlines your client's injuries and economic losses for presentation to the defendant's attorney.

Assisting at Trial.
If a trial is necessary, you will be responsible for contacting the client and all of your witnesses regarding the trial date and their testimony. You may also be asked to assist with the preparation of evidence that will be used at trial and to prepare a trial notebook. It will contain all of the litigation documents and can be prepared in a written or electronic format. During the trial, you may be asked to assist the attorney in the courtroom.

As you can see, your role in the litigation process is vital to the successful representation of the client's interests. Paralegals who are organized, are proficient in the use of technology, and possess strong communication skills are an important part of the litigation team.

Chapter 4), the number of paralegal education programs increased dramatically. According to the ABA's Standing Committee on Paralegals (formerly known as the ABA Standing Committee on Legal Assistants), there are now more than a thousand programs operating in the United States. A great deal of variety exists, however, in the types of programs offered and the quality of the education provided.

Educational Options

The role of higher education and formal paralegal education has become increasingly important in the growth and development of the paralegal profession. Numerous colleges, universities, and business and private schools now offer programs. Generally, paralegal education programs fall into one of five categories:

On the Web

Information on paralegal education programs is available on both the NALA and NFPA Web sites at **http://www.nala.org** and **http://www.paralegals.org**.

- Two-year community college programs, culminating in the award of an associate of arts degree or a paralegal certificate. Such programs usually require the completion of approximately 60 semester hours and include some general education requirements.
- Four-year bachelor's degree programs with a major or minor in paralegal studies. A bachelor's degree in paralegal studies usually requires the completion of about 120 semester hours, with 50 to 60 of these hours spent on general education courses. A person may select a minor field that enhances her or his desirability in the job market. Conversely, an individual who majors in another field—for example, nursing—and obtains a minor in paralegal studies will also be very marketable to potential employers.
- Certificate programs offered by private institutions, usually 3 to 18 months in length. Typically, this type of program requires only a high school diploma or the equivalent for admission.
- Postgraduate certificate programs, usually 3 to 12 months in length, culminating in the award of a paralegal certificate. These programs require that the individual already have a bachelor's degree in order to be admitted; some also require that the individual have achieved a certain grade point average.
- Master's degree programs, usually two years in length, which are offered by several universities. These programs prepare students to work as paralegals, paralegal supervisors, or law office administrators. Some master's degree programs offer specific concentrations—for example, dispute resolution or intellectual property. To be admitted to a master's degree program, an individual must already have a bachelor's degree.

Because those seeking to become paralegals have diverse educational backgrounds, capabilities, and work experience, no single type of program is best for everyone. Which program is most appropriate depends on the needs of the individual and the job market that he or she will enter.

Curriculum—A Blend of Substantive and Procedural Law

substantive law
Law that defines the rights and duties of individuals with respect to each other, as opposed to procedural law, which defines the manner in which these rights and duties are to be enforced.

A legal assistant's education includes the study of both substantive law and procedural law. Substantive law includes all laws that define, describe, regulate, and create legal rights and obligations. For example, a law prohibiting employment discrimination on the basis of age falls into the category of substantive law. Procedural law establishes the methods of enforcing the rights established by substantive law. Questions about what documents need to be filed to begin a lawsuit, when the documents should be filed, which court will hear the case, which witnesses will be called, and so on are all questions of procedural law. In brief, substantive law defines our legal rights and obligations; procedural law specifies what methods, or procedures, must be employed to enforce those rights and obligations.

procedural law
Rules that define the manner in which the rights and duties of individuals are to be enforced.

The Role of the AAfPE and ABA in Paralegal Education

American Association for Paralegal Education (AAfPE)
A national organization of paralegal educators; the AAfPE was established in 1981 to promote high standards for paralegal education.

The American Association for Paralegal Education (AAfPE) was formed in 1981 to promote high standards for paralegal education. The AAfPE and the ABA are the two major organizations responsible for developing the standards and curriculum for paralegal education programs across the nation. At present, the only state that requires a paralegal to meet certain minimum educational requirements is California.[5] Although education may not be mandated by the state, however, many employers today either require or prefer job candidates with a certain level of education. Some employers even select only graduates from well-established programs. A searchable database of schools offering paralegal programs is available at the AAfPE Web site, at **http://www.aafpe.org**, in the "Find a School" menu.

In 1974, the ABA first established a set of educational standards for paralegal training programs. Since then, the ABA guidelines have been revised several times to keep pace with changes in the paralegal profession. Paralegal schools are not required to be approved by the ABA. Rather, ABA approval is a voluntary process that gives extra credibility to the schools that successfully apply for it. Programs that meet the ABA's quality standards and that are approved by the ABA are usually referred to as **ABA-approved programs**. Of the paralegal education programs in existence today, the ABA has approved 260.

Certification

Certification refers to formal recognition by a professional group or state agency that an individual has met certain standards of proficiency specified by that group. Generally, this means passing an examination given by the organization and meeting certain requirements with respect to education and/or experience. Note that the term *certification,* as used here, does not refer to receiving a paralegal certificate. You may obtain a paralegal certificate after completing school, but you will not be considered a *certified paralegal* unless you complete the NALA, NFPA, NALS, AAPI, or state certification process. These certification programs are discussed in the following paragraphs. Currently, no state *requires* paralegals to take a certification examination. Although most employers also do not require certification, earning a voluntary certificate from a professional society or the state can offer a competitive advantage in the labor market and lead to a higher salary (see Chapter 2).

NALA and NFPA Certification

Paralegals who meet the standards set by NALA are eligible to take a two-day, comprehensive examination to become a **Certified Legal Assistant (CLA)**—or since 2004, a **Certified Paralegal (CP)** for those who prefer to use the term *paralegal.* For two decades, NALA also hosted Certified Legal Assistant Specialty (CLAS) exams at locations nationwide. In 2006, this program was replaced by the **Advanced Paralegal Certification (APC)** program. The APC program provides a series of courses composed of text lessons, slides, exercises, and interactive tests via the Internet. NALA offers APC certification to those who are already CLAs or CPs and who want to demonstrate special competence in a particular field of law.[6] Appendix G provides more detailed information on NALA certification and requirements.

Paralegals who have at least two years of work experience and who have met specific educational requirements can take the Paralegal Advanced Competency Exam (PACE) through NFPA. The PACE examination is broken down into two tests, one general and one specialized. Those who pass the examination use the designation **Registered Paralegal (RP)**. Further information on the PACE program is provided in Appendix H of this book.

Certification by Other Paralegal Organizations

NALS (the association for legal professionals)[7] offers three different certifications:

- Paralegals who have completed an accredited curriculum course or who have one year of work experience may take the basic certification exam for legal professionals.
- Paralegals who have three years of work experience or who have earned a prior certification may take the advanced certification exam for legal professionals.
- Paralegals who have five years of work experience may take an examination to obtain Professional Paralegal certification, which was developed by paralegals.

ABA-approved program
A legal or paralegal educational program that satisfies the standards for paralegal training set forth by the American Bar Association.

certification
Formal recognition by a private group or a state agency that an individual has satisfied the group's standards of proficiency, knowledge, and competence; ordinarily accomplished through the taking of an examination.

On the Web

You can learn more about the APC program at the NALA Web site at **http://www.nala.org/APC.htm**. For more information on NFPA's PACE program, go to **http://www.paralegals.org/displaycommon.cfm?an=17**.

Certified Legal Assistant (CLA) or Certified Paralegal (CP)
A legal assistant whose legal competency has been certified by the National Association of Legal Assistants (NALA) following an examination that tests the legal assistant's knowledge and skills.

Advanced Paralegal Certification (APC)
A credential awarded by the National Association of Legal Assistants to a Certified Paralegal (CP) or Certified Legal Assistant (CLA) whose competency in a legal specialty has been certified following an examination of the paralegal's knowledge and skills in the specialty area.

Registered Paralegal (RP)
A paralegal whose competency has been certified by the National Federation of Paralegal Associations (NFPA) after the paralegal's successful completion of the Paralegal Advanced Competency Exam (PACE).

NALA provides an online campus for continuing legal education (CLE) at **http://www.nalacampus.com**. For information on NFPA's online CLE offerings, go to **http://www.paralegals.org/displaycommon.cfm?an=18**.

**continuing legal
education (CLE) programs**
Courses through which attorneys and other legal professionals extend their education beyond school.

The American Alliance of Paralegals, Inc. (AAPI), also offers a certification program for paralegals who possess at least five years of work experience and have met specific educational requirements.

State Certification

Several states, including California, Florida, Louisiana, North Carolina, and Texas, have implemented voluntary, state-specific certification programs. Many more are considering implementing such programs. Generally, paralegal organizations (such as NALA and NFPA) are in favor of *voluntary* certification and oppose *mandatory* (legally required) certification or state licensing (as you will read in Chapter 3).

Continuing Legal Education

Paralegals, like attorneys, often supplement their formal education by attending **continuing legal education (CLE) programs**. CLE courses, which are offered by state bar associations and paralegal associations, often take the form of special seminars and workshops that focus on specific topics or areas of law. Such programs are a good way to learn more about a specialized area of law or keep up to date on the latest developments in the law and in technology. Many employers today encourage their paralegals to take CLE courses and often pay some or all of the costs involved.[8]

Additionally, some paralegal organizations require their members to complete a certain number of CLE hours per year as a condition of membership. Both NALA and NFPA require paralegals who are certified to take CLE courses every year in order to maintain their status. California is the only state, as yet, to require a minimum number of CLE hours from *all* individuals who work as paralegals. Paralegals in California are required to complete four CLE hours in legal ethics every three years and four CLE hours in either general law or a specialized area of law every two years.[9]

PARALEGAL SKILLS AND ATTRIBUTES

As noted earlier, paralegals today perform many tasks that lawyers used to perform. Thus, the demands on paralegals to be professional and efficient have increased. In order to be successful, a paralegal not only must possess specific legal knowledge but also should exhibit certain aptitudes and personality traits. For example, paralegals need to be able to think logically and to analyze complex issues of law and conflicting descriptions of fact. Some general characteristics that paralegals should have (or try to develop) are discussed below.

Analytical Skills

In any working environment, paralegals may be responsible for gathering and analyzing certain types of data. A corporate paralegal, for example, may be required to analyze new government regulations to see how they will affect the corporation. A paralegal working for the federal Environmental Protection Agency may be responsible for collecting and analyzing data on toxic waste disposal and drafting a memo setting forth his or her conclusions on the matter.

Legal professionals need to be able to take complex theories and fact patterns and break them down into smaller, more easily understandable components. That is how lawyers formulate arguments and judges decide cases. The process of legal analysis is critical to the paralegal's duties, especially when the paralegal is engaged in factual investigation, trial preparation, and legal research and writing. Analytical reasoning will be discussed in greater depth in Chapters 17 and 19 of this book. For now, it is important that you focus on developing a step-by-step approach to tackling each new subject or task that you encounter. Making analytical thinking a habit will improve your proficiency as a legal assistant.

REAL ESTATE PARALEGAL

Terry Prybylski is a real estate paralegal at a full-service law firm that has represented businesses and individuals since 1890, when the industrial age created a boomtown in the city of Detroit. The firm handled Detroit's incredible growth and survived and prospered during the trials of the twentieth century, including the stock market crash, two World Wars, the introduction of unions, race riots, and the onset of the information age and the explosion of technology. Today, the firm has approximately one hundred attorneys and twenty paralegals in offices located throughout Michigan. Prybylski works in the real estate group's transactional practice in downtown Detroit.

Prybylski has been a paralegal since 1992. She earned a postgraduate paralegal–legal assistant certificate from the American Institute for Paralegal Studies, Inc., and a master of business administration degree from the University of Detroit–Mercy.

Before specializing in real estate, Prybylski worked as a paralegal at a natural gas utility company and a national bank, where she was considered a "jack of all trades." At the bank, she worked in the areas of litigation and corporate, employment, banking, and regulatory law in addition to real estate law. She is a member of the State Bar of Michigan–Legal Assistants Section, Detroit Metropolitan Bar Association, and National Association of Legal Assistants (NALA) and is a notary public.

What do you like best about your work?

"What I like best about my work is the diversity of the client base and the variety of duties that I perform. I interact with developers, national banks, national and local tenants (particularly retail clients), corporate owners, individual buyers and sellers, surveyors, environmental consulting firms, title companies, and local governments. Each deal is unique, with its own specific set of circumstances, and each poses a challenge."

What is the greatest challenge that you face in your area of work?

"I am responsible for obtaining the title work, surveys, zoning letters, certificates of occupancy, corporate documents, and related due dili-

gence. It is not uncommon for a transaction to involve multiple properties located in a variety of states. It is often a challenge to coordinate the acquisition of all of the required information from the various sources in a timely manner. Time frames and closing dates do not always allow for the time desired, and it takes persistence and a great deal of organizational skill to guarantee that all of the required elements have been obtained, reviewed, and approved prior to the closing date."

What advice do you have for would-be paralegals in your area of work?

"You must recognize the important role you play in the grand scheme of things. Not all of your assignments will be glamorous, but your efforts are vital to the success of the matter. A simple mistake—such as an incorrect legal description of property, an incorrect tax parcel identification number, or failure to conform to geographical recording requirements—will result in a document's not being recorded in a timely manner. This may have serious consequences for the client. It is important to perform all job duties with professionalism. Even a mundane task, such as compiling the closing binder, must be done to the best of your ability because your work product reflects on you and your firm's reputation."

> *"Knowing how to navigate on the Internet is crucial."*

What are some tips for success as a paralegal in your area of work?

"Knowing how to navigate on the Internet is crucial. I have discovered valuable resources and obtained all sorts of useful information in a fraction of the time that more traditional methods would take to obtain the same results. Information on business entities, whom to contact for zoning approval at the county level, statutes, local surveyors, and other data are now available online. Being detail oriented and accurate is a necessity for a real estate paralegal. This comes into play in many aspects of the job, such as when reviewing surveys, title work, and legal descriptions. In any area of specialization, a good paralegal is a team player who is willing to go the distance to do whatever it takes to get the job done. Excellent verbal and written communication skills, as well as a willingness to learn and experience new challenges, will guarantee success in your profession."

Communication Skills

Good communication skills are critical to people working in the legal area. In fact, it is sometimes said that the legal profession is a "communications profession" because effective legal representation depends to a great extent on how well a legal professional can communicate with clients, witnesses, court judges and juries, opposing attorneys, and others. Poor communication can damage a case, destroy a client relationship, and harm the legal professional's reputation. Good communication, in contrast, wins cases, clients, and sometimes promotions.

Communication skills include reading skills, speaking skills, listening skills, and writing skills. We look briefly at each of these skills here. Although we focus on communication skills in the law office setting, realize that good communication skills are essential to success in any work environment.

Reading Skills

Reading skills involve more than just being able to decipher the meaning of written letters and words. Reading skills also involve understanding the *meaning* of a sentence, paragraph, section, or page. As a legal professional, you will need to be able to read and understand many different types of written materials, including statutes and court decisions. You will therefore need to become familiar with legal terminology and concepts so that you grasp the meaning of these legal writings. You will also need to develop the ability to read documents *carefully* so that you do not miss important distinctions, such as the difference in meaning that can result from the use of *and* instead of *or*.

Speaking Skills

Paralegals must also be able to speak well. In addition to using correct grammar, legal assistants need to be precise and clear in communicating ideas or facts to others. For example, when you discuss facts learned in an investigation with your supervising attorney, your oral report must communicate exactly what you found, or it could mislead the attorney. A mis-

Excellent reading skills are a plus in any profession, but they are especially important in the legal arena. As a paralegal, you must be able not only to read well but also to interpret what you are reading, whether it be a statute, a court's decision, or a contract's provisions.

(Courtesy of ®Royalty-Free/Corbis)

Developing Paralegal Skills

PROOFREADING LEGAL DOCUMENTS

Geena Northrop, a paralegal, works for a solo practitioner (a one-attorney law firm). Among her other duties, she handles a significant part of the legal writing for the attorney who owns the firm. Geena has learned that when creating a legal document, writing the document is only half the job. The rest is proofreading—and not just once. She has learned the hard way that one proofreading is simply not enough to catch every error or typo that may be in the document. Now she has adopted the motto of one of the instructors in her paralegal program: "Proof, proof, and proof again!"

Today, she has set aside some time to proofread carefully a last will and testament that she created yesterday for one of the firm's clients. Geena prints out a copy of the document for proofreading purposes, because she has learned that it is difficult to proofread a document on a computer screen. Moreover, style and formatting problems are often not as evident on even a high-resolution screen as they are on hard copy. Her first step in proofreading the document is to make sure that the document reflects all of the relevant information from her notes. Geena reviews her notes point by point from the client interview and from her later discussion with the attorney about the will and checks the document. All looks well in this respect, so she proceeds to her second step in proofreading: checking style and format. Are all of the headings in the correct size and font? Is the spacing between headings consistent? Are all of the paragraphs properly indented? She finds a couple of problems and marks her hard copy to make the appropriate changes. She then reads through the document word for word to ensure that there are no grammatical problems, spelling errors, or typos. Finally, she revises the document on her computer, prints it out, and takes it to the attorney for his review.

CHECKLIST FOR PROOFREADING LEGAL DOCUMENTS

- When you create a legal document, do not assume that one proofreading will be sufficient to catch all problems or errors that the document may contain.
- Read through the document again to make sure that the style and formatting elements are consistent throughout.
- Print out the document, and go through the contents line by line to make sure that it includes all required or relevant information.
- Finally, read through the document word for word to ensure that it is free of grammatical errors, misspelled words, and typos.

communication in this context could have serious consequences if it leads the attorney to take an action detrimental to the client's interests. Oral communication also has a nonverbal dimension—that is, we communicate our thoughts and feelings through gestures, facial expressions, and other "body language" as well as through words.

Listening Skills

Good listening skills are extremely important in the context of paralegal work. Paralegals must follow instructions meticulously. To understand the instructions that you receive, you must listen carefully. Asking follow-up questions will help you to clarify anything that you do not understand. In addition, repeating the instructions will not only ensure that you understand them but also give the attorney a chance to add anything that he or she may have forgotten to tell you initially. Listening skills are particularly important in the interviewing context. In Chapter 14, you will read in greater detail about different types of listening skills and techniques that will help you conduct effective interviews with clients or witnesses.

Technology and Today's Paralegal

PARALEGAL RESOURCES ONLINE

The Internet offers numerous resources that paralegals can use to enhance their professional skills and knowledge. Here, we look at some Web sites that can help paralegals continue their education, keep apprised of legal news, and conduct research.

PARALEGAL ASSOCIATIONS AND MAGAZINES

More than half of all paralegals are members of either the National Association of Legal Assistants (NALA) or the National Federation of Paralegal Associations (NFPA). At NALA's Web site, **http://www.nala.org**, you will find information on professional certification and continuing education programs. NALA Net also offers members updates about legislative activities, ethical issues, important cases, and current news related to the paralegal profession. NALA's magazine, *Facts and Findings*, is available online for NALA members.

NFPA, at **http://www.paralegals.org**, presents information about educational programs, offers articles about current issues within the paralegal community, and hosts a variety of listservs for members to discuss various legal topics. NFPA produces *Paralegal Reporter* magazine, with the current edition accessible online through NFPA's home page.

Similar to the magazines mentioned above, *Legal Assistant Today (LAT)* is one of the most prominent magazines dedicated to the paralegal profession. Many articles from previous issues of *LAT* are available online at **http://www.legalassistanttoday.com**.

THE AMERICAN BAR ASSOCIATION

The American Bar Association's Standing Committee on Paralegals, which reviews and approves paralegal programs nationally, provides a list of ABA-approved paralegal programs online at **http://www.abanet.org/legalservices/paralegals**. To discover what factors a lawyer may consider when employing a paralegal, click on "Information for Lawyers." This article discusses paralegal work assignments, ethical considerations, fees and compensation issues, recruitment, and education.

THE PARALEGAL GATEWAY

The Paralegal Gateway, at **http://www.paralegalgateway.com**, calls itself the place "where paralegals connect." The Paralegal Gateway offers a career center that displays winning résumés, shows examples of

Writing Skills

Finally, it is important for paralegals to have excellent writing skills. Legal assistants draft letters, memoranda, and a variety of legal documents. Letters to clients, witnesses, court clerks, and others must be clear and well organized and must follow the rules of grammar and punctuation. Legal documents must also be free of errors. Lawyers are generally scrupulously attentive to detail in their work, and they expect legal assistants to be equally so. Remember, you represent your supervising attorney when you write. You will learn more about writing skills in Chapter 19.

Computer Skills

In any workplace today, computer skills are essential. As mentioned earlier, advances in technology have transformed the way in which law firms and other organizations operate. At a minimum, you will be expected to have experience with word processing (generating and

successful interviews, and hosts a job bank. The Help Center provides legal forms, a legal dictionary, and discovery help. You will also find here the Paralegal Chat Center, legal humor, paralegal "superstars," and a list of links to other sites.

LEGAL NEWS AND RESOURCES

To keep abreast of legal news and information concerning the legal profession, you can go to **http://www.law.com**. Here, you will find daily headlines, court updates, legal surveys, a legal technology section, and a service for finding a legal expert.

Summaries of significant court decisions and legal developments that have been reported in news sources can be found through Cornell University's Legal Information Institute Web site at **http://www.law.cornell.edu**. This site also provides information on how to cite legal sources, direct access to the U.S. Constitution and U.S. legal codes, and an extensive law library. Cornell University's Web site also hosts Wex, a legal dictionary and encyclopedia, at **http://www.law.cornell.edu/wex**.

TECHNOLOGY TIP

For many paralegals, much of their work involves doing factual or legal research for their firm's clients. And research often entails extensive use of the Internet. As you begin your paralegal studies, you can begin becoming familiar with Internet resources for paralegals by exploring some of the Web sites discussed in this feature. In conducting research, however, you should realize that it is important to select credible online sources, because many information sites on the Internet are not reliable. Most Web sites have a link titled "About" or "About [company name]" that provides more information about the host of the Web site. It is often useful to analyze the URL as well. A site with ".edu" in the address is from an educational establishment in the United States, ".com" normally indicates a U.S.-based commercial establishment, and ".gov" signifies a U.S. government body. Try to use sources that provide the author's name, title, organization, and contact information. When possible, review the author's credentials, such as the author's education or experience in a field relevant to the information presented on the site. Also, be sure to note when the information was created and then decide whether it is still of value.

revising documents using a computer) and to have some data-entry skills. Realize, though, that paralegals who are well versed in computer technology will increasingly have an edge in the paralegal job market over those who are not. Already, some of the best-paying paralegal positions are held by paralegal specialists who know how to use sophisticated computer equipment and software, such as database-management systems, and how to adapt new technology to their workplace needs to improve efficiency.

We cannot stress enough that to become a successful paralegal, the best thing you can do during your paralegal training is to become as knowledgeable as possible about computer technology, including online communications. Throughout this book, you will read about how technology is being applied to all areas of legal practice. You will also learn how you can use technology, particularly the Internet, to perform various paralegal tasks and to keep up to date on the law. (See this chapter's *Technology and Today's Paralegal* feature for some online resources for paralegals.) As computer technology continues to advance, high-tech paralegals will increasingly be in demand.

Organizational Skills

Being a well-organized person is a plus for a legal assistant. Law offices are busy places. There are phone calls to be answered and returned, witnesses to get to court and on the witness stand on time, documents to be filed, and checklists and procedures to be followed. If you are able to organize files, create procedures and checklists, and keep things running smoothly, you will be doing a great service to the legal team and to clients.

If you work in a nontraditional setting, such as for a corporation or for the government, you will similarly find that good organizational skills are the key to success in your job. No matter where you work, you will need to organize files, certain types of data, and—most important—your time.

If organization comes naturally to you, you are ahead of the game. If not, now is the time to learn and practice organizational skills. You will find plenty of opportunities to do this as a paralegal student—by organizing your notebooks, devising an efficient tracking system for homework assignments, creating a study or work schedule and following it, and so on. Other suggestions for organizing your time and work, both as a student and as a paralegal on the job, are included at the beginning of this book. You will also find in any university or public library an abundance of books that offer guidelines on how to efficiently organize your work, your use of time, and your life generally.

Interpersonal Skills

The ability to communicate and interact effectively with other people is an important asset for the paralegal. Paralegals work closely with their supervising attorneys, and the capacity to cultivate a positive working relationship helps get tasks done more efficiently. Paralegals also work with legal secretaries and other support staff in the law office, with attorneys and paralegals from other firms, with court personnel, and with numerous other people. Paralegals frequently interview clients and witnesses. As you will read in Chapter 14, if you can relate well to the person whom you are interviewing, your chances of obtaining useful information are increased.

There may be times when you will have to deal with clients who are experiencing difficulties in their lives, such as a divorce or the death of a loved one. These people will need to be handled with sensitivity, tact, understanding, and courtesy. There will also be times when you will have to deal with people in your office who are under a great deal of stress or who for some other reason are demanding and less than courteous to you. You will need to know how to respond to these people in ways that promote positive working relationships.

The Ability to Keep Confidences

One of the requirements of being a paralegal is the ability to keep client information confidential. The word *requirement* is used here because being able to keep confidences is not just a desirable attribute in a paralegal, but a mandatory one. As you will read in Chapter 3, attorneys are ethically and legally obligated to keep all information relating to the representation of a client strictly confidential unless the client consents to the disclosure of the information.[10] The attorney may disclose this information only to people who are also working on behalf of the client and who therefore need to know it. Paralegals share in this duty imposed on all attorneys. If a paralegal reveals confidential client information to anyone outside the group working on the client's case, the lawyer (and the paralegal) may face legal consequences (including being sued by the client) if the client suffers harm as a result.

Keeping client information confidential means that you, as a paralegal, cannot divulge such information even to your spouse, family members, or closest friends. You should not talk about a client's case in hallways, elevators, or any areas in which others may overhear

Developing Paralegal Skills

INTERVIEWING A CLIENT

Brenda Lundquist is a paralegal in a one-attorney firm. Brenda has multiple responsibilities, including interviewing prospective divorce clients. Using a standard set of forms, Brenda meets with the prospective client and obtains information about the reasons for the divorce, finances and assets, and desired custody arrangements. This information is needed to assist the supervising attorney in determining whether to take the case. The information also will help Brenda in preparing the documents to be filed with the court should the attorney decide to represent the client. Brenda enjoys the work because she likes helping people, and often people who are getting divorced need both emotional and legal support.

CHECKLIST FOR CLIENT INTERVIEWS

- Plan the interview in advance.
- Print out forms and checklists to use during the interview.
- Introduce yourself as a paralegal or legal assistant.
- Explain the purpose of the interview to the client.
- Communicate your questions precisely.
- Listen carefully and be supportive, as necessary.
- Summarize the client's major concerns.
- Give the client a "time line" for what will happen next in the legal proceedings.

your conversation. Keeping work-related information confidential is an important part of being a responsible and reliable paralegal.

Professionalism

Paralegals should behave professionally at all times. That means you must be responsible and reliable in order to earn the respect and trust of the attorneys and clients with whom you work. It also means you must put aside any personal bias or emotion that interferes with your representation of a client or assessment of a case. Paralegals also need to be honest and assertive in letting others know what things paralegals can and cannot do (for example, they cannot give legal advice). This is particularly important because not everyone is sure what legal assistants are, and some people may have misconceptions about the role paralegals play.

As a paralegal, you will find that you are being judged not only by your actions and words but also by your appearance, demeanor, attitude, and a variety of other factors. When deadlines approach and the pace of office work becomes somewhat frantic, it can be difficult to meet the challenge of acting professionally. For example, you may have to complete a brief (a document to support an attorney's argument) and file it with the court by noon. It is 11 A.M., and you still have a considerable portion of the brief to finish. When the pressure is on, it is important to remain calm and focus on completing your task quickly and accurately to ensure quality work. If you are interrupted by a client's call or another attorney, be aware that the way you react to that interruption (your attitude and demeanor) is likely to affect whether others view you as professional. Strive to be courteous and

Today's Professional Paralegal

A WINNING COMBINATION

Susan Latham is a legal secretary for Melinda Oakwood, a real estate attorney who is a partner in the law firm of Morris, Crowther, Oakwood & Miller. The law firm is one of the largest in the state, employing over 300 attorneys, 75 paralegals, 130 secretaries, and many support staff members. Susan, who has become more of a legal assistant than a secretary to Melinda, has decided, at the age of forty, to return to the local university to obtain a paralegal degree. This way, Susan can be rewarded (in the form of higher wages) for the work that she actually does already and can seek advancement in the firm.

Susan has worked for Melinda for eleven years. She has been given increased responsibility because she has shown Melinda that she is dependable and reliable in handling her work assignments. Her work is always turned in on time, and it is always accurate.

LEARNING ON THE JOB

Susan is lucky to work for Melinda, who had been a teacher for ten years before she went to law school. Melinda instructs Susan on how to undertake new work assignments. When Susan has a new type of document to prepare at work, Melinda gives her a sample document and very good instructions. Now that Susan is studying to be a paralegal, Melinda has started giving her sample documents and copies of the laws that require those documents. Melinda also points out the differences between the class assignments and the sample documents and discusses with Susan why the differences matter from a legal perspective.

Additionally, Melinda encourages Susan to ask questions about school assignments and to take her time completing them so that when they are turned in, they are accurate. Susan has a strong sense of commitment, so she always sees a project through even if it seems to take forever.

USING PERSONAL ATTRIBUTES

Melinda is also lucky to employ Susan as her secretary and, eventually, as her paralegal. Susan has many personal attributes that help her on the job. She learns quickly and performs her work competently and efficiently. She also pays great attention to detail, which is one of the reasons Melinda encouraged Susan to get a paralegal degree. Unlike Melinda's former paralegal, who would send out letters and fail to include the documents that should have been enclosed, Susan is meticulous. And Melinda can always count on Susan to keep client information confidential.

Susan already had good computer and organizational skills when Melinda hired her. She did need to improve her analytical and listening skills, though. Susan's analytical skills are already getting better as a result of a course she is taking in legal research, which requires case analysis. Over time, Susan has learned to listen to Melinda's instructions and to ask questions when it is unclear what Melinda wants her to do.

THE RESULT: A WINNING TEAM

Melinda and Susan have developed a solid working relationship. It took time for Susan to develop some of the skills that she needed, but Melinda was a good and patient teacher. It also took time to develop a trusting relationship, but now Melinda can confidently delegate significant assignments to Susan, knowing that Susan will complete them accurately. Now that Susan is in a paralegal program, Melinda can also assign more challenging work to Susan, and Susan will eventually be promoted to paralegal status. Melinda and Susan work productively and efficiently together. They like and rely on each other and enjoy their work. Theirs is a winning combination of talents and skills.

respectful during such interruptions. Remember that it is imperative that the paralegal be detail oriented and accurate, even when working under pressure.

THE FUTURE OF THE PROFESSION

The paralegal profession is a dynamic, changing, and expanding field within the legal arena. Legal assistants continue to assume a growing range of duties in the nation's legal offices and perform many of the same tasks as lawyers. According to the U.S. Department of Labor, the number of paralegal and legal assistant positions is expected to increase by almost 30 percent between 2002 and 2012—faster than the average growth for all occupations. The Bureau of Labor Statistics projects that 57,000 new paralegal positions will have become available in the United States during this ten-year period. As suggested earlier, this growth stems from the fact that law firms and other employers with legal staffs are hiring more paralegals to lower the cost—and increase the availability and efficiency—of legal services. Those entering the profession today will find a broader range of career options than ever before. In addition, they will have the opportunity to help chart the course the profession takes in the future. The paralegal profession has become a popular career choice for many, so competition for jobs will continue, but formally trained and highly skilled paralegals will have excellent employment potential.

KEY TERMS AND CONCEPTS

ABA-approved program 9

Advanced Paralegal Certification (APC) 9

American Association for Paralegal Education (AAfPE) 8

American Bar Association (ABA) 3

certification 9

Certified Legal Assistant (CLA) 9

Certified Paralegal (CP) 9

continuing legal education (CLE) program 10

legal assistant 3

National Association of Legal Assistants (NALA) 3

National Federation of Paralegal Associations (NFPA) 3

paralegal 3

procedural law 8

Registered Paralegal (RP) 9

substantive law 8

chapter summary   Today's Professional Paralegal

What Is a Paralegal?

1. *Paralegal or legal assistant*—Many people use the terms *paralegal* and *legal assistant* interchangeably. Some persons trained as paralegals may use a different label, such as *legal technician* or *legal research specialist,* at their workplace, however. Paralegals perform many of the tasks traditionally handled by attorneys.

2. *Formal definition*—A legal assistant or paralegal is a person qualified by education, training, or work experience who is employed or retained by a lawyer, law office, corporation, governmental agency, or other entity who performs specifically delegated substantive legal work, for which a lawyer is responsible.

(Continued)

What Do Paralegals Do?

1. *Typical duties*—Legal assistants typically perform many of the following tasks: interviewing and maintaining general contact with clients and witnesses, locating and interviewing witnesses, conducting legal investigations, calendaring and tracking important deadlines, organizing and maintaining client files, conducting legal research, drafting legal documents, summarizing witness testimony, coordinating litigation proceedings, attending legal proceedings, and using computers and technology.

2. *Duties often vary*—Paralegals perform different functions depending on where they work and on their capabilities and experience. In law firms, paralegals' duties also vary according to the size of the firm and the kind of law practiced by the firm. Although their duties vary, paralegals commonly spend the bulk of their time performing document management, client relations, and research.

3. *Paralegals and technology*—Technology is the number-one area of expanding paralegal responsibility. Paralegals who are skilled in using newly available technologies to assist them in performing their duties will excel in the profession.

Paralegal Education

Higher education and paralegal education programs have become increasingly important in the growth and development of the profession.

1. *Educational options*—Colleges, universities, and private institutions now offer a wide variety of programs to train paralegals, ranging in length from three months to four years.

2. *ABA-approved programs*—Since 1974, the American Bar Association (ABA) has set educational standards for paralegal training programs. ABA-approved programs are those that meet with the ABA's approval. ABA approval is a voluntary process; paralegal programs are not required to be approved by the ABA.

3. *Certification*—The term *certification* refers to formal recognition by a professional group or state agency that an individual has met certain standards of proficiency specified by that group. Generally, this means passing an examination and meeting certain requirements with respect to education and/or experience. Paralegals may be certified by NALA, NFPA, or a state agency. Currently, no state requires paralegal certification.

4. *Continuing legal education (CLE)*—Continuing legal education courses are offered by state bar associations and paralegal associations. Such programs provide a way to learn more about a specialized area of law or keep up to date on the latest developments in law and technology.

Paralegal Skills and Attributes

Because paralegals today perform many of the tasks that lawyers used to perform, the demands on paralegals to be professional and efficient have increased. Paralegals also need to have a variety of skills. It is especially important for paralegals to have good analytical, communication, computer, organizational, and interpersonal skills and to be able to keep confidences.

QUESTIONS FOR REVIEW

1. What is a paralegal? Is there any difference between a paralegal and a legal assistant?

2. What kinds of tasks do paralegals perform?

3. What needs within the legal profession do paralegals help to meet?

4. Name the two largest national paralegal associations in the United States. What are the benefits of belonging to a paralegal association?

5. What types of educational programs and training are available to paralegals? Must a person meet specific educational requirements to work as a paralegal?

6. What role does the American Bar Association play in paralegal education?

7. What does *certification* mean? What is a CLA or a CP? What is the APC program? What does PACE stand for?

8. Name some states that have certification programs. Is state certification mandatory in those states?

9. List and describe the skills that are useful in paralegal practice. Do you have these skills?

10. List and describe some of the personal attributes of a professional paralegal. Do you feel that persons who do not have these attributes can cultivate them? If so, how?

ETHICAL QUESTIONS

1. Richard attends a six-month paralegal course and earns a certificate. In the West Coast city where he lives, certified paralegals—those with a CP or a CLA designation—are in great demand in the job market. Richard responds to a newspaper advertisement for a certified paralegal, indicating that he is one. Has Richard done anything unethical? What is the difference between a certificate and certification?

2. Paula Abrams works as a paralegal for a small law firm that specializes in tax law. Recently, Paula purchased some new tax-return software and was trained in how to use it. Last week, Paula used the software to prepare tax returns for the Benedetto family. Paula saved the forms on a disk. She then retrieved the Benedetto forms and used them for the Marshalls' tax return. Paula entered much of the Marshalls'

tax information into the computer. Mr. Marshall had not provided the children's Social Security numbers to Paula, though, so she decided to add the Social Security numbers later. In the meantime, Paula left the Benedetto children's Social Security numbers on the form.

In the tax-season rush, Paula inadvertently neglected to enter the children's Social Security numbers on the Marshalls' tax return. Several months later, the Marshalls received a letter from the Internal Revenue Service stating that their exemptions had been denied because their children's Social Security numbers had been claimed on someone else's tax return. How might this situation be resolved? What other kinds of ethical problems might result from using computer-generated forms?

PRACTICE QUESTIONS AND ASSIGNMENTS

1. Refer to Appendix F at the end of this book (or, if you have access to the Internet, go to **http://www.findlaw.com**), and find the answers to the following questions:

   a. Is there an affiliate of the National Association of Legal Assistants or the National Federation of Paralegal Associations in your city? Where is the nearest affiliate of either of these organizations located?

   b. Are there any regional or local paralegal associations in your area? If so, what are their names, street and e-mail addresses, and phone numbers?

2. Using the material on paralegal skills presented in the chapter, identify which of the following are skills that a paralegal should have, and explain why.

   a. Reading skills.   e. Math skills.
   b. Interpersonal skills.   f. Computer skills.
   c. Marketing skills.   g. Management skills
   d. Oral communication skills.

3. Which of the following personal attributes are helpful to a paralegal? Why?

   a. Insensitivity.   d. Unreliability.
   b. Commitment.   e. Objectivity.
   c. Integrity.   f. Inaccuracy.

QUESTIONS FOR CRITICAL ANALYSIS

1. Tom and Sandy are having coffee after their first paralegal class. The instructor discussed the ongoing debate within the profession about whether to use the term *paralegal* or *legal assistant*. Tom says he agrees with NFPA that the term *paralegal* is preferable because no one will confuse paralegals with legal secretaries. Sandy, who has been working as a legal secretary for the last few years, is offended by Tom's remarks. What label do you prefer—*legal assistant* or *paralegal*—and why? Is it an important issue, in your opinion?

2. Joan McMahon is meeting with an adviser at her local college to discuss the possibility of enrolling in the school's paralegal program. Joan has completed two years of college-level courses in general education, which she could transfer, but she has had no legal assistant classes. The adviser explains that there are three different degree options at the college: an associate's degree, a bachelor's degree, and a postgraduate certificate. Several for-profit business schools in the area offer certificate programs as well. How would you explain the differences in the degree and certificate options to Joan? Which options would Joan most likely favor? Why?

PROJECTS

1. Write or telephone the National Association of Legal Assistants and the National Federation of Paralegal Associations (see Appendix F for the addresses and telephone numbers of these associations). See if they have affiliates in your area. Also, see if there are any state or local paralegal organizations in your area. Contact them for membership information. Do they accept student members?

2. Arrange an interview with an experienced paralegal, such as a graduate of your program or another paralegal that you may know. Ask the paralegal what he or she thinks are the most important skills and characteristics that paralegals should have.

USING INTERNET RESOURCES

Browse through the materials on the Web sites of the National Association of Legal Assistants, or NALA (at **http://www.nala.org**), and the National Federation of Paralegal Associations, or NFPA (at **http://www.paralegals.org**). Then do the following:

1. Look closely at the benefits of membership listed by each of these organizations. How do they compare? Are there any significant differences?

2. Examine the information that is included on each site about the organization's certification program. For each program, summarize the requirements that a paralegal must meet to become certified.

3. Go to the Web site for Delmar, Cengage Learning Paralegal at **http://www.paralegal.delmar.cengage.com**. Click on "Student Center" and then on "Find State-Specific Resources and Forms" (at the bottom of the Student Center page). On the State Resources page, you will find links to relevant state-specific Web sites and to sites that furnish legal forms for individual states. Click on your state's Web links and browse through the resources available. List the Web sites you find and briefly describe the kind of information available at each site. Can you access your state's bar association? Is there a way to view any of your state's codes (laws) or judicial opinions? Does the state attorney general or secretary of state have a Web site listed?

4. Go to the NALA Web site (at **http://www.nala.org**). Roll your mouse over "General Information about NALA and the Paralegal Career Field" and then over "The Paralegal Profession." Then click on "What is a Paralegal?" Which of the following tasks might legal assistants perform, according to the information provided by NALA?

   a. Draft legal documents.
   b. Try cases in court.
   c. Locate witnesses.
   d. Give legal advice.
   e. Set legal fees.
   f. Interview clients.
   g. Perform legal investigations.

5.  For additional resources, visit our Web site at **http://www.paralegal.delmar.cengage.com**.

END NOTES

1. *Legal Assistant Today,* March/April 2006, pp. 49–50.

2. The members of NFPA voted to remove the term *legal assistant* from their definition of *paralegal* at the annual conference in May 2002. The American Association for Paralegal Education (AAfPE) took a similar position at its annual meeting in 2002.

3. This is according to a survey conducted by *Legal Assistant Today* magazine in 2004, reported in March/April 2005, p. 54.

4. This is according to a survey conducted by *Legal Assistant Today* magazine in 2003, reported in *Legal Assistant Today,* May/June 2004, p. 61.

5. California Business and Professions Code, Sections 6450–6456. Enacted in 2000.

6. California Advanced Specialist (CAS) certification is also available as a specialty exam through NALA to paralegals who possess CLA or CP certification. For more information on this state-specific NALA certification, see Appendix G.

7. Originally, *NALS* was an acronym for National Association of Legal Secretaries. The organization no longer regards the name *NALS* as an acronym and describes the association as "the association of legal professionals." For more information, go to the association's Web site at **http://www.nals.org** and select "About NALS."

8. According to a 2004 survey by *Legal Assistant Today,* 77.2 percent of employers paid at least part of the cost of continuing legal education. *Legal Assistant Today,* March/April 2005, p. 57.

9. California Business and Professions Code, Sections 6450–6456. Enacted in 2000.

10. Exceptions to the confidentiality rule are made in certain circumstances, as will be discussed in Chapter 3.

CAREER OPPORTUNITIES

CHAPTER

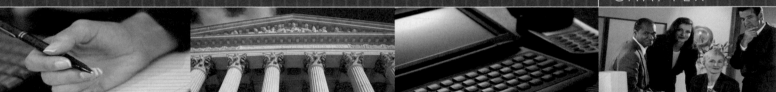

CHAPTER OUTLINE

Introduction

Where Paralegals Work

Paralegal Specialties

Paralegal Compensation

Planning Your Career

Locating Potential Employers

Reevaluating Your Career

AFTER COMPLETING THIS CHAPTER, YOU WILL KNOW:

▶ What types of firms and organizations hire paralegals.

▶ Some areas of law in which paralegals specialize.

▶ How much paralegals can expect to earn.

▶ How paralegals are compensated for overtime work.

▶ How to prepare a career plan and pursue it.

▶ How to search for an employer.

INTRODUCTION

Paralegals today enjoy a wide range of employment opportunities in both the private and the public sector. Competent paralegals are in demand in law firms because attorneys realize that the use of legal assistants enables them to provide superior legal services at a lower cost to clients. Furthermore, although the majority of legal assistants continue to work in law offices, virtually any business that uses legal services can utilize the services of persons with paralegal training. Corporations, insurance companies, banks, and real estate agencies regularly employ legal assistants. In addition, the government has created positions for paralegals at many agencies. Paralegals now work in many court systems, in county offices, and in legal-services clinics across the nation.

This chapter provides you with a starting point for planning your career. In the pages that follow, you will read about where paralegals work and what compensation paralegals receive. You will also learn about the steps you will need to follow to plan your career, locate potential employers, and find a job.

On the Web

For helpful information on all aspects of paralegal careers, go to the National Association of Legal Assistants' Web site at **http://www.nala.org** and the National Federation of Paralegal Associations' Web site at **http://www.paralegals.org**.

WHERE PARALEGALS WORK

Paralegal employers fall into a number of categories. This section describes the general characteristics of each of the major types of working environments.

Law Firms

When paralegals first established themselves within the legal community in the 1960s, they assisted lawyers in a law firm setting. Today, law firms continue to hire more paralegals than do any other organizations, and over two-thirds of all paralegals work in law firms.[1] Law firms vary in size from the small, one-attorney office to the huge "megafirm" with hundreds of attorneys. As you can see in Exhibit 2.1, the majority of paralegals work in settings that employ fewer than twenty attorneys.[2]

Working for a Small Firm

Many paralegals begin their careers working for small law practices, such as one-attorney firms or firms with just a few attorneys. To some extent, this is because small law firms simply outnumber large ones. It may also be due to geographic location. For example, a paralegal who lives in a relatively rural environment, such as a small community, may find that his or her only option is to work for a small legal practice.

On the Web

You can obtain a host of information on specific law firms by going to their Web pages. For example, go to the Web site for Wachtell, Lipton, Rosen & Katz at **http://www.wlrk.com**. (To find Web sites for law firms, check one of the legal directories discussed later in this chapter.)

NUMBER OF ATTORNEYS	PERCENTAGE OF PARALEGALS	AVERAGE COMPENSATION (salary plus bonuses)
1	14%	$44,850
2–5	30%	$45,950
6–10	16%	$45,250
11–20	14%	$46,350
21–50	13%	$49,950
51–100	6%	$53,050
Over 100	7%	$57,500

EXHIBIT 2.1

Paralegal Employment and Compensation by Size of Firm or Legal Department

The authors compiled this chart using data from a variety of sources, including NALA, *Legal Assistant Today* magazine, and the International Paralegal Management Association, or IPMA (formerly known as the Legal Assistant Management Association, or LAMA).

AVOIDING STRESS-RELATED MISTAKES

The paralegal profession can be very gratifying, but the demands can sometimes be stressful. And as everybody knows, it is easy to make mistakes when working under stress—for example, when rushing to meet deadlines. As you will learn in Chapter 3, attorneys have a duty to represent their clients competently. Errors or inaccuracies in legal documents can breach, or violate, that duty and be costly for the attorney—and for you. Because working under stress increases the chance of making a mistake, paralegals would be wise to experiment with stress-reduction strategies.

Consider a simple scenario. It is early in the afternoon, and you are in the process of filing some court documents online. The filing must be completed by the end of the day to meet the court's filing deadline. Just then, the managing partner of your firm tells you that he wants the billing statements for all of the firm's clients on his desk by the end of the day. Twenty minutes later, an associate attorney asks you to handle a complicated research assignment that she needs to have completed in three hours. You do not want to say "no" to either attorney, so you agree to do the work.

How can you avoid stressful situations such as this one? First, be candid about your workload when an attorney asks for your help. Second, prioritize your tasks. Determine (with your supervising attorney's assistance, if necessary) which project or projects should take priority over others. Third, consider asking your supervising attorney if it would be acceptable to ask another paralegal for assistance. Finally, keep in mind that simply becoming aware of how stressful situations arise is a major step in learning how to avoid them.

Working for a small firm offers many advantages to the beginning paralegal, and you should be aware of them. If the firm is a general law practice, you will have the opportunity to gain experience in many different areas of the law. You will be able to learn whether you enjoy working in one area (such as family law) more than another area (such as personal-injury law) in the event that you later decide to specialize. Some paralegals also prefer the often more personal and less formal environment of the small law office, as well as the variety of tasks and greater flexibility that frequently characterize this setting.

A characteristic of small firms that may prove challenging has to do with compensation. Small firms pay, on average, lower salaries than larger firms do. As Exhibit 2.1 on the previous page indicates, paralegal income is often related to firm size. Generally, the larger the firm, the higher the paralegal salaries. Small firms also may provide fewer employee benefits, such as pension or retirement plans.

Paralegals who work for small firms may also have less support staff to assist them. This means that if you work in a small law office, your job may involve a substantial amount of secretarial or clerical work.

Paralegals who work for large law firms often need to research statutes, court cases, or regulations in the firm's law library. Technological innovations in the past few decades, such as notebook computers and cell phones, have facilitated the ease with which paralegals can do research and communicate with attorneys, clients, and others.

(Courtesy of ©Steve Hamblin/Alamy)

Working for a Large Firm

In contrast to the (typically) more casual environment of the small law office, larger law firms usually are more formal. If you work for a larger firm, your responsibilities will probably be limited to specific, well-defined types of tasks. For example, you may work for a department that handles (or for an attorney who handles) only certain types of cases, such as real estate transactions. Office procedures and employment policies will also be more clearly defined and may be set forth in a written employment manual.

The advantages of the large firm include greater opportunities for promotions and career advancement, higher salaries and (typically) better benefits packages, more support staff for paralegals, and (often) more sophisticated computer technology and greater access to research resources.

You may view certain characteristics of large law firms as either advantages or disadvantages, depending on your personality and preferences. For example, if you favor the more specialized duties and more formal working environment of the large law firm, then you will view these characteristics as advantages. If you prefer to handle a greater variety of tasks and enjoy the more personal, informal atmosphere of the small law office, then you might view the specialization and formality of the large law firm as disadvantages.

Corporations and Other Business Organizations

As we've already mentioned, many paralegals work in business environments outside of law firms. Some of these businesses (such as insurance companies and banks) engage in activities that are highly regulated by government. Others (such as title insurance companies, law book publishers, legal-software companies, and law schools) are in some way related to the practice of law. In addition, a vast number of businesses that need legal assistance hire paralegals.

An increasing number of paralegals work for corporate legal departments. Most major corporations hire in-house attorneys to handle corporate legal affairs. Some extremely large corporations have hundreds of attorneys on their payrolls. Legal assistants who are employed by corporations ordinarily work under the supervision of in-house attorneys.

Developing Paralegal Skills

FINDING GOVERNMENT INFORMATION ONLINE

Sandy Benson has worked as a paralegal for a small law firm for several months. Her duties range from secretarial assistance to sophisticated legal research and legal writing. One day, she and her supervising attorney, John Allen, were discussing compensation issues, and Sandy mentioned the U.S. Department of Labor's 2004 FairPay rule. John knew that the rule had been issued to clarify the overtime-pay requirements under the Fair Labor Standards Act, but he had not looked closely at the rule. He asked Sandy to find out for him specifically what the rule said with respect to overtime pay for paralegals.

Sandy knew that she could quickly find this information on the Web without even consulting the URLs in a binder that she kept close at hand. She simply accessed **http://www.firstgov.gov**, the gateway to all federal government Web sites. She then selected the link to "Federal Executive," which took her to a page listing links for all of the cabinet departments. She clicked on the link to the Department of Labor and, reaching the home page for the department, accessed "wages" and then "overtime pay." Following further links to the FairPay rule, she found exactly the information she sought. She printed out the relevant pages and took them to John. All this took her less than five minutes. John was impressed and told her, "No wonder they call you a wizard!"

TIPS FOR ONLINE RESEARCH

- Keep close at hand a binder or notebook in which you list the URLs to frequently accessed Web sites.
- Keep in mind that **http://www.firstgov.gov** is a good starting point for locating and researching any government-issued materials.
- Memorize URLs for Web sites that you frequently use in your work if they are easy to remember.
- Always remember that the more quickly you can find information online, the more your employers will value your services—because you save valuable time.

Paralegals in a corporation perform a variety of functions, such as organizing corporate meetings and maintaining the necessary records, drafting employee contracts and benefit plans, and preparing financial and other reports for the corporation. Paralegals often are responsible for monitoring and reviewing government regulations to ensure that the corporation is operating within the law. When the corporation is involved in a lawsuit, paralegals may be assigned additional duties related to that lawsuit. (For more information on the duties of corporate paralegals, see Chapter 11.)

Nearly one-fifth of all paralegals now work in corporate environments. Paralegals who are employed by corporations frequently receive higher salaries than those working for law firms. In addition, paralegals who are employed by corporations normally work more regular hours and experience less stress than paralegals who work for law firms. For example, unlike the situation in law firms, in the corporate environment paralegals are not required to generate a specific number of "billable hours" per year (hours billed to clients for paralegal services performed, discussed in Chapter 4), because there are no clients to bill—the corporation is the client.

Government

Paralegals employed by government agencies work in various settings and often specialize in one aspect of the law.

Administrative Agencies

Most paralegals who work for the government work for administrative agencies, such as the federal Environmental Protection Agency or a state environmental resources department. Paralegals who work for government agencies may conduct legal research and analysis, investigate welfare eligibility and claims or disability claims, examine documents (such as loan applications), and engage in many other types of tasks. Within the federal government, the U.S. Department of Justice employs the largest number of paralegals, followed by the Social Security Administration and the Department of the Treasury. Your best source of information about employment positions in a particular administrative agency is the agency itself. You can find the names and telephone numbers of federal agencies, as well as a description of their functions, in the *United States Government Manual,* available in your public or college library.

Paralegals who work for government agencies normally work regular hours, tend to work fewer total hours per year (have more vacation time) than paralegals in other environments, and, like paralegals who work for corporations, do not have to worry about billable hours. Additionally, paralegals who work for the government usually enjoy comprehensive employment benefits. Salaries, however, are sometimes lower than those offered by traditional law firms and other employers in the private sector.

On the Web

You can locate information on government agencies at numerous Web sites, including that of FindLaw at **http://www.findlaw.com**.

Legislative Offices

Legislators in the U.S. Congress and in several state legislatures typically have staff members to help them with their various duties. These duties often include legal research and writing, and paralegals sometimes perform such services. For example, a senator who plans to propose an amendment to a law may ask a paralegal on her or his staff to research the legislative history of that law carefully (to discern the legislature's intention when passing the law—see Chapters 5 and 17) and write up a summary of that history.

Law Enforcement Offices and Courts

Many paralegals work for government law enforcement offices and institutions. As you will read in Chapter 16, which discusses criminal law and procedures in detail, a person accused of a crime is prosecuted by a *public prosecutor.* Public prosecutors (such as district attorneys, state attorneys general, and U.S. attorneys) are government officials who are paid by the government. Accused persons may be defended by private attorneys, or, if they cannot afford to hire a lawyer, by *public defenders*—attorneys paid for by the state to ensure that criminal defendants are not deprived of their constitutional right to counsel. Both public prosecutors and public defenders rely on paralegals to handle much of their legal work.

Paralegals also find work in other government environments, such as federal or state court administrative offices. Court administrative work ranges from recording and filing court documents (such as the documents filed during a lawsuit—see Chapter 13) to working for a local small claims court (a court that handles claims below a specified threshold amount—see Chapter 6). Paralegals may also work for bankruptcy courts (see page 35 for a discussion of bankruptcy law).

Legal Aid Offices

Legal aid offices provide legal services to those who find it difficult to pay for legal representation. During President Lyndon Johnson's "War on Poverty" in the 1960s, the government began to set aside funds for legal-services organizations around the country to help less advantaged groups obtain needed legal assistance at low or no cost. Most legal aid continues to be government funded, although some support comes from private legal foundations.

Many paralegals who work in this type of setting find their jobs rewarding, even though they often receive lower salaries than they would in other areas. In part, this is because of the nature of the work—helping needy individuals. Additionally, paralegals in legal aid offices generally assume a wider array of responsibilities than they would in a traditional law office or one of the other environments described earlier. For example, some federal and state administrative agencies, including the Social Security Administration at the federal level, allow paralegals to represent clients in agency hearings and judicial proceedings. As you will read in Chapter 3, paralegals normally are not allowed to represent clients—only attorneys can do so. Exceptions to this rule exist when a court or agency permits nonlawyers to represent others in court or in administrative agency hearings.

Freelance Paralegals

| **freelance paralegal**
A paralegal who operates his or her own business and provides services to attorneys on a contract basis. A freelance paralegal works under the supervision of an attorney, who assumes responsibility for the paralegal's work product.

A number of experienced paralegals operate as freelancers. **Freelance paralegals** (also called *independent contractors* or *contract paralegals*) own their own businesses and perform specified types of legal work for attorneys on a contract basis. Attorneys who need temporary legal assistance sometimes contract with freelance paralegals to work on particular projects. In addition, attorneys who need legal assistance but cannot afford to hire full-time paralegals might hire freelancers to work on a part-time basis. (The suggestions offered later in this chapter on how you can find work as a paralegal apply to freelance jobs as well.)

Freelancing as a paralegal has both advantages and disadvantages. Because freelancers are their own bosses, they can set their own schedules. Thus, they enjoy a greater degree of flexibility in their working hours. In addition, depending on the nature of their projects, they may work at home or in attorneys' offices. With flexibility, however, comes responsibility. A freelance paralegal's income depends on the paralegal's ability to promote and maintain his or her business. If the paralegal has no clients for the month, there will be no paycheck. Also, freelancers do not enjoy job benefits such as medical insurance, sick time, or vacation time. A freelance paralegal needs to be self-motivated and driven to make the business work.

| **legal technician or independent paralegal**
A paralegal who offers services directly to the public, normally for a fee, without attorney supervision. Independent paralegals assist consumers by supplying them with forms and procedural knowledge relating to simple or routine legal procedures.

Realize that freelance paralegals work under attorney supervision. Freelancers are not to be confused with **legal technicians**—often called **independent paralegals**—who do *not* work under the supervision of an attorney and who provide (sell) legal services directly to the public. These services include helping members of the public obtain and fill out forms for certain types of legal transactions, such as bankruptcy filings and divorce petitions. As you will read in Chapter 3, legal technicians run the risk of violating state statutes prohibiting the unauthorized practice of law.

PARALEGAL SPECIALTIES

While many paralegals work for small firms that offer a wide range of legal services, other paralegals have found it useful and satisfying to specialize in one area of law. The top five fields in which paralegals specialize, according to one survey, are litigation (45 percent), corporate law (29 percent), personal-injury law (26 percent), contract law (24 percent), and real estate law (23 percent).[3] Numerous other specialty areas exist, however. Some of these areas are listed in Exhibit 2.2, along with the average compensation for paralegals in that area. Here, we discuss just a few of the areas in which paralegals may specialize.

Litigation Assistance

| **litigation**
The process of working a lawsuit through the court system.

| **litigation paralegal**
A paralegal who specializes in assisting attorneys in the litigation process.

Working a lawsuit through the court system is called **litigation**. Paralegals who specialize in assisting attorneys in the litigation process are called **litigation paralegals**. Litigation paralegals work in general law practices, small litigation firms, litigation departments of larger

AREA OF SPECIALTY	AVERAGE COMPENSATION
Administrative/Government	$44,580
Bankruptcy	$39,710
Contracts	$51,240
Corporate	$50,450
Criminal	$40,300
Employment	$46,630
Environmental	$48,020
Family	$38,160
Insurance	$43,260
Intellectual property	$51,050
Litigation	$46,790
Medical malpractice	$43,250
Mergers and acquisitions	$55,610
Personal injury	$40,880
Probate (wills and estates)	$43,350
Real estate	$42,460

EXHIBIT 2.2
Average Compensation by Specialty

The authors compiled this chart using data from NALA and *Legal Assistant Today* magazine.

law firms, and corporate legal departments. Litigation paralegals often specialize in a certain type of litigation, such as personal-injury litigation (which will be discussed shortly) or product liability cases (which involve injuries caused by defective products).

Work performed by litigation paralegals varies with the substantive law area being litigated. Some litigation paralegals investigate cases, review documents containing evidence, interview clients and witnesses, draft documents to file with the courts, and prepare for hearings and trials. Note that the work performed by a litigation paralegal also varies depending on whether she or he works primarily on behalf of **plaintiffs** (those who bring lawsuits) or on behalf of **defendants** (those against whom lawsuits are brought). Lawyers in a personal-injury practice, for example, often represent plaintiffs. You will read in detail about litigation procedures and the important role played by paralegals in the litigation process in Chapters 13 through 16.

plaintiff
A party who initiates a lawsuit.

defendant
A party against whom a lawsuit is brought.

Corporate Law

Corporate law consists of the laws that govern the formation, financing, merger and acquisition, and termination of corporations, as well as the rights and duties of those who own and run the corporation. You will read in detail about the meaning of these terms and the tasks that corporate paralegals typically perform in Chapter 11.

Paralegals who specialize in corporate law may work for a corporation, in its legal department, or for a law firm that specializes in corporate law. Corporate paralegals often perform such tasks as preparing and filing documents with a state agency to set up corporations and to keep them in good standing, keeping corporate records, organizing and scheduling shareholders' meetings in accordance with state law, and preparing stock certificates. As you can see in Exhibit 2.2, which lists the average compensation by specialty, paralegals who work in corporate law generally receive higher salaries than paralegals in most other specialty areas. In addition, those corporate paralegals who further narrow their specialties to mergers and acquisitions are among the highest-paid paralegals today.

corporate law
Law that governs the formation, financing, merger and acquisition, and termination of corporations, as well as the rights and duties of those who own and run the corporation.

LITIGATION PARALEGAL

Michael Gaige is a legal assistant with OneBeacon Insurance Group in South Portland, Maine, where he specializes in civil litigation. Gaige received his B.A. degree from Lock Haven University in Pennsylvania in 1974 and his paralegal certificate from Bentley College in Waltham, Massachusetts, in 1979. He began working as a legal assistant in February 1980 and received his certified legal assistant (CLA) designation from the National Association of Legal Assistants in March 1985. Gaige has lectured at seminars on various litigation topics and teaches part of a CLA study course at Andover College in Portland. He was a founding member of the Maine State Association of Legal Assistants and has been a member of the board of directors of the National Association of Legal Assistants as a Region I director and as chair of several committees.

What do you like best about your work?

"The thing I like best is the constant learning process. Whether it is keeping up with advances in technology or gathering and organizing facts and documents about a particular case, litigation involves a constant learning process that is challenging and stimulating. Many cases require that you develop some degree of familiarity with an industry or a product or learn about something of which you had little or no previous knowledge. You can never acquire too much knowledge, and a law firm is a great place to do so—just 'bring your own container.'"

What is the greatest challenge that you face in your area of work?

"The greatest challenge in litigation is keeping everything organized. Whether it involves maintaining a database or keeping track of physical documents and other evidence, it is important that at least one person attempts to maintain control over the various components of a file at all times. Seldom does a day pass that I am not asked, 'Where can I find this?' or 'Can you bring me that?' When several people are working on delegated tasks related to the same file, it can be very challenging to keep track of and help coordinate everything related to one case, let alone the ten or twenty or thirty cases on which you are working."

What advice do you have for would-be paralegals in your area of work?

"Be as organized and proactive as possible. Learn to use the technology and software programs that can make your job easier. With experience comes the ability to anticipate what needs to be done. Don't wait to receive instructions to perform a task or a project if there are things you know need to be accomplished. Although preparing for and assisting at trial can be glamorous and exciting, it also requires long hours and generous helpings of stress. If you are looking for a nine-to-five job and are not particularly adept at coping with stress, you may be better suited to areas of the law other than litigation."

What are some tips for success as a paralegal in your area of work?

"Always reduce assignments to writing. Make certain you understand precisely what your assignment is and the time constraints associated with it. Few things are more frustrating to an attorney and more wasteful of time and energy than spending time on an assignment that does not result in what the attorney wanted accomplished. Make certain you have an understanding of all the factual and legal issues and the desired result. You may overlook important information if you perform isolated tasks with a limited understanding of the case. You never know when that seemingly unimportant point will become remarkably significant as the case develops."

> *"Make certain you understand precisely what your assignment is and the time constraints associated with it."*

Personal-Injury Law

Much litigation involves claims brought by persons who have been injured in automobile accidents or other incidents as a result of the negligence of others. *Negligence* is a *tort*, or civil wrong, and someone who has been injured as a result of another's negligence is entitled under tort law to obtain compensation from the wrongdoer. (Tort law, including negligence, will be discussed in Chapter 7.)

Paralegals who specialize in personal-injury litigation often work for law firms that concentrate their efforts on this domain. Legal assistants in this area obtain and review medical and employment records to determine the client's injuries and lost wages. These items are needed to ascertain the plaintiff's damages in a personal-injury lawsuit. Personal-injury paralegals are also hired by insurance companies to investigate claims. Defendants in personal-injury cases are typically insured by automobile or other insurance, and a defendant's insurance company therefore has a duty to defend an insured customer who is being sued.

Contract Law

A number of paralegals specialize in contract law. As you will read in Chapter 8, which looks at the law governing contracts in some detail, a **contract** is an agreement (based on a promise or an exchange of promises) that can be enforced in court. Paralegals who specialize in this area may work for a corporation's legal department, for a large law firm, or for a government agency.

contract
An agreement (based on a promise or an exchange of promises) that can be enforced in court.

The work of paralegals in the area of contract law typically involves preparing contracts and contract forms, and reviewing contracts to determine whether one of the parties to the contract has or has not complied with the terms of the contract. In a lawsuit for breach of contract, for example, a paralegal might be asked to look closely at the contract terms and do some factual investigation to find out whether the contract has indeed been breached, or broken. Contract specialists also may conduct research in the law governing contracts, either before a contract is formed or during litigation concerning the contract's provisions.

Paralegals who specialize in contract law typically obtain high salaries, as indicated in Exhibit 2.2 on page 31. In fact, as you can see in that exhibit, contract specialists earn more than specialists in any other area except mergers and acquisitions. Note, however, that because contracts are so prevalent in our legal environment, many paralegals—not just contract specialists—are involved with work relating to contracts.

Real Estate Law

Real estate, or *real property*, consists of land and all things permanently attached to the land, such as houses, buildings, and trees and foliage. Because of the value of real estate (for most people, a home is the most expensive purchase they will ever make), attorneys frequently assist persons or business firms that buy or sell real property to make sure that nothing important is overlooked. Paralegals who specialize in real estate may find employment in a number of environments, including small law firms that specialize in real estate transactions, real estate departments in large law firms, corporations or other business firms that frequently buy or sell real property, banking institutions (which finance real estate purchases), title companies, and real estate agencies. Paralegals working in the field of real estate law often draft contracts for the sale of real estate, draft mortgage agreements, draft and record deeds, and schedule closings on the sale of property. You will read in greater detail about real property law in Chapter 9.

real estate
Land and things permanently attached to the land, such as houses, buildings, and trees and foliage.

Insurance Law

A number of paralegals specialize in insurance law. **Insurance** is essentially a contract by which an insurance company (the insurer) promises to pay a sum of money or give something of value to another (either the insured or the beneficiary) to compensate the other for

insurance
A contract by which an insurance company (the insurer) promises to pay a sum of money or give something of value to another (either the insured or the beneficiary) to compensate the other for a specified loss.

a specified loss. Insurance protection may provide for compensation for the injury or death of the insured or another, for damage to the insured's property, or for other types of losses, such as those resulting from lawsuits. Paralegals who specialize in the area of insurance law may work for law firms that defend insurance companies in litigation brought against the companies. They may also work for insurance companies.

Paralegals who specialize in this area may be involved in reviewing government regulations concerning the insurance industry and monitoring an insurance firm's compliance with these regulations. Paralegals may also be asked to review insurance contracts, undertake factual and legal investigations relating to insurance claims, or provide litigation assistance in lawsuits involving the insurance company. Often, paralegals who do not specialize in this area may be asked to assist in litigation involving insurance claims. For example, a paralegal may be asked to provide investigative or litigation assistance for a client who is bringing or defending against a personal-injury, malpractice, or other type of lawsuit in which insurance may be an important factor.

Employment and Labor Law

As will be discussed in Chapter 11, laws governing employment relationships are referred to collectively as *employment and labor law.* Employment and labor law includes laws governing health and safety in the workplace, labor unions and union-management relations, employment discrimination, sexual harassment, wrongful termination, pension plans, retirement and disability income (Social Security), employee privacy rights, the minimum wage that must be paid, and overtime wages.

Paralegals who are experienced in one or more of these areas may work for law firms, corporations and other business entities, or government agencies. Often, paralegals specialize in just one area of employment law. For example, many paralegals specialize in the area of workers' compensation. Under state **workers' compensation statutes**, employees who are injured on the job are compensated from state funds (obtained from taxes paid by employers). Paralegals working in this area assist persons injured on the job in obtaining compensation from the state workers' compensation board. As mentioned earlier, some government agencies allow paralegals to represent clients during agency hearings, which are conducted by agencies to settle disputes, or during negotiations with the agencies. Many state workers' compensation boards allow paralegals to represent clients in such hearings.

Frequently, working in the area of employment law involves interacting with numerous administrative agencies, such as the Occupational Safety and Health Administration and the Equal Employment Opportunity Commission. Each governmental agency has its own set of rules, requirements, and legal procedures. Paralegals who work in employment or labor law need to be familiar with the relevant federal and state agencies, as well as with their specific roles in resolving disputes. Many of the administrative agencies that regulate employment issues also hire paralegals. You will learn more about employment law in Chapter 11 and administrative agencies in Chapter 5.

Estate Planning and Probate Administration

Estate planning and probate administration both have to do with the transfer of an owner's property, or *estate,* on the owner's death. Through **estate planning**, the owner decides, *before* death, how his or her property will be transferred to others. The owner may make a **will**, for example, to designate the persons to whom his or her property is to be transferred. If someone contests the validity of the will, or if the property in the deceased person's estate is of a certain value, the will must be **probated** (proved) in a **probate court**. Depending on the size of the estate, it may take months—in some cases, over a year—for the probate court to approve the property distribution and for the property to be transferred to the rightful heirs.

On the Web

Several law firms that specialize in labor and employment issues have posted their newsletters on the Web. One such firm is Ogletree Deakins, which you can access at **http://www.ogletreedeakins.com**.

workers' compensation statutes
State laws establishing an administrative procedure for compensating workers for injuries that arise in the course of their employment.

estate planning
Making arrangements, during a person's lifetime, for the transfer of that person's property or obligations to others on the person's death. Estate planning often involves executing a will, establishing a trust fund, or taking out a life insurance policy to provide for others, such as a spouse or children, on a person's death.

will
A document directing how and to whom the maker's property and obligations are to be transferred on his or her death.

probate
The process of "proving" the validity of a will and ensuring that the instructions in a valid will are carried out.

probate court
A court that probates wills; usually a county court.

Ethics Watch!

SERVING THE INTERESTS OF BEREAVED CLIENTS

One of the hardest events to cope with is the loss of a loved one, yet it is precisely at this time that bereaved persons must also cope with funeral arrangements and legal formalities. These formalities may include, for example, checking with an attorney, locating a will if one was made, and tending to the decedent's financial affairs. Undertaking these activities can be costly, and financial needs may cause further stress.

These are factors that paralegals should keep in mind when dealing with clients during the probate process. Probate proceedings always take time, but the duration may be reduced by the paralegal who files the necessary forms promptly and follows up on the status of the proceedings to make sure that there are no unnecessary delays. Your kind or sympathetic words may be appreciated by a bereaved client, but you can best serve his or her interests by doing your job efficiently and responsibly and by undertaking any action you can to speed up the probate process.

Furthermore, inheritance taxes and attorneys' fees (incurred in administering the estate) will reduce the value of the property that is given to heirs.

Because the probate process is time consuming and expensive, today many people engage in estate planning to avoid probate. For example, a person may opt to establish a **trust** agreement, which is a legal arrangement in which the ownership of property is transferred to a third person (the *trustee*) to be used for the benefit of another (the *beneficiary*). Paralegals often are responsible for interviewing clients to obtain information necessary to draft wills and trust agreements, for gathering information on debts and assets, and for locating heirs if necessary (see Chapter 10). A paralegal who is sensitive and caring toward the client, yet professional and conscientious in explaining and expediting procedures, is particularly well suited for this specialty.

Bankruptcy Law

Bankruptcy law is a body of law that allows debtors to obtain relief from their debts. Bankruptcy law is federal law, and bankruptcy proceedings take place in federal courts (see the discussion of the federal court system in Chapter 6). The twin goals of bankruptcy law are (1) to protect a debtor by giving him or her a fresh start, free from creditors' claims; and (2) to ensure that creditors who are competing for a debtor's assets are treated fairly. Bankruptcy law provides for several types of relief, and both individuals and business firms may petition for bankruptcy. Both large and small firms practice bankruptcy law and hire paralegals who specialize in this area.

In 2005, the laws pertaining to bankruptcy significantly changed. Debtors filing for ordinary bankruptcy now are required to receive credit counseling and to show that their income does not exceed the average income in their state of residence. Under the new law, attorneys handling bankruptcy cases must verify the accuracy of the information contained in their clients' forms.

trust
An arrangement in which title to property is held by one person (a trustee) for the benefit of another (a beneficiary).

bankruptcy law
The body of federal law that governs bankruptcy proceedings. The twin goals of bankruptcy law are (1) to protect a debtor by giving him or her a fresh start, free from creditors' claims; and (2) to ensure that creditors who are competing for a debtor's assets are treated fairly.

On the Web

If you are interested in bankruptcy law, a good site for learning about current bankruptcy issues is that of the American Bankruptcy Institute at **http://www.abiworld.org**.

The new rules mean that paralegals working in this area may also have more responsibilities than they would have had prior to 2005. The paralegal working in bankruptcy law today might be responsible for interviewing debtors to obtain information about their income, assets, and debts. The paralegal may verify the accuracy of the information provided by debtors and analyze whether a debtor's income exceeds the average for the state. The paralegal may also review the validity of creditors' claims, prepare the documents that must be submitted to the bankruptcy court, and arrange for debtors to receive credit counseling.

Intellectual Property Law

intellectual property
Property that results from intellectual, creative processes. Copyrights, patents, and trademarks are examples of intellectual property.

Intellectual property consists of the products of individuals' minds—products that result from intellectual, creative processes. Those who create intellectual property acquire certain rights over the use of that property, and these rights are protected by law. Literary and artistic works are protected by *copyright law.* *Trademark law* protects business firms' distinctive marks or mottos. Inventions are protected by *patent law.* The primary benefit of intellectual property rights to the owner is that he or she controls the commercial use of the property. The owner, for example, may sell the intellectual property rights to another, may collect royalties on the use of the property (such as a popular song) by others, and may prevent unauthorized publishers from reproducing the property (such as a novel). In Chapter 8, you will read in greater detail about laws governing intellectual property.

Many law firms (or special departments of large law firms) specialize in intellectual property law, such as patent law. Other firms provide a spectrum of legal services, of which intellectual property law is only a part. In addition, corporate legal departments may be responsible for registering copyrights, patents, or trademarks with the federal government.[4]

In the area of intellectual property, paralegals frequently research existing patents and trademarks. They also assist in compiling complex patent applications in accordance with detailed regulations, draft documents necessary to apply for trademark and copyright protection, and assist in litigating disputes. Because this area requires very specific knowledge, paralegal intellectual property specialists are paid more than specialists in most other areas (see Exhibit 2.2 on page 31). This is an especially good practice area for paralegals with a science background. In fact, anyone, including a paralegal, with three years of undergraduate science courses can apply to the U.S. Patent and Trademark Office to become a registered patent agent, who prepares patent applications.

On the Web

If you are interested in how cyberspace is affecting the laws governing intellectual property, a good general site covering current issues is that offered by the Bureau of National Affairs at **http://ipcenter.bna.com**.

Environmental Law

environmental law
All state and federal laws or regulations enacted or issued to protect the environment and preserve environmental resources.

Environmental law consists of all laws that have been created to protect the environment. Environmental law involves the regulation of air and water pollution, natural resource management, endangered species protection, hazardous waste disposal and the clean-up of hazardous waste sites, pesticide control, and nuclear power regulation.

Employers of paralegal specialists in environmental law include administrative agencies (such as the federal Environmental Protection Agency, state natural resource departments, and local zoning boards), environmental law departments of large law firms, law firms that specialize in environmental law, and corporations. For example, a corporation may employ a paralegal as an *environmental coordinator* to assist the corporation in maintaining compliance with government regulations, overseeing company environmental programs, and obtaining proper permits to use land in certain ways. Paralegals working in law firms that handle environmental matters often assist in litigation concerning alleged violations of environmental laws. They perform tasks similar to those described previously for litigation and personal-injury paralegals.

On the Web

For a comprehensive and up-to-date collection of news articles, laws, and agency regulations involving environmental law issues, go to the Environmental Law Net at **http://lawvianet.com**.

Ethics Watch!

QUESTIONS ABOUT CHILD CUSTODY

Divorcing clients frequently ask whether they can take their children out of the state while the mediation or divorce proceedings are under way. For example, suppose that Kerry Lynn, a paralegal, receives a call from a client who wants to know if it would be all right to take her children to her mother's home in another state over the weekend. Kerry tells the client that there is no problem with that.

Normally, there would be no problem, but what Kerry doesn't know is that in this case, just two days ago, the court ordered that the children could not leave the state. The client, relying on Kerry's answer, violates the order. Kerry has both given legal advice to a client (which only attorneys may do) and caused the client to suffer adverse legal consequences as a result of that advice.

In your work as a paralegal, you may face similar questions from divorcing parents. You should always let the client know that as a paralegal, you cannot give legal advice, which you would be doing if you answered such questions.

Family Law

Family law, as the term implies, deals with family matters, such as marriage, divorce, alimony, child support, and child custody. We discuss family law in detail in Chapter 10. Family law is governed primarily by state statutes. If you specialize in this area, you will need to become familiar with your state's requirements concerning marriage and divorce procedures, child support, and related issues.

As a family law specialist, you might work for a small family law practice, for a family law department in a large law firm, or with a state or local agency, such as a community services agency, that assists persons who need help with family-related problems. As a paralegal working in family law, you might research and draft documents that are filed with the court in divorce and adoption proceedings. You might also perform investigations into assets and the grounds for divorce. Paralegals in this area often have extensive contact with clients and need to be skilled at extracting relevant information from sometimes emotionally distraught persons. Those with a background or interest in social work or counseling are particularly well suited to this specialty.

family law
Law relating to family matters, such as marriage, divorce, child support, and child custody.

Criminal Law

Law is sometimes classified into the two categories of civil law and criminal law. **Civil law** is concerned with the duties that exist between persons or between citizens and their governments, excluding the duty not to commit crimes. Contract law, for example, is part of civil law. The whole body of tort law, which has to do with the infringement by one person of the legally recognized rights of another (see Chapter 7), is an area of civil law. **Criminal law**, in contrast, is concerned with wrongs committed against the public as a whole. Criminal acts are prohibited by federal, state, or local statutes (criminal law and procedures will be discussed in Chapter 16). In a criminal case, the government seeks to impose a penalty (a fine

civil law
The branch of law dealing with the definition and enforcement of private rights, as opposed to criminal matters.

criminal law
The branch of law that governs and defines those actions that are crimes and that subjects persons convicted of crimes to punishment imposed by the government (a fine or jail time).

Developing Paralegal Skills

WORKING FOR A PUBLIC DEFENDER

Michele Sanchez works as a paralegal for the public defender's office in her county. Today, she has been assigned to go to the county jail to meet with a new client, Geraldine Silverton. Silverton had been arrested for child abuse after the child's school notified the police. According to school officials, the child had bruises all over his body. The child also told his teacher that his mother frequently "beat him up" for no reason at all.

The client, Silverton, is very upset and tells Michele that "no way in the world would she harm her boy." Silverton claims that her son was hurt when he fell off the trampoline in their backyard and that he's just "making up" the abuse story to get attention.

Silverton demands to be released from jail immediately. Michele makes a note of Silverton's concerns and then explains the scheduling for the bail hearings.

TIPS FOR MEETING WITH A NEW CLIENT

*   Review the police report before meeting with the client.
*   During the interview with the client, ask the client for his or her side of the story.
*   Listen carefully and supportively to the client, and communicate with empathy.
*   Minimize note taking.
*   Do not appear to judge the client.

You can gain insight into criminal law and procedures by looking at some of the famous criminal law cases included on Court TV's Web site. Go to **http://www.courttv.com**.

or jail time) on a person who has committed a crime. In a civil case, one party tries to make the other party comply with a duty or pay for the damage caused by the failure to so comply.

Paralegals who specialize in criminal law may work for public prosecutors, public defenders, or criminal defense attorneys. A legal assistant working for the prosecutor's office, for example, might draft search or arrest warrants. A paralegal working for the defense attorney (public or private) might obtain police reports, conduct research, and draft documents to be filed with the court—for example, a document arguing that the police violated the defendant's constitutional rights. Although criminal law and civil law are very different, the trial process is similar, and paralegals perform similar types of tasks (investigation, summarizing witness testimony, and so forth) in preparation for litigation.

Additional Specialty Areas

The above listing of specialty areas is by no means exhaustive. In addition to these domains, other areas offer opportunities for paralegals who wish to specialize. For example, as the U.S. population ages, more and more attorneys are focusing on serving the needs of older clients. Elder law is the term used to describe this broad specialty. Paralegals who work in this practice area may be asked to assist in a variety of tasks, including those relating to estate planning (discussed earlier), age-discrimination claims, financial arrangements for long-term care, Medicare and Medicaid, abuse suffered by elderly persons, and the visitation rights of grandparents.

Additionally, many nurses have found profitable and challenging work as paralegals. A paralegal who is also a trained nurse is particularly well equipped to evaluate legal claims involving injuries, such as those involved in personal-injury, medical malpractice, or product liability lawsuits. A relatively new specialty area among nurses—and within the legal profes-

elder law
A relatively new legal specialty that involves serving the needs of older clients, such as estate planning and making arrangements for long-term care.

YEARS OF EXPERIENCE	AVERAGE SALARY
0–3	$38,196
3–5	$40,509
5–7	$42,146
7–10	$47,995
10–15	$49,192
15–20	$53,782
More than 20	$63,341

EXHIBIT 2.3
Paralegal Salary by Years of Experience

Legal Assistant Today, March/April 2006, p. 52, **http://www.legalassistanttoday.com**.

sion—is that of the **legal nurse consultant (LNC)**. An LNC consults with legal professionals and others on medical aspects of legal claims or issues. LNCs usually work independently (offering their services on a contract basis) and are typically well paid for their services—up to $200 per hour, in some cases. Some LNCs work for law firms, insurance companies, government offices, and risk management departments of companies as salaried employees. The American Association of Legal Nurse Consultants offers a certification program in which nurses who meet the eligibility criteria (including appropriate educational credentials and sufficient experience as a legal nurse) and pass an examination can become certified as LNCs.

Developments in technology are also opening doors to possible areas of specialization for paralegals. Paralegals who acquire expertise in high-tech equipment and software applications can perform valuable services for their employers and command high salaries. (For a discussion of career opportunities for paralegals with expertise in technology, see this chapter's *Technology and Today's Paralegal* feature on the following two pages.)

legal nurse consultant (LNC)
A nurse who consults with legal professionals and others about medical aspects of legal claims or issues. Legal nurse consultants normally must have at least a bachelor's degree in nursing and a significant amount of nursing experience.

On the Web

To learn more about the American Association of Legal Nurse Consultants and its certification programs, go to **http://www.aalnc.org**.

PARALEGAL COMPENSATION

What do paralegals earn? This is an important question for anyone contemplating a career as a paralegal. You can get some idea of what paralegals make, on average, from paralegal compensation surveys. Following a discussion of these surveys, we look at some other components of paralegal compensation, including job benefits and compensation for overtime work.

Compensation Surveys

Paralegal income is affected by a number of factors. We have already mentioned the effects of the size of the firm or legal department (see Exhibit 2.1 on page 25) and the specialty area in which the paralegal practices (see Exhibit 2.2 on page 31). Another income-determining factor is the paralegal's years of experience, which is shown in Exhibit 2.3. Typically, more experienced paralegals enjoy higher rates of compensation. This is particularly noticeable when a paralegal has worked for the same employer for a long period of time.

Another major factor that affects paralegal compensation is geographical location. The previous exhibits illustrate *national* averages. Exhibit 2.4, by contrast, shows *regional* averages of paralegal income. As you can see, paralegals who work in the West and in the Northeast generally enjoy

REGION	AVERAGE SALARY
West	$54,938
Northeast	$52,600
South	$49,860
Midwest	$46,989

EXHIBIT 2.4
Average Paralegal Salary by Region

Legal Assistant Today, March/April 2006, pp. 60–61, **http://www. legalassistanttoday.com**.

Technology and Today's Paralegal

MORE CAREER OPPORTUNITIES FOR TECH-SAVVY PARALEGALS

Today, more than ever, paralegals who possess superior computer and technological skills are in great demand in law firms across the nation. Nearly every person entering the paralegal profession will be required to use a computer on a daily basis. Knowing the basics—word processing, database management, computerized legal research, and navigating the Internet—is essential, but this knowledge may not be enough to give you a competitive edge in the marketplace. In this feature, we explore some of the skills that paralegals can master in order to secure their future in the job market.

MASTER KEYBOARDING SKILLS

Proficient keyboarding skills are an invaluable asset. The faster you can accurately key in data on a computer, the more work you can complete in a shorter period of time—and, consequently, the more valuable you are to an employer. This is true whether you are creating documents, scheduling court dates, managing calendars, or performing legal research. Make it a point, during your education, to practice your touch-typing skills (typing without looking at the keys) every day so that keyboarding becomes second nature to you. Practice entering numbers as well as letters so that you can accurately key in court dates and deadlines in calendaring programs and figures in billing programs. Many inexpensive typing programs are now available on CD-ROM or downloadable through the Internet.

BE PROFICIENT WITH TYPICAL OFFICE SOFTWARE

Most law firms use a variety of software applications daily, including computerized billing programs, e-mail, calendaring software, and legal research applications. To be competitive in the job market, paralegals should be skilled at using these programs and well versed in the alternatives. For example, paralegals are often responsible for keeping track of the deadlines for filing court documents, along with court filing fees and requirements. Local court rules specify the filing dates and applicable fees for different kinds of cases, but these rules change regularly. Failure to submit documents by the due date can result in a court's dismissing the case or the

higher levels of compensation than paralegals in other regions of the country. Remember, though, that these figures still represent averages and can therefore be deceptive. For example, a paralegal working in a rural area of Washington State may not earn as much as a paralegal who works in a city in the Plains states. Also, the compensation of a paralegal who works in a major city (such as Chicago or Detroit) may greatly exceed the average for that region.

Keep in mind, too, that salary statistics do not tell the whole story. Although paralegals earn more in California than in a midwestern state such as Nebraska, the cost of living is higher in California than in Nebraska. This means that your real income—the amount of goods and services that you can purchase with your income—may, in fact, be the same in both states despite the differences in salary. Salary statistics also do not reveal another important component of compensation—job benefits.

Job Benefits

Part of your total compensation package as an employee will consist of various job benefits. These benefits may include paid holidays, sick leave, group insurance coverage (life, disability, medical, dental), pension plans, and possibly others. Benefits packages vary from firm to

client's dismissing the firm. Moreover, missed deadlines are a leading cause of malpractice (professional negligence) lawsuits filed by clients against their attorneys.

Many firms have computerized calendaring software to help ensure that attorneys do not miss important dates and to calculate required fees based on the local court rules. Such software could suit the needs of a small law firm that handles only local cases, but it might not be adequate if the firm handles cases in numerous counties or states. Rather than buying a more comprehensive and expensive calendaring program and incurring the costs of installation and training, the firm could use an online calendaring service. A paralegal who knows about the availability of online calendaring applications could suggest that the firm use these services on a pay-per-use basis, which could save the firm time and funds. The paralegal might gain the respect and appreciation of the firm and might be asked for her or his input regarding future technology decisions.

CONTINUE TO TAKE ON NEW CHALLENGES

Many technologies now being developed are providing avenues for paralegals to advance their positions and become indispensable to their firms. For example, some courts now allow documents to be filed with the court electronically. Paralegals are often responsible for making sure that these documents are in the proper electronic format and that they include hyperlinks to relevant resources. In addition, every court now allows electronic discovery—that is, prior to a trial, a party can obtain evidence in electronic form from the opposing party's e-mails, cell phones, computers, Palm Pilots, and other electronic devices. Some law firms also take video depositions (testimony from witnesses) when witnesses are unable to appear in person. Paralegals with experience and skill in locating and obtaining electronic evidence or with the ability to film and produce videos are likely to be in demand.

TECHNOLOGY TIP

Along with technological advances come certain legal questions that are just being resolved by the courts. For example, how long does electronic evidence need to be retained on a computer system? Who should be required to pay for the discovery of electronic evidence? A paralegal who understands the various legal issues surrounding the use of new technologies and who knows how the courts in the area are resolving these disputes will likely become an invaluable member of the legal team.

firm. For example, one employer may pay the entire premium for your life and health insurance, while another employer may require you to contribute part of the cost of the insurance. Usually, the larger the firm, the greater the value of the benefits package. When evaluating any job offer, you need to consider the benefits that you will receive and what these benefits are worth to you. You will read more about the importance of job benefits later in this chapter, in the context of evaluating a job offer.

Salaries versus Hourly Wages

Some paralegals are salaried employees. In other words, they receive a specified annual salary regardless of the number of hours they actually work. Other paralegals are paid an hourly wage rate for every hour worked. Paralegals are frequently asked to work overtime, and how they are compensated for overtime work usually depends on whether they are salaried employees or are paid hourly wages. Many firms compensate their salaried paralegals for overtime work through year-end **bonuses**, which are special payments made to employees in recognition of their devotion to the firm and the high quality of their work. Paralegals often receive annual bonuses ranging from $1,500 to nearly $4,000, depending on years of

bonus
An end-of-the-year payment to a salaried employee in appreciation for that employee's overtime work, work quality, diligence, or dedication to the firm.

experience, firm size, and so forth. Some firms allow salaried employees to take compensatory time off work (for example, an hour off for every hour worked beyond usual working hours). Employees who are paid an hourly wage rate are normally paid overtime wages.

Federal Law and Overtime Pay

Compensation for overtime pay has been a major issue in the paralegal profession. Complicating the debate over this issue are the provisions of the Fair Labor Standards Act (FLSA) of 1938. This act requires employers to pay employees **overtime wages**—one and a half times their normal hourly rate—for all hours worked beyond forty hours per week. The act exempts certain types of employees from this overtime-pay requirement, however. *Exempt employees* include those who qualify under the terms of the act as holding "administrative," "executive," or "professional" positions.

The Professional Exemption

Paralegals whose duties are largely administrative or executive (managerial) in nature may qualify for the administrative or executive exemptions. If they do, then their employers are not required to pay them overtime wages. For a number of years, however, it was uncertain whether paralegals were exempt as professionals from FLSA provisions. The U.S. Department of Labor (DOL), which enforces the FLSA, had generally held that paralegals were not exempt as professional employees and thus should receive overtime pay for hours worked beyond forty hours per week. Nonetheless, many employers classified their paralegal employees as professionals to avoid the overtime-pay requirements of the act.

The paralegal profession was split on the issue. Some paralegals who received year-end bonuses questioned whether their bonuses sufficiently compensated them for the amount of overtime that they had worked. Other paralegals preferred year-end bonuses and their designation as professionals under the FLSA. In the early 1990s, the issue came before a federal court. A group of paralegals who worked for Page & Addison, a law firm in Dallas, Texas, sued their employer for $40,000 in back wages for overtime hours that they had worked. In a decision rendered in 1994, the court held that paralegals *could* be classified as professional (exempt) employees because they perform important work and exercise discretion and independent judgment.[5] This decision, while significant, did not resolve the problem in jurisdictions in which that court decision did not apply, and the debate continued.

The FairPay Initiative

In 2004, to provide a clearer test for determining which employees are exempt from the overtime provisions of the FLSA, the DOL issued a regulation concerning overtime pay known as the FairPay rule. Under this rule, any worker who is paid less than $23,660 per year, or $455 per week, must be paid overtime wages. To qualify under this rule for any of the three exemptions (executive, administrative, or professional), an employee's earnings must exceed this threshold.

The new rule also clarified the meaning of the term *professional*. To qualify for the professional exemption, the employee's work must require advanced knowledge in a field of science or learning, and the knowledge must normally have been acquired through a prolonged course of specialized intellectual instruction. The DOL's rule specifically addresses paralegal employees, stating as follows:

> Paralegals and legal assistants generally do not qualify as exempt learned professionals because an advanced specialized academic degree is not a standard prerequisite for entry into the field. Although many paralegals possess general four-year advanced degrees, most specialized paralegal programs are two-year associate degree programs from a community college or equivalent institution.[6]

overtime wages

Wages paid to workers who are paid an hourly wage rate to compensate them for overtime work (hours worked beyond forty hours per week). Under federal law, overtime wages are at least one and a half times the regular hourly wage rate.

For information on the DOL's FairPay rules, go to the DOL's FairPay Web site at **http://www.dol.gov/esa/ regs/compliance/whd/fairpay**.

Thus, most paralegals no longer qualify for the professional exemption under the FLSA. Realize, though, that paralegals remain professionals in the broader sense of the term, as well as under the criteria defined by the paralegal and legal professions.

PLANNING YOUR CAREER

Career planning involves essentially three steps. The first step is defining your long-term goals. The second step involves devising short-term goals and adjusting these goals to meet the realities of the job market. We look at these two steps of career planning in this section. (For some tips on how to succeed in your career, see this chapter's *Featured Guest* feature beginning on the next page.) Later in this chapter, we discuss the third step: reevaluating your career after you have had some on-the-job experience as a paralegal.

Defining Your Long-Term Goals

From the outset, you will want to define, as clearly as possible, your career goals, and this requires some personal reflection and self-assessment. What are you looking for in a career? Why do you want to become a paralegal? Is income the most important factor? Is job satisfaction (doing the kind of work you like) the most important factor? Is the environment in which you work the most important factor? What profession could best utilize your special talents or skills? Asking yourself these and other broad questions about your personal preferences and values will help you define more clearly your overall professional goals.

Do not be surprised to find that your long-term goals change over time. As you gain more experience as a paralegal and your life circumstances alter, you may decide that your former long-term goals are no longer appropriate. For example, the level of career involvement that suits you as a single person may not be appropriate should you marry and have children. Similarly, later in life, when your children leave home, you may have different goals with respect to your work.

Also, at the outset of your career, you cannot know what opportunities might present themselves in the future. Career planning is an ongoing challenge for paralegals, just as it is for everyone. Throughout your career as a paralegal, you will probably meet other paralegals who have made career changes. A high percentage of paralegals in today's workforce, for example, decided to become paralegals after several years of working in another profession, such as nursing, law enforcement, business administration, or accounting. Changes within the profession, your own experiences, and new opportunities constantly affect the career choices before you. The realities you face during your career may play a significant role in modifying your long-term goals.

Short-Term Goals and Job Realities

Long-term goals are just that—goals that we hope to achieve over the long run. It may take many years or even a lifetime to attain certain long-term goals that we set for ourselves. Short-term goals are the steps that we take to realize our long-term goals. As an entry-level paralegal, one of your short-term goals is simply to find a job.

Ideally, you will find a job that provides you with a salary commensurate with your training and abilities, a level of responsibility that is comfortable (or challenging) for you, and excellent job benefits. The realities of the job market are not always what we wish them to be, however. You should be prepared for the possibility that you might not find the "right" employer or the "perfect" job for you when you first start your job search. You may be lucky from the outset, but then again, it may take several attempts before you find the employer and the job that best suits your needs, skills, and talents. Remember, though, that even if you do not find the perfect job right away, you can gain valuable skills and experience in *any* job

Chere B. Estrin   FEATURED **Guest**

FOUR REASONS WHY LEGAL PROFESSIONALS SUCCEED (OR FAIL)

BIOGRAPHICAL NOTE

Chere B. Estrin, Ph.D., is the chief executive officer of Los Angeles–based EstrinLegalEd, a well-known paralegal training organization. She is founder of The Paralegal SuperConferences™ and its new division, **http://www. LegalProResumes.com**. *She has written eight books, including* The Successful Paralegal's Job Search Guide *(Thomson Delmar Learning) and* The Paralegal Career Guide *(Prentice Hall). A national seminar presenter and entrepreneur, Estrin has been interviewed by* Newsweek, *the* Los Angeles Times, *and the* Chicago Tribune, *among others. She is a founding member of the International Paralegal Management Association, a Lifetime Achievement Award recipient of the Los Angeles Paralegal Association, and a finalist for the* Inc. *magazine Entrepreneur of the Year award. Estrin can be reached at Chere@EstrinLegalEd.com.*

Often, we are so busy that we fail to take the time to learn basic life management principles that have been developed by highly success-

ful people in our industry. Many legal professionals are technical experts in their fields but fail at getting to the top of the fields, attaining job satisfaction, or just plain having fun at what they do. They fail not because of a weakness in their character but because their professional life was not properly managed.

Once a career has grown to a certain level, management of the career must change, or the career will run into trouble. Many legal professionals reach this level at between five and ten years of experience. Sometimes, the critical point comes earlier or later. Whenever it occurs, however, the legal professional must change from a floater (someone directed by his or her career) to a manager (someone who directs his or her career through strategic thinking).

How do successful people manage their careers? First, they invariably have a positive attitude toward their careers and life in general. They are committed to their effort, are patient, and are persistent. Furthermore, they constantly pursue additional training, because they understand that knowledge is a primary key to success.

Second, successful legal professionals have a strategic career plan that clearly describes their concept, philosophy, direction, and goals. Their positions, tasks, and responsibilities are defined. They know ahead of time what the next move will look like. If they don't, they spend time finding out.

environment—skills and experience that can help you achieve long-term goals in the future. In fact, you might want to "try on" jobs at different-sized firms and in different specialty areas to see how they "fit" with your particular needs.

LOCATING POTENTIAL EMPLOYERS

Looking for a job is time consuming and requires attention to detail, persistence, and creativity. Your paralegal education is preparing you, among other things, to do investigative research. The investigative skills that you will use on the job as a paralegal are the ones that you should apply when looking for a job.

Where do you begin your investigation? How can you find out what paralegal jobs are available in your area or elsewhere? How do you know which law firms practice the type of law that interests you? The following suggestions will help you find answers to all of these questions.

Once you have identified potential employers, you can begin the process of applying for jobs. The appendix following this chapter offers practical information and tips on how to market your skills effectively and find a job that is right for you.

Third, successful legal professionals have developed a "board of directors"—a group of advisers, not just one mentor, that consistently provides support and encouragement. Furthermore, these professionals view their colleagues as one of their most valuable resources.

Fourth, and last, successful legal professionals have developed strong support systems. These may be financial or nonfinancial, tangible or intangible, emotional, or educational. They are well organized; they take care of "red flags," know how to play office politics, and take timely action as change occurs.

In short, there are four keys to successful careers:

1. Successful professionals have developed habits and traits that are positive, committed, patient, and persistent.

2. They have a strategic career plan in place.

3. They have developed an organized board of directors to encourage them to be their best and to help them do so.

4. They have a strong support system.

> *"[S]uccessful legal professionals have a strategic career plan that clearly describes their concept, philosophy, direction, and goals."*

A little advance planning can go a long way toward making your life run smoothly, alleviating last-minute problems, and averting potential disasters. No matter what unforeseen problems or difficulties arise on the road to success, stay cool, calm, and professional. Even if you cannot solve the problem, your colleagues, friends, and family members will be impressed with your composure. If you remain confident and proceed with your program, your persistence should contribute to the success of your plan.

With hard work, thorough research, consistent testing, appropriate innovation, and enthusiasm, you should enjoy equal rewards. These simple but highly effective strategies can help you take advantage of the marketing potential of your plan and turn your program into a roaring success. Start fresh. Set up a new life file. There will be a new set of logistics to consider and work your way through. Start at the beginning and begin to fill in the detail. There is magic in the detail—the magic of memorable careers.

Networking

Career opportunities often go unpublished. Many firms post notices within their own organizations before publishing online or in the "Help Wanted" section of a newspaper or periodical. This opens doors to their own employees before the general public. It also spares employers from having to wade through hundreds of employment applications for a vacant position. If you have connections within an organization, you may be told that a position is opening up before other candidates are aware that an opportunity exists.

More paralegals report finding employment through networking than through any other means.[7] For paralegals, **networking** is the process of making personal connections with the other paralegals, paralegal instructors, attorneys, and others who are involved in (or who know someone who is involved in) the paralegal or legal profession. Professional organizations and internships offer two means of networkings.

networking
Making personal connections and cultivating relationships with people in a certain field, profession, or area of interest.

Join a Professional Association

Students can begin forming a network of paralegal connections through affiliation with professional associations and student clubs. You have already learned about NALA and NFPA, the two largest national associations for legal assistants. Many other organizations of paralegals exist across the country. Some of these organizations are listed in Appendix F at the end of this book. See if your local paralegal association allows students to be members. If it does, attend meetings and become acquainted with other paralegals, who may know of job opportunities in your area. Persons involved with other groups—such as the International Paralegal Management Association, or IPMA (an association of individuals who manage legal assistants), and the **state bar association** (a state-level association of attorneys)—can also provide valuable inside knowledge of potential job openings.

Network during Internships

Most paralegal education programs include an internship in which students are placed temporarily in a law firm or other work setting. Cultivate connections during your internship. The people you meet and deal with in these settings often turn out to be very beneficial to you in finding future employment. In many situations, an intern who has performed well is offered a full-time position after graduation. Even if you are not interested in working for the firm with which you do your internship at this time, be careful not to "burn your bridges." You will find that the legal community, even in cities, is relatively small and that lawyers are more inclined to hire paralegals about whom their colleagues have made positive remarks.

Finding Available Jobs

Your next effort should be to locate sources that list paralegal job openings. A good place to start is with the classified ads in your local newspaper. **Trade journals** and similar publications, such as your local or state bar association's journal or newsletters, usually list openings for legal professionals, including paralegals. Increasingly, employers advertise job openings in online publications and turn to online databases to find prospective employees. In fact, today the best starting point when launching your job search is probably the Internet.

Identifying Possible Employers

You should also identify firms and organizations for which you might like to work and submit an employment application to them. In a well-organized job search, you will locate and contact those organizations that offer the benefits, salary, opportunities for advancement, work environment, and legal specialty of your choice. Even though these organizations may not have vacancies in your field at the moment, you want your job application to be immediately available when an opening does occur. Most firms, if they are interested in your qualifications, will keep your application on file for six months or so and may contact you if a position becomes available.

It is a good idea to begin compiling employer information for your job search while you are still completing your paralegal studies. Many of the resources you will need are available at the college or university that you attend or through your paralegal program (and increasingly, online).

The Yellow Pages

An obvious source of information is the Yellow Pages of your local telephone directory. Look under "Attorneys" for the names of attorneys and law firms in your locale. If you want to work in a specialty area, such as real estate, you might look under other listings, such as "Title Companies." Many libraries have the Yellow Pages for major cities across the country, which allows you to broaden the geographic scope of your search. You may be able to find similar information in online Yellow Pages listings.

---

state bar association
An association of attorneys within a state. In most states, an attorney must be a member of the state bar association to practice law in the state.

trade journal
A newsletter, magazine, or other periodical that provides a certain trade or profession with information (products, trends, or developments) relating to that trade or profession.

On the Web

You can search the Yellow Pages online at a number of Web sites, including Yahoo's Yellow Pages at **http://yp.yahoo.com**.

Ethics Watch!

THE IMPORTANCE OF BEING HONEST

When looking for a job, always be honest with others about your skills and experience. Even though you may want to impress a prospective employer, never succumb to the temptation to exaggerate your qualifications. For example, suppose that you are working for a law firm during your internship and would really like to be hired by the firm in the future as a paralegal. In conversations with supervisors, or others in the firm, refrain from trying to impress them by making misleading statements about your academic qualifications or the skills that you possess. For instance, suppose that you mention to your supervisor that your GPA was 3.8 when in fact it was 3.4. This "little white lie" may come back to haunt you in the future. If the firm offers you a permanent job, it will likely check your credentials, including your transcripts. Any misrepresentation, no matter how minor it may seem, will create a negative impression. Professional responsibility requires, among other things, that you be honest and pay scrupulous attention to detail—not only on the job but also when you are looking for a job.

Legal Directories

There are numerous legal directories that provide lists of attorneys, their locations, and their areas of practice. The *Martindale-Hubbell Law Directory,* which you can find at most law libraries (and online at **http://www.martindale.com**), lists the names, addresses, telephone numbers, areas of legal practice, and other data for many lawyers and law firms throughout the United States. It is an excellent resource for paralegals interested in working for law firms or corporate legal departments. *Legal Directory* is another valuable source of information. It is on the Internet at **http://lawyers.findlaw.com**. The directory contains a detailed listing of U.S. attorneys and law firms, state and federal attorneys and offices, and corporate legal departments and general counsel.

Job-Placement Services

Throughout your job search, make full use of your school's placement service. Many paralegal programs provide job-placement services, and ABA-approved schools are required to provide ongoing placement services for students. Placement offices are staffed with personnel trained to assist you in finding a job, as well as in preparing job-search tools, such as your résumé and a list of potential employers.

A growing trend is to use legal staffing or placement companies (also known as *recruiters*) to locate employment. Usually, the employer pays the fees for the placement company's services, and the company recruits candidates for the paralegal position and arranges interviews. Placement services can be located through paralegal program directors, local paralegal associations, state bar associations, or on the Web.

Legal staffing companies place paralegal employees in both temporary (called "contract") and full-time (called "direct-hire") positions. Temporary contract employees are often used when a regular employee needs to take emergency or medical leave or when a special project requires additional paralegals, such as in large-scale litigation cases. Contract jobs can last from

On the Web

If you are looking for a job in a corporate legal department, Hoovers Online offers company and contact information for many public and private companies worldwide at **http://www.hoovers.com**.

a few days to over a year. Long-term contract opportunities can provide valuable work experience in a particular specialty. Direct-hire positions typically provide long-term employment with salary and benefits, which are not provided in most temporary employment contracts.

REEVALUATING YOUR CAREER

Once you have gained experience working as a paralegal, you can undertake the third step in career planning: reevaluation. Assume that you have worked for a long enough period (two to four years, for example) to have acquired experience in certain types of paralegal work. At this point, you should reevaluate your career goals and reassess your abilities based on your accumulated experience.

Paralegals who want to advance in their careers normally have three options: (1) being promoted or transferring to another department or branch office of the firm; (2) moving to another firm, and perhaps another specialty; and (3) going back to school for additional education.

Career Paths

Large firms often provide career paths for their paralegal employees. Moving from the entry-level position of *legal-assistant clerk* to the position of *legal-assistant manager,* for example, may be one career track within a large law firm. A career track with a state government agency might begin at a *legal-technician* level and advance to a *legal-specialist* level.

Creating Opportunities

Smaller firms, in contrast, usually have no predetermined career path or opportunities for promotion and career advancement. If you are the only paralegal in a small law firm, there will be no specified career path within the firm for you to follow. If you find yourself in this situation, you might consider staying with the firm and creating your own position or career ladder. Moving up the ladder is often a matter of bringing in someone new to assist you with your paralegal responsibilities. Are you prevented from taking on more complicated tasks (which you are capable of performing) because of your heavy workload, much of which could be handled by a paralegal with less experience? Suggest a plan to your employer that shows how you can provide more complex legal services if you delegate many of your existing responsibilities to a new paralegal employee. One of the advantages of working for a small firm is the lack of any set, formal structure for promotions. If the firm is expanding, the paralegal may have significant input into how and to whom responsibilities will be assigned as new people are hired.

You can also create opportunities by acquiring additional education. If you are interested in a particular specialty area, course work in that area, in addition to your existing paralegal training and experience, may help land a job that can advance your career ambitions. Alternatively, you might decide to work toward an advanced degree, such as a master's in business administration (MBA), to create new career opportunities. Some paralegals opt to go to law school and become attorneys.

Other Options

There are many other alternatives. You may apply for a job with another firm that offers you a better position or more advancement opportunities. You might apply for a position that has become available in a branch office of your firm. You might volunteer to speak to paralegal classes and seminars and, in so doing, establish new contacts and contribute to paralegal professional development. Researching and writing law-related articles for your paralegal association's newsletter or trade magazine improves your professional stature in the legal

Today's Professional Paralegal

A VIEW FROM THE INSIDE: ASSISTING A CIVIL LITIGATION PARALEGAL

One of the best ways for a paralegal student to get a sense of a professional paralegal's trial responsibilities is to assist with a case being tried in court. As a project concluding their Introduction to Paralegal Studies course, paralegal students Jay Herrera and Kelly Devon spent two weeks assisting in and observing a federal court case.

The case, conducted in a U.S. district court, originated when a union member brought a federal civil rights action against the Santa Corina Police Department (SCPD) and several officers. The lawsuit was the result of an altercation between a group of police officers and several union members who were picketing outside the gate of their employer, Duhaime News Service (DNS). The plaintiff was seeking to recover damages from the officers and the SCPD for excessive use of force, false arrest, and conspiring with DNS to suppress picketing activities.

Kelly and Jay worked with the state attorney general's office, which represented the police department in the case, both before and during the trial as paralegals. The project extended over two weeks. Kelly and Jay first assisted in the final trial-preparation work and then played supporting roles on the day of the trial.

ASSISTING WITH TRIAL PREPARATIONS

Shawna Jameson, a civil paralegal specialist for the state attorney general's office, talked with Jay and Kelly about the trial process and about Shawna's role as a paralegal. Shawna described her functions during the initial interview and explained how she conducted or assisted with other interviews and investigations. Shawna showed them how her office's filing system was organized. She then described how she assisted the attorneys by researching and organizing information to be used in drafting pretrial documents and requests for information from the opposing party. She also demonstrated how she compiled and organized litigation files.

The week before the trial, with Shawna's guidance, Kelly organized all of the photographs, diagrams, and other exhibits that would be used as evidence. Kelly then scanned the documents into the computer and helped Shawna set up a Microsoft PowerPoint presentation. Meanwhile, Jay organized all of the documents needed for the trial notebook according to Shawna's instructions. (Detailed information on a paralegal's role in pretrial preparation is provided in Chapter 13.)

THE DAY OF THE TRIAL

Kelly and Jay arrived early on the day of the trial. Jay sat next to Shawna and right behind the attorney representing the state, keeping a copy of the trial notebook in hand and following along as the trial progressed. Kelly sat at a nearby table with her laptop computer. As soon as she arrived, Kelly opened and tested her PowerPoint presentation. Jay watched as the room gradually filled with police officers, union representatives, corporate officers from DNS, and, finally, the judge.

Kelly ran the PowerPoint presentation software to display evidence when the attorney was presenting their side of the case. Jay was responsible for retrieving the proper documents for the attorney as they were needed during the trial. To stay on track and be prepared, each needed to follow the attorney's presentation carefully.

MEETING THE PARTICIPANTS

During the lunch break, Kelly and Jay had an opportunity to meet the attorneys briefly and talk with some of the police officers. Kelly briefly spoke with the judge. Both expressed excitement after meeting some of the players.

When the trial was over, Jay and Kelly each wrote a report for class describing their experiences and what they had learned. Over the two-week period, Jay and Kelly had gained many insights into the trial process and had expanded their understanding of a paralegal's role in a trial. At the conclusion of their project, Kelly and Jay both expressed gratitude to Shawna for this valuable window of insight into the paralegal profession. They also told Shawna how impressed they were with her ability to effectively manage all the aspects of her job.

community as well. Any of these activities will increase your visibility both inside and outside the firm. In a broad sense, these activities are part of networking. The people you meet when engaging in these activities may offer you employment opportunities that you did not even know existed but that are perfect for you.

KEY TERMS AND CONCEPTS

bankruptcy law   35

bonus   41

civil law   37

contract   33

corporate law   31

criminal law   37

defendant   31

elder law   38

environmental law   36

estate planning   34

family law   37

freelance paralegal   30

independent paralegal   30

insurance   33

intellectual property   36

legal nurse consultant (LNC)   39

legal technician   30

litigation   30

litigation paralegal   30

networking   45

overtime wages   42

plaintiff   31

probate   34

probate court   34

real estate   33

state bar association   46

trade journal   46

trust   35

will   34

workers' compensation statutes   34

chapter summary   Career Opportunities

Where Paralegals Work

1. *Law firms*—Today, over two-thirds of paralegals work in law firms. The majority of these paralegals work in small law firms—those employing fewer than twenty attorneys. Working for a small firm enables a legal assistant to gain experience in a number of areas of law and is characterized by a more personal and less formal environment. The drawback is that paralegals in small firms often earn less than those in larger firms and often need to perform secretarial duties. Paralegals working for larger firms tend to specialize in one or more areas of law, receive higher salaries, enjoy better employee benefits, and have more support staff.

2. *Corporations and other businesses*—About one-fifth of today's legal assistants work in corporations. Large corporate legal departments often have hundreds of attorneys and paralegals on their staffs. Paralegals working for corporations work regular hours, do not have to be concerned with billable hours (discussed in Chapter 4), and generally receive higher salaries than other paralegals. They may also specialize in certain aspects of corporate law. In addition, many other public and private institutions hire paralegals as a cost-saving measure and because of their legal and analytical skills. Paralegals work for insurance companies, banks, real estate companies, title insurance companies, law book publishers, legal-software companies, and law schools.

3. *Government*—Paralegals work in many government administrative agencies, such as the Environmental Protection Agency. Other employment opportunities exist with legislative offices, public prosecutors' offices, public defenders' offices, and federal and state courts.

4. *Legal aid offices*—Some paralegals find it rewarding to work in legal aid offices, which provide legal services to those who find it difficult to pay for legal representation. These offices are largely funded by the government, but some support comes from private legal foundations.

5. *Freelance paralegals*—Some experienced paralegals own their own businesses and perform legal work for attorneys on a contract basis. This type of work is more flexible with respect to working hours and can be done from a home office. Freelance paralegals work for only attorneys and thus are still supervised by attorneys. The success (and income) of a paralegal in this endeavor depends on the individual's skill, business sense, and motivation.

Paralegal Specialties

Many paralegals specialize in one area of law. The five areas in which the largest numbers of paralegals currently specialize are litigation, corporate law, personal-injury law, contract law, and real estate law. There are numerous other areas in which a legal assistant can specialize, including insurance law, employment and labor law, estate planning and probate administration, bankruptcy law, intellectual property law, environmental law, family law, criminal law, elder law, and legal nurse consulting.

Paralegal Compensation

Salaries and wage rates for paralegal employees vary substantially. Factors affecting compensation include geographical location, firm size, years of paralegal experience, and type of employer (law firm, corporation, or government agency). The issue of whether paralegals qualify for the professional exemption under the Fair Labor Standards Act (and thus are exempt from overtime-pay requirements of the act) was clarified by the U.S. Department of Labor's 2004 FairPay rule. Under this rule, most paralegals do not qualify for the professional exemption. When evaluating compensation, paralegals should consider not only salary or wages but also job benefits, such as insurance coverage, sick/vacation/holiday leave, and pension plans.

Planning Your Career

Career planning involves three steps: defining your long-term career goals, devising short-term goals and adjusting those goals to fit job realities, and reevaluating your career and career goals after you have had some on-the-job experience.

Locating Potential Employers

When looking for employment, paralegals should apply the investigative skills that they learned in their paralegal training.

1. *Networking*—Many paralegals learn of jobs through networking with other professionals. You can begin networking while you are still a paralegal student. If your local paralegal association allows students to become members, join the association. Knowing others in the legal community is an invaluable resource when looking for a job.

2. *Advertised job openings*—You can locate potential employers by reviewing published and posted information about law firms and other possible employers. Advertisements can be found in trade journals, in newspapers, on the Internet, and at your school's placement office.

(Continued)

3. *Legal directories*—Paralegals can also use the Yellow Pages of the phone book and numerous attorneys' directories to identify potential employers. Many of these resources can now be accessed via the Internet.

4. *Job-placement services*—

   a. School placement services—Paralegals should stay in contact with their school's placement office, which is typically staffed with personnel trained to assist paralegals with all aspects of job hunting.

   b. Legal staffing or private placement companies—Increasingly, paralegals are locating employment through private placement companies. Usually, the employer pays the placement company's fees and the company recruits candidates for the position and schedules interviews. Placements may be for temporary or long-term positions. Paralegals can find out about job-placement companies through school program directors, local paralegal associations, state bar associations, or the Web.

Reevaluating Your Career

Career goals change over time, as do job opportunities. Advancing in your career may mean educating your employer about your abilities so that you can take on more responsibility, looking for a job in a different department or branch office of the same firm or with another firm, or attending continuing education programs. Active participation in paralegal professional organizations or in paralegal education is a way to achieve higher visibility in the profession and to learn of new professional opportunities.

QUESTIONS FOR REVIEW

1. Name and describe five types of organizations that hire paralegals. Where do most paralegals work?

2. From your perspective, what would be the advantages and disadvantages of each of the following work settings?

   a. A small law firm.

   b. A large law firm.

   c. A corporation.

   d. A government agency or organization.

   e. A legal aid office.

   f. A freelance paralegal operation.

3. List and briefly describe each of the paralegal specialties discussed in this chapter. Which specialty area or areas interest you the most? Why?

4. How are paralegals compensated? What is the average paralegal salary in your region? On average, in what specialty area do paralegals receive the highest salaries?

5. What is the Department of Labor's FairPay rule of 2004? What is the professional exemption to this rule?

6. According to the 2004 FairPay rule, do most paralegals qualify for the professional exemption to the overtime-pay requirements under the Fair Labor Standards Act? Why or why not?

7. How can paralegals locate potential employers? What is networking? How might networking help paralegals find jobs?

8. Of the methods suggested in this chapter for locating potential employers, which method do you think would be the most effective in finding a job? Why?

9. Read through the appendix that follows this chapter and then respond to the following:

   a. List and describe the materials that are needed for the job-application process.

   b. What should you do before a job interview? What

types of questions may be asked during a job interview? What steps should you take after a job interview?

c. When are salary arrangements discussed during the job-application process? What factors other than

salary should you consider when determining what a job is worth?

10. What are some ways in which you can advance in your paralegal career?

ETHICAL QUESTIONS

1. Tom Brown is a legal assistant in a busy litigation firm. As Tom is walking in the door at 8:30 A.M., he passes Mike Walker, his supervising attorney, who is on his way to court to begin a trial. As they pass, Mike says to Tom, "I need a motion and a brief for the *Jones* case. I've left the file on your desk." Mike walks out the door and down the street to court. Tom becomes very anxious because he knows very little about the case and the law involved. Can Tom competently prepare the motion and brief? Why or why not? What should Tom do?

2. Laura Bronson has just started her first job with the firm of Thompson & Smith, a general law practice. Laura is asked to prepare articles of incorporation for one of the firm's corporate clients. Laura did not take corporate law

while studying to be a paralegal and has never prepared articles of incorporation before. Should Laura accept the assignment? If she does accept it, what obligations does she have?

3. Dennis Walker works at a very busy law firm. On each side of his desk, there are one-foot-high stacks of work, leaving only enough room for a small work space in the center of the desk and a spot for the telephone. His floor is likewise stacked high with legal documents. Dennis constantly misses deadlines and is often in trouble for turning work in late or doing work incorrectly. Dennis has tried to get organized but feels that it is impossible to do so because he has such a heavy workload. What are Dennis's ethical obligations in this situation?

PRACTICE QUESTIONS AND ASSIGNMENTS

1. In addition to the traditional law firm, for what types of employers do paralegals work?

2. Read through the appendix following this chapter. Using the sample résumé in Exhibit 2.A1 or Exhibit 2.A2 as a model, prepare a résumé. If possible, try creating a highly professional résumé using word-processing software or other technology. Also create a cover letter to accompany your résumé; the letter should highlight your strengths to a potential employer.

3. Which of the following factors would affect paralegal compensation?

a. Geographical location.

b. Job-interview preparation.

c. Type of employer.

d. Short-term goals.

e. Firm size.

f. The paralegal's specialty area.

4. What are some advantages and disadvantages of working for a small law firm? What are some advantages and disadvantages of working for a large law firm? Which would you prefer to do? Why?

QUESTIONS FOR CRITICAL ANALYSIS

1. If paralegals were deemed professionals under federal law (the Fair Labor Standards Act), how would this affect the way that paralegals were paid? Would it benefit most paralegals to be considered professionals under this law? Why or why not?

2. What are your long-term career goals? Do your short-term goals relate logically to the attainment of your long-term goals? Why or why not? Write one to two paragraphs explaining your long-term goals and how your short-term goals relate to them. Write these paragraphs to a potential employer.

PROJECTS

1. Locate the *Martindale-Hubbell Law Directory* in your school's library or your local law library. Find three law firms in your locale that practice areas of law in which you are interested. Write down the names and addresses of the firms. Also try to find the names of the hiring partners or human resources managers whom you could contact about a job in the future. Start your job file today!

2. Find out if your school has a placement office. If so, does it offer professional assistance or workshops in résumé preparation and interviewing? Find out at what point in your education you may use these services. Make a note of this information and keep it in your job file.

3. Ask your program director if your school has a legal-assistant student club and how you can get involved in it. Network with other students and consider how the club can be used to network on a broader scale—that is, to network with graduates, attorneys, and potential employers.

USING INTERNET RESOURCES

1. On the Internet, access LAWMATCH, an online résumé bank, at **http://www.lawmatch.com**. How do you use it? Would you post your résumé there? Why or why not? If you are currently looking for a position, try posting your résumé on that site.

2. Go to the Career Center of FindLaw at **http://careers. findlaw.com**. Under the heading "Find a Job," click on "Paralegal." Then select your state under the heading "Location," and click on "Search Jobs."

   a. How many positions are listed in your state?

   b. Pick one job listing. Does the description give the name of the firm or company, or is the listing with a legal staffing company?

   c. In which areas of law does the employer practice? Does the employer have a Web address listed? Can you submit a résumé online?

3. Visit the Web site for *Legal Assistant Today* magazine at **http://www.legalassistanttoday.com**. Under the heading "Becoming a Paralegal," you will find many useful articles about the paralegal profession, education, and employment. Select an article about paralegal education and write a three-paragraph summary of the article. Print and attach the first page of the article to submit with your summary.

4.  For additional resources, visit our Web site at **http://www.paralegal.delmar. cengage.com**.

END NOTES

1. NALA 2004 National Compensation and Utilization Survey Report, Section 2, p. 2. This information is available online at **http://www.nala.org/Survey_Table.htm**.

2. One of the difficulties in describing law firm environments is that the terms *small law firm* and *large law firm* mean different things to different people. In a large city, for example, a firm with twenty attorneys might qualify as a small law firm. In a smaller, more rural community, however, a firm with twenty attorneys would be considered a very large law firm. In this text, we refer to law firms with twenty or fewer attorneys as small law firms and firms with more than twenty attorneys as large firms.

3. NALA 2004 National Compensation and Utilization Survey Report, Section 2, p. 13. This information is available online at **http://**

www.nala.org/Survey_Table.htm. Note that the paralegals surveyed were able to select more than one specialty.

4. Copyrights are registered with the U.S. Copyright Office, Library of Congress, Washington, DC 20559. Patents and trademarks are registered with the Patent and Trademark Office, U.S. Department of Commerce, Washington, DC 20231.

5. *U.S. Department of Labor v. Page & Addison, P.C.,* U.S. District Court, Dallas, Texas, No. 91-2655, March 15, 1994.

6. 29 C.F.R. Section 541.301(e)(7). See Chapter 17 for a discussion of how to read citations to the *Code of Federal Regulations*.

7. *Legal Assistant Today,* March/April 2005, p. 58.

APPENDIX TO CHAPTER 2: MARKETING YOUR SKILLS

Once you have located potential employers, as described in the chapter text, the next step in your job search is to market your skills and yourself effectively to those employers. Marketing your skills involves three stages: the application process, interviewing for jobs, and following up on job interviews.

You should keep in mind throughout your job search that each personal contact you make, whether it results in employment or not, has potential for your future. A firm may not hire you today, for example, because you lack experience. But it may hire you a year from now if by then you have the experience that it is seeking. Therefore, always keep track of the contacts you make during your search, be patient, and be professional. You may be surprised how many doors will open for you; if not today, then tomorrow.

THE APPLICATION PROCESS

As a paralegal looking for professional employment, you will need to assemble and present professional application materials. The basic materials you should create are a résumé, a cover letter, a list of professional references, and a portfolio. The following discussion explains each of these documents and gives some practical tips on how to create them.

The Résumé

For almost all job applications, you must submit a personal *résumé,* which summarizes your employment and educational background. Your résumé is an advertisement, and you should invest the time to make that advertisement effective. Because personnel officers in law firms, corporations, and government agencies may receive a hundred or more résumés for each position they advertise, your résumé should create the best possible impression if you want to gain a competitive edge over other job seekers.

Either generate your résumé yourself, using a computer and a laser printer, or have a professional résumé-preparation service do it for you. Format each page so that the reader is able to scan it quickly and catch the highlights. You might vary the type size, but never use a type size or style that is difficult to read.

What to Include in Your Résumé

Your name, address, telephone number, e-mail address, and fax number belong in the heading of your résumé. The body of the résumé should be simple, brief, and clear. As a general rule, it should contain only information that is relevant to the job that you are seeking. A one-page résumé is usually sufficient, unless two pages are required to list relevant educational background and work experience. Exhibits 2A.1 and 2A.2 on pages 56 and 57 show two sample résumés—one of a person with paralegal experience and one of a person without paralegal experience. Note that you should avoid placing your name and address in the upper left-hand corner, as this area is often stapled.

Divide your résumé into logical sections with headings, such as those shown in Exhibits 2A.1 and 2A.2. Whenever you list dates, such as educational and employment dates, list them chronologically, in reverse order. In other words, list your most recent educational or work history first. When discussing your education, list the names, cities, and states of the colleges or universities that you have attended and the degrees that you have received. You may want to indicate your major and minor concentrations and those courses that are most related to your professional goal, such as "Major: Paralegal Studies" or "Minor: Political

EXHIBIT 2A.1
A Sample Résumé of a Person with Paralegal Experience

ELENA LOPEZ

1131 North Shore Drive
Nita City, NI* 48804
Telephone: (616) 555-0102 • Fax: (616) 555-2103 • E-mail: elopez@nitanet.net

EMPLOYMENT OBJECTIVE
A position as a paralegal in a private law firm that specializes in personal-injury practice.

EDUCATION

2002   Postbaccalaureate certificate
Midwestern Professional School for Paralegals, Green Bay, WI
Focus: Litigation Procedures, Legal Investigation, Torts, Arbitration and Mediation, Case Preparation, and Trial. GPA 3.8.

1999   Bachelor of Arts degree
University of Wisconsin, Madison, WI 53706.
Political Science major. GPA 3.5.

PARALEGAL EXPERIENCE

- Caldwell Legal Clinic, Nita City, NI
Paralegal: June 2004 to the present.
Responsibilities: Legal research and document review; drafting discovery documents, including interrogatories, deposition summaries, and requests for admissions; and trial preparation in personal-injury cases.

- Legal Aid Society, Green Bay, WI
Paralegal: June 2002 to May 2004.
Responsibilities: Part-time assistance to legal aid attorneys in their representation of indigent clients in matters such as divorce, abuse, child custody, paternity, and landlord/tenant disputes.

- University of Wisconsin, Madison, WI
Research Assistant: Political Science Department, January 1999 to May 2002.
Responsibilities: Research on the effectiveness of federal welfare programs in reducing poverty in the United States.

AFFILIATIONS
Paralegal Association of Wisconsin
National Association of Legal Assistants

*The abbreviation *NI* stands for Nita, a hypothetical state.

Science." When listing your work experience, specify what your responsibilities have been in each position that you have held. Also include any volunteer work that you have done.

Scholarships or honors should also be indicated. If you have a high grade point average (GPA), you should include the GPA in your résumé. Under the heading "Selected Accomplishments," you might indicate your ability to speak more than one language or other special skill, such as online research skills.

What if you are an entry-level paralegal and have no work experience to list? What can you include on your résumé to fill out the page? If you are facing this situation, add more information on your educational background and experience. You can list specific courses

EXHIBIT 2A.2
A Sample Résumé of a Person without Paralegal Experience

MARCUS BOHMAN

335 W. Alder Street
Gresham, CA 90650
Home Phone: (562) 555-6868 • Mobile Phone: (562) 555-2468 • E-mail: mboh44@gresham.net

OBJECTIVE

To obtain a paralegal position in a firm that specializes in real estate transactions.

QUALIFICATIONS

I am a self-motivated, certified paralegal (CLA 2005) with knowledge and background in real estate and a strong academic record (3.7 GPA). In addition to the education listed below, I have completed several courses on real estate financing and possess excellent accounting skills.

EDUCATION

2005	*Baccalaureate Degree*—ABA-Approved Program University of LaVerne, Legal Studies Program, LaVerne, CA Major: Paralegal Studies; Minor: Business Management Emphasis on Real Property and Land-Use Planning, Legal Research and Writing.

EMPLOYMENT

2005	*Intern, Hansen, Henault, Richmond & Shaw* Researched and drafted numerous real estate documents, including land sale contracts, commercial leases, and deeds. Scheduled meetings with clients. Participated in client interviews and several real estate closings. Filed documents with county.
2000–2004	*Office Assistant, Eastside Commercial Property* Maintained files and handled telephone inquiries at commercial real estate company. Coordinated land surveys and obtained property descriptions.
1999–2000	*Clerk, LandPro Title Company* Coordinated title searches and acted as a liaison among banks, mortgage companies, and the title company.
1997–1999	*Clerk, San Jose County Recorder's office* Handled inquiries from the public and provided instruction to those seeking to look up records via microfiche.

that you took, particular skills—such as computer skills—that you acquired during your paralegal training, and student affiliations.

Do Not Include Personal Data

Avoid including personal data (such as age, marital status, number of children, gender, or hobbies) in your résumé. Employers are prohibited by law from discriminating against employees or job candidates on the basis of race, color, gender, national origin, religion, age, or disability. You can help them fulfill this legal obligation by not including in your résumé any information that could serve as a basis for discrimination. For the same reason, you would be wise not to include a photograph of yourself with your résumé. Also, most prospective employers are not interested in such information as personal preferences, pastimes, or hobbies.

Proofread Your Results

Carefully proofread your résumé. Use the spelling checker and grammar checker on your computer, but do not totally rely on them. Have a friend or teacher review your résumé for punctuation, syntax, grammar, spelling, and content. If you find an error, you need to fix it, even if it means having new résumés printed. A mistake on your résumé tells the potential employer that you are a careless worker, and this message may ruin your chances of landing a job.

The Cover Letter

To encourage the recruiter to review your résumé, you need to capture his or her attention with a *cover letter* that accompanies the résumé. Because the cover letter often represents your first contact with an employer, it should be written carefully and precisely. It should be brief, perhaps only two or three paragraphs in length. Exhibit 2A.3 shows a sample cover letter. Whenever possible, you should learn the name of the individual in charge of hiring (by phone or e-mail, if necessary) and direct your letter to that person. If you do not know the name of the individual responsible for reviewing résumés, use a generic title, such as "Human Resources Manager" or "Legal Assistant Manager."

Your cover letter should point out a few things about yourself and your qualifications for the position that might persuade a recruiter to examine your résumé. As a recently graduated paralegal, for example, you might draw attention to your high academic standing at school, your eagerness to specialize in the same area of law as the employer (perhaps listing some courses relating to that specialty), and your willingness to relocate to the employer's city. Your job is to convince the recruiter that you are a close match to the mental picture that he or she has of the perfect candidate for the job. Make sure that the reader knows when and where you can be reached. Often this is best indicated in the closing paragraph of the letter, as shown in Exhibit 2A.3.

As with your résumé, you should read through your letter several times and have someone else read it also to make sure that it is free from mistakes and easily understood. You should use the same type of paper for your cover letter as you use for your résumé.

What about e-mailing your cover letter and résumé to prospective employers? This is a difficult question. On the one hand, e-mail is much faster than regular mail or express delivery services. On the other hand, an e-mail résumé does not look as nice. Furthermore, while some firms are accustomed to receiving applications by e-mail, others are not, and attorneys generally prefer traditional résumés. Generally, you need to use your own judgment. If the job you are applying for was advertised online or if the employer provided an e-mail address for interested job candidates to use, then e-mail is probably appropriate. Generally, though, job candidates who submit applications via e-mail should also send, via regular mail, printed copies of their letters and résumés.

List of Professional References

If a firm is interested in your application, you will probably be asked to provide a list of references—people whom the firm can contact to obtain information about you and your abilities. A paralegal instructor who has worked closely with you on an academic project, an internship supervisor who has firsthand knowledge of your work, or a past employer who has observed your problem-solving ability would all make excellent references. You should have at least three professionally relevant references, but no more than five references are necessary (if an interviewer needs additional references, he or she will ask for them). Never include the names of family members, friends, or others who will be clearly biased in your favor.

ELENA LOPEZ

1131 North Shore Drive
Nita City, NI 48804
Telephone: (616) 555-0102 • Fax: (616) 555-2103 • E-mail: elopez@nitanet.net

August 22, 2006

Allen P. Gilmore, Esq.
Jeffers, Gilmore & Dunn
553 Fifth Avenue, Suite 101
Nita City, NI 48801

Dear Mr. Gilmore:

I am responding to your advertisement in the *Vegas Law Journal* for a paralegal to assist you in personal-injury litigation. I am confident that I possess the skills and qualifications that you seek.

As you can see from the enclosed résumé, I received my paralegal certificate from Midwestern Professional School for Paralegals after obtaining a Bachelor of Arts degree from the University of Wisconsin. My paralegal courses included litigation procedures, legal research, legal investigation, and legal writing, and I graduated with a G.P.A. of 3.8.

After completing school, I obtained a position with a legal aid office, where I worked for several years and honed my legal research and writing skills. My current position with Caldwell Legal Clinic has provided me with valuable experience in preparing personal-injury cases for trial. I very much enjoy this area of law and hope to specialize in personal-injury litigation.

I am excited about the possibility of meeting with you to learn more about the position that you have available. I have enclosed my résumé, as well as a list of professional references and a brief writing sample for your perusal.

Please contact me to schedule an interview. I look forward to hearing from you.

Sincerely yours,

Elena Lopez

Elena Lopez

Enclosures

You should list your references on a separate sheet of paper, making sure to include your name, address, and telephone number at the top of the page, in the same format as on your résumé. For each person included on your list of references, include his or her current institutional affiliation or business firm, address, telephone number, fax number, and, if you know it, e-mail address. Generally, try to make it easy for prospective employers to contact and communicate with your references.

When creating your list of references, always remember the following rule: never list a person's name as a reference unless you have first obtained that person's permission to do so.

After all, it will not help you win the position if one of your references is surprised by the call or is unavailable, such as a paralegal instructor who is out of the country for the year. Such events raise a red flag to the interviewer and indicate that you are not concerned with details.

Obtaining permission from legal professionals to use their names as references also gives you an opportunity to discuss your plans and goals with them, and they may be able to advise you and assist you in your networking. Additionally, it gives you a chance to discuss with them the kinds of experience and skills in which a prospective employer may be interested.

Your Professional Portfolio

When a potential employer asks you for an interview, have your *professional portfolio* of selected documents ready to give to the interviewer. The professional portfolio should contain another copy of your résumé, a list of references, letters of recommendation written by previous employers or instructors, samples of legal documents that you have composed, college or university transcripts, and any other relevant professional information, such as proof of professional certification or achievement. This collection of documents should be well organized and professionally presented. Depending on the size of your portfolio, a cover sheet, a table of contents, and a commercial binder may be appropriate.

The interviewer may be very interested in your research and writing skills. Therefore, your professional portfolio should contain several brief samples of legal writing. If you are looking for your first legal position, go through your paralegal drafting assignments and pull out those that reflect your best work and that relate to the job skills you wish to demonstrate. Then, working with an instructor or other mentor, revise and improve those samples for inclusion in the portfolio. Documents that you have drafted while an intern or when working as a part-time or full-time paralegal might also be used. These documents make excellent writing samples because they involve real-life circumstances. Be careful, however, and always remember, on any sample document, to completely blacken out (or "white out") any identifying reference to a client unless you have the client's permission to disclose his or her identity or the information is not confidential.

Always include a résumé, as well as a list of references, in your professional portfolio, even though you already sent your résumé to the prospective employer with your cover letter. Interviewers may not have the résumé at hand at the time of the interview, and providing a second copy with your professional portfolio is a thoughtful gesture on your part.

Some interviewers may examine your professional portfolio carefully. Others may retain it to examine later, after the interview has concluded. Still others may not be interested in it at all. If there is a particular item in your portfolio that you would like the interviewer to see, make sure you point this out before leaving the interview.

THE INTERVIEW

Interviews with potential employers may be the most challenging (and most stressful) aspect of your search for employment. The interview ordinarily takes place after the employer has reviewed your cover letter and résumé. Often, if the employer is interested in your application, a secretary or legal assistant will contact you to schedule an interview.

Every interview will be a unique experience. Some interviews will go very well, but you may still lose out to another candidate. Nonetheless, you have made a good contact, and you may be able to use this interviewer as a resource for information about other jobs. Remember what went right about the interview, and try to use that information at the next one. Other interviews may go poorly. Good lessons can be learned from poor interviews, however.

You will also find that some interviewers are more skilled at interviewing than others. Some have a talent for getting applicants to open up and discuss candidly their work and backgrounds. Others are confrontational and put the already nervous candidate on the defensive. Still others may be unprepared for the interview. They may not have had time to compare applicants' qualifications with the job requirements, for example. Unfortunately, as the person being interviewed, you have no control over who will interview you. The following discussion will help you prepare for a first paralegal job interview and will also serve as a refresher for you when seeking a career change.

Before the Interview

You can do many things prior to the interview to enhance your chances of getting the job. First of all, you should do your "homework." Learn as much about the employer as possible. Check with your instructors or other legal professionals to find out if they are familiar with the firm or the interviewer. Check the employer's Web site, if there is one, and consult relevant directories, such as legal and company directories, as well as business publications, to see what you can learn about the firm and its members. When you are called for an interview, learn the full name of the interviewer, so that you will be able to address him or her by name during the interview and properly address a follow-up letter. During the interview, use Mr. or Ms. in addressing the interviewer unless directed by the interviewer to be less formal.

Anticipate and review in your mind the questions that you might be asked during the interview. Then prepare (and possibly rehearse with a friend) your answers to these questions. For example, if you did not graduate from high school with your class but later fulfilled the requirements to graduate and received a general equivalency diploma (GED), you might well be asked why you dropped out of school. If you have already prepared an answer for this question, it may save you the embarrassment of having to decide, on the spot, how to reduce a complicated story to a brief sentence or two.

You should also prepare yourself to be interviewed by a "team" of legal professionals, such as an attorney and another paralegal or perhaps two or more attorneys and/or paralegals. Many prospective employers today invite others who will be working with a new paralegal to participate in the interviewing process.

Promptness is an extremely important factor. Arrive for the interview at least ten minutes early, and allow plenty of extra time to get there. If the firm is located in an area that is unfamiliar to you, make sure that you know how to get there, how long it will take, and, if you are driving, whether parking space is available nearby.

Appearance is also important. Wear a relatively conservative suit or dress to the interview, and limit your use of jewelry or other flashy accents. You can find further tips on how to prepare for a job interview by checking online career sites or by looking at books dealing with careers and job hunting at a local bookstore or the library.

At the Interview

During the interview, pay attention and listen closely to the interviewer's questions, observations, and comments. The interviewer asks questions to learn whether the candidate will fit comfortably into the firm, whether the candidate is organized and competent and will satisfactorily perform the job, and whether the candidate is reliable and will apply himself or herself to mastering the tasks presented. Your answers should be directly related to the questions, and you should not stray from the point. If you are unsure of what the interviewer means by a certain question, ask for clarification.

Interviewers use certain question formats to elicit certain types of responses. Four typical formats for questions are the following:

- *Closed-ended questions*—to elicit simple "Yes" or "No" answers.
- *Open-ended questions*—which invite you to discuss, in some detail, a specific topic or experience.
- *Hypothetical questions*—to learn how you might respond to situations that could arise during the course of your employment.

EXHIBIT 2A.4
Objectionable or Illegal Questions and Possible Responses

> **Q. Are you married?**
>
> **A.** If you are concerned that my social life will interfere with work, I can assure you that I keep the two very distinct.
>
> **Q. Do you have any children yet?**
>
> **A.** That question leads me to believe that you would be concerned about my ability to prioritize my job and other responsibilities. Is that something that you are worried about?
>
> **Q. Are you or your husband a member of the Republican Party?**
>
> **A.** That is a private matter. Please realize that my family and political life will not interfere with my ability to do excellent work for your firm.
>
> **Q. You're quite a bit more mature than other applicants. Will you be thinking of retiring in the next ten years?**
>
> **A.** I don't understand how my age relates to my ability to perform this job.

- *Pressure questions*—to see how you deal with uncomfortable situations or unpleasant discussions.

You will learn more about question formats in Chapter 14, when we discuss some techniques that paralegals use when interviewing clients.

Be aware that certain types of questions are illegal, or at least objectionable. These include questions directed at your marital status, family, religion, race, color, national origin, age, health or disability, or arrest record. You do not have to answer such questions unless you choose to do so. Exhibit 2A.4 shows some examples of how you might respond to these types of questions.

As odd as it may seem, one of the most difficult moments is when the interviewer turns the inquiry around by asking, "Now then, do you have any questions?" Be prepared for this query. Before the interview, take time to list your concerns. Bring the list to the interview with you. Questioning the interviewer gives you an opportunity to learn more about the firm and how it uses paralegal services. Questioning the interviewer also may also give the interviewer an opportunity to see how you might interview a client on behalf of the firm. Exhibit 2A.5 lists some sample questions that you might ask the interviewer. Note that you should not raise the issue of salary at the first interview unless you are offered the job.

After the Interview

You should not expect to be hired as the result of a single interview, although occasionally this does happen. Often, two and even three interviews take place before you are offered a job. After leaving the interview, jot down a few notes to provide a refresher for your memory should you be called back for a second (or third) interview. You will impress the interviewer if you are able to "pick up where you left off" from a discussion initiated several weeks earlier. Also, list the names and positions of the people you met during the interview or just before or after it.

THE FOLLOW-UP/THANK-YOU LETTER

A day or two after the interview, but not longer than a week later, you should send a *follow-up letter* to the interviewer. In this brief letter, you can reiterate your availability and interest in the position, thank the interviewer for his or her time in interviewing you, and perhaps refer to a discussion that took place during the interview.

Questions that you might want to ask the interviewer include the following:

- What method does the firm use to assign duties to paralegals?
- How do paralegals function within the organization?
- What clerical support staff is available for paralegals?
- Does the job involve travel? How will travel expenses be covered?
- What computer technology is used by the firm?
- Does the firm support paralegal continuing education and training programs?
- Will client contact be direct or indirect?
- Does the firm have an in-house library and access to computerized research services that paralegals can use?
- Will the paralegal be assigned work in a given specialty, such as real estate or family law?
- When does the job begin?
- What method is used to review and evaluate paralegal performance?
- How are paralegals supervised, and by whom?
- Are paralegals classified as exempt employees by this firm?
- Is there a written job description or employee policy manual for the job that I may review?

You may have left the interview with the impression that the meeting went poorly. But the interviewer may have a different sense of what happened at the meeting. Interviewers have different styles, and what you interpreted to be a bad interview may just have been a reflection of that interviewer's approach or style. You simply have no way of being certain, so follow through and make yourself available for the job or at least for another meeting. For an example of a follow-up letter, see Exhibit 2A.6 on the following page.

JOB-HUNTING FILES

In addition to keeping your professional portfolio materials up to date, you need to create a filing system to stay abreast of your job-search activities. You should create a separate file for each potential employer and keep copies of your letters, including e-mail messages, to that employer in your file, along with any responses. You might also want to keep lists or notes for addresses, telephone numbers, e-mail addresses, dates of contacts, advantages and disadvantages of employment with the various firms that you have contacted or by which you have been interviewed, topics discussed at interviews, and so on. Then, when you are called for an interview, you will have information on the firm at your fingertips. Always keep in mind that when looking for paralegal employment, your "job" is finding work as a paralegal—and it pays to be efficient.

Your files will also provide you with an excellent resource for networking even after you have a permanent position. The files may also provide useful information for a career change in the future.

SALARY NEGOTIATIONS

Sometimes a firm states a salary or a salary range in its advertisement for a paralegal. During a first interview, a prospective employer may offer that information as well. In other situations, an applicant does not know what the salary for a certain position will be until he or she is offered the job.

EXHIBIT 2A.6
A Sample Follow-Up Letter

ELENA LOPEZ

1131 North Shore Drive
Nita City, NI 48804
Telephone: (616) 555-0102 • Fax: (616) 555-2103 • E-mail: elopez@nitanet.net

September 3, 2006

Allen P. Gilmore, Esq.
Jeffers, Gilmore & Dunn
553 Fifth Avenue, Suite 101
Nita City, NI 48801

Dear Mr. Gilmore:

Thank you for taking time out of your busy schedule to meet with me last Thursday
about your firm's paralegal position. I very much enjoyed our discussion, as well as
the opportunity to meet some of your firm's employees.

I am extremely interested in the possibility of becoming a member of your legal team
and look forward to the prospect of meeting with you again in the near future.

Sincerely yours,

Elena Lopez

Elena Lopez

When you are offered a job, be prepared for the prospective employer to indicate a
salary figure and ask you if that figure is acceptable to you. If it is acceptable, then you have
no problem. If you think it is too low, then the situation becomes more delicate. If you have
no other job offer and really need a job, you may not want to foreclose this job opportunity
by saying that the salary is too low. You might instead tell the prospective employer that the
job interests you and that you will consider the offer seriously. Also, remember that salary is
just one factor in deciding what a job is worth to you. In addition to salary, you need to consider job benefits and other factors, including those listed in Exhibit 2A.7.

Some prospective employers do not suggest a salary or a salary range but rather ask the
job applicant what kind of salary he or she had in mind. You should be prepared for this
question and should have researched paralegal salaries in the area.

Unless you are already familiar with the firm's salary structure, you should research the
compensation given to paralegals in similar job situations in your community before you
discuss salary with a prospective employer. You can find information on salaries by checking local, state, and national paralegal compensation surveys. Check first with your local
paralegal association to see if it has collected data on local paralegal salaries. You might also
find helpful information in your school's placement office.

Suppose that you have found in your research that paralegals in the community usually
start at $36,000 but that many with your education and training start at $43,000. If you ask

for an annual salary of $45,000, then you may be unrealistically expensive—and the job offer may be lost. If you ask for $43,000, then you are still "in the ballpark"—and you may win the job.

Negotiating salaries can be difficult. On the one hand, you want to obtain a good salary and do not want to underprice your services. On the other hand, overpricing your services may extinguish an employment opportunity or eliminate the possibility of working for an otherwise suitable employer. Your best option might be to state a salary range that is acceptable to you. That way, you are not pinned down to a specific figure. Note, though, that if you indicate an acceptable salary range, you invite an offer of the lowest salary—so the low end of the salary range should be the threshold amount that you will accept.

EXHIBIT 2A.7
Salary Negotiations: What Is This Job Worth to You?

BENEFITS

What benefits are included? • Will the benefits package include medical insurance? • Life insurance? • Disability insurance? • Dental insurance? • What portion, if any, of the insurance premium will be deducted from your wages? • Is there an employee pension plan? • How many paid vacation days will you have? • Will the firm cover your paralegal association fees? • Will the firm assist you with tuition and other costs associated with continuing paralegal education? • Will the firm assist with day-care arrangements and/or costs? • Will you have access to a company automobile? • Does the firm help with parking expenses (important in major cities)?

CAREER OPPORTUNITIES

Does the position offer you opportunities for advancement? You may be willing to accept a lower salary now if you know that it will increase as you move up the career ladder.

COMPENSATION

Will you receive an annual salary or be paid by the hour? • If you will receive an annual salary, will you receive annual bonuses? • How are bonuses determined? • Is the salary negotiable? (In some large firms and in government agencies, it may not be.)

COMPETITION

How stiff is the competition for this job? If you really want the job and are competing with numerous other candidates for the position, you might want to accept a lower salary just to land the job.

JOB DESCRIPTION

What are the paralegal's duties within the organization? Do you have sufficient training and experience to handle these duties? • Are you under- or overqualified for the job? • Will your skills as a paralegal be utilized effectively? • How hard will you be expected to work? • How much overtime work will likely be required? • How stressful will the job be?

JOB FLEXIBILITY

How flexible are the working hours? • If you work eight hours overtime one week, can you take a (paid) day off the following week? • Can you take time off during periods when the workload is less?

LOCATION

Do you want to live in this community? • What is the cost of living in this area? Remember, a $40,000 salary in New York City, where housing and taxes are very expensive, may not give you as much real income as a $30,000 salary in a smaller, midsized community in the Midwest.

PERMANENCE

Is the job a permanent or temporary position? Usually, hourly rates are higher for temporary assistance than for permanent employees.

TRAVEL

Will you be required to travel? • If so, how often or extensively? • How will travel expenses be handled? Will you pay them and then be reimbursed by the employer?

ETHICS AND PROFESSIONAL RESPONSIBILITY

CHAPTER OUTLINE

AFTER COMPLETING THIS CHAPTER, YOU WILL KNOW:

▶ Why and how legal professionals are regulated.

▶ Some important ethical rules governing the conduct of attorneys.

▶ How the rules governing attorneys affect paralegal practice.

▶ The kinds of activities that paralegals are and are not legally permitted to perform.

▶ Some of the pros and cons of regulation, including the debate over paralegal licensing.

INTRODUCTION

As discussed in the previous chapter, paralegals preparing for a career in today's legal arena have a variety of career options. Regardless of which career path you choose to follow, you should have a firm grasp of your state's ethical rules governing the legal profession. When you work under the supervision of an attorney, as most paralegals do, you and the attorney become team members. You will work together on behalf of clients and share in the ethical and legal responsibilities arising as a result of the attorney-client relationship.

In preparing for a career as a paralegal, you must know what these responsibilities are, why they exist, and how they affect you. The first part of this chapter is devoted to the regulation of attorneys because the ethical duties imposed on attorneys by state law affect paralegals as well. If a paralegal violates one of the rules governing attorneys, that violation may result in serious consequences for the client, for the attorney, and for the paralegal. As you read through the rules governing attorney conduct that are discussed in this chapter, keep in mind that these rules also govern paralegal practice, if indirectly.

Although attorneys are subject to direct regulation by the state, paralegals are not, except in California. Other states may directly regulate paralegals in the near future, however, in the form of licensing requirements. Paralegals are regulated indirectly both by attorney ethical codes and by state laws that prohibit nonlawyers from practicing law.[1] As the paralegal profession develops, professional paralegal organizations, the American Bar Association, and state bar associations continue to issue guidelines that also serve to indirectly regulate paralegals.

THE REGULATION OF ATTORNEYS

The term *regulate* derives from the Latin term *regula,* meaning "rule." According to Webster's dictionary, to regulate means "to control or direct in agreement with a rule." To a significant extent, attorneys engage in **self-regulation** because they themselves establish the majority of the rules governing their profession. One of the hallmarks of a profession is the establishment of minimum standards and levels of competence for its members. The accounting profession, for example, has established such standards, as have physicians, engineers, and members of virtually every other profession.

Attorneys are also regulated externally by the state, because the rules of behavior established by the legal profession are adopted and enforced by state authorities. The purpose of regulating attorney behavior is to protect the public interest. First, by establishing educational and licensing requirements, state authorities ensure that anyone practicing law is competent to do so. Second, by defining specific ethical requirements for attorneys, the states protect the public against unethical attorney behavior that may affect clients' welfare. We will discuss these requirements and rules shortly. Before we do, however, you should know how these rules are created and enforced.

> **self-regulation**
> The regulation of the conduct of a professional group by members of the group. Self-regulation usually involves the establishment of ethical or professional standards of behavior with which members of the group must comply.

Who Are the Regulators?

Key participants in determining what rules should govern attorneys and the practice of law, as well as how these rules should be enforced, are bar associations, state supreme courts, state legislatures, and, in some cases, the United States Supreme Court. Procedures for regulating attorneys vary, of course, from state to state. What follows is a general discussion of some of the possible regulators.

Bar Associations

Lawyers themselves determine the requirements for entering the legal profession and the rules of conduct they will follow. Traditionally, lawyers have joined together in professional groups, or bar associations, at the local, state, and national levels to discuss issues affecting the legal profession and to decide on standards of professional conduct.

On the Web

You can access information on state bar associations, legislatures, and courts, including the United States Supreme Court, at **http://www.findlaw.com**. The American Bar Association is online at **http://www.abanet.org**.

Although membership in local and national bar associations is always voluntary, membership in the state bar association is mandatory in many states. In these states, before an attorney can practice law, he or she must be admitted to the state's bar association. Approximately half of the lawyers in the United States are members of the American Bar Association (ABA), the voluntary national bar association discussed in Chapter 1. As you will read shortly, the ABA plays a key regulatory role by proposing model (uniform) codes, or rules of conduct, for adoption by the various states.

State Supreme Courts

Typically, the state's highest court, often called the state supreme court, is the ultimate regulatory authority in that state.[2] The court's judges decide what conditions (such as licensing requirements, discussed below) must be met before an attorney can practice law within the state and under what conditions that privilege will be suspended or revoked. In many states, the state supreme court works closely with the state bar association. The state bar association may recommend rules and requirements to the court. If the court so orders, these rules and requirements become state law. Under the authority of the courts, state bar associations often perform routine regulatory functions, including the initiation of disciplinary proceedings against attorneys who fail to comply with professional requirements.

State Legislatures

State legislatures regulate the legal profession by enacting legislation affecting attorneys—statutes prohibiting the unauthorized practice of law, for example. In a few states, the states' highest courts delegate significant regulatory responsibilities to the state legislatures, which may include the power to bring disciplinary proceedings against attorneys.

The United States Supreme Court

Occasionally, the United States Supreme Court decides issues relating to attorney conduct. For example, until a few decades ago, state ethical codes, or rules governing attorney conduct, prohibited lawyers from advertising their services to the public. These restrictions on advertising were later determined to be an unconstitutional limitation on attorneys' rights to free speech by the United States Supreme Court.[3]

Licensing Requirements

licensing
A government's official act of granting permission to an individual, such as an attorney, to do something that would be illegal in the absence of such permission.

The **licensing** of attorneys, which gives them the right to practice law, is accomplished at the state level. Each state has different requirements that individuals must meet before they are allowed to practice law and give legal advice. Generally, however, there are three basic requirements:

1. In most states, prospective attorneys must have obtained a bachelor's degree from a university or college[4] and must have graduated from an accredited law school (in many states, the school must be accredited by the ABA), which requires an additional three years of study.

2. In all states, a prospective attorney must pass a state bar examination—a very rigorous and thorough examination that tests the candidate's knowledge of the law and (in some states) of the state's ethical rules governing attorneys. The examination covers both state law (law applicable to the particular state in which the attorney is taking the exam and wishes to practice) and multistate law (law applicable in most states, including federal law).[5]

3. The candidate must pass an extensive personal background investigation to verify that he or she is a responsible individual and otherwise qualifies to engage in an ethical profession. An illegal act committed by the candidate in the past, for example, might disqualify the individual from being permitted to practice law.

Only when these requirements have been met can an individual be admitted to the state bar and legally practice law within the state.

Licensing requirements for attorneys are the result of a long history of attempts to restrict entry into the legal profession. The earliest of these restrictions date to the colonial era. During the 1700s, local bar associations began to form agreements to restrict membership to those who fulfilled certain educational and apprenticeship requirements. At the same time, to curb unnecessary litigation and the detrimental effects of incompetent legal practitioners, courts began to require that individuals representing clients in court proceedings had to be licensed by the court to do so.

Beginning in the mid-1850s, restrictions on who could (or could not) practice law were given statewide effect by state statutes prohibiting the **unauthorized practice of law (UPL)**. Court decisions relating to unauthorized legal practice also date to this period. By the 1930s, virtually all states had enacted legislation prohibiting anyone but licensed attorneys from practicing law. As you will see in subsequent sections, many of the regulatory issues facing the legal profession—and particularly paralegals—are directly related to these UPL statutes.

> **unauthorized practice of law (UPL)**
> The performance of actions defined by a legal authority, such as a state legislature, as constituting the "practice of law" without legal authorization to do so.

Ethical Codes and Rules

The legal profession is also regulated through ethical codes and rules adopted by each state—in most states, by order of the state supreme court. These codes of professional conduct—the names of the codes vary from state to state—evolved over a long period of time. A major step toward ethical regulation was taken in 1908, when the ABA approved the Canons of Ethics, which consisted of thirty-two ethical principles. In the following decades, various states adopted these canons as law.

Today's state ethical codes are based, for the most part, on two subsequent revisions of the ABA canons: the Model Code of Professional Responsibility (published in 1969) and the Model Rules of Professional Conduct (first published in 1983 to replace the Model Code and revised numerous times since then). Although most states have adopted laws based on the Model Rules, the Model Code is still in effect in some states. You should therefore be aware of both the Model Code and the Model Rules and become familiar with the set of rules that is in effect in your state.

The Model Code of Professional Responsibility

The ABA Model Code of Professional Responsibility, often referred to simply as the Model Code, consists of nine canons. In the Model Code, each canon is followed by sections entitled "Ethical Considerations" (ECs) and "Disciplinary Rules" (DRs). The ethical considerations are "aspirational" in character—that is, they suggest ideal conduct, not necessarily behavior that is required by law. For example, Canon 6 ("A lawyer should represent a client competently") is followed by EC 6–1, which states (in part) that a lawyer "should strive to become and remain proficient in his practice." In contrast, disciplinary rules are mandatory in character—an attorney may be subject to disciplinary action for breaking one of the rules. For example, DR 6–101 (which follows Canon 6) states that a lawyer "shall not . . . [n]eglect a legal matter entrusted to him."

The Model Rules of Professional Conduct

The 1983 revision of the Model Code—referred to as the Model Rules of Professional Conduct or, more simply, as the Model Rules—represented a thorough revamping of the code. The Model Rules replaced the canons, ethical considerations, and disciplinary rules of

On the Web

To read the ethics code adopted by your state, go to **http://www.law. cornell.edu/ethics** and click on "Listing by jurisdiction" under the heading "Ways to access material." Then click on the appropriate state. You can also access ethics opinions— formal statements addressing specific problem areas issued by the state bar association—on this site.

For a comprehensive collection of ethics articles and laws, as well as links to other ethics sources, go to **http://www.legalethics.com**.

On the Web

You can access the entire text of the Model Rules of Professional Conduct, along with an explanation of the 2002 revision and other changes to the rules, on the ABA's Web site at **http://www.abanet.org/ cpr/mrpc/model_rules.html**.

the Model Code with a set of rules organized under eight general headings, as outlined in Exhibit 3.1. Each rule is followed by comments shedding additional light on the rule's application and how it compares with the Model Code's treatment of the same issue.

EXHIBIT 3.1
The ABA Model Rules of Professional Conduct (Headings Only)

CLIENT-LAWYER RELATIONSHIP

1.1	Competence
1.2	Scope of Representation and Allocation of Authority between Client and Lawyer
1.3	Diligence
1.4	Communications
1.5	Fees
1.6	Confidentiality of Information
1.7	Conflict of Interest: Current Clients
1.8	Conflict of Interest: Current Clients: Specific Rules
1.9	Duties to Former Clients
1.10	Imputation of Conflicts of Interest: General Rule
1.11	Special Conflicts of Interest for Former and Current Government Officers and Employees
1.12	Former Judge, Arbitrator, Mediator, or Other Third-Party Neutral
1.13	Organization as Client
1.14	Client with Diminished Capacity
1.15	Safekeeping Property
1.16	Declining or Terminating Representation
1.17	Sale of Law Practice
1.18	Duties to Prospective Client

COUNSELOR

2.1	Advisor
2.2	(Deleted)
2.3	Evaluation for Use by Third Persons
2.4	Lawyer Serving as Third-Party Neutral

ADVOCATE

3.1	Meritorious Claims and Contentions
3.2	Expediting Litigation
3.3	Candor toward the Tribunal
3.4	Fairness to Opposing Party and Counsel
3.5	Impartiality and Decorum of the Tribunal
3.6	Trial Publicity
3.7	Lawyer as Witness
3.8	Special Responsibilities of a Prosecutor
3.9	Advocate in Nonadjudicative Proceedings

TRANSACTIONS WITH PERSONS OTHER THAN CLIENTS

4.1	Truthfulness in Statements to Others
4.2	Communication with Person Represented by Counsel
4.3	Dealing with Unrepresented Person
4.4	Respect for Rights of Third Persons

LAW FIRMS AND ASSOCIATIONS

5.1	Responsibilities of a Partner or Supervisory Lawyer
5.2	Responsibilities of a Subordinate Lawyer
5.3	Responsibilities Regarding Nonlawyer Assistant
5.4	Professional Independence of a Lawyer
5.5	Unauthorized Practice of Law; Multijurisdictional Practice of Law
5.6	Restrictions on Right to Practice
5.7	Responsibilities Regarding Law-Related Services

PUBLIC SERVICE

6.1	Voluntary *Pro Bono Publico* Service
6.2	Accepting Appointments
6.3	Membership in Legal Services Organization
6.4	Law Reform Activities Affecting Client Interests
6.5	Nonprofit and Court Annexed Limited Legal Services Programs

INFORMATION ABOUT LEGAL SERVICES

7.1	Communication Concerning a Lawyer's Services
7.2	Advertising
7.3	Direct Contact with Prospective Clients
7.4	Communication of Fields of Practice and Specialization
7.5	Firm Names and Letterheads
7.6	Political Contributions to Obtain Legal Engagements or Appointments by Judges

MAINTAINING THE INTEGRITY OF THE PROFESSION

8.1	Bar Admission and Disciplinary Matters
8.2	Judicial and Legal Officials
8.3	Reporting Professional Misconduct
8.4	Misconduct
8.5	Disciplinary Authority; Choice of Law

ABA, *Model Rules of Professional Conduct, 2004* Edition. ©2003 by the American Bar Association. Reprinted with permission. Copies of the ABA *Model Rules of Professional Conduct, 2004* are available from Service Center, American Bar Association, 321 North Clark Street, Chicago, IL 60610, 1-800-285-2221; orders@abanet.org.

Because the 1983 Model Rules serve as models for the ethical codes of most states, we use the 1983 rules as the basis for our discussion in this text. It is important to note, however, that the ABA's ethics commission periodically updates and revises the Model Rules as necessary in light of the realities of modern law practice. For example, in 2002, the ABA's ethics commission made several substantial revisions to the Model Rules to address new ethical concerns raised by technological developments (for example, e-mail and client confidentiality). Not all of the states have adopted these revised rules, however. We discuss the 2002 revisions as appropriate in the following subsections.

Sanctions for Violations

Attorneys who violate the rules governing professional conduct are subject to disciplinary proceedings brought by the state bar association, state supreme court, or state legislature—depending on the state's regulatory scheme. In most states, unethical attorney actions are reported (by clients, legal professionals, or others) to the ethics committee of the state bar association, which is obligated to investigate each complaint thoroughly. For serious violations, the state bar association or the court initiates disciplinary proceedings against the attorney.

Sanctions range from a **reprimand** (a formal "scolding" of the attorney—the mildest sanction[6]), to **suspension** (a more serious sanction by which the attorney is prohibited from practicing law in the state for a given period of time, such as one month or one year, or for an indefinite period of time), to **disbarment** (revocation of the attorney's license to practice law in the state—the most serious sanction).

In addition to these sanctions, attorneys may be subject to civil liability for negligence. As will be discussed in Chapter 7, *negligence* (called **malpractice** when committed by a professional, such as an attorney) is a tort (a wrongful act) that is committed when an individual fails to perform a legally recognized duty. Tort law allows one who is injured by another's wrongful or careless act to bring a civil lawsuit against the wrongdoer for **damages** (compensation in the form of money). Of course, a client is permitted to bring a lawsuit against an attorney only if the client has suffered harm because of the attorney's failure to perform a legal duty.

If a paralegal's breach of a professional duty causes a client to suffer substantial harm, the client may sue not only the attorney but also the paralegal. Although law firms' liability insurance policies typically cover paralegals as well as attorneys, if the paralegal is working on a contract (freelance) basis, he or she will not be covered under a liability policy covering the firm's employees. Just one lawsuit could ruin a freelance paralegal financially—as well as destroy that paralegal's reputation in the legal community. (Note that liability insurance is especially important not only for freelance paralegals but for independent paralegals, or legal technicians, as well.)

Attorneys and paralegals are also subject to potential criminal liability under criminal statutes prohibiting fraud, theft, and other crimes.

ATTORNEY ETHICS AND PARALEGAL PRACTICE

Because most state codes are guided by the Model Rules of Professional Conduct, the rules discussed in this section are drawn from the Model Rules. Keep in mind, though, that your own state's code of conduct is the governing authority on attorney conduct in your state.

As a paralegal, one of your foremost professional responsibilities is to meticulously follow the rules set forth in your state's ethical code. You will thus want to obtain a copy of your state's ethical code and become familiar with its contents. A good practice is to keep the code near at hand in your office (or on your desk).

---

reprimand
A disciplinary sanction in which an attorney is rebuked for his or her misbehavior. Although a reprimand is the mildest sanction for attorney misconduct, it is nonetheless a serious one and may significantly damage the attorney's reputation in the legal community.

suspension
A serious disciplinary sanction in which an attorney who has violated an ethical rule or a law is prohibited from practicing law in the state for a specified or an indefinite period of time.

disbarment
A severe disciplinary sanction in which an attorney's license to practice law in the state is revoked because of unethical or illegal conduct.

malpractice
Professional misconduct or negligence—the failure to exercise due care—on the part of a professional, such as an attorney or a physician.

damages
Money awarded as a remedy for a civil wrong, such as a breach of contract or a tort (wrongful act).

A paralegal discusses with her supervising attorney a potential conflict of interest with respect to a case that the attorney has agreed to accept. Attorneys and paralegals must be extremely careful to avoid violating the ethical rules of the legal profession, because violations of the rules can have serious consequences.

(Courtesy of ©Getty Images)

The ABA provides links to the rules of professional conduct of every state at **http://www.abanet.org/cpr/ links.html**.

Professional duties—and the possibility of violating them—are involved in virtually every task you will perform as a paralegal. Even if you memorize every one of the rules governing the legal profession, you can still quite easily violate a rule unintentionally (you should realize that paralegals rarely breach professional duties intentionally). To minimize the chances that you will unintentionally violate a rule, you need to know not only what the rules are but also how they apply to the day-to-day realities of your job.

The rules relating to competence, confidentiality, and conflict of interest deserve special attention here because they pose particularly difficult ethical problems for paralegals. Other important rules that affect paralegal performance—including the duty to charge reasonable fees, the duty to protect clients' property, and the duty to keep the client reasonably informed—will be discussed elsewhere in this text as they relate to special topics.

The Duty of Competence

Rule 1.1 of the Model Rules states one of the most fundamental duties of attorneys—the duty of competence. The rule reads as follows:

> A lawyer shall provide competent representation to a client. Competent representation requires the legal knowledge, skill, thoroughness and preparation reasonably necessary for representation.

breach
To violate a legal duty by an act or a failure to act.

Competent legal representation is a basic requirement of the profession, and **breaching** (failing to perform) this duty may subject attorneys to one or more of the sanctions discussed earlier. As a paralegal, you should realize that when you undertake work on an attorney's behalf, you share in this duty. If your supervising attorney asks you to research a particular legal issue for a client, for example, you must make sure that your research is careful and thorough—because the attorney's reputation (and the client's welfare) may depend on your performance. You should also realize that carelessly conducting research, if it results in substantial injury to the client's interests, can subject you personally to liability for negligence, not to mention the loss of a job or career opportunities.

How the Duty of Competence Can Be Breached

Most breaches of the duty of competence are inadvertent. Often, breaches of the duty of competence have to do with inadequate research, missed deadlines, and errors in legal documents filed with the court.

Ethics Watch!

MISSED DEADLINES

As a paralegal, you will find that one of your most useful allies is your calendar. Consistently entering important deadlines on a calendaring system (computerized or otherwise) will help to ensure that you and your supervising attorney do not breach the duty of competence simply because a document was not filed with the court on time. For example, if a *complaint* (the document that initiates a lawsuit—see Chapter 13) is served on one of your firm's clients, you must file with the court the client's *answer* to the complaint within a specified number of days. If you fail to file the answer during that time period, the court could enter a judgment in favor of the party bringing the lawsuit. As you might imagine, the consequences of this judgment—called a *default judgment*—can be extremely detrimental to the client. As a paralegal, you need to be aware of the seriousness of the consequences of missed deadlines for your clients, especially the consequences of failing to file an answer on time.

Inadequate Research. Paralegals frequently perform both legal and factual research for attorneys. Depending on the situation, an attorney's first step after meeting with a new client is often to have a paralegal research the facts or issues involved. The paralegal might be asked to investigate the facts to determine who did what to whom, when, where, and how. If the paralegal fails to discover a pertinent fact and the attorney then relies on the paralegal's research in advising the client, the result could be a breach of the duty of competence.

Similarly, a paralegal conducting legal research might breach the duty of competence by failing to find or report a specific court decision that controls the outcome of a client's case. For example, suppose that a paralegal performs initial research into the law surrounding a particular dispute and reports her findings to the attorney. Then, while the paralegal is working on an unrelated task, the state court rules on a case with issues very similar to those involved in the client's dispute. If the paralegal or the attorney does not go back and confirm that the initial research results are still accurate, he or she could overlook an authoritative ruling that would influence the client's case. This would breach the attorney's duty of competence to the client.

Although attorneys are ultimately responsible for competent representation, paralegals play an important role in providing accurate information to the attorneys for whom they work. If you are ever unsure of the accuracy of your research results, make sure to let the attorney know of your doubts. Also, keep good notes recording each step you took in conducting research so that you know what still needs to be done. Both of these measures will help prevent accidental breaches of the duty of competence.

Missed Deadlines. Paralegals frequently work on several cases simultaneously, and keeping track of every deadline in every case can be challenging—especially for paralegals who are pressed for time. Organization is the key to making sure that all deadlines are met. All important dates relating to every case or client should be entered on a calendar. Larger firms typically use computerized calendaring and "tickler" (reminder) systems. Even the smallest firm

On the Web

The Web sites of the two national paralegal associations, the National Association of Legal Assistants (NALA) and the National Federation of Paralegal Associations (NFPA), are good sources for information on the ethical responsibilities of paralegals, including new, technology-related ethical challenges. You can access NALA's site at **http://www.nala.org**. The URL for NFPA's site is **http://www.paralegals.org**.

normally has calendaring procedures and tickler systems in place. In addition to making sure that all deadlines are entered into the appropriate systems, you should also have your own personal calendar for tracking dates that are relevant to the cases on which you are working—and then make sure that you consistently use it. Develop a habit of checking your calendar every morning when you arrive at work or at some other convenient time. Also, you should check frequently with your attorney about deadlines that he or she may not have mentioned to you.

Errors in Documents.   Breaches of the duty of competence can also involve errors in documents. For example, erroneous information might be included (or crucial information omitted) in a legal document to be filed with the court. If the attorney fails to notice the error before signing the document, and the document is delivered to the court containing the erroneous information, a breach of the duty of competence has occurred. Depending on its legal effect, this breach may expose the attorney and the paralegal to liability for negligence. To prevent these kinds of violations, you need to be especially careful in drafting and proofreading documents.

Generally, if you are ever unsure about what to include in a document, when it must be completed or filed with the court, how extensively you should research a legal issue, or any other aspect of an assignment, you should ask your supervising attorney for additional instructions. You should also make sure that your work is adequately overseen by an attorney, to reduce the chances that it will contain costly mistakes or errors.

Attorney's Duty to Supervise

Rule 5.3 of the Model Rules defines the responsibilities of attorneys in regard to nonlawyer assistants. This rule states, in part, that "[a] lawyer having direct supervisory authority over the nonlawyer shall make reasonable efforts to ensure that the person's conduct is compatible with the professional obligations of the lawyer." The rule also sets forth the circumstances under which a lawyer will be held responsible for conduct of a nonlawyer that violates the standards set out for attorneys. The lawyer is responsible, for example, if she or he orders the conduct or ratifies (approves of) it, with knowledge of the specific conduct. Lawyers who have managerial authority in a law firm or have supervisory authority over the person can also be held responsible for a nonlawyer's unethical conduct if they knew about it and failed to take any action to prevent it.

The 2002 revision specifies that this rule applies not only to lawyers who work in private law firms but also to lawyers in corporate legal departments, government agencies, and elsewhere. In addition, in the statements outlining attorneys' responsibilities toward nonlawyer employees in this area, the ABA commission changed the word *should* to *must.* Attorneys must both instruct and supervise nonlawyer employees concerning the appropriate ethical conduct and can be held personally responsible for the ethical violations of their subordinates.

Inadequate Supervision

Because attorneys are held legally responsible for their assistants' work, it may seem logical to assume that attorneys will take time to direct that work carefully. In fact, paralegals may find it difficult to ensure that their work is adequately supervised. For one thing, most paralegals are kept very busy, and making sure that all their tasks are properly overseen can be time consuming. Similarly, an attorney often does not want to take the time to read through every document drafted by his or her paralegal—particularly if the attorney knows that the paralegal is competent. Nonetheless, as a paralegal, you have a duty to assist your supervising attorney in fulfilling his or her ethical obligations, including the obligation to supervise your work.

Developing Paralegal Skills

ADEQUATE SUPERVISION

Michael Patton is a paralegal in a small, busy, general-practice law firm. His supervising attorney, Muriel Chapman, answers his question about the specific information that he should insert into the complaints (the documents filed with the court to initiate a lawsuit) for two different clients' cases. Muriel is scheduled to attend a deposition (a pretrial procedure in which testimony is given under oath) in another matter this afternoon and has asked Michael to prepare the two complaints and file them with the court today. Muriel tells Michael to use a complaint from a previous client's case as a model for creating the new complaints, replacing that client's information as necessary.

Michael has drafted complaints before, and he is fairly certain that he knows what needs to be done. He leaves Muriel's office and starts revising the model document into a complaint for each of the clients. By the time he is finished, however, it is 4:00 P.M., and Muriel is involved in the deposition in the conference room. Michael needs to file the complaints at the courthouse by 5:00 P.M., but he remembers the adequate supervision rule and does not want to file the documents before Muriel has reviewed them. What should he do? He finally decides that he must interrupt the deposition so that Muriel can look over the complaints before they are filed with the court. He flags a few passages that he is unsure about and proceeds into the conference room. When Muriel sees him, she asks the opposing counsel if the group will agree to take a short break from the proceeding. Then Muriel and Michael step out of the room so that she can review the documents that he has prepared.

TIPS FOR OBTAINING ADEQUATE SUPERVISION

- Always request your supervising attorney to review your work.
- Use notes or ticklers as reminders to ask for a review.
- Try to make the review as convenient as possible for your supervising attorney, and point out or mark anything that needs particular attention.
- Discuss any ethical concerns with the attorney.
- Be persistent.

If you ever feel that your attorney is not adequately supervising your work, there are several things you can do. You can try to improve communications with the attorney—generally, the more you communicate with your supervising attorney, the more likely the attorney will take an active role in directing your activities. You can also ask the attorney for feedback on your work. Sometimes, it helps to place reminders on your personal calendar to discuss particular issues or questions with the attorney. Then, when an opportunity to talk to him or her arises, these issues or questions will be fresh in your mind. Another tactic is to attach a note to a document that you have prepared for the attorney, requesting him or her to review the document (or revised sections of the document) carefully before signing it.

Confidentiality of Information

Rule 1.6 of the Model Rules concerns attorney-client confidentiality. This rule is one of the oldest and most important rules of the legal profession, primarily because it would be difficult for a lawyer to properly represent a client without such a rule. A client must be able to confide in his or her attorney so that the attorney can best represent the client's interest. Because confidentiality is one of the easiest rules to violate, a thorough understanding of the rule is essential.

The general rule of confidentiality is that all information relating to representation of a client must be kept confidential. There are a number of exceptions to the rule, which we will discuss shortly.

Note that the rule does not make any qualifications about what kind of information is confidential. It simply states that a lawyer may not reveal "information relating to representation of a client." Does this mean that if a client tells you that he is the president of a local company, you have to keep that information confidential, even when the whole community knows that fact? For example, could you tell your spouse, "Mr. X is the president of XYZ Corporation"? It may seem permissible, because that fact is, after all, public knowledge. But in so doing, you must not indicate, by words or conduct, that Mr. X is a client of your firm. In such a situation, it is hard to know just what assumptions might be made based on what you have said. Consider another example. Suppose that one evening at dinner you told your spouse that you had met Mr. X that day. Your spouse might reasonably assume that your firm was handling some legal matter involving Mr. X. Because it may be difficult to decide what information is or is not confidential, a good rule of thumb is to regard all information about a client or a client's case as confidential information.

Exceptions to the Confidentiality Rule

Rule 1.6 provides for certain exceptions, each of which we look at here.

Client Gives Informed Consent to the Disclosure.   The rule indicates that an attorney can reveal confidential information if the client gives informed consent to the disclosure. The attorney must fully explain the risks and alternatives involved in the disclosure for the consent to be informed. For example, suppose that an attorney is drawing up a will for a client, and the client is making his only son the sole beneficiary under the will and leaving nothing to his daughter. The daughter calls and wants to know how her father's will reads. The attorney cannot divulge this confidential information to the daughter because the client has not consented to such disclosure. Now suppose that the attorney explains to the client that if his daughter does not learn about the provisions of the will until after her father's death, it is more likely that she will contest the will in court. After the attorney and client discuss the various alternatives and the risks of each, the client can given his informed consent to the attorney to disclose information to his daughter.

Impliedly Authorized Disclosures.   Rule 1.6 also states that an attorney can make "disclosures that are impliedly authorized in order to carry out the representation." This exception is clearly necessary. Legal representation of clients necessarily involves the attorney's assistants, and they must have access to the confidential information to do their jobs. If a paralegal is working on the client's case, for example, he or she must know what the client told the attorney about the legal matter and must have access to information in the client's file concerning the case.

Disclosures to Prevent Harm.   The Model Rules recognize that there are certain circumstances in which an attorney should be allowed to disclose confidential information when it is necessary to prevent harm to persons or property. Rule 1.6 specifically lists four exceptions to the confidentiality rule for this purpose:

1. An attorney is allowed to reveal a client's information to prevent reasonably certain death or substantial bodily harm. For example, suppose that the client confides in the attorney that he has assaulted and nearly killed several persons in the past. The

Developing Paralegal Skills

CLIENT INTENDS TO COMMIT A HARMFUL ACT

Samantha Serles, a legal assistant with a degree in psychology, is meeting with a client whom her firm is defending. The client, Jim Storming, has been charged with the murder of his mother-in-law. Samantha's job is to assess the client's mental state and consider whether he needs further evaluation. Samantha begins talking to Jim. She asks him how things are going and how he feels. He rolls his eyes at her questions and says, "How do you think I feel, being locked up in this place?" She decides to try to talk to him about the crime. "Jim," she says, "have you thought any more about how your mother-in-law died and about what happened that night?" "Yeah," he says. "I've thought about it plenty. I killed her, you know. But they aren't going to be able to prove that I did it."

Samantha just listens as he continues. "I hated her. She talked my wife into divorcing me, and then she and my ex-wife turned my kids against me. I'm going to get even with my ex-wife for that, too. I've been talking to some guys in here. They told me how I can have her taken care of while I'm in here. Then I won't have to take the rap for that one either." Samantha has seen enough to know that Jim needs psychiatric evaluation.

CHECKLIST FOR DETERMINING WHETHER A CLIENT INTENDS A HARMFUL ACT

* Ask the following questions:
    * ✓ Is the threat one of a criminal act?
    * ✓ If so, is it one that would cause bodily harm or death to another?
    * ✓ Is the threat real?
* Always inform your supervising attorney of the threat.

attorney is not allowed to disclose this information. If that same client then tells the attorney that he is going to physically assault a specific person in the future, however, the attorney can disclose this information to prevent reasonably certain bodily harm to the named person.

2. In certain situations, an attorney can also disclose confidential information to prevent a client from committing a crime or fraud. The crime or fraud must be reasonably certain to result in substantial injury to the financial interests or property of another. Also, the client must have used or be using the attorney's services to perpetrate the crime or fraud. If both these conditions are present, then the attorney can disclose information to the extent necessary to enable the affected person to contact the appropriate authorities. Even if the attorney does not learn of the client's crime or fraud until after it has occurred, the attorney may be able to disclose confidential information to mitigate, or reduce the severity, of the harm that results.

3. An attorney can disclose confidential information to the extent necessary to prevent substantial injury to the financial interests or property of another or to reduce its severity.

4. An attorney can also disclose confidential information to establish a defense to a criminal charge in a controversy between the attorney and the client based on conduct involving the client or to respond to allegations in any proceeding regarding the attorney's representation of the client.

Disclosures to Ensure Compliance with Model Rules.   If an attorney is unsure what is required to comply with the Model Rules of Professional Conduct in a particular situation, the attorney can seek legal advice from another lawyer without violating confidentiality. For example, suppose that an attorney who is representing a corporation becomes suspicious that the corporation is engaged in fraud. The attorney is not sure what her professional responsibilities are in that particular situation, so the attorney can seek confidential legal advice from another lawyer to assist her in complying with the Model Rules.

Defending against a Client's Legal Action.   An attorney may also disclose confidential information if the information is necessary to establish a defense in an action brought by the client against the attorney. For example, if the client sues the attorney for malpractice, it is essential for the lawyer to reveal confidential information to prove that he or she was not negligent. Note, though, that the attorney is permitted to disclose confidential information only to the extent that it is essential to defend against the lawsuit.

Disclosures to Comply with Court Order or Other Law.   An attorney may also reveal information relating to the representation of a client if ordered to do so by a court or other governmental entity. For example, suppose that one of the attorney's clients in a divorce case was allegedly hiding valuable assets from his wife. In that situation, a court could require the attorney to reveal any confidential information from the client related to the hidden assets. The attorney should first attempt to persuade the client to take suitable action (and disclose the location and value of the assets). Nevertheless, the attorney can reveal as much information as he or she deems reasonably necessary to satisfy the needs of the court or other governmental entity.

Violations of the Confidentiality Rule

Paralegals, like other professionals, spend a good part of their lives engaged in their work. Naturally, they are tempted to discuss their work at home, with spouses and family members, or with others, such as co-workers and good friends. As a paralegal, perhaps one of the greatest temptations you will face is the desire to discuss a particularly interesting case, or some aspect of a case, with someone you know. You can deal with this temptation in two ways: you can decide, as a matter of policy, never to discuss anything concerning your work; or you can limit your discussion to issues and comments that will not reveal the identity of your client. The latter approach is, for many paralegals, a more realistic solution, but it requires great care. Something you say may reveal a client's identity, even though you are not aware of it.

Conversations Overheard by Others.   Violations of the confidentiality rule can happen simply by oversight. For example, suppose that you and the legal secretary in your office are both working on the same case and continue, as you walk down the hallway toward the elevator, a conversation that you have been having about the case. You pause in front of the elevator, not realizing that your conversation is being overheard by someone around the corner from you. You have no way of knowing the person is there, and you have no way of knowing whether the confidential information that you inadvertently revealed will have any adverse effect on your client's interests. It is important for you to avoid the possibility of unwittingly revealing confidential information to **third parties** in such situations. Therefore, never discuss confidential information when you are in a common area, such as a hallway, an elevator, or a cafeteria, where a conversation might be overheard.

Electronic Communications and Confidentiality.   Whenever you talk to or about a client on the telephone, make sure that your conversation will not be overheard by a third party. You may be sitting in your private office, but if your door is open, someone may over-

third party
A person or entity not directly involved in an agreement (such as a contract), legal proceeding (such as a lawsuit), or relationship (such as an attorney-client relationship).

Ethics Watch!

SOCIAL EVENTS AND CONFIDENTIALITY

Assume that you are at a party with some other paralegals. You tell a paralegal whom you know quite well of some startling news—that a client of your firm, a prominent city official, is being investigated for drug dealing. Although your friend promises to keep this information strictly confidential, she nonetheless relays it to her husband, who in turn tells a co-worker, who in turn tells a friend, and so on. Within a few days, the news has reached the press, and the resulting media coverage results in irreparable harm to the official's reputation and standing in the community. If it can be proved that the harm is the direct result of your breach of the duty of confidentiality, the official could sue both you and the attorney for whom you work for damages.

hear the conversation. Paralegals should take special care when using cellular phones. Cellular phones are not secure. Although conversations on digital cellular phones are more difficult to intercept than conversations on analog phones (which can be overheard by anyone in the vicinity with a scanner), there is still a security risk. As a precaution, you should thus never disclose confidential information when talking on a cellular phone. Because of the widespread use of mobile phones, paralegals today often, as a routine precaution, ask a client who is calling whether he or she is calling from a mobile unit. If the client is using a mobile phone, the paralegal can caution the client that confidential information should not be discussed.

Even such a simple operation as sending a fax can pose ethical pitfalls. Generally, you should exercise great care to make sure that you (1) send the fax to the right person (for example, when a letter is addressed to an opposing party in a lawsuit but is supposed to be sent to the client for his or her approval) and (2) dial the correct fax number.

You also need to be cautious when sending e-mail messages. For example, suppose that you are asked by your supervising attorney to send an e-mail message to a client and to attach a document containing the attorney's analysis of confidential information submitted by the client. The client's e-mail address is in your e-mail "address book," along with other numbers. You click on the client's name, type a brief message, attach the document, and click "send." Too late, you realize that you accidentally clicked on the opposing counsel's name instead of your client's. By a click of the mouse, you have disclosed important confidential information. To avoid this kind of problem, before you click "send," you should take a minute not only to review the message—grammar, sentence structure, and spelling—but also to verify the recipient's name and/or address. (For a further discussion of confidentiality problems posed by the use of e-mail, see this chapter's *Technology and Today's Paralegal* feature on the following page.)

Other Ways of Violating the Confidentiality Rule. There are numerous other ways in which you can reveal confidential information without intending to do so. A file or document sitting on your desk, if observed by a third party, may reveal the identity of a client or enough information to suggest the client's identity. A computer screen, if visible to those passing by your desk, could convey information to someone who is not authorized to know

Technology and Today's Paralegal

IS E-MAIL "CONFIDENTIAL"?

The widespread use of the Internet by lawyers and paralegals has raised a host of ethical issues, many of which you will read about in later chapters of this book. Here, we look at a question of particular importance to all legal professionals, including paralegals: Does communicating with a client via e-mail constitute a violation of the confidentiality rule?

The problem with using e-mail to communicate with clients is that there is an increased risk that an unauthorized person will intercept (and read) the e-mail. When state bar associations first considered whether e-mail communications violate the duty of confidentiality, most concluded that lawyers should not use e-mail for sensitive client communications unless the e-mail is encrypted (encoded using some type of encryption software). In 1997, however, a number of states reached a different conclusion—finding that unencrypted e-mail communications with clients do not violate an attorney's ethical obligations, at least under normal circumstances.

THE ABA TAKES A STAND

In 1999, the ABA attempted to settle the controversy by issuing a formal opinion (Opinion No. 99-413), which concluded that "lawyers have a reasonable expectation of privacy in communications made by all forms of e-mail, including unencrypted e-mail sent on the Internet, despite some risk of interception and disclosure." This standard was then incorporated into the Model Rules of Professional Conduct in 2002. Under these guidelines, an attorney must take "reasonable precautions" to prevent information from falling into the wrong hands. What will be considered reasonable depends on the circumstances and the sensitivity of the information. The ABA commission has cautioned that in highly sensitive matters, lawyers must use enhanced security measures, which could include password protection or encryption. Note also that the ABA's guidelines apply to all forms of electronic communication (including faxes and cellular phones), not just e-mail.

STATES MAY HAVE STRICTER REQUIREMENTS THAN THE ABA

Many states have adopted the ABA's position, but some states require attorneys to follow additional security measures when sending electronic messages that contain confidential client information. For example, in some states, attorneys must discuss encryption options and obtain their clients' permission before sending any confidential information electronically. Some states require attorneys to include a disclaimer in their e-mail messages cautioning that the information is confidential. Other states require that specific procedures be followed if the message is sent to a client's workplace e-mail address as opposed to a home e-mail account. (This is because employers generally can access any e-mail sent to their employees without violating employees' rights to privacy, as will be discussed in Chapter 11.) Still other states have additional requirements for documents that are sent as attachments to a client's e-mail. For example, Iowa requires lawyers to use password protection in all documents that are attached to e-mail. As encryption software becomes less expensive and more commonplace, some states may eventually require all confidential client information sent via the Internet to be encrypted.

TECHNOLOGY TIP

Despite the trend toward acknowledging e-mail as a confidential medium, as a paralegal you should be very cautious when communicating with clients over the Internet. Know your state's rules and your employer's policies concerning e-mail transmissions of client information, and discuss any questions or concerns you have with your supervising attorney. The National Federation of Paralegal Associations (NFPA) advises that the best way to avoid possible confidentiality problems is simply not to put any confidential information on the Internet—which is precisely what some law firms have concluded. NFPA also suggests that legal professionals consider using encryption for e-mail with clients and establish office procedures regarding e-mail.

Ethics Watch!

PERSONAL VERSUS PROFESSIONAL ETHICS

What happens when a paralegal's personal ethical standards come into conflict with a professional duty, such as the duty of confidentiality? When this dilemma faced Merrell Williams, a paralegal with the Kentucky law firm of Wyatt, Tarrant & Combs, he decided to violate the duty of confidentiality to satisfy his conscience. From 1988 to 1992, he took over four thousand pages of confidential documents belonging to his firm's client, tobacco manufacturer Brown & Williamson (B&W), and gave them to the press and others. The documents immediately became a "smoking gun" for antismoking forces involved in litigation against the tobacco industry.

To some, Williams is a hero. After all, he sacrificed his job and faced a lawsuit by his former employer (which was settled in 1997) to help protect the public against the dangers of smoking. To others, Williams's actions were wrongful. Essentially, the question boils down to this: Is it ever in the public interest for a legal professional to violate an ethical duty, particularly when that duty was established by the legal profession to further its goal of protecting the public?

that information. You might be speaking to an expert witness about rescheduling a meeting and accidentally let something about the case slip out. Alternatively, you might be friendly with a paralegal at the opposing attorney's office because the two attorneys have worked on many cases together. You are on the phone trying to work out a date for an important meeting. This paralegal suggests a date and you tell her that the attorney that you work for is scheduled to be in court on a specific client's case that day. If you name the client, or indicate that the attorney will be arguing a particular type of motion in the case, you may breach the duty of confidentiality.

Confidentiality and the Attorney-Client Privilege

All information relating to a client's representation is considered confidential information. Some confidential information also qualifies as privileged information, or information subject to the **attorney-client privilege**.

The attorney-client privilege can be vitally important during the litigation process. As you will read in Chapter 13, prior to a trial each attorney is permitted to obtain information relating to the case from the opposing attorney and other persons, such as witnesses. This means that attorneys must exchange a certain amount of information relating to their clients. An attorney need not divulge privileged information, however—unless the client consents to the disclosure or a court orders the disclosure. Similarly, if an attorney is called to the witness stand during a trial, the attorney may not disclose privileged information unless the court orders him or her to do so.

What Kind of Information Is Privileged?

State statutes and court cases define what constitutes privileged information. Generally, any communications concerning a client's legal rights or problem fall under the attorney-client privilege. For example, suppose that an attorney's client is a criminal defendant. The client

attorney-client privilege
A rule of evidence requiring that confidential communications between a client and his or her attorney (relating to their professional relationship) be kept confidential, unless the client consents to disclosure.

tells the attorney that she was actually in the vicinity of the crime site at the time of the crime, but to her knowledge, no one noticed her presence there. This is privileged information that the attorney may disclose only with the client's consent or on a court's order to do so.

Other types of information, although confidential, are not necessarily privileged. For example, information relating to a client's identity is usually not privileged. Nor, as a rule, is information concerning client fees. Furthermore, information concerning the client's personal or business affairs is not privileged unless it is related to the legal claim. For example, suppose that a client who is bringing a malpractice suit against a physician mentions to the attorney that he is divorcing his wife. Unless the client's divorce is related in some way to the malpractice suit being handled by the attorney, the information about the divorce normally is not considered privileged.

Certain materials relating to an attorney's preparation of a client's case for trial are protected as privileged information under what is known as the **work product** doctrine. Usually, information concerning an attorney's legal strategy for conducting a case is classified as work product and, as such, may be subject to the attorney-client privilege. Legal strategy includes the legal theories that the attorney plans to use in support of the client's claim, how the attorney interprets the evidence relating to the claim, and so on. Certain evidence gathered by the attorney to support the client's claim, however, such as financial statements relating to the client's business firm, would probably not be classified as work product.

Because it is often difficult to tell what types of information (including work product) qualify as privileged, paralegals should consult closely with their supervising attorneys whenever issues arise that may require that such a distinction be made. It is also important to note that like any other confidential information relating to a client's case, privileged information is subject to the exceptions to the confidentiality rule discussed above.

> **work product**
> An attorney's mental impressions, conclusions, and legal theories regarding a case being prepared on behalf of a client. Work product normally is regarded as privileged information.

When the Attorney-Client Privilege Arises

The attorney-client privilege comes into existence the moment a client communicates with an attorney concerning a legal matter. People sometimes mistakenly assume that there is no duty to keep client information confidential unless an attorney agrees to represent a client and the client signs a retainer agreement. This is not so. The privilege—and thus the duty of confidentiality—arises even if the lawyer decides not to represent the client and even when the client is not charged any fee.

Duration of the Privilege

The client is the holder, or "owner," of the privilege, and only the client can waive (set aside) the privilege. Unless waived by the client, the privilege lasts indefinitely. In other words, the privilege continues even though the attorney has completed the client's legal matter and is no longer working on the case.

It is important to keep in mind that privileged information is confidential information. If confidential information is disclosed to others, it is no longer confidential and can no longer be considered privileged information. This is another reason why it is so important to guard against accidental violations of the confidentiality rule: if the rule is violated, information that otherwise might have been protected by the attorney-client privilege can be used in court, which may be harmful to the client's interests. For example, consider the e-mail example given earlier, in which the paralegal inadvertently sent a confidential document to opposing counsel instead of the client. The document, because it contained the attorney's analysis of confidential client information, might be classified as privileged information under the work product doctrine. The disclosure of the information to the opposing counsel destroyed its confidential character—and therefore any possibility that it might be protected as privileged information.

Conflict of Interest

If an attorney engages in an activity that adversely affects a client's interests, the attorney faces a **conflict of interest**. Model Rules 1.7, 1.8, 1.9, 1.10, and 1.11 all pertain to conflict-of-interest situations. The general rule is that an attorney should not represent a client if the representation of the client will be directly adverse to another client or if there is a significant risk that the attorney's ability to consider, recommend, or carry out an appropriate course of action for the client will be materially limited as a result of the attorney's other responsibilities or interests.

conflict of interest
A situation in which two or more duties or interests come into conflict, as when an attorney attempts to represent opposing parties in a legal dispute.

A classic example of a conflict of interest exists when an attorney simultaneously represents two adverse parties in a legal proceeding. Clearly, in such a situation, the attorney's loyalties must be divided. It would be as if a football player agreed to play on both teams during a game—half of the time with one team and half with the other.

Simultaneous Representation

If an attorney reasonably believes that representing two parties in a legal proceeding will not adversely affect either party's interest, then the attorney is permitted to do so—but only if both parties give informed consent. Normally, attorneys avoid this kind of situation because what might start out as a simple, uncontested proceeding could evolve into a legal battle. Divorce proceedings, for example, may begin amicably but end up in heated disputes over child-custody arrangements or property division. The attorney then faces a conflict of interest: assisting one party will necessarily be adverse to the interests of the other. Note that because of the potential for a conflict of interest in divorce proceedings, some courts do not permit attorneys to represent both spouses, even if the spouses consent to such an arrangement.

Similar conflicts arise when the "family attorney" is asked to handle a family matter and the family members eventually disagree on what the outcome should be. For example, consider a situation in which two adult children request the family lawyer to handle the procedures required to settle their deceased parent's estate. The parent's will favors one of the children, and the other child decides to challenge the will's validity. The attorney cannot represent both sides in this dispute without facing a conflict of interest.

Attorneys representing corporate clients may face conflicts of interest when corporate personnel become divided on an issue. For example, assume that ABC Corporation has retained Carl Finn, an attorney, to represent the corporation. Finn typically deals with the corporation's president, Julie Johnson, when rendering legal assistance and advice. At times, however, Finn deals with other corporate personnel, including Seth Harrison, the corporation's accountant. Harrison and Johnson disagree with each other on several major issues, and eventually Johnson arranges to have Harrison fired. Harrison wants attorney Finn to represent him in a lawsuit against the corporation for wrongful termination of his employment. Finn now faces a conflict of interest.

Former Clients

A conflict of interest may also involve former clients. Model Rule 1.9 states that "[a] lawyer who has formerly represented a client in a matter shall not thereafter represent another person in the same or substantially related matter in which that person's interests are materially adverse to the interests of the former client unless the former client gives informed consent, confirmed in writing." The rule regarding former clients is closely related to the rule on preserving the confidentiality of a client. The rationale behind the rule is that an attorney, in representing a client, is entrusted with certain information that may be unknown to others. That information should not be used against the client—even after the representation has ended.

For example, assume that a year ago an attorney defended a company against a lawsuit for employment discrimination brought by one of the company's employees. During the course of the representation, the attorney learned a great deal about the company. Now, someone who was injured while using one of that same company's products consults with the attorney about the possibility of bringing a product liability lawsuit against the company. The attorney normally must refuse to represent this person. Because the attorney has confidential information about the company that could be used to harm the company's interest, a conflict of interest exists.

Job Changes and Former Clients.

The rule concerning former clients does not prohibit an individual attorney or paralegal from working at a firm or agency that represents interests contrary to those of a former client. If that were the situation, many of those who have worked for very large firms would be unable ever to change jobs. Generally, the rules vary, depending on the specific circumstances. In some situations, when a conflict of interest results from a job change, the new employer can avoid violating the rules governing conflict of interest through the use of screening procedures. The new employer can erect an impenetrable screen, referred to as an **ethical wall**, around the new employee so that the new employee remains ignorant about the case giving rise to the conflict of interest.

Walling-Off Procedures.

Law offices usually have special procedures for "walling off" an attorney or other legal professional from a case when a conflict of interest exists. The firm may announce in a written memo to all employees that a certain attorney or paralegal should not have access to specific files, for example, and may set out procedures to be followed to ensure that access to those files is restricted. Computer documents relating to the case may be protected by warning messages or in some other way. Commonly, any hard-copy files relating to the case are flagged with a sticker to indicate that access to the files is restricted.

Firms normally take great care to establish and observe such procedures because if confidential information is used in a way harmful to a former client, the client may sue the firm seeking steep damages. In defending against such a suit, the firm will need to demonstrate that it took reasonable precautions to protect that client's interests.

Other Conflict-of-Interest Situations

Several other types of situations may give rise to conflicts of interest. Gifts from clients may create conflicts of interest, because they tend to bias the judgment of the attorney or paralegal. Some types of gifts are specifically prohibited. For example, the Model Rules prohibit an attorney from preparing documents (such as wills) for a client if the client gives the attorney or a member of the attorney's family a gift. (An exception to this rule exists, of course, when the attorney is a relative of the client.) Note that as a paralegal, you may be offered gifts from appreciative clients at Christmas or other times. Generally, such gifts pose no ethical problems. If a client offers you a gift that has substantial value, however, you should discuss the issue with your supervising attorney.

Attorneys also need to be careful about taking on a client whose case may create an "issue conflict" for the attorney. Generally, an attorney cannot represent a client with respect to a substantive legal issue if the client's position is directly contrary to that of another client being represented by the lawyer—or the lawyer's firm—in a case being brought within the same jurisdiction (the geographic area or subject matter over which a specific court has authority to decide legal disputes). The reason for this rule is that courts are obligated to follow precedents—earlier decisions on cases involving similar facts and issues (see Chapter 5). The court's ruling in one of the attorney's cases could therefore alter the outcome of the other case.

---

ethical wall
A term that refers to the procedures used to create a screen around a legal employee to shield him or her from information about a case in which there is a conflict of interest.

On the Web

To read an article by NFPA's ethics coordinator entitled, "The Ethical Wall: Its Application to Paralegals," go to **http://www.paralegals.org**. Then click on "Professional Development" in the left column, click the link to "Ethics," and click on the link to the article.

Developing Paralegal Skills

BUILDING AN ETHICAL WALL

Lana Smith, a paralegal, has been asked by her supervising attorney to set up an ethical wall because a new attorney, Sandra Piper, has been hired from the law firm of Nunn & Bush. While employed by Nunn & Bush, Piper represented the defendant, Seski Manufacturing, in the ongoing case of *Tymes v. Seski Manufacturing Co.* Lana's firm represents the plaintiff, Joseph Tymes, in that same case, so Piper's work for Nunn & Bush creates a conflict of interest, which Piper has acknowledged in a document signed under oath. Lana makes a list of the walling-off procedures to use to ensure that the firm cannot be accused of violating the rules on conflict of interest.

CHECKLIST FOR BUILDING AN ETHICAL WALL

- Prepare a memo to the office manager regarding the conflict and the need for special arrangements to ensure that Piper will have no involvement in the *Tymes* case.
- Prepare a memo to the team representing Tymes to inform them of the conflict of interest and the special procedures to be used.
- Prepare a memo to the firm giving the case name, the nature of the conflict, the parties involved, and instructions to maintain a blanket of silence with respect to Sandra Piper.
- Arrange for Piper's office to be on a different floor from the team (if possible) to demonstrate, if necessary, that the firm took steps to prevent Piper and the team from having access to one another or each other's files.
- Arrange with the office manager for special computer passwords to be issued to the team members so that access to computer files on the *Tymes* case is restricted to team members only.
- Place "ACCESS RESTRICTED" stickers on the files for the *Tymes* case.
- Develop a security procedure for signing out and tracking the case files in the *Tymes* case—to prevent inadvertent disclosure of the files to Piper or her staff members.

Occasionally, conflicts of interest may arise when two family members who are both attorneys or paralegals are involved in the representation of adverse parties in a legal proceeding. Because there is a significant risk that the family relationship will interfere with professional judgment, generally an attorney should not represent a client if the adverse party to the dispute is being represented by a member of the attorney's family (such as a spouse, parent, child, or sibling). If you, as a paralegal, are married to or living with another paralegal or an attorney, you should inform your firm of this fact if you ever suspect that a conflict of interest might result from your relationship. Similarly, if you discover that you may have a financial interest in the outcome of a lawsuit that your firm is handling, you should notify the attorney right away of the potential conflict.

Conflicts Checks

Whenever a potential client consults with an attorney, the attorney will want to make sure that no potential conflict of interest exists before deciding whether to represent the client. Running a **conflicts check** is a standard procedure in the law office and one that is frequently undertaken by paralegals. Before you can run a conflicts check, you need to know the name of the prospective client, the other party or parties that may be involved in the client's legal matter,

conflicts check
A procedure for determining whether an agreement to represent a potential client will result in a conflict of interest.

and the legal issue involved. Normally, every law firm has some established procedure for conflicts checks, and in larger firms there is usually a computerized database containing the names of former clients and the other information you will need in checking for conflicts of interest.

THE INDIRECT REGULATION OF PARALEGALS

Paralegals are regulated *indirectly* in several ways. Clearly, the ethical codes for attorneys just discussed indirectly regulate the conduct of paralegals. Additionally, paralegal conduct is regulated indirectly by standards and guidelines created by paralegal professional groups as well as guidelines for the utilization of paralegals developed by the American Bar Association and various states.

Paralegal Ethical Codes

Paralegals are becoming increasingly self-regulated. Recall from Chapter 1 that the two major national paralegal associations in the United States—the National Federation of Paralegal Associations, or NFPA, and the National Association of Legal Assistants, or NALA—were formed to define and represent paralegal professional interests on a national level. Shortly after they were formed, both of these associations adopted codes of ethics defining the ethical responsibilities of paralegals.

NFPA's Code of Ethics

In 1977, NFPA adopted its first code of ethics, called the Affirmation of Responsibility. The code has since been revised several times and, in 1993, was renamed the Model Code of Ethics and Professional Responsibility. In 1997, NFPA revised the code, particularly its format, and took the bold step of appending to its code a list of enforcement guidelines setting forth recommendations on how to discipline paralegals who violate ethical standards promulgated by the code. The full title of NFPA's current code is the Model Code of Ethics and Professional Responsibility and Guidelines for Enforcement.

    Exhibit 3.2 presents excerpts from Section 1 of the code, entitled NFPA Model Disciplinary Rules and Ethical Considerations. For reasons of space, only the rules are

On the Web

You can find NFPA's Model Code of Ethics and Professional Responsibility and Guidelines for Enforcement on the Web at **http://www.paralegals.org**. Click on "Professional Development" in the left column, click the link to "Ethics," and click on the link to the code.

EXHIBIT 3.2

Excerpts from Section 1 of NFPA's Code of Ethics and Professional Responsibility and Guidelines for Enforcement

Only the disciplinary rules are shown in this exhibit. The ethical considerations, which are important to a paralegal's understanding of these rules, can be read in Appendix C of this book.

§1.	NFPA MODEL DISCIPLINARY RULES AND ETHICAL CONSIDERATIONS
1.1	A PARALEGAL SHALL ACHIEVE AND MAINTAIN A HIGH LEVEL OF COMPETENCE.
1.2	A PARALEGAL SHALL MAINTAIN A HIGH LEVEL OF PERSONAL AND PROFESSIONAL INTEGRITY.
1.3	A PARALEGAL SHALL MAINTAIN A HIGH STANDARD OF PROFESSIONAL CONDUCT.
1.4	A PARALEGAL SHALL SERVE THE PUBLIC INTEREST BY CONTRIBUTING TO THE IMPROVEMENT OF THE LEGAL SYSTEM AND THE DELIVERY OF QUALITY LEGAL SERVICES, INCLUDING *PRO BONO PUBLICO* SERVICES.
1.5	A PARALEGAL SHALL PRESERVE ALL CONFIDENTIAL INFORMATION PROVIDED BY THE CLIENT OR ACQUIRED FROM OTHER SOURCES BEFORE, DURING, AND AFTER THE COURSE OF THE PROFESSIONAL RELATIONSHIP.
1.6	A PARALEGAL SHALL AVOID CONFLICTS OF INTEREST AND SHALL DISCLOSE ANY POSSIBLE CONFLICT TO THE EMPLOYER OR CLIENT, AS WELL AS TO THE PROSPECTIVE EMPLOYERS OR CLIENTS.
1.7	A PARALEGAL'S TITLE SHALL BE FULLY DISCLOSED.
1.8	A PARALEGAL SHALL NOT ENGAGE IN THE UNAUTHORIZED PRACTICE OF LAW.

Courtesy of the National Federation of Paralegal Associations, Inc.

included in the exhibit, not the ethical considerations that follow each rule. The ethical considerations are very important to paralegals, however, because they explain what conduct the rule prohibits. The full text of NFPA's code (including the rules, ethical considerations, and guidelines for enforcement) is presented in Appendix C of this book.

NALA's Code of Ethics

In 1975, NALA issued its Code of Ethics and Professional Responsibility, which, like NFPA's code, has since undergone several revisions. Exhibit 3.3 on the next page presents NALA's code in its entirety. Note that NALA's code, like the Model Code of Professional Responsibility discussed earlier in this chapter, presents ethical precepts as a series of "canons." (Prior to the 1997 revision of its code, NFPA also listed its ethical standards as "canons.")

Compliance with Paralegal Codes of Ethics

Paralegal codes of ethics state the ethical responsibilities of paralegals generally, but they particularly apply to members of paralegal organizations that have adopted the codes. Any paralegal who is a member of an organization that has adopted one of these codes is expected to comply with the code's requirements. Note that compliance with these codes is not legally mandatory. In other words, if a paralegal does not abide by a particular ethical standard of a paralegal association's code of ethics, the association cannot initiate state-sanctioned disciplinary proceedings against the paralegal. The association can, however, expel the paralegal from the association, which may have significant implications for the paralegal's future career opportunities. See this chapter's *Featured Guest* article on pages 90 and 91 for a further discussion on how setting high ethical standards can enhance a paralegal's career opportunities.

On the Web

You can find NALA's Code of Ethics and Professional Responsibility online by going to **http://www.nala. org/benefits.htm** and clicking the link title "NALA Code of Ethics."

Guidelines for the Utilization of Paralegals

As mentioned earlier in this chapter, the reason attorneys are regulated by the state is to protect the public from the harms that could result from incompetent legal advice and representation. Licensing requirements for attorneys thus serve the public interest. At the same time, they give lawyers something of a monopoly over the delivery of legal services—a monopoly that, in turn, may have detrimental effects on those who cannot afford to pay attorneys for their services. The increased use of paralegals stems, in part, from the legal profession's need to reduce the cost of legal services. The use of paralegals to do substantive legal work benefits clients because the hourly rate for paralegals is, of course, substantially lower than that for attorneys.

For this reason, bar associations (and courts, when approving fees) encourage attorneys to delegate work to paralegals whenever feasible to lower the costs of legal services for clients—and thus provide the public with greater access to legal services. In fact, some courts, when determining awards of attorneys' fees, have refused to approve fees at the attorney's hourly rate for work that could have been performed by a paralegal at a lower rate.

NALA, the ABA, and many of the states have adopted guidelines for the utilization of paralegal services. These guidelines were created in response to a variety of questions concerning the role and function of paralegals within the legal arena that had arisen during the 1970s and 1980s, including the following: What are paralegals? What kinds of tasks do they perform? What are their professional responsibilities? How can attorneys best utilize paralegal services? What responsibilities should attorneys assume with respect to their assistants' work?

NALA's Model Standards and Guidelines

In 1984, NALA adopted its Model Standards and Guidelines for the Utilization of Legal Assistants. This document addresses and provides guidance on several issues of paramount importance to legal assistants today. It begins by listing the minimum qualifications that

On the Web

NALA's Model Standards and Guidelines are online at **http://www. nala.org/98model.htm**.

EXHIBIT 3.3
NALA's Code of Ethics and Professional Responsibility

Preamble: A legal assistant must adhere strictly to the accepted standards of legal ethics and to the general principles of proper conduct. The performance of the duties of the legal assistant shall be governed by specific canons as defined herein so justice will be served and goals of the profession attained. (See Model Standards and Guidelines for Utilization of Legal Assistants, Section II.)

The canons of ethics set forth hereafter are adopted by the National Association of Legal Assistants, Inc., as a general guide intended to aid legal assistants and attorneys. The enumeration of these rules does not mean there are not others of equal importance although not specifically mentioned. Court rules, agency rules and statutes must be taken into consideration when interpreting the canons.

Definition: Legal assistants, also known as paralegals, are a distinguishable group of persons who assist attorneys in the delivery of legal services. Through formal education, training and experience, legal assistants have knowledge and expertise regarding the legal system and substantive and procedural law which qualify them to do work of a legal nature under the supervision of an attorney.

CANON 1.

A legal assistant must not perform any of the duties that attorneys only may perform nor take any actions that attorneys may not take.

CANON 2.

A legal assistant may perform any task which is properly delegated and supervised by an attorney, as long as the attorney is ultimately responsible to the client, maintains a direct relationship with the client, and assumes professional responsibility for the work product. (See NALA Model Standards and Guidelines, Section IV, Guideline 5.)

CANON 3.

A legal assistant must not: (See NALA Model Standards and Guidelines, Section IV, Guideline 2.)

   (a)   engage in, encourage, or contribute to any act which could constitute the unauthorized practice of law; and

   (b)   establish attorney-client relationships, set fees, give legal opinions or advice or represent a client before a court or agency unless so authorized by that court or agency; and

   (c)   engage in conduct or take any action which would assist or involve the attorney in a violation of professional ethics or give the appearance of professional impropriety.

NALA's Code of Ethics and Professional Responsibility ©1975; Revised 1979, 1988, 1995. Reprinted with permission.

legal assistants should have and then, in a series of guidelines, indicates what legal assistants may and may not do. We will examine these guidelines in more detail shortly. (See Appendix B for the complete text of the annotated version of NALA's Model Standards and Guidelines, as revised in 1997.)

The ABA's Model Guidelines

The ABA adopted its Model Guidelines for the Utilization of Legal Assistant Services in 1991. The ABA Standing Committee on Legal Assistants, which drafted the guidelines, based them on the NALA guidelines, various state codes and guidelines on the use of paralegals, and relevant state court decisions. The document consists of ten guidelines, each of which is followed by a lengthy comment on the derivation, scope, and application of the guideline.

The guidelines indicate, among other things, the types of tasks that a lawyer may not delegate to a paralegal and, generally, the responsibilities of attorneys with respect to para-

EXHIBIT 3.3
NALA's Code of Ethics and Professional Responsibility—Continued

---

CANON 4.

A legal assistant must use discretion and professional judgment commensurate with knowledge and experience but must not render independent legal judgment in place of an attorney. The services of an attorney are essential in the public interest whenever such legal judgment is required. (See NALA Model Standards and Guidelines, Section IV, Guideline 3.)

CANON 5.

A legal assistant must disclose his or her status as a legal assistant at the outset of any professional relationship with a client, attorney, a court or administrative agency or personnel thereof, or a member of the general public. A legal assistant must act prudently in determining the extent to which a client may be assisted without the presence of an attorney. (See NALA Model Standards and Guidelines, Section IV, Guideline 1.)

CANON 6.

A legal assistant must strive to maintain integrity and a high degree of competency through education and training with respect to professional responsibility, local rules and practice, and through continuing education in substantive areas of law to better assist the legal profession in fulfilling its duty to provide legal service.

CANON 7.

A legal assistant must protect the confidences of a client and must not violate any rule or statute now in effect or hereafter enacted controlling the doctrine of privileged communications between a client and an attorney. (See NALA Model Standards and Guidelines, Section IV, Guideline 1.)

CANON 8.

A legal assistant must do all other things incidental, necessary, or expedient for the attainment of the ethics and responsibilities as defined by statute or rule of court.

CANON 9.

A legal assistant's conduct is guided by bar associations' codes of professional responsibility and rules of professional

---

NALA's Code of Ethics and Professional Responsibility ©1975; Revised 1979, 1988, 1995. Reprinted with permission.

legal performance and compensation. For further detail on what is included in the guidelines, you can access them online at the ABA's Web site. Go to **http://www.abanet.org/legalservices/paralegals/downloads/modelguidelines.pdf.**

State Guidelines

Over two-thirds of the states have adopted some form of guidelines concerning the use of legal assistants by attorneys, the respective responsibilities of attorneys and legal assistants in performing legal work, the types of tasks paralegals may perform, and other ethically challenging areas of legal practice. Although the guidelines of some states reflect the influence of NALA's standards and guidelines, the state guidelines focus largely on state statutory definitions of the practice of law, state codes of ethics regulating the responsibilities of attorneys, and state court decisions. As a paralegal, you should make sure that you become familiar with your state's guidelines.

Lisa L. Newcity

FEATURED **Guest**

TEN TIPS FOR ETHICS AND THE PARALEGAL

BIOGRAPHICAL NOTE

*Lisa L. Newcity, J.D., is a full-time fac-
ulty member in the Legal Studies
Department at Roger Williams
University in Bristol, Rhode Island,
where she serves as the program
coordinator for the Legal Studies
Program. She also serves as a prelaw
adviser and as the faculty adviser and
coach to the Roger Williams
University Mock Trial Club. She is a
former chair of the NFPA Ethics
Board and teaches a number of courses with an ethics component.*

*Newcity was formerly a practicing attorney in Massachusetts concen-
trating in civil litigation in state and federal courts. Her areas of interest,
research, and publication include the licensing and regulation of paralegals, professional ethics, and the interdisciplinary study of law at the
undergraduate level.*

A paralegal with a clear understanding of the rules of ethics is an
invaluable asset to any law practice. Ethical behavior in the workplace
increases client satisfaction, reduces the risk of liability for the
employer, and, perhaps even more important, fosters a sense of
respect and pride for the profession. The following tips offer some
suggestions on how you can incorporate the rules of ethics and professional responsibility into your daily life as a practicing paralegal.

1. **Set a High Standard for Competence.** The best paralegals know that in order to remain current and productive, they
   must keep abreast of changes in the law, in law office technology,
   and in legal ethics. Attend CLE (continuing legal education) seminars in your area of practice, as well as in ethics. Read your local,
   state, and national legal newspapers and journals for updates and
   changes in these areas. Take advantage of the educational opportunities offered by paralegal associations and bar associations.
   Understand that your paralegal education and experience provide a foundation on which you are expected to build throughout your career. The codes of professional responsibility for

attorneys and paralegals require us to maintain a certain level of
competence. Do this at a minimum, but always strive for the
highest possible standard with respect to competence and skills.

2. **Demonstrate Respect for Others and for the Profession.**
   In recent years, there has been much discussion regarding the "lack
   of civility" within the legal profession. Do your part to promote an
   atmosphere of mutual respect and civility in your workplace by
   behaving professionally at all times. All legal professionals, attorneys
   and paralegals alike, should understand that clients and members of
   the public hold us to a higher standard of ethical conduct. We are
   expected to comport ourselves with dignity and to show respect
   for the law and for each other. Indeed, the codes of professional
   responsibility require us to avoid even the "appearance of impropriety." To that end, you must from time to time put your sense of professionalism and dignity before your own emotions when faced with
   uncivil conduct on the part of others. Do this for the good of your
   clients and for the good of the profession.

3. **Become Active in Local and National Professional
   Associations.** Collaborate with, and learn from, your colleagues
   as a member of a paralegal professional association, such as NFPA
   or NALA. Both organizations have made great strides in raising
   awareness about the paralegal profession, and both provide excellent sources of information for their members and for the public. In
   addition, these organizations (as well as state and local paralegal
   associations) have promulgated ethical guidelines for paralegals and
   publish ethics opinions and cases on ethics to guide their members.

4. **Understand and Observe the Rules of Confidentiality.**
   The ethical rules on confidentiality create the underpinnings of
   the attorney-client relationship. Our ability to provide the best
   possible legal services for our clients hinges on the trust and confidence that our clients place in us. Do nothing that could jeopardize this. Recognize common "danger zones" for paralegals in
   preserving confidentiality. Among other things, these danger
   zones include discussing clients and cases with family and friends,
   interviewing clients in your office when other clients' files and
   documents are in plain view, and discussing a client's case with a
   witness during an investigation.

The Increasing Scope of Paralegal Responsibilities

The ethical standards and guidelines just discussed, as well as court decisions concerning
paralegals, all support the goal of increasing the use of paralegals in the delivery of legal services. Today, paralegals can perform virtually any legal task as long as the work is super-

5. **Demonstrate Loyalty to the Client by Recognizing Potential Conflicts of Interest.** You know from studying the ethical rules concerning conflicts of interest that any conflict is a potential danger to the client and to your employer. Be diligent in following your firm's practices for conflict checking. Also, if you believe that a conflict may arise in a case that you are handling, speak to your supervising attorney immediately. It is always better to address conflict issues at the earliest possible opportunity. Waiting until later may result in unnecessary cost and embarrassment for you and for your employer.

6. **Demonstrate Loyalty to Your Employer through Your Professionalism.** As a legal professional and an employee, you are a representative of your firm or agency. Paralegals interact with clients, witnesses, and court personnel on a regular basis. Refrain from gossip or negative remarks about your firm or employer. Attorneys and paralegals work together as integral members of a team on behalf of their clients. If difficulties or conflicts arise with your supervisor, speak to that person directly in an effort to resolve them. Your professionalism will be respected and appreciated.

7. **Practice Diligence in Completing Your Work Promptly and Efficiently.** Prioritize your work to avoid neglecting important projects. Be scrupulous in maintaining your calendar and tickler system. Understand your own limits, and speak to your supervisor if the volume of work becomes so overwhelming that you run the risk of neglecting projects or missing deadlines. It is better to ask for assistance from your paralegal co-workers or from your supervisor than to ignore the problem until it is too late.

8. **Recognize Your Role as the Client's Contact, and Promote Responsiveness to the Client's Questions and Concerns.** Paralegals are often the persons within the firm to whom clients will look when questions arise. Unfortunately, one of the most common complaints about attorneys and their professional staff members is that they are unresponsive. Make it a point to return your clients' telephone calls in a prompt and courteous manner. When a client has a question calling for legal advice, bring it to the attorney's attention quickly, and encourage the attorney to respond to the client promptly. If the attorney is busy, offer to pass along the message (being careful to avoid giving legal advice yourself).

9. **Recognize "Pitfalls for Paralegals" in the Unauthorized Practice of Law (UPL).** As you gain the confidence and trust of your firm's clients, you will, on occasion, be faced with questions calling for legal advice. Learn to develop strategies for handling these situations with tact and empathy. Remember that if a client has a pressing problem that calls for immediate attention, it is not sufficient to tell him or her that as a paralegal you are not permitted to give legal advice. Inform the client that you will find an attorney who can assist the client and that either you or the attorney will get right back to the client. Then be sure to do just that. Of course, paralegals may face other situations with serious UPL implications as well. When in doubt, consult the rules for guidance and speak with your supervising attorney.

10. **Know When to Ask for Help and Where to Get It.** Every paralegal should have a copy of the ethical rules for attorneys and paralegals. Every paralegal should also regularly review ethics opinions, disciplinary proceedings, and cases interpreting the rules of professional conduct. Also, when questions or concerns about ethics arise, you should know where to turn for help. Many firms designate a particular individual within the firm as the "contact person" for ethical inquiries. Further, many state and local attorney licensing and regulatory agencies, bar associations, and paralegal associations provide services to legal professionals who have ethical questions. Inquire about your firm's policies regarding ethical questions, and take advantage of all available resources.

> *"Ethical behavior in the workplace increases client satisfaction, reduces the risk of liability for the employer, and, perhaps even more important, fosters a sense of respect and pride for the profession."*

vised by an attorney and does not constitute the unauthorized practice of law (to be discussed shortly).

Paralegals working for attorneys may interview clients and witnesses, investigate legal claims, draft legal documents for attorneys' signatures, attend will executions (in some states), appear at real estate closings (in some states), and undertake numerous other types of legal work, as long as the work is supervised by attorneys. When state or federal law allows them to do so, paralegals can also represent clients before government agencies. Paralegals are allowed to perform freelance services for attorneys and, depending on state law and the type of service, perform limited independent services for the public.

Legal assistants are also permitted to give information to clients on many types of matters relating to a case or other legal concern. When arranging for client interviews, they let clients know what kind of information is needed and what documents to bring to the office. They inform clients about legal procedures and what clients should expect to experience during the progress of a legal proceeding. For example, in preparing for trial, legal assistants instruct clients on trial procedures, what they should wear to the trial, and so on. Clearly, as a legal assistant, you will be permitted to give clients all kinds of information. Nonetheless, you must make sure that you know where to draw the line between giving permissible types of advice and giving "legal advice"—advice that only attorneys are licensed to give under state laws.

The specific types of tasks that paralegals are legally permitted to undertake are described throughout this book; it would be impossible to list them all here. As you can see from the ABA's guidelines, paralegals may not perform tasks that only attorneys can legally perform. If they do so, they risk liability for the unauthorized practice of law—an important topic to which we now turn.

THE UNAUTHORIZED PRACTICE OF LAW

On the Web

A good starting point for locating your state's UPL statute and UPL court cases is FindLaw's Web site at **http://www.findlaw.com/ casecode/state.html**.

Virtually every state has a statute that prohibits the unauthorized practice of law (UPL). Although state statutes vary, they all aim to prevent nonlawyers from providing legal counsel. It is vital that you be aware of your state's UPL law to avoid violating it. Note, however, that UPL statutes do not apply only to paralegals. Rather, they apply to all persons—including real estate agents, bankers, insurance agents, and accountants—who might provide services that are typically provided by licensed attorneys. For example, an insurance agent who offers advice to a client on a personal-injury claim might be liable for UPL.

Traditionally, state UPL statutes did not provide a clear definition of what constitutes the practice of law. Consequently, courts decided whether a person had engaged in UPL on a case-by-case basis. This made it difficult to know exactly what kinds of activities constituted UPL. To avoid violating UPL laws, a person had to be aware of the state courts' decisions on UPL. As you will read shortly, some states are working to address this problem.

Paralegals, of course, can also refer to the general guidelines for their profession provided by NALA. Guideline 2 in NALA's Model Standards and Guidelines prohibits a legal assistant from engaging in any of the following activities:

- Establishing attorney-client relationships.
- Setting legal fees.
- Giving legal opinions or advice.
- Representing a client before a court, unless authorized to do so by the court.
- Engaging in, encouraging, or contributing to any act that could constitute the unauthorized practice of law.

State UPL Statutes

Because of the difficulty in predicting with certainty whether a court would consider a particular action to be UPL, in recent years some states have made efforts to clarify what is meant by the "practice of law." According to one survey in 2004, nearly half of the states had

Developing Paralegal Skills

AVOIDING UPL PROBLEMS

Jenna Martin, a paralegal, is attending a client's holiday party. She is the first person from her firm to arrive at the party. As she enters the room, Mr. Holbrook, the president of the company, introduces himself to Jenna. She responds, saying, "It's nice to meet you. I'm Jenna Martin, with the firm of Atkins & White." Assuming that Jenna is an attorney, Holbrook begins to ask her for legal advice about a tax problem that the company is having. Jenna now needs to take action to avoid the unauthorized practice of law.

TIPS ON HOW TO AVOID UPL PROBLEMS

- Always introduce yourself as a paralegal or legal assistant.
- Always include your title when signing letters or other documents.
- If a letter contains information that may be construed as legal advice, make it clear that the attorney is the source of that advice.
- Make sure that your nonattorney status is clearly indicated on business cards and company letterhead.
- Always disclose your status to a court or other tribunal.
- If a client does not understand your role, explain it. Make it clear that paralegals may not give legal advice, and refer the client to an attorney.

adopted a definition of what constitutes the practice of law, either by statute or by court ruling.[7] For example, the Texas UPL statute provides, in part:

> the practice of law means the preparation of a pleading or other document incident to an action or special proceeding or the management of the action or proceeding on behalf of a client before a judge in court as well as a service rendered out of court, including the giving of advice or the rendering of any service requiring the use of legal skill or knowledge, such as preparing a will, contract, or other instrument, the legal effect of which under the facts and conclusions involved must be carefully determined.[8]

The Texas statute also states that this definition is not exclusive and that the state courts have the authority to determine that other activities, which are not listed, also constitute UPL. Other states' definitions of law practice focus on various factors, such as appearing in court or drafting legal papers, pleadings, or other documents in connection with a pending or prospective court proceeding. The enforcement of UPL statutes also varies widely among the states. In some states, the attorney general prosecutes violators; in others, the local or state prosecutor enforces UPL statutes; and in some states, the state bar association is in charge of enforcement.

In the following pages, we discuss some of the activities that are considered to constitute UPL in most states. It cannot be overemphasized, however, that a paralegal should know the parameters of the UPL statute in the state in which she or he works.

Giving Legal Opinions and Advice

Clearly, giving legal advice goes to the essence of legal practice. After all, a person would not seek out a legal expert if he or she did not want legal advice on some matter. Although a paralegal can communicate an attorney's legal advice to a client, a paralegal cannot give legal advice.

The Need for Caution

You need to be extremely careful to avoid giving legal advice even when discussing matters with friends and relatives. Although other nonlawyers often give advice affecting others' legal rights or obligations, paralegals should not do so. For example, when an individual receives a speeding ticket, a friend or relative who is a nonlawyer might suggest that the person should argue the case before a judge and explain his or her side of the story. When a paralegal gives such advice, however, he or she may be accused of engaging in the unauthorized practice of law. Legal assistants are prohibited from giving even simple, common-sense advice because of the understandably greater weight given to the advice of someone who has legal training.

Similarly, you need to be cautious in the workplace. Although you may have developed great expertise in a certain area of law, you must refrain from advising clients with respect to their legal obligations or rights. For example, suppose that you are a bankruptcy specialist and know that a client who wants to petition for bankruptcy has two realistic options to pursue under bankruptcy law. Should you tell the client about these options and their consequences? No, you should not. In effect, advising someone of his or her legal options is very close to advising a person of his or her legal rights and may therefore—in the view of many courts, at least—constitute the unauthorized practice of law. Also, even though you may qualify what you say by telling the client that he or she needs to check with an attorney, this does not alter the fact that you are giving advice on which the client might rely.

On the Web

For some tips on how to avoid UPL, go to **http://www.paralegals.org**. Click on "Professional Development" in the left column, scroll down to the link "Unauthorized Practice of Law," and read the article.

Be on the Safe Side

What constitutes the giving of legal advice can be difficult to pin down. As you read earlier, paralegals are permitted to advise clients on a number of matters, and drawing the line between permissible and impermissible advice may at times be difficult. To be on the safe side—and avoid potential liability for the unauthorized practice of law—never advise anyone regarding any matter if the advice may alter that person's legal position or legal rights.

Whenever you are pressured to render legal advice—as you surely will be at one time or another, by your firm's clients or others—say that you cannot give legal advice because it is against the law to do so. Offer to find an attorney who can answer the client's questions. Paralegals usually find that a frank and honest approach provides the best solution to the problem.

Representing Clients in Court

The rule that only attorneys—with limited exceptions—can represent others in court has a long history. Recall from the discussion of attorney regulation earlier in this chapter that attorney licensing was initially required only for court representation. In the last few decades, the ethical reasoning underlying this rule has been called into question by two developments.

First, in 1975 the United States Supreme Court held that people have a constitutional right to represent themselves in court.[9] Some people have questioned why a person can represent himself or herself in court but cannot hire a person more educated in the law to provide representation unless that person is a licensed attorney. Second, the fact that paralegals are allowed to represent clients before some federal and state government agencies, such as the federal Social Security Administration (as will be discussed in Chapter 5), has called into question the ethical underpinnings of this rule. Nonetheless, as a paralegal you should know that you are not allowed to appear in court on behalf of your supervising attorney—although local courts in some states are carving out exceptions to this rule for limited purposes.

Disclosure of Paralegal Status

Because of the close working relationship between an attorney and a paralegal, a client may have difficulty perceiving that the paralegal is not also an attorney. For example, a client's call to an attorney may be transferred to the attorney's paralegal if the attorney is not in the office. The paralegal may assume that the client knows that he or she is not an attorney and may speak freely with the client about a legal matter, advising the client that the attorney will be in touch with the client shortly. The client, however, may assume that the paralegal is an attorney and may make inferences based on the paralegal's comments that result in actions with harmful consequences—in which event the paralegal might be charged with the unauthorized practice of law. To avoid such problems, make sure that clients or potential clients know that you are a paralegal and, as such, are not permitted to give legal advice. Similarly, in correspondence with clients or others, you should indicate your nonattorney status by adding "Paralegal" or "Legal Assistant" after your name. If you have printed business cards or if your name is included in the firm's letterhead or other literature, also make sure that your nonlawyer status is clearly indicated there.

Guideline 1 of NALA's Model Standards and Guidelines emphasizes the importance of disclosing paralegal status by stating that all legal assistants have an ethical responsibility to "[d]isclose their status as legal assistants at the outset of any professional relationship with a client, other attorneys, a court or administrative agency or personnel thereof, or members of the general public." Disciplinary Rule 1.7 of NFPA's Model Code of Ethics and Professional Responsibility also stresses the importance of disclosing paralegal status. Guideline 4 of the ABA's Model Guidelines places on attorneys the responsibility for disclosing the nonattorney status of paralegals:

> A lawyer is responsible for taking reasonable measures to ensure that clients, courts, and other lawyers are aware that a paralegal, whose services are utilized by the lawyer in performing legal services, is not licensed to practice law.

Paralegals Freelancing for Attorneys

Some paralegals have their own businesses and work as freelance paralegals for attorneys, as you learned in the previous chapter. In the early 1990s, there was some concern over whether freelance paralegals were, by definition, sufficiently supervised by attorneys to avoid liability for the unauthorized practice of law. In a landmark decision in 1992, the New Jersey Supreme Court stated that it could find no reason why freelance paralegals could not be just as adequately supervised by the attorneys for whom they worked as those paralegals working in attorneys' offices. Since that decision, courts in several other states and ethical opinions issued by various state bar associations have held that freelance paralegals who are adequately supervised by attorneys are not engaging in the unauthorized practice of law.

In its opinion, the New Jersey Supreme Court also called for the establishment of a Committee on Paralegal Education and Regulation to study the practice of paralegals and make recommendations to the court. The committee's report, submitted to the court in 1998, recommended that paralegals in New Jersey should be subject to state licensing

Nancy B. Heller, RP

PARALEGAL **profile**

LITIGATION PARALEGAL

Nancy B. Heller, RP, is a litigation paralegal with the Columbus, Ohio, law firm of Vorys, Sater, Seymour, and Pease, LLP, where she special-izes in civil litigation, including toxic torts, employment, business and commercial law, personal-injury cases and medical malpractice, consumer practice, and insurance defense work. Heller received her B.A. degree from Indiana University in 1978 and her registered para-legal certificate (RP) from the National Federation of Paralegal Associations (NFPA) in 1999. In the early 1980s, Heller was active on the Lawyer/Legal Assistant Committee of the Columbus Bar Association (CBA) and co-authored a proposal for an associate membership category for paralegals, adopted in 1986. The CBA was the first bar association in the country to add such a category. Heller co-authored NFPA's Model Code of Ethics, served on the Professional and Ethics Standards Committee, and co-authored the ethics sections of the Paralegal Advanced Competency Exam (PACE) Study Manual.

From 1997 to 2003, Heller served as NFPA's representative to the American Bar Association Approval Commission. She has been a lec-turer on various litigation and ethics topics at seminars for more than twenty-five years and has served as an instructor in the Capital University Law School Paralegal Program.

In addition to her professional development endeavors, Heller has served pro bono as a court-appointed special advocate (CASA) and guardian ad litem for CASA of Franklin County. Another of her volunteer endeavors has been to provide respite care for terminally ill patients and their families through hospice.

What do you like best about your work?

"The ability to impose order on chaos and to create and develop a framework within which to work a litigation case is truly one of the great-est benefits and accomplishments of being a litigation paralegal. I have always enjoyed and appreciated the variety of work and cases, along with the opportunity to constantly learn new things. Solving problems, acting quickly on your feet, and helping to formulate and implement a plan that moves the case along all play into achieving that paralegal 'high.' For me, the ultimate highlight of my job comes at trial when all of the elements of the case come together and I play an integral role in the organization, coordination, and presentation of the case. The days and nights prepar-ing for and during trial are frenzied and intense—the adrenaline runs extremely high—but it is always the time when I pause to remember that this is why I love being a paralegal."

What is the greatest challenge that you face in your area of work?

"I have encountered numerous job challenges in the course of my career; however, I believe my greatest challenge came in 1998, when I worked on a customs investigation matter and had the opportunity

On the Web

To read an article discussing the report from the New Jersey Supreme Court's Committee on Paralegal Education and Regulation, go to **http://www. nala.org/LicIssues.htm**.

requirements. This recommendation caused widespread debate among legal professionals in New Jersey and elsewhere—as you will read shortly.

Legal Technicians (Independent Paralegals) and UPL

As mentioned in Chapter 2, legal technicians (also called independent paralegals) provide "self-help" legal services directly to the public. Since the 1970s, when these types of services began to spring up around the country, the courts have had to wrestle with questions such as the following: If an independent paralegal advises a customer on what forms are necessary to obtain a simple, uncontested divorce, how those forms should be filed with the court, how the court hearing should be scheduled, and so on, do those activities constitute the practice of law?

Generally, the mere dissemination of legal information does not constitute the unau-thorized practice of law. There is a fine line, however, between disseminating legal informato work in Asia. This highly sensitive matter, with strict deadlines, involved a detailed analysis of detainment orders and interviews with employees of a company and several of its divisions and subsidiaries. I gathered and organized the information and documents into databases and trained and supervised ten contract employees retained in Hong Kong to assist in the interview process. In addition, I helped to coordinate similar, simultaneous reviews and analyses in the company's U.S. offices. The challenges included extensive coordination of the work, adaptation to a foreign culture, and the ability to accomplish the work within that culture. Obvious cultural and language barriers and challenges inherent in working overseas were tests of careful planning, patience, and professionalism over several months. I will soon have another international opportunity to work in Seoul, South Korea, where I will take what I learned from my experience in Asia in 1998 as I begin another challenge."

What advice do you have for would-be paralegals in your area of work?

"Litigation calls for the refinement and application of all of your paralegal knowledge, with communication, organization, and time management being three of the most important elements of success. Of course, with the ever-changing world of technology, paralegals must keep updating their skills."

> *"Litigation calls for the refinement and application of all of your paralegal skills."*

What are some tips for success as a paralegal in your area of work?

"Develop an organizational method that works well for you. Keep yourself organized so that you are able to keep others organized. Utilize technology to maximize efficiency and accessibility. On every case, maintain a work file of each assignment so you will have a ready reference and will be able to respond to questions as they arise. To stay on top of deadlines, implement a tickler and docketing system. Always remember that the practice of law is a service profession. Communicate all interactions with the client to the supervising attorney so that there is no misunderstanding about what you have said to a client, or why. Lawyers must supervise and review your work, so be sure that you keep them fully informed. When using the Internet, do not overlook obvious sources of information. Each piece of information obtained usually leads to another lead. Do not forget to document all findings, along with the way in which you obtained them. Leave no stone unturned. Take advantage of classes, demonstrations, and online tutorials to learn all that you can."

Nancy Heller is also featured in the forthcoming book, Lessons from the Top Paralegal Experts, *by Carole Bruno.*

tion (by providing legal forms to a customer, for example) and giving legal advice (which may consist of merely selecting the forms that best suit the customer's needs)—and the courts do not always agree on just where this line should be drawn.

Early Cases

An early case on this issue was *The Florida Bar v. Brumbaugh*,[10] which was decided in 1978 by the Florida Supreme Court. The case was brought by the Florida Bar against Brumbaugh, who prepared legal documents for people who sought a simple, uncontested divorce. Brumbaugh prepared all the necessary court documents and told her customers how to file the documents with the court, how to schedule the court hearings, and—in a conference the day before the hearing—what would occur at the hearing.

SAYING "IF I WERE YOU . . ." AND THE UPL

Any time that a paralegal, in responding to someone concerned about legal rights, says, "If I were you, I would . . . ," the paralegal is, in effect, giving legal advice—and engaging in the unauthorized practice of law. For example, assume that a client calls your law office, and you take the call. The client, Mrs. Rabe, is an elderly woman who is very upset about the fact that an insurance company has not paid on a $3,000 life insurance policy that she purchased covering the life of her grandson, who has just died. Mrs. Rabe tells you all of the details, and you feel that even though she might win a lawsuit against the insurance company, she would probably spend a lot more than $3,000 in the process. Mrs. Rabe wants to know if your supervising attorney will see her about the case, and when you tell her the attorney is out of town, she presses you for advice. Finally, you say, "Well, if I were you, I'd take the case to small claims court. You would not have to hire an attorney, it would be less costly, and you might recover some of the money." What you have not told Mrs. Rabe is that if she sues the insurance company, she might win not just the $3,000 payment but also substantial punitive damages for the insurance company's wrongful behavior—and might also benefit from other penalties imposed under the state's insurance statute.

The Florida Bar claimed that Brumbaugh was engaging in the practice of law in violation of the state's UPL statute. The Florida Supreme Court held that Brumbaugh could sell legal forms and other printed information regarding divorces and other legal procedures, that she could fill in the forms as long as the customer provided the information in writing, and that she could advertise her services. She could not, however, advise customers of their legal rights; tell them which forms should be used, how they should be filled out, and where to file them; or tell customers how to present their cases in court.

A year later, the same court decided *The Florida Bar v. Furman,*[11] which involved a woman who performed legal services very similar to those performed by Brumbaugh. The court held that the woman, Furman, had engaged in the unauthorized practice of law by failing to comply with the decision in *Brumbaugh.* The *Furman* case received substantial publicity when Furman disobeyed an *injunction* (a court order to cease engaging in the prohibited activities) and was sentenced to prison for **contempt of court** (failing to cooperate with a court order).

An Ongoing Problem

Legal technicians continue to face UPL allegations brought against them primarily by UPL committees and state bar associations. In 1997, an Oregon appellate court upheld the conviction of Robin Smith for engaging in UPL. In that case, the bar association complained that Smith provided consumers with various legal forms, advised them on which forms to use, and assisted them in completing the documents. The court reasoned that by drafting and selecting documents and giving advice with regard to their legal effect, Smith was practicing law.[12]

contempt of court
The intentional obstruction or frustration of a court's attempt to administer justice. A party to a lawsuit may be held in contempt of court (punishable by a fine or jail sentence) for refusing to comply with a court's order.

In 1998, a number of legal technicians were facing UPL charges in one case in California when the legislature enacted Senate Bill 1418. The bill authorized nonlawyers to provide certain types of legal services directly to the public. Under that law, a person who qualifies and registers with the county as a "legal document assistant" (LDA) may assist clients in filling out legal forms but cannot advise clients which forms to use.[13] After the LDA law passed, the case was settled.

The Controversy over Legal Software

Notably, even publishers of self-help law books and computer software programs have come under attack for the unauthorized practice of law.[14] For example, in 1999 a Texas Court held that the legal software program *Quicken Family Lawyer* violated Texas's UPL statute. The program provided a hundred different legal forms (including contracts, real estate leases, and wills), along with instructions on how to fill out these forms. Because the program automatically adapted the content of a legal form to the responses of the user, the court held that it gave legal advice and thus constituted UPL.[15]

Shortly after the court's decision to prohibit the sale of the software, the Texas legislature amended the UPL statute to reverse the court's ruling. The new law in Texas explicitly authorizes the sale of legal self-help software, books, forms, and similar products to the public.[16] Note, however, that the Texas law authorizes these products to be used *only* for "self-help." The law does not permit persons who are not licensed to practice law (such as legal technicians) to utilize these programs to give legal advice or assistance to others.

Do Paralegals Who Operate as Legal Technicians Engage in UPL?

State courts and legislatures are still debating whether it is legal, at least in some situations, for legal technicians to operate without a lawyer's supervision. Generally, unless a state statute or rule specifically allows paralegals to assist the public directly without the supervision of an attorney, paralegals would be wise not to engage in such practices. Most state courts are much more likely to find that a paralegal is engaging in UPL than that a publisher of legal software is doing so. This is because of the special relationship of trust that develops between the paralegal and the client and the potential for abuse. In California, an LDA can assist a person by filling out forms, but the LDA must be careful not to suggest what forms to fill out or to select the appropriate forms to fill out based on the information provided by the client. A legal technician in Texas who uses a software program designed to help people file for bankruptcy may be engaging in UPL. The consequences of violating state UPL statutes can be very serious. Any paralegal who contemplates working as a legal technician (independent paralegal) therefore must thoroughly investigate the relevant state laws and court decisions on UPL before offering any services directly to the public and must rigorously abide by the letter of the law.

SHOULD PARALEGALS BE LICENSED?

One of the major issues facing legal professionals and other interested groups today is whether paralegals should be subject to direct regulation by the state through licensing requirements. Unlike certification, which was discussed in Chapter 1, licensing involves direct and mandatory regulation, by the state, of an occupational or professional group. When licensing requirements are established for a professional group, such as for attorneys, a license is required in order for a member of the group to practice his or her profession.

Movements toward regulation of paralegals have been motivated in large part by the activities of legal technicians, or independent paralegals—those who provide legal services directly to the public without attorney supervision. Many legal technicians call themselves paralegals even though they have little, if any, legal training, background, or experience. Yet at the same time, those who cannot afford to hire an attorney can benefit from the self-help services provided by legal technicians who do have training and experience.

General Licensing

general licensing

A type of licensing in which all individuals within a specific profession or group (such as paralegals) must meet licensing requirements imposed by the state in order to legally practice their profession.

A number of states—including Arizona, Florida, Hawaii, Maine, Minnesota, New Jersey, New York, Oklahoma, Rhode Island, South Dakota, Texas, Utah, and Wisconsin—have considered implementing a **general licensing** program. A general licensing program would require all paralegals to meet certain educational requirements and other specified criteria before being allowed to practice their profession.

For example, after five years of study, the New Jersey Supreme Court Committee on Paralegal Education and Regulation recommended that paralegals be licensed to practice their profession. The committee's report proposed that paralegals be subject to state licensure based on demonstrated educational requirements and knowledge of the ethical rules governing the legal profession. Less than one week later, however, the New Jersey Supreme Court declined to follow the committee's recommendations. The court concluded that direct oversight of paralegals is best accomplished through attorney supervision rather than through a state-mandated licensing system.

You can read the report issued by the New Jersey Supreme Court Committee on Paralegal Education and Regulation online at **http://www.judiciary. state.nj.us/pressrel/archives/ admpara.htm**.

Although other states are considering licensing for paralegals, California is the only state that currently makes it unlawful for persons to identify themselves as paralegals unless they meet certain qualifications. The California law requires paralegals to meet minimum education standards, work under lawyer supervision, and complete continuing education requirements (four hours of ethics courses every three years and four hours of either general or specialized law every two years). Individuals who are registered as legal document assistants (LDAs) cannot call themselves paralegals because they do not work under attorney supervision.[17] (Note that the California LDA law was amended in 2002 to allow LDAs who registered before 2001 and who had been using the term *paralegal* in their business name to continue to do so.)

Limited Licensing

limited licensing

A type of licensing in which a limited number of individuals within a specific profession or group (such as legal technicians within the paralegal profession) must meet licensing requirements imposed by the state in order to legally practice their profession.

As an alternative to general licensing, many states are considering **limited licensing**, which would limit licensing requirements to those paralegals (legal technicians, or independent paralegals) who wish to provide specified legal services directly to the public. With limited licensing, qualified paralegals would be authorized to handle routine legal services traditionally rendered only by attorneys, such as advising clients on simple divorces, will executions, bankruptcy petitions, incorporation, real estate transactions, selected tax matters, and other specified services as designated by the state licensing body. Already, a number of states allow some form of limited nonlawyer practice, and some states would like to establish a regulatory mechanism—such as a limited licensing program—to protect the consumers of these services.

Direct Regulation—The Pros and Cons

A significant part of the debate over direct regulation has to do with the issue of who should do the regulating. Certainly, state bar associations and government authorities would want to have a say in the matter. Yet paralegal organizations and educators, such as NALA, NFPA, and the American Association for Paralegal Education (AAfPE), would also want to play a leading role in developing the education requirements, ethical standards, and disciplinary procedures required by a licensing program. The problem is, NALA, NFPA, and the AAfPE have different views on these matters.

NFPA's Position

NFPA endorses the regulation of the paralegal profession on a state-by-state basis. Given that lower-cost legal services are in great demand, NFPA takes the position that the regulation of paralegals would improve consumers' access to quality legal services. NFPA favors establishing minimum education requirements to protect the public and to weed out the "bad apples" in the profession—those who call themselves paralegals but who do not have the necessary education or training to competently perform paralegal work.

NFPA contends that the licensing of paralegals would benefit both the public and attorneys because only demonstrably qualified paralegals would be licensed to practice the profession. Attorneys' search costs in finding competent assistants would be reduced. Moreover, licensing would be a step forward in the development of the paralegal profession, enhancing recognition and encouraging employers to give paralegals greater responsibilities. Also, because licensing would permit paralegals to perform specified tasks, there would be less chance of violating UPL laws.

NFPA proposes a two-tiered system of licensing: general licensing and specialty licensing. General licensing by a state board or agency would require all paralegals within the state to satisfy stipulated requirements in regard to education, experience, and continuing education; it would also subject practicing paralegals to disciplinary procedures by the licensing body. (As mentioned, NFPA has already developed a set of model enforcement guidelines—see Appendix C.) Specialty licensing would require paralegals who wish to practice in a specialized area to demonstrate, by an examination (see the discussion of the PACE examination in Chapter 1), their proficiency in that area.

NALA's Position

NALA supports voluntary certification (self-regulation) but opposes licensing requirements for paralegals. NALA takes the position that state licensing programs would only serve to control entry into the profession and would not improve the quality of the services that paralegals provide. Because a license merely grants a paralegal permission to work, NALA believes that licensing criteria would be kept at the lowest level of professional competency.

According to NALA, there is no demonstrated need to regulate paralegals at this time. Most paralegals work under the supervision of attorneys, who are already regulated by state ethical codes. NALA believes that regulation would increase the cost of paralegals to employers. This increase would then be passed on to consumers, resulting in higher-cost legal services. NALA therefore considers licensing an unnecessary burden to both employers and paralegals.

NALA further contends that licensing would not encourage the growth of the paralegal profession and would not expand the functions of paralegals. Paralegals already perform a wide range of tasks and work in a variety of settings. To impose mandatory, uniform requirements on all paralegals would be detrimental. Some paralegals who perform competently in one specified area (elder law, for example) might not qualify for a paralegal license (because they did not graduate from an ABA-accredited program, for example) and thus would be prohibited from employment as a paralegal.

NALA also objects to specific limited licensing proposals for legal technicians (independent paralegals). These objections, however, do not reflect opposition to the idea of limited licensing for legal technicians so much as disagreement with specific aspects of the proposed regulatory schemes.

Today's Professional Paralegal

WORKING FOR THE ATTORNEY DISCIPLINE BOARD

Denise James is a legal assistant who works for the attorney discipline board in her state. She has an interesting job that entails a variety of responsibilities. One of Denise's job responsibilities is to contact attorneys to sit on the attorney discipline board's hearing panel. She consults the list of attorneys who have volunteered to sit on the panel and calls them to make arrangements for the hearing panels. She forwards to them background information and briefs on the cases that they will hear. On the day of the hearing, she meets the attorneys, escorts them to the hearing room, provides them with hearing examiners' robes, and assists them in getting the hearing started.

PREPARING "NOTICES OF DISCIPLINE"

Another of Denise's duties is to prepare the "notices of discipline" that are published every month in the state bar association journal, a monthly publication that is sent to all licensed attorneys in the state. These notices identify which attorneys have been subject to disciplinary actions, and for what reasons. To prepare this month's notices, Denise pulls out all of the "final orders of discipline" that were entered this month. Then she reads and summarizes each order.

SUMMARIZING DISCIPLINARY PROCEEDINGS

Denise reads through a final order sanctioning an attorney. The attorney, who commingled a client's funds with her own personal funds, was suspended. The funds involved consisted of a check in the settlement of a personal-injury lawsuit. The attorney deposited the check to her personal checking account and then used the funds to pay her monthly bills. She did not issue a check to the client for the full amount until three months later. The client continually called the attorney's office and demanded the settlement check. The attorney kept stalling and then simply refused to return the client's phone calls.

Denise then summarized the disciplinary proceedings against the attorney as follows: "[attorney's name], P12345, Binghamton, by Attorney Discipline Board, Binghamton County, Hearing Panel #6, effective June 3, 2007. Respondent commingled client's funds by using the client's money, received in a settlement, to pay her personal bills, then paid the client three months later. The hearing panel found respondent's conduct to be in violation of Court Rule 1.15 and the state Rules of Professional Conduct. A suspension was issued and costs were assessed in the amount of $951.53."

There is never a dull moment working for the attorney discipline board. The unfortunate part is that Denise sees many cases in which clients have lost legal rights because their cases were neglected for a variety of reasons.

The AAfPE's Position

The American Association for Paralegal Education (AAfPE) does not take an official position on paralegal licensing. The major concern of the AAfPE is that if paralegals are regulated, certain educational standards should be required. Obviously, the AAfPE recommends that states adopt AAfPE's minimum educational standards in any regulatory plan they enact. It is the view of the AAfPE that paralegals (through associations such as NALA and NFPA) and paralegal educators should put aside their differences and present a united front in influencing licensing proposals. Otherwise, by default, the decision will not be theirs to make.

Other Considerations

While the positions taken by NFPA, NALA, and the AAfPE outline the main contours of the debate over regulation, other groups emphasize some different considerations. For example, one of the concerns of lawyers is that if legal technicians are licensed—through limited

On the Web

For updates on the positions taken by NFPA, NALA, and the AAfPE on regulation, as well as regulatory developments, check their Web sites: for NFPA, **http://www.paralegals. org**; for NALA, **http://www.nala.org**; for the AAfPE: **http://www.aafpe.org**.

licensing programs—to deliver low-cost services directly to the public, the business (and profits) of law firms would suffer. Many lawyers are also concerned that if paralegals are subject to mandatory licensing requirements, law firms will not be able to hire and train persons of their choice to become paralegals.

Some paralegals and paralegal associations are concerned that mandatory licensing would require all paralegals to be "generalists." As it is, a large number of paralegals specialize in particular areas, such as bankruptcy or family law, and do not need to have the broad knowledge of all areas of paralegal practice that licensing might require.

A FINAL NOTE

As a professional paralegal, you will have an opportunity to voice your opinion on whether paralegals should be directly regulated by state governments and, if so, what qualifications should be required. Whatever the outcome of the licensing debate, though, keep in mind that all of the issues discussed in this chapter are directly relevant to your paralegal career. The most important point to remember as you embark on a paralegal career is that you need to think and act in a professionally responsible manner in your particular workplace. Although this takes time and practice, in the legal arena there is little room for learning ethics by "trial and error." Therefore, you need to be especially attentive to the ethical rules governing attorneys and paralegal practice discussed in this chapter.

The *Ethics Watch!* features throughout this book offer further insights into some of the ethical problems that can arise in various areas of paralegal performance. Understanding how violations can occur will help you anticipate and guard against them as you begin your paralegal career. Once on the job, you can continue your preventive tactics by asking questions whenever you are in doubt and by making sure that your work is adequately supervised.

KEY TERMS AND CONCEPTS

attorney-client privilege 81	disbarment 71	reprimand 71
breach 72	ethical wall 84	self-regulation 67
conflict of interest 83	general licensing 100	suspension 71
conflicts check 85	licensing 68	third party 78
contempt of court 98	limited licensing 100	unauthorized practice of law (UPL) 69
damages 71	malpractice 71	work product 82

chapter summary   Ethics and Professional Responsibility

The Regulation of Attorneys

Attorneys are regulated by licensing requirements and by the ethical rules of their state. The purpose of attorney regulation is to protect the public against incompetent legal professionals and unethical attorney behavior.

1. *Self-regulation*—Lawyers themselves establish the majority of rules governing their profession through state bar associations and the American Bar Association (ABA), which has established model rules and guidelines relating to professional conduct.

(Continued)

2. *External regulation*—Other key participants in the regulation of attorneys are state supreme courts, state legislatures, and (occasionally) the United States Supreme Court.

3. *Model Code or Model Rules*—Most states have adopted a version of either the 1969 Model Code of Professional Responsibility or the 1983 revision of the Model Code, called the Model Rules of Professional Conduct, both of which were published by the ABA. The Model Rules were substantially amended by the ABA in 2002 to keep up to date with the realities of modern law practice. The majority of the states have adopted laws based on the Model Rules.

4. *Sanctions for violations*—The Model Code and Model Rules spell out the ethical and professional duties governing attorneys and the practice of law. Attorneys who violate the duties imposed by these rules may be subject to sanctions in the form of a reprimand, a suspension, or disbarment. Additionally, attorneys (as well as paralegals) face potential liability for malpractice or for violations of criminal statutes.

Attorney Ethics and Paralegal Practice

Some of the ethical rules governing attorney behavior pose particularly difficult problems for paralegals, and paralegals should consult their state's ethical code to learn the specific rules for which they will be accountable. The following rules apply in most states.

1. *Duty of competence*—This duty is violated whenever a client suffers harm as a result of the attorney's (or paralegal's) incompetent action or inaction.

   a. Breaching the duty of competence may lead to a lawsuit against the attorney (and perhaps against the paralegal) for negligence.

   b. Attorneys must adequately supervise a paralegal's work to ensure that this duty is not breached.

2. *Confidentiality*—The confidentiality rule requires that all information relating to a client's representation be kept in confidence and not revealed to third parties who are not authorized to know the information.

   a. Paralegals should be careful both on and off the job not to discuss client information with third parties.

   b. Client confidences can be revealed only in certain circumstances, such as when the client gives informed consent to the disclosure, when disclosure is necessary to represent the client or to prevent harm to persons or property, or when a court orders the attorney to reveal the information.

   c. Some client information is regarded as privileged information under the rules of evidence and receives even greater protection.

3. *Conflict of interest*—An attorney is prohibited from representing a client if the attorney's representation of that client will adversely affect the interests of another client, including a former client. An attorney is also prohibited from representing a client if there is a significant risk that the attorney's ability to consider, recommend, or carry out an appropriate course of action for the client will be materially limited as a result of the attorney's other responsibilities or interests.

   a. An attorney may represent both sides in a legal proceeding only if the attorney feels that neither party's rights will be adversely affected and only if both clients are aware of the conflict of interest and have given their informed consent to the representation. Paralegals also fall under this rule.

b. In the event that a firm is handling a case and one of the firm's attorneys or paralegals cannot work on the case because of a conflict of interest, that attorney or paralegal must be "walled off" from the case—that is, must be prevented from having any access to files or other information relating to the case.

c. Normally, whenever a prospective client consults with an attorney, a conflicts check is done to ensure that if the attorney or firm accepts the case, no conflict of interest will arise.

The Indirect Regulation of Paralegals

Paralegals are regulated indirectly by attorney ethical rules, by ethical codes created by NFPA and NALA, and by guidelines on the utilization of paralegals, which define the status and function of paralegals and the scope of their authorized activities. The ABA and several states have adopted guidelines on the utilization of paralegals. These codes and guidelines provide paralegals, attorneys, and the courts with guidance on the paralegal's role in the practice of law. The general rule is that paralegals can perform virtually any legal task that attorneys can (other than represent a client in court) as long as they work under an attorney's supervision. (Other exceptions to this rule are noted in the following section.)

The Unauthorized Practice of Law

Nearly every state has laws that prohibit nonlawyers from engaging in the unauthorized practice of law (UPL). Violations of these laws can have serious consequences.

1. *What constitutes UPL?*—Determining what constitutes UPL is complicated by the fact that many state UPL statutes offer only vague or very broad definitions of what constitutes the practice of law, although some states in recent years have made efforts to address this problem.

2. *The need for caution*—Paralegals working for attorneys and legal technicians (independent paralegals) need to be careful not to engage in activities that the state will consider UPL.

3. *Prohibited acts*—The consensus is that paralegals should not engage in any of the following acts:

   a. Establish an attorney-client relationship.

   b. Set legal fees.

   c. Give legal advice or opinions.

   d. Represent a client in court (unless authorized to do so by the court).

   e. Engage in, encourage, or contribute to any act that could constitute the unauthorized practice of law.

Should Paralegals Be Licensed?

A major concern today for both legal professionals and the public is whether paralegals should be directly regulated by the state through licensing requirements.

(Continued)

1. *General licensing*—General licensing would establish minimum standards that every paralegal would have to meet in order to practice as a paralegal in the state. California has adopted such a law, and other states may soon do so.

2. *Limited licensing*—Limited licensing would require paralegals wishing to offer routine legal services directly to the public in certain areas, such as family law and bankruptcy law, to demonstrate their proficiency in that area.

3. *The debate over licensing*—The pros and cons of direct regulation through licensing are being debated vigorously by the leading paralegal and paralegal education associations, state bar associations, state courts, state legislatures, and public-interest groups.

QUESTIONS FOR REVIEW

1. Why is the legal profession regulated? Who are the regulators? How is regulation accomplished?

2. What are the two primary sets of ethical rules that guide the legal profession in the United States? Who created these rules? Which set of rules has been modified recently? Why?

3. How is the paralegal profession regulated by attorney ethical codes?

4. What does the duty of competence involve? How can violations of the duty of competence be avoided?

5. What is the duty of confidentiality? What is the attorney-client privilege? What is the relationship between confidentiality and the attorney-client privilege? What are some potential consequences of violating the confidentiality rule?

6. What is a conflict of interest? How do law firms "wall off" an attorney or a paralegal when a conflict of interest arises?

7. How is the paralegal profession regulated by paralegal codes of ethics? Why have model guidelines been established on the utilization of paralegals?

8. What types of tasks can legally be performed by paralegals? What types of tasks can normally be performed only by attorneys?

9. What is the practice of law? What is the unauthorized practice of law (UPL)? How might paralegals violate state statutes prohibiting UPL?

10. What would the licensing of paralegals involve? What is limited licensing? What are some of the pros and cons in the debate over paralegal licensing?

ETHICAL QUESTIONS

1. Anton Snow, a paralegal, has been asked to research the cases decided by courts in his state to see if he can find a case in which a landlord was held liable for crimes caused by a third party (someone other than the landlord or the tenant) on leased premises. Anton finds a case in which the trial court held that a landlord was liable for harms suffered by a plaintiff when she was mugged and robbed in an apartment complex's parking lot. Anton does not take the time to update the case. He therefore fails to find out that the state court of appeals later reversed the trial court's decision. Thus, the trial court's decision, which Anton gives to his supervising attorney, is no longer "good law." The supervising attorney, relying on Anton's research, advises the client accordingly. Discuss the potential problems that the client, the attorney, and Anton

might face as a result of Anton's failure to update the trial court's decision.

2. Norma Sollers works as a paralegal for a small law firm. She is a trusted, experienced employee who has worked for the firm for twelve years. One morning, Linda Lowenstein, one of the attorneys, calls in from her home and asks Norma to sign Linda's name to a document that must be filed with the court that day. Norma has just prepared the final draft of the document and placed it on Linda's desk for her review and signature. Linda explains to Norma that because her child is sick, she does not want to leave home to come into the office. Norma knows that she should not sign Linda's name—only the client's attorney can sign the document. She mentions this to Linda, but

Linda says, "Don't worry. No one will ever know that you signed it instead of me." How should Norma handle this situation?

3. Matthew Hinson is a legal technician. He provides divorce forms and typing and filing services to the public at very low rates. Samantha Eggleston uses his services. She returns with the forms filled out, but she has one question: How much in monthly child-support payments will she be entitled to receive? How can Matthew legally respond to this question?

PRACTICE QUESTIONS AND ASSIGNMENTS

1. Kathryn Borstein works as a legal assistant for the legal department of a large manufacturing corporation. In the process of interviewing a middle-management accountant with the company about an employment-discrimination lawsuit, Kathryn discovers that a few of the top executives cheat on their income tax returns by not declaring a portion of their bonuses. Kathryn becomes disenchanted with her job with the corporation for these and other reasons and finds a new job with a law firm. Her supervising attorney in the new law firm is involved in a case against her former employer. The attorney tells Kathryn that the only way to deal with these big corporations is to get whatever dirt you can on them and then threaten to go to the press. He wants to know if she can give him any such information. Can she tell him the "dirt" about the executives who cheat on their income taxes? Why or why not? What ethical rules are involved in her decision?

2. Peter Smith, a paralegal, is using the Internet to find property tax records for a client. The client has come to the firm because he wants to buy a parcel of property, but he also wants to make sure that the property taxes have been paid. Peter finds a Web site for the county register of deeds. He locates the property and notes that, according to the information given on the Web page, the taxes have been paid. He prints the page and writes a brief memo to the attorney. The attorney then advises the client that the taxes have been paid and that it is okay to go ahead and purchase the property. The client does so, but several weeks later he receives a notice that he owes $6,500 in back taxes. The client, who is understandably upset, complains to Peter's boss. Peter is sent to the county register of deeds to look up the records relating to the property. Peter finds that the correct information was in the county's records but was not on the Web site. He makes a copy of what he finds and returns to the office. What ethical rule has been violated here? What do these "facts" reveal about the reliability of information posted on the Internet?

3. In which of the following instances may confidential client information be disclosed?

a. A client's daughter calls to find out whether her mother has left her certain property in her will. The mother does not want the daughter to know that the daughter has been disinherited until the will is read after the mother's death.

b. The client in a divorce case threatens to hire a hit man to kill her husband because she perceives that killing her husband is the only way that she can stop him from stalking her. It is clear that the client intends to do this.

c. A former client sues her attorney for legal malpractice in the handling of a breach-of-contract case involving her cosmetics home-sale business. The attorney discloses that the client is having an affair with her next-door neighbor, a fact that is unrelated to the malpractice or breach-of-contract case.

4. According to this chapter's text, which of the following tasks can a paralegal legally perform?

a. Draft a complaint at an attorney's request.

b. Interview a witness to a car accident.

c. Represent a client before an administrative agency.

d. Investigate the facts of a car accident case.

e. Work as a freelance paralegal for attorneys.

f. Work as a legal technician providing legal services directly to the public.

5. Review the facts in Ethical Question 3 above. What do the following ethical codes say about the unauthorized practice of law, and how would these statements apply to Hinson's situation? Could Hinson be disciplined if he gave Eggleston the information she requested?

a. NFPA's Model Code of Ethics and Professional Responsibility (see Appendix C or visit NFPA's Web site at **http://www.paralegals.org**).

b. NALA's Code of Ethics and Professional Responsibility (see Appendix A or visit NALA's Web site at **http://www.nala.org**).

Do your answers differ? If so, how?

QUESTIONS FOR CRITICAL ANALYSIS

1. Why are ethical rules needed? What could happen if the legal profession were not regulated? What might happen if, for example, there were no rule governing competence in the profession?

2. The material in the chapter indicates that lawyers are largely responsible for regulating their own conduct. What do you think of a system in which members of a profession regulate themselves? Is this a good system? Can you think of a better alternative?

3. An experienced legal secretary opened a business, Northside Secretarial Services, for the purpose of delivering certain legal services directly to the public. Specifically, she prepared legal documents—and provided detailed instructions for filing the documents with the court and for service of process—in divorce and adoption cases. She held briefing sessions during which she gave detailed instructions about trials and hearings, including the types of questions that the court would ask and the responses that her "clients" should give to the court. The secretary advertised her services in a local newspaper, holding herself out to be an "expert in family law." She also advertised the sale of "do-it-yourself" divorce kits. She charged no more than $50 for her services, and many of her "clients" were indigent and illiterate.

   The bar association in her state charged her with the unauthorized practice of law. A former client gave testimony that the secretary had advised her to lie about the date of her second marriage, because she could not remember it, in the complaint filed with the court to start divorce proceedings. Another former client testified that when he had found out that his wife was abusing the children, he had been advised he should not try to change the petition for divorce to seek custody of the minor children but should leave it to the state agency to handle abuse and custody issues.

   What was the likely result of the state bar association's filing of unauthorized-practice-of-law charges against the legal secretary? How might the legal secretary have responded to these charges? What would result if the legal secretary was enjoined by court order from engaging in these activities and continued to do so anyway?

4. In your view, are personal and legal ethics totally distinct? How, generally, do (or should) personal and legal ethical standards interrelate?

5. If it were up to you to devise a set of ethical standards for the legal profession, would they be any different from those presented in the chapter? If so, in what ways?

6. Compare the activities that constitute the unauthorized practice of law with the activities in which paralegals can lawfully engage under the guidelines for the utilization of legal assistants. Why do you think that the activities that constitute the unauthorized practice of law are prohibited for nonlawyers? Could someone with training as a legal assistant competently handle some of these activities? If so, which ones?

7. What is the difference between a freelance paralegal and a legal technician? What are the advantages and disadvantages of each type of status? Would you prefer to work as a freelance paralegal or as a legal technician? Why?

8. Do you think that paralegals should be licensed? Why or why not? If you think that they should be licensed, what type of license should they be granted—general or limited? What impact would this have on paralegals? What impact would it have on the legal profession as a whole?

PROJECTS

1. Go to the library or access your state's rules online to find out the requirements for becoming licensed to practice law in your state. Do your state's rules differ from the requirements mentioned in the text? If so, how?

2. Obtain a copy of your state's ethics rules for attorneys. These rules may be located in your state's court rules. How do the competence, confidentiality, and conflict-of-interest rules in your state compare with the ABA's Model Rules on these topics presented in this chapter? Using Microsoft's *PowerPoint* software or Corel's *Presentations*

software, prepare a slide show comparing the two sets of rules.

3. Look in your local telephone book or in a directory of attorneys issued by your state bar association for an agency or commission that is responsible for disciplining attorneys. Contact the agency or commission to find out how attorneys are disciplined in your state. Learn about the various degrees of discipline that may be imposed. If disciplinary hearings are open to the public, try to attend one of the hearings. What is your impression?

4. Contact your state bar association to find out if paralegals may join. If they may, present the material, including the requirements for admission and fees, to the class.

5. Go to the library or search the Web to find materials on the ethical standards of professions other than the legal profession. What ethical concerns do the rules of other professions cover? How are the rules of other professions similar to or different from the legal profession's ethical rules?

USING INTERNET RESOURCES

1. Go to **http://www.paralegals.org**, the home page for the National Federation of Paralegal Associations (NFPA). Click on "Positions & Issues," then click on "Ethics," and then click on "Opinions," this will take you to a page that lists, among other things, NFPA's ethics opinions. Then do the following:

   a. List five issues that NFPA has addressed in these opinions.

   b. Choose one opinion and write a paragraph explaining why the issue dealt with in the opinion is important for paralegals.

   c. Choose the same or a different opinion, read completely through it, and write a paragraph summarizing NFPA's advice on the issue being addressed in the opinion.

2. Go online and find the case *In re Powell*, 266 Bankr. 450 (N.D.Cal. 2001). It can be accessed through the Web site of the U.S. Bankruptcy Court for the Northern District of California at **http://www.canb.uscourts.gov**. Click on "Judges' Decisions," then click "Search." In the search box, type the name "Powell" and click "Search" again. Then select the link for "05/07/2001" to review the opinion titled "Memorandum of Decision Re: Unauthorized Practice of Law." Read through the court's opinion for *In re Powell* and answer the following questions:

   a. Why were Randy Wilson and Terry L. Clark (doing business as Professional Paralegal Services) charged with the unauthorized practice of law? What specific acts did they perform?

   b. Why is the case being heard by a bankruptcy court?

   c. From your reading of the case, are paralegals generally allowed to help members of the public fill out forms (bankruptcy petitions) to initiate bankruptcy proceedings? If so, what did these paralegals do wrong?

   d. What does the court say that Section 110 of the Bankruptcy Code requires of paralegals who prepare bankruptcy forms?

   e. What sanctions did the court impose on Wilson and Clark for engaging in the unauthorized practice of law?

3. Go online to **http://lp.findlaw.com**. Under the heading "Legal Careers & Services," click on the link to "State Bars," under the heading "Legal Organizations." Next, click on your state, and then click on the link to your state's bar association. Answer the following questions:

   a. What are the requirements for an attorney to become licensed to practice law in your state? (Hint: The way these requirements are listed varies from state to state. You may find them under such listings as "Admissions," "Board of Law Examiners," "Supreme Court Rules," or "Court of Appeals Rules.") Do they differ from the requirements described in this chapter? If so, how?

   b. Look up your state's ethical rules on competence, confidentiality, and conflict of interest. Are those rules the same as the rules discussed in this chapter? If not, what are the differences? Are the rules in your state stricter or more lenient?

   c. Look for rules on the admission of paralegals to the state bar association in your state. Also look for your state's guidelines on the utilization of legal assistants. What did you find?

4.  For additional resources, visit our Web site at **http://www.westlegalstudies.com**.

END NOTES

1. Some legal professionals maintain that statutes that prohibit nonlawyers from practicing law constitute a form of direct regulation, because paralegals who violate such statutes may be directly sanctioned (in the form of criminal penalties) under those laws. In this chapter, we use the term *direct regulation* to mean state regulation of a specified professional group, particularly through state licensing requirements.

2. There are exceptions, however. In some states, a lower state appellate court performs this function.

3. *Bates v. State Bar of Arizona*, 433 U.S. 350, 97 S.Ct. 2691, 53 L.Ed.2d 810 (1977). (See Chapter 17 for a discussion of how to read case citations.)

4. In a few states, one need not have completed a bachelor's degree but must have completed a specified number of credits toward a degree.

5. Note that a few states allow individuals who have not attended law school but who have undertaken a form of independent study and practice (usually as paralegals) to take the bar exam and be admitted to the practice of law.

6. Even this mildest sanction can seriously damage an attorney's reputation within the legal community. In some states, state bar associations publish in their monthly journals the names of violators and details of the violations for all members of the bar to read (see the discussion of attorney disciplinary proceedings in the *Today's Professional Paralegal* feature at the end of this chapter).

7. Thomas D. Zilavy and Andrew J. Chevrez, "The Unauthorized Practice of Law: Court Tells Profession, Show Us the Harm," *Wisconsin Lawyer* 78 (October 2005), p. 8. This article reports that a survey by the American Bar Association in December 2004 showed that the following jurisdictions have adopted a definition of the practice of law: Alabama, Alaska, Arizona, Colorado, District of Columbia, Hawaii, Idaho, Kentucky, Louisiana, Maine, Maryland, Michigan, Minnesota, Mississippi, Missouri, Nebraska, North Carolina, Oklahoma, Oregon, Pennsylvania, South Carolina, Utah, Virginia, Washington, West Virginia, and Wyoming.

8. Title 2 of the Texas Government Code, Section 81.101.

9. *Faretta v. California,* 422 U.S. 806, 95 S.Ct. 2525, 45 L.Ed.2d 562 (1975).

10. 355 So.2d 1186 (Fla. 1978).

11. 376 So.2d 378 (Fla. 1979).

12. *Oregon State Bar v. Smith,* 149 Or.App. 171, 942 P.2d 793 (1997).

13. This law is codified in California Business and Professions Code, Sections 6400–6416.

14. *In re Nolo Press/Folk Law, Inc.,* 42 Tex.Sup.Ct.J. 539, 991 S.W.2d 768 (1999).

15. *Unauthorized Practice of Law Committee v. Parsons Technology, Inc.,* 1999 WL 47235 (N.D.Tex. 1999). Note that this case has been overturned.

16. Texas Government Code Section 81.101(c) (Vernon Supp. 2000).

17. California Business and Professions Code, Sections 6450–6456. Enacted in 2000.

THE INNER WORKINGS
OF THE LAW OFFICE

CHAPTER OUTLINE

Introduction

The Organizational Structure of Law Firms

Law Office Management and Personnel

Employment Policies

Filing Procedures

Financial Procedures

Communicating with Clients

Law Office Culture and Politics

AFTER COMPLETING THIS CHAPTER, YOU WILL KNOW:

▶ How law firms are organized and managed.

▶ Some typical policies and procedures governing paralegal employment.

▶ The importance of an efficient filing system in legal practice and some typical filing procedures.

▶ How clients are billed for legal services.

▶ How law office culture and politics affect the paralegal's working environment.

INTRODUCTION

The wide variety of environments in which paralegals work makes it impossible to describe in any detail how the particular firm with which you find employment will be run. Typically, though, the way in which that firm operates will relate, at least in part, to the firm's specific form of business organization. Because most paralegals are employed by private law firms, this chapter focuses on the organization, management, and procedures characteristic of these firms.

In the beginning of the chapter, we look at how the size and organizational structure of a law firm affect the paralegal's working environment. As you might imagine, the working environment in a firm owned and operated by one attorney is significantly different from that in a large law firm with two or three hundred attorneys or a large corporate enterprise—or even a government agency.

We then look at other aspects of the working environment of paralegals. Typically, the firm you work for will have specific policies and procedures relating to employment conditions, filing systems, billing and timekeeping procedures, and financial procedures. We conclude the chapter with a brief discussion of law office culture and politics.

THE ORGANIZATIONAL STRUCTURE OF LAW FIRMS

Law firms range in size from the small, one-attorney firm to the huge megafirm that consists of hundreds of attorneys. Regardless of their size differences, though, in terms of business organization, law firms typically organize their businesses as sole proprietorships, partnerships, or professional corporations. Because the way in which a business is organized affects the office environment, we look briefly at each of the three major organizational forms here: sole proprietorships, partnerships (including limited liability partnerships), and professional corporations. These types of business organizations and others will be discussed in greater detail in Chapter 11.

Sole Proprietorships

sole proprietorship
The simplest form of business organization, in which the owner is the business. Anyone who does business without creating a formal business entity has a sole proprietorship.

personal liability
An individual's personal responsibility for debts or obligations. The owners of sole proprietorships and partnerships are personally liable for the debts and obligations incurred by their business firms. If their firms go bankrupt or cannot meet debts as they become due, the owners will be personally responsible for paying the debts.

Many law firms, particularly smaller firms, are **sole proprietorships**. Sole proprietorships are the simplest business form and are often used by attorneys when they first set up legal practices. In a sole proprietorship, one individual—the sole proprietor—owns the business. The sole proprietor is entitled to any profits made by the firm but is also personally liable for all of the firm's debts or obligations. **Personal liability** means that the business owner's personal assets (such as a home, automobile, savings or investment accounts, and other property) may have to be sacrificed to pay business obligations if the business fails.

An attorney who practices law as a sole proprietor is often called a *sole (solo) practitioner*. Although a sole practitioner may at times hire a staff attorney to help with the legal work, the attorney will be paid a specific sum for his or her time and will not share in the profits or losses of the firm itself.

Working for a sole practitioner is a good way for a paralegal to learn about law office procedures because the paralegal will typically perform a wide variety of tasks. Many sole practitioners hire one person to perform the functions of secretary, paralegal, administrator, and manager. Paralegals holding this kind of position would probably handle the following kinds of tasks: receiving and date-stamping the mail, organizing and maintaining the filing system, interviewing clients and witnesses, bookkeeping (receiving payments from clients, preparing and sending bills to clients, and so on), conducting investigations and legal research, drafting legal documents, assisting the attorney in trial preparation and perhaps in the courtroom, and numerous other tasks, including office administration.

Working for a sole practitioner is also a good way to find out which area of law you most enjoy because you will learn about procedures relating to many different areas of legal work. Alternatively, if you work for a sole practitioner who specializes in one area of law, you will have an opportunity to develop expertise in that area. In sum, working in a small law firm gives you a broad overview of law office procedures and legal practice. This knowledge will help you throughout your career.

Partnerships

The majority of law firms are organized as partnerships, limited liability partnerships, or professional corporations. In a **partnership**, two or more individuals undertake to do business jointly as **partners**. A partnership may consist of just a few attorneys or over a hundred attorneys. In a partnership, each partner owns a share of the business and shares jointly in the firm's profits or losses.

In smaller partnerships, the partners may participate equally in managing the partnership. They will likely meet periodically to make decisions relating to clients, policies, procedures, and other matters of importance to the firm. In larger partnerships, managerial decisions are usually made by a committee consisting of some of the partners, one of whom may be designated as the **managing partner**.

Partnerships (and professional corporations, which will be discussed shortly) frequently employ other attorneys who are not partners in the firm and thus do not share in the profits. Typically, these other attorneys are called **associate attorneys**. They are usually less experienced attorneys and may be invited to become partners after working for the firm for several years. Sometimes, firms hire **staff attorneys**, who work for the firm but will never become partners. Staff attorneys differ from *contract attorneys*, who provide services for busy firms on a project basis. Many firms also hire **law clerks** (sometimes called *summer associates*), law students who work for the firm during summers or part-time during school to gain practical legal experience. Law clerks who meet with the approval of the members of the firm are often offered positions as associates when they graduate and pass the bar exam.

Liability of Partners

Like sole proprietors, attorneys in a partnership are personally liable for the debts and obligations of the business if the business fails. In addition, a partner can be held personally responsible for the misconduct or debts of another partner. For example, suppose that a client sues one of the partners in the firm for malpractice and wins a large money judgment. The firm carries malpractice insurance, but the insurance is insufficient to pay the obligation. The court will first order the attorney who committed the wrongful act to pay the balance due. Once the responsible attorney's personal assets are exhausted, however, the personal assets of the other (innocent) partners can be used to pay the judgment. This unlimited personal liability of partners is a major disadvantage for law firms wishing to organize as partnerships.

Limited Liability Partnership (LLP)

During the 1990s and early 2000s, a new form of partnership called the **limited liability partnership (LLP)** became available to firms in many states. The LLP normally allows professionals to avoid personal liability for the malpractice of other partners. Although LLP statutes vary from state to state, generally each state statute limits the liability of partners in some way. For example, Delaware law protects each innocent partner from the "debts and

---

partnership
An association of two or more persons to carry on, as co-owners, a business for profit.

partner
A person who has undertaken to operate a business jointly with one or more other persons. Each partner is a co-owner of the business firm.

managing partner
The partner in a law firm who makes decisions relating to the firm's policies and procedures and who generally oversees the business operations of the firm.

associate attorney
An attorney working for a law firm who is not a partner and does not have an ownership interest in the firm. Associates are usually less experienced attorneys and may be invited to become partners after working for the firm for several years.

staff attorney
An attorney hired by a law firm as an employee. A staff attorney has no ownership rights in the firm and will not be invited to become a partner in the firm.

law clerk
A law student working as an apprentice with a law firm, during the summer or part-time during the school year, to gain practical experience. Some law firms refer to law clerks as *summer associates*.

limited liability partnership (LLP)
A business organizational form designed for professionals who normally do business as partners in a partnership. The LLP is a pass-through entity for tax purposes, like the general partnership, but limits the personal liability of partners.

obligations of the partnership arising from negligence, wrongful acts, or misconduct." You will read in greater detail about LLPs in Chapter 11. Note that professionals who are not attorneys can also organize as an LLP and that this form of business may provide certain tax advantages as well as limiting the partners' liability.

Professional Corporations

professional corporation (P.C.)
A firm that is owned by shareholders, so called because they have purchased the corporation's stock, or shares. The liability of shareholders is often limited to the amount of their investments.

shareholder
One who purchases corporate stock, or shares, and who thus becomes an owner of the corporation.

A **professional corporation (P.C.)** is owned by **shareholders**, so called because they have purchased the corporation's stock, or shares, and thus own a share of the business. The shareholders share in the profits and losses of the firm in proportion to how many shares they own. Their personal liability, unlike that of partners, may or may not be limited to the amount of their investments, depending on the circumstances and on state law. As you will read in Chapter 11, limited personal liability is one of the key advantages of the corporate form of business.

In many respects, the professional corporation is run like a partnership, and the distinction between these two forms of business organization is often more a legal formality than an operational reality. Because of this, attorneys who organize their business as a professional corporation are nonetheless sometimes referred to as partners. For the sake of simplicity, in this chapter we will refer to anyone who has ownership rights in the firm as a partner.

LAW OFFICE MANAGEMENT AND PERSONNEL

When you take a job as a paralegal, one of the first things you will want to learn is the relative status of the office personnel. Particularly, you will want to know who has authority over you and to whom you are accountable. You will also want to know who is accountable to you—whether you have an assistant or a secretary (or share an assistant or a secretary with another paralegal), for example. In a small firm, you will have no problem learning this information. If you work for a larger law firm, however, the lines of authority may be more difficult to perceive. Your supervisor will probably instruct you, either orally or in writing, on the relative status of the firm's personnel. If you are not sure about who has authority over whom and what kinds of tasks are performed by various employees, you should ask your supervisor.

The lines of authority and accountability vary from firm to firm, depending on the firm's size and its organizational and management preferences. A sample organizational chart for a relatively small law partnership is shown in Exhibit 4.1. The ultimate decision makers in the hypothetical firm represented by that chart are the partners. Next in authority are the associate attorneys and law clerks. The paralegals in this firm are supervised by both the attorneys (in regard to legal work) and the office manager (in regard to office procedural and paralegal staffing matters). In larger firms, there may be a **legal-assistant manager**, who coordinates and oversees paralegal staffing and various programs relating to paralegal educational and professional development.

legal-assistant manager
An employee in a law firm who is responsible for overseeing the paralegal staff and paralegal professional development.

legal administrator
An administrative employee of a law firm who manages the day-to-day operations of the firm. In smaller law firms, legal administrators are usually called office managers.

office manager
An administrative employee who manages the day-to-day operations of a business firm. In larger law firms, office managers are usually called legal administrators.

In addition to attorneys and paralegals, law firm employees include administrative personnel. In large firms, the partners may hire a **legal administrator** to run the business end of the firm. The legal administrator might delegate some of his or her authority to an office manager and other supervisory employees. In small firms, such as that represented by the chart in Exhibit 4.1, an **office manager** handles the administrative aspects of the firm. The legal administrator or office manager typically is in charge of docketing (calendaring) legal work undertaken by the attorneys; establishing and overseeing filing procedures; implementing new legal technology, such as new docketing software; ordering and monitoring supplies; and generally making sure that the office runs smoothly and that office procedures are established and followed. In a small firm, the office manager might also handle client

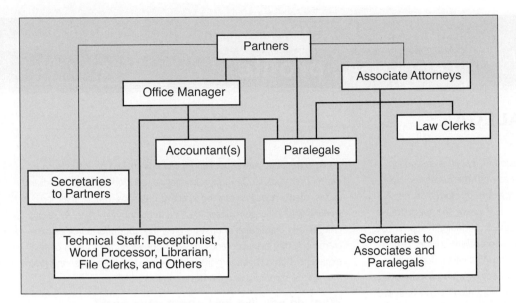

EXHIBIT 4.1
A Sample Organizational Chart for a Law Partnership

billing procedures. The hypothetical firm represented in Exhibit 4.1 has an accounting department to perform this function.

The **support personnel** in a large law office may include secretaries, receptionists, bookkeepers, file clerks, messengers, and others. Depending on their functions and specific jobs, support personnel may fall under the supervision of any number of other personnel in the firm. In a very small firm, just one person—the legal secretary, for example—may perform all of the above-mentioned functions.

support personnel
Employees who provide clerical, secretarial, or other support to the legal, paralegal, and administrative staff of a law firm.

EMPLOYMENT POLICIES

Employees of a law firm, which include all personnel other than the partners or those who work for the firm on a contract basis, are subject to the firm's specific employment policies and procedures. A firm's basic rules or policies governing employment relationships may be set forth in an **employment manual** in larger firms. In smaller firms, these rules and policies are often unwritten. In either situation, when you take a job as a paralegal, or perhaps before you accept a position, you will want to become familiar with the firm's basic conditions of employment. There will be an established policy, for example, on how much vacation time you are entitled to during the first year, second year, and so on. There will also be a policy governing which holidays are observed by the firm, how much sick leave you can take, when you are expected to arrive at the workplace, and what will serve as grounds for the employer to terminate your employment.

employment manual
A firm's handbook or written statement that specifies the policies and procedures that govern the firm's employees and employer-employee relationships.

Employment policies and benefits packages vary from firm to firm. A leading concern of paralegals (and employees generally) is how much they will be paid for their work, how they will be paid (that is, whether they will receive salaries or hourly wages), and what job benefits they will receive. These issues were discussed in detail in Chapter 2, so we will not examine them here. Rather, we look at some other areas of concern to paralegals in regard to employment policies, including performance evaluations and termination procedures.

Performance Evaluations

Many law firms have a policy of conducting periodic performance evaluations, and these evaluations are used to determine if the employee receives a raise. Usually, performance is evaluated annually, but some firms conduct evaluations every six months.

LITIGATION PARALEGAL

Susan G. Ippoliti is a litigation paralegal with the Rochester, New York, law firm of Harter, Secrest & Emery, LLP, where she specializes in civil litigation, including research; case investigations; client contact; expert retention and contact; document drafting, including pleadings, motions, and discovery requests; document analysis and management; and trial preparation. Her work experience includes plaintiff and defense litigation in areas such as product liability, labor and employment litigation, architectural design and construction malpractice, misappropriation of trade secrets, professional liability, intellectual property, asbestos litigation, personal injury, medical malpractice, and insurance defense.

Ippoliti is the vice president and director of membership for the National Federation of Paralegal Associations, Inc. (NFPA), and serves on its marketing committee. She previously served as the regulation review coordinator and special research coordinator for NFPA. In addition, Ippoliti has been a member of Paralegal Association of Rochester, Inc. (PAR), since 1998. She has enjoyed serving her association and the profession in capacities such as vice president of national affairs, vice president of professional development, chair of the Empire State Alliance of Paralegal Associations, member of the New York State Bar Association Law Practice Management Committee, and host coordinator of the NFPA Fall 2001 Convention.

As a frequent guest speaker, Ippoliti has spoken on topics such as ethical dilemmas facing today's paralegals, electronic filing in the district courts, media relations, running effective meetings, vendor selection, working with in-house counsel, legal drafting, and regulation. At several colleges and universities in upstate New York that offer paralegal programs, she has given presentations to students on topics such as her experiences as a litigation paralegal, how to draft pleadings, and proper methods of communication in the workplace.

What do you like best about your work?

"I enjoy the variety of the job. It offers a wide range of responsibilities that continue to challenge me. I love having the ability to be independent and advance my skills through education and research. I also like the fact that I can have a life outside of my job. I have been lucky enough to join my local and national paralegal associations and be very involved in the advancement of my profession. My firm has been supportive of that, and I have grown both personally and professionally because of it."

What is the greatest challenge that you face in your area of work?

"I find the greatest challenge is commanding the attention of my attorneys. The reason they have paralegals is that they are extremely busy people and need to utilize our skills to their greatest advantage to assist them in completing the work. With their busy schedules, it is sometimes difficult to find half an hour in a day to sit and discuss to-do's or how-to's. I do not always get all of the information I need, and I must check back constantly with the attorneys to be certain that

Know What Is Expected of You

Because paralegal responsibilities vary from firm to firm, no one evaluation checklist applies to every paralegal. Some of the factors that may be considered during a performance evaluation are indicated in Exhibit 4.2 on page 118. Note, though, that performance evaluations are much longer and more detailed than the list shown in the exhibit. For example, each major item in that list may have several subheadings and perhaps further subheadings under those subheadings. Normally, under each item listed on a performance evaluation is a series of options—ranging from "very good" to "unsatisfactory" or something similar—for the supervisor or attorney to check.

When you begin work as a paralegal, you should learn at the outset exactly what your duties will be and what performance is expected of you. This way, you will be able to prepare for your first evaluation from the moment you begin working. You will not have to wait

I am doing exactly as they desire and that they will get the outcome they want. Sometimes, they are just so busy that they are not able to provide all of the information at once."

What advice do you have for would-be paralegals in your area of work?

"Know what you do not know. You cannot be afraid to ask questions. It will be far more appreciated than taking on a task, assuming you know how to do it, and then finding out that you completely misunderstood what was desired. The task is always about the client, and you have to remember this when the day begins and the day ends. Did you act in the best interest of your client? Ask yourself this question. Do not be afraid to think outside the box. When attorneys ask for your suggestions or advice, tell them what you think. They really want to know. Find a mentor; that person will be your guardian angel. Every paralegal needs one or has had one at some point. That mentor is the person who will help you be the best paralegal you can be. Be creative. That is what makes a paralegal good at his or her job. We have the ability to act independently and use independent judgment on so many occasions."

What are some tips for success as a paralegal in your area of work?

"Challenge yourself to see the big picture. Look beyond the paper in the file and think about the overview of the case. Creativity is the key to any good method of case management. I always say to a new attor-

> *"Creativity is the key to any good method of case management."*

ney, "It's my job to make you look good." Always find new ways to develop your skills and improve them. Keep a calendar to track deadlines—it is a major element in any successful career. In fact, most firms now require it as part of their loss-prevention guidelines. Use or create many charts to keep track of medical records, workflow, exhibits, timelines, and so forth. For cases involving many documents, scanning and placing the documents into a database is the most efficient way to handle them.

Whether you are on a document-production site or getting ready for trial, it is important that you bring extra supplies along with you: staplers, hole punches, paper clips, pens, folders, anything you can think of, including medications such as Advil, Tylenol, and aspirin. Do not count on being able to buy what you need when you get there. If my trial is out of town, I usually create a shopping list, add to it daily, and then order everything well in advance of the date when I need it. This way, if I have forgotten anything, there is still time to purchase it.

Also, try to get to know everyone you will be working with, from the deputy to the judge's law clerk and secretary. Building these relationships will prove beneficial to you during the trial."

Susan Ippoliti is also featured in the forthcoming book, Lessons from the Top Paralegal Experts, *by Carole Bruno.*

six months or a year before you learn that you were supposed to be doing something that you failed to do.

Be Prepared

Make sure that you prepare for the evaluation and conduct yourself professionally at all times. Be your own advocate. Keep track of your accomplishments, such as the number of billable hours per week or month that you normally generate, so that you can point them out to your supervisor. If you were part of the team that worked many extra hours to win a big case for the firm, mention it during the evaluation. Make your supervisor aware of any way in which you have saved the firm money or contributed to the firm's success. If you have mastered a new software program or passed the CLA (or CP) or PACE exam, tell this to your supervisor.

EXHIBIT 4.2

Factors That May Be Considered in a Performance Evaluation

1. **RESPONSIBILITY**
   Making sure that all tasks are performed on time and following up on all pending matters.
2. **EFFICIENCY**
   Obtaining good results in the least amount of time possible.
3. **PRODUCTIVITY**
   Producing a sufficient quantity of work in a given time period.
4. **COMPETENCE**
   Knowledge level and skills.
5. **INITIATIVE**
   Applying intelligence and creativity to tasks and making appropriate recommendations.
6. **COOPERATION**
   Getting along well with others on the legal team.
7. **PERSONAL FACTORS**
   Appearance, grooming habits, friendliness, poise, and so forth.
8. **DEPENDABILITY**
   Arriving at work consistently on time and being available when needed.

Get the Most from Your Performance Evaluation

Both paralegals and their employers can benefit from the discussions that take place during a performance evaluation. In the busy workplace, you will probably not have much time available to talk with your supervisor about issues that do not relate to immediate work needs. Even if you do find a moment, you may feel awkward bringing up the topic of your performance or discussing a workplace problem. Performance evaluations are designed specifically to allow both sides to exchange their views on such matters.

During performance reviews, you will also learn how the firm rates your performance. You can gain valuable feedback from your supervisor, learn more about your strengths and weaknesses, and identify the areas in which you need to improve your skills. Be sure that you do not react negatively to any criticisms of your performance. Remember that even during an evaluation you are being evaluated. Adopting the right outlook and showing that you appreciate constructive criticism will impress your supervisor.

You can also utilize the evaluation to give your supervisor feedback on the workplace. This is especially useful if you feel you are capable of handling more complex tasks than you are being assigned. Attorneys sometimes underutilize paralegals simply because they do not know a paralegal's capabilities. If you gently suggest ways in which your knowledge and experience could be put to better use, sometimes that is all it takes to earn more challenging and rewarding job responsibilities. Also, if you and your supervising attorney never seem to have the time to meet face-to-face for the evaluation, consider writing up your own evaluation and presenting it to him or her for review.

Employment Termination

Virtually all policy manuals deal with the subject of employment termination. If you work for a firm that has prepared such a manual for its employees, the manual will likely specify what kind of conduct serves as a basis for firing employees. For example, the manual might specify that if an employee is absent more than twelve days a year for two consecutive years, the employer has grounds to terminate the employment relationship. The manual will also probably describe employment-termination procedures. For example, the firm might require that it be notified one month in advance if an employee decides to leave the firm; if the employee fails to give one month's notice, he or she may forfeit accumulated vacation time or other benefits on termination.

Employment Discrimination

Traditionally, employment relationships have been governed by the common law doctrine of employment at will. Under this doctrine, employers may hire and fire employees "at will"—that is, for any reason or no reason. Today, courts have created several exceptions to this doctrine, and state and federal statutes now regulate numerous aspects of the employment relationship. Under federal law (and many state statutes), employers may not refuse to hire job applicants, refuse to promote employees, or fire employees for discriminatory reasons—because of the employee's age, gender, or race, for example. These and other laws regulating employment relationships will be discussed in Chapter 11, but it should be mentioned here that virtually every large law firm today has special policies and procedures that must be followed with respect to claims of employment discrimination.

For example, an employee who experiences sexual harassment—a form of gender-based discrimination that is prohibited by federal law and most state laws—may be required by the firm's harassment policy to follow formal complaint channels to resolve the issue. If an employee fails to follow the required procedures, the firm may be able to avoid legal responsibility for the harassment. Similarly, if an employer does not have established procedures in place for dealing with harassment or other forms of discrimination, the employer may find it difficult to avoid liability for the harassment or discriminatory treatment initiated by supervisors or others against a particular employee.

On the Web

For information on federal laws governing employment discrimination, access the Equal Employment Opportunity Commission's Web site at **http://www.eeoc.gov**.

FILING PROCEDURES

Every law firm, regardless of its size or organizational structure, has some kind of established filing procedures. Efficient filing procedures are important in any law firm, because the paperwork generated by even a small firm can be substantial. Efficient filing procedures are particularly necessary in law offices because important and confidential documents must be safeguarded yet be readily retrievable when they are needed. If a client file is misplaced or lost, the client may suffer irreparable harm.

Additionally, documents must be filed in such a way as to protect client confidentiality. The duty of confidentiality was discussed at length in Chapter 3, but it deserves special mention here because of the extent to which it frames all legal work and procedures. This is particularly true of filing procedures. All information received from or about clients, including client files and documents, is considered confidential. A breach of confidentiality by a paralegal or other employee can cause the firm to incur potentially extensive liability.

If you work for a small firm, filing procedures may be rather informal, and you may even assume the responsibility for organizing and developing an efficient filing system. Larger firms normally have specific procedures concerning the creation, maintenance, use, and storage of office files. If you take a job with a large firm, a supervisor will probably spend some time training you in routine office procedures, including filing procedures. Although the trend today, particularly in larger firms, is toward computerized filing systems, firms routinely create "hard copies" to ensure that files are not lost if a computer system crashes.

Generally, law offices maintain several types of files. Typically, a law firm's filing system will include client files, work product files and reference materials, and forms files (as well as personnel files, which we do not discuss here).

Client Files

To illustrate client filing procedures, we present below the phases in the "life cycle" of a hypothetical client's file. The name of the client is Katherine Baranski; she has just retained one of your firm's attorneys to represent her in a lawsuit that she is bringing against Tony Peretto.

Developing Paralegal Skills

CLIENT FILE CONFIDENTIALITY

Robert James, a paralegal with the law firm of Jenkins & Fitzgerald, takes a client's file with him to the law library to do some legal research. While he walks several aisles away to look for a particular legal reference book, Lori Sanger, an attorney from another firm, walks by and notices the file. She can see on the file the law firm's name, the client's name (Purdy Contracting, Inc.), the court's docket number, and the firm's file number. Because she recognizes the client's name, she writes down the docket number, goes to the court clerk's office, and requests the court's file, which is public information. She reads through the file and sees that Purdy Contracting, Inc., a construction company, is being sued for a substantial amount of damages.

Lori has a client who is about to award a big construction project to Purdy Contracting. She calls her client and warns the client that this lawsuit could bankrupt Purdy. As a result, Purdy Contracting does not get the job and complains to Jenkins & Fitzgerald. The firm changes its policy so that client names no longer appear on the outside of client files.

CHECKLIST FOR CLIENT FILE CONFIDENTIALITY

- Create a confidential name for the client file, using alphabetical and/or numerical sequences.
- Do not leave files out in the open in public places, such as libraries or courts, where their contents can be observed by others.
- Do not leave files in areas within the law firm where other clients might observe a file and its contents.
- Follow the law firm's procedures for closing a file to ensure that extra copies of the documents and letters are destroyed.
- Destroy old files that are no longer needed by shredding them.

Because Baranski is initiating the lawsuit, she is referred to as the *plaintiff*. Peretto, because he has to defend against Baranski's claims, is the *defendant*. The name of the case is *Baranski v. Peretto*. Assume that you will be working on the case and that your supervising attorney has just asked you to open a new case file. Assume also that you have already verified, through a "conflicts check" (discussed in Chapter 3), that no conflict of interest exists.

Opening a New Client File

The first step that you (or a secretary, at your request) will take in opening a new file is to assign the case a file number. For reasons of both efficiency and confidentiality, many firms identify their client files by numbers or some kind of numerical and/or alphabetical sequence instead of the clients' names. The *Baranski v. Peretto* case file might be identified by the letters BARAPE—the first four letters of the plaintiff's name followed by the first two letters of the defendant's name.

Increasingly, law firms are using computerized databases to record and track case titles and files. For example, some firms have file labels containing bar codes in which are embedded attorney codes, subject-matter codes, the client's name and file number, and so forth.

Typically, law firms maintain a master client list on which clients' names are entered alphabetically and cross-referenced to the clients' case numbers. If file numbers consist of numerical sequences, there is also a master list on which the file numbers are listed in numerical order and cross-referenced to the clients' names.

Adding Subfiles

As the work on the *Baranski* case progresses and more documents are generated or received, the file will expand. To ensure that documents will be easy to locate, you will create subfiles. A special subfile might be created for client documents (such as a contract, will, stock certificate, or photograph) that the firm needs for reference or for evidence at trial. As correspondence relating to the *Baranski* case is generated, you will probably add a correspondence subfile. You will also want a subfile for your or the attorney's notes on the case, including research results.

As you will read in Chapters 13 through 15, litigation involves several stages. As the *Baranski* litigation progresses through these stages, subfiles for documents relating to each stage will be added to the *Baranski* file. Many firms find it useful to color-code or add tabs to subfiles so that they can be readily identified. Often, in large files, an index of each subfile's contents is created and attached to the inside cover of the subfile.

Documents are typically filed within each subfile in reverse chronological order, with the most recently dated document on the top. Usually, to safeguard the documents, they are punched at the top with a two-hole puncher so that they can be secured within the file with a clip. Note, though, that an original client document should not be punched or altered in any way. It should always be left loose within the file (or paper-clipped to a copy of the document that *is* punched and secured in the file). For example, if you were holding in the file a property deed belonging to a client, you would not want to alter that document in any way.

File Use and Storage

Often, files are stored in a central file room or area. Most firms have some kind of procedure for employees to follow when removing files from the storage area. For example, a firm might require the office staff to replace a removed file with an "out card" indicating the date, the name of the file, and the name or initials of the person who removed it.

Note that documents should never be removed from a client file or subfile. Rather, the entire file or subfile should be removed for use. This ensures that important documents will not be separated from the file and possibly mislaid or lost. Many paralegals make copies of documents in the file for their use. For example, if you are working on the *Baranski* case and need to review certain documents in the file, you might remove those documents from the file temporarily, copy them, and immediately return the file to storage.

Closing a File

Assume that the *Baranski* case has been settled out of court and that no further legal work on Baranski's behalf needs to be done. For a time, her file will be retained in the inactive files, but when it is fairly certain that no one will need to refer to it very often, if ever, it will be closed. Closed files are often stored in a separate area of the building or even off-site. Traditionally, many larger law firms stored the contents of old files on microfilm. Today, firms can use scanning technology to scan file contents for storage on CD-ROMs, DVDs, magnetic tapes, or other data-storage devices.

Specific procedures for closing files vary from firm to firm. Typically, when a case is closed, original documents provided by the client (for example, a deed to property) are returned to the client, and extraneous materials, such as extra copies of documents or cover letters, are destroyed.

Destroying Old Files

Law firms do not have to retain client files forever, and at some point, the *Baranski* case file will be destroyed. Old files are normally destroyed by shredding so that confidentiality is preserved. Law firms exercise great care when destroying client files because a court or government agency may impose a heavy fine on a law firm that destroys a file that should have been retained for a longer period of time. How long a particular file must be retained depends on many factors, including the nature of the client's legal matters and governing statutes, such as the statute of limitations.

Statutes of limitations limit the time period during which specific types of legal actions may be brought to court. Statutes of limitations for legal-malpractice actions vary from state to state—from six months to ten years after the attorney's last contact with the client. When the statute of limitations in your state expires is thus an important factor in determining how long to retain a client file, because an attorney or law firm will need the information contained in the client's file to defend against a malpractice action. If the file has been destroyed, the firm will not be able to produce any documents or other evidence to refute the plaintiff's claim.

Work Product Files and Reference Materials

Many law firms keep copies of research projects, legal memoranda, and various case-related documents prepared by the firm's attorneys and paralegals so that these documents can be referred to in future projects. In this way, legal personnel do not have to start all over again when working on a claim similar to one dealt with in the past.

Traditionally, hard copies of work product files, or legal-information files, were filed in the firm's law library with other reference materials and publications. Today, work product documents and research materials are often generated on computers and stored on CD-ROMs, DVDs, portable hard drives, flash cards, or other data-storage devices. Often, in large firms, these materials are kept in a central data bank that is readily accessible by the firm's personnel.

Forms Files

Every law firm keeps on hand various forms that it commonly uses. These forms are usually stored in a **forms file**. A forms file might include forms for retainer agreements (to be discussed shortly), for filing lawsuits in specific courts, for bankruptcy petitions, for real estate matters, and for numerous other types of legal matters. Often, to save time, copies of documents relating to specific types of cases are kept for future reference. Then, when the attorney or paralegal works on a similar case, those documents can serve as models, or guides. (These forms may also be kept in a work product file, as just mentioned.)

Increasingly, forms files are being computerized. Computerized forms have simplified legal practice by allowing legal personnel to generate customized documents within minutes. Forms for many standard legal transactions are now available from legal-software companies on CD-ROMs. They are also available online at an increasing number of Web sites, as you will read in Chapter 18.

FINANCIAL PROCEDURES

Like any other business firm, a law firm needs to at least cover its expenses or it will fail. In the business of law, the product is legal services, which are sold to clients for a price. A foremost concern of any law firm is therefore to establish a clear policy on fee arrangements and efficient procedures to ensure that each client is billed appropriately for the time and costs associated with serving that client. Efficient billing procedures require, in turn, that attorneys and paralegals keep accurate records of the time that they spend working on a given client's case or other legal matter.

---

statute of limitations
A statute setting the maximum time period within which certain actions can be brought to court or rights enforced. After the period of time has run, no legal action can be brought.

forms file
A reference file containing copies of the firm's commonly used legal documents and informational forms. The documents in the forms file serve as models for drafting new documents.

On the Web

For a sampling of the types of legal forms available on the Web, check the following sites: **http://www.lectlaw.com/form.html** and **http://www.legaldocs.com**.

Fee Arrangements

A major ethical concern of the legal profession has to do with the reasonableness of attorneys' fees and the ways in which clients are billed for legal services. Among other things, state ethical codes governing attorneys require legal fees to be reasonable. For example, Rule 1.5 of the Model Rules of Professional Conduct states, "A lawyer's fees shall be reasonable." The rule then lists the factors that should be considered in determining the reasonableness of a fee. The factors include the time and labor required to perform the legal work, the fee customarily charged in the locality for similar legal services, and the experience and ability of the lawyer performing the services.

Normally, fee arrangements are discussed and agreed on at the outset of any attorney-client relationship. Most law firms require each client to agree, in a signed writing called a **retainer agreement**, to whatever fee arrangements have been made. (Some states also require, by law, that fee arrangements be stated in writing.) The agreement specifies that the client is retaining (hiring) the attorney and/or firm to represent the client in a legal matter and states that the client agrees to the fee arrangements set forth in the agreement. Exhibit 4.3 on the following page shows a sample retainer agreement.

Basically, there are three types of fee arrangements: fixed fees, hourly fees, and contingency fees. We examine here each of these types of fees, as well as some alternative fee arrangements.

> **retainer agreement**
> A signed document stating that the attorney or the law firm has been hired by the client to provide certain legal services and that the client agrees to pay for those services in accordance with the terms set forth in the retainer agreement.

Fixed Fees

The client may agree to pay a **fixed fee** for a specified legal service. Certain procedures, such as incorporation and simple divorce filings, are often handled on a fixed-fee basis because the attorney can estimate fairly closely how much time will be involved in completing the work. Charging fixed fees is an increasingly popular method of billing. This is because it helps attorneys avoid lawsuits and other problems that can result when clients allege that their legal fees were excessive.

> **fixed fee**
> A fee paid to the attorney by his or her client for having rendered a specified legal service, such as the creation of a simple will.

Hourly Fees

Traditionally, with the exception of litigation work done on a contingency-fee basis (discussed below), most law firms have charged clients hourly rates for legal services. Hourly rates vary widely from firm to firm. Some litigation firms, for example, can charge extremely high hourly rates ($700 an hour or more) for their services because of their reputation for obtaining favorable settlements or court judgments for their clients. In contrast, an attorney just starting up a practice as a sole practitioner will have to charge a lower, more competitive rate (which may be as low as $100 per hour) to attract clients.

Today, law firms also bill clients for hourly rates for paralegal services. Because the hourly rate for paralegals is lower than that for attorneys, clients benefit from attorneys' use of paralegal services. Generally, the billing rate for paralegal services depends on the size and location of the firm. According to a biennial compensation survey conducted by the National Association of Legal Assistants in 2004, the average billing rate for paralegals ranges from $81 per hour in smaller firms to $113 per hour in larger firms. Also, the average billing rate for paralegals is generally higher ($106 per hour) in the far western region of the country than in any other area.

Note that although your services might be billed to the client at a certain hourly rate—say, $100—that does not mean that the firm will actually pay you $100 an hour as wages. The billable rate for paralegal services, as for attorney services, has to take into account the firm's expenses for overhead (rent, utilities, employee benefits, supplies, and so on).

EXHIBIT 4.3
A Sample Retainer Agreement

RETAINER AGREEMENT

I, Katherine Baranski, agree to employ Allen P. Gilmore and his law firm, Jeffers, Gilmore & Dunn, as my attorneys to prosecute all claims for damages against Tony Peretto and all other persons or entities that may be liable on account of an automobile accident that caused me to sustain serious injuries. The accident occurred on August 4, 2006, at 7:45 A.M., when Tony Peretto ran a stop sign on Thirty-eighth Street at Mattis Avenue and, as a result, his car collided with mine.

I agree to pay my lawyers a fee that will be one-third (33 percent) of any sum recovered in this case, regardless of whether the sum is received through settlement, lawsuit, arbitration, or any other way. The fee will be calculated on the sum recovered, after costs and expenses have been deducted. The fee will be paid when any money is actually received in this case. I agree that Allen P. Gilmore and his law firm have an express attorney's lien on any recovery to ensure that their fee is paid.

I agree to pay all necessary costs and expenses, such as court filing fees, court reporter fees, expert witness fees and expenses, travel expenses, long-distance telephone and facsimile costs, and photocopying charges. I understand that these costs and expenses will be billed to me by my attorney on a monthly basis and that I am responsible for paying these costs and expenses, even if no recovery is received.

I agree that this agreement does not cover matters other than those described above. It does not cover an appeal from any judgment entered, any efforts necessary to collect money due because of a judgment entered by a court, or any efforts necessary to obtain other benefits, such as insurance.

I agree to pay a carrying charge amounting to the greater of five dollars ($5.00) or four percent (4%) per month on the average daily balance of bills on my account that are thirty (30) days overdue. If my account is outstanding by more than sixty (60) days, all work by the attorney shall cease until the account is paid in full or a monthly paymenht plan is agreed on.

This contract is governed by the law of the state of Nita.

I AGREE TO THE TERMS AND CONDITIONS STATED ABOVE:

Date: ___2 / 4 / 2007___   *Katherine Baranski*
                                Katherine Baranski

I agree to represent Katherine Baranski in the matter described above. I will receive no fee unless a recovery is obtained. If a recovery is obtained, I will receive a fee as described above.

I agree to notify Katherine Baranski of all developments in this matter promptly, and I will make no settlement of this matter without her consent.

I AGREE TO THE TERMS AND CONDITIONS STATED ABOVE:

Date: ___2 / 4 / 2007___   *Allen P. Gilmore*
                                Allen P. Gilmore
                                Jeffers, Gilmore & Dunn
                                553 Fifth Avenue
                                Suite 101
                                Nita City, NI 48801

contingency fee
A legal fee that consists of a specified percentage (such as 30 percent) of the amount the plaintiff recovers in a civil lawsuit. The fee must be paid only if the plaintiff prevails in the lawsuit (recovers damages).

Contingency Fees

A common practice among litigation attorneys, especially those representing plaintiffs in certain types of cases (such as personal-injury or negligence cases) is to charge the client on a contingency-fee basis. A **contingency fee** is contingent (dependent) on the outcome of the

Ethics Watch!

HANDLING CLIENTS' QUESTIONS ABOUT FEES

Suppose that you work as a paralegal for a sole practitioner, Marina Tesner, who is just setting up practice. You know that the attorney is soliciting new clients and that she relies on you, when she is out of the office, to make sure that potential clients are not turned away for any reason. One day, while Tesner is out of town, a man named Henry Roth calls the office. He is purchasing a home and wants to consult with an attorney before signing the final papers four days from now. You explain that Tesner is out of the office but will return in two days and could see him then. Roth says he would wait for a couple of days if he could be certain of the hourly rate that Tesner would charge him for her services. Because Tesner has authorized you to tell potential clients her hourly rate, you indicate that she usually bills clients $150 an hour for her services. Roth then wants to know if she would reduce the rate for his "simple" legal matter. You know that Tesner has done this for clients in the past. What should you tell Roth? As discussed in Chapter 3, professional ethical codes prohibit anyone but an attorney from setting legal fees. If you told Roth what he wanted to know, you might be engaging in the unauthorized practice of law.

case. If the plaintiff wins the lawsuit and recovers damages or settles out of court, the attorney will be entitled to a certain percentage of the amount recovered (refer back to Exhibit 4.3 for an example of a contingency-fee retainer agreement). If the plaintiff loses the lawsuit, the attorney gets nothing—although the client normally will reimburse the attorney for the costs and expenses involved in preparing for trial (costs and expenses are discussed below, in regard to billing procedures).

Often, the attorney's contingency fee is one-fourth or one-third of the amount recovered. The agreement may provide for modification of the amount depending on how and when the dispute is settled. For example, an agreement that provides for a contingency fee of 33 percent of the amount recovered for a plaintiff may state that the amount will be reduced to a lower percentage if the case is settled out of court.

Do Contingency Fees Violate Ethics Rules?
Some people maintain that the use of contingency fees is ethically questionable because it encourages attorneys to resort to aggressive tactics in order to win a case. The legal profession points out, however, that contingency-fee arrangements allow clients who could not otherwise afford a lawyer to obtain competent representation. After all, litigation is adversarial by nature, and even clients who are economically deprived deserve a zealous advocate.

Limitations on Contingency Fees.
The law restricts the use of contingency-fee agreements to certain types of cases. An attorney can request a contingency fee only in civil matters, not in criminal cases. In a civil case, the plaintiff is often seeking money damages from

Ethics Watch!

TRUST ACCOUNTS

Suppose that a legal assistant who has access to funds held in trust for clients borrows from those funds for temporary personal use. Would such borrowing be unethical? Would it be illegal? The answer to both questions is a resounding "Yes!" By law, anyone who takes for personal use any property (including money) that is legally entrusted to his or her care commits a form of theft called embezzlement (see Chapter 16). It does not matter whether the person who used the funds intended to replace them the next day, week, or month. The fact is, a crime has been committed.

the defendant to compensate the plaintiff for injuries suffered. In criminal cases, as you will read in Chapter 16, the government is seeking to punish the defendant for a wrongful act committed against society as a whole. If the defendant is found not guilty of the charges, he or she will not receive money damages that the attorney could share.

Attorneys are also typically prohibited (by state law) from entering into contingency-fee agreements in divorce cases (see Chapter 10), probate cases (see Chapter 10), and workers' compensation cases (see Chapter 11). States usually prohibit contingency fees in these civil cases because lawmakers have determined that allowing attorneys to share in the proceeds recovered would be contrary to public policy.

Alternative Fee Arrangements

Some attorneys offer alternative fee arrangements to their clients. One alternative billing practice, called "task-based billing," is similar to a fixed-fee arrangement: fixed fees are charged for specific types of tasks that are involved in a legal matter. For example, the attorney might charge a flat fee for conducting a pretrial deposition (in which a party to a lawsuit or a witness gives sworn testimony—see Chapter 13). Another alternative billing practice is sometimes referred to as "value billing." When this arrangement is used, the fees charged to the client vary depending on the results of the representation—if a lawsuit is lost, won, or settled, for example.

Client Trust Accounts

retainer
An advance payment made by a client to a law firm to cover part of the legal fees and/or costs that will be incurred on that client's behalf.

trust account
A bank account in which one party (the trustee, such as an attorney) holds funds belonging to another person (such as a client); a bank account into which funds advanced to a law firm by a client are deposited. Also called an *escrow account*.

Law firms often require new clients to pay a **retainer**—an initial advance payment to the firm to cover part of the fee and various costs that will be incurred on the client's behalf (such as mileage or other travel expenses, phone and fax charges, and so on). Some businesses keep an attorney on retainer. This means that the client pays the attorney a fixed amount every month, and the attorney handles all necessary legal business that arises during the month. Retainer arrangements allow businesses to make legal costs even and predictable over time.

Funds received as retainers, as well as any funds received on behalf of a client (such as a payment to a client to settle a lawsuit), are placed in a special bank account. This account is usually referred to as a client **trust account** (or escrow account). It is extremely important that the funds held in a trust account be used *only* for expenses relating to the costs of serving that client's needs.

Misuse of client funds constitutes a breach of the firm's duty to its client. An attorney's personal use of the funds, for example, can lead to disciplinary action and possible disbarment, as well as criminal penalties. *Commingling* (mixing together) a client's funds with the firm's funds also constitutes abuse and is one of the most common ways in which attorneys breach their professional obligations. If you handle a client's trust account, you should be especially careful to document fully your use of the funds to protect yourself and your firm against the serious problems that may arise if there are any discrepancies in the account.

The Prohibition against Fee Splitting

An important ethical rule with which paralegals should be familiar is Rule 5.4 of the Model Rules of Professional Conduct. That rule states, "A lawyer or law firm shall not share legal fees with a nonlawyer." For this reason, paralegals cannot become partners in a law partnership (because the partners share the firm's income), nor can they have a fee-sharing arrangement with an attorney in any way.

One of the reasons for this rule is that it protects the attorney's independent judgment concerning legal matters. For example, if an attorney became partners with two or three nonattorneys, the nonattorneys would have a significant voice in determining the firm's policies. In this situation, a conflict might arise between a policy of the firm and the attorney's duty to exercise independent professional judgment in regard to a client's case. The rule against fee splitting also protects against the possibility that nonlawyers would indirectly, through attorneys, be able to engage in the practice of law, which no one but an attorney can do.

Billing and Timekeeping Procedures

As a general rule, a law firm bills its clients monthly. Each client's bill reflects the amount of time spent on the client's matter by the attorney or other legal personnel. In the context of legal work, client billing serves an obvious financial function (collecting payment for

A paralegal keeps track of the time she spent in the law office library. Later, she will enter the information into her firm's computerized billing program.

(Courtesy of ©Studio Photogram/Alamy)

Developing Paralegal Skills

CREATING A TRUST ACCOUNT

Louise Larson has been hired to work for Don Jones. Don is just starting his own sole practice of law after many years of working with a medium-sized law firm in which he had nothing to do with the firm's financial management. Louise's first assignment is to establish a client trust accounting system.

Don and Louise review the ethical rules regarding client property and funds. These rules require that client funds not be commingled with the lawyer's funds. "It's too easy to 'borrow' from a client's funds when they are in the lawyer's own bank account," explains Don. "Therefore," Don continues, "the first thing we need to do is open a checking account for client trust funds." Don and Louise then discuss what needs to be done in order to open the trust account and what other bookkeeping procedures will be involved in creating a client trust accounting system.

CHECKLIST FOR CREATING A CLIENT TRUST ACCOUNT

- Obtain and prepare the necessary forms from the bank in which the account will be maintained.
- Devise a bookkeeping method for tracking all fees and expenses for a particular case and/or client.
- Retain all deposit slips and canceled checks.
- Keep a record of payments made to clients.
- Decide who will have access to the account.

| **billable hours** |
Hours or fractions of hours that attorneys and paralegals spend in work that requires legal expertise and that can be billed directly to clients.

On the Web

You can obtain information on selected time-and-billing software at the following Web sites: **http://www.pclaw.com**, **http://www.timeslips.com**, and **http://www.tussman.com**.

---

services rendered). It also serves a communicative function (keeping the client informed of the work being done on his or her case), as you will learn later in this chapter.

Generally, client bills are prepared by a legal secretary or a bookkeeper or, in larger firms, by someone in the accounting department. The bills are based on the fee arrangements made with the client and the time slips collected from the firm's attorneys and paralegals. The time slips (discussed below) indicate how many hours are to be charged to each client at what hourly rate.

The *legal fees* billed to clients will be based on the number of billable hours generated for work requiring legal expertise. **Billable hours** are the hours or fractions of hours that attorneys and paralegals spend in client-related work that requires legal expertise and that can be billed directly to clients. The *costs* billed to clients will include expenses incurred by the firm (such as court fees, travel expenses, phone and fax charges, express-delivery charges, and copying costs) on the client's behalf. If an attorney is retained on a contingency-fee basis, the client is not billed monthly for legal fees. The client is normally billed monthly for any costs incurred on the client's behalf, however.

Typically, a preliminary draft of the client's bill will be given to the attorney responsible for that client's account. After the attorney reviews and possibly modifies the bill, the final draft of the bill is generated and sent to the client. Exhibit 4.4 illustrates a sample client bill in its final form.

Most law firms today have computerized their billing procedures and use time-and-billing software designed specifically for law offices. Time-and-billing software is based on traditional timekeeping and billing procedures. A familiarity with essential features of time-and-billing software programs, combined with a knowledge of the basic principles and pro-

EXHIBIT 4.4
A Sample Client Bill

Jeffers, Gilmore & Dunn
553 Fifth Avenue
Suite 101
Nita City, NI 48801

BILLING DATE: February 28, 2007

Thomas Jones, M.D.
508 Oak Avenue
Nita City, NI 48801

RE: Medical-Malpractice Action Brought against Dr. Jones,
       File No. 15789

DATE	SERVICES RENDERED	PROVIDED BY	HOURS SPENT	TOTAL
1/30/07	Initial client consultation	APG (attorney)	1.00	$200.00
1/30/07	Client interview	EML (paralegal)	1.00	74.00
1/30/07	Document preparation	EML (paralegal)	1.00	74.00
2/5/07	Interview: Susanne Mathews (nurse)	EML (paralegal)	1.50	<u>111.00</u>
	TOTAL FOR LEGAL SERVICES			<u>$459.00</u>

DATE	EXPENSES			
2/5/07	Hospital charges for a copy of the medical documents			<u>$75.00</u>
	TOTAL FOR EXPENSES			<u>$75.00</u>
	TOTAL BILL TO CLIENT			<u>$534.00</u>

cedures involved in client billing, will help you understand whatever type of time-and-billing software your employer may use.

Documenting Time and Expenses

Accurate timekeeping by attorneys and paralegals is crucial because clients cannot be billed for time spent on their behalf unless that time is documented. Attorneys and paralegals normally keep track of the time they spend on each client's work, as well as the time they spend on other tasks. Traditionally, **time slips** have been used for this purpose. Today, time slips are incorporated into timekeeping software programs. We look here at *Timeslips,* a software program created by Sage Software, Inc. This is the most commonly used time-and-billing software, according to a survey published in *Legal Assistant Today* magazine in 2004.

In the slip entry form shown in Exhibit 4.5 on the following page, the user inputs his or her name, the task being billed for, the client for whom the work is being performed, the case

time slip
A record documenting, for billing purposes, the hours (or fractions of hours) that an attorney or a paralegal worked for each client, the date on which the work was done, and the type of work that was undertaken.

EXHIBIT 4.5
Timeslips Slip Entry Form

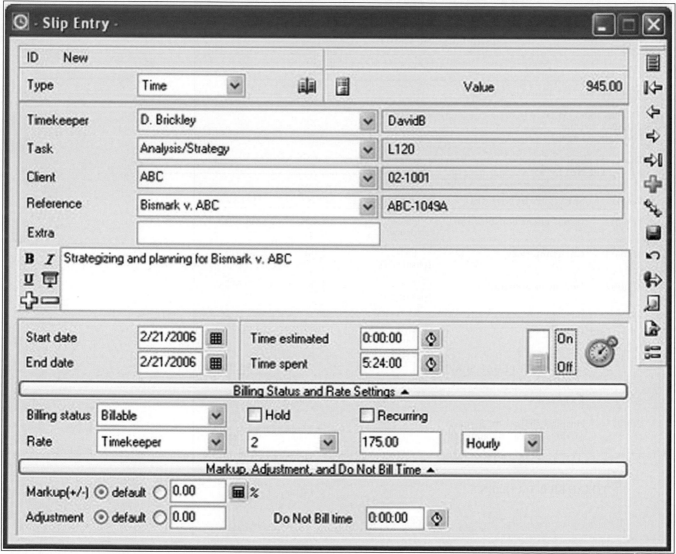

Screen shots from the Timeslips 2006 software are reprinted with the permission of Sage Software SB, Inc. Timeslips® is the registered trademark of Sage Software SB, Inc.

referenced, and a description of the task. The user then manually enters the time spent on the task or turns on an automated stopwatch timer—shown in Exhibit 4.6—to track the time spent on each task. Tasks can also be recorded as recurring, and rates can be adjusted according to any special agreements.

Costs incurred on behalf of clients have traditionally been entered on **expense slips**. Expenses are now usually entered into the billing program on a form similar to the time entry form shown in Exhibit 4.5. The form records a line-by-line description of each expense, along with the quantity and price of each item purchased on behalf of the client.

Billable versus Nonbillable Hours

The time recorded in timekeeping software is charged either to a client (billable hours) or to the firm (nonbillable hours). As mentioned, billable time generally includes the hours that attorneys and paralegals spend in client-related work that requires legal expertise. For exam-

expense slip
A slip of paper on which any expense, or cost, that is incurred on behalf of a client (such as the payment of court fees or long-distance telephone charges) is recorded.

EXHIBIT 4.6
Timeslips Timer

Screen shots from the Timeslips 2006 software are reprinted with the permission of Sage Software SB, Inc. Timeslips® is the registered trademark of Sage Software SB, Inc.

ple, the time you spend researching or investigating a client's claim is billable time. So is the time spent conferring with or about a client, drafting documents on behalf of a client, interviewing clients or witnesses, and traveling (to and from the courthouse to file documents, for example).

Time spent on other tasks, such as administrative work, staff meetings, or performance reviews, is nonbillable time. For example, suppose that you spend thirty minutes photocopying forms for the forms file, time sheets, or a procedures manual for the office. That thirty minutes is not considered billable time. In *Timeslips*, the user designates whether the task being recorded is billable, as you can see in the "Billing status" box in Exhibit 4.5.

Generally, law firms have a legitimate reason for wanting to maximize their billable hours: the financial well-being of a law firm depends to a great extent on how many billable hours are generated by its employees. Nonbillable time ultimately cuts into the firm's profits. Of course, as mentioned earlier, nonbillable time is factored into the hourly rate charged for legal services. But to remain competitive, a law firm cannot charge too high an hourly rate. Therefore, the more billable hours generated by the firm's legal professionals, the more profitable the business will be.

The Pressure to Generate Billable Hours

Law firms normally tell their paralegals and associate attorneys how many billable hours they are expected to produce and the consequences of not being able to meet that number. The majority of law firms require between 1,750 and 2,050 billable hours per year from attorneys; and at most firms, the base salary for associate attorneys is determined by a billable-hours target that the attorneys are expected to reach. Depending on the firm, a paralegal may be expected to generate between 800 and 2,000 billable hours per year.

Attorneys and paralegals face substantial pressure to produce billable hours for the firm. As a paralegal, you may be subject to this pressure and must learn how to handle it. For example, suppose that your employer expects you to produce 1,800 billable hours per year. Discounting vacation time and holidays (assuming a two-week vacation and ten paid holidays), this equates to 37.5 hours weekly. Assuming that you work 40 hours a week, you will have 2.5 hours a week for such nonbillable activities as interoffice meetings, performance reviews, coffee breaks, tidying up your desk, reorganizing your work area, and chatting with

Ethics Watch!

BACK UP YOUR WORK

Even a person who uses computers on a routine basis can easily forget—while the computer system is working—that a power failure or other problem can occur at any time. Should this happen, you may lose all current work that has not been saved to your hard disk. Surge protectors help to protect against "computer meltdown," but you should have, in addition, back-up copies of all of your work as well as a contingency plan—such as a second computer available to use.

Backing up your work frequently on a CD or other external storage device is particularly important and can "save the day" if the computer system crashes or fails to the extent that data on the hard drive cannot be retrieved. If you routinely back up documents, you may save yourself the hours of valuable time that could be required to re-create a document or file. You will also save yourself and the firm from the problem of deciding who will pay—the client or the law firm—for the extra time you had to spend to complete the work. Moreover, with back-up copies available, your employer will never have to be without a crucial document when it's needed. Another important precaution you can take to prevent loss of work is to have a crash-saving program, such as Symantec *LiveState Recovery,* available to recover lost data.

others in the office. As you can imagine, unless you are willing to work more than eight hours a day, you may have difficulty meeting the billable-hours requirement.

Ethics and Client Billing Practices

Because attorneys have a duty to charge their clients "reasonable" fees, legal professionals must be careful in their billing practices. They must not "pad" their clients' bills by including more billable hours than actually worked on behalf of those clients. They also must avoid **double billing**—billing more than one client for the same time.

double billing
Billing more than one client for the same billable time period.

Double Billing

Sometimes, situations arise in which it is difficult to determine which client should be billed for a particular segment of time. For example, suppose that you are asked to travel to another city to interview a witness in a case for Client A. You spend three hours traveling in an airplane, travel time that is necessary in working on behalf of Client A. You spend two hours in the airplane summarizing a document relating to a case for Client B. Who should pay for those two hours, Client A, Client B, or both? In this situation, you could argue—as many attorneys do in similar circumstances—that you generated five billable hours, three on Client A's work and two on Client B's case. This is an example of how double billing can occur.

Double billing also occurs when a firm bills a new client for work that was done for a previous client. For example, suppose that an attorney is working on a case for Client B that is very similar to a case handled by the firm a year ago for Client A. The firm charged Client A $2,000 for the legal services. Because much of the research, writing, and other work done on Client A's case can transfer over to Client B's case, the firm is able to complete the work for Client B in half the time. In this situation, would it be fair to bill Client B $2,000 also? After all, $1,000 of that amount represents hours spent on Client A's case (and for which Client A has already been billed). At the same time, would it be fair to Client A to bill Client B less for essentially the same services? Would it be fair to the firm not to allow it to profit from cost efficiencies generated by overlapping work?

Some firms today are tackling this ethical problem by splitting the benefits derived from cost efficiencies between the client and the firm. For example, the attorney in the above example might split the savings created by the overlapping research ($1,000) with Client B by billing Client B $1,500 instead of $2,000. Other firms still bill their clients for the time spent on previous work that transfers over to new clients' cases.

The American Bar Association's Response to Double Billing

The American Bar Association (ABA) addressed double billing in a formal ethical opinion issued in 1993. In that opinion, the ABA stated that attorneys are prohibited (under the Model Rules discussed in Chapter 3) from charging more than one client for the same hours of work. Additionally, the ABA rejected the notion that the firm, and not the client, should benefit from cost efficiencies created by the firm's work for previous clients. "The lawyer who has agreed to bill solely on the basis of time spent is obliged to pass the benefit of these economies on to the client."

Although ABA opinions are not legally binding on attorneys unless they are adopted by the states as law, they do carry significant weight in the legal community. Courts, for example, have tended to follow the ABA's position in resolving fee disputes. Typically, a court will not award attorneys' fees that it finds to be "excessive, redundant, or otherwise unnecessary."[1] In addition, some states will sanction or even disbar an attorney for double-billing a client.[2]

COMMUNICATING WITH CLIENTS

To succeed as a paralegal, excellent communication skills are a must. (See this chapter's *Featured Guest* feature on pages 136 and 137 for tips on effective communication.)

Sending monthly bills to clients is one way to keep attorney-client communication channels open. Such communication is important because attorneys have a duty to keep clients reasonably informed. Rule 1.4 of the Model Rules of Professional Conduct reads as follows:

> (a) A lawyer shall keep a client reasonably informed about the status of a matter and promptly comply with reasonable requests for information.
> (b) A lawyer shall explain a matter to the extent reasonably necessary to permit the client to make informed decisions regarding the representation.

As a paralegal, you need to be aware that keeping clients reasonably informed about the progress being made on their cases goes beyond courtesy and the cultivation of a client's goodwill—it is a legal duty of attorneys. The meaning of "reasonably informed" varies, of course, depending on the client and on the nature of the work being done by the attorney. In some cases, a phone call every week or two will suffice to keep the client informed. In other cases, the attorney may ask the paralegal to draft a letter to a client explaining the status of the client's legal matter. Some firms institute a regular monthly mailing to update clients on the status of their claims or cases. Generally, as a paralegal, you should discuss with your supervising attorney how each client should be kept informed of the status of his or her case.

Technology and Today's Paralegal

CYBERSPACE COMMUNICATIONS

E-mail has become a standard communication tool used by business and professional firms, including law firms. The reason why e-mail is so popular is simple: it is a quick, easy-to-use, and inexpensive way to communicate. In large law firms and corporate enterprises, as well as in government agencies, e-mail messages have largely replaced the printed interoffice memos of the past. E-mail is also a common way for attorneys and paralegals to communicate with clients, opposing counsel, witnesses, and others.

APPLY PROFESSIONAL STANDARDS TO E-MAIL COMMUNICATIONS

Because e-mail is transmitted almost instantaneously through an electronic medium—computer networks—it may be difficult to remember that it is also a *written communication*. People using e-mail have a tendency to adopt a casual, conversational tone and to ignore the traditional rules of writing, such as sentence structure, spelling, and capitalization. E-mail is still mail, however, and it should reflect the same professional tone and quality that you use in the firm's paper correspondence. If you want to convey a message to someone (especially a client), you need to use clear and effective language.

There are several things you can do to ensure that your e-mail messages are professional and error free. First, choose an e-mail program that has a spell checker. Typos, misspellings, punctuation errors, and grammatical problems all detract from the message and can easily be avoided. Make sure that you also proofread your e-mail carefully. Many times, it is helpful to print out an important message, let it sit for a while, and then review it later when you can see it from a fresh perspective. Also, make sure that you use the same form as you would in an ordinary letter (see Chapter 19), with perhaps a few variations—adding your e-mail address below your name in the closing and the word *confidential* at the top (when appropriate), for example.

TIPS FOR FORMATTING E-MAIL MESSAGES

Because e-mail often looks different on the recipient's computer screen than it does on your screen, keep the format as simple as possible. Use double spacing between paragraphs rather than indenting with tabs, and do not underline or boldface text (these features often do not transmit clearly from one e-mail system to another). If the message concerns a legal matter and is being sent to a client's workplace or a shared e-mail address, be careful what you identify in the subject line of the e-mail. For example, you could write "documents ready for signature" rather than "bankruptcy petition complete." Also, if your e-mail has an attachment, tell the recipient what word-processing program you used to create the attachment, and offer to resend it as a text document if the recipient cannot open it on his or her computer.

TECHNOLOGY TIP

Always print out a copy of your e-mail and retain it in the client's file so that a record exists of important communications. Be sure that any e-mail you send discloses your status as a paralegal (to avoid liability for the unauthorized practice of law). Request the recipient to verify that any important messages have been received (such as when you are notifying the person of a court date). E-mail systems often have a function that allows senders to request a "return receipt," which will confirm that the message you sent was received. You should also respond to incoming e-mail promptly so that the sender knows that you have received the e-mail. Finally, make sure that you know the policies of your firm regarding confidential e-mail. If used carefully, e-mail can be a very efficient way to fulfill your duties and communicate with the firm's clients.

Developing Paralegal Skills

ORGANIZING E-MAIL

Jolene Sandler works as a paralegal for a music distribution corporation that represents several thousand musical artists. Like most businesses today, Jolene's corporation relies very heavily on its computer network in conducting business.

Jolene receives over a hundred e-mails per day, including many unsolicited commercial messages (commonly called *spam*) that pass through her company's spam-filtering program. Jolene, like many paralegals, must keep track of and respond to a large volume of e-mail, so it is critical for her to maintain an organized e-mail system. Jolene learned how to manage her e-mails better at a workshop she attended. She now carefully follows a series of practical guidelines for responding to and organizing her e-mails. In addition, she learned to deal more effectively with spam and to guard against potentially dangerous e-mail attachments. After all, the company cannot afford a massive disruption of its computer system as a result of a malicious program, such as a virus, sent via e-mail.

TIPS FOR MANAGING E-MAIL

- Be as specific as possible in your e-mail subject lines. This allows you (and your recipients) to find specific messages quickly when necessary.

- Save time by keeping messages and replies as concise as possible and limiting the number of people to whom you send copies or forwarded messages so as to minimize the number of follow-up e-mails.

- Create folders in your e-mail program and name them clearly. For example, you might create folders to hold messages to or from specific persons. Subfolders within the folders can identify particular topics. You might also find it helpful to have a folder titled "Priority" or "Urgent" for messages that require immediate action.

- Make it a regular practice to clear messages from your Inbox after reading them. Delete messages you do not need to keep, and move others to the appropriate folders.

- If you suspect that e-mail could be spam, delete it without opening it. Also, do not click on anything in a suspicious e-mail, as you could inadvertently install a virus, spyware, or other harmful program by doing so.

- Do not reply to spam messages. A reply confirms to spammers that they have an active e-mail address, which they can then sell to other spammers.

- Only open e-mail attachments if you know the sender or are expecting to receive a specific attachment from the sender.

Copies of all letters to a client should, of course, be placed in the client's file. Additionally, the client's file should contain a written record of each phone call made to or received from a client. That way, there is a "paper trail" in the event it is ever necessary to provide evidence of communication with the client. (Actually, this is a good practice for all phone calls relating to a client's matter.) You will learn about the various forms of letters that attorneys send to clients in Chapter 19. Increasingly, attorneys and paralegals communicate with clients via e-mail, which can pose special problems—as discussed in this chapter's *Technology and Today's Paralegal* feature.

TEN TIPS FOR EFFECTIVE COMMUNICATION

BIOGRAPHICAL NOTE

Wendy B. Edson received her master's degree in library science (M.L.S.) from the University of Rhode Island and served as law librarian at the Buffalo, New York, firm of Phillips, Lytle, Hitchcock, Blain and Huber. In 1978, she joined the Paralegal Studies faculty at Hilbert College, in Hamburg, New York, and helped to develop an ABA-approved bachelor's degree program in 1992.

Edson teaches paralegalism and legal ethics, legal research and writing, law and literature, Internet research, and alternative dispute resolution (ADR). She also developed and coordinates the internship program. Edson reviews and publishes on the topics of paralegal education and legal research and writing. She has lectured to legal professionals on legal research, teaching skills, internships, legal ethics, and ADR. Edson is an AAfPE member and has presented papers at its national conferences.

Words! They are the building blocks of human communication. Whether words are exchanged face to face—or by e-mail, phone, fax, or letter—communication is a two-way street. But how do we become skilled at maneuvering the two-way traffic of interpersonal communication? As in driving, we need to follow the "rules of the road." The rules of the road in regard to communication traffic are embodied in the following ten tips.

1. Establish Communication Equality. Communication equality does not require that individuals hold equal status in an office or organization but requires that each party believe in *equal rights* to speak and listen. Observe someone whom you consider to be a good communicator. You will note that he or she demonstrates equality by actively listening and responding appropriately to whoever is speaking. Workplace problems often reflect communication ailments rooted in inequality. A firm belief in communication equality, despite job titles, will help to create a cooperative, productive working environment.

2. Plan for Time and Space. Effective communication requires *time*. Imagine your reaction to a request to work overtime if your supervising attorney took thirty seconds to order you to do the work versus taking two minutes to explain the reason for the request and listening to your response. In the first situation, the attorney saved one and a half minutes but scored "zero" in terms of communication skills. In today's rushed world, it is easy to overlook the importance of communication skills in morale building and creating a cooperative, efficient workforce.

Effective communicators are aware of how the physical environment in which a conversation takes place can affect the communication process. Communication is always enhanced when the parties have reasonable privacy and are not continually interrupted. Another important factor is physical comfort.

Choosing an inappropriate time and place for communication denies the importance of the matters being discussed and may send the wrong message to both the speaker and the listener.

3. Set the Agenda. Skilled communicators prepare an *agenda*—whether written or mental—of matters to be discussed in order of their priority. Frequently, both parties bring their respective agendas to a discussion, which means that priorities may need to be negotiated. A subordinate who brings up the topic of desired vacation time when the supervisor is preoccupied with a major project clearly demonstrates that his or her priorities are different from those of the supervisor.

Successful communication requires that the parties first negotiate a *common agenda*—that is, determine jointly the agenda for a particular discussion or meeting and what topics should take priority. Then, the topics can be dealt with one by one, in terms of their relative importance, to the satisfaction of both parties. *Agenda awareness* prevents parties from jumping from topic to topic without successfully resolving anything.

4. Fine-Tune Your Speaking Skills. Observe an individual whom you consider to be a good speaker, whether before a group of persons or on a one-on-one basis. What skills does that individual demonstrate? Effective speakers work hard to express thoughts clearly; sometimes, they refer to notes or lists to refresh their memories. Skilled speakers also try to communicate accurately and to talk about matters that they know will interest their listeners. They cultivate *communication empathy*—the sincere effort to put themselves in their listeners' shoes. As you speak to others, pause occasionally and ask yourself: "Would I enjoy listening to what I am saying and how I am saying it?"

5. Cultivate Listening Skills. Listening is not just refraining from speaking while another person is talking but is an *active* process—the other half of the communication partnership. An active listener does not interrupt the speaker. If you sense that the speaker is engaging in a monologue, you can use responsive behavior—including body language, attentiveness, and appropriate remarks—to steer the conversation back to a dialogue without cutting off the speaker.

An active listener realizes that listening is an investment in effective communication. By truly responding to what is being said, rather than regarding listening time as insignificant or as a time to plan his or her own remarks, the skilled listener establishes a bond of trust with the speaker. Active listeners avoid preconceived ideas about topics being discussed and assume that they do not know all the answers.

6. Watch for Body Language. Body language is nonverbal communication that reflects our emotional state. Physical positions, such as leaning forward or away from the speaker while listening, can reinforce or negate our spoken responses. Body attitudes, whether relaxed (comfortable posture, leaning forward, uncrossed arms and legs, relaxed neck and shoulders) or tense (stiff posture, backing away, crossed arms and legs, rigid neck and shoulders), vividly illustrate our responses before we utter a word. Eye contact is one of the most important tools in the body language tool kit for communication. Interviewers, social workers, and police officers have learned that steady and responsive eye contact means sincerity and credibility.

7. Put Note Taking in Perspective. Overinvolvement in note taking detracts from the communication process because opportunities to listen actively, speak responsively, and be sensitive to body language are reduced. The speaker may ramble while the listener records the ramblings in extensive notes.

When it is necessary to take notes, it is helpful to establish some rapport with the speaker or listener before launching the note-taking process. Alternatively, follow-up notes can be a workable solution to the problem. The note taker can devote the interview time to communication and, after the interview, record his or her general impressions of the interview and identify specific issues that need to be discussed further.

> *"Eye contact is one of the most important tools in the body language tool kit for communication."*

8. Recognize the Role of Criticism. *Constructive criticism* focuses on specific actions or behaviors rather than personalities. It is objective rather than subjective. Criticism that is stated calmly and objectively ("We need to rewrite the section on holographic wills") is much more palatable for the person being criticized than is criticism in the form of a personal attack ("You did a terrible job"). By placing emphasis on actions instead of personalities, the parties can more easily work toward a satisfactory solution. If both the critic and the person being criticized can remain calm and can separate actions from personalities, then criticism will usually produce the desired result and *mutual* satisfaction.

9. Aim for Satisfactory Closure. Closure means "wrapping up" the communication. Successful communicators know that handling closure properly can leave a participant with a good feeling even if the solution was not exactly what he or she initially desired. Summarizing the discussion and checking for agreement or a need for further discussion will encourage all participants to follow the tenth tip.

10. Commit to Communicate. Excellent speakers and listeners have positive, self-confident attitudes that problems can be solved if the "rules of the road" are followed. Skilled communicators cultivate open minds, self-knowledge, and the ability to tolerate differences and empathize with others. They are committed to exercising their rights and responsibilities as speakers and listeners in the communication process.

Today's Professional Paralegal

A PARALEGAL MANAGER AT WORK

The law firm of Brooks and Chandler employs over four hundred attorneys in four cities. Andrea Giancarlo, who works in the Chicago office, has been serving as a paralegal manager since 2001. Andrea is responsible for managing over eighty people in the Chicago office. Most of the people who work under her supervision are paralegals, but she also manages accountants, purchasing agents, and patent specialists. Additionally, she oversees those who work in the litigation technology department. Her job duties focus heavily on human resource issues and a variety of administrative responsibilities.

EXIT INTERVIEW

Andrea has a full schedule for today, but she must always remain flexible and be ready to change her schedule on short notice when necessary. Her morning begins with an exit interview with Maria Tullane, an insurance paralegal who has resigned after three years at the firm. Maria tells Andrea that she has enjoyed her work and the working environment generally at Brooks and Chandler but that another firm has offered her a job with a higher salary. Andrea assures Maria that she understands Maria's concerns about the pay level. She continues by saying that Maria has been a valued member of the insurance staff and that the partners at Brooks and Chandler would like her to continue working for them. She also tells Maria that the firm is rethinking the compensation of its paralegals with an eye toward a more competitive pay structure. Maria says that she has already accepted the offer from the other firm.

COMPENSATION ANALYSIS

After the meeting with Maria, Andrea remembers that she still needs to finish preparing for a meeting with the managers of the Chicago office that is scheduled for the following day. Andrea is meeting with the managers to discuss the new pay structure. Andrea has read many articles about law firm pay structures, analyzed compensation plans from other organizations, and attended a seminar on the subject. She is prepared to recommend a new pay structure based on market rates and objective performance standards. Andrea's recommendation will also factor in seniority, experience, and area of specialization. She spends the next half hour putting the finishing touches on the agenda for the meeting and copying documents to be distributed to the participants.

MANAGING EMPLOYEE CONFLICT

While Andrea is finishing her preparations for the meeting, one of the paralegals from the contracts section, Andrew Kirkland, appears in her doorway. He looks very upset and asks if he can talk to her. Andrea puts her meeting notes aside, invites him in, and asks him to close her office door behind him. Andrew sits down and explains that attorney David Blummer has repeatedly been flirting with some of Andrew's female co-workers while regularly demeaning Andrew and assigning him an excessive workload. Andrea spends over an hour discussing Andrew's concerns and assures him that she will look into this matter discreetly and will assess Andrew's workload. If appropriate, Andrea will also discuss with the managing attorneys possible disciplinary action against David. Andrew is calmer by the time he leaves Andrea's office. Andrea immediately begins making notes to prepare for interviews she will conduct with staff about the working environment in the contracts section.

CONNECTING WITH CO-WORKERS

While she is making notes, several co-workers show up for a lunch date with Andrea. After lunch, Andrea is scheduled to attend an important meeting with other administrative managers to plan the budget for technology purchases for the coming fiscal year. Andrea makes a note on her to-do list to follow up on Andrew's concerns after the technology meeting and heads to lunch.

LAW OFFICE CULTURE AND POLITICS

As a paralegal, you will find that each law firm you work for is unique. Even though two firms may be the same size and have similar organizational structures, they will have different cultures, or "personalities." The culture of a given legal workplace is ultimately determined by the attitudes of the firm's owners (the partners, for example) in regard to the fundamental goals of the firm.

Additionally, you will find that each firm has a political infrastructure that may have little to do with the lines of authority and accountability that are spelled out in the firm's employment manual or other formal policy statement. An up-and-coming younger partner in the firm, for example, may exercise more authority than one of the firm's older partners who is about to retire. There may be rivalry among associate attorneys for promotion to partnership status, and you may be caught in the middle of it. If you are aware (and you may not be) of the rivalry and your position relative to it, you may find yourself tempted to take sides—which could jeopardize your own future with the firm.

Unfortunately, paralegals have little way of knowing about the culture and politics of a given firm until they have worked for the firm awhile. Of course, if you know someone who works for or who has worked for a firm and value that employee's opinion, you might gain some advance knowledge about the firm's environment from that source. Otherwise, when you start to work for a firm, you will need to learn for yourself about interoffice politics. One way to do this is to listen carefully whenever a co-worker discusses the firm's staff and ask discreet questions to elicit information from co-workers about office politics and unwritten policies. This way, you can both prepare yourself to deal with these issues and protect your own interests. Ultimately, after you've worked for the firm for a time, you will be in a position to judge whether the company you have chosen is really the right firm for you.

KEY TERMS AND CONCEPTS

associate attorney 113	legal administrator 114	retainer 126
billable hours 128	legal-assistant manager 114	retainer agreement 123
contingency fee 124	limited liability partnership (LLP) 113	shareholder 114
double billing 132	managing partner 113	sole proprietorship 112
employment manual 115	office manager 114	staff attorney 113
expense slip 130	partner 113	statute of limitations 122
fixed fee 123	partnership 113	support personnel 115
forms file 122	personal liability 112	time slip 129
law clerk 113	professional corporation (P.C.) 114	trust account 126

chapter summary   The Inner Workings of the Law Office

The Organizational Structure of Law Firms

Law firms can be organized in the following ways:

1. *Sole proprietorship*—In a sole proprietorship, one individual attorney owns the business and is entitled to all the firm's profits. That individual also bears the burden of any losses and is personally liable for the firm's debts or other obligations.

(Continued)

2. *Partnership*—In a partnership, two or more individual lawyers jointly own the firm and share in the firm's profits and losses. Attorneys who are employed by the firm but who are not partners (such as associates and staff attorneys) do not share in the profits and losses of the firm.

   a. Generally, partners are subject to personal liability for all of the firm's debts or other obligations.

   b. In many states, firms can organize as *limited liability partnerships,* in which partners are not held personally liable for the malpractice of other partners in the firm.

3. *Professional corporation*—In a professional corporation, two or more individuals jointly own the business as shareholders. The owner-shareholders of the corporation share the firm's profits and losses (as partners do) but are not held personally liable for the firm's debts or obligations beyond the amount they invested in the corporation.

Law Office Management and Personnel

Each law firm has a unique system of management and lines of authority. Generally, the owners of the firm (partners, for example) oversee and manage all other employees. Law firm personnel include associate attorneys; law clerks (sometimes called summer associates); paralegals; administrative personnel, who are supervised by the legal administrator or the office manager; and support personnel, including receptionists, secretaries, file clerks, and others.

Employment Policies

Employment policies relate to compensation and employee benefits, performance evaluations, employment termination, and other rules of the workplace, such as office hours. Frequently (particularly in larger firms), the policies of the firm are spelled out in an employment manual or other writing. Most large firms today have specific policies and procedures that apply to discrimination in the workplace.

Filing Procedures

Every law firm follows certain procedures in regard to its filing system. In larger firms, these procedures may be written down. In smaller firms, procedures may be more casual and based on habit or tradition.

1. *Confidentiality*—Confidentiality is a major concern and a fundamental policy of every law firm. A breach of confidentiality by anyone in the law office can subject the firm to extensive legal liability. The requirement of confidentiality shapes, to a significant extent, filing procedures.

2. *Types of files*—A typical law firm has client files, work product files and reference materials, forms files, and personnel files.

3. *Objective*—Proper file maintenance is crucial to a smoothly functioning firm. An efficient filing system helps to ensure that important documents will not be lost or misplaced and will be available when needed. Filing procedures in a law office must also maximize client confidentiality and the safekeeping of documents.

Financial Procedures

A foremost concern of any law firm is to establish a clear policy on fee arrangements and efficient billing procedures so that each client is billed appropriately.

1. *Fee arrangements*—Types of fee arrangements include fixed fees, hourly fees, and contingency fees. Clients who pay hourly fees are billed monthly for the time spent by attorneys and other legal personnel on the clients' cases or projects, as well as all costs incurred on behalf of the clients.

2. *Client trust accounts*—Law firms are required to place all funds received from a client into a special account called a client trust account. This is to ensure that the client's money remains separate from the firm's money. It is extremely important that the funds held in the trust account be used only for expenses relating to the costs of serving that client's needs.

3. *Billing and timekeeping*—Firms require attorneys and paralegals to document how they use their time. Because the firm's income depends on the number of billable hours produced by the firm's employees, firms usually require attorneys and paralegals to generate a certain number of billable hours per year. This requirement subjects legal personnel to significant pressure. Double billing presents a major ethical problem for law firms.

Communicating with Clients

Attorneys have a duty to keep their clients reasonably informed on matters they are handling for the clients. Paralegals should be aware that this is a legal duty and that they can play a significant role in keeping clients informed. Sending billing statements to clients is one way to communicate with them. Periodic phone calls, letters, and e-mail messages are other ways to keep clients informed.

Law Office Culture and Politics

Each office has its own culture, or personality, which is largely shaped by the attitudes of the firm's owners and the qualities they look for when hiring employees. Each firm also has a political infrastructure that is not apparent to outsiders. Office culture and politics make a great difference in terms of job satisfaction and comfort. Wise paralegals will learn as soon as possible after taking a job, from co-workers or others, about these aspects of the law office.

QUESTIONS FOR REVIEW

1. What are the three basic organizational structures of law firms?

2. What is the difference between an associate and a partner?

3. Who handles the administrative tasks of a law firm? Who supervises the work performed by paralegals in a law firm?

4. Name some of the topics that might be included in an employment policy manual. How do firms evaluate paralegal performance?

5. Why is maintaining confidentiality so important in law offices? How does the confidentiality requirement affect law office procedures and practices?

6. What kinds of files do law firms maintain? What general procedures are typically followed in regard to client files?

7. How does a law firm arrange its fees with its clients? What ethical obligations do attorneys have with respect to legal fees?

8. How do lawyers and legal assistants keep track of their time? What is the difference between billable and nonbillable hours? What is a client trust account?

9. Describe some of the ways that attorneys communicate with clients. Why is communicating with clients important?

10. What is meant by the phrase "law office culture and politics"? How might law office culture and politics affect a paralegal?

 ## ETHICAL QUESTIONS

1. Catherine works as a paralegal for a sole practitioner. Catherine and the legal secretary both work in a large reception area. A client is waiting in the reception area to see the attorney. The legal secretary brings Catherine a fax of a real estate contract that she has just received from a client, Mrs. Henley, and then transfers Mrs. Henley's telephone call to her. Mrs. Henley tells Catherine that the attorney has promised to review the contract prior to the *closing* (the final step in the sale of real estate), which is scheduled for 4 P.M. today. Mrs. Henley is aware that Catherine, before she became a paralegal, worked as a real estate agent and is very experienced in real estate closings. Mrs. Henley insists that Catherine review and approve of the sales contract if the attorney is not available. What ethical problems is Catherine facing? What should she do?

2. Carla Seegen is an experienced legal assistant who is also a licensed real estate agent. She sold real estate for eight years before becoming a paralegal. Carla works in a small law firm and has recently been assigned to work for Mike McAllister, who is a new attorney and the son of one of the firm's founding partners, John McAllister. Mike is handling a real estate closing for the firm's biggest client. Mike is unfamiliar with the client's business and has no experience in real estate transactions. Carla soon learns of Mike's lack of knowledge and experience because he does not ask her to draft the appropriate documents and undertake the kinds of tasks that are necessary for the closing. Whenever she mentions these things to Mike, however, or offers to show him what must be done, Mike becomes annoyed. Carla likes her job and fears that if she continues to annoy Mike, she will be fired. At the same time, she is concerned about the client's welfare and legal protection. Should she talk to one of the partners about the problem? Should she discuss the issue with John McAllister, Mike's father? How would you handle the situation?

3. Roberta Miller works as a paralegal, secretary, and receptionist for a sole practitioner. She is working on a bankruptcy file for a client, Gina Thomas. Because Roberta is running late for a meeting with a client, James Archer, she leaves the file—which is clearly marked, "Gina Thomas/Bankruptcy"—on her desk. Mr. Archer comes into her office for the meeting. During the meeting, Roberta turns to her computer to print a document for Mr. Archer to sign. While her back is turned, Mr. Archer notices the Gina Thomas file on Roberta's desk. Gina Thomas is his neighbor. When Roberta turns around, Mr. Archer begins to ask her questions about the file. Has an ethical violation occurred? If so, what rule has been violated, and how could Roberta have avoided the situation?

4. Attorney Smith represents Mrs. White in a divorce and custody action against Mr. White. At the outset of the representation, Mrs. White makes it clear that all that she is interested in is obtaining custody of her children. She even suggests that they propose trading the house for custody of the children in the settlement of the dispute. Attorney Smith tells Mrs. White, "Don't worry, I can get your kids. I don't suggest offering to trade the house for the children, though, because custody rights can always change, and once you give away the house, it's gone and you have nothing." The case drags on for over three years. Mrs. White pays attorney Smith $30,000. At the end of the trial, which lasts for three months, the outstanding bill is over $100,000, and while Mrs. White loses custody of the children, she is awarded the house. The house has enough equity to pay attorney Smith's bill, including significant fees for his legal assistant's time. The attorney demands that Mrs. White give him a lien against her house. She refuses to do so, and they are thrown into a fee dispute. Mrs. White discovers that attorney Smith's fees for his services are significantly higher than what other family law attorneys in her area normally charge. What ethical rule comes into play here? What arguments would Mrs. White make against attorney Smith? What would be his counterarguments?

5. Sam Martin, an attorney, receives a settlement check for a client's case. It is made out jointly to Sam and his client. Sam signs it and instructs his paralegal to deposit it into his law firm's bank account, instead of the client's trust

account, because he wants to take out his fee before he gives the client his portion of the money. Can Sam do this? Why or why not? What should Sam's paralegal do?

6. Tom Baker, a paralegal, has been doing research for a client using Westlaw (a computerized research service discussed in Chapter 18). Tom's supervising attorney tells him to bill the Westlaw charges that he has just incurred on behalf of one client to both that client's and another client's account. The second client to be billed is a large and prosperous corporation, and the research applies to the second client as well. What ethical violation has occurred? What should Tom do?

PRACTICE QUESTIONS AND ASSIGNMENTS

1. Using the material presented in the chapter, identify the following law practices by their organizational structure:

   a. Bill James is an attorney who practices law on his own. He owns his legal practice, the building in which he works, and most of the office furniture. He leases his office equipment. Bill has one secretary and one paralegal who work for him.

   b. Roberta Wagner owns a law firm with Joe Rosen. They own equal interests in the firm, participate equally in the firm's management, and share jointly in its profits and losses. Wagner & Rosen has three associates, six secretaries, and three paralegals who work for the firm.

   c. Randall Smith and Susan Street own a law firm together as shareholders. They employ eight associate attorneys, twelve secretaries, and five legal assistants.

2. Using the material presented in the chapter, identify the following law office personnel:

   a. Martha Marsh worked as a paralegal in a large law firm. After thirteen years with the firm, Martha was promoted. She now oversees paralegal staffing, assignments, and professional development.

   b. Mark James was hired by the partners of a large law firm, Smith & Smith, to manage the day-to-day operations of the firm.

   c. Rhonda Allen is an attorney who works as an employee for Marsh & Martin, a law firm with 250 attorneys.

   d. Tom is a file clerk for Jepp & Allen, P.C.

   e. Michael O'Dowd is a lawyer. He owns O'Dowd & O'Dowd, P.C., with his sister, Jane.

3. Mary Anne is a paralegal student who has taken a job with a sole practitioner. The attorney has a general practice and handles legal matters relating to family law, real estate, estate planning and probate, and general civil litigation. He is very busy and, consequently, very disorganized. Mary Anne's first task is to help him organize his office, especially his client files. When Mary Anne arrives for her first day of work, she finds that he does not keep his files in the filing cabinets in the office. Rather, they are piled up on his desk, on the credenza, on the floor, and anywhere else that he happens to leave them. Using the material in this chapter, how would you create a filing system for the attorney's office? Be sure to include a discussion of how you would store, maintain, and destroy files.

4. Identify the type of billing that is being used in each of the following examples:

   a. The client is billed $150 per hour for a partner's time, $100 per hour for an associate attorney's time, and $70 per hour for a legal assistant's time.

   b. The attorney's fee is one-third of the amount that the attorney recovers for the client, either through a pretrial settlement or through a trial.

   c. The attorney charges $175 to change the name of a client's business firm.

5. Louise Lanham hires John J. Roberts, an attorney with the law firm of Sands, Roberts & Simpson, located at 1000 Plymouth Road, Phoenix, Arizona, to represent her in a divorce. She agrees to pay attorney Roberts a rate of $150 per hour and to pay a legal-assistant rate of $75 per hour. She also agrees to pay all costs and expenses, such as filing fees, expert-witness fees, court-reporter fees, and other fees incurred in the course of her representation. Using Exhibit 4.3 on page 124, A *Sample Retainer Agreement*, draft a retainer agreement between Louise Lanham and John J. Roberts.

QUESTIONS FOR CRITICAL ANALYSIS

1. Explain what *personal liability* means. What do you think of this concept? Is it fair to require that the personal assets of a partner, such as his or her house, be used to pay partnership debts?

2. Paralegals, who started out as support personnel in most law firms (because they evolved from the secretarial staff), are increasingly treated as professional staff members. Make a list of the reasons why paralegals should be

treated as professional staff members instead of support staff.

3. Do you think that performance evaluations are beneficial? What would happen if performance evaluations were not used? What types of information are included in them? What would you include to make them better?

4. Do you think that it is fair that employers are allowed to hire and fire employees for any reason or no reason under the employment-at-will doctrine? What might have led to the creation of the exceptions to the doctrine that now exist?

5. An employee who experiences sexual harassment may have to file a formal complaint and follow the firm's established procedures for resolving the issue. What impact might this requirement have on sexual-harassment complaints? What might happen if these procedures are not followed?

6. Why are efficient and confidential filing systems and procedures particularly necessary in law offices, more so than in other types of businesses? What might happen without them?

7. Why is it so important for members of a legal team to meticulously keep track of their hours? Why are some hours billable and others not? What happens if accurate billing records are not kept? Why are client trust funds required? Why are these accounts so important? What can happen if client funds are misused?

8. James Johnson is a sole practitioner. His office is about an hour's drive from the federal district court in which he files many of his lawsuits. He used to talk on his cell phone to clients as he traveled the two hours to and from the courthouse. He would then bill the client on whose behalf he was going to the courthouse for two hours and the clients with whom he talked on the phone for increments of the same two hours. When the American Bar Association issued its rule prohibiting double billing, he was concerned that the rule would drive him out of business. Johnson feels that there should be different billing rules for lawyers in large firms and lawyers in small practices, such as his. What do you think?

9. Many law firms require their legal assistants to meet a quota of billable hours. Often, legal assistants can only generate the number of billable hours required per week by working more than the number of hours that they are paid to work. This can lead to the temptation to "pad the bill." Can you think of ways to meet the quota without breaching ethical standards?

10. Other than courtesy and building good client relations, what are some primary reasons for communicating with clients? Make a list of the ways in which good client communication can be accomplished.

11. Every workplace, business, or law firm has its own personality or culture. How can you find out what a particular firm's culture is? Is this something you should try to determine before accepting employment with a particular firm? Why or why not?

 ## PROJECTS

1. Obtain a page from the "want ads" in your local newspaper or from another source that advertises for legal professionals. Try to determine from the ads whether the firms advertising openings are organized as sole proprietorships, partnerships, or professional corporations.

2. Research legal periodicals, such as *Legal Assistant Today* and the ABA's *Journal of Law Practice Management,* for articles on document/case management software. Write a one-page paper summarizing your findings. Be sure to describe how the software works and how its features and cost compare with other software on the market.

3. Research the online "Issue Archive" of *Law Office Computing* magazine, at **http://www.lawofficecomputing. com**, for articles on law office accounting software. Can you find any software specifically designed for trust accounts? Write a one-page paper summarizing your findings. Include a discussion of the pros and cons of each type of software, the cost, and which one was the most highly recommended.

4. Research various computer publications and Web sites, such as *PC World,* CNET.com, and *Law Office Computing,* for articles discussing presentation software programs. Write a one-page paper explaining how presentation programs could be useful in a law firm and discuss the capabilities of various presentation programs.

USING INTERNET RESOURCES

1. Go online and access the following Web site: **http://www.bizfilings.com**. Under the heading "Learn about Incorporating," click on the link for "Incorporating FAQs." Summarize in writing the answers given to the following questions:

   a. What are the advantages of incorporation?

   b. What are the disadvantages of incorporation?

   c. How many directors must a corporation have?

   d. What factors should be considered when deciding on a corporate name?

2. Find legal forms on the Internet by going to the following Web site: **http://www.legaldocs.com**. Make a general list of the types of forms that are available. Are they free? If not, how much do the forms cost? How can they be purchased? What methods of payment are accepted?

3. Research time-and-billing software on the Internet by going to the following Web site: **http://www.timeslips.com**. Under the pull-down menu for Products, select "Timeslips," then click "Product Features" to read about the latest version of Timeslips. What are some of the features of this software? Is it limited to one type of billing arrangement, or is it flexible? Can it create reports? What else can it do? Select "Online Demo" from the Products menu, if you want to try out the program for yourself.

4.  For additional resources, visit our Web site at **http://www.paralegal.delmar.cengage.com**.

END NOTES

1. *EEOC v. Clear Lake Dodge*, 60 F.3d 1146 (5th Cir. 1995).

2. See, for example, *In re Entin*, 732 N.Y.S.2d 648, 287 A.D.2d 943 (N.Y.A.D. 2001) (attorney disbarred for double-billing New York State).

INTRODUCTION TO LAW

PART

2

SOURCES OF AMERICAN LAW

CHAPTER OUTLINE

AFTER COMPLETING THIS CHAPTER, YOU WILL KNOW:

▶ The meaning and relative importance in the American legal system of constitutional law, statutory law, administrative law, and case law.

▶ How English law influenced the development of the American legal system.

▶ What the common law tradition is and how it evolved.

▶ The difference between remedies at law and equitable remedies.

▶ Some of the terms that are commonly found in case law.

▶ How national law and international law differ and why these bodies of law sometimes guide judicial decision making in U.S. courts.

INTRODUCTION

The American legal system is based largely on tradition. For the most part, the colonists who first came to America were governed by English law. As a result, the law of England continued to be the paramount model for American jurists and legislators after the colonists declared their independence from England in 1776. English common law from medieval times onward thus became part of the American legal tradition as well, modified as necessary to suit conditions unique to America.

This chapter opens with a discussion of the nature of law and then focuses on the sources of American law, including constitutional law, statutory law, administrative law, and case law. We then examine the common law tradition and its significance in the American legal system. We also explain how the law of other countries and international law affect judicial decision making in American courts. Another component of the American legal structure—the court system—will be examined in Chapter 6.

THE FRAMEWORK OF AMERICAN LAW

As you probably realize, the law means different things to different people. Before beginning your study of American law, it is therefore useful to have a basic understanding of what the law is and some of the different approaches to the law that influence judges' decisions. These topics are covered in the following subsections.

What Is the Law?

Most paralegals and lawyers can spend their entire careers dealing with legal matters and still not be able to provide you with a clear definition of the term *law*. How law is defined frequently depends on the speaker's personal views on such matters as morality, ethics, and truth. Generally, though, **law** can be defined as a body of rules of conduct established and enforced by the controlling authority (the government) of a society. These "rules of conduct" may consist of written principles of behavior, such as those established by a nomadic tribe. They may be set forth in a law code, such as the law code of one of today's European nations. They may consist of written laws and court decisions created by modern legislative and judicial bodies, as they do in the United States. Regardless of how such rules are created, they all have one thing in common: they establish rights, duties, and privileges that are consistent with the values and beliefs of their society or its ruling group.

One of the important functions of law in any society is to provide stability, predictability, and continuity so that people can be sure of how to order their affairs. If any society is to survive, its citizens must be able to determine what is legally right and legally wrong.

▶ **EXAMPLE 5.1** Citizens must know what sanctions will be imposed on them if they commit wrongful acts. If they suffer harm as a result of others' wrongful acts, they need to know whether and how they can receive compensation for their injuries. ◀ By setting forth the rights, obligations, and privileges of citizens, the law enables individuals to go about their business and personal lives with confidence and a certain degree of predictability. The stability and predictability created by the law provide an essential framework for all civilized societies.

Primary Sources of American Law

American law has numerous sources. **Primary sources of law**, or sources that establish the law, include the following:

1. The U.S. Constitution and the constitutions of the various states.
2. Statutory law—including laws passed by Congress, state legislatures, and local governing bodies.

On the Web

The University of Michigan maintains a useful site with links to almost all U.S. government Web sites and many foreign government Web sites at **http://www.lib.umich.edu/govdocs/ govweb.html**.

law
A body of rules of conduct established and enforced by the controlling authority (the government) of a society.

primary source of law
In legal research, a document that establishes the law on a particular issue, such as a case decision, legislative act, administrative rule, or presidential order.

3. Regulations created by administrative agencies, such as the U.S. Food and Drug Administration.

4. Case law and common law doctrines.

We describe each of these important sources of law in the following pages.

Secondary sources of law are books and articles that summarize and clarify the primary sources of law. Examples include legal encyclopedias, treatises, articles in law reviews, and compilations of law, such as the *Restatements of the Law* (which will be discussed later in this chapter). Courts often refer to secondary sources of law for guidance in interpreting and applying the primary sources of law discussed here.

secondary source of law
In legal research, any publication that indexes, summarizes, or interprets the law, such as a legal encyclopedia, a treatise, or an article in a law review.

CONSTITUTIONAL LAW

The federal government and the states have separate written constitutions that set forth the general organization, powers, and limits of their respective governments. **Constitutional law** is the law as expressed in these constitutions.

constitutional law
Law based on the U.S. Constitution and the constitutions of the various states.

The Federal Constitution

The U.S. Constitution, as amended, is the highest law of the land. This principle is set forth in Article VI of the Constitution, which provides that the Constitution, laws, and treaties of the United States are "the supreme Law of the Land." This provision is commonly referred to as the **supremacy clause**. A law in violation of the Constitution (including its amendments), no matter what its source, will be declared unconstitutional if it is challenged. For example, if a state legislature enacts a law that conflicts with the federal Constitution, a person or business firm that is subject to that law may challenge its validity in a court action. If the court agrees with the complaining party that the law is unconstitutional, it will declare the law invalid and refuse to enforce it.

The U.S. Constitution consists of seven articles. These articles, which are listed and summarized in Exhibit 5.1, set forth the powers of the three branches of government and the relationships among the three branches.

supremacy clause
The provision in Article VI of the U.S. Constitution that declares the Constitution, laws, and treaties of the United States "the supreme Law of the Land."

Constitutional Rights

The need for a written declaration of rights of individuals eventually caused the first Congress of the United States to submit twelve amendments to the Constitution to the states for approval. Ten of these amendments, commonly known as the **Bill of Rights**, were adopted in 1791 and embody a series of protections for individuals—and in some cases, business entities—against various types of interference by the federal government. Summarized below are the protections guaranteed by the Bill of Rights. The full text of the Constitution, including its amendments (of which there are now twenty-seven), is presented in Appendix J at the end of the book.

Bill of Rights
The first ten amendments to the U.S. Constitution.

1. The First Amendment guarantees the freedoms of religion, speech, and the press and the rights to assemble peaceably and to petition the government.

2. The Second Amendment guarantees the right to keep and bear arms.

3. The Third Amendment prohibits, in peacetime, the lodging of soldiers in any house without the owner's consent.

4. The Fourth Amendment prohibits unreasonable searches and seizures of persons or property.

On the Web

The Constitution Center provides extensive information on the U.S. Constitution, including its history and current debates over constitutional provisions, at **http://www. constitutioncenter.org**.

EXHIBIT 5.1
**The Articles
of the U.S. Constitution**

Article I creates and empowers the legislature. It provides that Congress is to consist of a Senate and a House of Representatives and fixes the composition of each house and the election procedures, qualifications, and compensation for senators and representatives. Article I also establishes the procedures for enacting legislation and the areas of law in which Congress has the power to legislate.

Article II establishes the executive branch, the process for electing and removing a president from office, the qualifications to be president, and the powers of the president.

Article III creates the judicial branch and authorizes the appointment, compensation, and removal of judges. It also sets forth the jurisdiction of the courts and defines *treason.*

Article IV requires that all states respect one another's laws. It also ensures citizens from one state the same rights and privileges as the citizens in any state they visit and requires that persons accused of crimes be returned to the state in which the crime was committed.

Article V governs how constitutional amendments are formally proposed and ratified.

Article VI establishes the Constitution as the supreme law of the land. It also requires that every federal and state official take an oath of office promising to support the Constitution and specifies that religion is not a required qualification to serve in any federal office.

Article VII required the consent of nine of the original thirteen states to ratify the Constitution.

5. The Fifth Amendment guarantees the rights to indictment by grand jury and to due process of law and prohibits compulsory self-incrimination and double jeopardy. (These terms and concepts will be defined in Chapter 16, which deals with criminal law and procedures.) The Fifth Amendment also prohibits the taking of private property for public use without just compensation.

6. The Sixth Amendment guarantees the accused in a criminal case the right to a speedy and public trial by an impartial jury and the right to counsel. The accused has the right to cross-examine witnesses against him or her and to solicit testimony from witnesses in his or her favor.

7. The Seventh Amendment guarantees the right to a trial by jury in a civil case involving at least twenty dollars.[1]

8. The Eighth Amendment prohibits excessive bail and fines, as well as cruel and unusual punishment.

9. The Ninth Amendment establishes that the people have rights in addition to those specified in the Constitution.

10. The Tenth Amendment establishes that those powers neither delegated to the federal government nor denied to the states are reserved for the states.

As originally intended, the Bill of Rights limited only the powers of the national government. Over time, however, the Supreme Court incorporated most of these rights into the protections against state actions afforded by the Fourteenth Amendment to the Constitution. That amendment, passed in 1868 after the Civil War, provides in part that "[n]o State shall . . . deprive any person of life, liberty, or property, without due process of law." Starting in 1925, the Supreme Court began to define various rights and liberties

On the Web

Information on the role of the United States Supreme Court in interpreting the Constitution is available at **http://www.usscplus.com**.

guaranteed in the national Constitution as comprising "due process of law," which was required of state governments under the Fourteenth Amendment. Today, most of the rights and liberties set forth in the Bill of Rights—such as the freedoms of speech and religion guaranteed by the First Amendment—apply to state governments as well as the national government.

The Courts and Constitutional Law

You should realize that the rights secured by the Bill of Rights are not absolute. The broad principles enunciated in the Constitution are given form and substance by the courts. Courts often have to balance the rights and freedoms enunciated in the Bill of Rights against other rights, such as the right to be free from the harmful actions of others. Ultimately, it is the United States Supreme Court, as the final interpreter of the Constitution, that both gives meaning to our constitutional rights and determines their boundaries.

Courts Balance the Right to Free Speech. An example of how the courts must balance the rights and freedoms granted by the Constitution can be found by looking at our right to free speech. Even though the First Amendment guarantees the right to free speech, we are not, in fact, free to say anything we want. ▶ **EXAMPLE 5.2** In interpreting the meaning of the First Amendment, the Supreme Court has made it clear that certain types of speech will not be protected. Speech that harms the good reputation of another, for instance, is commonly considered to be a tort, or civil wrong. If the speaker is sued, he or she may be ordered by a court to pay damages to the harmed person (as you will read in Chapter 7). ◀

Free Speech and the Internet. The Internet has raised new problems for the courts in determining how to define and apply the protections conferred by the Constitution, particularly with regard to free speech. For example, the Supreme Court has ruled that obscene speech, though difficult to define, is not entitled to First Amendment protection. Regulating obscene speech in the online environment, however, has proved to be difficult. ▶ **EXAMPLE 5.3** Congress first attempted to prohibit *online obscenity* in the Communications Decency Act (CDA) of 1996, which made it a crime to make available to minors online any "obscene or indecent" message.[2] Civil rights groups immediately claimed the act was an unconstitutional restraint on speech. The Supreme Court held that portions of the act were unconstitutional in *Reno v. American Civil Liberties Union.*[3] Subsequent attempts by Congress to curb pornography on the Internet have also encountered constitutional stumbling blocks.[4] ◀

On the Web

If you are interested in looking at state constitutions, including the one for your state, go to **http://www. findlaw.com/11stategov/ indexconst.html**.

State Constitutions

Each state also has a constitution that sets forth the general organization, powers, and limits of the state government. The Tenth Amendment to the U.S. Constitution, which defines the powers and limitations of the federal government, reserves all powers not granted to the federal government to the states. Unless they conflict with the U.S. Constitution, state constitutions are supreme within the states' respective borders. State constitutions are thus important sources of law.

CONSTITUTIONAL LAW AND THE PARALEGAL

Many paralegals assist attorneys in handling cases that involve constitutional provisions or rights. For example, a corporate client might claim that a regulation issued by a state administrative agency, such as the state department of natural resources, is invalid because it conflicts with a federal law or regulation. (Administrative agencies will be discussed later in this chapter.) You may be assigned the task of finding out which regulation takes priority. Many cases arise in which the plaintiff claims that his or her First Amendment rights have been violated. Suppose that a plaintiff's religious beliefs forbid working on a certain day of the week. If he or she is required to work on that day, the plaintiff may claim that the employer's requirement violates the First Amendment, which guarantees the free exercise of religion.

No matter what kind of work you do as a paralegal, you will find a knowledge of constitutional law beneficial. This is because the authority and underlying rationale for the substantive and procedural laws governing many areas of law are ultimately based on the Constitution. For example, knowledge of constitutional law is helpful to paralegals working in the area of criminal law, because criminal procedures are essentially designed to protect the constitutional rights of accused persons—as you will read in Chapter 16. (For a further discussion of the application of constitutional law concepts to legal work in other areas, see this chapter's *Featured Guest* article starting on the next page.)

STATUTORY LAW

Statutes, which are laws enacted by legislative bodies at any level of government, make up another source of law. The body of written laws created by the legislature is generally referred to as statutory law.

> **statute**
> A written law enacted by a legislature under its constitutional lawmaking authority.

> **statutory law**
> The body of written laws enacted by the legislature.

Federal Statutes

Federal statutes are laws that are enacted by the U.S. Congress and that apply to every state. As mentioned, any law—including a federal statute—that violates the U.S. Constitution will be held unconstitutional. Examples of federal statutes include laws protecting intellectual property rights (see Chapter 8), laws regulating the purchase and sale of corporate stock (see Chapter 11), statutes prohibiting employment discrimination (see Chapter 11), many environmental regulations (see Chapter 12), and consumer protection statutes (discussed in Chapter 7).

The Federal Government's Constitutional Authority to Enact Laws

In the federal system of government established by the founders, the national government (often called the federal government) and the state governments *share* sovereign power. The Constitution specifies, however, that certain powers can be exercised only by the national government. For example, the national government was authorized to regulate commerce among the states. Additionally, the president of the United States was declared to be the nation's chief executive and commander in chief of the armed forces. Finally, as already noted, the Constitution made it clear that laws made by the national government take priority over conflicting state laws. At the same time, the Constitution provided for numerous states' rights, including the right to control commerce within state borders and to exercise those governing powers that were not delegated to the national government.

> **federal system**
> The system of government established by the founders of the United States, in which the national government and the state governments share sovereign powers.

To prevent the possibility that the national government might use its power arbitrarily, the Constitution divided the national government's powers among three branches:

- The legislative branch, or Congress, which makes the laws.
- The executive branch, which enforces the laws.
- The judicial branch, which interprets the laws.

THE INTERRELATIONSHIP OF THE VARIOUS AREAS OF LAW

BIOGRAPHICAL NOTE

S. Whittington Brown earned a bachelor of arts degree from Rhodes College in 1981 and earned a law degree from the University of Arkansas in 1984. He is licensed to practice in the state of Arkansas, the United States District Court, and the United States Court of Appeals. He has served as an attorney and an attorney supervisor for the Arkansas Department of Human Services. He is currently the chief investigator for Developmental Disabilities Services and is a licensed polygraph examiner.

Brown has been an adjunct faculty member of Pulaski Technical College since 1999. He has taught American national government, legal terminology, legal research and writing, legal environment of business, business organizations, and torts. He is also the author of Legal Terminology, *published by Thomson Delmar Learning.*

Brown was recognized as an Outstanding Citizen of the State of Arkansas by then-governor Bill Clinton, has been commended by the Child Care Facility Review Board, and has been listed in Who's Who of America's Teachers, *Volumes 9 and 10.*

Law is divided into many different subject areas. An attorney may specialize in personal-injury, property, employment, or contract law, for example. None of these areas, however, exists in a vacuum. One legal principle may apply to many different areas of the law, and one subject area may influence others. An important skill that a paralegal must develop is the ability to see the relationships among areas of law that may appear to be totally unrelated. Consider just one example: the application of constitutional law concepts to the areas of criminal law and employment law. At first, it would appear that criminal law and employment law have nothing in common, but there are provisions of constitutional law that apply to both areas.

Article VI, Clause 2, of the Constitution of the United States states, "This Constitution and the Laws of the United States which shall be made in pursuance thereof . . . shall be the supreme Law of the Land." In other words, the Constitution is the highest source of law in the country, and other laws are inferior to the Constitution. Because of this clause, known as the supremacy clause, provisions of the U.S. Constitution can apply to many different areas of the law.

One of the main provisions of constitutional law is the principle of due process of law. According to the Fifth and Fourteenth Amendments to the Constitution, no person shall be deprived of life, liberty, or property, without due process of law. The concept of due process has two parts, substantive due process and procedural due process. *Substantive due process* means that the law itself, that which is being enforced, must be fair. The law must be applied the same way to every person and must not discriminate against anyone. *Procedural due process* means that the method used to enforce the law must be fair; it must be applied the same way to every person. One such element of due process of law is contained in the Fourth Amendment—the prohibition against unreasonable searches and seizures.

The application of this principle to the area of criminal law is fairly obvious. A person, because of an alleged violation of the law, faces the loss of property, liberty, or even life, depending upon the seriousness of the offense. Before the state can deprive the person of any of these things, the person is entitled to due process of law. This includes such rights as the right to be represented by an attorney, the

checks and balances
A system in which each of the three branches of the national government — executive, legislative, and judicial— exercises a check on the actions of the other two branches.

Each branch performs a separate function, and no branch may exercise the authority of another branch. Each branch, however, has some power to limit the actions of the other two branches. Congress, for example, can enact legislation relating to spending and commerce, but the president can veto that legislation. The executive branch is responsible for foreign affairs, but treaties with foreign governments require the advice and consent of members of the Senate. Although Congress determines the jurisdiction of the federal courts, the federal courts have the power to hold acts of the other branches of the federal government unconstitutional. Thus, with this system of **checks and balances**, no one branch of government can accumulate too much power.

right to a trial by a jury of his or her peers, the right to know the charges against him or her, the right to confront his or her accusers, and the right to present evidence in his or her defense. Also, any evidence seized in violation of the Fourth Amendment cannot be used against the defendant. A paralegal working in the area of criminal law must not only be aware of the crimes and what makes up each element of the crime but also must be aware of the due process rights guaranteed by the U.S. Constitution to a person who is accused of a crime.

Principles of constitutional law also apply to the employment relationship. The Fourth Amendment limitations on unreasonable searches and seizures apply to the workplace in combination with the right to privacy. The right to privacy—the right to be left alone and to be free from unwarranted publicity and interference—was created by the United States Supreme Court in the case of *Griswold v. Connecticut*.[a] The Court has stated that there are zones of privacy that apply to a person regardless of the situation in which a person may find himself or herself, including the workplace.

The limitations on searches and seizures and the right to privacy apply in the workplace when an employer wants to conduct searches of employees. An employer may have several reasons for wanting to conduct employee searches: to protect itself against employee theft, to protect sensitive material, and to ensure that illegal conduct is not occurring at the work site. An employee, however, is protected against unreasonable searches and seizures by the Fourth Amendment and

> *"An important skill that a paralegal must develop is the ability to see the relationships among areas of law that may appear to be totally unrelated."*

has an expectation of privacy, even in the workplace. In order for a workplace search to take place, certain criteria must be met.

The U.S. Supreme Court case of *O'Connor v. Ortega*[b] helped set out the criteria for when a search of an employee can take place. First, the employee's expectation of privacy must be reduced. In order to lessen the expectation, the employer is required to implement a policy establishing when and under what circumstances a search of the workplace may take place. Also, in order to conduct a valid workplace search, the search must be reasonable and based on allegations made against the employee, the purpose of the search should be clearly established, and the search should be limited in scope. The principles established by the limitation on searches and seizures and the right to privacy have also been applied to the use of lie-detector tests, drug tests, background checks, references, and credit checks in employment situations.

These are just two examples of how one area of law may interact with other areas. A basic principle of constitutional law applies to both criminal law and employment law. Employment law not only involves elements of constitutional law but also contains elements of contract law and agency law. Product liability and environmental protection laws are based in part on tort law principles, and insurance law contains elements of contract law and tort law. A paralegal must be able to see how the different areas of the law interact with each other and realize that no area of the law exists in a vacuum.

a. 381 U.S. 479 (1965).

b. 480 U.S. 708 (1987).

The Expansion of National Powers under the Commerce Clause

Article I, Section 8, of the Constitution expressly permits Congress to "regulate Commerce with foreign Nations, and among the several States, and with the Indian Tribes." This clause, which is known as the **commerce clause**, was initially interpreted to mean that the federal government's regulatory powers were limited to *interstate* commerce (commerce among the states) and not applicable to *intrastate* commerce (commerce within a state). In 1824, however, the United States Supreme Court concluded that commerce within a state could also be regulated by the national government as long as the commerce *substantially affected* commerce involving more than one state.[5]

commerce clause
The provision in Article I, Section 8, of the U.S. Constitution that gives the national government the power to regulate interstate commerce.

As the nation grew and faced new kinds of problems, this interpretation of the commerce clause became a vehicle for the additional expansion of the national government's regulatory powers. Even activities that seemed purely local came under the regulatory reach of the national government. ▶ **EXAMPLE 5.4**   In a landmark ruling in 1942, the Supreme Court held that wheat production by an individual farmer intended wholly for consumption on his own farm was subject to federal regulation.[6] ◀

Today, at least theoretically, the commerce power authorizes the national government to regulate every commercial enterprise in the United States. Indeed, many of the federal statutes that you will read about in this book rest on Congress's authority to regulate interstate commerce. Federal statutes now govern virtually every major activity conducted by businesses—from hiring and firing decisions to workplace safety, competitive practices, and financing.

The Federal Lawmaking Process

Each law passed by Congress begins as a *bill,* which may be introduced either in the House of Representatives or in the Senate. Often, similar bills are introduced in both chambers. In either chamber, the bill is then referred to a committee and its subcommittees for study, discussion, hearings, and rewriting. Next, it is scheduled for debate by the full chamber. Finally, a vote is taken, and the bill is either passed or defeated. If the two chambers pass similar bills containing somewhat different provisions, a *conference committee* is formed to write a compromise bill, which must then be approved by both chambers before it is sent to the president to sign. Once the president signs the bill, it becomes law.

During the legislative process, bills are identified by a number. A bill in the House of Representatives is identified by a number preceded by "HR" (such as HR 212), indicating that it is a House of Representatives bill. In the Senate, the bill's number is preceded by an "S" (such as S 212). When both chambers pass the bill and it is signed into law by the president, the statute is initially published in the form of a pamphlet or a single sheet, known as a *slip law.* The slip law is assigned a **public law number,** or P.L. number (such as P.L. 5030). At the end of the two-year congressional term, or session, the statute is published in the term's *session laws,* which are collections of statutes contained in volumes and arranged by year or legislative session. Ultimately, the statute is included in the *United States Code,* in which all federal laws are codified (systematized, or arranged in topical order) and published. (See Chapter 17 for further details on how federal statutes are published.)

public law number
An identification number assigned to a statute.

On the Web

A good starting point to access state statutes online is **http://www. law.cornell.edu/topics/ state_statutes.html.**

State Statutes

State statutes are laws enacted by state legislatures. Any state law that is found to conflict with the U.S. Constitution or with the state's constitution will be deemed unconstitutional. State statutes include state laws governing real property and insurance (see Chapter 9), estates and family law (discussed in Chapter 10), the formation of corporations and other business entities (see Chapter 11), and certain crimes (see Chapter 16), along with state versions of the Uniform Commercial Code (to be discussed shortly).

Conflicts between Federal and State Laws

If a state statute is found to conflict with a federal statute, the state law is rendered invalid. Because some powers are concurrent, however, it is necessary to determine which law governs in a particular circumstance. (*Concurrent* powers are powers that are shared by the federal government and the states, such as the power to levy taxes or to establish courts.)

Preemption occurs when Congress chooses to act exclusively in a concurrent area. In this circumstance, a valid federal law or regulation in the preempted area will take prece-

preemption
A doctrine under which a federal law preempts, or takes precedence over, conflicting state and local laws.

Developing Paralegal Skills

FINDING A RECENTLY ENACTED FEDERAL STATUTE

Joni Sullivan, a paralegal working for a midsized law firm, has been asked to research a statute on immigration law that was signed by the president just a few weeks ago. One of the firm's clients, a company that employs many immigrant workers, wants to know what documentation requirements will be imposed on employers under the new law. Joni knows that the law will not yet be included in the *United States Code,* in which all federal statutes are ultimately published (see Chapter 17), but the slip law should be available online.

Joni finds the title of the law through a general search on Google. Then, using Westlaw™, she finds the slip law, notes its public law (P.L.) number, and scans the bill looking for the section dealing with employer reporting requirements. Once she finds the section, she prints out a hard copy of that part of the statute for closer reading and analysis. To better understand Congress's intent in imposing these requirements, Joni locates and reads the relevant committee reports on the matter. She also finds important insights into Congress's intent by reading the transcripts of congressional debates on this issue. These transcripts are part of the *Congressional Record,* which is published daily while Congress is in session and is available via Westlaw. Joni concludes her task by printing out all relevant information and preparing a memorandum summarizing what she has learned for her supervising attorney.

TIPS FOR RESEARCHING RECENTLY ENACTED STATUTORY LAW

- If you do not know the title of the law that you need to locate, find the title either through a general online search or by consulting printed compilations of statutory materials (see Chapter 17).
- Find the slip law, which is cited by its P.L. number.
- If the congressional term has ended, search the session laws for the term to find the statute.
- To better understand Congress's intent in passing the law, check relevant committee reports and transcripts of congressional proceedings.

---

dence over a conflicting state or local law or regulation. Often, it is not clear whether Congress, in passing a law, intended to preempt an entire area. In these situations, it is left to the courts to determine Congress's intention. No single factor determines whether a court will find preemption. Generally, congressional intent to preempt will be found if a federal law regulating an activity is so pervasive, comprehensive, or detailed that the states have little or no room to regulate in that area. Also, when a federal statute creates an agency—such as the National Labor Relations Board—to enforce the law, matters that come within the agency's jurisdiction will likely preempt state laws.

The State Lawmaking Process

When passing laws, state legislatures follow procedures similar to those followed in Congress. All of the states except one have bicameral (two-chamber) legislatures. (Nebraska has a unicameral, or one-chamber, legislature.) Typically, bills may be introduced in either chamber, or both chambers, of the legislature. As in the U.S. Congress, if the two chambers pass similar bills that differ from one another in any respect, a conference committee works out a compromise, which must then be approved by both chambers before being sent to the state's governor to sign into law.

Developing Paralegal Skills

STATE VERSUS FEDERAL REGULATION

Stephanie Wilson works as a paralegal in the legal department of National Pipeline, Inc., whose business is transporting natural gas to local utilities, factories, and other sites throughout the country. Last month, one of National's pipelines, which ran under a residential street in Minneapolis, Minnesota, exploded, resulting in several severe injuries and one death.

The federal government has regulated pipeline safety and maintenance since 1968, under the Natural Gas Pipeline Safety Act. As a result of the explosion, the state of Minnesota wants to regulate pipeline safety as well. Stephanie's boss, the general counsel, and several other executives believe that the federal act preempts this field of law, preventing the state from enacting another layer of safety legislation. Stephanie is assigned the task of researching the statute and relevant case law to determine if the federal law does in fact preempt the state's regulation.

TIPS FOR DETERMINING FEDERAL PREEMPTION

- Read through the statute to see if it expressly states that Congress intended to preempt the relevant field (in this case, pipeline safety).

- Look for indications that Congress has impliedly occupied the field: Is the federal regulatory scheme pervasive? Is federal occupation of the field necessitated by the need for national uniformity? Is there a danger of conflict between state laws and the administration of the federal program?

- Locate and read cases discussing the issue of federal preemption in this area. Brief any cases that appear to be relevant to this issue. (See Chapter 17 for instructions on how to brief a case.)

Local Ordinances

ordinance
An order, rule, or law enacted by a municipal or county government to govern a local matter not addressed by state or federal legislation.

Statutory law also includes local ordinances. An **ordinance** is an order, rule, or law passed by a city or county government unit to govern matters not covered by federal or state law. Ordinances may not violate the U.S. Constitution, the relevant state constitution, or federal or state law. Local ordinances often have to do with land use (zoning ordinances), building and safety codes, construction and appearance of local housing, and other matters affecting the local unit. Persons who violate ordinances may be fined, jailed, or both.

Uniform Laws

A federal statute, of course, applies to all states. A state statute, in contrast, applies only within the state's borders. State laws thus vary from state to state. The differences among state laws were particularly notable in the 1800s, when conflicting state statutes frequently created problems for the rapidly developing trade and commerce among the states. To counter these problems, a group of legal scholars and lawyers formed the National Conference of Commissioners on Uniform State Laws (NCCUSL) in 1892 to draft uniform ("model") statutes for adoption by the states. The NCCUSL still exists today and continues to issue uniform statutes, often in conjunction with the American Law Institute.

Adoption of a uniform law is a state matter, and a state may reject all or part of the statute or rewrite it as the state legislature wishes. Hence, even when a uniform law is said to have been adopted in many states, those states' laws may not be entirely "uniform." Once adopted by a state legislature, a uniform act becomes a part of the statutory law of that state. A good example of a uniform law that has been adopted (at least in part) by all fifty states is the Uniform Commercial Code (UCC), which provides a uniform, yet flexible, set of rules governing commercial transactions and sales contracts. The UCC will be discussed in Chapter 8.

STATUTORY LAW AND THE PARALEGAL

As a paralegal, you may often deal with cases that involve violations of statutory law. If you work for a small law firm, you may become familiar with the statutory law governing a wide spectrum of activities. If you specialize in one area, such as bankruptcy law, you will become very familiar with the law governing that area. Here are just a few examples of areas in which you might work that are governed extensively by statutory law:

- *Corporate law*—governed by state statutes.
- *Patent, copyright, and trademark law*—governed by federal statutes.
- *Employment law*—governed to an increasing extent by federal statutes concerning discrimination in employment, workplace safety, labor unions, pension plans, Social Security, and other aspects of employment. Each state also has statutes governing certain areas of employment, such as safety standards in the workplace and employment discrimination.

- *Antitrust law*—governed by federal statutes prohibiting specific types of anticompetitive business practices.
- *Consumer law*—governed by state and federal statutes protecting consumers against deceptive trade practices (such as misleading advertising), unsafe products, and generally any activities that threaten consumer health and welfare.
- *Wills and probate administration* (relating to the transfer of property on the property owner's death)—governed by state statutes.

You will read about some of these areas of law in later chapters. A paralegal working in an area (or on a case) governed by statutory law needs to know how to both locate and interpret the relevant state or federal statutes. You will learn how to find and analyze statutory law in Chapter 17.

ADMINISTRATIVE LAW

Another important source of American law is **administrative law**, which consists of the rules, orders, and decisions of administrative agencies. An **administrative agency** is a federal, state, or local government agency established to perform a specific function, such as the regulation of food sold to consumers. Rules issued by various administrative agencies now affect virtually every aspect of a business's operation, including the firm's capital structure and financing, its hiring and firing procedures, its relations with employees and unions, and the way it manufactures and markets its products.

At the federal level, there are numerous federal administrative agencies, each of which has been established to perform specific governing tasks. ▶ **EXAMPLE 5.5** The federal Environmental Protection Agency coordinates and enforces federal environmental laws. The federal Food and Drug Administration enforces federal laws relating to the safety of foods and drugs. The Securities and Exchange Commission regulates purchases and sales of securities (corporate stocks and bonds). ◀

There are administrative agencies at the state and local levels as well. Commonly, a state agency (such as a state pollution control agency) is created as a parallel to a federal agency (such as the Environmental Protection Agency). Just as federal statutes take precedence over conflicting state statutes, so do federal agency regulations take precedence over conflicting state regulations. Because the rules of state and local agencies vary widely, we focus here exclusively on federal administrative law.

On the Web

The *United States Government Manual* describes the origins, purposes, and administrators of every federal department and agency. You can access this publication online at **http://www.gpoaccess.gov/gmanual**.

administrative law
A body of law created by administrative agencies in the form of rules, regulations, orders, and decisions in order to carry out their duties and responsibilities.

administrative agency
A federal or state government agency established to perform a specific function. Administrative agencies are authorized by legislative acts to make and enforce rules relating to the purpose for which they were established.

Debra Rudolph

PARALEGAL **profile**

GENERAL LAW PRACTICE PARALEGAL

Debra Rudolph earned a bachelor of arts degree in English literature from the University of Tennessee, Knoxville, and graduated summa cum laude from the paralegal studies program at Pellissippi State Technical Community College.

While a student in the paralegal studies program, Rudolph was the recipient of two paralegal scholarships and winner of West's Award for Outstanding Academic Achievement for 2000. She also was elected a member of Who's Who in American Junior Colleges *and the Lambda Chi honor society. She serves on the advisory committee for the paralegal studies program at Pellissippi State.*

Rudolph is editor-in-chief of The Paralegal Advocate, *a statewide newsletter for members of the Tennessee Paralegal Association. She has also taught a seminar for the Institute for Paralegal Education on the topics of depositions, legal research, and investigative techniques.*

Rudolph works in a small general law practice in downtown Knoxville, where she specializes in the areas of civil litigation, business organizations, and estate and inheritance taxes.

What do you like best about your work?

"I love the variety of assignments, cases, and clients that I've been exposed to while working in a small general law practice. In a typical week, I might be researching the side effects of a prescription drug, interviewing witnesses about a fatal train accident, reviewing discovery in a felony murder file, ordering forms for a tax return, summarizing lengthy pleadings, performing legal research on fiduciary relationships, and photographing a client's wrecked vehicle. I am very grateful for the continual opportunities to learn and experience new things as a paralegal in a general law practice."

What is the greatest challenge that you face in your area of work?

"There is a great deal of pressure and worry associated with supervising and tracking deadlines, statutes of limitations, task schedules, case status reports, and calendars. All of these functions are constantly and quickly changing, and it is a challenge to juggle and maintain these crucial administrative tasks while also working on legal projects."

What advice do you have for would-be paralegals in your area of work?

"Read! Being well read is vital to performing investigations, interviews, and legal research. Having an understanding of the human condition is the key to successfully working the legal arena. Also, knowledge of local, national, and world events will aid a paralegal in working with the variety of clients and cases encountered in a general law practice. An understanding of the business world is also an asset to a paralegal working in a general law practice because some of the work may relate to investments, taxes, estates, and business organizations."

> *"Keeping up with technology is a must in a general law practice."*

What are some tips for success as a paralegal in your area of work?

"Keeping up with technology is a must in a general law practice. In addition to strong keyboarding and Internet skills, knowledge of word processing, spreadsheets, and slide-show programs is a necessity. Strong organizational skills and the ability to think ahead are also important assets. A paralegal who really wants to shine will always maintain organized files and will anticipate anything his or her attorney may need. Things to anticipate may include summaries of pleadings, phone numbers and directions, and even the possibility of needing extra-large garbage bags when traveling with oversized exhibits in times of inclement weather."

Agency Creation

Because Congress cannot possibly oversee the actual implementation of all the laws it enacts, it must delegate such tasks to others, particularly when the issues relate to highly technical areas, such as air and water pollution. Congress creates an administrative agency by enacting **enabling legislation**, which specifies the name, composition, purpose, and powers of the agency being created.

▶ **EXAMPLE 5.6** The Federal Trade Commission (FTC) was created in 1914 by the Federal Trade Commission Act.[7] This act prohibits unfair and deceptive trade practices. It also describes the procedures the agency must follow to charge persons or organizations with violations of the act, and it provides for judicial review (review by the courts) of agency orders. Other portions of the act grant the agency powers to "make rules and regulations for the purpose of carrying out the Act," to conduct investigations of business practices, to obtain reports from interstate corporations concerning their business practices, to investigate possible violations of the act, to publish findings of its investigations, and to recommend new legislation. The act also empowers the FTC to hold trial-like hearings and to **adjudicate** (resolve judicially) certain kinds of trade disputes that involve FTC regulations. ◀

Note that the FTC's grant of power incorporates functions associated with the legislative branch of government (rulemaking), the executive branch (investigation and enforcement), and the judicial branch (adjudication). Taken together, these functions constitute *administrative process.*

Rulemaking

One of the major functions of an administrative agency is **rulemaking**—creating or modifying rules, or regulations, pursuant to its enabling legislation. The Administrative Procedure Act of 1946[8] imposes strict procedural requirements that agencies must follow in their rulemaking and other functions.

The most common rulemaking procedure involves three steps. First, the agency must give public notice of the proposed rulemaking proceedings, where and when the proceedings will be held, the agency's legal authority for the proceedings, and the terms or subject matter of the proposed rule. The notice must be published in the *Federal Register,* a daily publication of the U.S. government. Second, following this notice, the agency must allow ample time for interested parties to comment in writing on the proposed rule. After the comments have been received and reviewed, the agency takes them into consideration when drafting the final version of the regulation. The third and last step is the drafting of the final rule and its publication in the *Federal Register.* (See Chapter 17 for an explanation of how to find agency regulations.)

Investigation and Enforcement

Agencies have both investigatory and prosecutorial powers. In conducting an investigation, an agency can request that individuals or organizations hand over specified books, papers, records, or other documents. In addition, agencies may conduct on-site inspections, although a search warrant is normally required for such inspections. Sometimes, a search of a home, an office, or a factory is the only means of obtaining evidence needed to prove a regulatory violation. Agencies investigate a wide range of activities, including coal mining, automobile manufacturing, and the industrial discharge of pollutants into the environment.

After conducting an investigation of a suspected rule violation, an agency may begin to take administrative action against an individual or a business. Most administrative actions are resolved through negotiated settlements at their initial stages, without the need for formal

enabling legislation
A statute enacted by a legislature that authorizes the creation of an administrative agency and specifies the name, purpose, composition, and powers of the agency being created.

adjudicate
To resolve a dispute judicially.

rulemaking
The actions undertaken by administrative agencies when formally adopting new regulations or amending old ones.

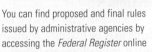

On the Web

You can find proposed and final rules issued by administrative agencies by accessing the *Federal Register* online at **http://www.gpoaccess. gov/cfr/index.html**.

adjudication. If a settlement cannot be reached, though, the agency may issue a formal complaint against the suspected violator, and the case may proceed to adjudication.

Adjudication

administrative law judge (ALJ)
One who presides over an administrative agency hearing and who has the power to administer oaths, take testimony, rule on questions of evidence, and make determinations of fact.

Agency adjudication involves a trial-like hearing before an **administrative law judge** (ALJ). The ALJ presides over the hearing and has the power to administer oaths, take testimony, rule on questions of evidence, and make determinations of fact. Although the ALJ works for the agency prosecuting the case, he or she is required by law to be an unbiased adjudicator (judge). Hearing procedures vary widely from agency to agency. They may be informal meetings conducted at a table in a conference room, or they may be formal adjudicatory hearings resembling trials. As you will read shortly, in some agencies, paralegals are allowed to represent clients at these hearings.

After the hearing, the ALJ renders a decision on the case. The ALJ may compel the charged party to pay a fine or may prohibit the party from carrying on some specified activity. Either side may appeal the ALJ's decision to the commission or board that governs the agency. If the party fails to get relief there, appeal can be made to a federal court. If no party appeals the case, or if the commission and the court decline to review the case, the ALJ's decision becomes final.

ADMINISTRATIVE LAW AND THE PARALEGAL

The functions of administrative agencies permeate almost every area of legal practice. No matter where you work, you should anticipate that sooner or later you will be interacting with a government agency. ▶ **EXAMPLE 5.7** Suppose you work for a small law firm that specializes in personal-injury claims. You may be required to communicate directly with an investigator for the Occupational Safety and Health Administration when the firm handles a personal-injury claim involving an employer's violation of workplace safety standards. ◀

Paralegals who work for law firms that have many corporate clients may be extensively involved in researching and analyzing agency regulations and their applicability to certain business activities. If you work in a corporate legal department, you may be asked to determine which agency regulations apply to the corporation and whether the corporation is complying with those regulations. Of course, if you work for an administrative agency, you may be involved in drafting new rules, analyzing survey results to see if a new regulation is necessary, mediating disputes between private parties and the agency, conducting investigations to gather facts about compliance with agency rules, and numerous other agency-related tasks.

Paralegals often become very familiar with the administrative process when helping clients obtain needed benefits from state or federal agencies. A paralegal helping homeless persons to obtain medical assistance, for example, would work closely with local agencies. As already mentioned, some administrative agencies, including the Social Security Administration and the Internal Revenue Service, allow paralegals to represent clients at agency hearings and other procedures. Finally, in any law practice, you may be asked to assist clients who are involved in disputes with administrative agencies.

CASE LAW AND THE COMMON LAW TRADITION

case law
Rules of law announced in court decisions.

Another important source of law consists of the decisions rendered by judges in cases that come before the courts. This body of law, called **case law**, arose from the English common law tradition. As mentioned earlier, because of our colonial heritage much of American law is based on the English legal system.

Developing Paralegal Skills

APPROVAL TO PRACTICE BEFORE THE IRS

Damian Forsythe has an associate's degree in accounting and is also interested in law. He has just completed Law 100, "Introduction to Law," and learned that some administrative agencies allow nonlawyers to practice before them. One of those agencies is the Internal Revenue Service (IRS). Damian would be allowed to represent clients before the IRS and to advise clients on tax matters without engaging in the unauthorized practice of law.

Damian contacts the Office of the Director of Practice in Washington, D.C. The administrative assistant who answers the telephone explains that the IRS allows nonlawyers and noncertified public accountants to practice before the agency. First, though, they must pass the "Enrolled Agents" exam and be admitted to practice. A person wishing to apply for admission to practice must submit Form 23 and must meet certain requirements, such as being current in personal income tax payments. There are no educational requirements, but the exam is very difficult and requires a knowledge of accounting, tax laws, and regulations. It is given only once a year, usually in September.

Damian is told that Form 2587, which he can use to register for the exam, is available online at the IRS's Web site at **http://www.irs.gov**. He can also obtain a copy of Form 23 from the Web site. Damian uses his computer to explore the possibility of representing clients before the IRS.

TIPS FOR CONTACTING AN ADMINISTRATIVE AGENCY

- Try to identify a person at the agency who can help you obtain the information you seek.
- Consider checking online sources to see if there is an agency directory that lists employee names and departments.
- If you place a blind call, think about your question ahead of time and about which department might be able to answer it.
- Obtain the name and telephone number of the person you are trying to reach before being transferred to that person.
- Be patient and polite.

Part of our English heritage was the **common law**—a body of general rules that prescribed social conduct and applied throughout the entire English realm. Courts developed the common law rules from the principles underlying judges' decisions in actual legal controversies. Judges attempted to be consistent. When possible, they based their decisions on the principles suggested by earlier cases. They sought to decide similar cases in a similar way and considered new cases with care because they knew that their decisions would make new law. Each interpretation became part of the law on the subject and served as a legal **precedent**. Later cases that involved similar legal principles or facts could be decided with reference to that precedent. The courts were thus guided by traditions and legal doctrines that evolved over time.

The Doctrine of *Stare Decisis*

The practice of deciding new cases with reference to former decisions, or precedents, eventually became a cornerstone of the English and American judicial systems. It forms a doctrine called *stare decisis*[9] ("to stand by things decided"). Under this doctrine, judges are

common law

A body of law developed from custom or judicial decisions in English and U.S. courts and not by a legislature.

precedent

A court decision that furnishes an example or authority for deciding subsequent cases in which identical or similar facts are presented.

stare decisis

The doctrine of precedent, under which a court is obligated to follow earlier decisions of that court or higher courts within the same jurisdiction. This is a defining characteristic of the common law system.

binding authority

Any source of law that a court must follow when deciding a case. Binding authorities include constitutions, statutes, and regulations that govern the issue being decided, as well as court decisions that are controlling precedents within the jurisdiction.

persuasive precedent

A precedent decided in another jurisdiction that a court may either follow or reject but that is entitled to careful consideration.

obligated to follow the precedents established by their own courts or by higher courts within their jurisdictions (the areas over which they have authority—see Chapter 6). These controlling precedents are referred to as binding authorities. A **binding authority** is any source of law that a court must follow when deciding a case. Binding authorities include constitutions, statutes, and regulations that govern the issue being decided, as well as court decisions that are controlling precedents within the jurisdiction. When no binding authority exists, courts will often review **persuasive precedents**, which are precedents decided in similar cases in other jurisdictions. The court may either follow or reject persuasive precedents, but these decisions are entitled to respect and careful consideration.

The doctrine of *stare decisis* performs many useful functions. It helps the courts to be more efficient because if other courts have carefully reasoned through a similar case, their legal reasoning and opinions can serve as guides. *Stare decisis* also creates consistency. It makes the law more stable and predictable, because if the law on a given subject is well settled, someone bringing a case to court can usually rely on the court to make a decision based on what the law has been.

Departures from Precedent

Sometimes a court will depart from the rule of precedent if it decides that the precedent should no longer be followed. If a court decides that a ruling precedent is simply incorrect or that technological or social changes have rendered the precedent inapplicable, the court might rule contrary to the precedent. Cases that overturn precedent often receive a great deal of publicity.

▶ **EXAMPLE 5.8** In *Brown v. Board of Education of Topeka*[10] (decided in 1954), for example, the United States Supreme Court expressly overturned precedent when it concluded that separate educational facilities for whites and African Americans, which had been upheld as constitutional in numerous previous cases,[11] were inherently unequal. The Supreme Court's departure from precedent in *Brown* received a tremendous amount of publicity as people began to realize the ramifications of this change in the law. It also spearheaded the civil rights movement, which led to further lawsuits involving claims of racial discrimination. ◀

On the Web

To learn how the Supreme Court justified its departure from precedent in the 1954 *Brown* decision, you can access the Court's opinion online at **http://www.law.cornell.edu/supct**.

Cases of First Impression

Sometimes, there is no precedent on which to base a decision. ▶ **EXAMPLE 5.9** In 1986, a New Jersey court had to decide whether a surrogate-parenting contract should be enforced against the wishes of the surrogate parent (the natural mother).[12] This was the first such case to reach the courts, and there was no precedent in any jurisdiction to which the court could look for guidance. ◀ Developments in technology, which often outpace the law, sometimes result in cases for which there is no precedent. ▶ **EXAMPLE 5.10** Suppose that an employee can see sexually offensive images on a co-employee's computer monitor, and the employee claims that this constitutes "hostile-environment" sexual harassment. There may be no controlling state or federal law that deals with the employee's complaint. ◀

case of first impression

A case presenting a legal issue that has not yet been addressed by a court in a particular jurisdiction.

public policy

A governmental policy based on widely held societal values.

When deciding cases such as these, called **cases of first impression**, or when there are conflicting precedents, courts may consider a number of factors, including legal principles and policies underlying previous court decisions or existing statutes, fairness, social values and customs, **public policy** (a governmental policy based on widely held societal values), and data and concepts drawn from the social sciences. Which of these sources is chosen or receives the greatest emphasis will depend on the nature of the case being considered and the particular judge hearing the case. (See this chapter's *Technology and Today's Paralegal* feature on pages 166 and 167 for a case of first impression involving defamation via the Internet and suggestions for how to proceed when researching cases of first impression.)

Ethics Watch!

LEGAL RESEARCH AND *STARE DECISIS*

One of the challenges faced by legal professionals is keeping up with the ever-changing law. For example, suppose that you are asked to do research on a case involving issues similar to those in a case you researched just three months ago. If you apply your previous research results to the current client's case, you need to verify that your earlier research still applies—that is, that previous case decisions are still "good law." In three months' time, an appeals court might have created a new precedent, and failure to update your research (how to do this is explained in Chapters 17 and 18) can lead to serious consequences for the client—and for you and the attorney, if the client decides to sue the attorney for negligence (specifically, for breaching the duty of competence).

Judges always strive to be free of subjectivity and personal bias in deciding cases. Each judge, however, has his or her own unique personality, set of values or philosophical leanings, and intellectual attributes—all of which necessarily frame the decision-making process.

Remedies at Law versus Remedies in Equity

In the early English king's courts, the kinds of **remedies** that the courts could grant were severely restricted. If one person wronged another in some way, the king's court could award as compensation only land, items of value, or money. The courts that awarded these things became known as **courts of law**, and the three remedies awarded by these courts—land, items of value, and money—became known as **remedies at law**.

Even though this system helped to standardize the ways in which disputes were settled, those parties who wanted a remedy other than economic compensation could not be helped. Because the courts of law could not grant noneconomic remedies, many disappointed litigants became very frustrated with the court system. Some of the more persistent parties petitioned the king for relief. Most of these petitions were decided by an adviser to the king, called a *chancellor*. The chancellor was said to be the "keeper of the king's conscience." When the chancellor thought that the claim was a fair one for which there was no adequate remedy at law, he would fashion new and unique remedies, called **remedies in equity**, to resolve the case. In this way, a new body of rules and remedies came into being and eventually led to the establishment of formal courts of chancery, or **courts of equity**.

Equity is that branch of law, founded on what might be described as notions of justice and fair dealing, that seeks to supply a remedy when there is no adequate remedy available at law. Once the courts of equity were established, plaintiffs could pursue their claims in either courts of law (if they sought money damages) or courts of equity (if they sought equitable remedies). Plaintiffs had to specify whether they were bringing an "action at law" or an "action in equity," and they chose their courts accordingly. Only one remedy could be granted for a particular wrong.

remedy
The means by which a right is enforced or the violation of a right is prevented or compensated for.

court of law
A court in which the only remedies that could be granted were things of value, such as money damages. In early England, courts of law were distinct from courts of equity.

remedy at law
A remedy available in a court of law. Money damages are awarded as a remedy at law.

remedy in equity
A remedy allowed by courts in situations where remedies at law are not appropriate. Remedies in equity are based on settled rules of fairness, justice, and honesty.

court of equity
A court that decides controversies and administers justice according to the rules, principles, and precedents of equity.

Technology and Today's Paralegal

CASES OF FIRST IMPRESSION AND THE INTERNET

The widespread use of the Internet for a variety of purposes has led to a number of cases of first impression. In this feature, we look at one such case—a case involving online defamation. (As you will read in Chapter 7, *defamation* occurs when someone publishes or publicly makes a false statement that harms another's good name, reputation, or character.) We also offer some helpful suggestions on how to proceed when you are asked to do research on a case of first impression.

Because the Internet knows no boundaries, online defamation across national borders can raise jurisdictional questions. *Jurisdiction* is an important legal concept that relates to the authority of a court to hear and decide a case. (You will read more about jurisdiction in Chapter 6.) In the United States, jurisdiction over individuals and businesses located in other states is based on the requirement of minimum contacts. Essentially, this requirement means that a defendant in a lawsuit (one against whom a lawsuit is brought) must have a minimum level of contact with residents of a particular state for that state's courts to exercise jurisdiction over the defendant. For example, suppose that a Wisconsin driver, while on vacation in California, crashes into a California resident's car. If the crash resulted from the Wisconsin driver's negligence, a *tort*, or civil wrong (see Chapter 7), will have been committed. The commission of the tort occurred in California, and that contact will be sufficient to allow a California court to exercise jurisdiction over the Wisconsin defendant.

Other countries' courts are applying the requirement of minimum contacts as developed by the U.S. courts. In the online context, however, determining *where* the defamation occurred presents a unique challenge.

DETERMINING WHERE THE ONLINE DEFAMATION OCCURRED

Suppose that a firm located in New Jersey posts a statement on its Web site that is defamatory. Further suppose that the person who has been defamed, or injured by the statement, lives in Australia. Can the Australian citizen sue the New Jersey firm in an Australian court? In other words, could an Australian court exercise jurisdiction over the New Jersey defendant? The answer to this question depends on two factors.

The first factor has to do with whether the Australian court has adopted the "minimum-contacts requirement" developed by U.S. courts. If it has, then the Australian court can exercise jurisdiction over the New Jersey defendant *if* it can be determined that the defendant had minimum contacts with Australia. The second factor stems from the first and involves determining *where* the tort of defamation occurred. If the tort occurred in Australia (where the defamatory message was viewed and was capable of being downloaded), an

Equitable Principles and Maxims

Courts of equity often supplemented the common law by making decisions based on considerations of justice and fairness. Today, the same court can award both legal and equitable remedies, so plaintiffs may request both equitable and legal relief in the same case. Yet judges continue to be guided by so-called **equitable principles and maxims** when deciding whether to grant equitable remedies. *Maxims* are propositions or general statements of rules of law that courts often use in arriving at a decision. Some of the most influential maxims of equity are the following:

equitable principles and maxims
Propositions or general statements of rules of law that are frequently involved in equity jurisdiction.

- Whoever seeks equity must do equity. (Anyone who wishes to be treated fairly must treat others fairly.)

- One who seeks the aid of an equity court must come to the court with clean hands. (The plaintiff must have acted fairly and honestly.)

Australian court could exercise jurisdiction based on the minimum-contacts requirement. After all, by committing a tort in Australia, the New Jersey firm opened the door to the possibility that it could be sued in an Australian court. If, however, the tort occurred in New Jersey (when the defamatory statement was posted on the New Jersey firm's Web site), the court could not exercise jurisdiction over the firm—because the New Jersey firm did not have sufficient contacts with Australia.

At least one nation's highest court—that of Australia—has ruled on this issue. The case involved a resident of Melbourne, Australia, who sued Dow Jones & Company, the U.S. publisher of the *Wall Street Journal,* for defamation. Dow Jones argued that the Australian court could not exercise jurisdiction over its U.S. servers, which were located in New Jersey. Ultimately, Australia's highest court rejected this argument. The court concluded that the tort had occurred in Australia, where the article had been downloaded and viewed, and thus the Australian court had jurisdiction over the dispute.[a]

RESEARCHING CASES OF FIRST IMPRESSION

Clearly, the Internet has posed many new difficulties for the courts in attempting to adapt traditional legal principles to cyberspace. Your approach to research thus needs to be flexible. First, look to see if there is any existing statutory law that the judge might determine *should* apply to your case (or that your supervising attorney can argue should apply). This is particularly important given that new technologies, and especially the Internet, have forced the courts to adapt many existing statutes, such as federal copyright law, to meet the needs of modern society. Second, look to see if any other court (in a different state or district, for example) has considered a similar legal issue and, if so, what that court concluded. Although cases decided in other jurisdictions will not be binding precedents, courts often look at the way other courts have handled an issue when deciding matters of first impression.

TECHNOLOGY TIP

Generally, when researching cases of first impression involving Internet transactions, you will need to broaden the scope of your search of the sources of law. A wise paralegal will be creative and adopt a research strategy that is aimed at discovering both which laws *may* apply and which laws *should* apply given the specific facts of the case.

a. *Dow Jones & Co., Inc. v. Gutnick,* HCA 56 (December 10, 2002).

- Equity will not suffer a right to exist without a remedy. (Equitable relief will be awarded when there is a right to relief and there is no adequate legal remedy.)
- Equity regards substance rather than form. (Equity is more concerned with fairness and justice than with legal technicalities.)
- Equity aids the vigilant, not those who slumber on their rights. (Individuals who fail to assert their legal rights within a reasonable period of time will not be helped.)

The last maxim listed above has become known as the equitable *doctrine of laches.* The doctrine of laches encourages people to bring lawsuits while the evidence is still fresh. What constitutes a reasonable time, of course, varies depending on the circumstances of the case. The time period for pursuing a particular claim against another party is now usually fixed by a statute of limitations (see Chapter 4). After the time allowed under the statute of limitations has expired, further action on that claim is barred.

ETHICS AND THE LAW

By now, you are probably well on your way toward understanding the importance of ethics in the legal profession and, consequently, in paralegal practice. What you might not realize, though, is that ethics is a pervasive element in the law itself. Keep this in mind as you study American law in this chapter and in the chapters that follow. You just read about equitable principles and maxims, which clearly illustrate the importance of ethics in the law. But ethics also provides the underpinnings for numerous laws that you will be researching and analyzing during your career as a paralegal.

Sometimes, the connection between a particular law and its ethical roots is not immediately apparent. But if you look closely, you will likely see the connection. For example, when you study contract law, which will be discussed in Chapter 8, consider that virtually every rule or legal doctrine in that area of the law ultimately stems from attempts to fairly balance the rights of the parties to a contract. Generally, understanding the ethical dimensions of particular laws helps you to better analyze those laws—and makes you a more valuable team member in your paralegal work.

For torts, or civil wrongs, the statute of limitations varies from state to state. It may be two years, three years, or even longer for certain types of wrongs. The statute of limitations for contracts involving the sale of goods is normally four years. In regard to criminal actions, the duration of the statute of limitations is often directly related to the seriousness of the offense. The statute of limitations for petty theft (the theft of an item of insignificant value), for example, may be a year while the statute of limitations for armed robbery might be twenty years. (For certain crimes, such as treason and first degree murder, there is no statute of limitations.)

Equitable Remedies

A number of equitable remedies are available. As mentioned above, equitable remedies are normally granted only if the court concludes that the remedy at law (money damages) is inadequate. Three equitable remedies—specific performance, rescission, and injunction—are briefly discussed here.

Specific Performance.   A judge's decree of **specific performance** is an order to perform what was promised. This remedy was, and still is, only available when the dispute before the court concerns a contractual transaction involving something unique and money damages are inadequate. Contracts for the sale of goods that are readily available on the market rarely qualify for specific performance. Money damages ordinarily are adequate in such situations because substantially identical goods can be bought or sold in the market.

specific performance
An equitable remedy requiring exactly the performance that was specified in a contract; usually granted only when money damages would be an inadequate remedy and the subject matter of the contract is unique (for example, real property).

Ethics Watch!

THE STATUTE OF LIMITATIONS AND THE DUTY OF COMPETENCE

The duty of competence requires, among other things, that attorneys and paralegals be aware of the statute of limitations governing a client's legal matter. Assume, for example, that a client of your firm, a restaurant owner, wants to sue a restaurant-supply company for breaking a contract for the sale of dishes. If the attorney asks you to look into the matter, the first thing you should check is your state's statute of limitations covering contracts for the sale of goods. If the time period has already expired, then your attorney will need to advise the client accordingly. If the time period is about to expire, then you and your supervising attorney need to act quickly to make sure that the complaint (the document that initiates a lawsuit) is filed before the time period expires.

If the goods are unique, however, a court of equity may grant specific performance. For example, paintings, sculptures, and rare books and coins are so unique that money damages will not enable a buyer to obtain substantially identical substitutes in the market. The same principle applies to contracts relating to sales of land or interests in land, because each parcel of land is unique.

Rescission. In certain situations, if the legal remedy of money damages is unavailable or inadequate, the equitable remedy of rescission may be given. Rescission[13] is an action to undo a contract—to return the parties to the positions they occupied before the contract was made. If a customer agrees to purchase a vacuum cleaner because the seller misrepresents its quality, for example, the buyer might want merely to rescind, or cancel, the agreement if he or she discovers the fraud before any money changes hands. If the money has already changed hands, rescission would also involve *restitution*—returning to each party any money or other items of value that had been exchanged by the parties.

> **rescission**
> A remedy whereby a contract is terminated and the parties are returned to the positions they occupied before the contract was made.

Injunction. An **injunction** is a court order directing the defendant to do or to refrain from doing a particular act. For example, an injunction may be obtained to stop a neighbor from burning trash in his or her yard or to prevent an estranged husband from coming near his wife. Persons who violate injunctions are typically held in *contempt of court* (see Chapter 3) and punished with a jail sentence or a fine.

> **injunction**
> A court decree ordering a person to do or refrain from doing a certain act.

The Merging of Law and Equity

During the nineteenth century, most states adopted rules of procedure that combined courts of law and equity—although some states, such as Arkansas, still retain the distinction. Today, as mentioned, a plaintiff may request both legal and equitable remedies in the same action, and the trial court judge may decide whether to grant either or both forms of relief.

Developing Paralegal Skills

REQUIREMENTS FOR SPECIFIC PERFORMANCE

Louise Lassen, a wealthy heiress, buys a painting from an artist in New York for $35,000. The artist agrees to ship the painting to Louise's home in Chicago within two weeks. After Louise returns home, she learns from the artist that he has changed his mind—he is no longer interested in selling the painting and is returning her payment.

Louise contacts the firm of Murdoch & Larson to have the contract enforced. Kevin Murdoch, one of the firm's partners, asks paralegal Bob Humboldt to assist him in determining whether the remedy of specific performance can be sought. Bob is to research case law on specific performance and prepare a research memorandum summarizing his results. Bob lets the attorney know that he will have the memorandum on the attorney's desk by the next morning.

CHECKLIST FOR ANALYZING A LEGAL PROBLEM

- Gather the facts involved in the problem.
- Determine whether unique or rare articles are involved.
- Find out what type of remedy the client wants.
- Determine whether an adequate legal remedy, such as money damages, will compensate the client.
- Apply the law to the client's facts to reach a conclusion regarding the appropriate remedy.

Despite the merging of the courts, remnants of the procedures used when law and equity courts were separate still exist. Courts continue to distinguish between remedies at law and equitable remedies, and differences in procedure sometimes also depend on whether a civil lawsuit involves an action in equity or an action at law. For example, in actions at law, a party has the right to demand a jury trial, but actions in equity are not decided by juries. (A judge may, however, call in a jury to serve in an advisory capacity.) The procedural differences between an action at law and an action in equity are summarized in Exhibit 5.2, which is applicable to most states.

The Common Law Today

The common law—which consists of the rules of law announced in previous court decisions—plays a significant role in the United States today. Federal and state courts frequently must interpret and enforce constitutional provisions, statutes enacted by legislatures, and regulations created by administrative agencies. For example, if a federal court interprets a regulation of the Environmental Protection Agency to be unconstitutional, the court's opinion becomes part of the common law. Courts looking at the same issue in other cases will then typically follow the ruling announced in the federal court.

To summarize and clarify common law rules and principles, the American Law Institute (ALI) has published a number of treatises called *Restatements of the Law*. The ALI, which was

PROCEDURE	ACTION AT LAW	ACTION IN EQUITY
Initiation of lawsuit	By filing a complaint	By filing a petition
Decision	By judge or jury	By judge (no jury)
Result	Judgment	Decree
Remedy	Monetary damages	Injunction, decree of specific performance, or rescission

EXHIBIT 5.2
Procedural Differences between an Action at Law and an Action in Equity

formed in the 1920s, is a group of practicing attorneys, legal scholars, and judges. *Restatements of the Law* generally summarize and explain the common law rules that are followed in most states with regard to a particular area of law, such as contracts or torts. Although the *Restatements* do not have the force of law, they are important secondary sources of legal analysis and opinion on which judges often rely in making their decisions. You will read more about the *Restatements of the Law* in Chapter 17, in the context of legal research.

Statutory Law and the Common Law

The common law governs all areas not covered by statutory law, which (as discussed previously) generally consists of those laws enacted by state legislatures and by the federal Congress. In the early years of this nation, the body of statutory law was relatively small compared with the body of common law principles and doctrines. The body of statutory law has expanded greatly since then, however, and continues to grow. To some extent, this expansion has resulted from the enactment of statutes that essentially codify common law doctrines. For example, criminal law was at one time governed extensively by common law. Over time, common law doctrines were codified, expanded on, and enacted in statutory form. Today, criminal law is primarily statutory law.

The expansion of statutory law has also resulted from the need to regulate business and other activities for various purposes. ▶ **EXAMPLE 5.11** Many federal and state statutes have been enacted in an attempt to protect consumers, employees, investors, and other groups from business practices that are potentially harmful to the rights or interests of these groups. Numerous statutes and regulations exist to protect the environment, and a whole body of law—antitrust law—is based on statutes passed to protect the public's interest in a freely competitive society. ◀ Another reason why the body of statutory law has expanded is to address the need for uniform laws among the states, such as the laws governing commercial transactions.

Even when legislation has been substituted for common law principles, a court's interpretation and application of a statute may become a precedent that lower courts in the jurisdiction must follow. Furthermore, courts often look to the common law when determining how to interpret a statute, on the theory that the people who drafted the statute intended to codify an existing common law rule. In a sense, then, common law and statutory law are never totally separate bodies of law.

The Terminology of Case Law

Throughout the remainder of this text, you will encounter various terms that have traditionally been used to describe parties to lawsuits, case titles, and the types of decisions that judges author. Although details on how to research case law will be given in Chapter 17, it is worthwhile at this point to explain some of the basic terminology of case law.

Case Titles

The title of a case, which is sometimes referred to as the *style* of the case, indicates the names of the parties to the lawsuit. Note that a case title, such as *Baranski v. Peretto,* includes only the parties' surnames, not their first names. The *v.* in the case title stands for *versus,* which means "against." In the trial court (the court in which a lawsuit is first brought and tried), Baranski is the plaintiff, so Baranski's name appears first in the case title. If the case is appealed to a higher court for review, however, the appeals court sometimes places the name of the party appealing the decision first, so that the case may be called *Peretto v. Baranski.* Because some appeals courts retain the trial court order of names, it is often impossible to distinguish the plaintiff from the defendant in the title of a reported appeals court decision. You must carefully read the facts of the case to identify the parties. Otherwise, the discussion by the appeals court will be difficult to understand.

Usually, whenever attorneys or paralegals refer to a court decision, they give not only the title of the case but also the case citation. The citation indicates the reports or reporters in which the case can be found (reports and reporters are volumes in which cases are published, or "reported"). For example, a citation to 251 Kan. 728 following a case title would indicate that the case could be found in volume 251 of the Kansas reports on page 728. You will read in further detail about how to read case citations and locate case law in Chapter 17.

citation
A reference that indicates where a particular constitutional provision, statute, reported case, or article can be found.

The Parties

The parties to a lawsuit are the plaintiff, who initiates the lawsuit, and the defendant, against whom the lawsuit is brought. Lawsuits frequently involve multiple parties—that is, more than one plaintiff or defendant. For example, a person who is injured by a defective product might sue both the manufacturer of the product and the retailer from whom the product was purchased to obtain compensation for injuries caused by the product. In this situation, the manufacturer and the retailer would be *co-defendants.*

party
With respect to lawsuits, the plaintiff or the defendant. Some cases involve multiple parties (more than one plaintiff or defendant).

Judges and Justices

The terms *judge* and *justice* are usually synonymous and represent two designations given to judges in various courts. All members of the United States Supreme Court, for example, are referred to as justices. Justice is also the formal title usually given to judges of appeals courts, although this is not always the case. Justice is commonly abbreviated to J., and justices to JJ. A Supreme Court case might refer to Justice Kennedy as Kennedy, J., or to Chief Justice Roberts as Roberts, C.J.

In a trial court, a case is heard by one judge. In an appeals court, normally a panel of three or more judges (or justices) sit on the bench. Most decisions reached by appeals courts are explained in written court opinions.

On the Web

If you are interested in learning more about the justices of the United States Supreme Court, go to the Legal Information Institute, sponsored by Cornell University, at **http://straylight. law.cornell.edu/supct/justices/ fullcourt.html**.

Decisions and Opinions

The opinion contains the court's reasons for its decision, the rules of law that apply, and the judgment. There are four types of opinions. When all judges or justices unanimously agree on an opinion, the opinion is written for the entire court and can be deemed a *unanimous opinion.* When there is not a unanimous opinion, a *majority opinion* is written, outlining the views of the majority of the judges or justices deciding the case. The name of the judge or justice immediately preceding the unanimous or majority opinion indicates the author of the opinion—that is, the judge or justice who wrote the opinion on behalf of the others.

Often, a judge or justice who feels strongly about making or emphasizing a point that was not made or emphasized in the majority opinion writes a *concurring opinion,* which

opinion
A statement by the court setting forth the applicable law and the reasons for its decision in a case.

appears just following the majority opinion. In a concurring opinion, the judge or justice agrees (concurs) with the decision given in the majority opinion but for different reasons. In other than unanimous opinions, a *dissenting opinion* may also be written by a judge or justice who does not agree with the majority. The dissenting opinion is important because it may form the basis of the arguments used years later in overruling the precedential majority opinion. The names of the judges or justices authoring any concurring or dissenting opinions are also indicated at the beginning of those opinions.

COMMON LAW AND THE PARALEGAL

As a paralegal, you will find that a basic understanding of the common law tradition is necessary whenever you need to research and analyze case law. The doctrine of *stare decisis* and the distinction between legal and equitable remedies are critical concepts when applied to real-life situations faced by clients.

For example, suppose that a client wants to sue another party for breaching a contract to perform computer consulting services. In this situation, the common law of contracts would apply to the case. (In contrast, as you will read in Chapter 8, contracts for the sale of *goods* are governed by statutory law in virtually all of the states.) If you were asked to research the case, you would search for previous cases dealing with similar issues to see how those cases were decided. You would want to know of any precedents set by a higher court in your jurisdiction—and, of course, by the United States Supreme Court—on that issue. Even in an area governed by statutory law, such as sales contracts, you will want to find out how the courts have interpreted and applied the relevant state statute or statutory provision.

In addition to lawsuits involving contract law, the common law also applies to *tort law* (the law governing civil wrongs, such as negligence or assault and battery, as opposed to criminal wrongs). As a paralegal, you may be working on behalf of clients bringing or defending against the following types of actions, all of which involve tort law:

- *Personal-injury lawsuits*—actions brought by plaintiffs to obtain compensation for injuries allegedly caused by the wrongful acts of others, either intentionally or through negligence.
- *Malpractice lawsuits*—actions brought by plaintiffs against professionals, such as physicians and attorneys, to obtain compensation for injuries allegedly caused by professional negligence (breach of professional duties).
- *Product liability lawsuits*—actions brought by plaintiffs to obtain compensation for injuries allegedly caused by defective products.

Numerous other areas, such as property law and employment law, are also still governed to some extent by the common law. Depending on the nature of your job as a paralegal, you may be dealing with many issues that are governed by the common law.

The Adversarial System of Justice

As discussed, the common law, or case law, is extremely important in defining what the law is in the United States. It is therefore important to keep in mind that U.S. courts, like English courts, follow the **adversarial system of justice**, in which the parties act as adversaries, or opponents. Parties to a lawsuit come before the court as contestants, both sides presenting the facts of their cases in the light most favorable to themselves, in an attempt to "win" the "battle." The parties do not come together in the courtroom with the idea of working out a compromise solution to their problems or of looking at the dispute from each other's point of view. Rather, they take sides, present their best case to the judge or jury (if it is a jury trial), and hope that this impartial decision maker rules in their favor.

adversarial system of justice
A legal system in which the parties to a lawsuit are opponents, or adversaries, and present their cases in the light most favorable to themselves. The impartial decision maker (the judge or jury) determines who wins and who loses based on the evidence presented.

The Goal Is to Win

Most people do not fully appreciate the impact that the adversarial nature of the legal system has on those who work within the system. For one thing, in an adversarial system, the goal of the attorneys (and paralegals) is not so much to determine the truth as to win the

Why is the common law important even in areas that are primarily governed by statutory law?

(Courtesy of ©Brand X Pictures/Alamy)

case. An attorney's job is not to seek out or reveal the truth to judges (although ethical rules clearly prohibit attorneys from presenting evidence that they know to be untrue). Rather, the role of the attorney is to discover and present the strongest legal argument on behalf of a client, regardless of the attorney's personal feelings about the client or the client's case. Because of the adversarial nature of our system, you may be asked to work on cases that you do not believe in or for clients whom you do not like.

Criticisms of the Adversarial System

The adversarial nature of proceedings frames the practice of law in many respects. Lawyers are under a great deal of pressure to win cases. Lawyers may also be pressured by the other attorneys in a law firm to win a particular client's case. Additionally, others who work in the lawyer's firm will likely be affected by the lawyer's success or failure in court.

Many people criticize our adversarial system of justice, believing that it contributes to a lack of integrity in the legal profession. After all, the idea is that a trial is supposed to lead to justice. Some attorneys in our system actually make higher incomes by prolonging disputes and obscuring the truth. The public may even view a lawyer who has successfully defended a criminal client as unethical because the client was found not guilty due to a "technicality."

Although our system is not perfect, most Americans agree that everyone should be allowed her or his "day in court" and should be given the opportunity to have legal advice and guidance in presenting her or his case. These are the foundations of the concept of due process of law (which you will read more about in Chapter 16). The adversarial system is therefore fundamental to what we consider to be justice in the United States.

NATIONAL AND INTERNATIONAL LAW

Because business and other activities are becoming increasingly global in scope, numerous cases now brought before U.S. courts relate to issues involving foreign parties or governments. The laws of other nations and international doctrines or agreements may affect the outcome of these cases, and thus those laws, doctrines, and agreements are also sources of law that guide judicial decisions in U.S. courts. Many paralegals, particularly those who work for law firms that service clients operating in foreign countries, may need to become familiar with the legal systems of other nations during the course of their careers. For example, if you work in a firm in Arizona, California, New Mexico, or Texas, you may assist in the representation of Mexican clients. In this situation, you will want to have some familiarity with Mexican law and any international agreements that regulate U.S.-Mexican relations, such as the North American Free Trade Agreement (NAFTA).

National Law

The law of a particular nation is referred to as national law. The laws of nations differ from country to country because each country's laws reflect that nation's own unique cultural, historical, economic, and political background. Broadly speaking, however, there are two types of legal systems used by the various countries of the world. We have already discussed one of these systems—the common law system of England and the United States. Generally, those countries that were once colonies of Great Britain retained their English common law heritage after they achieved their independence. Today, common law systems exist in several countries, including Australia, Canada, India, Ireland, and New Zealand.

In contrast to Great Britain and the common law countries, most of the other European nations base their legal systems on Roman *civil law,* or "code law." The term *civil law,* as used here, refers not to civil as opposed to criminal law but to *codified law*—an ordered grouping of legal principles enacted into law by a legislature or governing body. In a civil law system, the primary source of law is a statutory code, and case precedents are not judicially binding, as they normally are in a common law system. This is not to say that precedents are unimportant in a civil law system. On the contrary, judges in such systems commonly refer to previous decisions as sources of legal guidance. The difference is that judges in a civil law system are not obligated to follow precedent to the extent that judges in a common law system are; in other words, the doctrine of *stare decisis* does not apply.

Today, the civil law system is followed in most of the continental European countries, as well as in the Latin American, African, and Asian countries that were once colonies of the continental European nations. Japan and South Africa also have civil law systems. Ingredients of the civil law system are also found in the Islamic courts of predominantly Muslim countries. In the United States, the state of Louisiana, because of its historical ties to France, has in part a civil law system. The legal systems of Puerto Rico, Québec, and Scotland are similarly characterized as having elements of a civil law system.

International Law

Relationships among countries are regulated to an extent by international law. International law can be defined as a body of written and unwritten laws observed by independent nations and governing the acts of individuals as well as governments. The key difference between national law and international law is the fact that national law can be enforced by government authorities, whereas international law is enforced primarily for reasons of courtesy or expediency. In essence, international law is the result of centuries-old attempts to reconcile the traditional need of each nation to be the final authority over its own affairs with the desire of

---

On the Web

The Library of Congress offers extensive information on national and international law at **http://www.loc.gov**.

national law
Law that pertains to a particular nation (as opposed to international law).

civil law system
A system of law derived from that of the Roman Empire and based on a code rather than case law; the predominant system of law in the nations of continental Europe and the nations that were once their colonies.

international law
The law that governs relations among nations. International customs and treaties are generally considered to be two of the most important sources of international law.

nations to benefit economically from trade and harmonious relations with one another. Although no independent nation can be compelled to obey a law external to itself, nations can and do voluntarily agree to be governed in certain respects by international law for the purpose of facilitating international trade and commerce and civilized discourse.

Traditional sources of international law include the customs that have been historically observed by nations in their dealings with each other. Other sources are treaties and international organizations and conferences. A *treaty* is an agreement between two or more nations that creates rights and duties binding on the parties to the treaty, just as a private contract creates rights and duties binding on the parties to the contract. To give effect to a treaty, the supreme power of each nation that is a party to the treaty must ratify it. For example, the U.S. Constitution requires approval by two-thirds of the Senate before a treaty executed by the president will be binding on the U.S. government. *Bilateral agreements,* as their name implies, occur when two nations form an agreement that will govern their commercial exchanges or other relations with one another. *Multilateral agreements* are formed by several nations. The European Union, for example, which regulates commercial activities among its European member nations, is the result of a multilateral trade agreement. Other multilateral agreements have led to the formation of regional trade associations, such as the North American Free Trade Agreement (NAFTA), which was formed by Canada, Mexico, and the United States. More recently, Costa Rica, the Dominican Republic, El Salvador, Guatemala, Honduras, Nicaragua, and the United States signed a multilateral agreement creating the Central America–United States Free Trade Agreement (CAFTA-DR).

International organizations and conferences also play an important role in the international legal arena. International organizations and conferences adopt resolutions, declarations, and other types of standards that often require a particular behavior of nations. The General Assembly of the United Nations, for example, has adopted numerous resolutions and declarations that embody principles of international law and has sponsored conferences that have led to the formation of international agreements. The United States is a member of more than one hundred multilateral and bilateral organizations, including at least twenty through the United Nations.

treaty
An agreement, or compact, formed between two independent nations.

On the Web

To find information on the laws governing other nations, including constitutions around the world, go to **http://www.oefre.unibe.ch/law/icl**.

INTERNATIONAL LAW AND THE PARALEGAL

Communications technology, improved transportation facilities, and international organizations and treaties have all helped to form a global environment of business. What this means for attorneys and paralegals is that an increasing amount of legal work has an international dimension. As a paralegal, you may be asked to assist your supervising attorney in many tasks that involve an international aspect, including the following:

- Research the law of a foreign country on a particular issue, such as labor law, to determine whether a corporate client (or your corporate employer) with business operations overseas is complying with the laws of the host country.

- Assist a client who has a manufacturing plant overseas in forming employment policies that are consistent with the national law of the host country and (if U.S. employees work at the plant) with U.S. employment laws.

- Determine whether a client's patented product will be protected under the patent laws of a specific foreign country or whether an international treaty provides for such protection.

- Determine what special contractual provisions should be included in a client's contract for the international sale of goods to protect the client's interest.

- Send communications via mail, express delivery services, telephone, e-mail, or fax to the foreign offices of a U.S. firm or a foreign firm with which a U.S. client has business dealings.

Today's Professional Paralegal

WORKING FOR AN ADMINISTRATIVE AGENCY

The Environmental Protection Agency (EPA) employs several paralegals. One of them is Mary Ulrich, who works for the Freedom of Information Act (FOIA) officer. As you will read in Chapter 14, the Freedom of Information Act of 1966 requires federal government agencies to disclose certain records to any person on request. Some types of records, however, are exempt from the requirement. These records include those containing classified information (information concerning national security), confidential materials dealing with trade secrets, government personnel rules, and personal medical files.

A person wishing to obtain such records must submit a written request to the FOIA officer of the federal agency holding the records. The letter should indicate which records are being sought and why (although specifying the purpose of the request is optional). If the request is denied by the federal agency because an exemption applies, the agency must cite the specific exemption. (A sample letter for requesting information under the FOIA is also shown in Chapter 14.)

Mary Ulrich's job involves responding to FOIA requests on behalf of the EPA. FOIA requests must be made in writing, but often legal assistants or attorneys from law firms or corporations call before they submit written requests.

RECEIVING AN INFORMATION REQUEST

Mary's telephone rings. It is Scott Webb, a paralegal with Sims and Howard in Chicago. He wants to talk to Mary about the EPA's file on the Black Hole landfill, a toxic waste site to which one of Sims and Howard's clients has allegedly contributed hazardous waste. Scott wants to know the size of the file on the landfill and the type of information that it contains. If the EPA's file is small enough, Scott will request copies of most of its relevant contents. He will request the copies over the phone and will also follow up on the conversation with a letter. Mary will be able to tell Scott if there are documents in the file that might have to be reviewed by an agency attorney before they can be reproduced.

Mary pulls the file and finds that it contains at least ten thousand pages of documents. She informs Scott of this. Because the agency charges for copying costs, including the time that Mary spends copying the records, Scott asks for specific types of documents. One kind of record that he wants is a list of the types and quantities of hazardous waste that other parties have allegedly contributed to the site.

DEALING WITH FOIA EXEMPTIONS

Mary looks for this information in the file. She finds it but also sees that information on several of the alleged contributors is exempt from FOIA disclosure requirements under trade secrets exemptions. Mary informs Scott of this fact. Scott also wants information on why the agency decided to include his firm's client in the list of contributors to the toxic waste site. Mary reminds Scott that interagency memos are usually privileged and that his request will have to be reviewed by agency counsel to determine if the agency could disclose this information.

Mary and Scott finish their conversation. Mary decides to wait for Scott's formal FOIA letter before starting to work on the request because so many of the documents will have to be reviewed by counsel before they can be sent out. Maybe Scott and the attorney for whom he works will rethink their strategy or make a different request now that they know they will have to wait for a decision from the agency's counsel office, especially when a good part of their request might be denied.

KEY TERMS AND CONCEPTS

adjudicate 161

administrative agency 159

administrative law 159

administrative law judge (ALJ) 162

adversarial system of justice 173

Bill of Rights 150

binding authority 164

case law 162

case of first impression 164

checks and balances 154

citation 172

civil law system 175

commerce clause 155

common law 163

constitutional law 150

court of equity 165

court of law 165

enabling legislation 161

equitable principles and maxims 166

federal system 153

injunction 169

international law 175

law 149

national law 175

opinion 172

ordinance 158

party 172

persuasive precedent 164

precedent 163

preemption 156

primary source of law 149

public law number 156

public policy 164

remedy 165

remedy at law 165

remedy in equity 165

rescission 169

rulemaking 161

secondary source of law 150

specific performance 168

stare decisis 163

statute 153

statutory law 153

supremacy clause 156

treaty 176

chapter summary   Sources of American Law

The Framework of American Law

1. *Definition of law*—The law has been defined variously over the ages, yet all definitions of law rest on the following assumption about the nature of law: law consists of a body of rules of conduct established and enforced by the controlling authority (the government) of a society.

2. *Primary sources of American law*—There are four primary sources of American law: the U.S. Constitution and the constitutions of various states; statutory law, including laws passed by Congress, state legislatures, and local governing bodies; regulations created by administrative agencies; and the common law doctrines developed in cases.

Constitutional Law

Constitutional law is all law that is based on the provisions in the U.S. Constitution, as amended, and the various state constitutions. The U.S. Constitution creates and empowers the three branches of government, sets forth the relationship between the states and the federal government, and establishes procedures for amending the Constitution.

1. *Supremacy*—The U.S. Constitution is the supreme law of the land. A law in violation of the Constitution or one of its amendments, no matter what its source, will be declared unconstitutional and will not be enforced. A state constitution, so long as it does not conflict with the U.S. Constitution, is the supreme law within the state's borders.

2. *The Bill of Rights*—The first ten amendments to the federal constitution are known as the Bill of Rights. These amendments embody a series of protections for individuals— and in some instances, business entities—against various types of government actions. The Bill of Rights originally limited only the powers of the federal government. After the Fourteenth Amendment was passed, the Supreme Court began to apply the protections of the Bill of Rights against state government actions.

3. *The courts and constitutional law*—The rights secured by the constitution are not absolute. The courts, and ultimately the Supreme Court, interpret and define the boundaries of the rights guaranteed by the Constitution.

Statutory Law

Statutory law consists of all laws enacted by the federal Congress, a state legislature, a municipality, or some other governing body. Laws passed by Congress and state legislatures are called *statutes*. Laws passed by local governing units (cities and counties) are called *ordinances*. Statutory law takes precedence over the common law.

Administrative Law

Administrative law consists of the rules, regulations, and decisions of administrative agencies at all levels of government.

1. *Agency creation*—Congress (and state legislatures) create administrative agencies by passing enabling legislation, which specifies the name, purpose, function, and powers of the agency being created.

2. *Administrative process*—Administrative agencies exercise three basic functions:

    a. Rulemaking—Agencies make rules governing activities within the areas of their authority. Typically, rulemaking procedure involves publishing notice of the proposed rulemaking, allowing a comment period, and then drafting the final rule.

    b. Investigation and enforcement—Agencies conduct investigations of regulated entities both to gather information and to monitor compliance with agency rules. When a regulated entity fails to comply with agency rules, the agency can take administrative action. Most violations are resolved through negotiated settlements.

    c. Adjudication—If a settlement cannot be reached, the agency may issue a formal complaint, and an administrative law judge (ALJ) will conduct a hearing and decide the issue. Either party can appeal the ALJ's order to the board or commission that governs the agency if dissatisfied. Most agency decisions can also then be appealed to a court.

3. *State administrative agencies*—State administrative agencies regulate state affairs. Often, a state agency is created as a parallel to a federal agency. If the actions of parallel state and federal agencies come into conflict, the federal agency will prevail, based on the supremacy clause of the U.S. Constitution.

4. *Paralegals in agency hearings*—Paralegals and other nonlawyers are permitted to represent clients before certain federal and state agencies.

(Continued)

Case Law and the Common Law Tradition

Case law consists of the decisions rendered by judges in cases that come before the court. Case law evolved through the common law tradition, which originated in England and was adopted in America during the colonial era.

1. *Stare decisis*—*Stare decisis* means "to stand on things decided" and is the doctrine of precedent, which is a defining characteristic of the common law system. Under this doctrine, judges are obligated to follow the earlier decisions of that court or a higher court within their jurisdiction if the same points arise again in litigation.

   a. A court will depart from precedent if the court decides that the precedent should no longer be followed, such as if the ruling was incorrect or does not apply in view of changes in the social or technological environment.

   b. If no precedent exists, the court considers the matter as a case of first impression and looks to other areas of law and public policy for guidance.

2. *Remedies at law versus remedies in equity*—In medieval England, two types of courts emerged: courts of law and courts of equity. Courts of law granted remedies at law (such as money damages). Courts of equity arose in response to the need for other types of relief. In the United States today, the same court can typically grant either legal or equitable remedies.

3. *Remedies in equity*—Remedies in equity, which are normally available only when the remedy at law (money damages) is inadequate, include the following:

   a. Specific performance—A court decree ordering a party to perform a contractual promise.

   b. Injunction—A court order directing someone to do or refrain from doing a particular act.

   c. Rescission—An action to undo a contract and return the parties to their original positions; all duties under the contract are abolished.

4. *Statutory law and the common law*—The common law governs all areas of law not covered by statutory law. As the body of statutory law grows to meet different needs, the common law covers fewer areas. Even if an area is governed by a statutory law, however, the common law plays an important role because statutes are interpreted and applied by the courts, and court decisions may become precedents that must be followed by lower courts within the jurisdiction.

5. *Case law terminology*—

   a. Case title and citation—A case title consists of the surnames of the parties, such as *Baranski v. Peretto*. The *v.* stands for *versus*. The citation indicates the volume and page number of the reporter in which the case can be found.

   b. Party—The plaintiff or the defendant. Some cases involve multiple parties—that is, more than one plaintiff or defendant.

   c. Judge and justice—These terms are often used synonymously. Usage of the terms varies among courts. The term *justice* is traditionally used to designate judges who sit on the bench of the United States Supreme Court.

   d. Opinion—A document containing the court's reasons for its decision, the rules of law that apply, and the judgment. If the opinion is not unanimous, a majority opinion—reflecting the view of the majority of judges or justices—will be written. Concurring and dissenting opinions may also be written.

6. *The adversarial system of justice*—American courts, like English courts, follow a system of justice in which the parties to a lawsuit are opponents, or adversaries, and present their cases in the light most favorable to themselves. The impartial decision maker (the judge or jury) then determines who wins and who loses based on the evidence presented.

National and International Law

1. *National law*—The law of a particular nation. National law differs from nation to nation because each nation's laws have evolved from that nation's unique customs and traditions. Most countries have one of the following types of legal systems:

   a. The common law system—Great Britain and the United States have a common law system. Generally, countries that were once colonies of Great Britain retained their English common law heritage after achieving independence. Under the common law, case precedents are judicially binding.

   b. The civil law system—Many of the continental European countries and the nations that were formerly their colonies have civil law systems. Based on Roman codified law, civil law (or code law) is an ordered grouping of legal principles enacted into law by a governing body. The primary source of law is a statutory code. Although important, case precedents are not judicially binding.

2. *International law*—A body of laws that govern relationships among nations. International law allows nations to enjoy harmonious relations with each other and to benefit economically from international trade. Sources of international law include international customs and traditions developed over time, treaties among nations, and international organizations and conferences.

QUESTIONS FOR REVIEW

1. What is law? Does everyone agree on a single definition of law?

2. What is constitutional law? If a state constitution conflicts with the U.S. Constitution, which constitution takes priority?

3. What is a statute? How is statutory law created? What is an ordinance? What happens when a state statute conflicts with a federal statute?

4. What is an administrative agency? How and why are such agencies created? What are their primary functions?

5. Where, when, and how did the common law tradition begin?

6. What does *stare decisis* mean? Why is it said that the doctrine of *stare decisis* is the cornerstone of English and American law?

7. What is the difference between courts of law and courts of equity? Why did courts of equity evolve?

8. What kinds of remedies could be granted by courts of law? Name three remedies that could be granted by courts of equity.

9. How has statutory law affected the common law? What happens to a common law doctrine once it is codified in a statute?

10. What impact does the adversarial nature of our legal system have on court proceedings and attorneys in the United States? What are some pros and cons of the adversarial system?

ETHICAL QUESTIONS

1. Lon Thompson is a paralegal who works for a New York law firm. One of the firm's clients wants to open a chain of restaurants (including bars) in Michigan, and Lon has been asked to research the Michigan statutes to find out the legal drinking age in that state. Lon looks in the hardbound volume of the Michigan statutes and sees that the legal drinking age is eighteen. Lon forgets to check the "pocket part," which is inserted into a "pocket" in the inside back cover of the book. The pocket part contains amendments, indicates if a statute has been repealed, and generally updates the law as described in the volume. Because of this oversight, Lon does not learn that the legal drinking age in Michigan was recently raised to twenty-one. He tells his supervising attorney that the legal drinking age in Michigan is eighteen, and the attorney passes that information on to the client. Has Lon violated any ethical rule? If so, which one? What consequences might the attorney face as a result of Lon's oversight? What consequences might Lon face?

2. John Scott, an attorney, has asked his legal assistant, Nanette Lynch, to do some research. Nanette is to research the state statutes to find out how many persons are required to witness a will. Nanette looks up the relevant state statute and finds it difficult to understand because it is so poorly written. After studying the statute for a while, Nanette decides that two witnesses are required and conveys this information to John. Actually, the statute requires that a will be witnessed by three persons or it will not be valid. John, relying on Nanette's conclusion, has two per-

sons witness a client's will the next day. Have John and Nanette violated any ethical rules? Explain.

3. Marilyn Clark works as a paralegal in a small general law practice. After work one day, she receives a telephone call from her Aunt May, who is in distress. Her Aunt May and Uncle Bill went to open their summer cottage and found that beavers had made a dam in the lake, which caused severe flooding on their property and in their basement. Uncle Bill is threatening to take his rifle and put an end to the beavers and their mess. Aunt May, an environmentalist, does not want Uncle Bill to shoot the beavers, so she asks Marilyn if it is illegal to shoot beavers. Marilyn knows that beavers are protected as an endangered species under federal or state environmental statutes. How should Marilyn answer this question?

4. A legal assistant in your law firm is working on a case law research project for a class that she is taking. She spends two hours doing case law research for her personal project using a computerized legal-research service that charges the firm several dollars per minute of online time. The legal assistant bills the two hours to a major client's file, assuming that no one will ever learn what she has done. You happen to be sitting at the terminal next to her, and you notice that she bills the time to one of the firm's clients. What should you do? What would you do if you learned that your supervising attorney had billed personal research time to a client's file?

PRACTICE QUESTIONS AND ASSIGNMENTS

1. Identify the constitutional amendment being violated in the following hypothetical situations:

   a. Jeremy's boss threatens to fire him if he does not work on Saturday nights, even though that is when he attends worship services.

   b. The city proposes an ordinance requiring that anyone caught stealing be punished by having his or her hand cut off for the first offense and the other hand cut off for the second offense.

   c. Because Robert's house is located in a poor neighborhood, the police decide that he must be a drug dealer. The police burst in and tear the place apart searching for drugs. They find nothing.

   d. The federal government bans all advertising of cigarettes.

2. In the following hypothetical situations, identify the type of case (criminal or civil), the remedy being sought, and whether it is a remedy at law or a remedy in equity:

   a. Beth files a petition with the court. She is seeking a decree that would undo a contract into which she entered.

   b. Jim sues Bob, seeking to be compensated for the cost of replacing several trees that Bob's dog has destroyed.

   c. Laurie seeks to have a contract for the sale of an antique Mercedes enforced.

   d. Sam files a petition seeking to prevent the electric company from cutting down a large tree on his property.

3. Identify the type of law (common law, constitutional law, statutory law, or administrative law) that applies in each of the following scenarios:

   a. Jean Gorman strongly disagrees with the U.S. government's decision to declare war on a foreign country. She places an antiwar sign in the window of her home. The city passes an ordinance that bans all such signs.

   b. An official of the state department of natural resources learns that the Ferris Widget Company has violated the state's Hazardous Waste Management Act. The official issues a complaint against the company for not properly handling and labeling its toxic waste.

   c. Mrs. Sams was walking down a busy street when two teenagers on in-line skates crashed into her because they weren't watching where they were going. As a result of the teenagers' conduct, Mrs. Sams broke her hip, and according to her doctor, she will never walk normally again. She sues the teenagers for damages.

   d. Joseph Barnes is arrested and charged with the crime of murder.

4. Which of the following legal specialties are governed primarily by statutory law?

   a. Tort law.

   b. Family law.

   c. Corporate law.

   d. Property law.

5. Which of the following is an example of an administrative law case?

   a. An employment-discrimination case that is filed with the EEOC.

   b. A family law case pending in circuit court.

   c. A dispute pending before the Internal Revenue Service.

   d. An issue of securities law.

   e. A tax matter pending before the Court of Federal Claims.

6. Identify whether each of the following is a national or international law concept:

   a. The rule that in Germany there is no speed limit on the *autobahn*.

   b. The French legal system, in which the doctrine of *stare decisis* does not apply.

   c. The World Trade Organization, which governs trade among all member nations.

   d. The documents governing and establishing the European Union.

QUESTIONS FOR CRITICAL ANALYSIS

1. Rosa Jennings is an experienced paralegal. One day, one of Rosa's neighbors, Lori Dolan, asks Rosa some general questions about American law. Lori wants to know, for example, what the Bill of Rights is and what is meant by the common law tradition. Write one paragraph on each amendment in the Bill of Rights and a one-paragraph description of the common law tradition. Explain these concepts in your own words and include examples.

2. The rights guaranteed by the U.S. Constitution would be of little significance if they were not enforced by the government. In view of this fact, is a written constitution really necessary? Would the rights and privileges enjoyed by Americans be any different if we did not have a written constitution?

3. Locate *Clinton v. Jones,* 520 U.S. 681, 117 S.Ct. 1636, 137 L.Ed.2d 945 (1997). Answer the following questions about the case:

   a. Read the first paragraph of the Supreme Court's syllabus, or summary. Who filed the lawsuit in the federal district court? For what reason(s)? What did the federal district court decide?

   b. The Eighth Circuit Court of Appeals affirmed, or upheld, the district court's decision in part and reversed it in part. Using the syllabus, a case summary preceding the court's opinion, explain what the Eighth Circuit Court of Appeals did.

   c. Find the heading, "*Held.*" Paragraph 2 contains subparagraphs (a)–(d). This is a summary of the Supreme Court's reasons for affirming the decision of the Eighth Circuit Court of Appeals. For each subparagraph, summarize the Court's reasoning in one to two sentences.

4. Laws in the United States come primarily from four sources: the federal Constitution and state constitutions, statutes, administrative agencies, and the courts. Why are there so many different sources? What might happen if there were not? How could the law be changed if only courts made the law?

5. Judges, particularly the justices of the United States Supreme Court, play a paramount role in the American legal system. Why is this?

6. Why does the body of statutory law continue to expand?

7. Why do legislatures delegate authority to administrative agencies? How is the delegation of authority to agencies accomplished? Give examples of two federal administrative agencies and the type of work that paralegals might perform with respect to the areas regulated by these agencies.

8. Of what does law consist? How does common law fit intothe definition of law given in this chapter? How did the common law develop?

9. What does the phrase *stare decisis* mean? What obligation does *stare decisis* impose on judges? How did this doctrine develop? What do courts do when declining to follow precedent? What do they do when there is no precedent?

10. Why were the courts of law and the courts of equity separate? Are they still separate? How do legal and equitable remedies differ?

 ## PROJECTS

1. Look at the U.S. Constitution in Appendix J of this text. Identify the amendment and quote the relevant language in the Bill of Rights that gives U.S. citizens the following rights and protections:

   a. The right to freely exercise one's religion.

   b. Protection against unreasonable searches and seizures.

   c. Protection against self-incrimination.

   d. The right to counsel in criminal prosecutions.

   e. The right to free speech.

2. Look in the white pages of your local telephone directory for your U.S. representative and senator. Write down their names, addresses, and telephone numbers. Consider writing or calling their offices to request information on internships.

3. Look in your local telephone directory for listings under the name of your state. Write down the names of three administrative agencies listed there and see if you can determine from their names what areas or activities they regulate. Write down your conclusions.

4. Find out if your state's courts use different procedures for cases that involve equity matters than for cases that do not. Are there any trial courts in your state that cannot grant equitable remedies?

5. Read through the sample court case presented as Exhibit 17.10 in Chapter 17. Identify the case name, the citation, the parties, the judge or justice who authored the opinion, the type of opinion (for example, majority, unanimous, and so on), and the first five words of the opinion.

6. Research the North American Free Trade Agreement (NAFTA) in periodicals, such as *Time* magazine or *Newsweek*. Write a one-page paper explaining what the treaty involves and who the signatories are.

 ## USING INTERNET RESOURCES

1. Go to FindLaw's home page at **http://www.findlaw.com**. This site offers links to many of the federal and state sources of law that you have read about in this chapter. In this exercise, you will be examining state laws, so select "Cases and Codes" and then click on "U.S. State Laws." The page you reach will list all of the states in alphabetical order. Open the site for your state, browse through the state sources of law that can be accessed online, and then answer the following questions:

   a. Were you able to access the text of your state's constitution?

   b. Did the site include your state's code (compilation of statutes) and administrative regulations?

   c. What other primary materials were included in the site?

   d. Now browse through the site for three other states. How does your state's site compare with those of other states in terms of comprehensiveness and ease of use?

2. A database of the United States Supreme Court, located at **http://www.usscplus.com**, contains a description of the Court's role in interpreting the Constitution. Go to this

Web site, click on "Supreme Court FAQ," and then click on "The Court and Constitutional Interpretation." What is judicial review? What role did the case *Marbury v. Madison* have in shaping the Supreme Court's power of judicial review? Can the Supreme Court give "advisory opinions"? Why or why not?

3. Go to **http://www.psr.keele.ac.uk/const.htm**, a Web page that links users to international treaties and national constitutions. Select a country that interests you. Does the country have a constitution? When was it adopted? Can

you view it in any language other than English? How many categories of international treaties are available through this site? Click on "Guide to International Trade Conventions on the Internet" and explore the page that opens. How many multilateral and regional agreements are listed there? What other types of international resources can be accessed from this page?

4.  For additional resources, visit our Web site at **http://www.paralegal.delmar. cengage.com**.

END NOTES

1. Twenty dollars was forty days' pay for the average person when the Bill of Rights was written.

2. 47 U.S.C. Section 223(d)(1)(B). Specifically, the CDA prohibited any obscene or indecent message that "depicts or describes, in terms patently offensive as measured by contemporary community standards, sexual or excretory activities or organs." (You will read about the citation form for federal laws in Chapter 17.)

3. 521 U.S. 844, 117 S.Ct. 2329, 138 L.Ed.2d 874 (1997).

4. For example, the Child Online Protection Act (COPA) of 1998 banned material "harmful to minors" distributed without some kind of age-verification system to separate adult and minor users. In 2002, the Supreme Court upheld a lower court's injunction suspending the act. See *Ashcroft v. American Civil Liberties Union*, 535 U.S. 564, 122 S.Ct. 1700, 152 L.Ed.2d 771 (2002). See also *American Civil Liberties Union v. Ashcroft*, 322 F.3d 240 (3d Cir. 2003).

5. *Gibbons v. Ogden*, 22 U.S. (9 Wheat.) 1, 6 L.Ed. 23 (1824).

6. *Wickard v. Filburn*, 317 U.S. 111, 63 S.Ct. 82, 87 L.Ed. 122 (1942).

7. 15 U.S.C. Sections 41–48.

8. 5. U.S.C. Sections 551–706.

9. Pronounced *stahr-ee* dih-*si*-ses.

10. 347 U.S. 483, 74 S.Ct. 686, 98 L.Ed. 873 (1954).

11. See, for example, *Plessy v. Ferguson*, 163 U.S. 537, 16 S.Ct. 1138, 41 L.Ed. 256 (1896). In *Plessy*, the United States Supreme Court upheld a Louisiana statute providing for separate railway cars for whites and African Americans. The Court held that the statute did not violate the U.S. Constitution, which mandates equal protection under the laws, because the statute provided for equal facilities for African Americans. Lower courts interpreted this decision to apply to other types of facilities as well, and the "separate-but-equal doctrine" prevailed until the *Brown* decision in 1954.

12. *In re Baby M*, 217 N.J.Super. 313, 525 A.2d 1128 (1987).

13. Pronounced reh-*sih*-zhen.

THE COURT SYSTEM AND ALTERNATIVE DISPUTE RESOLUTION

CHAPTER

CHAPTER OUTLINE

Introduction

Basic Judicial Requirements

State Court Systems

The Federal Court System

Alternative Dispute Resolution

AFTER COMPLETING THIS CHAPTER, YOU WILL KNOW:

▶ The requirements that must be met before a lawsuit can be brought in a particular court by a particular party.

▶ The difference between jurisdiction and venue.

▶ The types of courts that make up a typical state court system and the different functions of trial courts and appellate courts.

▶ The organization of the federal court system and the relationship between state and federal jurisdiction.

▶ How cases reach the United States Supreme Court.

▶ The various ways in which disputes can be resolved outside the court system.

INTRODUCTION

As explained in Chapter 5, American law is based on numerous elements—the federal Constitution and state constitutions, statutes passed by federal and state legislatures, administrative law, the case decisions and legal principles that form the common law, and, to an extent, the laws of other nations and international law. But the laws would be meaningless without the courts to interpret and apply them, and for this reason the court system is a vital component of the American legal system.

Paralegals working in all areas of the law, and particularly litigation paralegals, need to have a basic understanding of the different types of courts that make up the American court system. Even though there are fifty-two court systems—one for each of the fifty states, one for the District of Columbia, and a federal system—similarities abound. Keep in mind that the federal courts are not superior to the state courts. They are simply an independent court system, which derives its authority from Article III, Section 2, of the U.S. Constitution.[1]

In the first part of this chapter, we examine the structure of the American court system. Because of the costs, in both time and money, and the potential publicity attending court trials, many individuals and firms today are turning to alternative methods of dispute resolution that allow parties to resolve their disputes outside of court. In some cases, parties are required by the courts to try to resolve their disputes by one of these methods before they can take their cases to court. In the latter part of this chapter, we provide an overview of these alternative methods of dispute resolution and the role that attorneys and paralegals play in facilitating out-of-court dispute settlements.

BASIC JUDICIAL REQUIREMENTS

Before a lawsuit can be brought before a court, certain requirements must be met. We examine here these important requirements and some of the basic features of the American system of justice.

Types of Jurisdiction

In Latin, *juris* means "law," and *diction* means "to speak." Thus, "the power to speak the law" is the literal meaning of the term **jurisdiction**. Before any court can hear a case, it must have jurisdiction over the person against whom the suit is brought or over the property involved in the suit. The court must also have jurisdiction over the subject matter.

jurisdiction
The authority of a court to hear and decide a specific action.

Jurisdiction over Persons

Generally, a court can exercise personal jurisdiction (*in personam* jurisdiction) over residents of a certain geographical area. A state trial court, for example, normally has jurisdictional authority over residents within the state or within a particular area of the state, such as a county or district. A state's highest court (often called the state supreme court[2]) has jurisdictional authority over all residents within the state.

In some cases, under the authority of a **long arm statute**, a state court can exercise personal jurisdiction over certain nonresident defendants based on activities that took place within the state. Before a court can exercise jurisdiction over a nonresident under a long arm statute, though, it must be demonstrated that the nonresident had sufficient contacts (*minimum contacts*) with the state to justify the jurisdiction. ▶ **EXAMPLE 6.1** If a California citizen committed a wrong within the state of Arizona, such as causing an automobile injury or selling defective goods, an Arizona state court usually could exercise jurisdiction over the California citizen. Similarly, a state may exercise personal jurisdiction over a nonresident defendant who is sued for breaching a contract that was formed within the state. ◀

long arm statute
A state statute that permits a state to obtain jurisdiction over nonresident individuals or corporations, however, must have certain "minimum contacts" with that state for the statute to apply.

In regard to corporations, the minimum-contacts requirement is usually met if the corporation does business within the state. ▶ **EXAMPLE 6.2** A Maine corporation that has a branch office or manufacturing plant in Georgia has sufficient minimum contacts with the state of Georgia to allow a Georgia court to exercise jurisdiction over the Maine corporation. If the Maine corporation advertises and sells its products in Georgia, those activities may also suffice to meet the minimum-contacts requirements. ◀ A state court may also be able to exercise jurisdiction over a corporation in another country if it can be demonstrated that the alien corporation has met the minimum-contacts test. ▶ **EXAMPLE 6.3** Suppose that an Italian corporation markets its products through an American distributor. If the corporation knew that its products would be distributed to local markets throughout the United States, it could be sued in any state by a plaintiff who was injured by one of the products. ◀

Jurisdiction over Property

A court can also exercise jurisdiction over property that is located within its boundaries. This kind of jurisdiction is known as *in rem* jurisdiction, or "jurisdiction over the thing." ▶ **EXAMPLE 6.4** Suppose that a dispute arises over the ownership of a boat in dry dock in Fort Lauderdale, Florida. The boat is owned by an Ohio resident, over whom a Florida court normally cannot exercise personal jurisdiction. The other party to the dispute is a resident of Nebraska. In this situation, a lawsuit concerning the boat could be brought in a Florida state court on the basis of the court's *in rem* jurisdiction. ◀

Jurisdiction over Subject Matter

Jurisdiction over subject matter is a limitation on the types of cases a court can hear. In both the state and federal court systems, there are courts of *general jurisdiction* and courts of *limited jurisdiction*. The basis for the distinction lies in the subject matter of cases heard. A probate court—a state court that handles only matters relating to the transfer of a person's assets and obligations on that person's death, including matters relating to the custody and guardianship of children—is an example of a court with limited subject-matter jurisdiction. One type of federal court of limited subject-matter jurisdiction is a bankruptcy court. Bankruptcy courts handle only bankruptcy proceedings, which are governed by federal bankruptcy law (bankruptcy law allows debtors to obtain relief from their debts when they cannot make ends meet). In contrast, a court of general jurisdiction can decide virtually any type of case.

The subject-matter jurisdiction of a court is usually defined in the statute or constitution creating the court. In both the state and federal court systems, a court's subject-matter jurisdiction can be limited not only by the subject of the lawsuit but also by the amount in controversy, by whether a case is a felony (a more serious type of crime) or a misdemeanor (a less serious type of crime), or by whether the proceeding is a trial or an appeal.

Original and Appellate Jurisdiction

The distinction between courts of original jurisdiction and courts of appellate jurisdiction normally lies in whether the case is being heard for the first time. Courts having original jurisdiction are courts of the first instance, or trial courts—that is, courts in which lawsuits begin, trials take place, and evidence is presented. In the federal court system, the *district courts* are trial courts. In the various state court systems, the trial courts are known by different names. The key point here is that normally, any court having original jurisdiction is known as a trial court. Courts having appellate jurisdiction act as reviewing courts, or appellate courts. In general, cases can be brought before them only on appeal from an order or a judgment of a trial court or other lower court. State and federal trial and appellate courts will be discussed more fully later in this chapter.

---

probate court
A court having jurisdiction over proceedings concerning the settlement of a person's estate.

bankruptcy court
A federal court of limited jurisdiction that hears only bankruptcy proceedings.

original jurisdiction
The power of a court to take a case, try it, and decide it.

trial court
A court in which cases begin and in which questions of fact are examined.

appellate jurisdiction
The power of a court to hear and decide an appeal; that is, the power and authority of a court to review cases that have already been tried in a lower court and to make decisions about them without actually holding a trial. This process is called *appellate review*.

appellate court
A court that reviews decisions made by lower courts, such as trial courts; a court of appeals.

Developing Paralegal Skills

CHOICE OF COURTS: STATE OR FEDERAL?

Susan Radtke, a lawyer specializing in the area of employment discrimination, and her legal assistant, Joan Dunbar, are meeting with a new client. The client wants to sue her former employer for gender discrimination. The client complained to her employer when she was passed over for a promotion. She was fired, she claims, as a result of her complaint. The client appears to have a strong case, because several of her former co-workers have agreed to testify that they heard the employer say on many occasions that he would never promote a woman to a managerial position.

Because both state and federal laws prohibit gender discrimination, the case could be brought in either state or federal court. The client tells Susan that because of Susan's experience, she wants her to decide whether the case should be filed in a state or federal court. Joan will be drafting the complaint, so Susan and Joan discuss the pros and cons of filing the case in each court. Joan reviews a list of considerations with Susan.

TIPS FOR CHOOSING A COURT

- Review the jurisdiction of each court.
- Evaluate the strengths and weaknesses of the case.
- Evaluate the remedy sought.
- Evaluate the jury pool available for each court.
- Evaluate the likelihood of winning in each court.
- Evaluate the length of time it will take each court to decide the case.
- Evaluate the costs and procedural rules involved in filing in each court.

Jurisdiction of the Federal Courts

Because the federal government is a government of limited powers, the jurisdiction of the federal courts is limited. Article III of the U.S. Constitution establishes the boundaries of federal judicial power. Section 2 of Article III states that "[t]he judicial Power shall extend to all Cases, in Law and Equity, arising under this Constitution, the Laws of the United States, and Treaties made, or which shall be made, under their Authority."

Federal Questions

Whenever a plaintiff's cause of action is based, at least in part, on the U.S. Constitution, a treaty, or a federal law, then a **federal question** arises, and the case comes under the judicial power of the federal courts. Any lawsuit involving a federal question can originate in a federal district (trial) court. People who claim that their constitutional rights have been violated can begin their suits in a federal district court.

Diversity Jurisdiction

Federal district courts can also exercise original jurisdiction over cases involving **diversity of citizenship**. Such cases may arise between (1) citizens of different states, (2) a foreign country and citizens of a state or of different states, or (3) citizens of a state and citizens or subjects of a foreign country. The amount in controversy must be more than $75,000 before a

federal question
A question that pertains to the U.S. Constitution, acts of Congress, or treaties. A federal question provides a basis for jurisdiction by the federal courts. This jurisdiction is authorized by Article III, Section 2, of the Constitution.

diversity of citzenship
Under Article III, Section 2, of the Constitution, a basis for federal district court jurisdiction over a lawsuit between (1) citizens of different states, (2) a foreign country and citizens of a state or states, or (3) citizens of a state and citizens or subjects of a foreign country. The amount in controversy must be more than $75,000 before a federal court can exercise jurisdiction in such cases.

federal court can take jurisdiction in such cases. For purposes of diversity-of-citizenship jurisdiction, a corporation is a citizen of the state in which it is incorporated and of the state in which its principal place of business is located. A case involving diversity of citizenship can be filed in the appropriate federal district court.

▶ **EXAMPLE 6.5** Maria Ramirez, a citizen of Florida, was walking near a busy street in Tallahassee, Florida, one day when a large crate flew off a passing truck and hit and seriously injured her. She incurred numerous medical expenses and could not work for six months. She now wants to sue the trucking firm for $500,000 in damages. The trucking firm's headquarters are in Georgia, although the company does business in Florida.

In this situation, Maria could bring suit in a Florida court because she is a resident of Florida, the trucking firm does business in Florida, and that is where the accident occurred. She could also bring suit in a Georgia court, because a Georgia court could exercise jurisdiction over the trucking firm, which is headquartered in that state. As a third alternative, Maria could bring suit in a federal court because the requirements of diversity jurisdiction have been met—the lawsuit involves parties from different states, Florida and Georgia, and the amount in controversy (the damages Maria is seeking) exceeds $75,000. ◀

Note that in a case based on a federal question, a federal court will apply federal law. In a case based on diversity of citizenship, however, a federal court will normally apply the law of the state in which the court sits. This is because cases based on diversity of citizenship generally do not involve activities that are regulated by the federal government. Therefore, federal laws do not apply, and state law will govern the issue.

Exclusive versus Concurrent Jurisdiction

When both federal and state courts have the power to hear a case, as is true in suits involving diversity of citizenship (such as Maria's case described in Example 6.5), **concurrent jurisdiction** exists. When cases can be tried only in federal courts or only in state courts, **exclusive jurisdiction** exists. Federal courts have exclusive jurisdiction in cases involving federal crimes, bankruptcy, patents, trademarks, and copyrights; in most class-action lawsuits[3]; in suits against the United States; and in some areas of admiralty law (law governing transportation on the seas and ocean waters). States also have exclusive jurisdiction in certain subject matters—for example, in divorce and adoptions. The concepts of concurrent and exclusive jurisdiction are illustrated in Exhibit 6.1.

concurrent jurisdiction
Jurisdiction that exists when two different courts have the power to hear a case. For example, some cases can be heard in either a federal or a state court.

exclusive jurisdiction
Jurisdiction that exists when a case can be heard only in a particular court, such as a federal court.

EXHIBIT 6.1
Exclusive and Concurrent Jurisdiction

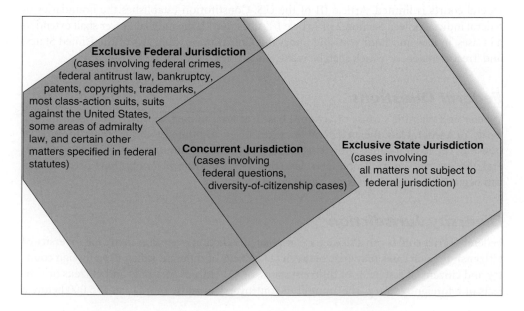

Exclusive Federal Jurisdiction
(cases involving federal crimes, federal antitrust law, bankruptcy, patents, copyrights, trademarks, most class-action suits, suits against the United States, some areas of admiralty law, and certain other matters specified in federal statutes)

Concurrent Jurisdiction
(cases involving federal questions, diversity-of-citizenship cases)

Exclusive State Jurisdiction
(cases involving all matters not subject to federal jurisdiction)

When concurrent jurisdiction exists, a party has a choice of whether to bring a suit in, for example, a federal or a state court. The party's lawyer will consider several factors in counseling the party as to which choice is preferable. The lawyer may prefer to litigate the case in a state court because he or she is more familiar with the state court's procedures, or perhaps the attorney believes that the state's judge or jury would be more sympathetic to the client and the case.

Alternatively, the lawyer may advise the client to sue in federal court. Perhaps the state court's **docket** (the court's schedule listing the cases to be heard) is crowded, and the case could be brought to trial sooner in a federal court. Perhaps some feature of federal procedure could offer an advantage in the client's case. Other important considerations include the law in an available jurisdiction, how that law has been applied in the jurisdiction's courts, and what the results in similar cases have been in that jurisdiction.

docket
The list of cases entered on the court's calendar and thus scheduled to be heard by the court.

Jurisdiction in Cyberspace

The Internet's capacity to bypass political and geographic boundaries undercuts traditional basic limitations on a court's authority to exercise jurisdiction. These limits include a party's contacts with a court's geographic jurisdiction. As already discussed, for a court to compel a defendant to come before it, there must be at least minimum contacts—the presence of a company's salesperson within the state, for example. Are there sufficient minimum contacts if the only connection to a jurisdiction is an ad on the Web originating from a remote location?

The "Sliding-Scale" Standard

Gradually, the courts are developing a standard—called a "sliding-scale" standard—for determining when the exercise of jurisdiction over an out-of-state party is proper. In developing this standard, the courts have identified three types of Internet business contacts: (1) substantial business conducted over the Internet (with contracts or sales, for example), (2) some interactivity through a Web site, and (3) passive advertising. Jurisdiction is proper for the first category, is improper for the third, and may or may not be appropriate for the second.

International Jurisdictional Issues

Because the Internet is international in scope, international jurisdictional issues understandably have come to the fore. As noted in Chapter 5, what seems to be emerging in the world's courts is a standard that echoes the requirement of minimum contacts applied by the U.S. courts. Most courts are indicating that minimum contacts—doing business within the jurisdiction, for example—are enough to compel a defendant to appear and that the defendant's physical presence is not required for the court to exercise jurisdiction.[4] The effect of this standard is that a company may have to comply with the laws of any jurisdiction in which it targets customers for its products.

Venue

Jurisdiction has to do with whether a court has authority to hear a case involving specific persons, property, or subject matter. **Venue**[5] is concerned with the most appropriate location for a trial. For example, two state courts may have the authority to exercise jurisdiction over a case, but it may be more appropriate or convenient to hear the case in one court than in the other.

venue
The geographical district in which an action is tried and from which the jury is selected.

Basically, the concept of venue reflects the policy that a court trying a suit should be in the geographic neighborhood (usually the county) in which the parties involved in the lawsuit reside or in which the incident leading to the lawsuit occurred. Pretrial publicity or other factors, though, may require a change of venue to another community, especially in criminal cases in which the defendant's right to a fair and impartial jury has been impaired.

▶ **EXAMPLE 6.6**   Suppose that a bomb has exploded in a federal building in Oklahoma City, killing more than 160 persons and injuring hundreds of others. Two defendants are indicted in connection with the bombing and scheduled for trial in an Oklahoma state court. Given these facts, the defense attorneys may argue—and the court will likely agree—that the defendants could not receive a fair trial in Oklahoma because an impartial jury could not be chosen. Although the Oklahoma court has jurisdiction, the court will order a change of venue to another location for trial. ◀

Standing to Sue

> **standing to sue**
> A sufficient stake in a controversy to justify bringing a lawsuit. To have standing to sue, the plaintiff must demonstrate that he or she has been either injured or threatened with injury.

To bring a lawsuit before a court, a party must have **standing to sue**, or a sufficient "stake" in a matter to justify seeking relief through the court system. In other words, a party must have a legally protected and tangible interest at stake in the litigation in order to have standing. The party bringing the lawsuit must have suffered a harm as a result of the action about which he or she complained. ▶ **EXAMPLE 6.7**   Assume that a friend of one of your firm's clients was injured in a car accident caused by defective brakes. The client's friend would have standing to sue the automobile manufacturer for damages. The client, however, would not have standing because the client was not injured and therefore has no legally recognizable stake in the controversy. ◀

Note that in some cases, a person has standing to sue on behalf of another person.

▶ **EXAMPLE 6.8**   Suppose that a child suffered serious injuries as a result of a defectively manufactured toy. Because the child is a minor, a lawsuit could be brought on his or her behalf by another person, such as the child's parent or legal guardian. ◀

Standing to sue also requires that the controversy at issue be justiciable. A **justiciable**[6] **controversy** is one that is real and substantial, as opposed to hypothetical or academic.

> **justiciable controversy**
> A controversy that is real and substantial, as opposed to hypothetical or academic.

▶ **EXAMPLE 6.9**   In the scenario discussed in Example 6.8, the child's parent could not sue the toy manufacturer merely on the ground that the toy was defective. The issue would become justiciable only if the child had actually been injured due to a defect in the toy as marketed. In other words, the parent normally could not ask the court to determine what damages might be obtained *if* the child had been injured, because this would be merely a hypothetical question. ◀

Judicial Procedures

On the Web

The Federal Rules of Civil Procedure are available online at **http://www.law.cornell.edu/rules/frcp/index.html**.

Litigation in court, from the moment a lawsuit is initiated until the final resolution of the case, must follow specifically designated procedural rules. The procedural rules for federal court cases are set forth in the Federal Rules of Civil Procedure. State rules, which are often similar to the federal rules, vary from state to state—and even from court to court within a given state. Rules of procedure also differ in criminal and civil cases. Paralegals who work for trial lawyers need to be familiar with the procedural rules of the relevant courts. Because judicial procedures will be examined in detail in Chapters 13 through 16, we do not discuss them here.

BASIC JUDICIAL REQUIREMENTS AND THE PARALEGAL

Paralegals should be familiar with the concepts of jurisdiction, venue, and standing to sue because these concepts affect pretrial litigation procedures. For example, a defendant in a lawsuit may claim that the court in which the plaintiff filed the lawsuit cannot exercise jurisdiction over the matter—or over the defendant or the defendant's property. If you are

Ethics Watch!

MEETING PROCEDURAL DEADLINES

One of the paralegal's most important responsibilities is making sure that court deadlines are met. For example, suppose that your supervising attorney asks you to file with the court a motion to dismiss (a document requesting the court to dismiss a lawsuit for a specific reason). You know that the deadline for filing the motion is three days away. You plan to deliver the motion to the court the next day, so you don't place a reminder note on your calendar. In the meantime, you place the motion in the client's file. The next morning, you arrive at work and immediately are called to help your supervising attorney with last-minute trial preparations on another case. You are busy all afternoon interviewing witnesses in still another case. You have totally forgotten about the motion to dismiss and do not think of it again until a week later—when the deadline for filing the motion has passed. Because you forgot to file the motion, your supervising attorney has breached the duty of competence. How can you make sure that you remember important deadlines? The answer is simple: *always* enter deadlines on the office calendaring system and *always* check your calendar several times a day. Also, realize that missed deadlines provide the basis for many malpractice suits against attorneys.

working on behalf of the defendant, you may be asked to draft a motion to dismiss the case on this ground. You may also be asked to draft a legal memorandum in support of the motion, outlining the legal reasons why the court cannot exercise jurisdiction over the case. (Motions to dismiss and supporting documents are discussed in Chapter 13.) Additionally, a party to a lawsuit may request that a case filed in a state court be "removed" to a federal court (if there is a basis for federal jurisdiction) or vice versa. You may be asked to draft a document requesting a change of venue (or objecting to an opponent's request for a change of venue) or requesting that the court dismiss the case because the plaintiff lacks standing to sue.

If you work for a plaintiff's attorney, you might be asked to draft a complaint to initiate a lawsuit. Once the attorney reviews the facts with you, he or she may expect you to know whether concurrent jurisdiction exists. If concurrent jurisdiction exists, the attorney may expect you to ask whether the suit should be filed in a state or a federal court. If concurrent jurisdiction does not exist, the attorney may assume that you know in which court the case will be filed and that you know how to prepare the complaint for the appropriate court.

Recall from Chapter 1 that paralegal education and training emphasize both substantive and procedural law. A paralegal can be a valuable member of a legal team if he or she has adequate knowledge of the procedural requirements relating to litigation and to different types of legal proceedings. You will read in detail about litigation procedures in Chapters 13 through 16.

STATE COURT SYSTEMS

Each state has its own system of courts, and no two state systems are the same. As Exhibit 6.2 on the next page indicates, there may be several levels, or tiers, of courts within a state court system: (1) state trial courts of general jurisidiction and limited jurisdiction, (2) appellate

EXHIBIT 6.2
Levels in a State Court System

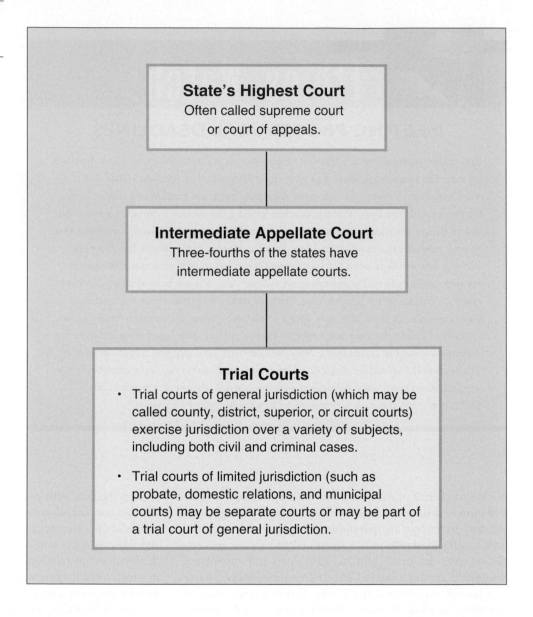

State's Highest Court
Often called supreme court
or court of appeals.

Intermediate Appellate Court
Three-fourths of the states have
intermediate appellate courts.

Trial Courts
- Trial courts of general jurisdiction (which may be called county, district, superior, or circuit courts) exercise jurisdiction over a variety of subjects, including both civil and criminal cases.

- Trial courts of limited jurisdiction (such as probate, domestic relations, and municipal courts) may be separate courts or may be part of a trial court of general jurisdiction.

On the Web

State court systems vary widely from state to state. To learn about your state's court system, go to the National Center for State Courts' Web site at **http://www.ncsconline.org** and select "Court Web Sites" at the bottom of the screen.

courts, and (3) the state's highest court (often called the state supreme court). Judges in the state court system are usually elected by the voters for a specified term.

Generally, any person who is a party to a lawsuit has the opportunity to plead the case before a trial court and then, if he or she loses, before at least one level of appellate court. Finally, if a federal statute or federal constitutional issue is involved in the decision of a state supreme court, that decision may be further appealed to the United States Supreme Court.

Trial Courts

Trial courts are exactly what their name implies—courts in which trials are held and testimony taken. You will read in detail about trial procedures in Chapter 15. In that chapter, we follow a hypothetical case through the various stages of a trial. Briefly, a trial court is presided over by a judge, who issues a decision on the matter before the court. If the trial is a jury trial (many trials are held without juries), the jury will decide the outcome of factual disputes, and the judge will issue a judgment based on the jury's conclusion. During the

LITIGATION PARALEGAL

Lee A. Paige, CLA, is a senior legal assistant in the Los Angeles office of the law firm of Morrison & Foerster, LLP, where he works in the intellectual property, labor, and litigation practice groups. Paige holds a bachelor's degree in journalism from Langston University and a master's degree in communications from the University of Oklahoma. He is also a graduate of the University of West Los Angeles School of Paralegal Studies and holds an ABA-approved paralegal certificate, as well as specialist certificates in civil litigation, environmental law, real estate, and intellectual property.

Paige has twenty years of paralegal experience. During those years, he has served the Office of the Los Angeles County District Attorney, the Los Angeles County Public Defender, and several prominent Los Angeles law firms. He served on the board of directors of the Los Angeles Paralegal Association (LAPA) for nine years and was president of LAPA in 1998.

Paige is a frequent guest speaker and lecturer for elementary schools, high schools, colleges, universities, and paralegal schools throughout Southern California. He has won several awards and honors for his excellent work and volunteer activities and was featured on the cover of the June 2000 issue of the national magazine Legal Assistant Today.

> *"One success tip that I always give to students and working paralegals is to never stop learning."*

What do you like best about your work?

"I very much enjoy research! To some paralegals, such a statement might sound a little crazy, but I really do enjoy researching more than any other part of my job. As a former news writer, my natural penchant for 'digging' for a story comes in quite handy. It is very gratifying to me for an attorney to give me a problem and rely on me to find the answer. I get quite an adrenaline rush from 'fact-finding' missions and a wealth of satisfaction from 'delivering the goods' that are the result of my computerized or manual research."

What is the greatest challenge that you face in your area of work?

"The greatest challenge I currently face is keeping ahead of our ever-mounting litigation schedule. I primarily assist a partner in my firm who juggles a huge caseload. My boss is an excellent attorney, but, as is the case with many litigators, he is frequently overloaded. His secretary and I must be constantly vigilant with his weekly calendar and daily schedule to prevent time conflicts and make sure that he does not miss any crucial dates or court appearances."

What advice do you have for would-be paralegals in your area of work?

"I frequently lecture at local paralegal schools, and the advice I normally give paralegal students is to focus their studies on areas of law that are of interest to them. This will give them an idea of where their real strengths are. I work in litigation, but it is not for everyone. Litigation is very complex and demanding, and if students go into it blindly they may be disappointed. Many people enter into the paralegal profession as a second career, perhaps as a result of a layoff, forced relocation, or downsizing. Other people see becoming a paralegal as a way of getting a 'foot in the door' of the legal profession, and still others use it as a proving ground in anticipation of going on to law school and becoming an attorney. Whatever their reasons for becoming paralegals, I always advise would-be paralegals to investigate the profession before they jump in, and to only attend an ABA-approved school."

What are some tips for success as a paralegal in your area of work?

"One success tip that I always give to students and working paralegals is to never stop learning. Paralegals should voluntarily take additional classes and seminars beyond their paralegal certificates. Such classes will keep them abreast of new developments in law and procedure that can affect their ability to assist their attorneys in the representation of their clients and increase their value to their employers."

trial, the attorney for each side introduces evidence (such as relevant documents, exhibits, and testimony of witnesses) in support of his or her client's position. Each attorney is given an opportunity to cross-examine witnesses for the opposing party and challenge evidence introduced by the opposing party.

State trial courts have either general or limited jurisdiction. Trial courts that have general jurisdiction as to subject matter may be called county, district, superior, or circuit courts.[7] The jurisdiction of these courts is often determined by the size of the county in which the court sits. State trial courts of general jurisdiction have jurisdiction over a wide variety of subjects, including both civil disputes (such as landlord-tenant matters or contract claims) and criminal prosecutions. In some states, trial courts of general jurisdiction may hear appeals from courts of limited jurisdiction.

Courts with limited jurisdiction as to subject matter are often called special inferior trial courts or minor judiciary courts. Courts of limited jurisdiction include small claims courts, which hear only civil cases involving claims of less than a certain amount, such as $5,000; domestic relations courts, which handle only divorce actions, paternity suits, and child-custody and support cases; local municipal courts, which mainly handle traffic violations; and probate courts, which, as previously mentioned, handle the administration of wills, estate-settlement problems, and related matters.

Appellate, or Reviewing, Courts

After a trial, the parties have the opportunity to file an appeal to a higher court if they are unsatisfied with the trial court's ruling. Practically speaking, however, parties are unlikely to file an appeal unless a reversible error was committed by the trial court that would cause the appellate court to overturn the trial court's decision. Usually, appellate courts do not look at questions of *fact* (such as whether a party did, in fact, commit a certain action, such as burning a flag) but at questions of *law* (such as whether the act of flag-burning is a form of speech protected by the First Amendment to the Constitution). Only a judge, not a jury, can rule on questions of law.

Appellate courts normally defer to a trial court's findings on questions of fact because the trial court judge and jury were in a better position to evaluate testimony by directly observing witnesses' gestures, demeanor, and nonverbal behavior during the trial. When a case is appealed, an appellate panel of three or more judges reviews the record (including the written transcript of the trial) of the case on appeal, and the record does not include these nonverbal elements. Generally, then, appellate courts look for errors of law rather than evaluating the trial court judge's or jury's conclusions on questions of fact.

Every state has at least one appellate court, which may be either an intermediate appellate court or the state's highest court.

Intermediate Appellate Courts

About three-fourths of the states have intermediate appellate courts, or courts of appeals. The subject-matter jurisdiction of these courts is substantially limited to hearing appeals. Usually, appellate courts review the records, read appellate briefs filed by the parties, and listen to the oral arguments presented by the parties' attorneys. Then the panel of judges renders a decision. If a party is unsatisfied with the appellate court's ruling, that party can appeal to the highest state court.

Highest State Courts

The highest appellate court in a state is usually called the supreme court but may be called by some other name. For example, in both New York and Maryland, the highest state court is called the court of appeals. The decisions of each state's highest court on all questions of

Ethics Watch!

EXPECT THE UNEXPECTED

For many paralegals, much of their time seems to be devoted to meeting deadlines. As you've learned in earlier chapters of this text, because every attorney has a duty to give competent representation, missing a deadline can subject an attorney to a lawsuit for breaching this duty. As a paralegal, you share in this duty. In other words, you are obligated to ensure that all deadlines are met. But how can you meet a deadline if it is changed unexpectedly?

For example, suppose that you are working on a set of jury instructions for a trial. It is now late Tuesday afternoon, and the attorney with whom you work has told you that he doesn't expect the judge to instruct the jury until Thursday. You decide to finish the jury instructions today, even though you could put it off until tomorrow. Before you leave, you place the completed instructions on the attorney's desk.

As it turns out, you made a wise decision. The next morning, just after you arrive at work at 9:00 A.M., the attorney informs you that the judge is starting the trial an hour earlier today because her docket is so congested. She plans to instruct the jury this morning between 9:30 and 10:00 A.M. Although you cannot prepare for all unexpected events, you can avoid many problems simply by not putting off work until the last minute.

state law are final. Only when issues of federal law are involved can a decision made by a state's highest court be overruled by the United States Supreme Court.

> **On the Web**
>
> Superior Information Services, a Michigan Internet consulting company, provides a single site from which you can access Web pages for trial courts. Go to **http://www.courts.net**.

STATE COURT SYSTEMS AND THE PARALEGAL

Because each state has its own unique system of courts, you will need to become familiar with the court system of your particular state. What is the official name of your state's highest court? How many intermediate state appellate courts are in your state, and to which of these courts should appeals from your local trial court or courts be appealed? What courts in your area have jurisdiction over what kinds of disputes?

In addition to knowing the names of your state's courts and their jurisdictional authority, you will also need to become familiar with the procedural requirements of specific courts. Paralegals frequently assist their attorneys in drafting legal documents to be filed in state courts, and the required procedures for filing these documents may vary from court to court. You will read more about court procedures in Chapters 13 and 15.

As indicated earlier and illustrated in Exhibit 6.1 on page 190, state courts exercise exclusive jurisdiction over all matters that are not subject to federal jurisdiction. Family law and probate law (both discussed in Chapter 10), for example, are two areas in which state courts exercise exclusive jurisdiction. If you work in an area of the law over which state courts exercise exclusive jurisdiction, you will need to be familiar with procedural requirements established by state (or local) courts relating to those areas.

Realize also that many paralegals work within the court system, in both state courts and county courts (which are part of the state court system). Some paralegals work as assistants to court clerks. In addition, many paralegals work for bankruptcy courts, which are part of the federal court system—a topic to which we now turn.

THE FEDERAL COURT SYSTEM

The federal court system is basically a three-tiered model consisting of (1) U.S. district courts (trial courts of general jurisdiction) and various courts of limited jurisdiction, (2) U.S. courts of appeals (intermediate courts of appeals), and (3) the United States Supreme Court, located in Washington, D.C. Exhibit 6.3 shows the organization of the federal court system.

According to the language of Article III of the U.S. Constitution, there is only one national Supreme Court. All other courts in the federal system are considered "inferior." Congress is empowered to create other inferior courts as it deems necessary. The inferior courts that Congress has created include those on the first and second tiers in our model— the district courts and various courts of limited jurisdiction, as well as the U.S. courts of appeals.

Unlike state court judges, who are usually elected, federal court judges—including the justices of the United States Supreme Court—are appointed by the president of the United States and confirmed by the U.S. Senate. Federal judges receive lifetime appointments (because under Article III they "hold their Offices during good Behavior").

On the Web

The Web site for the federal courts offers information on the federal court system and links to all federal courts at **http://www.uscourts.gov**.

U.S. District Courts

At the federal level, the equivalent of a state trial court of general jurisdiction is the district court. There is at least one federal district court in every state. The number of judicial districts can vary over time, primarily owing to population changes and corresponding caseloads. Currently, there are ninety-four judicial districts.

U.S. district courts have original jurisdiction in federal matters. Federal cases typically originate in district courts. There are other trial courts with original but special (or limited) jurisdiction, such as the federal bankruptcy courts and others shown in Exhibit 6.3.

EXHIBIT 6.3
The Organization of the Federal Court System

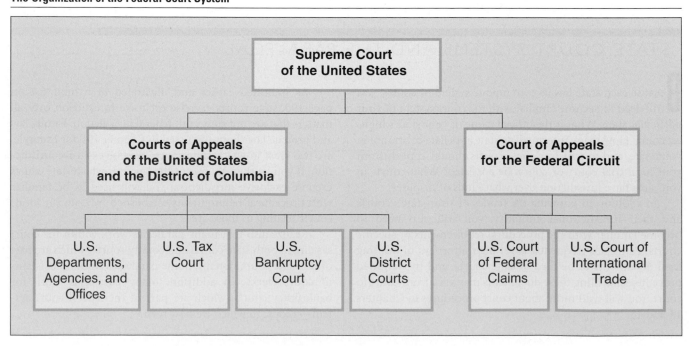

U.S. Courts of Appeals

In the federal court system, there are thirteen U.S. courts of appeals—also referred to as U.S. circuit courts of appeals. The federal courts of appeals for twelve of the circuits (including the District of Columbia Circuit) hear appeals from the federal district courts located within their respective judicial circuits. The court of appeals for the thirteenth circuit, called the Federal Circuit, has national appellate jurisdiction over certain types of cases, such as cases involving patent law and cases in which the U.S. government is a defendant.

A party who is dissatisfied with a federal district court's decision on an issue may appeal that decision to a federal circuit court of appeals. As in state courts of appeals, the decisions of the circuit courts are made by a panel of three or more judges. The judges review decisions made by trial courts to see if any errors of law were made, and the judges generally defer to a district court's findings of fact. The decisions of the circuit courts of appeals are final in most cases, but appeal to the United States Supreme Court is possible. Exhibit 6.4 shows the geographical boundaries of the U.S. circuit courts of appeals and the boundaries of the U.S. district courts within each circuit.

On the Web

At the following Web site, you can search the opinions of U.S. circuit courts: **http://www.law.cornell. edu/federal/opinions.html**.

EXHIBIT 6.4
Boundaries of the U.S. Courts of Appeals and U.S. District Courts

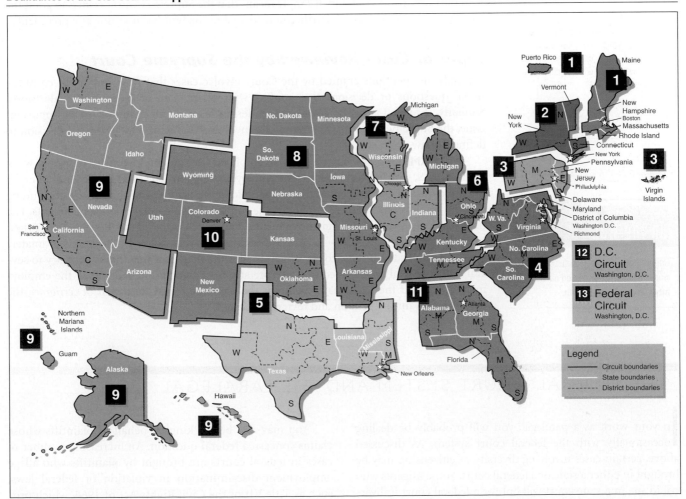

Source: Administrative Office of the United States Courts.

On the Web

An excellent site for information on the United States Supreme Court—including its basic functions and procedures, biographies and photographs of the justices, and even the history of the Supreme Court building—is the following:
http://www.usscplus.com/info.

writ of *certiorari*
A writ from a higher court asking the lower court to send it the record of a case for review. The United States Supreme Court uses *certiorari* to review most of the cases it decides to hear.

rule of four
A rule of the United States Supreme Court under which the Court will not issue a writ of *certiorari* unless at least four justices approve of the decision to issue the writ.

On the Web

United States Supreme Court cases since 1893 can be accessed online at **http://www.findlaw.com**.

The United States Supreme Court

The highest level of the three-tiered model of the federal court system is the United States Supreme Court. The Supreme Court consists of nine justices. Although the Supreme Court has original, or trial, jurisdiction in rare instances (set forth in Article III, Section 2, of the Constitution—see Appendix J), most of its work is as an appeals court. The Supreme Court can review any case decided by any of the federal courts of appeals, and it also has appellate authority over some cases decided in the state courts.

How Cases Reach the Supreme Court

Many people are surprised to learn that there is no absolute right of appeal to the United States Supreme Court. Thousands of cases are filed with the Supreme Court each year, yet in recent years, it has heard fewer than one hundred cases each year.

To bring a case before the Supreme Court, a party requests the Court to issue a writ of *certiorari*. A **writ of *certiorari***[8] is an order issued by the Supreme Court to a lower court requiring the latter to send it the record of the case for review. Parties can petition the Supreme Court to issue a writ of *certiorari*, but the Court will not issue a writ unless at least four of the nine justices approve of it. This is called the **rule of four**. Most petitions for writs are denied. A denial is not a decision on the merits of a case, nor does it indicate agreement with the lower court's opinion. It simply means that the Supreme Court declines to grant the request (petition) for appeal. Furthermore, denial of the writ has no value as a precedent.

Types of Cases Reviewed by the Supreme Court

Typically, the petitions granted by the Court involve cases that raise important constitutional questions or decisions that conflict with other state or federal court decisions. Similarly, if federal appellate courts are rendering inconsistent opinions on an important issue, the Supreme Court may review a case involving that issue and generate a decision to define the law on the matter.

▶ **EXAMPLE 6.10** Suppose that an employer fires an employee who refuses to work on Saturdays, which is forbidden by the employee's religion. The fired employee applies for unemployment benefits from the state unemployment agency, and the agency, concluding that the employer had good reason to fire the employee, denies unemployment benefits. The fired employee sues the state unemployment agency on the ground that the employee's right to freely exercise her religion—a constitutional right—was violated. The case is ultimately appealed to a state supreme court, which decides the issue in a way that is contrary to several recent federal appellate courts' interpretations of freedom of religion in the employment context. If the losing party petitions the Supreme Court for a writ of *certiorari*, the Court may grant the petition and review the case. ◀

THE FEDERAL COURT SYSTEM AND THE PARALEGAL

In your work as a paralegal, you will probably be dealing occasionally with the federal court system. As discussed above, certain cases involving diversity of citizenship may be brought in either a state or a federal court. Some litigants who could sue in a state court will opt for a federal court if diversity of citizenship exists for the reasons mentioned earlier.

You may also be working on behalf of plaintiffs whose claims concern a federal question. An increasing number of cases in federal courts are brought by plaintiffs who allege employment discrimination in violation of federal laws, such as Title VII of the Civil Rights Act of 1964, which prohibits employment discrimination based on race, color,

Developing Paralegal Skills

FEDERAL COURT JURISDICTION

Mona, a new client, comes to the law offices of Henry, Jacobs & Miller in Detroit, Michigan. She wants to file a lawsuit against a New York hospital where she had emergency gallbladder surgery. Mona contracted an infection as a result of the surgery and nearly died. She was so sick that she missed several months of work and lost wages of $18,000. She also has medical expenses exceeding $60,000. Jane Doyle, a paralegal, is asked to review the case to determine if it can be filed in federal court.

CHECKLIST FOR DETERMINING FEDERAL COURT JURISDICTION

- Is the case based, at least in part, on the U.S. Constitution, a treaty, or other question of federal law?
- If the case does not involve a question of federal law, does it involve more than $75,000 and one of the following:
  - ✓ Citizens of different states?
  - ✓ A foreign country and citizens of a state or different states?
  - ✓ Citizens of a state and citizens or subjects of a foreign country?

  If the case involves a combination of more than $75,000 and one of the citizenship requirements above, then diversity jurisdiction exists.

national origin, gender, or religion. Other federal laws prohibit discrimination based on age or disability. Sexual harassment and pregnancy discrimination are considered by the courts to fall under the protective umbrella of Title VII's prohibition against gender discrimination, and such cases frequently come before federal courts.

As indicated in Exhibit 6.1 on page 190, federal courts exercise exclusive jurisdiction over cases relating to bankruptcy, patents, copyrights, trademarks, federal crimes, and certain other claims. If you work on such cases, you will

be dealing with the federal court system and the court procedures set forth in the Federal Rules of Civil Procedure. As with state courts, you should make sure that you know the specific requirements of the particular federal court in which a client's lawsuit is to be filed, because each federal court has some discretionary authority over its procedural rules. (See the *Technology and Today's Paralegal* feature on the next page for a discussion of how to obtain court information online.) You will read in detail about the procedural rules governing litigation proceedings in federal courts in Chapters 13 and 15.

ALTERNATIVE DISPUTE RESOLUTION

Litigation is expensive. It is adversarial. It is also time consuming. Because of the backlog of cases pending in many courts, several years may pass before a case is actually tried. For these and other reasons, more and more individuals are turning to **alternative dispute resolution (ADR)** as a means of settling their disputes.

Methods of ADR range from neighbors sitting down over a cup of coffee in an attempt to work out their differences to huge multinational corporations agreeing to resolve a dispute through a formal hearing before a panel of experts. The great advantage of ADR is its

alternative dispute resolution (ADR)
The resolution of disputes in ways other than those involved in the traditional judicial process. Negotiation, mediation, and arbitration are forms of ADR.

Technology and Today's Paralegal

COURTS IN THE INTERNET AGE

Most courts today have sites on the Web. Some courts display only the names of court personnel, office phone numbers, and general information. Others add judicial decisions, electronic forms, court rules, filing guidelines and fees, legal resources, and employment opportunities within the court system. We look here at some useful Web sites for paralegals who wish to become familiar with the various court systems and their Internet interfaces. Experience with navigating pertinent court Web sites may give you an advantage in the employment market and make you a valued member of the legal team.

FEDERAL, STATE, AND LOCAL COURT STRUCTURES

It is important for paralegals to understand the structures of federal and state court systems so they know which types of cases are tried in which courts. You will find a description of the types of federal courts and links to all federal courts at the Federal Judiciary Web site, accessible at **http://www.uscourts.gov**. Villanova University hosts a federal court locator at **http://www.law.villanova.edu/library/researchandstudyguides/ federalcourtlocator.asp**, which includes links to related federal agencies and other legal information sources.

Each state's court system is structured uniquely. The National Center for State Courts (NCSC), a nonprofit organization dedicated to improving state courts, presents flowcharts depicting the structure of each state court system at **http://www.ncsconline.org/D_Research/Ct_Struct/Index.html**. The NCSC offers links to specific state court Web sites at **http://www.ncsconline.org/D_KIS/info_court_web_sites.html#State**. The NCSC's home page, at **http://www.ncsconline.org**, also displays state court statistics, articles about state court trends, and job announcements. Many state judicial systems have centralized Web sites with links to circuit and trial courts' Web sites. For example, the Web site for Michigan courts offers a directory of trial courts, maps of local court jurisdictions, and local trial court links at **http://courts.michigan.gov/scao/trial.htm**.

COURT DECISIONS

Paralegals are often called on to find court decisions on topics related to current or pending cases. Most state courts today include judicial decisions (often referred to as *opinions*) on their Web sites, and the majority of state courts provide case archives dating back several years. Decisions by the U.S. Supreme Court are posted on the Court's official Web site at **http://www.supremecourtus.gov** within hours after the decisions are rendered.

Even decisions that are designated as unpublished opinions by the appellate courts are often published online. "Unpublished" decisions generally do not contain the same detailed recital of facts or comprehensive legal analysis as published opinions. Today, some courts permit unpublished decisions to be cited, although usually as persuasive rather than binding authority. You may also sometimes cite *slip opinions*. A slip opinion (discussed further in Chapter 17) is the second version of an opinion, and it may contain corrections not appearing in the initial opinion. As a paralegal, it is important that you specify to the attorneys you are assisting whether any court opinions you refer to are unpublished decisions or slip opinions rather than published opinions.

TECHNOLOGY TIP

Paralegals in today's technologically oriented legal offices should be comfortable gathering court information through the Internet, and regular practice is the way to achieve such confidence. Use the links mentioned above to find Web sites for courts in your area, review various courts' rules, examine court dockets, and check out what forms are available online. As an example, use the NCSC Web site to locate the Web site for the California courts. From the California site, review some trial, pretrial, and probate rules. Then browse the dockets for the California appellate courts, including the Supreme Court. A paralegal should be comfortable with finding, filling out, and submitting court forms online. Click on "Forms" from the menu at the top of the California Courts Web site, read the instructions, choose a form from the list, and fill out the form. Then search the Web site to locate the specific procedures that are required for filing the documents with the court. You will find valuable court information through such exercises and be on the road to becoming the technology expert of your legal team.

flexibility. Normally, the parties themselves can control how the dispute will be settled, what procedures will be used, and whether the decision reached (either by themselves or by a neutral third party) will be legally binding or nonbinding.

Today, approximately 95 percent of cases are settled before trial through some form of ADR. Indeed, over half of the states either require or encourage parties to undertake ADR prior to trial. Several federal courts have instituted ADR programs as well. In the following pages, we examine various forms of ADR. Keep in mind, though, that new methods of ADR—and new combinations of existing methods—are continually being devised and employed. Additionally, ADR services are now being offered via the Internet. Paralegals who develop expertise in the area of ADR can greatly expand their future career opportunities (by becoming mediators, for example).

Negotiation

Negotiation is one alternative means of resolving disputes. Attorneys frequently advise their clients to try to negotiate a settlement of their disputes voluntarily before they proceed to trial. During pretrial negotiation, the parties and/or their attorneys may meet informally one or more times to see if a mutually satisfactory agreement can be reached.

▶ **EXAMPLE 6.11** Assume that Katherine Baranski is suing Tony Peretto for damages. Peretto ran a stop sign, and as a result, his van crashed into Baranski's car, causing her to sustain numerous injuries and damages exceeding $100,000. After pretrial investigations into the matter, both plaintiff Baranski and defendant Peretto realize that Baranski has a good chance of winning the suit. At this point, Peretto's attorney may make a settlement offer on behalf of Peretto. Baranski may be willing to accept a settlement offer for an amount lower than the amount of damages she claimed in her complaint simply to avoid the time, trouble, and expense involved in taking the case to trial.

To facilitate an out-of-court settlement, Baranski's attorney may ask his paralegal to draft a letter to Baranski pointing out the strengths and weaknesses of her case against Peretto, the ADR options for settling the case before trial, and the advantages and disadvantages associated with each ADR option. Additionally, the paralegal may be asked to draft a letter to Peretto's attorney indicating the strengths of Baranski's case against him and the advantages to Peretto of settling the dispute out of court. ◀

As a result of pretrial negotiations, such as those described in Example 6.11, a settlement agreement may be reached. In a **settlement agreement**, one party gives up the right to initiate or continue litigation in return for a sum of money to be paid by the other party. Exhibit 6.5 on the following page shows an example of a settlement agreement.

Mediation

Another alternative to a trial is mediation. In the **mediation** process, the parties themselves attempt to negotiate an agreement, but with the assistance of a neutral third party, a mediator. In mediation, the mediator talks with the parties separately as well as jointly. The mediator emphasizes points of agreement, helps the parties evaluate their positions, and proposes solutions. The mediator, however, does not make a decision on the matter being disputed.

The parties may select a mediator on the basis of his or her expertise in a particular field or reputation for fairness and impartiality. The mediator need not be a lawyer. The mediator may be one person, such as a paralegal, an attorney, or a volunteer from the community, or a panel of mediators may be used. Usually, a mediator charges a fee, which can be split between the parties. Many state and federal courts now require that parties mediate their disputes before being allowed to resolve the disputes through trials. In this situation, the mediators may be appointed by the court.

negotiation
A process in which parties attempt to settle their dispute informally, with or without attorneys to represent them.

You can find publications pertaining to ADR by accessing the Federal Judicial Center at **http://www.fjc.gov**.

settlement agreement
An out-of-court resolution to a legal dispute, which is agreed to by the parties in writing. A settlement agreement may be reached at any time prior to or during a trial.

mediation
A method of settling disputes outside of court by using the services of a neutral third party, who acts as a communicating agent between the parties; a method of dispute settlement that is less formal than arbitration.

EXHIBIT 6.5
A Sample Settlement Agreement

SETTLEMENT AGREEMENT

THIS AGREEMENT is entered into this twelfth day of May, 2007, between Katherine Baranski and Tony Peretto.

WITNESSETH

WHEREAS, there is now pending in the U.S. District Court for the District of Nita an action entitled *Baranski v. Peretto*, hereinafter referred to as "action."

WHEREAS, the parties hereto desire to record their agreement to settle all matters relating to said action without the necessity of further litigation.

NOW, THEREFORE, in consideration of the covenants and agreements contained herein, the sufficiency of which is hereby mutually acknowledged, and intending to be legally bound hereby, the parties agree as follows:

1. Katherine Baranski agrees to accept the sum of seventy-five thousand dollars ($75,000) in full satisfaction of all claims against Tony Peretto as set forth in the complaint filed in this action.

2. Tony Peretto agrees to pay Katherine Baranski the above-stated amount, in a lump-sum cash payment, on or before the first day of July, 2007.

3. Upon execution of this agreement and payment of the sum required under this agreement, the parties shall cause the action to be dismissed with prejudice.

4. When the sum required under this agreement is paid in full, Katherine Baranski will execute and deliver to Tony Peretto a release of all claims set forth in the complaint filed in the said action.

Katherine Baranski
Katherine Baranski

Tony Peretto
Tony Peretto

Sworn and subscribed before me this twelfth day of May, 2007.

Leela M. Shay
Leela M. Shay
Notary Public
State of Nita

Developing Paralegal Skills

TO SUE OR NOT TO SUE

Millie Burke, a paralegal, works for a sole practitioner. She has just been asked by the firm's owner, attorney Jim Wilcox, to draw up a checklist. The checklist is to consist of questions that clients should consider before initiating a lawsuit. Wilcox wants to have the checklist on hand when he first interviews clients who come to him for advice on whether to bring a lawsuit or to settle a dispute by some alternative means. Millie drafts a checklist for Wilcox's review.

CHECKLIST FOR DECIDING WHETHER TO SUE

* Now that you have a rough idea of what it might cost to litigate your dispute, are you still interested in pursuing a trial? If so, you will need to pay a retainer now from which I will pay the initial filing fees and court costs. You will also need to sign an agreement that you will pay me hourly rates if the costs exceed the amount of the retainer.

* Do you have the time and patience to follow a court case through the judicial system, even if it takes several years?

* Is there a way to settle your grievance privately, without going to court? Even if the settlement is less than you think you are owed, you may be better off settling now for the smaller figure. An early settlement will save time on future expenses and prevent the time loss and frustration associated with litigation.

* Can you use some form of alternative dispute resolution (negotiation, mediation, or arbitration) to settle the dispute? Before you say no, let's review these dispute-settlement methods and discuss the pros and cons of each alternative.

A Nonadversarial Forum

Mediation is not adversarial in nature, as lawsuits are. In litigation, the parties "do battle" with each other in the courtroom, while the judge is the neutral party. Because of its non-adversarial nature, the mediation process tends to reduce the antagonism between the parties and to allow them to resume their former relationship. For this reason, mediation is often the preferred form of ADR for disputes involving business partners, employers and employees, family members, or other parties involved in long-term relationships.

▶ **EXAMPLE 6.12** Suppose that two business partners have a dispute over how the profits of their firm should be distributed. If the dispute is litigated, the parties will be adversaries, and their respective attorneys will emphasize how the parties' positions differ, not what they have in common. In contrast, if the dispute is mediated, the mediator will emphasize the common ground shared by the partners and help them work toward agreement. ◀

Paralegals as Mediators

Because a mediator need not be a lawyer, this field is open to paralegals who acquire appropriate training and expertise. If you are interested in becoming a mediator, you might check with your local paralegal association or with one of the national paralegal associations to find out how you might pursue this career goal. You might also check with a county, state, or federal court in your area to see if you can qualify as a mediator for court-referred mediation (to be discussed shortly). Generally, any paralegal aspiring to work as a mediator must

A paralegal mediates a dispute by emphasizing the common ground shared by the parties as she proposes possible solutions.

(Courtesy of ©Blend Images/Alamy)

have excellent communication skills. This is because, as a mediator, it will be your job to listen carefully to each party's complaints and communicate possible solutions to a dispute in a way that is not offensive to either party. (See this chapter's *Featured Guest* article on pages 208 and 209 for further details on the functions performed by mediators and the role played by paralegals in the mediation process.)

Arbitration

arbitration
A method of settling disputes in which a dispute is submitted to a disinterested third party (other than a court), who renders a decision that may or may not be legally binding.

A more formal method of ADR is **arbitration**, in which an arbitrator hears a dispute and determines the outcome. The key difference between arbitration and the forms of ADR just discussed is that in arbitration, the third party hearing the dispute makes the decision for the parties—a decision that may be legally binding. In negotiation and mediation, in contrast, the parties decide for themselves, although a third party may assist them. In a sense, the arbitrator acts as a private judge, even though the arbitrator is not required to be a lawyer. Often, a panel of experts arbitrates the dispute.

In some respects, formal arbitration resembles a trial, although usually the procedural rules are much less restrictive than those governing litigation. In the typical hearing format, the parties present opening arguments to the arbitrator and state what remedies should or should not be granted. Evidence is then presented, and witnesses may be called and examined by both sides. The arbitrator then renders a decision.

Depending on the parties' circumstances and preferences, the arbitrator's decision may be legally binding or nonbinding on the parties. In nonbinding arbitration, the parties submit their dispute to a third party but remain free to reject the third party's decision. Nonbinding arbitration is more similar to mediation than to binding arbitration. As will be discussed later in this chapter, arbitration that is mandated by the courts is often not binding on the parties. If, after mandatory arbitration, the parties are not satisfied with the results of arbitration, they may then ignore the arbitrator's decision and have the dispute litigated in court. Even if the arbitrator's decision is legally binding, a party can appeal the decision to a court for judicial review—as will be discussed next.

Arbitration Clauses and Statutes

Virtually any commercial matter can be submitted to arbitration. When a dispute arises, parties can agree to settle their differences through arbitration rather than through the court system. Frequently, however, disputes are arbitrated because of an arbitration clause in a contract entered into before the dispute arose. An **arbitration clause** provides that any disputes arising under the contract will be resolved by arbitration. For example, an arbitration clause in a contract for the sale of goods might provide that "any controversy or claim arising under this contract will be referred to arbitration before the American Arbitration Association."[9]

Most states have statutes (often based in part on the Uniform Arbitration Act of 1955) under which arbitration clauses will be enforced, and some state statutes compel arbitration of certain types of disputes, such as those involving public employees. At the federal level, the Federal Arbitration Act (FAA) of 1925 enforces arbitration clauses in contracts involving maritime activity and interstate commerce. Because of the breadth of the commerce clause in the Constitution (see Appendix J), even business activities that have only remote or minimal effects on commerce between two or more states may be regarded as interstate commerce. Thus, arbitration agreements involving transactions only slightly connected to the flow of interstate commerce may fall under the FAA.

The FAA does not establish a set arbitration procedure. The parties themselves must agree on the manner of resolving their disputes. The FAA provides only that if the parties have agreed to arbitrate disputes arising in relation to their contract, through an arbitration clause, the arbitration clause will be enforced. In other words, arbitration must take place before a party can take a dispute to the courts.

arbitration clause
A clause in a contract that provides that, in case of a dispute, the parties will determine their rights through arbitration rather than the judicial system.

The Arbitration Process

The first step in the arbitration process is the **submission agreement**, in which the parties agree to submit their dispute for arbitration. (If an arbitration clause is included in a contract, the clause itself is the submission to arbitrate.) Most states require that an agreement to submit a dispute to arbitration must be in writing. The submission agreement typically identifies the parties, the nature of the dispute to be resolved, the monetary amounts involved in the dispute, the place of arbitration, and the powers that the arbitrator will exercise. Frequently, the agreement includes a signed statement that the parties intend to be bound by the arbitrator's decision.

The next step in the process is the *hearing*. Normally, the parties agree prior to arbitration—in an arbitration clause or in a submission-to-arbitrate agreement, for example—on what procedural rules will govern the proceedings. In a typical hearing, the parties begin as they would at a trial by presenting opening arguments to the arbitrator and stating what remedies should or should not be granted. After the opening statements have been made, evidence is presented. Witnesses may be called and examined by both sides. After all evidence has been presented, the parties give their closing arguments. Although arbitration is in some ways similar to a trial, the rules (such as those regarding what kinds of evidence may be introduced) are usually much less restrictive than those involved in formal litigation.

After each side has had an opportunity to present evidence and to argue its case, the arbitrator reaches a decision. The final decision of the arbitrator is called an **award**, even if no money is conferred on a party as a result of the proceedings. Under most arbitration statutes, the arbitrator must render an award within thirty days of the close of the hearing.

A paralegal may become extensively involved in preparations for arbitration, just as he or she would in preparing for a trial. The paralegal will assist in obtaining and organizing all evidence relating to the dispute, may interview witnesses and prepare them for the hearing, and generally will assist in other tasks commonly undertaken prior to a trial (see Chapter 13).

submission agreement
A written agreement to submit a legal dispute to an arbitrator or arbitrating panel for resolution.

award
In the context of ADR, the decision rendered by an arbitrator.

MEDIATION: CAREER OPPORTUNITIES FOR PARALEGALS

BIOGRAPHICAL NOTE

Fernaundra Ferguson is an assistant professor in the Criminal Justice and Legal Studies Division and the Diversity Studies Graduate Program of the University of West Florida. She earned a bachelor of arts degree in political science and history from Bennett College in 1976 and a J.D. degree from Howard University School of Law in 1979. Her current focus is in the area of conflict resolu-

tion; specifically, mediation, and she has published several articles on mediation. Ferguson serves on the Diversity and Equity executive committee and is past co-chair of the Training Section for the Association of Conflict Resolution. She is also a member of the Phi Delta Phi Legal Fraternity, the Southern Association for Pre-Law Advisors, and Societas Docta, Inc.

Litigation is costly and time consuming. For these and other reasons, the legal system in the United States is rapidly adopting alternative methods to the traditional adversarial process of litigation. Many state court systems, as well as the federal court system, now provide for one or more alternatives to litigation. Methods of alternative dispute resolution, or ADR, include negotiation, settlement conference, mediation, arbitration, mini-trial, summary jury trial, private judging, and conciliation.

Conflict resolution through mediation is often thought of as "win/win" resolution, because there is no winner or loser. Unlike litigation and some methods of alternative dispute resolution (such as arbitration), mediation is not adversarial in nature. This is because the focus of mediation is not on the parties' differences but on those points on which the parties agree.

THE MEDIATION PROCESS

Mediation is a voluntary and confidential process in which a neutral third party, the mediator, facilitates the resolution of a dispute between the parties. The mediator's role is to help the parties discuss difficult issues, propose solutions, and negotiate an agreement. The mediator does not have any decision-making power over the outcome; rather, it is up to the parties to decide which proposed solution to adopt. For the mediation process to work, the mediator must do the following:

- Gather information.
- Remain neutral and unbiased throughout the process.
- Be a good listener.
- Articulate the issues being disputed.
- Assess the interests of the parties and the realities they face.
- Obtain information from each party that will assist in resolving the dispute.
- Evaluate alternative solutions to the dispute.

The Role of the Courts in Prearbitration

The role of the courts in the arbitration process is limited. One important role is played at the prearbitration stage. When a dispute arises as to whether the parties have agreed in an arbitration clause to submit a particular matter to arbitration, one party may file suit to compel arbitration. The court before which the suit is brought will not decide the basic controversy but must decide whether the dispute is *arbitrable*—that is, whether the matter is one that can be resolved through arbitration. ▶ **EXAMPLE 6.13** Suppose that a dispute involves a claim of employment discrimination on the basis of age. If the issue of arbitrability reaches a court, the court will have to decide whether the Age Discrimination in Employment Act of 1967 (which protects persons forty years of age and older against employment discrimination on the basis of age) permits claims brought under this act to be arbitrated. ◀

- Identify the points on which the parties agree and propose solutions to the parties.
- Encourage the parties to settle their dispute.
- Formalize any agreement reached by the parties.
- Believe in the process.

ASSISTING ATTORNEYS IN THE MEDIATION PROCESS

Paralegals play a major role in assisting attorneys in the mediation of disputes, both before and during the mediation itself. Prior to the mediation, paralegals interview clients, assist in gathering any information (such as police reports, medical records, or child-care expenses) that will help the attorney when advising the client, draft documents that may be needed for the mediation, and prepare a list of mediators in the relevant geographic and specialty area. During the mediation, the paralegal may be asked to provide additional information and draft other documents (such as a settlement agreement). If the attorney serves as the mediator, the paralegal may be asked to schedule dates with the parties or their attorneys for the mediation, prepare any necessary forms, and draft a final settlement agreement.

> *"Paralegals play a major role in assisting attorneys in the mediation of disputes, both before and during the mediation itself."*

PARALEGALS AS MEDIATORS

Paralegals with mediation training are employed in a variety of dispute-resolution settings outside the law office. For example, some paralegals with mediation training work for administrative agencies that offer dispute-resolution services. Other paralegals who are trained in mediation have supervised and trained volunteer mediators in community centers. Increasingly, mediation is being utilized to address community issues, including hostilities leading to violence in the schools. Peer mediation, for example, helps to diffuse such feelings as anger, distrust, and fear before those feelings escalate into violent acts. Paralegals may also serve as mediators in disputes between communities and the local police force or between city governments and representatives of the local citizenry.

Organizations promoting community mediation have sprung up around the country. There is now a national association of such groups—the National Association for Community Mediation (NAFCM). The NAFCM is an association of community mediation centers, their staff and volunteer mediators, and other individuals and organizations interested in the community mediation movement. Paralegals who are interested in participating in community mediation should check to see what community mediation organizations exist in their city or state.

Mediation training also provides the paralegal with opportunities in international settings. Some paralegals have exciting careers as members of a team mediating disputes between countries.

If the court finds that the subject matter in controversy is covered by the agreement to arbitrate, then a party may be compelled to arbitrate the dispute. Even when a claim involves a violation of a statute passed to protect a certain class of people, such as a statute prohibiting age discrimination against employees in the workplace, a court may determine that the parties must nonetheless abide by their agreement to arbitrate the dispute. Usually, a court will allow the claim to be arbitrated if the court, in interpreting the statute, can find no legislative intent to the contrary.

No party, however, will be ordered to submit a particular dispute to arbitration unless the court is convinced that the party has consented to do so.[10] Additionally, the courts will not compel arbitration if it is clear that the prescribed arbitration rules and procedures are inherently unfair to one of the parties. ▶ **EXAMPLE 6.14** Suppose that an employer's arbitration agreement with an employee states that it is the employer's responsibility to establish the procedure and the rules for the arbitration. In this situation, the court may

Ethics Watch!

POTENTIAL ARBITRATION PROBLEMS

Many individuals and business firms prefer to arbitrate disputes rather than take them to court. For that reason, they often include arbitration clauses in their contracts. These clauses normally specify who or what organization will arbitrate the dispute and where the arbitration will take place. To safeguard a client's interests, when drafting and reviewing arbitration clauses in contracts, the careful paralegal will be alert to the possibility that those who arbitrate the dispute might not be totally neutral or that the designated place of arbitration is so geographically distant from the client's location that it may pose a great inconvenience and expense for the client should an arbitrable dispute arise. The paralegal should call any such problems to his or her supervising attorney's attention. The attorney can then discuss the problem with the client and help the client negotiate an arbitration clause that is more favorable to the client's position.

conclude that the rules are one sided and unfair and thus refuse to enforce the arbitration agreement.[11] ◀

The Postarbitration Role of the Courts

Courts also may play an important role at the postarbitration stage. If the arbitration has produced an award, one of the parties may appeal the award or may seek a court order compelling the other party to comply with the award. In determining whether an award should be enforced, a court conducts a review that is much more restricted in scope than an appellate court's review of a trial court decision. The general view is that because the parties were free to frame the issues and set the powers of the arbitrator at the outset, they cannot complain about the result. An arbitration award may be set aside, however, if the award resulted from the arbitrator's misconduct or "bad faith" or if the arbitrator exceeded his or her powers in arbitrating the dispute. An arbitrator is permitted to resolve only those issues that are covered by the agreement to submit to arbitration.

Other ADR Forms

The three forms of ADR just discussed are the oldest and traditionally the most commonly used forms. In recent years, a variety of new types of ADR have emerged. Some of them combine elements of mediation and arbitration. For example, in **binding mediation**, a neutral mediator tries to facilitate agreement between the parties, but if no agreement is reached the mediator issues a legally binding decision on the matter. In **mediation arbitration (med-arb)**, an arbitrator first attempts to help the parties reach an agreement, just as a mediator would. If no agreement is reached, then formal arbitration is undertaken, and the arbitrator issues a legally binding decision.

Other ADR forms are sometimes referred to as "assisted negotiation" because they involve a third party in what is essentially a negotiation process. For example, in **early neutral case evaluation**, the parties select a neutral third party (generally an expert in the subject matter of

binding mediation
A form of ADR in which a mediator attempts to facilitate agreement between the parties but then issues a legally binding decision if no agreement is reached.

mediation arbitration (med-arb)
A form of ADR in which an arbitrator first attempts to help the parties reach an agreement, just as a mediator would. If no agreement is reached, then formal arbitration is undertaken, and the arbitrator issues a legally binding decision.

early neutral case evaluation
A form of ADR in which a neutral third party evaluates the strengths and weaknesses of the disputing parties' positions; the evaluator's opinion forms the basis for negotiating a settlement.

the dispute) to evaluate their respective positions. The parties explain their positions to the case evaluator however they wish. The case evaluator then assesses the strengths and weaknesses of the parties' positions, and this evaluation forms the basis of negotiating a settlement.

The mini-trial is a form of assisted negotiation that is often used by business parties. In a **mini-trial**, each party's attorney briefly argues the party's case before representatives of each firm who have the authority to settle the dispute. Typically, a neutral third party (usually an expert in the area being disputed) acts as an adviser. If the parties fail to reach an agreement, the adviser renders an opinion as to how a court would likely decide the issue. The proceeding assists the parties in determining whether they should negotiate a settlement of the dispute or take it to court.

Still Another Approach—Collaborative Law

Still another method of resolving disputes is the collaborative law approach, which is increasingly being used by spouses during separation procedures. In *collaborative law,* both parties, their attorneys, and any professionals working with the parties agree to meet to resolve all of their issues without litigation. The lawyers act as negotiators and communication moderators while advising their clients about their legal rights, entitlements, and obligations. Both parties promise to take a reasoned stand on every issue, to keep discovery cooperative and informal, and to work together to craft an agreement. Any abusive communications are identified, discussed, and eliminated. Because the attorneys agree not to take part in any litigation that may occur if an agreement is not reached, the attorneys focus exclusively on settlement rather than on preparing documents or presentations for court. If either party seeks court intervention, both attorneys must withdraw from representation.

Court-Referred ADR

Today, the majority of states either require or encourage parties to undergo mediation or arbitration prior to trial. Generally, when a trial court refers a case for arbitration, the arbitrator's decision is not binding on the parties. If the parties do not agree with the arbitrator's decision, they can go forward with the lawsuit.

The types of court-related ADR programs in use vary widely. In some states, such as Missouri, ADR is voluntary. In other states, such as Minnesota, parties are required to undertake ADR before they can have their cases heard in court. Some states, such as Minnesota, offer a menu of options. Other states, including Florida (which has a statewide, comprehensive mediation program), offer only one alternative.

Today's courts are also experimenting with a variety of ADR alternatives to speed up justice and reduce its cost. Numerous federal courts now hold **summary jury trials (SJTs)**, in which the parties present their arguments and supporting evidence (other than witness testimony—witnesses are not called in an SJT). The jury renders a verdict, but unlike the verdict in an actual trial, the jury's verdict is not binding. The verdict does, however, act as a guide to both sides in reaching an agreement during the mandatory negotiations that immediately follow the SJT. If no settlement is reached, both sides have the right to a full trial later. Other alternatives being employed by the courts include summary procedures for commercial litigation and the appointment of special masters to assist judges in deciding complex issues.

Providers of ADR Services

ADR services are provided by both government agencies and private organizations. A major provider of ADR services is the **American Arbitration Association (AAA)**, which was founded in 1926. Most of the nation's largest law firms are members of this nonprofit association. Currently, about 200,000 disputes are submitted to the AAA for resolution each year

---

mini-trial
A private proceeding that assists disputing parties in determining whether to take their case to court. During the proceeding, each party's attorney briefly argues the party's case before the other party and (usually) a neutral third party, who acts as an adviser. If the parties fail to reach an agreement, the adviser renders an opinion as to how a court would likely decide the issue.

summary jury trial (SJT)
A method of settling disputes (used in some federal courts) in which a trial is held but the jury's verdict is not binding. The verdict acts only as a guide to both sides in reaching an agreement during the mandatory negotiations that immediately follow the trial. If a settlement is not reached, both sides have the right to a full trial later.

American Arbitration Association (AAA)
The major organization offering arbitration services in the United States.

To obtain information on the services offered by the American Arbitration Association (AAA), as well as forms used to submit a case for arbitration, go to the AAA's Web site at **http://www.adr.org**.

in its numerous offices around the country. Cases brought before the AAA are heard by an expert or a panel of experts in the area relating to the dispute and are usually settled quickly. Generally, about half of the panel members are lawyers. To cover its costs, the AAA charges a fee, paid by the party filing the claim. In addition, each party to the dispute pays a specified amount for each hearing day, as well as a special additional fee for cases involving personal injuries or property loss.

Hundreds of for-profit firms around the country also provide ADR services. Typically, these firms hire retired judges to conduct arbitration hearings or otherwise assist parties in settling their disputes. Private ADR firms normally allow the parties to decide on the date of the hearing, the presiding judge, whether the judge's decision will be legally binding, and the site of the hearing—which may be a conference room, a law school office, or a leased courtroom. The judges follow procedures similar to those of the federal courts and use similar rules. Usually, each party to the dispute pays a filing fee and a designated fee for a hearing session or conference.

As mentioned, courts also have ADR programs in which disputes are resolved by court-appointed attorneys or paralegals who are qualified to act as arbitrators or mediators in certain types of disputes. Many paralegals have found that becoming a mediator or an arbitrator is an especially rewarding career option.

Online Dispute Resolution

online dispute resolution (ODR)
The resolution of disputes with the assistance of an organization that offers dispute-resolution services via the Internet.

Today, a number of companies and organizations offer dispute-resolution services via the Internet. The settlement of disputes in these online forums is known as **online dispute resolution (ODR)**. The disputes resolved in these forums usually involve disagreements over the right to use a certain Web site address or the quality of goods purchased over the Internet (including goods sold through Internet auction sites). Those who do business in cyberspace (and the attorneys who represent them) should therefore be aware of this ADR option.

Most online forums do not automatically apply the law of any specific jurisdiction. Instead, results are often based on general, universal legal principles. As with offline methods of dispute resolution, a party normally may appeal to a court at any time. Negotiation, mediation, and arbitration services are all available to disputants over the Internet.

Online Negotiation

Several Web-based firms offer online forums for negotiating monetary settlements. Typically, one party files a complaint, and the other party is notified by e-mail. Password-protected access to the online forum site is available twenty-four hours a day, seven days a week. Fees are generally low (often 2 to 4 percent, or less, of the disputed amount). The parties can drop the negotiations at any time.

Online Mediation

Mediation providers have also tried resolving disputes online. SquareTrade, for example, has provided mediation services for the online auction site eBay and also resolves disputes among other parties. SquareTrade uses Web-based software that walks participants through a five-step e-resolution process. Negotiation between the parties occurs on a secure page within SquareTrade's Web site. The parties may consult a mediator. The entire process takes as little as ten to fourteen days, and there is at present no fee unless the parties use a mediator.

Online Arbitration

A number of organizations, including the American Arbitration Association, offer online arbitration services. For instance, Resolution Forum, Inc. (RFI), a nonprofit organization associated with the Center for Legal Responsibility at the South Texas College of Law, offers

Today's Professional Paralegal

ARBITRATING COMMERCIAL CONTRACTS

Julia Lorenz has worked as a legal assistant for International Airlines (IA) for ten years. She works in the legal department on the staff of the general counsel. Her job has been to work with Jim Manning, senior attorney. This attorney is responsible for all of the corporation's contracts, including the following: major contracts with jet manufacturers for the purchase of aircraft, contracts with catering companies to supply food during flights, fuel contracts, employment and labor contracts, and many small contracts for the purchase and lease of equipment and supplies for the numerous airline offices and ticket counters.

REVIEWING PROPOSED CONTRACTS

Julia's job is to review the provisions of proposed major contracts, such as contracts to purchase jet aircraft, and to provide Jim with an article-by-article summary of the contracts' provisions. Jim then negotiates these contracts to obtain the most favorable terms possible for the airline. Once he has negotiated a contract, Julia makes the final changes and forwards it to the appropriate IA corporate official to review and sign.

ATTENDING ARBITRATION PROCEEDINGS

All of the airline's major contracts contain arbitration clauses that require all contract disputes to be resolved through binding arbitration services provided by the American Arbitration Association (AAA). On numerous occasions, Julia has attended arbitration proceedings with Jim. In preparing for arbitration, Julia obtains affidavits, prepares subpoenas, and arranges for witnesses to be present to testify. During the arbitration proceedings, she assists in presenting material into evidence. She and Jim have developed a good rapport with several arbitrators at the local AAA office, and they usually request these arbitrators when they have a case that must be arbitrated.

BECOMING AN ARBITRATOR

Julia's knowledge of arbitration procedures and her outstanding work in preparing for arbitration, as well as during the proceedings, has won her significant recognition from this group of arbitrators. One of the arbitrators eventually approaches Julia and suggests that she apply for approval as an arbitrator. She says that she will consider it.

Julia later mentions the arbitrator's suggestion to Jim. He thinks that Julia has been paid quite a compliment and encourages her to contact the AAA to inquire about the possibility of being approved as an arbitrator. When Julia calls the AAA, she learns that arbitrators in the area of commercial arbitration are not required to be attorneys. She would need eight years of experience in her field and would have to meet certain educational requirements. When Julia realizes that she has the necessary qualifications, she submits an application. About two months later, she is approved as an arbitrator.

arbitration services through its CAN-WIN conferencing system. Using standard browser software and an RFI password, the parties to a dispute access an online conference room. When multiple parties are involved, private communications and breakout sessions are possible through private messaging facilities. RFI also offers mediation services.

ADR AND THE PARALEGAL

The time and monetary costs associated with litigating disputes in court continue to rise, and, as a result, disputing parties are increasingly turning to ADR as a means of settling their disagreements. As a way to reduce their caseloads, state and federal courts are also increasingly requiring litigants to undergo arbitration before bringing their suits in front of the courts. Although paralegals have always assisted attorneys in work relating to the negotiation of out-of-court settlements for clients, they may play an even greater role in the future. Some paralegals are qualified mediators and directly assist parties in reaching a mutually satisfactory agreement. Some paralegals serve as arbitrators. As more and more parties utilize ADR, paralegals will have increasing opportunities in this area of legal work.

If you are interested in becoming a mediator, you need to be thoroughly familiar with ADR law in the state in which you work. Some states do not require mediators to meet any special training requirements. For example, Florida law requires that a family mediator "shall be a person with the appropriate attributes who can demonstrate sensitivity toward the parties involved and facilitate solutions to the problem." Other states require mediators to have up to sixty hours of training in certain fields, such as family law, child development, or family dynamics.

KEY TERMS AND CONCEPTS

alternative dispute
   resolution (ADR)   201

American Arbitration
   Association (AAA)   211

appellate court   188

appellate jurisdiction   188

arbitration   206

arbitration clause   207

award   207

bankruptcy court   188

binding mediation   210

concurrent jurisdiction   190

diversity of citizenship   189

docket   191

early neutral case evaluation   210

exclusive jurisdiction   190

federal question   189

jurisdiction   187

justiciable controversy   192

long arm statute   187

mediation   203

mediation arbitration (med-arb)   210

mini-trial   211

negotiation   203

online dispute resolution (ODR)   212

original jurisdiction   188

probate court   188

rule of four   200

settlement agreement   203

standing to sue   192

submission agreement   207

summary jury trial (SJT)   211

trial court   188

venue   191

writ of *certiorari*   200

chapter summary   The Court System and Alternative Dispute Resolution

Basic Judicial Requirements

1. *Jurisdiction*—Before a court can hear a case, it must have jurisdiction over the person against whom the suit is brought (*in personam* jurisdiction) or the property involved in the suit (*in rem* jurisdiction), as well as jurisdiction over the subject matter.

   a. Limited versus general jurisdiction—Limited jurisdiction exists when a court is limited to a specific subject matter, such as probate or divorce. General jurisdiction exists when a court can hear any kind of case.

   b. Original versus appellate jurisdiction—Courts that have authority to hear a case for the first time (trial courts) have original jurisdiction. Courts of appeals, or reviewing courts, have appellate jurisdiction; generally, these courts do not have original jurisdiction.

c. *Federal jurisdiction*—Arises (1) when a federal question is involved (when the plaintiff's cause of action is based, at least in part, on the U.S. Constitution, a treaty, or a federal law) or (2) when a case involves diversity of citizenship (as in disputes between citizens of different states, between a foreign country and citizens of a state or states, or between citizens of a state and citizens or subjects of a foreign country) and the amount in controversy exceeds $75,000.

d. *Concurrent versus exclusive jurisdiction*—Concurrent jurisdiction exists when two different courts have authority to hear the same case. Exclusive jurisdiction exists when only state courts or only federal courts have authority to hear a case.

2. *Jurisdiction in cyberspace*—Because the Internet does not have physical boundaries, traditional jurisdictional concepts have been difficult to apply in cases involving activities conducted via the Web. Gradually, the courts are developing standards to use in determining when jurisdiction over a Web owner or operator in another state is proper.

3. *Venue*—Venue has to do with the most appropriate location for a trial, which is usually the geographic area where the event leading to the dispute took place or where the parties reside.

4. *Standing to sue*—A legally protected and tangible interest in a matter sufficient to justify seeking relief through the court system. The controversy at issue must also be a justiciable controversy—one that is real and substantial, as opposed to hypothetical or academic.

5. *Judicial procedures*—Rules of procedure prescribe the way in which disputes are handled in the courts. The Federal Rules of Civil Procedure govern all civil litigation in federal courts. Each state has its own procedural rules (often similar to the federal rules), and each court within a state has specific court rules that must be followed.

State Court Systems

1. *Trial courts*—Courts of original jurisdiction, in which legal actions are initiated. State trial courts have either general jurisdiction or limited jurisdiction.

2. *Intermediate appellate courts*—Many states have intermediate appellate courts that review the proceedings of the trial courts; generally, these courts do not have original jurisdiction. Appellate courts ordinarily examine questions of law and procedure while deferring to the trial court's findings of fact.

3. *Supreme (highest) courts*—Each state has a supreme court, although it may be called by some other name. Decisions of the state's highest court are final on all questions of state law. If a federal question is at issue, the case may be appealed to the United States Supreme Court.

4. *Judges and justices*—State court judges and justices are normally elected by the voters for specified terms.

The Federal Court System

1. *U.S. district courts*—The federal district court is the equivalent of the state trial court. The district court exercises general jurisdiction over claims arising under federal law

(Continued)

or based on diversity of citizenship. Federal courts of limited jurisdiction include the U.S. Tax Court, the U.S. Bankruptcy Court, and the U.S. Court of Federal Claims.

2. *U.S. courts of appeals*—There are thirteen intermediate courts of appeals (or circuit courts of appeals) in the federal court system. Of those courts, twelve hear appeals from the district courts within their circuits. The thirteenth circuit court has national appellate jurisdiction over certain types of cases, such as cases involving patent law and cases in which the U.S. government is a defendant.

3. *United States Supreme Court*—The United States Supreme Court is the highest court in the land and the final arbiter of the Constitution and federal law. There is no absolute right of appeal to the Supreme Court, and the Court hears only a fraction of the cases that are filed with it each year.

   a. Although the Supreme Court has original jurisdiction in some cases, it functions primarily as an appellate court.

   b. If the Supreme Court decides to review a case, it will issue a writ of *certiorari,* an order to a lower court requiring the latter to send it the record of the case for review. As a rule, only petitions that raise the possibility of important constitutional questions are granted.

4. *Judges and justices*—Federal court judges and justices are appointed by the president of the United States and confirmed by the Senate. They receive lifetime appointments.

Alternative Dispute Resolution

The costs and time-consuming character of litigation, as well as the public nature of court proceedings, have caused many to turn to various forms of alternative dispute resolution (ADR) for settling their disagreements. The methods of ADR include the following:

1. *Negotiation*—The simplest form of ADR, in which the parties come together, with or without attorneys to represent them, and try to reach a settlement without the involvement of a third party.

2. *Mediation*—A form of ADR in which the parties themselves reach an agreement with the help of a neutral third party, called a mediator, who proposes solutions and emphasizes areas of agreement.

3. *Arbitration*—The most formal method of ADR, in which the parties submit their dispute to a neutral third party, the arbitrator (or panel of arbitrators), who renders a decision. The decision may or may not be legally binding, depending on the circumstances.

   a. Arbitration clauses that are voluntarily agreed on in contracts require the parties to resolve their disputes in arbitration (rather than in court).

   b. Arbitrators' decisions, even when binding, may be appealed to the courts for review. The court's review, however, is much more restricted than an appellate court's review of a trial court record.

4. *Other types of ADR*—These include binding mediation, mediation arbitration (med-arb), early neutral case evaluation, mini-trials, and summary jury trials; generally, these are forms of "assisted negotiation."

5. *Collaborative law*—A form of ADR in which both parties, their attorneys, and any professionals working with the parties meet to resolve their issues without litigation. The lawyers act as negotiators and communication moderators while advising their clients

about their legal rights, entitlements, and obligations. If either party seeks court intervention, both attorneys must withdraw from representation.

6. *Providers of ADR services*—The leading nonprofit provider of ADR services is the American Arbitration Association. Hundreds of for-profit firms also provide ADR services.

7. *Online dispute resolution*—A number of organizations and firms offer negotiation, mediation, and arbitration services through online forums. To date, these forums have been a practical alternative for the resolution of disputes over the right to use a certain Web site address or the quality of goods purchased over the Internet.

QUESTIONS FOR REVIEW

1. Define *jurisdiction,* and explain why jurisdiction is important.

2. What is the difference between personal jurisdiction and subject-matter jurisdiction? What is a long arm statute?

3. Define *original jurisdiction* and *appellate jurisdiction.* What is the difference between the two?

4. Over what types of cases can federal courts exercise jurisdiction?

5. What is the relationship between state and federal jurisdiction?

6. What is venue? What is the difference between venue and jurisdiction?

7. Describe the functions of a trial court. How do they differ from the functions of an appellate court?

8. What are the typical courts in a state court system? What are the three basic tiers, or levels, of courts in the federal court system?

9. How do cases reach the United States Supreme Court?

10. List and explain the various methods of alternative dispute resolution.

ETHICAL QUESTIONS

1. Larry Simpson is working on a lawsuit that was recently filed in a federal district court on the basis of diversity-of-citizenship jurisdiction. Larry, a legal assistant, just received the plaintiff's answers to interrogatories (attorneys' written questions to the parties in a lawsuit), which he has been assigned by his supervising attorney to summarize. Larry discovers that the plaintiff's damages are nowhere near the $75,000 required for diversity jurisdiction. What should Larry do?

2. Diane Post, a paralegal, is working on the defense team in a civil lawsuit that has just been filed in the county court, which has limited jurisdiction over civil lawsuits. The plaintiff is seeking an injunction and $3,000 in damages. (Recall from Chapter 5 that an injunction is an equitable remedy in which a court orders a person to do or refrain from doing a particular act.) The superior court is the only court with jurisdiction over equitable remedies. No one but Diane has noticed that the plaintiff is seeking a remedy that the county court does not have the jurisdictional authority to grant. What should Diane do?

3. Suzanne Andersen's supervising attorney, Amy Lynch, works occasionally as a mediator for family law cases in the local courts. Amy has mediated a divorce case today

involving the property settlement of a wealthy businessperson, who happens also to be a defendant in another lawsuit in which Amy represents the plaintiff. As a result of her mediation today, Amy has learned some confidential financial information about this man. She now has come to Suzanne, her paralegal, and asked her to use this information to his disadvantage in the lawsuit. How should Suzanne handle this situation?

4. Steve is a paralegal with an Ohio law firm that specializes in intellectual property law. He is working on a case in which the client claims that a competitor misappropriated trade secrets in violation of the Uniform Trade Secrets Act. The supervising attorney asks Steve to prepare and submit a complaint with the federal court on behalf of the client. After the attorney has reviewed the complaint, Steve files it electronically, via the Internet, as is permitted by the court. The complaint is not encrypted (encoded) and contains confidential information about the client's company that pertains to the lawsuit. Has Steve or the attorney violated any ethical obligation? If so, which ethical rule has been violated? Can the client sue Steve or the firm for negligence? What could Steve and the attorney have done differently to better protect the client's interests?

PRACTICE QUESTIONS AND ASSIGNMENTS

1. A plaintiff and defendant are involved in an auto accident. Both are residents of the county and state in which the accident takes place. The plaintiff files an auto negligence lawsuit in the county circuit court where the trial will occur. What types of jurisdiction does the court have? (The types to be considered include *in personam* jurisdiction, *in rem* jurisdiction, subject-matter jurisdiction, limited jurisdiction, general jurisdiction, original jurisdiction, appellate jurisdiction, concurrent jurisdiction, and exclusive jurisdiction.)

2. The Brown family from Chicago, Illinois, owns a vacation home in Harbor Springs, Michigan. A dispute arises over the ownership of the property, and an action to partition, or divide, the ownership of the property is filed in the Michigan courts. What types of jurisdiction does the Michigan court have?

3. Renee Clark is a victim of gender discrimination in the workplace. She can file a lawsuit against her employer either under Title VII (a federal statute) in a federal district court or under her state's civil rights act in a state court. When both federal and state courts have authority to hear a case, as in this example, what kind of jurisdiction is involved?

4. Family courts hear cases involving divorce, custody, and other family matters. What types of jurisdiction do family courts have?

5. The court system in the state of Utopia has two levels of trial courts. The lower-level trial court has jurisdiction over civil cases involving damages under $25,000, misdemeanors, local ordinance violations, and small claims. The upper-level trial court has jurisdiction over civil cases involving damages exceeding $25,000, felonies and serious misdemeanors, divorce, and injunctions and can review the lower-level trial court's decisions. What are the various types of jurisdiction that each trial court in the state of Utopia has?

6. Marcia, who is from Toledo, Ohio, drives to Troy, Michigan, and shops at a popular mall. When leaving the parking lot, Marcia causes a car accident when she runs a stop sign. On what basis could a Michigan court obtain jurisdiction over Marcia?

7. Louise sues the manufacturer of her automobile, which is defective, under the Magnuson-Moss Warranty Act, a federal consumer protection statute. In which court can Louise bring her action, and on what jurisdictional basis?

8. Identify each of the following courts:

a. This state court takes testimony from witnesses and receives evidence. It may have either general or limited subject-matter jurisdiction.

b. This court has appellate jurisdiction and is part of a court system that is divided into geographical units called *circuits*.

c. This state court usually has a panel of three or more judges who review the record of a case for errors of law and procedure. It does not have original jurisdiction.

d. This court can exercise diversity-of-citizenship jurisdiction and receives testimony and other evidence.

e. The decisions of this court are usually final. It is the highest appellate court in its geographical area.

f. This federal court has nine justices. It has original jurisdiction over a few types of cases but functions primarily as an appellate court. There is no automatic right to appeal cases to this court.

9. Look at Exhibit 6.4 on page 199. In which federal circuit is your state located? How many federal judicial districts are located in your state? In which federal district is your community located?

10. Based on the information provided in this chapter, including the exhibits, determine which federal court (or courts) could hear the following cases and on what jurisdictional grounds:

a. A case in which the Internal Revenue Service sues a taxpayer for back taxes.

b. A case involving an automobile accident between a citizen of Chicago, Illinois, and a citizen of St. Louis, Missouri, in which the plaintiff is seeking damages of $100,000.

c. A bankruptcy case.

d. A lawsuit claiming sexual harassment in violation of Title VII of the federal Civil Rights Act of 1964.

e. A lawsuit claiming that the defendant violated the federal statute prohibiting racketeering crimes.

11. Suppose that you are a plaintiff in a case brought against the defendant for damages in the amount of $250,000. The case arose as a result of injuries and property damage that you incurred in a car accident caused by the defendant's reckless driving. You know that you have a good chance of winning that amount of damages if the case goes to trial. The defendant offers to settle the case for $175,000. Assume that it would take three years

before the court could hear the case. What factors would you consider in deciding this question? What would your decision be?

12. Using Exhibit 6.5 on page 204 as a model, draft a settlement agreement for a lawsuit involving the following facts:

Harry Jones is suing Burt Gaston in the U.S. District Court for the Western District of Kentucky, docket number 99-123456. On June 12, 2007, Harry agrees to accept $100,000 in settlement of the lawsuit. Harry's attorney will prepare a settlement agreement for their signatures on June 30. Harry will be paid in one lump-sum cash payment on the execution of the settlement agreement, and he will give up his right to all claims against Burt and release Burt from all future liability for all claims arising out of this occurrence.

13. Using the materials presented in the chapter, identify the following methods of alternative dispute resolution:

a. The parties to a divorce meet with a neutral third party who emphasizes points of agreement and pro-

poses solutions to resolve their dispute. After several hours, the parties come to a solution.

b. The parties to a contract dispute submit it to a neutral third party for a legally binding resolution. The neutral third party is not a court.

c. The plaintiff and defense attorneys in a personal-injury case propose settlement figures to one another and their clients in an effort to resolve the lawsuit voluntarily.

d. The attorneys from the personal-injury example above are able to reach an acceptable settlement figure of $100,000. They draft an agreement whereby the plaintiff gives up her right to sue in exchange for a payment of $100,000 by the defendant.

e. A commercial dispute involving $95,000 in damages is filed in a federal court. The judge requires the parties' attorneys to present their arguments and supporting evidence, excluding witnesses, to the jury. The jury then renders a nonbinding verdict. Once the nonbinding verdict is rendered, the parties reach a settlement.

QUESTIONS FOR CRITICAL ANALYSIS

1. Before a case can be heard by a court, the court must have jurisdiction to hear and decide the case. What types of jurisdiction exist? What would happen if a case were filed in a court that did not have jurisdiction over it?

2. The federal courts have jurisdiction primarily over diversity cases and over questions of federal law. State courts have jurisdiction over matters such as wills, divorces, and property concerns. Why? What would happen if federal courts decided divorce cases, for example? What would happen if state courts decided cases between a citizen of the state and a foreign citizen?

3. A change of venue from Oklahoma City to Denver, Colorado, was ordered for the trials of Timothy McVeigh and Terry Nichols after they had been indicted in connection with the 1995 bombing of the Alfred P. Murrah Federal Building in Oklahoma City, which killed more than 160 persons and injured hundreds of others. The decision changing the venue of the trial is *United States v. McVeigh*, 918 F.Supp. 1467 (1996). Review this case. What constitutional issues were involved in the court's decision allowing a change of venue? Do death penalty cases require a different standard? If so, what is the standard? What evidence did the court review in reaching its decision? Why did the court conclude that the federal district court in Denver, Colorado, met the requirements for an alternative venue?

Given the outcome of the case, was the change of venue effective? Given the pretrial publicity, would the defendants have been convicted if venue had been changed to Maine?

4. What is the difference in the roles that the trial and appellate courts play in a lawsuit? Why is it that appellate courts only rarely decide questions of fact? When does an appellate court review facts?

5. Most state court judges are elected, while federal court judges are appointed. Which system, in your opinion, is fairer? Does either system affect the quality of the judiciary?

6. Do you think that it is fair that in most cases there is no right to appeal to the United States Supreme Court? Should citizens have to petition for *certiorari* to be heard by the Supreme Court? What does the requirement of a grant of *certiorari*, coupled with the limited number of cases that the Supreme Court hears, tell you about the role and purpose of the Supreme Court?

7. Why are Americans increasingly turning to ADR as a way of settling their disputes? What are the implications of ADR, including the increased use of "private justice," for the American system of justice generally?

8. Some individuals have claimed that mandatory ADR infringes on a person's constitutional right to a jury trial. Do you agree with this view? Why or why not?

PROJECTS

1. Contact a local trial court and request a copy of a chart, pamphlet, or other publication that lists the courts in your state and describes the jurisdiction of each. Check with your instructor prior to undertaking this assignment for any special instructions.

2. Contact the local federal district court clerk's office and ask if electronic filings are accepted. If accepted, ask whether filings are accepted via e-mail or CD-ROM. Find out if electronic filing is limited to certain types of documents or cases. Check with your instructor prior to undertaking this assignment for any special instructions.

3. Review a local legal newspaper or bar association journal. Locate advertisements for firms offering ADR services.

Call one of these firms and find out what services are offered and what rates are charged.

4. Contact the American Arbitration Association and ask what kinds of disputes (contract disputes, employment disputes, and so on) it arbitrates. Request a copy of its procedural rules for the arbitration of disputes in one of the areas it handles. Review the rules and summarize the procedures involved.

5. Review the table of contents of the court rules of your state courts or the federal courts. What subjects are covered? How do these subjects relate to the topics discussed in this chapter? You should be able to locate these rules in your school's library or in a law school library.

USING INTERNET RESOURCES

1. Paralegals frequently assist in ADR proceedings and even, in some cases, serve as mediators or arbitrators. To learn more about ADR procedures, go to **http://www.adr.org**, the home page for the American Arbitration Association (AAA). Browse through the site's offerings and find the answers to the following questions:

   a. When was the AAA founded? What types of services does it offer?

   b. Where is the AAA regional office nearest you? Does the AAA engage in arbitration outside the United States?

   c. How many arbitration forms are available to download from this site? Is there any cost for downloading these forms? How many states provide state-specific forms on this site?

2. Go to the official site of the United States Supreme Court at **http://www.supremecourtus.gov**, and answer the following questions:

   a. Click on "About the Court," and then click on "The Court and Its Procedures." When does the Supreme Court session begin and end each year? How long does each side normally have to argue a case before the Supreme Court justices? When the Court is in recess, approximately how many petitions do the justices have to review per week to determine if they will hear the cases?

   b. Click on "Orders" from the home page menu, and then click on "Orders of the Court" from the most recent time period. What is an order in the language of the

Supreme Court? Do the justices sign orders? Are they used often?

   c. Click on "Opinions," and then click on "Latest Slip Opinions." What is a slip opinion? Select a Supreme Court opinion that contains a syllabus, or summary of the Court's opinion. Review it, and identify and briefly describe the parties, the general nature of the dispute, the dates the case was argued and decided, and the name of the justice who delivered the opinion of the Court and any justice(s) who dissented.

   d. Click on "Links." Can you access the executive and legislative branches of government through the links provided in this Web site?

3. Several businesses now offer clients the opportunity to settle, mediate, or otherwise resolve their legal disputes entirely online. To review one such Web site, go to **http://www.cybersettle.com**. Then answer the following questions:

   a. Roll your mouse over "About Us," then over "Company Information." Next, select "Company History" and read about Cybersettle's history and methods. For what types of disputes would Cybersettle's services be most useful?

   b. Roll your mouse over "System Demo" and click on "Interactive Demo." Go through the demonstration of how to use Cybersettle's services. How useful do you think Cybersettle's services are to business managers?

How important is it that Cybersettle's services be conducted online? Could the same techniques for settling disputes be used offline? How likely would you be to use the services of Cybersettle online? Would you feel that your information was secure and private?

c. Roll your mouse over "News and Information," click on the link to "Frequently Asked Questions (FAQs)," and

select the tab "Attorney FAQ." How does Cybersettle address concerns about security and privacy? Why might a party use Cybersettle's services instead of traditional ADR methods?

4.  For additional resources, visit our Web site at **http://www.paralegal.delmar. cengage.com**.

END NOTES

1. See Appendix J for the full text of the U.S. Constitution.

2. As will be discussed shortly, a state's highest court is often referred to as the state supreme court, but there are exceptions. For example, in New York the supreme court is a trial court.

3. Under the Class Action Fairness Act (CAFA) of 2005, it is likely that most class-action lawsuits will not qualify for state court jurisdiction.

4. Currently under negotiation is the Hague Convention on Jurisdiction, an international treaty intended to make civil judgments enforceable across national borders. One issue in the negotiations is whether to require that all disputes be settled in the country of the seller or the country of the buyer. It has also been suggested that mandatory jurisdiction provisions be left out of the treaty.

5. Pronounced *ven*-yoo.

6. Pronounced jus-*tish*-a-bul.

7. The name in Ohio is Court of Common Pleas; the name in New York is Supreme Court.

8. Pronounced sur-shee-uh-*rah*-ree.

9. As you will read later in the chapter, the American Arbitration Association is a leading provider of arbitration services in the United States.

10. See, for example, *Wright v. Universal Maritime Service Corp.,* 525 U.S. 70, 119 S.Ct. 391, 142 L.Ed.2d 361 (1998).

11. *Hooters of America, Inc. v. Phillips,* 173 F.3d 933 (4th Cir. 1999). See also *Circuit City Stores, Inc. v. Adams,* 279 F.3d 889 (2002).

TORT LAW, PRODUCT LIABILITY, AND CONSUMER LAW

CHAPTER OUTLINE

AFTER COMPLETING THIS CHAPTER, YOU WILL KNOW:

▶ What a tort is, the purpose of tort law, and the basic categories of torts.

▶ The four elements of negligence.

▶ What is meant by strict liability and the underlying policy for imposing strict product liability.

▶ What defenses can be raised in product liability actions.

▶ Some of the ways in which the government protects consumers against unfair business practices and harmful products.

INTRODUCTION

Torts are wrongful actions. In fact, the word *tort* is French for "wrong." Through tort law, society compensates those who have suffered injuries as a result of the wrongful conduct of others. Although some torts, such as trespass, originated in the English common law, the field of tort law continues to expand. As new ways to commit wrongs—such as the use of the Internet to commit wrongful acts—are discovered, the courts are extending tort law to cover these wrongs. Torts committed via the Internet are sometimes referred to as **cyber torts**.

In the pages that follow, we discuss some of the primary concepts of tort law and how they are being applied today in the context of the online environment, as well as other environments. We also discuss *product liability,* which is the area of tort law under which sellers can be held liable for defective products. In the final pages of the chapter, we look at a growing body of law designed to protect the health and safety of *consumers*—those who purchase goods and services from businesses.

▌ tort
A civil wrong not arising from a breach of contract; a breach of a legal duty that proximately causes harm or injury to another.

▌ cyber tort
A tort committed in cyberspace.

THE BASIS OF TORT LAW

Two notions serve as the basis of all torts: wrongs and compensation. Tort law recognizes that some acts are wrong because they cause injuries to others. In a tort action, one person or group brings a personal-injury suit against another person or group to obtain compensation (money damages) or other relief for the harm suffered. Because tort suits involve "private" wrongs, they are distinguishable from criminal actions, which involve "public" wrongs. The state prosecutor brings criminal actions against individuals who commit acts that are considered to be wrongs against society as a whole (crimes are usually defined by statute, as you will read in Chapter 16). Sometimes an act may result in both a tort lawsuit and a criminal prosecution.

Generally, the purpose of tort law is to provide remedies for the invasion of various interests—such as people's interests in their physical safety and security, privacy, freedom of movement, and reputation—that society seeks to protect. In this chapter, we first discuss two broad categories of torts: *intentional torts* and *negligence.* The classification of a particular tort depends largely on how the tort occurs (intentionally or unintentionally) and the surrounding circumstances. We then examine the concept of *strict liability,* a tort doctrine under which a defendant may be held liable for harm or injury to another regardless of intention or fault, and look at the application of this doctrine in the area of product liability.

On the Web

You can find cases and articles on torts in the tort law library at the Internet Law Library's Web site. Go to **http://www.lawguru.com/ilawlib**.

INTENTIONAL TORTS

An **intentional tort**, as the term implies, requires *intent.* In tort law, intent does not necessarily mean that the actor (who is sometimes referred to as the **tortfeasor**) intended to harm someone; rather, it means only that the actor intended the consequences of his or her act or knew with substantial certainty that certain consequences would result from the act. Note that the law generally assumes that individuals intend the *normal* consequences of their actions. Thus, forcefully pushing another—even if done in jest and without any evil motive—is an intentional tort (if injury results), because the object of a strong push can ordinarily be expected to go flying.

Intentional torts fall into two categories: intentional torts against persons and intentional torts against property. Next, we look at both of these categories.

▌ intentional tort
A wrongful act knowingly committed.

▌ tortfeasor
One who commits a tort.

Intentional Torts against Persons

Intentional torts against persons include assault and battery, false imprisonment, intentional infliction of emotional distress, defamation, invasion of the right to privacy, appropriation, misrepresentation, and wrongful interference.

Assault and Battery

assault

Any word or action intended to make another person apprehensive or fearful of immediate physical harm; a reasonably believable threat.

An **assault** is any word or action intended to make another person apprehensive or fearful of immediate physical harm. In other words, an assault is a reasonably believable threat. Note that apprehension is not the same as fear. If a contact is such that a reasonable person would want to avoid it, and if there is a reasonable basis for believing that the contact will occur, then the plaintiff suffers apprehension regardless of whether he or she is afraid. The interest protected by tort law concerning assault is the freedom from having to expect harmful or offensive contact. The occurrence of apprehension is enough to justify compensation.

battery

The intentional and offensive touching of another without lawful justification.

The *completion* of the fear-inducing act, if it results in harm to the plaintiff, is a **battery**, which is defined as harmful or offensive physical contact *intentionally* performed. ▶ **EXAMPLE 7.1** Suppose that Ivan threatens Jean with a gun, then shoots her. The pointing of the gun at Jean is an assault; the firing of the gun (if the bullet hits Jean) is a battery. ◀ The interest protected by tort law concerning battery is the right to personal security and safety. The contact can be harmful, or it can be merely offensive (such as an unwelcome kiss). Physical injury need not occur. The contact can involve any part of the body or anything attached to it—for example, a hat or other item of clothing, a purse, or a chair or an automobile in which one is sitting. Whether the contact is offensive or not is determined by the *reasonable person standard*.[1] The contact can be made by the defendant or by some force the defendant sets in motion—for example, a rock thrown, food poisoned, or a stick swung.

Compensation.   If the plaintiff shows that there was contact, and the jury agrees that the contact was offensive, the plaintiff has a right to compensation. There is no need to show that the defendant acted out of malice; the person could have just been joking or playing around. The underlying motive does not matter, only the intent to bring about the harmful or offensive contact to the plaintiff. In fact, proving a motive is never necessary (but is sometimes relevant). A plaintiff may be compensated for the emotional harm or loss of reputation resulting from a battery, as well as for physical harm.

defense

That which a defendant offers and alleges as a reason why the plaintiff should not recover what she or he seeks in a lawsuit.

Defenses to Assault and Battery.   A number of legally recognized **defenses** (reasons why plaintiffs should not obtain what they are seeking) can be raised by a defendant who is sued for assault, battery, or both:

- *Consent.* When a person consents to the act that damages her or him, there is generally no liability (legal responsibility) for the damage done. For example, if Sue consents to being kissed, Bryan can raise this as a defense if she sues for battery.

- *Self-defense.* An individual who is defending his or her life or physical well-being can claim self-defense. In situations of both *real* and *apparent* danger, a person may use whatever force is *reasonably* necessary to prevent harmful contact. Thus, if Simon is sexually assaulting Linda, she can claim this as a defense if Simon sues her for hitting him with a baseball bat.

- *Defense of others.* An individual can act in a reasonable manner to protect others who are in real or apparent danger—that is, if Fred offensively touches your wife and you hit Fred, you can raise this as a defense if Fred subsequently tries to sue you for battery.

- *Defense of property.* People can use reasonable force in attempting to remove intruders from their homes, although force that is likely to cause death or great bodily injury can never be used just to protect property. For example, if you catch someone in the act of breaking into your garage, you can use nondeadly force to stop that person without being liable for battery.

Developing Paralegal Skills

A CLAIM OF FALSE IMPRISONMENT

Julie Waterman works for a small law firm. She has just been asked to interview a new client. The client detained a customer in his video store for suspected shoplifting, and now he is facing a lawsuit brought by the customer for false imprisonment. Because Julie's supervising attorney has to go out of town unexpectedly, Julie will conduct the initial interview with the client, gather as much information as she can about the incident, and summarize what she learns in a memorandum for the attorney to review later. Before the interview, Julie checks the relevant state law governing false imprisonment. During the interview, Julie makes sure that she covers the topics on her checklist for determining false imprisonment.

CHECKLIST FOR DETERMINING FALSE IMPRISONMENT

- Did the client have reasonable grounds for believing that the customer was shoplifting? What were these grounds—that is, what specific behavior made the client suspect that the customer took merchandise without paying for it?
- Did the customer resist the detention?
- How long did the client detain the customer? Fifteen minutes? A half hour? An hour? Longer than an hour? Was the duration of the detention reasonable?
- Was the customer placed in a reasonably comfortable environment during the detention?
- Was the customer subjected to abusive or accusatory words or to any indignity while being confined?
- Were all procedures used to detain the client reasonable?

False Imprisonment

False imprisonment is defined as the intentional confinement or restraint of another person's activities without justification. False imprisonment interferes with the freedom to move without restraint. The confinement can be accomplished through the use of physical barriers, physical restraint, or threats of physical force. Moral pressure or threats of future harm do not constitute false imprisonment. It is essential that the person being restrained not comply with the restraint willingly.

Stores are often sued for false imprisonment after they have attempted to confine a suspected shoplifter for questioning. Under the "privilege to detain" granted to merchants in some states, a merchant can use the defense of *probable cause* to justify delaying a suspected shoplifter. Probable cause exists when the evidence to support the belief that a person is guilty outweighs the evidence against that belief. Although laws governing false imprisonment vary from state to state, generally they require that any detention be conducted in a *reasonable* manner and for only a *reasonable* length of time.

Intentional Infliction of Emotional Distress

The tort of *intentional infliction of emotional distress* can be defined as an intentional act that amounts to extreme and outrageous conduct resulting in severe emotional distress to another. ▶ **EXAMPLE 7.2** Suppose a prankster telephones an individual and says that the individual's spouse has just been in a horrible accident. As a result, the individual suffers intense mental pain or anxiety. The caller's behavior is deemed to be extreme and outrageous conduct that exceeds the bounds of decency accepted by society and is therefore **actionable** (capable of serving as the basis for a lawsuit). ◄ Note that courts in some jurisdictions require that the emotional distress be evidenced by some physical symptom or illness or some emotional disturbance that can be documented by a psychiatric consultant or other medical professional.

actionable
Capable of serving as the basis of a lawsuit. An actionable claim can be pursued in a lawsuit or other court action.

Defamation

defamation
Anything published or publicly spoken that causes injury to another's good name, reputation, or character.

slander
Defamation in oral form.

libel
Defamation in writing or some other form having the quality of permanence (such as videotape).

Wrongfully hurting a person's good reputation constitutes the tort of **defamation**. The law imposes a general duty on all persons to refrain from making false, defamatory statements about others. Breaching this duty orally involves the tort of **slander**; breaching it in writing involves the tort of **libel**. The tort of defamation also arises when a false statement is made about a person's product, business, or title to property.

The common law defines four types of false utterances that are considered slander *per se* (meaning that no proof of injury or harm is required for these false utterances to be actionable):

- A statement that another has a loathsome communicable disease.
- A statement that another has committed improprieties while engaging in a profession or trade.
- A statement that another has committed or has been imprisoned for a serious crime.
- A statement that an unmarried woman is unchaste.

The Publication Requirement.   The basis of the tort of defamation is the publication of a statement or statements that hold an individual up to contempt, ridicule, or hatred. *Publication* here means simply that the defamatory statements are communicated to persons other than the defamed party. ▶ **EXAMPLE 7.3**   If Sally writes Andrew a private letter accusing him of embezzling funds, the action does not constitute libel. If John calls Rita dishonest, unattractive, and incompetent when no one else is around, the action does not constitute slander. In neither case was the message communicated to a third party. ◄

The courts have generally held that even dictating a letter to a secretary constitutes publication, although the publication may be privileged (the meaning of privileged communications in defamation law will be discussed shortly). Moreover, if a third party overhears defamatory statements by chance, the courts usually hold that this also constitutes publication. Defamatory statements made via the Internet are actionable as well. Note further that any individual who republishes or repeats defamatory statements is liable even if that person reveals the source of the statements.

privilege
In tort law, the ability to act contrary to another person's right without that person's having legal redress for such acts. Privilege may be raised as a defense to defamation.

Defenses against Defamation.   Truth is normally an absolute defense against a defamation charge. In other words, if the defendant in a defamation suit can prove that his or her allegedly defamatory statements were true, the defendant will not be liable.

Another defense that is sometimes raised is that the statements were **privileged** communications and thus the defendant is immune from liability. Privileged communications are of two types: absolute and qualified. Only in judicial proceedings and certain legislative proceedings is an *absolute* privilege granted. For example, statements made in the courtroom by attorneys and judges during a trial are absolutely privileged, as are statements made by legislators during congressional floor debate. A *qualified,* or *conditional,* privilege applies when a statement is related to a matter of public interest or when the statement is necessary to protect a person's private interest and is made to another person with an interest in the same subject matter.

In general, false and defamatory statements that are made about *public figures* (public officials who exercise substantial governmental power and any persons in the public limelight) and that are published in the press are privileged if they are made without **actual malice**.[2] To be made with actual malice, a statement must be made *with either knowledge of falsity or a reckless disregard of the truth*. Statements made about public figures, especially when they are made via a public medium, are usually related to matters of general public interest; they are made about people who substantially affect all of us. Furthermore, public figures generally have some access to a public medium for responding to disparaging (belittling, discrediting) falsehoods about themselves; private individuals do not. For these reasons, public figures have a greater burden of proof in defamation cases (they must prove actual malice) than do private individuals.

> **actual malice**
> Real and demonstrable evil intent. In a defamation suit, a statement made about a public figure normally must be made with actual malice (with either knowledge of its falsity or a reckless disregard of the truth) for liability to be incurred.

Invasion of the Right to Privacy

A person has a right to solitude and freedom from prying public eyes—in other words, to privacy. The United States Supreme Court has held that a fundamental right to privacy is also implied by various amendments to the U.S. Constitution. Some state constitutions explicitly provide for privacy rights. In addition, a number of federal and state statutes have been enacted to protect individual rights in specific areas. Tort law also safeguards these rights through the tort of *invasion of privacy*. Four acts qualify as an invasion of privacy:

- *The use of a person's name, picture, or other likeness for commercial purposes without permission.* This tort, which is usually referred to as the tort of *appropriation*, will be examined shortly.

- *Intrusion in an individual's affairs or seclusion.* For example, invading someone's home or illegally searching someone's briefcase is an invasion of privacy. The tort has been held to extend to eavesdropping by wiretap, the unauthorized scanning of a bank account, compulsory blood testing, and window peeping.

- *Publication of information that places a person in a false light.* This could be a story attributing to the person ideas not held or actions not taken by the person. (Publishing such a story could involve the tort of defamation as well.)

- *Public disclosure of private facts about an individual that an ordinary person would find objectionable.* A newspaper account of a private citizen's sex life or financial affairs could be an actionable invasion of privacy.

On the Web

The Privacy Rights Clearinghouse offers numerous links to sources concerning privacy rights at **http://privacyrights.org/links.htm**.

Appropriation

The use by one person of another person's name, likeness, or other identifying characteristic, without permission and for the benefit of the user, constitutes the tort of **appropriation**. Under the law, an individual's right to privacy normally includes the right to the exclusive use of her or his identity.

▶ **EXAMPLE 7.4** A good example of appropriation can be found in the case brought by Vanna White, the hostess of the popular television game show *Wheel of Fortune*, against Samsung Electronics America, Inc. Without White's permission, Samsung included in an advertisement for its videocassette recorders a depiction of a robot dressed in a wig, gown, and jewelry, posed in a scene that resembled the *Wheel of Fortune* set, in a stance for which White is famous. The court held in White's favor, holding that the tort of appropriation does not require the use of a celebrity's name or likeness. The court stated that Samsung's robot ad left "little doubt" as to the identity of the celebrity whom the ad was meant to depict.[3] ◀

> **appropriation**
> In tort law, the use by one person of another person's name, likeness, or other identifying characteristic without permission and for the benefit of the user.

Ethics Watch!

ONLINE PRIVACY

A pressing issue in today's online world has to do with the privacy rights of Internet users, especially in the employment context. For example, law firms today routinely provide their paralegals and other employees with e-mail access to facilitate the performance of job duties. What if, however, a paralegal uses e-mail to spread rumors or to make sexually explicit or unprofessional comments about other employees? Can a paralegal claim a right to privacy in the personal e-mail sent from his or her office computer? Most courts that have considered the question have concluded that employees have no reasonable expectation of privacy in e-mails sent from their office computers. This is true even when employees were not informed that their e-mails could be read by the employer. After all, the employer has both a legal and an ethical obligation to prevent harassment and discrimination in the workplace. Although employers who provide Internet access to employees can usually monitor or access their employees' e-mail messages without liability for invasion of privacy, they would not be allowed by most courts to publicly disclose the contents of an employee's personal e-mail.

Misrepresentation (Fraud)

A misrepresentation leads another to believe in a condition that is different from the condition that actually exists. This is often accomplished through a false or an incorrect statement. The tort of **fraudulent misrepresentation**, or fraud, involves intentional deceit for personal gain— not misrepresentations innocently made by someone who is unaware of the existing facts.

> **fraudulent misrepresentation**
> Any misrepresentation, either by misstatement or omission of a material fact, knowingly made with the intention of deceiving another and on which a reasonable person would and does rely to his or her detriment.

Elements of Fraud.   The tort of fraudulent misrepresentation includes several elements:

- Misrepresentation of facts or conditions with knowledge that they are false or with reckless disregard for the truth.
- Intent to induce another to rely on the misrepresentation.
- Justifiable reliance by the deceived party.
- Damages suffered as a result of the reliance.
- Causal connection between the misrepresentation and the injury suffered.

Fraud exists only when a person represents as a fact something he or she knows is untrue. It is fraud to claim that a building does not leak when one knows it does. Facts are objectively ascertainable, whereas *seller's talk* is not. ▶ **EXAMPLE 7.5**   If Harry says, "I am the best accountant in town," that would be considered seller's talk, not fraud. The speaker is not trying to represent something as fact, because the term *best* is subjective (open to interpretation) and because a "reasonable person" would not rely on Harry's statement. ◀

Fact versus Opinion.   Normally, the tort of misrepresentation or fraud occurs only when there is reliance on a *statement of fact*. Sometimes, however, reliance on a *statement of opinion* may involve the tort of misrepresentation if the individual making the statement of

On the Web

The 'Lectric Law Library's Legal Lexicon includes an informative discussion of the elements of fraud as well as different types of fraud. To access this page, go to **http://www.lectlaw.com/def/f079.htm**.

opinion has a superior knowledge of the subject matter. ▶ **EXAMPLE 7.6** When a lawyer makes a statement of opinion about the law in a state in which the lawyer is licensed to practice, a court would construe reliance on such a statement to be equivalent to reliance on a statement of fact. ◀ (See this chapter's *Technology and Today's Paralegal* feature on pages 230 and 231 for a discussion of online fraud.)

Wrongful Interference

Today, many lawsuits involve situations in which an individual or business is accused of wrongfully interfering with the business of another. These **business torts** are generally divided into two categories: wrongful interference with a contractual relationship (contract law will be discussed in Chapter 8) and wrongful interference with a business relationship.

▌business tort
Wrongful interference with another's business rights.

Wrongful Interference with a Contractual Relationship.
The body of tort law relating to intentional interference with a contractual relationship has expanded greatly in recent years. Three elements are necessary to establish the tort of wrongful interference with a contractual relationship:

- A valid, enforceable contract must exist between two parties.
- A third party must know that this contract exists.
- The third party must *intentionally* cause either of the two parties to breach the contract.

The contract may be between a firm and its employees or a firm and its customers. Sometimes, for example, a competitor of a firm draws away one of the firm's key employees. If the original employer can show (1) that the competitor induced the employee to leave (a breach of the contract) and (2) that the employee would not otherwise have broken the contract, then the employer may be entitled to compensation from the competitor.

Wrongful Interference with a Business Relationship.
Wrongful interference with a business relationship involves situations in which a party unreasonably interferes with another's business in an attempt to gain a larger share of the market. There is a difference between competitive methods that do not give rise to tort liability and **predatory behavior**—actions undertaken with the intention of unlawfully driving competitors completely out of the market. The distinction usually depends on whether a business is attempting to attract customers in general or to solicit only those customers who have shown an interest in a similar product or service of a specific competitor. ▶ **EXAMPLE 7.7** If a shopping center contains two shoe stores, an employee of Store A cannot be positioned at the entrance of Store B for the purpose of diverting customers to Store A. This type of activity constitutes the tort of wrongful interference with a business relationship, which is commonly considered to be an unfair trade practice. If this type of activity were permitted, Store A would reap the benefits of Store B's advertising. ◀

▌predatory behavior
Business behavior that is undertaken with the intention of unlawfully driving competitors out of the market.

Defenses to Wrongful Interference.
A person will not be liable for the tort of wrongful interference with a contractual or business relationship if it can be shown that the interference was justified, or permissible. Good faith competitive behavior is a permissible interference even if it results in the breaking of a contract. ▶ **EXAMPLE 7.8** If Antonio's Meats advertises so effectively that it induces Beverly's Restaurant Chain to break its contract with Otis Meat Company, Otis Meat Company will be unable to recover against Antonio's Meats on a wrongful interference theory. After all, the public policy that favors free competition in advertising outweighs any possible instability that such competitive activity might cause in contractual relations. ◀

Technology and Today's Paralegal

THE LEGAL ISSUES REGARDING ONLINE SCAMS AND SPAM

Many people prefer to shop via the Web for the convenience of shopping at home and for the ease of comparing a wide range of products and prices. Consumers shopping online, however, may encounter some deceptive and fraudulent business practices unique to the world of Internet shopping. As a paralegal, you should be aware of the steps being taken to curb deceptive sales practices and online fraud, as well as efforts to control the onslaught of bulk, unsolicited e-mail, or spam.

KEEP ABREAST OF CURRENT SCAMS

You can find out about fraudulent schemes currently being perpetrated against consumers online by going to the "Consumer Alerts" page of the U.S. Consumer Gateway Web site at **http://www.consumer.gov**. You can also obtain information on online consumer fraud, including Internet fraud statistics, from the Web site of the National Consumers League at **http://www.fraud.org/internet/intinfo.htm**. This organization has developed Web pages to help consumers, as well as lawyers, who deal in Internet consumer fraud.

KNOW YOUR RESOURCES

The Federal Trade Commission (FTC) can bring actions against entities that make false or unsubstantiated claims in their Internet ads, and it has already done so on several occasions. The FTC has also provided "hot links" on Web sites that have engaged in deceptive advertising. A hot link takes the user to the FTC's own Web site, on which the complaint, restraining order, and other documents in the case can be read and downloaded. The FTC has also joined the Coupon Information Center to identify Internet advertisements that might be fraudulent coupon-related schemes.

THE FEDERAL CAN-SPAM ACT

Bulk, unsolicited e-mail ("junk" e-mail), often called *spam,* imposes a burden on an Internet service provider's equipment as well as on e-mail recipients' computer systems. Today, spam accounts for an estimated 60 percent of all e-mail. When dealing with clients who market goods or services through commercial e-mails, paralegals will need to understand recent laws regulating spam. In 2003, Congress enacted the Controlling the Assault of Non-Solicited Pornography and Marketing (CAN-SPAM) Act, which took effect on January 1, 2004. You can find information about the CAN-SPAM Act at the Federal Trade Commission's Web site at **http://www.ftc.gov/bcp/conline/pubs/buspubs/canspam.htm**.

Intentional Torts against Property

Intentional torts against property include trespass to land, trespass to personal property, and conversion. These torts are wrongful actions that interfere with individuals' legally recognized rights with regard to their land or personal property. The law distinguishes real property from personal property (see Chapter 9). *Real property* is land and things "permanently" attached to the land. *Personal property* consists of all other items, which are basically movable. Thus, a house and lot are real property, whereas the furniture inside a house is personal property. Money and stocks and bonds are also personal property.

The legislation applies to any "commercial electronic mail messages" that are sent to promote a commercial product or service. Generally, the act permits the use of unsolicited commercial e-mail but prohibits certain types of spamming activities, including the use of a false return address and the inclusion of false, misleading, or deceptive information. The statute also prohibits the use of "dictionary attacks"—sending messages to randomly generated e-mail addresses—and the "harvesting" of e-mail addresses from Web sites through the use of specialized software. Additionally, the law requires senders of commercial e-mail to do the following:

- Include a return address on the e-mail.
- Include a clear notification that the message is an ad and provide a valid physical postal address.
- Provide a mechanism that allows recipients to "opt out" of further e-mail ads from the same source.
- Take action on a recipient's "opt-out" request within ten days.
- Label any sexually oriented materials as such.

STATE STATUTES PREEMPTED

The CAN-SPAM Act preempted some stricter state antispam laws that were more favorable to the interests of consumers. California's law, for example, prohibited any person or business from sending e-mail ads to or from any e-mail address in California unless the recipient had expressly agreed to receive e-mail from the sender.

SPAMMING AS A TORT

Spamming might also constitute a tort if it interferes with a computer system's functioning. A number of plaintiffs have successfully sued, under tort law, when spam overloaded a business's computer system or impaired a business's computer equipment. In these cases, spamming was held to constitute unauthorized interference with the use of the personal property of another, which is a trespass to personal property.

TECHNOLOGY TIP

Consumers continue to face fraudulent online schemes, and spam continues to increase. Paralegals in consumer law therefore need to keep up to date on the types of scams that are being propagated over the Internet. Paralegals should also be familiar with the resources available to those with complaints of Internet fraud, which include the FTC and many state agencies. Finally, paralegals need to be familiar with laws regulating spam, such as the CAN-SPAM Act.

Trespass to Land

A **trespass to land** occurs whenever a person, without permission, enters onto land that is owned by another, causes anything to enter onto the land, remains on the land, or permits anything to remain on it. Actual harm to the land is not an essential element of this tort because the tort is designed to protect the right of an owner to exclusively possess his or her property. Common types of trespass to land include walking or driving on the land, shooting a gun over the land, throwing rocks at a building that belongs to someone else, causing water to back up on someone else's land, and placing part of one's building on an adjoining landowner's property.

trespass to land
The entry onto, above, or below the surface of land owned by another without the owner's permission or legal authorization.

Trespass Criteria, Rights, and Duties. The owner of the real property must show that a person is a trespasser. For example, if a person ignores "posted" trespass signs and enters onto the property, he or she is established as a trespasser. A guest in your home is not a trespasser—unless she or he has been asked to leave but refuses. Any person who enters onto your property to commit an illegal act (such as a thief) is established impliedly as a trespasser, without posted signs. Normally, a trespasser must pay for any damage caused to the property and can be removed from the premises through the use of reasonable force without the owner's being liable for assault and battery.

Defenses against Trespass to Land. The most common defense to trespass is that the trespass was warranted. For example, when a trespasser enters to assist someone in danger, a defense exists. Another defense exists when the trespasser can show that he or she had permission to come onto the land for a specified purpose, such as to read an electric meter. Note that the property owner can revoke such permission. If the property owner asks a meter reader to leave and the meter reader refuses, the meter reader at that point becomes a trespasser.

Trespass to Personal Property

| **trespass to personal property**
The unlawful taking or harming of another's personal property; interference with another's right to the exclusive possession of his or her personal property.

Whenever any individual unlawfully harms the personal property of another or otherwise interferes with the owner's right to exclusively possess that personal property, **trespass to personal property** occurs. ▶ **EXAMPLE 7.9** Suppose that a student takes another student's paralegal book as a practical joke and hides it so that the owner is unable to find it for several days prior to a final examination. In this situation, the student has engaged in a trespass to personal property. ◀

If it can be shown that trespass to personal property was warranted, then a complete defense exists. Most states, for example, allow automobile repair shops to hold a customer's car (under what is called an *artisan's lien*) when the customer refuses to pay for repairs already completed.

Conversion

| **conversion**
The act of wrongfully taking or retaining a person's personal property and placing it in the service of another.

Whenever personal property is wrongfully taken from its rightful owner, the act of **conversion** occurs. Conversion is any act depriving an owner of personal property without that owner's permission and without just cause. When conversion occurs, the lesser offense of trespass to personal property usually occurs as well. If the initial taking of the property was unlawful, there is trespass; retention of that property is conversion. Even if the owner permitted the initial taking of the property, failure to return it may still be conversion. Conversion is the civil side of crimes related to theft. A store clerk who steals merchandise from the store commits a crime and engages in the tort of conversion at the same time.

Even if a person mistakenly believed that she or he was entitled to the goods, a tort of conversion may occur. ▶ **EXAMPLE 7.10** Someone who buys stolen goods is guilty of conversion even if he or she did not know that the goods were stolen. If the true owner brings a tort action against the buyer, the buyer must either return the property to the owner or pay the owner the full value of the property (despite having already paid money to the thief). If the person accused of conversion can show that the purported owner did not in fact own the property, however, a defense exists. ◀ Necessity is another possible defense against conversion.

INTENTIONAL TORTS AND THE PARALEGAL

The common law of torts is an area of particular importance for paralegals. Tort lawsuits are frequent occurrences in the American legal arena, and many attorneys and paralegals devote a substantial amount of their time to serving clients who want to either bring or defend against tort lawsuits. The paralegal's tasks relating to a lawsuit for an intentional tort are similar to the tasks necessary for any litigation, including assisting with (or conducting) an interview with the client, investigating the client's claim, interviewing any witnesses to the alleged tort action, preparing documents to file with the relevant court, assisting at trial if the dispute is not settled out of court, and so on. You will become familiar with the types of work that paralegals perform before, during, and after a trial in later chapters. Although many tort lawsuits are brought for intentional torts, even more common are lawsuits for torts of negligence, a topic to which we now turn.

NEGLIGENCE

The tort of **negligence** occurs when someone suffers injury because of another's failure to live up to a required *duty of care*. In contrast to intentional torts, in torts involving negligence, the one committing the tort neither wishes to bring about the consequences of the act nor believes that they will occur. The actor's conduct merely creates a *risk* of such consequences. If no risk is created, there is no negligence. The risk must also be foreseeable— that is, it must be such that a reasonable person engaging in the same activity would anticipate the risk and guard against it.

Many of the actions discussed in the section on intentional torts constitute negligence if the element of intent is missing. ▶ **EXAMPLE 7.11** If Juan intentionally shoves Naomi, who falls and breaks an arm as a result, Juan will have committed the intentional tort of assault and battery. If Juan carelessly bumps into Naomi, however, and she falls and breaks an arm as a result, Juan's action will constitute negligence. In either situation, Juan has committed a tort. ◀

To succeed in a negligence action, the plaintiff must prove the following:

- That the defendant owed a duty of care to the plaintiff.
- That the defendant breached that duty.
- That the plaintiff suffered a legally recognizable injury.
- That the defendant's breach caused the plaintiff's injury.

We discuss here each of these four elements of negligence.

The Duty of Care and Its Breach

Central to the tort of negligence is the concept of a **duty of care**. The concept arises from the notion that if we are to live in society with other people, some actions can be tolerated and some cannot; some actions are right and some are wrong; and some actions are reasonable and some are not. The basic principle underlying the duty of care is that people are free to act as they please so long as their actions do not infringe on the interests of others.

The law of torts defines and measures the duty of care by the **reasonable person standard**. In determining whether a duty of care has been breached, for example, the courts ask how a reasonable person would have acted in the same circumstances. The reasonable person standard is said to be (though in an absolute sense it cannot be) objective. It is not necessarily how a particular person would act. It is society's judgment of how an ordinarily prudent person should act. If the so-called reasonable person existed, he or she would be careful, conscientious, prudent, even tempered, and honest. That individuals are required to exercise a reasonable standard of care in their activities is a pervasive concept in the law, and many of the issues dealt with in subsequent chapters of this text have to do with this duty.

In negligence cases, the degree of care to be exercised varies depending on the defendant's occupation or profession, her or his relationship with the plaintiff, and other factors. Generally, whether an action constitutes a breach of the duty of care is determined on a

negligence
The failure to exercise the standard of care that a reasonable person would exercise in similar circumstances.

duty of care
The duty of all persons, as established by tort law, to exercise a reasonable amount of care in their dealings with others. Failure to exercise due care, which is normally determined by the reasonable person standard, constitutes the tort of negligence.

reasonable person standard
The standard of behavior expected of a hypothetical "reasonable person"; the standard against which negligence is measured and that must be observed to avoid liability for negligence.

case-by-case basis. The outcome depends on how the trial court judge (or jury, if it is a jury trial) decides a reasonable person in the position of the defendant would have acted in the particular circumstances of the case. In the following subsections, we examine the degree of care typically expected of landowners and professionals.

The Duty of Landowners

Landowners are expected to exercise reasonable care to protect persons coming onto their property from harm. As suggested earlier, in some jurisdictions, landowners are held to owe a duty to protect even trespassers against certain risks. Landowners who rent or lease premises to tenants are expected to exercise reasonable care to ensure that the tenants and their guests are not harmed in common areas, such as stairways, entryways, laundry rooms, and the like.

Duty to Business Invitees.   Retailers and other firms that explicitly or implicitly invite persons to come onto their premises are usually charged with a duty to exercise reasonable care to protect those persons, who are considered **business invitees**. ▶ **EXAMPLE 7.12**   If you entered a supermarket, slipped on a wet floor, and sustained injuries as a result, the owner of the supermarket would be liable for damages if, when you slipped, there was no sign warning that the floor was wet. A court would hold that the business owner was negligent because the owner failed to exercise a reasonable degree of care in protecting the store's customers against foreseeable risks about which the owner knew or *should have known*. That a patron might slip on the wet floor and be injured as a result was a foreseeable risk, and the owner should have taken care to avoid this risk or to warn the customer of it. ◀ The owner also has a duty to discover and remove any hidden dangers that might injure a customer or other invitee.

business invitee
A person, such as a customer or a client, who is invited onto business premises by the owner of those premises for business purposes.

Open and Obvious Risks.   Some risks, of course, are so obvious that the owner need not warn of them. For instance, a business owner does not need to warn customers to open a door before attempting to walk through it. Other risks, however, even though they may seem obvious to a business owner, may not be so in the eyes of another, such as a child. ▶ **EXAMPLE 7.13**   A hardware store owner may not think it is necessary to warn customers that a stepladder leaning against the back wall of the store could fall down and harm them. It is possible, though, that a child could tip the ladder over and be hurt as a result and that the store could be held liable. ◀

The Duty of Professionals

On the Web

You can locate the professional standards for various organizations at **http://www.lib.uwaterloo.ca/ society/standards.html**.

If an individual has knowledge, skill, or intelligence superior to that of an ordinary person, the individual's conduct must be consistent with that status. Professionals—including physicians, dentists, psychiatrists, architects, engineers, accountants, lawyers, and others—are required to have a standard minimum level of special knowledge and ability. Therefore, in determining what constitutes reasonable care in the case of professionals, their training and expertise are taken into account. In other words, an accountant cannot defend against a lawsuit for negligence by stating, "But I was not familiar with that principle of accounting."

If a professional violates her or his duty of care toward a client, the professional may be sued for malpractice. For example, a patient might sue a physician for *medical malpractice*. A client might sue an attorney for *legal malpractice* (discussed in Chapter 3).

The Injury Requirement and Damages

To recover damages (receive compensation), the plaintiff in a tort lawsuit must prove that she or he suffered a *legally recognizable* injury—some loss, harm, wrong, or invasion of a protected interest. This is generally true in lawsuits for intentional torts as well as lawsuits for negligence. The facts of the case must clearly establish a basis for recovery.

Ethics Watch!

MALPRACTICE SUITS

Paralegals are not perfect and occasionally fail to perform a required duty. But the law will not "look the other way" if a client is harmed as a result of that negligence and then brings a malpractice suit against the attorney. It will not matter that the attorney specifically requested his or her paralegal to send a settlement letter to a defendant's attorney by a certain date. Nor will it matter that the attorney was under the impression that the letter had actually been sent by that date. The attorney, as the person responsible for the paralegal's work, will bear the legal consequences of the paralegal's negligent action if the client is harmed as a result and brings suit. The paralegal might also be held liable. As a paralegal, you should always make sure that you carry out instructions to the letter and perform your tasks accurately and in a timely manner, so that you do not expose your supervising attorney or yourself to liability for malpractice.

Essentially, the purpose of tort law is to compensate for legally recognized injuries resulting from wrongful acts. If no harm or injury results from a given negligent action, there is nothing to compensate—and no tort exists. ▶ **EXAMPLE 7.14** If you carelessly bump into a passerby, who stumbles and falls as a result, you may be liable in tort if the passerby is injured in the fall. If the person is unharmed, however, there normally could be no suit for damages, because no injury was suffered. Although the passerby might be angry and suffer emotional distress, few courts recognize negligently inflicted emotional distress as a tort unless it results in some physical disturbance or dysfunction. ◀

As already mentioned, the purpose of tort law is to compensate injured parties for damages suffered, not to punish people for the torts that they commit. **Compensatory damages** are intended to compensate, or reimburse, a plaintiff for actual losses—to make the plaintiff whole. Occasionally, however, punitive damages are also awarded in tort lawsuits. **Punitive damages** are intended to punish the wrongdoer and deter others from similar wrongdoing. Punitive damages are rarely awarded in lawsuits for ordinary negligence and usually are given only in cases involving intentional torts. They may be awarded, however, if the defendant's negligent conduct was particularly reckless or willful.

Causation

Another element necessary to a tort is *causation*. If a person fails in a duty of care and someone suffers injury, the wrongful activity must have caused the harm for a tort to have been committed. In deciding whether there is causation, the court must address two questions:

- *Is there causation in fact?* Did the injury occur because of the defendant's act, or would it have occurred anyway? If an injury would not have occurred without the defendant's act, then there is causation in fact. **Causation in fact** can usually be determined by the use of the *but for* test: "but for" the wrongful act, the injury

compensatory damages
A money award equivalent to the actual value of injuries or damages sustained by the aggrieved party.

punitive damages
Money damages that may be awarded to a plaintiff to punish the defendant and deter future similar conduct.

causation in fact
Causation brought about by an act or omission without which an event would not have occurred.

Paralegals who work in the area of tort law often assist in litigation involving automobile accidents. Investigating the facts of the accident and preparing sketches such as the one shown at right are often an important aspect of the paralegal's job.

(Courtesy of ©Royalty-Free/Corbis)

would not have occurred. Theoretically, causation in fact is limitless. One could claim, for example, that "but for" the creation of the world, a particular injury would not have occurred. Thus, as a practical matter, the law has to establish limits, and it does so through the concept of proximate cause.

proximate cause
Legal cause; exists when the connection between an act and an injury is strong enough to justify imposing liability.

- *Was the act the proximate cause of the injury?* **Proximate cause**, or legal cause, exists when the connection between an act and an injury is strong enough to justify imposing liability. ▶ **EXAMPLE 7.15** Suppose Arnie carelessly leaves a campfire burning. The fire not only burns down the forest but also sets off an explosion in a nearby chemical plant that spills chemicals into a river, killing all the fish for a hundred miles downstream and ruining the economy of a tourist resort. Should Arnie be liable to the resort owners? To the tourists whose vacations were ruined? These are questions of proximate cause that a court must decide. ◀

Both questions must be answered in the affirmative for liability in tort to arise. If a defendant's action constitutes causation in fact but a court decides that the action is not the proximate cause of the plaintiff's injury, the causation requirement has not been met—and the defendant normally will not be liable to the plaintiff.

Defenses to Negligence

Defendants often defend against negligence claims by asserting that the plaintiffs have failed to prove the existence of one or more of the required elements for negligence. Additionally, there are three basic *affirmative* defenses in negligence cases (defenses that defendants can use to avoid liability even if the facts are as the plaintiffs state): (1) assumption of risk, (2) superseding cause, and (3) contributory negligence.

assumption of risk
Voluntarily taking on oneself a known risk. Assumption of risk is a defense against negligence that can be used when the plaintiff has knowledge of and appreciates a danger and voluntarily exposes himself or herself to the danger.

Assumption of Risk

A plaintiff who voluntarily enters into a risky situation, knowing the risk involved, will not be allowed to recover. This is the defense of **assumption of risk**. The requirements of this defense are (1) knowledge of the risk and (2) voluntary assumption of the risk.

The risk can be assumed by express agreement, or the assumption of risk can be implied by the plaintiff's knowledge of the risk and subsequent conduct. For instance, a driver entering a race knows that there is a risk of being killed or injured in a crash. Of course, the plaintiff does not assume a risk different from or greater than the risk normally carried by the activity. In the scenario just mentioned, the race driver does not assume the risk that the banking in the curves of the racetrack will give way during the race because of a construction defect.

In emergency situations, risks are not considered assumed. Neither are they assumed when a statute protects a class of people from harm and a member of the class is injured by the harm. ▶ **EXAMPLE 7.16** Employees are protected by statute from harmful working conditions and therefore do not assume the risks associated with the workplace. If an employee is injured, he or she will generally be compensated regardless of fault under state workers' compensation statutes (discussed in Chapter 11). ◀

Superseding Cause

An unforeseeable intervening event may break the connection between a wrongful act and an injury to another. If so, it acts as a *superseding cause*—that is, it relieves a defendant of liability for injuries caused by the intervening event. ▶ **EXAMPLE 7.17** Suppose that Derrick keeps a can of gasoline in the trunk of his car. The presence of the gasoline creates a foreseeable risk and is thus a negligent act. If Derrick's car skids and crashes into a tree, causing the gasoline can to explode, Derrick will be liable for injuries sustained by passing pedestrians because of his negligence. If lightning striking the car causes the explosion, however, the lightning supersedes Derrick's original negligence as a cause of the damage, because the lightning was not foreseeable. ◀

Contributory Negligence

All individuals are expected to exercise a reasonable degree of care in looking out for themselves. In a few jurisdictions, recovery for injury resulting from negligence is prevented if the plaintiff was also negligent (failed to exercise a reasonable degree of care). This is the defense of **contributory negligence**. Under the common law doctrine of contributory negligence, no matter how insignificant the plaintiff's negligence is relative to the defendant's negligence, the plaintiff will be precluded from recovering any damages.

The majority of states now allow recovery based on the doctrine of **comparative negligence**. This doctrine enables both the plaintiff's and the defendant's negligence to be computed and the liability for damages distributed accordingly. Some jurisdictions have adopted a "pure" form of comparative negligence that allows the plaintiff to recover, even if the extent of his or her fault is greater than that of the defendant. For example, if the plaintiff was 80 percent at fault and the defendant 20 percent at fault, the plaintiff may recover 20 percent of his or her damages. Many states' comparative negligence statutes, however, contain a "50 percent" rule by which the plaintiff recovers nothing if she or he was more than 50 percent at fault.

Special Negligence Doctrines and Statutes

There are a number of special doctrines and statutes relating to negligence. We examine only a few of them here.

Negligence Per Se

Certain conduct, whether it consists of an action or a failure to act, may be treated as **negligence *per se*** (*per se* means "in or of itself"). Negligence *per se* may occur if an individual violates a statute or an ordinance providing for a criminal penalty and that violation

---

contributory negligence
A theory in tort law under which a complaining party's own negligence contributed to or caused his or her injuries. Contributory negligence is an absolute bar to recovery in a minority of jurisdictions.

comparative negligence
A theory in tort law under which the liability for injuries resulting from negligent acts is shared by all persons who were guilty of negligence (including the injured party) on the basis of each person's proportionate carelessness.

negligence *per se*
An action or failure to act in violation of a statutory requirement.

causes another to be injured. The injured person must prove (1) that the statute clearly sets out what standard of conduct is expected, when and where it is expected, and of whom it is expected; (2) that he or she is in the class intended to be protected by the statute; and (3) that the statute was designed to prevent the type of injury that he or she suffered. The standard of conduct required by the statute is the duty that the defendant owes to the plaintiff, and a violation of the statute is the breach of that duty.

▶ **EXAMPLE 7.18** A statute may require a landowner to keep a building in safe condition and may also subject the landowner to a criminal penalty, such as a fine, if the building is not kept safe. The statute is meant to protect those who are rightfully in the building. Thus, if the owner, without a sufficient excuse, violates the statute and a tenant is thereby injured, then a majority of courts will hold that the owner's unexcused violation of the statute conclusively establishes a breach of a duty of care—that is, that the owner's violation is negligence *per se.* ◀

Special Negligence Statutes

Good Samaritan statute
A state statute stipulating that persons who provide emergency services to others in peril—unless they do so recklessly, thus causing further harm—cannot be sued for negligence.

dram shop act
A state statute that imposes liability on the owners of bars and taverns, as well as those who serve alcoholic drinks to the public, for injuries resulting from accidents caused by intoxicated persons when the sellers or servers of alcoholic drinks contributed to the intoxication.

A number of states have enacted statutes prescribing duties and responsibilities in certain circumstances. For example, most states now have what are called **Good Samaritan statutes**. Under these statutes, persons who receive voluntary aid from others cannot turn around and sue the "Good Samaritans" for negligence. These laws were passed largely to protect physicians and medical personnel who voluntarily render their services in emergency situations to those in need, such as individuals hurt in car accidents.

Many states have also passed **dram shop acts**, under which a tavern owner or bartender may be held liable for injuries caused by a person who became intoxicated while drinking at the bar or who was already intoxicated when served by the bartender. In some states, statutes impose liability on *social hosts* (persons hosting parties) for injuries caused by guests who became intoxicated at the hosts' homes. Under these statutes, it is unnecessary to prove that the tavern owner, bartender, or social host was negligent.

NEGLIGENCE LAW AND THE PARALEGAL

Many paralegals become involved in tasks relating to lawsuits for negligence. If you work for a litigation firm, chances are that you will handle numerous assignments involving claims of negligence. Many law firms specialize in personal-injury litigation and represent plaintiffs who have been injured in car accidents or other incidents resulting from the defendant's alleged negligence.

If you work for a law firm that specializes in personal-injury litigation, you might be responsible for some of the following tasks:

- Interview a client (plaintiff) to obtain details about the accident and the injuries sustained in the accident.

- Locate and interview witnesses to gather additional information about the accident.

- Obtain medical reports from physicians and hospitals describing the plaintiff's injuries.

- Attend depositions, and summarize the testimony of witnesses, parties, and experts in the case.

- Obtain employment data to verify the amount of lost wages that should be claimed as damages if the client's current or future employment is affected by the injury.

- Obtain a copy of the police report, and, if necessary, consult with police officers and investigators who worked on the case.

- Prepare documents to initiate a lawsuit, respond to the other party's documents, and file documents and responses with the court.

- Prepare exhibits for trial, create a trial notebook for the attorney to refer to during the trial, and prepare the client and witnesses for trial.

- Generally, provide litigation assistance (litigation will be discussed at length in Chapters 13 through 15).

Many law firms or departments of law firms specialize in areas of tort litigation other than personal-injury liability, such as medical malpractice. This chapter's *Featured Guest* article on pages 240 and 241 focuses on the area of medical malpractice and offers some examples of paralegal duties in this area.

CYBER TORTS: DEFAMATION ONLINE

A significant issue that has come before the courts in recent years relates to the question of who should be held liable for *cyber torts,* or torts committed in cyberspace. For example, who should be held liable when someone posts a defamatory message online? Should an Internet service provider (ISP)—a company, such as America Online (AOL), that provides access to the Internet through a local phone line, cable, or DSL connection—be liable for the remark if the ISP was unaware that it was being made?

Cyber torts (like cyber crimes, which will be discussed in Chapter 16) are not new torts as much as they are new ways of committing torts that present special issues of proof. How, for example, can it be proved that an online defamatory remark was "published" (which requires that a third party see or hear it)? How can the identity of the person who made the remark be discovered? We explore some of these questions in this section. Generally, determining what tort duties apply in cyberspace and at what point one of those duties is breached is not an easy task for the courts.

Online forums allow anyone—customers, employees, or crackpots—to complain about a business firm's personnel, policies, practices, or products. Regardless of whether the complaint is justified or whether it is true, it might have an impact on the business of the firm. One of the early questions in the online legal arena was whether the providers of such forums could be held liable for defamatory statements made in those forums.

Liability of Internet Service Providers

Newspapers, magazines, and television and radio stations may be held liable for defamatory remarks that they disseminate, even if those remarks are prepared or created by others. Under the Communications Decency Act of 1996, however, Internet service providers, or "interactive computer service providers," are not liable for such material.[4]

Piercing the Veil of Anonymity

One initial problem for anyone who seeks to bring an action for online defamation is discovering the identity of the person who posted the defamatory message online. ISPs can disclose personal information about their customers only when ordered to do so by a court. Because of this, businesses and individuals are increasingly resorting to lawsuits against unidentified "John Does." Then, using the authority of the courts, they can obtain from the ISPs the identities of the persons responsible for the messages.

▶ **EXAMPLE 7.19** In one case, Eric Hvide, a former chief executive of a company called Hvide Marine, sued a number of "John Does" who had posted allegedly defamatory statements about his company on various online message boards. Hvide, who eventually lost his job, sued the John Does for libel in a Florida court. The court ruled that Yahoo! and AOL had to reveal the identities of the defendant Does.[5] ◀

In some other cases, though, the rights of plaintiffs in such situations have been balanced against the defendants' rights to free speech. For example, some courts have

Beth Walston-Dunham

FEATURED **Guest**

IS THERE A PLACE FOR PARALEGALS IN THE FIELD OF MEDICAL MALPRACTICE?

BIOGRAPHICAL NOTE

Beth Walston-Dunham has been publishing legal texts since 1990. She earned a bachelor of science degree in psychology and business from Central Missouri State University in 1981 and a J.D. degree from the Saint Louis University School of Law in 1984. She has been licensed in the states of Illinois, Missouri, Nebraska, and Texas, where her practice included plaintiffs' medical malpractice litigation. She has also held the position of administrative partner in a private medical practice and has worked as a consultant on risk management issues for health-care professionals. She served as the first director of paralegal studies, legal administration, and prelaw programs at the College of Saint Mary in Omaha, Nebraska. Her most recent book is Medical Malpractice Law and Litigation, *published in 2005 by Thomson Delmar Learning.*

The role of the paralegal in the justice system, and specifically the field of tort law, is filled with opportunities for development and advancement. Civil litigation has grown exponentially in recent years. As a result, a wide variety of doors have opened for the paralegal both within and outside the traditional law office setting. One particularly large area of growth has been that of medical malpractice law. Medical malpractice is nothing new. It has been a part of civil litigation in this country for nearly two hundred years. But today, variables such as rapidly developing technology, new health-care professions, scientific advances, the concept of insurance, and even the baby boom following World War II have contributed to a virtual explosion in the number of patients and treatments. These developments have resulted in a corresponding increase in the possibility of professional malfeasance and legal claims by those allegedly injured.

Without question, the paralegal has become an invaluable part of the legal team in the field of medical malpractice. Because of the high percentage of settled claims, a great deal of the work required to successfully litigate or defend a malpractice case comes in the pretrial stages. Of course, the qualified paralegal in the law firm can be a valuable asset in nearly every element of trial and pretrial preparation, with the exception of giving legal advice and advocacy. Common duties include, but are not limited to, the following:

- Gathering information about the incident that allegedly caused injury.

concluded that more than a bare allegation of defamation is required to outweigh an individual's right to anonymity in the exercise of free speech.

STRICT LIABILITY

▌**strict liability**
Liability regardless of fault. In tort law, strict liability may be imposed on a merchant who introduces into commerce a good that is so defective as to be unreasonably dangerous.

Intentional torts and torts of negligence involve acts that depart from a reasonable standard of care and cause injuries. Under the doctrine of **strict liability**, liability for injury is imposed for reasons other than fault. Strict liability for damages proximately caused by an abnormally dangerous or exceptional activity is one application of this doctrine.

Abnormally Dangerous Activities

Abnormally dangerous activities have three characteristics:

- The activity involves potential harm, of a serious nature, to persons or property.

- Interviewing potential witnesses.

- Preparing and responding to discovery materials such as interrogatories and requests for production, inspection, and physical examination.

- Securing expert witnesses.

- Preparing for depositions (both witness preparation and preparation of questions to be asked).

- Conducting legal research.

- Drafting pleadings, motions, discovery materials, and memoranda.

- Assembling evidence and preparing trial exhibits.

In addition to working in a law firm setting, paralegals have many opportunities within the health-care industry to participate in areas related to medical malpractice. A primary example is the field of risk management. In recent years, this relatively new profession has become deeply embedded in the field of health care. Whether risk management is conducted by an independent risk assessment company that works on a contract basis with providers, by an in-house risk management department for a health-care provider, or by a corporate legal department for providers of insurance, health care, or related products, the goal is the same: to identify vulnerable areas and to react accordingly. The response may range from changing policies and procedures, to providing education and training to employees, to collecting information about an incident that has already occurred. All of these are areas in which a paralegal can effectively function to meet the needs of the employer.

Clearly, the doors open to paralegals in tort law, and specifically medical malpractice, are boundless. The key is to have a thorough understanding of the legal system, and particularly the process of litigation.

Additionally, a paralegal should have the ability to examine the broad aspects of a case, think "outside the box," and use organizational skills to address issues related to litigation involving professional malfeasance.

> *"Clearly, the doors open to paralegals in tort law, and specifically medical malpractice, are boundless. The key is to have a thorough understanding of the legal system, and particularly the process of litigation."*

- The activity involves a high degree of risk that cannot be completely guarded against by the exercise of reasonable care.

- The activity is not commonly performed in the community or area.

Clearly, the primary basis of liability is the creation of an extraordinary risk. Even if blasting with dynamite is performed with all reasonable care, for instance, there is still a risk of injury. Balancing that risk against the potential for harm, it seems reasonable to ask the person engaged in the activity to pay for any injury it causes. Although there is no fault, there is still responsibility because of the dangerous nature of the undertaking.

Other Applications of Strict Liability

Strict liability may also apply to harm caused by animals. Persons who keep wild animals are strictly liable for any harm inflicted by the animals. The basis for applying strict liability is that wild animals, should they escape from confinement, pose a serious risk of harm to persons in the vicinity. An owner of domestic animals (such as dogs, cats, cows, or sheep) may be strictly liable for harm caused by those animals if the owner knew, or should have known, that the animals were dangerous or had a propensity to harm others.

A significant application of strict liability is in the area of *product liability*—liability of manufacturers and sellers for harmful or defective products. Because of the importance of product liability in tort litigation, we discuss this type of liability at length in the following section.

PRODUCT LIABILITY

product liability
The legal liability of manufacturers, sellers, and lessors of goods to consumers, users, and bystanders for injuries or damages that are caused by the goods.

Those who manufacture, sell, or lease goods can be held liable for injuries and damages caused by defective goods under the law of **product liability**. Liability here is a matter of social policy. It is based on the notion that manufacturers are better able to bear the cost of injury than innocent victims and that requiring them to pay for damages caused by their products encourages them to make safer products. Injured parties can sue under theories of negligence and misrepresentation, as well as strict liability.

Theories of Product Liability

A party who is injured by a defective product can bring a suit against the product's seller or manufacturer under several theories. These theories include negligence, misrepresentation, and strict product liability.

Product Liability Based on Negligence

If a manufacturer fails to exercise due care to make a product safe, *any person* who is injured by the product can sue the manufacturer for negligence. The plaintiff does not have to be the person who purchased the product. Due care must be exercised in designing the product, selecting the materials, producing and assembling the product, and placing adequate warnings on the label to inform the user of dangers. The duty of care also requires the inspection and testing of any item purchased that is incorporated into the final product.

Product Liability Based on Misrepresentation

When a manufacturer or seller misrepresents the quality, nature, or appropriate use of the product, and the user is injured as a result, the basis of liability may be the tort of fraud. Generally, the misrepresentation must have been made knowingly or with reckless disregard for the facts, and the party must have intended the user to rely on the statement. An example is the intentional concealment of a product's defects. In contrast to actions based on negligence and strict liability, the plaintiff does not have to show that the product was defective or malfunctioned in fraud cases.

Strict Product Liability

Under the doctrine of strict liability, a manufacturer that has exercised a reasonable degree of care can still be held liable if a product is defective and injures someone. Strict product liability reflects the general principle that the law should protect consumers from unsafe and dangerous products. The rule of strict liability is also applicable to the suppliers of component parts that are used in the final product.

Ethics Watch!

CONFIDENTIALITY AND PRODUCT LIABILITY

Recall from Chapter 3 that as a paralegal you are prohibited under ethical rules from revealing confidential client information. Although this sounds simple, paralegals in product liability firms may find themselves in a sticky situation. For example, suppose that your firm represents a particular toy manufacturer. The toy firm has produced and distributed a toy that is very popular for children two through four years of age. The toy, however, is apparently defective and has caused serious injuries to some children across the country. The product has not yet been recalled, and no information about the problems with the toy has appeared in the press. Everything you know about this toy you have learned from the work you have done on the case.

Now suppose that you are the parent of a child who is three years old, and many of your friends and family members have children around that age. Clearly, you would decide not to purchase that toy for your child, but what about telling others? Can you warn your friends and family about the defective toy? Can you tell your day-care provider? If you tell one person, even if it is a family member, you have technically violated the ethical rule of confidentiality. Yet what if you don't warn someone, and that person's child is injured as a result? This is just one example of ethical dilemmas that may arise for paralegals who work in the area of product liability. In circumstances such as these, it is advisable to consult your supervising attorney for direction.

Strict liability will be imposed only if the plaintiff can establish the following six requirements:

- The product must be in a defective condition when the defendant sells it.
- The defendant must normally be engaged in the business of selling (or otherwise distributing) that product.
- The product must be unreasonably dangerous to the user or consumer because of its defective condition (in most states).
- The plaintiff must incur physical harm to self or property by use or consumption of the product.
- The defective condition must be the proximate cause of the injury or damage.
- The goods must not have been substantially changed from the time the product was sold to the time the injury was sustained.[6]

On the Web

For news regarding safety and product liability cases, go to **http://www. safetyforum.com/news**.

Note that the plaintiff is not required to show why or in what manner the product became defective. The plaintiff must only prove that the product was so "defective" as to be "unreasonably dangerous"; that the product caused the injury; and that the condition of the product was essentially the same as when it was sold. A court will find the product to be an

unreasonably dangerous product

In product liability, a product that is defective to the point of threatening a consumer's health and safety. A product will be considered unreasonably dangerous if it is dangerous beyond the expectation of the ordinary consumer or if a less dangerous alternative was economically feasible for the manufacturer, but the manufacturer failed to produce it.

unreasonably dangerous product if either (1) the product is dangerous beyond the expectation of the ordinary consumer or (2) a less dangerous alternative was *economically* feasible for the manufacturer, but the manufacturer failed to produce it. A product may be unreasonably dangerous due to a flaw in the manufacturing process, a design defect, or an inadequate warning.

Manufacturing Defects.   A product that departs from its intended design, even though all possible care was exercised in the preparation and marketing of the product, has a manufacturing defect. Liability is imposed on the manufacturer (and on the wholesaler and retailer) regardless of whether the manufacturer acted "reasonably."

Design Defects.   A product has a design defect if the foreseeable risks of harm posed by the product could have been reduced or avoided by adopting a reasonable alternative design.

Warning Defects.   A product may also be deemed defective because of inadequate instructions or warnings in situations in which the risk of harm was foreseeable and could have been avoided if a proper warning had been given. In evaluating the adequacy of warnings, courts consider the risks of the product and whether the content of the warning was understandable and clear to the expected user.[7] For example, children would likely respond readily to bright, bold, simple warning labels, whereas educated adults might need more detailed information.

Note that there is no duty to warn about risks that are obvious or commonly known. Warnings about *obvious risks* do not add to the safety of a product and could even detract from it by making other warnings seem less significant. Also, a seller must warn those who purchase its product of the harm that can result from the *foreseeable misuse* of the product. The key is the foreseeability of the misuse; sellers are not required to foresee and take precautions against every conceivable mode of use and abuse to which their products might be put.

Defenses to Product Liability

To avoid liability under any theory of product liability, the defendant can show that there is no basis for the plaintiff's claim or that the plaintiff has not met the requirements for liability. For example, if the suit alleges negligence and the defendant proves that the product did not cause the plaintiff's injury, the defendant will not be liable. Additionally, if the defendant in a strict product liability suit can establish that the goods were subsequently altered, normally the defendant will not be held liable.[8] Defendants may also assert the affirmative defenses discussed next.

Assumption of Risk

The obviousness of a risk and a user's decision to proceed in the face of that risk may sometimes be a defense in a product liability suit. For example, if a buyer failed to heed a product recall by the seller, a court might conclude that the buyer had assumed the risk. To establish this defense, the defendant must show that (1) the plaintiff knew and appreciated the risk created by the product defect and (2) the plaintiff voluntarily assumed the risk, even though it was unreasonable to do so.

Product Misuse

Defendants can also claim that the plaintiff misused the product. This defense is similar to claiming that the plaintiff has assumed the risk. Here, however, the injured party *did not know that the product was dangerous for a particular use,* but the use was not the one for

On the Web

For information on product liability litigation against tobacco companies, including defenses raised by tobacco manufacturers in trial-related documents, go to the State Tobacco Information Center's Web site at **http://stic.neu.edu**.

which the product was designed. The courts have severely limited this defense. Even if the injured party does not know about the inherent danger of using the product in a wrong way, if the misuse is reasonably foreseeable, the seller must take measures to guard against it.

Comparative Negligence

Developments in the area of comparative negligence (discussed previously in this chapter) have affected the doctrine of strict liability—the most extreme theory of product liability. Previously, the plaintiff's conduct was not a defense to strict liability. Today, many jurisdictions consider the negligent or intentional actions of both the plaintiff and the defendant when apportioning liability and damages. Even if the plaintiff misused the product, though, she or he may be able to recover at least some damages for injuries caused by a defective product.

Commonly Known Dangers

As mentioned, the dangers associated with certain products (such as sharp knives and guns) are so commonly known that manufacturers need not warn users of those dangers. If a defendant shows that a plaintiff's injury resulted from a *commonly known danger,* the defendant normally will not be liable. A related defense is the *knowledgeable user* defense. If a particular danger (such as electrical shock) is or should be commonly known by particular users of the product (such as electricians), the manufacturer need not warn these users of the danger.

PRODUCT LIABILITY AND THE PARALEGAL

As a paralegal, you may often be intensively involved in product liability litigation. If you work for a law firm, you may be part of a legal team that is bringing a suit against a manufacturer or seller in a product liability action, or you may be part of the legal team defending the manufacturer or seller. If you work for a corporation, you may play a role in defending against product liability claims brought by users of a product made by the corporation.

Depending on the nature of the lawsuit, there may be thousands of documents to manage in a product liability case. For example, some such cases are brought as *class-action* lawsuits. In a class-action case, a plaintiff brings the suit on behalf of users of a product (such as tobacco) who claim that they were injured by the product. Cases of this kind can go on for years and typically involve mountains of documents that must be categorized, labeled, and catalogued so that they can be eas-

ily retrieved when needed. Often, paralegals involved in cases such as these must be experts in technology in order to manage the files and document presentations at trial.

Other product liability cases, of course, involve a single plaintiff. A plaintiff may claim that a design or manufacturing defect in a product, such as an automobile, was responsible for the plaintiff's injury or that a manufacturer's inadequate warning was responsible for an injury. Whether product liability litigation involves a single plaintiff or a class action, it will require extensive investigation into whether the product that allegedly caused the injury was in fact defective in any way or whether the defect, if there was one, actually caused the injury in question. Many of the specific tasks that paralegals perform in product liability litigation are similar to those described earlier for cases involving negligence.

CONSUMER LAW

Since the 1960s, many laws have been passed to protect the health and safety of consumers. A **consumer** is a person who purchases, for private use, goods or services from business firms. Sources of consumer protection exist at all levels of government. Exhibit 7.1 on page 247

consumer
An individual who purchases products and services for personal or household use.

PARALEGAL profile

Lori A. Gray

PRODUCT LIABILITY PARALEGAL

Lori A. Gray has worked in the legal profession for more than twenty years. She has been a paralegal specializing in product liability litigation since 1986. Gray began her career working on the plaintiff side and then defected to the defense side in 1995. In October 2002, Gray left traditional law firm practice and moved into the corporate legal environment at Rockwell Automation, Inc.

Gray attended Cuyahoga Community College and the American Institute for Paralegal Studies and is a member of the National Federation of Paralegal Associations. From 1998 to 2000, she served as the president of the Cleveland Association of Paralegals. She has taught many seminars and authored various articles for litigation paralegals.

What do you like best about your work?

"The most interesting aspect of my career has been learning about different products, including their design and application. It never ceases to amaze me how many hundreds of products we use in everyday life. Determining the cause of a product's failure is an exciting aspect of my work that allows me to continually build new skills. Every case is unique because of the product or combination of products involved. As modern technology continues to advance, this area of law will always offer fresh and exciting challenges."

What is the greatest challenge that you face in your area of work?

"One of the greatest challenges in my work lies in the investigation phase of every claim. Before I attend any site investigation, I learn all I can about the product, its history, and its application. Often, it is also helpful for me to research the design process and determine the original intended function of a product. This can sometimes be an arduous task, as a product may have originated long ago and its design may have changed dramatically since it entered the marketplace."

What advice do you have for would-be paralegals in your area of work?

"I have been fortunate throughout my career to have been surrounded by experts in the field. My paralegal education did not provide me with a background in engineering or product design. To excel in this area of the law, it is tremendously important to understand the product involved from the inception of its design through every possible application by the end user. It's always a great idea to see the product and even operate the product yourself, so you have firsthand knowledge. Also, it's important to know the applicable standards that govern the design and use of the product."

> *"To excel in this area of the law, it is tremendously important to understand the product involved from the inception of its design through every possible application by the end user."*

What are some tips for success as a paralegal in your area of work?

"Be open to learning everything you can about the product line, as well as similar and alternative designs. Also be aware of the human element involved in any product liability case. While a bad design can lead to a defective product, products are often altered and misused by the end user, resulting in serious injury or death. Never be afraid to ask questions of experts and engineers who are most familiar with the product."

indicates some of the areas of consumer law that are regulated by statutes. Federal administrative agencies, such as the Federal Trade Commission, also provide an important source of consumer protection. Nearly every agency and department of the federal government has an office of consumer affairs, and most states have one or more offices, including the offices of state attorneys general, to assist consumers.

Developing Paralegal Skills

PRODUCT LIABILITY PARALEGALS

Sylvia is a paralegal working in the legal department of an automobile company. The company is frequently the defendant in product liability lawsuits. In these lawsuits, during the discovery phase of the litigation (see Chapter 13), attorneys for the plaintiffs normally request information about the design and manufacturing process used by the company in producing its vehicles.

Sylvia's job is to work with the corporate attorneys to gather this information and provide it to the plaintiffs' attorneys, as allowed or required by court rules. Frequently, Sylvia meets with the company's engineers to discuss information requests and to obtain the necessary information. Sylvia then reviews with her supervising attorney the material to be sent out.

TIPS FOR OBTAINING INFORMATION

- Set up a meeting with the engineers.
- Provide the engineers with copies of the discovery request.
- Discuss with the engineers the scope of the discovery request.
- Review engineering files.
- Determine if a database will be needed to index the documents.
- Analyze the documents, looking for privileged or work-product documents (see Chapter 13) that should not be included in the response to the discovery request.
- Prepare a response to the discovery request.

All statutes, agency rules, and common law judicial decisions that serve to protect the interests of consumers are classified as **consumer law**. Because of the wide variation among state consumer protection laws, our primary focus here is on federal legislation—specifically, on legislation governing deceptive advertising, labeling and packaging, sales, health protection, product safety, and credit protection. Realize, though, that state laws often provide more sweeping and significant protections for the consumer than do federal laws.

consumer law
Statutes, agency rules, and judicial decisions protecting consumers of goods and services.

EXHIBIT 7.1
Selected Areas of Consumer Law Regulated by Statutes

Advertising
Example—The Federal Trade Commission Act of 1914

Labeling and Packaging
Example—The Fair Packaging and Labeling Act of 1966

Sales
Example—Uniform Commercial Code

Consumer Law

Consumer Health
Example—The Federal Food, Drug and Cosmetic Act of 1938

Product Safety
Example—The Consumer Product Safety Act of 1972

Credit Protection
Example—The Consumer Credit Protection Act of 1968

Deceptive Advertising

deceptive advertising
Advertising that misleads consumers, either by unjustified claims concerning a product's performance or by failure to disclose relevant information concerning the product's composition or performance.

Over the past several decades, consumers have received increased protection against deceptive advertising. This protection has come more from statutes and government agency rules than from the common law. Under the common law, if a seller misrepresented the quality, price, or availability of a certain product, the consumer's only recourse was to sue the seller for fraud. Fraud requires proof of *intent* to misrepresent the product's usefulness to the buyer. Frequently, the burden of having to prove intent was too great, and consumers were left with little or no legal recourse against deceptive practices.

Today, numerous government agencies, both federal and state, are empowered to protect consumers from deceptive advertising. At the federal level, the most important agency regulating advertising is the Federal Trade Commission (FTC). The Federal Trade Commission Act of 1914 authorizes the FTC to determine what constitutes a deceptive practice within the meaning of the act.

Deceptive advertising comes in many forms. Deception may arise from a false statement or claim about a company's own products or a competitor's products. Some advertisements contain "half-truths," meaning that the information presented is true but incomplete, leading consumers to a false conclusion. ▶ **EXAMPLE 7.20** The makers of Campbell's soups advertised that most Campbell's soups were low in fat and cholesterol and thus were helpful in fighting heart disease. What the ad did not say was that Campbell's soups are high in sodium and that high-sodium diets may increase the risk of heart disease. The FTC ruled that Campbell's claims were thus deceptive. ◀ Generally, the test for whether an ad is deceptive is *whether a reasonable consumer would be deceived by the ad.*

On the Web

A good source for information on the FTC, its regulations protecting consumers, and other government sites dealing with consumer issues is the FTC itself. You can access its home page at **http://www.ftc.gov**.

If a sufficient number of consumers complain to the FTC about the deceptive practices of a given retailer, the FTC has the power to investigate the problem and take action. If, after its investigation, the FTC believes that a given advertisement is unfair or deceptive, it drafts a formal complaint and sends it to the alleged offender. The company may agree to settle the complaint without further proceedings. If the company does not agree to a settlement, the FTC can conduct a hearing, at which the company can present its defense. If the FTC succeeds in proving that an advertisement is deceptive, it usually issues a **cease-and-desist order** requiring that the challenged advertising be stopped. It might also impose a sanction known as **counteradvertising** by requiring the company to supply new advertising—in print, on radio, and on television—to inform the public about the earlier misinformation.

cease-and-desist order
An administrative or judicial order prohibiting a person or business firm from conducting activities that an agency or court has deemed illegal.

counteradvertising
New advertising undertaken pursuant to a Federal Trade Commission order for the purpose of correcting earlier false claims that were made about a product.

Labeling and Packaging Laws

A number of federal and state laws deal specifically with the information given on labels and packages. In general, labels must be accurate, and they must use words that are easily understood by the ordinary consumer. For instance, a box of cereal cannot be labeled "giant" if that would exaggerate the amount of cereal contained in the box. In some instances, labels must specify the raw materials used in the product, such as the percentage of cotton, nylon, or other fiber used in a garment. In other instances, the product must carry a warning. Cigarette packages and advertising, for example, must include one of several warnings about the health hazards associated with smoking.

The Fair Packaging and Labeling Act of 1966 requires that products carry labels that identify the product; the net quantity of the contents, as well as the quantity of each serving, if the number of servings is stated; the manufacturer; and the packager or distributor. The act also establishes requirements concerning words used to describe packages, disclosure of ingredients of nonfood products, and the partial filling of packages.

Food products must bear labels detailing nutritional content, including how much fat the food contains and what kind of fat it is. The federal Food and Drug Administration (FDA) has guidelines to standardize nutritional information on packaged foods, and the

FTC plays a key role in enforcing the restrictions. The Nutrition Labeling and Education Act of 1990 requires standard nutrition facts (including fat content) on food labels; regulates the use of such terms as *fresh, low fat,* and *organic;* and, subject to FDA approval, authorizes certain health claims.

Sales Transactions

Many of the laws that protect consumers concern the disclosure of certain terms in sales transactions and provide rules governing the various forms of sales, such as door-to-door sales, mail-order sales, and the unsolicited receipt of merchandise. The FTC conducts most of the federal regulation of sales. One FTC regulation requires sellers to give consumers three days to cancel any door-to-door sale. In addition, the FTC rule requires that consumers be notified in Spanish of this right if the oral negotiations for the sale were in that language. The FTC also has rules requiring sellers of certain types of goods and services (such as used cars and funeral services) to disclose pertinent information to consumers.

Most states have enacted laws governing consumer sales transactions. Moreover, the Uniform Commercial Code (UCC), which will be discussed in Chapter 8 and has been adopted by every state, contains numerous provisions that protect consumers from unfair or deceptive trade practices.

Consumer Health and Safety

Laws discussed earlier regarding the labeling and packaging of products go a long way toward promoting consumer health and safety. But there is a difference between regulating the information dispensed about a product and regulating the content of the product. ▶ **EXAMPLE 7.21** Tobacco products have not been altered by regulation or banned outright despite their obvious hazards. What has been regulated are the warnings that producers are required to give consumers about the hazards of tobacco. ◀ We now look at several laws that regulate the actual products made available to consumers.

In 1906, Congress passed the Pure Food and Drug Act, which was the first step toward protecting consumers against adulterated and misbranded food and drug products. In 1938, the Federal Food, Drug and Cosmetic Act was passed to strengthen the 1906 legislation. These acts and subsequent amendments established standards for foods, specified safe levels of potentially dangerous food additives, and created classifications of foods and food advertising. They also required that drugs must be proved effective as well as safe before they are marketed. Also in 1906, Congress passed the Meat Inspection Act, the first of a series of laws that established inspection requirements for all meat and poultry sold for human consumption. Most of the statutes involving food and drugs are monitored and enforced by the Food and Drug Administration.

Congress has enacted a number of statutes in an attempt to protect individuals from harmful products as well. Statutes categorized as product-safety acts protect consumers by carefully regulating the distribution of hazardous or defective products. One example is the Flammable Fabrics Act of 1953, which prohibits the sale of highly flammable fabrics and clothing. Another is the Consumer Product Safety Act of 1972, which was enacted to protect consumers from unreasonably dangerous products. The Consumer Product Safety Commission, which was created by the act, conducts research on the safety of individual products and maintains a clearinghouse on the risks associated with various products. The Consumer Product Safety Act authorizes the commission to set standards for consumer products and to ban the manufacture and sale of any product that the commission deems to be potentially hazardous to consumers. Products banned by the commission include various types of unsafe fireworks, cribs, and toys, as well as many products containing asbestos or vinyl chloride.

Consumer Credit Protection

Because of the extensive use of credit by American consumers, credit protection has become an important area regulated by consumer protection legislation. One of the most significant statutes regulating the credit and credit-card industry is the Truth-in-Lending Act (TILA), the name commonly given to Title 1 of the Consumer Credit Protection Act, which was passed by Congress in 1968.

The Truth-in-Lending Act

The TILA is basically a *disclosure law.* It is administered by the Federal Reserve Board and requires sellers and lenders to disclose credit terms or loan terms so that individuals can shop around for the best financing arrangements. TILA requirements apply only to persons and entities that, in the ordinary course of business, lend money, sell on credit, or arrange for the extension of credit. Sales or loans made between two consumers do not come under the protection of the act. Additionally, the act only protects natural persons (as opposed to corporations or other business entities). Under the provisions of the TILA, all of the terms of a credit instrument must be clearly and conspicuously (obviously) disclosed. The TILA provides that a consumer can cancel a contract if a creditor fails to follow exactly the procedures required by the act.

In 1974, Congress enacted the Equal Credit Opportunity Act (ECOA) as an amendment to the TILA. The ECOA prohibits the denial of credit solely on the basis of race, religion, national origin, color, gender, marital status, or age. The act also prohibits credit discrimination on the basis of whether an individual receives certain forms of income, such as public-assistance benefits. Creditors are prohibited from requesting any information from a credit applicant that could be used for the type of discrimination covered by the act and its amendments. Under the ECOA, a creditor may not require the signature of an applicant's spouse, other than as a joint applicant, on a credit instrument if the applicant qualifies under the creditor's standards of creditworthiness for the amount and terms of the credit requested.

The TILA also contains provisions regarding credit cards. One provision limits the liability of a cardholder to $50 per card for unauthorized charges made before the creditor is notified that the card has been lost. Another provision prohibits a credit-card company from billing a consumer for any unauthorized charges on a credit card that was improperly issued by the company. ▶ **EXAMPLE 7.22** Suppose that a consumer receives an unsolicited credit card in the mail, and the card is later stolen and used by the thief to make purchases. In this situation, the consumer to whom the card was sent is not liable for the unauthorized charges. ◀ Further provisions of the act concern billing disputes related to credit-card purchases. A debtor may think that an error has occurred in billing or may wish to withhold payment for a faulty product purchased by credit card. The act outlines specific procedures for both the consumer and the credit-card company to follow in settling such a dispute.

Fair Credit Reporting

To protect consumers against inaccurate credit reporting, Congress enacted the Fair Credit Reporting Act in 1970. The act provides that consumer credit reporting agencies—such as Equifax, TransUnion, and Experian—may issue credit reports to users only for specified purposes. Authorized purposes include the extension of credit, the issuance of insurance policies, and compliance with a court order. A report may also be issued in response to a consumer's request for a copy of his or her own credit report. The act further provides that any time a consumer is denied credit or insurance on the basis of the consumer's credit report (or is charged more than others ordinarily would be), the consumer must be notified of that fact and of the name and address of the credit reporting agency that issued the credit report.

Under the act, consumers may request the source of any information being given out by a credit agency, as well as the identity of anyone who has received an agency's report. Consumers are also permitted to have access to the information contained about them in a credit reporting agency's files. If a consumer discovers that a credit reporting agency's files contain inaccurate information about the consumer's credit standing, the agency, on the consumer's written request, must investigate. If the investigation reveals that the information is unverifiable or inaccurate, the agency must delete it within a reasonable period of time.

Fair and Accurate Credit Transactions Act

In an effort to combat identity theft, Congress passed the Fair and Accurate Credit Transactions (FACT) Act of 2003. The act established a national fraud alert system so that consumers who suspect that they have been or may be victimized by identity theft can place an alert on their credit files. The act also requires the major credit reporting agencies to provide consumers with free copies of their own credit reports every twelve months. Another provision requires account numbers on credit-card receipts to be shortened ("truncated") so that merchants, employees, and others who may have access to the receipts do not have access to the consumers' names and full credit-card numbers. The act further mandates that financial institutions work with the Federal Trade Commission to identify "red flag" indicators of identity theft and to develop rules on how to dispose of sensitive credit information.

The FACT Act gives consumers who have been victimized by identity theft some assistance in rebuilding their credit reputations. For example, credit reporting agencies must stop reporting allegedly fraudulent account information once the consumer establishes that identify theft has occurred. Business owners and creditors are required to provide consumers with copies of any records that can help the consumer prove that a particular account or transaction is fraudulent (a forged signature, for example). In addition, the act allows consumers to report the accounts affected by identity theft directly to creditors in order to help prevent the spread of erroneous credit information.

Fair Debt-Collection Practices

In 1977, Congress passed the Fair Debt Collection Practices Act in an attempt to curb what were perceived to be abuses by collection agencies. The act applies only to debt-collection agencies that, usually for a percentage of the amount owed, regularly attempt to collect debts on behalf of someone else. Creditors who attempt to collect debts are not covered by the act unless, by misrepresenting themselves to the debtor, they cause the debtor to believe they are collection agencies.

The act prohibits such debt-collection practices as contacting the consumer at his or her place of employment if the employer objects, contacting the consumer at inconvenient or unusual times, and contacting the consumer if he or she is represented by an attorney. The act also prohibits debt-collection agencies from contacting third parties (other than parents, spouses, or financial advisers) about the payment of a debt unless authorized to do so by a court, using harassment and intimidation (such as abusive language), using false or misleading information (such as posing as a police officer), and communicating with the consumer after receipt of a notice that the consumer is refusing to pay the debt (except to advise the consumer of further action to be taken by the collection agency).

Garnishment Proceedings

Creditors have numerous remedies available to them when consumers fail to pay their debts. Among these remedies is garnishment. Garnishment occurs when a creditor, after complying with procedures mandated by state law, legally seizes a portion of a debtor's property (such as wages) in the possession of a third party (such as an employer). The creditor must first obtain an *order of garnishment* from the court, which allows the creditor to have access

garnishment
A proceeding in which a creditor legally seizes a portion of a debtor's property (such as wages) that is in the possession of a third party (such as an employer).

Developing Paralegal Skills

DISCHARGED FOR GARNISHMENT

Eva White works as a paralegal for a firm that specializes in labor law. A business client has called Eva's supervising attorney to ask for advice concerning garnishment. Basically, the client wants to know if he can fire an employee so that he can avoid having to comply with garnishment proceedings that have been initiated against the employee. The attorney, Melinda Jenks, has asked Eva to research recent case law on the question of whether an employer may fire an employee for such a reason.

Eva goes online to research the topic of garnishment and locates a case in which an employee was fired two days after his employer received notice of the garnishment. The case turned on whether the employer had notice that the garnishment proceedings had already been initiated against the employee. She reads through the case and finds a citation, or reference, to the statute. Eva's next step is to check the statute itself to ensure that she has up-to-date knowledge of how the statute is being applied.

CHECKLIST FOR LEGAL RESEARCH

- Locate case law.
- Locate statutes.
- Update your case law findings by checking a citator (see Chapters 17 and 18) to make sure that the holding in the case is still good law.
- Update the statute by using a citator to see if the statute has been amended or repealed.

to the debtor's wages while they are still in the control of the employer. State laws governing garnishment vary from state to state, and some states (for example, Texas) do not permit garnishment of wages by private parties except under a child-support order.

Garnishment can create a hardship for the consumer-debtor if he or she is relying on wages for support. To protect consumers, both federal and state laws limit the amount of income that can be taken from a debtor's weekly take-home pay. The federal Consumer Credit Protection Act of 1968 provides that a debtor can keep either 75 percent of the net earnings per week or a sum equivalent to the pay for thirty hours of work at federal minimum wage rates, whichever is greater. State laws also provide dollar exemptions, and these amounts are often larger than those provided by federal law. State and federal statutes can be applied together to create a pool of funds to enable a debtor to continue to provide for family needs while reducing the amount of the debt in a reasonable way.

Understandably, employers dislike garnishment proceedings. After all, such proceedings impose time costs on employers (appearance at court hearings, record-keeping costs, and so on). To protect the job security of employees whose wages are subject to garnishment, federal law provides that garnishment of an employee's wages for any one indebtedness cannot be grounds for that employee's dismissal.

CONSUMER LAW AND THE PARALEGAL

Because consumer laws protect all individuals, as a paralegal you may well encounter a client with a claim that falls under a federal or state consumer protection law. You might even find yourself working for a consumer group. In the area

Today's Professional Paralegal

DEVELOPING A LIFE-CARE PLAN

Attorney Long asks her paralegal, Jessica, to assist in developing a life-care plan for one of the firm's clients, Ashley. Ashley, a sixteen-year-old girl, passed out at school one day and was taken to Dr. Shafley, who diagnosed her as having the flu and sent her home. Less than a week later, Ashley's legs had to be amputated because of Dr. Shafley's failure to diagnose the symptoms of bacterial spinal meningitis. Dr. Shafley wishes to settle out of court to avoid the publicity of a trial (his brother is running for mayor). Attorney Long therefore needs to establish the amount of damages to be requested.

THE LIFE-CARE PLAN

Following a serious injury, health-care costs can accumulate into millions of dollars. An attorney who represents an injured plaintiff often must develop a plan that identifies and establishes the cost of the health care that the client will need for the rest of his or her life. The life-care plan is basically a tool used to quantify the health-care needs of a client and establish the amount of damages that the client will seek in any settlement or trial of the case. Typically, developing a life-care plan involves hiring an expert qualified to assess the plaintiff's limitations and care needs and assigning a paralegal to coordinate and assist.

MEETING WITH THE CLIENT

Jessica talks with the attorney, and they go together to meet Ashley and her parents at the hospital in which Ashley has been a patient for several months. Attorney Long tells Ashley that an expert will be coming to evaluate her condition and that Jessica will always be available to answer any questions she might have. After meeting Ashley, Jessica vows to do whatever she can to help Ashley receive the best possible care in the future. Jessica then contacts the expert whom the attorney has hired.

KEY COMPONENTS OF A LIFE-CARE PLAN

Jessica learns that there are several main components of any life-care plan. The first is what type of care is needed and where it will be provided. The options available include facility care, home care, and community care. The expert tells Jessica that as long as someone can be home with Ashley at all times and the house can be modified to accommodate her disabilities, home care is a good choice for Ashley.

The expert then tells Jessica that they need to assess the types of equipment, supplies, and medications that Ashley currently requires and what she will need in the future. For example, Ashley will be confined to a wheelchair until the proper prosthetics (artificial limbs) can be obtained. Her parents' house will need to have wheelchair ramps installed and other modifications made in order to accommodate Ashley's needs. The prosthetic devices, which are very expensive, will need to be replaced during Ashley's lifetime. Other supplies and medications will be required. The cost of all of these items must be estimated for the future.

Jessica also learns that the life-care plan must take into account long-term therapy and additional medical services. Ashley will need physical therapy on a regular basis to enable her to function with her limitations and to learn how to use the prosthetics. She will also need some psychological counseling and recreational therapy, given the extent of her injuries. Additionally, persons who have had their limbs amputated have an increased risk of infections, bedsores, and other problems, and the cost of treating these foreseeable medical problems must be included.

HOW A PARALEGAL CAN ASSIST

Paralegals can play a significant role by serving as a liaison among the expert and the client, the family, physicians, and educators. Injured plaintiffs benefit from knowing that someone can always be reached if they need assistance. Paralegals also can keep track of health-care bills, set up necessary appointments, research costs, and order equipment and supplies. If the case goes to trial, the paralegal can assist in formulating the questions to ask the expert and can create useful exhibits for the jury. Moreover, helping clients who have been seriously injured to regain a degree of independence and plan their futures can be very rewarding work.

of consumer law, paralegals may be asked to perform the following types of tasks:

- Investigate a client's complaint alleging deceptive advertising.
- Assist in work relating to a business client who has been charged with violating Federal Trade Commission rules governing deceptive trade practices.
- Develop acceptable standards for a food producer to ensure compliance with the labeling laws implemented by the Food and Drug Administration.
- Investigate a client's use of hazardous products to ensure compliance with Consumer Product Safety Commission standards.
- Draft a letter to a credit reporting agency to rectify an error on a client's credit report.
- Assist a client in collecting a debt through garnishment proceedings.
- Maintain and keep current the law firm's consumer law library.

KEY TERMS AND CONCEPTS

actionable 226
actual malice 227
appropriation 227
assault 224
assumption of risk 236
battery 224
business invitee 234
business tort 229
causation in fact 235
cease-and-desist order 248
comparative negligence 237
compensatory damages 235
consumer 245
consumer law 247
contributory negligence 237

conversion 232
counteradvertising 248
cyber tort 223
deceptive advertising 248
defamation 226
defense 224
dram shop act 238
duty of care 233
fraudulent misrepresentation 228
garnishment 251
Good Samaritan statute 238
intentional tort 223
libel 226
negligence 233
negligence *per se* 237

predatory behavior 229
privilege 226
product liability 242
proximate cause 236
punitive damages 235
reasonable person standard 233
slander 226
strict liability 240
tort 223
tortfeasor 223
trespass to land 231
trespass to personal property 232
unreasonably dangerous product 244

chapter summary   Tort Law, Product Liability, and Consumer Law

The Basis of Tort Law

Two notions serve as the basis of all torts: wrongs and compensation. Tort law recognizes that some acts are wrong because they cause injuries to others.

1. *Definition*—A *tort* is a civil wrong. In a tort action, one person or group brings a personal-injury suit against another person or group to obtain compensation (money damages) or other relief for the harm suffered.
2. *Objective of tort law*—Generally, the purpose of tort law is to provide remedies for the invasion of various interests, such as physical security, privacy, freedom of movement, and reputation.
3. *Classification of torts*—Torts fall into two broad classifications: *intentional torts* and *negligence*. In addition, in certain circumstances, defendants may be held liable for harm caused to others under the tort doctrine of *strict liability*.

Intentional Torts

1. *Intentional torts against persons*—

   a. Assault and battery—An assault is an intentional act that causes another person to be apprehensive or fearful of immediate harm. A battery is an assault that results in physical contact.

   b. False imprisonment—The intentional confinement or restraint of another person's movement without justification.

   c. Intentional infliction of emotional distress—An intentional act that amounts to extreme and outrageous conduct resulting in severe emotional distress to another.

   d. Defamation (libel or slander)—A false statement of fact, not made under privilege, that is communicated to a third person and that causes damage to a person's reputation. For public figures, the plaintiff must also prove actual malice.

   e. Invasion of the right to privacy—The use of a person's name or likeness for commercial purposes without permission, wrongful intrusion into a person's private activities, publication of information that places a person in a false light, or disclosure of private facts that an ordinary person would find objectionable.

   f. Appropriation—The use of another person's name, likeness, or other identifying characteristic without permission and for the benefit of the user.

   g. Misrepresentation (fraud)—A false representation made by one party, through misstatement of facts or through conduct, with the intention of deceiving another and on which the other reasonably relies to his or her detriment.

   h. Wrongful interference—Knowing, intentional interference by a third party with an enforceable contractual relationship or an established business relationship between other parties for the purpose of advancing the economic interests of the third party.

2. *Intentional torts against property*—

   a. Trespass to land—The invasion of another's real property without consent or privilege. Specific rights and duties apply once a person is expressly or impliedly established as a trespasser.

   b. Trespass to personal property—Unlawfully damaging or interfering with the owner's right to use, possess, or enjoy his or her personal property.

   c. Conversion—A wrongful act in which personal property is taken from its rightful owner.

Negligence

1. *Negligence*—The careless performance of a legally required duty or the failure to perform a legally required act. Elements that must be proved are that a legal duty of care exists, that the defendant breached that duty, and that the breach caused damage or injury to another.

2. *Defenses to negligence*—The basic affirmative defenses in negligence cases are assumption of risk, superseding cause, and contributory negligence.

3. *Special negligence doctrines and statutes*—

   a. Negligence *per se*—A type of negligence that may occur if a person violates a statute or an ordinance providing for a criminal penalty and the violation causes another to be injured.

(Continued)

b. Special negligence statutes—State statutes, such as dram shop acts and Good Samaritan laws, that prescribe duties and responsibilities in certain circumstances. The violation of such statutes will impose civil liability.

Cyber Torts: Defamation Online

General tort principles are being extended to cover cyber torts, or torts that occur in cyberspace, such as online defamation. Cyber torts often present special issues of proof. Federal and state statutes may also apply to certain forms of cyber torts.

Strict Liability

Under the doctrine of strict liability, a person or company may be held liable, regardless of the degree of care exercised, for damages or injuries caused by a product or activity. Strict liability includes liability for harms caused by abnormally dangerous activities, by dangerous animals, and by defective products (product liability).

Product Liability

1. *Theories of product liability*—
   a. Product liability based on negligence—Due care must be used by the manufacturer in designing the product; selecting materials; producing, assembling, and testing the product; and placing adequate warnings on the label or product.

   b. Product liability based on misrepresentation—When the seller misrepresents the quality, nature, or appropriate use of the product, and the user is injured as a result, the basis of liability may be the tort of fraud. The plaintiff does not have to show that the product was defective in such cases.

   c. Strict product liability—A manufacturer that has exercised a reasonable degree of care can still be held liable if a product is defective and injures someone. This reflects the general principle that the law should protect consumers from unsafe and dangerous products. Liability extends to suppliers of component parts.

2. *Defenses to product liability*—
   a. Assumption of risk—The user or consumer knew of the risk of harm and voluntarily assumed it.

   b. Product misuse—The user or consumer misused the product in a way unforeseeable by the manufacturer.

   c. Comparative negligence and liability—Liability may be distributed between the plaintiff and the defendant under the doctrine of comparative negligence if the plaintiff's misuse of the product contributed to the risk of injury.

   d. Commonly known dangers—If a defendant succeeds in convincing the court that a plaintiff's injury resulted from a commonly known danger, such as the danger associated with using a sharp knife, the defendant will not be liable.

Consumer Law

All statutes, agency rules, and common law judicial decisions that serve to protect the interests of consumers are classified as consumer law. Today, there are many federal consumer protection statutes, in addition to a wide variety of state consumer protection statutes. Some state statutes provide more protection than that afforded by the federal laws discussed below.

1. *Deceptive advertising*—Advertising that misleads consumers or that is based on false claims is prohibited by the Federal Trade Commission (FTC). Generally, the test for whether an ad is deceptive is whether a reasonable consumer would be deceived by the ad.

   a. Cease-and-desist orders—The FTC can require the advertiser to stop the challenged advertising.

   b. Counteradvertising—The FTC may also require the advertiser to advertise to correct the earlier misinformation.

2. *Labeling and packaging*—Manufacturers must comply with labeling or packaging requirements for their specific products. In general, labels must be accurate and not misleading. Food products must bear labels detailing their nutritional content, and standards must be met before a product can use terms like *fresh* and *organic* on the label.

3. *Sales transactions*—Many federal and state laws regulate the disclosure of terms to consumers in sales transactions, particularly in door-to-door and mail-order sales. The FTC conducts most of the federal regulation of sales. Numerous provisions of the Uniform Commercial Code also protect consumers from unfair trade practices at the state level.

4. *Consumer health and safety*—Laws protecting the health and safety of consumers regulate the content of a food, drug, or other item, as opposed to regulating what appears on the label.

   a. The Federal Food, Drug and Cosmetic Act protects consumers against adulterated and misbranded foods and drugs. The act establishes food standards, specifies safe levels of potentially hazardous food additives, and sets classifications of foods and food advertising.

   b. The Consumer Product Safety Act seeks to protect consumers from risk of injury from hazardous products. The Consumer Product Safety Commission has the power to remove products that are deemed imminently hazardous from the market and to ban the manufacture and sale of hazardous products.

5. *Consumer credit protection*—Credit protection has become an important area regulated by consumer protection legislation.

   a. Truth-in-Lending Act (TILA)—A disclosure law requiring sellers and lenders to disclose credit terms or loan terms so that individuals can shop around to compare terms. Also provides for the following:

      1. Equal credit opportunity—Prohibits creditors from discriminating on the basis of race, religion, national origin, color, gender, marital status, or age.

      2. Credit-card protection—Limits the liability of cardholders for unauthorized charges made on unsolicited credit cards.

      3. Credit-card rules—Allows credit-card users to withhold payment for faulty products purchased by credit card and to withhold payment for charges billed in error until disputes are resolved.

(Continued)

b. **Fair Credit Reporting Act**—Protects consumers against inaccurate credit reporting and provides that credit reports can only be issued for certain purposes. Consumers are entitled to receive a copy of their credit report on request and to be notified any time they are denied credit or insurance based on the report. The reporting agency must conduct an investigation if the consumer contests any information on the credit report.

c. **Fair and Accurate Credit Transactions Act**—Helps protect against identity theft by establishing a national fraud alert system for credit users, by requiring major credit reporting agencies to provide consumers with free copies of their credit reports every twelve months, by requiring that account numbers on credit-card receipts be shortened, and by assisting victims of identity theft in reestablishing their credit reputations.

d. **Fair Debt Collection Practices Act**—Prohibits debt collectors from using unfair debt-collection practices, such as contacting the debtor at his or her place of employment if the employer objects, contacting the debtor at unreasonable times, contacting third parties about the debt unless authorized to do so by a court, and harassing the debtor.

e. **Garnishment**—Allows a creditor to seize a portion of the debtor's property (such as wages) in the possession of a third party (such as an employer) to satisfy a debt. The creditor must comply with specific procedures mandated by state law.

QUESTIONS FOR REVIEW

1. What is a tort? What is the underlying purpose of tort law? What are the main categories of torts, and how do they differ?

2. List and describe some of the defenses available to defendants in intentional tort actions, such as assault and battery.

3. What are the four elements of negligence? Why is the duty of care for professionals different from the duty of an ordinary person?

4. What are the affirmative defenses to a negligence action? What is contributory negligence, and how is it different from comparative negligence?

5. What is meant by strict liability? In what circumstances is strict liability applied?

6. What is product liability? Under which tort theories

can product liability actions be brought? What elements must the plaintiff prove in a strict product liability action?

7. What are some of the defenses that can be raised in product liability actions? Can the plaintiff's negligent conduct be a defense in product liability cases?

8. What are some of the major federal statutes that were enacted to protect consumers of goods and services?

9. What is deceptive advertising? What agency of the federal government can take action against businesses that engage in such advertising?

10. What federal laws protect consumer health and safety? How has the federal government regulated the credit industry in the interests of protecting consumers?

ETHICAL QUESTIONS

1. Monica is a legal assistant in a law firm that specializes in representing business defendants in tort cases. Monica's supervising attorney has just been asked to defend a firm against a toxic tort claim. The attorney asks Monica to do

some legal research on toxic torts—an area with which she is not familiar. It takes Monica twelve hours to complete the research assignment, which is twice as long as the attorney told her to spend on the project. Monica is uncomfortable in billing the client for twelve hours of research time, and she is contemplating billing another client for six of the twelve hours. Should she? Why or why not?

2. Jeffrey Singleman is an experienced legal assistant in a tort law practice. He is given a great deal of responsibility and has minimal supervision. One day, Georgia Wellington, an associate with the firm, has two court appearances scheduled at the same time. One appearance is in federal court, which is on one side of town, and the other is in the county circuit court, which is on the other side of town. Georgia asks Jeffrey to handle the hearing in the county circuit court for her. What should Jeffrey do?

3. Dawn Mercer is a paralegal at Clarkson & Deichler, a firm that handles many tort law claims. Dawn is having dinner with Phil at a fish restaurant when a person sitting at a table near them begins to choke on a fish bone. When Phil stands up as if to go to the stranger's assistance, Dawn tells him not to—that he can be sued for negligence if something goes wrong. Dawn knows that the state they live in has not passed a Good Samaritan law. Because of Dawn's statements, Phil does not go to the individual's aid. Has Dawn violated any ethical duty? Does her statement constitute the unauthorized practice of law?

4. Claire is a new legal assistant interviewing a client who wants to sue the manufacturer of an allegedly defective treadmill. The client claims that while walking on the treadmill, he received an electrical shock that caused him to fall off and seriously injure his hip. Near the end of the interview, the client asks Claire whether she thinks he has a good case. Claire responds, "Well, as you know, I'm a paralegal, and I cannot give legal advice. Personally, though, I think that you do have a good case." Has Claire violated her ethical duties? How would you have handled the situation?

 ## PRACTICE QUESTIONS AND ASSIGNMENTS

1. Using the information on intentional torts and negligence presented in this chapter, identify the following torts:

   a. Mary receives a telephone call at 5:25 P.M. while she is making dinner for her husband, who will be home shortly. The caller says, "I've got your husband and his money, and I'm taking him to Brazil. You'll never see him again." In a panic, Mary, knowing that her husband has just received a large bonus from his employer, suffers a heart attack. The call was actually made by her husband's friend, Joe. Joe frequently plays practical jokes on Mary and her husband, and the call was another one of his pranks.

   b. Susan Stetson has difficulty paying a large bill for a business dinner in a restaurant because of an error by her credit-card company. The restaurant owner takes Susan's purse, which contains her car keys, and prevents Susan from leaving for over two hours while the matter is being resolved.

   c. The *Local Inquirer* publishes an article that claims that the sister of a famous movie star, whose name it mentions, is dying from AIDS. The article is false and is published without having been investigated by the reporter.

   d. Jennifer is driving her children home from school. The two oldest children are fighting in the backseat. She turns to scold them, taking her eyes off the road temporarily. When she turns back, there is a child on a bike crossing the street in front of her. Jennifer tries to swerve but is unable to avoid hitting the boy.

2. Shirley, an elderly woman, was taking a walk down the street in Santa Monica. Two teenaged boys confronted her, and one of the boys demanded that she hand over her purse. Shirley refused and began scolding the boys, telling them that their mothers would be ashamed of them. One of the boys then grabbed at the straps of her purse but was unable to dislodge it from her shoulder. When the boys realized they were not going to get the purse, they ran away. Does Shirley have a tort claim against the boys? Which tort or torts have been committed?

3. Sarah and David are divorced. While they were married, David continually accused Sarah in private of being "unfaithful" to him and sexually promiscuous. Now that the divorce is final, Sarah learns that David is sending e-mails to all their mutual friends claiming that she is promiscuous. Can Sarah sue David for defamation? Could she have brought a defamation action prior to the divorce? What would happen to Sarah's claim if David could prove that Sarah was, in fact, promiscuous?

4. Gerald Guerrero grew up in Small Town, U.S.A., where his family owned a local diner. He then moved to New York City and worked in retail for twenty years. After his father's death, Gerald inherited the business and returned to Small Town to reopen the diner as "Gerry's Place." Tourists have begun visiting Small Town because it is mentioned in a popular song. Gerald decides to capitalize on the new tourist industry by posting a three-foot wooden sign in front of the door to the diner that states "Gerald Guerrero

is the best cook in town" and presents testimonials of people who have supposedly eaten there and loved the food. The locals know that Gerald never cooked in the restaurant at all until last week, and no one has ever heard of any of the people named in the testimonials. One day, a group of tourists who have just eaten at Gerry's Place become seriously ill. While at the hospital, they speak to some locals and decide to file suit against Gerald Guerrero for fraudulent misrepresentation. Evaluate whether the facts presented meet the requirements of fraud.

5. In which of the following situations will the acting party be liable for the tort of negligence? Explain fully.

   a. Mary goes to the golf course on Sunday morning, eager to try out a new set of golf clubs she has just purchased. As she tees off on the first hole, the head of her club flies off and injures a nearby golfer.

   b. Mary's doctor gives her some pain medication and tells her not to drive after she takes it, as the medication induces drowsiness. In spite of the doctor's warning, Mary decides to drive to the store while on the medication. Owing to her lack of alertness, she fails to stop at a traffic light and crashes into another vehicle, injuring a passenger.

6. Ruth carelessly parks her car on a steep hill, leaving the car in neutral and failing to engage the parking brake. The car rolls down the hill, knocking down an electric line. The sparks from the broken line ignite a grass fire. The fire spreads until it reaches a barn one mile away. The barn houses dynamite, and the burning barn explodes, causing part of the roof to fall on and injure a passing motorist, Jim. Can Jim recover from Ruth? Why or why not?

7. Kim went to Ling's Market to pick up a few items for dinner. It was a rainy, windy day, and the wind had blown water through the door of Ling's Market each time the door opened. As Kim entered through the door, she slipped and fell in the approximately one-half inch of rainwater that had accumulated on the floor. The manager knew of the weather conditions but had not posted any sign to warn customers of the water hazard. Kim injured her back as a result of the fall and sued Ling's for damages. Can Ling's be held liable for negligence in this situation? Discuss.

8. Carmen buys a television set manufactured by AKI Electronics. She is going on vacation, so she takes the set to her mother's house for her mother to use. Because the set is defective, it explodes, causing considerable damage to her mother's house. Carmen's mother sues AKI for the damage to her house. Discuss the product liability theories under which Carmen's mother can recover from AKI.

9. When Patsy drove her new Chrysler, she sat very close to the steering wheel—less than a foot away from the steering-wheel enclosure of the driver's-side air bag. At the time, Chrysler did not provide any warning that a driver should not sit close to the air bag. In an accident with another car, Patsy's air bag deployed. The bag caused her elbow to strike the windshield pillar and fracture in three places, resulting in repeated surgery and physical therapy. Patsy filed a suit against Chrysler, alleging that her injuries had been caused by Chrysler's failure to warn consumers about sitting near the air bag. At the trial, an expert testified that the air bag was not intended to prevent arm injuries, which were "a predictable, incidental consequence" of the bag's deploying. Should Chrysler be required to pay for Patsy's injuries? Why or why not?

10. Ingersoll-Rand Co. makes a machine that is used for stripping asphalt from roads that are being repaved. The maintenance manual that comes with the machine warns that users should stay ten feet away from the rear of the machine while it is operating, verify that the back-up alarm is working, and check the area for the presence of others. There is also a sign on the machine that tells users to stay ten feet away. Terrill Wilson, a road worker, was operating the machine in the street one day. The alarm did not sound, and Cosandra Rogers, who was standing with her back to the machine, was run over and severely injured. Rogers filed a suit against Ingersoll-Rand, alleging strict liability on the basis of a design defect. The jury awarded Rogers $10.2 million in compensatory damages and $6.5 million in punitive damages. Ingersoll-Rand appealed, emphasizing the adequacy of its warnings. Can an adequate warning shield a manufacturer from liability for a defectively designed product? Explain your answer.

11. Using the material on consumer law presented in this chapter, identify the law that would apply to each of the following situations and explain how it would resolve the problem:

   a. Mary purchases a new computer system for $2,500 and pays for it with a credit card. The first week that Mary has her new computer, she has serious difficulty operating many of the programs, the computer constantly freezes up, and she loses work that she has prepared on the word processor. Mary complains to the company from which she purchased the computer. When the problem is not resolved, she withholds payment to her credit-card company and notifies it of the reason.

   b. Dick has a credit card with an $8,000 balance. He loses

his job and stops paying the credit-card company. A collection agency begins to harass him at all hours of the day and even calls his former employer to verify that Dick had been fired.

QUESTIONS FOR CRITICAL ANALYSIS

1. Tort law distinguishes between intentional acts that harm others and unintentional acts that harm others. How are they different? Are the consequences any different? Should they be?

2. The tort of intentional infliction of emotional distress imposes liability on a person who engages in extreme and outrageous conduct that causes another to suffer severe emotional distress. How can these types of "injuries" be measured? How can they be compensated for? Should this tort be allowed?

3. Negligence law imposes a duty on every member of society to act like a "reasonable person." How did the concept of a duty of care arise? What societal judgment does the reasonable person standard reflect?

4. A plaintiff in a negligence case must prove proximate cause, also known as legal cause, to succeed in the action. Foreseeability is one commonly used test of proximate cause. What impact does foreseeability have on the issue of causation? What might happen without such a test?

5. Mrs. Palsgraf was standing on a platform at a train station waiting for a train. Another train pulled up, and two men ran to catch it. The first man boarded the train without incident. The second man, however, ran into difficulty because the train had already begun to move. As he attempted to board the train, a guard on the train pulled him forward, and another guard on the platform pushed him from the platform onto the train. Unbeknownst to the guards, the package carried by the man, which was covered in newspaper, contained fireworks. When the package fell, it exploded. The explosion caused baggage scales some distance away to tip over and injure Palsgraf,

who was standing near the scales. Palsgraf sued the Long Island Railroad. Do you think a court would find that the railroad owed a duty of care to Palsgraf? How would a court view the issue of proximate cause in this case? Write two paragraphs, one analyzing the issue of duty of care and the other the issue of proximate cause.

6. Even if the elements of duty, breach of duty, and causation are met, there can be no recovery in a negligence action if the injury requirement is not met. Why not? Is this principle of tort law fair?

7. In a few states, if a plaintiff in a negligence case can be shown to have contributed at all to the injury, then the plaintiff is completely barred from recovering any damages by the defense of contributory negligence. Is this a fair outcome? With what doctrine have the majority of the states replaced the contributory negligence doctrine?

8. Strict liability imposes liability for injuries suffered by defendants without considering fault. Is this fair in any situation? If so, in which situations? What is the underlying rationale behind imposing strict product liability on defendants?

9. The United States has the strictest product liability laws in the world today. Why do you think many other countries, particularly developing countries, are more lax with respect to holding manufacturers liable for product defects?

10. Make a list of the consumer laws presented in this chapter. What rights do these laws protect? Why are they needed? What does the necessity for consumer protection laws say about our society?

PROJECTS

1. Find out what defenses against negligence are used in your state. Do the courts in your state allow the defense of contributory negligence, or have they adopted the comparative negligence doctrine?

2. Contact your local police department to find out what is required in your area to obtain a police report. Is there a

specific form that you need to fill out? Does the request have to be written and/or signed by an attorney, or can the request be made on the telephone or via e-mail? How much does it cost? How long does it take? Do you get a copy of any supplemental or investigative reports in addition to the original incident report?

3. Contact two local hospitals to find out what is required in order for them to release a person's medical records. Does one consent form authorize you to get all the medical records for an individual or only records within a specified time frame? What if the person had blood tests or other laboratory tests that were sent out of the hospital for processing—do you need a separate consent form for such tests? How much does the hospital charge to make copies of records? How long does it typically take to get medical records? Compare the information-release requirements of the two hospitals as well as the costs of obtaining the records and the time required.

4. Find a newspaper article on a serious-injury accident. Read the article carefully, and write a two-page memo evaluating the potential negligence claim and indicating what you think is needed to "work up" the case. For example, you might make a list of any witnesses that need to be interviewed and any reports that should be obtained. Make sure to attach the article, or a copy of it, to the memo you prepare.

5. Contact a credit reporting agency and obtain a credit report on yourself, if one exists. Does the report contain any inaccurate information about your credit transactions? If so, and if a denial of credit, employment, or insurance might have been based on the report, you can and should have it corrected, as permitted under the Fair Credit Reporting Act.

 ## USING INTERNET RESOURCES

1. Go to the Web site maintained by the Tobacco Control Resource Center at **http://www.library.ucsf.edu/tobacco/litigation** for information on state tobacco litigation. Click on the link for "Key Litigation Documents by State and Other Jurisdictions." Select a state. If there is more than one case listed, select one case, and click on "Full Text." You will find an electronic version of the complaint filed in the case. Use that document to answer the following questions:

   a. Who is the plaintiff in the action? How many tobacco companies are named as defendants in the complaint?

   b. How many "counts" or "causes of action" are listed in the complaint? (Hint: Usually the counts appear as headings.)

   c. What theory or theories of *tort* liability that were discussed in this chapter are alleged in the complaint?

2. Go to FindLaw's Injury and Tort Law Web Guide at **http://www.findlaw.com/01topics/22tort** to find answers to the following questions:

   a. Under the heading "Injury and Tort Law Web Guide," click on "Databases." What kind of information generally is available at this location? How might you use this information in a tort lawsuit? Can you access any data or reports from governmental agencies? Which agencies?

   b. Now click on "Software." What kinds of software are listed?

   c. Under the heading "Journals, Newsletters and Articles," you can find many articles on tort law. Read an article that interests you and write a one-page summary.

   d. Now click on "Web Sites" and browse through the listings. Note how many of the listings are dedicated to providing information about defective products and product liability actions. Explore one of the Web sites provided, and write a short synopsis of what you found at that site.

3. The Federal Trade Commission (FTC) provides information on consumer law issues through its Web site, located at **http://www.ftc.gov**. Access this Web site and then follow the instructions below.

   a. Select "About FTC" from the menu at the top of the screen. When the page opens, click on "A Guide to the Federal Trade Commission." When was the FTC created, and for what purpose? What subsequent laws have been passed to enhance the FTC's authority and the scope of its enforcement activities?

   b. Scroll down to the heading "Bureau of Consumer Protection" and read through the list of enforcement activities regulated by the Division of Advertising Practices. List five of these activities. How many other divisions are included in the Bureau of Consumer Protection?

   c. Scroll further down this page to the section titled "How the FTC Brings an Action." What types of events might trigger the FTC to take action on a given matter? Summarize the procedures that the FTC follows when taking an action against a company.

   d. Now look at the next section on the page, titled "FTC Offices You Should Know About." List and describe three of the offices discussed here.

   e. Next, read through the section titled "For More Information." Make a list of telephone numbers that you can call to obtain specific types of information.

4.  For additional resources, visit our Web site at **http://www.paralegal.delmar.cengage.com**.

END NOTES

1. The reasonable person standard is an objective test of how a reasonable person would have acted under the same circumstances. See the discussion under "The Duty of Care and Its Breach" later in this chapter.

2. *New York Times Co. v. Sullivan,* 376 U.S. 254, 84 S.Ct. 710, 11 L.Ed.2d 686 (1964).

3. *White v. Samsung Electronics America, Inc.,* 971 F.2d 1395 (9th Cir. 1992).

4. 47 U.S.C. Section 230.

5. *Does v. Hvide,* 770 So.2d 1237 (Fla.App.3d 2000).

6. *Restatement (Second) of Torts,* Section 402A.

7. *Restatement (Third) of Torts: Products Liability,* Section 2, Comment h.

8. Under some state laws, the failure to properly maintain a product may constitute a subsequent alteration.

CONTRACTS AND INTELLECTUAL PROPERTY LAW

CHAPTER OUTLINE

AFTER COMPLETING THIS CHAPTER, YOU WILL KNOW:

▶ The requirements for forming a valid contract and the kinds of circumstances under which contracts are not enforceable.

▶ The remedies available to the innocent party when a contract is breached, or broken.

▶ The nature of an electronic signature and the legal validity of such signatures.

▶ The nature of intellectual property and some forms of intellectual property.

▶ What conduct gives rise to a copyright infringement action.

INTRODUCTION

The law governs virtually every transaction or activity that individuals engage in across the nation. Simple, everyday transactions—such as purchasing a carton of milk from your corner grocer or installing a new software program on your home computer—are subject to specific laws that define the rights and duties of the parties involved. In this chapter, you will learn about two of the most important areas of law—contracts and sales. Paralegals routinely help attorneys deal with disputes involving contract and sales law. Because such disputes often deal with complicated issues, paralegals need a thorough understanding of the basic principles of these substantive law areas.

Another area of law that has become increasingly important involves the world's intellectual property, such as patents, trademarks, and copyrights. As you will learn later in the chapter, the value of intellectual property has become very important because of the freer flow of ideas throughout the world. Attorneys and their paralegals are frequently called on to help their clients register and protect some form of intellectual property.

On the Web

The 'Lectric Law Library provides information on many legal topics, including contracts. Click on **http://www.lectlaw.com/lay.html** to go to the "Laypeople's Law Lounge."

REQUIREMENTS TO FORM A VALID CONTRACT

Contract law deals with, among other things, the keeping of promises. A **promise** is an assurance that one will or will not do something in the future. As mentioned in Chapter 2, a *contract* is any agreement (based on a promise or an exchange of promises) that can be enforced in court. (Today, forms for numerous types of contracts are available online—see this chapter's *Technology and Today's Paralegal* feature on page 267 for information on how to access Web sites offering contract forms.)

If a client alleges that a party has breached (failed to perform) a contract, the first issue that you and your supervising attorney need to examine is whether a *valid contract* (a contract that will be enforced by a court) was ever formed. To form a valid contract, four basic requirements must be met:

> **promise**
> An assurance that one will or will not do something in the future.

- *Agreement.* An agreement includes an offer and an acceptance. One party must offer to enter into a legal agreement, and another party must accept the terms of the offer.

- *Consideration.* Any promises made by parties must be supported by legally sufficient and bargained-for consideration (which is something of value that is received or promised to convince a person to make a deal, as you will read shortly).

- *Contractual capacity.* Both parties entering into the contract must have the contractual capacity to do so; the law must recognize them as possessing characteristics that qualify them as competent parties.

- *Legality.* The contract's purpose must be to accomplish some goal that is legal and not against public policy.

If any of these four elements is lacking, no contract will have been formed. We look more closely at these requirements in the following subsections. It is important that you understand as you read these discussions that each requirement is separate and independent.

Agreement

A contract is, in essence, an **agreement** between two or more parties. Therefore, if the parties fail to reach an agreement on the terms of the contract, no contract exists. Ordinarily, agreement is evidenced by two events: an *offer* and an *acceptance*. One party offers a certain bargain to another party, who then accepts that bargain.

> **agreement**
> A meeting of the minds, and a requirement for a valid contract. Agreement involves two distinct events: an offer to form a contract and the acceptance of that offer by the offeree.

Offer

offer
A promise or commitment to do or refrain from doing some specified thing in the future.

offeror
The party making the offer.

offeree
The party to whom the offer is made.

An **offer** is a promise or commitment to do or refrain from doing some specified thing in the future. Three elements are necessary for an offer to be effective:

- The **offeror** (the party making the offer) must have the *intent to be bound* by the offer.

- The terms of the offer must be *reasonably certain, or definite*, so that the parties and the court can ascertain the terms of the contract. (Note that in contracts for the sale of goods, discussed later in this chapter, the requirement of definiteness is relaxed somewhat so that a contract can still arise even if certain terms are left "open," or unspecified.[1])

- The offer must be communicated to the **offeree** (the party to whom the offer is made).

Offers made in jest, in undue excitement, or in obvious anger do not meet the intent requirement. ▶ **EXAMPLE 8.1**   Suppose that Al and Sue ride to work together each day in Sue's car, which she bought for $18,000 six months ago. One cold morning, Al and Sue get into the car, but Sue cannot get it started. She yells in anger, "I'll sell you my car for $600!" Al writes Sue a check for $600. Has a contract to sell the car been formed? If Al consulted with your supervising attorney, claiming that Sue had breached a contract because she had refused to give him the car, what would the attorney say? Most likely, the attorney would tell Al that a reasonable person would have recognized under the circumstances that Sue's offer was not serious—she did not intend to be bound but was simply frustrated. Therefore, no valid contract was formed. ◀

Similarly, an offer will not be effective if it is too ambiguous in its terms. ▶ **EXAMPLE 8.2**   Suppose that Kim wants to sell her set of legal encyclopedias but has not mentioned a price. James then says to Kim, "I'll buy your encyclopedias and pay you some money for them next week." In this situation, no contract will result, because "some money" is not a definite term. ◀

A real estate paralegal reviews the terms of a purchase offer with a potential home buyer to ensure that all of the contract's terms are clear.

(Courtesy of ©Royalty-Free/Corbis)

Technology and Today's Paralegal

CONTRACT FORMS

Before the printing press was invented, every contract form had to be handwritten. Since the advent of printing, most standard contract forms have been readily available at low cost. The introduction of computers into legal practice obviated the need to use preprinted forms and further allowed attorneys and paralegals to customize contract forms for each situation. This procedure has been both simplified and expanded by the inclusion of contract forms on simple-to-use CD-ROMs.

ONLINE CONTRACT FORMS

Now the Internet has made available an even larger variety of contract forms, as well as other legal and business forms. For example, at **http://forms.lp.findlaw.com**, you can access over 25,000 legal forms for lawyers, businesses, and the public. The contracts range from basic sales contracts to sample software licensing agreements. Many are available free of charge. The Internet Legal Resource Group also offers a number of free contract forms and links to other online resources at **http://www.ilrg.com/forms/index.html#other**.

Yet another source for contract forms is 'Lectric Law Library's collection of forms at **http://www. lectlaw.com/formb.htm**. This site includes forms for the assignment of a contract, a contract for the sale of a business, and many others (some free, some for purchase). In addition, if you become a member of the 'Lectric Law Library, you can access document assembly software that uses the forms to build a final contract to suit your needs.

There are many other sources for contract forms on the Internet. For example, **http://www.uslegalforms. com** has numerous forms available in many areas of practice. Not only can you search for contracts by topic (such as corporate or construction contracts), but you can also look up state-specific forms (separation agreements, for example). Most of the forms are available for a nominal fee (ten to fifteen dollars) and can be obtained in printed form (mailed to you) or downloaded in the electronic format of your choice (*Microsoft Word, WordPerfect,* or rich text format). Similar types of services are available at many other sites, including **http://www.legal-forms-now.com**, **http://myshoppingonline.com/my/600forms1.htm** and **http://www.allaboutforms.com**.

TECHNOLOGY TIP

Online contract forms are a tremendous resource for paralegals. Thousands of forms can be easily accessed and customized for use in particular transactions. Keep in mind, though, that the contracts you find online will not necessarily be valid or upheld in your state or situation. You must always research the contract requirements in your state to verify that you are using the appropriate form.

Termination of the Offer

Once an offer has been communicated, the party to whom the offer was made can accept the offer, reject the offer, or make a counteroffer. If a party accepts the offer, a contract is formed (provided all the other requirements to form a contract are met). If the party rejects the offer, the offer is terminated. In other words, the offer no longer stands (and the offeree cannot take the offeror up on the offer). The offeree also has the option of rejecting the offer and simultaneously making another offer—called a counteroffer.

In a counteroffer, the offeree becomes the offeror—offering to form a contract with different terms. ▶ **EXAMPLE 8.3** Suppose that Dillon offers to perform work for Wayne for $50,000. Wayne responds, "Your price is too high. I'll hire you for $40,000." Wayne's response is a counteroffer, because it terminates Dillon's offer and creates a new offer by Wayne. ◀

Both a rejection of the offer and the making of a counteroffer terminate the original offer. The original offer can also be terminated if the party making the offer withdraws the offer before it has been accepted (which is called *revoking* the offer).[2] If the offer has already been accepted, however, then both parties are bound in contract. An offer will also terminate automatically in some circumstances, such as when the specific subject matter of the offer is destroyed, one of the parties dies or becomes incompetent, or a new law is passed that makes the contract illegal. Additionally, an offer will terminate if a period of time is specified in the offer and the offer is not accepted within that period. If no time for acceptance is specified in the offer, the offer expires when a *reasonable* period of time has passed. (What constitutes a reasonable period of time in the eyes of the court varies, depending on the circumstances.)

Acceptance

> **acceptance**
> In contract law, the offeree's indication to the offeror that the offeree agrees to be bound by the terms of the offeror's offer, or proposal to form a contract.

As mentioned, a party's **acceptance** of the offer results in a legally binding contract (if all of the other elements of a valid contract are present). The acceptance must be *unequivocal*— that is, the terms of the offer must be accepted exactly as stated by the offeror. This principle of contract law is known as the **mirror image rule**—the terms of the acceptance must be the same as ("mirror") the terms of the offer. If the acceptance is subject to new conditions or if the terms of the acceptance materially change the original offer, the acceptance may be deemed a counteroffer that implicitly rejects the original offer.

> **mirror image rule**
> A common law rule that requires that the terms of the offeree's acceptance adhere exactly to the terms of the offeror's offer for a valid contract to be formed.

Another requirement, for most types of contracts, is that the acceptance be communicated to the offeror. A significant problem with respect to contract formation has to do with the timeliness of acceptances. The general rule is that acceptance of an offer is timely if it is made before the offer is terminated. Problems arise, however, when the parties involved are not dealing face-to-face. In such cases, acceptance takes effect at the time the acceptance is communicated via the mode expressly or impliedly authorized by the offeror. This is the **mailbox rule**. Under this rule, if the offer states that it must be accepted by mail, the acceptance becomes valid the moment it is deposited in the mail (even if it is never received by the offeror).

> **mailbox rule**
> A rule providing that an acceptance of an offer takes effect at the time it is communicated via the mode expressly or impliedly authorized by the offeror, rather than at the time it is actually received by the offeror. If acceptance is to be by mail, for example, it becomes effective the moment it is placed in the mailbox.

Most of the time, the party making the offer does not indicate the preferred method of acceptance. In those cases, acceptance of an offer may be made by any medium that is *reasonable under the circumstances*. Several factors determine whether the acceptance was reasonable: the nature of the circumstances at the time the offer was made, the means used to transmit the offer, and the reliability of the offer's delivery. ▶ **EXAMPLE 8.4** Suppose that an offer was sent by FedEx overnight delivery because an acceptance was urgently required. In this situation, the offeree's attempt to accept by fax would be deemed reasonable. ◀ In contracts formed on the Internet, the issues of timeliness and method of acceptance usually do not arise. This is because persons often accept online offers simply by clicking on a box stating "I agree" or "I accept." Such **click-on agreements** are becoming widely used in the formation of contracts online (as discussed later in this chapter).

> **click-on agreement**
> An agreement that arises when a buyer, engaging in a transaction on a computer, indicates his or her assent to be bound by the terms of an offer by clicking on a button that says, for example, "I agree"; sometimes referred to as a *click-on license* or a *click-wrap agreement*.

Consideration

> **consideration**
> Something of value, such as money or the performance of an action not otherwise required, that motivates the formation of a contract. Each party must give consideration for the contract to be binding.

Another requirement for a valid contract is consideration. **Consideration** is usually defined as something of value—such as money or the performance of an action not otherwise required—that is given in exchange for a promise. No promise is enforceable without consideration. ▶ **EXAMPLE 8.5** Suppose that you give your friend $1,000 in exchange for her promise to take care of your house and garden for six months. This promise normally will be enforceable, because consideration has been given. Your consideration is $1,000; your friend's consideration is the assumption of an obligation (taking care of the house and garden) that she otherwise would not assume. ◀ Note that both parties to the contract must give consideration for the contract to be enforced.

Often, consideration is broken down into two parts: (1) something of *legal value* must be given in exchange for the promise, and (2) there must be a *bargained-for* exchange. The "something of legal value" may consist of a return promise that is bargained for. It may also consist of performance, which may be an act, a forbearance (refraining from action), or the creation, modification, or destruction of a legal relationship. ▶ **EXAMPLE 8.6** When you are twenty-one, your grandfather promises to pay you $10,000 if you agree not to smoke any cigarettes before the age of twenty-five. Your consideration in this situation is refraining from the act of smoking cigarettes. ◀

Once a contract has been formed, the general common law rule is that the terms of the contract cannot be modified without further consideration. For instance, after making the deal in the example just given, your grandfather cannot modify the terms by requiring you not to drink alcohol for the same $10,000—you would have to get additional consideration for this new agreement.

Legal Sufficiency of Consideration

For a binding contract to be created, consideration must be *legally sufficient*. To be legally sufficient, consideration for a promise must be either *legally detrimental to the promisee* or *legally beneficial to the promisor*. A party can incur legal detriment either by promising to give legal value (such as the payment of money) or by a forbearance or a promise of forbearance—that is, by refraining from or promising to refrain from doing something that the party had a legal right to do.

The requirement of consideration is what distinguishes contracts from gifts. ▶ **EXAMPLE 8.7** Suppose that you promise to give your friend $1,000 as a gift and she promises to accept your gift. In this situation, no contract results, because your friend has given no legally sufficient consideration for the contract. ◀

Adequacy of Consideration

Adequacy of consideration refers to the fairness of the bargain. In general, a court will not question the adequacy of consideration if the consideration is legally sufficient. Parties are normally free to bargain as they wish. If people could sue merely because they had entered into a bad bargain, the courts would be overloaded with frivolous suits. In other words, Jack is free to sell his 1999 Mercedes Benz, which is in perfect condition, to Herb for $1,000, even if the car is worth more (the court will not invalidate the contract).

In extreme cases, a court may consider the adequacy of consideration in terms of its amount or worth because inadequate consideration may indicate fraud, duress, undue influence, or a lack of bargained-for exchange. It may also reflect a party's incompetence (for example, an individual might have been too intoxicated or simply too young to make a contract).

Promissory Estoppel

In some circumstances, contracts will be enforced even though consideration is lacking. Under the doctrine of **promissory estoppel**, a person who has reasonably and substantially relied on the promise of another may be able to obtain some measure of recovery. The following elements are required:

- There must be a clear and definite promise.
- The promisee must justifiably rely on the promise.
- The reliance normally must be of a substantial and definite character.
- Justice will be better served by enforcement of the promise.

On the Web

To learn more about how the courts decide such issues as whether consideration was lacking for a particular contract, look at relevant case law, which you can access through Cornell University's School of Law site at **http://www.law.cornell.edu/wex/index.php/contracts**.

promissory estoppel
A doctrine under which a promise is binding if the promise is clear and definite, the promisee justifiably relies on the promise, the reliance is reasonable and substantial, and justice will be better served by enforcement of the promise.

If these requirements are met, a promise may be enforced even though it is not supported by consideration. In essence, the promisor will be *estopped* (prevented) from asserting the lack of consideration as a defense. ▶ **EXAMPLE 8.8** Suppose that your uncle tells you, "I'll pay you $500 a week so you won't have to work anymore." In reliance on your uncle's promise, you quit your job, but your uncle refuses to pay you. Under the doctrine of promissory estoppel, you may be able to enforce such a promise. ◀

Contractual Capacity

contractual capacity
The threshold mental capacity required by law for a party who enters into a contract to be bound by that contract.

For a contract to be deemed valid, the parties to the contract must have **contractual capacity**—the legal ability to enter into a contractual relationship. Courts generally presume the existence of contractual capacity, but there are some situations in which capacity is lacking or questionable. In many situations, a party may have the capacity to enter into a valid contract but also have the right to avoid liability under it.

Minors usually are not legally bound by contracts. Subject to certain exceptions, the contracts entered into by a minor are *voidable* (capable of being canceled, or avoided) at the option of that minor. The minor has the option of *disaffirming* (renouncing) the contract and setting aside the contract and all legal obligations arising from it. An adult who enters into a contract with a minor, however, cannot avoid his or her contractual duties on the ground that the minor can do so. Unless the minor exercises the option to set aside the contract, the adult party is bound by it.

Intoxication is a condition in which a person's normal capacity to act or think is inhibited by alcohol or some other drug. Under the common law rule, if the person was sufficiently intoxicated to lack mental capacity, the transaction is voidable at the option of the intoxicated person even if the intoxication was purely voluntary. Note that in spite of the common law rule, most courts today rarely permit contracts to be avoided because of a party's intoxication.

If a person has been adjudged mentally incompetent by a court of law and a guardian has been appointed, any contract made by the mentally incompetent person is *void*—no contract exists. Only the guardian can enter into binding legal duties on the incompetent person's behalf. Even if the court has not previously ruled that the person is mentally incompetent, the contract may be avoided if incompetence is proved. ▶ **EXAMPLE 8.9** Suppose that Rita, who suffers from Alzheimer's disease, signs a contract to buy ten new vacuums. If it can be proved that Rita did not understand what she was doing at the time she signed the contract, the contract will not be valid. ◀

Legality

A contract to do something that is prohibited by federal or state statutory law is illegal and, as such, void from the outset and thus unenforceable. For example, a contract to buy a kidney from another person is void because it is illegal. No court would enforce the contract if a lawsuit were brought for breach of contract. Any contract to commit a crime is unenforceable.

In some instances, the subject matter of the contract is not illegal, but one of the parties is not legally authorized to perform the contract. Consider an illustration. All states require that members of certain occupations—including physicians, lawyers, real estate brokers, architects, electricians, contractors, and stockbrokers—obtain licenses allowing them to practice. When a person enters into a contract with an unlicensed individual, the contract may still be enforceable, depending on the nature of the licensing statute. Some states expressly provide that the lack of a license in certain occupations (such as lawyers) bars the enforcement of work-related contracts. If the statute does not expressly declare this, one must look to the underlying purpose of the licensing requirements for a particular occupation. If the purpose is to protect the public from unauthorized practitioners, a contract involving an unlicensed individual normally is illegal and unenforceable. If the underlying

Developing Paralegal Skills

ASSESSING CONTRACTUAL CAPACITY

Suppose you are a legal assistant for Jeffrey Barlow. Barlow asks you to draft a contract for Margaret Klaus, a seventy-six-year-old widow. In the contract, Margaret will convey all of her shares in NAPO Corporation to her nephew Jeremy. In return, Jeremy will take care of Margaret for the rest of her life. The attorney is leaving on vacation and asks you to have the document completed and to arrange a meeting with the client and her nephew to sign the contract when he returns in two weeks.

While drafting the agreement, you learn that the stock being conveyed is worth a great deal of money. Also, you begin to have doubts about Margaret's mental status. She has called you at least once a day for the past week. During the conversations, she often calls you by different names, repeats herself, and does not remember what you just told her. Although you know that Jeremy has been living with Margaret for the past six months (and is unemployed), whenever Margaret calls, she is alone and seems to be frightened. Now that you have finished the contract, you wonder if Margaret is capable of consenting to it and whether Jeremy has exerted too much influence over her. What should you do?

TIPS FOR DEALING WITH SUSPICIONS OF INCOMPETENCE

- Document everything. Keep a record of all the conversations you had with the client that led you to suspect a lack of contractual capacity, as well as any other facts that contributed to your suspicions (if you discovered the person was taking medication for mental illness, for example).

- Do not discuss your suspicions with anyone except your supervising attorney (particularly not with the client or the client's family). Making such statements about a person can be very damaging to his or her reputation, and you may even be held liable for defamation.

- Remember that it is the attorney's job to evaluate the client's contractual capacity, not yours. You just want to make the attorney aware of the situation in an effort to protect the client's best interests.

purpose of the statute is to raise government revenues, however, a contract entered into with an unlicensed practitioner generally is enforceable—although the unlicensed person is usually fined.

Additionally, some contracts are not enforced because the court deems them to be contrary to public policy. For example, contracts that restrain trade (anticompetitive contracts) and contracts that are so oppressive to innocent parties that they are deemed *unconscionable* (unconscionable contracts will be discussed shortly) are not enforceable owing to the negative impact they would have on society.

DEFENSES TO CONTRACT ENFORCEABILITY

Two competent parties have entered into a contract for a legal purpose. The agreement is supported by consideration. The contract thus meets the four requirements for a valid contract. Nonetheless, the contract may be unenforceable if the parties have not genuinely assented (agreed) to its terms, if the contract is so oppressive to one of the parties that a court will refuse to enforce it, or if the contract is not in the proper form—such as in writing, if the law requires it to be in writing.

Genuineness of Assent

genuineness of assent
Knowing and voluntary assent to the contract terms. If a contract is formed as a result of mistake, misrepresentation, undue influence, or duress, genuineness of assent is lacking, and the contract will be voidable.

Lack of **genuineness of assent** can be used as a defense to the contract's enforceability. Genuineness of assent may be lacking because of a mistake, misrepresentation, undue influence, or duress.

Mistake

It is important to distinguish between *mistakes of fact* and *mistakes of value or quality*. If a mistake concerns the future market value or quality of the object of the contract, the mistake is one of *value*, and either party normally can enforce the contract. Each party is considered to have assumed the risk that the value would change or prove to be different from what he or she thought. Without this rule, almost any party who did not receive what he or she considered a fair bargain could argue mistake.

Only a mistake of fact allows a contract to be avoided. Mistakes of fact occur in two forms—*unilateral* and *mutual (bilateral)*. A **unilateral mistake** occurs when one party to the contract makes a mistake as to some **material fact**—that is, a fact important to the subject matter of the contract. The general rule is that a unilateral mistake does not afford the mistaken party any right to relief from the contract. There are some exceptions to this rule, however. ▶ **EXAMPLE 8.10**   Assume that a contractor's bid was significantly low because he or she made a mistake in addition when totaling the estimated costs. In this situation, any contract resulting from the bid normally can be rescinded. (**Rescission** is the act of canceling, or nullifying, a contract.) ◀

When *both* of the parties are mistaken about the same material fact, a **mutual mistake** has occurred, and either party can cancel the contract. ▶ **EXAMPLE 8.11**   Assume that at Perez's art gallery, Diana buys a painting of a landscape. Both Diana and Perez believe that the painting is by the artist Vincent van Gogh. Later, Diana discovers that the painting is a very clever fake. Because neither Perez nor Diana was aware of this material fact when they made their deal, Diana can rescind (cancel) the contract and recover the purchase price of the painting. ◀

unilateral mistake
Mistake as to a material fact on the part of only one party to a contract. In this situation, the contract is normally enforceable against the mistaken party, with some exceptions.

material fact
A fact that is important to the subject matter of the contract.

rescission
A remedy in which the contract is canceled and the parties are returned to the positions they occupied before the contract was made.

mutual mistake
Mistake as to the same material fact on the part of both parties to a contract. In this situation, either party can cancel the contract.

Fraudulent Misrepresentation

When an innocent party is fraudulently induced to enter into a contract, the contract usually can be avoided because that party has not *voluntarily* consented to its terms. Normally, the innocent party can either rescind (cancel) the contract and be restored to his or her original position or enforce the contract and seek damages for any injuries resulting from the fraud.

You read about the tort of fraudulent misrepresentation in Chapter 7. In the context of contract law, fraudulent misrepresentation occurs when one party to a contract misrepresents a material fact to the other party, with the intention of deceiving the other party, and the other party justifiably relies on the misrepresentation. To collect damages, a party must also have been injured. A party may still be able to avoid the contract in some states without proving that he or she was injured by the fraud, however.

Note that the misrepresentation may be based on conduct as well as oral or written statements. ▶ **EXAMPLE 8.12**   Suppose that Gene is contracting to buy Rachelle's horse for racing. While showing Gene the horse, Rachelle skillfully keeps the horse's head turned away so that Gene does not see that the horse is blind in one eye. Rachelle's conduct constitutes fraud. ◀

Undue Influence

Undue influence arises from special kinds of relationships in which one party can greatly influence another party, thus overcoming that party's free will. Elderly people may be unduly influenced by their caretakers, clients may be unduly influenced by their attorneys, and chil-

POTENTIAL CONFLICTS OF INTEREST

Many times in a law office, two parties come in together and want the attorney (and paralegal) to write a contract that represents their agreement. This raises an obvious conflict-of-interest issue. Can the attorney represent both parties in a contract? Recall from Chapter 3 that conflict rules prevent an attorney from simultaneously representing adverse parties in a legal proceeding. On the one hand, drafting a contract is not really a legal proceeding, since the parties could write up a legally binding contract without an attorney. On the other hand, should a dispute arise over the contract, assisting one party will necessarily be adverse to the other. In this situation, the attorney and paralegal need to carefully research the rules on waiving conflicts in their state. If the state has adopted the 2002 Revision of the Model Rules, then the attorney must obtain the informed consent of each party, and the consent must be confirmed in writing. This means the attorney must explain the risks of having one attorney draw up a contract for two people and also must discuss the alternatives. Then the attorney must have the two parties sign a consent form or, if the parties give consent orally, must promptly draft a written document evidencing the consent.

dren may be unduly influenced by their parents. The essential feature of undue influence is that the party being taken advantage of does not, in reality, exercise free will in entering into a contract. A contract entered into under excessive or undue influence lacks genuine assent and is therefore voidable.

Duress

Assent to the terms of a contract is not genuine if one of the parties is *forced* into the agreement. Forcing a party to do something, including entering into a contract, through fear created by threats is legally defined as *duress*. In addition, blackmail or extortion to induce consent to a contract constitutes duress. Duress is both a defense to the enforcement of a contract and a ground for the rescission of a contract.

Unconscionable Contracts or Clauses

Ordinarily, a court does not look at the fairness or equity of a contract; for example, a court normally will not inquire into the adequacy of consideration. Persons are assumed to be reasonably intelligent, and the court does not come to their aid just because they have made unwise or foolish bargains.

In certain circumstances, however, a bargain is so oppressive to one of the parties that the court will refuse to enforce the contract. Such a bargain is called an **unconscionable contract** (or **unconscionable clause**). Contracts entered into because of one party's vastly superior bargaining power may be deemed unconscionable. These situations usually involve an **adhesion contract**, which is a contract drafted by the dominant party and then presented to the other—the adhering party—on a "take-it-or-leave-it" basis.

unconscionable contract or unconscionable clause
A contract or clause that is so oppressive to one of the parties that the court will refuse to enforce the contract.

adhesion contract
A contract drafted by the dominant party and then presented to the other—the adhering party—on a "take-it-or-leave-it" basis.

The Statute of Frauds

An otherwise valid contract may be unenforceable if it is not in the proper form. To ensure that there is reliable proof of the agreement, certain types of contracts are required to be in writing. If a contract is required by law to be in writing and there is no written evidence of the contract, it may not be enforceable.

Every state has a statute (or more than one statute) that specifies what types of contracts must be in writing (or be evidenced by a written document). This statute is commonly referred to as the **Statute of Frauds**.[3] Although the state statutes vary slightly, the following types of contracts are normally required to be in writing:

- Contracts involving interests in land (or anything attached to land, such as buildings, plants, minerals, or timber).
- Contracts that cannot by their terms be performed within one year from the day after the date of formation.
- Collateral, or secondary, contracts, such as promises to answer for the debt or duty of another.
- Promises made in consideration of marriage, such as prenuptial agreements (which will be discussed in Chapter 10).
- Contracts for the sale of goods priced at $500 or more.

Note that the test for determining whether an oral contract is enforceable under the "one-year rule" stated in the second item above is not whether an agreement is *likely* to be performed within one year but whether performance is *possible* within one year. Also, the one-year period begins to run the day *after* the contract is formed. Exhibit 8.1 illustrates the one-year rule.

In some states, an oral contract that would otherwise be unenforceable under the Statute of Frauds may be enforced under the doctrine of promissory estoppel, based on detrimental reliance. Recall that if one party makes a promise on which the other party justifiably relies to his or her detriment, a court may prevent the party who made the promise from denying that a contract exists. In these circumstances, an oral promise may be enforceable if the reliance was foreseeable and if injustice can be avoided only by enforcing the promise.

Statute of Frauds
A state statute that requires certain types of contracts to be in writing to be enforceable.

EXHIBIT 8.1
The One-Year Rule

Under the Statute of Frauds, contracts that by their terms are impossible to perform within one year from the day after the date of contract formation must be in writing to be enforceable. Put another way, if it is at all possible to perform an oral contract within one year from the day after the contract is made, the contract will fall outside the Statute of Frauds and be enforceable.

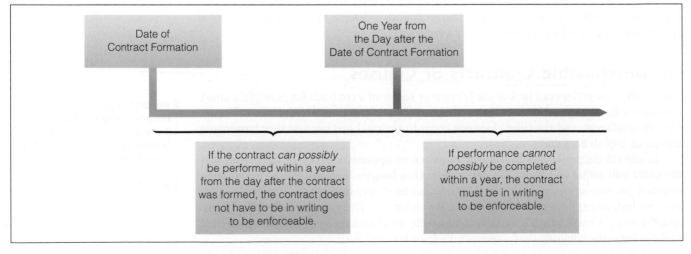

Date of Contract Formation

One Year from the Day after the Date of Contract Formation

If the contract *can possibly* be performed within a year from the day after the contract was formed, the contract does not have to be in writing to be enforceable.

If performance *cannot possibly* be completed within a year, the contract must be in writing to be enforceable.

SALES CONTRACTS AND WARRANTIES

Sales contracts, or contracts for the sale of goods, are governed by state statutes that are based on Article 2 of the **Uniform Commercial Code (UCC)**. The UCC is one of the many—and one of the most significant—uniform laws created by the American Law Institute and the National Conference of Commissioners on Uniform State Laws. The UCC was first issued in 1952 and has since been revised to reflect the changing customs and needs of business and society. The UCC has been adopted, in whole or in part, by all of the states. State statutory codes are not necessarily called the Uniform Commercial Code, however. In Ohio, for example, UCC provisions are incorporated into the Ohio Commercial Code.

The Scope of UCC Article 2

In regard to Article 2 of the UCC, two things should be kept in mind. First, Article 2 deals with the sale of *goods,* not real property (real estate), services, or intangible property. Second, the rules may vary quite a bit, depending on whether the buyer or seller is a merchant. You should always note the subject matter of a dispute and the people (merchants or consumers) involved when you are dealing with cases involving contractual disputes. If the subject is goods, then the UCC will govern. If it is real estate or services, then the common law principles discussed earlier will apply.

As under the common law of contracts, the parties to sales contracts are free to fashion the terms of their contracts as they wish. The UCC normally comes into play only when a dispute arises over ambiguous or missing terms. Note also that the UCC does not replace the common law of contracts—the body of contract law discussed in the previous sections. A contract for the sale of goods is also subject to the common law requirements of agreement, consideration, contractual capacity, and legality. Similarly, the common law defenses against contract formation or enforceability also apply to sales contracts. If the UCC has not modified a common law principle, then the common law governs. In other words, the general rule is that when the UCC addresses a particular matter, the UCC governs; when the UCC is silent, then the common law of contracts applies.

Warranties under the UCC

The UCC provides that a **warranty** of title arises in any sale of goods—that is, a seller automatically warrants (promises) to a buyer that the seller has good title to (legitimate ownership rights in) the goods being sold and can transfer that good title to the buyer. If the goods turn out to be stolen, for example, and the buyer has to return the goods to the real owner, the seller will be liable to the buyer for the value of the goods.

The UCC also contains provisions on express and implied warranties as to the quality or nature of the goods being sold. An *express warranty* is an oral or written promise made by a seller concerning the nature of the goods being sold. ▶ **EXAMPLE 8.13** The statement, "This is a new Black & Decker lawn mower" is an express warranty, or promise, that the lawn mower is indeed a Black & Decker lawn mower and that it is new. If you purchase the lawn mower and learn that it is not new but used, the seller has breached an express warranty. ◀

Under the UCC, implied warranties arise in all sales transactions. Every merchant makes an *implied warranty of merchantability* when goods are sold. The goods must be merchantable—that is, they must be "reasonably fit for the ordinary purposes for which such goods are used." Some examples of unmerchantable goods are a lightbulb that explodes when switched on, hamburger meat that contains fragments of glass, and a new boat that leaks. Goods sold by merchants must also be fit for the particular purpose for which they are sold. For this *implied warranty of fitness for a particular purpose* to arise, the buyer must rely on the seller's skill or judgment in selecting suitable goods.

---

sales contract
A contract for the sale of goods, as opposed to a contract for the sale of services, real property, or intangible property. Sales contracts are governed by Article 2 of the Uniform Commercial Code.

Uniform Commercial Code (UCC)
A uniform code of laws governing commercial transactions that has been adopted, in whole or in part, by all of the states. Article 2 of the UCC governs contracts for the sale of goods.

On the Web

You can access the Uniform Commercial Code (UCC), including Article 2, at the Web site of the Legal Information Institute. Go to **http://www.law. cornell.edu/ucc/ucc.table.html**.

warranty
An express or implied promise by a seller that specific goods to be sold meet certain criteria, or standards of performance, on which the buyer may rely.

Developing Paralegal Skills

CONTRACT REVIEW

Samantha Thompson works as a paralegal for a corporation. One of her jobs is to review contracts between the corporation and outside vendors. She is reviewing a contract for the corporation's purchase of fifty new personal computers from an outside vendor. The contract, which is a preprinted form contract, was submitted by the vendor and consists of thirty paragraphs of "fine print." The blanks in the form, for such terms as price and quantity, have been filled in by the vendor. As Samantha reads through the contract, she comes across a warranty disclaimer provision. Samantha realizes that this contract provision means that there will be no warranty of merchantability or fitness for a particular purpose for the new computers. She makes a note to tell her supervising attorney about this important provision. The attorney will want to inform management of this limitation on warranties.

TIPS FOR REVIEWING A CONTRACT

- Find out which contract provisions are acceptable to the client.
- Obtain the original copy of the contract.
- Read each provision carefully.
- Be certain you understand the meaning of each provision. If you are uncertain, find out what a provision means; do not rely on the formulaic language in standard contract forms.
- Prepare a memo explaining the client's rights and liabilities under the contract.
- In the memo, mention any contract terms and provisions that the client might find objectionable.

Law Guru can lead you to other sources of law relating to contract performance. Go to **http://lawguru.com**.

---

performance
In contract law, the fulfillment of duties arising under a contract; the normal way of discharging contractual obligations.

breach of contract
The failure, without legal excuse, of a contractual party to perform the obligations assumed in a contract.

The UCC permits express and implied warranties to be disclaimed, provided that the buyer is made aware of the disclaimers at the time the sales contract is formed. To disclaim an implied warranty of fitness for a particular purpose, the disclaimer must be in writing and be conspicuous (printed in larger or contrasting type or in a different color, for example). A merchantability disclaimer must mention the word *merchantability*, but it need not be in writing. If it is made in writing, the writing must be conspicuous. Generally speaking, unless circumstances indicate otherwise, the implied warranties are disclaimed by the expression "as is," "with all faults," or similar language that is commonly understood by both parties as meaning that there are no implied warranties.

CONTRACT PERFORMANCE AND REMEDIES

A party's contractual duties can be terminated in several ways. The most common way to terminate contractual duties, however, is by the **performance** of those duties. Failure to perform contractual duties as promised results in a **breach of contract**. When one party breaches a contract, the other party (the nonbreaching party) can seek remedies.

Contract Performance

Conditions expressly stated in a contract must be fully satisfied for complete performance to take place. A party who in good faith performs substantially all of the terms of a contract, however, can usually enforce the contract against the other party under the doctrine of *substantial performance.* Generally, performance that provides a party with the important and essential benefits of a contract, in spite of any omission or deviation from the terms, is substantial performance. Because substantial performance is not perfect, the other party is entitled to damages to compensate for the failure to comply with the contract.

After a contract has been made, performance may become impossible in an objective sense ("it can't be done," rather than "I can't do it"). For example, the subject matter of the contract may be destroyed, one of the parties to a personal contract may die or become incapacitated prior to performance, or performance may become illegal because of a change in the law. In these situations, the law excuses parties from their contractual performance duties under what is known as *impossibility of performance.*

Under the doctrine of *commercial impracticability,* courts may excuse parties from their performance obligations when the performance becomes much more difficult or expensive than contemplated at the time the contract was formed. For someone to invoke this doctrine successfully, however, the anticipated performance must become *extremely* difficult or costly.

Contract Remedies

A *remedy* is the relief provided for an innocent party when the other party has breached the contract. It is the means employed to enforce a right or to redress an injury. The most common remedies available to a nonbreaching party include damages, rescission, restitution, reformation, and specific performance.

On the Web

Information on contract law, including breach of contract and remedies, is available at **http://law.freeadvice. com/general_practice/ contract_law**.

Damages

A breach of contract entitles the nonbreaching party to sue for money damages (see Chapter 3). Damages are designed to compensate a party for the loss of the bargain. Generally, innocent parties are to be placed in the position they would have occupied had the contract been fully performed.

Compensatory Damages. Damages compensating the nonbreaching party for the loss of the bargain are known as *compensatory damages.* These damages compensate the injured party only for damages actually sustained and proved to have arisen directly from the loss of the bargain caused by the breach of contract. They simply replace what was lost because of the breach.

The amount of compensatory damages is the difference between the value of the breaching party's promised performance and the value of his or her actual performance. This amount is reduced by any loss that the injured party has avoided. In addition, the injured party may be able to recover *incidental damages*—expenses resulting directly from the breach of contract, such as those incurred to obtain performance from another source. ▶ **EXAMPLE 8.14** Suppose that you are hired to perform certain services during August for $3,000, but the employer breaches the contract and you find another job that pays only $500. You can recover $2,500 as compensatory damages. In addition, you can recover any expenses you incurred in finding the other job as incidental damages. ◀

Consequential Damages. Foreseeable damages that result from a party's breach of contract are called *consequential damages,* or *special damages.* They differ from compensatory damages in that they are caused by special circumstances beyond the contract itself. They flow from the consequences, or results, of a breach. To recover consequential damages, the breaching party must know (or have reason to know) that special circumstances will cause the nonbreaching party to suffer an additional loss. ▶ **EXAMPLE 8.15** Suppose that Glenda contracts with Eric to ship an item that she needs to repair her printing press. The contract states that Glenda must receive the item by Monday or she will not be able to print her paper and will lose $1,000. If Eric is late in shipping the item, Glenda normally can recover the consequential damages caused by the delay (that is, the $1,000 in losses). ◀

Punitive Damages.   *Punitive damages* are generally not awarded in an action for breach of contract. Punitive damages are designed to punish a guilty party and to make an example to deter similar conduct in the future. A breach of contract is not unlawful in a criminal sense. A contract is simply a civil relationship between the parties. The law may compensate one party for the loss of the bargain, no more and no less. In a few situations, though, if a tortious action—such as fraud or negligence—is connected to a breach of contract, punitive damages may be awarded.

Rescission, Restitution, and Reformation

As already discussed, *rescission* is essentially an action to undo, or terminate, a contract—to return the contracting parties to the positions they occupied prior to the transaction. When fraud, a mistake, duress, undue influence, misrepresentation, or lack of contractual capacity is present, rescission is available. The failure of one party to perform entitles the other party to rescind the contract.

> **restitution**
>
> An equitable remedy under which a person is restored to his or her original position prior to loss or injury, or placed in the position that he or she would have been in had the breach not occurred.

Generally, to rescind a contract, the parties must make **restitution** to each other by returning goods, property, or funds previously conveyed. If physical property or goods can be returned, they must be. If the property or goods have been consumed, the restitution must be made in an equivalent dollar amount.

When the parties have imperfectly expressed their agreement in writing, the equitable remedy of **reformation** may also be available. In cases involving breach of contract, this remedy occurs when the court revises a contract to reflect the true intention of the parties—if a mutual mistake occurred, for example.

> **reformation**
>
> An equitable remedy granted by a court to correct, or "reform," a written contract so that it reflects the true intentions of the parties.

Specific Performance

The equitable remedy of **specific performance** calls for the performance of the act promised in the contract. Normally, specific performance will not be granted unless the party's legal remedy (money damages) is inadequate. For this reason, contracts for the sale of goods rarely qualify for specific performance—substantially identical goods can be bought or sold in the market. If the contract involves unique goods, however, such as a painting or a rare book, a court will grant specific performance.

> **specific performance**
>
> An equitable remedy requiring exactly the performance that was specified in a contract; usually granted only when money damages would be an inadequate remedy and the subject matter of the contract is unique (for example, real property).

Generally, courts refuse to grant specific performance of contracts for personal services—contracts that require one party to work personally for another party. This is because public policy strongly discourages involuntary servitude, and ordering one party to perform personal services against his or her will amounts to a type of servitude.[4] Moreover, the courts do not want to monitor personal-service contracts. ▶ **EXAMPLE 8.16** If you contract with a brain surgeon to perform brain surgery on you and the surgeon refuses to perform, the court will not compel (and you certainly would not want) the surgeon to perform under these circumstances. The court cannot assure meaningful performance in such a situation.[5] ◀

Remedies for Breach of Sales Contracts

Remedies for breach of a contract for the sale of goods are designed to put the aggrieved party in as good a position as if the other party had fully performed. The seller's remedies for breach include the right to stop or withhold delivery of the goods and the right to recover damages or the purchase price of the goods from the buyer. The buyer's remedies include (1) the right to reject *nonconforming goods* (goods that do not conform to those specifically agreed on in the contract) or improperly delivered goods; (2) the right to *cover* (buy goods elsewhere and recover from the seller the extra cost of obtaining the substitute goods); (3) the right to recover damages; and (4) in certain circumstances, the right to obtain specific performance of the sales contract.

ELECTRONIC CONTRACTING AND ELECTRONIC SIGNATURES

Today, many contracts are formed over the Internet. How the courts apply the traditional principles of contract law in cyberspace is an increasingly important issue. Most disputes concerning contracts formed online tend to center on the specific terms of the contract and whether the parties voluntarily assented to those terms.

Online Offers and Acceptances

Generally, the terms of an online offer should be just as comprehensive as the terms in an offer made in a written (paper) document. All possible contingencies should be anticipated and provided for in the offer. Because jurisdictional issues often arise with online transactions, dispute-settlement provisions, such as arbitration clauses, are frequently used in electronic contracts. The offer should be displayed on the screen in such a way as to be easily readable and clear. An online offer should also include some mechanism, such as providing an "I agree" or "I accept" box, by which the customer can accept the offer.

Click-On Agreements

As described earlier, a click-on agreement (also sometimes called a *click-on license* or *click-wrap agreement*) arises when a buyer, completing a transaction on a computer, indicates his or her assent to be bound by the terms of an offer by clicking on a button that says "I agree" or "I accept." The terms may be contained on a Web site through which the buyer is obtaining goods or services, or they may appear on a computer screen when software is loaded. The courts have normally enforced click-on agreements.

▶ **EXAMPLE 8.17** Suppose that Aaron is downloading a new software program from the Internet. A message pops up on the screen with a small window through which Aaron can read the terms of the *licensing agreement*. (Note that a contract involving software usually grants a *license* by which a party is given the right to use the software but does not own the software.) Even if Aaron clicks on the "I agree" box below the window without reading the terms, he will be bound by the terms of that agreement. ◀

Shrink-Wrap Agreements

A **shrink-wrap agreement** is an agreement whose terms are expressed inside the box in which the goods are packaged. (The term *shrink-wrap* refers to the plastic that covers the box.) Usually, the party who opens the box is told that she or he agrees to the terms by keeping whatever is in the box. ▶ **EXAMPLE 8.18** Suppose that Rick orders a new computer from a national company, which ships the computer to Rick. Along with the computer, the box contains an agreement setting forth the terms of the sale, including what remedies are available. The document also states that Rick's retention of the computer for longer than thirty days will be construed as an acceptance of the terms. ◀

In most cases, a shrink-wrap agreement is an agreement between the manufacturer of the hardware or software and the ultimate buyer-user of the product (not between a retailer and a buyer). Thus, the terms typically concern warranties, remedies, and other issues associated with the use of the product.

▌shrink-wrap agreement
An agreement whose terms are expressed in a document located inside the box in which the goods (usually software) are packaged.

Generally, the courts have enforced the terms of shrink-wrap agreements the same as the terms of other contracts, with one exception: If a court finds that the buyer learned of the shrink-wrap terms *after* the parties entered into a contract, the court may conclude that those terms were proposals for additional terms and were not part of the contract unless the buyer expressly agreed to them. ▶ **EXAMPLE 8.19** Suppose that when Rick, in Example 8.18, entered into the contract to purchase his computer, he was not informed that any dispute regarding his purchase had to be arbitrated. Once the computer arrived and Rick was dissatisfied, he discovered that the shrink-wrap agreement included an arbitration clause. In that situation, a court may conclude that the arbitration clause—which Rick did not know about or consent to—was a proposal rather than part of the agreement. ◀

Browse-Wrap Terms

browse-wrap terms
Terms and conditions of use that are presented to an Internet user at the time the user downloads certain products, such as software, but that the user need not agree to (by clicking "I agree," for example) before being able to install or use the products.

Like the terms of a click-on agreement, "browse-wrap" terms can occur in a transaction conducted over the Internet. Unlike a click-on agreement, however, browse-wrap terms do not require an Internet user to assent to the terms before, say, downloading or using certain software. In other words, although the terms may appear on the computer screen, a person can use or install the software without clicking "I agree." Courts might not enforce browse-wrap terms because the user is unaware that he or she is entering into a contract.

E-Signatures

e-signature
An electronic sound, symbol, or process attached to or logically associated with a record and executed or adopted by a person with the intent to sign the record, according to the Uniform Electronic Transactions Act.

In many instances, a contract cannot be enforced unless it is signed by the party against whom enforcement is sought. A significant issue in the context of Internet transactions has to do with how electronic signatures, or e-signatures, can be created and verified on e-contracts.

In the days when many people could not write, documents were often signed with an "X." Then handwritten signatures become common, followed by typed signatures, printed signatures, and, most recently, digital signatures, which are transmitted electronically. Throughout the evolution of signature technology, the question of what constitutes a valid signature has arisen again and again, and with good reason—without some consensus on what constitutes a valid signature, little business or legal work could be accomplished.

Today, numerous technologies allow electronic documents to be signed. Since paralegals are frequently responsible for obtaining the necessary signatures on legal documents, some knowledge of digital signatures and alternative technologies is useful.

Digital Signatures

cybernotary
A legally recognized authority that can certify the validity of digital signatures.

The most prevalent e-signature technology today is the *asymmetric cryptosystem,* which creates a digital signature using two differently encoded "keys." With this system, a person attaches a digital signature to a document using a private key, or code. The key has a publicly available counterpart. Anyone with the appropriate software can use the public key to verify that the digital signature was made using the private key. A cybernotary, or legally recognized certification authority, issues the key pair, identifies the owner of the keys, and certifies the validity of the public key. The cybernotary also serves as a repository for public keys.

Signature Dynamics

With another type of signature technology, known as *signature dynamics,* a sender's signature is captured using a stylus (a tracing pen) and an electronic digitizer pad. A computer program takes the signature's measurements and records the sender's identity, the time and date of the signature, and the identity of the hardware. This information is then "encrypted" and attached to the document being transmitted. When this type of e-signature is used, it is not necessary to have a third party (cybernotary) verify the signature.

Other E-Signature Forms

Other forms of e-signatures have been—or are now being—developed as well. Some e-signatures use "smart cards." A *smart card* is a device the size of a credit card that is embedded with code and other data. Like credit and debit cards, this smart card can be inserted into computers to transfer information. Unlike those other cards, however, a smart card can be used to establish a person's identity as validly as a signature on a piece of paper. In addition, technological innovations now under way will allow an e-signature to be evidenced by an image of a person's retina, fingerprint, or face that is scanned by a computer and then matched to a numeric code. The scanned image and the numeric code are registered with security companies that maintain files on an accessible server that can be used to authenticate a transaction.

State Laws Governing E-Signatures

Most states have laws governing e-signatures. The problem is that state e-signature laws are not uniform. Some states—California is a notable example—provide that many types of documents cannot be signed with e-signatures, while other states are more permissive. Additionally, some states recognize only digital signatures as valid, while others permit other types of e-signatures.

In an attempt to create more uniformity among the states, in 1999 the National Conference of Commissioners on Uniform State Laws and the American Law Institute promulgated the Uniform Electronic Transactions Act (UETA). To date, the UETA has been adopted, at least in part, by more than forty states. Among other things, the UETA states that a signature or a contract may not be denied legal effect or enforceability solely because it is in electronic form.

Under the UETA, an *e-signature* is broadly defined as "an electronic sound, symbol, or process attached to or logically associated with a record and executed or adopted by a person with the intent to sign the record."[6] In other words, the signature does not have to be created by any specific technology and can be simply a person's name typed at the end of an e-mail message. The parties do have to agree to conduct their business electronically for the UETA provisions to apply, however. Also, the UETA states that it does not apply to (or change) the provisions of the Uniform Commercial Code (discussed earlier in this chapter) and does not apply to wills and trusts (see Chapter 10).

Federal Law on E-Signatures and E-Documents

In 2000, Congress enacted the Electronic Signatures in Global and National Commerce Act (E-SIGN Act)[7] to provide that no contract, record, or signature may be "denied legal effect" solely because it is in an electronic form. In other words, under this law, an electronic signature is as valid as a signature on paper, and an electronic document can be as enforceable as a paper one. For an electronic signature to be enforceable, the contracting parties must have agreed to use electronic signatures. For an electronic document to be valid, it must be in a form that can be retained and accurately reproduced.

The E-SIGN Act does not apply to all types of documents. Contracts and documents that are exempt include court papers, divorce decrees, evictions, foreclosures, health-insurance terminations, prenuptial agreements, and wills. Also, only certain agreements governed by the Uniform Commercial Code fall under this law.[8]

Despite these limitations, the E-SIGN Act has significantly expanded the possibilities for contracting online. From a remote location, a person can now open an account with a financial institution, obtain a mortgage or other loan, buy insurance, retain an attorney, and purchase real estate over the Internet. Payments and transfers of funds can be done entirely online. By using e-contracts, a person can thus avoid the time and costs associated with producing, delivering, signing, and returning paper documents.

CONTRACT LAW AND THE PARALEGAL

As a legal professional, it is vital that you have some knowledge of contract law. Regardless of where you work (for a large or a small law firm, for a corporation, or for the government) and regardless of your area of specialty as a paralegal, you may be asked to handle matters that require an understanding of the basic principles of contract law. This is because contracts are so pervasive in our society. Business firms and government agencies routinely form contracts. Individuals in all walks of life commonly make contracts with others for goods or services.

Here are just a few of the tasks you might perform, in any workplace and in any capacity, that involve contracts:

- Interview a client or other person to obtain information about a contract to be drafted or a claim for breach of contract.

- Review a contract to determine a client's rights and obligations as stated in the contract.

- Research previous cases decided by courts in your jurisdiction to determine whether a defense raised against a claim for breach of contract will likely succeed or to determine how the courts have interpreted a certain type of contract provision.

- Gather evidence to determine the amount of damages sustained as a result of a breach of contract.

- Assist in litigating a breach of contract.

- Draft a settlement letter to settle a contract dispute.

- Assist in arbitration or other proceedings held for the purpose of settling a contract dispute.

- Contact representatives of business firms (perhaps in foreign countries) for the purpose of contract negotiations or the settlement of contract disputes.

In addition to these tasks, you may be involved in legal work that arises only in relation to sales contracts. You may need to determine, for example, whether one of the parties to a contract qualifies as a "merchant" as defined by Article 2 of the UCC. If so, different rules may apply to the contract. You may be asked to investigate a claim for breach of warranty to determine whether a seller warranted the goods being sold and whether the seller's actions (or failure to act) constituted a breach of warranty.

INTELLECTUAL PROPERTY LAW

intellectual property
Property resulting from intellectual, creative processes.

The contract law that we have just discussed had its origins hundreds of years ago. Much of it is based on concepts developed in England. Now we move on to an area of law that, although it has existed for some time, has become a major concern in recent years. It has to do with the wealth created by people's minds. Most people think of wealth in terms of houses, land, cars, stocks, and bonds. Wealth, however, also includes **intellectual property**, which consists of the products that result from intellectual, creative processes. Although it is an abstract term for an abstract concept, intellectual property is nonetheless wholly familiar to virtually everyone. *Trademarks, service marks, copyrights,* and *patents* are all forms of intellectual property. The book you are reading is copyrighted. Undoubtedly, the personal computer you use at home is trademarked. The software you use, the movies you see, and the music you listen to are all forms of intellectual property.

The need to protect creative works was voiced by the framers of the U.S. Constitution over two hundred years ago: Article I, Section 8, of the Constitution authorized Congress "[t]o promote the Progress of Science and useful Arts, by securing for limited Times to Authors and Inventors the exclusive Right to their respective Writings and Discoveries." Laws protecting patents, trademarks, and copyrights are explicitly designed to protect and reward inventive and artistic creativity. Exhibit 8.2 offers a summary of the forms of intellectual property, how they are acquired, and what remedies are available for *infringement,* or unauthorized use.

EXHIBIT 8.2
Forms of Intellectual Property

	DEFINITION	HOW ACQUIRED	DURATION	REMEDY FOR INFRINGEMENT
Patent	A grant from the government that gives an inventor exclusive rights to an invention.	By filing a patent application with the U.S. Patent and Trademark Office and receiving its approval.	For inventions, 20 years from the date of application; for design patents, 14 years from the date of application.	Money damages, including royalties and lost profits, *plus* attorneys' fees. Damages may be tripled for intentional infringements.
Copyright	The right of an author or a creator of a literary or artistic work or other production (such as a computer program) to have the exclusive use of that work for a given period of time.	Automatic (once the work or creation is put in tangible form). Only the *expression* of an idea (and not the idea itself) can be protected by copyright.	For authors: the life of the author plus 70 years. For publishers: 95 years after the date of publication or 120 years after creation.	Actual damages plus profits received by the party who infringed *or* statutory damages under the Copyright Act, *plus* costs and attorneys' fees in either situation.
Trademark	A distinctive word, name, symbol, or device that an entity uses to distinguish its goods or services from those of others. The owner of a trademark has the exclusive right to use that mark.	1. At common law, created by use of the mark. 2. Registration with the appropriate federal or state office; mark must already be in use or be placed in use within the next six months.	Unlimited, as long as the mark is in use. To continue notice by registration, holder must renew between the fifth and sixth years and, thereafter, every ten years.	1. Injunction prohibiting future use of mark. 2. Actual damages plus profits received by the party who infringed. 3. Destruction of articles that infringed. 4. *Plus* costs and attorneys' fees.
Trade Secret	A business secret that makes a particular company or product unique and that would be of value to a competitor. Trade secrets include customer lists, plans, and research and development.	Through the development of the information and processes that constitute the business secret.	Unlimited, as long as not revealed to others (once a trade secret is revealed to others, it is no longer secret).	Money damages for misappropriation (the Uniform Trade Secrets Act also permits punitive damages if willful), *plus* costs and attorneys' fees.

The study of intellectual property law is important because intellectual property has taken on increasing significance, not only within the United States but globally as well. In today's information age, it should come as no surprise that the value of the world's intellectual property exceeds the value of physical property, such as machines and houses. Ownership rights in intangible intellectual property are more important to the prosperity of U.S. companies than are their tangible assets. Because of the importance of obtaining and protecting intellectual property rights in society today, attorneys and paralegals with specialized knowledge in this area are in great demand in law firms and in corporations. (See this chapter's *Featured Guest* article on pages 286 and 287 for information and suggestions on how to protect intellectual property.)

Ethics Watch!

Intellectual Property and Confidentiality

Working as a paralegal for an intellectual property firm can be an exciting profession. It can also present challenges for paralegals in the area of confidentiality. For example, suppose you are working for a firm that represents a motion picture company in an action against the creator of software that breaks the code of encrypted DVDs (digital versatile discs). The software is available free of charge on the Internet at a specific Web site and allows users to make "pirated" copies of DVD movies without the copyright owner's permission. Your brother, a computer wiz, has been making copies of DVDs from his home computer for the last six months. You don't know which software he uses, and you did not realize that he was violating copyright law until you began working on this case. The firm you work for is proposing to settle the case in exchange for the software creator's agreement to stop making the software available on the Internet and to hand over a list of all the users who have downloaded the software. Can you warn your brother about the proposed settlement? No, clearly you cannot divulge the client's information to anyone, including members of your own family. This is just one example of how paralegals working in intellectual property law might be tempted to disclose confidential information.

Patents

patent
A government grant that gives an inventor the exclusive right or privilege to make, use, or sell his or her invention for a limited time period.

A **patent** is a grant from the government that gives an inventor the exclusive right to make, use, and sell an invention for a period of twenty years from the date of filing the application for a patent. Patents for designs, as opposed to inventions, are given for a fourteen-year period. To secure a patent, the applicant must demonstrate to the satisfaction of the U.S. Patent and Trademark Office that the invention, discovery, process, or design is genuine, novel, useful, and not obvious in light of current technology. A patent holder gives notice to all that an article or design is patented by placing on it the word *Patent* or *Pat.* and the patent number. In contrast to patent law in other countries, U.S. patent law gives protection to the first person to invent a product or process, even though someone else may have been the first to file for a patent on that product or process.

If a firm makes, uses, or sells another's patented design, product, or process without the patent owner's permission, it commits the tort of patent infringement. Patent infringement may exist even though the patent owner has not put the patented product in commerce. Patent infringement may also occur even though not all features or parts of an invention are copied. (With respect to a patented process, however, all steps or their equivalent must be copied for infringement to exist.)

On the Web

A good online source for information on patents can be found at
http://www.oppedahl.com.

Copyrights

copyright
The exclusive right of an author (or other creator) to publish, print, or sell an intellectual production for a statutory period of time.

Literary or artistic productions (including computer software) are protected under copyright law. A **copyright** gives the creator of a work the right to the exclusive use of that work for a given period of time. Copyrights are governed by the Copyright Act of 1976,[9] as amended. Works created after January 1, 1978, are automatically given statutory copyright protection for the life of the author plus 70 years. For copyrights owned by publishing houses, the copyright expires 95 years from the date of publication or 120 years from the date of creation, whichever is first. For works by more than one author, the copyright expires 70 years after the death of the last surviving author.

Copyrights can be registered with the U.S. Copyright Office in Washington, D.C. (but registration is not required). A copyright owner also no longer needs to place a © or *Copyright* on the work to have the work protected against infringement. Chances are that if somebody created it, somebody owns it.

On the Web

For information on copyrights, go to the U.S. Copyright Office at **http://loc.gov/copyright**.

What Can Be Copyrighted?

Note that it is not possible to copyright an *idea*. Others may freely use the underlying ideas embodied in a work. What is copyrightable is the particular way in which an idea is *expressed*. Whenever an idea and an expression are inseparable, the expression cannot be copyrighted. Generally, anything that is not an original expression of an idea does not qualify for copyright protection. Facts widely known to the public are not copyrightable. Page numbers normally are not copyrightable because they follow a sequence known to everyone. Mathematical calculations are not copyrightable. The key requirement to obtain copyright protection is originality.

Copyright Infringement

Whenever the form or expression of an idea is copied, an infringement of copyright occurs. The reproduction does not have to be exactly the same as the original, nor does it have to reproduce the original in its entirety.

Penalties or remedies can be imposed on those who infringe copyrights. These range from actual damages (damages based on the actual harm caused to the copyright holder by the infringement) or statutory damages (damages provided for under the Copyright Act, not to exceed $100,000) to criminal proceedings for willful violations (which may result in fines and/or imprisonment).

An exception to liability for copyright infringement is made under the "fair use" doctrine. Under the Copyright Act, a person or organization can in certain situations reproduce copyrighted material without paying royalties (fees paid to the copyright holder for the privilege of reproducing the copyrighted material).[10] Generally, the courts determine whether a particular use is fair on a case-by-case basis.

Trademarks and Related Property

A **trademark** is a distinctive mark, motto, device, or emblem that a manufacturer stamps, prints, or otherwise affixes to the goods it produces so that those goods can be distinguished from the goods of other manufacturers and merchants. Examples of trademarks are brand-name labels on jeans, luggage, and other products. Generally, to be protected under trademark law, a mark must be distinctive. A distinctive mark might consist of an uncommon word (such as *Kodak, Xerox,* or *Google*) or words used in an uncommon or fanciful way (such as *English Leather* for an aftershave lotion instead of for leather processed in England).

Note that trademarks apply to *products.* The term **trade name** is used to indicate part or all of a business's name, such as McDonald's. Unless the trade name is also used as a trademark (as with Kodak, Xerox, and Coca-Cola, for example), the name is not protected under federal trademark law. Trade names are protected under the common law, however. Holiday Inns, Inc., for example, could sue a motel owner who used that name or a portion of it (such as "Holiday Motels") without permission. As with trademarks, words must be unusual or fanciful if they

trademark
A distinctive mark, motto, device, or emblem that a manufacturer stamps, prints, or otherwise affixes to the goods it produces so that they can be identified on the market and their origins made known. Once a trademark is established (under the common law or through registration), the owner is entitled to its exclusive use.

trade name
A term that is used to indicate part or all of a business's name and that is directly related to the business's reputation and goodwill. Trade names are protected under the common law (and under trademark law, if the business's name is the same as its trademark).

Deborah E. Bouchoux

FEATURED **Guest**

STRATEGIES FOR PROTECTING INTELLECTUAL PROPERTY: THE INTELLECTUAL PROPERTY AUDIT

BIOGRAPHICAL NOTE

Deborah E. Bouchoux is an attorney licensed to practice in the District of Columbia and the state of California (inactive). She has been involved in paralegal education for more than twenty years. Bouchoux currently teaches in the paralegal studies program at Georgetown University in Washington, D.C., and serves as a member of the advisory board for the paralegal studies program.

Prior to teaching at Georgetown University, Bouchoux was an instructor in the paralegal program at the University of San Diego. Bouchoux is a frequent lecturer for the National Capital Paralegal Association and is the author of Intellectual Property: The Law of Trademarks, Copyrights, Patents, and Trade Secrets; *and* Protecting Your Company's Intellectual Property: A Practical Guide to Trademarks, Copyrights, Patents, and Trade Secrets.

Because clients are often unaware of the value of their intangible assets or intellectual property, many law firms conduct intellectual property audits for their clients. The audit will identify the intellectual property owned by the client, and the legal team and the client will then develop a strategy to protect that property.

Audits are also conducted when a company sells its assets or merges with another entity. The buyer will want to know what type of intellectual property assets the company possesses so that it will know what assets it is acquiring and to ensure that it will not be inheriting infringement lawsuits. This type of audit is often referred to as a *due diligence review*.

THE NEED FOR INTELLECTUAL PROPERTY AUDITS

Clients may not understand the value of their intellectual property portfolios and the need to protect their rights. They may be using unique marketing materials that should be copyrighted, slogans that should be trademarked, and confidential information that should be protected as trade secrets. Without protection, valuable rights may be lost. For example, the disclosure of confidential information will lead to a loss of trade secret rights and result in declining profits. Moreover, once companies realize what intellectual property they own, they can use that intellectual property to create revenue. Trademarks, copyrights, patents, and trade secrets can all be licensed to others for fees to generate a continuing revenue stream for the company.

STRATEGIES FOR CONDUCTING AN INTELLECTUAL PROPERTY AUDIT

There are several steps in conducting a successful intellectual property audit. These steps are explored in the following subsections.

Designating the Team.   The law firm should designate an attorney and paralegal to serve as representatives of the firm, and the company should select an individual who will serve as the company's team leader. Together, these individuals will be primarily responsible for conducting the audit and can answer any questions that may arise in the course of the audit. The team should have a preliminary meeting to discuss the scope and nature of the audit. For example, the client will need to determine whether only U.S. materials will be reviewed or whether consideration will be given to seeking protection in foreign countries for certain trademarks and patents. The involvement of legal counsel ensures that any matters discussed are subject to the attorney-client privilege and remain confidential.

Preparing the Audit Questionnaire.   The legal team should prepare a worksheet or questionnaire for the client that is designed to elicit information from the client about its intellectual property assets. Paralegals play a significant role in drafting the audit questionnaire. The audit questionnaire will typically ask the following:

- Does the client use any specific names, logos, or slogans in advertising its products and services?

- Are any written materials used in marketing (such as brochures, newspaper advertisements, and slides and written materials used for presentations)?

- Has the client developed any products, software, or processes?

- Does the client use any software or products owned by another entity?

- Does the client use any confidential methods or processes in developing and marketing its products and services, including financial forecasts, marketing plans, and customer lists?

- Has the company ever been sued for or accused of infringing another party's intellectual property rights?

- How does the company control access to its valuable and proprietary materials?

The questionnaire should be tailored to the needs of the client. For example, companies engaged in telecommunications services or software development will need detailed sections designed to obtain information on software products and proprietary information. In contrast, companies engaged in consulting will likely have no "products" that need protection but will have a wealth of written materials that should be protected as trade secrets or registered as copyrights.

Conducting the Audit. On receiving the questionnaire, the client should begin gathering the materials that are responsive to the questionnaire. The legal team will then review the materials that the client has assembled to determine which materials can be protected under intellectual property law. If the client has a Web site, it should be carefully reviewed to ensure not only that the site is protected under copyright law but also that it does not infringe on the rights of another party. Paralegals often coordinate the time and manner of the audit by scheduling the audit date, arranging for a conference room, and ensuring that a photocopy machine is available to copy documents that are responsive to the questionnaire. Generally, the

audit is conducted at the client's office because this is where the pertinent materials and documents are located.

Writing the Audit Report. After conducting the audit, the legal team prepares a written report for the client summarizing the results of the audit. The report identifies all of the intellectual property owned by the client and makes recommendations for its continued protection and maintenance. For example, the audit may disclose that the client uses a distinctive slogan in its advertising materials. The legal team will then recommend that the slogan be registered as a trademark.

POSTAUDIT ACTIVITY

After the audit is complete, the legal team, and particularly the paralegal, will begin preparing applications to register trademarks, copyrights, and patents and will develop written policies to protect the client's trade secrets. Contracts will need to be drafted for the client to use when it hires independent contractors to develop certain products, such as software. Such contracts will clarify that the company will own all rights to any work products produced by those independent contractors. License agreements may need to be drafted so that the company can license its intellectual property to others to use. An Internet use policy may be needed so that all employees are aware of the confidential nature of the company's electronic communications.

> *"Paralegals play a significant role in drafting the audit questionnaire."*

The company will be advised to review materials used by its competitors to ensure that its competitors do not infringe on the company's valuable intellectual property rights—by using a trademark that is confusingly similar to one owned by the company, for example. Finally, the paralegal will create a docketing system to ensure that the client's intellectual property rights are maintained. For example, the paralegal should calendar the dates for maintenance and renewal of company trademarks. The paralegal should also schedule the date of the next intellectual property audit.

are to be protected as trade names. The word *Safeway,* for example, was considered by a court to be sufficiently fanciful to obtain protection as a trade name for a chain of food stores.

At common law, the person who used a symbol or mark to identify a business or product was protected in the use of that trademark. Today, trademarks may be registered with the state or with the federal government. Under current law, a mark can be registered federally (1) if it is already in commerce or (2) if the applicant intends to put the mark into commerce within six months.

Trademark Infringement

Registration of a trademark with the U.S. Patent and Trademark Office gives notice on a nationwide basis that the trademark belongs exclusively to the registrant. The registrant is also allowed to use the symbol ® to indicate that the mark has been registered. Whenever that trademark is copied to a substantial degree or used in its entirety by another (intentionally or unintentionally), the trademark has been infringed, and the owner can sue. A person need not have registered a trademark in order to sue for trademark infringement, but registration does furnish proof of the date the owner began using the trademark. Only those trademarks that are deemed sufficiently distinctive from all competing trademarks will be protected.

Trademark Dilution

Historically, federal trademark law prohibited the unauthorized use of the same mark on competing or "related" goods or services only when such use would be likely to confuse consumers. Trademark dilution laws, which have been passed by the federal government and about half of the states, extend that protection.

Trademark *dilution* occurs when a trademark is used, without authorization, in a way that diminishes the distinctive quality of the mark. Unlike trademark infringement, a dilution cause of action does not require proof that consumers are likely to be confused by a connection between the unauthorized use and the mark. For this reason, the products (or services) involved do not have to be similar.

In addition, a famous mark may be diluted not only by the use of an *identical* mark but also by the use of a *similar* mark. ▶ **EXAMPLE 8.20** Ringling Bros.–Barnum & Bailey, Combined Shows, Inc., brought a suit against the state of Utah, claiming that Utah's use of the slogan "The Greatest Snow on Earth"—to attract visitors to the state's recreational and scenic resorts—diluted the distinctiveness of the circus's famous trademark, "The Greatest Show on Earth." Utah moved to dismiss the suit, arguing that the law protected owners of famous trademarks only against the unauthorized use of identical marks. A federal court disagreed and refused to grant Utah's motion to dismiss the case.[11] ◀

Trade Secrets

Some business processes and information that are not (or cannot be) patented, copyrighted, or trademarked are nevertheless protected against appropriation by a competitor as trade secrets. **Trade secrets** consist of customer lists, plans, research and development, pricing information, marketing techniques, production techniques, and generally anything that makes an individual company unique and that would have value to a competitor.

What Is Protected?

Unlike copyright and trademark protection, protection of trade secrets extends both to ideas and to their expression. (For this reason, and because a trade secret involves no registration or filing requirements, trade secret protection may be well suited for software.) Of course,

trade secret
Information or processes that give a business an advantage over competitors who do not know the information or processes.

Allen F. Mihecoby   PARALEGAL **profile**

INTELLECTUAL PROPERTY PARALEGAL

Allen F. Mihecoby is employed in-house by a publicly traded corporation. His experience has been primarily in large firms, including multinational and publicly traded corporations. In 1997, he received a paralegal certificate from the ABA-approved program at Southeastern Paralegal Institute (now Southeastern Career Institute) in Dallas, Texas.

Mihecoby received both the PACE Registered Paralegal (RP) designation from NFPA and the Certified Legal Assistant (CLA) designation from NALA in 2002. In 2005, he received NALA's Certified Legal Assistant Specialist (CLAS) designation in corporate and business law. He is an associate member of the American Bar Association and a member of NALA; NFPA; the Paralegal Division of the State Bar of Texas; the College of the State Bar of Texas, Legal Assistants Division; the Dallas Area Paralegal Association; the Fort Worth Paralegal Association; and the Metroplex Association of Corporate Paralegals. He is a founding member of the Legal Assistants of North Texas (now North Texas Paralegal Association).

What do you like best about your work?

"I like the variety of my work. As an in-house paralegal, I am exposed to the full gamut of intellectual property law on a daily basis. My day may begin by drafting a trademark application and then progress to negotiating a license agreement for a celebrity endorsement. I might then review documents that are to be given over to the other side in litigation to ensure that we comply with our company's privacy policy. In the same day, I may contact a foreign correspondent to discuss use of a patent in the European Union, review a vendor contract providing for the electronic transmission of orders, and work with U.S. Customs to halt the influx of counterfeit merchandise into the United States. Each day, I am presented with unique challenges and opportunities to learn and expand my skills."

> *"Each day, I am presented with unique challenges and opportunities to learn and expand my skills."*

What is the greatest challenge that you face in your area of work?

"Intellectual property changes from day to day and is constantly evolving. I spend a lot of time attending continuing legal education events and reviewing court cases, as well as decisions from administrative agencies, such as the Trademark Trials and Appeals Board. Each morning, I review online resources to see what events transpired the day before. Keeping abreast of changes is particularly important in the areas of e-commerce and privacy regulation. You might become accustomed to drafting an e-contract in a specific way, only to discover that a decision in another jurisdiction changes the standard."

What advice do you have for would-be paralegals in your area of work?

"Find a seasoned, veteran paralegal to serve as your mentor. It is a great asset for me both personally and professionally to have a group of skilled paralegal friends that have over sixty years of combined experience in the field. Each practice area is demanding, so make sure that you choose the field that is right for you. Should you choose intellectual property, be prepared to be married to the field."

What are some tips for success as a paralegal in your area of work?

"Networking is vital. This is a dynamic field, and chances are that you will be presented with some of the same challenges that your colleagues have faced. There are many national and international organizations you can use to stay connected with others who can provide valuable guidance. Also, creative thinking is a must. Learn to think 'outside of the box.' You will often find that a specific project does not fit neatly within a particular 'box,' or category. Your job is to organize the abstract. Finally, learn from everyone—from the senior partner in a law firm, to the courier who delivers your office's documents, to the professional who handles the electronic data for your client or company."

the secret formula, method, or other information must be disclosed to some persons, particularly to key employees. Businesses generally attempt to protect their trade secrets by having all employees who use the process or information agree in their contracts, or in confidentiality agreements, never to divulge it.

Misappropriation of Trade Secrets

One who discloses or uses another's trade secret, without a privilege to do so, is liable to the other if (1) he or she discovered the secret by improper means or (2) the disclosure or use constitutes a breach of confidence. The theft of confidential business data through industrial espionage, such as when a business taps into a competitor's computer, is a theft of trade secrets and is actionable.

Until recently, virtually all law with respect to trade secrets was common law. In an effort to reduce the unpredictability of the law in this area, a model act, the Uniform Trade Secrets Act, was presented to the states for adoption in 1979. Parts of the act have been adopted in more than twenty states. In the states that have adopted the act, a plaintiff can also recover punitive damages for willful misappropriation of business secrets.

INTELLECTUAL PROPERTY AND THE PARALEGAL

Many lawsuits involve the alleged infringement of intellectual property rights. If you work for a general law practice, one of the firm's clients may seek legal assistance when the client discovers that someone has used, without permission, something that the client created—such as a software program, the words or music to a song, a novel, a patented invention, or a trademark.

Many law firms specialize in such areas as patent law or have special departments dealing with patent cases. Paralegals who work in such firms or departments may face the challenge of managing voluminous materials and paperwork for just one case. A lawsuit for the alleged infringement of patent rights in a sophisticated product, such as a genetically engineered drug for treating leukemia, can result in thousands of exhibits and other documents that must be organized, safeguarded, and retrievable at the right moment. A paralegal who can meet this challenge successfully will be a great asset to his or her firm.

An increasing number of paralegals are now working in the corporate environment. Many of today's corporations invest heavily in the development of new products. A major concern of such companies—and their legal departments—is to protect their investment in research and development by obtaining patents, trademarks, or copyrights. If you work for a corporation, you might be involved in researching and litigating cases concerning the infringement of intellectual property rights. The U.S. Patent and Trademark Office and the U.S. Copyright Office also employ paralegals. If you work for either

of these offices, you will be handling applications and other records relating to patents and trademarks or copyrights.

Here are some specific types of tasks that you might undertake in the area of intellectual property law:

- Interview a client (or a manager of a corporation for which you work) to obtain information regarding intellectual property to be registered.

- Contact the U.S. Patent and Trademark Office (by phone, by mail, or via the Internet) to find out if someone has applied for patent or trademark protection for a certain type of product that your firm's client (or your corporate employer) wants to develop and register.

- Draft the documents that are necessary to apply for patent, trademark, or copyright protection.

- Draft contracts that provide for another's authorized use of a copyrighted, patented, or trademarked product in return for royalties (a percentage of the proceeds received as a result of the authorized use of the intellectual property).

- Review marketing data and sales statements to verify royalties due for another's authorized use of your employer's trademarked, patented, or copyrighted product.

- Assist in litigation resulting from the infringement of rights in intellectual property.

Today's Professional Paralegal

CONFIDENTIALITY AGREEMENTS

Angela Dunn, a paralegal with the law firm of Carter, Plant, and Darrow, is in the process of training a paralegal whom the firm has just hired to assist Angela in the firm's intellectual property department. Today, Angela is showing the new paralegal, Cory Amundson, how to draft a confidentiality agreement. As a first step, Angela reviews with Cory the legal background for such agreements.

WHY DO FIRMS CREATE CONFIDENTIALITY AGREEMENTS?

Angela explains to Cory that most successful businesses have trade secrets. The law protects trade secrets indefinitely, provided that the information is not generally known, is kept secret, and has commercial value. Sometimes, of course, a business needs to disclose secret information to a party in the course of conducting business. For example, a company may need to hire a consultant to revamp a computer system, an engineer to design a manufacturing system, or a marketing firm to implement a sales program. All of these parties may need access to some of the company's trade secrets. Angela points out that one way to protect against the unauthorized disclosure of such information is through confidentiality agreements. Angela then proceeds to explain to Cory what a confidentiality agreement is and the necessity of defining the scope of the agreement.

WHAT IS A CONFIDENTIALITY AGREEMENT?

In a confidentiality agreement, one party promises not to divulge information about the other party to anyone else or to use the other party's confidential information for his or her own benefit. Confidentiality agreements are often included in licensing and employment contracts, but they can also be separate contracts. The key is to make sure that the agreement adequately protects the trade secrets and applies to any related transactions between the parties. For instance, assume that a business executes a separate confidentiality agreement with a marketing firm. In this situation, it is important to make sure that the agreement refers to any other contracts that the business has formed with the marketing firm prior to the confidentiality agreement. Also, subsequent contracts with the marketing firm should either refer back to the confidentiality agreement or include a new confidentiality provision.

DEFINING THE SCOPE OF A CONFIDENTIALITY AGREEMENT

Confidentiality agreements must be reasonable. When drafting a confidentiality agreement, you must be clear about what information needs to be protected, and for how long. Also, make certain that the client defines what is meant by *confidential information* and that this definition is included in the agreement. Does the client want to protect just a customer list or all financial, technical, and other business information? The confidentiality agreement must specify clearly what secrets are to be protected by the agreement.

   The duration of the agreement usually depends on the nature of the information. Very important secret information should remain confidential for a longer time than less important secrets. Sometimes, as with a marketing campaign, the time period for confidentiality may be self-evident (if the campaign ends in six months, for example). The agreement should be tailored to the client's needs as much as possible. If the party to whom the client is disclosing information will no longer need the information after a certain date—such as when the project is completed—include a provision requiring the return of confidential information after that date. This will alleviate concerns that the client's confidential trade secrets might later fall into the hands of a stranger.

DRAFTING THE AGREEMENT

Angela then shows Cory where to find some forms for, and examples of, confidentiality agreements. Angela suggests which form would be the most appropriate to the client's situation and also advises Cory to look at a confidentiality agreement that Angela previously drafted for another client. Cory thanks Angela, commenting that although he studied intellectual property during his paralegal program, the quick review of confidentiality agreements that Angela gave him was extremely helpful.

KEY TERMS AND CONCEPTS

chapter summary   Contracts and Intellectual Property Law

Requirements to Form a Valid Contract

A contract is any agreement (based on a promise or an exchange of promises) that can be enforced in court. To form a valid contract, four basic requirements must be met.

1. *Agreement*—An agreement includes an offer and an acceptance. One party must offer to enter into a legal agreement, and another party must accept the terms of the offer.

   a. An offer is a promise to do or to refrain from doing some specified thing in the future.

   b. The offeror must have the intent to be bound, the terms must be reasonably certain or definite, and the offer must be communicated to the offeree.

   c. Both a rejection of the offer and the making of a counteroffer terminate the original offer. The offer is also terminated if the party making the offer withdraws the offer before it has been accepted. Otherwise, the offer expires after a reasonable period of time has passed.

   d. An offer may automatically terminate by law if the subject matter is destroyed, one party dies or becomes incompetent, or the contract becomes illegal.

   e. The terms of the acceptance must be the same as ("mirror") the terms of the offer.

   f. Acceptance of an offer is timely if it is made before the offer is terminated. Acceptance takes effect at the time the acceptance is communicated via the mode expressly or impliedly authorized by the offeror. This is called the *mailbox rule*.

   g. If the contract does not specify the method of acceptance, an offer may be accepted by any means that is reasonable under the circumstances.

2. *Consideration*—Consideration is usually defined as "something of value"—such as money or the performance of an action not otherwise required—that is given in exchange for a promise.

   a. To be legally sufficient, consideration must involve a legal detriment to the promisee, a legal benefit to the promisor, or both.

   b. In general, a court will not question the adequacy of consideration (fairness of the bargain) if the consideration is legally sufficient. Courts will inquire into the adequacy of consideration only when fraud, undue influence, duress, or incompetence is involved.

   c. Some contracts may be enforced (or partially enforced) under the doctrine of promissory estoppel even though consideration is lacking.

3. *Contractual capacity*—The parties to the contract must have the legal ability to enter into a contractual relationship. Courts generally presume contractual capacity unless one party is a minor, intoxicated, or mentally incompetent.

4. *Legality*—A contract to do something that is prohibited by federal or state statutory law is illegal and, as such, void from the outset and thus unenforceable.

   a. Contracts entered into by persons who do not have a license, when one is required by statute, will not be enforceable *unless* the underlying purpose of the statute is to raise government revenues (and not to protect the public from unauthorized practitioners).

   b. Some contracts are not enforced because the court deems them to be contrary to public policy.

Defenses to Contract Enforceability

A contract that meets all the above requirements may not be enforceable if (1) the parties have not genuinely assented (agreed) to its terms, (2) the contract is so oppressive to one of the parties that a court will refuse to enforce it, or (3) the contract is not in the proper form.

1. *Mistake*—Generally, a contract can be avoided on the basis of mistake only if the mistake was one of material fact (not value) and only when both parties are mistaken (mutual mistake). An exception to this rule exists if one party made a mathematical error (unilateral mistake) in formulating a bid or estimating costs.

2. *Fraudulent misrepresentation*—When fraud occurs, usually the innocent party can enforce or avoid the contract.

3. *Undue influence*—Undue influence arises from special relationships in which one party's free will has been overcome by the undue influence exerted by the other party. Usually, the contract is voidable.

4. *Duress*—If one party forces the other to enter a contract under fear of a threat, the forced party can avoid the contract.

5. *Unconscionable contract*—When a contract is so oppressive to one of the parties that a court will refuse to enforce it, the oppressed party will be excused from performance. These situations usually involve an adhesion contract, which is a contract drafted by the dominant party and presented to the adhering party on a "take-it-or-leave-it" basis.

(Continued)

6. *Statute of Frauds*—Every state has a Statute of Frauds, which is a statute that specifies what types of contracts must be in writing (or be evidenced by a written document). The following types of contracts are normally required to be in writing:

   a. Contracts involving interests in land.

   b. Contracts that cannot by their terms be performed within one year from the day after the date of formation.

   c. Collateral, or secondary, contracts, such as promises to answer for the debt or duty of another.

   d. Promises made in consideration of marriage.

   e. Contracts for the sale of goods priced at $500 or more.

Sales Contracts and Warranties

State statutes that are based on Article 2 of the Uniform Commercial Code (UCC) govern contracts for the sale of goods (as opposed to real property or services). The UCC primarily comes into play when disputes arise over ambiguous or missing terms and when the buyer or seller is a merchant. If the UCC has not modified a common law rule, then the common law applies. The UCC also contains provisions on express and implied warranties that arise when goods are sold. For example, under the UCC, every merchant warrants that the goods are reasonably fit for the ordinary purpose for which such goods are used.

Contract Performance and Remedies

The most common way to terminate contractual duties is by the performance of those duties. Failure to perform contractual duties as promised results in a breach of the contract.

1. *Substantial performance*—Performance that provides a party with the important and essential benefits of a contract, in spite of any omission or deviation from the terms, is substantial performance. Because substantial performance is not perfect, the other party is entitled to damages to compensate for the failure to comply with the contract.

2. *Performance impossible or commercially impracticable*—If, after a contract has been made, performance becomes objectively impossible (the subject matter is destroyed, for example), then the parties' performance is excused. Also, if performance becomes extremely difficult or expensive due to some event, a court may excuse performance.

3. *Remedies for breach of contract*—

   a. Money damages are a legal remedy designed to compensate a party for the loss of the bargain.

      1. Compensatory damages compensate the injured party only for damages actually sustained.

      2. Incidental damages are for expenses caused directly by a breach of contract, such as the cost of obtaining performance from another source.

      3. Consequential damages flow from the party's breach and were foreseeable at the time the contract was formed.

b. The following equitable remedies are available only in limited circumstances:

1. Rescission is an action to undo or cancel the contract. When a contract is rescinded, restitution must be made.

2. Reformation is an action in which the court rewrites the contract to reflect the parties' true agreement.

3. Specific performance, which requires a party to perform the contract, is available only when money damages are inadequate and the contract is not for personal services.

c. In sales contracts, the UCC may provide additional remedies to buyers and sellers (such as the buyer's right to reject nonconforming goods).

Electronic Contracting and Electronic Signatures

Today many contracts are formed over the Internet. How the courts apply the traditional rules of contract law is an increasingly important issue. Generally, the terms of the offer should be just as comprehensive as in written documents. The method of acceptance should also be specified.

1. *Click-on agreement*—An agreement that arises when the buyer, completing a transaction on the computer, is required to indicate his or her assent to be bound by the terms of an offer by clicking on a button that says, for example, "I agree." The courts have enforced click-on agreements

2. *Shrink-wrap agreement*—An agreement whose terms are expressed inside the box in which the goods are packaged. The party who opens the box (the buyer) is informed that, by keeping the goods, she or he agrees to the terms of the agreement. Courts have enforced such agreements unless the buyer learned of the terms after entering the contract.

3. *Browse-wrap terms*—Terms and conditions of use that are presented to an Internet user but that do not require the user's assent. The courts have not enforced such terms.

4. *Electronic signature technologies*—Signatures verify the identity of parties to a contract. Today, a party's signature can be electronically encoded onto a key or card that is verified by a third party or can be digitally captured and attached to the electronic document. Additional technologies are currently being developed.

5. *State laws on e-signatures*—Most states have laws that specify which kinds of documents can be signed electronically. Some of these laws are based on the Uniform Electronic Transactions Act (UETA).

6. *Federal law on e-signatures and e-documents*—The Electronic Signatures in Global and National Commerce Act (E-SIGN Act) of 2000 gave validity to e-signatures by providing that no contract, record, or signature may be "denied legal effect" solely because it is in electronic form.

Intellectual Property Law

Intellectual property—the products that result from intellectual, creative processes—is becoming increasingly valuable. The following are the four basic types of intellectual property

(Continued)

rights. If a party infringes on these rights, the owner of the property can file suit and possibly obtain damages.

1. *Patent*—A grant from the government that gives an inventor the exclusive right to make, use, and sell an invention.

2. *Copyright*—The right of an author or a creator of a literary or artistic work or other production (such as a computer program) to have the exclusive use of that work for a given period of time.

3. *Trademark*—A distinctive mark or motto that a manufacturer stamps, prints, or affixes to goods so that its products are distinguishable from those of others. Trademarks apply to products, whereas trade names apply to business names.

4. *Trade secret*—A business secret that makes a particular company or product unique and that would be of value to a competitor (such as customer lists, plans, and research and development).

QUESTIONS FOR REVIEW

1. Name and describe the four basic requirements to form a valid contract. Are there any circumstances in which the court will enforce the parties' agreement even though it lacks consideration?

2. Under what circumstances are contracts that meet the four basic requirements generally unenforceable?

3. What is the Uniform Commercial Code (UCC), and to what types of contracts does it apply? How does the UCC affect the common law of contracts?

4. What is the doctrine of substantial performance? Why is it important in contract law? What happens if it becomes impossible to perform a contract? Are there any other situations in which performance will be excused?

5. What remedies are available to the innocent party when a contract is breached, or broken? What is specific performance, and in what kinds of circumstances is it available?

6. Explain what is meant by the terms *click-on agreement, shrink-wrap agreement,* and *browse-wrap terms.* How are they different? How are they similar? Which of the three do courts usually enforce?

7. What constitutes an electronic signature, and what is the legal validity of such signatures?

8. What is intellectual property, and why is it an important topic in the law today? Name four major forms of intellectual property.

9. What is a patent? How does one acquire a patent?

10. What types of property can be copyrighted? Must a copyright be registered with the U.S. Copyright Office in order to be protected under the law? What conduct gives rise to a copyright infringement action?

ETHICAL QUESTIONS

1. Douglas Coleman works as a paralegal for an oil company. The attorney he works for is responsible for negotiating franchise contracts with people who want to purchase gas-station franchises. Most of those applying for franchises have lawyers who negotiate for them. Bob Little is applying for a franchise without a lawyer to represent him. It is apparent from talking to Little that he does not have much education, and he has indicated that he has never owned a gas station before. He has, however, recently inherited some money, and he wants to achieve his lifelong dream of owning his own gas station.

He has been sent a copy of the standard-form franchise agreement. The standard-form contract is very one sided and unfair to the franchisee (the person purchasing the franchise). Little calls and says that he is ready to negotiate his franchise agreement with the oil company and asks Douglas to set up a telephone conference for that purpose. Douglas would like to tell Little that he really should have a lawyer represent his interests during the negotiations. Can he recommend to Little that he retain a lawyer? Should he give Little any tips about how to negotiate a franchising arrangement with the oil company? What might happen if Douglas does either of these things? What might happen if he does nothing?

2. Zachary Daniels is an experienced paralegal at a business law firm. He has drafted numerous contracts and is given a certain amount of independence in his work. Zachary frequently meets with clients without an attorney present. After each of these meetings, Zachary writes up a contract that reflects what the client is seeking and gives it to the attorney who is handling the case, along with a memorandum explaining why he has included certain provisions in the contract. Zachary is careful not to give legal advice to the clients during such meetings.

Today, Zachary is meeting with one of the firm's longtime clients, Jack Johnson, who owns a chain of well-known specialty stores worth several million dollars. With Jack is his fiancée, Oneida Kurtz, who is foreign born and speaks little English. Jack wants Zachary to draft a prenuptial agreement for him and his fiancée. In it, she will agree

not to pursue any of Jack's business assets in the event that their marriage ends in divorce. Oneida does not have an attorney and says little during the meeting. Zachary is concerned that Oneida might not fully understand the terms of the agreement. How should Zachary handle this situation? Can he draft a contract that represents the interests of both parties? Why or why not?

3. Joanne has been your best friend since the seventh grade. You and she share a lot of common interests, including music. She writes articles for the entertainment section of the local newspaper, and you recently landed a job as a paralegal with a firm that specializes in intellectual property. One day, you and Joanne are out to lunch discussing your favorite music group. She tells you that she heard from a reliable source that the lead guitarist, Jon, is leaving the group and going "solo" and will be playing the group's biggest hits on his first solo tour. You blurt out, "I know, my firm is representing the band" without thinking. Joanne then continues to question you and presses you to tell her the "scoop" about the case. What should you do? Have you revealed confidential client information just by telling her the band is a client? What might be the consequences of your actions? What could happen if you told her what the case was about?

 ## PRACTICE QUESTIONS AND ASSIGNMENTS

1. Using the material on contract law presented in this chapter, identify which defenses the defendants in the following hypothetical cases might use to defend against an action for breach of contract:

   a. Mrs. Martinez, a Spanish-speaking immigrant, buys a washing machine and signs a financing agreement that allows her to pay for it in monthly installments. The agreement contains a clause that allows the store to repossess the appliance if she misses a payment. Mrs. Martinez misses the next-to-the-last payment. The store notifies Mrs. Martinez that she has breached their contract and that it intends to repossess the washing machine. How might Mrs. Martinez defend against the store's action?

   b. Sally orally agrees to purchase a farm from her lifelong friend Fred. She promises to pay Fred $120,000 for the farm. She trusts Fred, so she does not put the deal in writing. A few days later, Fred sells the same property to Nell for $140,000. Fred and Nell put their agreement in writing. When Sally learns of Fred's contract with Nell, she sues Fred for breach of contract. What is Fred's defense?

   c. Rob enters into a contract with Tom to sell Tom fifty sweaters in Christmas colors and featuring Christmas designs. The first shipment of sweaters is due on October 1, 2007. When the sweaters are not delivered, Tom calls Rob and learns that the factory where the sweaters are produced has burned down. Tom, who is upset because he needed the sweaters for his Christmas catalogue sales, sues Rob for breach of contract. What is Rob's defense?

2. Using the material presented in this chapter on remedies for breach of contract, identify the remedies available to the innocent parties in the following situations:

   a. Mike sells two hundred computers to Heartland University for $100,000. Mike's secretary makes a typographical error when she types the contract, keying in $1,000,000 instead of $100,000. Heartland signs the contract without noticing the error but later refuses to pay more than $100,000. Mike, taking advantage of the error and Heartland's unwitting agreement to a price of $1,000,000 for the computers, sues Heartland for the full $1,000,000. What remedy will the court likely grant in this situation?

b. Mrs. Wilcox sells her house to a young couple, the Warners. Among other things, Mrs. Wilcox guarantees that the basement does not leak. Two weeks after the Warners move into the house, the basement floods severely during a rainstorm. The Warners are upset and investigate the problem. They learn that the foundation is cracked and that the basement has always leaked. They contact their lawyer, demanding to get their money back in exchange for returning the house to Mrs. Wilcox. What remedy will the Warners' lawyer seek?

c. Martha discovers an old painting in the attic of her grandmother's house. Martha has an antiques dealer come to the house and appraise the painting. The dealer offers her $1,000 for it. Martha accepts the dealer's offer and signs a contract of sale. The dealer is to pick up the painting, along with other items that Martha is selling to him, on the following Tuesday. Before the dealer returns, Martha's sister says that she would like to have the painting. Martha then calls the dealer and tells him that she will not be selling him the painting after all. The dealer sues Martha for breach of contract. What remedy might he seek?

3. On Saturday, Arthur mailed Tanya an offer to sell his car to her for $5,000. On Monday, having changed his mind and not having heard from Tanya, Arthur sent her a letter revoking his offer. On Wednesday, before she had received Arthur's letter of revocation, Tanya mailed a letter of acceptance to Arthur. When Tanya demanded that Arthur sell his car to her as promised, Arthur claimed that no contract existed because he had revoked his offer prior to Tanya's acceptance. Is Arthur correct? Explain.

4. Bernie, the sole owner of a small business, has a large piece of used farm equipment for sale. He offers to sell the equipment to Hank for $10,000. Discuss what happens to the offer in the following situations:

a. Bernie dies prior to Hank's acceptance; at the time he accepts, Hank is unaware of Bernie's death.

b. The night before Hank accepts, a fire destroys the equipment.

5. Jerome is an elderly man who lives with his nephew, Philip. Jerome is totally dependent on Philip's support. Philip tells Jerome that unless Jerome transfers a tract of land he owns to Philip for a price 30 percent below market value, Philip will no longer support and take care of him. Jerome enters into the contract. What defense can Jerome raise to set aside this contract?

6. Based on the material on intellectual property law presented in the chapter, in which of the following situations would a court likely hold Maruta liable for copyright infringement?

a. At the library, Maruta photocopies ten pages from a scholarly journal relating to a topic on which she is writing a term paper.

b. Maruta makes leather handbags and sells them in her small leather shop. She advertises her handbags as "Vutton handbags," hoping that customers might mistakenly assume that they were made by Vuitton, the well-known maker of high-quality luggage and handbags.

c. Maruta owns a video store. She purchases one copy of all the latest DVDs from various DVD manufacturers. Then, using blank discs, she makes copies to rent or sell to her customers.

7. Max plots a new Batman adventure and carefully and skillfully imitates the art of DC Comics to create an authentic-looking Batman comic book. Max is not affiliated with the owners of the copyright to Batman. Can Max publish the comic book without infringing on the owners' copyright?

8. Using the material on intellectual property presented in this chapter, identify the type of legal protection that applies to each form of intellectual property described below:

a. Karen Wilson designs book bags for students. Her logo is a small schoolhouse stamped on the book bag. Karen's logo distinguishes her book bags from those of other manufacturers.

b. Mike Pierson has developed a highly successful strategy for marketing his pizza and for locating his pizza shops. This strategy has made his company, Pizza Express, unique and prosperous.

c. Carol Garcia writes a textbook, which is published. The publisher's payments to Carol are in the form of royalties.

d. Dr. Alston invents a unique type of windshield wipers. He wants the right to sell his invention.

9. John and Andrew Doney invented a device for balancing rotors. Although they registered their invention with the U.S. Patent and Trademark Office, it was never put on the market as an automobile wheel balancer. Some time later, Exetron Corp. produced an automobile wheel balancer that used a device similar to that of the Doneys. Given the fact that the Doneys had not put the patented product in commerce, does Exetron's use of a similar device infringe on the Doneys' patent? Explain your answer.

QUESTIONS FOR CRITICAL ANALYSIS

1. Consideration, a requirement for a valid contract, is defined as *something of value.* What items, other than money, meet this definition? How does consideration distinguish a contract from a gift?

2. Under what circumstances should courts examine the adequacy of consideration?

3. Why are minors allowed to avoid contractual obligations by canceling or disaffirming contracts?

4. Contracts in violation of federal or state laws are illegal and void from the outset. Give examples of three different types of contracts that would violate federal or state laws.

5. Generally, courts hold that gambling contracts are illegal and thus void. Do you think that the advent of legalized forms of gambling, such as state-operated lotteries, is consistent with a continued public policy against the enforcement of gambling contracts? Why or why not?

6. Describe the types of individuals who might be capable of exerting undue influence on others.

7. The concept of substantial performance permits a party to be discharged from a contract even though the party has not fully performed his or her obligations according to the contract's terms. Is this fair? What policy interests are at issue here?

8. Many of our day-to-day transactions, such as buying a can of cola from a vending machine or purchasing groceries with a debit card, involve contracts. Explain how these contracts meet the requirements of a valid contract. Do they meet the requirements of the Statute of Frauds? Would a court enforce these contracts?

9. What does the Statute of Frauds require? How is it used in a contract dispute? Is the one-year rule fair? Why or why not?

10. Why are patents, trademarks, and copyrights known as intellectual property? What type of property is protected by a patent, a trademark, and a copyright, respectively? How is a trade secret protected?

PROJECTS

1. Find out what the law is in your state regarding surrogate-parenting contracts. Are they regulated at all? If so, are they legal or illegal? Write a one-page paper summarizing your state's law on this topic.

2. Obtain a copy of the *Wall Street Journal,* and find in it an article on a lawsuit involving breach of contract. Write a one-page paper explaining the issues in the dispute. Remember to note the name and date of the article for your instructor.

3. Using the requirements for an offer that are stated in the chapter, draft a simple offer to purchase a laptop computer (used, including software) from a fellow paralegal student. Make sure that the offer is definite and certain. Then write an explanation (in one or two paragraphs) of how you would communicate the offer to the person, how long the offer would remain open, and what method of acceptance you would prefer.

4. Interview a paralegal who works in an intellectual property firm. Find out what his or her day-to-day work entails. Draft an outline covering the topics you discussed, and then give an oral presentation to the class.

USING INTERNET RESOURCES

1. Go to an article in the FindLaw for Legal Professionals Library, which is located at **http://library.findlaw.com/ 1999/Jan/1/241463.html**.

   a. Scroll down to the heading "Consideration," and read the summary provided. How many examples are given? Then read the next section titled, "Typical Contract

Provisions." How many different types of clauses are discussed? Write down the types of clauses identified.

b. Go to FindLaw's main site on contracts, at **http://www.findlaw.com/01topics/07contracts**. Then click on "FindLaw Corporate Counsel Center—Sample Business Contracts." There, you can access contracts listed by industry, by type, or by company name, or you can browse through the most recent contracts added to the site. Using any of the methods available, select a contract to view. Note the name of the contract and its general purpose. Does the contract use all of the clauses you noted in Part A of this question (typical contract provisions)? Does it use any? If so, which of the typical clauses are used?

2. Go to the Web site of the U.S. Patent and Trademark Office (USPTO) at **http://www.uspto.gov**. This site offers a wealth of information concerning applying for patents and registering trademarks. You can also search existing patents and trademarks, get copies of records, and check the status of applications (among other things).

a. Click on "FAQ" on the top menu. Browse through the questions and answers for a few minutes, and then answer the following questions:

(1) What are the two categories of patents that are available? Briefly describe them.

(2) On average, how long does it take for a patent application to be processed?

(3) How long does it take to register a trademark?

(4) Can you download the forms to apply for a patent or register a trademark?

(5) Can you apply for a patent electronically?

(6) Can you apply for trademark protection electronically?

b. Although paralegals may fill out trademark registration documents, only paralegals who are authorized as "agents" by the USPTO can complete patent applications. You can find information about becoming a patent agent at the USPTO's Enrollment and Discipline Web site, located at **http://www.uspto.gov/web/offices/dcom/gcounsel/oed.htm**. Go to that page and review the links under "Exam Resources." What is generally required to become an agent? Must the applicant meet certain minimum educational requirements? Take a test? Pay a fee? Write a one-page summary of your findings. Conclude by stating whether you might be interested in becoming a patent agent in the future.

3.  For additional resources, visit our Web site at **http://www.paralegal.delmar.cengage.com**.

END NOTES

1. See Section 204 of Article 2 of the Uniform Commercial Code (UCC)—or, as citations to the UCC are usually given, UCC 2–204. You can access the UCC and its provisions by going to the Web site provided in this chapter in the *On the Web* feature on page 275.

2. Some offers are considered irrevocable—that is, they cannot be revoked by the offeror. For example, UCC 2–205 provides that a "merchant's firm offer," which arises when a merchant-offeror gives assurances in a signed writing that the offer will remain open, cannot be revoked during the time period stated in the offer or, if no time period is stated, for a reasonable period of time.

3. The name is misleading because the statute does not apply to fraud. Neither does it invalidate any type of contract. Rather, it denies *enforceability* to certain contracts that do not comply with its requirements in an effort to prevent fraud in the enforcement of contracts.

4. The Thirteenth Amendment to the U.S. Constitution prohibits

involuntary servitude, and thus a court will not order a person to perform under a personal-service contract. A court may grant an order (injunction) prohibiting that person from engaging in similar contracts in the future for a period of time, however.

5. Similarly, courts often refuse to order specific performance of construction contracts because courts are not set up to operate as construction supervisors or engineers.

6. UETA 102(8).

7. 15 U.S.C. Sections 7001 *et seq.*

8. The E-SIGN Act applies only to agreements covered by Articles 2 and 2A and UCC 1–107 and 1–206.

9. 17 U.S.C. Sections 101 *et seq.*

10. 17 U.S.C. Section 107.

11. *Ringling Bros.–Barnum & Bailey, Combined Shows, Inc. v. Utah Division of Travel Development*, 935 F.Supp. 763 (E.D.Va. 1996); *cert.* denied, 528 U.S. 923, 120 S.Ct. 286, 145 L.Ed.2d 239 (1999).

INSURANCE LAW AND REAL PROPERTY

CHAPTER OUTLINE

Introduction

Insurance Law

Real Property

AFTER COMPLETING THIS CHAPTER, YOU WILL KNOW:

▶ The terminology used in insurance contracts and the various classifications of insurance.

▶ What an insurable interest is and the difference between an insurance agent and an insurance broker.

▶ The types of provisions that are typically included in an insurance contract and the rights and duties of the parties under insurance contracts.

▶ The difference between real property and personal property.

▶ How one acquires, holds, and transfers ownership rights in property and what procedures are involved in the sale of real estate.

INTRODUCTION

As you study the areas of substantive law discussed in this unit, keep the following thought in mind: although these topics are treated individually, in relative isolation from one other, there is a great deal of overlap between them. For example, in tort and product liability cases, which you read about in Chapter 7, the defendant's insurance coverage—or lack of it—is typically an important element. Insurance and contract law also overlap significantly because insurance is a type of contract, one that is formed to guard against various risks. Insurance also plays an important role in other areas, such as business undertakings and the employment context.

In the first part of this chapter, we examine insurance law. It is important for paralegals to become familiar with this area, because nearly one-third of all paralegals spend most of their time on insurance law.[1] We then look at property law, an area in which many paralegals specialize. Again, although these two topics—insurance law and property law—are distinct bodies of law, in the real world they are often connected. Most buyers insure a home, a car, or other property as soon as they purchase it to protect themselves against possible losses due to fires, accidents, or other perils.

INSURANCE LAW

As you learned in Chapter 2, *insurance* is a contract in which the insurance company (the *insurer*), in return for consideration, promises to pay a sum of money to another (either the *insured* or the *beneficiary*) if the insured suffers harm or loss from a particular, stated peril. Basically, insurance is an arrangement for *transferring and allocating risk*. In many instances, **risk** can be described as a prediction concerning potential loss based on known and unknown factors. **Risk management** normally involves the transfer of certain risks from the insured individual to the insurance company by a contractual agreement. The insurance contract and its provisions will be examined shortly. First, however, we look at the different types of insurance that can be obtained, insurance terminology, and the concept of insurable interest.

Classifications of Insurance

Insurance is classified according to the nature of the risk involved. For instance, fire insurance, automobile insurance, and life insurance apply to different types of risk and protect against different types of loss. Exhibit 9.1 lists and describes a number of insurance classifications.

Insurance Terminology

An insurance contract is called a **policy**, the consideration paid to the insurer is called a **premium**, and the insurance company is sometimes called an **underwriter**. The parties to an insurance policy are the insurer (the insurance company) and the insured (the person covered by its provisions or the holder of the policy).

Insurance contracts are usually obtained through an *agent*, who ordinarily works for the insurance company, or through a *broker*, who is ordinarily an *independent contractor*. When a broker deals with an applicant for insurance, the broker is, in effect, the applicant's agent and not an agent of the insurance company. In contrast, an insurance agent is an agent of the insurance company, not of the applicant. As a general rule, the insurance company is bound by the acts of its insurance agents when they act within the agency relationship (agency relationships will be discussed in Chapter 11). In most situations, state law determines the status of all parties writing or obtaining insurance.

---

risk
A prediction concerning potential loss based on known and unknown factors.

risk management
Planning that is undertaken to reduce the risk of loss from known and unknown events. In the context of insurance, risk management involves transferring certain risks from the insured to the insurance company.

policy
In insurance law, a contract for insurance coverage. The policy spells out the precise terms and conditions as to what will and will not be covered under the contract.

premium
In insurance law, the price paid by the insured for insurance protection for a specified period of time.

underwriter
In insurance law, the insurer, or the one assuming a risk in return for the payment of a premium.

EXHIBIT 9.1
Selected Insurance Classifications

TYPE OF INSURANCE	COVERAGE
Automobile	May cover damage to automobiles resulting from specified hazards or occurrences (such as fire, vandalism, theft, or collision); normally provides protection against liability for personal injuries and property damage resulting from the operation of the vehicle.
Casualty	Protects against losses incurred by the insured as a result of being held liable for personal injuries or property damage sustained by others.
Fidelity or Guaranty	Provides indemnity against losses in trade or losses caused by the dishonesty of employees, the insolvency of debtors, or breaches of contract.
Fire	Covers losses incurred by the insured as a result of fire.
Group	Provides individual life, medical, or disability insurance coverage but is obtainable through a group of persons, usually employees; the policy premium is paid either entirely by the employer or partially by the employer and partially by the employee.
Health	Covers expenses incurred by the insured as a result of physical injury or illness and other expenses relating to health and life maintenance.
Homeowners'	Protects homeowners against some or all risks of loss to their residences and the residences' contents or liability arising from the use of the property.
Key-Person	Protects a business in the event of the death or disability of a key employee.
Liability	Protects against liability imposed on the insured as a result of injuries to the person or property of another.
Life	Covers the death of the policyholder. On the death of the insured, an amount specified in the policy is paid by the insurer to the insured's beneficiary.
Malpractice	Protects professionals (physicians, lawyers, and others) against malpractice claims brought against them by their patients or clients; a form of liability insurance.
Mortgage	Covers a mortgage loan; the insurer pays the balance of the mortgage to the creditor on the death or disability of the debtor.
Title	Protects against any defects in title to real property and any losses incurred as a result of existing claims against or liens on the property at the time of purchase.

Insurable Interest

A person can insure anything in which she or he has an **insurable interest**. Without an insurable interest, there can be no enforceable contract. In regard to real and personal property, an insurable interest exists when the insured derives a pecuniary (monetary) benefit from the preservation and continued existence of the property, such as a car, a home, business premises, or computer data. Put another way, a person has an insurable interest in property when he or she would sustain a financial loss from its destruction.

In regard to life insurance, a person must have a reasonable expectation of benefit from the continued life of another in order to have an insurable interest in that person's life. The benefit may be pecuniary (as with so-called *key-person insurance,* which insures the lives of important employees, usually in small companies), or it may be founded on the relationship between the parties (by blood or by affinity, such as marriage).

For property insurance, the insurable interest must exist at the time the loss occurs but need not exist when the policy is purchased. In contrast, for life insurance, the insurable interest must exist at the time the policy is obtained. The existence of an insurable interest is a primary concern in determining liability under an insurance policy.

insurable interest
An interest either in a person's life or well-being or in property that is sufficiently substantial to justify insuring against injury to or death of the person or damage to the property.

On the Web

The Web site of the Insurance Information Institute provides a wealth of news and information on insurance-related issues, including statistical data and a glossary of insurance terms. Go to **http://www.iii.org**.

The Insurance Contract

An insurance contract is governed by the general principles of contract law, although the insurance industry is heavily regulated by each state. In this section, we consider several aspects of the insurance contract, including the application for insurance, the date when the contract takes effect, and some of the important provisions typically found in insurance contracts. In addition, we discuss the cancellation of an insurance policy and defenses that insurance companies can raise against payment on a policy.

Application

The filled-in application form for insurance is usually attached to the policy and made a part of the insurance contract. Thus, an insurance applicant is bound by any false statements that appear in the application (subject to certain exceptions). Because the insurance company evaluates the risk factors based on the information included in the insurance application, misstatements or misrepresentations can void a policy, especially if the insurance company can show that it would not have extended insurance if it had known the true facts.

Effective Date

The effective date of an insurance contract—that is, the date on which the insurance coverage begins—is important. In some instances, the insurance applicant is not protected until a formal written policy is issued. In other situations, the applicant is protected between the time the application is received and the time the insurance company either accepts or rejects it. The following facts should be kept in mind:

- A broker is merely the agent of an applicant. Therefore, until the broker obtains a policy from the insurer, the applicant normally is not insured.
- A person who seeks insurance from an insurance company's agent will usually be protected from the moment the application is made, provided that some form of

Executives of a newly formed corporation consult with an attorney concerning the types of insurance they should purchase for the business. Many paralegals work in the area of insurance law and assist with tasks relating to insurance claims.

(Courtesy of ©Royalty-Free/Corbis)

premium has been paid. Between the time the application is received and either rejected or accepted, the applicant is covered (possibly subject to a medical examination). Usually, the agent will write a memorandum, or **binder**, indicating that a policy is pending and stating its essential terms.

binder
A written, temporary insurance policy.

- If the parties agree that the policy will be issued and delivered at a later time, the contract is not effective until the policy is issued and delivered or sent to the applicant, depending on the agreement. Thus, any loss sustained between the time of application and the delivery of the policy is not covered.

- The parties may agree that a life insurance policy will be binding at the time the insured pays the first premium, or the policy may be expressly contingent on the applicant's passing a physical examination. If the applicant pays the premium and passes the examination, the policy coverage is continuously in effect. If the applicant pays the premium but dies before having the physical examination, then in order to collect, the applicant's estate must show that the applicant *would have passed* the examination had he or she not died.

Coinsurance Clauses

Often, when taking out fire insurance policies, property owners insure their property for less than full value because most fires do not result in a total loss. To encourage owners to insure their property for an amount close to full value, fire insurance policies commonly include a coinsurance clause. Typically, a *coinsurance clause* provides that if the owner insures the property up to a specified percentage of its replacement value—usually 80 percent—she or he will be fully reimbursed for any loss. If the insurance is for less than the required percentage, the owner is responsible for a proportionate share of the loss.

▶ **EXAMPLE 9.1**   Assume that a property is valued at $100,000 and the owner insures this property for $80,000, satisfying the insurer's 80 percent coinsurance requirement. When the property suffers $50,000 in fire damages, the owner recovers the full $50,000. If the owner had insured the same property for only $40,000—half of the 80 percent ($80,000) coinsurance requirement—then the owner would have recovered only half of the $50,000 in fire damages, or $25,000. ◀

Indemnity Clauses

The term *indemnity* refers to a duty to make good on any loss, damage, or liability claims incurred by another. The term is used frequently in insurance law and insurance contracts because it involves the duty to compensate for loss. Under the principle of indemnity, the indemnified party is restored to the financial position that he or she was in before the loss or accident.

Indemnity clauses are frequently found in rental contracts. ▶ **EXAMPLE 9.2** Martinez is seeking to lease a building that is suitable for operating a dry-cleaning business. Commercial Property Management, Inc., a rental agency, has such a building for rent in the area in which Martinez desires to locate. Martinez signs a lease agreement with Commercial that contains an indemnity clause. Under the indemnity clause, if an employee is injured while using the dry-cleaning equipment, he or she cannot sue Commercial Property Management. In effect, Martinez has agreed to hold the rental agency harmless for any damages caused by use of the equipment. ◀ Because indemnity clauses protect specified parties from suffering financial loss due to lawsuits, they are sometimes referred to as *hold-harmless clauses*.

Corporations often indemnify their directors and officers for any legal costs and fees that they might incur if they become involved in lawsuits by virtue of their positions. (Corporate directors and officers will be discussed in Chapter 11.) ▶ **EXAMPLE 9.3** Patricia Harding files a product liability lawsuit against Repp, Inc., and its chief executive officer, James Kerr. If Kerr's employment contract includes an indemnity clause, Repp will assume responsibility for any costs that Kerr incurs in defending himself against this lawsuit. ◄

Subrogation Clauses

In simple terms, *subrogation* is the right to pursue another party's claim. In the context of insurance, subrogation deals with the right of the insurer to be put in the position of the insured in order to pursue recovery from a third party who is legally responsible to the insured for a loss paid by the insurer to the insured. If the insurance company has compensated the insured in full for a loss sustained, and then later receives recovery from a third party in the name of the insured, the company can ask a court to order reimbursement from the proceeds. ▶ **EXAMPLE 9.4**   Suppose that Ryan owns a building that he leases out to several businesses. A third party negligently causes a fire on the premises, which burns down the entire building. Ryan can sue the third party for damages. If Ryan does not file a claim against the party who caused the fire, a subrogation clause allows the insurance company to step into Ryan's shoes and file a negligence claim against the third party on Ryan's behalf. If the fire insurance company has fully compensated Ryan for the damages, and if the lawsuit is successful, the insurance company is entitled to be reimbursed from the proceeds in the amount that it paid to Ryan to cover his loss. ◄

Most insurance contracts contain explicit subrogation clauses, which often require the insured party to cooperate with the insurance company by providing documents, records, and whatever else is necessary for the company to pursue claims on behalf of the insured. Even if the contract does not contain a subrogation clause or does not use the word *subrogation*, however, courts often hold that insurance companies have a right to subrogation unless this right is explicitly waived (given up).

Other Provisions and Clauses

Some other important provisions and clauses contained in insurance contracts are defined in Exhibit 9.2. Paralegals are often responsible for analyzing the various insurance clauses and summarizing the contract terms for their employers or clients. The courts are aware that most people do not have the special training necessary to understand the intricate terminology used in insurance policies. Thus, the words used in an insurance contract have their

EXHIBIT 9.2
Insurance Contract Provisions and Clauses

Incontestability Clause	An incontestability clause provides that after a policy has been in force for a specified length of time—usually two or three years—the insurer cannot contest statements made in the application.
Appraisal Clause	Insurance policies frequently provide that if the parties cannot agree on the amount of a loss covered under the policy or the value of the property lost, an appraisal, or estimate, by an impartial and qualified third party can be demanded.
Arbitration Clause	Many insurance policies include clauses that call for arbitration of disputes that may arise between the insurer and the insured concerning the settlement of claims.
Antilapse Clause	An antilapse clause provides that the policy will not automatically lapse if no payment is made on the date due. Ordinarily, under such a provision, the insured has a *grace period* of thirty or thirty-one days within which to pay an overdue premium before the policy is canceled.
Multiple Insurance	Many insurance policies include a clause providing that if the insured has multiple insurance policies that cover the same property and the amount of coverage exceeds the loss, the loss will be shared proportionately by the insurance companies.

ordinary meanings. They are interpreted by the courts in light of the nature of the coverage involved. (For some online sources relating to policy interpretation and analysis, as well as sources relating to other aspects of insurance-related legal work, see this chapter's *Technology and Today's Paralegal* feature on the following two pages.)

When there is an ambiguity in the policy, the provision generally is interpreted against the insurance company. Also, when it is unclear whether an insurance contract actually exists because the written policy has not been delivered, the uncertainty normally is resolved against the insurance company. The court presumes that the policy is in effect unless the company can show otherwise. Similarly, an insurer must notify the insured of any change in coverage under an existing policy.

Cancellation

The insured can cancel a policy at any time, and the insurer can cancel under certain circumstances. When an insurance company can cancel its insurance contract, the policy or a state statute usually requires that the insurer give advance written notice of the cancellation to the insured.[2] The same requirement applies when only part of a policy is canceled. Any premium paid in advance may be refundable on the policy's cancellation. The insured may also be entitled to a life insurance policy's cash surrender value.

The insurer can cancel an insurance policy for various reasons, depending on the type of insurance. ▶ **EXAMPLE 9.5** Automobile insurance can be canceled for nonpayment of premiums or suspension of the insured's driver's license. Property insurance can be canceled for nonpayment of premiums or for other reasons, including the insured's fraud or misrepresentation, conviction for a crime that increases the hazard insured against, or gross negligence that increases the hazard insured against. Life and health policies can be canceled because of false statements made by the insured in the application, but cancellation can only take place before the effective date of an incontestability clause. ◀ An insurer cannot cancel—or refuse to renew—a policy for discriminatory reasons or other reasons that violate public policy or because the insured has appeared as a witness in a case against the company.

Good Faith Obligations

Both parties to an insurance contract are responsible for the obligations that they assume under the contract. In addition, both the insured and the insurer have an implied duty to act in good faith. Good faith requires the party who is applying for insurance to reveal everything necessary for the insurer to evaluate the risk. In other words, the applicant must disclose all material facts, including all facts that an insurer would consider in determining whether to charge a higher premium or to refuse to issue a policy altogether. Once the insurer has accepted the risk, and some event occurs that gives rise to a claim, the insurer has a duty to investigate to determine the facts.

When a policy provides insurance against third party claims, the insurer is obligated to make reasonable efforts to settle such a claim. If a settlement cannot be reached, then regardless of the claim's merit, the insurer must defend any suit against the insured. Usually, a policy provides that in this situation the insured must cooperate. A policy provision may expressly require the insured to attend hearings and trials, to help in obtaining evidence and witnesses, and to assist in reaching a settlement.

Defenses against Payment

To avoid paying on a claim, an insurance company can raise any of the defenses that would be valid in any ordinary action on a contract, as well as some defenses that do not apply in ordinary contract actions. If the insurance company can show that the policy was procured

Technology and Today's Paralegal

ONLINE RESOURCES CONCERNING INSURANCE CLAIMS

When a dispute arises between an insurance company and a policyholder regarding an insurance claim, attorneys are typically consulted to represent each party. In these situations, paralegals fulfill many functions for both sides, including analyzing insurance policies, researching the facts involved in the policyholder's claim, and locating experts. Here, we provide some practical Internet resources to assist with these functions.

ANALYZING CLAUSES IN INSURANCE POLICIES

In lawsuits regarding insurance claims, paralegals are commonly responsible for researching the provisions expressed in specific clauses of insurance policies. Consequently, it is beneficial for paralegals who deal with insurance law to understand how to read and analyze an insurance policy. FindLaw offers "a step by step method that insurance professionals and attorneys use to analyze a policy" at **http://library.findlaw.com/2000/Jan/1/130020.html**.

Insurance policies are sometimes written in terms that laypersons don't understand. To help people interpret various terms, InsWeb, an online insurance marketplace, offers an extensive glossary of insurance terms at **http://www.insweb.com/learningcenter/glossary/general-a.htm**. Another glossary of insurance terms is offered by the Insurance Information Institute (III) at **http://www.iii.org**.

INSURANCE COMPLAINTS AND INSURANCE FRAUD

A paralegal assisting a client with an insurance claim will sometimes need to research related complaints against the client's insurance company. The Web site of the National Association of Insurance Commissioners (NAIC) offers a good starting point for such research. NAIC's Consumer Information Source page, at **http://www.naic.org/cis**, allows users to search financial statements and consumer complaint reports for many insurance providers. NAIC's home page, **http://www.naic.org**, also furnishes an online fraud reporting system and links to state insurance department Web sites.

Paralegals sometimes assist clients who are dissatisfied with the claim payments offered by their insurance companies. A paralegal working with such a client may find helpful the many resources provided by the Fight Bad-Faith Insurance Companies (FBIC) Web site, at **http://www.badfaithinsurance.org**. FBIC posts a ranked list of the fifty worst bad faith insurers and the fifty best good faith insurers. FBIC also sponsors an extensive reference library of articles and downloadable videos on the subject of bad faith insurers, as well as a substantial list of insurance-related Internet links.

by fraud or misrepresentation, it may have a valid defense for not paying on a claim. (The insurance company may also have the right to disaffirm, or rescind, the insurance contract.) An absolute defense exists if the insurer can show that the insured lacked an insurable interest—thus rendering the policy void from the beginning. Improper actions, such as those that are against public policy or are otherwise illegal, can also give the insurance company a defense against the payment of a claim or allow it to rescind the contract.

An insurance company can be prevented from asserting some defenses that are normally available, however. ▶ **EXAMPLE 9.6** Suppose that a company tells an insured that information requested on a form is optional, and the insured provides it anyway. The company cannot use the information to avoid its contractual obligation under the insurance contract. Similarly, an insurance company normally cannot escape payment on the death of an insured on the ground that the person's age was stated incorrectly on the application. ◀

Paralegals working in the legal departments of insurance companies are frequently responsible for investigating potentially fraudulent claims by policyholders. To assist in the prevention and discovery of fraudulent insurance claims, the Coalition Against Insurance Fraud (CAIF) presents many resources at **http://www.insurancefraud.org**. Through CAIF's Web site, you can access state regulations related to insurance fraud and links to many antifraud associations, state fraud bureaus, and investigation tools. CAIF also posts many statistical reports and research articles related to insurance fraud offenses.

LOCATING ADJUSTERS AND APPRAISERS

When a loss occurs and a policyholder files a claim, the policyholder's insurance company will commonly employ the services of an *insurance adjuster*. An insurance adjuster is a person who inspects the damaged property, analyzes the insurance policy, and estimates the amount of loss. Paralegals sometimes assist attorneys in locating adjusters. The National Association of Independent Insurance Adjusters (NAIIA) is an association of independently owned property and casualty claims adjusting companies that have been approved by insurance carriers. Through the NAIIA's Web site, **http://www.naiia.com**, a claim can be assigned to an NAIIA adjuster in your area. This Web site also offers many industry links. Another resource is the National Association of Public Insurance Adjusters (NAPIA), **http://www.napia.com/search**. This organization accredits public insurance adjusters, who are hired to assist consumers. The NAPIA Web site offers a search engine to locate local public insurance adjusters.

In the case of an automobile insurance claim, it may be beneficial to utilize the online appraiser locator available through the Independent Automotive Damage Appraisers (IADA) Web site at **http://www.iada.org**. IADA is an association of automotive appraisers organized to protect insurance consumers from overpaying for auto body repairs.

TECHNOLOGY TIP

As a paralegal, make a habit of browsing the additional links listed on the Web pages you use as resources. In doing so, you may find sources of information more suitable to your individual research needs. If you are researching insurance claims, you will also find links to various service providers around the world through Insurance Adjusters Resource Center (IARC), at **http://www.adjust-it.com/findsite.asp?section=search**. Regularly browsing through "links" pages and resource centers like the IARC will keep you up to date on what information is available online and how to find it.

INSURANCE LAW AND THE PARALEGAL

Insurance is a pervasive aspect of American life. Nearly all citizens and businesses invest in some form of insurance, and often they have several types of insurance policies. Naturally, it follows that most paralegals work with matters related to insurance law at least some of the time. If you work for a general law practice, you may assist in bringing a client's claim against an insurance company if the company refuses to pay the claim. Paralegal work relating to insurance may involve representing people who have been involved in auto accidents; those who have lost homes or property to fire, floods, hurricanes, or theft; people who receive medical disability coverage; or people who have recently lost loved ones.

(Continued)

Developing Paralegal Skills

MEDICAL RECORDS

Derek Busset is a legal assistant for the small personal-injury firm of McNair and Iverson. Ralph McNair is handling a case in which Blanche Rosenthal's car was struck by an automobile driven by Daniel Gomez, who is insured by Reliable Insurance. The police report indicates that at the time of the accident, Gomez was speeding through a yellow light at the intersection when his car collided with Rosenthal's 2005 Cadillac, which had just entered the intersection on a green light. The insurance company has already compensated Rosenthal for the damage to her vehicle but disputes the amount she is claiming for medical bills. The insurance company believes that Rosenthal's back injury was a preexisting condition, not caused by the accident. After speaking with a representative from the insurance company, attorney McNair asks Derek to contact Rosenthal and acquire the medical records to support her claims. McNair also wants Derek to write up a summary of what the records show.

TIPS FOR OBTAINING AND EVALUATING MEDICAL RECORDS

- Find out from the client the names of all of the physicians who treated the client and the names of hospitals or other facilities in which the client received medical care.

- Prepare—and have the client sign—medical release forms, which authorize the treating physicians to provide the patient's medical records directly to the law firm.

- Keep a log of the records as they are received.

- If a claim involves the possibility of a preexisting condition, make certain to request the client's complete medical history (from before the injury as well as after it). You will need these records to determine whether a preexisting condition might have caused or contributed to the plaintiff's injury.

- Obtain a medical dictionary or reference book so that you can decipher the terminology and abbreviations frequently used by medical personnel in charts and records.

A paralegal working for an insurance company may be asked to research and analyze current legislation, assist in drafting insurance policies or amendments to those policies, and investigate the facts behind claims filed by policyholders. A paralegal working for a real estate investment firm may analyze insurance policies related to commercial property investments. Additionally, a paralegal might work for a state insurance regulatory agency. In this context, a paralegal may assist in drafting administrative procedures, investigating insurance fraud and licensing issues, and responding to consumers' insurance claims and questions—such as claims for workers' compensation (discussed in Chapter 11).

Paralegals who assist in insurance-related litigation involving torts will likely be involved in many of the same types of work that are required in the area of tort law (discussed in Chapter 7). Here is just a brief sampling of tasks related to insurance law that paralegals commonly manage:

- Research insurance clauses in relation to specific claims.

- Interact with experts, witnesses, and clients to obtain factual information about events giving rise to insurance claims.

- Work with representatives of an insurance company in defending an insured against a lawsuit brought against the insured.

- Obtain medical records concerning a client who needs assistance in obtaining payment from the insurer.

- Create, review, or prepare insurance application forms or insurance policies.

- Schedule medical appointments for health-insurance claimants.

Ethics Watch!

CLARIFYING INSTRUCTIONS

Attorneys and paralegals are usually busy. Often, attorneys give instructions to para-legals quickly and briefly, assuming that the instructions are understood as intended. Problems arise, however, if the instructions are not clear to the paralegal. If you ever find yourself in this position, make sure that the instructions are made clear. For example, suppose that your supervising attorney asks you to draft a letter to an insurance company, using as a model a letter recently sent to another insurance company on behalf of a client named Janine Lattimore. The name doesn't ring a bell with you, but you assume that you can find that letter quickly in the files. The attorney then leaves the office for the rest of the day, and you spend a miserable hour searching in vain through the files and the master client list for "Janine Lattimore."

The next morning, you explain the problem to the attorney and learn that Janine Lattimore is, in fact, the married name of a client whose files are under her maiden name, Janine Calvin. You are upset, the attorney is displeased, and the sending of the letter is delayed—all of which could have been avoided if you had asked the attorney "Who is Janine Lattimore?" when he was giving you instructions.

REAL PROPERTY

From an early period, the law has divided property into two classifications: real property and personal property. **Real property,** or *real estate,* is land and all things attached to the land (such as trees and buildings), as well as the minerals below the surface of the land and the air above the land. **Personal property** is all other property. Personal property can be either tangible or intangible. *Tangible* personal property, such as a television set or a car, has physical substance. *Intangible* personal property represents a set of rights and interests but has no real physical existence. Stocks, bonds, and intellectual property rights (discussed in Chapter 8) are examples of intangible personal property.

Ownership Rights in Property

Property ownership is often viewed as a "bundle of rights." One who owns the entire bundle of rights—ownership rights to the greatest degree possible—is said to own the property in **fee simple.** An owner in fee simple is entitled to use, possess, or dispose of the real or personal property (by sale, gift, or other means) however he or she chooses during his or her lifetime. On the owner's death, the interests in the property descend to the owner's heirs.

Of course, those who own real property even in fee simple may be subject to certain restrictions on their right to use the property absolutely as they choose. For example,

real property
Immovable property consisting of land and the buildings and plant life thereon.

personal property
Any property that is not real property. Generally, any property that is movable or intangible is classified as personal property.

fee simple
Ownership rights entitling the holder to use, possess, or dispose of the property however he or she chooses during his or her lifetime.

Kirtrena S. Deen

PARALEGAL **profile**

INSURANCE PARALEGAL

Kirtrena S. Deen received her bachelor of arts degree in legal administration from the University of West Florida in Pensacola, Florida, in 1996. On graduation, she worked at a large law firm as a legal assistant for approximately a year and a half in the area of personal-injury and employment law. She then accepted a position as a claims representative for a national automobile insurance company.

In September 1998, Deen received her Florida Department of Insurance Adjusters license. Additionally, she serves on the University of West Florida Legal Administration Program Advisory Board as a paralegal representative in the corporate/public sector.

What do you like best about your work?

"I enjoy the responsibility and exposure of investigating, evaluating, and negotiating a variety of automobile claims as opposed to adjusting only specific types of automobile claims. Some examples of the claims I am assigned to adjust include property, bodily injury, arson, theft, vandalism, and weather-related claims. I also enjoy the investigative process of meeting the parties involved, securing recorded statements, conducting scene investigations, and canvassing for witnesses."

What is the greatest challenge that you face in your area of work?

"Once a claim has been reported, the claims representative must investigate to establish coverage, finalize legal liability, and inspect the reported damage. Once the claim has been thoroughly investigated,

it must be evaluated to determine a fair settlement and negotiated accordingly. Therefore, the greatest challenge of adjusting claims is completing the investigation, evaluation, and negotiation process promptly and fairly while complying with the terms of the insurance policy and governing statutory laws."

What advice do you have for would-be paralegals in your area of work?

"My advice is to possess strong interpersonal skills, as well as superior writing and oral communication skills. Due to the variety of claims assigned, claims representatives in my area daily communicate and negotiate with insureds, claimants, and other claims representatives, as well as attorneys, regarding the settlement of claims. Additionally, regular meetings and communication with paint and body shop managers is needed regarding the assessment of automobile damage. Thus, the ability to communicate effectively with all kinds of people is a great asset to possess in my area of work."

> *"[T]he ability to communicate effectively with all kinds of people is a great asset to possess in my area of work."*

What are some tips for success as a paralegal in your area of work?

"Know the terms and conditions of the insurance policy and regularly refer to the policy to substantiate them. The insurance policy is the contract between the insurance company and the insured to which they must adhere. Know the statutory laws governing claims handling in your area and keep abreast of changes. Be detail oriented and analytical in the investigation process. Feel passionate about your work. Passion for your work will enable you to go that extra mile to handle claims promptly and fairly."

---

eminent domain
The power of a government to take land for public use from private citizens for just compensation.

easement
The right of a person to make limited use of another person's real property without taking anything from the property.

zoning laws may prohibit an owner of property in a given area from conducting certain types of activities (such as running a business) on the property. Also, under its power of **eminent domain**, the government has a right to take private property for public use (for a highway, for example), as long as the government compensates the owner for the value of the land taken.

Property owned in fee simple may also be subject to an **easement**, which is the right of another to use the owner's land for a limited purpose—a neighbor's right to use the land to reach a roadway, for example, or a utility company's right to erect and maintain power lines and poles or gas lines on the land.

In contrast to ownership in fee simple, other forms of ownership, including those discussed below, involve limited ownership rights.

Concurrent Ownership

Persons who share the bundle of ownership rights to either real or personal property are said to be concurrent owners. There are two principal types of concurrent ownership: tenancy in common and joint tenancy.

A **tenancy in common** is a form of co-ownership in which two or more persons own undivided interests in certain property. The interest is undivided because each tenant has rights in the whole property. ▶ **EXAMPLE 9.7** Rosa and Chad own a rare stamp collection together as tenants in common. This does not mean that Rosa owns certain stamps and Chad others. Rather, it means that each of them has rights in the *entire* collection. (If Rosa owned some of the stamps and Chad owned others, then the interest would be *divided*.) ◀ If a tenant in common dies, the tenant's ownership rights pass to his or her heirs.

A **joint tenancy** is also a form of co-ownership in which two or more persons own undivided interests in property. The key feature of a joint tenancy is the "right of survivorship." When a joint tenant dies, that tenant's interest passes to the surviving joint tenant or tenants and not to the deceased tenant's heirs, as it would with a tenancy in common. ▶ **EXAMPLE 9.8** Suppose that Rosa and Chad from the previous example held their stamp collection in a joint tenancy. If Rosa died before Chad, the entire collection would become the property of Chad. Rosa's heirs would receive no interest in the collection. ◀ If a joint tenant transfers his or her interest in the property, the transfer terminates the joint tenancy. The new co-owner (the one to whom the rights were transferred) and the other tenant or tenants become tenants in common.

Two other types of concurrent ownership are tenancy by the entirety and community property. A *tenancy by the entirety* is a form of co-ownership by husbands and wives that is similar to a joint tenancy, except that the spouses cannot separately transfer their interests in the property during their lifetimes. In several states, husbands and wives can hold property as community property. In those states, *community property* is all property acquired during the marriage; each spouse technically owns an undivided one-half interest in the property.

Life Estates

A *life estate* is an interest in real property that is transferred to another for the life of that individual. A conveyance "to Allison for her life" creates a life estate. In a life estate, the life tenant cannot injure the land in a manner that would adversely affect its value for the owner of the future interest in it.

Future Interests

When someone who owns real property in fee simple conveys the property to another conditionally or for a limited period of time (such as with a life estate), the original owner still retains an interest in the land. This interest is called a *future interest* because it will only arise in the future. The holder of a future interest may transfer it to another during his or her lifetime. If the interest is not transferred, it will pass to the owner's heirs on his or her death.

The Transfer and Sale of Real Property

Property can be transferred in numerous ways. Property can be given to another as a gift or transferred to another by inheritance, leased to another, or sold. Most commonly, property is transferred by sale. The sale of tangible personal property (goods) is covered by the

tenancy in common
A form of co-ownership of property in which each party owns an undivided interest that passes to his or her heirs at death.

joint tenancy
The joint ownership of property by two or more co-owners in which each co-owner owns an undivided portion of the property. On the death of one of the joint tenants, his or her interest automatically passes to the surviving joint tenant or tenants.

common law of contracts, as modified by Article 2 of the Uniform Commercial Code, which we discussed in Chapter 8. Rights in certain types of intangible property (such as checks, money orders, and other documents) are covered by other articles of the UCC. The sale of real property is governed by the common law of contracts as well as state (and, to a limited extent, federal) statutory law.

Here we look at some of the basic steps and procedures involved in the sale of real estate. These steps and procedures are summarized in Exhibit 9.3.

Contract Formation—Offer and Acceptance

The common law contractual requirements of agreement (offer and acceptance), consideration, contractual capacity, and legality all apply to real estate contracts. When a buyer wishes to purchase real estate, he or she submits an offer to the seller. The offer specifies all of the terms of the proposed contract—a description of the property, the price, and any other conditions that the buyer wishes to include. Often, a buyer conditions the offer on the buyer's ability to obtain financing. The offer might also specify which party will bear the cost of any repairs that need to be made. Typical provisions included in a real estate sales agreement are illustrated in Exhibit 9.4. When signed by the buyer and the seller, the offer constitutes a contract for the sale of land that is binding on the parties.

The buyer normally tenders a sum of money, called *earnest money,* along with the offer. By paying earnest money, the buyer indicates that he or she is making a serious offer. Normally,

EXHIBIT 9.3

Steps Involved in the Sale of Real Estate

BUYER'S PURCHASE OFFER

Buyer offers to purchase seller's property. The offer may be conditioned on buyer's ability to obtain financing, on satisfactory inspections of the premises, and so on. Included with the offer is earnest money.

SELLER'S RESPONSE

If seller accepts buyer's offer, then a contract is formed. Seller can also reject the offer or make a counteroffer that modifies buyer's terms. Buyer may accept or reject seller's counteroffer or make a counteroffer that modifies seller's terms.

PURCHASE AND SALE AGREEMENT

Once an offer or a counteroffer is accepted, a purchase and sale agreement is formed.

TITLE EXAMINATION AND INSURANCE

Title examiner investigates and verifies seller's rights in the property and discloses any claims or interests held by others. Buyer (and/or seller) may purchase title insurance to protect against a defect in title.

CLOSING

After financing is obtained and all inspections have been completed, the closing takes place. The escrow agent (such as a title company or a bank) transfers the deed to buyer and the proceeds of the sale to seller. The proceeds are the purchase price less any amount already paid by buyer and any closing costs to be paid by seller. Included in the closing costs are fees charged for services performed by the lender, escrow agent, and title examiner. The purchase and sale of the property is complete.

EXHIBIT 9.4
Typical Provisions in Real Estate Sales Agreements

- Names of parties and/or real estate agents.
- Date of agreement and how long seller has to accept agreement.
- Legal description of the property's location and size.
- Amount of the purchase offer.
- Amount of cash to be paid at the time of sale.
- Amount of earnest money deposit.
- Type of loan or financing the buyer plans to use.
- Whether the sale is contingent on the buyer's obtaining financing.
- Condition of the title and debt that buyer will assume.
- Warranties of title (restrictions, rights, or limitations).
- Condition of property and zoning or use rights.
- Prorations of taxes, insurance, or other obligations.
- Description of any fixtures, appliances, and furnishings that will be included in sale and any warranty as to the condition of such items.
- Inspection rights given to buyer (for example, water, well, mechanical, structural, electrical, termite), who will pay the costs of inspections, and whether the sale is contingent on inspector's approval.
- Statement of who will bear the cost for such items as transfer fees, abstracts of title, and closing costs.
- Conditions under which the offer may be canceled.

the offer will provide that if the seller accepts the offer (and forms a contract with the buyer), the buyer will forfeit this money if he or she breaches the contract. Other damages for breach might also be specified in the agreement. If the deal goes through, the earnest money is usually applied to the purchase price of the real estate.

Once the offer is submitted to the seller, the seller has three options: he or she can accept the offer, reject it, or modify its terms—thus creating a counteroffer. The buyer, in turn, can then accept, reject, or modify the terms of the counteroffer—thus creating yet another counteroffer for the seller to consider. In real estate transactions, bargaining over price and other conditions of the sale frequently involves the exchange of one or more counteroffers. Once one of the parties accepts an offer or counteroffer, a contract is formed by which both parties normally must abide.

The Role of the Escrow Agent

The sale of real property normally involves three parties: the seller, the buyer, and the escrow agent. Frequently, both the buyer and the seller are assisted by real estate agents, attorneys, and paralegals. The *escrow agent*, which may be a title company, bank, or special escrow company, acts as a neutral party in the transaction and facilitates the sale by allowing the buyer and the seller to complete the transaction without having to exchange documents and funds directly with each other.

To understand the vital role played by the escrow agent, consider the problems that might otherwise arise. Essentially, in the sale of property, the buyer gives the seller money, and the seller conveys (transfers) to the buyer a deed, representing ownership rights in the property (deeds will be discussed shortly). Neither the buyer nor the seller wishes to part with the money or the deed until all conditions of the sale and purchase have been met.

The solution is the use of an escrow agent. The escrow agent holds the deed until the buyer pays the seller for the property at the *closing* (the final step in the sale of real estate).

EXHIBIT 9.5
The Concept of Escrow

This exhibit illustrates the triangular relationship among the escrow agent, the seller, and the buyer in a transfer of real estate. As the exhibit indicates, the seller gives the escrow agent the deed, the buyer gives the escrow agent the money, and at the time of the closing, the escrow agent gives the seller the money and the buyer the deed—simultaneously.

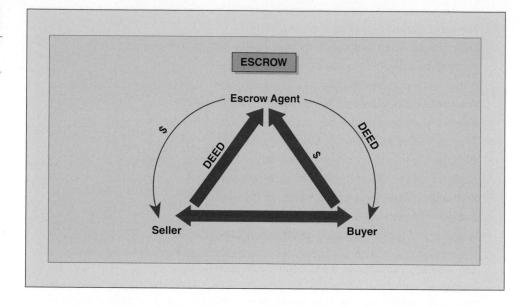

The escrow agent also holds any money paid by the buyer, including the earnest money mentioned above, until the sale is completed. At the closing, the escrow agent receives money from the buyer, the buyer is given the deed, and the seller is given the money. The triangular relationship that exists among the buyer, the seller, and the escrow agent is depicted in Exhibit 9.5.

Financing

Because few buyers want to, or can, pay cash for real property, buyers generally need to secure financing. Commonly, a buyer of real property finances the purchase by obtaining a loan (called a **mortgage**) from a bank, a mortgage company, or some other party. When a buyer obtains a mortgage, the bank or mortgage company takes a security interest in the property—that is, the bank or mortgage company secures the right to claim ownership of the property if the buyer fails to make the scheduled payments.

mortgage
A written instrument giving a creditor an interest in the debtor's property as security for a debt.

Inspection of the Premises

In addition to obtaining financing, buyers may have the premises inspected to see if there are any major electrical or plumbing problems, structural defects, termite or insect infestations, or other concerns. Often, the contract of sale is conditioned on the outcome of these inspections. If problems surface during the inspections, the buyer and seller may negotiate (or may have included in the contract) arrangements specifying which party will pay what portion of the costs of any necessary repairs.

Title Examination and Insurance

Whenever title to property is transferred from one party to another, that transfer is recorded by the county recording office. A *title examination* involves checking these records carefully to make sure that the seller is actually the owner of the property described in the purchase offer and to determine whether claims (such as a tax lien for overdue taxes) on the property

Ethics Watch!

ACCURATE PAPERWORK AND THE SALE OF REAL ESTATE

Art Guthrie, a paralegal, was drafting a real estate offer for one of the firm's clients. Instead of keying in $90,000 as the amount being offered for the property, Art accidentally entered $900,000. No one detected the error. The seller accepted the offer, and only when Art was reviewing the closing package did he notice the mistake and tell his supervising attorney about it. The seller agreed to cancel the contract (because in the meantime she had received an offer of $110,000 for the property). Eventually the client paid $115,000—$25,000 more than he otherwise would have had to pay—for the desired property. The client sued the attorney for negligence, alleging that the attorney had breached the duty of competence and seeking the extra $25,000 in damages. The picture emerging from this hypothetical scenario is clear: when handling paperwork relating to real estate transactions, as with other legal documents, the paralegal must make absolutely sure that the documents are accurate.

exist that were not disclosed by the seller. The title examination is an important task to be accomplished prior to the purchase of real estate. The title examination may be undertaken by the buyer or the buyer's attorney (paralegals frequently assume this responsibility) or by the lending institution, a title insurance company, or another party.

Normally, the history of past ownership and transfers of the property is already summarized in a document called an *abstract*, which may be in the possession of the seller (or the holder of the seller's mortgage or other company or institution). After examining the abstract, the title examiner gives an opinion as to the validity of the title. Title examinations are not foolproof, though, and buyers of real property generally purchase title insurance to protect their interests in the event that some defect in the title was not discovered during the examination.

The Closing

One of the terms specified in the contract is when the closing will take place. The *closing*—also called the settlement or the closing of escrow—is coordinated by the escrow agent. At the closing, several events happen nearly simultaneously: the buyer signs the mortgage note (if the purchase was financed by a mortgage), title insurance is obtained, the seller receives the proceeds of the sale (the purchase price less the amount previously paid by the buyer and less closing costs), and the deed to the property is delivered to the buyer.

A **deed** is the instrument of conveyance (transfer) of real property. As indicated on the sample deed in Exhibit 9.6 on the following page, a deed gives the names of the seller (*grantor*) and buyer (*grantee*), describes the property being transferred, evidences the seller's intent to convey (for example, "I hereby bargain, sell, grant, or give") the property, and contains the seller's signature.

deed
A document by which title to property is transferred from one party to another.

EXHIBIT 9.6
A Sample Deed

Date: May 31, 2007

Grantor: RAYMOND A. GRANT AND WIFE, JOANN H. GRANT

Grantor's Mailing Address (including county):
                         4106 North Loop Drive
                         Austin, Travis County, Texas
Grantee: DAVID F. HOGAN AND WIFE, RUTH E. HOGAN, AS
                         JOINT TENANTS WITH RIGHT OF SURVIVORSHIP
Grantee's Mailing Address (including county):
                         5929 Fuller Drive
                         Austin, Travis County, Texas

Consideration:
For and in consideration of the sum of Ten and No/100 Dollars ($10.00) and other
valuable consideration to the undersigned paid by the grantees herein named, the receipt
of which is hereby acknowledged, and for which no lien is retained, either express or
implied.

Property (including any improvements):
Lot 23, Block "A", Northwest Hills, Green Acres Addition, Phase 4, Travis County, Texas,
according to the map or plat of record in volume 22, pages 331-336, of the Plat Records
of Travis County, Texas.

Reservations from and Exceptions to Conveyance and Warranty:

This conveyance with its warranty is expressly made subject to the following:
Easements and restrictions of record in volume 7863, page 53, volume 8430, page 35,
volume 8133, page 152, of the Real Property Records of Travis County, Texas; and to
any other restrictions and easements affecting said property which are of record in
Travis County, Texas.

    Grantor, for the consideration and subject to the reservations from and exceptions to conveyance and
warranty, grants, sells, and conveys to Grantee the property, together with all and singular the rights and
appurtenances thereto in any wise belonging, to have and hold it to Grantee, Grantee's heirs, executors,
administrators, successors, or assigns forever. Grantor binds Grantor and Grantor's heirs, executors,
administrators, and successors to warrant and forever defend all and singular the property to Grantee and
Grantee's heirs, executors, administrators, successors, and assigns against every person whomsoever
lawfully claiming or to claim the same or any part thereof, except as to the reservations from and exceptions
to conveyance and warranty.

    When the context requires, singular nouns and pronouns include the plural.

                                                    BY: _Raymond A. Grant_
                                                        Raymond A. Grant
                                                    BY: _JoAnn H. Grant_
                                                        JoAnn H. Grant

STATE OF TEXAS
COUNTY OF TRAVIS
    This instrument was acknowledged before me on the   31st   day of   May 2007
by   Raymond A. and JoAnn H. Grant

                                                    Rosemary Potter
                                                    Notary Public, State of Texas
                                                    Notary's name (printed): ROSEMARY POTTER

Notary Seal
                                                    Notary's commission expires: 1/31/2009

Closing costs comprise fees for services, including those performed by the lender, escrow
agent, and title company. These costs can range from several hundred to several thousand
dollars, depending on the amount of the mortgage loan and other conditions of the sale, and
must be paid, in cash, at the closing. Usually, the buyer and seller can learn in advance, by

Developing Paralegal Skills

REVIEWING THE CLOSING PACKAGE

Andy Casmis, a paralegal, is reviewing a closing package for his supervising attorney, a sole practitioner. Andy's job is to request the closing package from the lender and review it before the closing takes place. The closing package consists of the purchaser's requirements, closing statement, settlement statement, deed, bill of sale, mortgage documents, and title insurance policy. Andy needs to make sure that there are no mistakes in the closing documents.

CHECKLIST FOR REVIEWING A CLOSING PACKAGE

- Order the closing package as far in advance as possible.
- Set aside uninterrupted time for reviewing the closing package.
- Review the address and legal description of the property in the mortgage note and the deed for accuracy.
- Using a calculator, review the purchaser's requirements sheet, the closing statement, the bill of sale, and the mortgage documents to make sure that there are no numerical errors.
- Review each document to make sure that the parties' names are listed and spelled correctly.
- Review the deed to ensure that the ownership rights are accurately listed and that the names are correct.
- Contact the client and remind him or her of the items that must be brought to the closing.

---

checking (or having their attorneys or real estate agents check) with the escrow agent handling the closing, what the closing costs will be. Also, under the federal Real Estate Settlement Procedures Act of 1974, lending institutions must notify—within a specified time period—each applicant for a mortgage loan of the precise costs that must be paid at the closing.

Leases

An owner of either personal or real property can lease, or rent, the property to another person or a business firm. A **lease** is a contractual agreement under which a property owner (the *lessor*) agrees to rent his or her property to another (the *lessee*) for a specified period of time. Leases of personal property (cars or equipment) are covered by the Uniform Commercial Code, which spells out the rights and duties of lessors and lessees.

Leases of real property are governed in part by the common law of contracts and in part (and to an increasing extent) by state statutory law. Although under the common law, an oral lease is valid, a party who seeks to enforce an oral lease may have difficulty proving its existence. In most states, statutes mandate that leases exceeding one year's duration must be in writing. When real property is leased, the lessor (landlord) retains ownership rights to the property, but the lessee (tenant) obtains the right to the exclusive possession of the property. Most leases, however, give the landlord the right to come onto the property for certain purposes—to make repairs, for example.

On the Web

If you are interested in learning why the Real Estate Settlement Procedures Act of 1974 was passed and what it requires of lending institutions, go to **http://www.hud.gov/offices/hsg/sfh/res/respa hm.cfm**. You can find the full act online at **http://www.fdic.gov/regulations/laws/rules**.

lease

In real property law, a contract by which the owner of real property (the landlord) grants to a person (the tenant) an exclusive right to use and possess the property, usually for a specified period of time, in return for rent or some other form of payment.

EXHIBIT 9.7
Typical Lease Terms

Term of lease: Indicates the duration of the lease, including the beginning and ending dates.

Rental: Indicates the amount of the rent payments and the intervals (monthly or yearly, for example) at which rent will be paid.

Maintenance and use of leased premises: Describes which areas will be repaired and maintained by the landlord and which by the tenant.

Utilities: Stipulates which utilities (electricity, water, and so forth) will be paid by the landlord and by the tenant.

Alterations: Normally states that no structural alterations to the property will be made by the tenant without the landlord's consent.

Assignment: States whether the tenant's rights in the lease can be assigned (transferred) by the tenant to a third party.

Insurance: Indicates whether the landlord or the tenant will insure the premises against damage. (Normally, the landlord secures insurance coverage for the building, and the tenant obtains a "renter's policy" for his or her own personal property—furniture and other possessions—that will be housed in the building.)

Taxes: Designates which party will be liable for taxes or special assessments on the property. (Normally, the landlord assumes this responsibility, but in some commercial leases, the tenant agrees to take on this obligation.)

Destruction: States what will happen in the event that the premises are totally destroyed by fire or other casualty.

Quiet enjoyment: A covenant (promise) by the landlord that the tenant shall possess and enjoy the premises without interference by any third party.

Termination: Usually specifies that the tenant's right to possession of the premises ends when the lease expires.

Renewal: Indicates that the tenant has an option to renew the lease if the landlord is notified of the intent to renew within a certain period of time (such as one month or three months) before the lease expires.

Paralegals frequently draft or review lease agreements for clients (or for corporate employers), and you should be familiar with the types of terms that are typically included in a lease agreement, or contract. Normally, a lease contract will specify the names of the lessor and lessee, the location of the premises being leased, the amount of rent to be paid by the lessee, the duration of the lease, and the respective rights and duties of the parties in regard to the use and maintenance of the leased premises. Exhibit 9.7 illustrates the kinds of provisions that are commonly included in lease agreements.

PROPERTY LAW AND THE PARALEGAL

Paralegals frequently undertake tasks that require an understanding of the law governing real property. If you work for a small legal practice, some of your work may involve assisting your supervising attorney in handling real estate transactions. If you work for a law firm (or a department within a law firm) that specializes in real estate transactions, you will have extensive contact with buyers and sellers of real property, as well as with real estate agents, title companies, banking institutions that finance real estate purchases, and the attorneys and paralegals who work on behalf of the other parties in real estate sales.

If a real estate agent is involved, the agent will assist the seller or the buyer in drawing up a purchase contract, in arranging for inspections, in having the title examined and title insurance procured, and in preparing the closing papers. In this situation, your job will be to assist the attorney in verifying, on behalf of your client, that all of the documents needed have been prepared and that the documents contain the correct purchase price, mortgage amount, property description, and other terms. Generally, you will be responsible for making sure that the documents are in order and that the client's interests are fully protected. (See this chapter's *Featured Guest* article on the following two pages for a discussion of the role of a legal due-diligence team in purchases of real estate.)

Here are just some of the types of tasks that you might perform as a real estate paralegal working for a law firm:

- Interview a client who wants to buy or sell property.
- Assist the client with the preliminary negotiations (offers and counteroffers) leading up to the purchase contract.
- Draft the offers and counteroffers, as well as other documents necessary to the sale.
- Conduct a title examination by going to the county courthouse and examining previous property transfers.
- Obtain or create a title abstract.
- Contact the title company to arrange for the closing.
- Handle the escrow account.
- Attend the closing. (In some states, paralegals are allowed to represent clients at closings.)

Corporations also purchase and sell property, and some larger corporations have real estate groups within their legal departments. If you work for a corporation that buys and sells a significant amount of property, your employer will be the "client," and you will perform similar tasks on the corporation's behalf.

The law governing real property also comes into play in contexts other than real estate purchases or sales. If you work in the area of probate administration, for example, you will need to have an understanding of how ownership rights in property are acquired and transferred.

FEATURED **Guest**

PROTECTING THE REAL ESTATE PURCHASER: THE LEGAL DUE-DILIGENCE TEAM

BIOGRAPHICAL NOTE

Daniel F. Hinkel earned a J.D. from the University of Illinois School of Law and a B.S. from Eastern Illinois University. He is vice president and corporate counsel for ING Investment Management, LLC, in Atlanta, Georgia.

Hinkel has taught in paralegal programs for a number of years. He is also the author of a number of books, including Practical Real Estate Law and Essentials of Practical Real Estate Law, both published by Thomson Delmar Learning.

Home ownership is at an all-time high, while commercial real estate has enjoyed increased demand from both domestic and foreign buyers. Whether the purchaser is acquiring a home for a residence or purchasing a shopping center as an investment, the transaction will be governed by the common law doctrine of *caveat emptor,* "let the buyer beware." This doctrine provides that a seller, absent an express warranty, is not liable to a buyer for any existing defects regarding the title to the land or any physical defects in the improvements located on the land. Even misrepresentations made by a seller concerning the property are generally not recoverable in an action for fraud if the purchaser could have discovered the truth from proper due diligence, such as a thorough inspection of the home or a title examination.

THE LEGAL DUE-DILIGENCE TEAM

A legal due-diligence team can save a real estate purchaser money and future headaches. Paralegals are important members of the legal

due-diligence team. The extent of the team's work will depend on the nature of the property being purchased. A home may require only a title and survey review. An investment property may require a review of title, survey, government regulations, leases, and other contracts that affect the use of the property.

TITLE DUE DILIGENCE

One of the main responsibilities of the legal due-diligence team is to determine that when the sale has been completed, the purchaser will have good title of ownership to the real property. The legal due-diligence team should require that the public real property title records be examined and the examination carefully reviewed to determine the title's marketability. It is common in many communities for a title insurance company to examine the public records and provide the legal due-diligence team with a title report or commitment to issue title insurance and copies of all the recorded documents listed in the title report. The team paralegal will review this report and, in consultation with the team attorney, determine if the title matters affect the marketability and the purchaser's proposed use of the property. The legal due-diligence team will also arrange for a title insurance policy insuring the purchaser's ownership to be issued at the time of purchase.

SURVEY DUE DILIGENCE

The legal due-diligence team should require a survey of the property. Most surveys are "as built," meaning the survey locates all physical improvements on the land in relation to the boundary lines of the land. The surveyor will locate all fences, walls, driveways, pavements, building structures, and natural features, such as streams and ponds. The survey will also indicate if the property is in a flood hazard area, which may require flood insurance.

The team paralegal may review the survey. A survey is usually reviewed in conjunction with the title commitment. This review will determine that all matters that would have a physical presence on the property, such as easements or building setback lines, are shown on the survey. The review will confirm that the description of the real property matches the description owned by the seller and that the description can be insured by the title insurance company. If there are differences between the description shown on the survey and in the title report, the legal due-diligence team will investigate the matter and determine why the differences exist and how they can be resolved.

In addition, the survey reviewer will note the location of improvements on the property and look for encroachments either onto or from the property or encroachments of buildings over easements. The reviewer will also determine if there is proper access to the property from a public street and if the necessary utilities, such as electricity, gas, and water, are available.

GOVERNMENT REGULATION DUE DILIGENCE

For an investment property, the legal due-diligence team will inquire into government regulations that affect the property. The team will obtain confirmation of the property's zoning status and determine if the purchaser's use or intended use of the property will comply with the uses permitted by the zoning.

LEASE REVIEW

The legal due-diligence team may review leases in connection with an investment property. The leases provide income to the purchaser,

> *"One of the main responsibilities of the legal due diligence team is to determine that when the sale has been completed, the purchaser will have good title of ownership to the real property."*

and the price of the property may be based on assumptions regarding the rental income contained in the leases. The team paralegal may review the leases and prepare an abstract, or summary, of the leases. The summary review will verify the terms of the lease, such as rental terms, the duration of the lease, and the various obligations and responsibilities of both the landlord and tenant. A lease will also be reviewed to determine if the tenant has an option to purchase the property. If the lease contains an option to purchase, the team attorney will carefully discuss the option with the purchaser to verify that it is acceptable.

The legal due-diligence team may prepare and require each tenant to sign an estoppel certificate. An estoppel certificate signed by the tenant generally confirms the basic facts regarding the lease, such as rental terms and duration and payment of security deposits. Also, it will state that there is no default under the lease and that the tenant has no defenses, setoffs, recoupments, claims, or counterclaims of any nature against the landlord.

THE LEGAL DUE-DILIGENCE TEAM PROVIDES VALUE

A legal due-diligence team made up of attorneys and paralegals performs an important role in protecting a purchaser from the harsh effects of the *caveat emptor* rule. A legal team's thorough investigation and competent review and analysis of supporting documents provide good value for the real property purchaser-client.

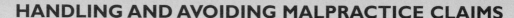

Today's Professional Paralegal

HANDLING AND AVOIDING MALPRACTICE CLAIMS

Delia Harmon works as a paralegal for the managing partner of Duke & Cruthers, LLP, a midsized law firm. The managing partner, Jeremy Wheaton, tells Delia that the partners are switching insurance companies for their malpractice insurance policy. The former company significantly increased its premium for malpractice coverage, and the partners decided that the firm could obtain similar coverage from another company at a much lower cost.

Jeremy hands the new policy to Delia and asks her to carefully review and then summarize in a memorandum the policy's major terms and conditions. Jeremy also hands Delia a handwritten list of ideas on how malpractice claims should be handled in the future and asks her to transform his notes into clear instructions to be included in the memorandum. Finally, Jeremy points out to Delia that the best way to handle malpractice claims is to avoid them to begin with. Jeremy asks Delia to draft a series of tips on this topic to include in the memorandum. "Can you finish this by tomorrow morning?" asks Jeremy. "I'd like to review it and have a final draft ready to circulate to the partners before I leave town tomorrow afternoon." "Well," responds Delia, "I could finish it by then if I could postpone the work on the research memorandum that I'm preparing for you on the *AlphaCom* case." Jeremy said that she could put off the *AlphaCom* case until the next day, so Delia cleared her desk and started reviewing the new malpractice policy.

DRAFTING THE MEMORANDUM

Once she has read the policy carefully, Delia begins to draft the memorandum to the partners. She summarizes the policy's terms and conditions in clear, concise language. Delia has had years of experience in reviewing and summarizing legal documents, so this part of the task comes easily for her. More difficult is trying to decipher Jeremy's handwritten notes on how the partners should handle malpractice claims. After she is certain that she understands Jeremy's thoughts on the matter, she creates a new subheading in the memorandum titled "How to Handle Malpractice Claims." Under the heading, she includes the following bulleted list:

- If a client brings a malpractice action, review the client's file immediately.
- Create a concise summary of the client's file so that you and the other partners can quickly review the nature of the client's case and the alleged basis for the client's claim of malpractice.

KEY TERMS AND CONCEPTS

- Determine how the partners and the firm can best respond to the claim. At a minimum, check the statute of limitations for malpractice claims to see if the client's delay in bringing the claim could bar the action from the outset.

- If the claim is justified, determine whether the firm should offer to settle the claim out of court. If so, decide on the amount the firm should offer to the client in settlement.

- Promptly report the claim to the malpractice insurance carrier, to prevent the insurance company from later using any delay in reporting the claim as a defense against payment under the policy.

TIPS ON HOW TO AVOID MALPRACTICE CLAIMS

Delia then turns to what, for her, is the most difficult aspect of her task—thinking of suggestions for how the partners can avoid malpractice claims. Finally, she comes up with the following tips:

- Cultivate a good relationship with clients by being sensitive to their needs and dealing with those needs courteously and promptly. A satisfied client will not likely wish to bring a malpractice action.

- If you are too busy to communicate with clients on the progress of their cases, ask the paralegal who works with you to do this and help keep the communication channels open.

- Make sure that all significant communications with clients are in writing. This includes keeping a written record of telephone conversations with clients. If questions arise later over what you did or did not say to a particular client on a specific matter, you can refer to your written notes.

- Before billing clients for overdue payments, try to wait until the statute of limitations on malpractice actions has passed. Then, if a client responds to the letter with a malpractice claim, it will have no legal effect.[a]

Delia can think of nothing more to say, so she prints out the draft of the memorandum and places it on Jeremy's desk for him to review the next morning.

a. The suggestions in this feature are based in part on a discussion of this topic in Abigail J. Gardner and Marcy L. Jankovich, "Avoiding Malpractice Claims," *Facts & Findings*, Vol. 32. No. 2 (August 2005), pp. 44–45.

chapter summary   Insurance Law and Real Property

Insurance Law

1. *Classifications*—See Exhibit 9.1 on page 303.
2. *Terminology*—
    a. Policy—The insurance contract.
    b. Premium—The consideration paid to the insurer for the policy.
    c. Underwriter—The insurance company.
    d. Insurer—The insurance company.
    e. Insured—The person covered by the insurance.

(Continued)

   f. Insurance agent—A representative of the insurance company.

   g. Insurance broker—Ordinarily, an independent contractor.

   h. Beneficiary—A person to receive payment under the policy.

3. *Insurable interest*—An insurable interest exists whenever an individual or entity benefits from the preservation of the property to be insured or the continued health or life of the person to be insured. For life insurance, an insurable interest must exist at the time the policy is issued. For property insurance, an insurable interest must exist at the time of the loss.

4. *The insurance contract*—

   a. Laws governing—The general principles of contract law are applied; the insurance industry is also heavily regulated by the states.

   b. Application—An insurance applicant is bound by any false statements that appear in the application (subject to certain exceptions), which is part of the insurance contract. Misstatements or misrepresentations may be grounds for voiding the policy.

   c. Effective date—Coverage on an insurance policy can begin when a binder (a written memorandum indicating that a formal policy is pending and stating its essential terms) is written; when the policy is issued; at the time of contract formation; or, depending on the terms of the contract, when certain conditions are met.

   d. Provisions and clauses—See Exhibit 9.2 on page 306. Words will be given their ordinary meanings, and any ambiguity in the policy will be interpreted against the insurance company. When the written policy has not been delivered and it is unclear whether an insurance contract actually exists, the uncertainty will be resolved against the insurance company. The court will presume that the policy is in effect unless the company can show otherwise.

   e. Defenses against payment to the insured—Defenses include misrepresentation, fraud, or violation of warranties by the applicant.

Real Property

Real property (also called real estate or realty) includes land and all things attached to the land (such as buildings and plants), as well as subsurface and air rights. All other types of property, both tangible and intangible, are personal property.

1. *Ownership rights in property*—

   a. Fee simple—The most complete form of ownership, entitling the holder to use, possess, or dispose of the property however he or she chooses during his or her lifetime.

   b. Tenancy in common—Co-ownership in which each party owns an undivided interest in the property that passes to his or her heirs at death.

   c. Joint tenancy—Co-ownership in which each party owns an undivided interest in the property that automatically passes to the surviving joint tenant or tenants on his or her death.

   d. Life estate—An interest in property that entitles a specified individual to possess, use, and benefit from the property for the duration of the person's life.

   e. Future interest—An interest in property that will arise in the future.

2. *The transfer and sale of real property*—Real property can be transferred as a gift, by inheritance, by lease, or by sale. Most of the time, real property is transferred by sale, which typically involves the following steps.

a. The buyer makes a purchase offer, often conditioned on obtaining financing, and pays an earnest money deposit.

b. If the seller accepts the offer, a contract is formed. Real estate agents may assist both the buyer and the seller in negotiating the terms.

c. An escrow agent acts as a neutral party in the transaction, holding the deed and any money paid by the buyer until the sale is completed.

d. Most buyers obtain a mortgage loan to finance the purchase. The holder of the mortgage then has a security interest in the property.

e. Often, the sale is contingent on certain inspections of the property.

f. A title examination is performed to ensure that the seller is actually the owner of the property and that no liens exist of which the buyer was not aware.

g. At the closing, the buyer signs the mortgage note (if the sale is financed), title insurance is obtained, the seller is paid the purchase price (less any closing costs), and the buyer is given the deed to the property.

3. *Leases*—The owner of real property (the lessor) may agree (contract) to rent the property out to another (the lessee) for a specified period of time. The lessee has the exclusive right to use the property. Leases are governed by contract law and by state statutes. Leases are usually in writing and must be written if the lease period exceeds one year.

QUESTIONS FOR REVIEW

1. What is insurance? How do insurance policies help to manage risk?

2. What are some classifications of insurance? What is an insurable interest? What is required for someone to have an insurable interest in property? in another's life?

3. What is the difference between an insurance agent and an insurance broker? Why is this difference significant for people seeking insurance coverage?

4. What might result if an insurance applicant makes false statements in an insurance application? In this situation, will the policy be enforceable? Explain.

5. What is an incontestability clause? What are some other types of clauses that are typically included in an insurance contract?

6. Under what circumstances can an insurer cancel an insurance policy?

7. What is the difference between real property and personal property? What is a fee simple? What are some other ways in which ownership rights in property can be held?

8. What is the most common way of transferring ownership rights in property?

9. What law governs the sale of real property? Describe the basic steps involved in the sale of real estate.

10. What is a lease? Describe some of the provisions that are typically included in lease contracts when real property is involved.

ETHICAL QUESTIONS

1. Joanne Dorman, a paralegal, works in the claims department of an automobile insurance company. One day, she is asked to review a claim brought by Derek Farmer, her nephew. Joanne's sister (Derek's mother) mentioned to Joanne that Derek broke his windshield recently when he accidentally ran into a mailbox beside the road leading to their rural home. In the claim that she is reviewing, however, Derek states that a rock hit his windshield. Joanne understands immediately what Derek is trying to do. Derek's policy states that his collision coverage (which would apply to the

mailbox accident) has a $500 deductible. His comprehensive coverage (which would apply if a rock had hit his windshield) has a deductible of only $50. It is clear to Joanne that Derek is trying to avoid having to pay the full $500 deductible. Joanne knows that Derek is a struggling college student with few financial resources. In contrast, the insurance company is a national entity that could easily absorb the extra cost. What should Joanne do in this situation?

2. Melinda Park, a paralegal, has been asked to review an offer to purchase real estate. The offer was made by a client who is a first-time buyer and has no experience in real estate transactions. The client wants to understand what the legal obligations of the buyer and the seller are before he signs the offer. Melinda is new to her job, and her supervising attorney, Chad Abraham, gives her the offer to review because he thinks it will be good experience for her. She is to go through the offer, summarize each provision, and note the legal effect of each provision on both the buyer and the seller.

Melinda begins to read the offer, and she sees a paragraph that states that the premises are being sold "as is." Melinda thinks that she understands what this provision means, so she doesn't check on its actual meaning. Instead, she writes, "The house is sold as it appears, and there is no legal effect on the buyer." (The "as is" clause in fact means that there is no warranty on the house; if there is anything wrong with it, such as a leaking roof, the seller is not obligated to cover repair costs. The buyer must pay for the repairs himself or herself.) What has Melinda done? How could she have better handled the situation?

3. Using the facts from the situation in the preceding question, assume that Melinda's supervising attorney does not have time to review her work before giving it to the client. Has the attorney violated any ethical or legal obligation? What effect might Melinda's explanation of the legal effect of the "as is" clause have on the client? On Melinda? On the attorney?

PRACTICE QUESTIONS AND ASSIGNMENTS

1. Review the diagram in Exhibit 9.5 on page 316. Explain the triangular relationship among the parties to an escrow agreement, and explain each party's responsibility.

2. Using the material presented in Exhibit 9.6 on page 318, "A Sample Deed," and the following facts, draft a deed to real property.

   - At a closing on January 22, 2007, Robert Smith and Sally Smith, husband and wife, of 987 Packard Street, Austin, Texas, transfer their summer cottage to John and William Jones, brothers, for consideration of $250,000.00 cash. John Jones lives at 10101 Summit Place, New City, Texas. William Jones's address is 99901 Hill Street, Casper, Texas. The Jones brothers will own the cottage as tenants in common.

   - The legal description of the property is Lot 91 of Whiteacre Subdivision, Amarillo County, Texas, according to the plat map contained in volume 89, pages 123–129, of the Plat Records of Amarillo County, Texas.

   - The conveyance with a warranty is expressly made subject to the Easements and Restrictions of Record in volume 7877, page 456, and volume 9988, page 431, of the Real Property Records of Amarillo County, Texas, and to any other restrictions and easements affecting the property that are of record in Amarillo County, Texas.

   - The notary public who will acknowledge the deed is Rosemary Potter, and her commission expires January 31, 2009.

3. Identify the insurance law terms that match the following definitions:

   a. A prediction concerning potential loss based on known and unknown factors.

   b. The one assuming a risk in return for the payment of a premium.

   c. A contract between the insurer and the insured in which, for consideration, the insurer agrees to compensate the insured for a specified loss.

   d. An interest either in a person's life or well-being or in property that is sufficiently substantial to justify insuring against injury to or death of the person or damage to the property.

   e. A written, temporary insurance policy.

4. Identify each of the following types of insurance based on the coverage that it provides:

   a. Protects against losses incurred by the insured as a result of being held liable for personal injuries or property damage sustained by others.

   b. Insures employers against liability for injuries or losses.

   c. Provides indemnity against losses in trade or losses caused by the dishonesty of employees, the insolvency of debtors, or breaches of contract.

   d. Protects the insured against some or all risks of loss to the insured's residence and its contents or liability arising from the use of the property.

   e. Protects against liability imposed on the insured as a result of injuries to the person or property of another.

f. Protects professionals (physicians, lawyers, and others) against claims brought against then by their patients or clients; a form of liability insurance.

5. Identify the following insurance contract provisions and clauses:

   a. The date on which the insurance coverage begins.

   b. A form that is filled out by the insured and made a part of the insurance contract.

   c. A clause that provides that if the owner insures the property up to a specified percentage of its replacement value, she or he will be reimbursed fully for any loss.

   d. A clause providing that after a policy has been in effect for a specified length of time, the insurer cannot contest statements made in the application.

   e. A clause requiring arbitration of disputes that may arise between the insurer and the insured concerning the settlement of claims.

6. List and explain the four important facts that affect the effective date of an insurance policy.

7. Identify the types of ownership rights described in the following statements.

   a. John and Linda, a brother and a sister, jointly own a cottage that they inherited from their mother. They have rights of survivorship.

   b. Jeannette conveys her beachfront property to her mother for as long as her mother lives. On her mother's death, the property is to go to Jeannette's daughter.

   c. Louise Winter owns her home, and she can use, possess, or dispose of it as she pleases. On Louise's death, the property will descend to her heirs.

   d. John Tully and Sam Marsh jointly own a large farm in Iowa. If either of them dies, the heirs of the deceased owner will inherit that owner's share of the farm.

8. Identify the following steps in a real estate sales transaction:

   a. An offer or counteroffer is accepted.

   b. Title to the property is reviewed to determine the seller's ownership interest and to determine if any liens against the property exist.

   c. The escrow agent transfers the deed to the buyer and the proceeds of the sale to the seller to complete the sale.

   d. The buyer tenders a sum of money, along with the offer.

9. Identify which of the following terms belong in a lease agreement:

   a. Buyer's purchase offer.

   b. Quiet enjoyment.

   c. Taxes.

   d. Closing.

   e. Termination.

   f. Title examination.

QUESTIONS FOR CRITICAL ANALYSIS

1. The insurance industry is subject to government regulation, particularly at the state level. Can you think of any reasons for this? What might happen if the industry were not regulated?

2. "When people obtain insurance to protect them against certain risks, they become more careless with respect to protecting against those risks themselves." Do you agree with this statement? Why or why not?

3. Statistics show that the extent of risk assumed by insurance companies varies depending on the gender of the insured. Many people contend that laws prohibiting gender-based insurance rates are thus fundamentally unfair. Do you agree with this contention? Explain your reasoning.

4. Who benefits from an incontestability clause, the insurer or the insured? Why are these clauses included in insurance contracts? What might result if they were not?

5. Why is property ownership described as a "bundle of rights"? What is one called who owns the entire bundle? Is it ever possible to own less than the entire bundle? How?

Give an example. Is it possible to share the bundle of rights? How? Give examples.

6. In a real estate sales transaction, the buyer is usually the offeror. Is there any situation in which the seller might become the offeror? Explain.

7. Assume that John submits an offer to Lisa to purchase Lisa's home for $300,000. Lisa responds to John's offer with a counteroffer: she will sell John her home for $325,000. John then offers to purchase the home for $325,000, and Lisa accepts the offer. In each of these transactions, who is the offeror and who is the offeree? At what point is a contract for the sale of the home formed?

8. Suppose that a certificate of deposit (CD) owned by two joint tenants is given by one of the joint tenants as security for a loan (without the other joint tenant's knowledge). Further suppose that the joint tenant dies after defaulting (failing to pay) on the loan. Who has superior rights in the CD, the creditor or the other surviving joint tenant? Why?

PROJECTS

1. Locate a homeowners' or renters' insurance policy. Find the effective date and determine whether a binder was initially issued. Also, try to locate coinsurance, cancellation, appraisal, antilapse, and multiple insurance clauses. Note that not all policies have the same coverage, so it is possible that not all of these clauses will be present in the insurance policy. Write a one-page description of the clauses that are included in the policy, including the effective date.

2. Call a local insurance agent to find out the cost and coverage of an automobile insurance policy for a 2006 Volvo S80 automobile that is driven to work—a total of 40 miles per day. Ask about different deductibles. Write a three-paragraph summary of the coverage and prices quoted. Include the factors (clauses and/or coverage) that make the price of the policy vary.

3. Visit the register of deeds office for your county. Ask to see how and where deeds are recorded. Find out what the term *liber* means. Write a one-page paper summarizing your visit and explaining the meaning of the term *liber*. Check with your instructor prior to undertaking this project for any special instructions or considerations for your county.

USING INTERNET RESOURCES

1. Go to the Web site of the Insurance Information Institute at **http://www.iii.org**. In the listing on the left side of the screen, select in turn the links to auto, home, and business insurance. Browse through the information given for each of these areas and then answer the following questions:

   a. What six types of coverage may be included in a basic auto policy?

   b. What is comprehensive coverage? What types of losses does this coverage protect against? What is uninsured or underinsured motorist coverage, and when does it come into play?

   c. What is covered by a standard homeowners' insurance policy? In the context of homeowners' insurance, what does liability coverage protect against?

   d. What two types of renters' insurance policies can be purchased? What is the difference between these two types of policies with respect to coverage? What is a floater policy?

   e. What does a business owner's insurance policy cover? What is business interruption insurance?

   f. What types of disasters typically are not covered by business (property) insurance?

2. Access the Web site of the National Association of Insurance Commissioners (NAIC) at **http://www.naic. org** and complete the following exercises:

   a. Select "About the NAIC" from the menu at the top of the screen and read through the NAIC's history and background. When was this organization formed, and why? How many states belong to the organization? What is the primary responsibility of state regulators of the insurance industry?

   b. Return to the home page and click on "NAIC States & Jurisdictions." Then select a particular state and explore the page that opens. List the titles of three articles that are linked to this page.

   c. Return again to the home page and select "Government Relations Office" from the menu at the top of the screen. When the page opens, click on one of the links under "Current Issues." On the page that opens, select one of the issues discussed, read through the site's description of the issue, and explore related legislative information and press releases. Write a one-paragraph summary of the kinds of information concerning this issue that are accessible via this page.

3.  For additional resources, visit our Web site at **http://www.paralegal.delmar. cengage.com**.

END NOTES

1. NALA 2004 National Compensation and Utilization Survey Report, Section 4, p. 15. This information is available online at **http://www.nala.org/Survey_Table.htm**.

2. In at least one case, a court held that a diskette containing a computerized document that could be printed out as "hard copy" was sufficient to constitute written notice of cancellation. See *Clyburn v. Allstate Insurance Co.*, 826 F.Supp. 955 (D.S.C. 1993).

ESTATES AND FAMILY LAW

10

CHAPTER

CHAPTER OUTLINE

Introduction

Family Law

Wills, Trusts, and Estates

AFTER COMPLETING THIS CHAPTER, YOU WILL KNOW:

► What estate planning is and why it is important.

► The various devices that are used in estate planning.

► The requirements for a valid will and the laws that govern property distribution when a person dies without a valid will.

► The legal rights and obligations of parents and children.

► How marital property and debts are divided when a marriage is dissolved.

(library)
a normal result

INTRODUCTION

All of the property that a person owns will be transferred to others on that person's death. For that reason, the laws governing the succession of property are a necessary corollary to the laws concerning private ownership of property. In the first part of this chapter, we examine various devices (procedures or techniques), including wills and trusts, that are often used to transfer a person's real and personal property, or *estate*, after death.

Property also generally plays a role in divorce proceedings, along with other matters, such as child custody and child and spousal support. In the latter part of this chapter, we look at these and other issues that arise in the area of what is generally called *family law*.

WILLS, TRUSTS, AND ESTATES

As mentioned in the chapter introduction, a person's real and personal property will be transferred to others when the person dies. People usually undertake *estate planning* to control how their property will be transferred. *Wills* and *trusts* are two basic devices used in the estate-planning process. We look at these devices, as well as others, in this section. We also discuss the process of *estate administration,* which involves collecting and transferring a decedent's (deceased person's) property.

Wills

testator
One who makes a valid will.

testate
The condition of having died with a valid will.

intestate
The state of having died without a valid will.

intestacy laws
State statutes that specify how property will be distributed when a person dies intestate (without a valid will).

executor
A person appointed by a testator to serve as a personal representative on the testator's death.

administrator
A person appointed by a court to serve as a personal representative for a person who died intestate (without a valid will), who made a will but failed to name an executor, or whose executor cannot serve.

probate
To prove and validate a will. The process of proving and validating a will and settling matters pertaining to the administration of a decedent's estate, guardianship of a decedent's children, and similar matters.

As you learned in Chapter 2, a *will* is the final declaration of how a person desires to have his or her property disposed of after death. The maker of a will is also called a **testator** (from the Latin *testari*, "to make a will"). A will is referred to as a *testamentary disposition* of property, and one who dies after having made a valid will is said to have died **testate**. If no valid will has been executed, a decedent is said to have died **intestate**. When a person dies intestate, state **intestacy laws** govern the distribution of the property among heirs or next of kin.

A will can serve other purposes besides the distribution of property. It can appoint a guardian for minor children or incapacitated adults. It can also appoint a *personal representative* to settle the affairs of the deceased. An **executor** is a personal representative named in a will. An **administrator** is a personal representative appointed by the court for a decedent who died without a will, who made a will but failed to name an executor, or whose executor is unable to serve.

Laws Governing Wills

The laws governing wills come into play when a will is probated. To **probate** (prove) a will means to establish its validity and carry the administration of the estate through a process supervised by a *probate court.* When drafting wills for clients, attorneys and paralegals must make sure that the wills meet the specific requirements imposed by state statute.

Probate laws vary from state to state. In 1969, however, the American Bar Association and the National Conference of Commissioners on Uniform State Laws approved the Uniform Probate Code (UPC). The UPC, which has since been significantly revised, codifies general principles and procedures for the resolution of conflicts in settling estates and relaxes some of the requirements for a valid will contained in earlier state laws. Like other "uniform" laws, the UPC is a model act that does not become law in a state until adopted by that state's legislature. Many states have enacted some part of the UPC and incorporated it into their own probate codes. Nonetheless, probate laws vary widely among states, and paralegals should always check the particular laws of the state involved.

Ethics Watch!

WILLS AND PARALEGAL SUPERVISION

It goes without saying that wills must accurately reflect the testator's wishes and that special care must be exercised in preparing a client's will. After all, unless the will is modified or revoked, it is indeed the "final word" on how the testator intends his or her property to be distributed. You will rest easier if you make sure that your supervising attorney reviews carefully any will that you draft, any subsequent modifications that are made, and particularly the document in its final form. Attorneys have a duty to supervise paralegal work. In regard to wills, as a paralegal you should remind your supervising attorney of this duty, if necessary.

Requirements for a Valid Will

A will must comply with state statutory requirements and formalities. If it does not, it will be declared void, and the decedent's property will be distributed according to state intestacy laws. Generally, most states uphold the following basic requirements for executing a will:

- *The testator must have testamentary capacity.* In other words, the testator must be of legal age (usually eighteen) and sound mind *at the time the will is made.*

- *Generally, a will must be in writing.* In some states, a will can be handwritten. In a few states, *nuncupative* wills (oral "deathbed" wills made before witnesses) that dispose of personal property are permitted.

- *A will must be signed by the testator, generally at the end of the document.*

- *A will must be witnessed.* The number of witnesses (often two, sometimes three), their qualifications, and the manner in which the witnessing must be done are generally determined by state law.

- *In some states, a will must be published.* A will is "published" by an oral declaration by the maker to the witnesses that the document they are about to sign is his or her "last will and testament."

The Probate Process

Typically, probate procedures vary depending on the size of the decedent's estate. For smaller estates, most state statutes provide for the distribution of assets without formal probate proceedings. Faster and less expensive methods are then used. ▶ **EXAMPLE 10.1** Property can be transferred by *affidavit,* which is a statement of facts written down and sworn to voluntarily in the presence of an official authorized to affirm it. Problems or questions can be handled during an administrative hearing. ◀ In addition, some state statutes provide that title to cars, savings and checking accounts, and certain other property can be passed merely by filling out forms.

A majority of states also provide for *family settlement agreements,* which are private agreements among the beneficiaries. Once a will is admitted to probate, the family members can agree to settle among themselves the distribution of the decedent's assets.

On the Web

To learn more about wills and probate procedures, you can access the UPC online at **http://www.law.cornell.edu/uniform**.

On the Web

To view the wills of various famous people, including Elvis Presley and Richard Nixon, go to **http://www.courttv.com/people/wills**.

Developing Paralegal Skills

DRAFTING A CLIENT'S WILL

Mr. Perkins has come to the law firm of Smith & Hardy to have his will prepared. He has previously met with attorney Jennifer Hardy, who has been assisting him in estate planning. Today, Perkins meets with Hardy's paralegal, James Reese, who will review the information that is needed to prepare the will with Perkins.

After the meeting, James returns to his office and begins drafting Perkins's will. Later in the week, after going over the will with Hardy, James will meet with Perkins again so that Perkins can review and sign the will.

CHECKLIST FOR DRAFTING A WILL

- Start with a computerized standard will form.
- Review each provision, or clause, in the standard form.
- Input the client's name, address, and other information.
- Modify the clauses as necessary to fit the client's needs.
- Specifically describe all of the client's assets in the will.
- Number each page and clause of the will.
- Print out the document and carefully proofread it.
- Make any necessary corrections and print out the final copy to be reviewed by your supervising attorney.

Although a family settlement agreement speeds the settlement process, a court order is still needed to protect the estate from future creditors and to clear title to the assets involved. The use of these and other types of summary procedures in estate administration can save time and money.

For larger estates, formal probate proceedings are normally undertaken, and the probate court supervises every aspect of the settlement of the decedent's estate. Additionally, in some situations—such as when a guardian for minor children or for an incompetent person must be appointed and a trust has been created to protect the minor or the incompetent person—more formal probate procedures cannot be avoided. Formal probate proceedings may take several months to complete. As a result, a sizable portion of the decedent's assets (up to perhaps 10 percent) may go toward payment of fees charged by attorneys and personal representatives, as well as court costs.

Trusts

trust
An arrangement in which property is transferred by one person (the grantor, or settlor) to another (the trustee) for the benefit of a third party (the beneficiary).

Trusts are important estate-planning devices that are being increasingly utilized to avoid the costs associated with probating a will. A **trust** involves any arrangement by which legal title to property is transferred from one person (the *settlor,* or *grantor*) to be administered by another (the *trustee*) for the benefit of still another party (the *beneficiary*). ▶ **EXAMPLE 10.2** If Mendel conveys (transfers) his farm to Western Bank to be held for the benefit of his daughters, Mendel has created a trust. Mendel is the *settlor,* or *grantor;* Western Bank is

TRUSTS AND ESTATES PARALEGAL

Susan J. Martin is a paralegal in the trusts and estates department of Devine, Millimet & Branch, a large law firm. Martin has offices in the firm's Manchester, New Hampshire, and Andover, Massachusetts, locations. She has been in the legal profession for over twenty-two years. She worked for nine years as a legal secretary before becoming a paralegal and has worked in both large and small law firms in New Hampshire, Maine, Florida, Colorado, and Montana.

Martin has a certificate from the National Association of Legal Secretaries, a certificate in paralegal studies from the University of New Hampshire, and a bachelor's degree from Franklin Pierce College in New Hampshire. She has been a member of the PACE Development Committee of the National Federation of Paralegal Associations (NFPA) and was an item writer/content area expert for the PACE exam.

Martin served as president of the Paralegal Association of New Hampshire in 1998–1999 and chaired its Committee on Paralegal Education. She was editor of the association's bimonthly newsletter, The Annotator, and also an adjunct member of the Delivery of Legal Services Committee of the New Hampshire Bar Association and a member of the bar association's Technology Section.

What do you like best about your work?

"One of the benefits of working in the trusts and estates field is that you are not involved in contentious lawsuits in which, in many cases, there is no winner and everyone is unhappy. Although estate clients are frequently dealing with grief and loss, they are not openly hostile or defensive. For the most part, clients view the trusts and estates team in a very positive way, and this makes the job very enjoyable."

What is the greatest challenge that you face in your area of work?

"Probably the greatest challenge of my job is keeping informed about the changes in federal and state tax law. The Internal Revenue Code is complex and convoluted, and new rules and regulations are promulgated daily. Also, it is not unusual to have an estate that is subject not only to federal tax laws but also to the tax laws of several states. Sorting out tax obligations and coordinating the timely filing of several tax returns can sometimes be a very difficult task."

What advice do you have for would-be paralegals in your area of work?

> *"To be successful in this field, you must be bright and articulate, and have a passion for detail."*

"To function well as a paralegal in the trusts and estates field, you must have a broad general knowledge of many other fields of law, including real estate, corporations, family law, and even civil litigation. You must also have some knowledge of basic accounting principles. People who function well as paralegals in this field usually have excellent quantitative skills, are extremely organized, are able to manage numerous files and deadlines simultaneously, can exercise sound independent judgment, and can work with a minimum of supervision. You must be computer literate and have proficient keyboarding skills."

What are some tips for success as a paralegal in your area of work?

"To be successful in this field, you must be bright and articulate and have a passion for detail. You should love working with people. Working with the elderly requires compassion, humility, and resourcefulness. In this field in particular, you will meet clients from every social stratum, ethnic background, and cultural association, and that requires patience, tolerance, and good humor."

EXHIBIT 10.1
A Trust Arrangement

In a trust, there is a separation of interests in the trust property. The trustee takes *legal* title, which appears to be complete ownership and possession but which does not include the right to receive any benefits from the property. The beneficiary takes *equitable* title, which is the right to receive all benefits from the property.

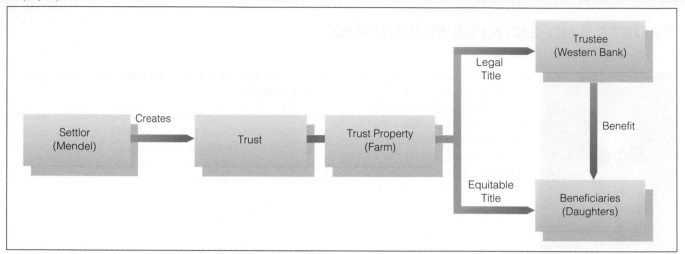

the *trustee;* and Mendel's daughters are the *beneficiaries* (Exhibit 10.1 illustrates this trust arrangement). ◀

There are numerous kinds of trusts, each with its own special characteristics. We look here at some of the most common types of trusts.

Living Trusts

> **inter vivos trust**
> A trust created by the grantor (settlor) and effective during the grantor's lifetime—that is, a trust not established by a will.

A living trust—or *inter vivos* trust (*inter vivos* is Latin for "between or among the living")—is a trust executed by a grantor during his or her lifetime. A living trust may be an attractive estate-planning option because living trusts are not included in the property of a decedent's estate that is probated.

Living trusts can be irrevocable or revocable. The distinction between these two types of living trusts is an important one for estate planners. In an *irrevocable* living trust, the grantor permanently gives up control over the property. In a *revocable* living trust, in contrast, the grantor retains control over the trust property during his or her lifetime.

To establish an irrevocable living trust, the grantor executes a trust deed, and legal title to the trust property passes to the named trustee. The trustee has a duty to administer the property as directed by the grantor for the benefit and in the interest of the beneficiaries. The trustee must preserve the trust property; make it productive; and, if required by the terms of the trust agreement, pay income to the beneficiaries, all in accordance with the terms of the trust. Once an irrevocable *inter vivos* trust has been created, the grantor has, in effect, given over the property for the benefit of the beneficiaries.

To establish a revocable living trust, the grantor deeds the property to the trust but retains the power to amend, alter, or revoke the trust during his or her lifetime. The grantor may also arrange to receive income earned by the trust assets during his or her lifetime. Unless the trust is revoked, the principal of the trust is transferred to the trust beneficiary on the grantor's death.

Testamentary Trusts

> **testamentary trust**
> A trust that is created by will and that does not take effect until the death of the testator.

A trust created by will to come into existence on the settlor's death is called a **testamentary trust**. Although a testamentary trust has a trustee who maintains legal title to the trust property, actions of the trustee are subject to judicial approval. This trustee can be named in the will or appointed by the court. Thus, a testamentary trust does not fail because a trustee has not been named in the will. The legal responsibilities of the trustee are the same as in an *inter vivos* trust.

If a will that establishes a testamentary trust is invalid, then the trust will also be invalid. The property that was supposed to be in the trust will then pass according to intestacy laws, not according to the terms of the trust.

Special Types of Trusts

A trust designed for the benefit of a segment of the public or the public in general is called a *charitable trust*. It differs from other types of trusts in that the identities of the beneficiaries are uncertain. Usually, to be deemed a charitable trust, a trust must be created for charitable, educational, religious, or scientific purposes.

In a *spendthrift trust*, the beneficiary is permitted to draw only a certain portion of the total amount to which he or she is entitled at any one time. This type of trust is used to protect the beneficiary from spending all that is in the trust. The majority of states allow spendthrift trust provisions to prohibit creditors from attaching such trusts. A divorced spouse or a minor child of the beneficiary may be permitted to obtain alimony or child-support payments, however.

A special type of trust created when one person deposits funds into an account, such as a savings account, in his or her own name as a trustee for another is a *Totten trust*.[1] This trust is tentative in that it is revocable at will until the depositor dies or completes the gift in his or her lifetime by some unequivocal act or declaration (for example, delivery of the funds to the intended beneficiary). If the depositor dies before the beneficiary dies and if the depositor has not revoked the trust, normally the beneficiary obtains property rights to the balance on hand. Totten trusts, like *inter vivos* trusts, are not included in probate property.

Other Estate-Planning Devices

Commonly, beneficiaries under a will must wait until the probate process is complete—which can take several months if formal probate proceedings are undertaken—to have access to money or other assets received under the will. For this and other reasons, some persons arrange to have property transferred in ways other than by will and outside the probate process. (For information on finding estate-planning options online, see this chapter's *Technology and Today's Paralegal* feature on the next page.)

One method of accomplishing this is by establishing a living trust, as has already been discussed. A person can also arrange to hold title to certain real or personal property as a joint tenant with a spouse or other person. Remember from Chapter 9 that in a joint tenancy, when one joint tenant dies, the other joint tenant or tenants automatically inherit the deceased tenant's share of the property. (This is true even if the deceased tenant has provided otherwise in his or her will.) Yet another way of transferring property outside the probate process is by making gifts to children or others while one is still living. Finally, to make sure that a spouse, child, or some other dependent is provided for, many people take out life insurance policies. On the death of the policyholder, the proceeds of the policy go directly to the beneficiary and are not involved in the probate process.

Estate Administration

Estate administration is the process of collecting a decedent's assets, settling his or her debts, and distributing all remaining assets. These tasks are undertaken by the decedent's personal representative. In every state, however, a special court, usually called a probate court, oversees the administration of decedents' estates. The rights of both creditors and beneficiaries must be protected during the estate-administration proceedings.

On the Web

You can find a broad array of useful information about estate planning at the Web site of the National Association of Financial and Estate Planning at **http://www.nafep.com**.

estate administration
The process in which a decedent's personal representative settles the affairs of the decedent's estate (collects assets, pays debts and taxes, and distributes the remaining assets to heirs); the process is usually overseen by a probate court.

Technology and Today's Paralegal

ONLINE HELP FOR ESTATE PLANNING

The Internet offers an abundance of estate-planning Web sites. Many of them, however, are aimed at consumers and laypersons. The trick for paralegals and attorneys who specialize in estate planning is to find sites that are useful to professionals. Today, a number of Web sites exist that can help estate planners perform research on tax and probate laws and stay current with legislation and developments in the field. These sites may also provide sample forms or estate plans, estate-tax calculators, and links to other Web sites of interest.

WHERE TO BEGIN

A good place to start your research is at **http://www.estateplanninglinks.com**. This site offers one of the most comprehensive collections of articles and links to Web sites pertaining to estate planning, probate, trusts, charitable trusts, IRAs (individual retirement accounts), tax law, and elder law. Created and maintained by lawyers, the site is geared toward professionals. Another good starting place is Cornell University's Legal Information Institute, from which you can access hypertext versions of relevant federal and state statutes and agency regulations (**http://www.law.cornell.edu/topics/estate_planning.html**). You can also read recent estate-planning cases decided by the United States Supreme Court, the federal circuit courts, and many state appellate courts at this site.

OTHER WEB SITES

Some of the best online assistance for estate planning comes from Web sites established by practitioners. For example, Florida attorney Jason Haven created a well-organized site called Legal Research for Estate Planners, located at **http://www.jasonhavens.net**. At this site, you will find estate-planning links arranged by topic, including both national and state-specific sites, up-to-date literature, and practice tools (including forms, memos, and samples). Obtaining state-specific information is crucial because laws governing wills, trusts, and some other estate-planning devices vary from state to state. Two other practitioners, Dan Brady (**http://www.danbrady.com**) and Layne Rushforth (**http://rushforth.net**), also offer helpful sites that provide sample forms, checklists, and questionnaires that can be used with estate-planning clients.

Paralegals and attorneys can also find practical information at **http://www.texasprobate.com**. This site has a state focus but presents articles, forms, and links that can be utilized by all. The site also offers a bill-tracking page for following state legislation. Many organizations also have useful Web sites (the American College of Trust and Estate Counsel at **http://www.actec.org**, for example).

SOFTWARE RECOMMENDATIONS

The Internet provides one of the best methods for finding software useful to an estate practice. Attorney Daniel B. Evans—a computer expert who frequently writes for the American Bar Association (ABA)—has created what is likely the definitive list of estate-planning software. The list was originally attached as Appendix A to the book *Wills, Trusts, and Technology*, published by the ABA and written by Evans. The appendix has been updated and is posted on Evans's Web site (**http://evans-legal.com/dan**), along with a great deal of other beneficial information. Evans categorizes numerous software programs by their features and functions. Paralegals who are asked to research and recommend software to the firm should find this list helpful.

Vendors maintain other Web sites that are useful for keeping up with technological developments. For example, RIA publishes a multitude of tax and estate-planning research products and software. Practitioners can go to the RIA Web site (**http://www.ria.thomson.com**) to order products or get free demonstrations and sample journal articles.

TECHNOLOGY TIP

Paralegals will find many good estate-planning resources and tools on the Web. Only a few are mentioned here. Once you find the sites that are most helpful to your practice, you can bookmark them for later reference.

Developing Paralegal Skills

ESTATE PLANNING

Sara Bloom is an experienced paralegal who has worked for the same small law firm for several years. One of the firm's clients, Arnold Thompson, has an appointment today with David Miller, Sara's supervising attorney, to discuss estate-planning options. Thompson, a widower, is particularly interested in how, on his death, his assets can be transferred outside the probate process to his three children. David asks Sara to sit in on this initial client interview and to take thorough notes. He also asks her to draw up a checklist of points to discuss with the client during the interview.

CHECKLIST FOR AVOIDING PROBATE

- *Life insurance*—If Thompson has a life insurance policy listing the children as beneficiaries, the proceeds will be distributed to the children immediately on his death (as soon as the insurance company has completed its investigation of the claim) and will not be subject to probate. The client should be informed, though, that life insurance proceeds normally are a part of the taxable estate.

- *Joint ownership of property*—Thompson can arrange to have his children become co-owners of his personal property (such as automobiles) and real property (such as his home). If property is held in joint tenancy with rights of survivorship, the property will pass to the children outside the probate process.

- *Trusts*—Assets can also be placed in a living trust for the children, allowing the assets to pass to the children outside the probate process. If Thompson wants to transfer funds in his bank account to his children on his death but wants to be able to access and use the funds if necessary until he dies, he can create a Totten trust.

- *Minimizing estate taxes*—Thompson can minimize estate and inheritance taxes by making tax-free gifts to his children each year, within the limits set by federal law.

If a will exists, it probably names a personal representative (executor) to administer the estate. If there is no will, if the will fails to name a personal representative, or if the personal representative named in the will cannot serve, then the court must appoint one (an administrator). The personal representative must inventory and collect the assets of the decedent and, if necessary, have them appraised to determine their value. In addition, the personal representative is responsible for managing the assets of the estate during the administration period and for preventing them from being wasted or unnecessarily depleted.

The personal representative pays debts owed by the decedent and also arranges for the estate to pay taxes. A federal tax is levied on the total value of the estate after debts and expenses for administration have been deducted and after various exemptions have been allowed. The tax is on the estate itself rather than on the beneficiaries. In most states, a state inheritance tax is imposed on the recipient of a decedent's property rather than on the estate. Some states also have a state estate tax similar to the federal estate tax. In general, inheritance tax rates are graduated according to the type of relationship between the beneficiary and the decedent. The lowest rates and largest exemptions are applied to a surviving spouse and the children of the decedent.

When the ultimate distribution of assets to the beneficiaries is determined, the personal representative is responsible for distributing the estate pursuant to the court order. Once the assets have been distributed, an accounting is rendered to the court, the estate is closed, and the personal representative is relieved of any further responsibility or liability for the estate.

WILLS, TRUSTS, AND ESTATES AND THE PARALEGAL

Paralegals are often involved in legal work relating to wills, trusts, other estate-planning devices, and estate administration. If you work for a general law practice, you may be required to assist in handling tasks relating to all of these areas at one time or another. If you specialize in estate planning and administration, you may be employed by a law firm or a probate court and work extensively with probate proceedings. Among other things, you might be responsible for coordinating the efforts of the personal representative with those of the probate court. An increasing number of paralegals today are specializing in trust law and finding career opportunities in trust departments of banking institutions.

Here is a sampling of the tasks paralegals perform in the areas of wills, trusts, and estates:

- Interview clients to obtain information about their assets and liabilities for estate-planning purposes.

- Draft a will for a client.

- Create the necessary documents to establish a trust for a client.

- Monitor a trust fund's investments to ensure that the funds are not unnecessarily depleted.

- Locate beneficiaries named in a will or the next of kin of a person who died intestate.

- File a will with the probate court to initiate probate procedures.

- Research laws governing estate and inheritance taxes to determine how they apply to a decedent's estate.

- Research state laws governing wills and probate procedures.

- Perform asset appraisals.

FAMILY LAW

Marriage, divorce, adoption, child support and custody, child and spousal abuse, and parental rights and duties are all areas of family law. Much of the legal work relating to family law has to do with marriage dissolution. Marriage is a status conferred by state law. Thus, when marriage ends, the state, through the court system, must become involved. Because of the high divorce rate in this country, many attorneys and paralegals deal with divorce cases. Such cases may include child-support and child-custody issues. In addition, the property owned by a divorcing couple must be divided between the spouses. In this section, you will read about some important legal concepts and doctrines governing family matters, including the matters surrounding marriage dissolution. (For a discussion of the important role that paralegals can play in the area of family law, see this chapter's *Featured Guest* article beginning on page 342.)

Marriage Requirements

Despite the fact that many couples today live together (cohabit) without first marrying, most Americans do marry at least once during their lifetimes. Marriage confers certain legal and practical advantages. The marriage establishes the rights and duties of the spouses, as well as of any children born during the marriage. Married couples may also have an easier time obtaining insurance and credit and adopting children. Additionally, many companies offer health insurance to spouses but not to unmarried partners.

States place some limitations on who can marry. The betrothed must be man and woman (except in Massachusetts, as you will read shortly), currently unmarried, not closely related by blood, and over a certain age—usually eighteen years. State laws vary, and some states prohibit marriage between those who are closely related even if the relation is only by marriage. Persons who are under the required age can marry with parental consent or if they are emancipated from their parents. (**Emancipation** normally occurs when a child leaves home to support himself or herself.) Below a certain age, such as fourteen or sixteen, marriage may be absolutely prohibited by state law except with court approval.

emancipation
The legal relinquishment by a child's parents or guardian of the legal right to exercise control over the child. Usually, a child who moves out of the parents' home and supports himself or herself is considered emancipated.

Procedural Requirements

Certain procedures are generally required for a legally recognized marriage to take place. The parties must first obtain a *marriage license* from the state government, usually through the county clerk's office. Many states also require a *blood test* to check for certain diseases, such as venereal disease and rubella. Some states require couples to go through a *waiting period* before getting the license or between the time of acquiring the license and officially getting married.

In the majority of the states, some form of *marriage ceremony* is also required. The parties must present the license to someone authorized by the state to perform marriages, such as a justice of the peace, a judge, or a member of the clergy. The marriage ceremony must involve a public statement of the agreement to marry. After the ceremony, the *marriage license must be recorded.*

Same-Gender Couples

One of the most controversial family law topics today involves the ability of gay or lesbian couples to marry. Many same-gender couples live in stable, long-term relationships. Sometimes, same-gender couples hold what are known as "commitment ceremonies," which are similar to marriage ceremonies, to formalize their relationships. Massachusetts is the only state that legally recognizes same-gender marriages; that state began issuing marriage licenses to state residents in May 2004. Forty-one other states expressly prohibit such marriages.

Civil Unions.   Two states have passed laws allowing same-gender couples to form "civil unions." Vermont passed such a law in 2000, entitling same-gender partners who form civil unions to receive many of the benefits available to married couples. These include the right to inherit a partner's property, to divorce, to be granted child custody, to receive alimony or child support, and to decide on medical treatment for an incapacitated partner. In 2005, Connecticut passed a law allowing same-gender couples to enter into civil unions and to receive all of the same rights as married couples.

Domestic Partnerships and Other Arrangements.   Three states have laws recognizing "domestic partnerships" for same-gender couples. Domestic partnerships allow same-gender couples to enjoy some of the same rights as married couples. In New Jersey, domestic partners and married couples have had the same rights with respect to medical decision making, insurance coverage, and filing joint state tax returns since 2004. California began allowing same-gender couples to register as domestic partners in 2005. Domestic partners in California have many of the same rights and obligations as married couples, including community property rights and the right to receive support from the former partner after a separation. Since 2005, domestic partners in Maine have had inheritance rights and the right to guardianship if one partner becomes disabled. Additionally, Hawaii passed a "reciprocal beneficiaries" law in 1997 allowing same-gender couples property inheritance, hospital visitation, and other rights.

Most of these state laws face legal challenges, and it remains to be seen what effect they may have on developments in federal law. Same-gender couples in all states may provide for some of these protections through contract.

Common Law Marriages

A **common law marriage** is one in which the parties become married solely by mutual consent and without a license or ceremony. At one time, common law marriages were frequent in Europe. England abolished the common law marriage in 1753, although it remained

common law marriage
A marriage that is formed solely by mutual consent and without a marriage license or ceremony. The couple must be eligible to marry, must have a present and continuing agreement to be husband and wife, must live together as husband and wife, and must hold themselves out to the public as husband and wife. Only fifteen states recognize common law marriages.

Nancy R. Gallo

FEATURED **Guest**

PARALEGALS IN FAMILY LAW PRACTICE

BIOGRAPHICAL NOTE

Nancy R. Gallo is a professor and the coordinator of legal studies programs at Sussex County Community College in Newton, New Jersey. She is also the author of the textbook Introduction to Family Law *(2004) and a frequent public speaker. A cum laude graduate of William Paterson University, Gallo was formerly a paralegal. She received her J.D. from Nova Southeastern University and is now licensed to practice law in both Florida and New Jersey. She has volunteered as an early-settlement panel member for the Sussex County Superior Court, and her practice has included family mediation. Gallo is a member of the Family Law Syllabus Task Force (2003) of the American Association*

for Paralegal Education, the Family Law Section of the American Bar Association, and the Elder Law Section of the New Jersey Bar.

An interesting development of late-twentieth-century legal practice was the creation of the *boutique* law firm. Boutique legal practices left behind the concept of a lone general practitioner handling the A to Z of a client's legal issues and instead moved toward the goal of having individual attorneys and their paralegals become specialists in one or two areas of practice. Family law is a good example of an area of the law that has flourished under specialist experts. Paralegals in this area are integral team members working with their employers toward a common goal of building and maintaining a respected and lucrative legal practice. Indeed, a new client's first contact with a law firm may be with one of the firm's paralegals. This is a very important first step in client relations, because there is a lot of truth in the maxim, "There's no second chance to make a good first impression."

lawful in Scotland and in the American colonies. Today, in the United States, only fifteen states[2] and the District of Columbia recognize common law marriage.

There are four general requirements for a common law marriage. The parties (1) must be eligible to marry, (2) must have a present and continuing intention and agreement to be husband and wife, (3) must live together as husband and wife, and (4) must hold themselves out to the public as husband and wife. Note that cohabitation alone cannot produce a common law marriage. The parties must additionally *hold themselves out to others as husband and wife*. Note that common law marriage does not require that a couple live together for a certain number of years.

A common law marriage is legal. Once a couple is regarded as married, they have all of the rights and obligations of a traditionally married couple—including the obligation to support each other and their children. Furthermore, those states that do not recognize common law marriages nonetheless acknowledge the validity of a common law marriage that was formed in one of the states that do permit common law marriages. Once a couple is regarded as married by common law, they must obtain a court decree to dissolve the marriage.

Marital Duties

In the old days, marriages were arranged between families through private contracts. Part of the contractual arrangement was that the husband would support and provide for his wife and children. The wife, in turn, had certain duties in the home. Although we still hear the term *marriage contract*, in fact, marriage represents a special type of contract that is gov-

The most typical comment about a family law practice is that there seldom is a typical day. Indeed, paralegals working with family law practitioners will find themselves dealing with cases reflecting a wide range of human experiences. Such a practice very often delves into a client's most personal issues. For example, a family law practice may involve the seemingly convoluted machinations of divorce and separation or the necessity of filing a restraining order. The drafting of prenuptial agreements, settlement agreements, and adoption paperwork may all occur in a typical day.

The statistical truth is that today, in the United States, over half of all marriages end in divorce. The high divorce rate may be good for business, but attorneys and paralegals practicing family law, more than those in most other areas of the law, must balance the client's legal needs with sensitivity to the client's emotional state. A well-trained paralegal can have a vital and important role in assisting the attorney with this dual responsibility. In fact, a paralegal may often be a client's closest link to a law firm during a very emotional time. The special emotional needs of family law clients will often inspire a paralegal to call on previously unknown reserves of patience and sensitivity.

One thing that is absolutely true is that law firms handling matters involving family law will heavily depend on paralegals to soothe often agitated clients and to keep a virtual mountain of paperwork moving efficiently. Paralegal work in a family law practice is seldom dull, usually involves very personal relationships with clients, and can result in life-changing benefits to clients. One cannot say that about too many areas of the law.

> *"The most typical comment about a family law practice is that there seldom is a typical day."*

erned not by contract law but by the state. In the United States, each state has laws that govern marriage and divorce and establish the spousal obligations of married partners.

Financial Support

Generally, spouses are allowed to arrange their own affairs however they see fit. Nonetheless, the law still holds that one spouse has a duty to support the other spouse and children financially by providing such basics as food, shelter, and medical care—insofar as the spouse is able to do so. In many states, this duty lasts throughout the marriage, even if the spouses are living apart. Failure to provide support for a child may be a criminal violation. Additional duties may be created by a separate agreement between the spouses. Some courts will not enforce certain types of agreements, though, such as agreements to dole out sexual relations in return for money or some other consideration.

Spousal Abuse

Each state creates its own definition of domestic violence through legislation and court decisions. In all states, however, it is illegal to batter a spouse. Unlawful abuse has been extended to include extreme cases of harassment and threats of physical beating or confinement. In some cases, an emergency restraining order may be necessary. A **restraining order** is a court order that requires one person (such as an abusing spouse) to stay away from another (such as the victim of spousal abuse). Many shelters are available to assist abused spouses.

restraining order
A court order that requires one person (such as an abusing spouse) to stay away from another (such as an abused spouse).

Ethics Watch!

DEALING WITH SPOUSAL ABUSE

In family law, situations often arise in which paralegals face a conflict between personal and legal ethics. For example, suppose that Lena, a paralegal, is asked to assist in a divorce case. Her firm's client is the divorcing husband. During an interview, the client not only admits to Lena that he has abused his wife but also appears proud of it. In the husband's mind, he's simply exercising his right as head of the household. Lena finds the man personally offensive and does not want to have anything further to do with him. What can she do in this situation? One option would be to explain her feelings to her supervising attorney and see if another paralegal might handle the work instead. Often, though, either there is no other paralegal available or the attorney will not agree to the replacement. If this is the case in Lena's situation, she will either have to work with the client or place her job in jeopardy. If you ever find yourself in this kind of situation, it may help to remind yourself that paralegals have a duty of loyalty to their employers. Additionally, part of the paralegal's job is to be professionally objective.

Parental Rights and Obligations

Legally, a child is defined as an unmarried minor (under the age of eighteen) who is not emancipated. Prior to a child's emancipation, parents have certain rights of control over the child. Parents can direct the upbringing of their children and control where they live, what school they attend, and even what religion they practice. Parents also generally control the medical care to be given, although a parent's refusal to provide for such care in life-threatening situations (usually for religious reasons) can be a crime. Parents have broad legal authority to control the behavior of their children and even physically punish them—so long as the punishment does not constitute child abuse (to be discussed shortly).

Parents also have obligations toward their children. Parents are obligated to provide food, shelter, clothing, medical care, and other necessities. Parents must also ensure that their children attend school (normally until the age of sixteen). If a couple is married, the law presumes that any newborn child was fathered by the husband, and the husband must support the child unless he can prove that he is not the biological father. (Some states do not allow the husband an opportunity to prove his lack of paternity, however.) Although parental duties to a child generally end when the child reaches the age of eighteen, these duties may continue for a longer period if the child is seriously disabled.

Liability for Children's Wrongful Acts

Generally, parents are not liable for the wrongful actions of their children, *unless the actions result from the parents' negligence.* ▶ **EXAMPLE 10.3** Vanessa Purdy permits her fourteen-year-old son, Jeremy, to drive the family car to the grocery store by himself, without supervision, although he has no driver's license. En route to the store, Jeremy causes an accident in which Thomas Boone, a passenger in the other car, is seriously injured. Boone would probably succeed in a negligence suit against Vanessa Purdy in this situation. ◀

Parents may also be liable for their children's intentional torts. About half of the states now provide for partial parental liability for children's intentional torts, up to a limit of about $10,000 (depending on state law).

Child Abuse and Neglect

All states allow parents to physically punish their children within reason. A parent, for example, may slap or spank a child without violating the laws prohibiting child abuse. Some states allow corporal (physical) punishment in the schools. In all states, however, laws prohibit sexual molestation and extreme punishment of children by anyone. For punishment to constitute physical child abuse, the punishment normally must result in injuries—such as broken skin or bones, excessive bruising, or swelling.

Child neglect is also a form of child abuse. Child neglect occurs when parents or legal guardians fail to provide for a child's basic needs, such as food, shelter, clothing, and medical treatment. Child abuse may even extend to emotional abuse, as when a person publicly humiliates a child in an extreme way.

Children Born out of Wedlock

Today, an increasing number of children are born to unmarried parents. In response, the law is evolving to provide added rights and protections for children born out of wedlock. One important right is the right of the child to be supported by the biological father. The biological father has a legal obligation to provide support for the child that is identical to that of a married father. The obligation usually lasts until the child is no longer a minor. The mother's subsequent marriage to another man does not necessarily extinguish the obligation of the biological father to support the child. In most states, the eventual marriage of the parents of a child born out of wedlock "legitimizes" the child.

Paternity Suits. An unmarried mother may file a **paternity suit** to establish that a certain person is the biological father of her child. If the unwed mother is on public-welfare assistance, the government may file a paternity suit on the mother's behalf to obtain reimbursement for welfare payments given to the mother. Fathers may also file paternity actions in order to obtain visitation rights or custody of the child. The paternity of a child can be proved scientifically. DNA testing or comparable procedures that check for genetic factors can now determine, with almost 100 percent accuracy, whether a person parented a particular child.

paternity suit
A lawsuit brought by an unmarried mother to establish that a certain person is the biological father of her child. DNA testing or a comparable procedure is often used to determine paternity.

Inheritance Rights. Under the common law, a child born out of wedlock (an illegitimate child) had no right to inherit. Today, inheritance laws governing illegitimate children vary from state to state. Generally, an illegitimate child is treated as the child of the mother and can inherit from her and her relatives. The child is usually not regarded as the legal child of the father unless paternity is established through some legal proceeding. Many state statutes permit the illegitimate child to inherit from the father if paternity has been established prior to the father's death. Even if paternity has been established, however, the illegitimate child will not necessarily have inheritance rights identical to those of legitimate children. Generally, the courts have upheld state probate statutes that discriminate between legitimate and illegitimate children for valid state purposes.

On the Web

The National Adoption Information Clearinghouse provides information on adoption laws and links to individual state statutes at **http://naic.acf. hhs.gov/general/legal**.

Adoption

In contrast to children born out of wedlock, adopted children normally have the same legal rights as the biological children of a married couple, including the right to inherit property from their adoptive parents on the parents' death. **Adoption** is a procedure in which persons

adoption
A procedure in which persons become the legal parents of a child who is not their biological child.

become the legal parents of a child that is not their biological child. Once an adoption is formally completed, the adoptive parents have all the responsibilities of biological parents. Should they divorce, each adoptive parent has all the child-support obligations of a biological parent. Note that adoption is not the same as foster care, which is a temporary arrangement in which a family is paid by the state to care for a child for a limited period of time, often pending adoption.

Requirements for Adoptions

Adoptions are governed by state laws, and these laws vary substantially from state to state. Generally, however, there are three minimum requirements for an adoption to be legal. First, the child's biological parents must give up their legal rights (either by consent, by death, or by order of the court). The adopting parents must then follow all procedures required by the state in which the adoption occurs. Finally, the adoption must be formally approved by a judge. There may be additional requirements in specific circumstances. For example, adopting a teenaged child generally requires the child's official consent.

All states permit single persons to adopt children, but married couples are generally preferred. Although some courts have approved adoptions by same-gender couples, generally such couples find it difficult to adopt children. Several states—including Florida, Mississippi, and Utah—have enacted laws that explicitly prohibit homosexual couples from adopting children.

Agency Adoptions

Adoption is often carried out through social-service agencies that are licensed by the state to place children for adoption. The biological parents terminate their parental rights, essentially giving up these rights to the agency and authorizing the agency to find legal parents for their child. Traditionally, in agency adoptions, the identities of the biological and the adoptive parents were kept confidential. Increasingly, though, state laws are allowing for the disclosure of this information in certain circumstances. In some states, for example, if an adopted child wants to meet with his or her birth parent or vice versa, the court will contact the child or parent to see if he or she will agree to such a meeting.

Independent Adoptions

Prospective adoptive parents may also pursue independent adoption. An independent adoption is one that is arranged privately, as when a physician, lawyer, or other individual puts a couple seeking to adopt a child in contact with a pregnant woman who has decided to give up her child for adoption. These parties make their own private arrangements. Usually, the adopting parents pay for the legal and medical expenses associated with the childbirth and adoption. The intermediary may also receive a fee. Because this method of adoption has the potential for abuse, it is prohibited by some states.

Stepparent Adoptions

Many adoptions today are stepparent adoptions, which occur when a married partner adopts his or her spouse's children from a former marriage. Usually, in such adoptions, the parental rights of the children's other biological parent are terminated either by consent or through a court proceeding.

Court Approval and Probation

All adoptions must be approved in court. The primary standard for approving an adoption is the "best interests of the child." Because this standard is so vague, the courts have a great deal of leeway in deciding whether to place children with prospective adoptive parents. The court considers the financial resources of the adopting parents, their family stability and

foster care
A temporary arrangement in which a family is paid by the state to care for a child for a limited period of time, often pending adoption.

independent adoption
A privately arranged adoption, as when a doctor, lawyer, or other individual puts a couple seeking to adopt a child in contact with a pregnant woman who has decided to give up her child for adoption.

home environment, their ages, their religious and racial compatibility, and other factors relevant to the child's future health and welfare.

After the adoption, many states place the new parents on probation for a time—usually from six months to one year. The agency or court appoints an individual to monitor developments in the home to ensure that the adoptive parents are caring appropriately for the child's well-being. If not, the child may be removed and returned to an agency for placement in another home.

Marriage Termination

A marriage can only be terminated by the state. In other words, even though partners want to end their marriage, and even though they separate and live apart, they will continue to have the legal rights and obligations of spouses until their marriage is legally terminated. There are two ways in which a marriage can be terminated: by annulment or by divorce.

Annulment

An **annulment** is a court decree that essentially invalidates (nullifies) a marriage. This means that the marriage was never effective in the first place. Today, annulments are rarely granted. Many of those seeking annulments do so because their religion does not condone divorce. In such situations, an annulment allows a subsequent marriage to be recognized as valid in the eyes of the church.

Grounds for invalidating a marriage through an annulment are similar to those for invalidating other contracts (even though marriage is not governed by contract law). If one of the parties did not genuinely assent to the marriage, if one of the parties lacked capacity, or if the marriage was based on fraud or duress, an annulment may be granted. An annulment may also be granted on other grounds, including **bigamy**, which is the act of marrying one person while already legally married to another.

Even though the marriage is deemed invalid, children born during the marriage are considered legitimate in the eyes of the law. Also, as in a divorce, when a marriage is annulled, issues involving child support, spousal support, child custody, and property settlement must be decided by the couple or by the court.

Divorce

The most common way to end a marriage is divorce. A **divorce** is a formal court proceeding that legally dissolves a marriage. Divorce laws vary among the states, with some states having much simpler divorce procedures than others.

Fault-Based versus No-Fault Divorces. Until the 1960s, to obtain a divorce a petitioning party had to allege reasons for the divorce—such as adultery, desertion, cruelty, or abuse—that were acceptable grounds for divorce under state law. This is called *fault-based divorce.* Unless the petitioning party could prove that his or her partner was "at fault" for the breakdown of the marriage in one of these ways, a divorce would not be granted. Eventually, changing economic and social conditions in America led to new attitudes toward divorce, which resulted in less stringent requirements for divorce. Thus arose the **no-fault divorce**—a divorce in which neither party is deemed to be at fault for the breakdown of the marriage.

Today, all states allow no-fault divorces. Generally, a no-fault divorce may be based on one of three grounds:

- Irreconcilable differences (the most common ground).
- Living separately for a period of time specified by state statute (ranging from six months to three years).
- Incompatibility.

annulment
A court decree that invalidates (nullifies) a marriage. Although the marriage itself is deemed nonexistent, children of a marriage that is annulled are deemed legitimate.

bigamy
The act of entering into marriage with one person while still legally married to another.

divorce
A formal court proceeding that legally dissolves a marriage.

no-fault divorce
A divorce in which neither party is deemed to be at fault for the breakdown of the marriage.

On the Web

The Legal Information Institute offers an excellent tool for finding information regarding each state's laws pertaining to marriage, grounds for divorce, and child custody, as well as links to other sites related to family law issues. Go to **http://www.law.cornell.edu/ topics/child_custody.html**.

petition for divorce
The document filed with the court to initiate divorce proceedings. The requirements governing the form and content of a divorce petition vary from state to state.

No-fault divorces make it practically impossible for one spouse to prevent a divorce desired by the other. Even in no-fault divorces, however, fault may be taken into consideration by the court in determining a couple's property settlement or spousal support arrangements.

The majority of the states permit *both* fault-based and no-fault divorces. Sometimes, a party may seek a fault-based divorce in an attempt to gain a more favorable property settlement (to be discussed shortly) than he or she could get in a no-fault divorce.

Divorce Procedures. The first step in obtaining a divorce is to file a **petition for divorce** with the appropriate state court. Although the form and content of the petition vary, generally the petition includes:

- The names and addresses of both spouses.
- The date and place of their marriage.
- The names and addresses of any minor children and whether the wife is currently pregnant.
- The reasons for the divorce.
- A summary of any arrangements made by the divorcing couple as to support, custody, or visitation.
- The relief sought.

The petition is served on the other spouse, who must file an answer to the petition within the number of days specified by state law. If the couple cannot agree on certain matters while the divorce is pending—such as who gets the children or who pays the mortgage—the court will hold a hearing to decide which partner should assume what responsibilities temporarily. Unless the case is settled through mediation or negotiation, a trial will be conducted, and the judge will decide the terms of the parties' final divorce decree.

Negotiation and Mediation. Very few divorces actually go to trial. Usually, the parties settle their differences themselves prior to trial—though often only after lengthy negotiations, which are facilitated by their attorneys. If the parties agree to a settlement concerning contested issues, the agreement will be put in writing and presented to the court for its approval.

A divorcing couple meet with a mediator in an attempt to resolve their dispute over child-custody arrangements. Couples are often required to mediate their disputes before being allowed to litigate them in court.

(Courtesy of ©Brand X Pictures/Alamy)

Divorcing spouses increasingly use mediation to settle disagreements, and in many states, mediation is mandatory in divorce cases. The mediator typically meets with the parties in the absence of lawyers and tries to guide the parties into agreeing on a mutually satisfactory settlement. Some paralegals are trained mediators and conduct mediation proceedings.[3]

Child Custody

In many divorces, the issue of child custody—the right to live with and to care for the children on an everyday basis—is the most contentious issue to be resolved. In some cases, a court may appoint a guardian *ad litem* for the child. A **guardian** *ad litem* is a person appointed by the court (often an attorney) to represent the interests of a child or a mentally incompetent person before the court.

> **guardian *ad litem***
> A person appointed by the court to represent the interests of a child or a mentally incompetent person before the court.

Factors Considered in Determining Child Custody

Traditionally, the mother almost always received custody. Mothers still usually receive custody, but courts now explicitly consider a number of factors when awarding custody. These factors include the following:

- The nature of the relationship and emotional ties with each parent.
- The ability of each parent to provide for the child's needs and education and each parent's interest in doing so.
- The ability of each parent to provide a stable environment for the child.
- The mental and physical health of each parent.
- The wishes of the child—especially older children.

In determining custody, courts may also consider other factors, such as whether one parent is a smoker (because secondary smoke can damage the child's lungs). Custodial arrangements are not permanent and may be changed by a court in view of the parents' changing circumstances.

Types of Custodial Arrangements

The parent who has **legal custody** of a child has the right to make major decisions about the child's life without consulting the other parent. Often, the parent who has legal custody also has physical custody.

> **legal custody**
> Custody of a child that confers on the parent the right to make major decisions about the child's life without consulting the other parent.

Many states now provide for **joint custody**—shared custody—of the children of divorcing parents. Joint *legal* custody means that both parents together make major decisions about the child. Some procedure, such as mediation, is usually available in the event of disagreement. In some states, including California, mediation is mandatory in child-custody disputes. Joint legal custody may also involve joint *physical* custody, in which both parents maintain a home for the child and have physical custody of the child for roughly comparable time periods. Joint physical custody usually works best if both parents live in the same school district or if the child attends a private school to which both parents have access.

> **joint custody**
> Custody of a child that is shared by the parents following the termination of a marriage.

Grandparents can petition the court to obtain custody of their grandchildren as well. In some situations, such as when a parent is disabled or when parents are not taking proper care of their children, a court may decide that grandparents should be granted custody of their grandchildren.

Visitation Rights

Typically, the noncustodial parent receives **visitation rights**—the right to have contact with the child. The parent may get to spend weekends, alternate holidays, or other time periods with the child. The times and duration of the noncustodial parent's visits are often stated in

> **visitation rights**
> The right of a noncustodial parent to have contact with his or her child. Grandparents and stepparents may also be given visitation rights.

CLIENT INFORMATION AND THE DUTY OF COMPETENCE

Paralegals who specialize in divorce law normally have frequent contact with divorcing clients. If you are a specialist in this area, you will probably come to know some of your clients quite well. You will also probably learn all kinds of information from them—about their lives, their spouses, and other things. What do you do with this information? Do you make a note of everything that a client tells you? Do you only record what you think is relevant to the case? How do you decide what is or is not relevant?

Many paralegals have solved this problem by taking thorough notes during interviews and following casual conversations with clients. Some paralegals even tape-record interviews. What seems irrelevant now may, in light of later developments, be very relevant. If you keep good notes on a case and review the notes as the case progresses, you can help to ensure that your supervising attorney will not breach the duty of competence.

the divorce settlement. In some situations, the court may order supervised visitation to ensure the child's safety. This means that the noncustodial parent's visits will take place in the presence of a third party. Only in extreme situations—such as when child abuse is involved—will a court completely deny visitation rights to the noncustodial parent.

In most states, courts can grant visitation rights to grandparents, although these laws vary from state to state. Many such laws require the visitation to be in the best interest of the child, and many require the grandparent to have an established or substantial relationship with the child. If the state's requirements are met, a court may set a schedule specifying the time that grandchildren are to spend with their grandparents.

Child Support

child support
The financial support necessary to provide for a child's needs. Commonly, when a marriage is terminated, the non-custodial spouse agrees or is required by the court to make child-support payments to the custodial spouse.

Regardless of the custody arrangements, a court must make some provision for **child support**—the financial support necessary to provide for the child's needs. States now have official, standardized guidelines determining child-support duties. These guidelines are often percentage formulas based on parental income. Judges must follow the guidelines, unless special circumstances justify a departure or the parents agree to a different arrangement. A child with a disability, for example, may require more support than provided for under the guidelines. Child-support orders may be revised and adjusted according to the changing needs of the child and incomes of the parents.

It is a common misconception that if one former spouse fails to meet his or her obligations under a divorce settlement or other court order (such as by withholding visitation rights), the other party can withhold payment of child support. Child support is a separate court order—it cannot be withheld because a former spouse does something that the other former spouse does not like. (Similarly, a parent cannot withhold visitation rights because the other parent did not pay support.)

Because so many noncustodial parents failed to make child-support payments in the past, state laws now provide for automatic withholding of support payments from the wages of the parent.

Spousal Support

In some situations, a divorce decree may also require that one spouse provide for the other spouse's support. **Alimony** (sometimes called *maintenance*) is money paid to support a former spouse. Historically, the husband was the wage earner and was expected to pay alimony to his former wife so that she could maintain her standard of living. Today, the law governing alimony has changed significantly, largely because so many couples are both income earners.

Alimony may be permanent or temporary. If a court orders one spouse to pay *permanent alimony* to the other, the alimony must be paid until the former spouse receiving the alimony remarries or dies (unless the court modifies the order for some reason). A more common form of alimony is temporary. This *rehabilitative alimony* is designed to provide the ex-spouse with the education, training, or job experience necessary to support himself or herself. In deciding whether rehabilitative alimony is appropriate, a court usually considers the recipient's prospects of developing a new career. If the recipient is relatively advanced in age, for example, the court may grant permanent rather than rehabilitative alimony.

The amount of alimony awarded usually depends on the specific circumstances of the parties—their age, education, and incomes, for example. In about half the states, courts may also consider the reason for the divorce. If one party was more responsible than the other for the breakdown of the marriage, the alimony paid by that spouse might be higher than it would otherwise have been. Courts will also consider whether one spouse supported the other through college or graduate school in determining alimony awards.

Property Division

When a marriage is terminated, the property owned by the couple (including their debts) must be divided. **Property settlement**—the division of property on divorce—is often a main area of disagreement. Although most divorcing couples eventually settle their financial disputes, the settlement reached is colored by the requirements of state law.

The way in which any court divides a couple's property depends largely on whether the property is considered marital property or separate property. **Marital property** is all property acquired during the course of a marriage (apart from inheritances and gifts received by one of the spouses). **Separate property** is property that a spouse owned before the marriage, plus inheritances and gifts acquired during the marriage. This property belongs to the spouse personally and not to the marital unit. On dissolution of the marriage, separate property is not divided but is retained by the owner.

The ownership right in separate property may be lost, however, if it is combined with marital property during marriage. ▶ **EXAMPLE 10.4** Hannah Olin owns a lot in Bangor, Maine. Hannah marries Mustafa Shamir, and they build a house together after their marriage. By building the house (thus creating marital property) on the lot, Hannah has lost her separate property rights in the land. ◀. Merely renovating separately held property (sprucing up a vacation home, for instance) may transform the separate property into joint property. Placing separate property (money) into a jointly held bank account may also transform the money into joint property.

Community Property

In ten states,[4] husbands and wives can hold property as community property. In those states, **community property** is all property acquired during the marriage (not including inheritances or gifts received by either party during the marriage). Even if only one party supplied

---

alimony
Money paid to support a former spouse after a marriage has been terminated. The alimony may be permanent or temporary (rehabilitative).

property settlement
The division of property between spouses on the termination of a marriage.

marital property
All property acquired during the course of a marriage, apart from inheritances and gifts made to one or the other of the spouses.

separate property
Property that a spouse owned before the marriage, plus inheritances and gifts acquired by the spouse during the marriage.

community property
Defined in ten states as all property acquired during the marriage, except for inheritances or gifts received during the marriage by either marital partner. Each spouse has a one-half ownership interest in community property.

Developing Paralegal Skills

PREPARING FOR PROPERTY-SETTLEMENT NEGOTIATIONS

Lea, a paralegal, works for a small law firm that specializes in divorce cases. One of the firm's clients, Mrs. Clark, is seeking a divorce. Tomorrow, her husband and his attorney will meet with Mrs. Clark and Lea's supervising attorney to negotiate a property settlement. Lea is preparing a settlement-agreement checklist for the attorney to take to the settlement meeting.

Lea makes a list of all of the property owned by the Clarks, along with the value of each item and outstanding liens (legal claims—to satisfy debts, for example) on the property. She also leaves blanks—after "H" for husband and "W" for wife—so that the attorney can write down to what division of property the parties agree. Lea also includes a list of the debts owed by the Clarks. Again, she leaves blanks so that the attorney can write in how much of each debt will be paid by each spouse.

Property	Value	Lien	Disposition	
Home	$500,000	$200,000	H ___	W ___
Cottage	$193,000	—	H ___	W ___
BMW	$52,000	$27,500	H ___	W ___
Savings Account	$9,500		H ___	W ___
Retirement (H)	$2,000,000		H ___	W ___
IRA (H)	$800,000		H ___	W ___
Life Insurance (H)	$1,000,000		H ___	W ___

Debts	Amount	Disposition	
Visa	$7,300	H ___	W ___
MasterCard	$2,500	H ___	W ___
Current Taxes (Due)	$9,456	H ___	W ___
Next Year's Taxes (Estimated)	$13,180	H ___	W ___

Lea goes over the checklist carefully to make sure that all of the Clarks' property and debts are included and that the amounts are accurate. Once she is satisfied that the checklist is accurate and complete, she takes it to her supervising attorney for review.

---

all of the income and assets during the marriage, both spouses share equally (half and half) in the ownership of that property. Property owned by either partner before the marriage—and inheritances or gifts that partner received during the marriage—remain the property of that individual, or separate property, however.

Equitable Distribution

All of the other states provide for the *equitable distribution* (fair distribution) of property to the divorcing spouses—that is, the marital property is divided according to the equities of the case (not necessarily split evenly). In some of these states, only the marital property is subject to distribution. In other states, all of the property owned by the couple, including separate property, may be factored into the property distribution. While in most cases, separate property remains with the owner, the courts exercise substantial discretion in deciding which person should receive what property. In deciding how to divide property between divorcing spouses, the courts consider a number of factors, including the following:

- The duration of the marriage.

- The health of the parties.
- The individuals' occupations and vocational skills.
- The individuals' relative wealth and income.
- The standard of living during the marriage.
- The relative contributions to the marriage (both financial and homemaker contributions).
- The needs and concerns of any children.
- Tax and inheritance considerations.

A typical property controversy in divorce cases concerns rights to the marital residence. If there are minor children, the house is usually given to the parent with custody of the children. It may be difficult to balance the grant of the house with other property (many families have few substantial assets other than their homes). Once the children are grown, the court may order the house to be sold and the proceeds divided to ensure that the property distribution is equitable.

Prenuptial Agreements

Increasingly, couples are using prenuptial agreements to avoid problems over property division that may arise in the future. A **prenuptial agreement** (also known as an *antenuptial agreement*) is a contract between the parties that is entered into before marriage and that provides for the disposition of property in the event of a divorce or the death of one of the spouses. Prenuptial agreements must be in writing to be enforceable.

Most states now uphold prenuptial agreements, even if the agreements eliminate financial support in the event of divorce. Courts do look closely at such agreements for evidence of unfairness, though. Often courts find a prenuptial agreement is unfair if the parties did not retain independent counsel prior to signing the agreement. To enforce a prenuptial agreement, a party must also show that the agreement was made voluntarily and without threats or unfair pressure. Courts have refused to enforce prenuptial agreements in some circumstances, such as when a party was pressured into signing the agreement or when a party failed to disclose all of his or her assets.

prenuptial agreement
A contract formed between two persons who are contemplating marriage to provide for the disposition of property in the event of a divorce or the death of one of the spouses after they have married.

FAMILY LAW AND THE PARALEGAL

The opportunities for paralegals in the area of family law are extensive and probably will continue to be so. The United States has the highest divorce rate in the world (statistically, one out of every two couples who marry end up getting a divorce), and there is no indication that this high rate will decline in the future. Many paralegals work for law practices that specialize in handling divorces and legal work related to divorces, such as child-custody arrangements and property settlements.

Divorce is just one specialty within the broad area of family law, however, and paralegals often work in other types of family law, such as adoptions. Paralegals today may work for state welfare departments, publicly sponsored legal aid foundations, or groups that assist persons of low income with family-related legal problems. Paralegals working in the area of probate and estate administration also deal with questions relating to inheritance by children. Finally, paralegals who work for general law practices will likely be involved in family law matters, such as prenuptial agreements, adoptions, and divorce cases.

Because the area of family law involves many special legal areas, paralegals working in family law perform many different types of work. Here are some examples of the kinds of tasks you might perform if you work in this area of the law:

- Interview a client who is seeking a divorce to obtain information about the married couple, their property

(Continued)

Today's Professional Paralegal

MEETING WITH THE PERSONAL REPRESENTATIVE

Jocelyn Furnow is a paralegal with a small law partnership, West & West. Terrence West, one of the two partners, told Jocelyn yesterday that a friend of his, Bob Milham, would be dropping by today. Bob's brother, Ralph Milham, died a few days ago in a car accident, and Bob, as Ralph's personal representative, wants to know what needs to be done to settle the estate.

JOCELYN'S ASSIGNMENT

Terrence tells Jocelyn that he will be out of the office all afternoon and that when Bob comes by, she should let him know what kinds of documents and information he needs to gather immediately. "Tell Bob," Terrence says to Jocelyn, "to collect these items as quickly as possible and then come in and see me. In fact, see if you can set up an appointment for this Thursday, and tell him he should try to have the necessary information by that time."

MEETING WITH THE CLIENT

That afternoon, Bob Milham enters the office, and Jocelyn greets him. She introduces herself as Terrence West's paralegal and explains that the attorney has authorized her to indicate the kinds of information that Bob should obtain right away. Jocelyn first asks Bob if he has brought his brother's will with him. Bob hands Jocelyn the will, which Jocelyn quickly scans. She notes that Bob's name is listed as Ralph's personal representative. She then hands Bob a prepared form—a worksheet that Bob can use to inventory his brother's assets and debts.

GOING OVER THE WORKSHEET

"Basically," explains Jocelyn, "you first need to list your brother's possessions, as the worksheet indicates. Do you know if he owned any real estate, such as a home or land?" Bob states that his brother owned a house and had a car and an airplane. He is fairly sure that Ralph also had some investment securities.

"Well," Jocelyn responds, "look through his personal papers. Try to find the deed to the house, the titles to the car and the airplane, and the certificates or other evidence of the securities he owned. These papers may be in a safe-deposit box, so you need to check with his bank to find out if he had one. Also locate his checkbook and any paperwork indicating whether he had a savings account or owned any certificates of deposit.

"The next step is to find out whether Ralph had any debts outstanding. When you look through his papers, find out how much, if anything, he still owed on the house and on his car and airplane. See if you can find evidence of any other loans that must be paid off."

Jocelyn continues to go over the items listed on the worksheet. Once she is sure that Bob understands what must be done, she schedules an appointment for the coming Thursday. At that time, Terrence can further advise Bob on the probate process and on Bob's duties as personal representative.

and debts, the reasons for the marriage breakdown, and their children, if any.

- Draft a petition for divorce and file divorce-related documents with the court.
- Assist in pretrial divorce proceedings, negotiations, and mediation.
- Assist in preparing a divorcing client for trial and in other trial-preparation matters.

- Draft a settlement agreement or prenuptial agreement.
- Assist in making arrangements for a private adoption.
- Research state laws governing marriage requirements, divorce procedures, child-custody arrangements, property settlements, and other matters.
- Help battered spouses obtain protection from their abusing spouses.

KEY TERMS AND CONCEPTS

chapter summary — Estates and Family Law

Wills, Trusts, and Estates

1. *Wills*—A will is the final declaration of how a person desires to have his or her property disposed of after death.

2. *Terminology*—A person who dies without leaving a will is said to have died intestate, and the decedent's property is distributed under state intestacy statutes. A person who makes a will is called a testator. The personal representative named in a will to settle the affairs of the decedent is called an executor. If the court appoints the personal representative, she or he is called an administrator.

3. *Requirements of a valid will*—A will must comply with state statutory requirements, which usually involve the following:

   a. The testator must have testamentary capacity (be of sound mind at the time the will is made).

   b. The will must be in writing (with some exceptions).

   c. The testator must sign the will.

   d. The will must be witnessed by a specified number of persons (usually two).

   e. In some states, the will must be published.

4. *Probate procedures*—To probate a will means to establish its validity and administer the estate through a court process. Probate laws vary from state to state. Procedures may be formal or informal, depending on the size of the estate and other factors, such as whether a guardian for minor children must be appointed.

5. *Trusts*—A trust is any arrangement by which property is transferred from one person (the grantor, or settlor) to be administered by another (the trustee) for the benefit of a third party (the beneficiary).

(Continued)

a. A living *(inter vivos)* trust is executed by the grantor during his or her lifetime and can be revocable or irrevocable.

b. A testamentary trust is created by will and comes into existence on the grantor's death.

c. Special types of trusts include charitable trusts, spendthrift trusts, and Totten trusts.

6. *Other estate-planning devices*—Several other strategies may be used to transfer property. These include owning property as joint tenants, giving gifts to children or others while one is still alive, and purchasing life insurance policies.

Family Law

1. *Marriage requirements*—Marriage is a status conferred by state law that establishes the rights and duties of spouses to one another and to any children born. Typically, the couple must be a man and a woman, currently unmarried, not closely related by blood, and over the age of eighteen (unless they have parental consent or are emancipated).

   a. Certain procedures may be required by the state in order for a marriage to be legally recognized. These procedures may involve a marriage license, a blood test, a waiting period, and a marriage ceremony, after which the license must be recorded.

   b. Only one state, Massachusetts, legally recognizes same-gender marriages. Forty-one states expressly prohibit such marriages. Two states (Connecticut and Vermont) recognize civil unions, three states (California, Maine, and New Jersey) recognize domestic partnerships, and Hawaii allows same-gender couples to enjoy some rights. Most of these state laws face challenges, however.

2. *Common law marriage*—A minority of states allow parties to be married solely by mutual consent and without a ceremony or license. Generally, the parties must be eligible to marry, must have an intention and agreement to be married, must live together as husband and wife, and must hold themselves out to others as husband and wife. If these requirements are met, the marriage is legal.

3. *Marital duties*—Spouses have the duty to support the other spouse and children financially by providing basic necessities. Abusing one's spouse is illegal in all states.

4. *Parental rights and obligations*—Parents have the legal right to control the upbringing of their minor children and to punish them within reason. They also must provide for the children's necessities and ensure that the children attend school (until the age of sixteen).

   a. Generally, parents are not liable for the wrongful actions of their children unless the actions result from the parents' negligence.

   b. Sexual molestation and extreme punishment of children are prohibited in all states.

   c. The biological father of a child born out of wedlock is obligated to support the child once paternity is established.

   d. An illegitimate child can usually inherit from the mother but not from the father unless paternity has been established. Even when paternity has been established, an illegitimate child may not have the same inheritance rights as legitimate children.

5. *Adoption*—Adoption is a procedure by which persons become the legal parents of a child who is not their biological child. An adopted child normally has the same legal rights as the biological children of a married couple, including inheritance rights. State law governs adoption, and procedures vary. The court must approve all adoptions.

   a. Agency adoptions are done through state-licensed social-service agencies.

   b. Independent adoptions are arranged privately, often through lawyers or doctors.

c. Stepparent adoptions are those in which a married partner adopts his or her spouse's children from a prior marriage.

6. *Marriage termination*—A marriage can only be terminated by the state, through annulment or divorce.

   a. Annulment is a court order invalidating a marriage. Annulments are rarely granted today.

   b. The most common way to end a marriage is by divorce. Divorce laws vary among states and may provide for either fault-based or no-fault divorces, or both. In a fault-based divorce, the petitioner must prove certain grounds for the divorce, such as adultery, cruelty, or abuse. Sometimes, a party may seek a fault-based divorce in the hope of gaining a more favorable property settlement. No-fault divorces are based on the grounds that the partners have irreconcilable differences, have been living separately for the length of time required by state statute, or are incompatible.

   c. The first step in obtaining a divorce is to file a petition for divorce with the appropriate state court. The petition is then served on the other spouse. If the parties cannot agree on certain matters (child custody, finances) in the interim, the court may hold a hearing to assign temporary responsibility for those matters. Many states require parties to attend mediation before trial.

7. *Child custody*—Which parent the child lives with is often fiercely contested in a divorce. The court sometimes appoints a guardian *ad litem* to protect the interests of the child. The court considers a number of factors when deciding custody.

   a. Parents granted joint legal custody make major decisions about the child together. Parents with joint physical custody have physical custody of the child for roughly comparable time periods. Many states now provide for joint custodial arrangements.

   b. Usually, one parent is awarded legal custody of the child and can make major decisions without consulting the other parent. The noncustodial parent receives visitation rights.

8. *Child support*—The noncustodial parent will be required to pay a certain sum monthly (often set according to standardized guidelines) as support for the child.

9. Spousal support—In some situations, one of the spouses is ordered to pay support (alimony) to the other. Alimony can be temporary (rehabilitative) or permanent.

10. *Property division*—

    a. Marital property is any property acquired during the marriage (except gifts or inheritances received by one spouse). It will be divided on divorce. Separate property is anything that a spouse owned prior to the marriage, plus inheritances and gifts received during the marriage. Separate property is usually not divided.

    b. In some states, all property acquired during the marriage is considered community property, even if only one party supplied all of the income and assets during the marriage. Each spouse has a one-half ownership interest in community property.

    c. All other states divide the divorcing couple's property by equitable (fair) distribution. The court decides how much of the marital property each spouse should receive given the circumstances of the parties and does not necessarily divide the property equally. In some states, only the marital property is divided; in others, separate property may also be included.

11. *Prenuptial agreements*—Agreements (contracts) made before marriage to provide for division of property in the event of divorce or death. Prenuptial agreements must be in writing. Most states enforce such agreements unless they are clearly unfair.

QUESTIONS FOR REVIEW

1. What is estate planning? What are the requirements of a valid will?

2. What is a trust? Name and describe two basic types of trusts.

3. Why and how are wills probated? What are the duties of a personal representative?

4. In the context of wills, what is the difference between an executor and an administrator?

5. Why is it important to check the law of your specific state when determining the requirements of a will? What laws govern the distribution of the estate of a person who dies without a valid will?

6. What procedures are involved in estate administration? Is a decedent's estate subject to taxation?

7. What are the rights and duties of parents with respect to their children? Can parents be held liable for their children's wrongful acts? What are the legal obligations of parents to children born out of wedlock and adopted children?

8. What two types of divorce may a court grant? Under the traditional (pre-1960s) type of divorce, what grounds must the petitioner prove to obtain a divorce?

9. On the termination of a marriage, how is a couple's property divided? What is separate property? What is community property?

10. What is a prenuptial agreement, and how does it affect a property settlement?

ETHICAL QUESTIONS

1. James Simpson, an attorney, has represented Miss Morgan for forty years. She is now eighty-three years old and is revising her will. She instructs the attorney to include in the will a bequest to James Simpson of $50,000. Can Simpson prepare this will? Why or why not?

2. Cynthia Warner works as a legal assistant for a sole practitioner, Samuel Weingarten. Weingarten's practice consists mainly of estate planning and probate. Today, Weingarten has received a check for $100,000 from the sale of real property that was in an estate that he is probating. Weingarten instructs Cynthia to deposit the check into the firm's bank account, not the client trust account, because he has some bills to pay. What should Cynthia do? How might she handle this situation?

3. During the course of their twenty-five-year marriage, Mr. and Mrs. Jones have had their family attorney, Mr. Shapiro, prepare their wills, handle their real estate purchases, and assist them with other legal matters. On Monday, Mrs. Jones calls Mr. Shapiro and makes an appointment. She explains that she wants to file a divorce action against Mr. Jones. On Wednesday, Mr. Jones calls

Mr. Shapiro. He wants to make an appointment to discuss filing a divorce action against Mrs. Jones. May the attorney, Mr. Shapiro, represent both Mr. Jones and Mrs. Jones in the divorce action?

4. Brenda Bates, a paralegal, works for a large, prestigious law firm. Today, Brenda and her supervising attorney, Michael Leason, have an initial client interview with the mayor's wife. During the interview, they learn that the mayor's wife wants to initiate divorce proceedings against her husband. The mayor's wife shows them evidence, in the form of photographs, of the mayor's infidelity. In addition, they learn that the mayor cheats not only on his wife but also on his tax returns. When Brenda returns home after a busy day at the office, she turns on the television. The lead story is about the mayor and all of the charitable acts that he has performed over the past several months. Brenda starts to tell her husband what she learned about the mayor today from the mayor's wife. Brenda stops midsentence, realizing that she has violated an important ethical duty. What ethical duty has she violated?

PRACTICE QUESTIONS AND ASSIGNMENTS

1. Identify the term that is normally used to describe each of the following persons (indicated by italics):

   a. *Helen* died without a valid will.

   b. *Anne* is appointed by the court to settle the affairs of her sister, Helen, who died without having made a will.

   c. *Mark* died after having created a valid will.

   d. *Bill*, Mark's brother, had been appointed by Mark to settle Mark's affairs on Mark's death.

2. Identify each of the following types of trusts:

   a. Barbara inserts a trust provision in her will requiring that all of her property be held in trust for her children until they reach the age of thirty.

   b. Steve, who is seventy years old, transfers his home into a trust for the benefit of his children and their spouses.

   c. Kathy creates a trust in her will for cancer research.

3. Identify which of the following types of estate-planning devices allow property to be transferred outside of the probate process:

   a. Living trusts.

   b. Life insurance.

   c. Testamentary trusts.

   d. Holding property as joint tenants with rights of survivorship.

   e. Gifts to children.

4. Identify which of the following requirements need *not* be met for a valid will to be created.

   a. The testator must have testamentary capacity.

   b. The will must be witnessed.

   c. The will must provide for an equitable distribution of the testator's property.

   d. The will must be approved by the state attorney-general.

   e. The testator must sign the will.

5. Identify which of the following scenarios best describes the creation of a Totten trust:

   a. Jason deposits funds into his savings account in his own name as a trustee for his daughter, Lucy. The trust is revocable by Jason during his lifetime.

   b. Jason creates a trust for the benefit of his nephew, Alvin. Under the terms of the trust, Alvin is entitled to have only a part of the funds at any one time.

   c. Jason provides in his will that the bulk of his wealth will be held in trust for his daughter, Geena. The trust funds will be transferred to Geena on Jason's death.

   d. Jason provides in his will that the bulk of his wealth will be held in trust for his sister's school, New Horizons.

6. Identify which of the following factors will generally *not* be considered by the courts when determining child custody:

   a. The nature of the relationship and emotional ties between the child and each parent.

   b. The ability of each parent to provide for the child's needs and education.

   c. The ability of the parents of each spouse to support and care for the child if the spouse has a full-time job.

   d. The ability of each parent to provide a stable environment for the child.

7. Identify which of the following are required under most state laws for marriage:

   a. The couple must be man and woman.

   b. The couple must be unmarried.

   c. The couple must not be closely related by blood.

   d. The couple must obtain a marriage license.

   e. A wedding ceremony must be performed by a member of the clergy.

   f. The wedding must result in a common law marriage.

8. Identify which of the following are legally recognized methods for dividing marital property at the time of a divorce:

   a. Equitable distribution.

   b. Community property.

   c. Prenuptial agreement.

   d. Palimony.

QUESTIONS FOR CRITICAL ANALYSIS

1. Why do people make wills? What happens if a person does not make a will? Is it more advantageous for those inheriting property to inherit it by will or through state laws governing intestate succession? Explain.

2. What is the difference between an *inter vivos* trust and a testamentary trust? When would each type of trust be used? Give an example of each.

3. Many attorneys have probate practices in which they administer estates, with paralegals assisting in collecting a decedent's assets, settling the debts of the estate, or working with the personal representative to accomplish these tasks on behalf of the decedent. How do you feel about performing these types of tasks? Would you be interested in the area of probate administration? Why or why not?

4. What is a nuncupative will? Should nuncupative wills ever be valid? Explain the reasoning behind your answer.

5. Suppose that a wealthy testator has a son who suffers from a severe disability that requires costly medical monitoring and treatment. Because the son can earn no income and has no independent wealth, the state assumes the costs of his treatment. If the testator's will provides that all of his wealth and property should go to charity, can the son successfully contest the will? Can the state intervene to obtain compensation for the costs associated with the son's medical care? Why or why not?

6. Before they marry, Ron and Jolene form a written agreement providing that Jolene will inherit nothing on Ron's death. Ron is a billionaire, whereas Jolene has no independent source of income. What is this agreement called? Is it enforceable? Are there any circumstances in which a court might refuse to enforce the agreement?

7. Until the 1960s, to obtain a divorce, a person had to allege grounds for divorce, such as adultery, desertion, cruelty, or abuse. Today, all states allow no-fault divorces. Since the 1960s, the divorce rate has continually risen. It has now reached 50 percent—in other words, today, one out of every two marriages ends in divorce. Explain how no-fault divorce laws might have affected the divorce rate. What other social changes in the past three decades might have contributed to the increase in the divorce rate?

8. Parents are increasingly being awarded joint legal custody and joint physical custody of their children. What are some of the advantages of joint custody? Are there any disadvantages?

9. A woman agrees that in exchange for $10,000, she will be artificially inseminated, conceive a child, carry the child to term, and after delivery of the baby surrender it to the father and his wife. The mother will terminate her parental rights, and the father's wife will adopt the child. Is this a valid contract? What are the arguments in favor of its being upheld as valid? What are the arguments favoring its invalidation?

 PROJECTS

1. One task performed by paralegals in a probate law practice is locating the heirs of a person who died without a will, or intestate. Occasionally, these heirs are unknown or difficult to find. In these instances, a law firm may hire a search business to locate missing heirs. One such firm is International Genealogical Search, Inc. Contact the firm at **http://www.heirsearch.com** or by telephone at 1-800-663-2255 to find out what services the company provides and what its rates are. Write a three-paragraph summary of your findings.

2. Contact your local courthouse or family law court (the court that has jurisdiction over family law matters), and determine the answers to the following questions. Then write a one-page paper summarizing your findings.

   a. What are the requirements for divorce in your state?

   b. What is the typical procedure?

   c. How long does a person have to live in the state before the court will have jurisdiction to hear a family law case (such as divorce or child custody) involving that person?

   d. Can a person petition for a divorce without an attorney?

   e. Is there any state office (or state-funded office) that will help those who cannot afford an attorney?

3. Obtain a copy of your local newspaper, and skim through the classifieds. Are there any advertisements for adoption services? How many? What type of adoption is being offered? Is the service provider located in your city or state? Now check whether any parents who wish to adopt a child have placed an advertisement in the paper. (Hint: Such ads sometimes appear in the "personals" section of the classifieds.) How many parents (if any) are advertising? What do their ads say? Write a few paragraphs describing your findings (and the name and date of the newspaper you used).

4. Call the clerk of your local court to find out when and where family court will be in session. Spend some time observing the court's proceedings. Write a one-page summary of what took place during your visit, including your personal observations concerning the proceedings.

USING INTERNET RESOURCES

1. To learn more about intestacy laws, access the Uniform Probate Code (UPC) at the Web site given below, offered by Cornell University, and then answer the questions that follow.

   http://www.law.cornell.edu/uniform/probate.html

   a. How many states have adopted the UPC in its entirety?

   b. How many states have adopted it in part or with modifications?

2. You can view the wills of famous people by accessing the wills section of the Court TV Web site at **http://www.courttv.com/people/wills**. Go to this Web site, scroll down the page that opens, and click on the will of Jacqueline Kennedy Onassis. Then answer the following questions:

   a. What did she leave to her children?

   b. What did she leave to Maurice Templesman?

   c. Were any trusts established in her will? If so, for whom? What are the terms of the first trust that was created in her will?

   d. What is a residuary clause? Was one included in this will?

3. Nolo.com, Inc., owned by a group of attorneys, has long provided legal do-it-yourself books and kits for creating wills, marital or divorce documents, and a variety of other legal documents. Nolo also provides information on a wide variety of legal topics on its Web site at **http://www.nolo.com**. Access this site and then select "Family Law and Immigration" from the "Main Topics" menu. On the page that opens, click on "Divorce and Child Custody." On that page, under "Featured Articles," select "Establishing and Calculating Child Support FAQ," browse through its contents, and then answer the following questions:

   a. How do courts calculate child support? In most states, what four factors must the courts consider when making these calculations?

   b. Is there a significant amount of uniformity among the states in terms of the amount of child support awarded?

   c. If a spouse feels that the amount of child support awarded is unfair, what can he or she do about it?

   d. What are two circumstances in which a court may grant a permanent modification of child support?

4.  For additional resources, visit our Web site at **http://www.paralegal.delmar.cengage.com**.

END NOTES

1. This type of trust derives its unusual name from *In the Matter of Totten*, 179 N.Y. 112, 71 N.E. 748 (1904).

2. Alabama, Colorado, Georgia, Idaho, Iowa, Kansas, Nevada, New Hampshire, Oklahoma, Oregon, Pennsylvania, Rhode Island, South Carolina, Texas, and Utah.

3. See the discussion of mediation and negotiation in Chapter 6 for additional information on these two methods of dispute settlement.

4. Alaska, Arizona, California, Idaho, Louisiana, Nevada, New Mexico, Texas, Washington, and Wisconsin. Spouses can also hold property as community property in Puerto Rico.

LAWS AFFECTING BUSINESS

11

CHAPTER

CHAPTER OUTLINE

Introduction

Agency Law

Negotiable Instruments

Forms of Business Organization

Employment Law

AFTER COMPLETING THIS CHAPTER, YOU WILL KNOW:

▶ What agency relationships are and the significance of agency law for business relationships.

▶ What negotiable instruments are and how the rights and duties accompanying checks and other instruments are transferred from one party to another.

▶ The most common forms of business organizations and how each type of business organizational form is created and operated.

▶ How profits, losses, risks, and liabilities are distributed in each business organizational form.

▶ How the government regulates employer-employee relationships.

INTRODUCTION

An understanding of the laws affecting business will benefit not only paralegals who work in the business environment but also paralegals whose tasks require some knowledge of business structures and relationships. In this chapter, we cover several legal topics that are central to business operations. We begin by discussing agency law, a concept that permeates the business world. Next, we examine negotiable instruments, including checks and promissory notes, which are routinely used in business transactions as a substitute for cash. Then we focus on how business organizations are formed and structured. We conclude our review of laws affecting business with a discussion of employment law, an area in which many paralegals specialize.

AGENCY LAW

The common law of agency involves concepts and principles with which all paralegals should be familiar. Agency is a pervasive concept in our society because little work could get done without agents. An **agency** relationship exists when one party, called the **agent**, agrees to represent or act for another party, called the **principal**. If you are working as a paralegal employee, in essence you are an agent of your employer. Attorneys, because they represent and act for their clients, are agents of those clients. All forms of business organizations involve agents. Indeed, a business world without agents is hard to imagine. Picture Henry Ford trying to design, produce, and sell all of the cars that Ford Motor Company manufactured. Obviously, other people must be appointed to fill in—act as agents—for the owner of a large company—the principal.

agency
A relationship between two persons in which one person (the agent) represents or acts in the place of the other (the principal).

agent
A person who is authorized to act for or in the place of another person (the principal).

Employees and Independent Contractors

Normally, all employees who deal with third parties are deemed to be agents.
▶ **EXAMPLE 11.1** A salesperson in a department store is an agent of the store's owner (the principal) and acts on the owner's behalf. Any sale of goods made by the salesperson to a customer is binding on the principal. Similarly, most representations of fact made by the salesperson with respect to the goods sold are binding on the principal. ◀

Agency relationships can also arise between employers and independent contractors (such as real estate agents) who are hired to perform special tasks or services (such as the sale of property). An **independent contractor** is a person who is hired to perform a specific undertaking but who is free to choose how and when to perform the work. ▶ **EXAMPLE 11.2** Building contractors and subcontractors are independent contractors because the property owner does not control the acts of either of these professionals. Truck drivers who own their equipment and hire themselves out on a per-job basis are independent contractors, but truck drivers who drive company trucks on a regular basis are usually classified as employees. ◀ Generally, courts look at the degree of control and supervision the employer exercised over the work performed to determine if the individual was an employee or an independent contractor. *An independent contractor may or may not be an agent.*

principal
In agency law, a person who, by agreement or otherwise, authorizes another person (the agent) to act on the principal's behalf in such a way that the acts of the agent become binding on the principal.

independent contractor
A person who is hired to perform a specific undertaking but who is free to choose how and when to perform the work. An independent contractor may or may not be an agent.

Agency Formation

Normally, agency relationships come about voluntarily by agreement of the parties. Although the parties often sign a contract (such as an agreement to list a house for sale with a real estate agent), the agreement need not be in writing. For example, if Deborah asks Ling, a gardener, to contract with others to landscape her yard, and Ling agrees, an agency relationship is created. If Ling then enters into a contract with a landscape architect to design Deborah's yard, Deborah, as the principal, is legally bound by that contract.

An agency agreement can also be implied by conduct. Suppose that a hotel allows Dwight to park cars, even though Dwight does not have an employment contract there. The hotel's manager tells Dwight when to work, as well as where and how to park the cars. The hotel's conduct implies that Dwight has authority to act as a parking valet, and Dwight will be considered the hotel's agent for that purpose.

An agency relationship can also arise if the *principal* causes a third person to reasonably believe that another person is his or her agent, thus creating the *appearance* of an agency that does not in fact exist.[1] ▶ **EXAMPLE 11.3**   Carmen, a sales representative, brings her friend with her to solicit orders from a customer and repeatedly refers to her friend as her assistant. The customer reasonably believes that the friend works with Carmen and proceeds to place orders with the friend. Carmen will not be allowed to deny that the friend is her agent. ◀ Similarly, if a principal approves or affirms a contract after the fact—by filling orders placed with a person who was not truly an agent, for example—an agency relationship is created.

Fiduciary Duties

❚ fiduciary relationship
A relationship involving a high degree of trust and confidence.

An important concept in agency law is that an agency is a **fiduciary relationship**—one involving a high degree of trust and confidence. Because of this, certain fiduciary duties arise whenever an agency relationship comes into existence. Basically, this means that each party owes the other the duty to act honestly and to pursue faithfully the objective of the agency.

The principal is obligated to cooperate with the agent, provide safe working conditions for the agent, and reimburse the agent for work performed and for any expenses incurred while working on the principal's behalf. The agent, in turn, must perform his or her tasks competently and must obey and be loyal to the principal. The duty of loyalty means that the agent's actions must be strictly for the benefit of the principal and must not result in any secret profit for the agent. In addition, the agent cannot represent two principals in the same transaction unless both know of the dual capacity and consent to it. The agent also has a duty to notify the principal of all matters that come to her or his attention concerning the subject matter of the agency and to render an accounting to the principal of all property and money received and paid out on behalf of the principal.

Duties also imply rights. In general, the agent has a right corresponding to every duty owed by the principal, and vice versa. Consider that when an attorney serves as an agent for a client (the principal), the attorney has a duty of loyalty to the client. The client, therefore, has a right to the attorney's loyalty. If you read through your state's ethical rules governing attorneys, you will find that many of the rules governing attorney-client relationships are rooted in these agency concepts.

Agency Relationships and Third Parties

Agency law also comes into play when disputes arise over who should be liable—the principal, agent, or both—when an agent either forms a contract with a third party or causes injury to a third party. Generally, a principal is liable only for the authorized actions of his or her agent. Because the principal is frequently an employer or company that has greater resources with which to pay damages (has "deeper pockets") than the employee, the injured party usually seeks to hold the principal liable for the loss or damage caused by an agent.

Contract Liability

If an agent is not authorized to enter into a contract on behalf of the principal, then normally the principal will not be bound by the contract unless he or she voluntarily accepts (ratifies) it. An agent may be clearly authorized, either orally or in writing, to form certain

Ethics Watch!

THE PARALEGAL AS AGENT AND SUBAGENT

Whenever an attorney agrees to represent a client, the attorney becomes an agent of the client. But what is the status of the paralegal who works for the attorney-agent on the client's behalf? In this situation, the paralegal becomes both an agent (of the attorney) and a subagent (of the client). Subagents also owe fiduciary duties to the principal. A paralegal who works for a law firm thus has fiduciary duties (as an agent) to the firm and (as a subagent) to the client. As a general rule, you should treat both your attorney and the client as principals and serve their interests with the utmost loyalty and care.

contracts. The agent's authority may also be implied by custom—that is, an agent normally has the authority to do whatever is customary or necessary to fulfill the purpose of the agency. A paralegal office manager, for example, has the implied authority to enter into a contract to purchase office supplies on behalf of the firm because the authority to purchase supplies is necessary to the duties of office manager.

Tort Liability

Obviously, any person, including an agent, is liable for her or his own torts. Whether a principal can also be held liable for an agent's torts depends largely on whether the agent was an employee and whether the agent was acting within the scope of his or her employment at the time of committing the tort.

Under the doctrine of *respondeat superior*,[2] the principal-employer is liable for any harm caused to a third party by an agent-employee *acting within the scope of employment*. The doctrine imposes **vicarious liability** on the employer—that is, liability without regard to the personal fault of the employer—for torts committed by an employee in the course or scope of employment. The theory of *respondeat superior* is similar in this respect to the theory of strict liability covered in Chapter 7.

Today's courts consider a number of factors in determining whether a particular act occurred within the course and scope of employment. If the employer authorized the act or had reason to know that the employee would do the act in question, if the injury occurred during work hours, or if the employer furnished the means or tools (for example, a truck or a machine) that caused the injury, that fact would point toward employer liability. In contrast, if the injury occurred after work hours or while the employee was on a "frolic" of his or her own, having substantially abandoned the employer's business, the employer might not be held responsible.

Liability for Independent Contractors' Torts

Generally, the principal is not liable for physical harm caused to a third person by the negligent act of an independent contractor in the performance of the contract. This is because the employer does not have the right to control the details of an independent contractor's

On the Web

To learn more about how agency doctrines apply to sexual harassment in today's workplace, access the United States Supreme Court's opinions at **http://www.findlaw.com/casecode/ supreme.html**, and use the "Party Name Search" box to find the following two cases decided by the Court in 1998: *Burlington Industries, Inc. v. Ellerth* and *Faragher v. City of Boca Raton.*

respondeat superior
A doctrine in agency law under which a principal-employer may be held liable for the wrongful acts committed by agents or employees acting within the scope of their agency or employment.

vicarious liability
Legal responsibility placed on one person for the acts of another.

Developing Paralegal Skills

A CASE OF *RESPONDEAT SUPERIOR*

Rosie Ball, a single parent, and her son Steven were driving home from the grocery store one winter evening in their late-model Volkswagen. They were slowly making their way down an icy street. As they approached an intersection with a stop sign for oncoming traffic, their car was hit by a Jaguar, which failed to stop at the stop sign. The car was speeding, and the driver went through the stop sign at forty-five miles per hour. In the accident, Steven sustained a severe head injury that resulted in irreparable brain damage. The wealthy occupants of the Jaguar, a married couple, had gone out for dinner, had several drinks, and then stopped to purchase Christmas cards for clients of the husband's employer, a multimillion-dollar business.

Seeking legal representation, Rosie contacted the office of attorney Jared Mills, who is a partner in a law firm serving plaintiffs in personal-injury litigation. Jared is the supervising attorney for paralegal Tom Mintin. After meeting with Rosie, the attorney asks Tom to research the issue of whether the multimillion-dollar business can be held liable for the car accident under a theory of *respondeat superior*. Tom researches the issue and learns that an employer is liable under *respondeat superior* for the negligent acts of an employee if the acts are committed in the scope of his or her employment. The employer may also be liable for an employee's acts if the acts occur while the employee is on a brief "detour" from the employer's work—such as when a paralegal employee stops by the dry cleaner's for personal reasons while on the way to the court-house for his or her employer. The employer is not liable, however, if the employee is on a "frolic" of his or her own and is not pursuing work that he or she was hired to perform.

CHECKLIST FOR DETERMINING LIABILITY UNDER THE DOCTRINE OF *RESPONDEAT SUPERIOR*

- Did the employee's act constitute a tort?
- Did the employee commit the act within the course and scope of his or her employment?
- Was the act committed during work hours or after work hours?
- Did the employer authorize the act or have reason to know that the employee would do the act?
- Did the employer furnish the means by which the injury was inflicted (the car, for example)?
- Was the act committed during a brief detour from the employee's course of employment, or was the employee on a "frolic" of his or her own when the act occurred?

performance. Exceptions to this rule are made in certain situations, however, as when exceptionally hazardous activities are involved or when the employer does in fact exercise a significant degree of control over the contractor's performance.

AGENCY LAW AND THE PARALEGAL

A knowledge of agency law is important for the paralegal for several reasons. As a paralegal employee, you will be directly involved in an agency relationship, and it is to your advantage to know what kinds of rights and duties are involved in that relationship. A knowledge of agency law also helps you understand the ethical rules of the legal profession, many of which are derived from the common law of agency.

Furthermore, in your work as a paralegal, you will often be dealing with agents and issues of agency. As you will read shortly, for example, each partner in a partnership is considered an agent of every other partner in the firm and thus has fiduciary duties to the other partners. Corporate officers (such as corporate presidents and vice presidents) are agents of the corporation and, as such, assume the fiduciary duties that arise in agency relationships. Paralegals who work on behalf of corporate clients or who specialize in the area of corporate law will find that agency law permeates the corporate environment.

For paralegals working in the employment context, the doctrine of *respondeat superior* is particularly important because the outcome of many employment cases is influenced by this legal concept. For example, when an employee sues an employer for a supervisor's harassment, the employer may have to pay damages to the employee even though the employer was unaware of the supervisor's actions.

NEGOTIABLE INSTRUMENTS

Most modern commercial transactions would be inconceivable without negotiable instruments. A **negotiable instrument** is a signed writing (record) that contains an unconditional promise or order to pay an exact sum of money on demand or at a specified future time to a specific party or to bearer. A *bearer* is a person in possession of an instrument. The checks you write to pay for groceries and other items are negotiable instruments. Sometimes negotiable instruments are referred to as *commercial paper* because they are normally written on paper and traded commercially.

Negotiable instruments are governed by Articles 3 and 4 of the Uniform Commercial Code (UCC). (As you learned in Chapter 5, the UCC is one of a number of uniform laws drafted by legal experts and submitted to the states for adoption. Uniform laws are *model* laws. They become *actual* laws only when adopted by the states.) Article 3 of the UCC establishes the requirements that an instrument must meet to be negotiable and governs the process of negotiation (the transfer of an instrument from one party to another). Article 4 of the UCC governs bank deposits and collections.

A negotiable instrument can function as a substitute for money or as an extension of credit. For a negotiable instrument to operate *practically* as either a substitute for money or a credit device, or both, it is essential that the instrument be easily transferable without danger of being uncollectible.

> **negotiable instrument**
> A signed writing (record) that contains an unconditional promise or order to pay an exact sum of money on demand or at an exact future time to a specific person or order or to bearer.

Requirements for Negotiability

For an instrument to be negotiable, it must:

- *Be in written form.* The instrument can be written on anything that is readily transferable and has a degree of permanence.

- *Be signed by the maker or the drawer.* The UCC defines a **signature** as any symbol executed or adopted by a party with a present intention to authenticate a writing. The signature can be in any form (such as a word, mark, or rubber stamp) that purports to be a signature and authenticates the writing. It can be anyplace on the face of the instrument. A signature may also be made by an agent.

- *Be a definite promise or order to pay.* A promise must be more than a mere acknowledgment of a debt. The words "I/We promise" or "Pay" meet this criterion.

- *Be an unconditional promise or order to pay.* Payment normally cannot be conditional on the occurrence of an event and cannot be subject to or governed by another agreement.

- *State a fixed amount of money to be paid.* An amount may be considered a fixed sum even if payable in installments, at a stated discount, at an exchange rate, or with a fixed or variable rate of interest.

- *Be payable in money.* Any medium of exchange recognized as the currency of a government is money. The maker or drawer cannot retain the option to pay the instrument in money *or* something else.

> **signature**
> As defined by the UCC, any symbol executed or adopted by a party with a present intention to authenticate a writing

- *Be payable on demand or at a definite time.* Any instrument that is payable on sight, presentation, or issue or that does not state any time for payment is a demand instrument. An instrument is considered payable at a definite time even if it is payable on or before a stated date, if it is payable within a fixed period after sight, or if the drawer or maker has an option to extend the time for a definite period.

- *Be payable to order or to bearer.* An *order instrument* is one that identifies the payee with reasonable certainty. In contrast, a *bearer instrument* does not designate a specific payee and is payable to the person in possession of the instrument (the bearer). An instrument containing such terms as "Payable to bearer," "Payable to James Ried or bearer," or "Payable to cash" is a bearer instrument.

The UCC specifies four types of negotiable instruments: promissory notes, certificates of deposit (CDs), drafts, and checks. Promissory notes and CDs are *promises to pay.* Promissory notes include notes that people sign when they take out a car loan or a home mortgage loan. A CD represents a promise by a bank to repay the person purchasing the CD the amount of the CD, plus interest, on a certain future date. Drafts and checks are *orders to pay.* In the remainder of this section on negotiable instruments, we focus mainly on drafts and checks, because, depending on their jobs, paralegals may have responsibility for managing bank accounts in the course of their work.

Drafts and Checks (Orders to Pay)

A **draft** (bill of exchange) is an unconditional written order that involves three parties. The party creating the draft (the **drawer**) orders another party (the **drawee**) to pay money, usually to a third party (the **payee**).

The most commonly used type of draft is a check. A **check** is a special type of draft that is drawn on a bank, ordering the bank to pay a fixed amount of money on demand. The writer of the check is the drawer, the bank on which the check is drawn is the drawee, and the person to whom the check is payable is the payee. ▶ **EXAMPLE 11.4** Suppose that Anita Cruzak writes a check from her checking account to pay her college tuition. In this situation, Anita is the drawer, her bank is the drawee, and her college is the payee. ◀ Exhibit 11.1 shows a sample check.

draft

An unconditional written order by which a party (the drawer) orders another party (the drawee) to pay money, usually to a third party (the payee).

drawer

The party that issues a draft (such as a check), thereby ordering the drawee to pay.

drawee

The party that is ordered to pay a draft (such as a check). With a check, a bank or a financial institution is always the drawee.

payee

The party to whom a negotiable instrument, such as a check, is made payable.

check

A draft drawn on a bank by which the drawer orders the bank to pay a fixed amount of money on demand.

EXHIBIT 11.1
A Sample Check

payee

Venita Davies
234 A Street
Nita City, NI 83956

4378

DATE *June 1, 2008*

PAY
TO THE ORDER OF *The Corner Flower Shop* $57⁰⁰

Fifty Seven and ⁰⁰/₁₀₀   DOLLARS

First National Bank of Whiteacre
Whiteacre, Nita 83850

⑆000234123⑆ 1010 010 222 4378

Venita Davies

drawee   *drawer*

Transfer of Instruments by Negotiation

The UCC defines **negotiation** as the transfer of an instrument in such form that the transferee (the one to whom the instrument is transferred) receives, at the very least, the rights of the previous possessor of the instrument. As you will read shortly, in some circumstances, a transfer by negotiation can make it possible for the transferee to receive even *more* rights in the instrument than the prior possessor had.

There are two methods of negotiating an instrument. The method used depends on whether the instrument is an order instrument or a bearer instrument.

negotiation
The transfer of an instrument in such a way that the transferee (the person to whom the instrument is transferred) receives, at the very least, the rights of the previous possessor of the instrument.

Negotiating Order Instruments

An *order instrument* clearly identifies the name of the payee, such as "Pay to the order of Lloyd Sorenson." If the instrument is an order instrument, it is negotiated by delivery to the payee with any necessary indorsements. An **indorsement** is a signature, with or without additional words or statements, that is most often written on the back of an instrument.

▶ **EXAMPLE 11.5** National Express Corporation issues a payroll check "to the order of Lloyd Sorenson." Sorenson takes the check to the supermarket, signs his name on the back (an indorsement), gives it to the cashier (a delivery), and receives cash. Sorenson has *negotiated* the check to the supermarket. ◀

indorsement
A signature, with or without additional words or statements, that is most often written on the back of an instrument.

Four types of indorsements can be used to negotiate an instrument. The most common type is a *blank indorsement,* which consists only of the person's signature (for example, "Alan Luberda") and does not specify the party to whom the instrument is being transferred. A *special indorsement,* in contrast, identifies the person to whom the indorser intends to make the instrument payable (for example, "Pay to Anthony Bartomo"). A *qualified indorsement* (for example, "Pay to Elvie Ling without recourse") limits the liability of the person who indorsed the instrument—usually someone acting as an agent. A *restrictive indorsement* (for example, "Pay to Ada Johnson in trust for Sarah Emerson" or "For deposit only") requires the person to whom the instrument is payable to comply with certain instructions regarding the funds involved. Exhibit 11.2 on the following page provides examples and descriptions of these types of indorsements.

Negotiating Bearer Instruments

If an instrument is payable to bearer, it is negotiated simply by delivery—that is, by transfer into another person's possession. Indorsement is not necessary. The use of bearer instruments thus involves more risk through loss or theft than the use of order instruments.

▶ **EXAMPLE 11.6** Assume that Richard Kray writes a check "payable to cash" and hands it to Jessie Arnold (a delivery). Kray has issued the check (a bearer instrument) to Arnold. Arnold places the check in her wallet, which is later stolen. The thief now in possession of the check has no rights to it. If the thief "delivers" the check to an innocent third person, however, negotiation will be complete. All rights to the check will be passed absolutely to that third person, and Arnold will lose all rights to recover the proceeds of the check from that person. Of course, Arnold could attempt to recover the money from the thief, providing that the thief, can be found. ◀

Unauthorized Signatures

The key to liability on a negotiable instrument is a signature. As a general rule, people are not liable to pay on negotiable instruments unless their signatures appear on the instruments. An unauthorized signature will not bind the person whose name is forged.

▶ **EXAMPLE 11.7** Parker finds Dolby's checkbook lying in the street, writes out a check to himself, and forges Dolby's signature. If a bank fails to ascertain that Dolby's signature is

EXHIBIT 11.2
Types of Indorsements

TYPE OF INDORSEMENT	EXAMPLE	EXPLANATION
Blank	*Alan Luberda*	Consists only of a signature and does not specify the party to whom the instrument is being transferred.
Special	*Pay to Anthony Bartomo* *Peter Rabe*	Identifies the person to whom the indorser intends to make the instrument payable.
Qualified	*Pay to Elvie Ling without recourse.* *Bridget Cage*	Often used by agents to limit their personal liability in the event that the instrument is not honored (not paid by the drawee bank, for example).
Restrictive	FOR DEPOSIT ONLY *Stephanie Mullah* *Pay to Ada Johnson in trust for Sarah Emerson* *Robert Emerson*	Requires the party to whom the instrument is payable to comply with certain instructions regarding the funds involved. For example, a "For deposit only" indorsement prohibits further negotiation except by the bank. An indorsement to pay funds "in trust" or "as agent" for another requires the payee to use the funds only for the benefit of the named person.

not genuine (which banks normally have a duty to do) and cashes the check for Parker, the bank will generally be liable to Dolby for the amount.

A principal can, however, ratify (make valid) an unauthorized signature made by an agent (as a mother might do if her daughter forged the mother's name). Also, a person whose name is forged may not be able to deny liability if the person's own negligence substantially contributed to the forgery. ▶ **EXAMPLE 11.8** Suppose that the owner of a business, Rob, leaves his signature stamp and a blank check on an office counter. An employee, using the stamp, fills in and cashes the check. Because Rob's negligence contributed to the forgery, he may be prevented from denying liability on the check.

Holder versus Holder in Due Course (HDC)

holder
As defined by the UCC, any person in possession of an instrument drawn, issued, or indorsed to him or her, to his or her order, to bearer, or in blank.

holder in due course (HDC)
A holder of a negotiable instrument who has acquired the instrument for value; in good faith; and without notice that the instrument is overdue, that it has been dishonored, that any person has a defense against it or a claim to it, or that the instrument contains unauthorized signatures, has been altered, or is so irregular or incomplete as to call into question its authenticity.

The UCC defines a **holder** as a person in the possession of an instrument drawn, issued, or indorsed to him or her, to his or her order, to bearer, or in blank. An ordinary holder obtains only those rights that the transferor had in the instrument. A holder normally is also subject to the same defenses (legal reasons why a party need not pay on the check) that could be asserted against the transferor.

Problems sometimes arise when a holder seeking payment of a negotiable instrument learns that a defense to payment exists or that another party has a prior claim to the instrument. In such situations, for the person seeking payment, it becomes important to have the rights of a **holder in due course (HDC)**. By meeting certain requirements, an HDC takes a negotiable instrument free of all claims and most defenses of other parties.

A holder of a negotiable instrument must meet three requirements to be an HDC. She or he must take the instrument:

- *For value.* An HCD must have given *value* for the instrument. A holder takes an instrument for value only to the extent that the promise for which the instrument was given has been performed. A promise to give value in the future normally does not constitute value sufficient to make a person an HDC. Also, a person who receives an instrument as a gift has not met the requirement of giving value and thus does not become an HDC.

- *In good faith.* The holder must have acted honestly in the process of acquiring the instrument. It is immaterial whether the transferor acted in good faith. Thus, even a person who takes a negotiable instrument from a thief may become an HDC if the person acquires the instrument in good faith.

- *Without notice.* A holder will not receive HDC protection if he or she acquires an instrument and is *on notice* (knows or has reason to know) that it is defective. The instrument may be defective if it is overdue, it has been dishonored, it contains unauthorized signatures or alterations, or any person has a defense against it or a claim to it. An instrument is also considered defective if it is so irregular or incomplete as to call into question its authenticity.

Checks and the Banking System

As mentioned earlier, checks are the most commonly used type of draft. The use of checks, of course, involves the relationship between banks and their customers. The bank-customer relationship begins when the customer opens a checking account and deposits funds that the bank will use to pay for checks written by the customer. When the customer writes a check on his or her account, an agency relationship arises between the customer and the bank. In effect, the customer is ordering the bank to pay the amount specified on the check when a holder of the check presents it to the bank for payment. In this situation, the bank becomes the customer's agent and is obligated to honor the customer's request. Similarly, if

A bank officer welcomes a new customer. When the customer writes a check on his checking account, an agency relationship will arise between the bank and the customer.

(Courtesy of ®Comstock Images/Alamy)

the customer deposits a check into her or his account, the bank, as the customer's agent, is obligated to collect payment on the check from the bank on which the check was drawn.

Insufficient Funds

When a banking institution provides checking services, the customer agrees to keep sufficient funds on deposit with the bank to cover all checks written. If the bank receives an item properly payable from a customer's checking account but the account contains insufficient funds to cover the amount of the check, the bank can pursue either of two options:

- *The bank can dishonor the item.* If a check "bounces"—is dishonored for insufficient funds—the holder can resubmit the check, hoping that at a later date sufficient funds will be available to pay it. The holder must notify any indorsers on the check of the first dishonor, however; otherwise, they will be discharged from liability for payment of the check. The writer of the dishonored check is liable to the payee or to the holder of the check in a civil suit.

- *The bank can pay the item and charge the customer's account, thus creating an overdraft.* If the customer has authorized the bank to do so and the practice does not violate any bank-customer agreement, the bank can subtract the amount of the overdraft (plus a service charge) from the customer's next deposit (or from the customer's other accounts).[3]

Stop-Payment Orders

stop-payment order
An order by a bank customer to his or her bank not to pay or certify a certain check.

A **stop-payment order** is an order by a customer to his or her bank not to pay a certain check. When a stop-payment order is given orally, it is binding on the bank for only fourteen calendar days unless confirmed in writing.[4] A written stop-payment order or an oral order confirmed in writing is effective for six months, at which time it must be renewed in writing. The customer-drawer must have a *valid legal ground* for issuing such an order; otherwise, the holder can sue the drawer for payment. A person who wrongfully stops payment on a check will be liable to the payee for the amount of the check and also may be liable for consequential damages incurred by the payee as a result of the wrongful stop-payment order.

Checks Bearing Forged Drawers' Signatures

When a bank pays a check on which the drawer's signature is forged, generally the bank is liable. A bank, however, may be able to recover at least some of the loss from the customer (if the customer's negligence contributed to the making of the forgery), from the forger of the check (if he or she can be found), or from the holder who presented the check for payment (if the holder knew that the signature was forged).

Because a forged signature on a check has no legal effect as the signature of the drawer, banks require each customer who opens a checking account to sign a signature card. Signature cards allow the bank to verify whether the signatures on their customers' checks are genuine. The general rule is that the bank must recredit the customer's account when it pays a check with a forged signature. (Note that banks today normally verify signatures only on checks that exceed a certain threshold, such as $1,000, $2,500, or some higher amount. Even though a bank sometimes incurs liability costs when it has paid forged checks, the costs involved in verifying the signature on every check would be much higher.)

Timely Examination of Bank Statements Required.
When the customer's negligence substantially contributed to the forgery, the bank normally will not be obligated to recredit the customer's account for the amount of the check.[5] Banks typically send or make available to their customers monthly statements detailing activity in their checking accounts. The customer has a duty to examine bank statements (and canceled checks or photocopies, if they are

included with the statements) promptly and with reasonable care and to promptly report any alterations or forged signatures (including any forged signatures of indorsers) to the bank.

If the customer fails to fulfill this duty and the bank suffers a loss as a result, the customer will be liable for the loss. Even if the customer can prove that she or he took reasonable care against forgeries, the UCC provides that the customer must discover the forgeries and notify the bank within a period of one year to require the bank to recredit her or his account. In some smaller law offices, reviewing the firm's bank statements is a paralegal's responsibility. It is important to review each bank statement promptly and thoroughly to prevent a possible loss of funds due to forgeries.

Consequences of Failing to Detect Forgeries.   When the same wrongdoer has committed a series of forgeries, the UCC provides that the customer, to recover for all of the forged items, must discover and report the first forged check to the bank within thirty calendar days of the receipt of the bank statement (and canceled checks or copies, if they are included).

Checks Bearing Forged Indorsements

A bank that pays a customer's check bearing a forged indorsement must recredit the customer's account or be liable to the customer-drawer for breach of contract. The customer, however, has a duty to report forged indorsements promptly. Failure to report forged indorsements within a three-year period after the forged items have been made available to the customer relieves the bank of any liability.

Altered Checks

The customer's instruction to the bank is to pay the exact amount on the face of the check to the holder. The bank has a duty to examine each check before making final payment. If it fails to detect an alteration, it is liable to its customer for the loss because it did not pay as the customer ordered. The loss is the difference between the original amount of the check and the amount actually paid. ▶ **EXAMPLE 11.9** Suppose that a check written for $11 is altered to read $111. The customer's account will be charged $11 (the amount the customer ordered the bank to pay). The bank will normally be responsible for the $100. ◀

As in a situation involving a forged drawer's signature, a customer's negligence can shift the loss when payment is made on an altered check (unless the bank was also negligent). A common example occurs when a person carelessly writes a check and leaves large gaps around the numbers and words where additional numbers and words can be inserted (see Exhibit 11.3). As a paralegal, if you are asked to write checks to a law firm's creditors, be sure to begin writing at the far left on each line and draw a line through the remaining space to the right.

EXHIBIT 11.3
A Poorly Filled-Out Check

XYZ CORPORATION
10 INDUSTRIAL PARK
ST. PAUL, MINNESOTA 56561

2206

June 8 20 07   22-1/960

P AY TO THE ORDER OF _____ John Doe _____ $ 100.00

One hundred and 70/100 _____ DOLLARS

THE FIRST NATIONAL BANK OF MYTOWN
332 MINNESOTA STREET
MYTOWN, MINNESOTA 55555

Stephanie Roe, President

⑆94⑈77577⑈ 0885

Electronic Fund Transfers

Increasingly, credit cards, debit cards, and other devices and methods to transfer funds electronically are being used to pay for goods and services. The application of computer technology to banking has helped to relieve banking institutions of the burden of having to move mountains of paperwork to process electronic fund transfers. An **electronic fund transfer (EFT)** is a transfer of funds through the use of an electronic terminal, a telephone, a computer, or magnetic tape.

electronic fund transfer (EFT)
A transfer of funds through the use of an electronic terminal, a telephone, a computer, or magnetic tape.

Types of EFT Systems

Most banks today offer EFT services to their customers. The four most common types of EFT systems used by bank customers are the following:

- *Automated teller machines (ATMs).* Automated teller machines are connected online to a bank's computers. Customers insert a plastic card issued by the bank and key in a personal identification number (PIN) to access their accounts and conduct banking transactions.

- *Point-of-sale systems.* In point-of-sale systems, online terminals located at checkout counters allow consumers to use debit cards to transfer funds to merchants to pay for purchases.

- *Direct deposits and withdrawals.* Customers can authorize a bank to allow another party—such as the government or an employer—to make direct deposits into their accounts. Similarly, a customer can request the bank to make automatic payments from the customer's funds to a third party at regular, recurrent intervals (insurance premiums or loan payments, for example).

- *Pay-by-Internet systems.* Many financial institutions permit their customers to access the institution's computer system via the Internet and direct a transfer of funds between accounts or pay a particular bill, such as a utility bill.

Consumer Fund Transfers

The Electronic Fund Transfer Act (EFTA) of 1978 provides a basic framework for the rights, liabilities, and responsibilities of consumers who use EFT systems. The EFTA governs financial institutions that offer EFTs involving consumer accounts. The types of accounts covered include checking accounts, savings accounts, and any other asset accounts established for personal, family, or household purposes. Telephone transfers are covered by the EFTA only if they are made in accordance with a prearranged plan under which periodic or recurring transfers are contemplated.

The EFTA is essentially a disclosure law benefiting consumers. The act requires financial institutions to inform consumers of their rights and responsibilities, including those listed here, with respect to EFT systems.

- If a customer's debit card is lost or stolen and used without the customer's permission, the customer may be required to pay no more than $50. The customer, however, must notify the bank of the loss or theft within two days of learning about it. Otherwise, the liability increases to $500. The customer may be liable for more than $500 if he or she does not report the unauthorized use within sixty days after it appears on the customer's statement. (If a customer voluntarily gives his or her debit card to another, who then uses it improperly, the protections just mentioned do not apply.)

- The customer must notify the bank of any error on the monthly statement within sixty days. The bank then has ten days to investigate and must report its conclusions to the customer in writing. If the bank takes longer than ten days, it must return the disputed amount to the customer's account until it finds the error. If there is no error, the customer has to give the money back to the bank.

- The bank must furnish receipts for transactions made through customer terminals, but it is not obligated to do so for telephone transfers.

- The bank must provide a monthly statement for every month in which there is an electronic transfer of funds. Otherwise, the bank must provide statements every quarter. The statement must show the amount and date of the transfer, the names of the retailers or other third parties involved, the location or identification of the terminal, and the fees. Additionally, the statement must give an address and a phone number for inquiries and error notices.

- Any authorized prepayment for utility bills and insurance premiums can be stopped three days before the scheduled transfer.

Unauthorized EFTs. Under the EFTA, a transfer is unauthorized if (1) it is initiated by a person who has no actual authority to initiate it, (2) the consumer receives no benefit from it, and (3) the consumer did not furnish the person "with the card, code, or other means of access" to his or her account. Unauthorized access to an EFT system constitutes a federal crime, and those convicted may be sentenced to a fine of up to $10,000 and imprisonment for up to ten years.

Violations and Damages. If a bank violates the EFTA, a consumer may recover both actual damages (including attorneys' fees and costs) and punitive damages of not less than $100 and not more than $1,000. Failure to investigate an error in good faith makes the bank liable for treble damages (three times the amount of damages). Even when a customer has sustained no actual harm, the bank may be liable for legal costs and punitive damages if it fails to follow the error-resolution procedures outlined by the EFTA.

Commercial Transfers

The volume of payments transferred electronically, or "by wire," between commercial parties amounts to more than a trillion dollars a day—an amount that far exceeds the dollar volume of payments made by other means. Commercial wire transfers are governed by Article 4A of the UCC, which has been adopted by most states. In a wire transfer transaction, a customer instructs his or her bank to transfer funds from the customer's account to another party's account in a bank located elsewhere. Depending on the complexity of the transaction (if it involves overseas banks, for example), additional banks may be involved in the process.

NEGOTIABLE INSTRUMENTS AND THE PARALEGAL

It is estimated that over sixty-five billion personal and commercial checks are written each year in the United States. For virtually all businesses, issuing and receiving negotiable instruments, particularly checks, are common parts of their operations. As a paralegal, whether you work for a law firm or a corporation, your employer will routinely issue and receive checks (and other negotiable instruments). Because of the extensive use of negotiable instruments, the types of disputes that may arise—and may require legal assistance to resolve—

are wide ranging. Here is just a sampling of the type of work that paralegals may undertake with respect to negotiable instruments:

- Assist in litigation to recover damages for a bank's wrongful dishonor of a check presented for payment by a client.

- Write checks for an employer's signature and review bank statements as they arrive.

(Continued)

- Indorse checks as they arrive so that they can be deposited in the firm's bank account.
- Research the UCC provisions relating to the rights and liabilities of parties to negotiable instruments to determine whether a client can be held liable for a forged check.
- Assist an executor of a will in organizing the decedent's bank accounts and determining if the decedent paid certain debts.

- Help a recently divorced or widowed client who has never managed his or her financial affairs to set up and maintain a checking account.
- Organize a law firm's banking files and devise procedures to protect against negligence in the handling of checks.
- Make arrangements for electronic fund transfers.
- Locate indorsers of a check to obtain payment on an instrument that has been dishonored.

FORMS OF BUSINESS ORGANIZATION

Traditionally, there were three basic forms of business organization: the sole proprietorship, the partnership, and the corporation. These forms continue to be used. In addition, today's business owners and professionals are turning to newer, alternative business organizational forms known as limited liability companies and limited liability partnerships.

Each business form involves different relationships, rights, obligations, and regulatory schemes. In your work as a paralegal, you will want to have some idea of what rights and duties accompany each of these business forms when you work on behalf of clients.

Sole Proprietorships

Remember from Chapter 4 that the simplest form of business is the *sole proprietorship,* in which one person—the sole proprietor—owns the business. The sole proprietor is entitled to all of the business's profits and bears personal responsibility for all of the business's debts and other obligations. Sole proprietors can own and manage any type of business, from an informal, home-office undertaking to a large restaurant or construction firm. Sole proprietorships are very common. In fact, they constitute over two-thirds of all American businesses. They are also usually small enterprises—only about 1 percent of the sole proprietorships in the United States earn over $1 million per year.

Formation of a Sole Proprietorship

The sole proprietorship is usually easier and less costly to start than any other kind of business, as few legal forms are involved. No partnership agreement need be devised, because there are no partners. No papers need be filed with the state (as when a corporation is formed) to establish the business. At most, there will be only minor paperwork involved, depending on the law of the city in which the business is located.

Because it is the simplest business form to create, persons first starting up businesses often choose to operate as sole proprietors. An attorney or a freelance paralegal might begin doing business as a sole proprietor. (Recall from Chapter 4 that an attorney who practices law as a sole proprietor is often called a *sole practitioner.*)

Advantages of Sole Proprietorships

A major advantage of the sole proprietorship is that the sole proprietor is entitled to all the profits made by the firm (because he or she takes all the risk). The sole proprietor is also free to make any decision he or she wishes concerning the business—whom to hire, when to take a vacation, what kind of business to pursue, and so on. Additionally, sole proprietors are

PARALEGAL **profile**

Melissa L. Howe

PARALEGAL ENTREPRENEUR

Melissa L. Howe worked for many years as a paralegal for private attorneys before founding two paralegal-related businesses. The first, a paralegal freelance business, was opened in 1999. She sold this business in 2001 and opened a private paralegal college licensed by the Oklahoma Board of Private Vocational Schools. The college has a very successful job-placement program for students.

Howe takes great pride in her students' accomplishments and is always willing to give them advice on how to open and operate their own businesses successfully. She is a former associate director of Women of Vision, a group that seeks to assist women in meeting their career challenges. In addition to running the paralegal college, Howe works as a consultant in the paralegal job field and consults and trains individuals on various legal-software programs. She has also written a book, The Paralegal Entrepreneur, published by Thomson Delmar Learning.

In 2005, Howe received her bachelor's degree in criminal justice from Cameron University in Lawton, Oklahoma. She hopes to complete her studies toward a master of business administration (MBA) degree in the spring of 2007.

What do you like best about your work?

"I derive great pleasure from working in a business organization and assisting others with paralegal career training and employment. I am able to work with a variety of clients daily. I also enjoy the fact that I am able to use my own ideas and business plans and turn these ideas into profits. Each time my profits grow, or I find employment for a graduating paralegal student, I feel good inside."

What is the greatest challenge that you face in your area of work?

"The greatest challenge is meeting deadlines on a tight schedule. Another important challenge is staying current with certain permits, licenses, and business regulations. Sometimes it is difficult when you are very busy to take the time to complete these types of documents, but all successful organizations must update them on a regular basis."

What advice do you have for would-be paralegals in your area of work?

> *"The greatest challenge is meeting deadlines on a tight schedule. Another important challenge is staying current with certain permits, licenses, and business regulations."*

"You must possess excellent oral communication skills as well as writing skills. Stay on top of deadlines associated with regulations, licenses, and permits. Begin preparing these documents long before they are actually due. Preparing ahead will allow you to make last-minute changes and correct mistakes. Meeting these deadlines is very important to the organizations that need to approve or certify a license renewal."

What are some tips for success as a paralegal in your area of work?

"Tips for success are to not only dress professionally but act professionally and maintain ethical standards. Stay current with ever-changing laws and administrative regulations. Make it a priority to know in what type of organization you are working. There are several types of business organization, and each has certain rules and regulations that must be followed. You should become very familiar with these rules and regulations, as well as with the expirations of certain permits and licenses. You should also have strong interpersonal skills and be able to work with all types of people. You should be a good troubleshooter for human resource and other computer software programs."

allowed to establish tax-exempt retirement accounts, such as Keogh plans. (A *Keogh plan* is a retirement program designed for self-employed persons by which such persons can shelter a certain percentage of their income from taxation. The principal and interest earnings are not taxed until funds are withdrawn from the plan.)

Disadvantages of Sole Proprietorships

A major disadvantage of the sole proprietorship is that the proprietor alone, as the firm's sole owner, is personally liable for any losses, debts, and obligations incurred by the business enterprise. As discussed in Chapter 4, *personal liability* means that the personal assets of the business owner (such as a home, car, savings account, or other tangible or intangible property) may be subject to creditors' claims if the business fails.

As a paralegal, if you are asked to do a preliminary investigation of a client's claim against a business entity, one of the first things you should check is the form of the business. ▶ **EXAMPLE 11.10** Your firm's client wants to sue a business firm for damages. If you learn that the firm is a sole proprietorship, then you will know that if the firm itself has insufficient assets to pay damages to the client (should the client win in court), the firm's owner will personally be liable for the damages. Depending on what you learn about the firm's financial condition, you may want to investigate the owner's personal financial position as well. ◀

Another disadvantage of the sole proprietorship is that it may be difficult to obtain capital for expansion. The sole proprietor is dependent on loans made by lending institutions and others. For this reason, sole proprietors sometimes decide to take on partners, who will contribute capital to the business, or to incorporate and sell shares in the business to raise funds.

Taxation and Sole Proprietorships

A sole proprietor must pay income taxes on business profits, but he or she does not have to file a separate tax return for the business. Rather, the profits are reported on the sole proprietor's personal tax return and taxed as personal income.

Termination of the Sole Proprietorship

In a sole proprietorship, the owner is the business. For that reason, when the owner dies, so does the business—it is automatically dissolved. If the business is transferred to family members or other heirs, a new proprietorship is created. Similarly, if the proprietor sells the business, whoever purchases it must establish either a new sole proprietorship or some other business form, such as a partnership or a corporation.

Partnerships

On the Web

You can review the text of the Uniform Partnership Act, summaries of the amendments, and legislative facts about the bill by clicking on the various links at **http://www.nccusl.org**.

As discussed in Chapter 4, many law firms organize their business in the form of a *partnership*, which arises when two or more individuals undertake to do business together as *partners*. Each partner owns a portion of the business and shares jointly in the firm's profits or losses. Partners are personally liable for the debts and obligations of the business if the business fails, just as sole proprietors are.

The Uniform Partnership Act (UPA) governs the operation of partnerships *unless the partners have expressly agreed otherwise.* Like the UCC, the UPA is a model law that becomes actual law only when adopted by a state legislature. The majority of the states adopted the most recent version of the UPA in 1994 and the amended version in 1997.

Partnership Formation

Under the UPA, a partnership is defined as "an association of two or more persons to carry on as co-owners a business for profit." To create a partnership, two or more persons interested in establishing a profit-making business simply agree to do so, as partners. The partnership agreement can be expressed orally or in writing, or it can be implied by conduct. If the partnership is to continue for over a year, then the agreement must be in writing to satisfy the Statute of Frauds, a state statute that specifies what types of contracts must be in writing to be enforceable (discussed in Chapter 8).

Rights and Duties of Partners

When two or more persons agree to do business as partners, they enter into a special relationship with one another. To an extent, their relationship is similar to an agency relationship because each partner is deemed the agent of the other partners and of the partnership.

Partnership law is distinct from agency law in one significant way, however. A partnership is based on a voluntary contract between two or more competent persons who agree to place some or all of their money or other assets, labor, and skill in a business, with the understanding that profits and losses will be proportionately shared. In a nonpartnership agency relationship, the agent usually does not have an ownership interest in the business, nor is he or she obligated to bear a portion of the ordinary business losses.

The rights of partners are often written into the partnership agreement. If the agreement does not specify these rights, then the UPA comes into play (the state's version of the UPA, as adopted). Some of the important rights of partners are listed in Exhibit 11.4.

Liability of Partners

Historically, a partnership could not be sued or initiate a lawsuit in its own name. This traditional rule treated all partnerships as aggregates of individuals. Under this rule, which is still followed in some states, only the individual partners—not the partnership—can be sued. Because this approach is so cumbersome, most states today recognize the partnership as an entity that can sue or be sued and collect judgments in the partnership's name.

A distinguishing feature of the partnership, and one that is often regarded as a disadvantage of this form of business, is the potentially extensive personal liability faced by partners for partnership obligations and for the actions of the other partners. Partners have **joint liability**, or shared liability. In other words, partners may be held personally liable not only for their own actions and those of the partnership as an entity but also for the actions of other partners.

Partners may also be subject to **joint and several liability**—*several* liability means *individual* liability.[6] Joint and several liability means that a third party may sue all of the partners (jointly) or one or more of the partners separately (severally) at his or her option. This is true even if one of the partners sued did not participate in, ratify, or know about whatever gave rise to the cause of action.

▶ **EXAMPLE 11.11** Suppose that a plaintiff wants to recover for damages allegedly caused by a physician's negligence (medical malpractice). The physician is one of four partners who own a partnership. Because partners are jointly and severally liable, the plaintiff could sue the physician who allegedly caused the harm, the partnership, one of the other physicians (even if that physician had nothing to do with the plaintiff's treatment), or all of the physicians to recover damages. ◀ The liability faced by partners is a major reason for the rapid growth of a new form of partnership, the limited liability partnership, which will be discussed later.

joint liability
Shared liability. In partnership law, partners incur joint liability for partnership obligations and debts.

joint and several liability
Shared and individual liability. In partnership law, joint and several liability means that a third party may sue all of the partners (jointly) or one or more of the partners separately (severally) at his or her option. This is true even if one of the partners sued did not participate in, ratify, or know about whatever gave rise to the cause of action.

EXHIBIT 11.4
Rights of Partners

PARTNERS HAVE THE RIGHT:

- To hold an ownership interest in the firm and to receive a share of the profits.
- To inspect partnership books and records.
- To an accounting of partnership assets and profits (for example, to determine the value of each partner's share in the partnership). An accounting can be performed voluntarily or can be compelled by a court order. Formal accounting occurs by right in connection with partnership dissolution proceedings.
- To participate in the management of the business operation unless the partnership agreement specifies otherwise.

THE PARALEGAL AS AN APPARENT PARTNER

If you work as a paralegal for a law partnership, you need to be especially careful to ensure that clients do not mistakenly conclude that you are an attorney-partner in the firm. For example, assume that you and your supervising attorney are waiting for a client to arrive for an intake interview. You are sitting in the attorney's office talking about another matter when the client arrives. During the course of the interview, the attorney asks you about an ordinance just passed by the city that might affect the client's planned renovations of an office building. Your answer indicates that you are knowledgeable in the law. The client leaves the office assuming that you are an attorney, even though you were introduced as the attorney's legal assistant. Should the client ever sue the firm and/or the partners, you may be subject to liability as an "apparent partner" if the client convinces the court that you "held yourself out as an attorney."

Taxation of Partnerships

The partnership itself, as an entity, does not pay federal income taxes. The partnership as an entity files an information return with the Internal Revenue Service on which the income received by the partnership is reported. The partners declare their shares of the partnership's profits on their personal income tax returns and pay taxes accordingly.

Partnership Termination

The partnership agreement may specify the duration of the partnership by indicating that the partnership will end on a certain date or on the occurrence of a certain event. It would be a breach of the partnership agreement for one partner to withdraw from the partnership before the specified date arrived or the specified event occurred. The withdrawing partner would be liable to the remaining partners for any related losses.

When an agreement does not specify the duration of the partnership, the partners are free to withdraw at any time without incurring liability to the remaining partners. Under the UPA, withdrawal by a partner results in the **dissolution** (the formal disbanding) of the partnership (although a new partnership may arise among those who stay with the enterprise). Under the revised UPA, however, the withdrawal of a partner causes a partnership to be dissolved only if the withdrawal results in the breakup of the partnership itself and the business cannot continue. The occurrence of certain events also results in partnership termination. The death or bankruptcy of a partner, for example, terminates the partnership.

Partnership termination is a two-step process. Dissolution is the first step in the process. The second step is the **winding up** of partnership affairs. Once the firm is dissolved, it continues to exist legally until the process of winding up all business affairs (collecting and distributing the firm's assets) is complete.

Limited Partnerships

Ordinary partnerships, such as those just discussed, are often referred to as *general partnerships*. The **limited partnership**, in contrast, is a special form of partnership involving two different types of partners—general partners and limited partners. The **general partners**

---

dissolution
The formal disbanding of a partnership or a corporation.

winding up
The process of winding up all business affairs (collecting and distributing the firm's assets) after a partnership or corporation has been dissolved.

limited partnership
A partnership consisting of one or more general partners and one or more limited partners.

general partner
A partner who participates in managing the business of a partnership and has all the rights and liabilities that arise under traditional partnership law.

manage the business and have the rights and liabilities of partners in a general partnership. The **limited partners** are, for the most part, simply investors in the business. A limited partnership may be formed, for example, to purchase and develop real estate. The limited partners play a passive role. Their funds help to finance the venture, and they receive a share of the profits in return.

The limited partner does not participate in the management of the partnership and, in return, enjoys limited liability status. Unlike general partners, who are personally liable for partnership obligations, limited partners are liable only up to the amounts that they have invested. In other words, if the partnership goes bankrupt they will lose their investments but cannot be held liable for partnership debts beyond that amount.

In contrast to the informal, private, and voluntary agreement that usually suffices to create a general partnership, the formation of a limited partnership is a public and formal proceeding that must follow state statutory requirements. The partners must sign a *certificate of limited partnership,* which requires information similar to that found in a corporate charter. The certificate must be filed with the designated state official (usually, the secretary of state). In this respect, the limited partnership resembles the corporation—another creature of statute.

> **limited partner**
> One who invests in a limited partnership but does not play an active role in managing the operation of the business. Unlike general partners, limited partners are only liable for partnership debts up to the amounts that they have invested.

Corporations

Paralegals frequently work on behalf of corporate clients or on legal matters involving corporations. An increasing number of paralegals are also now working for corporate employers. As a paralegal, you should thus have a basic knowledge of how corporations are formed and operated. You should also be familiar with the basic rights and responsibilities of corporate personnel. Corporate personnel include the **shareholders** (the owners of the business, called shareholders because they purchase corporate **shares,** or stock), the **directors** (persons elected by the shareholders to direct corporate affairs), and the **officers** (persons hired by the directors to manage the day-to-day operations of the corporation). Corporate officers include the corporate president, vice president, secretary, treasurer, and possibly others, such as a chief financial officer and chief executive officer. Corporate officers are employees of the corporation and subject to employment contracts.

Although it is owned by individuals, the corporation is a separate legal entity, which is created and recognized by state law. In the eyes of the law, a corporation is a legal "person" that enjoys many of the rights and privileges that U.S. citizens enjoy, such as the right of access to the courts as an entity that can sue or be sued. It also has, among other rights, the right to due process of law and the right to freedom from unreasonable searches and seizures.

The Model Business Corporation Act (MBCA) is a codification of modern corporation law that has been influential in the codification of corporation statutes. Today, the majority of state statutes are guided by the revised version of the MBCA, known as the Revised Model Business Corporation Act (RMBCA). There is, however, considerable variation among the statutes of the states that have based their statutes on the MBCA or the RMBCA, and several states do not follow either act. Because of this, as a paralegal you will need to rely on individual state corporation laws rather than the MBCA or RMBCA. We look next at a number of characteristics of corporations.

> **shareholder**
> One who has an ownership interest in a corporation through the purchase of corporate shares, or stock.
>
> **share**
> A unit of stock, a measure of ownership interest in a corporation.
>
> **director**
> A person elected by the shareholders to direct corporate affairs.
>
> **officer**
> A person hired by corporate directors to assist in the management of the day-to-day operations of the corporation.

Corporate Formation

Generally, forming a corporation involves two steps. The first step consists of preliminary organizational and promotional undertakings—particularly, obtaining capital for the future corporation. Before a corporation becomes a reality, people invest in the proposed corporation as *subscribers.* The subscribers become the shareholder-owners of the corporation when the corporation becomes a legal entity.

On the Web

Corporate statutes for all but a few states are online at **http://www. law.cornell.edu/topics/ state_statutes.html**.

EXHIBIT 11.5
Articles of Incorporation

Filed with Secretary of State
_____, 20_____

SHORT FORM
ARTICLES OF INCORPORATION
OF
_____Hiram, Inc._____

ARTICLE I

The name of this corporation _____Hiram, Inc._____

ARTICLE II

The purpose of this corporation is to engage in any lawful act or activity for which a corporation may be organized under the General Corporation Law of New Pacum other than the banking business, the trust company business, or the practice of a profession permitted to be incorporated by the New Pacum Corporation Code.

ARTICLE III

The name and address in the State of New Pacum of this corporation's initial agent for service of process is: _____Hiram Galliard,_____
8934 Rathburn Avenue, North Bend, New Pacum 98754

ARTICLE IV

The corporation is authorized to issue only one class of shares of stock; and the total number of shares that this corporation is authorized to issue is ____10,000_____ .

ARTICLE V

The corporation is a close corporation. All the corporation's issued shares of stock shall be held of record by not more than ten (10) persons.

DATED: __June 3, 2007_____

Hiram Galliard   _Martha Bonnell_
_____
[Signature(s) of Incorporator/Directors(s)]

I (we) hereby declare that I (we) am (are) the person(s) who executed the foregoing Articles of Incorporation, which execution is my (our) act and deed.

Hiram Galliard   _Martha Bonnell_

prospectus
A document that discloses relevant facts about a company and its operations so that those who wish to purchase stock (invest) in the corporation have a basis for making an informed decision.

articles of incorporation
The document filed with the appropriate state official, usually the secretary of state, when a business is incorporated. State statutes usually prescribe what kind of information must be contained in the articles of incorporation.

Contracts to purchase corporate shares are frequently made by *promoters* on behalf of the future corporation. Promoters are those who, for themselves or others, take the preliminary steps in organizing a corporation. One of the tasks of the promoter is to issue a prospectus. A **prospectus** is a document that describes the corporation and its operations so that those who wish to purchase stock (invest) in the corporation have a basis for making an informed decision.

The second step in forming a corporation is the process of incorporation. Exact procedures for incorporation differ among states, but the basic requirements are similar. The primary document needed to begin the incorporation process is called the **articles of incorporation** (see Exhibit 11.5 for sample articles of incorporation for a small corpo-

Developing Paralegal Skills

RESERVING A CORPORATE NAME

Jon Thomas is a paralegal in a law firm that specializes in corporate law. Jon and his supervising attorney have just concluded a meeting with new clients who want to incorporate their existing partnership. They want to use their current name, L&J Building Construction. Jon's assignment is to find out if the name is available and then, if it is, to reserve it. Jon knows that in his state he must contact the secretary of state's Department of Business Services to perform a preliminary inquiry regarding corporate name availability. He can do this in three ways: by telephone, by a search of the department's online database, or by e-mail using the department's corporate name availability inquiry form. Jon decides to search the online database at the department's Web site and discovers that the name is available. He then downloads and prints the corporate name reservation form, prepares it, and immediately faxes it to the Department of Business Services.

TIPS FOR RESERVING A CORPORATE NAME

- Have the preferred name and several alternatives available.
- Make sure the client understands that the name selected may not be available.
- Determine whether the name is available before reserving it.
- Once you learn that the name is available, file the corporate name reservation form immediately.
- Let your supervising attorney know that you have filed the form.
- Let the client know that the corporate name reservation form has been filed with the Department of Business Services.

---

ration). The articles include basic information about the corporation and serve as a primary source of authority for its future organization and business functions. Once they have been filed in the appropriate state office, the articles of incorporation become a public record.

Paralegals frequently assist their supervising attorneys in preparing incorporation papers and filing them with the appropriate state office. (See this chapter's *Technology and Today's Paralegal* feature on pages 386 and 387 for a discussion of online incorporation.) Also, as a paralegal, you may need to obtain information about a corporation—for example, when you are conducting an investigation. For both of these reasons, you should know what information is generally included in the articles of incorporation. Exhibit 11.6 on the next page lists and describes this information.

After the articles of incorporation have been prepared, signed, and authenticated by the incorporators, they are sent to the appropriate state official, usually the secretary of state, along with the appropriate filing fee. In many states, the secretary of state then issues a **certificate of incorporation** representing the state's authorization for the corporation to conduct business. (This may be called the **corporate charter**.) The certificate and a copy of the articles are returned to the incorporators, who then hold the initial organizational meeting that completes the details of incorporation. At this first organizational meeting, the corporation adopts a set of rules to govern the management of the corporation, called the **bylaws**. These bylaws grant or restrict the powers of the corporation.

certificate of incorporation (corporate charter)
The document issued by a state official, usually the secretary of state, granting a corporation legal existence and the right to function.

bylaws
A set of governing rules adopted by a corporation or other association.

EXHIBIT 11.6

Information Generally Included in the Articles of Incorporation

THE NAME OF THE CORPORATION

- The choice of a corporate name is subject to state approval to ensure against duplication or deception. State statutes usually require that the secretary of state run a check on the proposed name in the state of incorporation. Once cleared, a name can be reserved for a short time, for a fee, pending the completion of the articles of incorporation.

THE NATURE AND PURPOSE OF THE CORPORATION

- The intended business activities of the corporation must be specified in the articles, and, naturally, they must be lawful. Stating a general corporate purpose (for example, "to engage in the production and sale of agricultural products") is usually sufficient to give rise to all of the powers necessary or convenient to the purpose of the organization.

THE DURATION OF THE CORPORATION

- A corporation can have perpetual existence under most state corporation statutes. A few states, however, prescribe a maximum duration, after which the corporation must formally renew its existence.

THE CAPITAL STRUCTURE OF THE CORPORATION

- The capital structure of the corporation is generally set forth in the articles. A few state statutes require a relatively small capital investment (for example, $1,000) for ordinary business corporations but a greater capital investment for those engaged in insurance or banking. The number of shares of stock authorized for issuance, their valuation, the various types or classes of stock authorized for issuance, and other relevant information concerning equity, capital, and credit must be outlined in the articles.

THE INTERNAL ORGANIZATION OF THE CORPORATION

- Whatever the internal management structure of the corporation, it should be described in the articles, although it can be included in bylaws adopted after the corporation is formed.

THE REGISTERED OFFICE AND AGENT OF THE CORPORATION

- The corporation must indicate the location and address of its registered office within the state. Usually, the registered office is also the principal office of the corporation. The corporation must give the name and address of a specific person who has been designated as an agent and who can receive legal documents (including service of process) on behalf of the corporation.

THE NAMES AND ADDRESSES OF THE INCORPORATORS

- Each incorporator must be listed by name and must indicate an address. An incorporator is a person—often the corporate promoter—who applies to the state on behalf of the corporation to obtain its corporate charter. The incorporator need not be a shareholder and need not have any interest at all in the corporation. Many states do not impose residency or age requirements for incorporators. States vary on the required number of incorporators; it can be as few as one or as many as three. Incorporators are required to sign the articles of incorporation when they are submitted to the state; often, this is their only duty. In some states, they participate at the first organizational meeting of the corporation.

Classifications of Corporations

How a corporation is classified depends on its purpose, ownership characteristics, and location. A *private corporation* is, as the term indicates, a corporation that is privately owned. A *public corporation* is formed by the government for a political or governmental purpose, as when a town incorporates. Note that a public corporation is not the same as a publicly held corporation. A **publicly held corporation** is any corporation whose shares are publicly traded in securities markets, such as the New York Stock Exchange.

Corporations may also be classified as either *for-profit corporations* or *not-for-profit* (or *nonprofit*) *corporations*. A not-for-profit corporation may be formed by a group—such as a charitable association, a hospital, or a religious organization—to conduct its business without exposing the individual owners to personal liability.

Corporations owned by a small group of shareholders, such as family members, are called **close corporations**, or *closely held corporations*. Unlike large corporations, close corporations cannot sell their shares on public securities markets and usually place restrictions on the transfer of corporate shares—to keep the business in the family, for example, or for some other reason. State laws may provide more flexibility for close corporations, in terms of statutory formalities that must be observed, than for other corporations. Also, certain close corporations are permitted to elect a special corporate tax status under Subchapter S of the Internal Revenue Code. These corporations are called *S corporations*.

Lawyers, physicians, accountants, architects, engineers, and other professionals frequently incorporate as *professional corporations*. As discussed in Chapter 4, law firms often prefer to incorporate as professional corporations (P.C.s) rather than operate as partnerships.

Directors and Officers

The articles of incorporation name the initial board of directors, which is appointed by the incorporators. Thereafter, the board of directors is elected by a majority vote of the shareholders. The board holds formal meetings and records the minutes (formal notes of what transpired at the meetings). Each director has one vote, and generally the majority rules. The directors' rights include the right to participate in board meetings and the right to inspect corporate books and records. The directors' responsibilities to the corporation and its shareholders include declaring and paying **dividends** (payments to shareholders representing their share of corporate profits), appointing and removing officers, and making significant policy decisions.

The board of directors appoints the corporate officers, who manage the day-to-day operations of the firm. As previously mentioned, the officers are employees of the corporation and are subject to employment contracts. As employees, they are also agents of the corporation.

Directors and officers have fiduciary duties to the corporation and its shareholder-owners, including the duty of loyalty and the duty to exercise reasonable care when conducting corporate business. The duty of loyalty is breached when an officer or director uses corporate funds or confidences for personal gain, as when an officer discloses company secrets (such as a proposed merger) to an outsider. The duty of care is breached when a director's or officer's negligence—failure to make informed and reasonable decisions—results in harmful consequences for the corporate entity. Under modern criminal law, corporate directors and officers can also face criminal penalties, including imprisonment, for their actions or for the actions of employees under their supervision. In addition, a corporation may be held financially liable for any criminal acts or torts committed by its agents or officers within the course and scope of their employment.

In 2002, after a series of corporate scandals involving companies that used deceptive accounting practices to hide their actual financial positions from shareholders and investors, Congress passed the Sarbanes-Oxley Act. This act imposed numerous disclosure requirements

publicly held corporation
A corporation whose shares are publicly traded in securities markets, such as the New York Stock Exchange.

close corporation
A corporation owned by a small group of shareholders, often family members; also called a *closely held corporation*. Shares in close corporations cannot be publicly traded on the stock market, and often other restrictions on stock transfer apply. Some close corporations qualify for special tax status as *S corporations*.

dividend
A distribution of profits to corporate shareholders, disbursed in proportion to the number of shares held.

On the Web

For a site that offers online incorporation services, go to **http://www.bizfilings.com**.

Technology and Today's Paralegal

ONLINE INCORPORATION

Today, just about anybody can form a corporation for any lawful purpose in any state. The requirements differ from state to state. As a paralegal, your supervising attorney may ask you to assist a client who wishes to incorporate his or her business. The client may wish to incorporate in the state in which he or she already does business, in another state (such as Delaware), or even in another country. As a paralegal, you may not advise clients on where to form a corporation. You can, however, assist in the process by using the Internet to find out the formal requirements and cost of incorporation in various states. You can also help to locate potential investors for the corporation online. In addition, you can find numerous online providers of company formation and registered agent services. (The *registered agent* acts as the original incorporator, files the articles of incorporation, and remains the registered agent for the life of the corporation.)

RESEARCHING STATE REQUIREMENTS

Nearly every state has a Web site at which you can find out the state's requirements for incorporation. Typically, incorporation is handled by the secretary of state's office. You can locate the state's site by performing a general search using the state's name, or you can go to a directory site such as that offered by the Library of Congress (**http://www.loc.gov/rr/news/stategov**) or Piper Resources (**/http://www.statelocalgov.net**). Most state sites post guidelines or instructions on forming corporations (and other business entities), fee schedules, and frequently asked questions (FAQs). Many also provide downloadable corporate forms. The majority of states also have searchable databases of corporate names and registered agents.

LOCATING POTENTIAL INVESTORS

The Internet allows promoters and others to access, easily and inexpensively, a large number of potential investors. Several online services specialize in matching potential investors with companies (or future companies) that are seeking investors. For example, the American Venture Capital Exchange, or AVCE (at **http://www.avce.com**), lists hundreds of companies that seek financing. Some of these companies are just starting up, while others are existing firms that wish to expand their businesses. AVCE provides a summary of each company's business plan for potential investors to review. Potential investors can then contact the companies in which they are interested. AVCE's listings include companies in Asia, Australia, Canada, Europe, Mexico, Russia, and South America as well as the United States.

on corporate directors and officers in an attempt to prevent similar activities in the future. Chief corporate executives—and the lawyers and accountants who work for them—must now take responsibility for the accuracy of their financial statements and reports or risk steep penalties for violating the act.

Shareholders

Any person who purchases a share in a corporation becomes an owner of the corporation. Through shareholders' meetings, the shareholders play an important role in the corporate entity—they elect the directors who control the corporation, and they have a right to vote (one vote per share) on decisions that significantly affect the corporation. They also have a right to share in corporate profits proportionate to the number of shares they hold. Shareholders do not manage the daily affairs of the corporation, nor are they liable for corporate debts or other obligations beyond the amounts of their investments. Corporate own-

Some companies specialize in matching entrepreneurs in specific industries with potential investors. For example, Garage.com (at **http://www.garage.com**) provides a list of start-up high-tech companies and summaries of their business plans and a list of potential investors. Potential investors who are interested in one of the listed start-up companies can contact the company directly. The site also features articles of interest, research materials, and forums where users can ask questions of experts in certain areas. Other companies, such as BizWiz (**http://www.clickit.com/capitalist**), introduce capital seekers (companies) to capital sources (investors) worldwide.

ONLINE INCORPORATION SERVICES

Hundreds of companies provide incorporation services online that will assist you with incorporation. Although many sites are aimed at persons seeking to incorporate, some target law firms as clients and provide additional beneficial services. For example, if your client is interested in forming a Delaware corporation, Harvard Business Services (**http://www.delawareinc.com**) offers a fast and efficient way to incorporate. In addition, it provides free downloadable forms and will act as the corporation's registered agent for a fixed annual fee of fifty dollars.

Another Web site of use to corporate attorneys and paralegals is that of the Corporation Service Company (CSC) at **http://www.incspot.com/public**. CSC, a company with more than a hundred years' experience, offers an extensive range of services, including corporate formation and registered agent services. In addition, the company will scan and upload all the documents related to a transaction or litigation into an online database, providing centralized access to important documents for authorized users anywhere in the world and allowing multiple parties to track ongoing negotiations. Useful news and substantive law updates (federal and state) are provided at this site as well. CSC also sponsors the Paralegal Leadership Institute, which provides educational seminars (and CLE credits) to paralegals at locations across the country.

TECHNOLOGY TIP

The Web can assist paralegals with the incorporation process in many ways. It provides an efficient means of finding out state requirements, obtaining the proper forms, locating investors, and keeping abreast of current developments affecting corporations. The usefulness of a particular site will depend on the paralegal's level of experience and the individual needs of the client or firm. In some cases, it may be more cost-effective for a firm to hire a service provider than to conduct the research and prepare the paperwork for start-up companies.

ers, or shareholders, thus have *limited liability*— a key advantage of the corporate form of business.

Corporate Taxation

The corporation as an entity pays income taxes on corporate profits. Then, when the profits are distributed to the shareholders in the form of dividends, the shareholders pay personal income taxes on the income they receive. This double-taxation feature of the corporate form of business is one of its major disadvantages.

Some small (close) corporations are permitted to avoid the double taxation of corporate profits by electing S corporation status under Subchapter S of the Internal Revenue Code. An S corporation, like a partnership, is a "pass-through" entity for tax purposes. This means that the corporation itself does not pay income taxes. Instead, it files an information return only, as a partnership does, indicating the corporation's net profits. The S corporation shareholders declare their proportionate shares of the corporation's net income on their personal tax returns and pay taxes on that income accordingly.

Corporate Merger and Consolidation

As a paralegal, you may be asked to help corporate clients in procedures relating to major corporate changes, such as mergers and consolidations. A **merger** is a process through which one corporation (the surviving corporation) acquires all of the assets and liabilities of another corporation (the merged corporation). The shareholders of the merged corporation receive payment for their shares, either in cash or in shares in the surviving corporation. A **consolidation** is a similar process. The difference is that in a consolidation, both existing corporate entities disappear and a completely new corporation is formed. The differences between a merger and a consolidation are illustrated graphically in Exhibit 11.7.

State laws vary somewhat as to the procedures that must be undertaken to accomplish a merger or a consolidation. As a paralegal, you will need to find out what the specific requirements are in your state. Generally, the following requirements must be met:

- The boards of directors and the shareholders of each corporation involved must approve the merger or consolidation.
- Once the merger or consolidation is approved by these groups, articles of merger or articles of consolidation must be filed with the state, usually with the secretary of state's office.
- When state formalities have been satisfied, the state issues a certificate of merger to the surviving corporation or a certificate of consolidation to the newly consolidated corporation.

merger

A process in which one corporation (the surviving corporation) acquires all of the assets and liabilities of another corporation (the merged corporation).

consolidation

A process in which two or more corporations join to become a completely new corporation. The original corporations cease to exist.

EXHIBIT 11.7
Merger and Consolidation

A *merger* involves the legal combination of two or more corporations in such a way that only one of the corporations continues to exist. For example, Corporation A and Corporation B decide to merge. It is agreed that A will absorb B, so after the merger, B ceases to exist as a separate entity, and A continues as the surviving corporation. *Consolidation* occurs when two or more corporations combine in such a way that both corporations cease to exist and a new one emerges. For example, Corporation A and Corporation B consolidate to form an entirely new organization, Corporation C. In the process, both A and B are terminated as legal entities, and C comes into existence as an entirely new entity.

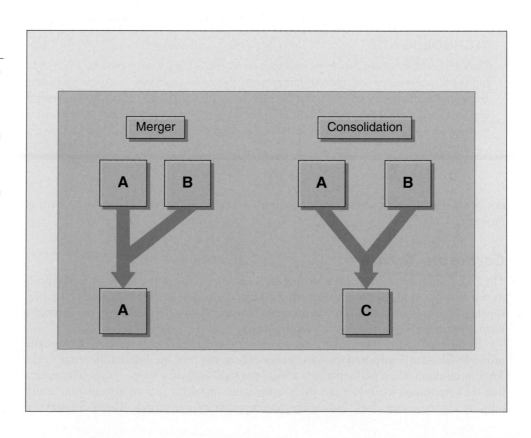

As a paralegal, you should realize the difference in legal effect between a merger or a consolidation and an *acquisition,* which occurs when one corporation acquires or purchases all or almost all of the assets of another company. In a merger or a consolidation, the surviving corporation or the newly consolidated corporation assumes not only the assets but also the liabilities of the previously existing entities. If a person has a valid claim against one of those entities, this claim is a liability that will be assumed by the surviving or newly consolidated corporation. A person injured by a defective product manufactured by one of the previously existing corporations, for example, could sue the surviving or new corporation and recover damages. In contrast, if an acquisition has occurred, the acquiring corporation has acquired the assets of the other corporation but normally has not assumed responsibility for the liabilities of that corporation.

Corporate Termination

Like partnership termination, corporate termination involves two steps. The first step, dissolution, extinguishes the legal existence of the corporation. The second step, **liquidation**, involves the winding up of the corporation's business affairs. After creditors have been paid, all remaining assets are distributed to the shareholders.

Corporations can be terminated at a time specified in the articles of incorporation or by the agreement of the shareholders and the board of directors. In certain circumstances, a court may dissolve a corporation. For example, if the directors are deadlocked and cannot agree on the management of the corporation, a court may grant a shareholder's petition to dissolve the corporation. A corporation may also be terminated by law if it fails to meet certain statutory requirements, such as the payment of taxes or annual fees.

Limited Liability Organizations

In the late 1990s and early 2000s, two new forms of limited liability business organizations emerged, the limited liability company and the limited liability partnership. The use of these new forms is spreading quickly because of the advantages they offer to businesspersons in regard to business taxation and liability—advantages not available through the partnership and corporate forms of business.

For example, one of the major tax advantages of a partnership is that the partnership's income passes through to the partners as personal income. Consequently, partners avoid the double-taxation feature of the corporate form of business. But there is a price to pay for this tax advantage: partners face unlimited personal liability. The partners can avoid unlimited personal liability by incorporating their business, because corporate owners (shareholders) have limited liability. But again, there is a price to pay for this limited liability: the double taxation of profits characteristic of the corporate form of business.

As mentioned, one way to achieve both goals—limited liability and single taxation of profits—is to elect S corporation status. Certain requirements must be met, however, before a corporation can qualify for S corporation status. One requirement is that the corporation have one hundred or fewer shareholders, thus excluding very large firms. Another requirement is that an S corporation may have only one class of stock (meaning that there is little flexibility in how corporate profits are distributed). Additionally, certain entities (such as partnerships and, with some exceptions, corporations) cannot be shareholders in an S corporation.

Limited Liability Companies

The **limited liability company (LLC)** is a hybrid form of business enterprise that combines the pass-through tax benefits of S corporations and partnerships with the limited liability of limited partners and corporate shareholders. Like the limited partnership and the corporation, an

On the Web

Hoover's Online has an extensive collection of data on U.S. corporations at **http://www.hoovers.com**.

liquidation
In regard to corporations, the process by which corporate assets are converted into cash and distributed among creditors and shareholders according to specific rules of preference.

limited liability company (LLC)
A hybrid form of business organization authorized by a state in which the owners of the business have limited liability and taxes on profits are passed through the business entity to the owners.

LLC must be formed and operated in compliance with state law. To form an LLC, *articles of organization* must be filed with a central state agency, such as the secretary of state's office. The business's name must include the words "Limited Liability Company" or the initials "L.L.C."

A major advantage of the LLC is that, as indicated, it does not pay taxes as an entity. Rather, profits are "passed through" the LLC and paid personally by the owners of the company, who are called *members* instead of shareholders. Another key advantage is that the liability of members is limited to the amounts of their investments. In an LLC, members are also allowed to participate fully in management activities, and under some state statutes, the firm's managers need not even be members of the LLC. Yet another advantage is that corporations and partnerships, as well as foreign investors, can be LLC members. Additionally, in contrast to S corporations, there is no limit on the number of members of the LLC. Finally, part of the LLC's attractiveness to businesspersons is the flexibility it offers. The members can themselves decide how to operate the various aspects of the business through a simple operating agreement.

The disadvantages of the LLC are relatively few. Generally, the major disadvantage has been the lack of uniformity among state statutes with respect to LLCs. The differences among the states are rapidly disappearing, however.

Limited Liability Partnerships

limited liability partnership (LLP)
A hybrid form of business organization authorized by a state that allows professionals to enjoy the tax benefits of a partnership while limiting in some way the normal joint and several liability of partners.

The **limited liability partnership (LLP)** is similar to the LLC. The difference is that the LLP is designed more for professionals, such as attorneys, who normally do business as partners in a partnership. Like LLCs, LLPs must be formed and operated in compliance with state statutes. The appropriate form must be filed with a central state agency, usually the secretary of state's office, and the business's name must include either "Limited Liability Partnership" or the initials "L.L.P."

The major advantage of the LLP is that it allows a partnership to function as a pass-through entity for tax purposes but limits the personal liability of the partners for partnership tort liability. Although LLP statutes vary from state to state, generally each state statute limits in some way the liability of partners. In most states, it is relatively easy to convert a traditional partnership into an LLP because the firm's basic organizational structure remains the same. Additionally, all of the laws governing partnerships still apply (apart from those modified by the LLP statute). Normally, an LLP statute is simply an amendment to a state's already existing partnership law.

A few states provide for a specific type of limited partnership called a *limited liability limited partnership* (LLLP).[7] In an LLLP, the liability of all partners is limited to the amounts of their investments in the firm.

BUSINESS ORGANIZATIONS AND THE PARALEGAL

We have already mentioned many of the ways in which paralegals benefit from a knowledge of business organizations. (For a discussion of some of the ethical issues confronting lawyers and paralegals in the business organization context, see this chapter's *Featured Guest* article on pages 392 and 393.) Because so much legal work has to do with business clients, it is impossible to summarize the many tasks involving business organizations that paralegals carry out. The following list, however, will give you an idea of some of the types of work that paralegals frequently perform in this area:

- Reserve a corporate name for an incorporator.
- Draft a partnership agreement and the documents necessary to form a limited partnership or limited liability company. File the required papers with the appropriate state office.

- Prepare articles of incorporation or articles of consolidation or merger and file them with the appropriate state office.

- Prepare minutes of corporate meetings and maintain a minutes binder.

- Draft a corporate prospectus, corporate bylaws, or a stock option agreement for corporate clients. (A *stock option agreement* is an option to purchase the corporation's stock at a specified price.)

- Review or prepare documents relating to the sale of corporate securities (stocks and bonds); assist a supervising attorney in making sure that federal and state requirements relating to the sale of corporate securities are met.

- Assist in the dissolution of a partnership or corporation.

- Assist in litigation relating to a corporation or other form of business.

- Research state laws governing partnerships, corporations, and limited liability organizations.

EMPLOYMENT LAW

Whenever a business organization hires an employee, an employment relationship is established. In the United States, employment relationships traditionally have been governed primarily by the common law. Today, though, federal and state statutes regulate the workplace extensively and provide employees with many rights and protections. Common law doctrines apply to areas *not* covered by statutory law.

Because attorneys and paralegals are frequently involved in legal work relating to employment relationships, you should have a basic understanding of employment law. In this section, we look at the common law doctrine governing employment relationships and at some of the ways in which the government regulates today's workplace.

Employment at Will

Traditionally, employment relationships have been governed by the common law doctrine of employment at will, as well as by the common law rules governing contracts, torts, and agency (discussed previously). Under the doctrine of **employment at will**, either party may terminate an employment relationship at any time and for any reason, unless a contract or statute specifically provides otherwise. Today, the majority of American workers continue to have the legal status of "employees at will." In other words, this common law doctrine is still in widespread use, and only one state (Montana) does not apply the doctrine.

Nonetheless, there are many situations in which the doctrine is not applied. Sometimes, an employment contract specifies the circumstances under which an employee can be fired. Even in the absence of an express employment contract, some courts have held that an *implied* contract exists—for example, when an employee manual states that, as a matter of policy, workers will be dismissed only for "good cause."[8] (For this reason, it is often important for a paralegal to read the employee manual when researching an employee's termination.) Also, as mentioned, federal and state statutes governing employment relationships prevent the at-will doctrine from being applied in a number of circumstances. Today's employer is not permitted to fire an employee if to do so would violate a federal or state employment statute, such as one prohibiting employment termination for discriminatory reasons (to be discussed shortly).

employment at will
A common law doctrine under which employment is considered to be "at will"—that is, either party may terminate the employment relationship at any time and for any reason, unless a contract or statute specifies otherwise.

John E. Moye

FEATURED **Guest**

ETHICAL CONSIDERATIONS FOR THE CORPORATE PARALEGAL: WHOM DO YOU REPRESENT?

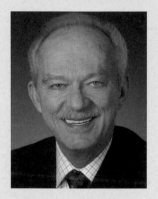

BIOGRAPHICAL NOTE

John E. Moye is a founding partner in the law firm of Moye White, LLP. The firm acts as general counsel for corporate, commercial, and nonprofit clients on a regional, national, and international basis. The firm's areas of specialization include commercial transactions, banking, corporations, nonprofit corporations, business planning, securities, taxation, estate planning, litigation, and real estate.

Moye graduated from the University of Notre Dame and received his law degree from Cornell University (with distinction). He is admitted to practice in New York and in Colorado. Moye has served on the faculty of Southern Methodist University and the University of Denver College of Law, where he has also served as Associate Dean for Academic Affairs. He lectures and teaches extensively throughout the United States in the areas of contract, corporate, commercial, banking, and partnership law.

He has written several books, including legal texts on corporations, business organizations, partnerships, federal jurisdiction, and the Uniform Commercial Code. His third edition of Colorado Business Organizations Forms and Practice *has recently been published by Lexis Law Publishing, and his sixth edition of* The Law of Business Organizations *has just been completed for Thomson Delmar Learning.*

He is past president of the Colorado Bar Association and was recently awarded the Colorado Bar Association Award of Merit, the highest award given by that organization for professional and community service.

In today's modern law practice, a paralegal plays an important role as a member of a professional team providing legal services to a business organization client. In working with clients to form a business, paralegals collect information pertaining to the formation of the business entity, meet with clients to discuss their plans and potential structures, and prepare documents and certificates for public filings. As a member of the professional staff of a law firm, paralegals must abide by and observe the ethical rules of lawyers relating to representation of clients. In a business organization context, the identification of the client and the representation of the client's specific objectives raise important ethical issues for lawyers and paralegals.

THE FORMATION OF A BUSINESS

The formation of a business entity may begin with promoters—people who make arrangements for the business to be conducted in the pre-formation stage. These people hire employees, negotiate leases, purchase property and equipment, and research the market for the business. Often, several promoters seek to form a business together and need legal advice concerning the appropriate form of business entity. When several individuals approach a law firm for advice about the appropriate form of an entity, it creates a potential ethical problem concerning whom to represent. The ethical approach to this situation is to clarify with each participant the terms of the representation and identify the client at the early stages of the representation.

When forming a business entity, paralegals and lawyers can represent clients in various capacities as follows:

- The law firm may represent the entity to be formed.
- The law firm may represent one of the promoters who will have a majority interest in the business and wants the business formed according to his or her instructions.
- The law firm may represent more than one promoter in developing a structure that suits their collective interests, but only with full disclosure.

The preferable approach is for the law firm to represent the entity to be formed. In such a case, each of the individual promoters should be instructed to seek separate legal advice, if they wish, concerning their own individual interests in the ongoing business of the entity. It would be a conflict of interest for the law firm to attempt to represent the entity and the individual promoters at the same time. Thus, in the preparation of the organizational documents for a business entity, the paralegal's work will be for the benefit of and consistent with the objectives of the entity.

When a partnership is formed, however, the identity of the client is more difficult, since each individual partner has managerial responsibilities and ownership interests, and the partnership itself has historically been regarded as an aggregation of these persons. Under modern statutes, partnerships are treated as entities as well, and the paralegal and law firm should represent the entity in preparing the organizational documents for the partnership. The prospective partners should seek separate legal advice concerning the effect of the partnership agreement (which should be drafted to protect the interests of the business) on their individual rights as partners.

If the paralegal and law firm are asked to represent several individuals who are seeking advice about forming a business and the firm agrees to represent their individual interests in forming the entity, additional disclosure is required. Under normal ethical rules, whenever a lawyer undertakes multiple representation of several individuals, the lawyer and paralegal must disclose the following:

- That the representation of multiple clients may result in a conflict among the clients on certain issues in the formation of the entity.

- That such conflicts may result in the need to obtain independent counsel at a later time and result in additional expense for that purpose.

- That independent counsel should be consulted to determine whether the joint representation of several individuals in the formation of the entity is appropriate.

- That the attorney-client privilege will be compromised because of the need for full disclosure of all facts to all clients represented.

- That each client will be requested to provide written acknowledgment that there is multiple representation and that these issues could arise.

"Paralegals must be aware of the ethical rules that apply when several individuals are attempting to form and operate a business entity."

client. The individual officer or director may, however, be seeking representation that would conflict with the interests of the business entity (or that could have a detrimental effect on the business of the entity even if not directly in conflict). In that case, the firm should either decline the representation and refer the individual to another lawyer or seek the consent of a disinterested management group of the business entity for the continued representation of the individual.

In situations in which an individual who is involved with the business entity seeks advice against another individual who is involved in the business entity, as when one shareholder seeks advice concerning a buy-sell agreement with another shareholder, the following ethical obligations arise:

- If the entity client could be adversely affected by the advice given, both individuals need to be referred to other counsel.

- If the law firm was involved in the preparation of the document concerning which the individual owners are now seeking advice, the firm can ethically explain what it understands the document to say but cannot represent an individual party to the document against another party in a dispute over the language.

OPERATIONAL ISSUES IN A BUSINESS CONTEXT

When a law firm represents a business entity, often the officers and owners of that entity contact the law firm for individual advice. The advice may relate to the business of the entity, or it may concern a completely unrelated matter. If the business entity is a client, the lawyer and paralegal must be careful to distinguish between:

- Individual questions that are completely unrelated to the business of the entity client.

- Individual questions that are directly related to the business of the entity client.

- Individual questions related to the relationship of an individual with another owner or officer of the entity client.

- Individual questions that are directly in conflict with the entity client.

Certainly, a lawyer and paralegal can assist an entity's individual officer or director on a personal matter that is unrelated to the entity

Often, law firms are asked to draft documents that affect several individuals, such as shareholder buy-sell agreements, partnership agreements among partners, or operating agreements among members of a limited liability company. In these cases, the law firm is generally regarded as representing the entity. In any written and oral communications with the individual owners, the lawyer and the paralegal should make sure these individual owners understand that the law firm represents the entity and is protecting the interests of the entity in drafting the documents. The individual owners should consult independent counsel to protect their individual interests.

CONCLUSION

Paralegals must be aware of the ethical rules that apply when several individuals are attempting to form and operate a business entity. The paralegal and the lawyer should consult early in the representation to be certain that all members of the professional legal team understand the identity of the client and any associated needs for disclosure or written acknowledgments.

Wrongful Discharge

wrongful discharge
An employer's termination of an employee's employment in violation of the law.

Whenever an employer discharges an employee in violation of an employment contract or a statutory law protecting employees, the employee may bring an action for **wrongful discharge**. For example, most states have a statute prohibiting employers from discharging or taking other actions against an employee because the employee has filed a workers' compensation claim. If an employee who was injured on the job files a claim for workers' compensation, and the employer then fires the employee, the employee can sue for wrongful discharge.

Even in situations in which an employer's actions do not violate an employment contract or statute, an employee may be able to bring a wrongful discharge action. This is particularly true if the employer has violated some common law principle of contract, tort, or agency law. ▶ **EXAMPLE 11.12** Suppose that an employer makes defamatory statements about an employee who is being terminated. In this situation, the employee may sue for wrongful discharge under tort theories. ◀

Sometimes, employees claim that they were "constructively discharged" from their jobs. **Constructive discharge** occurs when the employer causes the employee's working conditions to be so intolerable that a reasonable person in the employee's position would feel compelled to quit.

constructive discharge
A termination of employment that occurs when the employer causes the employee's working conditions to be so intolerable that a reasonable person in the employee's position would feel compelled to quit.

Labor Laws

In the early decades of the twentieth century, employees began to organize to protect their interests. They formed associations called *labor unions* and elected union representatives to bargain with employers for improved wages and working conditions. The ultimate weapon of the labor union was, of course, the *strike*. By their organized refusal to work, employees could bring their employer's operations to a halt—to the financial detriment of the employer.

In 1932, Congress established the legal right of employees to organize labor unions with the passage of the Norris-LaGuardia Act. The act protected peaceful strikes, picketing, and boycotts and restricted the power of the federal courts to enjoin (stop or prohibit) labor unions from engaging in peaceful strikes.

collective bargaining
The process by which labor and management negotiate the terms and conditions of employment, including wages, benefits, working conditions, and other matters.

The Norris-LaGuardia Act was strengthened by the enactment of the National Labor Relations Act (NLRA) of 1935. The twin goals of the NLRA were to protect workers' efforts to organize into unions and to promote **collective bargaining** (bargaining between union representatives and employers) as a peaceful method of dispute resolution. The NLRA sought to curb activities that would discourage or prevent collective bargaining efforts conducted on behalf of the workers. The NLRA also created the National Labor Relations Board (NLRB) to oversee the enforcement of the statute. Congress gave the NLRB the power to investigate alleged NLRA violations and to prevent continued violations by particular employers.

Another law to protect workers was the Fair Labor Standards Act (FLSA) of 1938. Among other things, the act prohibited the oppression or exploitation of children by regulating the employment of minors. For example, under the act, children below the age of sixteen cannot be employed on a full-time basis except in very limited circumstances. The FLSA also established guidelines regulating overtime pay and minimum hourly wages. The act provided that if in any week an employee works more than forty hours, the hours in excess of the first forty must be compensated at one and a half times the employee's regular hourly rate. As for the minimum hourly wage, it represents the absolute minimum amount that an employer can pay an employee per hour. The minimum wage rate, which is set by Congress, is changed periodically to reflect inflation.

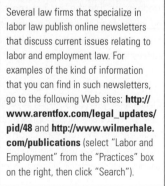

On the Web

Several law firms that specialize in labor law publish online newsletters that discuss current issues relating to labor and employment law. For examples of the kind of information that you can find in such newsletters, go to the following Web sites: **http://www.arentfox.com/legal_updates/pid/48** and **http://www.wilmerhale.com/publications** (select "Labor and Employment" from the "Practices" box on the right, then click "Search").

Ethics Watch!

THE UNAUTHORIZED PRACTICE OF LAW

To illustrate how easy it is to give legal advice without intending to, consider this example. Lara, a paralegal, was interviewing a client who was considering petitioning for bankruptcy. The client's right arm was in a sling. After Lara asked him about the injury, he described how it had happened. He also said that he had been unable to work at his job as a mechanic for two weeks and that he was worried because his employer was threatening to fire him if he couldn't return to work within another week or two. When Lara looked puzzled at this news, the client asked her what was wrong. She said, "Well, I'm wondering how you could be fired, because employers are required by law to give their employees medical leave for up to twelve weeks during any one-year period." Lara said that she would check with her supervising attorney about that matter, and then she continued the interview. In the meantime, what if the client, relying on Lara's statement, later confronted his employer and demanded a twelve-week leave? What if the employer fired him on the spot? What if the employer had only a few employees and was not subject to the leave requirements of the Family and Medical Leave Act of 1993? As you can see, Lara's "legal advice" might have caused the client to suffer harm.

Family and Medical Leave

In 1993, Congress passed the Family and Medical Leave Act (FMLA) to protect employees who need time off work for family or medical reasons. A majority of the states also have legislation allowing for employment leave for family or medical reasons, and many employers maintain private family-leave plans for their workers.

The FMLA requires employers who have fifty or more employees to provide employees with up to twelve weeks of family or medical leave during any twelve-month period. During the employee's leave, the employer must continue the worker's health-care coverage and guarantee employment in the same position or a comparable position when the employee returns to work. An important exception to the FMLA, however, allows the employer to avoid reinstatement of a *key employee*—defined as an employee whose pay falls within the top 10 percent of the firm's workforce. Additionally, the act does not apply to employees who have worked less than one year or less than twenty-five hours a week during the previous twelve months.

Generally, an employee may take family leave when he or she wishes to care for a newborn baby, a newly adopted child, or a foster child just placed in the employee's care. An employee may take medical leave when the employee or the employee's spouse, child, or parent has a "serious health condition" requiring care. For most absences, the employee must demonstrate that the health condition requires continued treatment by a health-care provider and includes a period of incapacity of more than three days. Employees suffering from certain chronic health conditions, such as asthma and diabetes, as well as employees who are pregnant, may take FMLA leave for their own incapacities that require absences of less than three days.

Remedies for violations of the FMLA include (1) damages for unpaid wages (or salary), lost benefits, denied compensation, and actual monetary losses (such as the cost of providing for care) up to an amount equivalent to the employee's wages for twelve weeks; (2) job reinstatement; and (3) promotion. The successful plaintiff is entitled to court costs, attorneys' fees, and—in cases involving bad faith on the part of the employer—double damages. Supervisors may also be subject to personal liability, as employers, for violations of the act.[9]

State Workers' Compensation Laws

▌**workers' compensation laws**
State statutes that establish an administrative procedure for compensating workers for injuries that arise out of or in the course of their employment, regardless of fault.

State **workers' compensation laws** establish an administrative procedure for compensating workers injured on the job. Instead of suing, an injured worker files a claim with the administrative agency or board that administers the local workers' compensation claims. State workers' compensation statutes normally allow employers to purchase insurance from a private insurer or a state fund to pay workers' compensation benefits in the event of a claim. Most states also allow employers to be *self-insured*—that is, employers who show an ability to pay claims do not need to buy insurance.

In general, the right to recover benefits is based wholly on the existence of an employment relationship and the fact that the injury was *accidental* and *occurred on the job or in the course of employment,* regardless of fault. Intentionally inflicted self-injury, in contrast, would not be considered accidental and hence would not be covered. If an injury occurred while an employee was commuting to or from work, it usually would not be considered to have occurred on the job or in the course of employment and hence would not be covered.

An employee must notify his or her employer of an injury promptly (usually within thirty days of the injury's occurrence). Generally, an employee also must file a workers' compensation claim with the appropriate state agency or board within a certain period (sixty days to two years) from the time the injury is first noticed, rather than from the time of the accident.

An employee's acceptance of workers' compensation benefits bars the employee from suing for injuries caused by the employer's negligence. By barring lawsuits for negligence, workers' compensation laws also bar employers from raising common law defenses to negligence, such as contributory negligence. For example, an employer can no longer raise such defenses as contributory negligence or assumption of risk (see Chapter 7) to avoid liability for negligence. A worker may sue an employer who *intentionally* injures the worker, however.

Employment Discrimination

Federal laws prohibiting employment discrimination have done much to further employees' rights to fair treatment in the workplace. State laws also protect employees from discriminatory treatment, sometimes to a greater extent than federal laws do. The major federal laws prohibiting employment discrimination are the following:

- Title VII of the Civil Rights Act of 1964 (prohibits discrimination based on race, color, national origin, religion, and gender).

- The Age Discrimination in Employment Act of 1967 (prohibits discrimination based on age).

- The Americans with Disabilities Act of 1990 (prohibits discrimination based on disability).

Title VII of the Civil Rights Act of 1964

The most significant federal law prohibiting discrimination is the Civil Rights Act of 1964. The law was enacted to protect certain groups from the discriminatory practices of business owners, educational institutions, employers, and other groups. One section of the act, known as Title VII, pertains to employment practices. Title VII prohibits

Developing Paralegal Skills

ASSISTING WITH A WORKERS' COMPENSATION CLAIM

David Calloway, an employee of GearHead Outlet, was on a ladder arranging boxes of tools when a box split open and the contents knocked him to the concrete floor. His wrist was broken in three places. Calloway submitted a workers' compensation claim to GearHead's personnel department two days after the incident. When the cast was removed from Calloway's arm, his wrist had swollen significantly. His physician prescribed physical therapy to alleviate the intense pain he experienced and to restore function to Calloway's wrist. GearHead's workers' compensation insurance provider, Delacroix Mutual, refused to authorize the therapy treatment and sent Calloway to another physician, who prescribed pain medication and declared the alternative therapy unnecessary. Calloway's wrist continued to swell, and the pain in his wrist increased.

Two weeks after the injury, Calloway contacted the law firm of Shapiro and Masters, which specializes in workers' compensation litigation, to assist with his claim. Attorney Daniel Shapiro conducted an initial interview with Calloway and accepted Calloway's case. After the interview, Shapiro asked his legal assistant, Geena Tulane, to gather evidence and prepare for a hearing before a workers' compensation judge.

CHECKLIST FOR A WORKERS' COMPENSATION CLAIM

- Review the employer's worker's compensation insurance policy with the attorney to clarify coverage terms.
- Collect all medical records and compensation claim forms from the client or employer.
- Assemble as much evidence as possible regarding the medical condition the client has as a result of the work-related injury or illness. If possible, photograph the scene where the injury occurred or the illness was caused, as well as any visible injuries that may assist in proving the claim. Gather statements from any witnesses.
- Contact state insurance regulators to research any prior complaints against the insurer.
- Compile an estimate of all medical costs. Call the offices of the physicians to whom the client has been referred for treatment of the injury or illness to inquire about their fees for specific treatments.
- Keep a log of all communications with the insurer and save e-mails and any recorded phone messages from the insurer. Document when the claim was submitted to the insurer, how and when the insurer responded, what the insurer asked for, and what was provided.
- Draft a request for a workers' compensation hearing with the state commission or court responsible for settling workers' compensation claims.
- Before submitting claim information for the hearing, compile the information in a coherent, organized presentation. A well-documented claim generally will be paid faster than a disorganized claim.

employers from discriminating against employees or potential employees on the basis of race, color, national origin, religion, or gender. The Pregnancy Discrimination Act of 1978 amended Title VII to expand the definition of gender-based discrimination to include discrimination based on pregnancy.

Title VII has been interpreted by the courts to prohibit both intentional and unintentional discrimination. The latter occurs when certain employer practices or procedures have a discriminatory effect, even though they were not intended to be discriminatory. ▶ **EXAMPLE 11.13** A city requires all of its firefighters to be at least six feet tall. In effect, that job requirement discriminates against women, because few women are that tall. The effect of the rule is discriminatory, even though the intent in adopting the rule might have been merely to ensure an able-bodied firefighting crew. ◀

Sexual Harassment.   The courts have also extended Title VII protection to those who are subject to sexual harassment in the workplace. There are two types of sexual harassment. *Quid pro quo harassment* occurs when a superior doles out awards (promotions, raises, benefits, or other advantages) to a subordinate in exchange for sexual favors. (*Quid pro quo*, a Latin term, means "this for that" or "something for something.") In contrast, *hostile-environment harassment* occurs when an employee is subjected to offensive sexual comments, jokes, or physical contact in the workplace that makes it difficult or impossible for the employee to perform a job satisfactorily.

Generally, under the doctrine of *respondeat superior* (discussed earlier in this chapter), an employer is held responsible (liable) for the conduct of certain employees, such as managers and supervisors, even if the employer was unaware of the conduct. In a sexual-harassment case, if an employee in a supervisory position did the harassing, the employer will usually be held liable *automatically* for the behavior. If the person who did the harassing was not a supervisor but a co-worker, the employer will be held liable only if the employer knew, or should have known, about the harassment and failed to take immediate corrective action. An employer may even be held liable at times for the actions of nonemployees (customers or clients, for example) if the employer knew about the harassment and let it continue.

Note that Title VII prohibits not only sexual harassment but also the harassment of any employee on the basis of race, color, national origin, religion, age, or disability. In other words, racial or ethnic slurs against an employee may give rise to a hostile work environment claim under Title VII, just as sexually offensive comments would.

The Equal Employment Opportunity Commission.   The Equal Employment Opportunity Commission (EEOC) is a federal agency that administers and enforces Title VII and the laws prohibiting employment discrimination based on disability or age (to be discussed shortly), as well as some other federal antidiscrimination laws. Claims of Title VII violations must first be filed with the EEOC. The EEOC will either investigate and take action on the claim on behalf of the employee or allow the employee to file a civil suit against the employer. The EEOC also has established guidelines that are often used by the courts to determine if the actions complained of constitute harassment under the law.

Employers' Liability under Title VII.   An employer's liability under Title VII can be extensive. In general, the court can order injunctive relief against the employer (a judicial order to prevent future discrimination), retroactive promotions that were wrongfully withheld from the employee, and past wages to compensate the employee for any time he or she was wrongfully unemployed. Damages are also available in cases involving *intentional* discrimination.

Discrimination Based on Age

The Age Discrimination in Employment Act (ADEA) of 1967 prevents employers from discriminating against workers who are forty years of age or older on the basis of their age. The act was passed, in part, in response to an increasing tendency on the part of employers to reduce costs by excluding older workers from their workforces and hiring younger workers (at lower salaries) instead. For the ADEA to apply, however, an employer must have twenty or more employees, and the employer's business activities must affect interstate commerce.

Discrimination Based on Disability

Congress enacted the Americans with Disabilities Act (ADA) in 1990 to strengthen existing laws prohibiting discrimination in the workplace against individuals with disabilities. Employers with fifteen or more employees are obligated to satisfy the requirements of the ADA.

sexual harassment
In the employment context, (1) the hiring or granting of job promotions or other benefits in return for sexual favors (*quid pro quo* harassment) or (2) language or conduct that is so sexually offensive that it creates a hostile working environment (hostile-environment harassment).

On the Web

You can find the complete text of Title VII, the ADEA, and the ADA (and other federal antidiscrimination laws), as well as information about the activities of the EEOC, at the EEOC's Web site. Go to **http://www.eeoc.gov**.

Today's Professional Paralegal

DEVELOPING A POLICY ON SEXUAL HARASSMENT

Erika Delong, a legal assistant, works in the office of the general counsel at ABC Manufacturing Corporation. She works closely with the personnel department. Today, she is attending a meeting with her supervisor, Gene Tompkins, who is the general counsel, to discuss the company's policy on sexual harassment with the vice president of human resources, the president of the corporation, and the vice presidents of several of the corporation's divisions. Erika has been asked to attend the meeting because her supervisor will ultimately be responsible for preparing the policy and he wants her to draft it. Erika has already obtained copies of other companies' policies to use as samples in the meeting.

The meeting is held in a large conference room. The president opens the meeting by explaining its purpose—to develop a policy on sexual harassment. "We want to discourage it and to have a written policy that includes reporting and investigation procedures. Erika and Gene have several samples that we can review," says the president.

SETTING POLICY GOALS AND DEFINING SEXUAL HARASSMENT

Erika passes out the sample policies. The group then reviews the various policies, with Gene explaining the legal ramifications of each one. The president remarks that he thinks the policy should begin with a statement that the corporation wants to promote an atmosphere in which authority and power are not abused and in which sexual harassment is not condoned. He points out some language that he likes in one of the samples. Erika highlights it so she will have an idea of how to draft the introduction.

Gene then states, "After an introduction and general statement of the corporation's policy, we should give the legal definition of what constitutes sexual harassment. The definition in sample three is very good from both a legal and a practical point of view because it also gives examples." Erika highlights the definition paragraph in sample three and puts a number 2 next to it, so she knows that it should come second. She flips back to the sample the president referred to and puts a number 1 next to it.

DEVELOPING PROCEDURES

As the discussion continues, the vice president of human resources comments on the procedure for filing a complaint, the investigation that will take place, and the disciplinary measures that will be imposed for sexual harassment. The vice president does not like any of the samples, and the group spends quite a bit of time working through specific language to pin down what he wants. When the meeting is over, the group goes to lunch in the executive dining room. After lunch, Gene informs the others that Erika will prepare a draft of the policy and will circulate it among them for review and comment. Once all of their comments have been collected, the group will meet again to decide on the final provisions. Erika will then prepare and circulate a final draft of the policy. Erika returns to her office to begin working on the initial draft.

As defined by the 1990 statute, disabilities include heart disease, cancer, blindness, paralysis, acquired immune deficiency syndrome (AIDS), emotional illnesses, and learning disabilities. Under the ADA, an employer is not permitted to discriminate against a person with a disability if *reasonable accommodations* can be provided to assist the worker in satisfactorily performing the job. An employer is not required to accommodate a worker with a disability if the accommodation would constitute an undue hardship for the employer, however. For example, if the cost of accommodating the employee is extremely high, that high cost might constitute an undue hardship for the employer. Although enforcement of the ADA falls within the jurisdiction of the EEOC, the paralegal should note that the worker alleging discrimination in violation of the ADA may also file a civil lawsuit against the employer for violation of the act.

EMPLOYMENT LAW AND THE PARALEGAL

Employment law necessarily affects the paralegal. As an employee, you will be subject to the laws governing employment relationships. As a legal professional, you may be extensively involved in tasks relating to labor and employment laws. You may work in the corporate counsel's office of a large corporate enterprise, for example. If the corporation's employees belong to a labor union, the corporate counsel's office will handle matters governed by labor laws, such as collective bargaining agreements and labor-management disputes. As a paralegal in a law firm or a government agency, you might assist in work relating to claims of employment discrimination, which might require you to interact with the EEOC or a relevant state agency. Here are a few tasks that paralegals commonly undertake in the area of labor and employment law:

- Draft employment contracts for an employer.
- Assist with contract negotiations between labor and management.
- Prepare for arbitration proceedings before the NLRB.
- Respond to inquiries from the NLRB regarding a client's alleged unfair labor practices.
- Prepare for and attend administrative hearings before the EEOC.
- Gather factual information to counter or support a claim of employment discrimination.
- Prepare reports and furnish documentation in response to an EEOC investigation into an employee's claim of employment discrimination.
- Draft a policy manual for a business client concerning what actions constitute discriminatory employment practices.
- Research the EEOC's guidelines on sexual harassment and relevant case law to determine what types of policies and procedures will help a client avoid liability for sexual harassment.
- Prepare notices regarding a firm's employment policies, important changes in employment laws, and so on.
- Assist in litigation involving multiple plaintiffs who are suing the same employer.

KEY TERMS AND CONCEPTS

chapter summary   Laws Affecting Business

Agency Law

An agency relationship arises when one person (called the *agent*) agrees to act for or in the place of another person (called the *principal*).

1. *Employees versus independent contractors*—Employees who deal with third parties are normally considered to be agents of their employers. An independent contractor differs from an employee in that the employer does not control the details of the independent contractor's job performance. The independent contractor may or may not be an agent.

2. *Agency formation*—An agency relationship may be formed by express agreement (oral or written) or implied by conduct. It can also arise if the principal causes a third party to believe the agency existed.

3. *Duties of the principal*—The principal must cooperate with the agent, provide safe working conditions for the agent, and reimburse the agent for work performed and for any expenses incurred on the principal's behalf.

4. *Duties of the agent*—The agent must perform his or her tasks competently, obey and be loyal to the principal, notify the principal of matters concerning the agency, and render an accounting to the principal of how and for what purpose the principal's funds were used.

5. *Liability for an agent's contracts*—The principal normally is bound by any contract formed by the agent on behalf of the principal, as long as the action was authorized. If the action was not authorized, the principal will not be liable unless he or she voluntarily agrees to be bound by (ratifies) the contract.

6. *Liability for an agent's torts*—Agents are personally liable for the torts that they commit. If an agent commits a tort within the scope of his or her employment as an agent, the principal may also be held liable under the doctrine of *respondeat superior*.

7. *Liability for independent contractor's torts*—A principal is not liable for harm caused by an independent contractor's negligence, unless hazardous activities are involved (in which situation the principal is strictly liable for any resulting harm) or other exceptions apply.

Negotiable Instruments

1. *Definition*—A negotiable instrument is a signed writing that contains an unconditional promise or order to pay an exact sum of money on demand or at a specified future time to a specified person or order or to bearer.

2. *Requirements for negotiability*—

   a. Must be in writing.

(Continued)

b. Must be signed by the maker or drawer.

c. Must be a definite promise or order to pay.

d. Must be unconditional.

e. Must state a fixed amount of money to be paid.

f. Must be payable in money.

g. Must be payable on demand or at a definite time.

h. Must be payable to order or to bearer.

3. *Drafts and checks*—A draft is an unconditional written bill of exchange involving three parties. The party creating the draft is called the drawer. The party that pays the draft is called the drawee. The party receiving the payment is called the payee. A check is a special type of draft that is drawn on a bank to pay a fixed amount of money on demand.

4. *Transfer of instruments by negotiation*—Negotiation is the transfer of an instrument in such form that the transferee becomes a holder. An order instrument contains the name of the payee capable of indorsing it and is negotiated by delivery with any necessary indorsements. An instrument payable to the bearer is negotiated simply by delivery, without indorsement.

5. *Types of indorsements*—

   a. Blank indorsement—Specifies no particular indorsee and can consist of a mere signature.

   b. Special indorsement—Names the indorsee with words such as "Pay to the order of Clay."

   c. Qualified indorsement—Contains a qualifying statement to disclaim the indorser's liability in certain circumstances.

   d. Restrictive indorsement—Requires the indorsee to comply with certain instructions regarding the funds involved.

6. *Unauthorized signatures*—The key to liability on a negotiable instrument is a signature. An unauthorized signature will not bind the person whose name was forged. An exception may arise when a person ratifies an agent's unauthorized signature or when a person's own negligence contributed substantially to the forgery.

7. *Holder in due course (HDC)*—An ordinary holder obtains only those rights that the transferor had in the instrument. In contrast, an HDC can normally acquire a higher level of immunity in regard to defenses against payment on the instrument or ownership claims to the instrument by other parties. A holder of a negotiable instrument becomes an HDC by taking the instrument in good faith without notice of any defects in the instrument and by giving something of value.

8. *Checks and the banking system*—When a customer writes a check, the bank (as the customer's agent) is responsible for paying the amount specified on the check to the holder when it is presented to the bank.

   a. When a customer holds insufficient funds in his or her checking account, the bank can either dishonor the check or pay the item and charge the customer's account for the overdraft.

   b. A stop-payment order is an order by a customer to his or her bank not to pay or certify a certain check. An oral stop-payment order is binding for fourteen days in states where such stop-payment orders are allowed. A written stop-payment order is effective for six months, at which time it must be renewed in writing.

c. When a bank pays a check on which the drawer's signature has been forged, generally the bank is liable. Banks typically send their customers monthly statements detailing activity in their checking accounts. The customer has a duty to examine bank statements and report any alterations or forged signatures promptly.

d. A bank that pays a customer's check bearing a forged indorsement must recredit the customer's account or be liable to the customer-drawer for breach of contract. The customer has a duty to report a forged indorsement within three years after the forged item became available to the customer.

9. *Electronic fund transfers (EFTs)*—

a. Consumer EFT systems include ATMs, point-of-sale systems (with debit cards), direct deposits and withdrawals, and pay-by-Internet systems. The Electronic Fund Transfer Act of 1978 sets forth consumers' rights and responsibilities with respect to EFTs, rules concerning unauthorized EFTs, and the amount of damages available for a bank's violation of the act.

b. Commercial electronic transfers are governed by Article 4A of the UCC.

Forms of Business Organization

1. *Sole proprietorships*—The simplest form of business organization; used by anyone who does business without creating a separate business entity. The owner is the business, even though he or she may hire employees to run the business.

a. The owner is personally liable for all business debts and obligations.

b. The owner pays personal income taxes on all profits.

c. The proprietorship terminates on the death of the sole proprietor or the sale or transfer of the business.

2. *Partnerships*—Created by the written or oral agreement of the parties to do business jointly as partners. All partners share equally in management, unless otherwise provided for in the partnership agreement. The partners may hire employees to assist them in running the business.

a. Partners are personally liable for partnership debts and obligations.

b. The partnership as an entity does not pay income taxes but files an informational tax return with the Internal Revenue Service each year. Each partner pays personal income tax on his or her share of the profits of the partnership.

c. A partnership may be terminated by the agreement of the partners or by the occurrence of certain events, such as the death or bankruptcy of a partner.

d. The creation of a limited partnership is a formal proceeding that must comply with state statutory requirements. Only the general partners may participate in management in a limited partnership, and only the general partners have unlimited personal liability; the liability of limited partners is limited to the amount of their investments.

3. *Corporations*—

a. A corporation is created by a state-issued charter. The shareholders elect directors, who set policy and appoint officers to manage day-to-day corporate affairs.

b. Shareholders have limited liability and are not personally liable for the debts of the corporation (beyond the amount of their investments).

(Continued)

    c. The corporation pays income tax on net profits; shareholders again pay income tax on profits distributed as dividends.

    d. A corporation may be terminated at the time specified in the articles of incorporation, by agreement of the shareholders and the board of directors, or by court decree.

4. *Limited liability organizations*—Two relatively new forms of business organization are the limited liability partnership (LLP) and the limited liability company (LLC). Generally, these organizations allow business owners to combine the tax advantages of the partnership with the limited liability of limited partners or corporate shareholders.

Employment Law

1. *Employment at will*—Traditionally, the employment relationship has been governed by the doctrine of "employment at will"—that is, the relationship can be terminated at any time for any reason by either the employer or the employee—as well as by common law rules relating to contracts, torts, and agency. Today, most Americans continue to have the legal status of "employees at will," but federal and state statutes prevent the doctrine from being applied in some circumstances.

2. *Wrongful discharge*—Wrongful discharge occurs whenever an employer discharges an employee in violation of the law or of an employment contract.

3. *Labor laws*—The Norris-LaGuardia Act of 1932 gave employees the legal right to organize into unions and to engage in peaceful strikes. The National Labor Relations Act of 1935 strengthened it by protecting workers' efforts to organize into unions and by promoting collective bargaining. The act also created the National Labor Relations Board to oversee enforcement of the statute.

4. *Family and medical leave*—The Family and Medical Leave Act of 1993 requires employers with fifty or more employees to provide their employees (except for key employees) with up to twelve weeks of unpaid family or medical leave during any twelve-month period for the following reasons:

    a. Family leave may be taken to care for a newborn baby, a newly adopted child, or a foster child just placed in the employee's care.

    b. Medical leave may be taken when the employee or the employee's spouse, child, or parent has a serious health condition requiring care.

5. *State workers' compensation laws*—Every state has an administrative procedure for compensating workers injured on the job.

6. *Employment discrimination*—Both federal and state laws prohibit discrimination against employees in the workplace. State laws sometimes afford greater protection. The major federal laws are:

    a. Title VII of the Civil Rights Act (1964), which prohibits employment discrimination against job applicants and employees on the basis of race, color, national origin, gender, or religion. The courts have interpreted Title VII to prohibit both intentional and unintentional discrimination, as well as pregnancy discrimination and sexual harassment.

    b. The Age Discrimination in Employment Act (ADEA) of 1967, which prohibits employment discrimination against employees who are forty years of age or older.

    c. The Americans with Disabilities Act (ADA) of 1990, which prohibits discrimination on the basis of disability against individuals qualified for a given job. Employers must reasonably accommodate the needs of persons with disabilities.

QUESTIONS FOR REVIEW

1. What is an agency relationship? How is an agency formed? What fiduciary duties arise in an agency relationship?

2. When is a principal liable for the contracts formed by an agent? Under what common law doctrine may a principal be held liable for the torts of the agent?

3. What a negotiable instrument? What law governs negotiable instruments? How are negotiable instruments transferred from one party to another?

4. What are the four common types of electronic fund transfers? What law governs these types of transfers of funds?

5. What are the three most common traditional forms of business organization? How is each form created and terminated?

6. How are the profits distributed in each of the three major traditional forms of business organization? How do the

three forms compare in terms of the liability of the owners and taxation?

7. What is a limited liability company? What advantages does this business organizational form offer to businesspersons?

8. What are limited liability partnerships?

9. What is meant by employment at will? When did the government begin to regulate employment relationships? What was the purpose of the National Labor Relations Act, and what agency administers and enforces the act's provisions?

10. What federal statutes prohibit employment discrimination? What kinds of discrimination are prohibited under these statutes? What federal agency handles claims of employment discrimination?

ETHICAL QUESTIONS

1. Peter works as a legal assistant for a law firm. The firm's client is suing her former employer for wrongful termination of the employment relationship. The employee-plaintiff has financial records that prove that her supervisor authorized nondisclosure of income to the Internal Revenue Service. Disclosing these records would seriously affect her supervisor's credibility and would strengthen the employee-plaintiff's case. Peter contacts the client to obtain the records. She refuses, fearing the effect it might have on her ability to find another job. Peter's supervising attorney is adamant about the need to obtain these records. The attorney is concerned that the firm might be guilty of malpractice if it failed to introduce this evidence. To whom is Peter obligated, the client or the firm? Why? How should Peter resolve this conflict?

2. Trevor Holland is an independent paralegal who is interested in the area of workers' compensation. He contacts the state workers' compensation board to request information on whether a nonlawyer may represent clients who have workers' compensation claims. He is told that nonlawyers are not allowed to practice before the agency. What would happen if he began practicing in this area anyway?

3. Amy Mehall is a paralegal in the legal department of a large corporation. One day, her good friend Sarah, who works in the company's purchasing department, asks Amy for help. Sarah is being sexually harassed by her boss. Amy tells

Sarah that she cannot give her any legal advice. Sarah asks Amy to make an appointment for her with Amy's supervising attorney, so that she can get the legal advice that she needs. May employees of a corporate legal department represent other employees of the corporation? Why or why not?

4. Mark Anderson has been the operations manager of Division B of the Wicks Co. for fifteen years. The Wicks Co. is now undergoing a reorganization and is combining the management of Division B with that of Division A. The operations manager of Division A, a younger man who has been with the firm for only three years, has been asked to take over Mark's responsibilities. The net result for Mark is that he has been given the choice of retiring earlier than planned (with a special retirement bonus) or taking another job with the company with less pay and little job security. Mark has always received favorable performance evaluations and does not want to retire. He concludes that he is being discriminated against on the basis of age and calls to make an appointment with an attorney to seek legal advice. His main question is whether the company would have a legitimate reason to fire him if he discussed the matter with the Equal Employment Opportunity Commission. The attorney is out of town, and the attorney's paralegal, June Carter, takes the call. How should June respond to Mark's question?

PRACTICE QUESTIONS AND ASSIGNMENTS

1. Identify the parties involved in the relationships described below as either principals or agents:

   a. Bob drives a delivery van for a retail florist chain, Forget-Me-Not Flowers, Inc. Forget-Me-Not Flowers, Inc., owns the delivery truck and provides Bob with a delivery schedule.

   b. Tim owns Forget-Me-Not Flowers, Inc. He hired Bob to drive the delivery van.

   c. Attorney Mary Hacker represents Tom Smith in a drunk-driving case.

   d. Attorney Hacker's paralegal, Amy Wilson, files a motion with the court in Tom Smith's case.

2. Explain why the principal is (or is not) liable for the actions of the agent in each of the following situations:

   a. Attorney Tom Moran tells his paralegal, Jane Davis, to purchase litigation software.

   b. Attorney Jane Smith leaves a written memo to her paralegal, David Hayes, instructing David to solicit bids for a computer network for the law firm from three computer consulting firms. David not only obtains three bids but also hires one of the firms to set up the network at a cost of $10,000.

   c. Paralegal Megan Meldrum works for a sole practitioner and has office management duties in addition to her paralegal responsibilities. When the photocopier no longer functions, she enters into a lease for a new machine without discussing it with her supervising attorney. The cost of the new machine is the same as the cost of the old machine. Would it make any difference if the cost of the new machine were significantly greater than the cost of the old one?

3. Using the material on negotiable instruments presented in the chapter, identify which of the following are requirements for negotiability:

   a. Must be payable in money.

   b. Must have a blank indorsement.

   c. Must be in written form.

   d. Must have a restrictive indorsement.

   e. Must be signed by the maker or drawer.

4. Identify the following types of indorsements:

   a. An indorsement that does not specify the party to whom the instrument is being transferred.

   b. An indorsement requiring the party to whom the instrument is payable to comply with certain instructions.

   c. An indorsement often used by agents to limit their personal liability for paying on the instrument.

   d. An indorsement that identifies the person to whom the indorser intends to make the instrument payable.

5. Identify whether each of the business firms described below is a sole proprietorship, a partnership, or a corporation, and explain why:

   a. Terrence and Lars have owned a business together for three months. Terrence contributed 60 percent of the capital needed to start the business, and Lars contributed the other 40 percent. Each owner is responsible for a proportionate share of the profits and losses of the business, and each owner participates in managing the business.

   b. Four wealthy individuals create a business for the purpose of funding the construction of a new commerce center to revitalize the downtown business district in their city. Each individual contributes 25 percent of the funds necessary for the project, and each individual is liable for only 25 percent of the firm's losses. They all sign an agreement.

   c. Anne Hall, Joe Richie, and Mike Werner are all certified public accountants. They decide to do business together. By the end of its first year, the firm has become very profitable. As a result, the firm has to pay a substantial amount in income taxes on its profits.

   d. Dr. Menendez practices medicine on his own; he has not incorporated his business.

   e. The Pear Co. is a for-profit business that has a charter issued by the state. The charter provides for the limited liability of the company's owners.

6. Using Exhibit 11.5, *Articles of Incorporation,* on page 382, draft a set of short-form articles of incorporation using the following facts:

   Richard Hart, Steve Grable, and Lucy White decide to incorporate the restaurant that they have been operating for the past six months. All three will be the incorporators. The name of the corporation, which is available, is Lucy's Tavern. Steve Grable will be the registered agent, and the address for service of process will be the restaurant's address, 1000 Audubon Road, Anytown, Anystate 10010. The purpose of the corporation will be any lawful act or activity for which a corporation may be organized under the general corporation law of Anystate. The corporation will be for profit, and 15,000 shares of stock will be issued.

7. Identify each of the following labor laws or employment doctrines:

   a. A federal statute regulating minimum hourly wages and overtime pay.

   b. A federal statute prohibiting age discrimination.

   c. A federal statute allowing employees to organize into unions and to strike.

   d. A federal statute prohibiting employment discrimination on the basis of race, color, national origin, gender, or religion.

   e. A federal statute authorizing collective bargaining and strikes and establishing an agency to oversee union elections and other union activities.

   f. A doctrine allowing employment relationships to be terminated at any time for any reason by either party.

   g. A federal statute prohibiting employment discrimination on the basis of disability.

   h. State statutes that allow workers to be compensated for on-the-job injuries.

8. Identify what type of employment discrimination, if any, is being practiced in each of the following hypothetical situations:

   a. Lana Ronsky, a legal assistant in an all-male law firm, is the object of frequent sexual jokes and comments and occasional uninvited touching—all of which are offensive to her and make it difficult for her to do her job.

   b. Monica Pierson, a partner in a large law firm, interviews seven potential legal assistants, including an Asian American. Although the Asian American is the best qualified for the job, Monica does not hire him because he speaks English with an accent, which might offend some of the firm's clients.

   c. Diana Bekins, the manager of an insurance agency, makes it clear to Jack McBride, a new sales representative, that she will promote him only if he provides sexual favors in return.

   d. A post office has a rule that all mail carriers must be able to bench-press two hundred pounds, because the mailbags are so heavy. As a result, only 3 out of 150 mail carriers are women.

QUESTIONS FOR CRITICAL ANALYSIS

1. What is a fiduciary relationship? Why does the law impose such a relationship on parties involved in agency relationships?

2. Attorneys are agents of their clients and thus are governed by the principles of agency law discussed in this chapter. Do you see any similarities between the duties of agents to their principals and the ethical rules governing attorneys (discussed in Chapter 3)? If so, what are the similarities? In other words, which duties of agents, if any, correspond to the specific ethical rules discussed in Chapter 3?

3. One of the goals of Article 3 of the Uniform Commerical Code (UCC) is to facilitate the negotiability of instruments and to balance the rights of parties to negotiable instruments. How does the concept of holder in due course further these general goals?

4. Review the *Developing Paralegal Skills* feature entitled "A Case of *Respondeat Superior*" on page 366. Apply the requirements for determining liability given in the checklist to the facts of the case. Make a list of arguments for and against finding liability under the theory of *respondeat superior*. Which arguments should prevail? Why?

5. What protection does the corporation provide that sole proprietorships and partnerships do not? Why might this protection have come into existence? Whom does it favor? Is is detrimental to anyone?

6. What are the advantages of running a business as a sole proprietorship? How do these advantages compare with the costs and risks involved?

7. How do the rights among partners under partnership law differ from the rights of agents under agency law? What is the reason for these differences?

8. How do sole proprietorships, partnerships, and corporations pay income taxes? When would it be advantageous, for tax purposes, to be incorporated? When would it be more advantageous not to be incorporated?

9. What types of duties do directors and officers owe to a corporation? How do these duties compare with those of an agent? Is it possible for an individual to serve as an officer and a director of a corporation at the same time?

10. What are limited liability companies and limited liability partnerships? What are the advantages of these forms of business organization? Give an example of a situation in which each type of entity would be used.

11. Employers typically want their employees to be bright young people who are dedicated to their work. Some

employers do not want to hire people who need to take family or maternity leaves, who are old, or whose racial or ethnic background is dissimilar to theirs. Should employers be allowed to hire only the people they want to hire? Should they be able to limit their employees to certain age groups or ethnic backgrounds? Should they be able to refuse to hire job candidates with disabilities?

Why or why not? What laws protect people in these groups from employment discrimination?

12. What laws resulted from the efforts of labor unions? What other benefits have workers realized as a result of labor unions' efforts? What might happen if labor unions did not exist?

PROJECTS

1. Find out if your state's corporation statute is based on the Model Business Corporation Act or the Revised Model Business Corporation Act.

2. Look in your telephone directory or in a state administrative agency manual in your library for the name and telephone number of the state department or agency that regulates businesses and accepts corporate filings, such as articles of incorporation. Call this department for information about a company located in your area. See how much information you can acquire about that company from the government office.

3. Call the agency you located in response to question 2 above. Find out if it requires forms to be filed to establish a partnership. If they are required, request a copy of the forms.

4. Locate your state employment agency in the telephone directory. Contact the agency, and find out whether your state adheres to the employment-at-will doctrine. Also find out if, and in what circumstances, exceptions to this doctrine are made.

5. Call the Equal Employment Opportunity Commission at 1-800-669-4000 and find out where the nearest regional office of the agency is located. Also find out what the time frames and procedures are for filing claims of gender-based discrimination, age discrimination, and disability-based discrimination.

6. Contact your bank and find out what its procedures are when (a) the bank receives a check for an account containing insufficient funds, (b) a customer requests a stop-payment order, and (c) a customer claims that the bank paid a check on which the customer's signature was forged.

USING INTERNET RESOURCES

1. Go online, and access the following site: **http://www.bizfilings.com**. Click on the heading "Learn About Incorporating." There you will find a series of frequently asked questions (FAQs) about incorporation. Summarize in writing the answers given on the Web page to the following questions:

   a. What are the advantages of incorporation?

   b. What are the disadvantages of incorporation?

   c. How many directors must a corporation have?

   d. What factors should be considered in deciding on a corporate name?

2. Research the Cornell Law Library Web site at **http://www.law.cornell.edu**, and find your state's corporation statute. What are the requirements for corporate formation?

3. Many paralegals, at one time or another, are asked to assist in cases dealing with employment discrimination. For that reason, it is a good idea to become familiar with the agency that administers federal laws prohibiting various forms of employment discrimination, the Equal Employment Opportunity Commission (EEOC). This exercise will help you learn more about this agency and its activities. First, access the EEOC's Web site at **http://www.eeoc.gov**. Browse through the site, and then find answers to the following questions:

   a. What federal law (enabling legislation) established the EEOC? What federal acts does the EEOC enforce?

   b. Within how many days after a discriminatory action must an employee file a charge (claim) with the EEOC? Can the employee first file a charge with a state or local agency that implements state and local laws?

c. How many charges of discrimination were filed with the EEOC in the most recent year listed? What percentage of the total annual claims dealt with each of the following types of discrimination: gender-based discrimination, disability-based discrimination, and race-based discrimination?

d. Give the titles of two recent enforcement guidelines issued by the EEOC.

4.  For additional resources, visit our Web site at **http://www.paralegal.delmar. cengage.com**.

END NOTES

1. Note that it is the conduct and statements of the *principal* that will create an agency rather than the acts or declarations of a purported *agent*.

2. Pronounced ree-*spahn*-dee-uht soo-*peer*-ee-your.

3. With a joint account, the bank cannot hold the nonsigning customer liable for payment of an overdraft unless that person benefited from its proceeds [UCC 4–401(b)].

4. Some states do not recognize oral stop-payment orders; they must be in writing.

5. Note that banks can shift some of the risk of forged checks to the customer by contract, such as the risk of forged signatures created by the use of facsimile or other nonmanual signature devices. See, for example, *Arkwright Mutual Insurance Co. v. Nations Bank*, 212 F.3d 1224 (11th Cir. 2000).

6. The term *several* stems from the medieval English term *severall*, which meant "separately," or "severed from" one another. As used here, *several* liability means *separate* (individual) liability.

7. See, for example, Colorado Revised Statutes Annotated Section 7-62 109. Other states that provide expressly for limited liability limited partnerships include Delaware, Florida, Missouri, Pennsylvania, Texas, and Virginia.

8. See, for example, *Kuest v. Regent Assisted Living, Inc.*, 111 Wash.App. 36, 43 P.3d 23 (2002).

9. See, for example, *Rupnow v. TRC, Inc.*, 999 F.Supp. 1047 (N.D. Ohio 1998).

BANKRUPTCY AND ENVIRONMENTAL LAW

CHAPTER OUTLINE

AFTER COMPLETING THIS CHAPTER, YOU WILL KNOW:

▶ The various types of relief available for debtors under federal bankruptcy law.

▶ The basic procedures involved in an ordinary, or straight, bankruptcy proceeding.

▶ How bankruptcy law provides relief for corporate debtors and what basic procedures are involved in corporate reorganizations.

▶ The major laws regulating environmental pollution.

▶ The basic purpose and provisions of Superfund.

INTRODUCTION

Historically, debtors had few rights. At one time debtors who could not pay their debts as they came due faced harsh consequences, including imprisonment and involuntary servitude. Today, in contrast, debtors have numerous rights. One of these rights is the right to petition for bankruptcy relief under federal law.

In the past twenty years, the number of petitions for bankruptcy filed each year has risen dramatically. In fact, the number of people who have filed personal bankruptcies has increased every year since 1980 (from fewer than 300,000 per year to over 1.6 million per year). For paralegals, this means that bankruptcy law is an area in which they will be increasingly in demand.

In this chapter, you will read about the different types of relief offered under federal bankruptcy law and about the basic bankruptcy procedures required for specific types of relief. You will also learn in this chapter about the major laws regulating environmental pollution. Although bankruptcy and environmental law are quite distinct areas of law, both are based largely on federal legislation, and both are areas in which many paralegals specialize.

THE BANKRUPTCY CODE

Bankruptcy relief is provided under federal law. Although state laws may play a role in bankruptcy proceedings, particularly state laws governing property, the governing law is based on federal legislation.

Congressional authority to provide bankruptcy relief for debtors is based on Article I, Section 8, of the U.S. Constitution, which gives Congress the power to establish "uniform laws on the subject of bankruptcies throughout the United States." Federal bankruptcy legislation was first enacted in 1898 and since then has undergone several modifications.

Bankruptcy law prior to 2005 was based on the Bankruptcy Reform Act of 1978, as amended—hereinafter called the Bankruptcy Code, or more simply, the Code. In 2005, Congress enacted the Bankruptcy Reform Act, which became effective in October 2005.[1] As you will see, the 2005 act significantly overhauled certain provisions of the Bankruptcy Code.

Goals of Bankruptcy Law

Modern bankruptcy law is designed to accomplish two main goals. The first is to provide relief and protection to debtors who have "gotten in over their heads." The second is to provide a fair means of distributing a debtor's assets among all creditors. Thus, the law attempts to protect the rights of both the debtor and the creditor.

Although the twin goals of bankruptcy remain the same, the balance between them has shifted somewhat. There was growing criticism after the 1978 act that too many debtors were able to avoid paying their debts. Thus, one of the major goals of the 2005 reform legislation was to require consumers to pay as many of their debts as they possibly could instead of having those debts fully extinguished in bankruptcy.

Bankruptcy Courts

Bankruptcy proceedings are held in federal bankruptcy courts, which are under the authority of U.S. district courts, and rulings from bankruptcy courts can be appealed to the district courts. Essentially, a bankruptcy court fulfills the role of an administrative court for the federal district court concerning matters in bankruptcy. The bankruptcy court holds proceedings dealing with the procedures required to administer the estate of the debtor in bankruptcy. Bankruptcy court judges are federally appointed. A bankruptcy court can conduct a jury trial if the appropriate district court has authorized it and the parties to the bankruptcy consent. Bankruptcy courts follow the Federal Rules of Bankruptcy Procedure rather than the Federal Rules of Civil Procedure (see Chapter 13).

Types of Bankruptcy Relief

The Bankruptcy Code is contained in Title 11 of the United States Code (U.S.C.) and has eight chapters.[2] Chapters 1, 3, and 5 of the Code include general definitional provisions and provisions governing case administration, creditors, the debtor, and the estate. These three chapters apply generally to all kinds of bankruptcies. The next five chapters of the Code set forth the different types of relief that debtors can seek:

- Chapter 7 provides for **liquidation** proceedings (the selling of all nonexempt assets and the distribution of the proceeds to the debtor's creditors).
- Chapter 9 governs the adjustment of debts of a municipality.
- Chapter 11 governs reorganizations.
- Chapters 12 and 13 provide for the adjustment of debts by parties with regular incomes (family farmers and family fishermen under Chapter 12 and individuals under Chapter 13).

In the following pages, we look at the specific type of bankruptcy relief provided under Chapters 7, 11, and 13 of the Code. To fully inform a **consumer-debtor** (defined as an individual whose debts are primarily consumer debts) of the types of relief available, the Code requires that the clerk of the court give all consumer-debtors written notice of the general purpose, benefits, and costs of each chapter under which they might proceed. In addition, under the 2005 act, the clerk must provide consumer-debtors with information on the types of services available from credit-counseling agencies.

LIQUIDATION PROCEEDINGS

Liquidation under Chapter 7 of the Bankruptcy Code is probably the most familiar type of bankruptcy proceeding and is often referred to as *ordinary,* or *straight,* bankruptcy. Put simply, a debtor in a liquidation bankruptcy states his or her debts and turns all assets over to a *bankruptcy trustee.* The trustee sells the nonexempt assets and distributes the proceeds to creditors (the trustee's role will be discussed in more detail later in this chapter). With certain exceptions, the remaining debts are then **discharged** (extinguished), and the debtor is relieved of his or her obligation to pay the debts.

Any "person"—defined as including individuals, partnerships, and corporations—may be a debtor in a liquidation proceeding. A husband and wife may file jointly under a single petition. Railroads, insurance companies, banks, savings and loan associations, investment companies licensed by the Small Business Administration, and credit unions *cannot* be debtors in a liquidation bankruptcy, however. Rather, other chapters of the Bankruptcy Code or federal or state statutes apply to them.

A straight bankruptcy can be commenced by the filing of either a voluntary or an involuntary **petition in bankruptcy**—the document that is filed with a bankruptcy court to initiate bankruptcy proceedings. If a debtor files the petition, it is a *voluntary bankruptcy.* If one or more creditors file a petition to force the debtor into bankruptcy, it is an *involuntary bankruptcy.* We discuss both voluntary and involuntary bankruptcy proceedings under Chapter 7 in the following subsections.

liquidation
A proceeding under Chapter 7 of the Bankruptcy Code (often referred to as *ordinary,* or *straight,* bankruptcy) in which a debtor states his or her debts and turns all assets over to a trustee, who sells the nonexempt assets and distributes the proceeds to creditors. With certain exceptions, the remaining debts are then discharged, and the debtor is relieved of the obligation to pay the debts.

consumer-debtor
A debtor whose debts are primarily consumer debts—that is, debts for purchases that are primarily for household or personal use.

discharge
The termination of an obligation. A discharge in bankruptcy terminates the debtor's obligation to pay the debts discharged by the court.

petition in bankruptcy
An application to a bankruptcy court for relief in bankruptcy; a filing for bankruptcy. The official forms required for a petition in bankruptcy must be completed accurately, sworn to under oath, and signed by the debtor.

Voluntary Bankruptcy

To bring a voluntary petition in bankruptcy, the debtor files official forms designated for that purpose in the bankruptcy court. The Bankruptcy Reform Act of 2005 specifies that before debtors can file a petition, they must receive credit counseling from an approved non-profit agency within the 180-day period (roughly six months) preceding the date of filing. A debtor filing a Chapter 7 petition must include a certificate proving that he or she has received individual or group counseling from an approved agency within the last 180 days. One of your tasks as a paralegal may be to assist the debtor in locating and completing the required credit counseling course.

The Code requires a consumer-debtor who has opted for liquidation bankruptcy proceedings to confirm the accuracy of the petition in bankruptcy that he or she has filed. The debtor must also state in the petition, at the time of filing, that he or she understands the relief available under other chapters of the Code and has chosen to proceed under Chapter 7. If an attorney is representing the consumer-debtor, the attorney must file an affidavit stating that she or he has informed the debtor of the relief available under each chapter of the Bankruptcy Code. In addition, the 2005 act requires the attorney to reasonably attempt to verify the accuracy of the consumer-debtor's petition and schedules (described below). Failure to do so is considered perjury.

Chapter 7 Schedules

The voluntary petition must contain the following schedules:

1. A list of both secured and unsecured creditors, their addresses, and the amount of debt owed to each. A **secured creditor** is one who has a security interest in the collateral that secures the debt. For example, a lending institution that finances the purchase of an automobile normally takes a security interest in the automobile—the collateral for the loan.

2. A statement of the financial affairs of the debtor.

secured creditor
A lender, seller, or any other person in whose favor there is a security interest.

A paralegal meets with a couple filing for Chapter 7 (liquidation) bankruptcy to obtain information about their financial situation. Under the Bankruptcy Reform Act of 2005, debtors must meet stricter requirements to be eligible for Chapter 7 bankruptcy.

(Courtesy of ©Comstock Images/Alamy)

3. A list of all property owned by the debtor, including property that the debtor claims is exempt.

4. A listing of current income and expenses.

5. A certificate from an approved credit counseling agency (as discussed previously).

6. Proof of payments received from employers within sixty days prior to the filing of the petition.

7. A statement of the amount of monthly income, itemized to show how the amount is calculated.

8. A copy of the debtor's federal income tax return (or a transcript of the return) for the year ending immediately before the filing of the petition.

The official forms must be completed accurately, sworn to under oath, and signed by the debtor. To conceal assets or knowingly supply false information on these schedules is a crime under the bankruptcy laws.

U.S. trustee
A government official who performs appointing and other administrative tasks that a bankruptcy judge would otherwise have to perform.

Additional Information May Be Required.   At the request of the court, of the U.S. trustee (a government official who performs appointing and other administrative tasks that a bankruptcy judge would otherwise have to perform), or of any party in interest (a party, such as a creditor, who has a valid interest in the outcome of the proceedings), the debtor must file a tax return at the end of each tax year while the case is pending and provide a copy to the court. This requirement also applies to Chapter 11 and 13 bankruptcies (discussed later in this chapter). Also, if requested by the U.S. trustee or bankruptcy trustee, the debtor must provide a photo document (such as a driver's license or passport) or other personal identifying information to establish his or her identity.

Time Period for Filing Schedules.   With the exception of tax returns, the required schedules must be filed within forty-five days after the filing of the petition (unless an extension of up to forty-five days is granted). Failure to file on time will result in an automatic dismissal of the petition. The debtor has up to seven days before the date of the first creditors' meeting (to be discussed later in the chapter) to provide a copy of the most current tax returns to the trustee.

Substantial Abuse and Means Testing

Prior to 2005, a bankruptcy court could dismiss a Chapter 7 petition if the use of Chapter 7 would constitute a "substantial abuse" of that chapter. The Bankruptcy Reform Act of 2005 established a new system of "means testing" (evaluating the debtor's income) to determine whether a debtor's petition is presumed to be a "substantial abuse" of Chapter 7.

When Abuse Will Be Presumed.   Means testing is now based on whether the debtor's family income is greater than the median family income in the state in which the petition is filed. Median incomes vary from state to state and are calculated and reported by the U.S. Bureau of the Census. The debtor's current monthly income is calculated based on the last six months' average income, less certain "allowed expenses" reflecting the basic needs of the debtor.[3] The monthly amount is then multiplied by twelve. If the resulting income exceeds the state median income by $6,000 or more,[4] abuse is presumed, and the trustee or any creditor can file a motion to dismiss the petition. A debtor can rebut (refute) the presumption of abuse "by demonstrating special circumstances that justify additional expenses or adjustments of current monthly income for which there is no reasonable alternative." (One example might be anticipated medical costs not covered by health insurance.) These additional expenses or adjustments must be itemized, and the debtor must attest under oath to their accuracy.

When Abuse Will Not Be Presumed.   If the debtor's income is below the state median (or if the debtor has successfully rebutted a presumption of abuse based on the means test), abuse will not be presumed. In these situations, the court may still find substantial abuse, but the creditors will not have standing to file a motion to dismiss. Basically, this leaves intact the prior law on substantial abuse, which allowed the court to consider such factors as the debtor's bad faith or circumstances when determining whether a Chapter 7 bankruptcy would constitute substantial abuse.

Additional Grounds for Dismissal

As noted, a debtor's voluntary petition for Chapter 7 relief may be dismissed for substantial abuse or for failing to provide the necessary documents (such as schedules and tax returns) within the specified time. In addition, a motion to dismiss a Chapter 7 filing may be granted in two other situations under the Bankruptcy Reform Act of 2005. First, if the debtor has been convicted of a violent crime, the victim can file a motion to dismiss the voluntary petition.[5] Second, if after filing a petition the debtor fails to pay domestic-support obligations (which include child and spousal support), the court may dismiss the petition.

Order for Relief

If the voluntary petition for bankruptcy is found to be proper, the filing of the petition will itself constitute an **order for relief**. (An order for relief is a court's grant of assistance to a bankruptcy petitioner.) Once a consumer-debtor's voluntary petition has been filed, the clerk of the court or other appointee must give the trustee and creditors notice of the order for relief by mail not more than twenty days after entry of the order.

order for relief
A court's grant of assistance to a complainant.

Involuntary Bankruptcy

An involuntary bankruptcy occurs when the debtor's creditors force the debtor into bankruptcy proceedings. An involuntary case cannot be commenced against a farmer[6] or a charitable institution. For an involuntary action to be filed against other debtors, the following requirements must be met: If the debtor has twelve or more creditors, three or more of these creditors having unsecured claims totaling at least $12,300 must join in the petition. If a debtor has fewer than twelve creditors, one or more creditors having a claim of $12,300 may file.

If the debtor challenges the involuntary petition, a hearing will be held, and the bankruptcy court will enter an order for relief if it finds either of the following:

1. The debtor is generally not paying debts as they become due.
2. A general receiver, assignee, or custodian took possession of, or was appointed to take charge of, substantially all of the debtor's property within 120 days before the filing of the petition.

If the court grants an order for relief, the debtor will be required to supply the same information in the bankruptcy schedules as in a voluntary bankruptcy.

An involuntary petition should not be used as an everyday debt-collection device, and the Code provides penalties for the filing of frivolous petitions against debtors. Judgment may be granted against the petitioning creditors for the costs and attorneys' fees incurred by the debtor in defending against an involuntary petition that is dismissed by the court. If the petition is filed in bad faith, damages can be awarded for injury to the debtor's reputation. Punitive damages may also be awarded.

Automatic Stay

The moment a petition in bankruptcy—either voluntary or involuntary—is filed, there exists an **automatic stay**, or suspension, of virtually all litigation and other action by creditors against the debtor or the debtor's property. In other words, once a petition has been

automatic stay
A suspension of all judicial proceedings upon the occurrence of an independent event. Under the Bankruptcy Code, the moment a petition to initiate bankruptcy proceedings is filed, all litigation or other legal action by creditors against a debtor and the debtor's property is suspended.

filed, creditors cannot contact the debtor by phone or mail or start any legal proceedings to recover debts or to repossess property. In some circumstances, a creditor may petition the bankruptcy court for relief from the automatic stay, however.

The Code provides that if a creditor *knowingly* violates the automatic stay (a willful violation), any party injured, including the debtor, is entitled to recover actual damages, costs, and attorneys' fees and may be entitled to recover punitive damages as well.

Exceptions to the Automatic Stay

The 2005 Bankruptcy Reform Act provides several exceptions to the automatic stay. A new exception is created for domestic-support obligations, which include any obligation owed to a spouse, a former spouse, a child of the debtor, a child's parent or guardian, or a governmental unit. In addition, proceedings against the debtor related to divorce, child custody or visitation, domestic violence, and support enforcement are not stayed. Also excepted are investigations by a securities regulatory agency, proceedings to establish certain claims against real property (including property taxes), eviction actions on judgments obtained prior to the filing of the petition, and withholding from the debtor's wages for repayment of a retirement account loan.

Limitations on the Automatic Stay

Under the 2005 act, if a creditor or other such party requests relief from the stay, the stay will automatically terminate sixty days after the request, unless the court grants an extension or the parties agree otherwise. Also, the automatic stay on secured debts will terminate thirty days after the petition is filed if the debtor filed a bankruptcy petition that was dismissed within the prior year. (This is true unless the dismissal was based on the means test and the current petition was filed under a different chapter.) Any party with a legitimate interest can request the court to extend the stay by showing that the filing is in good faith.

If the debtor filed two or more bankruptcy petitions that were dismissed during the prior year, the Code presumes bad faith, and the automatic stay does not go into effect until the court orders that the filing was made in good faith. In addition, if the petition is subsequently dismissed (because the debtor failed to file the required documents within thirty days of filing, for example), the stay is terminated.

Finally, the automatic stay on secured property terminates forty-five days after the creditors' meeting (to be discussed shortly) unless the debtor redeems (pays for) the property or reaffirms (agrees to pay) the debt. In other words, the debtor cannot keep secured property, such as a financed automobile—even if she or he continues to make payments on it—without reinstating the rights of the secured party to collect on the debt.

The Estate in Property

estate in property
In bankruptcy proceedings, all of the debtor's interests in property currently held and wherever located, as well as interests in certain property to which the debtor becomes entitled within 180 days after filing for bankruptcy.

On the commencement of a liquidation proceeding under Chapter 7, an **estate in property** (sometimes called an *estate in bankruptcy*) is created. The estate consists of all the debtor's interests in property currently held, wherever located. Interests in certain property—such as gifts, inheritances, property settlements (divorce), and life insurance death proceeds—to which the debtor becomes entitled *within 180 days after filing* may also become part of the estate. In addition, under the 2005 act, contributions that the debtor has already made to an employee benefit plan are excluded from the estate. Generally, though, the filing of a bankruptcy petition fixes a dividing line: property acquired prior to the filing of the petition becomes property of the estate, and property acquired after the filing of the petition remains the debtor's.

Creditors' Meeting and Claims

Within a reasonable time after the order for relief has been granted (not less than twenty days or more than forty days), the U.S. trustee must call a meeting of the creditors listed in the schedules filed by the debtor. The bankruptcy judge does not attend this meeting.

Debtor's Presence Required

The debtor is required to attend the meeting (unless excused by the court) and to submit to examination under oath by the creditors and the trustee. Failing to appear when required or making false statements under oath may result in the debtor's being denied a discharge in bankruptcy. At the meeting, the trustee ensures that the debtor is aware of the potential consequences of bankruptcy and of his or her ability to file for bankruptcy under a different chapter of the Bankruptcy Code.

Creditors' Claims

To be entitled to receive a portion of the debtor's estate, each creditor normally files a **proof of claim** with the bankruptcy court clerk within ninety days of the creditors' meeting.[7] The proof of claim lists the creditor's name and address, as well as the amount that the creditor asserts is owed to the creditor by the debtor. A creditor need not file a proof of claim if the debtor's schedules list the creditor's claim as liquidated (exactly determined) and the creditor does not dispute the amount of the claim. A proof of claim is necessary if there is any dispute concerning the claim. If a creditor fails to file a proof of claim, the bankruptcy court or trustee may file the proof of claim on the creditor's behalf but is not obligated to do so.

Generally, any legal obligation of the debtor is a claim (except claims for breach of employment contracts or real estate leases for terms longer than one year). When a claim is disputed, or unliquidated, the bankruptcy court will set the value of the claim. Any creditor holding a debtor's obligation can file a claim against the debtor's estate. These claims are automatically allowed unless contested by the trustee, the debtor, or another creditor. A creditor who files a false claim commits a crime.

proof of claim
A document filed with a bankruptcy court by a creditor to inform the court of a claim against a debtor's property. The proof of claim lists the creditor's name and address, as well as the amount that the creditor asserts is owed to the creditor by the debtor.

Exemptions

As mentioned, the bankruptcy trustee takes control over the debtor's property in a Chapter 7 bankruptcy, but an individual debtor is entitled to exempt (exclude) certain property from the bankruptcy. The Bankruptcy Code exempts the following property:[8]

1. Up to $18,450 in equity in the debtor residence and burial plot (the *homestead exemption,* which will be discussed shortly).

2. Interest in a motor vehicle up to $2,950.

3. Interest, up to $475 for a particular item, in household goods and furnishings, wearing apparel, appliances, books, animals, crops, and musical instruments (the aggregate total of all items is limited, however, to $9,850).

4. Interest in jewelry up to $1,225.

5. Interest in any other property up to $975, plus any unused part of the $18,450 homestead exemption up to $9,250.

6. Interest in any tools of the debtor's trade up to $1,850.

7. Any unmatured life insurance contract owned by the debtor.

8. Certain interests in accrued dividends and interest under life insurance contracts owned by the debtor, not to exceed $9,850.

9. Professionally prescribed health aids.

10. The right to receive Social Security and certain welfare benefits, alimony and support, certain retirement funds and pensions, and education savings accounts held for specific periods of time.

11. The right to receive certain personal-injury and other awards up to $18,450.

Individual states have the power to pass legislation precluding debtors from using the federal exemptions within the state; a majority of the states have done this. In those states, debtors may use only state, not federal, exemptions. In the rest of the states, an individual debtor (or a husband and wife filing jointly) may choose either the exemptions provided under state law or the federal exemptions.[9]

Note also that the 2005 Bankruptcy Reform Act clarified specifically what is included in "household goods and furnishings" (referred to in item 3 in the above list). ▶ **EXAMPLE 12.1** The category includes one computer, one radio, one television, one videocassette recorder, educational materials or equipment primarily for use by minor dependent children, and furniture that is used exclusively by a minor dependent (or by an elderly or disabled dependent). Other items—including works of art; electronic entertainment equipment with a fair market value of over $500; antiques and jewelry (except wedding rings) valued at more than $500; and motor vehicles, tractors, lawn mowers, watercraft, and aircraft—are not included in household goods. ◀

The Homestead Exemption

homestead exemption
A law permitting the debtor to retain the family home, either in its entirety or up to a specified dollar amount, free from the claims of unsecured creditors or trustees in bankruptcy.

The 2005 Bankruptcy Reform Act significantly changed the law for debtors seeking to use state **homestead exemption** statutes. In six states, among them Florida and Texas, state homestead exemptions allow debtors petitioning for bankruptcy to shield unlimited amounts of equity in their homes from creditors. The Bankruptcy Code previously required that the debtor have lived in the state for at least six months to apply any of the state exemptions. Under the 2005 act, however, the period is two years. In other words, the debtor must have lived in the state for two years prior to filing the petition to be able to use the state homestead exemption.

In addition, if the homestead was acquired within three and a half years preceding the date of filing, the maximum equity exempted is $125,000, even if the state law would permit a higher amount. (This does not apply to equity that has been rolled over during the specified period from the sale of a previous homestead in the same state.) Also, if the debtor owes a debt arising from a violation of securities law or if the debtor committed certain criminal or tortious acts in the previous five years that indicate the filing constituted substantial abuse, the debtor cannot exempt any amount of equity.

The Bankruptcy Trustee

bankruptcy trustee
A person appointed by the bankruptcy court to administer the debtor's estate in the interests of both the debtor and the creditors. The basic duty of the bankruptcy trustee is to collect and reduce to cash the estate in property and to close up the estate as speedily as is compatible with the best interests of the parties.

Promptly after the order for relief in the liquidation proceeding has been entered, an interim, or provisional, **bankruptcy trustee** is appointed by the U.S. trustee. The bankruptcy trustee may be a bankruptcy attorney (one who is not involved in the case).

The basic duty of the bankruptcy trustee is to collect and reduce to cash the estate in property and to close up the estate as speedily as is compatible with the best interests of the parties. The trustee is held accountable for administering the debtor's estate in the interests of *both* the debtor and the creditors.

New Duties under the 2005 Act

The Bankruptcy Reform Act of 2005 imposes new duties on trustees with regard to means testing for debtors who file Chapter 7 petitions. Under the new law, the trustee is required to review promptly all materials filed by the debtor. Not later than ten days after the first meeting of the creditors, the trustee must file a statement as to whether the case is presumed to be an abuse under the means test. The trustee must then provide a copy of this statement to all creditors within five days. Not later than forty days after the first creditors' meeting, the trustee must either file a motion to dismiss the petition (or convert it to a Chapter 13 case) or file a statement setting forth the reasons why the motion would not be appropriate.

The trustee also has new duties under the 2005 act designed to protect domestic-support creditors (those to whom a domestic-support obligation is due). The trustee is required to provide written notice of the bankruptcy to the claim holder (a former spouse who is owed child support, for example). The notice must also include certain information, such as the debtor's address, the name and address of the debtor's last known employer, and the address and phone number of the state child-support enforcement agency. (Note that these requirements are not limited to Chapter 7 bankruptcies, and the trustee may have additional duties in other types of bankruptcies to collect assets for distribution to the domestic-support creditor.)

Trustee's Powers

The trustee has the power to require persons holding the debtor's property at the time the petition is filed to deliver the property to the trustee. To enable the trustee to implement this power, the Code provides that the trustee occupies a position equivalent in rights to that of certain other parties. ▶ **EXAMPLE 12.2** The trustee has the same rights to obtain the debtor's property as certain types of creditors do. The trustee also has rights equivalent to those of the debtor. ◀

In addition, the trustee has specific *powers of avoidance*—that is, the trustee can set aside (avoid) a sale or other transfer of the debtor's property, taking it back as a part of the debtor's estate. These powers include voidable rights available to the debtor, preferences, and fraudulent transfers by the debtor. Each is discussed in more detail below. Additionally, certain statutory liens (creditors' claims against the debtor's property) may be avoided by the trustee.

The debtor shares most of the trustee's avoidance powers. Thus, if the trustee does not take action to enforce one of the rights just mentioned, the debtor in a liquidation bankruptcy can nevertheless enforce that right. Note that under the 2005 act, neither the debtor nor the trustee has the power to avoid any transfer that was a bona fide payment of a domestic-support debt.

Voidable Rights

A trustee steps into the shoes of the debtor. Thus, any reason that a debtor can use to obtain the return of his or her property can be used by the trustee as well. These grounds include fraud, duress, incapacity, and mutual mistake (see Chapter 8 for definitions of these terms).

▶ **EXAMPLE 12.3** Barry sells his boat to Zach. Zach gives Barry a check, knowing that there are insufficient funds in his bank account to cover the check. Zach has committed fraud. Barry has the right to avoid that transfer and recover the boat from Zach. Once an order for relief under Chapter 7 of the Code has been entered for Barry, the trustee can exercise the same right as Barry could to recover the boat from Zach, and the boat becomes a part of the debtor's estate. ◀

Preferences

A debtor is not permitted to transfer property or to make a payment that favors— or gives a preference to—one creditor over others. The trustee is allowed to recover payments made both voluntarily and involuntarily to one creditor in preference over another.

To have made a preferential payment that can be recovered, a debtor generally must have transferred property, for a preexisting debt, within *ninety days* of the filing of the petition in bankruptcy. The transfer must give the creditor more than the creditor would have

preference
In bankruptcy proceedings, the debtor's favoring of one creditor over others by making payments or transferring property to that creditor at the expense of the rights of other creditors. The bankruptcy trustee is allowed to recover payments made to one creditor in preference over another.

Ethics Watch!

DIVIDED LOYALTIES

As a paralegal, if you learn that a fraudulent transfer of property was made by a debtor, you have an ethical obligation to inform your supervising attorney of the debtor's illegal action. But what if the debtor is also your friend? What if you know that the debtor is concealing certain personal property (her grand piano, two valuable paintings inherited from her father, and so on)? When you ask her about these items during the intake interview, she confides in you that she "gave" them to her sister to hold for her so they wouldn't be subject to creditors' claims. What do you do? On the one hand, you know how important these items of personal property are to your friend and are sympathetic to her plight. On the other hand, you know that it is unfair to her creditors to conceal this property and that you would be violating your ethical obligations if you said nothing about it to your supervising attorney. This is another example of how, as a paralegal, your personal loyalties and professional commitments may come into conflict. Harsh as it may sound, you should abide by your professional duties in such situations. Remember, if you do not report the fraudulent concealment of assets, you are, in essence, participating in this wrongdoing.

received as a result of the bankruptcy proceedings. Sometimes the creditor receiving the preference is an *insider*—an individual, a partner, a partnership, or an officer or a director of a corporation (or a relative of one of these) who has a close relationship with the debtor. In this situation, the avoidance power of the trustee usually is extended to transfers made within *one year* before filing.

If a preferred creditor (one who has received a preference) has sold the transferred property to an innocent third party, the trustee cannot recover the property from the innocent party. The creditor, however, generally can be held accountable for the value of the property.

Fraudulent Transfers

The trustee can avoid fraudulent transfers or obligations if they were made within two years of the filing of the petition or if they were made with actual intent to hinder, delay, or defraud a creditor. ▶ **EXAMPLE 12.4** Suppose that a debtor who is thinking about petitioning for bankruptcy sells his stamp collection, worth several thousand dollars, to a friend for $500. The friend agrees that in the future he will "sell" the collection back to the debtor for the same amount of money. This is a fraudulent transfer. ◀

When a fraudulent transfer is made outside the Code's two-year limit, creditors may seek alternative relief under state laws. State laws often allow creditors to recover for transfers made up to three years prior to the filing of a petition.

Distribution of Property

In the distribution of the debtor's estate in property, secured creditors take priority over unsecured creditors. The Code provides that a consumer-debtor, within thirty days of filing a liquidation petition or before the date of the first meeting of the creditors (whichever is first), must file with the clerk a statement of intention with respect to the secured collateral.

The statement must indicate whether the debtor will retain the collateral or surrender the collateral to the secured party. Also, if applicable, the debtor must specify whether the collateral will be claimed as exempt property and whether the debtor intends to redeem the property or reaffirm the debt secured by the collateral. The trustee is obligated to enforce the debtor's statement within forty-five days after it is filed. (This chapter's *Featured Guest* article on pages 422 and 423 discusses the statement of intention in more detail.)

Distribution to Secured Creditors

If the collateral is surrendered to the secured party, the secured creditor can enforce the security interest either by accepting the property in full satisfaction of the debt or by selling the collateral and using the proceeds to pay off the debt. Thus, the secured party has priority over unsecured parties as to the proceeds from the disposition of the collateral. Indeed, the Code provides that if the value of the collateral exceeds the secured party's claim, the secured party also has priority as to the proceeds in an amount that will cover reasonable fees and costs incurred because of the debtor's default. Any excess over this amount is used by the trustee to satisfy the claims of unsecured creditors. Should the collateral be insufficient to cover the secured debt owed, the secured creditor becomes an unsecured creditor for the difference.

Distribution to Unsecured Creditors

Bankruptcy law establishes an order of priority for classes of debts owed to unsecured creditors, and they are paid in the order of their priority. Each class of unsecured creditors must be fully paid before the next class is entitled to any of the remaining proceeds. If there are insufficient proceeds to pay fully all the creditors in a class, the proceeds are distributed proportionately to the creditors in the class, and classes lower in priority receive nothing. The new bankruptcy law elevated domestic-support obligations to the highest priority of unsecured claims. The order of priority among classes of unsecured creditors is as follows:

1. Claims for domestic-support obligations, such as child support and alimony (subject to the priority of the administrative costs that the trustee incurred in administering assets to pay the obligations).

2. Administrative expenses—including court costs, trustee fees, and attorneys' fees.

3. In an involuntary bankruptcy, expenses incurred by the debtor in the ordinary course of business from the date of the filing of the petition up to the appointment of the trustee or the issuance by the court of an order for relief.

4. Unpaid wages, salaries, and commissions earned within ninety days of the filing of the petition, limited to $4,925 per claimant. Any claim in excess of $4,925 or earned before the ninety-day period is treated as a claim of a general creditor (listed as number 10 below).

5. Unsecured claims for contributions to be made to employee benefit plans, limited to services performed during 180 days prior to the filing of the bankruptcy petition and $4,925 per employee.

6. Claims by farmers and fishermen, up to $4,925, against debtor operators of grain storage or fish storage or processing facilities.

7. Consumer deposits of up to $2,225 given to the debtor before the petition was filed in connection with the purchase, lease, or rental of property or purchase of services that were not received or provided. Any claim in excess of $2,225 is treated as a claim of a general creditor (number 10 below).

8. Certain taxes and penalties due to government units, such as income and property taxes.

Sidney K. Swinson

FEATURED **Guest**

THE STATEMENT OF INTENTION UNDER THE BANKRUPTCY REFORM ACT OF 2005

BIOGRAPHICAL NOTE

Sidney K. Swinson is a shareholder and director of the Tulsa, Oklahoma, firm of Gable & Gotwals, P.C. He earned a bachelor's degree in business administration in 1977 from the University of Notre Dame and a J.D. from the University of Tulsa College of Law in 1980. Swinson is an Adjunct Professor of Law at the University of Tulsa College of Law and is co-author of An Introduction to Bankruptcy Law, *Fifth Edition (Thomson Delmar Learning).*

THE STATEMENT OF INTENTION BEFORE THE 2005 BANKRUPTCY REFORM ACT

When a debtor files for bankruptcy, Section 362(a) of the Bankruptcy Code[a] imposes an automatic stay that prevents creditors from taking certain actions to collect debts that arose prior to the bankruptcy filing. Creditors with collateral securing their claims are understandably anxious to know a debtor's intentions. Is the debtor going to keep the collateral or surrender it? Section 521 addresses this issue by requiring an individual debtor, within thirty days after filing a petition, to file a statement of intention "with respect to the retention or surrender of such property and, if applicable, specifying that such property is claimed as exempt, that the debtor intends to redeem such property [pay the creditor in a lump sum an amount equal to the value of the collateral], or that the debtor intends to reaffirm [sign a written agreement to remain obligated on the debt despite receiving a discharge] debts secured by such property."

Despite this mandate, debtors sometimes keep collateral and refuse to either reaffirm the debt or redeem the collateral, claiming that filing for bankruptcy has not placed them in default under the terms of the security agreement. Courts are not in agreement about whether a debtor who is current on his or her loan payments can be compelled to reaffirm the debt or redeem the collateral. The reason is that the statute is ambiguous about whether the debtor's only options are to reaffirm, redeem, or surrender, and the statute itself provides no remedy if the debtor retains the collateral without redeeming or reaffirming.[b]

Furthermore, creditors who include a provision in their security agreements (the agreements that give the creditors a security interest in the collateral) that the act of filing bankruptcy is an event of default have had mixed success. Some courts have found such a provision unenforceable because it is inconsistent with the fresh-start policy of the Bankruptcy Code.[c]

---

a. References are to the United States Bankruptcy Code, Sections 11 U.S.C.A §101 et seq.

b. See *In re Boodrow*, 126 F.3d 43 (2d Cir. 1997). In this case, a debtor who was not in default was permitted to retain collateral and keep making payments.

c. *Riggs National Bank v. Perry*, 729 F.2d 982 (4th Cir. 1984).

---

9. Claims for death or personal injury resulting from the operation of a motor vehicle or vessel if such operation was unlawful because the debtor was intoxicated as a result of using alcohol, a drug, or another substance. (This provision was added by the 2005 act.)

10. Claims of general creditors.

If any amount remains after the priority classes of creditors have been satisfied, it is turned over to the debtor.

Discharge

From the debtor's point of view, the primary purpose of liquidation is to obtain a fresh start through a discharge of debts. Certain debts, however, are not dischargeable in bankruptcy. Also, certain debtors may not qualify to have all debts discharged in bankruptcy. These situations are discussed below.

THE STATEMENT OF INTENTION AFTER THE 2005 BANKRUPTCY REFORM ACT

For cases filed on or after October 17, 2005, the Bankruptcy Abuse Prevention and Consumer Protection Act (BAPCA, or Bankruptcy Reform Act) of 2005 forbids an individual Chapter 7 debtor from retaining collateral securing a purchase-money loan in certain circumstances. (A *purchase-money loan* is one in which a lender extends credit for the borrower to use to purchase specific goods that serve as collateral for the loan.) Under the BAPCA, the debtor cannot retain collateral secured by such a loan unless the debtor, within forty-five days after the meeting of creditors, either reaffirms the debt under Section 524(c) or redeems the collateral under Section 722. If the debtor does not reaffirm the debt or redeem the collateral, the automatic stay is terminated, and the property is removed from the bankruptcy estate. In that event, the creditor may proceed to exercise its rights under the security agreement with respect to the collateral. Those rights generally include the right to repossess the collateral, sell it in a commercially reasonable manner, and apply the proceeds to the debt.

This relief may be of little value to the secured creditor if the debtor is not otherwise in default under the security agreement. Historically, courts have disagreed about the enforceability of a provision in a security agreement making a bankruptcy filing an event of

default. Section 521(d) now provides additional assistance to creditors by making enforceable a provision in a lease or security agreement that renders a debtor in default "by reason of the occurrence, pendency, or existence of a proceeding under [the Bankruptcy Code] or the insolvency of the debtor."

CONCLUSION

A paralegal assisting an attorney in representing an individual debtor in bankruptcy must be particularly mindful not only of the debtor's duty to file a statement of intention but also of the ramifications of the debtor's failure to timely perform his or her intentions. In addition, when assisting a party in a bankruptcy case, a paralegal must pay careful attention to the default provisions in a security agreement, regardless of whether the client is a debtor or a secured creditor. A provision that makes bankruptcy filing an event of default may cause an unsuspecting debtor to lose his or her car even if the debtor wants to keep it. Conversely, such a provision will enable a secured creditor to force a recalcitrant debtor to reaffirm or redeem as a condition of keeping the collateral. Properly serving a client's needs requires careful attention to such detail.

> *"Properly serving a client's needs requires careful attention to ... detail."*

Exceptions to Discharge

Discharge of a debt may be denied because of the nature of the claim or the conduct of the debtor. Claims that are not dischargeable in a liquidation bankruptcy include the following:

1. Claims for bank taxes accruing within two years prior to bankruptcy.

2. Claims for amounts borrowed by the debtor to pay federal taxes or any nondischargeable taxes.

3. Claims against property or funds obtained by the debtor under false pretenses or by false representations.

4. Claims by creditors who were not notified of the bankruptcy; these claims did not appear on the schedules the debtor was required to file.

5. Claims based on fraud or misuse of funds by the debtor while he or she was acting in a fiduciary capacity or claims involving the debtor's embezzlement or larceny.

6. Domestic-support obligations and property settlements as provided for in a separation agreement or divorce decree.

7. Claims for amounts due on a retirement account loan.

8. Claims based on willful or malicious conduct by the debtor toward another or the property of another.

9. Certain government fines and penalties, which under the 2005 act also include penalties imposed under federal election laws.

10. Certain student loans or obligations to repay funds received as an educational benefit, scholarship, or stipend—unless payment of the loans imposes an undue hardship on the debtor and the debtor's dependents.

11. Consumer debts of more than $500 for luxury goods or services owed to a single creditor incurred within ninety days of the order for relief. (Prior to the passage of the 2005 act, the amount was $1,150 and the period was sixty days.) This denial of discharge is a rebuttable presumption (that is, the denial can be challenged by the debtor), however, and any debts reasonably incurred to support the debtor or dependents are not classified as luxuries.

12. Cash advances totaling more than $750 that are extensions of open-end consumer credit obtained by the debtor within seventy days of the order for relief. (The prior law allowed $1,150 in cash advances obtained within sixty days of the order.) A denial of discharge of these debts is also a rebuttable presumption.

13. Judgments or consent decrees against a debtor as a result of the debtor's operation of a motor vehicle or any vessel or aircraft while intoxicated.

14. Fees or assessments arising from a lot in a homeowners' association, as long as the debtor retained an interest in the lot.

15. Failure of the debtor to provide required or requested tax documents. (This exception to discharge also applies to Chapter 11 and Chapter 13 bankruptcies.)

Objections to Discharge

In addition to the exceptions to discharge just listed, a bankruptcy court may also deny the discharge based on the debtor's conduct. In such a situation, the assets of the debtor are still distributed to the creditors, but the debtor remains liable for the unpaid portion of all claims. Some grounds for the denial of discharge based on the debtor's conduct follow:

1. The debtor's concealment or destruction of property with the intent to hinder, delay, or defraud a creditor.

2. The debtor's fraudulent concealment or destruction of financial records.

3. The granting of a discharge to the debtor within eight years of the filing of the petition. (This period was increased from six to eight years by the 2005 act.)

4. Failure of the debtor to complete the required credit counseling course (unless such a course is unavailable). (This ground for denial was provided for by the 2005 act and also applies to Chapter 13 petitions.)

5. The institution of proceedings in which the debtor could be found guilty of a felony. (Basically, the 2005 act states that a court cannot discharge any debt until the completion of felony proceedings against the debtor.)

Effect of Discharge

The primary effect of a discharge is to void, or set aside, any judgment on a discharged debt and prohibit any action to collect a discharged debt. A discharge does not affect the liability of a co-debtor.

Revocation of Discharge

The Code provides that a debtor's discharge may be revoked. On petition by the trustee or a creditor, a bankruptcy court may, within one year, revoke the discharge decree if it is discovered that the debtor acted fraudulently or dishonestly during the bankruptcy proceedings. The revocation renders the discharge void, allowing creditors not satisfied by the distribution of the debtor's estate to proceed with their claims against the debtor.

Reaffirmation of Debt

A debtor may voluntarily agree to pay a debt—for example, a debt owed to a family member, family physician, close friend, or some other party—notwithstanding the fact that the debt could be discharged in bankruptcy. An agreement to pay a debt dischargeable in bankruptcy is referred to as a **reaffirmation agreement**. To be enforceable, reaffirmation agreements must be made before the debtor is granted a discharge. The agreement must be signed and filed with the court. Court approval is required unless the debtor is represented by an attorney during the negotiation of the reaffirmation and submits the proper documents and certifications. Even then, court approval may be required if it appears that the reaffirmation will result in undue hardship on the debtor. When court approval is required, a separate hearing will take place. The court will approve the reaffirmation only if it finds that the agreement will not result in undue hardship to the debtor and that the reaffirmation is consistent with the debtor's best interests.

reaffirmation agreement
An agreement between a debtor and a creditor in which the debtor reaffirms, or promises to pay, a debt dischargeable in bankruptcy. To be enforceable, the agreement must be made prior to the discharge of the debt by the bankruptcy court.

Presumption of Undue Hardship

Under the provisions of the 2005 act, if the debtor's monthly income minus the debtor's monthly expenses is less than the scheduled payments on the reaffirmed debt, undue hardship will be presumed. A presumption of undue hardship can be rebutted, however. The debtor can either file a written statement with the court or explain to the court in person how she or he will be able to make future payments on the debt.

If the debtor has an attorney, the attorney must certify in writing that he or she has fully advised the debtor of the legal effect and consequences of reaffirmation. In addition, to rebut the presumption of undue hardship, the attorney must certify that, in the attorney's opinion, the debtor will be able to make the payments.

New Reaffirmation Disclosures

To discourage creditors from engaging in abusive practices, the 2005 act added new requirements for reaffirmation. The Code now provides the specific language for several pages of disclosures that must be given to debtors entering reaffirmation agreements. Among other things, these disclosures explain that the debtor is not required to reaffirm any debt but that liens on secured property, such as mortgages and cars, will remain in effect even if the debt is not reaffirmed. The reaffirmation agreement must disclose the amount of the debt reaffirmed, the rates of interest, the date payments begin, and the right to rescind. The disclosures also caution the debtor, "Only agree to reaffirm a debt if it is in your best interest. Be sure you can afford the payments you agree to make." The original disclosure documents must be signed by the debtor, certified by the debtor's attorney, and filed with the court at the same time as the reaffirmation agreement. A reaffirmation agreement that is not accompanied by the original signed disclosures will not be effective.

If the debtor is represented by an attorney and no presumption of undue hardship arises, then the reaffirmation becomes effective immediately on filing with the court. If the debtor is not represented, the reaffirmation is not effective until the court approves it. The debtor can rescind, or cancel, the agreement at any time before the court enters a discharge order or within sixty days of the filing of the agreement, whichever is *later*.

Ethics Watch!

THE PERILS OF INDEPENDENT PRACTICE

As you read in Chapter 2, independent paralegals, or legal technicians, provide services directly to the public (without attorney supervision). Often, independent paralegals assist debtors by selling them "do-it-yourself" bankruptcy kits, typing up bankruptcy forms, and so on.

Although the Bankruptcy Code allows paralegals to act as bankruptcy petition preparers without attorney supervision, it also contains very strict requirements that paralegals must follow. The law specifically prohibits petition preparers from advising bankruptcy debtors about numerous issues and from offering legal advice. For example, petition preparers may not tell a debtor whether he or she will be able to retain certain property, such as a house or car, after filing for bankruptcy. They may not say whether a particular debt will or can be discharged. They may not tell debtors how to characterize an interest in property when filling out the forms, whether to reaffirm a particular debt, or what tax consequences might be involved.

Violators may be subject to a fine; may be required to forfeit the fees they received from, or pay damages to, the debtor; and may even be ordered not to prepare bankruptcy petitions in the future. Because of the dangers involved, paralegals who prepare bankruptcy petitions without attorney supervision must be exceedingly careful to avoid pitfalls and potential lawsuits.

REORGANIZATIONS

The type of bankruptcy proceedings used most commonly by a corporate debtor is the Chapter 11 *reorganization*. In a reorganization, the creditors and the debtor formulate a plan under which the debtor pays a portion of his or her debts and is discharged of the remainder. The debtor is allowed to continue in business. Although this type of bankruptcy is commonly a corporate reorganization, any debtor (except a stockbroker or a commodities broker) who is eligible for Chapter 7 relief is eligible for relief under Chapter 11. Railroads are also eligible. In 1994, Congress established a "fast-track" Chapter 11 procedure for small-business debtors whose liabilities do not exceed $2 million and who do not own or manage real estate. This procedure does not require the appointment of committees and can save time and costs.

The same principles that govern the filing of a liquidation (Chapter 7) petition apply to reorganization proceedings. The case may be brought either voluntarily or involuntarily. The same principles govern the entry of the order for relief. The automatic-stay provision is also applicable in reorganizations. Under the 2005 act, an exception from the automatic stay is triggered in the event that the debtor files for bankruptcy again within two years, and new grounds for dismissal (such as substantial abuse) or conversion of the case are established. Also, the 2005 act contains specific rules and limitations for *individual* debtors who file a Chapter 11 petition. For example, an individual debtor's postpetition acquisitions and earnings become the property of the bankruptcy estate.

Workouts

In some instances, creditors may prefer private, negotiated adjustments or creditor-debtor relations, also known as **workouts**, to bankruptcy proceedings. Often these out-of-court workouts are much more flexible and thus more conducive to a speedy settlement. Speed is critical, because delay is one of the most costly elements in any bankruptcy proceeding. Another advantage of workouts is that they avoid the various administrative costs of bankruptcy proceedings.

workout
An out-of-court negotiation in which a debtor enters into an agreement with a creditor or creditors for a payment or plan to discharge the debtor's debt.

Must Be in the Best Interests of the Creditors

A bankruptcy court, after notice and a hearing, may dismiss or suspend all proceedings in a case at any time if dismissal or suspension would better serve the interests of the creditors. The Code also allows a court, after notice and a hearing, to dismiss a case under reorganization "for cause." Cause includes the absence of a reasonable likelihood of rehabilitation, the inability to effect a plan, and an unreasonable delay by the debtor that is prejudicial to (may harm the interests of) creditors.

Debtor in Possession

On entry of the order for relief, the debtor generally continues to operate his or her business as a **debtor in possession (DIP)**. The court, however, may appoint a trustee (often referred to as a *receiver*) to operate the debtor's business if gross mismanagement of the business is shown or if appointing a trustee is in the best interests of the estate.

debtor in possession (DIP)
In Chapter 11 bankruptcy proceedings, a debtor who is allowed, for the benefit of all concerned, to maintain possession of the estate in property (the business) and to continue business operations.

The DIP's role is similar to that of a trustee in a liquidation. The DIP is entitled to avoid preferential payments made to creditors and fraudulent transfers of assets that occurred prior to the filing of the Chapter 11 petition. The DIP has the power to decide whether to cancel or assume obligations under executory contracts (contracts that have not yet been performed) that were made prior to the filing.

Collective Bargaining Agreements

The Code attempts to reconcile federal policies favoring collective bargaining with the need to allow a debtor company to reject executory labor contracts while trying to reorganize. The Code sets forth standards and procedures under which collective bargaining contracts can be assumed or rejected under a reorganization filing. In general, a collective bargaining contract can be rejected if the debtor has first proposed necessary contractual modifications to the union and the union has failed to adopt them without good cause. The company is required (1) to provide the union with the relevant information needed to evaluate the proposal and (2) to confer in good faith in attempting to reach a mutually satisfactory agreement on the modifications.

Creditors' Committees

As soon as practicable after the entry of the order for relief, a creditors' committee of unsecured creditors is appointed. The committee may consult with the trustee or the DIP concerning the administration of the case or the formulation of the reorganization plan. Additional creditors' committees may be appointed to represent special interest creditors. Generally, no orders affecting the estate will be entered without either the consent of the committee or a hearing in which the judge hears the position of the committee.

As mentioned, businesses with debts of less than $2 million that do not own or manage real estate can avoid creditors' committees. In these cases, orders can be entered without a committee's consent.

The Reorganization Plan

A reorganization plan to rehabilitate the debtor is a plan to conserve and administer the debtor's assets in the hope of an eventual return to successful operation and solvency. The plan must be fair and equitable and must do the following:

1. Designate classes of claims and interests.
2. Specify the treatment to be afforded the classes. (The plan must provide the same treatment for each claim in a particular class.)
3. Provide an adequate means for execution. (The 2005 Bankruptcy Reform Act requires individual debtors to utilize postpetition assets as necessary to execute the plan.)
4. Provide for payment of tax claims over a five-year period.

Filing the Plan

Only the debtor may file a plan within the first 120 days after the date of the order for relief. Under the 2005 act, the 120-day period may be extended, but not beyond eighteen months from the date of the order for relief. If the debtor does not meet the 120-day deadline or obtain an extension, and if the debtor fails to obtain the required creditor consent within 180 days, any party may propose a plan. The plan need not provide for full repayment to unsecured creditors. Instead, creditors receive a percentage of each dollar owed to them by the debtor. If a small-business debtor chooses to avoid creditors' committees, the time for the debtor's filing is 180 days.

Acceptance and Confirmation of the Plan

Once the plan has been developed, it is submitted to each class of creditors for acceptance. For the plan to be adopted, each class that is adversely affected by the plan must accept it. A class has accepted the plan when a majority of the creditors, representing two-thirds of the amount of the total claim, vote to approve it. Confirmation is conditioned on the debtor's certifying that all postpetition domestic-support obligations have been paid in full.

Even when all classes of creditors accept the plan, the court may refuse to confirm it if it is not "in the best interests of the creditors." A former spouse or child of the debtor can block the plan if it does not provide for payment of his or her claims in cash. Under the 2005 act, the plan can also be modified at the request of the debtor, the trustee, the U.S. trustee, or a holder of an unsecured claim. If an unsecured creditor objects to the plan, specific rules apply to the value of property to be distributed under the plan. Tax claims must be paid over a five-year period.

Even if only one class of creditors has accepted the plan, the court may still confirm the plan under the Code's so-called **cram-down provision**. In other words, the court may confirm the plan over the objections of a class of creditors. Before the court can exercise this right of cram-down confirmation, it must be demonstrated that the plan "does not discriminate unfairly" against any creditors and that the plan is "fair and equitable."

cram-down provision
A provision of the Bankruptcy Code that allows a court to confirm a debtor's Chapter 11 reorganization plan even though only one class of creditors has accepted it. To exercise the court's right under this provision, the court must demonstrate that the plan does not discriminate unfairly against any creditors and is fair and equitable.

Discharge

The plan is binding on confirmation. The Bankruptcy Reform Act of 2005, however, provides that confirmation of a plan does not discharge an individual debtor. For individual debtors, execution of the plan must be completed before discharge will be granted, unless the court orders otherwise. For all other debtors, the court may order discharge at any time after the plan is confirmed. The debtor at this time is given a reorganization discharge from all claims not protected under the plan. This discharge does not apply to any claims that would be denied discharge under liquidation.

OFF-THE-JOB CONFIDENCES AND THE DUTY OF LOYALTY

What if, as a paralegal, you learn—off the job—that one of your firm's clients is planning to petition for bankruptcy? For instance, suppose that you are having dinner with a friend at Tina's Italian Restaurant. Your friend knows the owner, Tina, very well and tells you that Tina is planning to petition for bankruptcy because business is so bad. He asks you to keep this information in the "strictest confidence." You are shocked at the information because the sole practitioner for whom you work has handled Tina's legal affairs for years. You know that Tina not only owes the firm money for previous services but also wants your supervising attorney to defend her in a case of racial discrimination brought by a job applicant. Should you let your employer know about Tina's apparent intention to file for bankruptcy? Yes, you should. Although you have a moral duty to your friend to keep the information confidential, you have a legal duty, as an agent of your employer, to notify your employer of information relevant to the agency (the employment relationship). You also have a duty to be loyal to your employer's interests.

INDIVIDUAL REPAYMENT PLANS

Chapter 13 of the Bankruptcy Code provides for "Adjustment of Debts of an Individual with Regular Income." Individuals (not partnerships or corporations) with regular income who owe fixed unsecured debts of less than $307,675 or fixed secured debts of less than $922,975 may take advantage of bankruptcy repayment plans. Among those eligible are salaried employees; sole proprietors; and individuals who live on welfare, Social Security, fixed pensions, or investment income. Many small-business debtors have a choice of filing a plan for reorganization or for repayment. There are several advantages to repayment plans. One is that they are less expensive and less complicated than reorganization proceedings or liquidation proceedings.

Filing the Petition

A repayment-plan case can be initiated only by the filing of a voluntary petition by the debtor. In addition, certain liquidation and reorganization cases may be converted to repayment-plan cases with the consent of the debtor.

A Chapter 13 repayment plan case may also be converted to a Chapter 7 case at the request of either the debtor or, under certain circumstances, a creditor. A Chapter 13 repayment-plan case may be converted to a Chapter 11 case after a hearing.

Upon the filing of a repayment-plan petition, a trustee, who will make payments under the plan, must be appointed. The automatic stay previously discussed also takes effect. Although the stay applies to all or part of a consumer debt, it does not apply to any business debt incurred by the debtor.

Developing Paralegal Skills

PREPARING A PROOF OF CLAIM

Lee Smith works as a paralegal for a bankruptcy attorney. Today, Lee has been assigned the task of preparing a proof-of-claim form to be filed with the bankruptcy court for a client. The client is Bill Peaslee, a farmer who supplies a number of local restaurants with organic produce. One of Peaslee's customers, Fred Burke (the sole owner of Greenleaf Restaurant and Grill) owes Peaslee nearly $10,000 for orders that were placed in the previous nine months. Three weeks ago, when attempting to collect the past-due balance from Burke, Peaslee learned that Burke had filed for relief under Chapter 13 of the Bankruptcy Code. Peaslee, as a creditor of an individual debtor filing for bankruptcy protection, must file a proof of claim with the bankruptcy court to establish the amount of his claim against Burke. After Lee's supervising attorney provides the necessary information, Lee turns to his computer.

CHECKLIST FOR PREPARING A PROOF-OF-CLAIM FORM

* Retrieve the proof-of-claim form from the firm's forms database.
* Key in the client-creditor's name and address.
* Insert the amount that the debtor owes to the client.
* Enter the date, the debtor's name, and other required data.
* Print out the completed form and proofread it carefully.
* Give the completed form to the supervising attorney to review.
* After the attorney has reviewed the form, make copies of it to send to the court for filing.

Filing the Plan

Only the debtor may file a repayment plan. This plan may provide either for payment of all obligations in full or for payment of a lesser amount. Prior to the 2005 act, the time for repayment was usually three years unless the court approved an extension for up to five years. Under the new code, the duration of the payment plan (three or five years) is determined by the debtor's median family income. If the debtor's family income is greater than the state median family income under the means test (previously discussed), the proposed time for repayment must be five years. The term may not exceed five years.

The Code requires the debtor to make "timely" payments from the debtor's disposable income, and the trustee is required to ensure that the debtor commences these payments. The debtor must begin making payments under the proposed plan within thirty days after the plan has been filed with the court. If the plan has not been confirmed, the trustee is instructed to retain the payments until the plan is confirmed and then distribute them accordingly. If the plan is denied, the trustee will return the payments to the debtor less any costs. Failure of the debtor to make timely payments or to begin payments within the thirty-day period will allow the court to convert the case to a liquidation bankruptcy or to dismiss the petition.

Confirmation of the Plan

After the plan is filed, the court holds a confirmation hearing, at which interested parties may object to the plan. Under the 2005 act, the hearing must be held at least twenty days, but no more than forty-five days, after the meeting of the creditors. Confirmation of the plan is dependent on the debtor's certification that postpetition domestic-support obligations have been paid in full and all prepetition tax returns have been filed. The court will confirm a plan with respect to each claim of a secured creditor under any of the following circumstances:

1. If the secured creditors have accepted the plan.
2. If the plan provides that secured creditors retain their claims against the debtor's property until payment is made in full or until the debtor receives a discharge.
3. If the debtor surrenders the property securing the claim to the creditors.

Objections to the Plan

Unsecured creditors do not have a vote to confirm a repayment plan, but they can object to it. The court can approve a plan over the objection of the trustee or any unsecured creditor only in either of the following situations:

1. When the value of the property to be distributed under the plan is at least equal to the amount of the claims.
2. When all the debtor's projected disposable income to be received during the plan period will be applied to making payments. Disposable income is all income received *less* amounts needed to pay domestic-support obligations and/or amounts needed to meet ordinary expenses to continue the operation of a business. The 2005 act also excludes from disposable income charitable contributions up to 15 percent of the debtor's gross income and the reasonable and necessary costs for health insurance for the debtor and his or her dependents.

Modification of the Plan

Prior to completion of payments, the plan may be modified at the request of the debtor, the trustee, or an unsecured creditor. If any interested party objects to the modification, the court must hold a hearing to determine approval or disapproval of the modified plan.

Discharge

After the completion of all payments, the court grants a discharge of the debts provided for by the repayment plan. Not all debts are dischargeable, however. Under prior law, a discharge under Chapter 13 was sometimes referred to as a "superdischarge" because certain debts were discharged that would not have been dischargeable in a Chapter 7 bankruptcy. The 2005 Bankruptcy Reform Act has done away with most of these superdischarge provisions. Today, nondischargeable debts in a Chapter 13 bankruptcy include allowed claims not provided for by the plan; certain long-term debts provided for by the plan; claims for domestic-support obligations; payments on retirement accounts; and debts for trust fund taxes, taxes for which returns were never filed or filed late (within two years of the bankruptcy filing), student loans, and injury or property damage from driving under the influence of alcohol or drugs. Also excluded are debts arising from fraudulent tax obligations, criminal fines and restitution, fraud by a person acting in a fiduciary capacity, and restitution for willfully and maliciously causing personal injury or death.

If the debtor does not complete the plan, a hardship discharge may be granted if failure to complete the plan was due to circumstances beyond the debtor's control and if the value of the property distributed under the plan was greater than creditors would have received in a liquidation proceeding. A discharge can be revoked within one year if it was obtained by fraud.

BANKRUPTCY LAW AND THE PARALEGAL

Today, roughly one in every five paralegals spends at least half of his or her work time on bankruptcy law. Opportunities have expanded in recent years for independent paralegals who specialize in bankruptcy law. Indeed, much of the work previously handled by attorneys can now be done by paralegals with expertise in this area. For example, a debtor-client who wants to petition for bankruptcy relief must provide the court with numerous forms stating in detail the debtor's assets and liabilities. These forms must be filled out accurately and thoroughly.

Paralegals familiar with the requirements imposed by bankruptcy law know what information must be included with the petition for bankruptcy and can assist attorneys in collecting this information from clients. Paralegals may be involved in evaluating and verifying the debtor's financial statements, researching the law governing certain types of claims, and locating and perhaps appraising certain property belonging to the debtor. In addition, paralegals often help draft bankruptcy petitions and schedules and file them with the court.

As a paralegal, you may be dealing with bankruptcy cases periodically as part of your work for a general law practice. If you work for a firm that specializes in bankruptcy law, you may be working on behalf of either debtors or creditors who are involved in bankruptcy proceedings. Bankruptcy trustees also require paralegal assistance. In assisting a bankruptcy trustee, you would be working in the interests of both debtors and creditors during the administration of the debtor's estate in property. In any of these situations, a paralegal well trained in the substantive and procedural laws governing bankruptcy can provide invaluable assistance.

The specific types of work handled by bankruptcy paralegals vary, of course, depending on whether they work on behalf of the debtor, a creditor, or the bankruptcy trustee. Here are a few examples of paralegal tasks that you might be asked to perform if you were assisting a debtor-client (which could be an individual or a corporate representative) in petitioning for bankruptcy relief:

- Conduct an intake interview—and follow-up interviews as necessary—to obtain information concerning the debtor's income, debts, and assets.
- Verify the accuracy of the debtor's financial statements.
- Make arrangements for the debtor to receive credit counseling from an approved nonprofit agency (as required under the 2005 Bankruptcy Reform Act).
- Draft the bankruptcy petition based on the information obtained from the client.
- Verify the validity of creditors' claims that have been submitted to the bankruptcy court.
- Prepare the client for bankruptcy proceedings, such as creditors' meetings.
- Assist in work on the debtor's behalf in any legal actions relating to the bankruptcy proceedings.
- Research the Bankruptcy Code to verify that certain provisions are still effective and keep up to date on bankruptcy law.
- Research state statutes governing property exemptions.
- Research case law to see how the courts have applied a certain provision of the Bankruptcy Code or a state law applicable to the bankruptcy proceedings.

ENVIRONMENTAL LAW

We now turn to a discussion of the various ways in which businesses are regulated by the government in the interest of protecting the environment. Remember from Chapter 2 that *environmental law* is defined as all law pertaining to environmental protection.

Environmental law is not new. Indeed, the federal government began to regulate some activities, such as those involving the pollution of navigable waterways, in the late 1800s. In the last few decades, however, the body of environmental law has expanded substantially as the government has attempted to control industrial waste and to protect dwindling natural resources and endangered species. Today, businesses face the task of complying with numerous environmental regulations. Because of the complexity of many of these regulations, businesses often need legal assistance to make sure that they meet environmental requirements imposed by law. For this reason, many attorneys and paralegals now specialize in environmental law. (This chapter's *Technology and Today's Paralegal* feature on pages 434 and 435 discusses a number of helpful online resources that paralegals can turn to for detailed information on environmental laws and compliance requirements.)

In this section, we first discuss the common law actions that can be brought against business firms and individuals for damage caused by polluting activities. We then look at some of the most significant statutes and regulations that have been created to protect the environment.

Common Law Actions

Common law remedies against environmental pollution originated centuries ago in England. Today, injured individuals continue to rely on the common law to obtain damages and injunctions against business polluters. For example, an injured party may sue a business polluter in tort under the negligence and strict liability theories discussed in Chapter 7. A developing area of tort law, and legal practice, involves **toxic torts**—actions against toxic polluters.

Businesses that engage in ultrahazardous activities—such as the transportation of radioactive materials—are strictly liable for whatever injuries the activities cause. In a strict liability action, the injured party does not need to prove that the business failed to exercise reasonable care.

toxic tort
A wrongful act (tort) that occurs when a person or business fails to properly use or clean up toxic chemicals that cause harm to a person or to society; also used to refer to an action brought against a toxic polluter.

Federal Regulation of the Environment

Congress has passed a number of statutes to control the impact of human activities on the environment. Some of these statutes were passed in an attempt to improve the quality of air and water. Some of them specifically regulate toxic chemicals, including pesticides, herbicides, and hazardous wastes.

Environmental Regulatory Agencies

Much of the body of federal law governing business activities consists of the regulations issued and enforced by administrative agencies. The most well known of the agencies regulating environmental law is, of course, the Environmental Protection Agency (EPA), which was created in 1970 to coordinate federal environmental responsibilities. Other federal agencies with authority to regulate specific environmental matters include the Department of the Interior, the Department of Defense, the Department of Labor, the Food and Drug Administration, and the Nuclear Regulatory Commission. These regulatory agencies—and all other agencies of the federal government—must take environmental factors into consideration when making significant decisions. Most federal environmental laws also provide that citizens can sue to enforce environmental regulations if government agencies fail to do so—or to limit enforcement if agencies go too far in their enforcement actions.

On the Web

For information on the standards, guidelines, and regulations of the Environmental Protection Agency, go to **http://www.epa.gov**.

Environmental Impact Statements

The National Environmental Policy Act (NEPA) of 1969 requires that for every major federal action that significantly affects the quality of the environment, an **environmental impact statement (EIS)** must be prepared. Construction by a private developer of a ski resort on federal land, for example, may require an EIS. Building or operating a nuclear power plant, which requires a federal permit, or constructing a dam as part of a federal project would require an EIS. An EIS must analyze (1) the impact on the environment that the action will have, (2) any adverse effects on the environment and alternative actions that might be taken, and (3) irreversible effects the action might generate. EISs have become instruments used by private citizens, consumer interest groups, businesses, and others to challenge federal agency actions on the basis that the actions improperly threaten the environment.

environmental impact statement (EIS)
A statement required by the National Environmental Policy Act for any major federal action that will significantly affect the quality of the environment. The statement must analyze the action's impact on the environment and explore alternative actions that might be taken.

Technology and Today's Paralegal

ENVIRONMENTAL COMPLIANCE

One of the challenges for lawyers and paralegals today is keeping abreast of environmental laws and regulations. Environmental regulations affect virtually all businesses at one point or another, and violations of these regulations can be costly. Moreover, those who violate environmental laws may face criminal penalties as well as civil sanctions. As a paralegal, you may need to know what those laws are, how to monitor them, and what requirements they impose on businesses. With today's easy access to Internet resources, paralegals can quickly find an abundance of information not only on environmental laws but also on what businesses must do to comply with these laws. Here, we look at just a few online resources that paralegals can use to obtain such information.

ENVIRONMENTAL LAWS AND REGULATIONS

A primary source for environmental laws and regulations is, of course, the U.S. Environmental Protection Agency (EPA), which coordinates and enforces many of these laws and regulations. You can go directly to a page on the EPA's Web site titled "Laws and Regulations" at **http://www.epa.gov/epahome/lawreg.htm**. This Web page contains links to a number of information sources, including the major environmental laws and regulations, new regulations and proposed rules, proposed environmental legislation in Congress, an explanation of how the EPA writes regulations, and a "plain English" guide to the Clean Air Act.

You can read the EPA's regulations and other information concerning wetlands at **http://www.epa.gov/owow/wetlands**. Another helpful Web site can be found at **http://enviro.blr.com**, which is hosted by Business & Legal Reports, Inc. Here, you can find information on environmental laws and regulatory activity, as well as the full text of federal and state environmental regulations. You can also find various tools (such as special forms and checklists) for monitoring and implementing a firm's compliance with regulatory requirements.

COMPLIANCE ASSISTANCE

There are a number of online environmental compliance resources. You can directly access the EPA's National

Air Pollution

Federal involvement with air pollution goes back to the 1950s, when Congress authorized funds for air-pollution research. In 1963, the federal government passed the Clean Air Act, which focused on multistate air pollution and provided assistance to states. Subsequent amendments to the act strengthened the government's authority to regulate air quality. These laws provide the basis for issuing regulations to control air pollution. The EPA attempts to update pollution-control standards when new scientific information becomes available.

Mobile and Stationary Sources of Pollution

The Clean Air Act covers both mobile and stationary sources of pollution. Mobile sources include automobiles and other moving sources. The Clean Air Act of 1970 and its amendments require automobile manufacturers to cut new automobiles' exhaust emissions by a

Environmental Compliance Assistance Clearinghouse by going to **http://cfpub.epa.gov/clearinghouse**. This site includes an interactive online guide to environmental compliance requirements.

The Environmental Compliance Assistance Platform, at **http://www.envcap.org**, is designed to help businesses comply with environmental regulations. This site includes links to compliance assistance for various industries and groups (for example, for the construction, health-care, and automotive recycling industries). Through this site, you can also access state regulations and other information. The Small Business Environmental home page (**http://www.smallbiz-enviroweb.org/compliance/compliance.html**) will also take you to numerous compliance resources.

ENVIRONMENTAL SOFTWARE AND VIDEOS

A growing number of firms offer special software designed to help businesses monitor and comply with environmental regulations. One software company, PrismSystems, Inc., at **http://www.prismsystems.com/environmental.htm**, offers environmental management solutions and tools. At this site, you can download a free demonstration CD illustrating the features of the software. Another software company, Environmental Software Providers (**http://www.esp-net.com**), has software products designed to manage environmental performance and risk. Commonwealth Films, Inc., provides videos to help companies train their employees in environmental compliance. You can access Commonwealth's Web site at **http://www.commonwealth.com**.

TECHNOLOGY TIP

Creating a list of URLs for helpful Web resources is a must for most paralegals. To minimize the time you spend finding specific Web sites in your list, make sure that the list is well organized. For example, including subject headings in your list and sorting the headings alphabetically will help you locate Web sites more easily. Also, when you are searching for government resources and do not have a URL at hand, remember that **http://firstgov.gov** is a gateway to *all* federal agencies and institutions.

certain percentage by a given date. For example, the 1990 amendments to the Clean Air Act required manufacturers to reduce new automobiles' exhaust emissions of nitrogen oxide by 60 percent and of other pollutants by 35 percent by 1998. Regulations that took effect beginning with 2004 model cars called for nitrogen oxide tailpipe emissions to be cut by nearly 10 percent by 2007. For the first time, sport utility vehicles and light trucks were required to meet the same standards as automobiles.

Stationary sources include manufacturing plants, electric utilities, and other nonmoving sources of pollution. The Clean Air Act authorizes the EPA to establish air-quality standards for these sources. The EPA sets the maximum levels of certain pollutants that may be emitted by stationary sources, and the states formulate plans to achieve those standards. Different standards apply to sources of pollution in clean areas and sources in polluted areas. Different standards also apply to existing sources of pollution and major new sources. Performance standards for major sources require the use of "maximum achievable control technology" to reduce emissions from the combustion of fossil fuels (coal and oil). The EPA issues guidelines as to what equipment meets this requirement.

On the Web

The Virtual Law Library of the Indiana University School of Law provides numerous links to online environmental law resources. Go to **http://www.law.indiana.edu**.

Penalties for Violating the Clean Air Act

The EPA can assess civil penalties of up to $25,000 per day for violations of emission limits under the Clean Air Act. Additional fines of up to $5,000 per day can be assessed for other violations, such as failing to maintain required records. To penalize those for whom it is more cost-effective to violate the act than to comply with it, the EPA is authorized to obtain a penalty equal to the violator's economic benefits from noncompliance. Persons who provide information about violators may be paid up to $10,000. Private citizens can also sue violators. Those who knowingly violate the act may be subject to criminal penalties, including fines of up to $1 million and imprisonment for up to two years (for false statements or failures to report violations). Corporate officers are among those who may be subject to these penalties.

Water Pollution

Federal regulations governing water pollution can be traced back to the Rivers and Harbors Appropriation Act of 1899. These regulations prohibited ships and manufacturers from discharging or depositing refuse in navigable waterways.

Navigable Waters

Navigable waters include coastal waters, freshwater wetlands, and lakes and streams used by interstate travelers and industry. In 1948, Congress passed the Federal Water Pollution Control Act (FWPCA), but its regulatory system and enforcement proved inadequate. In 1972, amendments to the FWPCA—known as the Clean Water Act—were enacted to (1) make waters safe for swimming, (2) protect fish and wildlife, and (3) eliminate the discharge of pollutants into the water. The amendments required that municipal and industrial polluters apply for permits before discharging wastes into navigable waters.

They also set forth specific time schedules, which were extended by amendment in 1977 and by the Water Quality Act of 1987. Under these schedules, the EPA establishes limits for discharges of different types of pollutants based on the technology available for controlling them. Regulations, for the most part, specify that the "best available control technology" be installed. The EPA issues guidelines as to what equipment meets this standard, which essentially requires the most effective pollution-control equipment available.

Under the Clean Water Act, violators are subject to a variety of civil and criminal penalties. Civil penalties for each violation range from a maximum of $10,000 per day, and not more than $25,000 per violation, to as much as $25,000 per day. Criminal penalties range from a fine of $2,500 per day and imprisonment for up to one year to a fine of $1 million and fifteen years' imprisonment. Injunctive relief and damages can also be imposed. The polluting party can be required to clean up the pollution or pay for the cost of doing so. Criminal penalties apply only if a violation was intentional.

Drinking Water

Another statute governing water pollution is the Safe Drinking Water Act of 1974, which requires the EPA to set maximum levels for pollutants in public water systems. Operators of public water supply systems must come as close as possible to meeting the EPA's standards by using the best available technology that is economically feasible. The EPA is particularly concerned about contamination from underground sources. Pesticides and wastes leaked from landfills or disposed of in underground injection wells are among the more than two hundred pollutants known to exist in groundwater used for drinking in at least thirty-four

Deanna (Sami) L. Falzone

PARALEGAL **profile**

LITIGATION PARALEGAL

Deanna (Sami) L. Falzone has worked as a paralegal in a number of areas, including insurance defense work, personal-injury litigation, and workers' compensation claims. Since joining the law firm of Holland & Hart, LLP, in 1991, Falzone has specialized in general, commercial, and bankruptcy litigation; labor law; business transactions; natural resources; and environmental litigation. Since 1995, she has been the corporate and natural resource paralegal for the firm's Cheyenne office.

Falzone has been involved in the research, writing, and editing of several publications. Since 1996, she has assisted in the research and writing of Wyoming's Oil and Natural Gas Update, *published annually in the American Bar Association's* Natural Resources, Energy and Environmental Law Year in Review. *She is an instructor at Laramie County Community College and a member of the advisory board for its legal assistant program, as well as a member of Legal Assistants of Wyoming.*

What do you like best about your work?

"My favorite part of my work in the environmental law field is the variety of my assignments—preparing pleadings, briefs, graphics, and exhibits; assisting with witness preparation; going through relevant files at state agencies; and researching new legislation (and actually taking part in the formation of new legislation by attending legislative committee meetings and working with clients to prepare comments and proposed legislative language). I never have a "typical" day! I also love the "digging" part—trying to find the one missing piece of information needed to support our case. I like organizing documents so they can be readily used. Working with our clients is another great perk."

What is the greatest challenge that you face in your area of work?

"The topics in environmental law are ever changing, and instantly becoming knowledgeable about the newest hot topic can be challeng-

ing. As an example, coal bed methane (CBM) production has been around for many years but was not taken seriously until about six years ago, when *energy crisis* became a household term. Suddenly, CBM wells were sprouting up throughout our state. With this new energy source came many problems: access issues involving federal and state lands, water quality and storage of water used to bring the methane to the surface, and many other environmental issues. Educating yourself while agency personnel are trying to develop new agency rules and regulations is a terrific asset to your clients."

What advice do you have for would-be paralegals in your area of work?

"Develop great writing and comprehension skills, computer skills, and people skills, and be detail oriented. Working in the environmental law field will necessitate spending a great deal of time in agency offices wading through records, so developing good relationships with agency personnel is a must. They can be your greatest resource. You will also spend considerable time in your clients' offices, so develop superb organizational skills and work ethics. Remember that you are a mirror of your law firm, and client satisfaction is the key to success. Any project you work on is a team effort that includes not only the attorney but the paralegal and staff as well. I am very fortunate to work with a firm that strongly believes in teamwork—no one team member is more important than another."

What are some tips for success as a paralegal in your area of work?

"Success hinges on a willingness to undertake any task, work independently with little direction, complete tasks accurately the first time, think ahead, use common sense, and build strong client relationships. Another key to success is building strong relationships with contacts in the various state and federal agencies with which you work. Cultivate these allies! If possible, intern with a law firm with a strong practice in natural resource and environmental law. Look at the issue before you from both sides. Take ownership of your assignments, and love what you do!"

> *"The topics in environmental law are ever changing, and instantly becoming knowledgeable about the newest hot topic can be challenging."*

states. The act was amended in 1996 to give the EPA more flexibility in setting regulatory standards governing drinking water.

Ocean Dumping

The Marine Protection, Research, and Sanctuaries Act of 1972 (known popularly as the Ocean Dumping Act), as amended in 1983, prohibits entirely the ocean dumping of certain materials, including chemical and high-level radioactive waste. The act establishes a permit program for transporting and dumping other materials. There are specific exemptions, including pollutants subject to the permit provisions of other environmental legislation.

Each violation of any provision or permit may result in a civil penalty of not more than $50,000 or revocation or suspension of the permit. A knowing violation is a criminal offense that may result in a $50,000 fine, imprisonment for not more than a year, or both. An injunction may also be imposed.

Oil Pollution

In 1989, the supertanker *Exxon Valdez* caused the worst oil spill in North American history in the waters of Alaska's Prince William Sound. A quarter of a million barrels of crude oil—more than ten million gallons—leaked out of the ship's broken hull. In response to the *Exxon Valdez* oil-spill disaster, Congress passed the Oil Pollution Act of 1990. Any onshore or offshore oil facility, oil shipper, vessel owner, or vessel operator that discharges oil into navigable waters or onto an adjoining shore may be liable for clean-up costs, as well as damages. The act created a $1 billion oil clean-up and economic compensation fund and decreed that by 2011, oil tankers using U.S. ports must be double hulled to limit the severity of accidental spills.

Under the act, damage to natural resources, private property, and the local economy, including the increased cost of providing public services, is compensable. The act provides for civil penalties of $1,000 per barrel spilled or $25,000 for each day of the violation. The party held responsible for the clean-up costs can bring a civil suit for contribution from other potentially liable parties.

Toxic Chemicals

Originally, most environmental clean-up efforts were directed toward reducing smog and making water safe for fishing and swimming. Over time, however, control of toxic chemicals became an important part of environmental law.

Pesticides and Herbicides

The first toxic chemical problem to receive widespread public attention was that posed by pesticides and herbicides. Using these chemicals to kill insects and weeds has increased agricultural productivity, but their residue remains in the environment. In rare instances, accumulations of this residue have killed animals, and scientists have identified potential long-term effects that are detrimental to humans. Under the Federal Insecticide, Fungicide, and Rodenticide Act of 1947, pesticides and herbicides must be registered before they can be sold, used only for approved applications, and used in limited quantities when applied to food crops. If a substance is identified as harmful, the EPA can cancel its registration.

Under 1996 amendments to the act, for a pesticide to remain on the market, there must be a "reasonable certainty of no harm" to people from exposure to the pesticide. This means that there must be no more than a one-in-a-million risk to people of developing cancer from exposure in any way, including eating food that contains residues from the pesticide.

Penalties for registrants and producers for violating the act include imprisonment for up to one year and a fine of no more than $50,000. Penalties for commercial dealers include imprisonment for up to one year and a fine of no more than $25,000. Farmers and other private users of pesticides or herbicides who violate the act are subject to a $1,000 fine and imprisonment for up to thirty days.

Toxic Substances

The Toxic Substances Control Act of 1976 regulates chemicals and chemical compounds that are known to be toxic (such as asbestos and polychlorinated biphenyls, popularly known as PCBs) and authorizes investigation of any possible harmful effects from new chemical compounds. The regulations permit the EPA to require that manufacturers, processors, and other organizations determine the effects of chemicals on human health and the environment before using them. The EPA may require special labeling, limit the use of a substance, set production quotas, or prohibit the use of a substance altogether.

Hazardous Wastes

Some industrial, agricultural, and household wastes pose more serious threats than others. If not properly disposed of, these toxic chemicals may present a substantial danger to human health and the environment. If released into the environment, they may contaminate public drinking water resources.

Resource Conservation and Recovery Act. In 1976, Congress passed the Resource Conservation and Recovery Act (RCRA) in reaction to ever-increasing concern about the effects of hazardous waste materials on the environment. The RCRA required the EPA to establish regulations to monitor and control hazardous waste disposal and to determine which forms of solid waste should be considered hazardous and thus subject to regulation. The act authorized the EPA to promulgate various technical requirements for some types of facilities for storage and treatment of hazardous waste. The act also requires all producers of hazardous waste materials to label and package properly any hazardous waste that is to be transported.

The RCRA was amended in 1984 and 1986 to decrease the use of land containment in the disposal of hazardous waste and to require compliance with the act by some generators of hazardous waste—such as those generating less than 1,000 kilograms (2,200 pounds) a month—that had previously been excluded from regulation under the RCRA.

Under the RCRA, a company may be assessed a civil penalty based on the seriousness of the violation, the probability of harm, and the extent to which the violation deviates from RCRA requirements. The assessment may be up to $25,000 for each violation. Criminal penalties include fines up to $50,000 for each day of violation, imprisonment for up to two years (in most instances), or both. Criminal fines and the time of imprisonment can be doubled for certain repeat offenders.

Superfund. In 1980, Congress passed the Comprehensive Environmental Response, Compensation, and Liability Act (CERCLA), commonly known as Superfund. The basic purpose of Superfund, which was amended in 1986, is to regulate the clean-up of disposal sites in which hazardous waste is leaking into the environment. A special federal fund was created for this purpose.

Superfund provides that when a release or a threatened release of hazardous chemicals from a site occurs, the following persons are responsible for cleaning up the site: (1) the

Developing Paralegal Skills

MONITORING THE *FEDERAL REGISTER*

Robin Hayes is a legal assistant for CARCO, Inc., a large company that manufactures automobile parts. She works in the environmental law practice group within the corporation's legal department. One of her responsibilities is to monitor the *Federal Register* on a daily basis for newly proposed environmental regulations and for changes to existing rules. Today, Robin notices a change to the hazardous waste manifest, a form that CARCO is required to use when shipping hazardous waste to a disposal facility. The change requires the company to certify its efforts in reducing the amount of hazardous waste that it generates. Robin prepares a memo to the attorneys in the group, because they will need to inform management of the change.

CHECKLIST FOR MONITORING THE *FEDERAL REGISTER*

* Review the *Federal Register* every day without fail.
* Next, review the topics and subtopics to determine if notices, rules, or proposed rules have been issued on topics affecting your client.
* Skim through any notices, rules, and proposed rules that may apply to your client.
* Read in detail the relevant notices, rules, and proposed rules that may apply to your client.
* Print out relevant notices, rules, and proposed rules for circulation to the attorneys and others who should be advised of this information.
* Notify the attorneys and others of upcoming deadlines for comments on proposed rules and changes.

---

potentially responsible party (PRP)

A party who may be liable under the Comprehensive Environmental Response, Compensation, and Liability Act, or Superfund. Any person who generated hazardous waste, transported hazardous waste, owned or operated a waste site at the time of disposal, or currently owns or operates a site may be responsible for some or all of the clean-up costs involved in removing the hazardous chemicals.

person who generated the wastes disposed of at the site, (2) the person who transported the wastes to the site, (3) the person who owned or operated the site at the time of the disposal, and (4) the current owner or operator. A person falling within one of these categories is referred to as a **potentially responsible party (PRP)**. If the PRPs do not clean up the site, Superfund authorizes the EPA to clean up the site and recover clean-up costs from the PRPs.

Superfund imposes strict liability on PRPs. Also, liability under Superfund is usually joint and several—that is, a PRP who generated only a fraction of the hazardous waste disposed of at the site may nevertheless be liable for all of the clean-up costs. CERCLA authorizes a party who has incurred clean-up costs to bring a "contribution action" against any other person who is liable or potentially liable for a percentage of the costs.

State and Local Regulation

Many states regulate the degree to which the environment may be polluted. Thus, for example, even when state zoning laws permit a business's proposed development, the proposal may have to be altered to change the development's impact on the environment. State laws may restrict a business's discharge of chemicals into the air or water or regulate its disposal of toxic wastes. States may also regulate the disposal or recycling of other wastes, including glass, metal, and plastic containers and paper. Additionally, states may restrict emissions from motor vehicles.

Today's Professional Paralegal

GATHERING INFORMATION FOR A BANKRUPTCY PETITION

Jeff Jones, a paralegal, works for Colin Peters, an attorney who specializes in bankruptcy cases. Today, Jeff is meeting with Mike Hammersmith, a client who wants to file a voluntary petition for bankruptcy under Chapter 7 of the Bankruptcy Code. Mike owns the Corner Liquor Store, a retail liquor and convenience store, and is facing serious financial difficulties. Mike owns the store as a sole proprietor.

The receptionist announces Mike's arrival, and Jeff meets him in the lobby. They walk to the conference room, which Jeff previously reserved, and sit down at the conference table. Jeff removes a checklist from a file folder that he brought with him into the conference room. The same checklist was given to Mike last week, at the end of the initial client interview. Jeff attended that interview with his supervising attorney, so he is already familiar with Mike's case.

REVIEWING THE LIST OF CREDITORS

"First, I'll need a list of your creditors, with their addresses and the amount that you owe to each," says Jeff. Mike hands Jeff a handwritten list, which is somewhat difficult to read. Jeff reviews the list and asks Mike if he owes $5,000 or $8,000 to the National Bank. "It's hard to tell which it is," says Jeff. Mike clarifies that the amount of the debt is $5,000.

REVIEWING THE LIST OF ASSETS

The next item that Jeff needs is a list of all of the assets—both personal and real property—that Mike owns. Mike hands Jeff another handwritten list, and the first thing Jeff notices is that the list is incomplete: it does not include Mike's home or his car. Jeff asks, "Didn't you tell Mr. Peters and me last week that you owned a home and a car?" "That's correct," answers Mike. "But I thought that property would be exempt." "We need to list those items here," Jeff says. "We have to disclose all of your property, including exempt property." Mike then gives Jeff the necessary information about the home and the car, and Jeff adds the information to the list.

REVIEWING THE LIST OF INCOME AND EXPENSES

"The last item that I need is the list of your income and expenses," states Jeff. Mike hands his list to Jeff. Jeff reviews it and does not find anything that is inconsistent with what Mike said in the initial client interview.

CONCLUDING THE INTERVIEW

"That's all I need for today. I'll give this information to Mr. Peters. After he reviews it, he'll want to discuss with you how the 2005 Bankruptcy Reform Act's provisions may affect your case. Depending on your income level, you may not be able to file under Chapter 7 of the Bankruptcy Code. Can you come by tomorrow—say, at two o'clock?" Jeff asks. "Yes, I think so," Mike responds.

"Thanks for your help," says Mike, as he shakes Jeff's hand. "Come with me and I'll show you out," says Jeff.

City, county, and other local governments control some aspects of the environment. For instance, local zoning laws control some land use. These laws may be designed to inhibit or direct the growth of cities and suburbs or to protect the natural environment. Numerous other environmental concerns, including methods of waste and garbage removal, are typically subject to local regulation.

ENVIRONMENTAL LAW AND THE PARALEGAL

Paralegals who specialize in environmental law find employment in a number of settings. A paralegal specialist in this area may work for a federal or state environmental agency, a local government agency concerned with natural resources, a law firm's environmental department, or a corporate legal department.

If you work for a government environmental agency, you may be involved in the research and writing necessary to create new rules or revise existing ones. You may be asked to assist in monitoring compliance with a particular regulation. You may draft documents relating to legal actions brought against violators. In a corporate environment, you may be asked to help draft the firm's environmental policies and procedures or to obtain and fill out forms the firm is required to submit to an environmental agency.

Some paralegals working in the area of environmental law may be involved in extensive litigation concerning environmental claims. For example, a government agency may bring an action against a business that has failed to comply with a particular law or regulation. One company may sue another company that refuses to contribute to the cost of cleaning up a hazardous site to which it furnished materials. An individual or group of individuals may sue a company for health injuries suffered because of the company's polluting activities. Often, such litigation involves massive amounts of paperwork and exhibits, and case management becomes a challenge. A paralegal who can meet this challenge will be a valuable asset to his or her employer.

Here are some of the many types of tasks that you might perform as a paralegal working in the area of environmental law:

- Draft and file permits with federal, state, or local environmental agencies to use property in certain ways (such as clearing trees or filling wetlands).

- Draft and file the documents necessary to include another polluting company as a defendant in an action brought by a government agency.

- Monitor the *Federal Register* on a routine basis to determine if new environmental regulations have been proposed by the EPA.

- Research the scope and applicability of a particular regulation to find out whether a client's planned action may violate that rule, whether a permit is required, and so on.

- Prepare for and perhaps attend hearings before environmental agencies.

- Assist in negotiations between an environmental agency and a business firm or group of firms to settle a dispute over a claimed violation of an environmental law or regulation.

- Coordinate a corporate employer's environmental programs and policies and monitor corporate activities to ensure proper compliance with environmental laws.

KEY TERMS AND CONCEPTS

automatic stay 415	estate in property 416	proof of claim 417
bankruptcy trustee 418	homestead exemption 418	reaffirmation agreement 425
consumer-debtor 412	liquidation 412	secured creditor 413
cram-down provision 428	order for relief 415	toxic tort 433
debtor in possession (DIP) 427	petition in bankruptcy 412	U.S. trustee 414
discharge 412	potentially responsible party (PRP) 440	workout 427
environmental impact statement (EIS) 433	preference 419	

chapter summary   Bankruptcy and Environmental Law

Forms of Bankruptcy Relief Compared

	Chapter 7	Chapter 11	Chapter 13
Purpose	Liquidation.	Reorganization.	Adjustment of debts.
Who Can Petition	Debtor (voluntary) or creditors (involuntary).	Debtor (voluntary) or creditors (involuntary).	Debtor (voluntary) only.
Who Can Be a Debtor	Any "person" (including partnerships and corporations) except railroads, insurance companies, banks, savings and loan institutions, investment companies licensed by the Small Business Administration, and credit unions. Farmers and charitable institutions cannot be involuntarily petitioned. If the court finds the petition to be a substantial abuse of the use of Chapter 7, the debtor may be required to convert to a Chapter 13 repayment plan.	Any debtor (except a stockbroker or a commodities broker) eligible for Chapter 7 relief; railroads are also eligible.	Any individual (not partnerships or corporations) with regular income who owes fixed unsecured debts of less than $307,675 or fixed secured debts of less than $922,975.
Procedure Leading to Discharge	Nonexempt property is sold with proceeds to be distributed (in order) to priority groups. Dischargeable debts are terminated.	Plan is submitted; if it is approved and followed, debts are discharged.	Plan is submitted (must be approved if debtor turns over disposable income for a three-year or five-year period); if it is approved and followed, debts are discharged.
Advantages	On liquidation and distribution, most debts are discharged, and the debtor has the opportunity for a fresh start.	Debtor continues in business. Creditors can accept the plan, or it can be "crammed down" on them. Plan allows for reorganization and liquidation of debts over the plan period.	Debtor continues in business or possession of assets. If plan is approved, most debts are discharged after the plan period.

Environmental Law

    1. *Common law actions*—Parties can recover damages for injuries sustained as a result of a firm's pollution-causing activities under the theories of negligence and strict

(Continued)

liability. Businesses engaging in ultrahazardous activities are liable for whatever injuries the activities cause, regardless of whether they exercise reasonable care.

2. *Federal regulation of the environment*—

   a. The federal Environmental Protection Agency (EPA) was created in 1970 to coordinate federal environmental programs. The EPA administers most federal environmental policies and statutes.

   b. The National Environmental Policy Act of 1969 imposes environmental responsibilities on all federal agencies and requires the preparation of an environmental impact statement (EIS) for every major federal action. An EIS must analyze the action's impact on the environment, its adverse effects and possible alternatives, and its irreversible effects on environmental quality.

3. *Important areas regulated by federal law*—

   a. Air pollution—Regulated under the authority of the Clean Air Act of 1963 and its amendments, particularly those of 1970 and 1990.

   b. Water pollution—Regulated under the authority of the Rivers and Harbors Appropriation Act of 1899, as amended, and the Federal Water Pollution Control Act of 1948, as amended by the Clean Water Act of 1972.

   c. Toxic chemicals and hazardous waste—Pesticides and herbicides, toxic substances, and hazardous waste are regulated under the authority of the Federal Insecticide, Fungicide, and Rodenticide Act of 1947, the Toxic Substances Control Act of 1976, and the Resource Conservation and Recovery Act of 1976, respectively. The Comprehensive Environmental Response, Compensation, and Liability Act (CERCLA) of 1980, as amended, regulates the clean-up of hazardous waste sites.

4. *State and local regulation*—Activities affecting the environment are controlled at the local and state levels through regulations relating to land use, the disposal and recycling of garbage and waste, and pollution-causing activities in general.

 QUESTIONS FOR REVIEW

1. What are the two major goals of bankruptcy law? What law governs bankruptcy matters, and in which courts are bankruptcy cases filed?

2. What types of relief are available under the Bankruptcy Code?

3. How is a liquidation proceeding under Chapter 7 initiated? What is the difference between a voluntary bankruptcy and an involuntary bankruptcy? What is "means testing"?

4. What effect does the filing of a bankruptcy petition have on creditors? What is an automatic stay?

5. How does Chapter 7 bankruptcy differ from Chapter 13 bankruptcy? What happens if a company files for reorganization under Chapter 11?

6. How is the debtor's estate distributed in a Chapter 7 liqui-

dation? What is the difference between a secured creditor and an unsecured creditor? Is this difference significant in bankruptcy proceedings?

7. What is a discharge in bankruptcy? What is the difference between an "exception to discharge" and an "objection to discharge"?

8. What are the major federal statutes that protect the environment? What federal agency is charged with administering federal environmental laws? Do states also pass laws and issue regulations protecting the environment?

9. What is an environmental impact statement (EIS), and when is one required? What factors does an EIS evaluate?

10. What is Superfund? What parties are responsible for the clean-up of hazardous waste sites?

ETHICAL QUESTIONS

1. Marla, an independent paralegal, provides a variety of services for the public. Among other things, she provides debtors with bankruptcy forms and types of bankruptcy petitions. Mr. Ford has sought Marla's services in filing for bankruptcy. He takes home a set of Chapter 7 forms, reads through them, and begins to provide the information needed. He is not certain that he qualifies for Chapter 7 liquidation. He calls Marla and asks her if he has any other options. How should Marla answer Mr. Ford's questions?

2. Tom, a paralegal, meets Mr. Simpson, a client of the law firm for which Tom works, in the elevator. Tom knows that Mr. Simpson has an appointment to see Tom's supervising attorney regarding a bankruptcy petition. There is only one other man on the elevator, whom Tom does not recognize. Tom begins to ask Mr. Simpson about his appointment. Mr. Simpson reveals that he intends to file for bankruptcy.

The other passenger on the elevator happens to work for the bank where the client does most of his business. He returns to the bank and informs his supervisor of Mr. Simpson's intention to file for bankruptcy. Have any ethical rules been breached? If so, which one(s)?

3. The state Department of Environmental Quality is holding a hearing. FastCar, an automobile manufacturing company, has been accused of violating the air-emissions standards in the state. An administrative law judge (ALJ) is presiding over the hearing. The ALJ makes several comments about lawless corporate polluters and refers to the state's environmental laws as "polluter pay acts." Julie Marks, a paralegal, is attending the hearing with Jeffrey Nelson, a FastCar attorney. How should they respond to the ALJ's remarks?

PRACTICE QUESTIONS AND ASSIGNMENTS

1. Douglas Worth earns a salary of $30,000 a year as a sales representative. In addition to his salary, he is entitled to a 10 percent commission on what he sells. Over the past five years, Douglas earned annual commissions of $80,000 to $100,000. Because the economy was booming and Douglas was making such large commissions, he purchased a $50,000 Cadillac and a $25,000 boat and incurred credit-card debts totaling $35,000. This year, the economy has slowed down, and Douglas has made only $10,000 in commissions in the last six months. He still owes $40,000 on the Cadillac and $20,000 on the boat. In all, he owes $95,000 to creditors. Douglas cannot pay his debts as they become due, and it does not appear that his financial situation will improve over the next two years. As a result, he is thinking about filing for bankruptcy. If the median income in Douglas's state is $35,000 a year, would he be able to obtain a Chapter 7 liquidation under the 2005 Bankruptcy Reform Act? Explain your answer.

2. John and Mary Bogen have filed for voluntary bankruptcy under Chapter 7. They own a car, which was financed by the First American Bank and in which the bank took a security interest. They still owe about $10,000 to the bank. They will owe attorneys' fees, trustee fees, and court costs for the bankruptcy action. John owes alimony and child support to his former wife and children. John and Mary also owe income taxes and penalties from 1995. List the priority in which the creditors will be paid.

3. Jon Goulet attended the University of Wisconsin in Eau Claire and Regis University in Denver, Colorado, from which he earned a bachelor's degree in history in 1972. Over the next ten years, he worked as a bartender and restaurant manager. In 1984, he became a life insurance agent, and his income ranged from $20,000 to $30,000. In 1989, however, his agent's license was revoked for insurance fraud, and he was arrested for cocaine possession. From 1991 to 1995, Goulet was again at the University of Wisconsin, working toward, but failing to obtain, a master's degree in psychology. To pay for his studies, he took out student loans totaling $76,000. Goulet then returned to bartending and restaurant management and tried real estate sales. His income for the year 2000 was $1,490, and his expenses, excluding a child-support obligation, were $5,904. When the student loans came due, Goulet filed a petition for bankruptcy. On what ground might the loans be dischargeable? Should the court grant a discharge on this ground? Why or why not?

4. Runyan voluntarily petitions for bankruptcy. He has three major claims against his estate. One is by Calvin, a friend who holds Runyan's negotiable promissory note for $2,500; one is by Kohak, an employee who is owed three months' back wages of $4,500; and one is by the First Bank of Sunny Acres on an unsecured loan of $5,000. In addition, Martinez, an accountant retained by the trustee, is owed $500, and property taxes of $1,000 are owed to Micanopa County. Runyan's nonexempt property has

been liquidated, with the proceeds totaling $5,000. Discuss fully what amount each party will receive, and why.

5. Greers Ferry Lake is in Arkansas, and its shoreline is under the management of the U.S. Army Corps of Engineers, which is part of the U.S. Department of Defense (DOD). The Corps's 2000 Shoreline Management Plan (the Plan) rezoned numerous areas along the lake and authorized the Corps to issue permits for the construction of new boat docks in the rezoned areas. The Plan also increased by 300 percent the area around habitable structures that could be cleared of vegetation and instituted a Wildlife Enhancement Permit to allow limited modifications of the shoreline. The Corps issued a Finding of No Significant Impact, which declared that no environmental impact statement (EIS) was necessary. The Corps issued thirty-two boat dock construction permits under the SMP before Save Greers Ferry Lake, Inc., filed a suit in a federal district court against the DOD, asking the court to, among other things, stop the Corps from acting under the SMP and order it to prepare an EIS. What are the requirements for an EIS? Is an EIS needed in this case? Explain.

6. Identify the environmental law that applies to each of the following situations and explain how it would resolve the problem:

a. The foreman at a manufacturing plant disposes of a fifty-five-gallon drum of spent solvents, a toxic waste, every week by pouring it on the ground "out back."

b. An investigation reveals that the local gas utility company has PCBs in its pipeline in excess of those allowed.

c. An oil company releases hundreds of gallons of oil into a local river, contaminating the river, which is a major source of drinking water for the area.

d. A manufacturing plant that produces metallic paint for use on motor vehicles releases more pollutants into the air than the allowable emissions limits for its vicinity.

e. In the 1950s, five large manufacturing companies disposed of hazardous waste by burying the waste on the property of a farmer forty miles away from the city and its inhabitants. The rural farm is now part of a suburb. The suburb's groundwater and drinking water are found to be contaminated by the waste buried on the site of the former farm. The citizens demand that the site be cleaned up.

 ## QUESTIONS FOR CRITICAL ANALYSIS

1. Do your think that people should be able to avoid paying their debts by filing for bankruptcy? Does a person have a moral responsibility to pay his or her debts, even if it takes years and years to pay them off entirely?

2. Why is certain property exempt from the debtor's estate in property? Are these exemptions unduly harsh to creditors? What would result if such exemptions were not allowed?

3. Do you think that our bankruptcy laws are too lenient or too harsh for debtors? Do bankruptcy laws adequately balance the needs of debtors "who have gotten in over their heads" and creditors?

4. In setting standards governing air quality, traditionally the Environmental Protection Agency (EPA) has not been required to take costs into account. Rather, the emphasis is on the benefits. For example, when the EPA issued new rules on particulate matter and ozone, the head of the EPA claimed that the new standards would save 15,000 lives a year. Given that the EPA values a human life at $5 million, the agency calculated that the lives saved and medical expenses avoided by the strict standards would amount to $100 billion a year in benefits. Nothing was said about the costs of implementing these rules, though. Do you think that the costs of EPA regulations should be weighed against their prospective benefits?

5. It has been estimated that for every dollar spent cleaning up hazardous waste sites, administrative agencies spend seven dollars in overhead. Can you think of any way to trim the administrative costs associated with the clean-up of contaminated sites?

6. The Clean Air Act, the Clean Water Act, and the Toxic Substances and Control Act, among others, regulate the amount of pollution allowed into the air, water, and other aspects of the environment. Should any pollution be allowed into the environment? Who should determine how "clean" air or water should be? What might happen if no pollution at all were allowed?

7. In addition to imposing joint liability, Superfund also imposes strict liability—that is, liability without regard to fault—on generators and transporters of hazardous waste and on those who own and operate the site at the time of the disposal and at the time of the clean-up. Is it fair to hold companies liable if they did not know that the waste they were disposing of was harmful? Is it fair to hold a subsequent purchaser of contaminated property liable if the purchaser did not know that the property was polluted when he or she purchased it? Who ultimately pays for the clean-up costs?

PROJECTS

1. If there is a federal bankruptcy court located near you, attend a bankruptcy proceeding for a day or part of a day. Write a one-page summary of your experience.

2. Review your state's bankruptcy laws to determine what property is exempt from the debtor's estate in property. Does your state prohibit debtors from using the federal exemptions within the state, or is a debtor allowed to choose between state and federal exemptions? Write a one-page summary of your findings.

3. Using a telephone book or a state directory (or an online directory of state agencies), determine whether your state has any agencies that regulate environmental issues such as air and water quality. Call each agency and ask if nonlawyers are allowed to practice before it. Record your results, and report them to the class. Discuss with others in the class what agency each would prefer to work for, and why.

4. Contact one of the agencies identified in your answer to Project 3. Arrange to visit the agency to observe what kind of work paralegals perform at that agency. Discuss this project with your instructor before you undertake it to learn if any limitations apply.

 USING INTERNET RESOURCES

1. The Legal Information Institute (LII) at Cornell University's Web site contains resource material on bankruptcy. Go to **http://www.law.cornell.edu/wex/index.php/Bankruptcy**, read the overview, and then answer the following questions:

   a. What title of the United States Code governs bankruptcy law? Who are trustees? Who promulgates bankruptcy rules?

   b. Describe the two basic types of bankruptcy proceedings. Can creditors initiate a bankruptcy proceeding? Can creditors make an effort to collect debts outside of the bankruptcy proceedings?

2. Go to **http://www.abiworld.org**, the Web site of the American Bankruptcy Institute. Place your mouse over the heading "Online Resources" at the top of the page and select "Bankruptcy Statistics" from the drop-down menu. Browse through the bankruptcy statistics and charts included on this page, and then answer the following questions:

   a. According to this page, which state had the most personal (nonbusiness) bankruptcy filings during the most recent year mentioned? Which state had the fewest?

   b. How many bankruptcy filings occurred in the most recent quarter? Are most of these filings business filings or nonbusiness filings?

   c. Click on the link titled "Bankruptcy Today Program." What is this program?

   d. What information is available from this site that might be useful to you as a paralegal working in the area of bankruptcy law?

3. It can be a difficult task for paralegals to keep up with the many environmental regulations and make sure that a client's company does not violate these regulations. For an interesting article by Stephen Forbes on environmental compliance and management benefits, go to **http://www.trst.com/IsoArticleSF.htm**. Read through the article and then answer these questions.

   a. Generally, what types of businesses are subject to environmental regulations? List some of the companies mentioned by the author.

   b. According to the author, are environmental regulatory agencies generally cooperative? Is the initiation of a substantial enforcement action by an agency a common or an uncommon course of action?

   c. What is a common reason for a regulatory agency to inspect a low-profile company? How do environmental agencies learn about violations?

4.  For additional resources, visit our Web site at **http://www.paralegal.delmar.cengage.com**.

END NOTES

1. The full title of the act is the Bankruptcy Abuse Prevention and Consumer Protection Act of 2005, Pub. L. No. 109-8, 119 Stat. 23 (April 20, 2005). The bulk of the act became effective in October 2005. (Bankruptcy petitions that were filed before the act became effective continued to be administered and governed by the 1978 Bankruptcy Reform Act, as amended.)

2. There are no Chapters 2, 4, 6, 8, or 10 in Title 11. Such "gaps" are not uncommon in the U.S.C. This is because chapter numbers (or other subdivisional unit numbers) are sometimes reserved for future use when a statute is enacted. (A gap may also appear if a law has been repealed.)

3. Section 707 of the Bankruptcy Reform Act of 2005 describes the means test and provides a detailed listing of the expenses allowed under the act.

4. This amount ($6,000) is the equivalent of $100 per month for five years, indicating that the debtor could pay at least $100 per month under a Chapter 13 five-year repayment plan.

5. Note that the court may not dismiss a case due to a prior conviction if the debtor's bankruptcy is necessary to satisfy a claim for a domestic-support obligation.

6. The definition of *farmer* includes persons who receive more than 50 percent of their gross income from farming operations, such as tilling the soil, dairy farming, ranching, or the production or raising of crops, poultry, or livestock. Corporations and partnerships may qualify under certain conditions.

7. This ninety-day rule applies in Chapter 12 and Chapter 13 bankruptcies as well.

8. The dollar amounts stated in the Bankruptcy Code are adjusted automatically every three years on April 1 based on changes in the Consumer Price Index. The adjusted amounts are rounded to the nearest $25. The amounts stated in this chapter are in accordance with those computed on April 1, 2004.

9. State exemptions may or may not be limited with regard to value. Under state exemption laws, a debtor may enjoy an unlimited value exemption on a motor vehicle, for example, even though the federal bankruptcy scheme exempts a vehicle only up to a value of $2,950. A state law may also define the property coming within an exemption differently than the federal law or may exclude, or except, specific items from an exemption, making it unavailable to a debtor who fits within the exception.

LEGAL PROCEDURES AND PARALEGAL SKILLS

PART

3

CIVIL LITIGATION— BEFORE THE TRIAL

CHAPTER

CHAPTER OUTLINE

AFTER COMPLETING THIS CHAPTER, YOU WILL KNOW:

▶ The basic steps involved in the civil litigation process and the types of tasks that may be required of paralegals during each step of the pretrial phase.

▶ What a litigation file is, what it contains, and how it is organized, maintained, and reviewed.

▶ How a lawsuit is initiated and what documents are filed during the pleadings stage of the civil litigation process.

▶ What a motion is and how certain pretrial motions, if granted by the court, will end the litigation before the trial begins.

▶ What discovery is and what kinds of information attorneys and their paralegals obtain from parties to the lawsuit and from witnesses when preparing for trial.

INTRODUCTION

The paralegal plays a particularly important role in helping the trial attorney prepare for and conduct a civil trial. Preparation for trial involves a variety of tasks. The law relating to the client's case must be carefully researched. Evidence must be gathered and documented. The litigation file must be created and carefully organized. Procedural requirements and deadlines for filing certain documents with the court must be met. Witnesses—persons asked to testify at trial—must be prepared in advance and be available to testify at the appropriate time during the trial. Any exhibits, such as charts, photographs, or videotapes, to be used at the trial must be properly prepared, mounted, scanned into the computer, or filmed. Arrangements must be made to have any necessary equipment, such as a DVD or CD-ROM player and projector, available for use at the trial. The paralegal's efforts are critically important in preparing for trial, and attorneys usually rely on paralegals to ensure that nothing has been overlooked.

Attorneys may request that their paralegals assist them during the trial as well. In the courtroom, the paralegal can perform numerous tasks. For example, the paralegal can locate documents or exhibits as they are needed. The paralegal can also observe jurors' reactions to statements made by attorneys or witnesses, check to see if a witness's testimony is consistent with sworn statements made by the witness before the trial, and perhaps give witnesses some last-minute instructions outside the courtroom before they are called to testify.

The complexity of even the simplest civil trial requires that the paralegal have some familiarity with the litigation process and the applicable courtroom procedures. Much of this expertise, of course, can only be acquired through hands-on experience. Yet every paralegal should be acquainted with the basic phases of civil litigation and the forms and terminology commonly used in the process. In this chapter, you will learn about the pre-trial stages of a civil lawsuit, from the initial attorney-client meeting to the time of trial. In the next chapter, you will read about conducting investigations and interviews prior to trial.

> **witness**
> A person who is asked to testify under oath at a trial.

> **On the Web**
>
> For a summary of the step-by-step procedures followed during a civil law case in one state (Arizona), go to **http://www.supreme.state.az.us/ guide/How_Case.htm**.

CIVIL LITIGATION—A BIRD'S-EYE VIEW

Although civil trials vary greatly in terms of complexity, cost, and detail, they all share similar structural characteristics. They begin with an event that gives rise to the legal action, and (provided the case is not settled by the parties at some point during the litigation process—as most cases are) they end with the issuance of a judgment, the court's decision on the matter. In the interim, the litigation itself may involve all sorts of twists and turns. Even though each case has its own "story line," most civil lawsuits follow some version of the course charted in Exhibit 13.1 on the following page.

> **judgment**
> The court's final decision regarding the rights and claims of the parties to a lawsuit.

Pretrial Settlements

As just mentioned, in most cases, the parties reach a *settlement*—an out-of-court resolution of the dispute—before the case goes to trial. Lawsuits are costly in both time and money, and it is usually in the interest of both parties to settle the case out of court. Throughout the pre-trial stage of litigation, the attorney will therefore attempt to help the parties reach a settlement. At the same time, though, the attorney and the paralegal will operate under the assumption that the case will go to trial because if it does, all pretrial preparation must be completed prior to the trial date.

EXHIBIT 13.1
A Typical Case Flowchart

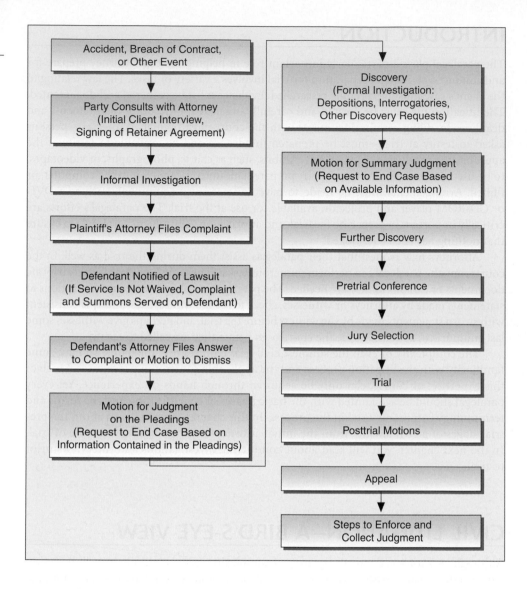

Accident, Breach of Contract, or Other Event

↓

Party Consults with Attorney
(Initial Client Interview, Signing of Retainer Agreement)

↓

Informal Investigation

↓

Plaintiff's Attorney Files Complaint

↓

Defendant Notified of Lawsuit
(If Service Is Not Waived, Complaint and Summons Served on Defendant)

↓

Defendant's Attorney Files Answer to Complaint or Motion to Dismiss

↓

Motion for Judgment on the Pleadings
(Request to End Case Based on Information Contained in the Pleadings)

Discovery
(Formal Investigation: Depositions, Interrogatories, Other Discovery Requests)

↓

Motion for Summary Judgment
(Request to End Case Based on Available Information)

↓

Further Discovery

↓

Pretrial Conference

↓

Jury Selection

↓

Trial

↓

Posttrial Motions

↓

Appeal

↓

Steps to Enforce and Collect Judgment

Federal Rules of Civil Procedure (FRCP)
The rules controlling all procedural matters in civil trials brought before the federal district courts.

On the Web

The Federal Rules of Civil Procedure are available online at the Legal Information Institute Web site at **http://www.law.cornell.edu/ rules/frcp**.

You can also access the rules governing civil procedure in most states at **http://www.law.cornell. edu/topics/state_statutes. html#civil_procedure**.

Procedural Requirements

Understanding and meeting procedural requirements is essential in the litigation process. These requirements are spelled out in the procedural rules of the court in which a lawsuit is brought. All civil trials held in federal district courts are governed by the **Federal Rules of Civil Procedure (FRCP)**.[1] These rules specify what must be done during the various stages of the federal civil litigation process. For example, FRCP 4 (Rule 4 of the FRCP) describes the procedures that must be followed in notifying the defendant of the lawsuit. Each state also has its own rules of civil procedure (which in many states are similar to the FRCP). In addition, many courts have their own local rules of procedure that supplement the federal or state rules. The attorney and the paralegal must comply with the rules of procedure that apply to the specific court in which the trial will take place.

A Hypothetical Lawsuit

To illustrate the procedures involved in litigation, we present a hypothetical civil lawsuit. The case involves an automobile accident in which a car driven by Tony Peretto collided with a car driven by Katherine Baranski. Baranski suffered numerous injuries and incurred substantial medical and hospital costs. She also lost wages for the five months that she was unable to work. Baranski has decided to sue Peretto for damages. Because Baranski is the person initiating the lawsuit, she is the plaintiff. Peretto, because he must defend against Baranski's claims, is the defendant. The plaintiff and the defendant are referred to as the *parties* to the lawsuit, as discussed in Chapter 5. (Some cases involve several plaintiffs and/or defendants.)

The attorney for the plaintiff (Baranski) is Allen P. Gilmore. Gilmore is assisted by paralegal Elena Lopez. The attorney for the defendant (Peretto) is Elizabeth A. Cameron. Cameron is assisted by paralegal Gordon McVay. Throughout this chapter and the following two chapters, *Case at a Glance* features in the page margins will remind you of the names of the players in this lawsuit.

Case at a Glance

The Plaintiff—
Plaintiff: Katherine Baranski
Attorney: Allen P. Gilmore
Paralegal: Elena Lopez

The Defendant—
Defendant: Tony Peretto
Attorney: Elizabeth A. Cameron
Paralegal: Gordon McVay

THE PRELIMINARIES

Katherine Baranski arranges to meet with Allen P. Gilmore, an attorney with the law firm of Jeffers, Gilmore & Dunn, to see if Gilmore will represent her in the lawsuit. Gilmore asks paralegal Elena Lopez to prepare the usual forms and information sheets, including a retainer agreement and a statement of the firm's billing procedures, and to bring them with her to the initial interview with Baranski. Gilmore also asks Lopez to run a conflicts check (see Chapter 3) to ensure that representing Baranski in this action will not create a conflict of interest.

The Initial Client Interview

Most often, an initial client interview is conducted by the attorney—for several reasons. First, if attorney Gilmore is interested in taking on a new client, he will want to explain to the client the value of his services and those of his firm. Second, only an attorney can agree to represent a client. Third, only an attorney can set fees, and if Gilmore decides to take Baranski on as a client, fee arrangements will be discussed, and possibly agreed on, during the initial client interview. Finally, only an attorney can give legal advice, and the initial client interview may involve advising Baranski of her legal rights and options. In short, what transpires during the initial client interview normally falls under the umbrella of "the practice of law," and, as you read in Chapter 3, only attorneys are permitted to practice law.

Because attorney Gilmore and paralegal Lopez will be working together on the case, however, Gilmore will ask Lopez to sit in on the interview. Gilmore will want Lopez to meet Baranski, become familiar with Baranski's claim, and perhaps make arrangements for follow-up interviews with Baranski should Gilmore decide to take the case.

During the initial client interview, Katherine Baranski explains to attorney Gilmore and paralegal Lopez the facts of her case as she perceives them. Baranski tells them that Tony Peretto, who was driving a Dodge van, ran a stop sign and crashed into the driver's side of her Ford Escort as she was driving through the intersection of Mattis Avenue and Thirty-eighth Street in Nita City, Nita. The accident occurred at 7:45 A.M. on August 4, 2006. Baranski has misplaced Peretto's address, but she knows that he lives in another state, the state of Zero.[2] Baranski claims that as a result of the accident, she has been unable to work for five months and has lost approximately $20,000 in wages. Her medical and hospital expenses total $95,000, and the property damage to her car is estimated to be $15,000. Throughout the initial interview, Lopez takes notes to carefully record the details of the case as relayed by Baranski.

Gilmore agrees to represent Baranski in the lawsuit against Peretto. He explains the fee structure to Baranski, and she signs the retainer agreement.[3] He also has Baranski sign forms authorizing Gilmore to obtain relevant medical, employment, and other records relating to the claim. (These forms, which are called *release forms*, will be discussed in Chapter 14.) At

Ethics Watch!

THE UNAUTHORIZED PRACTICE OF LAW

When a paralegal conducts an initial client interview, the paralegal must be constantly aware of the ethical pitfalls inherent in such situations. Suppose that attorney Gilmore is out of town but wants to obtain information about Baranski's legal matter as soon as possible. In this situation, he might ask Lopez to conduct an initial interview solely for the purposes of gaining information from Baranski about her claim. To avoid potential liability for the unauthorized practice of law, Lopez must be careful not to advise Baranski in regard to fees or her legal rights and obligations.

the end of the interview, Gilmore also asks Lopez to schedule a follow-up interview with Baranski. Lopez will conduct the follow-up interview and obtain more details from Baranski about the accident and its consequences.

Preliminary Investigation

After Baranski leaves the office, attorney Gilmore asks paralegal Lopez to undertake a preliminary investigation to glean as much information as possible concerning the factual circumstances of Baranski's accident. Sources of this information will include the police report of the accident, medical records, employment data, and eyewitness accounts of the accident.

You will read in Chapter 14 about the steps that a paralegal can take when investigating the facts of a client's case, and therefore we will not discuss investigation here. Bear in mind, though, that at this point in the pretrial process, the paralegal may engage in extensive investigation. Legal investigation is an important part of pretrial work, and facts discovered (or not discovered) by the legal investigator may play an important role in determining the outcome of the lawsuit.

Creating the Litigation File

Attorney Gilmore also asks paralegal Lopez to create a litigation file for the case. As the litigation progresses, Lopez will carefully maintain the file to make sure that such items as correspondence, bills, research and investigation results, and all documents and exhibits relating to the litigation are in the file and segregated in an organized manner.

Each law firm or legal department has its own specific organizational scheme to follow when creating and maintaining client files. Recall from Chapter 4 that there are three goals of any law office filing system: to preserve confidentiality, to safeguard legal documents, and to ensure that the contents of files can be easily and quickly retrieved when needed. Usually, it is the paralegal's responsibility to make sure that the litigation file is properly created and maintained.

As a case progresses through the litigation process, subfiles may be created for documents relating to the various stages. For example, at this point in the Baranski case, the litigation file will contain notes taken during the initial client interview, the signed retainer agreement, and information and documents gathered by paralegal Lopez during her prelim-

Litigation files can easily expand into thousands of documents. Part of the paralegal's job is to file and organize these documents in such a way that they can be quickly retrieved when needed.

(Courtesy of ©Blend Images/Alamy)

inary investigation of the claim. As the lawsuit progresses, Lopez will make sure that special subfiles are created for documents relating to the pleadings and discovery stages (to be discussed shortly). Depending on the office filing system, the file folders for these subfiles may be color coded or numbered so that each subfile can be readily recognized and retrieved. Lopez will also prepare an index for each subfile to indicate what documents are included in it. The index will be placed at the front of the folder for easy reference.

A properly created and maintained litigation file will provide a comprehensive record of the case so that others in the firm who become involved with it can quickly acquaint themselves with the progress of the proceedings. Because well-organized files are critical to the success of any case, Lopez should take special care to properly maintain the file.

THE PLEADINGS

The next step will be for plaintiff Baranski's attorney (Gilmore) to file a complaint in the appropriate court. The **complaint**[4] is a document that states the claims the plaintiff is making against the defendant. The complaint also contains a statement regarding the court's jurisdiction over the dispute and a demand for a remedy (such as money damages).

The filing of the complaint is the initial step that begins the legal action against the defendant, Peretto. The plaintiff's complaint and the defendant's answer—both of which are discussed below—are **pleadings**. The pleadings inform each party of the claims of the other and specify the issues (disputed questions) involved in the case. We examine here the complaint and answer, two basic pleadings.

The complaint must be filed within the period of time allowed by law for bringing legal actions. The allowable period is fixed by state statutes of limitations (discussed in Chapter 5), and this period varies for different types of lawsuits. For example, actions concerning breaches of sales contracts must usually be brought within four years. For negligence lawsuits, statutes of limitations vary from state to state. After the time allowed under a statute of limitations has expired, normally no action can be brought, no matter how strong the case was

complaint
The pleading made by a plaintiff or a charge made by the state alleging wrongdoing on the part of the defendant.

pleadings
Statements by the plaintiff and the defendant that detail the facts, charges, and defenses involved in the litigation.

Developing Paralegal Skills

FILE WORKUP

Once a litigation file has been created, the paralegal typically "works up" the file. In the Baranski case, after paralegal Lopez has completed her initial investigation into Baranski's claim, she will review and summarize the information that she has amassed so far, including the information that she has gathered through the initial client interview, subsequent client interviews, and any investigation that she has conducted.

Lopez will also identify areas that might require the testimony of an expert witness. For example, if Baranski claimed that as a result of the accident she had broken her hip and would always walk with a limp, Gilmore would want a medical specialist to give expert testimony to support Baranski's claim. (How to locate expert witnesses will be discussed in later chapters.) Lopez would prepare a list of potential experts for Gilmore to review.

Once Lopez has worked up the file, she will prepare a memo to Gilmore summarizing the file. This memo will provide Gilmore with factual information for deciding which legal remedy or strategy to pursue, what legal issues need to be researched, and generally how to proceed with the case.

TIPS FOR PREPARING A FILE WORKUP MEMO

- Summarize the information that has been obtained about the case.
- Suggest a plan for further investigation in the case (you will read about investigation plans in Chapter 14).
- Suggest additional information that might be obtained during discovery (discussed later in this chapter).
- Include a list of expert witnesses to contact, explaining which witnesses might be preferable, and why.

---

originally. For example, if the statute of limitations covering the auto-negligence lawsuit that plaintiff Baranski is bringing against defendant Peretto allows two years for bringing an action, Baranski normally has to initiate the lawsuit within that two-year period or forgo (give up) forever the possibility of suing Peretto for damages caused by the car accident.

Drafting the Complaint

The complaint itself may be no more than a few paragraphs long, or it may be many pages in length, depending on the complexity of the case. In the Baranski case, the complaint will probably be only a few pages long unless special circumstances justify additional details. The complaint will include the following sections, each of which we discuss below:

- Caption.
- Jurisdictional allegations.
- General allegations (the body of the complaint).
- Prayer for relief.
- Signature.
- Demand for a jury trial.

Exhibit 13.2 on pages 458 and 459 shows a sample complaint. The sections of the complaint are indicated in the marginal annotations.

Baranski's case is being filed in a federal court, so the Federal Rules of Civil Procedure (FRCP) apply. If the case were being filed in a state court, paralegal Lopez might need to

LITIGATION PARALEGAL

Janet M. Powell is a commercial litigation paralegal specializing in computerized litigation support, case management, and trial support in Miami, Florida. She has been working in the legal field for more than twenty years. She is an adjunct professor in the paralegal studies program at Miami-Dade College and focuses her teaching on online public records and other investigation resources. She obtained her NALA certification in 1991 and served in the Miami–Dade County guardian ad litem program. She is the case manager in the Miami office of Ogletree, Deakins, Nash, Smoak & Stewart, a national firm specializing in management consulting and labor and employment case representation.

What do you like best about your work?

"Litigation has always interested me because it is intellectually stimulating. In order to understand the documentation and the investigation stream in cases, often you have to learn quite a bit about various other kinds of businesses, industries, products, and commercial transactions. This depth of understanding is important if you are involved in the discovery process, as investigation and strategizing are generally necessary for successful handling. I am always learning something new; it makes each day different. Boredom is out of the question."

What is the greatest challenge that you face in your area of work?

"My greatest challenge specific to my profession is to keep current with emerging technologies, specifically various computer-based case management and practice management tools. In many instances, litigation paralegal roles are evolving into positions that are more technical. If you work at a firm that will invest in your continuing education, that is a huge benefit. Regardless of whether your firm offers such training, however, we all have to take responsibility for continuing to build our knowledge base and manage our own professionalism. I am a great believer in taking charge of one's own educa-

> *"My greatest challenge ... is to keep current with emerging technologies...."*

tion, as it builds self-confidence and enhances future employability and prospects. Education is available today through many avenues, such as continuing legal education (CLE) seminars sponsored by associations, schools, and independent paralegal organizations."

What advice do you have for would-be paralegals in your area of work?

"My role as a paralegal is to support the needs and anticipated needs of the attorneys I work for and to tailor my output accordingly. To that end, it is helpful to have a supportive, caring disposition. Some people may need help defining what their case needs are, and being willing to go the extra mile goes a long way toward establishing professional friendships that can turn into personal ones. Generally, you should be as adaptable and as helpful as you can be. You must also think deeply about what is truly important, and keep your priorities clearly in mind. You can be a top-notch paralegal and a valued member of your firm, but if you do not have balance in your work and personal life, it will be difficult to be happy and successful."

What are some tips for success as a paralegal in your area of work?

"Learn to manage yourself, your projects, and your time well. Be reasonable in understanding your limitations, and ask for help or relief when it looks like you might be getting overwhelmed. Trying to do too much in too short a time will not let you produce your best work, and it will reflect poorly on you. Learn to communicate effectively, be appreciative for projects and work assigned to you, and take pride in your work product. Double-check your work for accuracy; proofread everything backwards. If there are few or no in-house educational opportunities, take charge of your own professional development. Set your own professional goals, and do not wait for permission to better yourself. Learn from everyone, especially your co-workers and colleagues. Attend your local association's meetings and luncheons. The more paralegals you know, the more you will learn."

Janet Powell is also featured in the forthcoming book, Lessons from the Top Paralegal Experts, *by Carole Bruno.*

EXHIBIT 13.2
The Complaint

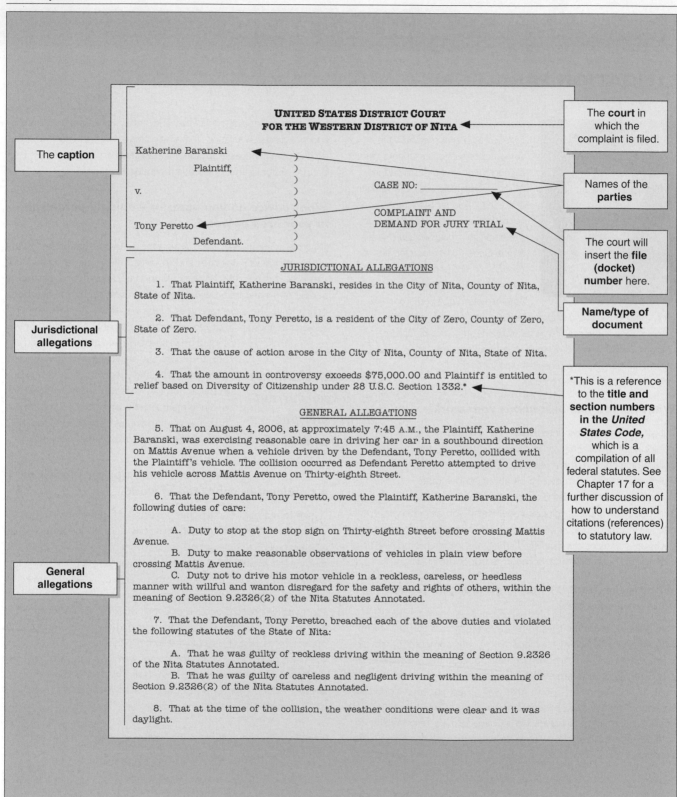

The **caption**

UNITED STATES DISTRICT COURT
FOR THE WESTERN DISTRICT OF NITA

The **court** in which the complaint is filed.

Katherine Baranski

     Plaintiff,

v.

Tony Peretto

    Defendant.

CASE NO: _____

COMPLAINT AND
DEMAND FOR JURY TRIAL

Names of the **parties**

The court will insert the **file (docket) number** here.

Name/type of document

Jurisdictional allegations

JURISDICTIONAL ALLEGATIONS

1. That Plaintiff, Katherine Baranski, resides in the City of Nita, County of Nita, State of Nita.

2. That Defendant, Tony Peretto, is a resident of the City of Zero, County of Zero, State of Zero.

3. That the cause of action arose in the City of Nita, County of Nita, State of Nita.

4. That the amount in controversy exceeds $75,000.00 and Plaintiff is entitled to relief based on Diversity of Citizenship under 28 U.S.C. Section 1332.*

*This is a reference to the **title and section numbers** in the *United States Code,* which is a compilation of all federal statutes. See Chapter 17 for a further discussion of how to understand citations (references) to statutory law.

GENERAL ALLEGATIONS

5. That on August 4, 2006, at approximately 7:45 A.M., the Plaintiff, Katherine Baranski, was exercising reasonable care in driving her car in a southbound direction on Mattis Avenue when a vehicle driven by the Defendant, Tony Peretto, collided with the Plaintiff's vehicle. The collision occurred as Defendant Peretto attempted to drive his vehicle across Mattis Avenue on Thirty-eighth Street.

6. That the Defendant, Tony Peretto, owed the Plaintiff, Katherine Baranski, the following duties of care:

    A. Duty to stop at the stop sign on Thirty-eighth Street before crossing Mattis Avenue.
    B. Duty to make reasonable observations of vehicles in plain view before crossing Mattis Avenue.
    C. Duty not to drive his motor vehicle in a reckless, careless, or heedless manner with willful and wanton disregard for the safety and rights of others, within the meaning of Section 9.2326(2) of the Nita Statutes Annotated.

General allegations

7. That the Defendant, Tony Peretto, breached each of the above duties and violated the following statutes of the State of Nita:

    A. That he was guilty of reckless driving within the meaning of Section 9.2326 of the Nita Statutes Annotated.
    B. That he was guilty of careless and negligent driving within the meaning of Section 9.2326(2) of the Nita Statutes Annotated.

8. That at the time of the collision, the weather conditions were clear and it was daylight.

EXHIBIT 13.2

The Complaint—Continued

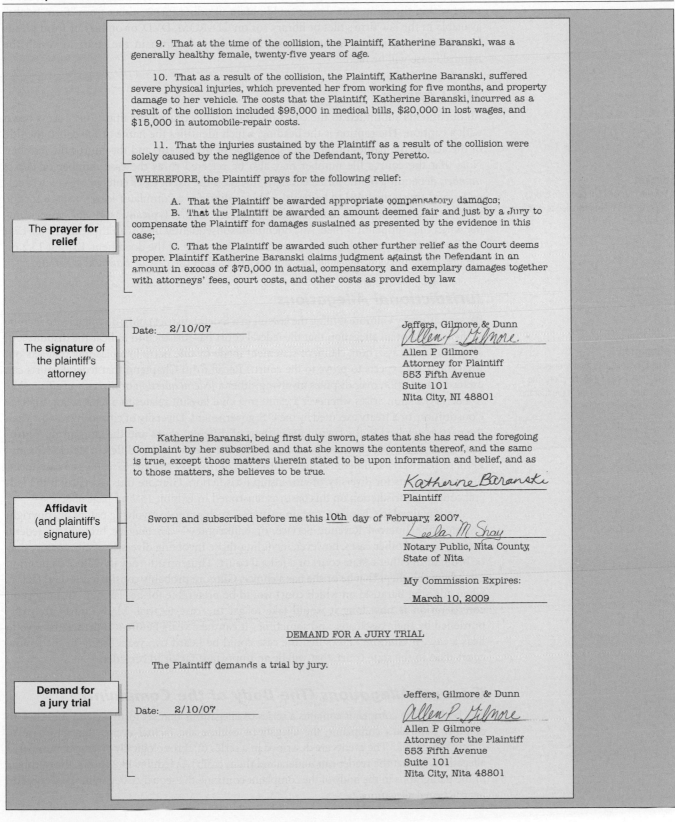

9. That at the time of the collision, the Plaintiff, Katherine Baranski, was a generally healthy female, twenty-five years of age.

10. That as a result of the collision, the Plaintiff, Katherine Baranski, suffered severe physical injuries, which prevented her from working for five months, and property damage to her vehicle. The costs that the Plaintiff, Katherine Baranski, incurred as a result of the collision included $95,000 in medical bills, $20,000 in lost wages, and $15,000 in automobile-repair costs.

11. That the injuries sustained by the Plaintiff as a result of the collision were solely caused by the negligence of the Defendant, Tony Peretto.

WHEREFORE, the Plaintiff prays for the following relief:

The prayer for relief

A. That the Plaintiff be awarded appropriate compensatory damages;
B. That the Plaintiff be awarded an amount deemed fair and just by a Jury to compensate the Plaintiff for damages sustained as presented by the evidence in this case;
C. That the Plaintiff be awarded such other further relief as the Court deems proper. Plaintiff Katherine Baranski claims judgment against the Defendant in an amount in excess of $75,000 in actual, compensatory, and exemplary damages together with attorneys' fees, court costs, and other costs as provided by law.

The signature of the plaintiff's attorney

Date: 2/10/07

Jeffers, Gilmore, & Dunn

Allen P. Gilmore

Allen P Gilmore
Attorney for Plaintiff
553 Fifth Avenue
Suite 101
Nita City, NI 48801

Affidavit (and plaintiff's signature)

Katherine Baranski, being first duly sworn, states that she has read the foregoing Complaint by her subscribed and that she knows the contents thereof, and the same is true, except those matters therein stated to be upon information and belief, and as to those matters, she believes to be true.

Katherine Baranski
Plaintiff

Sworn and subscribed before me this 10th day of February, 2007.

Leela M Shay
Notary Public, Nita County,
State of Nita

My Commission Expires:

March 10, 2009

DEMAND FOR A JURY TRIAL

The Plaintiff demands a trial by jury.

Demand for a jury trial

Date: 2/10/07

Jeffers, Gilmore & Dunn

Allen P Gilmore

Allen P Gilmore
Attorney for the Plaintiff
553 Fifth Avenue
Suite 101
Nita City, Nita 48801

review the appropriate state rules of civil procedure. The rules for drafting pleadings in state courts differ from the FRCP. The rules also differ from state to state and even from court to court within the same state. Lopez could obtain pleading forms, either from "form books" available in the law firm's files or library (or on CD-ROM, DVD, or online) or from pleadings drafted previously in similar cases litigated by the firm in the court in which the Baranski case will be filed.

The Caption

All documents submitted to the court or other parties during the litigation process begin with a caption. The caption is the heading, which identifies the name of the court, the title of the action, the names of the parties, the type of document, and the court's file number. Note that the court's file number may also be referred to as the case number or *docket number,* depending on the jurisdiction. (A **docket** is the list of cases entered on a court's calendar and thus scheduled to be heard.) The caption for a complaint leaves a space for the court to insert the number that it assigns to the case. Courts typically assign the case a number when the complaint is filed. Any document subsequently filed with the court in the case will list the file, case, or docket number on the front page of the document. Exhibit 13.2 on the preceding pages shows how the caption will read in the case of *Baranski v. Peretto.*

docket
The list of cases entered on a court's calendar and thus scheduled to be heard by the court.

Jurisdictional Allegations

Because attorney Gilmore is filing the lawsuit in a federal district court, he will have to include in the complaint an allegation that the federal court has jurisdiction to hear the dispute. (An **allegation** is an assertion, claim, or statement made by one party in a pleading that sets out what the party expects to prove to the court.) Recall from Chapter 6 that federal courts can exercise jurisdiction over disputes involving either a *federal question* or *diversity of citizenship.* A federal question arises whenever a claim in a civil lawsuit relates to a federal law, the U.S. Constitution, or a treaty executed by the U.S. government. Diversity of citizenship exists when the parties involved in the lawsuit are citizens of different states and the amount in controversy exceeds $75,000. Because Baranski and Peretto are citizens of different states (Nita and Zero, respectively) and because the amount in controversy exceeds $75,000, the case meets the requirements for diversity-of-citizenship jurisdiction. Gilmore thus asserts that the federal court has jurisdiction on this basis, as illustrated in Exhibit 13.2 on page 458.

allegation
A party's statement, claim, or assertion made in a pleading to the court. The allegation sets forth the issue that the party expects to prove.

As explained in Chapter 6, certain matters—such as those involving patent or copyright disputes, the Internal Revenue Service, or bankruptcy—can *only* be brought in federal courts. Certain other cases, however, including those involving diversity of citizenship, may be brought in either a state court or a federal court. Thus, an attorney in Gilmore's position can advise the client that he or she has a choice. Gilmore probably considered several factors when advising Baranski on which court would be preferable for her lawsuit. An important consideration is how long it would take to get the case to trial. Many courts are overburdened by their caseloads, and sometimes it can take years before a court will be able to hear a case. If Gilmore knows that the case could be heard two years earlier in the federal court than in the state court, that will be an important factor to consider.

General Allegations (The Body of the Complaint)

The body of the complaint contains a series of allegations that set forth a claim for relief. In plaintiff Baranski's complaint, the allegations outline the factual events that gave rise to Baranski's claims.[5] The events are described in a series of chronologically arranged, numbered allegations so that the reader can understand them easily. As Exhibit 13.2 shows, the numbers of the paragraphs in the body of the complaint continue the sequence begun in the section on jurisdictional allegations.

Advocate Plaintiff's Position. When drafting the complaint, paralegal Lopez will play the role of advocate. She must present the facts forcefully and in a way that supports and strengthens the client's claim. The recitation of the facts should demonstrate that defendant Peretto engaged in conduct that entitles plaintiff Baranski to relief. Even though she will want to present the facts in a light most favorable to Baranski, Lopez must be careful not to exaggerate the facts or make false statements. Rather, she must present the facts in such a way that the reader could reasonably infer that defendant Peretto was negligent and that Peretto's negligence caused Baranski's injuries and losses.

What if her research into the case had given Lopez reason to believe that a fact was probably true even though she could not be certain as to its validity? She could still include the statement in the complaint by prefacing it with the phrase, "On information and belief . . . ." This language would indicate to the court that the plaintiff, Baranski, had good reason to believe the truth of the statement but that the evidence for it either had not yet been obtained or might not hold up under close scrutiny.

Be Clear and Concise. The most effective complaints are those that are clear and concise. Moreover, brevity and simplicity are required under FRCP 8(a). As in all legal writing, Lopez should strive for clarity. When drafting the complaint, Lopez should use clear language and favor simple and direct statements over more complex wording. This is because the court may, at the request of opposing counsel, strike (delete) from the complaint ambiguous phrases—phrases whose meaning is unclear or that could be interpreted in more than one way. Lopez should also resist the temptation to include facts that are not absolutely necessary for the complaint. By reducing the body of the complaint to the simplest possible terms, Lopez will not only achieve greater clarity but also minimize the possibility of divulging attorney Gilmore's trial strategies or hinting at a possible defense that the opponent might use to defeat the claim.

Outline the Harms Suffered and the Remedy Sought. After telling plaintiff Baranski's story, paralegal Lopez will add one or more paragraphs outlining the harms suffered by the plaintiff and the remedy (in money damages) that the plaintiff seeks. In general, it is preferable that all allegations of damages—such as hospital costs, lost wages, and auto-repair expenses—be included in a single paragraph, as in Exhibit 13.2 in Paragraph 10. Lopez should check the relevant court rules, however, to see whether the court requires that certain types of damages (Baranski's lost wages, for example) be alleged in a separate paragraph.

Prayer for Relief

Paralegal Lopez will include at the end of the complaint a paragraph, similar to that shown in Exhibit 13.2 on page 459, asking that judgment be entered for the plaintiff and appropriate relief be granted. This **prayer for relief** will indicate that plaintiff Baranski is seeking money damages to compensate her for the harms that she suffered.

prayer for relief
A statement at the end of the complaint requesting that the court grant relief to the plaintiff.

Signature

In federal practice, the signature following the prayer for relief certifies that the plaintiff's attorney (or the plaintiff, if he or she is not represented by an attorney) has read the complaint and that the facts alleged are true to the best of his or her knowledge. In addition to the attorney's signature, some state courts require an affidavit signed by the plaintiff verifying that the complaint is true to the best of the plaintiff's knowledge. **Affidavits** are sworn statements attesting to the existence of certain facts. They are acknowledged by a notary public or another official authorized to administer such oaths or affirmations. Exhibit 13.2, on page 459, illustrates an affidavit for the Baranski complaint.

affidavit
A written statement of facts, confirmed by the oath or affirmation of the party making it and made before a person having the authority to administer the oath or affirmation.

Demand for a Jury Trial

A trial can be held with or without a jury. If there is no jury, the judge determines the truth of the facts alleged in the case. The Seventh Amendment to the U.S. Constitution guarantees the right to a jury trial in federal courts in all "suits at common law" when the amount in controversy exceeds $20. Most states have similar guarantees in their own constitutions, although many states put a higher minimum dollar restriction on the guarantee (for example, in Maryland the minimum amount is $10,000). If this threshold requirement is met, either party may request a jury trial.

The right to a trial by jury does not have to be exercised, and many cases are tried without one. In most states and in federal courts, one of the parties must request a jury trial, or the right is presumed to be waived (that is, the court will presume that neither party wants a jury trial). The decision to exercise the right to a jury trial usually depends on what legal theory the party is using and which judge is assigned to the trial. In the Baranski case, plaintiff Baranski's attorney, Gilmore, may advise Baranski to demand a jury trial if he believes that a jury would be sympathetic to Baranski's position. If plaintiff Baranski wants a jury trial, Gilmore will ask paralegal Lopez to include a demand for a jury trial (similar to the one illustrated in Point "B" of Exhibit 13.2 on page 459) with the complaint.

Filing the Complaint

Once the complaint has been prepared, carefully checked for accuracy, and signed by attorney Gilmore, paralegal Lopez will file the complaint with the court in which the action is being brought. To file the complaint, Lopez will either deliver the paper document to the court—the traditional method—or file the complaint with the court electronically via e-mail, fax, or CD-ROM.

Traditional Method of Filing

Traditionally, a person filing a complaint personally delivers the complaint to the clerk of the court, together with a specified number of copies of the complaint and a check payable to the court in the amount of the required filing fee. Usually, a summons (which will be discussed shortly) is also attached. If Lopez uses this method of filing, she can either deliver the complaint to the court clerk or have someone deliver it for her. If she is not aware of the court's specific procedures for filing the complaint, she will need to contact the court to verify the amount of the filing fee and how many copies of the complaint need to be filed. Typically, the original (signed) complaint is filed with at least two copies (the court keeps the original, and the plaintiff and defendant receive a copy), although additional copies may be required, particularly if there are multiple plaintiffs or defendants in the case.

The court clerk files the complaint by stamping the date on the first page of all the documents (original and copies); assigning the case a file number, or docket number; and assigning the case to a particular judge. (In some state courts, the file number or judge may not be assigned until later.) The clerk then returns the date-stamped copies to the person who delivered the documents for service on the defendant (to be discussed shortly).

Electronic Filing

Instead of delivering a paper document to the court, Lopez may be able to file the complaint electronically. Indeed, electronic filing is becoming more and more common. Because of the reduced time and paperwork involved, electronic filing can result in substantial savings for attorneys, their clients, and the courts.

The Federal Courts. The FRCP provides that federal courts may permit filing by electronic means that are consistent with any technical standards established by the Judicial

Developing Paralegal Skills

FEDERAL COURT RULES—CREATING A COMPLAINT CHECKLIST

Ann Marston is a paralegal who works in a firm with a federal court practice. A new paralegal, Brian Blake, is joining the firm, and Ann has been asked to train Brian. Her supervising attorney has suggested that she create a checklist for drafting federal court complaints. The checklist could be used to train not only Brian but also new associates in the firm.

Before she begins drafting the checklist, Ann meets with Brian and explains what she does. Ann tells Brian that she starts by getting the file and reviewing her notes, memos from the client interview, and any reports (such as police reports) that are in the file. She explains that these sources will assist her in describing how, for example, a personal injury occurred in an accident case. She also checks to see if she made any notes, during her meeting with the attorney who will handle the case, regarding the court in which the case will be filed, because in some cases the state and federal courts have concurrent jurisdiction. Next, she finds out the plaintiff's and the defendant's correct legal names. If necessary, she contacts the secretary of state to obtain the legal name of a corporation. Last, she takes out her copy of the Federal Rules of Civil Procedure and reviews Rules 8, 10, and 11, which specify the kind of information that should be included in complaints filed in a federal court.

CHECKLIST FOR DRAFTING A COMPLAINT

- Determine when the statute of limitations expires by checking the file for the relevant dates.

- Locate a previously drafted complaint form for the type of cases involved.

- Determine the court's basis for jurisdiction in the case, and draft an allegation explaining it.

- Determine the facts that create the cause of action, or the legal basis for the lawsuit.

- Draft the "general allegations," or the body of the complaint. If the plaintiff has more than one legal basis for the relief sought, draft as many "counts" as the plaintiff has.

- Determine the specific type of relief, such as money damages, that the plaintiff is seeking, and draft a prayer for relief.

- Insert a signature block for an attorney to sign after conducting a reasonable inquiry into the facts that support the claim.

- Determine if a jury trial is desired, and draft a demand for a jury trial if needed.

Conference, which sets policy for the administration of the federal courts. The federal court system first experimented with an **electronic filing (e-filing) system** in January 1996. E-filing systems are now used in more than 130 courts. To initiate an e-filing system, each court goes through an implementation process that takes about ten months. With e-filing, registered attorneys can file case documents over the Internet twenty-four hours a day, seven days a week, right up to the filing deadline, with no additional filing fees. At last count, tens of millions of documents had been filed electronically by more than 150,000 attorneys, paralegals, and others. The e-filing system for federal district courts was initiated nationally in May 2002 and now extends to most district courts. Implementation of an electronic filing system for appellate courts began in late 2004.

State and Local Courts. State and local courts are also setting up electronic filing systems. Since the late 1990s, the court system in Pima County, Arizona, has been accepting

electronic filing (e-filing) system
A computer system that enables attorneys to file case documents with courts over the Internet twenty-four hours a day, seven days a week.

Ethics Watch!

ELECTRONIC FILING AND PRIVACY ISSUES

One major concern about electronic filing is how to protect the privacy of client information that is sent via the Internet. Electronic filing on a nationwide basis would open up all trial court documents to anyone with an Internet connection and a Web browser. Utilizing special software, anyone could go online and within just a few minutes access information—ranging from personal health records, to financial reports, to criminal violations—from dozens of courts. This means that serious privacy issues are at stake. How should a paralegal deal with these privacy issues? Clearly, that is a matter that you and your supervising attorney need to discuss with the client. Usually, at least to date, the courts that allow electronic filing require the parties' consent before any documents are electronically filed. The attorney will therefore have an opportunity to discuss with the client the privacy implications of filing documents electronically at the time of obtaining his or her consent.

On the Web

To find out whether a particular court permits documents to be filed electronically and, for some courts, to obtain the appropriate forms, visit that court's Web page (or the home page for the state court system). You can find links to federal and state courts at **http://www.findlaw.com**.

---

service of process
The delivery of the summons and the complaint to a defendant.

summons
A document served on a defendant in a lawsuit informing the defendant that a legal action has been commenced against him or her and that the defendant must appear in court or respond to the plaintiff's complaint within a specified period of time.

---

pleadings via e-mail. The supreme court of the state of Washington also now accepts online filings of litigation documents. In addition, electronic filing projects are being developed in other states, including California, Idaho, Kansas, Maryland, Michigan, Texas, Utah, and Virginia. The state of Colorado implemented the first statewide court e-filing system and currently allows e-filing in over sixty courts. Generally, when electronic filing is available, it is optional. In early 2001, however, a trial court judge in the District of Columbia launched a pilot project that *required* attorneys to use electronic filing for all documents relating to certain types of civil cases.

Service of Process

Before the court can exercise jurisdiction over the defendant—in effect, before the lawsuit can begin—the court must have proof that the defendant was notified of the lawsuit. Serving the summons and complaint—that is, delivering these documents to the defendant in a lawsuit—is referred to as **service of process**.

The Summons

The **summons** identifies the parties to the lawsuit, as well as the court in which the case will be heard, and directs the defendant to respond to the complaint within a specified period of time. In the Baranski case, paralegal Lopez will prepare a summons by filling out a form similar to that shown in Exhibit 13.3. Lopez will also prepare a cover sheet for the case (a preprinted form), which is required in the federal courts and in most state courts.

If the case were being brought in a state court, paralegal Lopez would deliver the summons to the court clerk at the same time she delivered the complaint. (In federal court cases, as will be discussed, the complaint may already have been filed under the FRCP provisions relating to waiver of notice.)

EXHIBIT 13.3
A Summons in a Civil Action

**UNITED STATES DISTRICT COURT
FOR THE WESTERN DISTRICT OF NITA**

Katherine Baranski)	**Civil Action, File Number 07-14335-NI**
Plaintiff,)	
v.)	*Summons*
)	
Tony Peretto)	
Defendant.)	

To the above-named Defendant:

You are hereby summoned and required to serve upon A. P. Gilmore, Jeffers, Gilmore & Dunn, plaintiff's attorney, whose address is 553 Fifth Avenue, Suite 101, Nita City, NI 48801, an answer to the complaint which is herewith served upon you, within 20 days after service of this summons upon you, exclusive of the day of service. If you fail to do so, judgment by default will be taken against you for the relief demanded in the complaint.

C. H. Hynek   February 10, 2007

CLERK   DATE

John Dolan

BY DEPUTY CLERK

After the clerk files the complaint and signs, seals, and issues the summons, attorney Gilmore will be responsible for making sure that the summons and complaint are served on defendant Peretto. The service of the complaint and summons must be effected within a specified time—120 days under FRCP 4(m)—after the complaint has been filed.

Serving the Complaint and Summons

How service of process occurs depends on the rules of the court or jurisdiction in which the lawsuit is brought. Under FRCP 4(c)(2), service of process in federal court cases may be effected "by any person who is not a party and who is at least 18 years of age." Paralegal Lopez, for example, could serve the summons by personally delivering it to defendant Peretto. Alternatively, she could make arrangements for someone else to do so, subject to the approval of attorney Gilmore. Many law firms contract with independent companies that provide process service in the local area. In some types of cases, the attorney might request that the court have a U.S. marshal or other federal official serve the summons.

Under FRCP 4(e)(1), service of process in federal court cases may also be effected "pursuant to the law of the state in which the district court is located." Some state courts require that the complaint and summons be served by a public officer, such as a sheriff.

Alternative Service Methods. Although the most common way to serve process on a defendant is through personal service, or actual delivery, as described above, other methods of service are permissible at times, depending on the jurisdiction. *Substituted service* is any method of service allowed by law in place of personal service, such as service by mail, fax, or e-mail. Most states allow a process server to effect service by leaving a copy of the documents at the defendant's place of work, at his or her home address, or with someone else who

EXHIBIT 13.4
A Return-of-Service Form

RETURN OF SERVICE

Service of the Summons and Complaint was made by me	DATE 2/11/07

NAME OF SERVER Elena Lopez	TITLE Paralegal

Check one box below to indicate appropriate method of service

☒ Served personally upon the defendant. Place where served: _Defendant Peretto's Home: 1708 Johnston Drive, Zero City, Zero 59806_
_____

☐ Left copies thereof at the defendant's dwelling house or usual place of abode with a person of suitable age and discretion then residing therein.
Name of person with whom the summons and complaint were left: _____

☐ Returned unexecuted: _____
_____
_____

☐ Other (specify): _____
_____

DECLARATION OF SERVER

I declare under penalty of perjury under the laws of the United States of America that the foregoing information contained in the Return of Service and Statement of Service Fees is true and correct.

Executed on ___2/11/07_____   *Elena Lopez*_____
             Date   *Signature of Server*

308 University Avenue, Nita City, Nita 48804
_____
Address of Server

| **return-of-service form**
A document signed by a process server and submitted to the court to prove that a defendant received a summons.

resides in the home (such as a wife or an older child). In some circumstances, if the defendant cannot be physically located, the law may allow the process server to effect service by mailing a copy of the summons and complaint to the defendant's last known address and/or publishing a notice in the local newspaper. In other situations, delivering the documents to an authorized agent is sufficient. The paralegal and attorney thus need to know the types of service authorized by the laws of civil procedure in their own state.

Proof of Service.   Regardless of how the summons is served, attorney Gilmore will need some kind of proof that defendant Peretto actually received the summons. In federal court cases, unless service is made by a U.S. marshal or other official, proof of service is established by having the process server fill out and sign a form similar to the **return-of-service form** shown in Exhibit 13.4. This form is then submitted to the court as evidence that service has been effected.

Jurisdictions May Vary.   Paralegal Lopez must be very careful to comply with the service requirements of the court in which plaintiff Baranski's suit has been filed. If service is not properly made, defendant Peretto will have a legal ground (basis) for asking the court to dismiss the case against him, thus delaying the litigation. As mentioned earlier, the court will not be able to exercise jurisdiction over Peretto until he has been properly notified of the lawsuit being brought against him.

Serving Corporate Defendants

In cases involving corporate defendants, the summons and complaint may be served on an officer or a *registered agent* (representative) of the corporation. The name of a corporation's registered agent is usually obtainable from the secretary of state's office in the state in which the company incorporated its business (and, usually, the secretary of state's office in any state in which the corporation does business).

Finding the Defendant

Because some defendants may be difficult to locate, paralegals sometimes have to investigate and attempt to locate a defendant so that process can be served. Helpful information sources include telephone directories, banks, former business partners or fellow workers, credit bureaus, Social Security offices, insurance companies, landlords, state and county tax rolls, utility companies, automobile-registration bureaus, bureaus of vital statistics, and the post office. (Chapter 14 discusses these and other possible sources, including various online sources, that the paralegal might consult when trying to locate parties or witnesses involved in lawsuits.)

The Defendant Can Waive Service

In many instances, the defendant is already aware that a lawsuit is being filed (often the plaintiff's attorney has been in contact with the defendant and has indicated that a complaint would be filed). In such cases, a plaintiff can request the defendant to *waive* (give up) her or his right to be formally served with a summons. FRCP 4(d) sets forth the procedure by which a plaintiff's attorney can request the defendant to accept service of the documents through the mail or "other reliable means." Many states have similar rules.

The aim of FRCP 4(d) is to eliminate the costs associated with service of process and to foster cooperation among adversaries. As an incentive, defendants who agree to waive formal service of process under the federal rules receive additional time to respond to the complaint (sixty days, compared with the twenty days that a defendant normally has to respond to the complaint under FRCP 12). Some state rules of civil procedure provide other types of incentives, such as making a party who will not agree to waive service pay for reasonable expenses thereafter incurred in serving or attempting to serve the party.

The Defendant's Response

Once a defendant receives the plaintiff's complaint, the defendant must respond to the complaint within a specified time period (typically twenty to thirty days). If the defendant fails to respond within that time period, the court, on the plaintiff's motion, will enter a **default judgment** against the defendant. The defendant will then be liable for the entire amount of damages that the plaintiff is claiming and will lose the opportunity to either defend against the claim in court or settle the issue with the plaintiff out of court.

In the Baranski case, assume that defendant Peretto consults with an attorney, Elizabeth A. Cameron, to decide on a course of action. Before Cameron advises Peretto on the matter, she will want to investigate plaintiff Baranski's claim and obtain evidence of what happened at the time of the accident. She may ask her paralegal, Gordon McVay, to call anyone who may have witnessed the accident and any police officers who were at the scene. Attorney Cameron will also ask McVay to gather relevant documents, including the traffic ticket that Peretto received at the time of the accident and any reports that might have been filed by the police. If all goes well, attorney Cameron and paralegal McVay will complete their investigation in a few days and then meet to assess the results.

As mentioned earlier, most cases are settled out of court before they go to trial. But even if Peretto's attorney suspects that an out-of-court settlement might be financially preferable

default judgment
A judgment entered by a clerk or court against a party who has failed to appear in court to answer or defend against a claim that has been brought against him or her by another party.

Case at a Glance

The Plaintiff—
Plaintiff: Katherine Baranski
Attorney: Allen P. Gilmore
Paralegal: Elena Lopez

The Defendant—
Defendant: Tony Peretto
Attorney: Elizabeth A. Cameron
Paralegal: Gordon McVay

answer
A defendant's response to a plaintiff's complaint.

affirmative defense
A response to a plaintiff's claim that does not deny the plaintiff's facts but attacks the plaintiff's legal right to bring an action.

counterclaim
A claim made by a defendant in a civil lawsuit against the plaintiff; in effect, a counterclaiming defendant is suing the plaintiff.

cross-claim
A claim asserted by a defendant in a civil lawsuit against another defendant or by a plaintiff against another plaintiff.

to a trial, she will still draft a response to plaintiff Baranski's claim. She knows that if defendant Peretto does not respond to the plaintiff's complaint within the proper time period, the court will enter a default judgment against Peretto. In deciding how best to respond to the complaint, Peretto's attorney, Cameron, must consider whether to file an answer or a motion to dismiss the case.

The Answer

A defendant's **answer** must respond to each allegation in the plaintiff's complaint. FRCP 8(b) permits the defendant to admit or deny the truth of each allegation. Defendant Peretto's attorney may advise Peretto to admit to some of the allegations in plaintiff Baranski's complaint, because doing so narrows the number of issues in dispute. Any allegations that are not denied by the defendant will be deemed to have been admitted.

If defendant Peretto has no knowledge as to whether a particular allegation is true or false, then his attorney, Cameron, may indicate that in the answer. This puts the burden of proving the allegation on plaintiff Baranski, just as if it were an outright denial. It is not necessary for Peretto's attorney to include in the answer any of the reasons for the denial of particular allegations in Baranski's complaint. These reasons may be revealed during the discovery phase of the litigation process (discussed later in this chapter).

Exhibit 13.5 illustrates the types of responses that defendant Peretto might make in his answer. Like the complaint, the answer begins with a caption and ends with the attorney's signature. It may also include, following the attorney's signature, an affidavit signed by the defendant, as well as a demand for a jury trial, as in Exhibit 13.5.

Answer and Affirmative Defenses.   A defendant may assert, in the answer, a reason why he or she should not be held liable for the plaintiff's injuries even if the facts, as alleged by the plaintiff, are true. This is called raising an **affirmative defense**.

For example, Peretto might claim that someone else was driving his Dodge van when it crashed into Baranski's car. Peretto's attorney might also raise the defense of *contributory negligence.* That is, she could argue that even though defendant Peretto's car collided with Baranski's, plaintiff Baranski was also negligent because she was exceeding the speed limit when the accident occurred and was thus unable to avoid being hit by Peretto's car. As discussed in Chapter 7, in a few states, if it can be shown that the plaintiff was contributorily negligent, the plaintiff will be completely barred from recovery. Most states, however, have abandoned the doctrine of contributory negligence in favor of a *comparative negligence* standard. In these states, a plaintiff whose own negligence contributed to an injury can still recover damages, but the damages are reduced by a percentage that represents the degree of the plaintiff's negligence. Although affirmative defenses are directed toward the plaintiff, the plaintiff is not required to file additional pleadings in response to these defenses.

Answer and Counterclaim.   Peretto's attorney may follow the answers to the plaintiff's allegations with one or more counterclaims. A **counterclaim** is like a reverse lawsuit in which the defendant asserts a claim against the plaintiff for injuries that the defendant suffered from the same incident. For example, defendant Peretto might contend that plaintiff Baranski lost control of her car and skidded into Peretto's car, causing Peretto to be injured. This allegation would be a counterclaim. The plaintiff is required to reply to any counterclaims made by the defendant.

Answer and Cross-Claim.   In cases in which a complaint names multiple defendants, the answer filed by one defendant might be followed by a **cross-claim**, in which the defendant asserts a claim against another defendant. (Note that cross-claims may also be filed by one plaintiff against another plaintiff in the same case.) For example, suppose that plaintiff

EXHIBIT 13.5
The Answer

UNITED STATES DISTRICT COURT
FOR THE WESTERN DISTRICT OF NITA

Katherine Baranski)
)
           Plaintiff,)   CASE NO. 07-14335-NI
)   Honorable Harley M. Larue
v.   )
)
)   ANSWER AND
Tony Peretto   )   DEMAND FOR JURY TRIAL
           Defendant.)

JURISDICTIONAL ALLEGATIONS

1. Defendant lacks sufficient information to form a belief as to the truth of the allegations contained in paragraph 1 of Plaintiff's Complaint.

2. Defendant admits the allegations contained in paragraph 2 of Plaintiff's Complaint.

3. Defendant admits the allegations contained in paragraph 3 of Plaintiff's Complaint.

4. Defendant lacks sufficient information to form a belief as to the truth of the allegations contained in paragraph 4 of Plaintiff's Complaint.

GENERAL ALLEGATIONS

5. Defendant admits the allegations contained in paragraph 5 of Plaintiff's Complaint.

6. Defendant admits the allegations contained in paragraph 6 of Plaintiff's Complaint.

7. Defendant contends that he was operating his vehicle properly and denies the allegations contained in paragraph 7 of Plaintiff's Complaint for the reason that the allegations are untrue.

8. Defendant admits the allegation contained in paragraph 8 of Plaintiff's Complaint.

9. Defendant lacks sufficient information to form a belief as to the truth of the allegation contained in paragraph 9 of Plaintiff's Complaint.

10. Defendant lacks sufficient information on the proximate cause of Plaintiff's injuries to form a belief as to the truth of the averments contained in paragraph 10 of Plaintiff's Complaint.

11. Defendant denies the allegation of negligence contained in paragraph 11 of Plaintiff's Complaint.

(Continued)

EXHIBIT 13.5
The Answer—Continued

NEW MATTER AND AFFIRMATIVE DEFENSES

Although denying that the Plaintiff is entitled to the relief prayed for in the Plaintiff's Complaint, Defendant further states that the Plaintiff is barred from recovery hereunder by reason of the following:

1. That the Plaintiff's injuries were proximately caused by her own contributory negligence and want of due care under the circumstances prevailing at the time of the accident.

2. That the Plaintiff was exceeding the posted speed limit at the time and place of the accident and therefore was guilty of careless and negligent driving within the meaning of Section 9.2325(1) of the Nita Statutes Annotated.

3. That the Plaintiff failed to exercise that standard of care that a reasonably prudent person would have exercised under the same or similar conditions for her own safety and that her own negligence, contributory negligence, and/or comparative negligence caused or was a contributing factor to the incident out of which the Plaintiff's cause of action arises.

4. The Defendant reserves the right, by an appropriate Motion, to move the Court to amend the Defendant's Answer to the Plaintiff's Complaint, to allege other New Matters and Affirmative Defenses as may be revealed by discovery yet to be had and completed in this case.

WHEREFORE, the Defendant prays for a judgment of no cause of action with costs and attorneys' fees to be paid by the Plaintiff.

Cameron & Strauss, P.C.

Elizabeth A. Cameron

Date: 2/25/07

Elizabeth A. Cameron
Attorney for the Defendant

310 Lake Drive
Zero City, ZE 59802

Tony Peretto, being first duly sworn, states that he has read the foregoing Answer by him subscribed and that he knows the contents thereof, and the same is true, except those matters therein stated to be upon information and belief, and as to those matters, he believes to be true.

Tony Peretto

Defendant

Sworn and subscribed before me this 25th day of February, 2007.

Laura Curtis

Notary Public, Zero County,
State of Zero

My Commission Expires:
December 8, 2008

DEMAND FOR A JURY TRIAL

The Defendant demands a trial by jury.

Cameron & Strauss, P.C.

Elizabeth A. Cameron

Date: 2/25/07

Elizabeth A. Cameron
Attorney for the Defendant
310 Lake Drive
Zero City, Zero 59802

Baranski had been struck by two vehicles, one belonging to defendant Peretto and one belonging to Leon Balfour. If Peretto and Balfour had been named as co-defendants in Baranski's complaint, Peretto's attorney might have filed an answer to Baranski's complaint that included a cross-claim against Balfour. The party against whom the cross-claim is brought is required to reply to (answer) the claim.

Under the federal rules, a defendant who has a claim against the plaintiff related to the same incident is normally required to file a counterclaim within the defendant's pleading. A party who fails to file such a counterclaim in a pleading may forgo the possibility of asserting the claim at a later date. This requirement to file a counterclaim is intended to prevent multiple lawsuits between the same parties.

Motion to Dismiss

A **motion** is a procedural request submitted to the court by an attorney on behalf of his or her client. When one party files a motion with the court, that party must also send to, or serve on, the opposing party a *notice of motion*. The notice of motion informs the opposing party that the motion has been filed and indicates when the court will hear the motion. The notice of motion gives the opposing party an opportunity to prepare for the hearing and argue before the court why the motion should not be granted.

The **motion to dismiss**, as the phrase implies, requests the court to dismiss the case for reasons provided in the motion. Defendant Peretto's attorney, for example, could file a motion to dismiss if she believed that Peretto had not been properly served, that the complaint had been filed in the wrong court, that the statute of limitations for that type of lawsuit had expired, or that the complaint did not state a claim for which relief (a remedy) could be granted. See Exhibit 13.6 for an example of a motion to dismiss.

Case at a Glance

The Plaintiff—
Plaintiff: Katherine Baranski
Attorney: Allen P. Gilmore
Paralegal: Elena Lopez

The Defendant—
Defendant: Tony Peretto
Attorney: Elizabeth A. Cameron
Paralegal: Gordon McVay

motion
A procedural request or application presented by an attorney to the court on behalf of a client.

motion to dismiss
A motion filed by the defendant in which the defendant asks the court to dismiss the case for a specified reason, such as improper service, lack of personal jurisdiction, or the plaintiff's failure to state a claim for which relief can be granted.

EXHIBIT 13.6
A Motion to Dismiss

UNITED STATES DISTRICT COURT
FOR THE WESTERN DISTRICT OF NITA

Katherine Baranski)
        Plaintiff,)
) CASE NO. 07-14335-NI
v.) Honorable Harley M. Larue
)
) MOTION TO DISMISS
Tony Peretto)
        Defendant.)

    The Defendant, Tony Peretto, by his attorney, moves the court to dismiss the above-named action because the statute of limitations governing the Plaintiff's claim has expired, as demonstrated in the memorandum of law that is being submitted with this motion. The Plaintiff therefore has no cause of action against the Defendant.

                    Cameron & Strauss, P.C.

                    Elizabeth A. Cameron
Date: 2/20/07   Elizabeth A. Cameron
                    Attorney for the Defendant
                    310 Lake Drive
                    Zero City, ZE 59802

supporting affidavit
An affidavit accompanying a motion that is filed by an attorney on behalf of his or her client. The sworn statements in the affidavit provide a factual basis for the motion.

memorandum of law
A document (known as a *brief* in some states) that delineates the legal theories, statutes, and cases on which a motion is based.

If defendant Peretto's attorney decides to file a motion to dismiss plaintiff Baranski's claim, she may want to attach one or more supporting affidavits—sworn statements as to certain facts that may contradict the allegations made in the complaint. Peretto's attorney may also have her paralegal draft a memorandum of law (which is called a *brief* in some states) to be submitted along with the motion to dismiss and the accompanying affidavits. The memorandum of law will present the legal basis for the motion, citing any statutes and cases that support it. A supporting affidavit gives factual support to the motion to dismiss, while the memorandum of law provides the court with the legal grounds for the dismissal of the claim.

The Scheduling Conference

After the complaint and answer have been filed, the court will typically schedule a conference to consult with the attorneys for both sides. (A party who is not represented by an attorney will attend the conference himself or herself.) Following this meeting, the judge will enter a *scheduling order* that sets out the time limits within which pretrial events (such as the pleadings, the discovery, and the final pretrial conference) must be completed, as well as the date of the trial. Under FRCP 16(b), the scheduling order should be entered "as soon as practicable but in any event within 90 days after the appearance of a defendant and within 120 days after the complaint has been served on a defendant." The purpose of this meeting is to enable the court to manage the case efficiently and establish time restrictions that are appropriate given the specific facts and circumstances involved in the case.

Amending the Pleadings

An attorney may be called on by a client to file a complaint or an answer without having much time to become familiar with the facts of the case. Because no attorney can anticipate how a case will evolve, the complaint or answer may have to be amended to account for newly discovered facts or evidence. Amendments may also be desirable when circumstances dictate that a different legal theory or defense be put forward.

PRETRIAL MOTIONS

Many motions may be made during the pretrial litigation process, including those listed and described in Exhibit 13.7. Some pretrial motions, if granted by the court, will end a case before trial. These motions include the motion to dismiss (which has already been discussed), the motion for judgment on the pleadings, and the motion for summary judgment. Here we examine the latter two motions.

Motion for Judgment on the Pleadings

motion for judgment on the pleadings
A motion that may be filed by either party in which the party asks the court to enter a judgment in his or her favor based on information contained in the pleadings. A judgment on the pleadings will only be made if there are no facts in dispute and the only question is how the law applies to a set of undisputed facts.

Once the two attorneys in the Baranski case, Gilmore and Cameron, have finished filing their respective pleadings and amendments, either one of them may file a motion for judgment on the pleadings. Motions for judgment on the pleadings are often filed when the pleadings indicate that no facts are in dispute and the only question is how the law applies to a set of undisputed facts. For example, assume for a moment that in the Baranski case, defendant Peretto admitted to all of plaintiff Baranski's allegations in his answer and raised no affirmative defenses. In this situation, Baranski's attorney, Gilmore, would file a motion for judgment on the pleadings in Baranski's favor.

EXHIBIT 13.7
Pretrial Motions

MOTION TO DISMISS

A motion filed by the defendant in which the defendant asks the court to dismiss the case for a specified reason, such as improper service, lack of personal jurisdiction, or the plaintiff's failure to state a claim for which relief can be granted.

MOTION TO STRIKE

A motion filed by the defendant in which the defendant asks the court to strike (delete) from the complaint certain of the paragraphs contained in the complaint. Motions to strike help to clarify the underlying issues that form the basis for the complaint by removing paragraphs that are redundant or irrelevant to the action.

MOTION TO MAKE MORE DEFINITE AND CERTAIN

A motion filed by the defendant to compel the plaintiff to clarify the basis of the plaintiff's cause of action. The motion is filed when the defendant believes that the complaint is too vague or ambiguous for the defendant to respond to it in a meaningful way.

MOTION FOR JUDGMENT ON THE PLEADINGS

A motion that may be filed by either party in which the party asks the court to enter a judgment in his or her favor based on information contained in the pleadings. A judgment on the pleadings will only be made if there are no facts in dispute and the only question is how the law applies to a set of undisputed facts.

MOTION TO COMPEL DISCOVERY

A motion that may be filed by either party in which the party asks the court to compel the other party to comply with a discovery request. If a party refuses to allow the opponent to inspect and copy certain documents, for example, the party requesting the documents may make a motion to compel production of the documents.

MOTION FOR SUMMARY JUDGMENT

A motion that may be filed by either party in which the party asks the court to enter judgment in his or her favor without a trial. Unlike a motion for judgment on the pleadings, a motion for summary judgment can be supported by evidence outside the pleadings, such as witnesses' affidavits, answers to interrogatories, and other evidence obtained prior to or during discovery.

Motion for Summary Judgment

A **motion for summary judgment** is similar to a motion for judgment on the pleadings in that the party filing the motion is asking the court to grant a judgment in its favor without a trial. As with a motion for judgment on the pleadings, a court will only grant a motion for summary judgment if it determines that no facts are in dispute and the only question is how the law applies to a set of facts agreed on by both parties.

When the court considers a motion for summary judgment, it can take into account *evidence outside the pleadings.* This distinguishes the motion for summary judgment from the motion to dismiss and the motion for judgment on the pleadings. To support a motion for summary judgment, one party can submit evidence obtained at any point prior to trial (including during the discovery stage of litigation—to be discussed shortly) that refutes the other party's factual claim. In the Baranski case, for example, suppose that Peretto was in

motion for summary judgment
A motion that may be filed by either party in which the party asks the court to enter judgment in his or her favor without a trial. Unlike a motion for judgment on the pleadings, a motion for summary judgment can be supported by evidence outside the pleadings, such as witnesses' affidavits, answers to interrogatories, and other evidence obtained prior to or during discovery.

Ethics Watch!

DEADLINES AND THE DUTY OF COMPETENCE

Experienced paralegals often emphasize how easy it is to miss deadlines. A very important deadline that the paralegal should always check is when the statute of limitations expires for the type of claim being made. For example, suppose that the state of Nita's statute of limitations requires Baranski to file her complaint against Peretto within two years or forever forgo the right to sue him. Also suppose that Baranski did not realize that she would always have a limp until a year or so after the accident. Baranski consults with attorney Gilmore about the matter a month before the two-year statute of limitations expires. Gilmore and his paralegal, Lopez, should immediately check the statute of limitations to make sure that they do not miss any deadlines. Otherwise, by the time Lopez completes her initial investigation into the matter, has further consultations with Baranski, and completes other preliminaries—including the drafting of the complaint—the statute might expire before the complaint is filed. All attorneys (and their paralegals) are charged with a duty of competence, and a breach of this duty (such as failing to notice and advise a client of the date on which a statute of limitations expires) may subject the attorney to a lawsuit for professional negligence (malpractice).

another state at the time of the accident. Defendant Peretto's attorney could make a motion for summary judgment in Peretto's favor and attach to the motion a witness's sworn statement that Peretto was in the other state at the time of the accident. Unless plaintiff Baranski's attorney could bring in sworn statements by other witnesses to show that Peretto was at the scene of the accident, Peretto would normally be granted his motion for summary judgment.

A motion for summary judgment would be particularly appropriate if plaintiff Baranski had previously signed a release waiving her right to sue defendant Peretto on the claim. In that situation, Peretto's attorney, Cameron, would attach a copy of the release to the motion before filing the motion with the court. Cameron would also prepare and attach a memorandum of law in support of the motion. When the motion was heard by the court, Cameron would argue that the execution of the waiver barred plaintiff Baranski from pursuing her claim against defendant Peretto.

The burden would then shift to plaintiff Baranski's attorney, Gilmore, to demonstrate that the release was invalid or otherwise not binding on Baranski. If the judge believed that the release had been voluntarily signed by plaintiff Baranski, then the judge might grant the motion for summary judgment in Peretto's favor. If attorney Gilmore convinced the judge that the release signed by Baranski had been procured by coercive or fraudulent practices, however, then the judge would deny the motion for summary judgment and permit the case to go to trial.

TRADITIONAL DISCOVERY TOOLS

Before a trial begins, the parties can use a number of procedural devices to obtain information and gather evidence about the case. Plaintiff Baranski's attorney, for example, will want to know how fast defendant Peretto was driving, whether he had been drinking, and whether

Case at a Glance

The Plaintiff—
Plaintiff: Katherine Baranski
Attorney: Allen P. Gilmore
Paralegal: Elena Lopez

The Defendant—
Defendant: Tony Peretto
Attorney: Elizabeth A. Cameron
Paralegal: Gordon McVay

Ethics Watch!

KEEPING CLIENT INFORMATION CONFIDENTIAL

As it happens, attorney Gilmore's legal assistant, Lopez, is a good friend of plaintiff Baranski's sister. Lopez learns from the results of Baranski's medical examination that Baranski has a terminal illness. Lopez is sure that the sister, who quarreled with Baranski two months ago and hasn't spoken to her since, is unaware of the illness and would probably be very hurt if she learned that Lopez knew of it and didn't tell her. Should Lopez tell her friend about the illness? No. This is confidential information at this point, which Lopez only became aware of by virtue of her job. Should the information be revealed publicly during the course of the trial, then Lopez would be free to disclose it to her friend if the friend still remained unaware of it. In the meantime, Lopez is ethically (and legally) obligated not to disclose the information to anyone who is not working on the case, including her friend.

FRCP
Federal Rules of
Civil procedures

he saw the stop sign. The process of obtaining information from the opposing party or from other witnesses is known as **discovery**.

Discovery serves several purposes. It preserves evidence from witnesses who might not be available at the time of the trial or whose memories will fade as time passes. It can pave the way for summary judgment if both parties agree on all of the facts. It can lead to an out-of-court settlement if one party decides that the opponent's case is too strong to challenge. Even if the case does go to trial, discovery prevents surprises by giving parties access to evidence that might otherwise be hidden. This allows both parties to learn as much as they can about what to expect at a trial before they reach the courtroom. It also serves to narrow the issues so that trial time is spent on the main questions in the case.

The FRCP and similar rules in the states set forth the guidelines for discovery activity. Discovery includes gaining access to witnesses, documents, records, and other types of evidence. The rules governing discovery are designed to make sure that a witness or a party is not unduly harassed, that **privileged information** (communications that ordinarily may not be disclosed in court) is safeguarded, and that only matters relevant to the case at hand are discoverable. The trend today is toward allowing more discovery and thus fewer surprises.

Traditional discovery devices include interrogatories, depositions, requests for production and physical examination, and requests for admission. Each of these discovery tools is examined below.

Interrogatories

Interrogatories are written questions that must be answered, in writing, by the parties to the lawsuit and then signed by the parties under oath. Typically, the paralegal drafts the interrogatories for the attorney's review and approval. In the Baranski case, for example, attorney Gilmore will probably ask paralegal Lopez to draft interrogatories to be sent to defendant Peretto.

discovery
Formal investigation prior to trial. During discovery, opposing parties use various methods, such as interrogatories and depositions, to obtain information from each other and from witnesses to prepare for trial.

privileged information
Confidential communications between certain individuals, such as an attorney and his or her client, that are protected from disclosure except under court order.

interrogatories
A series of written questions for which written answers are prepared and then signed under oath by a party to a lawsuit (the plaintiff or the defendant).

P. David Palmiere   FEATURED **Guest**

TEN TIPS FOR THE EFFECTIVE USE OF INTERROGATORIES

BIOGRAPHICAL NOTE

P. David Palmiere received his bachelor's degree magna cum laude in economics from the University of Michigan in 1972 and his law degree from the University of Michigan Law School in 1975. Palmiere, currently a member of the firm of Secrest, Wardle, Lynch, Hampton, Truex & Morley in Farmington Hills, Michigan, has practiced litigation for more than twenty-five years in courts from California to New York.

For the past twenty-four years, Palmiere has also been an adjunct professor in an ABA-accredited legal assistant program at Oakland University in Rochester, Michigan, where he teaches litigation and also assisted in designing the litigation specialty curriculum. Palmiere has been a guest lecturer at Wayne State University School of Law and a featured speaker at the state convention of the Legal Assistants Association of Michigan.

Interrogatories are written questions to an opposing party requiring written answers. Interrogatories are a mainstay of discovery, but often interrogatory effort is wasted because of poor topic selection or ineffective drafting. Here are some guidelines for the effective use of interrogatories.

1. Interrogatories and Answers Are a Struggle between Adversaries.   Good answers start with good questions. An interrogatory (question) is wasted if the answer is not meaningful. There are sanctions for bad faith answers to good questions. Ambiguous questions, however, allow the opponent to dodge the question without incurring sanctions. The more direct, crisp, and clear your phras-

ing, the more a fear of sanctions will compel informative answers. Always assume that your opponent will seize any excuse to decline to answer, and minimize such opportunities. If your questions pass the clarity test, they will probably be effective.

2. Limit Interrogatories to Appropriate Subjects.   There are five basic discovery tools: interrogatories, requests for production of documents and things, requests for admission, depositions, and physical or mental examinations of persons. Each tool has its own role in discovery. Interrogatories are best used to elicit concrete items of factual information, such as names, addresses, dates, times, and places. Interrogatories are usually ineffective in asking for narrative accounts of complex facts or for the basis for opinions—tasks that are more appropriate to a deposition. Similarly, instead of wasting interrogatories asking for specifics about documents (other than who has them), it is better practice to join the interrogatories to a request for production of the documents themselves. Limit interrogatories to their most appropriate purpose—learning hard, factual data.

3. Use Contention Interrogatories.   One exception to the foregoing is a "contention interrogatory," which asks the opponent for all facts supporting some assertion from the opponent's pleading. If the defendant asserts that the plaintiff's claim is barred by the statute of limitations, the plaintiff's contention interrogatory says, "Please state each fact that supports your contention that the plaintiff's claim is barred by the statute of limitations." Contention interrogatories can effectively smoke out and dispose of sham issues. Note, however, that contention interrogatories have a major blind spot: they do not elicit, except indirectly, information to *refute* the opponent's contentions. Other questions are needed for that.

4. Use Several Sets of Interrogatories at Strategic Points during the Discovery Process.   Interrogatories are primarily used early in the case to gather leads for further investigation. But interrogatories are not "just for breakfast." They are also useful to

Drafting Interrogatories

All discovery documents, including interrogatories, normally begin with a caption similar to the complaint caption illustrated earlier in this chapter. Following the caption, Lopez will add the name of the party who must answer the interrogatories, instructions to be followed by the party, and definitions of certain terms that are used in the interrogatories. The body of the document consists of the interrogatories themselves—that is, the questions that the opposing party must answer. The interrogatories should end with a signature line for the attorney, followed by the attorney's name and address.

follow up on leads developed in other discovery, such as document productions or depositions. As you read every new document and deposition, list new or unanswered questions, and consider interrogatories as the tool of choice for following up on the matter.

5. Be Aware of Court Rules Concerning Interrogatories. The court hearing the case will have rules about interrogatories. Know those rules. For example, the Federal Rules of Civil Procedure allow interrogatories only *after* the lawyers have conferred about a discovery schedule. The federal rules also require court permission to ask more than twenty-five questions, including subparts. State courts have their own rules limiting or affecting the use of interrogatories. These limitations must be observed.

6. Each Interrogatory Must Stand on Its Own—The "Stranger in the Street" Test. Interrogatory questions are often flawed because they lack context. Give every question this test: If a stranger approached you in the street, and asked the question just as you have written it, without more, could you answer it? For example, a stranger approaches you and says, "What time was it?" Your natural response would be, "What time was *what*?" or "What are you talking about?" This question does not pass the "stranger in the street" test. Any question that fails the test will probably not bring a meaningful answer from the opponent.

7. Use Definitions to Supply Context for Questions. Open your interrogatories with definitions of terms to be used, such as "the incident." Be sure that your definitions are nonargumentative—for example, if a plaintiff defines "the incident" as "the collision caused by defendant's negligence," the defendant will object to every question using the term. Then, in the interrogatories, you can ask what time "the incident" took place or who saw any part of "the

incident" without having to repeat the entire description to supply the necessary context. Once you define a term, however, use it consistently. Remember that this word now has a special meaning and cannot be used as if it were ordinary English.

8. Some Questions You *Always* Ask. Questions that you should always ask include questions about eyewitnesses, about the opponent's trial witnesses, and about the opponent's expert witnesses. Ask these even if you ask nothing else.

"Limit interrogatories to their most appropriate purpose—learning hard, factual data."

9. Master Standard Phrasing. Like other legal drafting, interrogatories tend to fall into standard patterns and phrases. Master these. Many lawyers begin each interrogatory, "Please state . . . ." If you do so, each item that follows must be an item of information. (Students often submit questions reading, "Please state each car that you own." One cannot "state" a car, but only information about the car, which is not what the question asks.) When an interrogatory contains a condition, description, or qualification, place it at the beginning of the question: "For each lawsuit to which you have ever been a party, please state . . . ." This phrasing is an effective substitute for questions that would otherwise have an "if-then" structure ("If you have ever been a party to a lawsuit, then please state . . ."). Drafting will be simpler if you use singular word forms rather than plural. When using subparts, make sure each one follows grammatically from the body of the main question.

10. Make Effective Use of the Duty to Supplement Responses. Federal Rule 26(e) and many state rules establish a duty to supplement interrogatory responses. This duty is often overlooked. Send periodic letters to the opposition, requesting supplements of prior interrogatory answers under the applicable rule. This places your side in a strong position to object if surprises are sprung at the trial.

Before drafting the questions, Lopez will want to review carefully the contents of the case file (including the pleadings and the evidence and other information that she obtained during her preliminary investigation into plaintiff Baranski's claim) and consult with attorney Gilmore on what litigation strategy should be pursued. For further guidance, she might consult form books containing sample interrogatories as well as interrogatories used in similar cases previously handled by the firm. (For tips on how to draft effective interrogatories, see this chapter's *Featured Guest* article beginning on the facing page.)

Depending on the complexity of the case, interrogatories may be few in number, or they may run into the hundreds. Exhibit 13.8 on the next two pages illustrates the types of

EXHIBIT 13.8
Sample Interrogatories

UNITED STATES DISTRICT COURT
FOR THE WESTERN DISTRICT OF NITA

Katherine Baranski)
       Plaintiff,)
)
v.   )
)
)
Tony Peretto   )
      Defendant.)

CASE NO. 07-14335-NI
Honorable Harley M. Larue

PLAINTIFF'S FIRST
INTERROGATORIES
TO DEFENDANT

    PLEASE TAKE NOTICE that the following Interrogatories are directed to you under the provisions of Rule 26(a)(5) and Rule 33 of the Federal Rules of Civil Procedure. You are requested to answer these Interrogatories and to furnish such information in answer to the Interrogatories as is available to you.

    You are required to serve integrated Interrogatories and Answers to these Interrogatories under oath, within thirty (30) days after service of them upon you. The original answers are to be retained in your attorney's possession, and a copy of the answers is to be served upon Plaintiff's counsel.

    The answers should be signed and sworn to by the person making answer to the Interrogatories.

    When used in these Interrogatories the term "Defendant," or any synonym thereof, is intended to and shall embrace and include, in addition to said Defendant, all agents, servants and employees, representatives, attorneys, private investigators, or others who are in possession of or who may have obtained information for or on behalf of the Defendant.

    These Interrogatories shall be deemed continuing, and supplemental answers shall be required immediately upon receipt thereof if Defendant, directly or indirectly, obtains further or different information from the time answers are served until the time of trial.

1.   Were you the driver of an automobile involved in an accident with Plaintiff on August 4, 2006, at about 7:45 A.M. at the intersection of Mattis Avenue and Thirty-eighth Street, in Nita City, Nita? If so, please state:

    (a) Your name;
    (b) Every name you have used in the past;
    (c) The dates you used each name;
    (d) The date and place of your birth.

2.   Please list your current residence and all residences you occupied in the five years preceding your move to your current residence, including complete addresses, dates of residence, and names of owners or managers.

3.   Please indicate where you are presently employed and where you were employed during the five years preceding the beginning of your current employment. In so doing, please indicate the following:

    (a) The names, addresses, and telephone numbers of each employer or place of business, including the dates during which you worked there;
    (b) How many hours you worked, on average, per week;
    (c) The names, addresses, and telephone numbers of your supervisors (or owners of the business);
    (d) The nature of the work that you performed.

EXHIBIT 13.8
Sample Interrogatories—Continued

4. At the time of the incident, were you acting as an agent or employee for any person? If so, state:

   (a) The name, address, and telephone number of that person;
   (b) A description of your duties.

5. At the time of the incident, did you have a driver's license? If so, state:

   (a) The state or other issuing entity;
   (b) The license number and type;
   (c) The date of issuance and expiration;
   (d) Any violations, offenses, or restrictions against your license.

6. Indicate whether you have ever had your driver's license suspended, revoked, or canceled and whether you have ever been denied the issuance of a driver's license for mental or physical reasons. If you have, please indicate the date and state of such occurrence as well as the reasons for it.

7. At the time of the incident, did you or any other person have any physical, emotional, or mental disability or condition that may have contributed to the occurrence of the incident? If so, for each person state:

   (a) The name, address, and telephone number;
   (b) The nature of the disability or condition;
   (c) The name, address, and telephone number of any qualified person who treated or diagnosed the condition and the dates of such treatment;
   (d) The manner in which the disability or condition contributed to the occurrence of the incident.

8. Within twenty-four hours before the incident, did you or any person involved in the incident use or take any of the following substances: alcoholic beverage, marijuana, or other drug or medication of any kind (prescription or not)? If so, for each person state:

   (a) The name, address, and telephone number;
   (b) The nature or description of each substance;
   (c) The quantity of each substance used or taken;
   (d) The date and time of day when each substance was used or taken;
   (e) The address where each substance was used or taken;
   (f) The name, address, and telephone number of each person who was present when each substance was used or taken;
   (g) The name, address, and telephone number of any health-care provider that prescribed or furnished the substance and the condition for which it was prescribed or furnished.

9. For each time you have had your vision checked within the last five years, please indicate the following:

   (a) The date and reason for the vision examination;
   (b) The name, address, and telephone number of the examiner;
   (c) The results and/or actions taken.

10. For each time you have had your hearing checked within the last five years, please indicate the following:

    (a) The date and reason for the hearing examination;
    (b) The name, address, and telephone number of the examiner;
    (c) The results and/or actions taken.

[Additional questions would be asked relating to the accident, including questions concerning road conditions and surface, posted speed limits, shoulders and curbs on the road, general character of the neighborhood, when the defendant noticed the plaintiff's vehicle, where it was located and the speed at which the plaintiff was traveling, whether there were other vehicles between the plaintiff's and the defendant's vehicles, and so forth.]

Dated: _____

Allen P. Gilmore
Attorney for Plaintiff

interrogatories that have traditionally been used in cases similar to the Baranski-Peretto case. Depending on the rules of the court in which the Baranski case is being filed, paralegal Lopez might draft similar interrogatories for defendant Peretto to answer. Realize that many state courts limit the number of interrogatories that can be used. FRCP 33 limits the number of interrogatories in federal court cases to twenty-five (unless a greater number is allowed by stipulation of the parties or by court order). Therefore, before drafting interrogatories, the paralegal should always check the rules of the court in which an action is being filed to find out if that court limits the number of interrogatories that can be used.

Answering Interrogatories

After receiving the interrogatories, defendant Peretto must answer them within a specified time period (thirty days under FRCP 33) in writing and under oath, as mentioned above. Very likely, he will have substantial guidance from his attorney and his attorney's paralegal in forming his answers. Peretto must answer each question truthfully, of course, because he is under oath. His attorney and her paralegal will counsel him, though, on how to phrase his answers so that they are both truthful and strategically sound. For example, they will advise Peretto on how to limit his answers to prevent disclosing more information than necessary.

Depositions

> **deposition**
>
> A pretrial question-and-answer proceeding, usually conducted orally, in which a party or witness answers an attorney's questions. The answers are given under oath, and the session is recorded.

> **deponent**
>
> A party or witness who testifies under oath during a deposition.

Like interrogatories, **depositions** are given under oath. Unlike interrogatories, however, depositions are usually conducted orally (except in certain circumstances, such as when the party being deposed is at a great distance and cannot be deposed via telephone). Furthermore, they may be taken from witnesses. As indicated earlier, interrogatories can only be taken from the parties to the lawsuit.

When an attorney takes the deposition, the attorney is able to question the person being deposed (the **deponent**) *in person* and then follow up with any other questions that come to mind. The attorney is not limited in the number of questions that she or he may ask in a deposition, whereas many courts limit the number of interrogatory questions. Moreover, because the questioning is usually done in person, the deponent must answer the questions without asking an attorney or paralegal how he or she should respond. Thus, the answers to deposition questions are not filtered through counsel in the same way answers to interrogatories are.

Normally, the defendant's attorney deposes the plaintiff first, and then the plaintiff's attorney deposes the defendant. Following these depositions, the attorneys may depose witnesses and other parties to obtain information about the event leading to the lawsuit. When both the defendant and the plaintiff are located in the same jurisdiction, the site of the deposition will usually be the offices of the attorney requesting the deposition. When the parties are located in different jurisdictions, other arrangements may be made. In the Baranski case, attorney Gilmore will travel to defendant Peretto's city, which is located in another state, and depose Peretto in the office of Peretto's attorney, Cameron.

Procedure for Taking Depositions

> **subpoena**
>
> A document commanding a person to appear at a certain time and place to give testimony concerning a certain matter.

The attorney wishing to depose a party or witness must give reasonable notice in writing to all other parties in the case. This is done by serving the opposing attorney (or attorneys) with a notice of taking deposition, which states the time and place of the deposition and the name of the person being examined (see Exhibit 13.9).

If the person scheduled to be deposed would not attend voluntarily, a paralegal may also need to prepare a subpoena for deposition and submit it to the court for signature. Generally, a **subpoena** is an order issued by the court clerk directing a party to appear and

EXHIBIT 13.9
Notice of Taking Deposition

UNITED STATES DISTRICT COURT
FOR THE WESTERN DISTRICT OF NITA

Katherine Baranski)
   Plaintiff,)
) CASE NO. 07-14335-NI
) Honorable Harley M. Larue
v.   )
) NOTICE OF TAKING
) DEPOSITION
Tony Peretto   )
   Defendant.)

TO: Elizabeth A. Cameron
   Cameron & Strauss, P.C.
   310 Lake Drive
   Zero City, ZE 59802

  PLEASE TAKE NOTICE that Katherine Baranski, by and through her attorneys, Jeffers, Gilmore & Dunn, will take the deposition of Tony Peretto on Wednesday, April 15, 2007, at 1:30 P.M., at the law offices of Cameron & Strauss, P.C., 310 Lake Drive, Zero City, ZE 59802, pursuant to the Federal Rules of Civil Procedure, before a duly authorized and qualified notary and stenographer.

Dated: March 20, 2007   Jeffers, Gilmore & Dunn

           Allen P. Gilmore
           Allen P. Gilmore
           Attorney for Katherine Baranski
           553 Fifth Avenue, Suite 101
           Nita City, NI 48801

to testify at trial, as will be discussed in Chapter 15. A *subpoena for deposition* orders the person to appear at a deposition rather than in a court proceeding. A subpoena should also be prepared if the attorney wants the deponent to bring certain documents or tangible things to the deposition (this is called a *subpoena duces tecum*).

Under FRCP 30 and 31, court permission is required for depositions to be taken before the parties have made the initial disclosures required by Rule 26 (discussed later in this chapter). Also, court approval may be required if either party wants to take more than one deposition from the same person or more than a total of ten depositions in the case.

Drafting Deposition Questions

Depositions are conducted by attorneys. Although paralegals may attend depositions, they do not ask questions. Deposition questions are often drafted by paralegals, however. In the Baranski case, for example, attorney Gilmore might ask paralegal Lopez to draft questions for a deposition of defendant Peretto or someone else, such as an eyewitness to the accident. For Peretto's deposition, Lopez might draft questions similar to those presented in Exhibit 13.10 on the next page. Attorney Gilmore can then use Lopez's questions as a kind of checklist during the deposition. Note, though, that Gilmore's questions will not be limited to the questions included in the list. Other, unforeseen questions may arise as Gilmore learns new information during the deposition. Also, the deponent's answer to one question may reveal the answer to another, so that not all questions will need to be asked.

EXHIBIT 13.10
Sample Deposition Questions

DEPOSITION QUESTIONS

1. Please state your full name and address for the record.
2. Please state your age, birth date, and Social Security number.
3. What is your educational level, and what employment position do you hold?
4. Do you have a criminal record, and if so, for what?
5. Have you been involved in previous automobile accidents? What driving violations have you had? Has your driver's license ever been suspended?
6. What is your medical history? Have you ever had health problems? Are you in perfect health? Were you in perfect health at the time of the accident?
7. Do you wear glasses or contact lenses? If so, for what condition? Were you wearing your glasses or contacts at the time the accident occurred?
8. Do you take medication of any kind?
9. Do you have any similar lawsuits or any claims pending against you?
10. Who is your automobile insurer? What are your policy limits?
11. Were there any passengers in your vehicle at the time of the accident?
12. Describe your vehicle. What was the mechanical condition of your vehicle at the time of the accident? Do you do your own mechanical work? If so, what training do you have in maintaining and repairing automobiles? Had you taken your vehicle to a professional mechanic's shop prior to the accident?
13. Please state the date on which the accident occurred.
14. Where were you prior to the accident, for at least the six hours preceding the accident?
15. Where were you going when the accident occurred, and for what purpose?
16. What were you doing during the last few moments before the accident? Were you smoking, eating, drinking, or chewing gum?
17. What were you thinking about just before the accident occurred?
18. What route did you take to reach your destination, and why did you take this particular route?
19. Describe the weather conditions at the time of the accident.
20. Please recite the facts of how the accident occurred.
21. Please describe the area in which the accident occurred. Were there many cars and pedestrians on the streets? Were there traffic controls, obstructions, or the like?
22. What was your location, and in what direction were you going?
23. When did you see the plaintiff's automobile approaching?
24. How far away were you when you first saw the auto? What was your rate of speed?
25. Did your vehicle move forward or was it pushed backward by the impact?
26. When did you first apply your brakes? Were your brakes functioning properly?
27. Did you attempt to avoid the accident? If so, how?
28. Did you receive a traffic ticket as a result of the accident?
29. Do you own the vehicle that you were driving at the time of the accident?
30. Were you acting within the scope of your employment when the accident occurred?
31. What were the conditions of the parties affected by the accident just after the accident occurred?
32. Did you attempt to provide first aid to any party?
33. How did the plaintiff leave the scene, and what was the plaintiff's physical condition?
34. What was the damage to your vehicle, and has it been repaired?

Preparing the Client for a Deposition

No attorney can predict a deponent's answers beforehand. Spontaneous and perhaps even contradictory statements can seriously damage the deponent's case. For this reason, the deposed party and his or her lawyer will want to prepare for the deposition by formulating mock answers to anticipated questions. For example, if defendant Peretto's attorney plans to depose plaintiff Baranski, attorney Gilmore and paralegal Lopez might have Baranski come into their office for a run-through of possible questions that Peretto's attorney might ask her

Developing Paralegal Skills

DEPOSITION SUMMARIES

After a deposition is taken, each attorney orders a copy of the deposition transcript. Copies may be obtained in printed form or on a CD-ROM, a DVD, or online. When the transcript is received, the legal assistant's job is to prepare a summary of the testimony that was given. The summary is typically only a few pages in length.

The legal assistant must be very familiar with the lawsuit and the legal theories that are being pursued so that he or she can point out inconsistencies in the testimony or between the testimony and the pleadings. The paralegal might also give special emphasis to any testimony that will help to prove the client's case in court.

After the deposition summary has been created, the paralegal places the summary in the litigation file, usually in a special discovery folder or binder within the larger file. The deposition summary will be used to prepare for future depositions, to prepare pretrial motions, and to impeach witnesses at the trial, should they give contradictory testimony.

TIPS FOR SUMMARIZING A DEPOSITION

- Find out how the deposition is to be summarized—by chronology, by legal issue, by factual issues, or otherwise.
- Read through the deposition transcript and mark important pages.
- Using a dictaphone or dictation software, dictate a summary of the information on the marked pages.
- Be sure to include a reference to the page and line that is being summarized.
- Take advantage of software that will assist in summarizing the deposition transcript.

---

during the deposition. This kind of preparation does not mean that the lawyer tells the deponent what to say. Instead, the lawyer offers suggestions as to how the answers to certain questions should be phrased. The answers must be truthful, but the truth can be presented in many ways.

Gilmore would also caution Baranski to limit her responses to the questions and not to engage in speculative answers that might prejudice her claim. If plaintiff Baranski was asked whether she had ever been involved in an automobile accident before, for example, Gilmore would probably caution her to use a simple (but truthful) "yes" or "no" answer. Attorney Gilmore normally would permit Baranski to volunteer additional information only in response to precisely phrased questions.

The Role of the Deponent's Attorney

The deponent's attorney will attend the deposition, but the attorney's role will be limited. Under FRCP 30, the attorney may instruct a deponent not to answer a question only when necessary to preserve a privilege, to enforce a limitation directed by the court, or to present a motion to terminate the deposition. In other words, if plaintiff Baranski was being deposed by defendant Peretto's attorney, Cameron, she would have to answer Cameron's questions even if the questions were not clearly relevant to the issues of the case—unless the court had previously limited this line of questioning. The deponent's attorney, Gilmore, could object only to questions that called for privileged information to be disclosed. Under Rule 30, that attorney is also required to state objections concisely, in a nonargumentative and nonsuggestive manner.

Case at a Glance

The Plaintiff—
 Plaintiff: Katherine Baranski
 Attorney: Allen P. Gilmore
 Paralegal: Elena Lopez

The Defendant—
 Defendant: Tony Peretto
 Attorney: Elizabeth A. Cameron
 Paralegal: Gordon McVay

As will be discussed shortly, deposition proceedings are recorded. If both attorneys agree to do so, however, they can go "off the record" to clarify a point or discuss a disputed issue. Depositions are stressful events, and tempers often flare. In the event that the deposition can no longer be conducted in an orderly fashion, the attorney conducting the deposition may have to terminate it.

The Deposition Transcript

deposition transcript
The official transcription of the recording taken during a deposition.

Every utterance made during a deposition is recorded. A court reporter will usually record the deposition proceedings and create an official **deposition transcript**. Methods of recording a deposition include stenographic recording (a traditional method that involves the use of a shorthand machine), tape recording, videotape or digital recording, or some combination of these methods. Rule 30(b)(2) of the FRCP states that unless the court orders otherwise, a deposition "may be recorded by sound, sound-and-visual, or stenographic means."

impeach
To call into question the credibility of a witness by challenging the truth or accuracy of his or her trial statement.

The deposition transcript may be used by either party during the trial to prove a particular point or to **impeach** (call into question) the credibility of a witness who says something during the trial that is different from what he or she stated during the deposition. For example, a witness in the Baranski case might state during the deposition that defendant Peretto *did not* stop at the stop sign before proceeding to cross Mattis Avenue. If, at trial, the witness states that Peretto *did* stop at the stop sign before crossing Mattis Avenue, plaintiff Baranski's attorney (Gilmore) could challenge the witness's credibility on the basis of the deposition transcript. Exhibit 13.11 shows a page from a transcript of a deposition conducted by attorney Gilmore in the Baranski case. The deponent was Julia Williams, an eye-witness to the accident. On the transcript, the letter "Q" precedes each question asked by Gilmore, and the letter "A" precedes each of Williams's answers.

Summarizing and Indexing the Deposition Transcript

On the Web

If you are interested in the history of court reporting, visit the Web site of the National Court Reporters Association at **http://www.ncraonline.org/ aboutNCRA/History**.

Typically, the paralegal will summarize the deposition transcript. The summary, which along with the transcript will become part of the litigation file, allows the members of the litigation team to review quickly the information obtained from the deponent during the deposition.

In the Baranski case, assume that paralegal Lopez is asked to summarize the deposition transcript of Julia Williams. Typically, the transcript is summarized sequentially—that is, in the order in which it was given during the deposition—as shown in Exhibit 13.12 on page 486. Notice that the summary includes the page and line numbers in the deposition transcript where the full text of the information can be found.

Often, in addition to summarizing the transcript, the paralegal provides an index to the document. The index consists of a list of topics (such as education, employment status, injuries, and medical costs) followed by the relevant page and line numbers of the deposition transcript. Together, the summary and the index allow anyone involved in the case to locate information quickly. Today, key-word indexes allow attorneys and paralegals to locate within seconds deposition testimony on a particular topic. Often, court reporters will provide key-word indexes on request.

Requests for Production and Physical Examination

Another traditional method of discovery is the request for the production of documents or tangible things or for permission to enter on land or other property for inspection and other purposes. FRCP 34 authorizes each party to request documents and other forms of evidence from any other party. If the item requested is very large or cannot be "produced" for some reason (Baranski's car, for example), then the party can request permission to enter on the other party's land to inspect, test, sample, and photograph the item. In federal courts,

EXHIBIT 13.11
A Deposition Transcript (Excerpt)

67	Q: Where were you at the time of the accident?
68	A: I was on the southwest corner of the intersection.
69	Q: Are you referring to the intersection where Thirty-eighth Street crosses Mattis Avenue?
70	A: Yes.
71	Q: Why were you there at the time of the accident?
72	A: Well, I was on my way to work. I usually walk down Mattis Avenue to the hospital.
73	Q: So you were walking to work down Mattis Avenue and you saw the accident?
74	A: Yes.
75	Q: What did you see?
76	A: Well, as I was about to cross the street, a dark green van passed within three feet of me and ran the
77	stop sign and crashed into another car.
78	Q: Can you remember if the driver of the van was a male or a female?
79	A: Yes. It was a man.
80	Q: I am showing you a picture. Can you identify the man in the picture?
81	A: Yes. That is the man who was driving the van.
82	Q: Do you wear glasses?
83	A: I need glasses only for reading. I have excellent distance vision.
84	Q: How long has it been since your last eye exam with a doctor?
85	A: Oh, just a month ago, with Dr. Sullivan.

page 4

the duty of disclosure under FRCP 26 (to be discussed shortly) has greatly decreased the need to file such production requests.

When the mental or physical condition of a party is in controversy, the opposing party may also request the court to order the party to submit to a physical or mental examination by a licensed examiner. For example, if defendant Peretto claims that plaintiff Baranski's injuries were the result of a preexisting medical condition, rather than the collision, defense attorney Cameron may file a request to have Baranski examined by a licensed physician. Because the existence, nature, and extent of Baranski's injuries are important in calculating the damages that she might be able to recover from Peretto, the court may order Baranski to undergo a physical examination if requested.

Requests for Admission

During discovery, a party can also request that the opposing party admit the truth of matters relating to the case. For example, plaintiff Baranski's attorney can request that defendant Peretto admit that he did not stop at the stop sign before crossing Mattis Avenue at Thirty-eighth Street.

Case at a Glance

The Plaintiff—
Plaintiff: Katherine Baranski
Attorney: Allen P. Gilmore
Paralegal: Elena Lopez

The Defendant—
Defendant: Tony Peretto
Attorney: Elizabeth A. Cameron
Paralegal: Gordon McVay

EXHIBIT 13.12
A Deposition Summary (Excerpt)

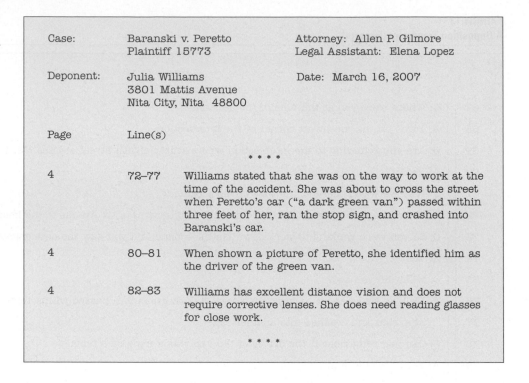

Case:	Baranski v. Peretto Plaintiff 15773	Attorney: Allen P. Gilmore Legal Assistant: Elena Lopez
Deponent:	Julia Williams 3801 Mattis Avenue Nita City, Nita 48800	Date: March 16, 2007

Page	Line(s)	
		* * * *
4	72–77	Williams stated that she was on the way to work at the time of the accident. She was about to cross the street when Peretto's car ("a dark green van") passed within three feet of her, ran the stop sign, and crashed into Baranski's car.
4	80–81	When shown a picture of Peretto, she identified him as the driver of the green van.
4	82–83	Williams has excellent distance vision and does not require corrective lenses. She does need reading glasses for close work.
		* * * *

Such admissions save time at trial because the parties will not have to spend time proving facts on which they already agree. Any matter admitted under such a request is conclusively established as true for the trial. FRCP 36 permits requests for admission but stipulates that a request for admission cannot be made, without the court's permission, prior to the prediscovery meeting of the attorneys. In view of the limitations on the number of interrogatories under the FRCP (and under some state procedural rules), requests for admission are a particularly useful discovery tool.

THE DUTY TO DISCLOSE UNDER FRCP 26

In federal courts prior to 1993, if an attorney wanted to obtain information or evidence that was in the possession of another party, she or he had to ask for it using one of the traditional discovery methods already discussed. In 1993, amendments to the FRCP significantly changed the discovery rules in federal courts, and these changes have influenced state rules on civil procedure. Today, each party to a lawsuit has a duty to disclose to the other party specified types of information prior to the discovery stage of litigation. Under Rule 26(f), once a lawsuit is brought, the parties (the plaintiff and defendant and/or their attorneys, if the parties are represented by counsel) must schedule a prediscovery meeting to discuss the nature of the lawsuit, any defenses that may be raised against the claims being brought, and possibilities for promptly settling or otherwise resolving the dispute. The meeting should take place as soon as practicable but at least fourteen days before a scheduling conference is held or a scheduling order issued. Either at this meeting or within ten days after it, the parties must also make the initial disclosures described below and submit to the court a plan for discovery. As the trial date approaches, the attorneys must make subsequent disclosures relating to witnesses, documents, and other information that is relevant to the case.

These rules do not replace the traditional methods of discovery discussed in the preceding section. Rather, the rules impose a duty on attorneys to disclose specified information automatically to opposing counsel early in the litigation process so that the time and costs of traditional discovery methods can be reduced. Attorneys may still use the traditional discovery tools (depositions and interrogatories, for instance) to obtain information, but they cannot use these methods until the prediscovery meeting has been held and initial disclosures have been made. Also, to save the court's time, the rules give attorneys a freer hand in crafting a discovery plan that is appropriate to the nature of the claim and the parties' needs.[6]

Initial Disclosures

FRCP 26(a)(1) requires each party to disclose the following information to the other party either at an initial meeting of the parties or within ten days following the meeting:

- The name, address, and telephone number of any person who is likely to have "discoverable information" and the nature of that information.
- A copy or "description by category and location" of all documents, data, and other "things in the possession, custody, or control of the party" that are relevant to the dispute.
- A computation of the damages being claimed by the disclosing party. The party must make available to the other party, for inspection and copying, documents and other materials on which the computation of damages is based, "including materials bearing on the nature and extent of injuries suffered."
- Copies of any insurance policies that cover the injuries or harms alleged in the lawsuit and that may pay part or all of a judgment (damages, for example) resulting from the dispute.

In the Baranski case, attorney Gilmore and paralegal Lopez must work quickly to assemble all relevant information, documents, and other evidence that Lopez has gathered during client interviews and during her preliminary investigation into the case. Lopez will prepare copies of the documents or other information—or a description of them—for attorney Gilmore's review and signature. The copies or descriptions will then be filed with the court and delivered to defendant Peretto's attorney.

Note that in the information disclosed to defendant Peretto's attorney, paralegal Lopez must include even information that might be damaging to Baranski's position. Lopez need not disclose *privileged information,* however, such as confidential discussions between Baranski and attorney Gilmore. If defendant Peretto's attorney seeks information that attorney Gilmore claims is privileged, Peretto's attorney will be able to obtain that information only through a court order.

Failure to Disclose

A party will not be excused from disclosing relevant information simply because the party has not yet completed an investigation into the case or because the other party has not yet disclosed the required information. FRCP 37(c) makes it clear that the failure to make these initial disclosures can result in serious sanctions. If a party fails to disclose certain relevant information, that party will not be able to use the information as evidence at trial. In addition, the court may impose other sanctions, such as ordering the party to pay reasonable expenses, including attorneys' fees, created by the failure to disclose. In sum, attorney Gilmore and paralegal Lopez need to make sure that all relevant information (that is not privileged) is disclosed, or Gilmore will not be able to use it in court (and may face other sanctions as well).

Discovery Plan

As mentioned above, at the initial meeting of the parties, the attorneys must work out a **discovery plan** and submit a report describing the plan to the court within ten days of the meeting. The type of information to be included in the discovery plan is illustrated in

discovery plan
A plan formed by the attorneys litigating a lawsuit, on behalf of their clients, that indicates the types of information that will be disclosed by each party to the other prior to trial, the testimony and evidence that each party will or may introduce at trial, and the general schedule for pretrial disclosures and events.

EXHIBIT 13.13
Form 35—Report of Parties' Planning Meeting (Discovery Plan)

[Caption and Names of Parties]

1. Pursuant to Fed. R. Civ. P. 26(f), a meeting was held on _____(date)_____ at _____(place)_____ and was attended by:

_____(name)_____ for plaintiff(s) _____(party name)_____
_____(name)_____ for defendant(s) _____(party name)_____
_____(name)_____ for defendant(s) _____(party name)_____

2. Pre-Discovery Disclosures. The parties [have exchanged] [will exchange by _____(date)_____] the information required by [Fed. R. Civ. P. 26(a)(1)] [(local rule _____)].

3. Discovery Plan. The parties jointly propose to the court the following discovery plan: [Use separate paragraphs or subparagraphs as necessary if parties disagree.]

Discovery will be needed on the following subjects:
_____(brief description of subjects on which discovery will be needed)_____
All discovery commenced in time to be completed by __(date)__. [Discovery on__(issue for early discovery)__ to be completed by _____(date)_____.]
Maximum of ____ interrogatories by each party to any other party. [Responses due ____ days after service.]
Maximum of ____ requests for admission by each party to any other party. [Responses due ____ days after service.]
Maximum of ____ depositions by plaintiff(s) and ____ by defendant(s).
Each deposition [other than of _____] limited to maximum of ____ hours unless extended by agreement of parties.
Reports from retained experts under Rule 26(a)(2) due:
     from plaintiff(s) by _____(date)_____.
     from defendant(s) by _____(date)_____.
Supplementations under Rule 26(e) due (time(s) or intervals(s)).

4. Other Items. [Use separate paragraphs or subparagraphs as necessary if parties disagree.]

The parties [request] [do not request] a conference with the court before entry of the scheduling order.
The parties request a pretrial conference in____(month and year)____.
Plaintiff(s) should be allowed until __(date)__ to join additional parties and until __(date)__ to amend the pleadings.
Defendant(s) should be allowed until __(date)__ to join additional parties and until __(date)__ to amend the pleadings.
All potentially dispositive motions should be filed by__(date)__.
Settlement [is likely] [is unlikely] [cannot be evaluated prior to __(date)__] [may be enhanced by use of the following alternative dispute resolution procedure: _____].
Final lists of witnesses and exhibits under Rule 26(a)(3) should be due
     from plaintiff(s) by __(date)__.
     from defendant(s) by __(date)__.
Parties should have _____ days after service of final lists of witnesses and exhibits to list objections under Rule 26(a)(3).
The case should be ready for trial by __(date)__ [and at the time is expected to take approximately __(length of time)__].
[Other matters.]

Date: _____

Exhibit 13.13, which shows Form 35, a form generated for this purpose. As indicated by the form, Rule 26(f) allows the attorneys substantial room to negotiate the details of discovery, including the time schedules to be followed.

In the Baranski case, paralegal Lopez will make sure that attorney Gilmore takes a copy of Form 35 with him to the initial prediscovery meeting of the parties to use as a checklist. After the attorneys decide on the details of the plan to be proposed to the court, attorney Gilmore will probably have paralegal Lopez draft a final version of the plan for his review and signature.

Subsequent Disclosures

In addition to the initial disclosures just discussed, each party must make other disclosures prior to trial. All subsequent disclosures must also be made in writing, signed by the attorneys, and filed with the court. Subsequent disclosures include information relating to expert witnesses and other witnesses and exhibits that will or may be used at trial.

Expert Witnesses

Under FRCP 26(a)(2), each party must disclose to the other party the names of any expert witnesses who may be called to testify during the trial. Additionally, the following information about each expert witness must be disclosed in a report signed by the expert witness:

- A statement by the expert witness indicating the opinions that will be expressed, the basis for the opinions, and the data or information considered by the witness when forming the opinions.

- Any exhibits that will be used to summarize or support the opinions.

- The qualifications of the expert witness, including a list of all publications authored by the witness within the preceding ten years.

- The compensation to be paid to the expert witness.

- A list of any other cases in which the witness has testified as an expert at trial or by deposition within the preceding four years.

These disclosures must be made either at times set by the court or, if the court does not indicate any times, at least ninety days prior to the trial date.

Other Pretrial Disclosures

Under revised FRCP 26(a)(3), each party must also disclose to the other party the following information about other witnesses that will testify at trial or any exhibits that will or may be used:

- A list containing the names, addresses, and telephone numbers of other witnesses that may or will be called during the trial to give testimony. The witness list must indicate whether the witness "will be called" or "may be called."

- A list of any witnesses whose deposition testimony may be offered during the trial and a transcript of the relevant sections of the deposition testimony, if the testimony was not taken stenographically.

- A list of exhibits that indicates which exhibits will be offered and which exhibits may be offered if the need arises.

These disclosures must be made at least thirty days before trial, unless the court orders otherwise. Once the disclosures have been made, the opposing party has fourteen days within which to file with the court any objections to the use of any deposition or exhibit. If objections are not made, they are deemed to be waived (unless a party can show good cause why he or she failed to object to the disclosures within the fourteen-day time period).

An attorney's duty to disclose relevant information is ongoing throughout the pretrial stage. Any time an attorney learns about relevant supplemental information concerning statements or responses made earlier, that information must be disclosed to the other party.

DISCOVERY OF ELECTRONIC EVIDENCE

Over the last decade, electronic evidence has significantly changed litigation and has become a major consideration in pretrial discovery. Electronic evidence, or e-evidence, consists of all computer-generated or electronically recorded information, such as e-mail, voice mail, spreadsheets, word-processing documents, and other data. E-evidence has become increasingly important because it can reveal significant facts that are not discoverable by other means. The Federal Rules of Civil Procedure and most state rules (as well as court decisions) specifically allow discovery of electronic "data compilations" (or e-evidence).

The discovery of e-evidence is fundamentally different from the discovery of paper documents and physical evidence, although traditional discovery methods, such as interrogatories and depositions, are still used in obtaining it. The following subsections describe the features of e-evidence that make it uniquely important. They are intended only as an introduction to the rapidly advancing area of electronic evidence. For a discussion of the costs of electronic discovery, see this chapter's *Technology and Today's Paralegal* feature.

The Advantages of Electronic Evidence

E-evidence has several distinct advantages over paper discovery. People and businesses use computers to store and communicate enormous amounts of data. A great deal of the information stored on computers (20 to 30 percent) is never printed on paper. In addition, whenever a person is working on a computer, information is being recorded on the hard drive without being saved by the user. This information, called **metadata**, is the hidden data kept by the computer about a file, including location, path, creator, date created, date last accessed, hidden notes, earlier versions, passwords, and formatting. It reveals information about how, when, and by whom a file was created, accessed, modified, and transmitted. This information can only be obtained from the file in its electronic format—not from printed versions.

metadata

Embedded electronic data recorded by a computer in association with a particular file, including location, path, creator, date created, date last accessed, hidden notes, earlier versions, passwords, and formatting. Metadata reveal information about how, when, and by whom a document was created, accessed, modified, and transmitted.

E-Mail Communications

Today, millions of e-mail messages are sent each year, and it is commonplace to use e-mail at work and at home. Because e-mail is so widespread, it has become a fertile ground for gathering evidence in litigation. In fact, some believe that e-mail is the "smoking gun" of the future. This is largely due to the fact that most people converse freely and informally in their e-mail communications, as if talking to a close friend or business associate. This makes e-mail very believable and compelling evidence—evidence that can be very damaging if discovered by outsiders.

In addition, in its electronic form, e-mail contains information that provides links to other e-mails, e-mail attachments, erased files, and metadata. These metadata reveal the identity of any person who received copies of an e-mail message (even "blind" copies). Thus, e-evidence can be used to trace a message to its true originator, reconstruct an e-mail conversation, and establish a timeline of the events in dispute (who knew what, when). Attorneys also use it to verify the client's claims or discredit the claims of the opposition. Whether it is evidence of adultery, sexual harassment, employment discrimination, fraud, or the theft of trade secrets, e-mail often contains the most compelling evidence in a case.

Deleted Files Can Be Retrieved

Another major advantage of e-evidence is that even deleted files can often be retrieved from the "residual data" within the computer. This is because deleting a file does not actually destroy the data but simply makes the space occupied by those data available to be overwritten by new information. Until that space is actually used for new data (which may be in weeks, in months, or never), the deleted record can be retrieved with special software.

Technology and Today's Paralegal

WHO BEARS THE COSTS OF ELECTRONIC DISCOVERY?

Traditionally, the party responding to a discovery request has had to pay the expenses involved in obtaining the requested materials. If compliance would be too burdensome or too costly, however, the judge could either limit the scope of the request or shift some or all of the costs to the requesting party. How do these traditional rules governing discovery apply to requests for electronic evidence?

WHY COURTS MIGHT SHIFT THE COSTS OF ELECTRONIC DISCOVERY

Electronic discovery has dramatically increased the costs associated with complying with discovery requests. It is no longer simply a matter of photocopying paper documents. Now the responding party may need to hire computer forensics experts to make "image" copies of desktop, laptop, and server hard drives, as well as removable storage media (including CD-ROMs, DVDs, and flash drives), back-up tapes, voice mail, cell phones, and any other form of digitally stored data.

   In cases involving multiple parties or large corporations with many offices and employees, the electronic discovery process can easily run into hundreds of thousands—if not millions—of dollars. In one case, for example, concert promoters alleged that thirty separate defendant companies had engaged in discriminatory practices. The federal district court hearing the case found that the complete restoration of the back-up tapes of just one of those defendants would cost $9.75 million. Acquiring 200,000 e-mail messages from another defendant would cost between $43,000 and $84,000, with an additional $247,000 required to pay an attorney to review the retrieved documents. Restoring the 523 back-up tapes of a third defendant would cost $395,000 plus $120,000 for the attorney to review them. The judge hearing the case decided that the plaintiffs and defendants would share in these discovery costs.[a]

WHAT FACTORS DO COURTS CONSIDER IN DECIDING WHETHER TO SHIFT COSTS?

Increasingly, the courts are shifting part of the costs of obtaining electronic discovery to the party requesting it (which is usually the plaintiff). At what point, however, should this cost-shifting occur? In *Zubulake v. UBS Warburg LLC,*[b] the court identified a three-step analysis for deciding disputes over discovery costs. First, if the data are kept in an accessible format, the usual rules of discovery apply: the responding party should pay the costs of producing the data. A court should consider cost-shifting only when electronic data are in a relatively inaccessible form, such as in back-up tapes or deleted files.

   Second, the court should determine what data may be found on the inaccessible media and whether a sampling of the data might be sufficient. Requiring the responding party to restore and produce documents from a small sample of the requested medium is a sensible approach in most cases. Third, the court should consider a series of other factors, including, for example, the availability of the information from other sources, the total cost of producing the information compared with the amount in controversy, and each party's ability to pay these costs.

TECHNOLOGY TIP

Paralegals should keep in mind not only the high costs of some electronic discovery requests but also the possibility that the court may shift some of these costs to the party requesting discovery. Suppose, for example, that you are assisting a corporate defendant in a product liability lawsuit brought by a plaintiff who was seriously harmed by one of the defendant's products. If the plaintiff requests extensive electronic evidence during discovery, the defendant corporation may be required to pay a significant portion of the costs of the discovery.

a. *Rowe Entertainment, Inc. v. William Morris Agency,* 2002 WL 975713 (S.D.N.Y. 2003).
b. 2003 WL 21087884 (S.D.N.Y. 2003).

Developing Paralegal Skills

ELECTRONIC DISCOVERY

Paralegals, particularly litigation paralegals, need to be prepared to deal with electronic discovery. This means not only formulating electronic discovery plans but also making sure to preserve the integrity of any electronic evidence acquired. It is important, too, to remember that e-evidence is fragile. Although—as discussed in the chapter text—it may be difficult to truly delete files from a computer system, it is certainly not impossible. Every time a user enters new data, loads new software, or performs routine maintenance procedures, the data on the computer are permanently altered. Just booting up a computer can change dates and times on numerous files. The following are some general guidelines to follow in conducting e-discovery.

TIPS FOR CONDUCTING E-DISCOVERY

- Write a preservation-of-evidence letter to all parties involved, including your own client, at the outset of discovery. This letter informs the parties that they have a duty to take immediate action to preserve the evidence.

- Use interrogatories to gather information about the opposing party's computer system so that you can learn as much as you can about the system with which you are dealing.

- Follow up with depositions. Once you know the names of the parties who oversee the system or have special knowledge of it, take depositions from them.

- After you have found out the details of where electronic evidence is located, draft a request for production of the evidence.

- When the e-evidence is acquired, determine how best to manage, review, and interpret the data, which may involve using the services of an outside company that specializes in this field.

Most people believe that when they delete a record or e-mail and empty the recycle bin, the message is gone from their computer. This increases the probability of candid e-mail communications. As just described, however, deleted data remain on the computer until overwritten by new data (or wiped out by certain utility software). In fact, experts have even been able to retrieve data, in whole or in part, from computers that have been damaged by water, fire, or severe impact. Therefore, don't assume that e-evidence is not available just because a file was deleted, a computer was damaged, or a utility program was run.

The Sources of Electronic Evidence

Key to conducting electronic discovery is developing an understanding of the kinds of information that computers can provide so that you will know where to look for particular kinds of information. Generally, computer data can be located in active files, in back-up files, or as residual data. Active files are those currently accessible on the computer (word-processing documents, e-mail, and spreadsheets, for example). Back-up files are those that have been copied to removable media such as flash pen drives, CDs, or DVDs. As mentioned, residual data are data that appear to be gone but are still recoverable from somewhere on the computer system. Residual data no longer have pointers to indicate their location and can only be retrieved by special software.

Back-Up Data

Back-up files can be a source of hidden treasure for the legal team. Reviewing back-up copies of documents and e-mail provides useful information about how a particular matter progressed over several weeks or months.

Many companies back up data at routine intervals (weekly or monthly), while others have no formal back-up schedule. Some companies have back-up routines for word-processing documents but not for e-mail. Back-up copies may also be made automatically by word-processing software or individually by a user. Sometimes, a person makes back-up copies of work files for use on his or her home computer. Because the current location of the data depends on which back-up process is used, you need to find out the individual's or business's back-up policy (or practice) as soon as you can during discovery.

Note that back-up files contain not only the e-mail messages and word-processing documents but also other embedded information that can be useful. For example, when computers are networked, computer logs and audit trails that keep track of network usage may be available. An audit trail will tell you who accessed the system, when it was accessed, and whether those who accessed the system copied, downloaded, modified, or deleted any files. In addition, back-up data files include certain nonprinting information, such as the date and time the files were created. Some word-processing software allows users to insert hidden comments or track changes while drafting and revising documents. These comments and revisions can also be accessed from the electronic version of the back-up file.

Other Sources of E-Evidence

It is important to remember that electronic evidence is not limited to the data found on computer systems. As stated, e-evidence includes *all* electronically recorded information, such as voice mail; back-up voice mail; video; electronic calendars; phone logs; Palm Pilots, Blackberries, and other personal digital assistants; laptops; cell phones; and any other devices that digitally store data. You should not overlook any possible sources of e-evidence during discovery. Use traditional discovery tactics (such as interrogatories and depositions) to find out about other sources of potential e-evidence. Consider and ask about all possible sources that might prove fruitful.

The Special Requirements of Electronic Evidence

The law has been developing to accommodate electronic evidence. It is clear that while most courts allow discovery of electronic evidence, judges also recognize that electronic evidence can be easily manipulated. To ensure that the evidence you obtain during discovery will be admissible as evidence in court, you must do two things. First, make sure that you obtain an exact image copy of the electronic evidence, as described shortly. Second, make sure that you can prove that nothing has been altered or changed from the time the image copy was made.

Acquiring an Image Copy

In order to use any evidence in court, you must convince the court that the evidence is authentic. In the case of electronic evidence, you must show that the electronic version of the evidence that you have acquired is exactly the same as the version that was present on the target system. The only way to do this is to have an image copy made.

Suppose the target system is a computer hard drive. Making an image copy would involve creating a sector-by-sector mirror image of the drive being copied. The image copy would capture all data, including residual data. This is much different from the usual file-by-file back-up copying method.

Today's Professional Paralegal

WITNESS COORDINATION

Barbara Lyons works as a paralegal for a busy litigation firm. Today she is assisting with a medical-malpractice trial. Susan Weiss, the attorney for whom Barbara works, has asked Barbara to coordinate Susan's witnesses. It is 8:30 A.M., and Barbara and Susan are waiting in the courtroom for Dr. Max Brennan, the first witness that Susan will call today.

PLANNING A WITNESS'S ARRIVAL TIME

While they are waiting, Susan fills Barbara in on how the trial went yesterday and what she expects to happen today. Susan tells Barbara that she expects Dr. Brennan to be on the stand testifying from 9 A.M. until at least the lunch break. Then she expects that he will be cross-examined for an hour or two after lunch. Susan wants Barbara to have the next witness, Laura Lang, at the courthouse and ready to testify by 11 A.M., though, in the event that Dr. Brennan is excused earlier than expected.

Barbara has already arranged with the witness to arrive at the courthouse by 11 A.M. but is concerned that Lang will not be on time. Barbara has met with Lang two times to review her testimony and prepare her for the trial experience, and Lang has always been late. Barbara tells Susan about her concerns. Susan tells Barbara to go out into the hallway at 9 A.M. and call Lang. "Tell her that things are moving along more quickly than planned and to be here at ten o'clock. That should help to make sure that she will be here by eleven."

A WITNESS IS DELAYED

It is 8:35 A.M., and Dr. Brennan has not yet arrived. Susan asks Barbara to go out to the hallway and call him, first in his car and then in his office, to find out where he is. Barbara opens her trial notebook to the witness section. Dr. Brennan's page is first because he is the first witness scheduled to appear. She locates the number for his cell phone, jots it down on a scrap of paper, and leaves the courtroom. As she starts dialing Dr. Brennan's number, she sees him walk out of the elevator. Barbara puts the phone back and greets Dr. Brennan. "Sorry I'm running late, but I had an emergency this morning and I had to stop by the hospital before I came here," explains Dr. Brennan.

"I'm just glad to see you!" exclaims Barbara. "Let's go into the courtroom. You are the first witness, and Susan wants to see you." Barbara and Dr. Brennan enter the courtroom, and Susan and Dr. Brennan talk briefly before the judge enters. The court is called to order, and the trial resumes. Barbara sits at the counsel table while Susan questions Dr. Brennan on the stand. At 9 A.M., Barbara leaves the courtroom and calls Laura Lang.

TAKING PRECAUTIONS—ARRANGING FOR A WITNESS TO ARRIVE EARLY

Lang answers the phone. "Hello Ms. Lang. It's Barbara Lyons from Smith, White & White. Susan Weiss asked me to call you and tell you that the trial is moving faster than we anticipated. Susan would like you to be here at ten o'clock instead of eleven, if that's possible," advises Barbara. "Oh. Well, I suppose I can be there by then," responds Lang. "Do you remember how to get here?" asks Barbara. "Yes, I have the directions," answers Lang. "Good. I'll see you soon then, at ten o'clock," says Barbara. She returns to the courtroom.

At 9:55 A.M., Barbara leaves the courtroom again to wait in the hallway for Laura Lang. By 10:15 A.M., Lang has still not arrived. Barbara opens the courtroom door to listen. The testimony is going faster than Susan had anticipated, and Barbara can tell that Susan will probably be ready to put Lang on the stand in another thirty minutes or so. Barbara closes the courtroom door. She gets out her cell phone and dials Lang's telephone number. There is no answer. "I hope that she is on her way," thinks Barbara.

A TIMELY ARRIVAL

Now it is 10:45 A.M., and Lang has still not arrived. Barbara opens the courtroom door again and can tell that there is only about five minutes left in Dr. Brennan's testimony. She dials Lang's number again. No answer. Barbara continues to wait in the hallway, and a few minutes later Lang appears. Barbara breathes a sigh of relief. She opens the courtroom door, catches Susan's eye, and nods her head.

Making an image copy of a computer drive is complicated and is best left to an expert in computer forensics. Computer forensics experts collect, preserve, and analyze electronic evidence and testify in court if needed. Unskilled attempts to acquire an image of a computer's drive can easily lead to disaster, wrecking the evidence and rendering it inadmissible at trial.

Preserving the Chain of Custody

Once you have acquired an exact copy of the electronic evidence, you must establish and maintain a chain of custody to avoid any claims that the evidence has been tampered with. The phrase **chain of custody** refers to the movement and location of evidence from the time it is obtained to the time it is presented in court. It is particularly crucial when dealing with electronic evidence to make sure that you can track the evidence from its original source to its admission in court. This will provide the court with the necessary assurance that nothing has been added, changed, or deleted. The original image copy should be write-protected so that it is tamperproof, labeled as the original, and kept in a secure location. Typically, a forensic specialist will make working copies of the original data that are write-protected and scanned for viruses. You should always use the working copies rather than the original when reviewing e-evidence.

> **chain of custody**
> A series describing the movement and location of evidence from the time it is obtained to the time it is presented in court. The court requires that evidence be preserved in the condition in which it was obtained if it is to be admitted into evidence at trial.

KEY TERMS AND CONCEPTS

chapter summary   Civil Litigation—Before the Trial

Civil Litigation— A Bird's-Eye View

1. *Pretrial settlements*—Throughout the pretrial stage of litigation, the attorney and paralegal will attempt to help the parties reach a settlement at the same time as they are preparing the case for trial.

(Continued)

2. *Procedural requirements*—Although civil lawsuits vary from case to case in terms of complexity, cost, and detail, all civil litigation involves similar procedural steps, as described in Exhibit 13.1 on page 452.

   a. The Federal Rules of Civil Procedure (FRCP) govern all civil cases heard in federal courts and specify what must be done during the various stages of litigation.

   b. Each state has adopted its own rules of civil procedure, which in many states are similar to the FRCP.

   c. Many courts also have (local) rules of procedure that supplement the federal or state rules.

The Preliminaries

1. *The initial client interview*—The first step in the civil litigation process occurs when the attorney initially meets with a client who wishes to bring a lawsuit against another party or parties. Before the meeting, the paralegal will conduct a conflicts check to ensure that representing the client would not create a conflict of interest. The attorney normally conducts the initial client interview, although the paralegal often attends the interview and may make arrangements with the client for subsequent interviews.

2. *Preliminary investigation*—Once the attorney agrees to represent the client in the lawsuit and the client has signed the retainer agreement, the attorney and the paralegal undertake a preliminary investigation to ascertain the facts alleged by the client and gain other factual information relating to the case.

3. *The litigation file*—A litigation file is created to hold all documents and records pertaining to the lawsuit. Each law firm or legal department has its own specific procedures for organizing and maintaining litigation files. Generally, the file will expand, as the case progresses, to include subfiles for the pleadings, discovery, and other documents and information relating to the litigation.

The Pleadings

The pleadings inform each party of the claims of the other and detail the facts, charges, and defenses involved in the litigation. Pleadings typically consist of the plaintiff's complaint, the defendant's answer, and any counterclaim or cross-claim.

1. *The complaint*—A complaint states the claim or claims that the plaintiff is making against the defendant. A lawsuit in a federal or state court normally is initiated by the filing of a complaint with the clerk of the appropriate court.

   a. The complaint includes a caption, jurisdictional allegations, general allegations (body of the complaint) detailing the cause of action, a prayer for relief, a signature, and, if appropriate, a demand for a jury trial.

   b. A complaint can be filed either by personal delivery of the papers to the court clerk or, if the court permits, by electronic filing via e-mail, fax, or CD-ROM. The procedural requirements of courts that allow electronic filing vary and should be researched prior to any electronic filing.

2. *Service of process*—Typically, the defendant is notified of a lawsuit by delivery of the complaint and a summons (which is called service of process). The summons identifies the parties to the lawsuit, identifies the court in which the case will be heard, and directs the defendant to respond to the complaint within a specified time period.

a. Although often the complaint and summons are personally delivered to the defendant, other methods of service are allowed in some cases, depending on the jurisdiction.

b. In federal cases and in many states, the defendant can waive or give up the right to be personally served with the summons and complaint (and accept service by mail, for example).

c. Under FRCP 4, if the defendant waives service of process, the defendant receives additional time to respond to the complaint.

3. *The defendant's response*—On receiving the complaint, the defendant has several options.

a. The defendant may submit an answer. The answer may deny any wrongdoing or may assert an affirmative defense against the plaintiff's claim, such as the plaintiff's contributory negligence. The answer may be followed by a counterclaim, in which the defendant asserts a claim against the plaintiff arising out of the same incident; or it may be followed by a cross-claim, in which the defendant makes claims against another defendant named in the complaint.

b. Alternatively or simultaneously, the defendant may make a motion to dismiss the case. A motion to dismiss asserts that, even assuming that the facts of the complaint are true, the plaintiff has failed to state a cause of action or there are other grounds for dismissal of the suit.

Pretrial Motions

1. *Motion for judgment on the pleadings*—A pretrial motion that may be filed by either party after all pleadings and amendments have been filed. The motion asks the court to enter a judgment in favor of one party based on information contained in the pleadings alone. A judgment on the pleadings will only be made if there are no facts in dispute and the only question is how the law applies to the facts.

2. *Motion for summary judgment*—A motion that may be filed by either party during or after the discovery stage of litigation. This motion, like the motion for judgment on the pleadings, asks the court to enter judgment without a trial. Unlike a motion for judgment on the pleadings, however, a motion for summary judgment can be supported by evidence outside the pleadings (including affidavits, depositions, and interrogatories). The motion for summary judgment will not be granted if any facts are in dispute.

Traditional Discovery Tools

In preparing for trial, the attorney for each party undertakes a formal investigative process called discovery to obtain evidence helpful to his or her client's case.

1. *Interrogatories*—Interrogatories are written questions that the parties to the lawsuit must answer, in writing and under oath. The FRCP and some states' rules limit the number of questions that may be asked, as well as the total number of interrogatories that may be filed.

2. *Depositions*—Like interrogatories, depositions are given under oath, but unlike interrogatories, depositions may be taken from witnesses as well as from the parties to the lawsuit. Also, the attorney is able to question the deponent (the person being deposed) in person. There is no limit on the number of questions that may be asked. Usually, a court reporter records the official transcript of the deposition.

(Continued)

3. *Requests for production*—During discovery, the attorney for either side may request another party to produce documents or tangible things or to allow him or her access to documents or tangible things for inspection and other purposes.

4. *Physical or mental examinations*—When the mental or physical condition of a party is in controversy, the opposing party may request the court to order the party to submit to an examination by a licensed examiner.

5. *Requests for admission*—A party can request the opposing party to admit the truth of matters relating to the case. Such admissions save time at trial because the parties do not have to spend time proving facts on which they agree.

The Duty to Disclose under FRCP 26

In federal court cases, FRCP 26 requires that the attorneys cooperate in forming a discovery plan early in the litigation process. The rule also requires attorneys to disclose relevant information *automatically*. Under FRCP 26, only after initial disclosures have been made can attorneys resort to the use of traditional discovery tools. An attorney's duty to disclose relevant information under FRCP 26 is ongoing throughout the pretrial stage.

Discovery of Electronic Evidence

Electronic evidence consists of all computer-generated or electronically recorded information, such as e-mail, voice mail, spreadsheets, and word processing documents. The federal rules and most state rules allow discovery of evidence in electronic form. E-evidence has significantly changed discovery in civil litigation because it can reveal facts not discoverable by other means.

1. *Advantages of e-evidence*—Electronic evidence often provides more information than paper discovery, because many data that are on the computer are never printed out. In addition, the computer records hidden data (called metadata) about documents and e-mail, which can be very useful to the legal team. Even files that were deleted by the user can be retrieved from the residual data within the computer.

2. *Sources of e-evidence*—E-evidence may be located in the active data of the computer, the back-up data that have been copied to removable media, or the residual data that appear to be gone from the computer. Back-up data are particularly useful to the legal team. Not all e-evidence is located on computers, and you should investigate other potential sources, such as voice mail, phone logs, personal digital assistants, and so forth.

3. *Requirements of e-evidence*—In order to ensure that e-evidence will be admissible as evidence in the trial, you must obtain an exact image copy of the original data and then preserve the chain of custody until the time of trial, making sure to do nothing that will alter the evidence.

 QUESTIONS FOR REVIEW

1. What happens during the initial client interview? Who normally conducts this interview, the attorney or the paralegal? Why?

2. What are the basic steps in the litigation process prior to the trial? How does the paralegal assist the attorney in each of these steps?

3. What kinds of documents are contained in a litigation file? How might these documents be classified, or organized, within the file?

4. What documents constitute the pleadings in a civil lawsuit? What is the effect of each type of document on the litigation?

5. How are defendants notified of lawsuits that have been brought against them? What procedures are required under FRCP 4 for notifying the defendant in a lawsuit?

6. What is service of process? Why is it important?

7. Name three pretrial motions, and state the purpose of each.

8. What is a counterclaim? What is an affirmative defense? What is the effect of each of these on the litigation?

9. What is discovery? When does it take place? List three discovery devices that can be used to obtain information prior to trial.

10. How has the duty to disclose under FRCP 26 changed the discovery process in federal court cases?

ETHICAL QUESTIONS

1. Pamela Hodges has just started working as a paralegal for Lawyers, Inc., a high-volume, low-overhead law firm that handles mostly simple and routine litigation. Her supervising attorney, Carol Levine, has two initial client meetings scheduled at the same time. Carol tells Pam to handle one, and she (Carol) will come in to sign the retainer agreement. After one and a half hours, Carol is still tied up, and the client is demanding that Pam sign the retainer agreement or he will find another attorney. Should Pam let the client leave and risk losing his business, or should Pam sign the retainer agreement? Does she have other options?

2. Your next-door neighbor's son was beaten up while at school. The boy's mother is facing over $3,000 in medical and dental expenses as a result of his injuries, which she cannot afford to pay. She knows that you work as a paralegal in a law firm that specializes in personal-injury litigation, so she asks you if you will help her. She wants you to write a letter threatening legal action, which she will then sign, and she also wants to know whether she can sue the parents of the boys who beat up her son. Should you write the letter? Should you advise her on what action she might take against the other boys' parents? What are your ethical obligations in this situation? How could you help her without violating professional ethical standards?

3. Bruce Miller, a paralegal, is meeting with a client, Callie Nelson, to prepare answers to interrogatories. In the course of preparing the answers, Callie asks Bruce if he thinks that she has a good case, if there are better legal theories that she could pursue to win her case, and what her options are if she loses. How should Bruce answer these questions?

4. Scott Emerson takes a job as a paralegal with a large law firm that specializes in defending clients against product liability claims. The firm's clients are some of the largest manufacturing companies in the country. Mark Jones, an associate attorney, assigns Scott the job of drafting and sending out interrogatories to the plaintiff in a case brought against one of the firm's clients. Specifically, Scott is told to send out a standard set of one hundred interrogatories, each with five parts. Scott eventually learns that one of the favorite discovery tactics of the firm is to inundate plaintiffs with discovery requests, interrogatories, and depositions to cause continuous delays and to outspend the plaintiffs. Scott knows that the relevant state court rules do not limit the number of interrogatories that can be used, but he suspects that the firm's tactics are ethically questionable. Are they? What should Scott do?

PRACTICE QUESTIONS AND ASSIGNMENTS

1. Assume that you work for attorney Tara Jolans of Adams & Tate, 1000 Town Center, Suite 500, White Tower, Michigan. Jolans has decided to represent Sandra Nelson in her lawsuit against David Namisch. Based on the following information, draft a complaint to be filed in the U.S. District Court for the Eastern District of Michigan.

Sandra Nelson is a plaintiff in a lawsuit resulting from an automobile accident. Sandra was turning left at a traffic light at the intersection of Jefferson and Mack Streets, while the left-turn arrow was green, when she was hit from the side by a car driven by David Namisch, who failed to stop at the light. The accident occurred on June 3, 2007, at 11:30 P.M. David lives in New York, was visiting his family in Michigan, and just prior to the accident had been out drinking with his brothers. Several witnesses saw the accident. One of the witnesses called the police.

Sandra was not wearing her seat belt at the time of the accident, and she was thrown against the windshield, sustaining massive head injuries. When the police and ambulance arrived, they did not think that she would make it to the hospital alive, but she survived. She wants to claim damages of $500,000 for medical expenses, $65,000 for lost wages, and $55,000 for property damage to her Rolls Royce. The accident was reported in the local newspaper, complete with photographs.

2. Using Exhibit 13.3, *A Summons in a Civil Action,* on page 465, draft a summons to accompany the complaint against David Namisch. David's address is 1000 Main Street, Apartment 63, New York, NY 10009. The court clerk's name is David T. Brown.

3. Using Exhibit 13.4, *A Return-of-Service Form,* on page 466, draft a form to show that you, a paralegal for Whitman, Schultz & Horowitz, 325 Cleveland Avenue, Suite 407, New York, NY 10009, personally delivered a complaint and summons to Jarred Ramul at his residence. Jarred's address is 10833 Main Street, Apartment 63, on the sixth floor of the Baker Building in New York City, 10009. Include all required information.

4. Draft the first ten questions for a set of interrogatories to be directed to the plaintiff, Sandra Nelson, based on the facts given in Question 1 above.

5. Using Exhibit 13.9, *Notice of Taking Deposition,* on page 481, draft a notice that Sandra Nelson's attorneys will be taking the deposition of David Namisch on September 10, 2007, at 9:00 A.M., at the law offices of Adams & Tate. Mr. Namisch's attorney is Mark Simmons of Simmons & Smith, 444 Park Avenue, New York, NY 10007.

6. Using the material presented in the chapter on pretrial motions, identify each of the following motions:

   a. Tom Smith is a defendant in an auto-negligence case. His attorney files a motion requesting that a judgment be granted in Tom's favor without a trial. He attaches to the motion an affidavit of an eyewitness, who saw the plaintiff run a stop sign.

   b. Dr. Higgins is sued for medical malpractice. The plaintiff recovered completely and has no damages. Dr. Higgins's attorney files a motion asking that the case against his client be dismissed for failure to state a claim on which relief can be granted.

   c. After the answer is filed in a case brought by a plaintiff who slipped on a broken egg and fell on a grocery store floor, her attorney files a motion requesting that the court enter a judgment in the plaintiff's favor based on the undisputed facts contained in both the answer and the complaint.

   d. Dr. Higgins's attorney loses the motion discussed above. When the plaintiff's attorney requests medical records, Dr. Higgins instructs his attorney to refuse to provide the records. The plaintiff's attorney files a motion to obtain the records.

 ## QUESTIONS FOR CRITICAL ANALYSIS

1. Most cases are settled before trial. Why is this? What does it say about our system of justice? Does it place certain parties at a disadvantage? Why or why not?

2. What is the difference between preliminary investigation and discovery? What impact does this difference have on a case? Which would you prefer to undertake to determine the facts of a case?

3. A complaint must be served on the defendant in a lawsuit. What happens if the defendant is not properly served? Is this a fair result? Why or why not?

4. Why are defendants in federal courts and some state courts allowed to waive service of process? What is it that these defendants actually waive?

5. Why does a complaint contain jurisdictional allegations and general allegations? What is the difference between these types of allegations? Why is each type necessary?

What might happen if jurisdictional allegations were not included in a complaint?

6. How can a legal professional include a fact in a complaint if he or she has reason to believe that the fact is true but is uncertain as to its truth? Does including such a fact have any impact on the attorney's signing of the complaint or an affidavit?

7. If a defendant fails to respond to the plaintiff's complaint within a specified time period, what can happen? Is this a fair rule? Why?

8. What happens if a defendant fails to deny an allegation in answering a complaint? Is this fair to the defendant? What happens if a defendant is uncertain as to the truth of a matter being alleged by a plaintiff in a complaint?

9. What is the difference between a motion for summary judgment and a motion for judgment on the pleadings?

Is one motion preferable to the other? Give an example of how each motion is used.

10. What is the difference between interrogatories and depositions? Which is more efficient? Which is more cost-effective? Which would you prefer to use?

11. Some state court rules require the use of traditional dis-covery tools. The FRCP, in contrast, imposes a duty on parties and their attorneys to disclose certain information automatically, without waiting for traditional discovery requests. Which system of discovery is better, and why? Which is faster? Which is more realistic?

PROJECTS

1. Litigation is paper and document intensive, and computers can help tame the "paper dragon." Software has been developed and is constantly being updated that can organize and coordinate various pieces of evidence and testimony by using a combination of imaging software, database software, and full-text searching. This allows evidence, including documents and deposition transcripts, to be scanned into the computer, indexed, and easily located or retrieved. Two of the companies that sell the software are CT Summation and Inmagic, Inc. Contact one of these companies for a free demonstration CD or free online demonstration. CT Summation can be reached at 1-800-735-7866 or via the Internet at **http://www.summation.com**. Inmagic can be reached at 1-800-229-8398 or online at **http://www.inmagic.com**. After trying a demonstration of one of these companies' products, write a one-page paper describing how the software works.

2. Visit the county court clerk's office (or the clerk's office of a local court) and obtain the following: local court rules, summons and return-of-service forms, and a filing-fee schedule.

3. Review your state's court rules to determine which, if any, of the pretrial motions covered in this chapter are used in the courts in your state. Are the rules the same for all courts in your state? If not, what are some differences among courts?

4. Find out when a local court's "motion day" is, and attend court for two to three hours on that day. Observe as many motions as possible. Write a one-page summary of what you observed. Be sure to include the name of the court you visited, the date, and the judge's name.

USING INTERNET RESOURCES

1. Access the Web site of the National Court Reporters Association at **http://www.ncraonline.org**.

   a. Click on "Site Map" at the bottom of the screen. Under the heading "About NCRA," click on "History of Court Reporting." Read the article, and then answer the following questions:

   - When was the stenotype first invented? How does this machine work?

   - What is computer-aided transcription? What is "real-time" translation?

   b. Now click on "Find Reporters or Captioners," and search for your city (if you live in a smaller community, enter the name of a large city in your area or state).

   - How many court reporters or court-reporting firms offer services in that area?

   - List five types of services that one (or more) of these court reporters or firms offer.

2. The legal documents in the case brought by Paula Corbin Jones against former U.S. president Bill Clinton for sexual harassment can be found at a site maintained by the *Washington Post*. Go to this site at **http://www.washingtonpost.com/wp-srv/politics/special/pjones/legal.htm**, and answer the following questions:

   a. Under the heading "Complaint and Responses," go to the complaint filed by Paula Corbin Jones.

   - In what court was the complaint filed?

   - Who were the defendants?

   - How many causes of action did plaintiff Jones allege?

- What was the amount of the damages (compensatory and punitive) that the plaintiff requested?
- Did the plaintiff ask for a jury trial?

b. Under the heading "Complaint and Responses," go to President Clinton's response (answer).

- What case number was assigned to the case?
- Does the president admit to or deny the allegations of the complaint?
- How many affirmative defenses does the president's answer raise?

c. Scroll down to "President Clinton's Deposition," and click on it to view excerpts from the deposition. Find the part of the deposition titled "Events at the Excelsior Hotel." Answer the following questions:

- When was the president's deposition taken?
- Where was the president's deposition taken?
- How many objections were made by the president's attorney during this section of the deposition?
- What did the president say about his relationship with Paula Jones?

3.  For additional resources, visit our Web site at **http://www.paralegal.delmar.cengage.com**.

END NOTES

1. Some practitioners use the abbreviation FRCivP to distinguish the Federal Rules of Civil Procedure from the Federal Rules of Criminal Procedure.

2. Nita and Zero are fictitious states invented for the purpose of this hypothetical.

3. See Chapter 4 for a discussion of legal fees and the form and function of the retainer agreement.

4. In some courts and in certain types of cases, this document may be called a *petition*.

5. The body of the complaint described in this section is a *fact pleading*, in which sufficient factual circumstances must be alleged to convince the court that the plaintiff has a cause of action. State courts often require fact pleadings, whereas federal courts only require *notice pleading*. FRCP 8(a) requires only that the complaint have "a short and plain statement of the claim showing that the pleader is entitled to relief." Fact pleading and notice pleading are not totally different—that is, the same allegation of facts could be in the body of a complaint submitted to either a federal or a state court. Federal courts simply have fewer requirements in this respect, and therefore they are often more attractive to litigants.

6. Under the provisions of the FRCP, federal district courts can modify or opt not to follow the rules requiring early disclosures.

CONDUCTING INTERVIEWS AND INVESTIGATIONS

14

CHAPTER

CHAPTER OUTLINE

Introduction

Planning the Interview

Interviewing Skills

Interviewing Clients

Interviewing Witnesses

Planning and Conducting Investigations

AFTER COMPLETING THIS CHAPTER, YOU WILL KNOW:

▶ How to prepare for an interview and the kinds of skills employed during the interviewing process.

▶ The common types of client interviews paralegals may conduct and the different types of witnesses paralegals may need to interview during a preliminary investigation.

▶ How to create an investigation plan.

▶ The variety of sources that you can use to locate information or witnesses.

▶ Rules governing the types of evidence that are admissible in court.

▶ How to summarize investigation results.

INTRODUCTION

Paralegals frequently interview clients. After the initial client interview (which is usually conducted by the supervising attorney), the paralegal may conduct one or more subsequent interviews to obtain detailed information from the client. How the paralegal relates to the client has an important effect on the client's attitude toward the firm and the attorney or legal team handling the case.

Additionally, paralegals often conduct pretrial investigations. As part of a preliminary investigation into a client's claim, the paralegal may interview one or more witnesses to gain as much information as possible. The more factual evidence that can be gathered in support of a client's claim, the better the client's chances in court—or in any other dispute-settlement proceeding.

Learning how to conduct interviews and investigations is thus an important part of preparing for your career as a paralegal. In this chapter, you will read about the basic skills and concepts that you can apply when interviewing clients or witnesses and when conducting investigations.

PLANNING THE INTERVIEW

Planning an interview involves organizing many details. As a paralegal, you may be responsible for locating a witness, scheduling the interview, determining where the interview should take place, arranging for the use of one of the firm's conference rooms or other office space for the interview, and managing additional related details. Crucial to the success of any interview is how well you prepare for it.

Know What Information You Want to Obtain

interviewee
The person who is being interviewed.

Prior to any interview, you should have clearly in mind the kind of information you want to obtain from the client or witness being interviewed—the **interviewee**. If possible, discuss with your supervising attorney the goal of the interview and the type of information that the attorney hopes to obtain. This will ensure that you and the attorney share an understanding of what topics need to be covered in the interview. Once you know the questions that you want to ask, prepare a checklist or outline in advance so that you can refer to it during the interview.

Preprinted Interview Forms

Many law firms have created preprinted or computerized forms indicating the kinds of information that should be gathered during client interviews relating to particular types of claims. Firms that frequently handle personal-injury claims, for example, often use a personal-injury intake sheet such as that shown in Exhibit 14.1 on pages 506 and 507. Standardized client intake forms are also available as part of many legal software programs and from a variety of online sources. Using preprinted forms helps to ensure that all essential information will be obtained, especially for the beginning interviewer.

In some cases, the information needed will be clear from the legal forms or documents that will ultimately be filed with the court. For example, a paralegal interviewing a client who is petitioning for bankruptcy or divorce can look at the bankruptcy or divorce court forms during the interview to make sure all required information is obtained.

Remain Flexible

Keep in mind, however, that prepared questions and preprinted forms should only be used as guidelines during the interview. Do not simply read the questions word for word from a prepared list or stick rigidly to a planned outline of topics. If you do, you throw away an opportunity to interact with the interviewee and gain the interviewee's trust, and he or she will probably not disclose any information other than what is specifically asked for.

During any interview, the interviewer should remain flexible, listen carefully to the interviewee's responses, and let those responses guide the questioning. (Remember that you can always ask the interviewee to return to a certain topic later on in the interview.) By focusing too much on your own role and on what your next question will or should be, you can easily overlook the importance of what the client or witness is saying right now. Therefore, make sure that you listen to the interviewee's responses and modify your questions accordingly. Effective listening techniques are discussed later in this chapter.

Plan to Ask Follow-Up Questions

Another important point to remember is to ask for details and clarification after the interviewee has made a statement. Find out who, what, when, where, and how. If an interviewee says, for example, that he saw someone hit Jane in the face, you will need to ask for more specifics, such as:

- How far away was he at the time?
- What exactly did he see?
- How many times was she hit and with what (open hand, fist, weapon)?
- Who else was present?
- Was it light or dark? Inside or outside?
- From what angle did he view the incident?
- Does he know Jane or her assailant? How?
- What were Jane and the assailant doing before and after the incident?
- What was the witness doing before the incident?

Also, although you should read the case file thoroughly before the interview, try to set aside what you have read or heard about the case. Let the interviewee tell you the story from his or her own perspective and avoid preconceived notions about what the person will say. One approach is to pretend that you know nothing about the case and let the interviewee tell you her or his version of the facts. Then, as the interview unfolds, think about what the person is saying from the perspective of your opponent—why should anyone believe that story? Ask follow-up questions aimed at establishing what makes the person's story more or less believable. If a witness says a car was going fifty-five miles per hour, for example, ask how he or she could tell the speed. If it turns out the witness has been racing cars recreationally for the past fifteen years, this fact can be used to help make the witness's testimony more believable.

Recording the Interview

Some interviewers record their interviews. Before you record an interview, you should always obtain permission to do so from both your supervising attorney and the person being interviewed. When you are using a recorder, you should state or include at the beginning of the recording the following identifying information:

- The name of the person being interviewed and any other relevant information about the interviewee.
- The name of the person conducting the interview.
- The names of other persons present at the interview, if any.
- The date, time, and place of the interview.
- On the record, the interviewee's consent to having the interview recorded.

EXHIBIT 14.1
Personal-Injury Intake Sheet

PERSONAL-INJURY INTAKE SHEET

Prepared for Clients of
Jeffers, Gilmore & Dunn

1. **Client Information:**

   Name: Katherine Baranski

   Address: 335 Natural Blvd.

                         Nita City, NI   48802

   Social Security No.: 206-15-9858

   Marital Status: Married   Years Married: 3

   Spouse's Name: Peter Baranski

   Children: None

   Phone Numbers: Home (616) 555-2211   Work (616) 555-4849

   Employer: Nita State University

                         Mathematics Department

   Position: Associate Professor of Mathematics

   Responsibilities: Teaching

   Salary: $58,000

2. **Related Information:**

   Client at Scene: Yes

   Lost Work Time: 5 months

   Client's Habits: Normally drives south on Mattis Avenue on way to

                         university each morning at about the same time.

If more than one recording file is used, you should indicate at the end of each file that the interview will be continued on the next file in the series, and each subsequent file should contain identifying information.

There are several advantages to recording an interview. For one thing, having a digital audio record of the interview reduces the need to take extensive notes during the interview. You can either have the audio file transcribed for future reference or listen to the file later (when creating an interview summary, for example, as discussed later) to refresh your memory of how the interviewee responded to certain questions. You may also want to have other members of the legal team read the transcript or listen to the file. Sometimes, what seemed insignificant to you may seem significant to someone else working on the case. Also, as a case

EXHIBIT 14.1
**Personal-Injury Intake
Sheet—Continued**

3. Incident/Accident:

Date: August 4, 2006   Time: 7:45 A.M.

Place: Mattis Avenue and 38th Street, Nita City, Nita

Description: Mrs. Baranski was driving south on Mattis Avenue
when a car driven by Tony Peretto, who was
attempting to cross Mattis at 38th Street, collided
with Mrs. Baranski's vehicle.

Witnesses: None known by Mrs. Baranski

Defendant: Tony Peretto

Police: Nita City

Action Taken: Mrs. Baranski was taken to City Hospital
by ambulance (Nita City Ambulance Co.).

4. Injuries Sustained:

Nature: Multiple fractures to left hip and leg; lacerations
to left eye and left side of face; multiple contusions
and abrasions

Medical History: No significant medical problems prior to the
accident

Treating Hospital: Nita City Hospital

Treating Physician: Dr. Swanson

Hospital Stay: August 4, 2006   to November 20, 2006

Insurance: Southwestern Insurance Co. of America

Policy No: 00631150962 -B

Interview Conducted by:

Allen P. Gilmore   January 30, 2007
Attorney   Date

Elena Lopez   January 30, 2007
Paralegal/Witness   Date

progresses, a remark made by an interviewee that did not seem important at the time of the interview may take on added significance in view of evidence gathered later.

There are also some disadvantages to recording interviews. A major disadvantage is that clients and witnesses may feel uncomfortable and be less willing to disclose information freely if they know everything they are saying is being recorded. Such reluctance is understandable in view of the fact that the interviewee does not know what exactly will transpire during the course of the interview or how the audio file may later be used. When asking an interviewee for his or her permission to record an interview, you should therefore evaluate carefully how the interviewee responds to this question. Depending on the interviewee's response, you might consider taking notes instead of recording the session. Another option is to go through the questions you will ask with the interviewee once before asking permission to turn on the recorder.

INTERVIEWING SKILLS

Interviewing skills are essentially any skills—particularly interpersonal and communication skills—that help you to conduct a successful interview. In this section, you will learn how the use of interpersonal and communication skills can help you establish a comfortable relationship with the interviewee. Then, you will read about specific questioning and listening techniques that can help you control the interview and elicit various types of information.

Interpersonal Skills

At the outset of any interview, remember that your primary goal is to obtain information from the client or witness being interviewed. Although some people communicate information and ideas readily and effectively, others may need considerable prompting and encouragement. If they feel comfortable in your presence and in the interviewing environment, they will generally be more willing to disclose information.

As you begin an interview, you should remember that the interviewee may be very nervous or at least uncomfortable. Because the time you have to talk with a client or witness will be limited, you should put that individual at ease as quickly as possible. A minute or two spent chatting casually with the client or witness is time well spent. Also, saying or doing something that shows your concern for the interviewee's physical comfort helps to make the interviewee feel more relaxed. For example, you might offer the individual a cup of coffee or other beverage.

Using language that the interviewee will understand is essential in establishing a good working relationship with that person. If you are interviewing a client with only a grade-school education, for example, do not use the phrase "facial lacerations" when talking about "cuts on the face." If you are interviewing a witness who does not speak English very well, arrange to have an interpreter present unless you are fluent in the witness's native language. Because most clients and witnesses are not familiar with legal terminology, you should always avoid using legal terms that will not be clearly understood by the interviewee. If you must use a specific legal term to express an idea, be sure that you define the term and that it is clearly understood.

Questioning Skills

When questioning witnesses or clients, you should remember to remain objective at all times and gather as much relevant factual information as possible. Sometimes, you may have difficulty remaining objective when questioning witnesses because you sympathize with the client and may not want to hear about facts that are contrary to the client's position. But relevant factual information includes those details that adversely affect the client's case as well as those that support his or her position. Indeed, your supervising attorney must know *all* of the facts, especially any that might damage the client's case in court.

In some situations, it may be difficult to remain objective not because of your sympathy *for* the client but because of your own personal biases *against* the client, the witness, or the case. Interviewers must be especially careful to evaluate their own feelings prior to conducting an interview. If you feel a person's conduct or situation is morally reprehensible, you may convey those feelings during the interview either verbally or nonverbally. Once the interviewee senses your disapproval, he or she is likely to limit the information disclosed. For example, suppose that you are interviewing Sandra, a client who is trying to regain custody of her children. The state took Sandra's children away because she abused "crack" cocaine and failed to properly care for them. You have read through the file and strongly disapprove of Sandra's past conduct. You also have doubts about whether she has sufficiently recovered from her drug problem. If you do not set aside your personal feelings prior to meeting with Sandra, they may unconsciously affect your interaction and thwart the success of the interview.

The experienced legal interviewer uses certain questioning techniques to prompt interviewees to communicate the information needed. There are several types of questions, including open-ended, closed-ended, leading, and hypothetical questions. Exhibit 14.2 provides some examples of the types of questions discussed in the following subsections.

Open-Ended Questions

The **open-ended question** is a broad, exploratory question that invites any number of possible responses. The open-ended question can be used when you want to give the interviewee an opportunity to talk at some length about a given subject. "What happened on the night of October 28—the night of the murder?" is an open-ended question. Other examples of open-ended questions are "And what happened next?" and "What did you see as you approached

open-ended question
A question phrased in such a way that it elicits a relatively unguided and lengthy narrative response.

EXHIBIT 14.2
Types of Interview Questions

TYPE OF QUESTION	OPEN-ENDED QUESTION	CLOSED-ENDED QUESTION	LEADING QUESTION	HYPOTHETICAL QUESTION
Definition	A broad, exploratory question that elicits a lengthy response.	A question phrased in such a way that it elicits a "yes" or "no" response.	A question phrased in such a way that it suggests the desired answer.	A question that asks the interviewee to assume a certain set of facts in forming an answer.
Typical Uses	Used mostly with friendly witnesses and clients.	Used to clarify a witness's statement or to keep her or him on track. Used with adverse or reluctant witnesses.	Used at times with adverse witnesses in interviews. Used often by attorneys to cross-examine witnesses at trial (see Chapter 15).	Used primarily with expert witnesses in interviews and during trial.
Examples	• Describe the morning of the accident. What did you do that morning? • What did you observe prior to entering the intersection? • When did you first observe the defendant's car and where was it? • How fast was the defendant going at the time of the accident?	• Were you late for work that morning? • Was there anyone in the car with you at the time? • Were you already in the intersection at the time you first saw the plaintiff's car? • Were you exceeding the speed limit at the time the accident occurred?	• You were running late for work that morning, correct? • You saw that the light had turned red before you entered the intersection, didn't you? • Isn't it true that you were driving in excess of the speed limit at the time of the accident? • Isn't it true that you had been out drinking at a bar until late on the night before the accident?	• If a full-sized van is traveling at fifty-five miles per hour, how far before an intersection must the driver apply the brakes in order to stop the vehicle? • If a 200-pound man consumed fourteen beers in six hours, how long would it take before the alcohol was out of his system so that it would not affect his ability to drive? • What type of treatment does a person who has suffered the kinds of

the intersection?" When you ask a question of this kind, be prepared for a lengthy response. If a witness has difficulty narrating the events he or she observed or if a lull develops during the explanation, you will need to encourage the witness to continue through the use of various prompting responses (which will be discussed shortly in the context of listening skills).

Open-ended questions are useful in interviewing clients or friendly witnesses (witnesses who favor the client's position). This is because these kinds of interviewees are usually forthcoming, and you will be able to gain information from them by indicating in broad terms what you want them to describe. Open-ended questions are also a good way for the interviewer to evaluate whether the interviewee's demeanor and overall effectiveness would make him or her a good witness at trial.

Closed-Ended Questions

closed-ended question
A question phrased in such a way that it elicits a simple "yes" or "no" answer.

The **closed-ended question**, in contrast, is intended to elicit a "yes" or "no" response from the interviewee. "Did you see the murder weapon?" is an example of a closed-ended question. Although closed-ended questions tend to curb communication, they are useful in some situations. For example, if an interviewee tends to digress frequently from the topic being discussed, using closed-ended questions can help keep him or her on track. Closed-ended questions, because they invite specific answers, also may be useful to clarify the interviewee's previous response and to relax the interviewee in preparation for more difficult questions that follow. In addition, closed-ended questions may help to elicit information from adverse witnesses (those who are not favorable to the client's position), who may be reluctant to volunteer information.

Leading Questions

leading question
A question that suggests, or "leads to," a desired answer. Interviewers may use leading questions to elicit responses from witnesses who otherwise would not be forthcoming.

The **leading question** is one that suggests to the listener the answer to the question. "Isn't it true that you were only ten feet away from where the murder took place?" is a leading question. This question, of course, invites a "yes" answer. Leading questions can be very effective for drawing information out of eyewitnesses or clients, particularly when they are reluctant to disclose information. They can also be useful for interviewing adverse witnesses who are hesitant to communicate information that may be helpful to the client's position. (In fact, they are the primary method of questioning used by attorneys when cross-examining witnesses at trial, as you will read in Chapter 15.) When used with a client or friendly witnesses, however, leading questions have a major drawback. They may lead to distorted answers because the client or witness may tailor the answer to fit his or her perception of what the interviewer wants to know. For this reason, in the interviewing context, leading questions should be used cautiously and only when the interviewer is fully aware of the possible distortions that might result.

Hypothetical Questions

hypothetical question
A question based on hypothesis, conjecture, or fiction.

As a paralegal, you may be asked to interview an expert witness either to gather information about a case or to evaluate whether that person would be an effective expert witness at trial (*expert witnesses* will be discussed later in this chapter). The **hypothetical question** is frequently used with expert witnesses. Hypothetical questions allow you to obtain an answer to an important question without giving away the facts (and confidences) of a client's case. For example, you might invent a hypothetical situation involving a certain type of knee injury (the same kind of injury as that sustained by a client) and then ask an orthopedic surgeon what kind of follow-up care would ordinarily be undertaken for that type of injury.

Listening Skills

The interviewer's ability to listen is perhaps the most important communication skill used during the interviewing process. Whenever you conduct an interview, you will want to absorb fully the interviewee's verbal answers, as well as his or her nonverbal messages. Prior to the interview, you should make sure that the room in which it is to be held will be free of noises, phone calls, visitors, and other interruptions or distractions. During the interview itself, you can use several listening techniques to maximize communication and guide the interviewee toward the fullest disclosure of needed information.

Passive Listening

As mentioned earlier, the interviewer should listen attentively when the interviewee is answering questions. It is extremely important that the client or witness gets the impression that the interviewer is interested in what he or she is saying. If the interviewee pauses briefly or there is a lull in the conversation, the interviewer can use **passive listening** techniques, which are verbal or nonverbal cues that encourage the speaker to continue. For example, the interviewer might say, "I'm listening, please go on" or "And then what happened?" A nonverbal cue can be any facial expression or body language that shows you are interested in what is being said. Nodding positively, for example, is an effective nonverbal way to convey your interest. Maintaining eye contact is another nonverbal cue to indicate your interest in the interviewee's statements.

passive listening
The act of listening attentively to the speaker's message and responding to the speaker by providing verbal or nonverbal cues that encourage the speaker to continue; in effect, saying, "I'm listening, please go on."

Active Listening

For communication to be truly an interactive process, the listener must engage in active listening. **Active listening** involves not only paying close attention to what the speaker is saying but also providing appropriate feedback to show that you *understand* what is being said. Because people do not always say what they mean to say—or what they think they are saying—active listening is critical to a productive interview. Active listening allows the interviewer to clarify and confirm the interviewee's statements throughout the interview.

active listening
The act of listening attentively to the speaker's message and responding by giving appropriate feedback to show that you understand what the speaker is saying; restating the speaker's message in your own words to confirm that you accurately interpreted what was said.

Paraphrasing

Reflecting Back.   One very effective active listening technique is for the interviewer to "reflect back," or "mirror," what the interviewee has already said. For example, after the interviewee has conveyed her or his thoughts on a particular topic, you might say, "Let me see if I understand you correctly" and then summarize your impression of what she or he has said. If your interpretation is incorrect, the interviewee now has the opportunity to make you understand what she or he meant to say. This technique is useful for clarifying the person's statement. In addition, it reinforces the idea that you are listening carefully and are interested in what the interviewee has to say.

Controlling the Flow of the Interview.   Active listening also enables the interviewer to put the person's statements into the context of the larger picture and facilitates smooth transitions between interview topics. For example, suppose you are interviewing a client who is suing her former employer. After telling you about the rude and offensive behavior of her co-workers, she indicates that she just couldn't go back to work and starts to cry. You can restate what she has told you in a way that makes the client feel you support and identify with her: "I understand that you did not return to work because of the hostility of your co-workers toward you." You might then move into a discussion of damages by saying, "It sounds as if you've been through a lot. Did you go see a counselor or get help from anyone during that time?" The interviewer who engages in active listening can thus direct the flow of the interview according to the reactions and responses of the person being interviewed.

INTERVIEWING CLIENTS

Typically, the paralegal interviews either clients or witnesses. Here, we look at client interviews. (We will discuss witness interviews shortly.) The various types of client interviews include the initial client interview, subsequent client interviews to obtain further information, and informational interviews, or meetings, to inform the client of the status of his or her case and to prepare the client for trial or other legal proceedings. See this chapter's *Featured Guest* article on pages 512 and 513 for additional tips on conducting client interviews.

Daniel G. Cantone FEATURED **Guest**

TEN TIPS FOR EFFECTIVE CLIENT-CENTERED INTERVIEWING

BIOGRAPHICAL NOTE

Daniel G. Cantone is a sole practitioner concentrating primarily on all aspects of matrimonial law. He has been a lawyer in small firms in the Syracuse, New York, area for over twenty years. Cantone teaches legal research and writing, family and domestic relations, and introduction to law and ethics as an adjunct professor at Syracuse University, where he received his cum laude *undergraduate and juris doctor degrees.*

As an individual member of the AAfPE, Cantone writes and lectures regionally and nationally, and he serves as faculty adviser to the LEX paralegal honor society chapter at his alma mater. Cantone's law office staff includes a general practice legal assistant who has frequent personal contact with clients of the firm.

The practice of law is inherently a combination of human service and business for profit. Clients are served well, of course, by competent legal professionals skilled in their area of expertise. Successful interpersonal contact with clients increases their satisfaction with the law firm, leading to more gratified and contented contributors to the office's "bottom line." Genuine rapport with clients begins with the initial telephone inquiry or the first handshake at the reception desk. Effective (or ineffective) fact gathering and communication can literally make (or break) a positive relationship with a client.

In most firms, lawyers are regularly in court, at closings, or dealing with other matters outside the office for extended periods. Having paralegals conduct interviews is convenient for clients and enhances responsiveness to the clients' interests. With experience, a legal assistant will inevitably develop an interviewing style that is comfortable, adaptable, and efficient.

The following ten tips are gleaned from many years of meeting and communicating with hundreds of individuals seeking legal services. Some of the tips are perhaps quite obvious; others, however, are more subtle.

1. Use Direct Eye Contact. Sitting face to face with a person needing legal representation provides a legal professional with a prime opportunity to "connect with" the interviewee. Often, interviewers are so focused on recording facts that they lose sight of the human subjects before them. For the client, eye contact means that the legal assistant is truly in tune with the problem presented. For the paralegal, eye-to-eye communication compels truthfulness and candor from the client. This golden rule of interviewing—to maximize eye contact with the client—is usually far easier said than done. Practicing with friends or family members in mock interviews can be helpful in gaining feedback about your skills. Avoid the inclination to write absolutely everything down. Let your client's eyes give you insight into the whole story.

2. Prevent Possible Interruptions. Perhaps nothing is more intrusive and disruptive to a smooth interview than phone calls or other interruptions. Cellular devices and beepers should be turned off. Staff members must be alerted that you are in a conference with a client. The setup of the interview room needs to preserve privacy. If the area is surrounded by glass, close the blinds, if possible. Otherwise, seat the client so that he or she faces away from the highly visible office areas. Should your work space be an open cubicle, reserve a closed meeting area for the time allotted in advance. Interviews at law firms must be free from distractions, even from well-intentioned colleagues.

3. Show Empathy and Compassion. A good interviewer must be able, at least to some degree, to walk in the shoes of the client. Legal problems are sometimes embarrassing. Suppose that you were the client. How would you want to be treated? Empathy comes from really understanding the client's plight or misfortune. Compassion comes from truly caring about the situation. A successful interviewer is a skilled listener who values service to others. Try to use open-ended questions allowing for narrative answers so that the interviewee can vent, explain, and express himself or herself completely.

4. Obtain Background Information on the Client. Whether compiled by your supervising attorney, by your secretary, or through your own contact with the client, facts known up front will save time and help to create an orderly progression for the interview. Sometimes, firms send biographical forms to be completed and returned before an appointment. Generally, the more a paralegal knows about a person prior to an interview, the more helpful and streamlined the session will be.

5. Be Aware of Time, Timing, and Timeliness. Always allot sufficient time to conduct any interview. Clients do not want to be rushed or feel like they are part of an assembly line. Set appointments when they are most convenient for the clients. Be prompt in your own arrival for all client meetings. Do not forget that clients normally pay by the hour, so time is indeed a precious commodity for interviewees. A keen understanding of the value of your own time will lead to much more productive interviews. If your work schedule is rigid because of office policy or personal commitments, suggest a midday time frame for client contact. Interviewees and their employers are usually more likely to be able to make time for professional appointments around the lunch hour.

6. Clarify Your Role. No matter where you work, the unauthorized practice of law is illegal. Clients, especially when they become acquainted with a particular paralegal, may be lulled into a sense that they can bypass more expensive consultation time with the lawyer overseeing their cases. This is absolutely never an acceptable outlook. Clients must be reminded of your status as a paralegal and of the proper chain of command with respect to obtaining actual legal advice. Be sure that you are well versed in the statutory, regulatory, and common law definitions of what constitutes the practice of law in your state, and have your supervising attorney explain carefully the expectations about client contact *before* you begin. Clients will respect a forthright discussion about your inability to render legal counsel and the benefits of having a paralegal involved.

7. Have Supplies at Hand. Sometimes, the most obvious types of preparation for a productive interview are those that are most overlooked. Depending on the nature of the case, certain supplies and office equipment ought to be readily accessible in the interview room itself. For instance, if an intake meeting concerns tax returns or bankruptcy, a calculator or an adding machine should be nearby. For marital matters, a box of tissues is a proverbial tool of the trade. In automobile-accident cases, an ample supply of blank paper and multicolored pens allows the client to sketch the accident scene for your file. Items that are used repeatedly, such as a calendar and

"Having paralegals conduct interviews is convenient for clients and enhances responsiveness to the clients' interests."

your notary stamp, should be at your disposal. Having the right supplies at hand will help to minimize the time you spend exiting and returning to the interview room.

8. Provide Helpful Documents. Clients often leave meetings conducted by paralegals or attorneys with unresolved questions that come to mind at some later time. Giving the client preprinted or self-prepared documents can satisfy many such questions. Firm brochures, newsletters, relevant articles, and bar association pamphlets are usually good sources of information. Many paralegals create checklists or time lines for clients during the interview itself. Any written data that can be taken and reviewed by clients at their leisure tend to reinforce the discussion in the office and clarify topics that were not already addressed.

9. Strive to Instill Confidence. No matter how new you may be to the interviewing process, you need to project confidence in your demeanor and attitudes. Giving the impression that "I've done this before" puts the client at ease. Keep in mind that clients do not always communicate clearly. When you are confused about something, ask the client to reiterate relevant facts and specifics. Your first concern is to get the story right, in a logical, methodical, and honest fashion. An ability to do this builds confidence in both yourself and the client.

10. Follow Up on the Interview. Details are best remembered immediately after an interview. Make it a habit to decipher your own shorthand notes right away so that others in the firm can benefit from your efforts. The preparation of comprehensive typed summaries serves this purpose. Prompt contact with the attorney assigned to the matter is also crucial to ensure that a proper course of action is taken. Perhaps the most important thing in following up on an interview is to make an unsolicited phone call or write a brief letter to the client. Continuing communication with the client makes for positive sentiments about the paralegal and creates long-term personal relationships—relationships that are vital to the ongoing economic welfare and goodwill of the firm.

The Initial Client Interview

As discussed in previous chapters, when a client seeks legal advice from an attorney, the attorney normally holds an initial interview with the client. During this interview, the client explains his or her legal problem so that the attorney can advise the client on possible legal options and the legal fees that may be involved. Either then or at a later time, the client and the attorney will agree on the terms of the representation, if the attorney decides to take the case.

Paralegals often attend initial client interviews. Although the attorney normally conducts this first interview, the paralegal plays an important role. Usually, you will observe the client, take notes on what the client is saying, and provide the client with forms, statements explaining the firm's fees, and other prepared information normally given to new clients. Following the interview, you and the attorney may compare your impressions of the client and of what the client said during the interview.

All of the people present at the interview should be introduced to the client, their titles given, and the reason for their presence at the interview made known to the client. In introducing you, the paralegal, to the potential client, the attorney will probably stress that you are not a lawyer and cannot give legal advice. If your supervising attorney does not indicate your nonattorney status to the client, you should do so. If a firm decides to take a client's case, the client should be introduced to every member of the legal team who will be working on the case.

A follow-up letter, such as the one shown in Exhibit 14.3, will be sent to the client after the interview. The letter will state whether the attorney has decided to accept the case or, if the attorney orally agreed during the initial client interview to represent the client, will confirm the oral agreement in writing.

Subsequent Client Interviews

Paralegals are often asked to conduct additional interviews with clients whose cases have been accepted. For example, assume that a client wants to obtain a divorce. After the initial interview, your supervising attorney may ask you to arrange for an interview with the client to obtain all the information necessary to prepare the divorce pleadings. When scheduling the interview, you should tell the client what kinds of documents or other data he or she should bring to the interview. Then send the client a letter confirming the date and time of the interview and listing all the items you would like the client to bring. During the interview, you will fill out the form that the firm uses to record client information in divorce cases. Paralegals often assume responsibility for gathering most of the information needed to file for a divorce or to begin child-custody proceedings.

When conducting a client interview, the paralegal should disclose his or her nonlawyer status if this fact was not made clear at an earlier session. Remember, even if you have been introduced to the client as a legal assistant, the client may not realize that a legal assistant is not an attorney. To protect yourself against potential claims that you have engaged in the unauthorized practice of law, you should clearly state to the client that you are not an attorney and cannot give legal advice.

The Informational Interview

The informational interview, or meeting, is an interview in which the client is brought in to discuss upcoming legal proceedings. Most clients know very little about the procedures involved in litigation, and firms often have their paralegals explain these procedures to clients and prepare clients for the trial experience. For example, the paralegal can describe to clients what will take place during the trial, how to dress and conduct themselves appropriately for trial, where to look when they testify, and so forth. The informational interview

EXHIBIT 14.3
A Sample Follow-Up
Letter to a Client

Jeffers, Gilmore & Dunn
553 Fifth Avenue
Suite 101
Nita City, NI 48801

Telephone: (616) 555-9690
Fax: (616) 555-9679
e-mail: jgd@nitanet.net

February 2, 2007

Ms. Katherine Baranski
335 Natural Boulevard
Nita City, Nita 48802

Dear Ms. Baranski:

It was a pleasure to meet and talk with you on January 30. Jeffers, Gilmore & Dunn will be pleased to act as your representative in your action against Tony Peretto to obtain compensation for your injuries.

I am enclosing a fee agreement for your review. If you wish this firm to act as your legal counsel, please sign and date the agreement and return it to me as soon as possible. A self-addressed, stamped envelope is enclosed for your convenience. As soon as I receive the completed agreement, we will begin investigating your case.

As I advised during our meeting, to protect your rights, please refrain from speaking with the driver of the vehicle, his lawyer, or his insurance company. If they attempt to contact you, simply tell them that you have retained counsel and refer them directly to me. I will handle any questions that they may have.

If you have any questions, please do not hesitate to call me or my paralegal, Ms. Elena Lopez.

Sincerely,

Allen P. Gilmore

Allen P. Gilmore
Attorney at Law

APG/db

Encs.

helps the client understand why certain proceedings are taking place and his or her role in those proceedings.

Summarizing the Interview

The interviewing process does not end with the close of the interview. A final and crucial step in the process involves summarizing the results of the interview for the legal team working on the case. As a paralegal, you may be asked to create an intake memorandum following each initial client interview. If the firm has a prepared intake form for particular types of cases, such as the personal-injury intake sheet referred to earlier and illustrated in Exhibit 14.1 on pages 506 and 507, the completed form might constitute the interview summary.

Ethics Watch!

HANDLING CLIENT DOCUMENTS

Clients frequently give paralegals important documents relating to their cases during interviews. A client might, for example, give you the only copy she has of her divorce agreement. State codes of ethics impose strict requirements on attorneys in regard to the safekeeping of clients' funds and other property, including documents. You should never rely on memory when it comes to client documents. Instead, immediately after the conclusion of the interview, record the receipt of any documents or other items received from the client. The information may be recorded in an evidence log (discussed later in this chapter) or in some other way, depending on the procedures established by your firm to govern the receipt and storage of such property. An evidence log or its equivalent provides you with evidence—should it be necessary—of what you did (or did not) receive from a client.

Information obtained during any subsequent interviews with a client should be analyzed and summarized in a memo for your supervising attorney or other team members to review and for later inclusion in the client's file.

Your interview summary should be created immediately after the interview, while the session is still fresh in your mind. When summarizing the results of a client interview, you should carefully review your notes and, if the session was recorded, review the file. Never rely totally on your memory of the statements made during the interview. It is very easy to forget the client's specific words, and it may be very important later to know exactly how the client phrased a certain comment or response. Relying on memory is also risky because, as mentioned earlier, sometimes a statement that seemed irrelevant at the time of the interview may turn out to be very important to the case. You should thus make sure that the facts are accurately recorded and are as reliable as possible. Also note your general impressions of the client and the client's nonverbal behaviors.

Depending on the nature of the legal claim being made by the client, you may want to include a visual element or two in your summary. For example, if the claim concerns an automobile accident, you might consider creating a graphic depiction of the accident to attach to the summary. (For a further discussion of the value of visual communications, see this chapter's *Technology and Today's Paralegal* feature.)

INTERVIEWING WITNESSES

Witnesses play a key role in establishing the facts of an event. As a legal investigator, your goal is to elicit as much relevant and reliable information as possible from each witness about the event that you are investigating. Interviewing witnesses is in many ways similar to interviewing clients, and many of the interviewing skills, such as listening skills, that we have already discussed apply to interviews of witnesses. A major difference between clients and witnesses, however, is that the latter may not always be friendly to the client's position. Here

Technology and Today's Paralegal

COMMUNICATING WITH GRAPHICS

We have all heard the saying, "A picture is worth a thousand words." This adage is worth remembering when you are interviewing clients or witnesses concerning an accident or other event that can be displayed graphically.

THE VALUE OF CHARTS AND DIAGRAMS

Suppose that you work for a law firm specializing in personal-injury cases. You are asked to interview a client to obtain details about an automobile accident. The client was injured in the accident and wishes to sue the driver of the other car for damages. When you conduct the interview, keep in mind that a visual depiction of the accident can communicate to the attorney, quickly and clearly, how the client described the accident. During your interview, you might ask the client to draw a diagram of the accident, urging the client to provide details to clarify certain points as necessary. You might ask, for example, whether a street was a two-lane or a four-lane street and then include that detail on the diagram.

Later, after you've concluded your interview and are summarizing the interview, you can attach the diagram to the memorandum you will provide to your supervising attorney. The diagram will allow the attorney to quickly grasp, at a glance, what essentially happened during the accident.

Visual communications can often convey concepts much more simply and clearly than the written or spoken word. This is why exhibits are prepared for presentation at trial. Yet you need not wait until trial preparations begin to create charts, diagrams, and flowcharts to communicate events and situations pertaining to a client's case. Indeed, as just described, using charts at the beginning stages of a lawsuit, even during an initial client interview, can be helpful as well.

DRAWING SOFTWARE

Today, numerous computer programs are available to help you prepare visual exhibits. For example, SmartDraw® markets a drawing tool that helps users create a variety of different types of charts and diagrams, including flowcharts and organization charts. The *SmartDraw Legal Solution* is designed to meet the needs of legal professionals, including attorneys and paralegals. SmartDraw's Web site (at **http://www. smartdraw.com**) offers free tutorials for different types of charts and allows you to download software for a free trial.

SerifSoftware.com also offers a drawing program, called *DrawPlus 4*, via its Web site at **http://www. freeserifsoftware.com/software/DrawPlus**. You can download this software from the Web site at no charge. Still another program is provided by The CAD Zone, Inc., at **http://www.cadzone.com/ products.htm**. The CAD Zone offers a variety of programs for different uses, including law enforcement uses. For example, the *Crash Zone* and the *Quick Scene* programs are designed for users who wish to reconstruct accidents. The Crime Zone is an easy-to-use drawing program for creating crime-scene diagrams. The CAD Zone offers live online training sessions in how to use its programs.

TECHNOLOGY TIP

Regardless of where you work as a paralegal or the type of work you perform, you may be able to use charts and other graphics to enhance the clarity and neatness of your work product. It is certainly worth exploring some of the drawing and graphics software available online to see if there is a program that you could easily adapt to your needs.

Ethics Watch!

THE UNAUTHORIZED PRACTICE OF LAW

Paralegals must be especially careful not to give legal advice when interviewing clients. Suppose that you are conducting a follow-up interview of a client, Sue Collins. Collins was injured in a car accident and is suing the driver of the other car involved for negligence. During the initial client interview, Collins told you and your supervising attorney that the accident was totally the result of the other driver's negligence. During the course of your follow-up interview, however, Collins presents you with an interesting hypothetical. She says to you, "What would happen, in a lawsuit such as mine, if the plaintiff was not watching the road when the accident occurred? What if the plaintiff was looking in the backseat to see why her baby was crying? Could the plaintiff still expect to win in court?" You know that under the laws of your state, contributory negligence on the part of the plaintiff (discussed in Chapter 7) is an absolute bar to the recovery of damages. Should you explain this to Collins? No. Even though the question is phrased as a hypothetical, it is possible that your answer could affect Collins's future actions. Your best option is to tell Collins that you are not permitted to give legal advice but that you will relay the "hypothetical" question to your supervising attorney.

On the Web

You can find databases containing the names of numerous expert witnesses at various Web sites, including **http://www.experts.com**, **http://www.hgexperts.com**, and **http://www.claims.com**.

❚ expert witness
A witness with professional training or substantial experience qualifying him or her to testify as to his or her opinion on a particular subject.

❚ lay witness
A witness who can truthfully and accurately testify on a fact in question without having specialized training or knowledge; an ordinary witness.

we describe the various types of witnesses as well as some basic skills and principles that are particularly relevant to investigative interviews.

Types of Witnesses

Witnesses include expert witnesses, lay witnesses, and eyewitnesses. Witnesses are also sometimes classified as friendly witnesses or hostile (adverse) witnesses.

Expert Witnesses

An **expert witness** is an individual who has professional training, advanced knowledge, or substantial experience in a specialized area, such as medicine, computer technology, ballistics, or construction techniques. Paralegals often arrange to hire expert witnesses either to testify in court or to render an opinion on some matter relating to the client's case. Expert witnesses are often used in cases involving medical malpractice and product liability to establish the duty, or standard of care, that the defendant owed to the plaintiff. For example, if a client of your firm is suing a physician for malpractice, your supervising attorney might arrange to have another physician testify as to the standard of care owed by a physician to a patient in similar circumstances.

Lay Witnesses

Most witnesses in court are lay witnesses. In contrast to expert witnesses, **lay witnesses** do not possess any particular skill or expertise relating to the matter before the court. They are people who happened to observe or otherwise have factual knowledge about an event. A

Ethics Watch!

KEEPING THE CLIENT INFORMED

Attorneys have a duty to keep their clients reasonably informed about their cases or claims. As a paralegal, you should assume the responsibility for making sure that the attorney does not breach this duty. Periodic notes or phone calls to the client not only keep the client informed about progress on the case but also keep you in touch with the case status—and you and your supervising attorney will be less likely to miss important deadlines relating to the litigation. Frequent communications with clients also cultivate goodwill. Clients generally welcome any news from their attorneys' offices. Even a letter saying "nothing is happening" is usually appreciated. To make sure that the client is kept informed, you will want to have some kind of a tickler system to remind you to contact the client at periodic intervals.

professional or expert in one field may be a lay witness in another field about which he or she does not have expert knowledge. A physician involved in a fraud claim, for example, might give testimony about the fraud as a lay witness but not as an expert witness.

Eyewitnesses

In attempting to gain more information about an event relating to a client's legal claim, paralegals may be required to interview eyewitnesses. **Eyewitnesses** are lay witnesses who have witnessed an event and who may testify in court as to what they observed. The term *eyewitness* is deceiving; a better term might be "sense" witness. This is because an eyewitness's firsthand knowledge of an event need not have been derived from the sense of sight—that is, from actually seeing the event. An eyewitness may be someone who listened in on a telephone conversation between an accused murderer and his or her accomplice. A blind man may have been an eyewitness to a car crash, because he heard it.

> **eyewitness**
> A witness who testifies about an event that he or she observed or experienced firsthand.

In interviews, eyewitnesses are ordinarily asked to describe an event, in their own words and as they recall it, that relates to the client's case. Eyewitness accounts may be lengthy, and the paralegal may want to record the interview session to ensure accuracy. The experienced paralegal may also find that different eyewitnesses to the same event have contradictory views on what actually took place. People's perceptions of reality differ, as paralegals often find when comparing eyewitness reports.

Friendly Witnesses

Some witnesses to an event may be the client's family members, friends, co-workers, neighbors, or other persons who know the client and who want to be helpful in volunteering information. These witnesses are regarded as **friendly witnesses.** You may think that friendly witnesses are the best kind to interview, and they often are. They may also be biased in the client's favor, however, so the paralegal should look closely for the actual facts (and not the witness's interpretation of the facts) when interviewing friendly witnesses.

> **friendly witness**
> A witness who is biased against your client's adversary or sympathetic toward your client in a lawsuit or other legal proceeding.

❚ hostile witness
A witness who is biased against your client or friendly toward your client's adversary in a lawsuit or other legal proceeding; an adverse witness.

Hostile Witnesses

Witnesses who may be prejudiced against your client or friendly to your client's adversary are regarded as **hostile witnesses** (or *adverse witnesses*). Interviewing hostile witnesses can be challenging. Sometimes the witness has an interest in the outcome of the case and would be in a better position if your client lost in court. For example, if the client is a tenant who refuses to pay rent until the landlord makes a structural repair to the roof, then the paralegal interviewing the landlord's manager should be prepared to deal with that person as a potentially hostile witness.

Sometimes, hostile witnesses refuse to be interviewed. On learning that the alternative might be a subpoena, however, a hostile witness may consent to at least a limited interview. If you plan to interview hostile witnesses, contact and interview them in the early stages of your investigation. The longer you wait, the greater the chance that they may be influenced by the opposing party's attorney or the opinions of persons sympathetic to the opposing party.

When interviewing hostile witnesses, you need to be especially careful to be objective, fair, and unbiased in your approach. This does not mean that you have to ignore your client's interests. On the contrary, you will best serve those interests by doing all you can to keep from further alienating a witness whose information might ultimately help your client's case.

Questioning Witnesses

When you are asking questions as a legal investigator, you should phrase your questions so that they lead to the most complete answer possible. Investigative questions should thus be open ended. Compare, for example, the following two questions:

1. "Did you see the driver of the green van run the stop sign?"
2. "What did you see at the time of the accident?"

The first question calls for a "yes" or "no" answer. The second question, in contrast, invites the witness to explain fully what he or she actually saw. Something else that the witness saw could be important to the case—but unless you allow room for the witness's full description, you will not learn about this information.

Notice that the first question also assumes a fact—that the driver of the green van ran the stop sign. The second question, however, makes no assumptions and conveys no information to the witness that may influence his or her answer. Generally, the less the witness knows about other witnesses' descriptions, the better, because those other descriptions could influence the witness's perception of the event. You want to find out exactly what the witness observed, in his or her own words.

Checking a Witness's Qualifications

When you are interviewing a witness during the course of an investigation, you often will not know whether the testimony of that witness will be needed in court or even whether the claim you are investigating will be litigated. Nonetheless, you should operate under the assumption that each witness is a potential court witness. Thus, you should make sure that the witness is competent to testify, reliable, and credible.

Competence

Under the Federal Rules of Evidence, any person is competent to be a lay witness as long as the individual has personal knowledge of the matter. Thus, only if a potential witness did not actually see, hear, or perceive the events in some way (because of a physical or mental disability, for example) will that person be judged incompetent to testify. Although state

As part of a factual investigation into a client's legal claim, a paralegal may contact witnesses or other sources for information about the matter. Although a restaurant is not an ideal setting for discussing confidential information, sometimes it is not possible to meet a witness or other information source in an office environment.

(Courtesy of ©Royalty-Free/Corbis)

rules of evidence vary, most states also define competence for lay witnesses broadly. Expert witnesses are qualified only if they possess special knowledge, skill, experience, training, or education.

Credibility

Because it is easy to establish competence for most witnesses, the primary issue with respect to most witnesses' qualifications is not whether they can testify but whether the testimony will be credible, or believable. The parties to a lawsuit can attack the credibility of an opponent's witness and try to show that the witness is not telling the truth or is unreliable. In federal courts and most state courts, the credibility or reliability of a witness's testimony can be called into question by evidence, in the form of opinion or reputation, that points to the witness's character for truthfulness or untruthfulness. Thus, the paralegal investigating the case should inquire into any matters that tend to show whether the witness is honest. For example, does the witness abuse drugs or have a reputation in the community as a troublemaker or liar? Has the witness been convicted of a crime? If so, was it a felony, or did it involve any dishonesty or false statement? How long ago was the conviction? (Under the federal rules, a witness's credibility can be attacked by evidence of a conviction for a crime punishable by incarceration for over one year or a conviction for any crime involving dishonesty or false statements that occurred within the last ten years.)

Bias

The paralegal should also investigate the witness's possible bias. Does the witness have an interest in the claim being investigated that would tend to make his or her testimony prejudicial? Is the witness a relative or close friend of one of the parties involved in the claim? Does the witness hold a grudge against one of the parties? If the answer to any of these questions is yes, the witness's testimony may be discredited in court. In any event, it will probably not be as convincing as testimony given by a neutral, unbiased witness.

EXHIBIT 14.4
**Information Contained
in a Witness Statement**

1. **Information about the Witness**
   —Name, address, and phone number.
   —Name, address, and phone number of the witness's employer or
     place of business.
   —Interest, if any, in the outcome of the claim being investigated.

2. **Information about the Interview**
   —Name of the interviewer.
   —Name of the attorney or law firm for which the claim is
     being investigated.
   —Date, time, and place of the interview.

3. **Identification of the Event Witnessed**
   —Nature of the action or event observed by the witness.
   —Date of the action or event.

4. **Witness's Description of the Event**

5. **Attestation Clause**
   —Provision or clause at the end of the statement affirming the truth of the witness's
     description as written in the statement.

                                                          [Witness's Signature]

Winding Up the Interview

At the conclusion of an interview, the paralegal should ask the witness if there is anything
else the witness would like to add to his or her statement. This gives the witness the opportunity to expand on areas not previously discussed or explain an answer previously given.
The paralegal should verify the witness's complete mailing address, physical address, and
telephone number. It is also a good idea to get the name and telephone number of a friend
or relative living in the immediate area whom you can contact to locate the witness in the
event that he or she moves prior to the trial.

Witness Statements

Whenever you interview a witness, you should take thorough and accurate notes and prepare a memo to your supervising attorney. Include in the memo your evaluation of the witness's credibility and a description of any nonverbal communication that you felt was
relevant (if the witness seemed uncomfortable with some aspect of the interview or became
nervous when asked questions about a particular topic, for example).

You may also prepare a formal witness statement. Make sure to check with your supervising attorney before preparing such a statement, because formal witness statements may
have to be given to the opposing party under applicable discovery rules (as discussed in
Chapter 13). A **witness statement** is a written document setting forth what the witness said
during the interview. The witness is given an opportunity to review the contents of the statement and then signs the statement to verify its contents. Exhibit 14.4 shows the type of
information normally contained in a witness statement, and Exhibit 14.5 presents excerpts
from a sample witness statement.

Statutes and court rules vary as to the value of witness statements as evidence. Usually,
statements made by witnesses during interviews cannot be introduced as evidence in court,

witness statement
The written record of the statements
made by a witness during an interview,
signed by the witness.

EXHIBIT 14.5
A Sample Witness Statement (Excerpt)

STATEMENT OF JULIA WILLIAMS

I, Julia Williams, am a thirty-five-year-old female. I reside at 3765 Mattis Avenue, Nita City, Nita 48800, and my home telephone number is (616) 555-8989. I work as a nurse at the Nita City Hospital & Clinic, 412 Hospital Way, Nita City, Nita 48802. My work telephone number is (408) 555-9898. I am making this statement in my home on the afternoon of February 8, 2007. The statement is being made to Elena Lopez, a paralegal with the law firm of Jeffers, Gilmore & Dunn.

In regard to the accident on the corner of Mattis Avenue and Thirty-eighth Street on August 4, 2006, at approximately 7:45 A.M. on that date, I was standing at the southwest corner of that intersection, waiting to cross the street, when I observed . . .

* * * *

I affirm that the information given in this statement is accurate and true to the best of my knowledge.

Julia Williams
Julia Williams

---

but they can be used for other purposes. For example, if a hostile witness's testimony in court contradicts something he or she said during your interview, the witness statement may be used to impeach the witness—that is, to call into question the witness's testimony or demonstrate that the witness is unreliable. Witness statements also can be used to refresh a witness's memory.

PLANNING AND CONDUCTING INVESTIGATIONS

Because factual evidence is crucial to the outcome of a legal problem, investigation is necessarily an important part of legal work. Attorneys often rely on paralegals to conduct investigations, and you should be prepared to accept the responsibility for making sure that an investigation is conducted thoroughly and professionally. In the following pages, you will read about the basics of legal investigation—how to plan and undertake an investigation, how the rules of evidence shape the investigative process, and the importance of carefully documenting the results of your investigation.

Of course, you have already read about one aspect of investigations—interviewing witnesses. A preliminary investigation, however, can involve much more. For one thing, before witnesses can be interviewed, they must be located. Information relating to the case may also have to be obtained from a police department, weather bureau, or other source.

Where Do You Start?

Assume that you work for Allen Gilmore, the attorney representing the plaintiff in the hypothetical case discussed in Chapter 13. Recall that the plaintiff in that case, Katherine Baranski, is suing Tony Peretto for negligence. Peretto ran a stop sign at an intersection, and

Developing Paralegal Skills

CHECKING THE ACCIDENT SCENE

Gina Hubbard, a paralegal, works for a small law firm. She and her supervising attorney, John Calpert, have just concluded an intake interview with a new client. The client was involved in an automobile accident, and the driver of the other car, who sustained serious injuries, is suing the client for damages. The client maintains that the accident was not his fault and has asked Calpert to defend him in the lawsuit. The attorney asks Gina to first obtain a copy of the police report on the accident to verify the exact location of the accident, along with other pertinent information, such as photographs taken by police officers. Then, Gina should go to the accident site to learn what she can about the site.

Both Gina and the attorney know that this case may be settled early on, and therefore it may be too soon to hire a private investigator to investigate the accident scene. Even if the case is not settled before trial and an investigator is hired later, months may have passed, and the scene may be considerably changed. Road repairs may alter the area, new signs may be installed, the street may be widened, and so on. It is therefore important that Gina visit the site right away. She makes a list of the equipment she needs to take with her to use when checking the site.

TIPS FOR CHECKING AN ACCIDENT SCENE

- Take a camera to the accident site. A digital camera may be preferable, because it will enable you to include the photos in computer documents relating to the case.
- Consider taking a digital camcorder if one is available.
- Take an audio recorder as well. You may want to dictate notes about your observations or record an interview with an eyewitness should you encounter someone at the site who saw the accident.
- Take a pencil and pad of paper to create sketches of the area, and be sure to include in the sketches any obstacles that could interfere with visibility.
- Include a tape measure or other measuring device in the tool kit as well. This will allow you to obtain precise measurements so that you can create a scale for your photographs and sketches.

as a result, his car collided with Baranski's. Further assume that the case is still in its initial stages. Attorney Gilmore has just met with Katherine Baranski for the initial client interview. You sat in on the interview, listened carefully to Baranski's description of the accident and of the damages she sustained as a result (medical expenses, lost wages, and so on), and took thorough notes.

After the interview, Gilmore asks you to do a preliminary investigation into Baranski's claim. It is now your responsibility to find the answers to a number of questions. Did the accident really occur in the way perceived by the client, Katherine Baranski? Exactly where and when did it happen? How does the police report describe the accident? Were there any witnesses? Was Tony Peretto insured, and if so, by what insurance company? What other circumstances (such as weather) are relevant? Your supervising attorney will want to know the answers to these and other questions before advising Baranski as to what legal action should be pursued.

In undertaking any legal investigation, your logical point of departure is the information you have already acquired about the legal claim or problem. In the Baranski case, this information consists of the statements made by Baranski during the initial client interview and summarized in your notes. Baranski described what she remembered about the accident, including the date and time it occurred. She said she thought that the police investigator had the names of some persons who had witnessed the accident. She also stated that she was employed as an associate professor in the math department at Nita State University, earning approximately $58,000 a year. By using common sense and a little imagination, you can map out a fairly thorough investigation plan based on this information.

Creating an Investigation Plan

An **investigation plan** is simply a step-by-step list of the tasks that you plan to undertake to verify or obtain factual information relating to a legal problem. In the Baranski case, the steps in your investigation plan would include those summarized in Exhibit 14.6 on pages 526 and 527 and discussed next. The paralegal should make sure that his or her supervising attorney approves the investigation plan. Generally, throughout the investigation, it is important to keep in close touch with your supervising attorney about progress being made.

Contacting the Police Department

The initial step in your plan should be to contact the police department. You will want to look at a copy of the police report of the accident, view any photographs that were taken at the scene, obtain the names of persons who may have witnessed the accident, and, if possible, talk to the investigating officer.

Contacting and Interviewing Witnesses

Next, you will want to contact and interview any known witnesses and document their descriptions of what took place at the time of the accident. Known witnesses include the driver (Tony Peretto) of the vehicle that hit Katherine Baranski, the police officer at the scene, and the other witnesses noted in the police investigation report. Keep in mind that if Tony Peretto is aware of Baranski's intention to sue him, he will probably have retained an attorney. If he has, then you are not permitted to contact him directly—all communications with him will have to be through his attorney.

Obtaining Medical and Employment Records

To justify a claim for damages, you will need to ascertain the nature of the injuries sustained by Baranski as a result of the accident, the medical expenses that she incurred, and her annual or monthly income (to determine the amount of wages she lost as a result of the accident). To obtain this information, you will need copies of her medical and employment records.

Note that the institutions holding these records will not release them to you unless Katherine Baranski authorizes them to do so. Therefore, you will also need to arrange with Baranski to sign release forms to include with your requests for copies. A sample authorization form to release medical records is shown in Exhibit 14.7 on page 528. You should make sure that Baranski signs these forms before she leaves the office after the initial interview. Otherwise, waiting for her to return the signed forms may delay your investigation. In addition to obtaining medical records, you may be asked to do some research on the type of injury sustained by Baranski and related statistical or other information.

Contacting the National Weather Service

Weather conditions at the time of the accident may have an important bearing on the case. If it was raining heavily at the time of the accident, for example, Peretto's attorney may argue that Peretto did not see the stop sign or that water on the road prevented him from stopping. You will therefore want to ascertain what the weather conditions were at the time of

investigation plan
A plan that lists each step involved in obtaining and verifying facts and information relevant to the legal problem being investigated.

The National Weather Service is online at **http://www.nws.noaa.gov**.

EXHIBIT 14.6
An Investigation Plan

INVESTIGATION PLAN
File No. 15773

	Date Requested	Date Received
1. Contact Police Department		
—To obtain police report	____	____
—To ask for photographs of accident scene	____	____
—To talk with investigating officer	____	____
—SOURCE: Nita City Police Dept.		
—METHOD: Request in person or by mail		
2. Contact Known Witnesses		
—Tony Peretto, van driver		
—Michael Young, police officer at accident scene	____	____
—Julia Williams, witness at accident scene	____	____
—Dwight Kelly, witness at accident scene	____	____
—SOURCE: Police report		
—METHOD: Contact witnesses by initial phone call and personal interview when possible		
3. Obtain Employment Records		
—To learn Baranski's employment status and income	____	____
—SOURCE: Nita State University		
—METHOD: Written request by mail with Baranski's release enclosed		
4. Obtain Hospital Records		
—To learn necessary information about Baranski's medical treatment and costs	____	____
—SOURCE: Nita City Hospital		
—METHOD: Written request by mail with Baranski's release enclosed		

the accident by contacting the National Weather Service. When you interview eyewitnesses, you should ask them about weather conditions at the place and time of the accident as well.

Obtaining Vehicle Title and Registration Records

To verify that Tony Peretto owns the vehicle that he was driving at the time of the accident, you will need to obtain title and registration records. Usually, these can be acquired from the state department of motor vehicles, although in some states the secretary of state's office handles such records. The requirements for obtaining such information vary from state to state and may include the submission of special forms and fees. Therefore, you should call the relevant state department or office in advance to find out what procedures should be followed.

Contacting the Insurance Company

If you learned the name of Peretto's insurance company from Baranski or from the police report, you will want to contact that company to find out what kind of insurance coverage Peretto has and the limits of his liability under the insurance policy. Insurance companies usually are reluctant to give this information to anyone other than the policyholder. They

On the Web

Relevant driving and vehicle registration records may be on the Web. See, for example, the list of licensed drivers in the state of Texas at **http://www. publicdata.com**. To find the home pages of your state's government agencies, go to **http://www. firstgov.gov** and click on "State Government."

EXHIBIT 14.6
An Investigation Plan—Continued

	Date Requested	Date Received
5. Contact National Weather Service —To learn what the weather conditions were on the day of the accident	_____	_____
—SOURCE: National Weather Service or newspaper —METHOD: Phone call or written request		
6. Obtain Title and Registration Records —To verify Peretto's ownership of the vehicle	_____	_____
—SOURCE: Department of Motor Vehicles —METHOD: Order by mail		
7. Contact Peretto's Insurance Company —To find out about insurance coverage —To check liability limits	_____ _____	_____ _____
—SOURCE: Insurance company —METHOD: Written request by mail		

8. Use a Professional Investigator
—To contact such witnesses as
  –ambulance attendants
  –doctors
  –residents in neighborhood of accident scene
—To inspect vehicle
—To take photos of accident site
—To investigate accident scene, and so on
	_____
	
	_____
	_____
	_____
		_____
		
		_____
		_____
		_____

—SOURCE: Regular law firm investigator —METHOD: In person		

sometimes cooperate with such requests, however, because they know that if they do not, the information can be obtained during discovery, should a lawsuit be initiated.

Using a Professional Investigator's Services

Some law firms routinely use the services of professional investigators. Depending on the circumstances, your supervising attorney may decide to use a professional investigator for certain tasks, including those just described. An experienced professional investigator will often have developed many useful contacts with law enforcement officers, subject-matter experts, coroners, and other sources. This familiarity can expedite an investigation and allow a professional investigator to obtain information that others cannot access. In addition, certain government and private databases are restricted to government agents and licensed investigators. Attorneys also sometimes hire professional investigators to obtain facts omitted from police reports, search public records, serve subpoenas, evaluate trial presentations, and conduct surveillance.

Locating certain witnesses may be difficult and time consuming. Your supervising attorney may therefore prefer that the professional investigator handle this task as well, particularly if the attorney needs your assistance in the office. The investigator might locate

EXHIBIT 14.7
Authorization to
Release Medical Records

TO: Nita City Hospital & Clinic   PATIENT: Katherine Baranski
      Nita City, NI 48803   335 Natural Boulevard
                                                                              Nita City, NI 48802

     You are hereby authorized to furnish and release to my attorney, Allen P. Gilmore of Jeffers, Gilmore & Dunn, all information and records relating to my treatment for injuries incurred on August 4, 2006. Please do not disclose information to insurance adjusters or to other persons without written authority from me. The foregoing authority shall continue in force until revoked by me in writing, but for no longer than one year following the date given below.

Date: January 30, 2007   *Katherine Baranski*
                                                Katherine Baranski

Please attach your invoice for any fee or photostatic costs and send it with the information requested above to my office.

Thank you,

Allen P. Gilmore

Allen P. Gilmore
Jeffers, Gilmore & Dunn
Attorneys at Law
553 Fifth Avenue
Suite 101
Nita City, NI 48801

Helena Moritz

Helena Moritz
Notary Public State of Nita
Nita County
My Commission Expires: November 12, 2008

witnesses such as the ambulance driver, physicians who treated Baranski, residents in the area who might have observed the accident, and witnesses who have moved.

     You may be responsible for working with the investigator. For example, your supervising attorney may ask you to arrange for the investigator to inspect and take photographs of the accident scene. You will then also work cooperatively with the investigator to determine the credibility and effectiveness of certain witnesses. In addition, you will meet with the investigator to review discovery documents in order to provide additional insight or generate investigative leads.

Locating Witnesses

Perhaps one of the most challenging tasks for the legal investigator is locating a witness whose address is unknown or who has moved from a previous, known address. Suppose, for example, that in the Baranski case the police investigation report lists the name, address, and telephone number of Edna Ball, a witness to the accident. When you call her number, a recording informs you that the phone has been disconnected. You go to her address, and the house appears to be vacant. What is your next step?

At this point, many paralegals suggest to their supervising attorneys that a professional investigator take over the search. But if you alone must locate the witness, there are several sources to which you can turn. A good starting point is to visit other homes in the neighborhood. Perhaps someone living nearby knows Edna Ball and can give you some leads as to where she is or what happened to her. Other sources are discussed below.

Telephone and City Directories

The telephone directory can sometimes be a valuable source of information for the investigator. In trying to locate Edna Ball, for example, you might check to see if her name is listed in the current directory and, if so, whether it is listed jointly with someone, such as her husband. Your local telephone information service might have a new number listed for her. If the information operator indicates that the number is unlisted, you can explain the nature of your concern and request that the operator phone Edna Ball at that number to see if she is willing to call you.

City directories are also good potential sources of information. Such directories may be available in the local library, the law firm's library, or on the Web. A city directory generally contains more information than a phone book. For example, some city directories list places of employment and spouses' names in addition to addresses and telephone numbers. Typically, city directories provide a listing of names and phone numbers by street address. In the Baranski case, if you wanted to obtain the telephone numbers of persons who live in the area of the Baranski-Peretto accident, you could consult a city directory for addresses near the intersection where the accident occurred.

Online People Finders

Today, paralegals can use one of the numerous Internet people-finding services to locate witnesses (and witnesses' assets, if needed). Some of these online services charge a nominal fee (ranging from three dollars to seventy dollars) for each search, depending on the type of report requested (simple address record, background check, e-mail address, assets). The services will check public records, telephone directories, court and criminal records, and a variety of other sources and provide results quickly and efficiently. (For an example, go to **http://www.people-finder.com**, **http://bigfoot.com**, or **http://www.searchbug.com/peoplefinder** and enter the name, city, and state of a person you wish to locate.) Both of the largest online legal research services (Westlaw® and Lexis®, which will be discussed in Chapter 18) offer people-finding services as well. In addition, several software programs that conduct Internet searches, such as *NetDetective* and *OnlineDetective*, are available for a one-time charge.

On the Web

To find Web sites that provide telephone book listings, you can do a broad search using a search engine, such as Lycos, at **http://www.lycos.com**.

Other Information Sources

Other sources of information include media reports (newspaper and magazine articles and television videos covering the event being investigated); court records (probate proceedings, lawsuits, and so on); deeds to property (usually located in the county courthouse); birth, marriage, and death certificates; voter-registration lists; the post office (at which the witness may have left a forwarding address); credit bureaus; the tax assessor's office; and city utilities, such as the local electric or water company.

Professional organizations may be useful sources as well. For example, if you have learned from one of Edna Ball's neighbors that she is a paralegal, you can check with state and local paralegal associations to see if they have current information on her. You might

Charisse A. Charles

PARALEGAL **profile**

LITIGATION PARALEGAL

Charisse A. Charles received her bachelor of arts degree, cum laude, in legal administration in December 1993 from the University of West Florida. Her first paralegal job was as an intern for a judge. After graduation, she was hired by a small law firm as a workers' compensation litigation paralegal and is currently working as a litigation paralegal, primarily in the area of personal injury.

She is an active member of the Northwest Florida Paralegal Association, serves on the University of West Florida Legal Studies Advisory Board, and is very active in her community with a group called the Pensacola Community Arts and Recreation Association, a nonprofit organization.

What do you like best about your work?

"What I like best about my work is being able to communicate with people in various offices to assist our clients in defending their claims. I have met a lot of people via the telephone and in so doing, have established great working relationships with many doctors' offices, judges' offices, clerks at the courthouse, and adjusters at various insurance companies, to just list a few. My working relationships with these people make my job much easier when I need to call on their assistance for our clients."

What is the greatest challenge that you face in your area of work?

"The greatest challenge for me is playing the role of both a plaintiff's paralegal and a defense paralegal. Some days it is very hard to empathize with clients who I know in my heart are not seriously injured and are only looking for a handout. On the flip side, it is sometimes very difficult to not allow my emotions to come into play when defending a matter for an insurance company regarding an individual who has been seriously injured."

What advice do you have for would-be paralegals in your area of work?

"Communication can help you or destroy you."

"I suggest that they focus heavily on their communication skills. Communication can help you or destroy you. I encourage them to attend workshops that focus on communicating with clients who are both difficult and not so difficult. I also encourage would-be paralegals to be detail oriented. Last, I suggest that they welcome challenges, big or small."

What are some tips for success as a paralegal in your area of work?

"Tips for success as a personal-injury paralegal include good communication skills, organizational skills, computer skills, timeliness, a willingness to accept changes, and a willingness to make changes that will benefit all parties involved."

---

also check with federal, state, or local governmental agencies or bureaus (discussed in the following section) to see if the information contained in public records will be helpful in locating Edna Ball.

Accessing Government Information

Records and files acquired and stored by government offices and agencies can be a tremendous resource for the legal investigator. Public records available at local government buildings or offices (such as the county courthouse or post office) were mentioned above. Additionally, it is possible to obtain information from federal agencies, such as the Social Security Administration, and from state departments or agencies, such as the state revenue department or the secretary of state's office. If you wish to obtain information from any gov-

On the Web

You can access the home pages of federal agencies by going to **http://www.firstgov.gov** and clicking on the "A–Z Agency Index."

EXHIBIT 14.8
**Freedom of Information
Act Request Form**

Agency Head or FOIA Officer
Title
Name of Agency
Address of Agency
City, State, ZIP Code

Re: Freedom of Information Act Request.

Dear_____:

    Under the provisions of the Freedom of Information Act, 5 U.S.C. 552, I am
requesting access to [identify the records as clearly and specifically as possible].
    If there are any fees for searching for, or copying, the records I have requested, please
inform me before you fill the request. [Or: . . . please supply the records without informing
me if the fees do not exceed $_____.]
    [Optional] I am requesting this information [state the reason for your request if you think
it will assist you in obtaining the information].
    [Optional] As you know, the act permits you to reduce or waive fees when the release
of the information is considered as "primarily benefiting the public." I believe that this
request fits that category and I therefore ask that you waive any fees.
    If all or any part of this request is denied, please cite the specific exemption(s) that
you think justifies your refusal to release the information, and inform me of the appeal
procedures available to me under the law.
    I would appreciate your handling this request as quickly as possible, and I look foward
to hearing from you within ten days, as the law stipulates.

Sincerely,

Signature
Name
Address
City, State, ZIP Code

On the Web

For further information on how to
make an FOIA request, go to **http://
www.nist.gov/admin/foia/foia.htm**.

ernment files or records, you should check with the specific agency or department to see
what rules apply.

    The Freedom of Information Act (FOIA), which was enacted by Congress in 1966,
requires the federal government to disclose certain records to any person on request. A
request that complies with the FOIA procedures need only contain a reasonable description
of the information sought. Exhibit 14.8 illustrates the proper format for a letter requesting
information under the FOIA. Note that the FOIA exempts some types of information from
the disclosure requirement, including classified information (information concerning
national security), confidential material dealing with trade secrets, government personnel
rules, and personal medical files.

Investigation and the Rules of Evidence

Because an investigation is conducted to obtain information and verify facts that may eventually be introduced as evidence at trial, you should know what kind of evidence will be
admissible in court before undertaking your investigation.

    Evidence is anything that is used to prove the existence or nonexistence of a fact.
Whether evidence will be admitted in court is determined by the **rules of evidence**—rules
that have been created by the courts to ensure that any evidence presented in court is fair

evidence
Anything that is used to prove the
existence or nonexistence of a fact.

rules of evidence
Rules governing the admissibility of
evidence in trial courts.

Developing Paralegal Skills

ACCESSING GOVERNMENT INFORMATION

Ellen Simmons has started a new job as a paralegal for Smith & Case, a law firm that handles Superfund cases (see Chapter 12). Ellen is about to request copies of documents from the Environmental Protection Agency (EPA). Ellen calls and speaks to Christopher Peter, a paralegal with the EPA. She identifies herself as a paralegal from Smith & Chase, which is representing a client involved at the Suburban Landfill Superfund site. Ellen is greeted with an icy silence and wonders what she might have said to offend Christopher. She asks if the EPA has the waste-in/waste-out report that gives the total volume of hazardous waste at the site and lists the potentially responsible parties.

Christopher responds, in a surprised voice, that the EPA does have the documents. "Are you new?" asks Christopher. "Is it that obvious?" jokes Ellen. Christopher responds that it's not really that obvious and explains that her predecessor always just sent in FOIA requests for everything that the EPA had in its files and that it took weeks to respond to these requests. "Believe me, your firm has quite a reputation around here," says Christopher.

Ellen knows that she is off to a good start in her new job and with an important legal assistant at the EPA. She smiles to herself as she promises to submit the FOIA request for only the waste-in/waste-out report.

TIPS FOR WORKING WITH GOVERNMENT AGENCIES

- Review the file to familiarize yourself with the case before calling the agency.
- Review the agency's regulations to ascertain which documents the agency prepares in specific types of cases, such as Superfund cases.
- Make a list of the various documents.
- Determine in advance (from the list) which documents you will be requesting.
- Develop a list of alternatives to use in the event that the documents that you request have not been prepared or are not available.
- Make reasonable requests from the agency.
- Cultivate good working relationships with agency staff members.

and reliable. The Federal Rules of Evidence govern the admissibility of evidence in federal courts. For cases brought in state courts, state rules of evidence apply. (Many states have adopted evidence rules patterned on the federal rules.) Of course, you will not need to become an expert in evidentiary rules, but a basic knowledge of how evidence is classified and what types of evidence are admissible in court will greatly assist your investigative efforts.

Direct versus Circumstantial Evidence

direct evidence
Evidence directly establishing the existence of a fact.

circumstantial evidence
Indirect evidence offered to establish, by inference, the likelihood of a fact that is in question.

Two types of evidence may be brought into court—direct evidence and circumstantial evidence. **Direct evidence** is any evidence that, if believed, establishes the truth of the fact in question. For example, bullets found in the body of a shooting victim provide direct evidence of the type of gun that fired them. **Circumstantial evidence** is indirect evidence that, even if believed, does not establish the fact in question but only the degree of likelihood of the fact. In other words, circumstantial evidence can create an inference that a fact exists.

For example, suppose that your firm's client owns the type of gun that shot the bullets found in the victim's body. This circumstantial evidence does not establish that the client shot the victim. Combined with other circumstantial evidence, however, it could help to

Developing Paralegal Skills

KEEPING AN EVIDENCE LOG

Steve Fessler works as a paralegal for Marty Melman, a sole practitioner. Marty is representing June Linden, the plaintiff in a personal-injury case. Marty has asked Steve to obtain X-rays of the plaintiff's fractured ankle. The fracture occurred as a result of an auto accident.

Steve receives a phone call from the hospital indicating that the X-rays are ready to be picked up. Steve drives to the hospital, picks up the X-rays, and brings them back to the office. He places them in a special folder and applies an exhibit label to the folder. The label contains a thorough description of the X-rays for purposes of identification. The special folder will preserve the X-rays. Next, he places the folder in the evidence cabinet, which is kept locked so that access to the cabinet is controlled. He takes out a notebook entitled "Evidence Log" and places a clean log sheet in it.

TIPS FOR CREATING AN EVIDENCE LOG

- The log-sheet form should contain blanks for the file name, a description of the evidence, and information about its acquisition, such as the date on which it was acquired, how it was acquired, and who acquired it.

- Additionally, the form should contain blanks for identifying marks on the evidence, where the evidence is kept within the firm, and the name of the evidence custodian.

- The form should include columns that show the chain of custody of the evidence, such as columns for the name, date, and purpose of each release of the evidence.

- The form should prominently state that anyone removing the evidence must safeguard it and return it unchanged. Anyone removing the evidence should be required to sign this statement.

- Consider taking a Polaroid or digital snapshot before and after each transfer of the evidence.

Maintaining an evidence log enables the law firm to keep track of evidence in its possession. If the evidence needs to be removed and reviewed by someone, such as an expert witness, there will be a record of the evidence and who has or had custody of it. Maintaining an evidence log also helps to protect against claims that the evidence is not authentic or has been altered while in the law firm's possession.

convince a jury that the client committed the crime. For instance, if other circumstantial evidence indicates that your firm's client had a motive for harming the victim and that the client was at the scene of the crime at the time the crime was committed, a jury might conclude that the client committed the crime.

Relevance

Evidence will not be admitted in court unless it is relevant. **Relevant evidence** is evidence that tends to prove or disprove the fact in question. For example, evidence that the gun belonging to your firm's client was in the home of another person when the victim was shot would be relevant, because it would tend to prove that the client did not shoot the victim.

Even relevant evidence may not be admitted in court if its probative (proving) value is substantially outweighed by other important considerations. For example, even though evidence is relevant, it may not be necessary—the fact at issue may have been sufficiently proved or disproved by previous evidence. In that situation, the introduction of further evidence would be a waste of time and would cause undue delay in the trial proceedings. Relevant evidence may also be excluded if it would tend to distract the jury from the main issues of the case, mislead the jury, or cause the jury to decide the issue on an emotional basis.

relevant evidence
Evidence tending to prove or disprove the fact in question. Only relevant evidence is admissible in court.

Authentication of Evidence

authentication

The process of establishing the genuineness of an item that is to be introduced as evidence in a trial.

At trial, an attorney must lay the proper foundation for the introduction of certain evidence, such as documents, exhibits, and other objects, and must demonstrate to the court that the evidence is what the attorney claims.[1] The process by which this is accomplished is referred to as **authentication**. The authentication requirement relates to relevance, because something offered in evidence becomes relevant to the case only if it is authentic, or genuine. As a legal investigator, you therefore need to make sure that the evidence you obtain is not only relevant but also capable of being authenticated if introduced at trial.

Commonly, evidence is authenticated by the testimony of witnesses. For example, if an attorney wants to introduce an autopsy report as evidence in a case, he or she can have the report authenticated by the testimony of the medical examiner who signed it. Generally, an attorney must offer enough proof of authenticity to convince the court that the evidence is, in fact, what it is purported to be.

The rules of evidence require authentication because certain types of evidence, such as exhibits and objects, cannot be cross-examined by opposing counsel, as witnesses can, yet such evidence may have a significant effect on the jury. The authentication requirement provides a safeguard against the introduction of nonverified evidence that may strongly influence the outcome of the case.

The Federal Rules of Evidence provide for the self-authentication of specific types of evidence. In other words, certain documents or records need not be authenticated by testimony. Certified copies of public records, for example, are automatically deemed authentic. Other self-authenticating evidentiary documents include official publications (such as a report issued by the federal Environmental Protection Agency), documents containing a notary public's seal or the seal of a public official, newspaper or magazine articles, and manufacturers' trademarks or labels.

Hearsay

hearsay

Testimony that is given in court by a witness who relates not what he or she knows personally but what another person said. Hearsay is generally not admissible as evidence.

When interviewing witnesses, keep in mind that the witness's testimony *in court* must be based on the witness's own knowledge and not hearsay. **Hearsay** is defined as testimony that is given in court by a witness who relates not what he or she knows personally but what another person said. Literally, it is what someone heard someone else say. Hearsay is generally not admissible in court when offered to prove the truth of the matter asserted.

For example, a witness in the Baranski case cannot testify in court that she heard another observer say, "That van is going ninety miles per hour"—even if the other observer was a police officer. Such testimony would be inadmissible under the hearsay rule. The witness can only testify about what she personally observed regarding the accident. Of course, during the investigation, witnesses often tell you what other people said (and you should not discourage them from doing so). If you wish to use information obtained this way as evidence in court, however, you need to find an alternative method of proving it (such as by the testimony of the people who made the original statements).

Policy underlying the Hearsay Rule.   There are several reasons why hearsay is generally not allowed. First, the person who made the out-of-court statements (referred to as the *declarant*) was not under oath at the time of making the statements. Second, the witness who is testifying may have misunderstood what the other person said. Third, because there is no opportunity to cross-examine the person who actually made the statements, there is no way to verify that the statements were actually made, much less that the witness heard them correctly. In other words, hearsay evidence is inadmissible because it is unreliable, not because it is irrelevant.

Exceptions to the Hearsay Rule.   Exceptions to the hearsay rule are made in specific circumstances, often because the statements are made in situations that indicate a high degree of reliability. For example, a witness is usually allowed to testify about what a dying person said concerning the cause or circumstances of his or her impending death. This is because the courts have concluded that a person facing imminent death will usually not lie about who or what caused that death. Similarly, if a person makes an excited statement at the time of a stressful or startling event (such as "Oh no! That woman has just dropped her baby out the window"), a witness can usually testify as to that statement in court. If one of the parties to a lawsuit makes an out-of-court admission (for example, if defendant Peretto in the Baranski case admits to his friends that he was driving too fast at the time of the accident), a witness's testimony about what the party said will be admissible.[2] Exhibit 14.9 lists and describes some of the traditional exceptions to the hearsay rule.

EXHIBIT 14.9
Some Exceptions to the Hearsay Rule

Present Sense Impression—A statement describing an event or condition made at the time the declarer perceived the event or condition or immediately thereafter [FRE 803(1)].* Example: "I smell smoke."

Excited Utterance—A statement relating to a startling event or condition made while the declarer was under the stress or excitement caused by the startling event or condition [FRE 803(2)]. Example: "Oh no! The brakes aren't working!"

State of Mind—A statement of the declarer's then-existing state of mind, emotion, sensation, or physical condition (such as intent, plan, motive, design, mental feeling, pain, or bodily health). Such statements are considered trustworthy because of their spontaneity [FRE 803(3)]. Example: "My leg is bleeding and hurts terribly."

Recorded Recollection—A memorandum or record indicating a witness's previous statements concerning a matter that the witness cannot now remember with sufficient accuracy to testify fully about the matter. If admitted in court, the memorandum or record may be read into evidence but may not itself be received as an exhibit unless offered by an adverse party [FRE 803(5)]. Example: An employer's memo to one of his or her employees in which the employer responds to the employee's complaint about safety violations in the workplace.

Former Testimony—Testimony that was given at another hearing or deposition by a witness who is now unavailable, if the party against whom the testimony is now offered was a predecessor in interest and had an opportunity to examine the witness in court during the previous hearing or deposition [FRE 804(b)(1)]. Example: An employee's testimony about his or her employer that was introduced at a trial brought by the employee's co-worker against that employer for sexual harassment. The employer is now being sued by another employee for sexual harassment, and the employee who testified in the previous trial is out of the country. The employee's testimony in the previous trial may be admissible.

Business Records—A document or compilation of data made in the course of a regularly conducted business activity, unless the source of the information or the method or circumstances of the document's preparation indicate that it is not trustworthy as evidence. The source of information must be from a person with firsthand knowledge, although this person need not be the person who actually made the entry or created the document [FRE 803(6)]. Example: Financial statement of a business firm.

Dying Declarations—In a prosecution for homicide or in a civil proceeding, a statement made by a person who believes that his or her death is impending about the cause or circumstances of his or her impending death [FRE 804(b)(2)]. Example: Derek said just before he died, "Jethro stabbed me."

Statement against Interest—A statement that was made by someone who is now unavailable and that was, at the time of its making, so far contrary to the declarer's financial, legal, or other interests that a reasonable person in the declarer's position would not have made the statement unless he or she believed it to be true [FRE 804(b)(3)]. Example: Sanchez says that Jackson, who is now missing, made the following statement to Sanchez just before leaving town: "I committed the perfect crime!"

Miscellaneous Exceptions—Miscellaneous exceptions include records of vital statistics [FRE 803(9)]; records of religious organizations [FRE 803(11)]; marriage, baptismal, or similar certificates [FRE 803(12)]; family records (including charts, engravings on rings, inscriptions on family portraits, and engravings on tombstones) [FRE 803(13)]; and statements offered as evidence of a material fact that are trustworthy because of the circumstances in which they were uttered [FRE 804(b)(5) and FRE 803(24)].

---

*Federal Rules of Evidence.

Today's Professional Paralegal

INTERVIEWING A CLIENT

Amanda Blake, a paralegal, works for John Kerrigan, a sole practitioner. A new client, Joel Sontag, calls for an appointment to make his will. The attorney has to go out of town for a court hearing. Because Sontag seems to be anxious to get the will done, the attorney asks Amanda to meet with Sontag and interview him to obtain some basic information. The attorney will review the information when he returns from his trip and then call Sontag to advise him on the will and other estate-planning possibilities.

PREPARING FOR THE INTERVIEW

Amanda reserves the conference room. On the day of Sontag's visit, she has it set up for the interview. She has already made a copy of the will and estate-planning checklist that she will use to ensure that she gets all of the essential information from Sontag. The secretary shows Sontag into the conference room when he arrives.

MEETING THE CLIENT

Amanda introduces herself, saying, "Hello, Mr. Sontag, I'm Amanda Blake, John Kerrigan's legal assistant. I'll be meeting with you today to obtain the estate-planning information that Mr. Kerrigan needs if he is to advise you." Sontag responds, "Mr. Kerrigan told me that we would be meeting today. He also told me how capable you are." Amanda smiles and says, "Thanks. And did Mr. Kerrigan explain to you that I'm not an attorney?" Sontag responds, "Yes, he did." Amanda then removes her checklist and note pad from her file.

OBTAINING INFORMATION ABOUT THE CLIENT

"I'll be reviewing this checklist to make sure that we obtain all of the information that we need for your will," Amanda informs Joel. "First, I need you to fill out the client information form," instructs Amanda. "As you can see, it requires you to give us personal information, such as your name, legal residence, date of birth, and other data." Joel takes the form and fills it out. When he is finished, he hands it to Amanda.

"Now I need some other information. First, I need to know if you're married," states Amanda. "Yes, I am," responds Joel. "Your wife's name is?" asks Amanda. "Nicole Lynn Sontag," answers Joel. "And your wife resides

Summarizing Your Results

The final step in any investigation is summarizing the results. Generally, your investigation report should provide an overall summary of your findings, a summary of the facts and information gathered from each source that you investigated, and your general conclusions and recommendations based on the information obtained during the investigation.

Overall Summary

The overall summary of the investigation should thoroughly describe for the reader all of the facts you have gathered about the case. This section should be written in such a way that someone not familiar with the case could read it and become adequately informed of the case's factual background.

Source-by-Source Summaries

You should also create a list of your information sources, including witnesses, and summarize the facts gleaned from each of these sources. Each "source section" should contain all of the information gathered from that source, including direct quotes from witnesses. Each

with you at the address that you've given on the client information form?" asks Amanda. "Yes, she does," Joel states. "When was she born, and what's her Social Security number?" asks Amanda. "She was born on January 17, 1968, and her Social Security number is 363-46-2350," says Joel.

"Now, Joel, do you have any children?" asks Amanda. "Yes, we have one son, Joel, Jr., aged four," answers Joel. "Do you want to provide for both of them in your will?" asks Amanda. "Yes," responds Joel. "Do you have any other relatives for whom you want to provide?" asks Amanda. "Yes, I have a brother, Alfred Sontag, who lives in a home for autistic people," answers Joel. "I'll need the address for the home," responds Amanda. Joel takes an address book out of his briefcase and gives her the address. "Is there anyone else whom you want to provide for in your will?" asks Amanda. "No," responds Joel.

OBTAINING INFORMATION ABOUT THE CLIENT'S PROPERTY

"Now we need to discuss property," Amanda informs Joel. "Do you own a home?" she asks. "Yes," he answers. Amanda says, "I need to know if the home is located at the address you gave on the form, when you bought it, what it cost, what its present approximate market value is, whether you own it jointly with your wife, and the balance on your mortgage." Joel gives her all of the requested information. Amanda continues questioning Joel about his property holdings until she has covered all the items on her checklist.

CONCLUDING THE INTERVIEW

"Well," says Amanda, "we've covered everything on the checklist. Now we need to set up a time for you to meet with Mr. Kerrigan to discuss estate-planning procedures and your will. Because you jointly own property with your wife, Mr. Kerrigan may want both of you to meet with him. Would two o'clock next Tuesday afternoon be a good time for you both to come in to meet with Mr. Kerrigan?" Joel tells Amanda that he thinks that both he and his wife could arrange to meet with the attorney at that time. They tentatively schedule an appointment for that date. Joel will call Amanda if the appointment must be changed. Joel gets up to leave the office, saying that he'll probably see her again next Tuesday. "I'll look forward to that," says Amanda. Amanda then begins to prepare a detailed summary of the interview to give to her supervising attorney on his return.

source section should also contain a subsection giving your personal comments on that particular source. You might comment on a witness's demeanor, for example, or on whether the witness's version of the facts was consistent or inconsistent with those of other witnesses. Your impressions of the witness's competence or reliability could be noted. If the witness provided you with further leads to be explored, this information could also be included.

General Conclusions and Recommendations

In the final section, you will present your overall conclusions about the investigation, as well as any suggestions that you have on the development of the case. Attorneys rely heavily on their investigators' impressions of witnesses and evaluations of investigative results because the investigators have firsthand knowledge of the sources. Your impression of a potentially important witness, for example, may help the attorney decide whether to arrange for a follow-up interview with the witness. Usually, the attorney will want to interview only the most promising witnesses, and your impressions and comments will serve as a screening device. Based on your findings during the investigation, you might also suggest to the attorney what further information can be obtained during discovery, if necessary, and what additional research needs to be done.

KEY TERMS AND CONCEPTS

active listening 511

authentication 534

circumstantial evidence 532

closed-ended question 510

direct evidence 532

evidence 531

expert witness 518

eyewitness 519

friendly witness 519

hearsay 534

hostile witness 520

hypothetical question 510

interviewee 504

investigation plan 525

lay witness 518

leading question 510

open-ended question 509

passive listening 511

relevant evidence 533

rules of evidence 531

witness statement 522

chapter summary — Conducting Interviews and Investigations

Planning the Interview

Paralegals often interview clients and witnesses. Prior to the interview, the paralegal should prepare the interview environment to ensure that interruptions, noises, and delays will be minimized, that the client will be comfortable, and that any necessary supplies, forms, and equipment are at hand.

1. *Planning the questions*—In preparing for an interview, the interviewer should have in mind the kind of information being sought from the interviewee. Preprinted interview forms provide helpful guidelines, but the interviewer should remain flexible during the interview, tailor questions to the interviewee's responses, and ask follow-up questions.

2. *Recording the interview*—Some paralegals record their interviews for future reference. If you do, make sure to obtain permission from your supervising attorney and the person being interviewed before recording. Also, keep in mind that some clients and witnesses will be less willing to disclose information freely when being recorded. If the interviewee appears hesitant, consider taking notes instead.

Interviewing Skills

Interviewing skills include interpersonal skills, questioning skills, and communication skills, particularly listening skills.

1. *Interpersonal skills*—The interviewer should put the interviewee at ease, use language that the person will understand, and avoid using legal terms.

2. *Questioning skills*—Types of questions used during the interviewing process include open-ended, closed-ended, leading, and hypothetical questions. The questioning technique will depend on the person being interviewed and the type of information sought (see Exhibit 14.2 on page 509).

3. *Communication skills*—The ability to listen is perhaps the most important skill for an interviewer to develop.

   a. Passive listening involves listening attentively to the speaker and using either verbal or nonverbal cues (such as nodding) to encourage him or her to continue.

   b. Active listening involves not just listening attentively but also giving feedback that indicates to the speaker that you understand what he or she is saying.

c. One effective active listening technique is for the interviewer to "reflect back," or restate, what the interviewee has said. This gives the speaker an opportunity to clarify or correct previous statements.

d. Active listening enables the interviewer to control the flow of the interview. It allows the interviewer to put the interviewee's statements into the larger context and facilitates smooth transitions between topics.

Interviewing Clients

There are three types of client interviews: initial interviews (usually conducted by the attorney but often attended by the paralegal), subsequent interviews (often conducted by the paralegal), and informational interviews (or meetings, also typically handled by the paralegal).

1. *Scheduling interviews*—In setting up an interview, the paralegal should tell the client what documents to bring to the interview and follow up with a confirmation letter giving the date and time of the interview and listing the items the client is to bring.

2. *Summarizing the interview*—As soon as possible after an interview is concluded, the paralegal should summarize in a written memorandum the information gathered in the interview. The memorandum should include the paralegal's general impressions of the client's statements and nonverbal behaviors.

Interviewing Witnesses

1. *Types of witnesses*—Types of witnesses include expert witnesses (who have specialized training that qualifies them to testify as to their opinion in a given area), lay witnesses (ordinary witnesses who have factual information about the matter being investigated), eyewitnesses (who have firsthand knowledge of an event—because they saw it happen, for example), friendly witnesses (who are favorable to the client's position), and hostile witnesses (who are biased against the client, friendly to the opponent, or resent being interviewed for other reasons).

2. *Questioning witnesses*—Investigative questions should be open ended so that they elicit the most complete answers possible. Additional questions should ascertain whether the witness is competent, credible, and reliable and whether the witness has any bias relevant to the case.

3. *Winding up the interview*—The paralegal should ask the witness at the end of the interview if the witness would like to add anything to her or his statement. This gives the witness an opportunity to explain an answer or expand on the areas discussed.

4. *Witness statements*—Following an interview of a witness, the paralegal should prepare a memo to the supervising attorney relating what the witness said during the interview and asking if the attorney wants a formal witness statement prepared. The formal witness statement identifies the witness, discloses what was discovered during the interview, and is signed by the witness.

Planning and Conducting Investigations

Factual evidence is crucial to the outcome of a legal problem, and paralegals are often asked to conduct investigations to discover any factual evidence that supports (or contradicts) a

(Continued)

client's claims. Before starting an investigation, the paralegal should create an investigation plan—a step-by-step list of what sources will be investigated to obtain specific types of information (police reports, medical and employment records, and so forth). The paralegal should discuss the plan with his or her supervising attorney before embarking on the investigation.

1. *Locating witnesses*—Sources of factual information regarding witnesses or other persons include telephone and city directories; online people finders; media reports; court records; utility companies; professional organizations; and information recorded, compiled, or prepared by federal, state, and local government entities. The Freedom of Information Act of 1966 requires that federal agencies disclose certain records to any person on request, provided that the form of the request complies with the procedures mandated by the act.

2. *Rules of evidence*—Evidence is anything that is used to prove the existence or nonexistence of a fact. Rules of evidence established by the federal and state courts spell out what types of evidence may or may not be admitted in court.

   a. Direct evidence is any evidence that, if believed, establishes the truth of the fact in question.

   b. Circumstantial evidence is evidence that does not directly establish the fact in question but that establishes, by inference, the likelihood of the fact.

   c. Only relevant evidence, which tends to prove or disprove a fact in question, is admissible as evidence in court.

   d. For evidence to be admitted at trial, the attorney must prove to the court that the evidence is what it purports to be. This is called *authentication*.

   e. Hearsay is testimony given in court by a witness who relates not what he or she knows personally, but what someone else said. Generally, hearsay evidence is not admissible in court. Exceptions are made in circumstances that indicate a high degree of reliability—for example, when the hearsay involves a party's out-of-court admissions or a dying person's statement about who caused his or her death.

3. *Summarizing results*—When the investigation is complete, the paralegal should summarize the results. The summary should include an overall summary, a source-by-source summary, and a final section giving the paralegal's conclusions and recommendations.

QUESTIONS FOR REVIEW

1. What kinds of skills do interviewers employ during interviews?

2. What are the types of questions that can be used in an interview? When would you use each type?

3. What takes place during the initial client interview? What is the paralegal's role at this interview? What other types of client interviews are commonly conducted by paralegals? What is the purpose of each type?

4. List and describe the various types of witnesses. In what kinds of situations might each of these types of witnesses be used?

5. What is a witness statement? How is it used?

6. Why and how do you create an investigation plan? What types of actions might be included in an investigation plan?

7. List five sources that you would consult in attempting to locate a witness. Which would be the most useful? Which would be the least useful? Why?

8. What is evidence? How are the rules of evidence used?

9. Define and give examples of the following types of evidence: direct evidence, circumstantial evidence, relevant evidence, authenticated evidence, and hearsay.

10. What is included in an investigation summary? Why should one be prepared?

ETHICAL QUESTIONS

1. Leah Fox, a legal assistant, has been asked by the attorney for whom she works to contact several potential witnesses to see what they know about an event. The first witness that Leah calls says, "I don't know if I should get involved. I don't want to get in trouble. You see, I was supposed to be at work, but I called in sick. If I get involved and my employer finds out where I really was, I might get fired. You're a lawyer, what do you think?" How should Leah respond?

2. Kirsten Piels, a legal assistant, is conducting a follow-up interview with a new client, who is seeking a divorce. Kirsten is asking the client about the couple's marital property. According to the client, both spouses want to divide the property evenly on their divorce. When Kirsten asks the client about checking or savings accounts, the client says to Kirsten, "You know, Kirsten, I have this 'secret' savings account, but I don't want anybody to know about it. Please don't tell Mr. Harcourt [Kirsten's supervising attorney] what I've just told you." What should Kirsten do in this situation?

3. Jeffrey Jones starts a new job as a paralegal. He reviews a file and notices that the client has not been contacted and updated on the status of the case in three months. He also notices that there is a settlement conference scheduled for tomorrow and that the client needs to be in court. What should Jeffrey do?

4. Peter Romano is asked to review the *Clemmons v. Auto Manufacturer of America* file and to investigate the case. His boss represents the auto manufacturer in this product liability case and believes, based on the evidence uncovered so far, that he has an open-and-shut case against the plaintiff, who claims that her husband was killed when the car exploded on impact during an auto accident. Peter

begins interviewing witnesses, including an engineer who works for the company. The engineer states that he knew the car was defective and would explode on impact. Peter is worried that his boss will be upset about this fact, because it damages his "open-and-shut" case. What should Peter do?

5. Thomas Lent is a new legal assistant with a law firm that specializes in personal-injury cases. He is reviewing a request to produce documents that was recently received in a case that his supervising attorney is handling for the plaintiff. The document requests the plaintiff's medical records, but it does not state specifically which records or for what injuries. Thomas's supervising attorney instructs Thomas to obtain copies of all of the plaintiff's medical records. The plaintiff's medical-records file is several inches thick because the plaintiff is an elderly person and has various medical problems. Thomas is instructed to bury the relevant medical records in the stack and not to make them obvious to the defendant's attorney. If she wants these records, she will have to sort through the file, says the attorney. What should Thomas do? Can the attorney be disciplined for this kind of behavior?

6. In response to a discovery request, Lynnette Banks, a paralegal in a corporate law firm, receives a package of documents in the mail. She opens the package and begins to read through the documents. As she does so, she discovers some that have the words "Privileged and Confidential" stamped on them. She scans a document and realizes that it is a letter from the opposing counsel to his client. The letter reveals the opposing attorney's legal strategy for the case on which Lynnette is now working. What should Lynnette do?

PRACTICE QUESTIONS AND ASSIGNMENTS

1. Review the Baranski-Peretto hypothetical case discussed in Chapter 13. Then write sample questions that you would ask when interviewing eyewitnesses to the accident. Phrase at least one question in each of the question formats discussed in this chapter.

2. Using the information in this chapter on questioning skills, identify the following types of questions:

   a. "Did you go on a cruise in the Bahamas with another woman, Mr. Johnson?"

   b. "Isn't it true, Mr. Johnson, that someone other than your wife accompanied you on a cruise in the Bahamas?"

   c. "Mr. Johnson, will you please describe your whereabouts between January 10 and January 17, 2007?"

3. Lena Phillips, a fifty-two-year-old, self-employed seamstress, fell down the three steps in front of her house and fractured her right wrist. She was treated in the emergency room at the Neighborhood Hospital by Dr. Ralph

Dean on the day that she fell (January 10, 2006) and released. On January 17, January 25, and February 11, 2006, she visited Dr. Dean's office for follow-up care to make sure that the wrist was healing properly. It appeared that the wrist was healing properly during the month in which she was treated by Dr. Dean. She noticed, however, that even though she had a full range of motion in her wrist, the wrist angled inward somewhat. When she queried Dr. Dean about this, he told her that some angling of the wrist was inevitable.

Over the course of the following year, her wrist became increasingly crooked and bent inward. She went to an orthopedist, Dr. Alicia Byerly, on March 30, 2007. Dr. Byerly tried a splint, but without success. Dr. Byerly eventually performed surgery on the wrist at the Neighborhood Hospital on May 3, 2007, but was unable to correct the problem. Dr. Byerly told Ms. Phillips that she should have had surgery on the wrist during the first three weeks after it was broken to correct the angling problem.

Lena Phillips has come to the firm for which you work, the law firm of Samson & Gore, 5000 West Avenue, Northville, NH 12345, because she wants to sue Dr. Dean for medical malpractice. On May 15, 2007, you are asked to investigate her case. Draft an investigation plan.

4. Using Exhibit 14.3 on page 515, *A Sample Follow-Up Letter to a Client,* as an example, draft a follow-up letter to Lena Phillips based on the facts in Question 3 above. The attorney who gave you the assignment is Alan Samson. You will need to include a retainer agreement and instruct the client not to talk to Dr. Dean.

5. Using the factual background presented in Question 3, draft an "Authorization to Release Medical Information" letter for Lena Phillips to sign. Her name and address are Lena A. Phillips, 150 North Street, Northville, NH 12345.

6. Using the format in Exhibit 14.4 on page 522, *Information Contained in a Witness Statement,* and Exhibit 14.5 on page 523, *A Sample Witness Statement (Excerpt),* draft a witness statement based on the following facts:

   a. You work for the law firm of Thomas & Snyder. On April 1, 2007, you are interviewing a witness to a car-train accident that happened a few hours ago. The interview takes place at the police station. The witness's name is Henry Black. Henry is retired and lives at 2002 Stephens Road, Clinton Township, Pennsylvania. His telephone number is (123) 456-7890.

   b. Henry was in his Cadillac, stopped in front of the railroad tracks on Jefferson Avenue in Clinton Township, Pennsylvania, at approximately 10:00 A.M., when a red 2006 Ford Windstar minivan sped past him and

across the tracks. He was very surprised that the minivan did not stop at the tracks because the train was only about thirty feet away and was blowing its whistle. There were no gates or guard rails in front of the tracks. Henry looked over at the driver of the minivan and saw that she was talking on a cellular phone as she was driving. She did not appear to hear the train. As her minivan crossed the tracks, the train struck the passenger side of her vehicle. Fortunately, there appeared to be no one else in the vehicle.

7. Assume that a witness is being questioned about statements that she heard a third party make. Determine which of the following statements would qualify as exceptions to the hearsay rule:

   a. The third party exclaimed, "Watch out, he's not stopping at the red light!"

   b. The third party apologized, "Are you all right? I am so sorry. I didn't mean to hurt you."

   c. The third party uttered just before he died, "Make sure you find Joe. He is the one who shot me. Tom didn't have anything to do with this."

   d. The third party exclaimed, "I smell gas fumes!"

8. During the course of a murder trial, a prosecuting attorney paraded through the courtroom carrying a hand that had been unearthed the day before and that had been widely publicized as belonging to the murder victim. The defense attorney strenuously objected on the ground that the hand was not relevant. Should the judge sustain the objection?

9. Determine whether each of the following statements is a statement of fact or a statement of opinion, and explain why:

   a. "I am sure that the suspect took the money because when I saw him near the cash register, he looked around suspiciously and then tried to sneak away without being seen."

   b. "The man who took the money from the cash register was wearing a green trench coat, brown pants, and black boots and was carrying a large tan briefcase."

10. Working in groups of three, role-play the initial client interview described in Chapter 13 between Katherine Baranski and the legal team—attorney Allen Gilmore and paralegal Elena Lopez. Attorney Gilmore will need to prepare a list of questions and will ask most of the questions during the interview. Paralegal Lopez will take notes during the interview, provide the retainer agreement and release forms, and schedule the follow-up interview. Change roles if time allows.

QUESTIONS FOR CRITICAL ANALYSIS

1. Some attorneys ask their legal assistants to conduct initial client interviews alone, without the attorneys' being present. During these types of interviews, clients often ask legal assistants for legal advice. Is it fair to put the legal assistant in this position? How would you handle an attorney who asked you to conduct an initial client interview? How would you handle a client who asked for legal advice?

2. Why do you think you need to obtain the client's or witness's permission to record an interview? What might happen if you did not obtain permission?

3. Leading questions tend to lead to distorted answers and are typically used only on cross-examination. Why would an attorney want to use this type of question? Is the use of leading questions ethical?

4. There are several different types of client interviews. Make a list of the different types of client interviews and the kinds of questions that would be most effective to use during each one.

5. Expert witnesses give testimony relating to incidents they have not observed or people they may never have met. What, then, is the value of expert testimony? Why do courts allow expert witnesses to testify?

6. Several types of witnesses were described in this chapter (expert witnesses, lay witnesses, eyewitnesses, friendly witnesses, hostile witnesses). Do any of these categories overlap—that is, could one witness fall into more than one of the categories? Explain.

7. Hostile witnesses are often interviewed, but usually they are not called to testify at trial by the party to whom they are hostile. Why is this? How would an attorney handle a witness who is hostile to his or her client's case?

8. Witnesses' qualifications are checked out during the course of investigation. Why is this? What might happen if a witness's qualifications were not checked?

9. Why should you use an investigation plan? What might happen without one? What if you find information that requires you to drastically modify your plan? How should you proceed?

10. Clients are often required to sign releases authorizing an entity (such as a hospital) to turn over information to a particular party (such as an attorney). Why is this? What might happen if releases were not required?

PROJECTS

1. Watch an interview on television. Write a two-page, double-spaced paper describing the interview. Include in your description the following information:

    a. The names of the interviewer and the interviewee.

    b. The subject of the interview.

    c. The date and time of the interview and the television channel over which it was broadcast.

    d. The different types of questions (open ended, closed ended, and so on) used by the interviewer and the types of responses elicited by the different kinds of questions.

    e. The ways in which the interviewer and interviewee communicated nonverbally.

    f. Your overall evaluation of the interviewer's skill at interviewing this particular interviewee.

2. Locate law libraries in your city or county that are open to the public. What resources does each library have that would help you locate expert witnesses?

3. Call the county offices for your county and ask if they give tours. If they do, arrange to go on a tour of the offices. Find out what information is kept there, such as data on births, deaths, marriages, and property. Also find out what information is available to the public and what procedures must be followed to obtain this information.

4. Go to a library and do some research on listening skills. Write a one-page, double-spaced paper giving additional information on the listening techniques discussed in this chapter.

USING INTERNET RESOURCES

1. Access the following Web site to find the Federal Rules of Evidence: **http://www.law.cornell.edu/rules/fre**. Browse through these rules, and then respond to the following:

   a. How do the Federal Rules of Evidence define "relevant evidence"?

   b. Name and briefly describe four types of documents that the Federal Rules of Evidence consider to be self-authenticating (under Rule 902).

   c. Look at Rule 803, which lists several exceptions to the "hearsay rule." List and describe five of these exceptions.

2. KnowX.com is a public records Web site. Much of the information that can be located at this site is information that a private investigator (or a paralegal) might want to find when investigating a case. Access the site at **http://www.KnowX.com** and select "Site Map" from the menu at the top of the screen. Based on the information contained on the site map, what can you find using KnowX.com?

   a. Click on "Ultimate People Finder" and select "Database Info." What databases does KnowX.com search to find people? Is there any cost involved? If so, how much?

   b. Return to the site map and select "The Ultimate Business Finder." What databases does KnowX.com search for business information?

   c. Return to the site map and choose "Run a Background Check." What types of background checks does KnowX.com perform? What databases does it search? Is there any cost involved? If so, how much?

   d. Return to the site map and click on "Business Background Check." Key in the name and state for a business. What is the charge for viewing the results of the background check?

3.  For additional resources, visit our Web site at **http://www.paralegal.delmar. cengage.com**.

END NOTES

1. The legal phrase *laying a foundation* means introducing evidence or testimony that establishes certain facts needed to render later evidence in a lawsuit relevant, material, or competent so that the evidence will be admissible.

2. Note that in some jurisdictions, a party's out-of-court admissions are not considered to be hearsay, whereas in others, such admissions are considered hearsay.

TRIAL PROCEDURES

CHAPTER

CHAPTER OUTLINE

AFTER COMPLETING THIS CHAPTER, YOU WILL KNOW:

- ► How attorneys prepare for trial and how paralegals assist in this task.
- ► How jurors are selected and the role of attorneys and their legal assistants in the selection process.
- ► The various phases of a trial and the kinds of trial-related tasks that paralegals often perform.
- ► The options available to the losing party after the verdict is in.
- ► How a case is appealed to a higher court for review.

INTRODUCTION

Trials are costly in terms of both time and money. For this reason, parties to lawsuits often try to avoid going to trial. Pretrial negotiations between the parties and their respective attorneys may lead to an out-of-court settlement. Using the pretrial motions discussed in Chapter 13, the parties may attempt to end the litigation after the pleadings are filed or while discovery takes place. In many cases, parties opt for alternative methods of dispute resolution, such as mediation or arbitration, to avoid the time, expense, and publicity of courtroom trials. Recall from Chapter 6 that alternative dispute resolution is not always optional—many state and federal courts *mandate* that a dispute be mediated or arbitrated by the parties before they are permitted to bring the dispute before a court. If the parties fail to settle their dispute through any of these means, the case will go to trial.

To illustrate how attorneys and paralegals prepare for trial, we will continue using the hypothetical scenario developed in Chapter 13, in which Katherine Baranski (the plaintiff) is suing Tony Peretto (the defendant) for negligence. In the Baranski-Peretto case, Allen P. Gilmore is the attorney for plaintiff Baranski, and Gilmore's legal assistant is Elena Lopez. Defendant Peretto's attorney is Elizabeth A. Cameron, and Cameron's legal assistant is Gordon McVay.

Case at a Glance

The Plaintiff—
Plaintiff: Katherine Baranski
Attorney: Allen P. Gilmore
Paralegal: Elena Lopez

The Defendant—
Defendant: Tony Peretto
Attorney: Elizabeth A. Cameron
Paralegal: Gordon McVay

PREPARING FOR TRIAL

As the trial date approaches, the attorneys for the plaintiff and the defendant and their respective paralegals complete their preparations for the trial. The paralegals collect and organize all of the documents and other evidence relating to the dispute. They may find it useful to create a trial-preparation checklist similar to the one in Exhibit 15.1. Even though settlement negotiations may continue throughout the trial, both sides assume, for planning purposes, that the trial court will have to decide the issue.

At this point in the litigation process, plaintiff Baranski's attorney, Gilmore, will focus on legal strategy and how he can best use the information learned during the pleadings and discovery stages when presenting Baranski's case to the court. He will meet with his client and with his key witnesses to make last-minute preparations for trial. He might also meet with defendant Peretto's attorney to try once more to settle the dispute. Gilmore's legal assistant, Elena Lopez, will be notifying witnesses of the trial date and helping Gilmore prepare for trial. For example, she will make sure that all exhibits to be used during the trial are ready and verify that the trial notebook (to be discussed shortly) is in order.

Contacting and Preparing Witnesses

Typically, the paralegal is responsible for ensuring that witnesses are available and in court on the day of the trial. As mentioned in previous chapters, a witness is any person asked to testify at trial. The person may be an eyewitness, an official witness (such as a police officer), an expert witness, or anyone with knowledge relevant to the lawsuit.

Several types of negligence lawsuits require expert witnesses. As discussed in Chapters 13 and 14, an expert witness is one who has specialized knowledge in a particular field. Such witnesses are often called to testify in negligence cases, because one element to be proved in a negligence case is the reasonableness of the defendant's actions. In medical-malpractice cases, for example, it takes someone with specialized knowledge in the defendant physician's area of practice to establish the reasonableness of the defendant's actions.

EXHIBIT 15.1
Trial-Preparation Checklist

TWO MONTHS BEFORE THE TRIAL

____ Review the status of the case and inform the attorney of any depositions, interrogatories, or other discovery procedures that need to be undertaken prior to trial.
____ Interview witnesses and prepare witness statements.
____ Review deposition transcripts/summaries, answers to interrogatories, witness statements, and other information obtained about the case. Inform the attorney of any further discovery procedures that should be undertaken prior to trial.
____ Begin preparing the trial notebook.

ONE MONTH BEFORE THE TRIAL

____ Make a list of the witnesses who will testify at the trial for the trial notebook.
____ Prepare a subpoena for each witness, and arrange to have the subpoenas served.
____ Prepare any exhibits that will be used at trial and reserve any special equipment (such as for a PowerPoint presentation) that will be needed at the trial.
____ Draft *voir dire* (jury selection) questions and perhaps prepare a jury profile.
____ Prepare motions and memoranda.
____ Continue assembling the trial notebook.

ONE WEEK BEFORE THE TRIAL

____ Check the calendar and call the court clerk to confirm the trial date.
____ Complete the trial notebook.
____ Make sure that all subpoenas have been served.
____ Prepare the client and witnesses for trial.
____ Make the final arrangements (housing, transportation, and so on) for the client or witnesses, as necessary.
____ Check with the attorney to verify how witnesses should be paid (for lost wages, travel expenses, and so on).
____ Make final arrangements to have all equipment, documents, and other items in the courtroom on the trial date.

ONE DAY BEFORE THE TRIAL

____ Meet with others on the trial team to coordinate last-minute efforts.
____ Have a final pretrial meeting with the client.

Contacting Witnesses and Issuing Subpoenas

In the Baranski case, attorney Gilmore and paralegal Lopez will have lined up witnesses to testify on behalf of their client, plaintiff Baranski. In preparing for the trial, Lopez will inform the witnesses that the trial date has been set and that they will be expected to appear at the trial to testify. A *subpoena* (an order issued by the court clerk directing a person to appear in court—see Chapter 13) will be served on each of the witnesses to ensure the witness's presence in court. A subpoena to appear in a federal court is shown in Exhibit 15.2 on page 549. (Although not shown in the exhibit, a return-of-service form, similar to the one illustrated in Chapter 13, will be attached to the subpoena to verify that the witness received it.)

Unless she is already familiar with the court's requirements, paralegal Lopez will want to check with the court clerk to find out about what fees and documents she needs to take to the court to obtain the subpoena. The subpoena will then be served on the witness. Most subpoenas to appear in federal court can be served by anyone who is eighteen years of age or older, including paralegals, who often serve subpoenas. Subpoenas to appear in state court are often served by the sheriff or other process server.

Developing Paralegal Skills

POWERPOINT PRESENTATIONS

Joanna Newcomb, a paralegal manager, works for a large law firm. The paralegals under her supervision often assist attorneys in trial preparations, and Joanna has decided to host a series of workshops for the paralegals on trial presentation techniques. She has decided that the focus of the first workshop will be on the basics of PowerPoint presentations. She prepares a list of suggestions to hand out to the paralegals during the workshop.

TIPS FOR POWERPOINT PRESENTATIONS

- Plan your PowerPoint presentation carefully. Keep in mind that the display should clarify your presentation, not muddle it.

- Many presenters write out their presentations beforehand in a compatible word-processing program and transfer the contents to the slides.

- Consider using preset animations, a PowerPoint feature that allows you to show one line or one point at a time as you are speaking. (You can select this feature from the "Slide Show" menu.)

- Use the "four-by-four rule"—limit the text on each slide to four lines of no more than four words of text. This will keep your message simple and focused.

- The audience cannot hear your main points if they are reading your visuals, so stop speaking when a slide or individual line is loading.

- The background color should be geared to your audience. Some studies have shown that blue is most people's favorite color, so consider using that color for a background.

- The color of the text should be easy to read from afar.

- Simple fonts, such as Arial or Times New Roman, are best.

- Images and graphics can enhance your presentation, but do not "paste" images into your PowerPoint file. Instead, from the "Insert" menu, select "Picture" and then "From File" to insert a graphic.

- Always rehearse your PowerPoint presentation ahead of time, *on the equipment that you will be using.* Nothing will make you look less professional than a sloppy PowerPoint presentation. Audiences understand equipment breakdowns but are not as kind when it comes to poor preparation.

- Bring photocopies of the slides or other handouts to distribute in case for some reason you cannot use the PowerPoint presentation that you prepared.

When contacting *friendly witnesses* (those favorable to Baranski's position), Lopez should take care to explain that all witnesses are served with subpoenas, as a precaution, and to tell each witness when he or she can expect to receive the subpoena. Otherwise, a friendly witness might assume that Gilmore and Lopez did not trust the witness to keep his or her promise to appear in court.

Preparing Witnesses for Trial

No prudent attorney ever puts a party or a witness on the stand unless the attorney has discussed the testimony beforehand with the party or witness. Good advance preparation can make a tremendous difference to the testimony that a witness provides in a case. The amount of time spent preparing a witness will vary depending on the size of the case, the importance of the witness's testimony, and whether the attorney believes the witness will

EXHIBIT 15.2
A Subpoena

AO 88 (Rev. 2/06) Subpoena in a Civil Case

Issued by the
UNITED STATES DISTRICT COURT

WESTERN DISTRICT OF NITA

Katherine Baranski **V.** Tony Peretto	**SUBPOENA IN A CIVIL CASE** CASE NUMBER 07-14335-NI

TO: Julia Williams
     3765 Mattis Avenue
     Nita City, NI 48803

[X] YOU ARE COMMANDED to appear in the United States District Court at the place, date, and time specified below to testify in the above case.

PLACE OF TESTIMONY 4th and Main Nita City, NI	COURT ROOM B
	DATE AND TIME 8/4/07 10:00 A.M.

[ ] YOU ARE COMMANDED to appear at the place, date, and time specified below to testify at the taking of a deposition in the above case.

PLACE OF DEPOSITION	DATE AND TIME

[ ] YOU ARE COMMANDED to produce and permit inspection and copying of the following documents or objects at the place, date, and time specified below (list documents or objects):

PLACE	DATE AND TIME

[ ] YOU ARE COMMANDED to permit inspection of the following premises at the date and time specified below.

PREMISES	DATE AND TIME

    Any organization not a party to this suit that is subpoenaed for the taking of a deposition shall designate one or more officers, directors, or managing agents, or other persons who consent to testify on its behalf, and may set forth, for each person designated, the matters on which the person will testify. Federal Rules of Civil Procedure, 30(b)(6).

ISSUING OFFICER SIGNATURE AND TITLE (INDICATE IF ATTORNEY FOR PLAINTIFF OR DEFENDANT) *Allen P. Gilmore*, Attorney for the Plaintiff	DATE July 13, 2007

ISSUING OFFICER'S NAME, ADDRESS AND PHONE NUMBER
Allen P. Gilmore, Jeffers, Gilmore & Dunn,
553 Fifth Avenue, Suite 101, Nita City, NI 48801   (616) 555-9690

(See Rule 45, Federal Rules of Civil Procedure, Parts C & D on Reverse)

If action is pending in district other than district of issuance, state district under case number.

Ethics Watch!

WHY SUBPOENA FRIENDLY WITNESSES?

The beginning paralegal might logically ask why it is necessary to subpoena friendly witnesses. The answer to this question is threefold. First, subpoenas make it easier for witnesses to be excused from their jobs and any other obligations on the date they are to appear in court. Second, in many courts, serving a subpoena on a witness entitles him or her to receive a witness fee (usually a small sum, but at least some encouragement to appear in court). Third, and most important, attorneys must take reasonable steps (and serving witnesses with subpoenas is a reasonable measure) to ensure that clients' interests are best served. If a witness has not been subpoenaed and for some reason fails to appear at trial, the lack of his or her crucial testimony may jeopardize the client's chances of winning the case. By serving the witness with a subpoena, the attorney has proof that he or she has not breached the duty of competence to the client.

be able to communicate clearly and effectively in court. Additional time will be needed to prepare witnesses who are relatively inexperienced, are not very articulate, or are especially nervous about testifying.

Tell Witnesses What to Expect.   Prior to trial, attorney Gilmore and paralegal Lopez will meet with each witness to prepare her or him for trial. Gilmore will discuss with the witness the types of questions that he intends to ask the witness in court and the questions that he expects the opposing attorney to ask. He will also tell the witness that during cross-examination opposing counsel will ask leading questions and may try to confuse the witness or attack his or her statements. The attorney may recommend, for example, that the witness answer the opponent's questions in as few words as possible while not appearing to be overly defensive. (The attorney may not, of course, tell the witness what to say in response to questions.)

Gilmore will also review with the witness any statements the witness has made with regard to the case, particularly if the statements were given under oath (such as during a deposition). It is important that a witness understand that during the trial, he or she may be asked about any inconsistent statements previously given. Additionally, Gilmore may want to review the substantive legal issues involved in the case and emphasize how the witness's testimony will affect the outcome of those issues.

Role-Playing.   If the witness needs additional preparation, either attorney Gilmore or paralegal Lopez may engage in some role-playing with the witness. This type of rehearsal is often valuable in helping the witness to understand more fully how the questioning will proceed and what types of tactics may be involved in the opposing attorney's questions. It also serves to alleviate some of the witness's fears. In addition, Lopez might take the witness to the courtroom in which the trial will take place to familiarize the witness with the trial setting. Testifying can be a very stressful experience. Anything that the paralegal can do to reduce a witness's discomfort will enable the witness to better control his or her responses when testifying and thus will ultimately benefit the client.

Other Details. Paralegals are often responsible for handling all the details involved in preparing witnesses for court. For example, Lopez might recommend appropriate clothing and grooming or tell the witness where to look and how to remain calm and composed when speaking to the court. If the witness will be asked about any exhibits or evidence (such as photographs or documents), Lopez will show these items to the witness. Lopez will continually update the witness as to when he or she will probably be called to testify.

Exhibits and Displays

Paralegals frequently prepare exhibits or displays that will be presented at trial. Attorney Gilmore may wish to present to the court a photograph of plaintiff Baranski's car taken after the accident occurred, a diagram of the intersection, an enlarged document (such as a police report), or other relevant evidence. Paralegal Lopez will be responsible for making sure that all exhibits are properly prepared and ready to introduce at trial. If any exhibits require special equipment, such as an easel, DVD player, or laptop computer, Lopez must also make sure that these will be available in the courtroom and properly set up when they are needed. Increasingly, attorneys are using high-tech equipment to prepare their trial presentations. For a discussion of how high-tech presentations are altering the paralegal's trial-preparation tasks, see the *Technology and Today's Paralegal* feature on pages 552 and 553.

The Trial Notebook

To present plaintiff Baranski's case effectively, attorney Gilmore will need to have all of the relevant documents in the courtroom; he will also need to be able to locate them quickly. To accomplish these goals, Lopez will prepare a trial notebook. Typically, the **trial notebook** is a three-ring binder (or several binders, depending on the complexity of the case) in which trial-related materials are separated by tabbed divider sheets. (Note that some attorneys use an expandable file folder instead of a notebook for organizing trial documents and insert manila folders for each subject within the expandable folder.)

Paralegal Lopez meets with attorney Gilmore to discuss what Gilmore wants to include in the trial notebook for Baranski's case and how the notebook should be organized. Gilmore instructs Lopez that the organization of the notebook should make it possible to find quickly whatever documents they may need during the trial. Gilmore explains that Lopez should include the following materials in the notebook:

- Copies of the pleadings.
- Interrogatories.
- Deposition transcripts and summaries.
- Pretrial motions.
- A list of exhibits and a case outline indicating when they will be used.
- A witness list, the order in which the witnesses will testify, and the questions that will be asked of each witness.
- Relevant cases or statutes that Gilmore plans to cite.
- Any additional documents or information that will be important to have close at hand during the trial.

Lopez will create a general index to the notebook's contents and place this index at the front of the notebook. She may also create an index for each section of the binder and place those indexes at the beginnings of the sections. Paralegals sometimes use a computer notebook and a software retrieval system to help them quickly locate documents, especially in complicated cases involving thousands of documents.

trial notebook
A binder that contains copies of all of the documents and information that an attorney will need to have at hand during the trial.

Case at a Glance

The Plaintiff
Plaintiff: Katherine Baranski
Attorney: Allen P. Gilmore
Paralegal: Elena Lopez

The Defendant—
Defendant: Tony Peretto
Attorney: Elizabeth A. Cameron
Paralegal: Gordon McVay

Technology and Today's Paralegal

COURTROOM TECHNOLOGY

In the past, attorneys and paralegals involved in complex litigation had to carry boxes of papers into the courtroom and then, during trial, search through them for key documents and exhibits. Visual presentations were usually limited to enlarged photographs or text displayed on an easel. Today, advances in technology give paralegals and attorneys numerous other options.

DIGITAL RECORDS AND VIDEO

A major challenge for the paralegal in complex litigation is keeping the mountains of evidence organized, cross-referenced, and easily accessible to the attorney during the trial. Suppose, for example, that a witness is making certain statements on the stand and the paralegal wishes to compare them with statements on the same topic made by that witness in a deposition prior to trial. Finding these earlier statements quickly can be difficult. If the documents have been scanned into a computer, however, the paralegal using litigation support software can search through *all* the documents in the case in a matter of seconds. This means that counsel will not need to bring numerous copies of deposition transcripts, records, and reports to court. Instead, one laptop computer can access thousands of documents quickly and efficiently.

Other technologies being utilized in courts today involve digital video recording and court reporting. For example, when depositions in the case are digitally recorded and loaded on a computer, that video file can be combined on a split screen with the transcript of the written words. This can be an effective way for the lawyer to demonstrate inconsistencies in a witness's statements. Rather than reading the deposition transcript in court (as traditionally has been done), the jurors are able to see the person's face and demeanor as they hear and read what the witness previously said.

In addition, "real-time," or computer-assisted, court reporting is now available. When real-time court reporting is used, the transcript appears on the computer screen as the person is speaking. Real-time videoconferencing can also be used to bring into the courtroom the "live" testimony of experts and other witnesses who cannot be physically present. A judge's permission may be required to use these technologies in the courtroom.

When preparing the trial notebook, always remember that the documents in the notebook should not be the original documents but rather copies of them. The original documents (unless they are needed as evidence at trial) should always remain in the firm's files, both for reasons of security (should the trial notebook be misplaced) and to ensure that Lopez or others in the office will have access to the documents while the notebook is in court with the attorney.

Paralegal Lopez will not wait until the last minute to prepare the trial notebook. Rather, at the outset of the lawsuit, she will make copies of the pleadings and other documents as they are generated to include in the notebook. That way, she will not have to spend valuable time just before the trial, when there are other pressing needs, to do work that could have been done earlier. For further suggestions on what might be contained in a trial notebook, see this chapter's *Featured Guest* article on pages 554 and 555.

PRETRIAL CONFERENCE

pretrial conference
A conference prior to trial in which the judge and the attorneys litigating the suit discuss settlement possibilities, clarify the issues in dispute, and schedule forthcoming trial-related events.

Before the trial begins, the attorneys usually meet with the trial judge in a **pretrial conference** to explore the possibility of resolving the case and, if a settlement is not possible, at least agree

TRIAL PRESENTATION SOFTWARE

Using trial presentation software can help the legal team to create a more effective, persuasive, and visually stimulating presentation of its case. Most people absorb and retain information better when it is presented visually as well as verbally. Visual information is also more engaging for jurors than long recitations of detailed facts by witnesses (and attorneys). By providing visual displays, then, the legal team's presentation can have a greater impact on juries.

For example, the legal team can create a mixed-media presentation (including video and sound) and store it on CD-ROM for use at trial. The order and elements of the presentation can be manipulated in a variety of ways to maximize its effectiveness. A person preparing digital images to be included in a presentation, for instance, could highlight certain portions of an image and dim others to help the jury focus on the desired part. He or she could also zoom in on part of an image, insert a box containing an enlargement of part of the image, or add arrows, labels, titles, or symbols to an image.

Presentation software also makes it easy to create diagrams of an accident scene, graphic illustrations of scientific evidence, medical models and diagrams to help explain medical procedures and injuries, and schematics of mechanical or physical evidence. Rather than simply telling the jury how a particular product or machine caused a client's injuries, for example, an attorney can show how the injury occurred. The legal team can also create flow charts to indicate the relationships between events and bulleted lists to highlight the strengths of its case or the weaknesses of the opponent's case. These exhibits can be modified easily if necessary during the trial.

TECHNOLOGY TIP

Computers and courtroom technologies can make a litigation paralegal's job easier, especially in cases that involve extensive documentation. Make sure to obtain the court's permission, if required, to use a specific technology in the courtroom, however. Make sure, too, that all presentations and diagrams are accurate, are reliable, and comply with the rules of evidence. Keep a back-up copy of all documents, cross-referenced the old-fashioned way, in the event the computer crashes. Finally, if you are working with an outside vendor to provide support or presentation services, be careful not to breach confidentiality rules.

on the manner in which the trial will be conducted. In particular, the parties may attempt to clarify the issues in dispute and establish ground rules to restrict such matters as the admissibility of certain types of evidence. For example, attorney Gilmore might have paralegal Lopez draft a **motion *in limine***[1] (a motion to limit evidence) to submit to the judge at this time. The motion will request the judge to order that certain types of evidence not be brought out at trial.

To illustrate: Suppose that plaintiff Baranski had been arrested in the past for illegal drug possession. Gilmore knows that evidence of the arrest, if introduced by the defense at trial, might prejudice the jury against Baranski. In this situation, Gilmore might submit a motion *in limine* to keep the defense from presenting the evidence. Exhibit 15.3 on page 556 presents a sample motion *in limine*. Note that with the motion Gilmore would include affidavits and/or a memorandum of law (a brief)—these documents were discussed in Chapter 13—to convince the judge that the motion should be granted.

Once the pretrial conference has concluded, both parties turn their attention to the trial itself. Assuming that the trial will be heard by a jury, however, one more step is necessary before the trial begins: selecting the jurors who will hear the trial and render a verdict on the dispute.

> **motion *in limine***
> A motion requesting that certain evidence not be brought out at the trial, such as prejudicial, irrelevant, or legally inadmissible evidence.

Ken Rosenblum   FEATURED **Guest**

THE TRIAL NOTEBOOK

BIOGRAPHICAL NOTE

Ken Rosenblum is assistant dean of academic affairs at Ivy Tech Community College Northwest in Valparaiso, Indiana. Before becoming assistant dean, he served the college as both program chair of the Paralegal Studies Program and division chair of the Public Service Division. He received a bachelor's degree in philosophy from the University of Wisconsin and a J.D. from DePaul University Law School. Before joining Ivy Tech, he practiced law in Chicago and was engaged in a wide variety of civil litigation for thirty years. Although much of his work today is administrative, he continues to teach his favorite course: Litigation—Advanced Trial Technique. There, his students select one case and, from drafting the complaint to jury instructions and closing argument, prepare it for trial using the trial notebook as the framework. He says that in this way, his students are exposed to the creativity, intensity, scope, and discipline that litigation requires before they graduate.

The foundation of litigation is preparation and, by implication, organization. While the attorney and paralegal are engaged in pretrial work, however, the elements of the case usually reside in numerous folders carrying various and sometimes unique labels identifying the contents. Generally, these components are separate from each other and from the case as a whole. This disarrangement, at times, cannot be avoided. Cases seem to be organic—they grow at speeds and in directions that are unpredictable and often uncontrollable. But there comes a time when the paralegal and the supervising attorney must organize all these separate parts into a useful working composite of all that has gone before. The vehicle often recommended for optimum organization and management is a *trial notebook.*

Simply put, a trial notebook is an organizational system. The pretrial work is reviewed, synthesized, and categorized to facilitate further trial preparation as well as easy location and reference during the trial. Physically, the trial notebook frequently is a three-ring binder or at times multiple binders, perhaps color coded. The contents can also outgrow the notebook and employ physical files or computer folders. But some words of caution! A trial notebook does not contain all of the material accumulated in either the pretrial or trial stage. It is instead a road map to the location of the work product amassed, as well as a resource for quick orientation, support, and functionality for the future.

The contents, design, and arrangement of a trial notebook are dictated by the type of case and the idiosyncrasies of the trial attorney. Whatever organizational scheme you use, however, make sure that it provides quick and accurate access to the notebook's contents. Additionally, be flexible. Just as the case itself may have developed in

On the Web

Numerous firms offer trial consulting services, including assistance in jury selection. You can access the Web site of one such firm, Jury Research Institute, at **http://www.jri-inc.com**.

voir dire
A proceeding in which attorneys for the plaintiff and the defendant ask prospective jurors questions to determine whether any potential juror is biased or has any connection with a party to the action or with a prospective witness.

JURY SELECTION

Before the trial gets under way, a panel of jurors must be assembled. The clerk of the court usually notifies local residents by mail that they have been selected for jury duty. The process of selecting prospective jurors varies, depending on the court, but often they are randomly selected by the court clerk from lists of registered voters or those to whom driver's licenses have been issued. The persons selected then report to the courthouse on the date specified in the notice. At the courthouse, they are gathered into a single pool of jurors, and the process of selecting those jurors who will actually hear the case begins. Although some types of trials require twelve-person juries, civil matters can be heard by a jury of as few as six persons in many states.

Voir Dire

Both the plaintiff's attorney and the defendant's attorney have some input into the ultimate make-up of the jury. Each attorney will question prospective jurors in a proceeding known as *voir dire.*[2] Experienced litigators know how important the *voir dire* process is—not only ways you did not predict, so too may the trial, requiring that you adapt as events and circumstances unfold.

At a minimum, an acceptable trial notebook should contain the following sections:

- *Directory.* The names, phone numbers, fax numbers, and e-mail addresses of all parties, attorneys, paralegals, court personnel, and witnesses.

- *Pleadings.* All operative pleadings, motion for summary judgment, and all applicable pretrial orders.

- *Discovery.* Interrogatories and answers, production requests and replies, requests to admit and responses, requests for examination and orders, and deposition digests/abstracts or summaries (if available).

- *Trial motions.* Motion to separate witnesses, motion *in limine,* motion to bar witnesses, and motion to amend the pleadings.

- *Witness identification and testimony.* A list of all witnesses for your case in order of presentation, followed by their direct examination.

- *Witness cross-examination.* Cross-examination of adverse parties and witnesses.

> *"Whatever the situation, there is no substitute for preparation and no excuse for disorganization. There is no dress rehearsal in a trial!"*

- *Demonstrative evidence and exhibit treatment.* A list of all of the exhibits to be offered into evidence and an exhibit grid containing sectors for a description of each item, identification number, means of authentication, and whether admitted or refused, plus date.

- *Jury voir dire.* Panel grid forms and juror profile list.

- *Jury instructions.* Prepare these instructions early to be certain that all elements are reviewed and covered.

- *Legal research.* Internal memorandum and/or external memorandum, case law pertinent to trial issues, and evidentiary issues anticipated, plus briefs.

- *Opening statement.*

- *Closing argument.*

- *Negotiations, notes, and memos.*

You may become a paralegal who writes the closing argument before preparing testimony and uses it as a template, or one who creates applicable jury instructions at the first hint of a trial and then superimposes those instructions over the facts, or one who undertakes the responsibilities chronologically, step by step. Whatever the situation, there is no substitute for preparation and no excuse for disorganization. There is no dress rehearsal in a trial!

---

to picking the right jury but also as a time for attorneys to introduce themselves and their clients and make a favorable impression on the jury before the trial begins.

Legal assistants often work with their attorneys to write up the questions that will be asked of jurors during *voir dire.* Because all of the jurors will have previously filled out forms giving basic information about themselves, the attorneys and their paralegals can tailor their questions accordingly. They fashion the questions in such a way as to uncover any biases on the part of prospective jurors and to find persons who might identify with the plights of their respective clients.

Typically, the legal team for each side has already developed an idea of what kind of person would be most sympathetic toward or most likely to vote in favor of its client. Indeed, sometimes experts are hired to help create a juror profile (see the *Today's Professional Paralegal* feature later in this chapter on page 572). The paralegals and attorneys then formulate questions based on this notion of the ideal juror in the case.

Jury selection may last a few hours or many days, depending on the complexity of the case and the rules and preferences of the particular court or judge. In some courts, the judge queries prospective jurors using questions prepared and submitted by the attorneys. In other

On the Web

You can read the *Handbook for Trial Jurors Serving in the United States District Courts* at **http://www.mnd. uscourts.gov/jury_handbook.htm**.

EXHIBIT 15.3
Motion *in Limine*

A. P. Gilmore
Jeffers, Gilmore & Dunn
553 Fifth Avenue
Suite 101
Nita City, NI 48801
(616) 555-9690

Attorney for Plaintiff

UNITED STATES DISTRICT COURT
FOR THE WESTERN DISTRICT OF NITA

Katherine Baranski	)	
Plaintiff,	)	CASE NO. 07-14335-NI
	)	Honorable Harley M. Larue
v.	)	
	)	MOTION IN LIMINE
	)	
Tony Peretto	)	
Defendant.	)	

The Plaintiff respectfully moves the Court to prohibit counsel for the Defendant from directly or indirectly introducing or making any reference during the trial to the Plaintiff's arrest in 1997 for the possession of illegal drugs.

The grounds on which this motion is based are stated in the accompanying affidavits and memorandum.

Date: 6/18/07

Allen P. Gilmore
Allen P. Gilmore
Attorney for the Plaintiff

courts, the judge has each juror answer a list of standard questions and then gives each attorney a small amount of time to ask follow-up questions. When large numbers of prospective jurors are involved, the attorneys (or judge) may direct their questions to groups of jurors as opposed to individual jurors in order to minimize the time spent choosing a jury.

Challenges during *Voir Dire*

During *voir dire,* the attorney for each side will decide if there are any individuals he or she would like to prevent from serving as jurors in the case. The attorney may then exercise a **challenge** to exclude a particular person from the jury. There are two types of challenges available to both sides in a lawsuit: challenges for cause and peremptory challenges.

Challenges for Cause

The attorney can exercise a **challenge for cause** if the prospective juror is biased against the client or case for some reason. For example, if a juror states during *voir dire* that he or she hates all immigrants and the client is foreign born, the attorney can exercise a challenge for cause. Each side's attorney can exercise an *unlimited* number of challenges for cause. Because

challenge
An attorney's objection, during *voir dire,* to the inclusion of a particular person on the jury.

challenge for cause
A *voir dire* challenge to exclude a potential juror from serving on the jury for a reason specified by an attorney in the case.

Developing Paralegal Skills

TRIAL SUPPORT

Scott Greer, a paralegal with the firm of Dewey & Stone, is helping an attorney prepare for a trial in a personal-injury lawsuit. The client was injured in an automobile accident and is now a paraplegic. Scott has received a memo from his supervising attorney requesting that he prepare a diagram of the accident and arrange to have a "day in the life" recording made with a digital video camera. Scott can then edit the recording on his computer and have it stored on a DVD for use at trial. The DVD will show what a typical day in the life of the plaintiff is like as a result of the injuries sustained in the accident. Scott contacts Trial Support Services, Inc., a firm that specializes in litigation support, to make the recording. Scott also obtains permission to have Trial Support Services, Inc., create the diagram as well.

TIPS FOR CREATING A TRIAL DVD

- Use a reliable trial support services provider or vendor.
- Arrange to meet the vendor at the location where the recording will be made.
- Make sure that the recording is realistic, so that the court will allow its use.
- Preview and edit the recording before giving it to the attorney.
- After the attorney has approved the recording, store it on a DVD for presentation to the jury at the trial.
- Make sure that the vendor is paid on time.

most people are not forthcoming about their biases, the attorney must be able to prove sufficiently to the court that the person cannot be an objective juror in the case. Often, the judge will ask the challenged juror follow-up questions and then determine that the juror can be objective after all.

Peremptory Challenges

Both attorneys may exercise a *limited* number of **peremptory challenges** without giving any reason to the court as to why they object to a particular juror. In most cases, peremptory challenges are the only challenges exercised (because there is no proof that an individual juror is biased). A juror may thus be excused from serving on the jury for any reason, including his or her facial expressions or nonverbal behavior during the questioning. Peremptory challenges based on racial criteria or gender, however, are illegal.[3]

Because the number of peremptory challenges is limited (a court may allow only three, for example), attorneys must exercise peremptory challenges carefully. Experienced litigators try to conserve their peremptory challenges so that they can eliminate the prospective jurors who appear the most hostile.

> **peremptory challenge**
> A *voir dire* challenge to exclude a potential juror from serving on the jury without any supporting reason or cause. Peremptory challenges based on racial or gender criteria are illegal.

Procedure for Challenges

Typically, *voir dire* takes place in the courtroom, and the attorneys question the six to twelve prospective jurors who are seated in the jury box. Other prospective jurors may be seated in the audience area of the courtroom, so that as one person is excused, another person can

Ethics Watch!

SHOULD YOU TELL YOUR SUPERVISING ATTORNEY WHAT YOU KNOW ABOUT A PROSPECTIVE JUROR?

During *voir dire*, paralegal Lopez notices one of her neighbors among the prospective jurors. Lopez knows that her neighbor is strongly biased against foreigners and will probably not be an impartial juror in the case against Tony Peretto, who has a slight foreign accent. Lopez also knows that she and attorney Gilmore want their client, plaintiff Baranski, to win the case, and a juror biased against Peretto would definitely help them achieve this goal. Should Lopez tell Gilmore what she knows about this prospective juror? Yes. It is to Gilmore's—and his client's—advantage to know all he can about the prospective jurors, and it is up to Gilmore to decide how to use whatever information he obtains. Furthermore, Lopez has no legal duty to keep confidential any information that she has learned about her neighbor.

walk up to take his or her place in the jury box. The procedure varies, of course, depending on the jurisdiction. Often, rather than making challenges orally in front of the jury, the attorneys simply write down on a piece of paper which juror they wish to challenge and the paper is given to the judge. The judge thanks and dismisses the prospective juror, and the process starts over again with the next individual. When this method is used, the remaining prospective jurors do not know which side dismissed the individual and so are less likely to make guesses about the underlying reasons.

The Paralegal's Role during *Voir Dire*

As mentioned, paralegals help develop a jury profile and draft questions that will be asked during *voir dire*. In addition, a paralegal can assist an attorney by providing another pair of eyes and ears during the jury selection process. Attorneys frequently rely on the observations of other members of the legal team (including paralegals) who are present during the questioning.

If paralegal Lopez attends *voir dire* with attorney Gilmore in the Baranski case, for example, she will carefully watch all of the jurors as the attorneys question them. Lopez, because she is not participating in the questioning, is free to observe the prospective jurors more closely than Gilmore. She will then report to Gilmore any verbal or nonverbal response she observed that Gilmore might not have noticed. For example, suppose that as Gilmore is questioning one juror, another juror is staring at plaintiff Baranski and frowning with disapproval. Gilmore might not notice this behavior, and Lopez can bring it to his attention.

Alternate Jurors

Because unforeseeable circumstances or illness may necessitate that one or more of the sitting jurors be dismissed, the court seats several *alternate jurors* who will also hear the entire trial. Depending on the rules of the particular jurisdiction, a court might have two or three

---

Case at a Glance

The Plaintiff—
  Plaintiff: Katherine Baranski
  Attorney: Allen P. Gilmore
  Paralegal: Elena Lopez

The Defendant—
  Defendant: Tony Peretto
  Attorney: Elizabeth A. Cameron
  Paralegal: Gordon McVay

alternate jurors present throughout the trial. If a juror has to be excused in the middle of the trial, then an alternate can take his or her place without disrupting the proceedings. Unless they replace jurors, alternate jurors do not participate in jury deliberations at the end of the trial.

THE TRIAL

Once the jury members are seated, the judge swears in the jury, and the trial itself can begin. During the trial, the attorneys, Allen Gilmore and Elizabeth Cameron, will present their cases to the jury. Because the attorneys will be concentrating on the trial, it will fall to their paralegals to coordinate the logistical aspects of the trial and observe as closely as possible the trial proceedings. Because paralegal Lopez is thoroughly familiar with the case and Gilmore's legal strategy, she will be a valuable ally during the trial. She will be able to anticipate Gilmore's needs and provide appropriate reminders or documents as Gilmore needs them.

Prior to each trial day, for example, Lopez will assemble the documents and materials that will be needed in court. During the court proceedings, Lopez will make sure that attorney Gilmore has within reach any documents or exhibits that he needs for questioning parties or witnesses. When attorney Gilmore no longer needs the documents or exhibits, Lopez will put them aside in an appropriate place. At the end of the day, she will again organize the documents and materials, decide what will be needed for the next day, and file the documents that can remain in the office.

Paralegal Lopez must also monitor each witness's testimony to ensure that it is consistent with previous statements made by the witness. Lopez will have the relevant deposition transcript (and summary) at hand when a witness takes the stand. She will follow the deposition transcript (or summary) of each witness as that witness testifies. This way, she can pass a note to Gilmore if he misses any inconsistencies in the witness's testimony.

Lopez will also observe how the jury is responding to various witnesses and their testimony or to the attorneys' demeanor and questions. She will take notes during the trial on these observations as well as on the points being stressed and the types of evidence introduced by the opposing counsel, Cameron. At the end of the day, Lopez and Gilmore may review the day's events, and Lopez's "trial journal" will provide a ready reference to the major events that transpired in the courtroom.

Opening Statements

The trial both opens and closes with attorneys' statements to the jury. In their **opening statements**, the attorneys will give a brief version of the facts and the supporting evidence that they will use during the trial. Because some trials can drag on for weeks or even months, it is extremely helpful for jurors to hear a summary of the story that will unfold during the trial. Otherwise, they may be left wondering how a particular piece of evidence fits into the dispute.

In short, the opening statement is a kind of "road map" that describes the destination that each attorney hopes to reach and outlines how he or she plans to reach it. Plaintiff Baranski's attorney, Gilmore, will focus on such things as his client's lack of fault and the injuries that she sustained when she was hit by defendant Peretto's car. Peretto's attorney, Cameron, will highlight the points that weaken plaintiff Baranski's claim (for example, Cameron might point out that Baranski was speeding) or otherwise suggest that defendant Peretto did not commit any wrongful act. Note that the defendant's attorney has the right to reserve her or his opening statement until after the plaintiff's case has been presented.

opening statement
An attorney's statement to the jury at the beginning of the trial. The attorney briefly outlines the evidence that will be offered during the trial and the legal theory that will be pursued.

Dwayne E. Krager

PARALEGAL **profile**

LITIGATION PARALEGAL

Dwayne E. Krager received his bachelor of arts degree from Southern Illinois University in Carbondale, Illinois, and his paralegal certification from Roosevelt University in Chicago. In 1995, Krager received Legal Assistant Today's "Paralegal of the Year Award," and he has served as president of the Wisconsin Paralegal Association. For about two years, he wrote a column entitled "Creative Computing" for Legal Assistant Today, offering tips on how to work with technology.

By 1989, several companies were in the early stages of creating two of the most widely used litigation support programs in today's legal marketplace. One of these programs is Summation. While working in the thirty-attorney litigation department of Reinhart Boerner Van Deuren, SC, a large law firm in Milwaukee, Wisconsin, Krager was able to implement the use of Summation as the main software program used at the firm.

Reinhart, a technologically progressive law firm, allowed Krager to implement a firmwide docket system and an in-house imaging center. He also designed, built, promoted, and then ran one of the first mock courtrooms, known as the Trial Science Institute, LLC (TSI), which was one of his greatest achievements. Today, Krager teaches other paralegals how

to use technological tools to help make their firms more successful.

What do you like best about your work?

"I enjoy my entire myriad of responsibilities. The autonomy that I have received because of my work in creating the Trial Science Institute has brought me recognition among my peers and in the legal world. In addition, the possibilities for a challenging future are constantly expanding. I am excited about continuing to operate and coordinate all activities associated with TSI as one important aspect of my job. However, I still enjoy another equally significant part of my job— mentoring and training the paralegals and attorneys in our firm on the use of litigation, imaging, and trial support programs. Because there are constant changes in the field of technology, the litigation process, and the use of litigation support, I think I will always enjoy my work."

What is the greatest challenge that you face in your area of work?

"The creation of the Trial Science Institute was one of my most exciting ventures. Utilizing the same skills as a litigation paralegal, I conducted extensive research to determine what the courtroom of the future would look like. In addition to conferring with architects and coordinating the bidding process for the construction of the facilities, I performed my normal paralegal duties. This required me to schedule my time and to focus specifically on the tasks that I had to complete. While this pro-

The Plaintiff's Case

Once the opening statements have been made, Gilmore will present the plaintiff's case first. Because he is the plaintiff's attorney, he has the burden of proving that defendant Peretto was negligent.

Direct Examination

direct examination
The examination of a witness by the attorney who calls the witness to the stand to testify on behalf of the attorney's client.

Attorney Gilmore will call several eyewitnesses to the stand and ask them to tell the court about the sequence of events that led to the accident. This form of questioning is known as **direct examination**. For example, Gilmore will call Julia Williams, an eyewitness who saw the accident occur, and ask her questions such as those presented in Exhibit 15.4 on page 562. He will also call other witnesses, including the police officer who was summoned to the accident scene and the ambulance driver. Gilmore will try to elicit responses from these witnesses that strengthen plaintiff Baranski's case—or at least that do not visibly weaken the claim.

cess was time consuming, one of the greatest challenges of the project was to gain approval from one of the founders of the firm, Richard Van Deuren. Before meeting with Mr. Van Deuren, I learned that he was a man who appreciated having everything presented to him in an orderly fashion. Using my litigation skills, I made sure that every supporting document was organized and indexed for Van Deuren's review. This undertaking enabled me to acquire significant knowledge about how to proceed with the project and get the task at hand done."

What advice do you have for would-be paralegals in your area of work?

"Today's litigation paralegal is faced with learning much more than procedure and how to organize a case. Because technology now offers the most efficient tools to organize the litigation process, it is imperative that litigation paralegals learn what these tools are and how to work with them. To be most effective as a litigation paralegal, paralegals must know how to use litigation support, time management, and trial presentation software; they should also have a thorough working knowledge of imaging and the electronic discovery process. Cases that have multitudinous documents require the use of a litigation support software program that will create a document database and allow for the use of imaging/OCR (optical character recognition)

> *"Out of all the paralegal skills, organization and time management are the most critical for litigation paralegals."*

technology. Paralegals who are not using a litigation support program are not working efficiently. Out of all the paralegal skills, organization and time management are the most critical for litigation paralegals."

What are some tips for success as a paralegal in your area of work?

"The first step is planning. A firm should either choose someone from its staff or use an outside trial consultant when deciding to present evidence electronically at trial. If you help present evidence electronically at trial, it is extremely important that you know as much as possible about the case (including the type of lawsuit, the number of plaintiffs and defendants, and the trial location) and the parties involved (attorneys, paralegals, and support staff). To help avoid miscommunication among team members, there must be a close working relationship among the members of the trial team who assist in accessing materials. It is important to identify vendors who can easily help with any last-minute concerns, which may arise at midnight on the day before the trial begins. If the trial is taking place outside of your normal location, it is imperative to locate nearby vendors to provide litigation support."

Dwayne Krager is also featured in the forthcoming book, Lessons from the Top Paralegal Experts, *by Carole Bruno.*

During direct examination, attorney Gilmore usually will not be permitted to ask *leading questions,* which are questions that lead the witness to a particular desired response (see Chapter 14). A leading question might be something like the following: "So, Mrs. Williams, you noticed that the defendant ran the stop sign, right?" If Mrs. Williams answers "yes," she has, in effect, been "led" to this answer by Gilmore's leading question. The fundamental purpose behind a trial is to establish what actually happened, not to tell witnesses what to say. Leading questions may distort the testimony by discouraging witnesses from telling their stories in their own words.

When Gilmore is dealing with *hostile witnesses* (uncooperative witnesses or those who are testifying on behalf of the other party), however, he is normally permitted to ask leading questions. This is because hostile witnesses may be uncommunicative and unwilling to describe the events they witnessed. If Gilmore asked a hostile witness what he or she observed on the morning of August 4 at 7:45 A.M., for example, the witness might respond, "I saw two trucks driving down Mattis Avenue." That answer might be true, but it has

EXHIBIT 15.4
Direct Examination—
Sample Questions

ATTORNEY:	Mrs. Williams, please explain how you came to be at the scene of the accident.
WITNESS:	Well, I was walking north on Mattis Avenue toward Nita City Hospital, where I work as a nurse.
ATTORNEY:	Please describe for the court, in your own words, exactly what you observed when you reached the intersection of Mattis Avenue and Thirty-eighth Street.
WITNESS:	I was approaching the intersection when I saw the defendant run the stop sign on Thirty-eighth Street and crash into the plaintiff's car.
ATTORNEY:	Did you notice any change in the speed at which the defendant was driving as he approached the stop sign?
WITNESS:	No. He didn't slow down at all.
ATTORNEY:	Mrs. Williams, are you generally in good health?
WITNESS:	Yes.
ATTORNEY:	Have you ever had any problems with your vision?
WITNESS:	No. I wear reading glasses for close work, but I see well in the distance.
ATTORNEY:	And how long has it been since your last eye examination?
WITNESS:	About a month or so ago, I went to Dr. Sullivan for an examination. He told me that I needed reading glasses but that my distance vision was excellent.

nothing to do with the Baranski-Peretto accident. Therefore, to elicit information from this witness, Gilmore would be permitted to use leading questions, which would force the witness to respond to the question at issue.

Cross-Examination

After attorney Gilmore has finished questioning a witness on direct examination, defendant Peretto's attorney, Cameron, will begin her **cross-examination** of that witness. During her cross-examination, Cameron will be primarily concerned with reducing the witness's credibility in the eyes of the jury and the judge. Attorneys typically use leading questions during cross-examination (since the witness is obviously hostile). Generally, experienced trial attorneys will ask only questions to which they know the answers—because otherwise a question might elicit testimony from the witness that further supports the opponent's case.

Cameron will formulate questions for Gilmore's witnesses based on the witnesses' previous answers in depositions and interrogatories. Discovery usually provides attorneys with a fairly good idea as to what areas of questioning may prove fruitful. Moreover, if a witness's testimony on the witness stand differs considerably from the answers he or she previously gave, or contradicts some other item of evidence (some physical evidence or the testimony of another witness), the attorney can use this discrepancy to attack the witness's credibility.

The defendant's attorney, Cameron, must generally confine her cross-examination to matters that were brought up during direct examination or that relate to a witness's credibility. This restriction is not followed in all states, however, and ultimately both the nature and extent of the cross-examination are subject to the discretion of the trial judge.[4] In any

cross-examination
The questioning of an opposing witness during the trial.

Case at a Glance

The Plaintiff—
Plaintiff: Katherine Baranski
Attorney: Allen P. Gilmore
Paralegal: Elena Lopez

The Defendant—
Defendant: Tony Peretto
Attorney: Elizabeth A. Cameron
Paralegal: Gordon McVay

EXHIBIT 15.5
Cross-Examination—
Sample Questions

ATTORNEY:	You have just testified that you were approaching the intersection when the accident occurred. Isn't it true that you stated earlier, under oath, that you were at the intersection at the time of the accident?
WITNESS:	Well, I might have, but I think I said that I was close to the intersection.
ATTORNEY:	In fact, you said that you were at the intersection. Now, you say that you were approaching it. Which is it?
WITNESS:	I was approaching it, I suppose.
ATTORNEY:	Okay. Exactly where were you when the accident occurred?
WITNESS:	I think that I was just in front of the Dairy Queen when the accident happened.
ATTORNEY:	Mrs. Williams, the Dairy Queen on Mattis Avenue is at least seventy-five yards from the intersection of Mattis Avenue and Thirty-eighth Street. Is it your testimony today that you noticed the defendant's car from seventy-five yards away as it was approaching the intersection on Mattis Avenue?
WITNESS:	Well, no, I guess not.
ATTORNEY:	Isn't it true that there were a lot of other cars driving on the road that morning?
WITNESS:	Yes.
ATTORNEY:	And you had no reason to be paying particular attention to the defendant's car, did you?
WITNESS:	Not really.
ATTORNEY:	In fact, you did not see the defendant's car until after the collision occurred, did you, Mrs. Williams?

event, Cameron's interrogation may not extend to matters unrelated to the case. She normally may not introduce evidence that a witness for the plaintiff is a smoker or dislikes children, for example, unless she can demonstrate that such facts are relevant to the case. In general, Cameron will try to uncover relevant physical infirmities of the plaintiff's witnesses (such as poor eyesight or hearing), as well as any evidence of bias (such as a witness's habit of playing a friendly round of golf with plaintiff Baranski every Saturday). Some questions that Cameron might ask Julia Williams, Gilmore's eyewitness, are presented in Exhibit 15.5.

Redirect and Recross

After defendant Peretto's attorney, Cameron, has finished cross-examining each witness, plaintiff Baranski's attorney, Gilmore, will try to repair any damage done to the credibility of the witness's testimony—or, indeed, to the case itself. Gilmore will do this by again questioning the witness and allowing the witness to explain his or her answer. This process is known as **redirect examination**.

If Cameron's cross-examination revealed that one of Gilmore's eyewitnesses to the accident had vision problems, for example, Gilmore could ask the witness whether he or she was wearing corrective lenses at the time of the accident. Gilmore might also have the witness demonstrate to the court that he or she has good vision by having the witness identify a letter or object at the far end of the courtroom. Because redirect examination is primarily used to improve the credibility of cross-examined witnesses, it is limited to matters raised during

redirect examination
The questioning of a witness following the adverse party's cross-examination.

At trial, attorneys and paralegals must have close at hand all of the documents and information that they may need to refer to during the proceedings. Typically, these materials are contained in the trial notebook, which may consist of several binders. Increasingly, for complex litigation, attorneys and paralegals retrieve necessary documents from offline or online databases using laptop computers.

(Courtesy of ©Royalty-Free/Corbis)

cross-examination. (If attorney Cameron chooses not to cross-examine a particular witness, then, of course, there can be no redirect examination by Gilmore.)

Following Gilmore's redirect examination, defendant Peretto's attorney, Cameron, will be given an opportunity for **recross-examination**. When both attorneys have finished with the first witness, Gilmore will call the succeeding witnesses in plaintiff Baranski's case, each of whom will be subject to cross-examination (and redirect and recross, if necessary).

recross-examination
The questioning of an opposing witness following the adverse party's redirect examination.

Motion for a Directed Verdict

After attorney Gilmore has presented his case for plaintiff Baranski, then Cameron, as counsel for defendant Peretto, may decide to make a **motion for a directed verdict** (now also known as a *motion for judgment as a matter of law* in federal courts). Through this motion, attorney Cameron will be saying to the court that the plaintiff's attorney, Gilmore, has not offered enough evidence to support a claim against defendant Peretto. If the judge agrees to grant the motion, then a judgment will be entered for defendant Peretto, plaintiff Baranski's case against him will be dismissed, and the trial will be over. A sample motion for judgment as a matter of law is shown in Exhibit 15.6.

motion for a directed verdict
A motion (also known as a *motion for judgment as a matter of law* in the federal courts) requesting that the court grant a judgment in favor of the party making the motion on the ground that the other party has not produced sufficient evidence to support his or her claim.

The motion for a directed verdict (judgment as a matter of law) is seldom granted because only those cases that involve genuine factual disputes are permitted to proceed to trial in the first place. If the judge had believed that Baranski's case was that weak before the trial started, then the judge would probably have granted a pretrial motion to dismiss the case, thereby avoiding the expense of a trial. Occasionally, however, the occurrence of certain events—such as the death of a key witness—might mean the plaintiff has no evidence at all to support his or her allegations. In that event, the court may grant the defendant's motion for a directed verdict, or judgment as a matter of law.

The Defendant's Case

Assuming that the motion for directed verdict (motion for judgment as a matter of law) is denied by the court, the two attorneys, Gilmore and Cameron, will now reverse their roles. Attorney Cameron will begin to present evidence demonstrating the weaknesses of plaintiff

EXHIBIT 15.6
Motion for Judgment as a Matter of Law

Elizabeth A. Cameron
Cameron & Strauss, P.C.
310 Lake Drive
Zero City, ZE 59802
(616) 955-6234

Attorney for Defendant

UNITED STATES DISTRICT COURT
FOR THE WESTERN DISTRICT OF NITA

Katherine Baranski)
            Plaintiff,)   CASE NO. 07-14335-NI
)   Honorable Harley M. Larue
v.)
)
)   MOTION FOR JUDGMENT
Tony Peretto)   AS A MATTER OF LAW
           Defendant.)

     The Defendant, Tony Peretto, at the close of the Plaintiff's case, moves the court to withdraw the evidence from the consideration of the jury and to find the Defendant not liable.

     As grounds for this motion, Defendant Peretto states that:

     (1) No evidence has been offered or received during the trial of the above-entitled cause of action to sustain the allegations of negligence contained in Plaintiff Baranski's complaint.

     (2) No evidence has been offered or received during the trial proving or tending to prove that Defendant Peretto was guilty of any negligence.

     (3) The proximate cause of Plaintiff Baranski's injuries was not due to any negligence on the part of Defendant Peretto.

     (4) By the uncontroverted evidence, Plaintiff Baranski was guilty of contributory negligence, which was the sole cause of the Plaintiff's injuries.

Date: 7/21/07

Elizabeth A Cameron
Elizabeth A. Cameron
Attorney for the Defendant

Baranski's claims against defendant Peretto. She will essentially follow the same procedure used by Gilmore when he presented plaintiff Baranski's side of the story. Cameron will call witnesses to the stand and question them. After Cameron's direct examination of each witness, that witness will be subject to possible cross-examination by Gilmore, redirect examination by Cameron, and recross-examination by Gilmore.

     In her presentation of the defendant's case, attorney Cameron will attempt to counter the points made by attorney Gilmore during his presentation of plaintiff Baranski's side of the story. To that end, Cameron and her paralegal, Gordon McVay, may have to prepare

Ethics Watch!

COMMUNICATING WITH JURORS

Suppose that you are the paralegal working on the Baranski case with attorney Allen Gilmore, and one of your neighbors is a juror in the case. One evening, while you are gardening in your backyard, your neighbor approaches you and says, "You know, I didn't really understand what that witness, Williams, was saying. Did she really see the accident? Also, is it true that Mrs. Baranski will never be able to walk normally again?" You know the answers to these questions, and you would like the juror to know the truth. You also know that it would enhance Baranski's chances of winning the case if this juror were as familiar with the factual background as you are. What should you do? First, you should inform your neighbor that as a paralegal, you have an ethical duty to abide by the professional rules of conduct governing the legal profession. One of these rules prohibits *ex parte* (private) communications with jurors about a case being tried. Second, you should remind your neighbor that jurors are not permitted to discuss a case they are hearing with anyone.

exhibits and assorted memoranda of law in addition to those originally prepared. The need to prepare additional exhibits and memoranda sometimes arises when the plaintiff's attorney pursues a strategy different from the one anticipated by the defense team. Depending on Cameron's preference or strategy, she may choose to begin by exposing weaknesses in the plaintiff's case (by asserting that the plaintiff was speeding, for example) or by presenting defendant Peretto's version of the accident. Regardless of the procedure used, however, paralegal McVay, like paralegal Lopez, will have to keep track of the materials brought to court each day to faciliate Cameron's presentation.

Once Cameron has finished presenting her case on behalf of defendant Peretto, Gilmore will be permitted to offer evidence to *rebut* (refute) evidence introduced by Cameron in Peretto's behalf. After Gilmore's rebuttal, if any, both attorneys will make their closing arguments to the jury.

Closing Arguments

closing argument
The argument made by each side's attorney after the cases for the plaintiff and defendant have been presented. Closing arguments are made prior to the jury charge.

In their **closing arguments**, the attorneys summarize their presentations and argue in their clients' favor. A closing argument should include all of the major points that support the client's case. It should also emphasize the shortcomings of the opposing party's case. Jurors will view a closing argument with some skepticism if it merely recites the central points of a party's claim or defense without also responding to the unfavorable facts or issues raised by the other side. Of course, neither attorney wants to focus too much on the other side's position, but the elements of the opposing position do need to be acknowledged and their flaws highlighted.

Both attorneys will want to organize their presentations so they can explain to the jury their respective arguments and show how their arguments are supported by the evidence. Once both attorneys have completed their remarks, the case will be submitted to the jury, and the attorneys' role in the trial will be finished.

EXHIBIT 15.7
Jury Charge—Request
for Findings of Fact

The jury is requested to answer the following questions:

(1) Was the defendant negligent?

Answer: (yes or no) _____

(2) If your answer to question (1) is "yes," then you must answer this question: Was the defendant's negligence a proximate (direct) cause of the plaintiff's injuries?

Answer: (yes or no) _____

(3) Was the plaintiff negligent?

Answer: (yes or no) _____

(4) If your answer to question (3) is "yes," then you must answer this question: Was the plaintiff's negligence a proximate (direct) cause of the accident and injuries that she suffered?

Answer: (yes or no) _____

(5) If your answer to either question (1) or question (3) is "yes," then answer the following:

Taking 100% as the total fault causing the accident and injuries, what percentage of the total fault causing the accident and injuries do you attribute to:

_____ the defendant

_____ the plaintiff

(If you find that a party has no fault in causing the accident, then attribute 0 percentage of the fault to that party.)

(6) Regardless of how you answered the previous questions, answer this question:

Disregarding any negligence or fault on the part of the plaintiff, what sum of money would reasonably compensate the plaintiff for her claimed injury and damage?

Answer: $ _____

Jury Instructions

Before the jurors begin their deliberations, the judge gives the jury a **charge**, in which the judge sums up the case and instructs the jurors on the rules of law that apply to the issues involved in the case. (Note that in some courts, jury instructions are given prior to closing arguments and may even be given at some other point during trial proceedings.) Because the jury's role is to serve as the fact finder, the factual account contained in the charge is not binding on the jurors. Indeed, they may disregard the facts as noted in the charge. They are *not* free to ignore the statements of law, however. The charge contains a request for findings of fact, which is typically phrased in an "if, then" format. For example, in the charge presented in Exhibit 15.7, the jury is first asked to decide if the defendant was negligent. The next question states that *if* the jury decides that the defendant was negligent, *then* the jury must decide whether the defendant's negligence caused the plaintiff's injuries. This format helps to channel the jurors' deliberations.

charge
The judge's instruction to the jury, following the attorneys' closing arguments, setting forth the rules of law that the jury must apply in reaching its decision, or verdict.

Charges, which are also called jury instructions, are usually drafted by the attorneys and discussed with the judge before the trial begins, and an attorney's trial strategy will likely be linked to the charges. Often, the paralegal drafts the instructions for the attorney's review. The judge, however, has the final decision as to what instructions will be submitted to the jury.

The Verdict

Following its receipt of the charge, the jury begins its deliberations. Once it has reached a decision, the jury issues a **verdict** in favor of one of the parties. If the verdict is in favor of the plaintiff, the jury will specify the amount of damages to be paid by the defendant. Following the announcement of the verdict, the jurors are discharged. Usually, immediately after the verdict has been announced and the jurors discharged, the party in whose favor the verdict was issued makes a motion asking the judge to issue a *judgment*—which is the court's final word on the matter—consistent with the jury's verdict. For example, if the jury in the Baranski case finds that defendant Peretto was negligent and awards plaintiff Baranski damages in the amount of $85,000, the judge will order defendant Peretto to pay the plaintiff that amount.

POSTTRIAL MOTIONS AND PROCEDURES

Every trial must have a winner and a loser. Although civil litigation is an expensive and cumbersome process, the losing party may wish to pursue the matter further after the verdict has been rendered. Assume that plaintiff Baranski wins at trial and is awarded $85,000 in damages. Cameron, as defendant Peretto's attorney, may wish to file a posttrial motion or appeal the decision to a higher court. Note that plaintiff Baranski, even though she won the case, could also appeal the judgment. For example, she might appeal the case on the ground that she should have received $130,000 in damages instead of $85,000, arguing that the latter amount inadequately compensates her for the harms that she suffered as a result of defendant Peretto's negligence.

Posttrial Motions

Assume that defendant Peretto's attorney, Cameron, believes that the verdict for plaintiff Baranski is not supported by the evidence. In this situation, she may file a **motion for judgment notwithstanding the verdict** (also known as a *motion for judgment as a matter of law* in the federal courts).[5] By filing this motion, attorney Cameron asks the judge to enter a judgment in favor of defendant Peretto on the ground (basis) that the jury verdict in favor of plaintiff Baranski was unreasonable and erroneous. Cameron may file this motion only if she previously filed a motion for a directed verdict (or judgment as a matter of law) during the trial and the motion was denied at that time. If she decides to file this motion, she must file it within ten days following the entry of judgment against defendant Peretto. Like virtually all motions in federal court, this motion must be accompanied by a supporting affidavit or a memorandum of law, or brief (these documents were discussed in Chapter 13). The judge will then determine whether the jury's verdict was reasonable in view of the evidence presented at trial.

Rule 50 of the Federal Rules of Civil Procedure permits either party to file a **motion for a new trial**. Such a motion may be submitted along with a motion for a judgment notwithstanding the verdict. A motion for a new trial is a far more drastic tactic because it asserts that the trial was so pervaded by error or otherwise fundamentally flawed that a new trial should be held. Because such a motion reflects adversely on the way in which the judge conducted the trial, it should be filed only if the attorney truly believes that a miscarriage of justice will otherwise result.

---

verdict
A formal decision made by a jury.

On the Web

To find information on jury verdicts in assorted trials throughout the country, including the amount of damages awarded in each case, go to **http://www.morelaw.com**.

Case at a Glance

The Plaintiff—
　Plaintiff: Katherine Baranski
　Attorney: Allen P. Gilmore
　Paralegal: Elena Lopez

The Defendant—
　Defendant: Tony Peretto
　Attorney: Elizabeth A. Cameron
　Paralegal: Gordon McVay

motion for judgment notwithstanding the verdict
A motion (also referred to as a *motion for judgment as a matter of law* in federal courts) requesting that the court grant judgment in favor of the party making the motion on the ground that the jury verdict against him or her was unreasonable or erroneous.

motion for a new trial
A motion asserting that the trial was so fundamentally flawed (because of error, newly discovered evidence, prejudice, or other reason) that a new trial is needed to prevent a miscarriage of justice.

EXHIBIT 15.8
**Motion for Judgment as a
Matter of Law or for a New Trial**

Elizabeth A. Cameron
Cameron & Strauss, P.C.
310 Lake Drive
Zero City, ZE 59802
(616) 955-6234

Attorney for Defendant

UNITED STATES DISTRICT COURT
FOR THE WESTERN DISTRICT OF NITA

Katherine Baranski	)	CASE NO. 07-14335-NI
Plaintiff,	)	Honorable Harley M. Larue
	)	
v.	)	
	)	MOTION FOR JUDGMENT AS
	)	A MATTER OF LAW OR, IN
Tony Peretto	)	THE ALTERNATIVE,
Defendant.	)	MOTION FOR A NEW TRIAL

The Defendant, Tony Peretto, moves this Court, pursuant to Rule 50(b) of the
Federal Rules of Civil Procedure, to set aside the verdict and judgment entered
on August 15, 2007, and to enter instead a judgment for the Defendant as a
matter of law. In the alternative, and in the event the Defendant's motion for
judgment as a matter of law is denied, the Defendant moves the Court to order
a new trial.

The grounds for this motion are set forth in the attached memorandum.

Date: 8/16/07

Elizabeth A. Cameron
Elizabeth A. Cameron
Attorney for the Defendant

For a motion for a new trial to have a reasonable chance of being granted, the motion
must allege such serious problems as jury misconduct, prejudicial jury instructions, excessive or inadequate damages, or the existence of newly discovered evidence (but not if the evidence could have been discovered earlier through the use of reasonable care). Like other
posttrial motions in federal courts, the motion for a new trial must be filed within ten days
following the entry of the judgment. Exhibit 15.8 illustrates a motion for judgment as a matter of law or, in the alternative, for a new trial.

Appealing the Verdict

If attorney Cameron's posttrial motions are unsuccessful or if she decides not to file them,
she may still file an **appeal**. The purpose of an appeal is to have the trial court's decision
either reversed or modified by an appellate court. As discussed in Chapter 6, appellate
courts, or courts of appeals, are *reviewing* courts, not trial courts. In other words, no new
evidence will be presented to the appellate court, and there is no jury. The appellate court
will review the trial court's proceedings to decide whether the trial court erred in applying

On the Web

The Federal Rules of Appellate
Procedure are online at **http://www.
law.cornell.edu/wex/index.php/
Appellate_procedure**.

appeal
The process of seeking a higher court's
review of a lower court's decision for the
purpose of correcting or changing the
lower court's judgment or decision.

the law to the facts of the case, in instructing the jury, or in administering the trial generally. Appellate courts rarely tamper with a trial court's findings of fact because the judge and jury were in a better position than the appellate court to evaluate the credibility of witnesses, the nature of the evidence, and so on.

As grounds for the appeal, defendant Peretto's attorney, Cameron, might argue that the trial court erred in one of the ways mentioned in the preceding paragraph. Unless she believes that a reversal of the judgment is likely, however, she will probably advise Peretto not to appeal the case, as an appeal will simply add to the costs and expenses already incurred by Peretto in defending against plaintiff Baranski's claim.

Notice of Appeal

When the appeal involves a federal district court decision, as in the Baranski case, the **appellant** (the party appealing the decision) must file a notice of appeal with the district court that rendered the judgment. The clerk of the court then notifies the **appellee** (the party against whom the appeal is taken) as well as the court of appeals. The clerk also forwards to the appellate court a transcript of the trial court proceedings, along with any related pleadings and exhibits; these materials together constitute the **record on appeal**.

The Appellate Brief and Oral Arguments

When a case is appealed, the attorneys for both parties submit written *briefs* that present their positions regarding the issues to be reviewed by the appellate court. The briefs outline each party's view of the proper application of the law to the facts.

After the appellate court has had an opportunity to review the briefs, the court sets aside a time for both attorneys to argue their positions before the panel of judges. The attorneys will then present their arguments and answer any questions that the judges might have. Generally, the attorneys' arguments before an appellate court are limited in terms of both the time allowed for argument and the scope of the argument. Following the oral arguments, the judges will decide the matter and then issue a formal written opinion, which normally will be published in the relevant reporter (see Chapter 17 for a detailed discussion of how court opinions are published).

The Appellate Court's Options

Once they have reviewed the record and heard oral arguments, the judges have several options. For example, in the Baranski case, if the appellate court decided to uphold the trial court's decision, then the judgment for plaintiff Baranski would be **affirmed**. If the judges decided to **reverse** the trial court's decision, however, then Peretto would no longer be obligated to pay the damages awarded to Baranski by the trial court. The court might also affirm or reverse a decision *in part*. For example, the judges might affirm the jury's finding that Peretto was negligent but **remand** the case—that is, send it back to the trial court—for further proceedings on another issue (such as the extent of Baranski's damages). An appellate court can also *modify* a lower court's decision. If, for example, the appellate court decided that the jury awarded an excessive amount in damages, the appellate court might reduce the award to a more appropriate, or fairer, amount.

The decision of the appellate court may sometimes be appealed further. A state appellate court's decision, for example, may be appealed to the state supreme court. A federal appellate court's decision may be appealed to the United States Supreme Court. It will be up to these higher courts to decide whether they will review the case. In other words, these courts normally are not *required* to review cases. Recall from Chapter 6 that although thousands of cases are submitted to the United States Supreme Court each year, it hears less than

---

appellant
The party who takes an appeal from one court to another; sometimes referred to as the *petitioner*.

appellee
The party against whom an appeal is taken—that is, the party who opposes setting aside or reversing the judgment; sometimes referred to as the *respondent*.

record on appeal
The items submitted during the trial (pleadings, motions, briefs, and exhibits) and the transcript of the trial proceedings that are forwarded to the appellate court for review when a case is appealed.

affirm
To uphold the judgment of a lower court.

reverse
To overturn the judgment of a lower court.

remand
To send a case back to a lower court for further proceedings.

Developing Paralegal Skills

LOCATING ASSETS

Paralegal Myra Cullen works for a law firm that represented Jennifer Roth in a lawsuit brought against Best Eatery, a local restaurant. Roth won $100,000 in a lawsuit for damages she suffered when she fell and broke her leg in the restaurant's lobby on a rainy morning. Best Eatery's only insurance coverage is a small liability policy that will only pay a portion of Roth's award. Myra has been assigned the task of investigating Best Eatery's assets to determine how the judgment can be collected. Myra learned through pretrial discovery that John Dobman owns Best Eatery as a sole proprietor, which means that he is personally liable for the debts of the business. Myra now contacts the county register of deeds to research the value of the property on which Best Eatery is located and any other property owned by John Dobman. In Myra's county, the county clerk's deed records can be searched via the Internet. Myra knows, however, that after conducting an online search she will need to verify the information obtained. She therefore writes down the document numbers provided online so that she can quickly access the information at the clerk's office. Myra determines that Dobman's equity (market value minus mortgage outstanding) in the property on which Best Eatery is located is $110,000, which will cover any shortfall in the damages. Because the equity is sufficient to cover the award, Myra simply notes the record number of Dobman's other real property (his house) in the client's file.

TIPS FOR LOCATING ASSETS

- Ask what property the defendant owns during discovery, such as in interrogatories.
- Ask for the address of the property.
- Go to the register of deeds to learn about any liens filed against the property and the amount of any mortgage loan.
- Check with a real estate agent or an appraiser as to the market value of the property.
- Deduct the liens and the mortgage debt from the market value to determine the defendant's equity.

one hundred. (An action decided in a state court, however, has a somewhat greater chance of being reviewed by the state supreme court.)

ENFORCING THE JUDGMENT

The uncertainties of the litigation process are compounded by the lack of guarantees that any judgment will be enforceable. It is one thing to have a court enter a judgment in your favor; it is quite another to collect the funds to which you are entitled from the opposing party. Even if the jury awarded Baranski the full amount of damages requested ($130,000), for example, she might not, in fact, "win" anything at all. Peretto's auto insurance coverage might have lapsed, in which event the company would not cover any of the damages. Alternatively, Peretto's insurance coverage might be limited to $30,000, meaning that Peretto would have to pay the remaining $100,000 personally. If Peretto did not have that amount available, then Baranski would need to go back to court and request that the court issue a **writ of execution**—an order, usually issued by the clerk of the court, directing the sheriff to seize (take temporary ownership of) and sell Peretto's assets. The proceeds of the sale would then be used to pay the damages owed to Baranski. Any excess proceeds of the sale would be returned to Peretto.

writ of execution
A writ that puts in force a court's decree or judgment.

Today's Professional Paralegal

DRAFTING *VOIR DIRE* QUESTIONS LIKE A PRO

Andrea Leed, a legal assistant, is preparing for trial. Her boss is a famous trial attorney, Mary Marshall. Mary rarely loses a case. One of the many secrets of her success is that she always draws up a jury profile and prepares carefully for *voir dire*.

Mary is defending a corporation in an environmental liability case. The case involves many complex engineering and scientific issues that the jury will need to understand in order to reach its verdict. It is a common practice in these types of cases to select a "blue ribbon" jury—a jury consisting of persons who are very well educated. Mary has suggested that Andrea locate and hire a psychologist to prepare a jury profile.

CONSULTING WITH AN EXPERT WITNESS

Andrea contacts TrialPsych, Inc., a consulting firm headed by Dr. Linda Robertson, who specializes in jury selection. Dr. Robertson would be delighted to work on the case, but her services are very expensive, and Andrea must find out whether the client is willing to pay Dr. Robertson's fee. The client agrees to pay the fee, so Andrea meets with Dr. Robertson to discuss the case. Andrea explains that the client is a corporation and that the case involves complex scientific and engineering issues. Dr. Robertson consults her files for statistical information on these types of cases. She finds that the ideal jury would be made up of white-collar professionals holding advanced degrees in engineering or another applied science. Also, the prospective jurors would ideally be against extensive government regulation of the corporate world.

DRAFTING *VOIR DIRE* QUESTIONS

Andrea returns to the office and discusses with Mary the results of her consultation with Dr. Robertson. Mary and Andrea decide to draft questions for *voir dire* that are designed to elicit the type of information recommended by Dr. Robertson. Andrea then drafts a list of about twenty questions, including the following:

1. Please state your name and address.
2. Where are you employed, and how long have you been employed there?
3. What is the highest level of education that you have attained: high school diploma, some college but no degree, college degree, advanced degree (please specify)?
4. If you have attended college or received a college degree, what was your field of study?
5. Have you ever been fired by a corporate employer in a way that you believed was unfair?
6. Have you ever worked for a government regulatory agency, and, if so, what were your responsibilities in that position?
7. Have you, or persons or business firms with whom you are or have been associated, ever been sued for violating environmental statutes or regulations? If so, what were the violations?
8. In your opinion, what should be the government's role in regulating a company's operations?

REVIEWING THE *VOIR DIRE* QUESTIONS

Andrea faxes the list of questions to Dr. Robertson, who reviews them and faxes back some suggested changes, which Andrea incorporates. When the final list of questions is drawn up, Andrea presents it to Mary and places a copy of the list in the trial notebook. Mary asks Andrea to call Dr. Robertson and ask her if she is available to sit in on the actual *voir dire* process to ensure that jury selection goes smoothly.

Even as a **judgment creditor** (one who has obtained a court judgment against his or her debtor), Baranski may not be able to obtain the full amount of the judgment from Peretto. Laws protecting debtors provide that certain property (such as a debtor's home up to a specific value, tools used by the debtor in his or her trade, and so on) is *exempt*. Exempt property cannot be seized and sold to pay debts owed to judgment creditors. Similar exemptions would apply if Peretto declared bankruptcy. Thus, even though Baranski won at trial, she, like many others who are awarded damages, might not be able to collect them. Realize, though, that judgments constitute liens (legal claims) for significant time periods. If the financial circumstances of the debtor—such as Peretto—change in the future, recovery may be possible.

The difficulty of enforcing court judgments, coupled with the high costs accompanying any litigation (including attorneys' fees, court costs, and the litigants' time costs), is a major reason why most disputes are settled out of court, either before or during the trial.

| **judgment creditor**
A creditor who is legally entitled, by a court's judgment, to collect the amount of the judgment from a debtor.

KEY TERMS AND CONCEPTS

affirm   570

appeal   569

appellant   570

appellee   570

challenge   556

challenge for cause   556

charge   567

closing argument   566

cross-examination   562

direct examination   560

judgment creditor   573

motion for a directed verdict   564

motion for a new trial   568

motion for judgment notwithstanding
   the verdict   568

motion *in limine*   553

opening statement   559

peremptory challenge   557

pretrial conference   552

record on appeal   570

recross-examination   564

redirect examination   563

remand   570

reverse   570

trial notebook   551

verdict   568

voir dire   554

writ of execution   571

chapter summary   Trial Procedures

Preparing for Trial

1. *Trial-preparation checklist*—Before the trial begins, attorneys for both sides and their paralegals gather and organize all evidence, documents, and other materials relating to the case. It is helpful to create a checklist to ensure that nothing is overlooked during this stage.

2. *Witnesses and subpoenas*—Paralegals often assist in contacting and issuing subpoenas to witnesses, as well as in preparing witnesses for trial.

3. *Prepare exhibits and trial notebook*—Paralegals also assume responsibility for making sure that all exhibits and displays are ready by the trial date and that the trial notebook is complete.

Pretrial Conference

Prior to the trial, the attorneys for both sides meet with the trial judge in a pretrial conference to decide whether a settlement is possible or, if not, to decide how the trial will be conducted and what types of evidence will be admissible.

(Continued)

1. *Motions in limine*—One or both of the attorneys may make a motion *in limine,* which asks the court to keep certain evidence from being offered at the trial.

Jury Selection

1. *Voir dire*—During the *voir dire* process, attorneys for both sides question potential jurors to determine whether certain potential jurors should be excluded from the jury.

2. *Challenges for cause*—Attorneys for both sides can exercise an unlimited number of challenges for cause on the basis of prospective jurors' bias against the client or case.

3. *Peremptory challenges*—Both attorneys can exercise a limited number of peremptory challenges without giving any reason to the court for excluding a particular juror.

The Trial

Once the jury has been selected and seated, the trial begins. The paralegal, if he or she attends the trial, coordinates witnesses' appearances, tracks the testimony of witnesses and compares it with sworn statements that the witnesses made prior to the trial, and provides the attorney with appropriate reminders or documents when necessary.

1. *Opening statements*—The trial begins with opening statements in which the attorneys briefly outline their versions of the facts of the case and the evidence they will offer to support their views.

2. *Plaintiff's case*—Following the attorneys' opening statements, the plaintiff's attorney presents evidence supporting the plaintiff's claims, including the testimony of witnesses.

   a. The attorney's questioning of a witness whom he or she calls is referred to as direct examination.

   b. Following direct examination by the plaintiff's attorney, the defendant's attorney may cross-examine the witness.

   c. If the witness was cross-examined, the plaintiff's attorney may question the witness on redirect examination, after which the defendant's attorney may question the witness on recross-examination.

3. *Motion for a directed verdict*—After the plaintiff's attorney has presented his or her client's case, the defendant's attorney may make a motion for a directed verdict, also called a motion for judgment as a matter of law. This motion asserts that the plaintiff has not offered enough evidence to support the validity of the plaintiff's claim against the defendant. If the judge grants the motion, the case will be dismissed.

4. *Defendant's case*—The attorneys then reverse their roles, and the defendant's attorney presents evidence and testimony to refute the plaintiff's claims. Any witnesses called to the stand by the defendant's attorney will be subject to direct examination by that attorney, cross-examination by the plaintiff's attorney, and possible redirect examination and recross-examination.

5. *Closing arguments*—After the defendant's attorney has finished his or her presentation, both attorneys give their closing arguments. A closing argument includes all the major points that support the client's case and emphasizes shortcomings in the opposing party's case.

6. *Jury instructions*—Following the attorneys' closing arguments (or, in some courts, at some other point in the proceedings), the judge instructs the jury in a charge—a document that includes statements of the applicable law and a review of the facts as they were presented during the trial. The jury must not disregard the judge's instructions as to what the applicable law is and how it should be applied to the facts of the case as interpreted by the jury.

7. *Verdict*—Once the jury reaches a decision, it issues a verdict in favor of one of the parties and is discharged. The court then enters a judgment consistent with the jury's verdict.

Posttrial Motions and Procedures

After the verdict has been pronounced and the trial concluded, the losing party's attorney may file a posttrial motion or an appeal.

1. *Motion for judgment notwithstanding the verdict*—A motion for judgment notwithstanding the verdict (also called a motion for judgment as a matter of law) asks the judge to enter a judgment in favor of the losing party in spite of the verdict because the verdict was not supported by the evidence or was otherwise erroneous.

2. *Motion for a new trial*—A motion for a new trial asserts that the trial was so flawed—by judge or juror misconduct or other pervasive errors—that a new trial should be held.

3. *Appealing the verdict*—The attorney may, depending on the client's wishes, appeal the decision to an appellate court for review. Appeals are usually filed only when the attorney believes that a reversal of the judgment is likely.

   a. If an appeal is pursued, the appellant must file a notice of appeal with the court that rendered the judgment. Then the clerk will forward the record on appeal to the appropriate reviewing court.

   b. The parties then file appellate briefs arguing their positions. Later, they will be given the opportunity to present oral arguments before the appellate panel.

   c. The appellate court decides whether to affirm, reverse, remand, or modify the trial court's judgment.

   d. The appellate court's decision may sometimes be appealed further (to the state supreme court, for example).

Enforcing the Judgment

Even though a plaintiff wins a lawsuit for damages, it may be difficult to enforce the judgment against the defendant, particularly if the defendant has few assets. The paralegal is often involved in locating assets so that the attorney can request a writ of execution (court order to seize property) in an attempt to collect the amount the client is owed.

QUESTIONS FOR REVIEW

1. What role does the paralegal play in preparing witnesses, exhibits, and displays for trial? How can the paralegal assist the attorney in preparing the trial notebook?

2. What is a pretrial conference? What issues are likely to be raised and decided at a pretrial conference?

3. How are jurors selected? What role does the attorney play

in the selection process? Does the paralegal play a role in the process?

4. What is the difference between a peremptory challenge and a challenge for cause?

5. What role might the paralegal play during the trial? What types of trial-related tasks may the paralegal perform?

6. How are witnesses examined during trial? What is the difference between direct examination and cross-examination?

7. What is a jury charge? Can the jury decide matters of law?

8. Name the posttrial motions that are available. In what situation is each of them used?

9. Describe the procedure for filing an appeal. What factors does an attorney consider when deciding whether a case should be appealed?

10. Why do appellate courts defer to trial courts' findings of fact? What options might an appellate court pursue after it has completed its review of a case?

ETHICAL QUESTIONS

1. Anthony Paletti, a paralegal, is attending a trial with his supervising attorney. Anthony leaves the courtroom to meet a witness. On his way down the hall, he runs into the defendant in the case. The defendant says to Anthony, "You work for the plaintiff's attorney, don't you? I have a question for you about that contract that your attorney offered into evidence." Should Anthony answer the defendant's question? Why or why not?

2. A client claiming to have severely injured his back at work comes into the office of a law firm. The client, in a wheelchair, seeks legal advice about filing a lawsuit, and the attorney decides to take the case. Two days later, Alvin Kerrigan, the attorney's paralegal, sees the new client on the roof of a building installing shingles. What should Alvin do?

3. During a lunch break in the course of a trial, Louise Lanham, a paralegal, was washing her hands in the rest room. One of the members of the trial jury came up to her and said, "I don't understand what negligence is. Can you explain it to me?" How should Louise answer this question?

PRACTICE QUESTIONS AND ASSIGNMENTS

1. Paralegal Patricia Smith is assisting her supervising attorney, who has received a trial date for an auto accident case. The trial is set to begin in ten weeks. Discovery has been completed in the case. The depositions of the plaintiff and defendant have been taken, along with those of two eyewitnesses, a police officer, and Dr. Black, the plaintiff's physician. Additionally, the plaintiff and the defendant have answered interrogatories. Patricia's firm represents the plaintiff, and her supervising attorney plans to call not only the client but also the defendant, an eyewitness (Mr. Sams), and the police officer to testify. All of the witnesses are local. The case file contains police reports, newspaper articles about the accident, and medical records in addition to the deposition and interrogatory materials. Using the material presented in Exhibit 15.1 on page 547, *Trial-Preparation Checklist*, prepare a checklist for Patricia to complete.

2. A product liability trial is about to begin. It involves the death of Tom Bert, which resulted from a defective industrial press. The plaintiff's wife is suing as Tom's personal representative. One of her claims is for *loss of consortium*, which is a claim for the loss of her relationship with her husband. Tom's wife remarried three weeks after his funeral, however, and there exists evidence that she was having an affair with her second husband prior to Tom's death. The defense attorney wants to be able to address the plaintiff as Mrs. Ross, her new name resulting from her recent marriage, throughout the trial. Calling the wife by her new name in front of the jury will emphasize to the jury that she did not have much of a relationship with Tom Bert. The defense attorney hopes that this will significantly decrease any damages that might be awarded to Mrs. Ross on the loss-of-consortium claim. The plaintiff's attorney assigns you the task of drafting a motion *in limine* to keep the defense attorney from addressing the plaintiff as Mrs. Ross during the trial. Prepare an outline of the argument that would be included in the motion.

3. Using Exhibit 15.2 on page 549, *A Subpoena*, draft a subpoena for a friendly witness using the following facts:

   Simon Kolstad, whose address is 100 Schoolcraft Road, Del Mar, California, is a witness to be subpoenaed in *Sumner v. Hayes*, a civil lawsuit filed in the U.S. District Court for the Eastern District of Michigan, case number

06–123492. He is being subpoenaed by the plaintiff's attorney, Marvin W. Green, whose office is located at 300 Penobscot Building, Detroit, Michigan. Kolstad is to appear in room number 6 of the courthouse, which is located at 231 Lafayette Boulevard, Detroit, Michigan, at 2:30 P.M. on January 10, 2007.

4. Draft a series of questions for the plaintiff's attorney and for the two defendants' attorneys (the attorneys representing the doctor and the pharmaceutical company) to use during *voir dire* in a case involving the following facts:

   The plaintiff's daughter died five days after starting a regimen of taking weight-loss pills. The daughter died because the pills were incompatible with her blood type. Prior to taking the pills, she was a perfectly healthy twenty-five-year-old law student. The mother is bringing a medical-malpractice suit against the doctor for prescribing the wrong type of pill. The mother is also suing the pharmaceutical company that manufactured the pill on the ground that it failed to warn of the dangers of its pill for those persons, including her daughter, whose blood types were incompatible with the pill.

5. Using the scenario from Question 4 above, involving the law student who died after taking weight-loss pills that were incompatible with her blood type, conduct the *voir dire*. Plaintiff and defense teams, each consisting of at least one attorney and one paralegal, will need to be selected. The rest of the class will serve as the jury pool to be questioned during *voir dire*. Each legal team, using the questions drafted for Question 4 above, is to select the jurors most favorable to its client's position. Additional factual information relating to the two defendants includes the following:

   a. The physician has prescribed this pill on numerous occasions and has never had a patient die as a result of taking it. The doctor did not take a thorough medical history of the plaintiff, nor did he note her blood type.

   b. The pharmaceutical company does include a package insert warning physicians of the dangers involved in taking the drug and instructing them as to the types of tests that should be undertaken before the pill is prescribed.

6. Your client, a surgeon, is suing a lawyer for slander (a tort arising when someone makes a verbal statement that harms another's good name or reputation—see Chapter 7). The lawyer was representing the surgeon in a malpractice case. In the presence of several other physicians, the lawyer told the surgeon that he "ought to have his head examined" and that he was "so incompetent at his job" that the lawyer

had decided not to defend him against the malpractice claim. The surgeon is suing the lawyer for slander because, as a result of the lawyer's comments, the physician's staff privileges at a major hospital have been suspended and he can no longer perform surgery there.

Using the material presented in the chapter, draft questions for your supervising attorney to ask your client, the surgeon, during trial.

7. Identify the motion that would be filed in each of the following situations:

   a. A plaintiff's attorney loses a case, and she believes that her loss is due to prejudicial jury instructions given by the judge.

   b. The defendant's key witness was hospitalized during a trial and was unable to testify. As a result, key evidence was not presented, and the defendant was unable to prove his case.

   c. In the example given in item b above, the plaintiff's attorney made the appropriate motion, which was not granted, and ultimately lost the lawsuit. Thus, according to the plaintiff's attorney, the judgment was not supported by the evidence.

   d. The defense attorney has seen grisly photographs of an accident that the plaintiff's attorney has in her file. The defense attorney is concerned that these photographs would unfairly prejudice a jury against the defendant during the trial.

8. Indicate whether the appellate court will affirm, modify, or reverse the trial court's decision or remand the case for further proceedings:

   a. A trial court finds for the plaintiff in the amount of $150,000 in a case in which the plaintiff slipped and fell in a grocery store. The court of appeals finds that while the plaintiff is entitled to damages, the damages awarded by the jury are excessive. The appellate court sends the case back to the trial court for reevaluation of the amount of damages awarded.

   b. A trial court finds that the plaintiff was slandered by the defendant. On appeal, the court of appeals finds that the trial court admitted evidence that it should not have allowed and holds that without this evidence, there was no slander.

   c. A trial court finds that the defendant breached a contract and owes the plaintiff $1,000,000 in damages. The defendant appeals, claiming that the damages are not supported by the evidence. The court of appeals agrees with the trial court's decision.

QUESTIONS FOR CRITICAL ANALYSIS

1. Typically, all witnesses called to appear at a trial are served with subpoenas, even friendly witnesses. Why is this? What might happen if they were not subpoenaed? How can the service of subpoenas be handled with friendly witnesses so that they are not offended?

2. Most prudent attorneys do not put a witness on the stand without discussing the witness's testimony beforehand or at least learning what the witness will say. What might happen if a witness whose testimony has not been discussed ahead of time, or whose testimony is unknown, takes the stand? What effect might this have on the outcome of the case?

3. Much preparation and organization go into trial work, from preparing witnesses and trial notebooks, to drafting questions, to creating exhibits and displays. Why is this done? What impact do these preparations have on the jury? What impact would (or do) disorganization and lack of preparation have on the jury?

4. Certain types of cases, such as product liability cases, require complex evidence. Should certain types of jurors be required in these complex cases? Why or why not?

5. What is the difference between redirect examination and recross-examination? When is each type of examination used? What is allowed during each type of examination?

6. Why are leading questions not allowed during direct examination? Why are leading questions allowed during cross-examination? Is the use of leading questions fair to the witness being cross-examined?

7. What is the basis for a motion for a directed verdict? Why would a trial start if the grounds for a motion for a directed verdict existed? Are these motions frequently granted?

8. Why do you think that attorneys and paralegals, instead of judges, draft jury instructions? Does this surprise you? Why or why not?

9. Is there a difference between a verdict and a judgment? If so, what is the difference? Who do you think drafts the judgment? Why?

10. After a trial, the losing party may file a motion for a judgment notwithstanding the verdict and/or a motion for a new trial. What is the likelihood that a judge will grant such motions? Why would a losing party file these types of motions as opposed to appealing the case?

11. How is a judgment paid when there is no insurance or other cash assets available to pay the judgment? Is all of a defendant's property subject to the judgment? If not, what property is exempt? Why might these exemptions have been created?

PROJECTS

1. Call a local court clerk or administrator (not a judge) to obtain a list of the cases on the court's trial docket. Arrange to attend a trial that is not expected to last longer than a few days. Attend the trial for as many days as you can, and observe carefully the following proceedings: *voir dire,* opening statements, the presentation of evidence, and closing arguments. Also note how paralegals are used. Prepare a three-page summary of your observations, making sure to include the name and docket number of the case, the name of the court, and the name of the judge.

2. Look up your state's court rules and find out how many challenges for cause are allowed during *voir dire.* How many peremptory challenges are permitted during *voir dire*?

3. Call your local sheriff's office and find out what happens when a writ of execution is carried out. Ask if any printed information on this procedure is available. If so, request a copy. Share the results of your research with the class. (Discuss this assignment with your instructor prior to undertaking it.)

4. Look through some computer magazines, such as *Law Office Computing* and *Law Technology News,* for articles on the use of technology, such as digital cameras or scanners, to prepare or present evidence during a trial. If possible, obtain demo discs or videos of the technology. Present your findings to the class.

USING INTERNET RESOURCES

1. If you are assisting an attorney in litigating a case, you may be asked to do some research on jury verdicts in similar cases. To date, not many fully searchable databases that contain this information are available on the Web, although the number is expanding. One site is that offered by MoreLaw at **http://www.morelaw.com**. Access this site, and spend some time browsing through its offerings. Then click on "Case by Subject," and select a topic, such as "Divorce."

   a. How many cases/verdicts were listed for the topic you selected?

   b. Choose five cases. For each case, describe briefly what it was about, who "won" the case (the plaintiff or the defendant), and, if the plaintiff won, what amount of damages was awarded.

   c. Choose one of these cases, and describe it in further detail. Who initiated the lawsuit? Why? Who was the defendant? What general area of law was involved (torts, product liability, contracts, and so on)? How did the jury decide the issue? Did the jury award damages? If so, in what amount? Were punitive damages also awarded?

   d. Generally, what are the advantages of this site for paralegals doing research on jury verdicts? What are the disadvantages?

2. Do a general search on the Internet for vendors of trial support services, such as imaging and coding. Pick two of the vendors, and browse through their Web sites.

   a. Write a one-page summary of the services that each company provides.

   b. Write an additional two paragraphs comparing the vendors' services and stating which of the two companies you would recommend, and why.

3. ONLINE COMPANION™ For additional resources, visit our Web site at **http://www.paralegal.delmar.cengage.com**.

END NOTES

1. Pronounced in *lim*-uh-nay.

2. Pronounced vwahr *deer*. These old French verbs mean "to speak the truth." In legal language, the phrase refers to the process of questioning jurors to learn about their backgrounds, attitudes, and similar attributes.

3. Discriminating against prospective jurors on the basis of race was prohibited by the United States Supreme Court in *Batson v. Kentucky*, 476 U.S. 79, 106 S.Ct. 1712, 90 L.Ed.2d 69 (1986). Discriminating against prospective jurors on the basis of gender was prohibited by the Supreme Court in *J.E.B. v. Alabama ex rel. T.B.*, 511 U.S 127, 114 S.Ct. 1419, 128 L.Ed.2d 89 (1994). See Chapter 17 for an explanation of how to read court citations.

4. Tennessee, for example, follows the "English rule," which allows a litigant to prove elements of his or her own case during the cross-examination of the opponent's witnesses. Moreover, most states that limit cross-examination to matters brought up during direct examination do not rigidly enforce the rule. Rather, as mentioned, the decision as to what can be brought up during cross-examination is subject to the discretion of the trial judge.

5. Amendments to the Federal Rules of Civil Procedure designated both the motion for a directed verdict and the motion for judgment notwithstanding the verdict as motions for judgment as a matter of law. One of the reasons for the change was to make evident the common identity of these motions (both motions claim, at different times during the proceedings, that there is insufficient evidence against the defendant to justify a claim—or a verdict against the defendant). Many judges and attorneys continue to use the former names of these motions, however, so we include them in our discussion.

CRIMINAL LAW AND PROCEDURES

16

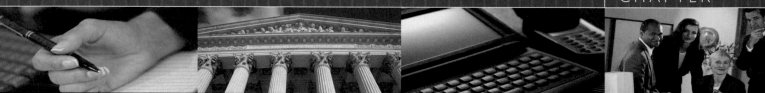

CHAPTER OUTLINE

AFTER COMPLETING THIS CHAPTER, YOU WILL KNOW:

▶ The difference between crimes and other wrongful acts.

▶ The two elements that are required for criminal liability and some of the most common defenses that are raised in defending against criminal charges.

▶ Five broad categories of crimes and some common types of crimes.

▶ The constitutional rights of persons accused of crimes.

▶ The basic steps involved in criminal procedure from the time a crime is reported to the resolution of the case.

▶ How and why criminal litigation procedures differ from civil litigation procedures.

INTRODUCTION

More than one million people are arrested for crimes and enter the criminal justice system each year. While the crime rate has declined during some recent years, a large number of attorneys and paralegals continue to work on criminal law cases. In fact, about one in every five paralegals spends most of her or his work time on criminal law.

Criminal cases are prosecuted by **public prosecutors**, who are employed by the government. The public prosecutor in federal criminal cases is called a U.S. attorney. In cases tried in state or local courts, the public prosecutor may be referred to as a *prosecuting attorney, state prosecutor, district attorney, county attorney,* or *city attorney.* Defendants in criminal cases may hire private attorneys to defend them. If a defendant cannot afford to hire an attorney, the court will appoint one for him or her. Everyone accused of a crime that may result in a jail sentence has a right to counsel, and this right is ensured by court-appointed attorneys, called **public defenders**, who are paid by the state.

Many employment opportunities exist for paralegals interested in working for public prosecutors or public defenders across the country. Private criminal defense attorneys also utilize paralegals. In addition, victims' rights organizations and police departments may employ legal assistants. Paralegals may also come into contact with criminal defendants in the course of their work in a general law practice or in a corporate legal department. A client of the firm may be arrested for driving while intoxicated or for possessing illegal drugs, for example, or a corporation might have to defend against alleged criminal violations of federal environmental laws.

In this chapter, we provide an overview of criminal law and procedure. We begin by explaining the nature of crime and the key differences between criminal law and civil law. We then discuss the elements of criminal liability and some of the many types of crime. Throughout the chapter, we emphasize the constitutional protections that come into play when a person is accused of a crime and focus on how and why criminal procedures differ from civil procedures.

WHAT IS A CRIME?

What is a crime? To answer that question, we begin by distinguishing crimes from other wrongs, such as torts—and, hence, criminal law from tort, or civil, law. Major differences between civil law and criminal law are summarized in Exhibit 16.1. After discussing these

public prosecutor
An individual, acting as a trial lawyer, who initiates and conducts criminal cases in the government's name and on behalf of the people.

public defender
A court-appointed attorney who is paid by the state to represent a criminal defendant who is unable to hire private counsel.

EXHIBIT 16.1
Civil Law and Criminal Law Compared

ISSUE	CIVIL LAW	CRIMINAL LAW
Area of concern	Rights and duties between individuals and between persons and their government	Offenses against society as a whole
Wrongful act	Harm to a person or to a person's property	Violation of a statute that prohibits some type of activity
Party who brings suit	Person who suffered harm	The state
Standard of proof	Preponderance of the evidence	Beyond a reasonable doubt
Remedy	Damages to compensate for the harm or a decree to achieve an equitable result	Punishment (fine, removal from public office, imprisonment, or death)

differences, we explain how one act can qualify as both a crime and a tort. We then describe classifications of crimes and jurisdiction over criminal acts.

Key Differences between Civil Law and Criminal Law

crime

A broad term for violations of law that are punishable by the state and are codified by legislatures. The objective of criminal law is to protect the public.

A **crime** can be distinguished from other wrongful acts, such as torts, in that a crime is an *offense against society as a whole.* Criminal defendants are prosecuted by public officials on behalf of the state, as mentioned above, not by their victims or other private parties. In addition, those who have committed crimes are subject to penalties, including fines, imprisonment, and, in some cases, death. As discussed in Chapter 7, tort remedies—remedies for civil wrongs—are generally intended to compensate the injured party (by awarding money damages, for example). Criminal law, however, is concerned with punishing the wrongdoer in an attempt to deter others from similar actions.

Another factor distinguishing criminal law from tort law is that criminal law is primarily statutory law. Essentially, a crime is whatever a legislature has declared to be a crime. Although federal crimes are defined by the U.S. Congress, most crimes are defined by state legislatures.

As mentioned in Chapter 5, at one time criminal law was governed primarily by the common law. Over time, common law doctrines and principles were codified, expanded on, and enacted in statutory form. Although many crimes were originally defined by the common law, the statutory definitions of those crimes may differ significantly from the related common law definitions.

Many state criminal codes are now online. To find your state's code, go to **http://www.findlaw.com/ casecode/#statelaw**.

For example, under the common law, in order to be guilty of *burglary,* a person had to break into and enter another person's dwelling at night with intent to commit a felony. Today, under most state statutes, a burglary need not take place at night, and the building entered need not be a person's home. Statutes have thus modified the common law definition of burglary.

The standards of proof required in criminal and civil cases represent another area of difference. Because the state has extensive resources at its disposal when prosecuting criminal cases, there are numerous procedural safeguards to protect the rights of defendants. One of these safeguards is the higher standard of proof that applies in a criminal case. In a civil case, the plaintiff usually must prove his or her case by a *preponderance of the evidence.* Under this standard, the plaintiff must convince the court that, based on the evidence presented by both parties, it is more likely than not that the plaintiff's allegation is true.

beyond a reasonable doubt

The standard used to determine the guilt or innocence of a person charged with a crime. To be guilty of a crime, a suspect must be proved guilty "beyond and to the exclusion of every reasonable doubt."

In a criminal case, in contrast, the state must prove its case **beyond a reasonable doubt**—that is, every juror in a criminal case must be convinced, beyond a reasonable doubt, of the defendant's guilt. The higher standard of proof in criminal cases reflects a fundamental social value—a belief that it is worse to convict an innocent individual than to let a guilty person go free. We will look at other safeguards later in the chapter, in the context of criminal procedure.

Yet another factor that distinguishes criminal law from tort law is the fact that a criminal act does not necessarily involve a victim, in the sense that the act directly and physically harms another. If Marissa grows marijuana in her backyard for her personal use, she may not be physically or directly harming another's interests, but she is nonetheless committing a crime (in most states and under federal law). Why? Because she is violating a rule of society that has been enacted into law by duly elected representatives of the people.

Civil Liability for Criminal Acts

Note that those who commit crimes may be subject to both civil and criminal liability. For example, suppose Joe is walking down the street, minding his own business, when suddenly a person attacks him. In the ensuing struggle, the attacker stabs Joe several times, seriously

EXHIBIT 16.2
Tort (Civil) Lawsuit and Criminal Prosecution for the Same Act

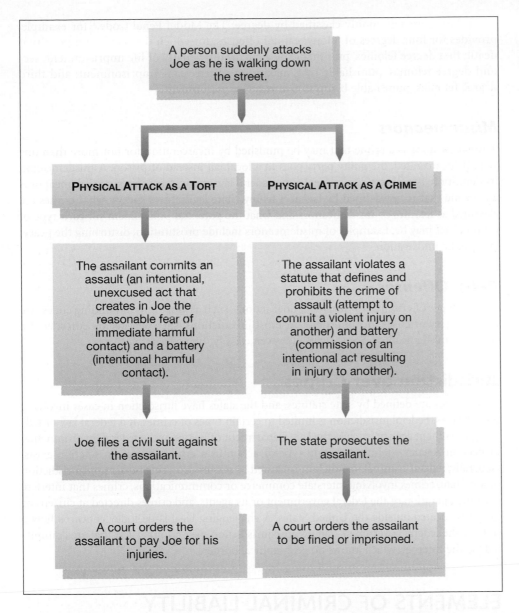

injuring him. A police officer restrains and arrests the wrongdoer. In this situation, the attacker may be subject both to criminal prosecution by the state and to a tort lawsuit brought by Joe. Exhibit 16.2 illustrates how the same act can result in both a tort action and a criminal action against the wrongdoer.

Classifications of Crimes

Crimes are generally divided into two broad classifications: felonies and misdemeanors.

Felonies

A **felony** is a serious crime that may be punished by imprisonment for more than one year. In some states, certain felonies are punishable by death. Examples of felonies include murder, rape, robbery, arson, and grand larceny. (You will read more about these and other crimes later in the chapter.)

felony
A crime—such as arson, murder, rape, or robbery—that carries the most severe sanctions. Sanctions range from one year in a state or federal prison to life imprisonment or (in some states) the death penalty.

Felonies are commonly classified by degree. The Model Penal Code,[1] for example, provides for four degrees of felony: capital offenses, for which the maximum penalty is death; first degree felonies, punishable by a maximum penalty of life imprisonment; second degree felonies, punishable by a maximum of ten years' imprisonment; and third degree felonies, punishable by up to five years' imprisonment.

Misdemeanors

> **misdemeanor**
> A less serious crime than a felony, punishable by a fine or incarceration for up to one year in jail (not a state or federal penitentiary).

A **misdemeanor** is a crime that may be punished by incarceration for not more than one year. If incarcerated, the guilty party goes to a local jail instead of prison. A misdemeanor, by definition, is a less serious crime. Under federal law and in most states, a misdemeanor is any crime that is not defined by law as a felony. State legislatures specify what crimes are classified as felonies or misdemeanors and what the potential punishment for each type of criminal act may be. Examples of misdemeanors include prostitution, disturbing the peace, and public intoxication.

Petty Offenses

> **petty offense**
> In criminal law, the least serious kind of wrong, such as a traffic or building-code violation.

Certain types of criminal or quasi-criminal actions, such as violations of building codes, are termed **petty offenses**, or *infractions*. In most jurisdictions, such actions are considered a subset of misdemeanors. Some states, however, classify them separately.

Jurisdiction over Crimes

Most crimes are defined by state statutes, and the states have jurisdiction in cases involving these crimes. Federal jurisdiction is limited to certain types of crimes. If a federal law or federal government agency (such as the U.S. Department of Justice or the federal Environmental Protection Agency) defines a certain type of action as a crime, federal jurisdiction exists. Generally, federal criminal jurisdiction is limited to crimes occurring outside the jurisdiction of any state, crimes involving interstate commerce or communications, crimes that interfere with the operation of the federal government or its agents, and crimes directed at citizens or property located outside the United States. A challenging legal issue today concerns how a state or the federal government can exercise jurisdiction over criminal acts that are committed via the Internet, which knows no geographical borders.

ELEMENTS OF CRIMINAL LIABILITY

For a person to be convicted of a crime, two elements must exist simultaneously: (1) the performance of a criminal act and (2) a specified state of mind, or intent. This section describes these two elements of criminal liability and some of the defenses that can be used to avoid liability for crimes.

The Criminal Act

> **actus reus**
> A guilty (prohibited) act. The commission of a prohibited act is one of the two essential elements required for criminal liability; the other element is the intent to commit a crime.

A criminal act is known as the *actus reus,*[2] or guilty act. Most crimes require an act of *commission;* that is, a person must *do* something in order to be accused of a crime. In some cases, an act of *omission* can be a crime, but only when a person has a legal duty to perform the omitted act. Failure to file a tax return is an example of an omission (failure to act) that is a crime.

The guilty-act requirement is based on one of the premises of criminal law—that a person is punished for harm done to society. Thinking about killing someone or about stealing a car may be wrong, but the thoughts do no harm unless they are translated into action. Of

On the Web

A good source for statistical data and other information on crime is the Federal Bureau of Investigation, which is online at **http://www.fbi.gov**.

course, a person can be punished for *attempting* murder or robbery, but normally only if substantial steps toward the criminal objective have been taken.

State of Mind

Even a completed act that harms society is not legally a crime unless the court finds that the second element—the required state of mind—was present. A wrongful mental state, or *mens rea*,[3] is as necessary as a wrongful act in establishing criminal liability. What constitutes such a mental state varies according to the wrongful action. For murder, the criminal act is the taking of a life, and the mental state is the intent to take life. For theft, the guilty act is the taking of another person's property, and the mental state involves both the knowledge that the property belongs to another and the intent to steal that property. Without the mental state required by law for a particular crime, there is no crime.

The same criminal act can result from varying mental states, and how a crime is defined and punished depends on the degree of "wrongfulness" of the defendant's state of mind. For example, taking another's life is *homicide,* a criminal act. The act can be committed coldly, after premeditation, as in *murder in the first degree,* which carries the most severe criminal penalty. The act can be committed in the heat of passion, as in *voluntary manslaughter,* which carries a less severe penalty than murder. Or the act can be committed as a result of criminal negligence (reckless driving or driving while intoxicated, for example), as in *involuntary manslaughter.* In each of these situations, the law recognizes a different degree of wrongfulness, and the harshness of the punishment depends on the degree to which the act of killing another was an *intentional* act.

> **mens rea**
> A wrongful mental state, or intent. A wrongful mental state is a requirement for criminal liability. What constitutes a wrongful mental state varies according to the nature of the crime.

Corporate Criminal Liability

At one time, it was thought that a corporation could not incur criminal liability because, although a corporation is a legal person, it can act only through its agents (corporate directors, officers, and employees). Therefore, the corporate entity itself could not "intend" to commit a crime. Under modern criminal law, however, a corporation may be held liable for crimes. Obviously, corporations cannot be imprisoned, but they can be fined or denied certain legal privileges. Today, corporations are normally liable for the crimes committed by their agents and employees within the course and scope of their employment.

Corporate directors and officers are personally liable for the crimes they commit, regardless of whether the crimes were committed for their personal benefit or on the corporation's behalf. Additionally, corporate directors and officers may be held liable for the actions of employees under their supervision. Under what has become known as the **responsible corporate officer doctrine**, a court may impose criminal liability on a corporate officer regardless of whether she or he participated in, directed, or even knew about a given criminal violation.

For example, in one case the chief executive officer of a national supermarket chain was held personally liable for sanitation violations in corporate warehouses, in which the food was exposed to contamination by rodents. The court imposed personal liability on the corporate officer not because he intended the crime or even knew about it but because he was in a "responsible relationship" to the corporation and had the power to prevent the violation.[4] Courts have used similar reasoning to impose criminal liability on corporate managers whose negligence causes harm to the environment in violation of federal law, such as the Clean Water Act (discussed in Chapter 12).

> **responsible corporate officer doctrine**
> A common law doctrine under which the court may impose criminal liability on a corporate officer for actions of employees under her or his supervision regardless of whether she or he participated in, directed, or even knew about those actions.

Defenses to Criminal Liability

Asserting that a defendant lacks the required degree of criminal intent for a specific crime is, of course, one way of defending against criminal liability. This defense and other defenses against criminal liability are discussed below.

The Required Mental State Is Lacking

Proving that a defendant did or did not possess the required mental state for a given crime is difficult because a person's state of mind is, by nature, a subjective attribute. For example, assume that Jackson shot and killed Avery. Jackson is arrested and charged with the crime of murder. Jackson contends that he did not commit murder because he was too drunk to know what he was doing and thus lacked the required mental state for murder—intent to kill. Jackson may have committed a criminal act (homicide). In view of his mental state, however, he committed not the crime of murder but (probably) the crime of involuntary manslaughter. Of course, there will most certainly have to be some facts in evidence tending to show that Jackson was indeed so drunk that he could not have intended to kill Avery.

Criminal defendants may assert that they lacked the required degree of criminal intent for other reasons, including *insanity* (the inability to distinguish between right and wrong due to diminished mental capacity), *duress* (which exists when one is forced to commit a specific act), or *mistake* (for example, taking someone else's property, such as a briefcase, thinking that it is one's own).

Protection of Persons or Property

self-defense
The legally recognized privilege to protect oneself or one's property against injury by another. The privilege of self-defense only protects acts that are reasonably necessary to protect oneself or one's property.

We all have the right to protect ourselves from physical attacks by others; this is the right of **self-defense**. The force we use to protect ourselves must be reasonable under the circumstances, though. The force used must be justified by the degree of threat posed in a given situation. If someone is about to take your life, the use of *deadly force* (shooting that person with a gun, for example) might be deemed reasonable, depending on the circumstances. If, however, someone in a shopping mall tries to pick your pocket to steal your wallet, you normally do not have a right to shoot him or her, because there was no physical threat to your person.

defense of others
The use of reasonable force to protect others from harm.

Similarly, we have the right to use force in **defense of others** if they are threatened with imminent harm. If you and a friend are walking down a city street one night and someone attacks and threatens to kill your friend, you are justified in using whatever force is reasonable under the circumstances to protect your friend. As with self-defense, it must be shown that the force used was reasonable in view of the nature of the threat.

defense of property
The use of reasonable force to protect one's property from the harm threatened by another. The use of deadly force in defending one's property is seldom justified.

We also have the right to use reasonable force in the **defense of property**. In particular, if someone is illegally trespassing on our property or is stealing our property, we have the right to use force to stop the trespassing or prevent the theft; again, the amount of force used must be reasonable. Because human life has a higher value than property, deadly force is normally not allowed in the protection of property unless the thief or trespasser poses a threat to human life.

Statutes of Limitations

With some exceptions, such as for the crime of murder, statutes of limitations apply to crimes just as they do to civil wrongs. In other words, criminal cases must be prosecuted within a certain number of years. If a criminal action is brought after the statutory time period has expired, the accused person can raise the statute of limitations as a defense.

Other Defenses

Further defenses include *mistaken identity* and other reasons why the criminal charges might not be valid. For example, a defendant may offer an *alibi* (proof that the defendant was somewhere else at the time of the crime, for example) as a defense. Still other defenses to criminal liability have to do with violations of procedural law. For example, the police officer or officers who arrested the defendant must have had the proper authority to do so,

Jena Parker

PARALEGAL **profile**

CRIMINAL LAW PARALEGAL

Jena Parker, CP, has worked as a criminal law paralegal for over eleven years. Parker received her associate's degree in applied science in 1992 from Tarrant County Junior College in Fort Worth, Texas, and became a certified paralegal in January 1997. She has been involved in the Fort Worth Paralegal Association, serving as president in 2005, and was nominated as paralegal of the year for two years in a row.

She has also been active in the National Association of Legal Assistants (NALA), the State Bar of Texas Paralegal Division, and the College of the State Bar of Texas.

Parker works primarily one on one with her attorney-employer. This close working relationship has enabled her to have significant responsibility, which she enjoys. She meets with clients, performs legal research, handles discovery, interviews witnesses, and drafts memoranda of law, as well as other legal documents. Parker helps her attorney-employer with all stages of his representation of a client, from the initial interview through the trial, in both federal and state courts.

What do you like best about your work?

"My days are never the same. I work for an attorney who is supportive and will let me work closely with him on all cases, from beginning to end. I am able to do everything that an attorney does, except represent someone in court, quote fees, and give legal advice. My supervising attorney utilizes my experience and knowledge as a paralegal and, most important, treats me with respect; he is confident that my work is accurate. We have had cases in state court ranging from charges of driving while intoxicated to capital murder and have handled both trials and appeals. In federal court, we have had cases in California, Colorado, Texas, and West Virginia. Those cases have ranged from a death penalty case to tax evasion and, again, from trials to appeals through the United States Supreme Court."

What is the greatest challenge that you face in your area of work?

"It is a great challenge to have the responsibility of drafting various documents—such as petitions, motions and orders, discovery doc-

> *"To work as a criminal law paralegal, you must be flexible.... Your priorities will change regularly."*

uments, and legal memoranda—and to be trusted to handle client and witness interviews. We typically have many cases that are in different stages of the process of preparation for trial. Therefore, I am generally working on several cases at once. Prior to the start of the day, I will plan, in my mind, what I need to work on that day. But it never seems that I can work on what I plan. Something may come up on a different case, or a new case may take priority. At the same time, I must answer the telephone and handle everyday situations of our clients. So remembering what I was doing prior to starting a new project can be a challenge. I have learned to write plenty of notes."

What advice do you have for would-be paralegals in your area of work?

"To work as a criminal law paralegal, you must be flexible and talented in many areas. Your priorities will change regularly. You need to have a handle on your tasks. Take good notes, and do your follow-up. You must keep a tight calendar for your attorney and yourself and be organized. In addition, one of the most important pieces of advice I can give is to know the court rules, whether in state or federal court. Each federal court has its own local rules, and it is extremely important that a paralegal follow each one. Keep the rules in a binder, and update them as you receive notices."

What are some tips for success as a paralegal in your area of work?

"To be successful in this area of the law, you must have good communication skills and the ability to handle details. You must be able to keep track of where you are on each task, take good notes, and have an excellent memory, backed up by your notes. You must be open to new approaches to your tasks. It is important that you have excellent professional skills in criminal law and treat your clients with respect, regardless of how you may feel. In addition, excellent computer skills are necessary to perform your work well. Keep in touch with other paralegals in your specialty to learn new ways of doing your work."

Jena Parker is also featured in the forthcoming book, Lessons from the Top Paralegal Experts, *by Carole Bruno.*

and the court in which the action is brought must have jurisdiction over the subject matter of the case and over the person brought before the court.

Because criminal law brings the force of the state, with all its resources, to bear against the individual, law enforcement authorities must be sure they abide by the letter of procedural law when arresting and prosecuting a person accused of a crime. If they do not, the defendant may be able to use the prosecution's violations of procedural laws as a defense against criminal liability, depending on the nature of the defendant's right that was violated and the degree of violation.

TYPES OF CRIMES

The number of acts that are defined as criminal is nearly endless. Federal, state, and local laws provide for the classification and punishment of hundreds of thousands of different criminal acts. Traditionally, though, crimes have been grouped into five broad categories, or types: violent crime (crimes against persons), property crime, public order crime, white-collar crime, and organized crime. Cyber crime—which consists of crimes committed in cyberspace with the use of computers—is less a category of crime than a new way to commit crime. We will examine cyber crimes in the next section.

Violent Crime

Crimes against persons, because they cause others to suffer harm or death, are referred to as *violent crimes.* Murder is a violent crime. So is sexual assault, or rape. Assault and battery, which were discussed in Chapter 7 in the context of tort law, are also classified as violent crimes. Robbery—defined as the taking of money, personal property, or any other article of value from a person by means of force or fear—is another violent crime. Typically, states have more severe penalties for *aggravated robbery*—robbery with the use of a deadly weapon.

Each of these violent crimes is further classified by degree, depending on the circumstances surrounding the criminal act. These circumstances include the intent of the person committing the crime, whether a weapon was used, and (in cases other than murder) the level of pain and suffering experienced by the victim. For example, at common law, killing another human being could result in one of three different offenses, depending on the defendant's intent: murder (if the killing was intentional), voluntary manslaughter (if intentional but provoked), or involuntary manslaughter (if the killing was unintentional but resulted from criminal negligence or an unlawful act, such as drunk driving).

Most states follow the common law classifications of homicide but add degrees of murder to provide penalties of different severity. For example, deliberate and premeditated killing is usually first degree murder (a *capital offense*—a crime punishable by death). First degree murder may also include killings committed during certain types of felonies, such as arson, burglary, rape, or robbery. When a person is killed during other types of felonies, the charge is likely to be second degree murder, which is typically not punishable by death.

Property Crime

The most common type of criminal activity is property crime—a crime in which the goal of the offender is some form of economic gain or damage to property. Robbery is a form of property crime, as well as a violent crime, because the offender seeks to gain the property of another. Other property crimes are discussed next.

▌robbery
The taking of money, personal property, or any other article of value from a person by means of force or fear.

Burglary

As mentioned, most state statutes have modified the common law definition of burglary. Today, burglary usually involves breaking and entering onto the property of another with the intent to commit a felony. (Note that a burglary does not necessarily involve theft. The defendant may have intended to commit some other felony and still be guilty of burglary.)

burglary
Breaking and entering onto the property of another with the intent to commit a felony.

Larceny

Any person who wrongfully or fraudulently takes and carries away another person's personal property is guilty of larceny. In other words, larceny is "stealing." To be guilty of larceny, the person must have intended to deprive the owner permanently of the property. Larceny does not involve force or fear (as in robbery) or breaking into a building (as in burglary). Picking pockets is larceny. Taking company products and supplies home for personal use, if one is not authorized to do so, is also larceny. In addition, many states have expanded the definition of larceny to encompass thefts of services, such as computer programs, computer time, and utilities. Although the common law distinguished between grand larceny (a felony) and petit larceny (a misdemeanor) depending on the value of the property taken, many states have abolished this distinction.

larceny
The wrongful or fraudulent taking and carrying away of another person's personal property with the intent to deprive the person permanently of the property.

Obtaining Goods by False Pretenses

It is a criminal act to obtain goods by means of false pretenses—for example, buying groceries with a check, knowing that one has insufficient funds to cover it. Statutes dealing with such illegal activities vary widely from state to state.

Receiving Stolen Goods

It is a crime to receive stolen goods. The recipient of such goods need not know the true identity of the owner or the thief. All that is necessary is that the recipient knew or *should have known* that the goods were stolen (which implies the intent to deprive the owner of those goods). In other words, if someone sells you a new digital camera for ten dollars from the back of a truck full of new digital cameras, you may be guilty of receiving stolen property.

Arson

The willful and malicious burning of a building (and, in some states, personal property) owned by another is the crime of arson. At common law, arson traditionally applied only to burning down another person's house. Today, arson statutes have been extended to cover the destruction of any building, regardless of ownership, by fire or explosion. Every state also has a special statute that covers a person's burning a building for the purpose of collecting insurance.

arson
The willful and malicious burning of a building (and, in some states, personal property) owned by another; arson statutes have been extended to cover the destruction of any building, regardless of ownership, by fire or explosion.

Forgery

The fraudulent making or altering of any writing in a way that changes the legal rights and liabilities of another is forgery. If, without authorization, Tyler signs Ben's name to the back of a check made out to Ben, Tyler is committing forgery. Forgery also includes changing trademarks, falsifying public records, counterfeiting, and altering a legal document.

forgery
The fraudulent making or altering of any writing in a way that changes the legal rights and liabilities of another.

Public Order Crime

Historically, societies have always outlawed activities considered to be contrary to public values and morals. Today, the most common public order crimes include public drunkenness, prostitution, gambling, and illegal drug use. These crimes are sometimes referred to as victimless crimes because they potentially could harm only the offender. From a broader perspective, however, they are deemed detrimental to society as a whole because they are thought to create an environment that gives rise to property and violent crimes.

White-Collar Crime

white-collar crime
A crime that typically occurs only in a business context; popularly used to refer to an illegal act or series of acts committed by an individual or business entity using nonviolent means.

Crimes that typically occur only in the business context are commonly referred to as white-collar crimes. Although there is no official definition of white-collar crime, the term is popularly used to mean an illegal act or series of acts committed by an individual or business entity using some nonviolent means. Usually, this kind of crime is committed in the course of a legitimate occupation. Corporate crimes fall into this category.

Embezzlement

embezzlement
The fraudulent appropriation of the property or money of another by a person entrusted with that property or money.

When a person entrusted with another person's property or funds fraudulently appropriates it, embezzlement occurs. Typically, embezzlement involves an employee who steals funds. Banks face this problem, and so do a number of businesses in which corporate officers or accountants "jimmy" the books to cover up the fraudulent conversion of funds for their own benefit. Embezzlement is not larceny, because the wrongdoer does not physically take the property from the possession of another, and it is not robbery, because force or fear is not used.

Mail and Wire Fraud

One of the most potent weapons against white-collar criminals is the Mail Fraud Act of 1990.[5] Under this act, it is a federal crime (mail fraud) to use the mails to defraud the public. Illegal use of the mails must involve (1) mailing or causing someone else to mail something written, printed, or photocopied for the purpose of executing a scheme to defraud and (2) a contemplated or an organized scheme to defraud by false pretenses. If, for example, Johnson advertises by mail the sale of a cure for cancer that he knows to be fraudulent because it has no medical validity, he can be prosecuted for fraudulent use of the mails.

Federal law also makes it a crime (called *wire fraud*) to use the telephone to defraud. In addition, under the same statute, it is a crime to use virtually any means of public communication, such as radio or television, to defraud. Violators may be fined up to $1,000, imprisoned for up to five years, or both. If the violation affects a financial institution, the violator may be fined up to $1 million, imprisoned for up to thirty years, or both.

Bribery

Basically, three types of bribery are considered crimes: bribery of public officials, commercial bribery, and bribery of foreign officials. The attempt to influence a public official to act in a way that serves a private interest is a crime. As an element of this crime, intent must be present and proved. The bribe can be anything the recipient considers to be valuable. Realize that *the crime of bribery occurs when the bribe is offered.* It does not matter whether the bribe is accepted. *Accepting a bribe* is a separate crime.

Typically, people make commercial bribes to obtain information, cover up an inferior product, or secure new business. For example, a person in one business may offer an employee in a competing business some type of payoff in exchange for trade secrets or pricing schedules. So-called *kickbacks,* or payoffs for special favors or services, are a form of commercial bribery in some situations. Bribing foreign officials to obtain favorable business contracts is also a crime.

Bankruptcy Fraud

Today, federal bankruptcy law allows individuals and businesses to be relieved of oppressive debt through bankruptcy proceedings, as explained in Chapter 12. Numerous white-collar crimes may be committed during the many phases of a bankruptcy proceeding. A creditor, for example, may file a false claim against the debtor, which is a crime. Also, a debtor may fraudulently transfer assets to favored parties before or after the petition for bankruptcy is filed. For example, a company-owned automobile may be "sold" at a bargain price to a trusted friend or relative. It is also a crime for the debtor to fraudulently conceal property during bankruptcy, such as by hiding gold coins.

The Theft of Trade Secrets

As discussed in Chapter 8, trade secrets constitute a form of intellectual property that for many businesses can be extremely valuable. The Economic Espionage Act of 1996[6] made the theft of trade secrets a federal crime. The act also made it a federal crime to buy or possess trade secrets of another person, knowing that the trade secrets were stolen or otherwise acquired without the owner's authorization.

Violations of the act can result in steep penalties. An individual who violates the act can be imprisoned for up to ten years and fined up to $500,000. If a corporation or other organization violates the act, it can be fined up to $5 million. Additionally, the law provides that any property acquired as a result of the violation and any property used in the commission of the violation are subject to criminal *forfeiture*—meaning that the government can take the property. A theft of trade secrets conducted via the Internet, for example, could result in the forfeiture of every computer, printer, or other device used to commit or facilitate the violation.

Insider Trading

An individual who obtains "inside information" about the plans of a publicly listed corporation can often make stock-trading profits by using the information to guide decisions relating to the purchase or sale of corporate securities. **Insider trading** is a violation of securities law that subjects the violator to criminal penalties. One who possesses inside information and who has a duty not to disclose it to outsiders may not profit from the purchase or sale of securities based on that information until the information is available to the public.

Organized Crime

As mentioned, white-collar crime takes place within the confines of the legitimate business world. *Organized crime,* in contrast, operates *illegitimately* by, among other things, providing illegal goods and services. For organized crime, the traditional preferred markets are gambling, prostitution, illegal narcotics, pornography, and loan sharking (lending funds at higher-than-legal interest rates), along with more recent ventures into counterfeiting and credit-card scams.

Money Laundering

The profits from illegal activities, particularly illegal drug transactions, amount to billions of dollars a year. Under federal law, banks and other financial institutions are required to report currency transactions involving more than $10,000. Consequently, those who engage in illegal activities face difficulties in depositing their cash profits from illegal transactions.

As an alternative to simply storing cash from illegal transactions in a safe-deposit box, wrongdoers and racketeers have invented ways to launder "dirty" money to make it "clean." This **money laundering** is done through legitimate businesses. For example, suppose that

insider trading
Trading in the stock of a publicly listed corporation based on inside information about the corporation that is not available to the public. One who possesses inside information and has a duty not to disclose it to outsiders may not profit from the purchase or sale of securities based on that information until the information is available to the public.

money laundering
Falsely reporting income that has been obtained through criminal activity, such as illegal drug transactions, as income obtained through a legitimate business enterprise to make the "dirty" money "clean."

Matt, a successful drug dealer, becomes a partner with a restaurateur. Little by little, the restaurant shows an increasing profit (because Matt is falsely reporting income obtained through drug dealing as the restaurant's income). As a partner in the restaurant, Matt is able to report the "profit" as legitimate income on which he pays federal and state taxes. He can then spend that income without worrying that his lifestyle may exceed the level possible with his reported income.

The Racketeer Influenced and Corrupt Organizations Act (RICO)

In 1970, in an effort to curb the apparently increasing entry of organized crime into the legitimate business world, Congress passed the Racketeer Influenced and Corrupt Organizations Act (RICO).[7] The act makes it a federal crime to (1) use income obtained from racketeering activity to purchase any interest in an enterprise, (2) acquire or maintain an interest in an enterprise through racketeering activity, (3) conduct or participate in the affairs of an enterprise through racketeering activity, or (4) conspire to do any of the preceding activities. Today, RICO is used more often to attack white-collar crime than organized crime.

Racketeering activity is not a new type of crime created by RICO; rather, RICO incorporates by reference twenty-six separate types of federal crimes and nine types of state felonies[8] and declares that if a person commits *two* of these offenses, he or she is guilty of "racketeering activity." Any individual found guilty of a violation is subject to a fine of up to $25,000 per violation, imprisonment for up to twenty years, or both. Additionally, the statute provides that those who violate RICO may be required to forfeit any assets, in the form of property or cash, that were acquired as a result of the illegal activity or that were "involved in" or an "instrumentality of" the activity.

CYBER CRIMES

Today, many crimes are committed with computers and occur in cyberspace. These crimes fall under the broad label of **cyber crime**. As we mentioned earlier, most cyber crimes are not "new" crimes. Rather, they are existing crimes in which the Internet is the instrument of wrongdoing. The challenge for law enforcement is to apply traditional laws—which were designed to protect persons from physical harm or to safeguard their physical property—to crimes committed in cyberspace. Here, we look at several types of cyber crimes against persons and property.

cyber crime
A crime that occurs online, in the virtual community of the Internet, as opposed to the physical world.

Cyber Theft

In cyberspace, thieves are not subject to the physical limitations of the "real" world. A thief with dial-in access can steal data stored in a networked computer from anywhere on the globe. Only the speed of the connection and the thief's computer equipment limit the quantity of data that can be stolen.

Financial Crimes

Computer networks provide opportunities for employees to commit crimes that can involve serious economic losses. For example, employees of a company's accounting department can transfer funds among accounts with little effort and often with less risk than would be involved in paper transactions. Generally, the dependence of businesses on computer operations has left many companies vulnerable to sabotage, fraud, embezzlement, and the theft of proprietary data, such as trade secrets or other intellectual property (discussed in Chapter 8).

On the Web

The Bureau of Justice Statistics of the U.S. Department of Justice offers an impressive collection of statistics on crime, including cyber crime, at the following Web site: **http://www.ojp.usdoj.gov/bjs**.

Identity Theft

A form of cyber theft that has become particularly troublesome in recent years is identity theft. Identity theft occurs when the wrongdoer steals a form of identification—such as a name, date of birth, or Social Security number—and uses the information to access the victim's financial resources. This crime existed to a certain extent before the widespread use of the Internet. Thieves would "steal" calling-card numbers by watching people using public telephones, or they would rifle through garbage to find bank account or credit-card numbers. The Internet, however, has turned identity theft into perhaps the fastest-growing financial crime in the United States. The Internet provides those who steal information offline with an easy medium for using items such as stolen credit-card numbers and e-mail addresses while protected by anonymity. An estimated 700,000 Americans are victims of identity theft each year.

Cyberstalking

Most states have laws against stalking. These laws make it a crime to harass or follow a person while making a "credible threat" that puts that person in reasonable fear for his or her safety or the safety of his or her immediate family. Traditionally, these laws required a physical act (following the victim). Cyberstalkers are stalkers who commit their crimes in cyberspace—usually finding their victims through Internet chat rooms, newsgroups, bulletin boards, or e-mail. To close this "loophole" in existing stalking laws, more than three-fourths of the states now have laws specifically designed to combat cyberstalking and other forms of online harassment.

Note that cyberstalking can be even more threatening than physical stalking in some respects. While it takes a great deal of effort to stalk physically, it is relatively easy to harass a victim with electronic messages. Furthermore, the possibility of personal confrontation may discourage a stalker from actually following a victim. This disincentive is removed in cyberspace. Finally, there is always the possibility that a cyberstalker will eventually pose a physical threat to her or his target.

Hacking

Persons who use one computer to break into another are sometimes referred to as hackers. Hackers who break into computers without authorization often commit cyber theft. Sometimes, however, the principal aim of hackers is to cause random data errors on others' password-protected computers or to make telephone calls through an organization's computerized telephone switchboard.

It is difficult to know how frequently hackers succeed in breaking into databases across the United States. The Federal Bureau of Investigation estimates that only 25 percent of all corporations that suffer such security breaches report the incident to a law enforcement agency. For one thing, corporations do not want it to become publicly known that the security of their data has been breached. For another, admitting to a breach would be admitting to a certain degree of incompetence, which could damage their reputations.

Prosecuting Cyber Crimes

The Internet has raised new issues in the investigation of crimes and the prosecution of offenders. As discussed in Chapter 6, the issue of jurisdiction presents difficulties in cyberspace. Identifying the wrongdoers can also be difficult. Cyber criminals do not leave physical traces, such as fingerprints or DNA samples, as evidence of their crimes. Even electronic "footprints" can be hard to find and follow. For example, e-mail can be sent through a remailer, an online service that guarantees that a message cannot be traced to its source.

identity theft
The theft of a form of identification, such as a name, date of birth, or Social Security number, which is then used to access the victim's financial resources.

On the Web

For information on identity theft and actions taken by the Federal Trade Commission to curb this form of crime, go to **http://www.consumer. gov/idtheft/id_federal.htm**.

cyberstalker
A person who commits the crime of stalking in cyberspace. The cyberstalker usually finds the victim through Internet chat rooms, newsgroups, bulletin boards, or e-mail and proceeds to harass that person or put the person in reasonable fear for his or her safety or the safety of his or her immediate family.

hacker
A person who uses one computer to break into another.

For these reasons, laws written to protect physical property are difficult to apply in cyberspace. Nonetheless, governments at both the state and federal levels have taken significant steps toward controlling cyber crime, both by applying existing criminal statutes and by enacting new laws that specifically address wrongs committed in cyberspace.

The Computer Fraud and Abuse Act

Perhaps the most significant federal statute specifically addressing cyber crime is the Counterfeit Access Device and Computer Fraud and Abuse Act of 1984. This act, as amended,[9] provides, among other things, that a person who accesses or attempts to access a computer online, without authority, to obtain classified, restricted, or protected data is subject to criminal prosecution. Such data could include financial and credit records, medical records, legal files, military and national security files, and other confidential information in government or private computers. The crime has two elements: accessing a computer without authority and taking the data. This theft is a felony if it is committed for a commercial purpose or for private financial gain or if the value of the stolen data (or computer time) exceeds $5,000. Penalties include fines and imprisonment for up to twenty years. A victim of computer theft can also bring a civil suit against the violator to obtain damages, an injunction, and other relief.

Other Federal Statutes

The federal wire fraud statute, the Economic Espionage Act of 1996, and RICO, all of which were discussed earlier, extend to crimes committed in cyberspace as well. Two other federal statutes that may apply are the Electronic Fund Transfer Act of 1978, which makes unauthorized access to an electronic fund transfer system a crime, and the Anticounterfeiting Consumer Protection Act of 1996, which increased penalties for stealing copyrighted or trademarked property.

CONSTITUTIONAL SAFEGUARDS

From the very moment a crime is reported until the trial concludes, law enforcement officers and prosecutors must be careful to abide by the specific criminal procedures that have been established to protect an accused person's constitutional rights. Before allowing a case to go to trial, the prosecutor and paralegals assigned to the case review all pretrial events very closely to make sure that all requirements have been properly observed. Defense attorneys and their legal assistants also investigate and review closely the actions of arresting and investigating police officers in an attempt to obtain grounds for a dismissal of the charges against their clients.

The U.S. Constitution provides specific procedural safeguards to protect persons accused of crimes against the potentially arbitrary or unjust use of government power. These safeguards are stated in the first ten amendments to the Constitution, which constitute the Bill of Rights. As you will see in the following pages, criminal procedure is rooted in the constitutional rights and protections spelled out in the Fourth, Fifth, Sixth, and Eighth Amendments. These rights and protections are summarized below. The full text of the U.S. Constitution, including the Bill of Rights, is presented in Appendix J.

1. The Fourth Amendment prohibits unreasonable searches and seizures and requires a showing of probable cause (which will be discussed shortly) before a search or an arrest warrant may be issued.

2. The Fifth Amendment requires that no one shall be deprived of "life, liberty, or property without due process of law." **Due process of law** means that the govern-

On the Web

The American Civil Liberties Union (ACLU) has long acted as a guardian of Americans' civil liberties. You can learn about some of the constitutional questions raised by various criminal laws and procedures by going to the ACLU's Web site at **http://www. aclu.org**.

due process of law
Fair, reasonable, and standard procedures that must be used by the government in any legal action against a citizen. The Fifth Amendment to the U.S. Constitution prohibits the deprivation of "life, liberty, or property without due process of law."

ment must follow a set of reasonable, fair, and standard procedures (that is, criminal procedural law) in any action against a citizen.

3. The Fifth Amendment prohibits **double jeopardy** (trying someone twice for the same criminal offense).

4. The Fifth Amendment guarantees that no person shall be "compelled in any criminal case to be a witness against himself." This is known as the privilege against compulsory **self-incrimination**.

5. The Sixth Amendment guarantees a speedy and public trial, a trial by jury, the right to confront witnesses, and the right to a lawyer at various stages in some proceedings.

6. The Eighth Amendment prohibits excessive bail and fines and cruel and unusual punishment.

The Exclusionary Rule

Under what is known as the **exclusionary rule**, all evidence obtained in violation of the constitutional rights spelled out in the Fourth, Fifth, and Sixth Amendments normally must be excluded from the trial, along with all evidence derived from the illegally obtained evidence. Evidence derived from illegally obtained evidence is known as the "fruit of the poisonous tree." For example, if during an illegal search drugs are obtained, the search is "the poisonous tree," and the drugs are the "fruit," which normally will be excluded from evidence if the case is brought to trial.

The purpose of the exclusionary rule is to deter police from conducting warrantless searches and from engaging in other misconduct. The rule is sometimes criticized because it can lead to injustice. Many a defendant has "gotten off on a technicality" because law enforcement personnel failed to observe procedural requirements. Even though a defendant may be obviously guilty, if the evidence of that guilt was obtained improperly (without a valid search warrant, for example), it normally cannot be used against the defendant in court.

The *Miranda* Rule

In *Miranda v. Arizona*,[10] a case decided in 1966, the United States Supreme Court established the rule that individuals who are arrested must be informed of certain constitutional rights, including their Fifth Amendment right to remain silent and their Sixth Amendment right to counsel. These rights, which have come to be called the *Miranda* **rights**, are listed in Exhibit 16.3. If the arresting officers fail to inform a criminal suspect

double jeopardy
To place at risk (jeopardize) a person's life or liberty twice. The Fifth Amendment to the Constitution prohibits a second prosecution for the same criminal offense in all but a few circumstances.

self-incrimination
The act of giving testimony that implicates oneself in criminal wrongdoing. The Fifth Amendment to the Constitution states that no person "shall be compelled in any criminal case to be a witness against himself."

exclusionary rule
In criminal procedure, a rule under which any evidence obtained in violation of the accused's constitutional rights, as well as any evidence derived from illegally obtained evidence, will not be admissible in court.

Miranda rights
Certain constitutional rights of accused persons taken into custody by law enforcement officials, such as the right to remain silent and the right to counsel, as established by the United States Supreme Court's decision in *Miranda v. Arizona*.

EXHIBIT 16.3
The *Miranda* Rights

On taking a criminal suspect into custody and before any interrogation takes place, law enforcement officers are required to communicate the following rights and facts to the suspect:

1. **The right to remain silent.**
2. **That any statements made may be used against the person in a court of law.**
3. **The right to talk to a lawyer and have a lawyer present while being questioned.**
4. **If the person cannot afford to hire a lawyer, the right to have a lawyer provided at no cost.**

In addition to being advised of these rights, the suspect must be asked if he or she understands the rights and whether he or she wishes to exercise the rights or waive (not exercise) the rights.

If you are interested in reading the Supreme Court's opinion in *Miranda v. Arizona*, go to **http://www.law. cornell.edu/supct/cases/name.htm**. Select "M" from the menu at the top of the page, scroll down to find the case name, and click on it.

of these constitutional rights, any statements the suspect makes normally will not be admissible in court. It is important to note that the police are not required to give *Miranda* warnings until the individual is placed in custody. Thus, if a person who is not in custody makes voluntary admissions to an officer, these statements are admissible.

Challenges to the Miranda Rule

The Supreme Court's *Miranda* decision was controversial, and in 1968 Congress attempted to overrule the decision when it enacted Section 3501 of the Omnibus Crime Control Act. Essentially, this act reinstated the rule that had been in effect for 180 years before *Miranda*—namely, that statements by defendants can be used against them as long as the statements are made voluntarily. The U.S. Justice Department immediately disavowed the act as unconstitutional, however, and the section has never been enforced. Although the U.S. Court of Appeals for the Fourth Circuit attempted to enforce the provision in 1999, the court's decision was reversed by the United States Supreme Court in 2000. The Supreme Court held that the *Miranda* rights enunciated by the Court in the 1966 case were constitutionally based and thus could not be overruled by a legislative act.[11] Today, both on television and in the real world, police officers routinely advise suspects of their "*Miranda* rights" on arrest.

Exceptions to the Miranda Rule

Over time, as part of a continuing attempt to balance the rights of accused persons against the rights of society, the United States Supreme Court has carved out numerous exceptions to the *Miranda* rule. In 1984, for example, the Court recognized a "public safety" exception. The need to protect the public warranted the admissibility of statements made by the defendant (in this case, indicating where he placed a gun) as evidence at trial, even though the defendant had not been informed of his *Miranda* rights.[12]

In 1985, the Supreme Court further held that a confession need not be excluded even though the police failed to inform a suspect in custody that his attorney had tried to reach him by telephone.[13] In an important 1991 decision, the Court stated that a suspect's conviction will not be overturned solely on the ground that the suspect was coerced into making a confession by law enforcement personnel. If other, legally obtained evidence admitted at trial is strong enough to justify the conviction without the confession, then the fact that the confession was obtained illegally can, in effect, be ignored.[14]

In yet another case, in 1994, the Supreme Court ruled that a suspect must unequivocally and assertively request to exercise his or her right to counsel in order to stop police questioning. Saying, "Maybe I should talk to a lawyer" during an interrogation after being taken into custody is not enough. The Court held that police officers are not required to decipher the suspect's intentions in such situations.[15]

CRIMINAL PROCEDURES PRIOR TO PROSECUTION

Although the Constitution guarantees due process of law to individuals accused of committing crimes, the actual steps involved in bringing a criminal action vary significantly depending on the jurisdiction and type of crime. In this section, we provide an overview of the basic procedures that take place before an individual is prosecuted for a crime. Exhibit 16.4 illustrates a general outline of criminal procedure in both federal and state cases. Because of the many procedural variations, however, a paralegal involved in a criminal case will need to research the specific procedural requirements that apply to the case. (The many roles paralegals can play in criminal cases are described in this chapter's *Featured Guest* article on pages 598 and 599.)

EXHIBIT 16.4

**Major Procedural
Steps in a Criminal Case**

ARREST

Police officer takes suspect into custody. Most arrests are made without a warrant. After the arrest, the officer searches the suspect, who is then taken to the police station.

BOOKING

At the police station, the suspect is searched again, photographed, fingerprinted, and allowed at least one telephone call. After the booking, charges are reviewed, and if they are not dropped, a complaint is filed and a magistrate reviews the case for probable cause.

INITIAL APPEARANCE

The suspect appears before the magistrate, who informs the suspect of the charges and of his or her rights. If the suspect requires a lawyer, one is appointed. The magistrate sets bail (conditions under which a suspect can obtain release pending disposition of the case).

GRAND JURY

A grand jury determines if there is probable cause to believe that the defendant committed the crime. The federal government and about half of the states require grand jury indictments for at least some felonies.

PRELIMINARY HEARING

In a court proceeding, a prosecutor presents evidence, and the judge determines if there is probable cause to hold the defendant over for trial.

INDICTMENT

The grand jury formally charges a criminal suspect by issuing an indictment.

INFORMATION

The prosecutor formally charges a criminal suspect by filing an information, or criminal complaint.

ARRAIGNMENT

The suspect is brought before the trial court, informed of the charges, and asked to enter a plea.

PLEA BARGAIN

The prosecutor may offer a plea bargain. A plea bargain is a prosecutor's promise to make concessions (or promise to seek concessions) in return for a suspect's guilty plea. Concessions may include a reduced charge or a lesser sentence.

GUILTY PLEA

In most jurisdictions, most cases that reach the arraignment stage do not go to trial but are resolved by a guilty plea, often as a result of a plea bargain. The judge sets the case for sentencing.

TRIAL

Generally, most felony trials are jury trials, and most misdemeanor trials are bench trials (trials before judges). If the verdict is "guilty," the judge sets the case for sentencing. Everyone convicted of a crime has the right to an appeal.

Pamela Poole Weber

FEATURED **Guest**

PARALEGALS AND CRIMINAL LITIGATION

BIOGRAPHICAL NOTE

Pamela Poole Weber graduated from Stetson University College of Law and is licensed to practice law in Florida. In 1989, after working in both the corporate and public sectors as a litigator, she joined Seminole Community College in Central Florida. There, she developed and was the director of a two-year legal assistant program as well as serving as the executive director of the Seminole Community College Foundation. Weber has been active in various legal areas, including teaching police recruits in the area of juvenile law and lecturing to seniors on issues relating to the rights of elderly persons.

The gavel strikes, the trial is over, and the jury is escorted to the jury room to deliberate. Your pulse begins to pound, and the gravity of the situation overwhelms you. This is the first time that you, as a paralegal, have assisted your supervising attorney in a criminal case. Now comes the most difficult time—waiting for the decision. But you take satisfaction in knowing that you have done the best job you can.

* * * *

Criminal litigation is a very fast-paced area of law that is continually changing. Many people do not understand what is involved in defending or prosecuting someone accused of a crime. First and foremost, both sides must be familiar with current laws and especially with changes or new interpretations of those laws. Attorneys do not always have the time required to keep up with these changes. A paralegal can be a valuable asset to a law office by keeping informed on current developments—by reading current court decisions, by reviewing summaries of new laws or modifications to existing laws, by being alert for emerging trends reported in the media, and by generally keeping eyes and ears open. This behind-the-scenes work is in many ways just as interesting as the spectacular trial scenes on television, and a paralegal's input with respect to current law may well determine the outcome of a case.

Both the defense and the prosecution must review every aspect of the case. This requires combining legal research with critical analysis. Attorneys and paralegals work together in planning a course of action for each case, regardless of whether the case is simple or highly complex. This team approach is becoming more widely accepted because of the results it generates. As the old saying goes, "Two heads are better than one."

OPPORTUNITIES FOR PARALEGALS

Criminal litigation may present paralegals with a variety of opportunities, although paralegals are not utilized as extensively in criminal litigation as they are in civil litigation. Some attorneys do not use paralegals to their fullest capabilities because they do not know how to maximize paralegal services. Often, paralegals must suggest tasks that they can perform or, if appropriate, must simply go ahead and perform the tasks on their own. Remember, though, that paralegals cannot engage in any actions that only attorneys are licensed to perform.

What are some of the services that paralegals can provide? Obviously, legal research is critical to successful criminal litigation, and paralegals can perform this research for attorneys. Such research may involve a review and analysis of the law or laws that allegedly have been violated by the defendant, various defense strategies, procedural problems, and evidentiary problems—just to name a few. Sometimes, research is very detailed, requiring days and even weeks to complete. At other times, research may have to be done at the last minute.

Paralegals who want more contact with people can involve themselves in the evidentiary side of the case. Both the defense attorney and the prosecuting attorney in a criminal case have some sort of evidence—physical evidence, witnesses' testimony, or confessions, for example—with which to work. The paralegal may interview witnesses, prepare deposition questions, review police and laboratory reports, or identify photographs that may be useful at trial.

Many paralegals enjoy the challenge of critical analysis and strategic thinking. The criminal litigation paralegal is continually provided with challenges in this respect. In this area, the paralegal can assist in actually preparing the case for trial. The paralegal may be asked to draft pretrial motions, review the available research and documents, draft responses to the opposing side's motions, prepare questions for jury selection, and prepare jury instructions for the conclusion of the case.

HOW CAN I ASSIST IN THE DEFENSE OF A CRIMINAL?

This question, long asked by attorneys, is now being asked by paralegals. Many people look at this area of law and say that they could never represent such defendants as Ted Bundy and Jeffrey Dahmer (convicted serial killers). Perhaps these people believe that by representing such defendants, the attorneys are somehow condoning their criminal actions. Or perhaps they detest those defendants so much that they want them convicted and punished without the benefit of due process. But attorneys and their legal assistants must remind themselves that until the verdict is in, the defendants are only *accused* of committing the criminal acts. They are guilty of no crime until the jury decides they are guilty *beyond a reasonable doubt.* Our country's criminal justice system is founded on the principle that a person is "innocent until proven guilty." The paralegal must remember that his or her job is not to decide the guilt or innocence of an accused person. Rather, it is to ensure that *justice* is being served.

A paralegal working for the prosecutor will strive to ensure that the people of a particular city, county, or state, or even the United States, are having their interests protected. The prosecution does not represent the victim of a criminal act but rather the citizens of a community.

The defense paralegal will work to ensure the protection of the rights of the accused. The U.S. Constitution guarantees that all persons have certain rights, including the right to a trial in which they may confront their accusers and the right to be represented by legal counsel during that trial. These rights apply to everyone—including those who actually commit the crimes with which they are charged. It is up to the defense team to make sure that the defendant has not been deprived of any of his or her constitutional rights.

The defense attorney and his or her legal assistants will examine closely all the circumstances, procedures, and evidence involving the defendant to make sure that the defendant has been allowed to exercise these rights. It may be the task of the paralegal to determine if evidence, including a confession, was properly obtained. If it was not, the paralegal may assist in drafting motions to bring this to the attention of the court. The defense team will also explore various defenses that may be available to the accused.

Paralegals who wish to work in the area of criminal justice must be prepared to be highly objective about criminal proceedings. They must be able to separate their personal and emotional responses to a particular defendant's alleged criminal acts from their professional goal of serving that defendant's best interests by doing all they can to ensure that his or her rights have been observed.

> *"The defense paralegal will work to ensure the protection of the rights of the accused."*

CONCLUSION

Criminal litigation offers numerous opportunities for legal assistants, but it is important to remember that in some cases it may be difficult to achieve the necessary personal and emotional distance from a case to deal with it objectively and professionally.

* * * *

The bailiff returns and announces that the jury has reached a verdict. Your heart leaps into your throat. You take a deep breath and wait. The jury returns a verdict for your side, and you realize that you have just experienced a first victory as a paralegal. After all, you say to yourself, your efforts were crucial to the success of your attorney's case. You know that not all future cases will be "won," but you experience the rewarding feeling of being an integral part of the system seeking justice for all Americans.

arrest
To take into custody a person suspected of criminal activity.

booking
The process of entering a suspect's name, offense, and arrival time into the police log (blotter) following his or her arrest.

probable cause
Reasonable grounds to believe the existence of facts warranting certain actions, such as the search or arrest of a person.

Arrest and Booking

An **arrest** occurs when police officers take a person into custody and charge him or her with a crime. After the arrest, the police typically search the suspect and take the suspect to a *holding facility* (usually at the police station or a jail), where booking occurs. **Booking** refers to the process of entering a suspect's name, the offense for which the suspect is being held, and the time of arrival into the police log (computer). The suspect is then finger-printed and photographed, told the reason for the arrest, and allowed to make a phone call. If the crime is not serious, the officer may then release the suspect on personal recog-nizance—that is, on the suspect's promise to appear before a court at some later date. Otherwise, the suspect may be held in custody pending his or her initial appearance (which generally occurs within a few days).

Obviously, law enforcement personnel are in control of the arrest and booking of sus-pects. Paralegals and attorneys are not usually involved until after an arrest has been made. The defense will, however, look closely to see that the proper procedure was followed in the arrest of the client. An officer can legally arrest a person with or without a warrant, as long as the officer has probable cause to believe that the person committed a crime (discussed shortly). Before an officer questions a suspect who has been arrested, the officer must give the *Miranda* warnings discussed earlier.

Detention Is Not an Arrest

Before we discuss probable cause, it is important to note that an arrest differs from a *stop* or *detention,* such as a traffic stop. Police officers have a right to stop and detain a person if they have a *reasonable suspicion* that the person committed, or is about to commit, a crime. Reasonable suspicion is a much lower standard than probable cause—because stopping a person is much less invasive than arresting the person. That means, for example, that an offi-cer can stop a person who matches the description of an assailant in the neighborhood based on reasonable suspicion. The officer can even "frisk" the person being detained (pat down the person's clothes) to make sure the person is not carrying a weapon. The officer cannot legally arrest any person, however, without probable cause.

Probable Cause

The requirement of **probable cause** is a key factor that is assessed repeatedly throughout the various stages of criminal proceedings. The first stage, arrest, requires probable cause. In the context of arrest, probable cause exists if there is a substantial likelihood that both of the fol-lowing events occurred:

1. A crime was committed.
2. The individual committed the crime.

Note that probable cause involves a *likelihood*—not just a possibility—that the suspect com-mitted the crime. It is not enough that the police officer suspects that the individual has committed a crime. It must be likely. The probable cause requirement stems from the Fourth Amendment, which prohibits unreasonable searches and seizures.

If a police officer observes a crime being committed, the officer can arrest the wrong-doer on the spot without a warrant, because the probable cause requirement is met. If a vic-tim or some other person reports a crime to the police, the police must decide whether there is enough information about the alleged wrongdoer's guilt to establish probable cause to arrest. What is and is not considered probable cause can vary depending on the case law in the particular jurisdiction. Usually, if the suspect is at his or her home at the time of the arrest, the police will need to obtain an arrest warrant (unless the police pursued the suspect to the home or some other emergency circumstance exists).

Developing Paralegal Skills

THE PROSECUTOR'S OFFICE—WARRANT DIVISION

Kathy Perello works as a legal assistant in the warrant division of the county prosecutor's office. Officer Ryan McCarthy is at her door with a burglary report. The police have a suspect they want to arrest. Officer McCarthy presents the paperwork from the prosecutor that authorizes the arrest and requests that Kathy prepare an arrest warrant. Officer McCarthy will then take the warrant to the court, swear to the truth of its contents, and ask the judge to sign the warrant so that he can make the arrest.

CHECKLIST FOR PREPARING A WARRANT

- Obtain written authorization from a prosecutor before initiating the warrant procedure.
- Obtain a copy of the suspect's criminal history.
- Use the above to prepare the warrant.
- Verify that the criminal history matches the suspect.
- Make sure that the crime and the suspect are both specifically described.
- Review the typed warrant to ensure that it includes any other required terms.
- Call the officer to pick up the warrant and take it to a judge for a determination of probable cause.

Warrants

Often, the police try to gather more information to help them determine whether a suspect should be arrested. If, after investigating the matter, the police decide to arrest the suspect, they must obtain an **arrest warrant** from a judge or other public official. To obtain this warrant, the police will have to convince the official, usually through supporting affidavits, that probable cause exists.

Probable cause is also required to obtain a **search warrant**, which authorizes police officers or other criminal investigators to search specifically named persons or property for evidence and to seize the evidence if they find it (see Exhibit 16.5 on the following two pages). Probable cause requires law enforcement officials to have trustworthy evidence that would convince a reasonable person that the proposed search or seizure is more likely justified than not. Furthermore, the Fourth Amendment prohibits general warrants. It requires a particular description of that which is to be searched or seized. Once a warrant is obtained, the search cannot extend beyond what is described in the warrant. General searches through a person's belongings are impermissible.

There are exceptions to the requirement for a search warrant. For example, if an officer is arresting a person (either with an arrest warrant or sufficient probable cause) and sees drug paraphernalia "in plain view," no search warrant is required to seize that evidence. Another exception exists when it is likely that the items sought will be removed or destroyed before a warrant can be obtained.

arrest warrant
A written order, based on probable cause and issued by a judge or public official (magistrate), commanding that the person named on the warrant be arrested by the police.

search warrant
A written order, based on probable cause and issued by a judge or public official (magistrate), commanding that police officers or criminal investigators search a specific person, place, or property to obtain evidence.

EXHIBIT 16.5
A Search Warrant

Ch. 89   **SEARCH AND SEIZURE**   **§ 7942**
Rule 41

§ 7942.   **Search Warrant**

AO 93 (Rev. 5/85)   Search Warrant   ⊕

United States District Court

_____ DISTRICT OF_____

In the Matter of the Search of
(Name, address or brief description of person or property to be searched)

                       SEARCH WARRANT

             CASE NUMBER:

TO: _____ and any Authorized Officer of the United States

Affidavit(s) having been made before me by_____who has reason to
                                      Affiant

believe that ☐ on the person of or ☐ on the **premises known as** (name, description and/or location)

in the _____ District of_____ there is now
concealed a certain person or property, namely (describe the person or property)

I am satisfied that the affidavit(s) and any recorded testimony establish probable cause to believe that the person
or property so described is now concealed on the person or premises above-described and establish grounds for
the issuance of this warrant.

YOU ARE HEREBY COMMANDED to search on or before _____
                                                  Date
(not to exceed 10 days) the person or place named above for the person or property specified, serving this warrant
and making the search (in the daytime—6:00 A.M. to 10:00 P.M.) (at any time in the day or night as I find
reasonable cause has been established) and if the person or property be found there to seize same, leaving a copy
of this warrant and receipt for the person or property taken, and prepare a written inventory of the person or property seized and promptly return this warrant to _____
as required by law.   U.S Judge or Magistrate

_____ at _____
Date and Time Issued   City and State

_____   _____
Name and Title of Judicial Officer   Signature of Judicial Officer   [G13950]

Investigation after the Arrest

As already mentioned, when a suspect is "caught red-handed," the police may arrest the suspect without an arrest warrant and may not have to undertake much of an investigation of
the alleged offense after the arrest. In other cases, however, the police must find and interview witnesses and conduct searches (of the suspect's home or car, for example) to collect
evidence. Witnesses may view the suspect individually in a *lineup,* in which the suspect
appears with a group of several others. In more serious cases, detectives may take charge of
the investigation.

EXHIBIT 16.5
A Search Warrant—Continued

§ 7942
Rule 41

SPECIAL PROCEEDINGS

Ch. 89

AO 93 (Rev. 5/85) Search Warrant

RETURN

DATE WARRANT RECEIVED	DATE AND TIME WARRANT EXECUTED	COPY OF WARRANT AND RECEIPT FOR ITEMS LEFT WITH

INVENTORY MADE IN THE PRESENCE OF

INVENTORY OF PERSON OR PROPERTY TAKEN PURSUANT TO THE WARRANT

CERTIFICATION

    I swear that this inventory is a true and detailed account of the person or property taken by me on the warrant.

_____

Subscribed, sworn to, and returned before me this date.

_____   _____
U.S. Judge or Magistrate   Date

[G13951]

As the police review the evidence at hand, they may conclude there is insufficient evidence to justify recommending the case for prosecution. If so, the suspect is released, and no charges are filed. This does not preclude the police from recommending prosecution later if more evidence is obtained. Alternatively, the police may decide to change the offense with which the suspect is being charged. The police may also decide to release the suspect with a warning or a referral to a social-service agency. Unless the suspect is released, at this point in the criminal process, control over the case moves from the police to the public prosecutor.

On the Web

You can find summaries of famous criminal cases, and sometimes related pleadings and other documents, at the Web site of Court TV. Go to **http://www.courttv.com/trials**.

THE PROSECUTION BEGINS

The prosecution of a criminal case begins when the police inform the public prosecutor of the alleged crime, provide the reports written by the arresting and investigating officers, and turn over evidence relating to the matter. The prosecutor may choose to investigate the case further by personally interviewing the suspect, the arresting and investigating officers, and witnesses, and gathering other evidence. The prosecutor's legal assistants often participate in these tasks. Based on a review of the police file or an investigation, the prosecutor decides whether to take the case to trial or drop the case and allow the suspect to be released. Major reasons for releasing the suspect include insufficient evidence and unreliable witnesses.

The prosecutor has broad discretion. If the prosecutor decides to pursue the case, he or she also decides what charges to file against the defendant. Because prosecutions are expensive and resources are limited, most prosecutors do not go forward with a case unless they think they can prove the case in court. Typically, if the prosecutor decides to file the case, he or she will allege as many criminal offenses as could possibly be proved based on the facts. If the defendant is facing numerous charges, the likelihood is greater that the prosecutor will get a conviction on at least one of them (the chances are also greater that the defendant will plead guilty to one or more of the offenses in exchange for having the others dropped).

If the decision is made to prosecute the case, then the prosecutor must undertake the necessary procedures to formally charge the person before the court. These procedures vary depending on the court and the type of case. Often, misdemeanor charges are handled somewhat differently than felony charges. In some states, prosecutors may file complaints involving misdemeanor charges, but a grand jury indictment (which will be discussed shortly) is required for felony charges. The way a criminal case is initiated is one area of criminal procedure that varies substantially among the states. Keep this in mind as you read the following subsections.

Complaint and Initial Appearance

The criminal litigation process may begin with the filing of a *complaint* (see Exhibit 16.6). The complaint includes a statement of the charges that are being brought against the suspect. The suspect now becomes a criminal defendant. Because the defendant is in the court system, prosecutors must show that they have legal grounds to proceed. They must show probable cause that a crime was committed and that the defendant committed the crime.

In most jurisdictions, defendants are taken before a judge or magistrate (public official) very soon after arrest. During this *initial appearance,* the judge makes sure that the person appearing is the person named in the complaint, informs the defendant of the charge or charges made in the complaint, and advises the defendant of the right to counsel and the right to remain silent. If a defendant cannot afford to hire an attorney, a public defender or member of the private bar may be appointed to represent the defendant at this time (or the defendant may be asked to fill out an application for appointed counsel).

The judge must also make a decision whether to set bail in the case or release the defendant until the next court date. **Bail** is an amount paid by the defendant to the court as insurance that the defendant will show up for future court appearances. If the defendant shows up as promised, the court returns the funds. Courts often use standard bail schedules, which set the bail for specific kinds of cases, and may deny bail for very serious crimes. The Eighth Amendment prohibits "excessive bail," and the defendant has a right to a bail hearing to reduce the amount set by the court. If the court sets bail in an amount that the defendant is unable to pay, the defendant (or his or her attorney or paralegal) can arrange with a *bail bondsperson* to post a bail bond on the defendant's behalf. The bail bondsperson promises to pay the bail amount to the court if the defendant fails to return for further proceedings. In return, the bail bondsperson receives a payment from the defendant, usually 10 percent of the bail amount.

bail

The amount of money or conditions set by the court to assure that an individual accused of a crime will appear for further criminal proceedings. If the accused person provides bail, whether in cash or by means of a bail bond, then the person is released from jail.

EXHIBIT 16.6
A Complaint

United States District Court

DISTRICT OF _____

UNITED STATES OF AMERICA
V.

CRIMINAL COMPLAINT

CASE NUMBER:

(Name and Address of Defendant)

I, the undersigned complainant being duly sworn state the following is true and correct to the best of my

knowledge and belief. On or about _____ in _____ county, in the

_____ District of _____ defendant(s) did, (Track Statutory Language of Offense)

in violation of Title _____ United States Code, Section(s) _____.

I further state that I am a(n) _____ and that this complaint is based on the following
                                        Official Title

facts:

Continued on the attached sheet and made a part hereof: ☐ Yes   ☐ No

_____
Signature of Complainant

Sworn to before me and subscribed in my presence,

_____ at _____
Date   City and State

Preliminary Hearing

The defendant again appears before a magistrate or judge at a **preliminary hearing**. During
this hearing, the magistrate or judge determines whether the evidence presented is sufficient
to establish probable cause to believe the defendant committed the crime with which he or
she is charged. This may be the first adversarial proceeding in which both sides are represented by counsel. Paralegals may become extensively involved in the process at this point by
assisting in preparation for the hearing. The prosecutor may present witnesses, who may be
cross-examined by defense counsel (the defense rarely presents its witnesses prior to trial).
If the defendant intends to plead guilty, he or she usually waives the right to a preliminary

preliminary hearing
An initial hearing in which a judge or
magistrate decides if there is probable
cause to believe that the defendant
committed the crime with which he or
she is charged.

At a preliminary hearing, a judge or a magistrate evaluates the evidence against the defendant. If the evidence is sufficient to establish probable cause (reasonable grounds to believe that the defendant committed the crime with which he or she is charged), the prosecutor issues an *information,* and the defendant is bound over for further proceedings. Paralegals often assist either the defendant or the prosecutor in preparing for preliminary hearings.

(Courtesy of ©Brand X Pictures/Alamy)

hearing to help move things along more quickly. In many jurisdictions, however, the preliminary hearing is required in certain felony cases.

If the magistrate finds the evidence insufficient to establish probable cause, either the charge is reduced to a lesser one or charges are dropped altogether and the defendant is released. If the magistrate believes there is sufficient evidence to establish probable cause, the prosecutor issues an information. The **information** is the formal charge against the defendant and binds over the defendant for further proceedings, which usually means that the defendant is arraigned and the case proceeds to trial.

Grand Jury Review

The federal government and about half of the states require a grand jury, and not the prosecutor, to make the decision as to whether a case should go to trial. In other words, a grand jury's indictment is an alternative to a prosecutor's information to initiate the criminal litigation process.

A **grand jury** is a group of citizens called to decide whether there is probable cause to believe that the defendant committed the crime with which he or she is charged and therefore should go to trial. Even in cases in which grand jury review is not required, the prosecutor may call a grand jury to evaluate the evidence against a suspect, which will indicate to the prosecutor the relative strength or weakness of the case.

The grand jury sits in closed session and hears only evidence presented by the prosecutor—the defendant cannot present evidence at this hearing. Normally, the defendant and his or her attorney are not even allowed to attend grand jury proceedings—although in some cases the defendant may be required to testify. The prosecutor presents to the grand jury whatever evidence the state has against the defendant, including photographs, documents, tangible objects, test results, the testimony of witnesses, and other items. If the grand jury finds that probable cause exists, it issues an **indictment** against the defendant called a *true bill.* Over 97 percent of the cases that prosecutors bring to grand juries result

information
A formal criminal charge made by a prosecutor without a grand jury indictment.

grand jury
A group of citizens called to decide whether probable cause exists to believe that a suspect committed the crime with which he or she has been charged and should stand trial.

indictment
A charge or written accusation, issued by a grand jury, that probable cause exists to believe that a person has committed a crime for which he or she should stand trial.

EXHIBIT 16.7
An Indictment

[Title of Court and Cause]

The Grand Jury charges that:

On or about _____ , 20__, at _____ , _____ , in the _____ District of _____ , _____ having been convicted of knowingly acquiring and possessing food stamp coupons in a manner not authorized by the provisions of Chapter 51, Title 7, United States Code, and the regulations issued pursuant to said chapter, a felony conviction, in the federal district court for the _____ District of _____ , and sentenced on _____ , 20__, did knowingly possess a firearm that had been transported in and affecting commerce, to wit: an OMC Pistol, Back Up 380 Caliber, serial number _____ ; all in violation of Section 1202(a)(1) of Title 18, United States Code, Appendix.

A True Bill

_____,
Foreperson.

_____,
United States Attorney.

in an indictment. The indictment is filed with the trial court and becomes the formal charge against the defendant. An example of an indictment is shown in Exhibit 16.7.

Arraignment

At the **arraignment**, the defendant is informed of the charges against him or her and must respond to the charges by entering a plea. Three possible pleas can be entered: guilty, not guilty, and *nolo contendere,* which is Latin for "I will not contest it" and is often called a no-contest plea. A plea of no contest is neither an admission of guilt nor a denial of guilt—but it operates like a guilty plea in that the defendant is convicted. The primary reason for pleading no contest is so that the plea cannot later be used against the defendant in a civil trial. For example, if a defendant pleads guilty to assault, the admission of guilt can be used to impose civil liability, whereas with a no-contest plea, the plaintiff in the civil suit must prove the defendant's guilt. No-contest pleas are thus useful for the defendant who could be sued in a civil action for damages caused to a person or property.

At the arraignment, the defendant can move to have the charges dismissed, which happens in a fair number of cases for a variety of reasons. The defendant may claim, for example, that the case should be dismissed because the statute of limitations for the crime in question has lapsed. Most frequently, however, the defendant pleads guilty to the charge or to a lesser charge that has been agreed on through **plea bargaining** between the prosecutor and the defendant. If the defendant pleads guilty, no trial is necessary, and the defendant is sentenced based on the plea. If the defendant pleads not guilty, the case is set for trial.

Pretrial Motions

Defense attorneys and their paralegals will search for and be alert to any violation of the defendant's constitutional rights. Many pretrial motions are based on possible violations of the defendant's rights as provided by the Constitution and criminal procedural law. We

arraignment
A court proceeding in which the suspect is formally charged with the criminal offense stated in the indictment. The suspect then enters a plea (guilty, not guilty, or *nolo contendere*) in response.

nolo contendere
Latin for "I will not contest it." A criminal defendant's plea in which he or she chooses not to challenge, or contest, the charges brought by the government. Although the defendant will still be convicted and sentenced, the plea neither admits nor denies guilt.

plea bargaining
The process by which the accused and the prosecutor in a criminal case work out a mutually satisfactory disposition of the case, subject to court approval. Usually, plea bargaining involves the defendant's pleading guilty to a lesser offense in return for a lighter sentence.

Ethics Watch!

THE ETHICS OF PLEA BARGAINING

Paralegals who work on criminal cases may be ethically troubled by plea bargaining. In such situations, it may be helpful to view the issues in the larger context of the American justice system and American society. American courts are overburdened with cases, and it is in the public interest to reduce their caseloads. American jails and prisons are overcrowded, and reducing prison sentences is one way to deal with this issue. In the larger context, then, the ethical issue is whether you believe that it is fair to balance society's interest in obtaining strict justice against society's interest in lowering the social costs (more prisons, more courts, more judges, and so on) of that justice. Also, and more directly to the point, your job as a paralegal is to serve the client's best interests—and it may be in the client's best interests to plea-bargain. In such a situation, you will need to set your personal feelings aside.

discuss here a few of the most common motions filed in a criminal case. Note, however, that the specific requirements for pretrial motions vary depending on the jurisdiction. Not every jurisdiction allows every type of pretrial motion, and the standards used by judges to evaluate such motions may differ as well. Also keep in mind that a motion is generally accompanied by a separate pleading that sets forth the legal argument in support of the motion; this pleading may be called a memorandum of law, a brief, or supporting points and authorities.[16] Affidavits may also be attached.

Motions to Suppress

motion to suppress evidence
A motion requesting that certain evidence be excluded from consideration during the trial.

One of the most common and effective motions made by defense attorneys is the **motion to suppress evidence**. A motion to suppress asserts that the evidence against the defendant was illegally obtained and should be excluded (inadmissible). Typically, this motion is filed when the officer performs a search without probable cause, seizes evidence, and then arrests the defendant based on that evidence. For example, suppose an officer stops the defendant's vehicle because his taillight is out and then proceeds to search through the contents of the defendant's trunk, finding illegal narcotics. The defendant is subsequently charged with possession. A motion to suppress would be appropriate here (and probably successful) because the officer did not have probable cause to search the trunk in carrying out a traffic stop.

The defense attorney normally prepares the motion and submits a memorandum of law (legal argument) with the motion. (Often, these motions are drafted by paralegals.) Exhibit 16.8 on pages 610 and 611 shows a sample memorandum. Often, the attorney will request the court to allow oral argument on the motion, although in some jurisdictions it is automatic. The court will then conduct a hearing on the motion. The attorneys for both sides may call witnesses (police officers and others who were present) to testify, and the judge will make a ruling. If the judge agrees that the evidence should be excluded and grants the motion, the defendant may be able to avoid trial. This is because frequently, without the evidence, the prosecution will not be able to prove its case against the defendant and will thus drop the charges.

Motions to Dismiss

A motion can be filed to dismiss all of the charges or only some of the charges pending against the defendant (if multiple offenses are alleged). There are many grounds for filing a motion to dismiss. Motions to dismiss in criminal cases often assert that the defendant's constitutional rights—or criminal procedures stemming from the Constitution—have been violated. For example, the defense might argue that the prosecution has waited too long to prosecute the case in violation of the defendant's Sixth Amendment right to a speedy and public trial (sometimes called a *speedy trial motion*). The defense will file the motion along with a supporting memorandum, which may argue that the defendant has been prejudiced by the delay, that witnesses are no longer available, and that a fair trial cannot be had. If the judge grants the motion, the case is dismissed.

Because it may eliminate charges against a client without subjecting the client to the risks of a jury trial, the motion to dismiss is one of the most useful motions for the defense to file. A paralegal who becomes skilled at writing persuasive motions to dismiss will thus be a valuable asset to the defense team.

Other Common Motions

Just as in civil cases, attorneys in criminal cases often file motions *in limine* (discussed in Chapter 15) to keep certain evidence out of the trial. For example, a defense attorney whose client has prior criminal convictions may file a motion *in limine* requesting the court to prevent any evidence of these convictions from being offered by the prosecution. The prosecutor may also file such motions to keep possibly prejudicial evidence from being admitted (concerning a victim's reputation, for example).

Sometimes—when there is a good deal of pretrial publicity, for instance—the defense may make a **motion for a change of venue** asking the court to relocate the trial. Other times, the defense may file a **motion to recuse** asking the trial judge to remove himself or herself from the case. Such a motion usually is filed only when the judge has publicly displayed some bias or personally knows the parties or witnesses in the case. If the motion is granted, a different judge will hear the defendant's case. When a case involves more than one defendant, the defense counsel may file a **motion to sever** (separate) the cases for purposes of trial.

Various other motions—including motions to reduce the charges against the defendant, to obtain evidence during discovery, or to extend the trial date—may also be made prior to the trial. As with motions made during the civil litigation process, each motion must be accompanied by supporting affidavits and/or legal memoranda.

motion for a change of venue
A motion requesting that a trial be moved to a different location to ensure a fair and impartial proceeding, for the convenience of the parties, or for some other acceptable reason.

motion to recuse
A motion to remove a particular judge from a case.

motion to sever
A motion to try multiple defendants separately.

Discovery

In preparing for trial, public prosecutors, defense attorneys, and paralegals engage in discovery proceedings (including depositions and interrogatories), interview and subpoena witnesses, prepare exhibits and a trial notebook, examine relevant documents and evidence, and do other tasks necessary to most effectively prosecute or defend the defendant. Although similar to civil litigation in these respects, criminal discovery is generally more limited, and the time constraints relating to discovery are different in criminal cases.

During discovery, defendants are generally entitled to obtain *any* evidence in the possession of the prosecutor relating to the case, including statements previously made by the defendant, objects, documents, and reports of tests and examinations. The prosecutor must hand over evidence that tends to show the defendant's innocence as well as evidence of the defendant's guilt. Defendants are given this right to offset the fact that the prosecution (the state) has more resources at its disposal than the defendant (an individual citizen).

EXHIBIT 16.8
Memorandum in Support of Motion to Suppress

[Attorney for Defendant]

SUPERIOR COURT OF THE STATE OF NITA
FOR THE COUNTY OF NITA

THE PEOPLE OF THE STATE OF NITA,	)	Case No.: C45778
Plaintiff,	)	D.A. No.: A39996
	)	
	)	**MEMORANDUM OF LAW IN SUPPORT**
v.	)	**OF MOTION TO SUPPRESS**
	)	
	)	DATE: 10-27-07
	)	TIME: 1:15
Eduardo Jose Mendez,	)	Estimated Time: 45 min.
Defendant.	)	No. of Witnesses: 1

Defendant, Eduardo Jose Mendez, by and through his attorney the Public Defender of the County of Nita, respectfully submits the following memorandum of law in support of his motion to Suppress.

STATEMENT OF FACTS

On or about September 23, 2007, at approximately 02:15, Officer Ramirez observed Mr. Mendez riding his bicycle in the area of 1300 Elm St. and 500 C St. It was drizzling, and few people walked the streets. Officer Ramirez indicated that the area is known for narcotic activity and that he believed Mr. Mendez had been participating or was about to participate in narcotic activity.

Mr. Mendez was on his bicycle at the corner of Elm and C St. when Officer Ramirez approached him. He indicated that Mr. Mendez appeared to be nervous and was sweating profusely. He asked Mr. Mendez what he was doing, and Mr. Mendez responded that he was waiting for his girlfriend. Officer Ramirez conducted a pat-down search for weapons. He felt several hard objects inside Mr. Mendez's pants pockets and asked Mr. Mendez if he had a knife in his pocket. Mr. Mendez consented to a search of his pockets, and Officer Ramirez found only a wooden pencil.

Without asking for permission, and without notice, Officer Ramirez reached for and grabbed Mr. Mendez's baseball cap. The officer took the cap off of Mr. Mendez's head. He felt the outside of the cap and with his fingers manipulated a small soft lump in Mr. Mendez's cap. He went through the cap and moved the side material of the cap. He found a small plastic package burnt on one end. He opened the package. Officer Ramirez found a small amount of an off-white powder substance inside the package.

ARGUMENT

I. MR. MENDEZ'S FOURTH AMENDMENT RIGHT TO PRIVACY WAS VIOLATED BECAUSE THE OFFICER'S DETENTION OF MR. MENDEZ WAS NOT JUSTIFIED BY REASONABLE SUSPICION

A person has been seized within the meaning of the Fourth Amendment if, in view of all the circumstances surrounding the incident, a reasonable person would have believed that he was not free to leave. *United States v. Mendenhall,* 446 U.S. 544, 554 (1980). Here, Officer Ramirez seized Mr. Mendez when he stopped to question him. Mr. Mendez submitted to Officer Ramirez's show of authority when he responded to the questioning. Mr. Mendez's belief that he was not free to leave is evidenced by his actions during the seizure. He appeared nervous and kept looking around in all directions as if looking for someone to help him. A reasonable person such as Mr. Mendez, in view of all of the circumstances, would have believed and in fact did believe he was not free to leave. Therefore, the officer's initial stop was a seizure.

* * * *

EXHIBIT 16.8
Memorandum in Support of Motion to Suppress—Continued

Officer Ramirez did not have reasonable suspicion to stop Mr. Mendez. He fails to point to specific facts causing him to suspect criminal activity was afoot. Officer Ramirez notes in his police report that he "felt" that defendant "had been participating or was about to participate in narcotic activity." The officer also indicated that he believed the area was known for narcotic activity. However, "Persons may not be subjected to invasions of privacy merely because they are in or are passing through a high-crime area." *McCally-Bey v. Kirner*, 24 F.Supp.3d 389 (N.D. Nita 2002).

These observations taken as a whole and Officer Ramirez's explanation do not rise to the requisite level of reasonable suspicion necessary to invade the privacy of a citizen.

II. OFFICER RAMIREZ'S PAT-DOWN SEARCH EXCEEDED ITS SCOPE WHEN HE SEARCHED THE BASEBALL CAP AND MANIPULATED ITS CONTENTS

Under the *Terry* doctrine, a search is referred to as a "frisk." *Terry v. Ohio*, 392 U.S. 1 (1968). A *frisk* is justified only if the officer reasonably believes that the person is armed and dangerous. A frisk is a pat-down of a person's outer clothing. It is limited in scope to its purpose, which is to search for weapons. Even slightly lingering over a package because it feels like it contains drugs exceeds the scope of the search. *Minnesota v. Dickerson*, 508 U.S. 366 (1993). An officer cannot manipulate a package or a substance that is clearly not a weapon through an individual's clothing during a *Terry* pat-down search.
* * * *

III. OFFICER RAMIREZ DID NOT HAVE PROBABLE CAUSE TO CONDUCT A WARRANTLESS SEARCH OF MR. MENDEZ
* * * *

IV. ALL EVIDENCE OBTAINED AS A RESULT OF AN UNLAWFUL DETENTION MUST BE SUPPRESSED AS TAINTED EVIDENCE; FRUIT OF THE POISONOUS TREE
* * * *
* * * *

As discussed above, the detention of Mr. Mendez did not meet constitutionally established standards of reasonableness. Hence, all evidence obtained as a result of such unlawful detention is inadmissible. In addition, all evidence seized as a result of the arrest that followed from his unlawful detention is inadmissible as fruit of the poisonous tree.
* * * *

For the above-mentioned reasons, all evidence obtained as a result of Mr. Mendez's detention, illegal search, and subsequent arrest in this case must be suppressed.

Dated:

Respectfully submitted,

_____
Attorney for Defendant

Developing Paralegal Skills

DISCOVERY IN THE CRIMINAL CASE

The law firm of McCoy & Warner is defending Taylor Rogers in a case of attempted murder. Rogers allegedly shot a person in a drive-by shooting on the expressway. Lee Soloman, a paralegal, is working on the case. Today, as the result of a discovery motion that his supervising attorney won in court, Lee has received copies of all of the evidence that the prosecuting attorney has in his file. Lee's job is to create the discovery file and then to work with the material in the file to prepare the case.

TIPS FOR CRIMINAL DISCOVERY

- Create a discovery file containing sections for the defendant's statements, witnesses' statements, police reports, tests, and other evidence.
- Review the evidence and prepare a memo summarizing it.
- Review the memo and/or evidence with your supervising attorney.
- If the supervising attorney agrees, contact witnesses and obtain statements.
- Interview the police officers who were involved in the arrest or who were at the crime scene.

Some state statutes allow the prosecutor access to materials that the defense intends to introduce as evidence in the trial. Also, in some jurisdictions, when the defense attorney requests discovery of case materials from the prosecutor, the defense is required to disclose similar materials to the prosecutor in return. In the absence of such statutes, courts have generally refused discovery to the prosecution. This judicial restraint is intended to protect the defendant from self-incrimination, as guaranteed by the Fifth Amendment to the U.S. Constitution (see Appendix J).

THE TRIAL

Only a small fraction of the criminal cases brought by the state actually go to trial. Some defendants are released, or the charges against them are dropped. Most defendants plead guilty to the offense or to a lesser offense prior to trial. Plea bargaining occurs at every stage of criminal proceedings, from the arraignment to the date of trial (even during a trial, defendants can accept a plea bargain). Because a trial is expensive and the outcome uncertain, both sides in criminal cases have an incentive to negotiate a plea and thus avoid the trial—just as both sides in a civil dispute are motivated to reach a settlement.

Although some criminal trials go on for weeks and are highly publicized, most criminal trials last less than one week (often only a few days). The trial itself is conducted in much the same way as a civil trial. The prosecutor and the defense attorney make their opening statements, examine and cross-examine witnesses, and summarize their positions in closing

Ethics Watch!

THE IMPORTANCE OF ACCURACY

In preparing exhibits for trial, especially when creating an exhibit from raw data, it is important that the paralegal ensure that the exhibit is accurate and not misleading. An attorney has a duty not to falsify evidence, and if erroneous evidence is introduced in court and challenged by opposing counsel, your supervising attorney may face serious consequences. By preparing an inaccurate exhibit (for example, by miscalculating a column of figures), the paralegal may jeopardize the attorney's professional reputation by causing the attorney to breach a professional duty.

arguments. The jury is instructed and sent to deliberate. When the jury renders a verdict, the trial comes to an end. There are, however, a few major procedural differences between criminal trials and civil trials, including those discussed below.

The Presumption of Innocence

In criminal trials, the defendant is innocent until proven guilty. The prosecutor bears the burden of proving the defendant is guilty of the offenses with which he or she is charged. The defendant does not have to prove that he or she did not commit the offenses. In fact, the defendant is not required to present any evidence whatsoever to counter the state's accusations (although clearly it might be in the defendant's best interests to put on a defense). Even if a defendant actually committed the crime, he or she will be innocent in the eyes of the law unless the prosecutor can substantiate the charges with sufficient evidence to convince the jury or judge of the defendant's guilt.

Not only does the state bear the burden of proving the defendant guilty, but it also is held to a very high standard of proof. Remember that in criminal cases the prosecution must prove its case *beyond a reasonable doubt*. It is not enough for the jury (or judge) to think that the defendant is probably guilty; the members of the jury must be firmly convinced of the defendant's guilt. The jurors receive instructions such as "If you think there is a real possibility that he [or she] is not guilty, you *must* give him [or her] the benefit of the doubt and find him [or her] not guilty." The presumption of innocence and the high burden of proof are designed to protect the individual from the state.

The Privilege against Self-Incrimination

As already mentioned, the Fifth Amendment to the U.S. Constitution states that no person can be forced to give testimony that might be self-incriminating. Therefore, a defendant does not have to testify at trial. Witnesses may also refuse to testify on this ground. For example, if a witness, while testifying, is asked a question and answering the question would reveal his or her own criminal wrongdoing, the witness may "take the Fifth" and refuse to testify on the ground that the testimony may incriminate him or her.

Developing Paralegal Skills

PREPARING GRAPHIC PRESENTATIONS

Melanie Hofstadter, a paralegal who is about to retire from her job, is training her replacement. Melanie has worked for Johnson & Bott, a criminal law practice, for nearly twenty years and has assisted the attorneys countless times with trial preparations. Today, she is instructing the new paralegal, Kyra Mason, on how to prepare graphic presentations for the attorneys to use in the courtroom.

Melanie first explains to Kyra that trial graphics are classified into three main types: fact graphics, concept graphics, and case graphics. Fact graphics show only the facts on which both parties agree—for example, a time line indicating the order in which events occurred. Concept graphics are used to educate the judge and jury about ideas with which they may not be familiar—such as the general procedures involved in DNA fingerprinting. Case graphics, or analytical graphics, illustrate the basis of the defense or allegation—for example, a flowchart showing how certain facts are related and how they lead to a specific conclusion.

Melanie then gives Kyra a document that Melanie has prepared. The document contains a list of tips and suggestions that Kyra should keep in mind when preparing trial graphics.

TIPS FOR PREPARING A GRAPHIC PRESENTATION

- Remember that less is often more. A good graphic presentation should be simple and straightforward. Trim excess words and punctuation from charts, lists, and diagrams; using incomplete sentences and simple phrases is acceptable in graphic presentations.

- Use boldfaced text and easy-to-read fonts.

- Keep plenty of "white space" in the graphic displays.

- Know what you want the reader to focus on, and eliminate all distractions.

- Remember that it is your job to make it easy for the jury to see, read, and understand your points. Don't overburden the graphic displays with too much information or detail.

- Keep in mind that the main purpose of trial graphics is to focus attention on the points that you want to emphasize or highlight, not to focus attention on the actual presentation or display.

The Right to a Speedy Trial

The Sixth Amendment requires a speedy and public trial for criminal prosecutions but does not specify what is meant by "speedy." Courts interpret whether a defendant's right to a speedy trial has been violated on a case-by-case basis. (Usually, the issue is raised in pretrial motions, as discussed earlier.) Generally, however, criminal cases are brought to trial much more quickly than civil cases. A defendant who remains in custody prior to trial, for example, will often be tried within thirty to forty-five days from the date of arraignment. If the defendant (or the defendant's attorney) needs more time to prepare a defense, the defendant may give up the right to be tried within a certain number of days but will still go to trial within a relatively short period of time (a few months, typically).

As noted in Chapter 5, the Sixth Amendment also guarantees an accused person the right to confront and cross-examine witnesses against him or her. Does a witness's testimony via two-way video teleconferencing satisfy this constitutional mandate? For a discussion of this issue, see the *Technology and Today's Paralegal* feature on pages 616 and 617.

The Requirement for a Unanimous Verdict

Of the criminal cases that go to trial, the majority are tried by a jury. In most jurisdictions, jury verdicts in criminal cases must be *unanimous* for **acquittal** or conviction. In other words, all twelve jurors (or all six jurors, if the state allows six-person juries) must agree that the defendant is either guilty or not guilty. If the jury cannot reach unanimous agreement on whether to acquit or convict the defendant, the result is a **hung jury**. When the jury is hung, the defendant may be tried again (although often the case is not retried). The requirement for unanimity is important because if even one juror is not convinced of the defendant's guilt, the defendant will not be convicted. Thus, the prosecuting attorney must make as strong a case as possible, while the defense attorney can aim at persuading one or more jurors to have doubts.

Sentencing

When a defendant is found guilty by a trial court (or pleads guilty to an offense without a trial), the judge will pronounce a **sentence**, which is the penalty imposed on anyone convicted of a crime. Often, the sentence is pronounced in a separate proceeding at a later date.

Unless the prosecutor is seeking the death penalty, the jury normally is not involved in the sentencing of the defendant. Jurors are dismissed after they return a verdict, and the judge either sentences the defendant on the spot or schedules a future court appearance for sentencing. At the sentencing hearing, the judge usually listens to arguments from both attorneys concerning the factors in "aggravation and mitigation" (which involve why the defendant's punishment should be harsh or lenient).

Most criminal statutes set forth a maximum and minimum penalty that should be imposed for a violation. Thus, judges often have a range of options and a great deal of discretion in sentencing individual defendants. The judge typically sentences the offender to one or more of the following:

- Incarceration in a jail or a prison.
- Probation (formal or informal).
- Fines or other financial penalties.
- Public work service (for less serious offenders).
- Classes (for certain types of offenses, such as domestic violence and alcohol- or drug-related crimes).
- Death (in some states).

Incarceration

Defendants sentenced to incarceration will go to a county jail for less serious offenses (involving sentences of less than one year) or a state prison for serious crimes (involving sentences of more than one year). In some cases, the judge may consider alternatives to jail time. A defendant may be placed on house arrest (and in many jurisdictions wear an electronic device around her or his ankle that will notify the authorities if she or he leaves a designated area). A defendant who has an alcohol or drug problem may sometimes be allowed to satisfy the incarceration portion of a sentence in an inpatient rehabilitation program. In some states, a defendant may be allowed to satisfy short periods of custody time (ten to thirty days) by checking into the jail on weekends only or by participating in a supervised release program, which enables the defendant to stay employed.

Probation

A standard part of almost every sentence (in both felony and misdemeanor cases) is probation. Typically, a person will be sentenced to substantially less than the maximum penalty and placed on probation with certain conditions for at least two or three years (depending

---

acquittal
A certification or declaration following a trial that the individual accused of a crime is innocent, or free from guilt, in the eyes of the law and is thus absolved of the charges.

hung jury
A jury whose members are so irreconcilably divided in their opinions that they cannot reach a verdict. The judge in this situation may order a new trial.

sentence
The punishment, or penalty, ordered by the court to be inflicted on a person convicted of a crime.

On the Web

The U.S. Sentencing Guidelines can be found online at **http://www.ussc.gov**.

Technology and Today's Paralegal

TECHNOLOGY AND THE SIXTH AMENDMENT

As you read in Chapter 6 and in the chapters on civil litigation (Chapters 13 and 15), technology has significantly altered many aspects of litigation and court proceedings. Electronic filing of legal actions, electronic discovery, and high-tech courtrooms are but a few examples of how technological innovations are affecting the way in which cases are litigated. Technology has also affected criminal procedures. For example, in some areas, arraignments of criminal suspects have taken place via video conferencing between the courtroom and the facility in which the suspects are being held.

Suppose, though, that the prosecution in a criminal trial wishes to have witnesses in another country testify against the defendant through two-way video conferencing. How does this use of technology affect a defendant's Sixth Amendment right "to be confronted with the witnesses against him [or her]"? Does this constitutional provision, sometimes called the *confrontation clause,* mean that defendants have the right to a physical, face-to-face confrontation with witnesses who testify against them? Or is a two-way video teleconference sufficient to satisfy the Sixth Amendment's mandate? In an increasingly technological and global environment, how this question is answered can have serious practical implications. Here, we look at a decision on the issue rendered in 2006 by a federal appellate court.

THE *YATES* CASE

The 2006 case, *United States v. Yates,*[a] involved Anton Pusztai and Anita Yates. Pusztai and Yates had been charged in a federal district trial court with mail fraud and other crimes, including prescription-drug–related offenses in connection with their involvement in an Internet pharmacy based in Alabama. Two potential witnesses in the case lived in Australia. One of the witnesses had allegedly processed customers' Internet payments for Pusztai and Yates. The other witness's name had allegedly been used on Internet drug prescriptions.

The government prosecutors considered the testimony of these two witnesses to be crucial to their case. The witnesses, however, were unwilling to travel to the United States for the trial, and they were beyond the reach of the government's subpoena power. Thus, the government urged the court to accept the two witnesses' testimony

a.   438 F.3d 1307 (11th Cir. 2006).

on the maximum allowed by statute). If the person fails to meet the conditions of her or his probation, probation may be revoked, and the person may be sentenced to custody time up to the maximum for the offense.

For example, if convicted of driving while under the influence, a defendant might be sentenced to two days in custody, three years of informal probation, a fine of $3,000, ten days of public work service (picking up roadside trash), and a first-offenders program (meeting twice a week for six to eight weeks and costing several thousand dollars). If the defendant does not do all of the things he or she has been sentenced to do, the court can revoke probation and sentence the person to spend up to a year in jail.

Probation can be either formal or informal. In formal probation, which is typical in felony cases, the defendant is required to meet regularly with a probation officer, who monitors his or her progress. The defendant may be required to submit to drug and alcohol testing, to possess no firearms, and to avoid socializing with those who might be engaging in criminal activity, for example. Defendants on informal probation do not have a probation officer, but they may be required to comply with certain conditions, such as paying a fine, performing public work service, participating in specified programs (such as attending Alcoholics Anonymous meetings or anger management classes), and not violating the law.

by means of a live, two-way video teleconference. Although Yates argued that allowing the two witnesses to testify in this way would violate her Sixth Amendment right to confront witnesses, the court disagreed. The court allowed the witnesses to testify via video teleconference, and the jury found Pusztai and Yates guilty. Pusztai and Yates appealed the district court's decision to the U.S. Court of Appeals for the Eleventh Circuit.

THE APPELLATE COURT'S CONCLUSION

The federal appellate court held that the admission of the teleconferenced testimony violated the defendants' Sixth Amendment right to confront witnesses. The appellate court emphasized that a defendant has a right to a physical, face-to-face confrontation of witnesses against him or her in a criminal trial. This right can be denied, but only if the denial is necessary to further an important public policy. The trial court had concluded that the video teleconference *did* further an important public policy—the government's stated interest in providing the court with crucial evidence and in resolving the case "expeditiously and justly." The appellate court, however, stated that "the prosecutor's need for the video conference testimony to make a case and to expeditiously resolve it are not the type of public policies that are important enough to outweigh the defendants' right to confront their accusers face to face." According to the appellate court, if it were to approve the introduction of testimony in this manner in this case, "every prosecutor wishing to present testimony from a witness overseas would argue that providing crucial prosecution evidence and resolving the case expeditiously are important public policies that support the admission of testimony by two-way video conference." The appellate court vacated (nullified) the trial court's decision and sent the case back to the trial court for a new trial.

TECHNOLOGY TIP

Whether other federal jurisdictions will agree with the appellate court in this case remains to be seen. If federal courts come into conflict over the issue, the United States Supreme Court may ultimately have to render a final decision on the matter. In the meantime, paralegals should keep this decision in mind if an opposing party in a criminal case wants to introduce testimony via a two-way video teleconference. Paralegals should also realize the importance of constitutional rights in the area of criminal law. This case serves as a reminder that regardless of how technologically advanced our society becomes, constitutional rights continue to form the backbone of all criminal procedures.

Diversion

In many states, **diversion programs** are available to defendants charged with certain types of offenses specified by statute. Diversion is an alternative to prosecution. Diversion programs vary. Basically, however, these programs suspend criminal prosecution for a certain period of time and require that the defendant complete specified conditions—such as attending special classes and not having contact with the police—during that time. If the person fulfills *all* of the requirements of diversion, the case will be dismissed. If the defendant fails to complete the diversion satisfactorily, the criminal prosecution springs back to life, and the defendant is prosecuted for the crime. The objective is to deter the defendant from further wrongdoing by offering an incentive—namely, a way to avoid any record of conviction. In essence, diversion is similar to a sentencing without a conviction.

A defendant who is charged with a first offense of driving under the influence, for example, may qualify for diversion on the charge (eligibility requirements vary among states). The defendant might be required to (1) attend an eight-month-long course educating him or her on the dangers of drunk driving, (2) pay for that course, (3) pay a certain sum to a victims' restitution fund, and (4) not have any contact with the police for a period of two years. If the defendant complies with all of the conditions, then after two years, the

diversion program
In some jurisdictions, an alternative to prosecution that is offered to certain felony suspects to deter them from future unlawful acts.

Ethics Watch!

THE BENEFITS OF GOOD RECORD KEEPING

One of your jobs as a paralegal is to make sure that witnesses are in court at the proper time. This job relates to the attorney's duty of competence, which, if breached, could expose the attorney to potential liability for malpractice. For all your efforts, however, a key witness fails to appear in court. Your supervising attorney is understandably upset about this and asks you how it could have happened. You show the attorney the memorandum of your interview with the client, in which you noted that the witness was willing to testify; the receipt from the certified letter that you sent to the witness, which contained the subpoena, indicating that the witness had received it; and a telephone memo of a call that you made to the witness a week prior to the trial in which the witness agreed to be in court on the date of the trial. Although your documentation is not a cure for the problem presented by the missing witness, it does provide evidence—should it be necessary—that neither you nor the attorney was negligent.

case will be dismissed. If the person completes only seven of the eight months required by the course, or is charged with another crime six months later, he or she will fail to complete the diversion successfully, and the charges against him or her will be reinstated immediately (or as soon as the court or prosecutor discovers the failure).

Diversion is a good option for the defendant who is guilty of the crime alleged and wants to avoid having a criminal conviction on her or his record. Most of the time, defendants who are eligible for diversion choose that option at the arraignment or soon after and thus do not proceed to trial. On occasion, however, judges may allow a person to divert even after a trial.

Appeal

On the Web

For an example of an appeal petition in an actual criminal case, go to **http://www.courttv.com/trials/woodward/appeal.html**.

Persons convicted of crimes have a right of appeal. (The prosecution may appeal certain types of decisions, but it may not appeal a verdict of not guilty.) Most felony convictions are appealed to an intermediate court of appeal. In some states, however, there is no intermediate court of appeal, so the appeal goes directly to the state's highest appellate court, usually called the supreme court of the state. Most convictions that result in supervised release or fines are not appealed, but a high percentage of the convictions that result in prison sentences are appealed. About 10 to 20 percent of such convictions are reversed on appeal. The most common reason for reversal is that the trial court admitted improper evidence, such as evidence obtained by a search that did not meet constitutional requirements.

If a conviction is overturned on appeal, the defendant may or may not be tried again, depending on the reason for the reversal and on whether the case was reversed with or without prejudice. A decision reversed "with prejudice" means that no further action can be taken on the claim or cause. A decision reversed "without prejudice" may be tried again.

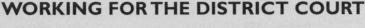

Today's Professional Paralegal

WORKING FOR THE DISTRICT COURT

Amanda Bowin is a legal assistant who is assigned to work for six of the twelve judges who serve on the district court. Today is "criminal call," and she is in the courtroom observing an arraignment. She has in front of her a docket sheet for the defendant. She listens while the judge explains the criminal charges. The defendant pleads not guilty, and the date for the pretrial hearing is set. (If the defendant had pled guilty, then a sentencing date and probation interview would have been scheduled.) Amanda notes the plea and the pretrial hearing date on the docket sheet. She then observes five more arraignments and notes the defendants' pleas on their respective docket sheets.

"SHOW CAUSE" MOTIONS

Several attorneys enter the courtroom. They are present for "show cause" motions. A "show cause" motion is made when a defendant has violated the terms of his or her probation or sentence. The first motion is made by an assistant prosecutor against a defendant who was stopped on the highway for speeding and was found to be carrying a handgun. The judge evaluates the evidence and gives the defendant the option of either pleading guilty to the violation of probation or going to trial on the issue. The defendant chooses to plead guilty and is sentenced by the judge. Amanda notes all of the information on her docket sheet for this case. She listens to the remaining "show cause" motions and makes notes on the pleas and sentences.

SENTENCING HEARINGS

Next, the sentencing hearings begin. Amanda listens and notes the sentences on the relevant docket sheets. The last item up this morning is the sentencing of a woman who has been convicted for criminal neglect—she abandoned her two-year-old child at a gas station. The child has been placed in a foster home. The defense attorney is allowed to call a witness to testify as to the defendant's character and how well she cared for her daughter. This is an attempt to convince the judge to impose the lightest possible sentence allowable for this crime.

The attorney calls a social worker to the stand. The social worker testifies that the defendant-mother had previously had a drug problem for which she had sought treatment. There had been no place for her to go for treatment where she could take her baby, and she had no one with whom she could leave her baby. For those reasons, she had opted for an outpatient program, a less effective form of treatment. She had tried hard to fight her addiction to "crack" cocaine and had been doing well, but sometimes it takes more than one attempt at treatment to succeed. The social worker continues by telling the court that unfortunately, the defendant-mother had strayed from her treatment and was under the influence of cocaine at the time that her friend talked her into abandoning her child.

The mother is very remorseful and regrets her actions. She truly loves her daughter and does not want to lose custody of her permanently. If the judge gives her a long jail sentence, she is afraid that she will ultimately lose custody of her child. After this testimony, the social worker steps down from the stand.

The judge considers the testimony. He knows that if he puts the defendant-mother in jail, she will not receive the treatment that she needs. This will not help either the defendant or her daughter. He sentences her to one year of drug rehabilitation in a live-in facility. This means that her child will remain in foster care for that time. The decision regarding her daughter's custody after that time will be left up to the agency that placed the daughter in the foster home. If the mother's treatment is successful, the agency might consider returning the child to the mother's custody. The defendant is to appear before the court every three months and give a progress report.

CRIMINAL CALL ENDS

Amanda notes this sentence on her docket sheet. She leaves the courtroom now that the criminal call is over. She takes the files containing the docket sheets and her notes for the cases to the Records Department. There the information will be entered into the county's computer system to update the status of these cases.

KEY TERMS AND CONCEPTS

acquittal 615

actus reus 584

arraignment 607

arrest 600

arrest warrant 601

arson 589

bail 604

beyond a reasonable doubt 582

booking 600

burglary 589

crime 582

cyber crime 592

cyberstalker 593

defense of others 586

defense of property 586

diversion program 617

double jeopardy 595

due process of law 594

embezzlement 590

exclusionary rule 595

felony 583

forgery 589

grand jury 606

hacker 593

hung jury 615

identity theft 593

indictment 606

information 606

insider trading 591

larceny 589

mens rea 585

Miranda rights 595

misdemeanor 584

money laundering 591

motion for a change of venue 609

motion to recuse 609

motion to sever 609

motion to suppress evidence 608

nolo contendere 607

petty offense 584

plea bargaining 607

preliminary hearing 605

probable cause 600

public defender 581

public prosecutor 581

responsible corporate officer
doctrine 585

robbery 588

search warrant 601

self-defense 586

self-incrimination 595

sentence 615

white-collar crime 590

chapter summary Criminal Law and Procedures

What Is a Crime?

1. *Key differences between civil and criminal law*—Crimes are distinguished from other types of wrongs, such as torts, in several ways:

   a. Crimes are deemed to be offenses against society as a whole.

   b. Whereas tort (civil) litigation involves lawsuits between private parties, criminal litigation involves the state's prosecution of a wrongdoer.

   c. Crimes are defined as such by state legislatures or the federal government.

   d. The burden of proof in criminal cases is higher than for civil cases. The state must prove the defendant's guilt beyond a reasonable doubt. In civil cases, the plaintiff need only prove his or her case by a preponderance of the evidence.

   e. A criminal act need not involve a victim.

2. *Civil liability for criminal acts*—Those who commit crimes may be subject to both criminal and civil liability, as when a defendant commits an assault.

3. *Classification of crimes*—Crimes fall into two basic classifications: felonies and misdemeanors.

   a. Felonies are more serious crimes (such as murder, rape, and robbery) for which penalties may range from imprisonment for a year or longer to (in some states) death.

b. Misdemeanors are less serious crimes (such as prostitution, disturbing the peace, and public intoxication) for which penalties may include imprisonment for up to a year. Petty offenses, or infractions, such as violations of building codes, are usually a subset of misdemeanors.

Elements of Criminal Liability

Two elements are required for criminal liability to exist: a wrongful act (*actus reus*) and a specified state of mind (*mens rea*).

1. *Actus reus*—Most crimes require that the defendant commit an act, although sometimes a person may commit a crime by failing to do something that is required, such as filing a tax return.

2. *Mens rea*—Even a wrongful act that harms society will not be punished unless the defendant had the required state of mind, or intent. What constitutes the required intent varies according to the action.

3. *Corporate criminal liability*—Under modern law, corporations may be held liable for crimes, and corporate officers and directors may sometimes be held personally liable for the crimes of the corporation.

4. *Defenses to criminal liability*—Criminal liability may be avoided if the state of mind required for the crime was lacking or some other defense against liability can be raised. Defenses include self-defense, defense of others, defense of property, the running of a statute of limitations, and others (procedural violations and alibis, for example).

Types of Crimes

The number of acts defined as criminal by federal, state, and local laws is nearly endless. The five traditional categories of crimes are as follows:

1. *Violent crime*—Crimes that cause another person to suffer harm or death are violent crimes, such as murder, rape, robbery, and assault and battery.

2. *Property crime*—The most common criminal activities are those in which the offender either takes or damages the property of another. Property crimes include burglary, larceny (stealing), obtaining goods by false pretenses, receiving stolen goods, arson, and forgery.

3. *Public order crimes*—Crimes that do not cause direct harm to others but involve behavior that society has deemed inappropriate or immoral, such as public drunkenness and illegal drug use, are public order crimes.

4. *White-collar crime*—Illegal acts committed by individuals or business entities in the course of legitimate business—for example, embezzlement, mail or wire fraud, bribery, theft of trade secrets, and insider trading—are considered white-collar crimes.

5. *Organized crime*—The criminal enterprises that make up organized crime are operated illegitimately, usually providing illegal goods and services. Preferred markets have traditionally included gambling, prostitution, illegal narcotics, and the like.

(Continued)

Cyber Crimes

Cyber crimes are crimes that are committed with computers and occur in cyberspace. They are not new crimes but existing crimes in which the Internet is the instrument of wrongdoing. Cyber crimes include theft of money or data, identity theft, cyberstalking, and hacking. Prosecuting cyber crimes presents special challenges.

Constitutional Safeguards

Specific procedures must be followed in arresting and prosecuting a criminal suspect to safeguard the suspect's constitutional rights. The U.S. Constitution guarantees that every person accused of a crime has certain rights and protections, including protection against unreasonable searches and seizures, the right to due process of law, protection against double jeopardy, protection against self-incrimination (the right to remain silent), the right to a speedy and public trial, the right to confront witnesses and be represented by an attorney, and protection against excessive bail and cruel and unusual punishment.

1. *Exclusionary rule*—All evidence obtained in violation of the defendant's constitutional rights normally must be excluded from the trial, along with evidence derived from illegally obtained evidence.

2. *Miranda rule*—At the time a criminal suspect is taken into custody, the arresting officers must inform the suspect of his or her rights by reading the *Miranda* warnings. Any evidence or confession obtained in violation of the suspect's rights will normally not be admissible in court. The Supreme Court has made numerous exceptions to the *Miranda* rule, such as when public safety is at stake.

Criminal Procedures prior to Prosecution and at the Beginning of Prosecution

The initial procedures undertaken by the police after a crime is reported include arrest, booking, and investigation after arrest. Criminal litigation against a suspect begins when the prosecutor decides to prosecute the case and files a complaint. See Exhibit 16.4 on page 597 for a summary of the major steps in the criminal justice process.

1. *Pretrial motions*—The defendant's attorney may file pretrial motions based on possible violations of the defendant's rights. For example, defense attorneys often file a motion to suppress evidence if probable cause for the search is questionable. Motions to dismiss may be filed for any number of reasons, including a violation of the defendant's right to a speedy trial.

2. *Discovery*—In criminal cases, the defendant is entitled to obtain any evidence relating to the case possessed by the prosecution, including documents, statements previously made by the defendant, objects, reports of tests or examinations, and other evidence. In some cases, the prosecutor is entitled to obtain certain evidence related to the case possessed by the defense as well.

The Trial

Most criminal cases are settled before they get to trial through plea bargaining or other means. Most criminal trials last less than one week and are similar to civil trials, except in a few major ways.

1. *The presumption of innocence*—The defendant is innocent until the prosecutor proves the defendant's guilt to the jury (or judge) beyond a reasonable doubt. The defendant is not required to present any evidence at the trial.

2. *Self-incrimination*—The defendant and witnesses cannot be forced to testify if such testimony would be incriminating.

3. *Speedy trial*—Criminal defendants have a right to a speedy and public trial. Even if they waive (give up) that right, criminal cases usually go to trial more quickly than civil cases.

4. *Unanimous jury*—Most criminal cases are tried by juries. Generally, all of the jurors must reach agreement in order to acquit or convict the defendant (whereas civil trials typically do not require unanimous agreement).

5. *Sentencing*—The judge sentences a defendant who has been found guilty (or who pleads guilty or no contest), often at a separate proceeding. Most criminal statutes set forth a range of penalties that can be imposed, and judges are free to select the appropriate penalty within that range. Typically, sentences involve fines, imprisonment, and probation (including conditions of probation). In some cases (in some states), the death penalty may be imposed. Jurors are often involved in determining whether the death penalty is appropriate in a particular case.

6. *Diversion*—Alternatively, the defendant may be sentenced to a diversion program, which will result in a dismissal of the case provided that the defendant complies with all the requirements of diversion (which vary by state).

7. *Appeal*—If the defendant loses at trial, he or she may appeal the case to a higher court. A small percentage of criminal cases are reversed on appeal.

 ## QUESTIONS FOR REVIEW

1. How does a crime differ from a tort? What are the major classifications of crimes?

2. What two elements are required for criminal liability? What defenses can be raised against criminal liability?

3. What are five broad categories of crimes? What is white-collar crime? What is cyber crime?

4. What are the constitutional rights of a person accused of a crime? Which constitutional amendments provide these rights?

5. What are the basic steps involved in criminal procedure from the time a crime is reported to the resolution of the case?

6. How is probable cause defined? Who determines whether probable cause exists?

7. What is the difference between an indictment and an information? When is each used?

8. What different pleas may a defendant enter during an arraignment? What is plea bargaining, and when does it typically occur?

9. What types of pretrial motions may be filed in a criminal case?

10. What are the major procedural differences between civil litigation and criminal litigation? What are the reasons for these differences?

ETHICAL QUESTIONS

1. Linda Lore is an experienced paralegal who works for a criminal defense firm. The lawyers trust her implicitly and feel that she is as knowledgeable as they are. One Monday morning, John Dodds, an attorney with the firm, is scheduled to be in court for a motion and, at the same time, at a deposition. John calls Linda into his office and asks her to take the deposition. Should Linda take it? Why or why not?

2. Janice Henley is a legal assistant to a criminal defense attorney. They are defending a notorious drug dealer who was arrested in a huge drug bust. The drug bust was videotaped by the agents of the Drug Enforcement Administration who carried it out. The videotape is their best evidence against the client.

   In the hall outside the courtroom, Janice observes the girlfriend of the defendant approach the federal prosecutor and talk to him. He happens to be holding the videotape, along with some papers, in his hand. The girlfriend pulls what appears to be a large magnet from her oversized purse and leans toward the videotape. If the magnet makes contact with the tape, it will erase it. What should Janice do?

3. Larry Dow works as a paralegal for the criminal defense firm of Rice & Rowen. He and his boss have just met with Joe Dollan, an attorney from another well-known law firm. Joe has been arrested for embezzling funds from an estate he was managing for a client and needs a criminal defense attorney to handle the case. Embezzlement is a felony, and if convicted, Joe will lose his license to practice law. Larry knows that a good friend of his recently retained Joe to handle the estate of her uncle. Should Larry tell his friend that Joe has been charged with embezzlement? Is there anything that Larry can do to help his friend?

4. Melinda Johns works as a legal assistant for the county prosecutor. She is working with Ms. Roberts, the victim of a robbery. They are preparing for trial. The prosecutor gives Ms. Roberts several options for proving the case and tells her to think about it overnight. The next morning, Ms. Roberts, still undecided, asks Melinda which strategy she should pursue. How should Melinda answer Ms. Roberts's question?

PRACTICE QUESTIONS AND ASSIGNMENTS

1. Identify each of the following crimes by its classification:

   a. Jerry refuses to mow his lawn, and it grows to a height of seven inches. The local police department receives complaints from his neighbors and gives Jerry a citation for violating the local lawn-height ordinance.

   b. Nancy is arrested for being drunk in public. She faces a possible jail sentence of six months.

   c. Susan is arrested for arson. The penalty includes confinement for over one year in prison on conviction.

2. The following situations are similar (all involve the theft of Makoto's television set), yet they represent three different crimes. Identify which crime has been committed, noting the differences among them.

   a. While passing Makoto's house one night, Sarah sees a portable television set left unattended on Makoto's lawn. Sarah takes the television set, carries it home, and tells everyone she owns it.

   b. While passing Makoto's house one night, Sarah sees Makoto outside with a portable television set. Holding Makoto at gunpoint, Sarah forces him to give up the set. Then Sarah runs away with it.

   c. While passing Makoto's house one night, Sarah sees a portable television set in a window. Sarah breaks the front-door lock, enters, and leaves with the set.

3. Which, if any, of the following crimes necessarily involve illegal activity on the part of more than one person?

   a. Bribery.

   b. Forgery.

   c. Embezzlement.

   d. Larceny.

   e. Receiving stolen property.

4. Rafael stops Laura on a busy street and offers to sell her an expensive wristwatch for a fraction of its value. After some questioning by Laura, Rafael admits that the watch is stolen property, although he says he was not the thief. Laura pays for and receives the wristwatch. Has Laura committed any crime? Has Rafael? Explain.

5. Review the material presented in this chapter on the *Miranda* rights. Summarize these rights. Now review Appendix J, which includes the Bill of Rights. From which amendment(s) are the *Miranda* rights derived?

6. Review the material presented in the chapter on the major procedural steps in a criminal case. Prepare a one-page summary of these steps. Identify the steps that involve constitutional rights and the amendments on which these rights are based.

7. A suspect is arrested, taken into custody, and interrogated at the police station. The police are determined to get him to confess to a murder. They confront him with an accomplice who accuses him of having committed the murder. The accused denies the allegation and says, "I didn't do it, you did." The police then take him, hand-cuffed, into an interrogation room and question him for hours until he confesses. He is never told that he has the right to remain silent or to consult an attorney. Additionally, they refuse him the right to talk to his attorney when he requests to do so during the interrogation, and they refuse to allow his attorney to speak with him when his attorney arrives at the police station.

   Using the material presented in the chapter, analyze the facts of this situation, and explain what rights the accused should have been accorded, and why.

8. Using the material presented in the chapter on state of mind, identify the type of homicide committed in each of the following situations:

   a. David, while driving in an intoxicated state, crashes into another car and kills its occupants.

   b. David, after pulling up next to his wife at a stoplight and observing her passionately kissing another man, smashes into her car and kills her.

   c. David, who is angry with his boss for firing him, plans to kill his boss by smashing his car into his boss's car, killing his boss and making it look like a car accident. David carries out his plan, kills his boss, and survives the accident.

9. Discuss the following defenses:

   a. Mary is waiting for a bus at a dimly lit bus stop at 6:30 A.M. A man approaches her from behind and pulls out a gun. He puts the gun to her head and starts laughing, telling her that there is one bullet in the barrel and that he is going to pull the trigger until it goes off. Mary pulls a gun out of her pocket, puts her hand behind her back, and shoots her assailant in the stomach, killing him.

   b. Jennifer and Kathy are walking on a crowded downtown street. Suddenly, from behind, someone grabs Jennifer's purse. Kathy pulls a gun out of her pocket and shoots and kills the purse snatcher.

   c. Joan is lying in bed at night, drifting off to sleep, when her bedroom window breaks. A man dressed in black with a stocking over his head jumps through it and attacks her. Joan, aware that a serial rapist has attacked several of her neighbors, pulls out a gun from under her mattress and shoots and kills her assailant.

   d. Jan arrives home from grocery shopping on a Tuesday morning at 10:00 A.M. and enters her house through the kitchen door. She hears a noise upstairs and goes to investigate. She finds a burglar loading her jewelry into a small felt bag. Jan pulls out a handgun and shoots and kills the burglar.

10. Identify the following criminal procedures:

    a. Tom is charged with the crime of arson. He pleads not guilty and is bound over for trial in the district court.

    b. Ned is taken to the police station, searched, photographed, fingerprinted, and allowed to make one telephone call.

    c. A jury of Barbara's peers reviews the evidence against her and determines whether probable cause exists and whether the prosecutor should proceed to trial for manslaughter.

    d. Police officers stop Larry on the street because his description matches that of a reported gas-station robber. He is three blocks from the gas station when they stop him. They question him, search him, and find that he has a pocketful of $20 and $50 bills—the same denominations that were reported by the gas-station attendant as having been stolen. The police read Larry his rights and take him into the station.

    e. Larry is taken before a magistrate, where the charges against him are read and counsel is appointed. His request to be set free on bail is denied.

    f. In exchange for a guilty plea to manslaughter, the prosecutor agrees to drop the more serious murder charges against Mary.

QUESTIONS FOR CRITICAL ANALYSIS

1. Crimes are classified into two major categories: felonies and misdemeanors (including petty offenses). What is the difference between these classifications? What does the difference indicate about the reasons for the classifications?

2. When is a crime a federal crime? Why is there a difference between state and federal crimes? Should there be?

3. A guilty act is typically required in order for a crime to be committed. Is it ever possible for a crime to be committed without a guilty act? If so, how? Give an example of such a crime.

4. What role does the mental state of an accused play in the definition of a crime? How does the degree of wrongfulness affect the crime? What would be the result if intent were not considered? Would this be a fair outcome for the accused? For society?

5. Should cyber crimes include the elements of traditional crimes (*actus reas* and *mens rea*)? Why or why not? Do you think the punishment for crimes committed in cyberspace should be more severe than the punishment for traditional crimes? Why or why not?

6. Should people who are insane be convicted of crimes? If so, should they be convicted of all crimes or only certain types of crimes? What should the test be for determining if someone is insane? Should insane persons who are convicted of crimes be placed in mental institutions instead of prisons?

7. The statute of limitations is a defense to some crimes. Should it be allowed as a defense to all crimes? What about the crime of murder?

8. Why do you think so many procedural safeguards were included in the Constitution for the protection of criminal defendants?

9. Look at the U.S. Constitution in Appendix J. Is there anything in the Bill of Rights that requires the police to give criminal suspects the *Miranda* warnings on arrest?

10. The United States Supreme Court has made numerous exceptions to the *Miranda* rule. Additionally, juries are permitted to accept confessions without being convinced that they were voluntarily made. What does this say about the way in which the rule has been applied? What does it say about the way in which criminals' rights are enforced by the courts in general?

11. How is *probable cause* defined? What might be the historical reasons for this requirement?

12. Make a list of the differences between the requirements for a civil trial and for a criminal trial. What is the reason for these differences?

13. On conviction in federal court, the defendant is sentenced by a judge who applies the federal sentencing guidelines. These guidelines provide a range of penalties from which the judge may choose. Should the judge be able to choose a sentence, or should sentences be mandatory? Should the defendant be given the opportunity to present evidence to minimize his or her sentence?

14. Timothy McVeigh was sentenced to death for the 1995 bombing of a federal building in Oklahoma City, Oklahoma, that killed 168 people. Do you think that this was a fair penalty for the crime committed? Why or why not? He appealed his conviction and sentence to the United States Supreme Court, which ruled against him. What arguments might he have made in an attempt to persuade the Supreme Court to rule against the death penalty?

PROJECTS

1. Call the state court in your city that handles pretrial criminal procedures, such as initial hearings and arraignments. Arrange to be in court when these matters are being heard.

2. Call the state court in your city that handles the most serious crimes (felonies and/or serious misdemeanors), and obtain a list of the criminal trials that are on the docket. Arrange to attend one of the trials for as long as possible. Observe how legal assistants are used by the trial attorneys.

3. Call the county prosecutor's office in your area, and ask if it gives tours to students. If so, arrange to go on a tour of the prosecutor's office, and try to learn how warrants are issued and how the prosecutor prepares for trial. Also observe how paralegals are utilized in the office.

4. Contact your local police department, and ask if it gives tours to students. If so, arrange to take a tour of the department and learn, to the extent possible, what procedures are followed in regard to booking and investigation.

5. Call your local criminal court. Ask if it has a copy of the state court's standard criminal search warrant. Request a copy. Compare the state court forms with the standard federal court search warrant presented in the chapter as Exhibit 16.5 on pages 602 and 603. Write a one-page paper summarizing the differences and similarities.

6. Review your state's court rules to see how the rules for criminal cases differ from those for civil cases. List and describe the major differences.

USING INTERNET RESOURCES

1. Go to **http://library.thinkquest.org/2760**. This site, which has become well known primarily for its "Anatomy of a Murder," also provides a list of "Landmark Supreme Court Cases" in criminal law. Select "Rockin' Supreme Court Cases" to view a list of these cases. Select one of the cases, scan through it, and then answer the following questions:

   a. Who was the defendant, and with what crime or crimes was he or she charged?

   b. What defenses were raised by the defendant?

   c. What constitutional issue was involved?

   d. What was the Supreme Court's decision?

2. Learn more about the Federal Bureau of Investigation (FBI). Go to **http://www.fbi.gov**, and click on "History" under "Learn about Us" in the left column. Browse through the history pages, and then answer the following questions:

   a. When was the FBI founded, and by whom?

   b. What was the agency's original name? When and how was it changed?

   c. Prior to 1920, what types of crimes did the FBI investigate? Were there many crimes to be investigated? Why or why not?

   d. When did the FBI become a large agency? Why?

3.  For additional resources, visit our Web site at **http://www.paralegal.delmar. cengage.com**.

END NOTES

1. The American Law Institute (mentioned in Chapter 5) issued the Official Draft of the Model Penal Code in 1962. The Model Penal Code was designed to assist state legislatures in reexamining and recodifying state criminal laws. Uniformity among the states is not as important in criminal law as in other areas of the law. Crime varies with local circumstances, and it is appropriate that punishments vary accordingly.

2. Pronounced *ak-*tus *ray us.*

3. Pronounced menz *ray-uh.*

4. *United States v. Park,* 421 U.S. 658, 95 S.Ct. 1903, 44 L.Ed.2d 489 (1975).

5. 18 U.S.C. Sections 1341–1342.

6. 18 U.S.C. Sections 1831–1839.

7. 18 U.S.C. Sections 1961–1968.

8. See 18 U.S.C. Section 1961(1)(A).

9. The National Information Infrastructure Protection Act of 1996, 18 U.S.C. Section 1030, amended the Computer Fraud and Abuse Act of 1984.

10. 384 U.S. 436, 86 S.Ct. 1602, 16 L.Ed.2d 694 (1966).

11. *Dickerson v. United States,* 530 U.S. 428, 120 S.Ct. 2326, 147 L.Ed.2d 405 (2000).

12. *New York v. Quarles,* 467 U.S. 649, 104 S.Ct. 2626, 81 L.Ed.2d 550 (1984).

13. *Moran v. Burbine,* 475 U.S. 412, 106 S.Ct. 1135, 89 L.Ed.2d 410 (1985).

14. *Arizona v. Fulminante,* 499 U.S. 279, 111 S.Ct. 1246, 113 L.Ed.2d 302 (1991).

15. *Davis v. United States,* 512 U.S. 452, 114 S.Ct. 2350, 129 L.Ed.2d 362 (1994).

16. At a minimum, the following states, as well as the District of Columbia, refer to the pleading that accompanies a motion as a memorandum of law: Alaska, Connecticut, Illinois, Maryland, Massachusetts, Michigan, Missouri, Montana, New York, North Carolina, Oregon, and Texas.

LEGAL RESEARCH AND ANALYSIS

17
CHAPTER

CHAPTER OUTLINE

Introduction

Researching Case Law—The Preliminary Steps

Finding Relevant Cases

The Case Reporting System

Analyzing Case Law

Researching Statutory Law

Analyzing Statutory Law

Researching Administrative Law

Finding Constitutional Law

Updating the Law—Learning to Use Citators

AFTER COMPLETING THIS CHAPTER, YOU WILL KNOW:

▶ How primary and secondary sources of law differ and how to use each of these types of sources in the research process.

▶ How court decisions are published and how to read case citations.

▶ How to analyze case law and summarize, or brief, cases.

▶ How federal statutes and regulations are published and the major sources of statutory and administrative law.

▶ How to interpret statutory law and understand what kinds of resources are available for researching the legislative history of a statute.

▶ Why finding current law is important and how to verify that your research results are up to date.

INTRODUCTION

For many paralegals, legal research is a fascinating part of their jobs. They find it intrinsically interesting to read the actual words of a court's opinion on a legal question or the text of a statute. Additionally, they acquire a firsthand knowledge of the law and how it applies to actual people and events. Research is also a crucial part of the paralegal's job, and the ability to conduct research thoroughly yet efficiently enhances a paralegal's value to the legal team.

As a paralegal, you may be asked to perform a variety of research tasks. Some research tasks will be simple. You may be asked to locate and print out a court case, for example. Other research tasks may take days or even weeks to complete. In almost all but the simplest of research tasks, legal research overlaps extensively with legal analysis. To find relevant case law, for example, you need to be able to analyze the cases you find to ensure that they are indeed relevant.

Many paralegals conduct research without even entering a law library. Computerized legal services such as Westlaw® and Lexis® allow legal professionals to find the text of cases, statutes, and other legal documents without leaving their desks. Indeed, according to a 2006 survey conducted by *Legal Assistant Today,* over 90 percent of paralegals today use the Internet for most of their legal research.[1] (See Chapter 18 for a discussion of online legal research.) Regardless of whether you conduct legal research online or in a law library using printed volumes, however, it is essential to know what sources to consult for different types of information. In this chapter, you will learn about these sources. You will also learn how to make sure that the law you find is up to date and still "good law."

RESEARCHING CASE LAW— THE PRELIMINARY STEPS

To illustrate how to research case law, we use a hypothetical case. The case involves one of your firm's clients, Trent Hoffman, who is suing Better Homes Store for negligence. During the initial client interview, Hoffman explained to you and your supervising attorney that he had gone to the store to purchase a large mirror. As he was leaving the store through the store's side entrance, carrying the bulky mirror, he ran into a large pole just outside the door. He did not see the pole because the mirror blocked his view. On hitting the pole, the mirror broke, and a piece of glass entered Hoffman's left eye, causing permanent loss of eyesight in that eye. Hoffman claims that the store was negligent in placing a pole so close to the exit and is suing the store for $3 million in damages.

You have already undertaken a preliminary investigation into the matter and obtained evidence supporting Hoffman's account of the facts. Your supervising attorney now asks you to do some research. Your job is to research case law to find other cases with similar fact patterns and see how the courts decided the issue in those cases.

Before you begin your research, though, you need to define the issue to be researched and determine your research goals. We look now at these two preliminary steps in researching case law.

Defining the Issue

In defining the legal issue that you need to research, your first task will be to examine closely the facts of Hoffman's case to determine the nature of the legal issue involved. Based on Hoffman's description of the factual circumstances (verified through your preliminary investigation) and on his allegation that Better Homes Store should not have placed a pole just outside one of the store's entrances, you know that the legal issue relates to the tort of negligence. As a starting point, you should therefore review what you know about negligence theory.

Ethics Watch!

EFFICIENCY IN RESEARCH

Attorneys have a duty to charge their clients reasonable fees. As a paralegal, you help your attorney fulfill this duty by working efficiently so as to minimize the number of hours you spend on work relating to the client's matter. Legal research can be extremely time consuming, as every paralegal knows. To reduce the time spent in researching a particular legal issue, start out on your quest with a clear idea of your research task. After all, your time is expensive not only for the client (who pays for it) but also for your supervising attorney (who may need your assistance on other cases as well). By knowing as precisely as possible what the goal of your research is, you can reach that goal more quickly and thus better serve the interests of both the client and your supervising attorney.

Recall from Chapter 7 that the tort of negligence is defined as the failure to exercise reasonable care. To succeed in a negligence action, a plaintiff must establish that (1) the defendant had a duty of care to the plaintiff, (2) the defendant breached that duty, (3) the plaintiff suffered a legally recognizable injury, and (4) the injury was caused by the defendant's breach of the duty of care. A knowledge of these elements will help you determine the issue that needs to be researched in Hoffman's case. There is little doubt that the third requirement has been met—Hoffman's loss of sight in his left eye is a legally recognizable injury for which he can be compensated—*if* he succeeds in proving the other three elements of negligence. Proving the fourth element, causation, is largely dependent on proving the first two

Although today most legal research is carried out using online resources, some paralegals still consult printed legal volumes when conducting legal research.

(Courtesy of Sean Nel, 2006. Used under license from ShutterStock, Inc.)

Developing Paralegal Skills

DEFINING THE ISSUES TO BE RESEARCHED

Federal government agents observed David Berriman in his parked car talking on his cellular phone. Later, other cars were seen driving up to David's car and stopping. The drivers received brown paper bags in exchange for money. David was questioned, and his car was searched. Cocaine was found in the car. He was arrested for transporting and distributing cocaine, and the police took his car and cellular phone. David 's lawyer is arguing that the government agents did not have the authority to seize David's car and cellular phone and force him to forfeit this property. Natalie Martin, a legal assistant with the U.S. attorney's office, has been assigned the task of researching the federal statutes and cases on this issue.

Before Natalie can begin her research project, she must thoroughly review the case to determine what specific issues need to be researched. Using a checklist method that she learned in school, she breaks the facts of the case down into five categories and inserts the relevant facts from her assignment. Now Natalie is ready to begin her research.

CHECKLIST FOR DEFINING RESEARCH ISSUES

- Parties: Who are the people involved in the action or lawsuit?

- Places and things: Where did the events take place, and what items are involved in the action or lawsuit?

- Basis of action or issue: What is the legal claim or issue involved in the action or lawsuit?

- Defenses: What legal justification did the police have for seizing David's car and cellular phone? Will this justification still exist if David is found not guilty of the underlying charges, or will the police be required to return the forfeited property?

- Relief sought: What is the legal remedy or penalty sought in the case?

elements. In your research, you will therefore want to focus on the first two elements. Specifically, you need to find answers to the following questions:

- Did Better Homes Store owe a duty of care to its customer, Hoffman? You might phrase this question in more general terms: Do business owners owe a duty of care to **business invitees**—customers and others whom they invite onto their premises?

- If so, what is the extent of that duty, and how is it measured? In other words, are business owners always liable, in all circumstances, when customers are injured on their premises? Or must some condition be met before store owners will be liable? For example, must a customer's injury be a *foreseeable* consequence of a condition on the premises, such as the pole outside the store's door, for the store owner to be liable for the injury?

- If the injury must be a foreseeable consequence of a condition, would a court find that Hoffman's injury in this case was a foreseeable consequence of the pole's placement just outside the store's door?

| **business invitee** |
| A person, such as a customer or client, who is invited onto business premises by the owner of those premises for business purposes. |

These, then, are the issues you need to research. Notice how the term *issue* has become plural. You will find that this is a common occurrence in legal research—only rarely will you be researching a single legal issue.

Determining Your Research Goals

Once you have defined the issue or issues to be researched, you will be in a better position to determine your research goals. Remember that you are working on behalf of a client, who is paying for your services. Your overall goal is thus to find legal support for Hoffman's claim. To achieve this goal, you will want to find two things: cases on point and cases that are binding authorities. Depending on what you find, you may also need to look for persuasive authorities.

Cases on Point

One of your research goals is to find a case (or cases) on point in which the court held for the plaintiff. A **case on point** is a previous case involving fact patterns and legal issues that are similar to those in the case you are researching. In regard to Hoffman's negligence claim, a case on point would be one in which the plaintiff alleged that he or she was injured while on a store's premises because of a dangerous condition on those premises.

The ideal case on point would be a case in which all four elements of a case (the parties, the circumstances, the legal issues involved, and the remedies sought by the plaintiff) are very similar to those in your case. Such a case is called a **case on "all fours"**.[2] In regard to Hoffman's claim, a case on "all fours" would be a case on point, such as just described, in which the plaintiff-customer did not expect a condition (such as an obstacle in his or her path) to exist and was prevented from seeing the condition by some action that a customer would reasonably undertake (such as carrying a large box out of a store). The parties and the circumstances of the case would thus be very similar to those in Hoffman's case. In addition, the plaintiff would have sustained a permanent injury, as Hoffman did, and sought damages for negligence.

Binding Authorities

In researching Hoffman's case, another goal is to find cases that are binding authorities. As discussed in Chapter 5, a *binding authority* is any authority that the court must follow in deciding the issue. A binding authority may be a statute, regulation, or constitution that governs the issue, or it may be a previously decided court case that is controlling in your jurisdiction.

For a case to serve as a binding authority, it must be on point and must have been decided by a superior court. A superior court, in the sense used here, refers to the tiers in a court system. Recall from Chapter 6 that both the federal and state court systems consist of several levels, or tiers, of courts. *Trial courts,* in which evidence is presented and testimony given, are on the bottom tier (which also includes lower courts handling specialized issues). Decisions from a trial court can be appealed to a higher court, which commonly is an intermediate *court of appeals,* or *appellate court.* Decisions from these intermediate courts of appeals may be appealed to an even higher court, such as a state supreme court or, if a federal question is involved, the United States Supreme Court.

A lower court is bound to follow the decisions set forth by a higher court in the same jurisdiction. An appellate court's decision in a case involving facts and issues similar to a case brought in a trial court in the same jurisdiction would thus be a binding authority—the trial court would be bound to follow the appellate court's decision on the issue. A higher court is never required to follow an opinion written by a lower court in the same jurisdiction, however. When you are performing research, look for cases on point decided by the highest court in your jurisdiction, because those cases carry the most weight.

State courts have the final say on state law, and federal courts have the final say on federal law. Thus, except in deciding an issue that involves federal law, state courts do not have to follow the decisions of federal courts. In deciding issues that involve federal law, however, state courts must abide by the decisions of the United States Supreme Court.

Persuasive Authorities

A **persuasive authority** is not binding on a court. In other words, the court is not required to follow that authority in making its decisions. Examples of persuasive authorities include:

- Persuasive precedents—previous court opinions from other jurisdictions, as discussed in Chapter 5.

---

case on point
A case involving factual circumstances and issues that are similar to those in the case being researched.

case on "all fours"
A case in which all four elements (the parties, the circumstances, the legal issues involved, and the remedies sought by the plaintiff) are very similar to those in the case being researched.

persuasive authority
Any legal authority, or source of law, that a court may look to for guidance but on which it need not rely in making its decision. Persuasive authorities include cases from other jurisdictions, discussions in legal periodicals, and so forth.

- Legal periodicals, such as law reviews, in which the issue at hand is discussed by legal scholars.

- Encyclopedias summarizing legal principles or concepts relating to a particular issue.

- Legal dictionaries that describe how the law has been applied in the past.

Often, a court refers to persuasive authorities when deciding a *case of first impression,* which is a case involving an issue that has never been addressed by that court before. For example, if in your research into Hoffman's claim you find that no similar cases have ever reached a higher court in your jurisdiction, you will look for similar cases decided by courts in other jurisdictions. If courts in other jurisdictions have faced a similar issue, the court may be guided by those other courts' decisions when deciding Hoffman's case. Your supervising attorney will want to know about these persuasive authorities so that she can present them to the court for consideration.

FINDING RELEVANT CASES

When conducting legal research, you need to distinguish between two basic categories of legal sources: primary sources and secondary sources. As discussed in Chapter 5, *primary sources of law* include court decisions, statutes enacted by legislative bodies, rules and regulations created by administrative agencies, presidential orders, and generally any documents that *establish* the law. *Secondary sources of law* consist of books and articles that summarize, systematize, compile, or otherwise interpret the law.

Generally, when embarking on research projects, paralegals look first to secondary sources of law to help them find relevant primary sources. For this reason, secondary sources of law are often referred to as *finding tools.* Consider the research project before you involving the Hoffman claim. How can you find cases on point and binding authorities on this issue? The body of American case law consists of over five million court decisions, to which more than forty thousand decisions are added each year. Because judicial decisions are published in chronological order, finding relevant precedents would be a Herculean task if it were not for secondary sources of law that classify decisions according to subject. Two important finding tools that are helpful in researching case law are legal encyclopedias and case digests, which we describe next. We also look at some other secondary sources that may be helpful to paralegals who are researching case law.

Legal Encyclopedias

In researching Hoffman's claim, you might look first at a legal encyclopedia to learn more about the topic of negligence and the duty of care that business owners owe to business invitees. A popular legal encyclopedia is *American Jurisprudence,* Second Edition, commonly referred to as *American Jurisprudence 2d* or, more briefly, as *Am. Jur. 2d.* (An excerpt from this encyclopedia is shown in Exhibit 17.1 on the following page.) *American Jurisprudence* covers more than four hundred topics in eighty-three volumes. The topics are presented alphabetically, and each topic is further divided into subtopics describing general rules of law that have emerged from generations of court decisions. The encyclopedia also provides cross-references to specific court cases, statutory law, and relevant secondary sources of law. Additionally, each volume includes an index, and a separate index covers the entire encyclopedia. As is typical with many printed legal compilations, the volumes are kept current through supplements called **pocket parts.** Pocket parts, so named because they slip into a pocket in the front or back of the volume, contain changes and additions to various topics and subtopics.

pocket part
A separate pamphlet containing recent cases or changes in the law that is used to update hornbooks, legal encyclopedias, and other legal authorities. It is called a "pocket part" because it slips into a sleeve, or pocket, in the front or back binder of the volume.

EXHIBIT 17.1

Excerpt from *American Jurisprudence 2d*

Reprinted with permission of Thomson/West.

PREMISES LIABILITY

by

Irwin J. Schiffres, J.D. and Sheila A. Skojec, J.D.

Scope of topic: This article discusses the principles and rules of law applicable to and governing the liability of owners or occupants of real property for negligence causing injury to persons or property by reason of defects therein or hazards created by the activities of such owners or occupants or their agents and employees. Treated in detail are the classification of persons injured as invitees, licensees, or trespassers, and the duty owed them, as well as the rules applicable in those jurisdictions where such status distinctions are no longer determinative of the duty owed the entrant; the effect of "recreational use" statutes on the duty owed persons using the property for such purposes; the greater measure of duty owed by the owner to children as compared to adult licensees and trespassers, including the attractive nuisance doctrine; and the specific duties and liabilities of owners and occupants of premises used for business or residential purposes. Also considered is the effect of the injured person's negligence on the plaintiff's right to recover under principles of contributory or comparative negligence.

Federal aspects: One injured on premises owned or operated by the United States may seek to recover under general principles of premises liability discussed in this article. Insofar as recovery is sought under the Federal Torts Claims Act, see 35 Am Jur 2d, FEDERAL TORTS CLAIMS ACT § 73.

Treated elsewhere:

Mutual obligations and liabilities of adjoining landowners with respect to injuries arising from their acts or omissions, see 1 Am Jur 2d, ADJOINING LANDOWNERS AND PROPERTIES §§ 10, 11, 28 et seq., 37 et seq.

Liability for the acts or omissions of the owners or occupants of premises abutting on a street or highway which cause injury to those using the way, see 39 Am Jur 2d, HIGHWAYS, STREETS, AND BRIDGES §§ 517 et seq.

Liability for violation of building regulations, see 13 Am Jur 2d, BUILDINGS §§ 32 et seq.

Liability of employer for injuries caused employees on the employer's premises, see 53 Am Jur 2d, MASTER AND SERVANT §§ 139 et seq.

Liability for injuries caused by defective products on the premises, see 63 Am Jur 2d, PRODUCTS LIABILITY

Respective rights and liabilities of a landlord and tenant where one is responsible for an injury suffered by the other, or by a third person, on leased premises or on premises provided for the common use of tenants, see 49 Am Jur 2d, LANDLORD AND TENANT §§ 761 et seq.

Liability of a receiver placed in charge of property for an injury sustained thereby or thereon by someone other than the persons directly interested in the estate, see 66 Am Jur 2d, RECEIVERS § 364

Duties and liabilities of occupiers of premises used for various particular types of businesses or activities, see 4 Am Jur 2d, AMUSEMENTS AND EXHIBITIONS §§ 51 et seq.; 14 Am Jur 2d, CARRIERS §§ 964 et seq.; 38 Am Jur 2d, GARAGES, AND FILLING AND PARKING STATIONS §§ 81 et seq.; 40 Am Jur 2d, HOSPITALS AND ASYLUMS § 31; 40 Am Jur 2d, HOTELS, MOTELS, AND RESTAURANTS §§ 81 et seq.; 50 Am Jur 2d, LAUNDRIES, DYERS, AND DRY CLEANERS §§ 21, 22; 54 Am Jur 2d, MOBILE HOMES, TRAILER PARKS, AND TOURIST CAMPS § 17; 57 Am Jur 2d, MUNICIPAL, COUNTY, SCHOOL, AND STATE TORT LIABILITY; AND 59 Am Jur 2d, PARKS, SQUARES, AND PLAYGROUNDS §§ 43 et seq.

Duties and liabilities with respect to injuries caused by particular agencies, such as

317

Another helpful encyclopedia is *Corpus Juris Secundum*, or *C.J.S.* Like *Am. Jur. 2d*, this encyclopedia provides detailed information on almost every area of the law and includes indexes for each volume as well as for the entire set. Its 101 volumes cover 433 topics, which are presented alphabetically and further divided into subtopics. One of the volumes of this set is depicted in Exhibit 17.2.

Still another encyclopedia is *Words and Phrases*, which offers definitions and interpretations of legal terms and phrases. Each term or phrase in this forty-six-volume set is followed by brief summary statements from federal or state court decisions in which the word or phrase has been interpreted or defined. The summary statements also indicate the names of the cases and the reporters in which they can be located. **Reporters** are publications containing the actual text of court cases, as will be discussed later.

All of these encyclopedias are published by West Group. When beginning your research into the Hoffman claim, you could use any of these secondary sources, or finding tools, to lead you to the primary sources (cases) that you will need to read and analyze. You could search any of the sources for such terms as *premises liability, business invitees, duty of care,* and *landowners,* for example. Remember, though, that legal encyclopedias contain only general rules of law. They do not include specific rules of law from your state, which you will need to locate.

Case Digests

In researching the issue in Hoffman's case against Better Homes Store, you might want to check a case digest as well as a legal encyclopedia for references to relevant case law. **Digests,** which are produced by various publishers, are helpful research tools because they provide indexes to case law—from the earliest recorded cases through the most current opinions. Case digests arrange topics alphabetically and provide information to help you locate referenced cases, but they do not offer the detail found in legal encyclopedias. Collected under each topic heading in a case digest are annotations. **Annotations** are comments, explanatory notes, or case summaries. In case digests, annotations consist of very short statements of relevant points of law in reported cases. The digests published by West Group offer the most comprehensive system for locating cases by subject matter. Exhibit 17.3 on the next page shows some excerpts from one of West's federal digests on the topic of negligence.

The West Key-Number System

West's key-number system has simplified the task of researching case law. The system divides all areas of American law into specific categories, or topics, arranged in alphabetical order. The topics are further divided into many specific subtopics, each designated by a **key number,** which is accompanied by the West key symbol: 🔑 You can see the use of this key symbol in Exhibit 17.3. Exhibit 17.4 on page 637 shows some of the key numbers used for other subtopics under the general topic of negligence.

The key-number system organizes millions of case summaries under specific topics and subtopics. For example, in researching the Hoffman claim, suppose that you locate a negligence case on point decided by a court in your state five years ago. Your goal is to find related—and perhaps more recent—cases that support Hoffman's claim. Here is how the key-number system can help. When you read through any case in a West's case reporter, you will find that a series of **headnotes** precedes the court's actual opinion. Each headnote contains a summarized statement of one portion of the court's opinion in the case. West editors create each headnote and assign it to a particular topic with a key number.

Key numbers correlate the headnotes in cases to the topics in digests and can be very useful in finding cases on a particular subject. Once you find the key number in a case that discusses the issue you are researching, you can easily find every other case in your state or region that discusses this issue. You simply go to the West case digest and locate the particular key number and topic. Beneath the key number, the digest provides case summaries, titles, and citations to all the cases discussing the issue in the area covered by the digest. When you find a case that seems on point, you know exactly where to find it because you have the citation.

Types of Digests

As mentioned, West offers a comprehensive system of digests. West publishes digests of both federal court opinions and state court opinions, as well as regional digests and digests that correspond with its reporters covering specialized areas, such as bankruptcy. For example,

EXHIBIT 17.2
Corpus Juris Secundum

Reprinted with permission of Thomson/West.

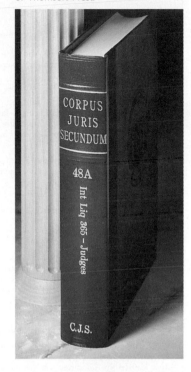

▌ **reporter**
A book in which court cases are published, or reported.

▌ **digest**
A compilation in which brief summaries of court cases are arranged by subject and subdivided by jurisdiction and court.

▌ **annotation**
A brief comment, an explanation of a legal point, or a case summary found in a case digest or other legal source.

▌ **key number**
A number (accompanied by the symbol of a key) corresponding to a specific topic within West's key-number system to facilitate legal research of case law.

▌ **headnote**
A note near the beginning of a reported case summarizing the court's ruling on an issue.

EXHIBIT 17.3
Excerpts from a *West's Federal Digest*

Reprinted with permission of Thomson/West.

77A F P D 4th—173

NEGLIGENCE ☞ 1037(4)

For references to other topics, see Descriptive-Word Index

E.D.Mich. 1998. Under Michigan law, a property owner is not an absolute insurer of the safety of invitees.

> Meyers v. Wal-Mart Stores, East, Inc., 29 F.Supp.2d 780.

E.D.Mich. 1995. under Michigan law, property owner is not insurer of safety of invitees.

> Bunch v. Long John Silvers, Inc., 878 F.Supp. 1044.

E.D.Mich. 1994. Under Michigan law, property owner is not insurer of safety of invitees.

> Dose v. Equitable Life Assur. Soc., 864 F.Supp. 682.

E.D.N.C. 1993. Premises owner does not automatically insure safety of invitees and is not liable in absence of negligence.

> Faircloth v. U.S., 837 F.Supp. 123.

E.D.Va. 1999. Under Virginia law, owner of premises is not insurer of his invitees safety; rather, owner must use ordinary care to render premises reasonably safe for invitee's visit.

> Sandow-Pajewski v. Busch Entertainment Corp., 55 F.Supp.2d 422.

☞ **1037(4). Care required in general.**

C.A.7 (Ill.) 1986. Under Illinois law, landowner is liable for physical harm to his invitees caused by condition on his land: where landowner could by exercise of reasonable care have discovered condition; where landowner should realize that condition involves unreasonable risk to harm to invitees; where landowner should expect that invitees will not discover danger or will fail to protect against it; and where landowner fails to exercise reasonable care to protect invitees.

> Higgins v. White Sox Baseball Club, Inc., 787 F.2d 1125.

C.A.7 (Ind.) 1994. Under Indiana law, landowner's duty to invitee while that invitee is on premises is that of reasonable care.

> Salima v. Scherwood South, Inc., 38 F.3d 929.

Under indiana law, landowner is liable for harm caused to invitee by condition on land only if landowner knows of or through exercise of reasonable care would discover condition and realize that it involves unreasonable risk of harm to such invitees, should expect the invitee will fail to discover or realize danger or fail to protect against it, and fails to exercise reasonable care in protecting invitee against danger.

> Salima v. Scherwood South, Inc., 38 F. 3d 929.

Under Indiana law, landowner is not liable for harm caused to invitees by conditions whose

For cited U.S.C.A. sections and legislative histo[ry]

danger is known or obvious unless landowner could anticipate harm despite obviousness.

> Salima v. Scherwood South, Inc., 38 F.3d 929.

C.A.6 (Mich.) 1998. Under Michigan law, where invitor has reason to expect that, despite oper[...] neve[...] have[...] step[...]

NEGLIGENCE

77A F P D 4th—542

XVI. DEFENSES AND MITIGATING CIRCUMSTANCES.—Continued.

     570. _____ Professional rescuers; "firefighter's rule."
     575. Imputed contributory negligence.

XVII. PREMISES LIABILITY.

  (A)   IN GENERAL.
      ☞ 1000. Nature.
      1001. Elements in general.
      1002. Constitutional, statutory and regulatory provisions.
      1003. What law governs.
      1004. Preemption.

  (B)   NECESSITY AND EXISTENCE OF DUTY.
      ☞ 1010. In general.
      1011. Ownership, custody and control.
      1012. Conditions known or obvious in general.
      1013. Conditions created or known by defendant.
      1014. Foreseeability.
      1015. Duty as to children.
      1016. _____ In general.
      1017. _____ Trespassing children.
      1018. Duty to inspect or discover.
      1019. Protection against acts of third persons in general.
      1020. Duty to warn.
      1021. Duty of store and business proprietors.
      1022. _____ In general.
      1023. _____ Duty to inspect.
      1024. _____ Protection against acts of third persons.
      1025. Duty based on statute or other regulation.

  (C)   STANDARD OF CARE.
      ☞ 1030. In general.
      1031. Not insurer or guarantor.
      1032. Reasonable or ordinary care in general.
      1033. Reasonably safe or unreasonably dangerous conditions.
      1034. Status of entrant.
      1035. _____ In general.
      1036. _____ Care dependent on status.
      1037. _____ Invitees.
         (1). In general.
         (2). Who are invitees.
         (3). Not insurer as to invitees.
         (4). Care required in general.
         (5). Public invitees in general.
         (6). Implied invitation.
         (7). Persons working on property.
         (8). Delivery persons and haulers.
     1040. _____ Licensees.
         (1). In general.
         (2). Who are licensees.

EXHIBIT 17.4
Subtopics and Key
Numbers in a West Digest

Reprinted with permission
of Thomson/West.

NEGLIGENCE

SUBJECTS INCLUDED

General civil negligence law and premises liability, including duty, standards of care, breach of duty, proximate cause, injury, defenses, and comparative fault, whether based on the common law or statute, as well as procedural aspects of such actions

General civil liabilities for gross negligence, recklessness, willful or wanton conduct, strict liability and ultrahazardous instrumentalities and activities

Negligence liabilities relating to the construction, demolition and repair of buildings and other structures, whether based on the common law or statute

General criminal negligence offenses and prosecutions

SUBJECTS EXCLUDED AND COVERED BY OTHER TOPICS

Accountants or auditors, negligence of, see ACCOUNTANTS ⏃8,9

Aircraft, accidents involving, see AVIATION ⏃141–153

Attorney's malpractice liability, see ATTORNEY AND CLIENT ⏃105–129.5

Banks, liabilities of, see BANKS AND BANKING ⏃100

Brokers, securities and real estate, liabilities of, see BROKERS

Car and highway accidents, see AUTOMOBILES

Common carriers, liabilities to passengers, see CARRIERS

Domestic animals, injuries by or to, see ANIMALS

Dram Shop liability and other liabilities for serving alcohol, see INTOXICATING LIQUORS ⏃282–324

* * * *

For detailed references to other topics, see Descriptive-Word Index

Analysis

 I. IN GENERAL, ⏃200–205.

 II. NECESSITY AND EXISTENCE OF DUTY, ⏃210–222.

 III. STANDARD OF CARE, ⏃230–239.

 IV. BREACH OF DUTY, ⏃250–259.

 V. HEIGHTENED DEGREES OF NEGLIGENCE, ⏃272–276.

 VI. VULNERABLE AND ENDANGERED PERSONS; RESCUES, ⏃281–285.

 VII. SUDDEN EMERGENCY DOCTRINE, ⏃291–295.

 VIII. DANGEROUS SITUATIONS AND STRICT LIABILITY, ⏃301–307.

the *Lawyers' Edition of the Digest of the Supreme Court Reports* corresponds to decisions listed in the West case reporter entitled *Lawyers' Edition of the Supreme Court Reports.*

 Other publishers also publish digests. For instance, Callahan's *Michigan Digest* is a digest specific to Michigan courts. Note that other publishers' digest do not use the key-number system.

D. Grace Carter   PARALEGAL **profile**

LITIGATION PARALEGAL

D. Grace Carter, CP, received her B.S. degree from Florida State University in Tallahassee, Florida. Her first position was as a word processor, but she focused on becoming a paralegal. When she moved to North Carolina in 1990, she found a mentor in patent attorney James D. Myers, who introduced her to the world of intellectual property litigation. Carter discovered that intellectual property law allowed her to stretch her intellectual muscles. Carter remained at Myers Bigel Sibley & Sajovec until April 2004. After a brief foray into products liability at Nelson Mullins Riley & Scarborough, she finally found a home at Syngenta Biotechnology, Inc., in Research Triangle Park, North Carolina.

Currently, Carter serves as an intellectual property litigation paralegal and as a corporate records manager, chief archivist, and information security officer for Syngenta. The wide range of her duties includes legal research and analysis (electronic and traditional) and specifically relates to corporations, experts, and other entities.

Carter is also an adjunct instructor for the Meredith College paralegal program in Raleigh, North Carolina, where she teaches law office management. Carter works with attorneys and paralegals across the state of North Carolina in maintaining practice standards for the paralegal profession.

What do you like best about your work?

"The vision of Syngenta Biotechnology, Inc., is 'to deliver better food to a better world through extensive crop solutions.' Understandably, my work revolves around the work of scientists, and this is the best part of my job. The work begins at a lab bench and marches on through various laboratories and departments. Along the way, data are mined, protocols archived, and patent applications filed. Seeing the law through a scientist's eyes requires patience and a willingness to learn scientific methods, while keeping in mind official company policies and procedures. Complex databases hold raw data and complement work performed in collaborative document management platforms, such as *Documentum,* which allows users to create, manage, and archive documents. Of course, no paralegal job seems complete without paper. As corporate records manager, I assist employees and departments in the proper maintenance, storage, and destruction of their company information in accordance with the company's record retention policies, procedures, and schedules. Again, working across diverse backgrounds and experiences, I utilize the most fundamental skill paralegals have in their tool kits—organizational skills and attention to detail."

Annotations: *American Law Reports*

The *American Law Reports (A.L.R.)* and *American Law Reports Federal (A.L.R. Federal),* published by West Group, are also useful resources for the legal researcher. These multivolume sets present the full text of selected cases in numerous areas of the law. They are helpful in finding cases from jurisdictions throughout the country with similar factual and legal issues.

There are five different series of *American Law Reports,* covering case law since 1919. The first and second series contain separate digests that provide references to cases and also have word indexes to assist the researcher in locating specific areas. The remaining sets of *A.L.R.* volumes use a different approach, called a *Quick Index,* which allows the user to quickly access cases and information on a particular topic. The cases presented in these reporters are followed by annotations—that is, references to articles that explain or comment on the specific issues involved in the cases. These reporters can therefore be a good source to turn to for an overview of a specific area of law or current trend in the law.

What is the greatest challenge that you face in your area of work?

"My greatest challenge as a paralegal is staying current with local and federal laws and keeping my skills at an effective level. One solution is to read professional publications, such as *Legal Assistant Today* or the National Association of Legal Assistants' *Facts & Findings*. Another is utilizing the Internet to check court Web sites and professional Web sites. Blogs (short for 'Weblogs') have become an invaluable source of up-to-the-minute information. I recommend the Intellectual Property Owners Association blog (**http://www.ipoa.typepad.com**) and the Acrobat for Legal Professionals blog (**http://www.blogs.adobe.com/acrolaw**). Attending continuing legal education classes and participating in professional organizations is another way to keep current and stay in touch with your colleagues."

What advice do you have for would-be paralegals in your area of work?

"Keep your outlook positive. Demonstrate your willingness to do whatever it takes to complete the task. Be thorough and persistent. Meet your deadlines, and do not make unrealistic commitments. Be confident that you can do the job. Keep current with the latest on the Internet. Know how to do more than the basics on Microsoft Word or WordPerfect, Excel, PowerPoint, and Access. Understand databases—take a class, ask questions, and build your own. Learning to operate deposition summary programs such as *Concordance* and *Summation* will be a plus as well. Take free training from your Westlaw or Lexis representative. Utilize the 800 number on the back of your account information card for assistance. Never be afraid to ask for help. Do not hesitate to call a colleague to ask a question; he or she will be flattered. You can figure out the details as you work with others to complete the task."

> *"Never be afraid to ask for help."*

What are some tips for success as a paralegal in your area of work?

"When you are doing research, monitor your steps so you do not have to retrace steps and find yourself going over the same path. Make yourself a research chart, and keep good notes. Define the issues, and make sure you understand the assignment. Review relevant pleadings and documents. Make a research plan and keep your attorney informed of your progress. This will help you avoid progressing in the wrong direction and wasting valuable time. Check your citations to ensure that they are correct. Do not embarrass yourself or your attorney with an overruled citation. Do not be afraid to do some manual research, if necessary."

D. Grace Carter is also featured in the forthcoming book, Lessons from the Top Paralegal Experts, *by Carole Bruno.*

When using any of the volumes of *A.L.R.,* the researcher must be sure to update her or his results. *A.L.R.* annotations are periodically updated by the addition of relevant cases. For the first series, the annotations are updated in a set of books called the *A.L.R. Blue Book of Supplemental Decisions.* The second series is updated in the *A.L.R. Later Case Service,* and the remaining series are made current by pocket-part supplements located in the front of each volume. In addition, the researcher can consult the annotation history table located at the end of the Quick Index to see whether any new annotations supplement or change an earlier annotation.

Other Secondary Sources

There are a number of other secondary sources that you may wish to refer to when conducting legal research. We look here at three of these sources: treatises, *Restatements of the Law,* and legal periodicals. Like other secondary sources of law, these sources do not in themselves

EXHIBIT 17.5

A Page from the *Hornbook* on the Law of Torts

Reprinted with permission of Thomson/West.

Chapter 11

NEGLIGENCE: DEFENSES

Table of Sections

Sec.
65. Contributory Negligence.
66. Last Clear Chance.
67. Comparative Negligence.
68. Assumption of Risk.

§ 65. Contributory Negligence

The two most common defenses in a negligence action are contributory negligence and assumption of risk. Since both developed at a comparatively late date in the development of the common law,[1] and since both clearly operate to the advantage of the defendant, they are commonly regarded as defenses to a tort which would otherwise be established. All courts now hold that the burden of pleading and proof of the contributory negligence of the plaintiff is on the defendant.[2]

Contributory negligence is conduct on the part of the plaintiff, contributing as a legal cause to the harm he has suffered, which falls below the standard to which he is required to conform for his own protection.[3] Unlike assumption of risk, the defense does not rest upon the idea that the defendant is relieved of any duty toward the plaintiff. Rather, although the defendant has violated his duty, has been negligent, and would oth-

---

§ 65

1. The earliest contributory negligence case is Butterfield v. Forrester, 1809, 11 East 60, 103 Eng.Rep. 926. The first American case appears to have been Smith v. Smith, 1824, 19 Mass. (2 Pick.) 621. Assumption of risk first appears in a negligence case in 1799. See infra, § 68 n. 1.

2. E.g., Wilkinson v. Hartford Accident & Indemnity Co., La.1982, 411 So.2d 22; Moodie v. Santoni, 1982, 292 Md. 582, 441 A.2d 323; Addair v. Bryant, 1981, ___ W.Va. ___, 284 S.E.2d 374; Pickett v. Parks, 1981, 208 Neb. 310, 303 N.W.2d 296; Hatton v. Chem-Haulers, Inc., Ala.1980, 393 So.2d 950; Sampson v. W. F. Enterprises, Inc., Mo.App.1980, 611 S.W.2d 333; Howard v. Howard, Ky.App.1980, 607 S.W.2d 119; cf. Reuter v. United States, W.D.Pa.1982, 534 F.Supp. 731 (presumption that person killed or suffering loss of memory was acting with due care).

Illinois and certain other jurisdictions held to the contrary for some time. See West Chicago Street Railroad Co. v. Liderman, 1900, 187 Ill. 463, 58 N.E. 367; Kotler v. Lalley, 1930, 112 Conn. 86, 151 A. 433; Dreier v. McDermott, 1913, 157 Iowa 726, 141 N.W. 315. See Green, Illinois Negligence Law II, 1944, 39 Ill.L.Rev. 116, 125–130.

3. Second Restatement of Torts, § 463. See generally, Malone, The Formative Era of Contributory Negligence, 1946, 41 Ill.L.Rev. 151; James, Contributory Negligence, 1953, 62 Yale L.J. 691; Bohlen, Contributory Negligence, 1908, 21 Harv.L.Rev. 233; Lowndes, Contributory Negligence, 1934, 22 Geo.L.J. 674; Malone, Some Ruminations on Contributory Negligence, 1981, 65 Utah L.Rev. 91; Schwartz, Contributory and Comparative Negligence: A Reappraisal, 1978, 87 Yale L.J. 697; Note, 1979, 39 La.L.Rev. 637.

451

---

have the force of law. They are important sources of legal analysis and opinion, however, and are often cited as persuasive authorities.

Treatises

treatise

In legal research, a work that provides a systematic, detailed, and scholarly review of a particular legal subject.

hornbook

A single-volume scholarly discussion, or treatise, on a particular legal subject (such as property law).

A **treatise** is a formal scholarly work by a law professor or other legal professional that treats a particular subject systematically and in detail. Some treatises are published in multivolume sets, while others are contained in a single book. Single-volume treatises that synthesize the basic principles of a given legal area are known as **hornbooks**. These texts are useful to paralegals who want to familiarize themselves with a particular area of the law, such as torts or contracts. For example, in researching the issue in Hoffman's negligence case, you might want to locate the treatise entitled *Prosser and Keeton on the Law of Torts*, Fifth Edition, which is included in West's Hornbook Series, and read the sections on negligence in that volume. (Exhibit 17.5 shows the page of this book that opens the chapter on defenses to negligence.) In addition to providing a clear and organized discussion of the subject matter, hornbooks such as *Prosser and Keeton on the Law of Torts* present many examples of case law and references to cases that may be helpful to a researcher.

Restatements of the Law

The *Restatements of the Law* are also a helpful resource, and one on which judges often rely as a persuasive authority when making decisions. The *Restatements* are compilations of the common law that have been drafted and published by the American Law Institute. There are *Restatements* in the areas of contracts, torts, agency, trusts, property, restitution, security, judgments, and conflict of laws. Many of the *Restatements* are now in their second or third editions. Exhibit 17.6 shows a volume of the *Restatement (Third) of Torts*. Each section in the *Restatements* contains a statement of the principles of law that are generally accepted by the courts or embodied in statutes, followed by a discussion of those principles. The discussions present particular cases as examples and also discuss variations.

Legal Periodicals

Legal periodicals, such as law reviews and law journals, are also important secondary sources of law that can be very helpful to paralegals. If an article in a legal periodical deals with the specific area that you are researching, the article will likely include footnotes citing cases relating to the topic. These references can save you hours of research time in finding relevant case law.

To locate articles that are relevant to the area you are researching, you can look in the *Index to Legal Periodicals* (see Exhibit 17.7). This index, which is available in law libraries as well as online, lists articles by subject, title, and author. Another popular index to legal periodicals is the *Current Legal Index*.

THE CASE REPORTING SYSTEM

The primary sources of case law are, of course, the cases themselves. Once you have learned what cases are relevant to the issue you are researching, you need to find the cases and examine the exact words of the court opinions. (See the *Featured Guest* article on pages 644 and 645 for tips on conducting legal research.) Assume, for example, that in researching the issue in Hoffman's case, you learn that your state's supreme court issued a decision a few years ago on a case with a very similar fact pattern. In that case, the state supreme court upheld a lower court's judgment that a retail business owner had to pay extensive damages to a customer who was injured on the store's premises. You know that the state supreme court's decision is a binding authority, and to your knowledge, the decision has not been overruled or modified. Therefore, the case will likely provide weighty support to your attorney's arguments in support of Hoffman's claim.

At this point, however, you have only read *about* the case in secondary sources. To locate the case itself and make sure it is applicable, you need to understand the case reporting system and the legal "shorthand" employed in referencing court cases.

State Court Decisions

Most state trial court decisions are not published. Except in New York and a few other states that publish selected opinions of their trial courts, decisions from state trial courts are merely filed in the office of the clerk of the court, where the decisions are available for public inspection.

EXHIBIT 17.6
Restatement (Third) of Torts: Products Liability

Reprinted with permission of Thomson/West.

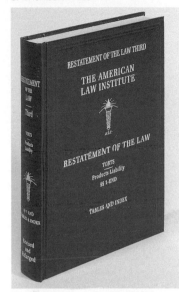

On the Web

You can learn more about the American Law Institute (ALI) and its publications, including information on which *Restatements of the Law* are in the process of being revised, by accessing the ALI's Web site at **http://www.ali.org**.

EXHIBIT 17.7
Index to Legal Periodicals

Reprinted with permission of H.W. Wilson Company.

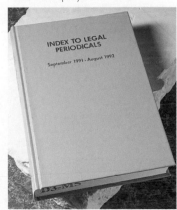

USING SECONDARY SOURCES

When rushing to meet a deadline, you may be tempted to avoid a critical step in the research process—checking primary sources. For example, suppose that a firm's client complains that a publisher of his novels is now publishing the novels online, as e-books. The client wants to know if the online publication constitutes copyright infringement. At issue is whether the publisher, which has the right to publish the printed texts, also has the right to publish the books online. An attorney for the firm asks Sarah, a paralegal, to research case law to see how the courts have dealt with this issue.

Sarah has just finished reading a lengthy, detailed article in a law journal about a similar case that was recently decided by the United States Supreme Court. Sarah rereads the article carefully. Without taking the time to look up and read the case itself, she relies on the author's conclusions in the article. She prepares a memo to the attorney presenting her "research" results. In the memo, she summarizes the background and facts of the case, the issue before the Court, the Court's holding, and the reasoning behind the Court's decision.

Based on Sarah's research conclusions, the attorney advises the client that the publisher had no right to publish the client's works online. The client decides to sue the publisher. During Sarah's more extensive pretrial research, she finds and reads the case itself. Unfortunately for Sarah (and the client and the attorney), the author of the article did not discuss an important qualification made by the Court in its ruling relating to the terms of the publishing contract. It turns out that the Court's decision does not apply to the client's situation, and the case cannot be used as a binding authority after all!

State Reporters

Written decisions of the appellate, or reviewing, courts, however, are published and distributed. The reported appellate decisions are published chronologically in volumes called *reports* or *reporters,* which are numbered consecutively. State appellate court decisions are found in the state reporters of that particular state. The reporters may be either the "official" reporters, designated as such by the state legislature, or "unofficial" reporters, published by West Group. Although some states still have official reporters (and a few states, such as New York and California, have more than one official reporter), many states have eliminated their own official reporters in favor of West's National Reporter System, discussed next.

Regional Reporters

State court opinions also appear in regional units of the National Reporter System, published by West Group. Many lawyers and libraries have the West reporters because they report cases more quickly and are distributed more widely than the state-published reports. Also, the lawyer can look up cases in other neighboring states in the same book (thus saving the cost of buying multiple state-published reports).

Ethics Watch!

AVOIDING PLAGIARISM

Plagiarism—copying the exact, or nearly exact, words of another without acknowledging the author of those words—may constitute a violation of federal copyright law (discussed in Chapter 8). You should realize that it is possible to plagiarize another's words *unintentionally*. Suppose, for example, that you are taking notes from a legal treatise, such as a hornbook on the law of torts, and you copy several paragraphs word for word for your future reference. You don't enclose the paragraphs in quotation marks because you know you will remember that those are not your words but the words of the hornbook's authors. A week or so later, you are preparing a brief and, referring to your notes, you include those paragraphs, assuming that they are your own version of what the authors said in the hornbook. In short, you have plagiarized a substantial portion of another's copyrighted work without even being aware of it. To ensure that your employer will not face a lawsuit for copyright infringement, always remember to include quotation marks (and the exact source of the quoted material) when copying another's words.

The National Reporter System divides the states into the following geographic areas: *Atlantic* (A. or A.2d), *South Eastern* (S.E. or S.E.2d), *North Eastern* (N.E. or N.E.2d), *North Western* (N.W. or N.W.2d), *Pacific* (P., P.2d, or P.3d), *South Western* (S.W., S.W.2d, or S.W.3d), and *Southern* (So. or So.2d). The *2d* and *3d* in the abbreviations refer to *Second Series* and *Third Series,* respectively. The states included in each of these regional divisions are indicated in Exhibit 17.8 on page 646, which illustrates West's National Reporter System. Note that the names of the areas may not be the same as what we commonly think of as a geographical region. For example, the *North Western* reporter does not include the Pacific Northwest but does include states, such as Iowa, that most people do not think of as being in the Northwest.

Citation Format

In order to locate a case, you must know where to look. After an appellate decision has been published, it is normally referred to (cited) by the name of the case, the volume number and the abbreviated name of the book in which the case is located, the page number on which the case begins, and the year. In other words, there are five parts to a standard **citation**:

Case name	Volume number	Name of book	Page number	(Year)

This basic format is used for every citation regardless of whether the case is published in an official state reporter or a regional reporter (or both). When more than one reporter is cited for the same case, each reference is called a **parallel citation** and is separated from the next citation by a comma. The first citation is to the state's official reporter (if there is one), although the text of the court's opinion will be the same (parallel) at any of the listed locations.

citation
In case law, a reference to a case by the name of the case, the volume number and name of the reporter in which the case can be found, the page number on which the case begins, and the year. In statutory and administrative law, a reference to the title number, name, and section of the code in which a statute or regulation can be found.

parallel citation
A second (or third) citation for a given case. When a case is published in more than one reporter, each citation is a parallel citation to the other(s).

E. J. Yera   FEATURED **Guest**

TEN TIPS FOR EFFECTIVE LEGAL RESEARCH

BIOGRAPHICAL NOTE

In 1987, E. J. Yera graduated from the University of Miami School of Law, where he subsequently served as a research instructor until 1989.

After clerking for the U.S. District Court for the Southern District of Florida, Yera served as corporate counsel for Holmes Regional Medical Center in Melbourne, Florida, and its affiliates until 1995. He then became a member of the Health Care Task Force in the Antitrust Division of the U.S. Department of Justice in Washington, D.C.

In 1997, Yera became a member of the U.S. Attorney's Office in the Southern District of Florida. He has taught and lectured in various paralegal programs and has published several articles.

If you perform legal research frequently, you will develop a routine. The purpose of this article is not to give you ironclad rules but to set out ten guidelines that will help you find the routine that is most comfortable for you. You may come back to this article and reread it over time. Now, however, as you read it for the first time, think about how you can use the tips in your future research tasks.

1. Before You Start, Make Sure You Know the Exact Legal Issue You Will Be Researching. You would be surprised at how many students, paralegals, and lawyers research a question for hours only to discover they were not researching the correct legal question. Before you start your research, you should determine the legal question or issue that needs to be researched. You might learn this from reviewing information you already have available, such as a summary of a client interview. If you have an opportunity to ask questions of the attorney giving you a research assignment, do so. What counts, in the end, is coming back with the correct answers, not impressing the attorney by appearing to understand the research task completely when you first

hear about it. It will take you twice as long to finish the assignment if you research the wrong issue or if you are unsure what the issue is.

2. Understand the Language of the Issue. Often, the researcher finds that he or she cannot find the answer because the legal terms used in defining the problem are unfamiliar to him or her. Legal terms, or "terms of art," as they are often called, are as unfamiliar to many people as a foreign language. If you are uncertain about the meaning of any term or phrase, look it up in a law dictionary or encyclopedia to get a general idea of its meaning. Depending on how broad the term is, you may want to read a hornbook on the topic to give you a basic understanding of it. For example, assume you are researching an issue relating to securities law. If you do not have a clear understanding of what securities are, there is no way in the world that you can conduct effective research on the issue. You will need to acquire some background knowledge before you focus on the particular research topic.

3. Be Aware of the Circular Nature of Legal Research and Use It to Your Advantage. Students often ask whether primary or secondary sources should be researched first. The answer is that it does not matter, as long as you always research both types of sources. By researching both primary and secondary sources on a topic, you can be assured that you are almost always double-checking your own work. For example, in a case (primary source of law) on a particular issue, the judge writing the opinion will discuss any pertinent statutes on the issue. Similarly, most annotated versions of a statute (annotations are secondary sources of law) give a listing, following the text of the statute, of cases applying the statute and the context in which the statute was applied. The reason you check both sources is to make sure you have found all of the relevant materials.

4. Until You Submit the Assignment, Always Assume There Are Additional Relevant Materials to Find. You need to keep on your toes until you complete your research task. Always assuming that further relevant materials must be located will help you do this. Of course, there comes a point when you have to assume that you *have* covered the research territory, and knowing when to

To illustrate how to find case law from citations, suppose you want to find the following case: *Marycle, LLC v. First Choice Internet,* 166 Md.App. 481, 890 A.2d 818 (2006). You can see that the opinion in this case can be found in Volume 166 of the official *Maryland Appellate Reports,* on page 481. The parallel citation is to Volume 890 of the *Atlantic Reporter, Second Series,* page 818. In some cases, additional information may appear in stop doing research is perhaps one of the hardest things to learn. Certain legal issues can be researched for months and even years. The intent of this tip, though, is to encourage you not to cut corners when conducting research.

5. Keep a List of What Sources You Have Found and Where They Have Led You. You do not want to spend valuable time wondering if you have already checked certain sources. Therefore, it is important to construct a "road map" of where you have been and where you are going.

6. Take the Time to Become Familiar with the Sources You Are Using. It probably seems obvious that you need to become familiar with your sources, yet this requirement is sometimes overlooked. For example, a case digest (a volume summarizing cases) may indicate on its spine that the digest covers the years "1961 to Date." "To Date," however, does not mean that it is the most current digest; it only means that the digest covers cases up to the date of publication. You should take the time to read the first few pages of the digest to verify its contents. This is true generally for any source you are using—look it over carefully before assuming it contains the sources you need.

7. Be Aware of the Jurisdiction and the Time Frame You Are Researching. If you are researching an issue that will be resolved by a Florida state court, then your emphasis should be on Florida cases. Of course, there are times when no case law is available, and you must then find cases on point from other states to use as persuasive authorities. You must also be aware of the time frame covered by the source you are using (as mentioned in Tip 6). Be aware when researching any area of the law that very often there is either a loose-leaf service or a pamphlet or pocket part (a small booklet that slips into a pocket of the bound volume) containing newer information. Always ask yourself the following question: Where can the most up-to-date material be found? If you don't know, ask a law librarian who does.

> *"What counts, in the end, is coming back with the correct answers . . . ."*

8. Always Refer to *Shepard's* to Make Sure the Cases You Are Using Are Up to Date. *Shepard's Citations* is a set of volumes that helps the researcher of case law in two ways. First, it lists other cases that have cited the cases you have found. This information is helpful because if another case has cited a case you have found, that other case may also be relevant to your issue, and thus you may be able to use it. Also, cases that cite your case are more recent, and using one or more of those cases may thus be advantageous. Second, *Shepard's* tells you, among other things, whether the cases that you have found are still "good law"—that is, whether the cases have been overruled, reversed, or the like. Knowing this information is crucial—because presenting a case to your attorney that no longer represents good law could well be a short cut to the unemployment line.

9. Use Computerized Legal Research Services to Update Your Research Results. Computerized legal databases such as Westlaw and Lexis allow you to update your research results by using online citators. Also, these services allow you to search the available case law for words or phrases. By doing so, you can actually create your own indexing system. Additionally, the Internet is a great source for legal materials. Several state and federal courts, government agencies, law schools, and bar associations have developed Web sites containing different types of primary and secondary legal materials.

10. Twice a Year, Take Three or Four Hours and Browse through Your Local Law Library. You cannot use sources effectively if you do not know that they exist. You should periodically—say, twice a year—spend an afternoon in the law library browsing through the shelves. Read the first few pages of each new source; then make a note of what the source contains. Ask the librarian for new sources in your area. The time you save later will more than compensate for an afternoon's time spent in the library. You will be surprised at how quickly the new sources you discovered or were told about at the law library come to mind when you receive a research assignment, and they may figure significantly in your research.

parentheses at the end of a citation, usually indicating the court that heard the case (if that information is not clear from the citation alone). Exhibit 17.9 on pages 647 through 649 further illustrates how to read case citations.

When conducting legal research, you should write down the citations to the cases or other legal sources that you have consulted, quoted, or want to refer to in a written summary of your

EXHIBIT 17.8
National Reporter System—Regional and Federal

Regional Reporters	Coverage Beginning	Coverage
Atlantic Reporter (A. or A.2d)	1885	Connecticut, Delaware, Maine, Maryland, New Hampshire, New Jersey, Pennsylvania, Rhode Island, Vermont, and District of Columbia.
North Eastern Reporter (N.E. or N.E.2d)	1885	Illinois, Indiana, Massachusetts, New York, and Ohio.
North Western Reporter (N.W. or N.W.2d)	1879	Iowa, Michigan, Minnesota, Nebraska, North Dakota, South Dakota, and Wisconsin.
Pacific Reporter (P., P.2d, or P.3d)	1883	Alaska, Arizona, California, Colorado, Hawaii, Idaho, Kansas, Montana, Nevada, New Mexico, Oklahoma, Oregon, Utah, Washington, and Wyoming.
South Eastern Reporter (S.E. or S.E.2d)	1887	Georgia, North Carolina, South Carolina, Virginia, and West Virginia.
South Western Reporter (S.W., S.W.2d, or S.W.3d)	1886	Arkansas, Kentucky, Missouri, Tennessee, and Texas.
Southern Reporter (So. or So.2d)	1887	Alabama, Florida, Louisiana, and Mississippi.

Federal Reporters		
Federal Reporter (F., F.2d, or F.3d)	1880	U.S. Circuit Court from 1880 to 1912; U.S. Commerce Court from 1911 to 1913; U.S. District Courts from 1880 to 1932; U.S. Court of Claims (now called U.S. Court of Federal Claims) from 1929 to 1932 and since 1960; U.S. Court of Appeals since 1891; U.S. Court of Customs and Patent Appeals since 1929; and U.S. Emergency Court of Appeals since 1943.
Federal Supplement (F.Supp. or F.Supp.2d)	1932	U.S. Court of Claims from 1932 to 1960; U.S. District Courts since 1932; and U.S. Customs Court since 1956.
Federal Rules Decisions (F.R.D.)	1939	U.S. District Courts involving the Federal Rules of Civil Procedure since 1939 and Federal Rules of Criminal Procedure since 1946.
Supreme Court Reporter (S.Ct.)	1882	U.S. Supreme Court since the October term of 1882.
Bankruptcy Reporter (Bankr.)	1980	Bankruptcy decisions of U.S. Bankruptcy Courts, U.S. District Courts, U.S. Courts of Appeals, and U.S. Supreme Court.
Military Justice Reporter (M.J.)	1978	U.S. Court of Military Appeals and Courts of Military Review for the Army, Navy, Air Force, and Coast Guard.

NATIONAL REPORTER SYSTEM MAP

EXHIBIT 17.9
How to Read Citations

From Instructor's Edition (with *Online Legal Research Guide* and *Instructor's Course Planning Guide*) for *West's Business Law*, 10th edition by CLARKSON/JENTZ/CROSS/MILLER. ©2006. Reprinted with permission of South-Western, Cengage Learning. **www.cengage.com/permissions**

State Courts

269 Neb. 82, 690 N.W.2d 778 (2005)[a]

N.W. is the abbreviation for West's publication of state court decisions rendered in the *North Western Reporter* of the National Reporter System. *2d* indicates that this case was included in the *Second Series* of that reporter. The number 690 refers to the volume number of the reporter; the number 778 refers to the first page in that volume on which this case can be found.

Neb. is an abbreviation for *Nebraska Reports,* Nebraska's official reports of the decisions of its highest court, the Nebraska Supreme Court.

125 Cal.App.4th 949, 23 Cal.Rptr.3d 233 (2005)

Cal.Rptr. is the abbreviation for West's unofficial reports—titled *California Reporter*—of the decisions of the California Supreme Court and California appellate courts.

1 N.Y.3d 280, 803 N.E.2d 757, 771 N.Y.S.2d 484 (2003)

N.Y.S. is the abbreviation for West's unofficial reports—titled *New York Supplement*—of the decisions of New York courts.

N.Y. is the abbreviation for *New York Reports,* New York's official reports of the decisions of its court of appeals. The New York Court of Appeals is the state's highest court, analogous to other states' supreme courts. (In New York, a supreme court is a trial court.)

267 Ga.App. 832, 600 S.E.2d 800 (2004)

Ga.App. is the abbreviation for *Georgia Appeals Reports,* Georgia's official reports of the decisions of its court of appeals.

Federal Courts

543 U.S. 447, 125 S.Ct. 847, 160 L.Ed.2d 881 (2005)

L.Ed. is an abbreviation for *Lawyers' Edition of the Supreme Court Reports,* an unofficial edition of decisions of the United States Supreme Court.

S.Ct. is the abbreviation for West's unofficial reports—titled *Supreme Court Reporter*—of decisions of the United States Supreme Court.

U.S. is the abbreviation for *United States Reports,* the official edition of the decisions of the United States Supreme Court.

a. The case names have been deleted from these citations to emphasize the publications. It should be kept in mind, however, that the name of a case is as important as the specific numbers of the volumes in which it is found. If a citation is incorrect, the correct citation may be found in a publication's index of case names. The date of a case is also important because, in addition to providing a check on error in citations, the value of a recent case as an authority is likely to be greater than that of an earlier case.

(Continued)

EXHIBIT 17.9
How to Read Citations—Continued

Federal Courts (continued)

394 F.3d 520 (7th Cir. 2005)

7th Cir. is an abbreviation denoting that this case was decided in the
United States Court of Appeals for the Seventh Circuit.

340 F.Supp.2d 1051 (D.S.D. 2004)

D.S.D. is an abbreviation indicating that the United States District Court
for the District of South Dakota decided this case.

English Courts

9 Exch. 341, 156 Eng.Rep. 145 (1854)

Eng.Rep. is an abbreviation for *English Reports, Full Reprint,* a
series of reports containing selected decisions made in English
courts between 1378 and 1865.

Exch. is an abbreviation for *English Exchequer Reports,* which included the
original reports of cases decided in England's Court of Exchequer.

Statutory and Other Citations

18 U.S.C. Section 1961(1)(A)

U.S.C. denotes *United States Code,* the codification of *United States
Statutes at Large.* The number 18 refers to the statute's U.S.C. title number
and 1961 to its section number within that title. The number 1 refers to a subsection
within the section and the letter A to a subdivision within the subsection.

UCC 2–206(1)(b)

UCC is an abbreviation for *Uniform Commercial Code.* The first number 2 is a
reference to an article of the UCC and 206 to a section within that article.
The number 1 refers to a subsection within the section and the letter b to a
subdivision within the subsection.

Restatement (Second) of Contracts, Section 162

Restatement (Second) of Contracts refers to the second edition of the American
Law Institute's *Restatement of the Law of Contracts.* The number 162 refers to a
specific section.

17 C.F.R. Section 230.505

C.F.R. is an abbreviation for *Code of Federal Regulations,* a compilation of
federal administrative regulations. The number 17 designates the regulation's
title number, and 230.505 designates a specific section within that title.

EXHIBIT 17.9
How to Read Citations—Continued

Westlaw® Citations[b]

2005 WL 27554

WL is an abbreviation for Westlaw. The number 2005 is the year of the document that can be found with this citation in the Westlaw database. The number 27554 is a number assigned to a specific document. A higher number indicates that a document was added to the Westlaw database later in the year.

Uniform Resource Locators (URLs)

http://www.westlaw.com[c]

The suffix *com* is the top level domain (TLD) for this Web site. The TLD *com* is an abbreviation for "commercial," which normally means that a for-profit entity hosts (maintains or supports) this Web site.

westlaw is the host name—the part of the domain name selected by the organization that registered the name. In this case, West Group registered the name. This Internet site is the Westlaw database on the Web.

www is an abbreviation for "World Wide Web." The Web is a system of Internet servers that support documents formatted in *HTML* (hypertext markup language). HTML supports links to text, graphics, and audio and video files.

http://www.uscourts.gov

This is "The Federal Judiciary Home Page." The host is the Administrative Office of the U.S. Courts. The TLD *gov* is an abbreviation for "government." This Web site includes information and links from, and about, the federal courts.

http://www.law.cornell.edu/index.html

This part of a URL points to a Web page or file at a specific location within the host's domain. This page is a menu with links to documents within the domain and to other Internet resources.

This is the host name for a Web site that contains the Internet publications of the Legal Information Institute (LII), which is a part of Cornell Law School. The LII site includes a variety of legal materials and links to other legal resources on the Internet. The TLD *edu* is an abbreviation for "educational institution" (a school or a university).

http://www.ipl.org/ref

ref is an abbreviation for "Internet Public Library Reference Center," which is a map of the topics into which the links at this Web site have been categorized.

ipl is an abbreviation for "Internet Public Library," which is an online service that provides reference resources and links to other information services on the Web. The IPL is supported chiefly by the School of Information at the University of Michigan. The TLD *org* is an abbreviation for "organization" (normally nonprofit).

b. Many court decisions that are not yet published or that are not intended for publication can be accessed through Westlaw, an online legal database.
c. The basic form for a URL is "service://hostname/path." The Internet service for all of the URLs in this text is *http* (hypertext transfer protocol). Most Web browsers will add this prefix automatically when a user enters a host name or a hostname/path.

research results. Several guides have been published on how to cite legal sources. Traditionally, the most widely used guide has been a book entitled *The Bluebook: A Uniform System of Citation,* which is published by the Harvard Law Review Association. This book explains the proper format for citing cases, statutes, constitutions, regulations, and other legal sources. It is a good idea to memorize the basic format for citations to cases and statutory law because these legal sources are frequently cited in legal writing. An increasingly popular guide is a booklet entitled *ALWD Citation Manual: A Professional System of Citation,* which is published by the Association of Legal Writing Directors and Darby Dickerson. One of the ways in which the *ALWD Citation Manual* differs from the *Bluebook* is that the *ALWD Manual* uses the same citation format for law journal articles as it does for articles in other periodicals. Today, many law schools and legal professionals prefer to use the *ALWD Manual,* which is now in its second edition.

Federal Court Decisions

On the Web

To find Supreme Court opinions and opinions issued by the federal appellate courts, as well as information on the federal court system, a good starting point is the official U.S. courts Web site at **http://www.uscourts.gov**.

Court decisions from the U.S. district courts (federal trial courts) are published in West's *Federal Supplement* (F.Supp. or F.Supp.2d), and opinions from the circuit courts of appeals are reported in West's *Federal Reporter* (F., F.2d, or F.3d). These are both unofficial reporters (there are no official reporters for these courts). Both the *Federal Reporter* and the *Federal Supplement* incorporate decisions from specialized federal courts. West also publishes separate reporters, such as its *Bankruptcy Reporter,* that contain decisions in certain specialized fields under federal law.

United States Supreme Court Decisions

Opinions from the United States Supreme Court are published in several reporters, including the *United States Reports,* West's *Supreme Court Reporter,* and the *Lawyers' Edition of the Supreme Court Reports,* each of which we discuss below. A sample citation to a Supreme Court case was also included in Exhibit 17.9 on page 647. This chapter's *Technology and Today's Paralegal* feature explains how you can find information online about new legal developments, including cases pending before the Supreme Court.

The United States Reports

The *United States Reports* (U.S.) is the official edition of all decisions of the United States Supreme Court for which there are written opinions. Published by the federal government, the series includes reports of Supreme Court cases dating from the August term of 1791. Approximately two to four weeks after the Supreme Court issues a decision, the official slip opinion is published by the U.S. Government Printing Office. The **slip opinion** is the first authoritative text of the opinion and is printed as an individual pamphlet. After a number of slip opinions have been issued, the advance sheets of the official *United States Reports* appear. These are issued in pamphlet form to provide a temporary resource until the official bound volume is finally published.

The Supreme Court Reporter

Supreme Court cases are also published in West's *Supreme Court Reporter* (S.Ct.), which is an unofficial edition of Supreme Court opinions dating from the Court's term in October 1882. In this reporter, the case report—the formal court opinion—is preceded by a brief **syllabus** (summary of the case) and headnotes with key numbers (used throughout the West reporters and digests) prepared by West editors.

The Lawyers' Edition of the Supreme Court Reports

The *Lawyers' Edition of the Supreme Court Reports* (L.Ed. or L.Ed.2d), also published by West Group, is an unofficial edition of the entire series of the Supreme Court reports containing many decisions not reported in early official volumes. The advantage offered to the legal

---

slip opinion
A judicial opinion published shortly after the decision is made and not yet included in a case reporter or advance sheets.

syllabus
A brief summary of the holding and legal principles involved in a reported case, which is followed by the court's official opinion.

Technology and Today's Paralegal

LOOKING AHEAD

Every day, it seems, legislatures propose or pass new laws, administrative agencies propose or issue new regulations, and new cases begin to work their way through the court system. A few of these may reach the nation's highest court. As a paralegal, you can perform a valuable service for your supervising attorney by keeping up with new developments in the legal arena or in your specialty area. Online sources can help you in this task.

WHAT NEW FEDERAL STATUTES ARE LIKELY TO BE ENACTED?

You can keep up to date on what bills are pending in Congress by subscribing to national law journals. Law journals such as the *National Law Journal* (a monthly publication) and *Lawyers USA* (issued weekly by Lawyers Weekly, Inc.) discuss new developments in the law, including legislation that is being seriously considered by Congress. To find out more about these two publications, go to their home pages at **http://www.law.com/jsp/nlj** and **http://www.lawyersweekly.com**, respectively. Both sites offer a wealth of information on new statutes, cases, regulations, and other developments of interest to legal professionals, as well as information about how to subscribe. You can get an idea of the coverage of the journals by viewing the most recent issues online at **http://www.law.com/jsp/nlj/thisweek.jsp** and **http://www.lawyersweeklyusa.com**. An advantage of the online publications is that the Web sites offer searchable databases of previously published articles. To search past issues, you need a password, which in turn requires a subscription.

ARE ANY NEW UNIFORM LAWS BEING DEVELOPED?

To find out about new uniform laws being developed by the National Conference of Commissioners on Uniform State Laws (NCCUSL), you can visit its Web site at **http://www.nccusl.org**. There, you will find the full text of all uniform acts, including every draft of the final uniform act. You can also find out which states have already adopted an act and which states have adoption legislation pending. In addition, the site provides comprehensive legislative reports by act or by state so that you can see the status of bills that are being considered by legislatures across the country. The site also includes the text of all in-process drafts and proposed revisions to existing uniform laws. While these drafts are just that—they are not yet law—they may become law in the future once approved by the NCCUSL and submitted to the states for adoption. In the meantime, provisions in these drafts may serve as persuasive authorities.

WHAT CASES ARE ON THE SUPREME COURT DOCKET?

You can find out what cases are pending before the Supreme Court from a number of online sources. For example, at **http://washingtonpost.findlaw.com/supreme_court/docket**, you will find a subject index that tells you if the Supreme Court has heard or is scheduled to hear in the current term any cases that involve a specific area of law. Once you click on the area you are interested in, you will find the case name(s) and docket number(s) of interest. You can then access the Court's decision (if a decision has been reached), the briefs submitted by the parties (and others), the transcripts of oral arguments, and the case history (what the lower courts held, and why). You can also search the Supreme Court's database by docket number or case name and view case information and decisions at **http://www.supremecourtus.gov/docket/docket.html**.

TECHNOLOGY TIP

Paralegals today can readily access information online to stay current on new developments in the law. More difficult is sorting through the wealth of information available. Search for Web sites that will quickly and efficiently provide information that is pertinent to the area of law in which you are interested. After identifying a site as useful, bookmark it and check it regularly.

researcher by the *Lawyers' Edition* is its research tools. In its second series, it precedes each case report with a full summary of the case and discusses in detail selected cases of special interest to the legal profession. Also, the *Lawyers' Edition* is the only reporter of Supreme Court opinions that provides summaries of the briefs presented by counsel.

Unofficial Loose-Leaf Service

United States Law Week, published by the Bureau of National Affairs (BNA), is an unofficial loose-leaf service that publishes decisions rendered by the federal appellate courts and the United States Supreme Court the day after a decision is announced. BNA lawyer-editors select and summarize federal, state, and administrative law cases that establish new precedents, address new statutes, or address current controversies.

ANALYZING CASE LAW

Attorneys often rely heavily on case law to support a given position or argument. One of the difficulties all legal professionals face in analyzing case law is the sheer length and complexity of some court opinions. While certain court opinions may be only two or three pages long, others can occupy hundreds of pages. Understanding the components of a case—that is, the basic format in which cases are presented—can simplify your task of reading and analyzing case law. You will find that over time, as you acquire experience, case analysis becomes easier. This section focuses on how to read and analyze cases, as well as how to summarize, or *brief,* a case.

The Components of a Case

Reported cases contain much more than just the court's decision. Cases have many different parts, and you should understand why each part is there and what information it communicates. To illustrate the various components of a case, we present an annotated sample court case in Exhibit 17.10 starting on the next page. This exhibit shows an actual case that was decided by the U.S. Court of Appeals for the Sixth Circuit in 2005.

Important sections, terms, and phrases in the case are defined or explained in the margins. You will note also that triple asterisks (* * *) and quadruple asterisks (* * * *) frequently appear in the exhibit. The triple asterisks indicate that we have deleted a few words or sentences from the opinion for the sake of readability or brevity. Quadruple asterisks mean that an entire paragraph (or more) has been omitted. Also, when the opinion cites another case or legal source, the citation to the referenced case or source has been omitted to save space and to improve readability.

We discuss below the various components of a case. As you read through the descriptions of these components, refer to Exhibit 17.10, which illustrates most of them. Remember, though, that the excerpt presented in Exhibit 17.10, because it has been pared down for illustration, may be much easier to read than some court opinions that you will encounter.

Case Title

The title of a case indicates the names of the parties to the lawsuit, and the *v.* in the case title stands for *versus,* or "against." In the trial court, the plaintiff's last name appears first, and the second name is the defendant's. If the case is appealed, however, the appellate court will *sometimes* place the name of the party appealing the decision first, so the parties' names

EXHIBIT 17.10
A Sample Court Case

This section contains the case citation—the name of the case, the name of the court that heard the case, the year of the court's decision, and the reporter in which the court's decision can be found.	D.A.B.E., Inc., d/b/a Arnie's Saloon, Plaintiffs-Appellants v. City of Toledo, Defendant-Appellee United States Court of Appeals for the Sixth Circuit, 2005 393 F.3d 692
The *docket number* assigned by the Court of Appeals for the Sixth Circuit.	No. 03-4462
The *syllabus*—a brief summary of the issues and decisions in the case. Prepared by West Group editors.	**Background:** Restaurant and bar owners brought action against city, seeking declaratory judgment that city ordinance restricting smoking in enclosed public places was void and unenforceable, and seeking injunction to prohibit its enforcement. The United States District Court for the Northern District of Ohio, James G. Carr, J[udge], 292 F.Supp.2d 968, denied injunction, and entered judgment in favor of city. Restaurant and bar owners appealed. **Holdings:** The Court of Appeals, Martin, Circuit Judge, held that: (1) owners failed to establish that city ordinance denied them economically viable use of their property, as required to prove that ordinance effected a regulatory taking, and (2) Ohio statute regulating smoking in places of public assembly did not preempt city ordinance.
The U.S. Court of Appeals for the Sixth Circuit concluded that the lower court was correct in its interpretation of the law.	Affirmed.
Names of counsel for the appellants and the appellee.	Richard M. Kerger, Kerger & Kerger, Toledo, Ohio, for Appellants. Keith A. Wilkowski, Vassar, Dills & Dawson, Toledo, Ohio, for Appellee.

(Continued)

EXHIBIT 17.10
A Sample Court Case—Continued

This line gives the name of the judge who authored the opinion of the court.	BOYCE F. MARTIN, JR., Circuit Judge.

* * * *

I.

The court divides the opinion into three parts, headed by Roman numerals. The first part of the opinion summarizes the factual background of the case.	

The City of Toledo has regulated smoking in public places since 1987 * * *. In early 2003, the City Council * * * enacted a new Clean Indoor Air Ordinance, No. 509-03.

Ordinance No. 509-03 regulates the ability to smoke in public places, such as retail stores, theaters, courtrooms, libraries, museums, health-care facilities, and—most relevant to the **instant** case—restaurants and bars. In enclosed public places,

Present or current.	

smoking is generally prohibited except in a "separate smoking lounge" that is designated for the exclusive purpose of smoking * * *.

* * * *

* * * Appellants * * * [challenge] the ordinance on two grounds: first, that it constitutes a * * * taking of their property in violation of the Fifth [Amendment to the U.S. Constitution] * * *; and second, that it is **preempted**

Prevented from taking effect.	

by Section 3791.031 of the Ohio Revised Code, a state law that regulates smoking in places of public assembly but that does not apply to restaurants, bowling alleys, and bars.

* * * *

The second major section of the opinion sets out and applies the law to the plaintiffs' arguments.	**II.**

* * * *

The first part of this section addresses the claim that the ordinance is a taking of the plaintiffs' property.	**A.** * * * **Taking Claim**

The * * * Fifth Amendment * * * provides that private property shall not "be taken for public use, without just compensation." * * * [A] statute regulating the uses that can be made of property effects a taking if it denies an owner

Financially sustainable; capable of working, functioning, or developing adequately.	**economically viable** use of his land. * * *

The words of a writing in their apparent or obvious meaning.	The evidence presented in this case fails to establish that, **on its face**, the Clean Indoor Air Ordinance denies appellants economically viable use of their respective properties. Appellants have submitted affidavits alleging that they have lost—or fear they will lose—customers as a result of the ordinance, because smoking is an

EXHIBIT 17.10
A Sample Court Case—Continued

activity in which many customers wish to engage while patronizing their establishments. * * *

 * * * First, there is nothing on the face of the Clean Indoor Air Ordinance that prevents the beneficial use of appellants' property. To the contrary, the ordinance has absolutely no effect on any aspect of appellants' businesses other than to restrict the areas in which appellants' patrons may smoke. Second, the ordinance does not

> **Absolutely, unqualifiedly.**

categorically prohibit smoking inside appellants' establishments; it merely regulates the conditions under which smoking is permitted. We recognize that the construction of separate smoking lounges in most cases will require some financial investment, but an ordinance does not effect a taking merely because compliance with it requires the expenditure of money. Finally, for obvious reasons, the ordinance does not purport to regulate alternative uses of appellants' respective properties. Therefore, * * * it is clear that appellants have failed to establish that the Clean Indoor Air Ordinance, on its face, effects a * * * taking of their property.

> **The second part of this section addresses the assertion that the city ordinance is void because a state statute already covers the subject and thus takes precedence.**

B. Preemption Claim

 Appellants' second argument is that the Clean Indoor Air Ordinance conflicts with—and, therefore, is preempted by—Section 3791.031(A) of the Ohio Revised Code.

 A state statute takes precedence over a local ordinance when * * * the ordinance is in conflict with the statute * * *.

 * * * [T]he test is whether the ordinance permits or licenses that which the statute forbids or prohibits, and vice versa. To the extent that the statute does not address or apply to an item or issue, however, an ordinance regulating the excluded item or issue does not conflict with the statute, even if it deals with the same general subject matter. * * *

 In this case, Section 3791.031 of the Ohio Revised Code regulates indoor smoking throughout the State of Ohio within "places of public assembly." It explicitly provides, however, that "[r]estaurants, food service establishments, dining rooms, cafes, cafeterias, or other rooms used primarily for the service of food, as well as bowling alleys and places licensed by the division of liquor control

(Continued)

EXHIBIT 17.10
A Sample Court Case—Continued

to sell intoxicating beverages for consumption on the premises, are not places of public assembly." * * *

Appellants argue that because smoking is allowed in their establishments under state law but not under the ordinance, there is a conflict that renders the ordinance preempted by state law. The City argues, by contrast, that the statute "simply does not regulate the establishments" that are subject to the ordinance and, therefore, municipalities within the State of Ohio are free to regulate smoking within these establishments * * *.

* * * [B]y stating that certain types of establishments—such as restaurants, bars, bowling alleys, etc.—"are not places of public assembly," the legislature indicated not that these establishments were immune to smoking-related regulation, but that they simply did not fall within the * * * statute.

Our independent research reveals that other courts that have considered whether smoking-related ordinances are preempted by state law have reached similar conclusions. * * * The [statute] prohibits smoking in certain locations; it does not contain the slightest hint that the legislature intended to create a positive right to smoke in all public places where it did not expressly forbid smoking. Nothing in the [statute] is inconsistent with a

> A government body with the authority to act within a certain geographic area.

local jurisdiction's decision to impose greater limits on public smoking. * * *

* * * *

> In the third major section of this opinion, the court states its decision and gives its order.

III.

For these reasons, the district court's judgment is AFFIRMED.

---

may be reversed. Because some appellate courts retain the trial court order of names, it is often impossible to distinguish the plaintiff from the defendant in the title of a reported appellate court decision. You must therefore carefully read the facts of each case to identify the parties.

Case Citation

Typically, the citation to the case is found just above or just below the case title (and often at the tops of consecutive printed or online pages). If the citation appears on Westlaw and one of the parallel citations is not yet available, the citation may include underlined spaces for the volume and page numbers to be filled in once they become available (such as "___ U.S. ___").

Docket Number

The docket number immediately follows the case title. Recall from Chapter 13 that a docket number is assigned by the court clerk when a case is initially filed. The number serves as an identifier for all papers submitted in connection with the case. A case published in a reporter should not be cited by its docket number, but the docket number may serve as a valuable tool in obtaining background information on the case. Cases appearing in slip-opinion form (cases that have been decided but not yet published in a reporter) are usually identified, filed, and cited by docket number. After publication of the decision, the docket number may continue to serve as an identifier for appellate records and briefs (appellate briefs will be discussed in Chapter 19).

Dates Argued and Decided

An important component of a case is the date on which it was decided by the court. Usually, the date of the decision immediately follows the docket number. In addition to the date of the court's decision on the matter, the date on which the case was argued before the court (in appellate court cases) may also be included here.

Syllabus

Following the docket number is the *syllabus*—a brief synopsis of the facts of the case, the issues analyzed by the court, and the court's conclusion. In official reporters, the courts usually prepare the syllabi; in unofficial reporters, the publishers of the reporters usually prepare them. The syllabus is often a helpful research tool. It provides a clear overview of the case and points out various legal issues discussed by the court. But always keep in mind that reading the syllabus is not a substitute for reading the case.

Headnotes

Often, unofficial reporters, such as those published by West Group, make extensive use of case *headnotes*. As discussed earlier, headnotes are short paragraphs that serve to highlight and summarize specific rules of law mentioned in the case. In reporters published by West Group, they are correlated to the comprehensive West key-number system. In Exhibit 17.10, the headnotes were deleted for reasons of space.

Names of Counsel

The published report of the case usually contains the names of the lawyers (counsel) representing the parties. The attorneys' names are typically found just following the syllabus (and headnotes, if any).

Name of Judge or Justice Authoring the Opinion

The name of the judge or justice who authored the opinion in the case will also be included in the published report of the case, just before the court's opinion. In some cases, instead of the name of a judge or justice, the decision will be authored *per curiam* (Latin for "by the court"), which means that the opinion is that of the whole court and not the opinion of any one judge or justice. Sometimes the phrase is used to indicate that the chief justice or presiding judge wrote the opinion. The phrase also may be used for an announcement of a court's disposition of a case that is not accompanied by a written opinion.

Opinion

As you may have noted in previous chapters, the term *opinion* is often used loosely to refer to a court case or decision. In fact, the term has a precise meaning. The formal opinion of the court contains the analysis and decision of the judge or judges who heard and decided the case. Most opinions contain a brief statement of the facts of the case, a summary of the legal issues raised by the facts, and the remedies sought by the parties. In appellate court cases, the court summarizes the errors of the lower court, if any, and the impact of these errors on the case's outcome. The main body of the court's opinion is the application of the law to the particular facts. The court often mentions case precedents, relevant statutes, and administrative rules and regulations to support its reasoning. Additionally, court opinions often contain discussions of policy and other factors that clarify the underlying reason for the court's decision.

When all of the judges unanimously agree in their legal reasoning and their decision, the opinion is deemed a *unanimous* opinion. When the opinion is not unanimous, a *majority* opinion is written, outlining the views of the majority of the judges deciding the case. If a judge agrees, or concurs, with the majority's decision, but for different reasons, that judge may write a *concurring opinion*. A *dissenting opinion* presents the views of one or more judges who disagree with the majority's decision. The dissenting opinion is important because it may form the basis of the arguments used years later in overruling the precedential majority opinion.

The Court's Conclusion

In the opinion, the judges indicate their conclusion, or decision, on the issue or issues before the court. If several issues are involved, as often happens, there may be a conclusion at the end of the discussion of each issue. Often, at the end of the opinion, the conclusions presented within the opinion are briefly reiterated and summarized. If no conclusions have yet been presented, they are presented in the concluding section of the opinion.

An appellate court also specifies what the *disposition* of a case should be. If the appellate court agrees with a lower court's decision, it will *affirm* that decision, which means that the decision of the lower court remains unchanged. If the appellate court concludes that the lower court erred in its interpretation of the law, the court may *reverse* the lower court's ruling. Sometimes, if an appellate court concludes that further factual findings are necessary or that a case should be retried and a decision made that is consistent with the appellate court's conclusions of law, the appellate court will *remand* the case to the lower court for further proceedings consistent with its opinion. In the sample case presented in Exhibit 17.10 on pages 654 through 656, the U.S. Court of Appeals for the Sixth Circuit affirmed the lower court's decision.

Analyzing Cases

When you are researching case law, your main focus should be on the opinion—the words of the court itself. You will inevitably find that some opinions are easier to understand than others. Some judges write more clearly and logically than others do. You may need to reread a case (or a portion of a case) to understand what is being said, why it is being said at that point in the case, and what the judge's underlying legal reasoning is. Some cases contain several pages describing facts and issues of previous cases and how those cases relate to the one being decided by the court. You might want to reread these discussions several times to distinguish between comments made in the previous case and comments that are being made about the case at bar (before the court).

Look for Guideposts in the Opinion

Often, the judge writing the opinion provides some guideposts, perhaps by indicating sections and subsections within the opinion by numbers, letters, or subtitles. Note that in Exhibit 17.10, Roman numerals are used to divide the opinion into basic sections. Scanning through the opinion for these types of indicators can help orient you to the opinion's format.

In cases that involve dissenting or concurring opinions, you need to make sure that you identify these opinions so that you do not mistake one of them for the majority opinion. Generally, you should scan through the case a time or two to identify its various components and sections and then read the case (or sections of the case) until you understand the facts and procedural history of the case, the issues involved, the applicable law, the legal reasoning of the court, and how the reasoning leads to the court's conclusion on the issue or issues.

Distinguish the Court's Holding from Dicta

In reading and analyzing cases, you should also be able to determine which statements of the court are legally binding and which are not. Only the **holding** (the legal principle to be drawn from the court's decision) is binding. Other views expressed in the opinion are referred to as *dicta* and are not binding in subsequent cases. *Dicta* is the plural of *dictum*. As used here, *dictum* is an abbreviated form of the Latin term *obiter dictum*, which means "a remark by the way." *Dicta* are any statements made by a judge that go beyond the facts of the case or that do not directly relate to the facts of the case or to the resolution of the issue being addressed. *Dicta* include comments used by the court to illustrate an example and statements concerning a rule of law that is not essential to the case at hand. You can probably assume that statements are *dicta* if they begin with "If the facts were different" or "If the plaintiff had . . ." or some other "if/then" phrase.

> **holding**
> The binding legal principle, or precedent, that is drawn from the court's decision in a case.

> **dicta**
> A Latin term referring to nonbinding (nonprecedential) judicial statements that are not directly related to the facts or issues presented in the case and thus not essential to the holding.

Summarizing and Briefing Cases

After you have read and analyzed a case, you may decide that it is on point and that you want to include a reference to it in your research findings. If so, you will want to summarize in your notes the important facts and issues in the case, as well as the court's decision, or holding, and the reasoning used by the court. This is called **briefing a case**.

There is a fairly standard procedure that you can follow when you brief any court case. You must first read the case opinion carefully. When you feel you understand the case, you can begin to prepare the brief. Typically, a brief presents the essentials of the case under headings such as those listed below. Many researchers conclude their briefs with an additional section in which they note their own comments or conclusions about the case.

> **briefing a case**
> Summarizing a case. A typical case brief will indicate the full citation for the case, the factual background and procedural history of the case, the issue or issues raised in the case, the court's decision, the court's holding, and the legal reasoning on which the court based its decision. The brief may also include conclusions or notes concerning the case made by the one briefing it.

1. **Citation.** Give the full citation for the case, including the name of the case, the date it was decided, and the court that decided it.

2. **Facts.** Briefly indicate (a) the reasons for the lawsuit (who did what to whom) and (b) the identity and arguments of the plaintiff(s) and defendant(s).

3. **Procedure.** Indicate the procedural history of the case in a sentence or two. What was the lower court's decision? What did the appellate court do (affirm, reverse, remand)? How did the matter arrive before the present court?

4. **Issue.** Concisely phrase, in the form of a question, the essential issue before the court. (If more than one issue is involved, you may have two—or even more—questions here.)

5. **Decision.** Indicate here—with a "yes" or "no," if possible—the court's answer to the question (or questions) that you noted in the *Issue* section.

6. **Reasoning.** Summarize as briefly as possible the reasons given by the court for its decision (or decisions) and the case or statutory law relied on by the court in arriving at its decision.

7. **Holding.** Succinctly state the rule of law for which the case stands.

Exhibit 17.11 presents a briefed version of the sample court case presented in Exhibit 17.10 to illustrate the typical format used in briefing cases.

RESEARCHING STATUTORY LAW

Up to this point in our discussion of primary sources of law, we have been discussing case law, which is sometimes referred to as *judge-made* law because it is made by the judges and justices of the American court system. Judge-made law is also known as the common law, as explained in Chapter 5. Another primary source of law is *statutory law*—the statutes and ordinances enacted by legislative bodies, such as the U.S. Congress, state legislatures, and town governments.

Some statutes serve to supplement the common law, while other statutes replace it. Legislative bodies have broad power in establishing law, and if a common law principle conflicts with a statutory provision, the statute will normally take precedence. Additionally, a legislature may create statutes that deal with areas, such as age discrimination, that are not covered by the common law.

Statutes are codified and published in compilations referred to as **codes**, which arrange materials by topic. Most statutory codes are updated through the issuance of supplemental pocket parts or by loose-leaf services. Paralegals conducting research on statutory law should begin by reviewing the index for the relevant statutory code.

> **code**
> A systematic and topically organized presentation of laws, rules, or regulations.

Federal Statutes

On the Web

You can access and search (by title and section number) the *United States Code* online at **http://www.law. cornell.edu/uscode**.

Federal statutes are contained in the *United States Code,* or U.S.C. This official compilation of federal statutes is published by the U.S. government every six years and is updated annually. The U.S.C. is divided into fifty topic classifications. As shown in Exhibit 17.12 on page 662, each of these topics, called *titles,* carries a descriptive name and a number. For example, laws relating to commerce and trade are collected in Title 15. Laws concerning the courts and judicial procedures are collected in Title 28. Titles are subdivided into chapters (sections) and subchapters. A citation to the U.S.C. includes title and section numbers. Thus, a reference to "28 U.S.C. Section 1346" means that the statute can be found in Section 1346 of Title 28. "Section" may also be designated by the symbol §, and "Sections" by §§.

Statutes are listed in the U.S.C. by their official names. Many legislative bills enacted into law are commonly known by a popular name, however. Some have descriptive titles reflecting their purpose; others are named after their sponsors. Sometimes a researcher may know the popular name of a legislative act but not its official name. In this situation, the researcher can consult the U.S.C. volume entitled *Popular Name Table,* which lists statutes by their popular names. For example, suppose you have learned that the Landrum-Griffin Act governs an issue that you are researching. You know that this is the popular name for the act, not the official name. You can consult the *Popular Name Table* to find the act's official title, which is the Labor-Management Reporting and Disclosure Act of 1959.

There are also two unofficial versions of the federal code, each of which contains additional information that can be helpful to researchers. West's *United States Code Annotated* (*U.S.C.A.)* contains the full text of the U.S.C., the U.S. Constitution, the Federal Rules of

EXHIBIT 17.11
**A Briefed Version of
the Sample Court Case**

D.A.B.E., INC. v. CITY OF TOLEDO

393 F.3d 692 (6th Cir. 2005).

FACTS The city of Toledo, Ohio, has regulated smoking in public places since 1987. In 2003, Toledo's city council enacted a new Clean Indoor Air Ordinance. The ordinance restricts the ability to smoke in public places—stores, theaters, courtrooms, libraries, museums, health-care facilities, restaurants, and bars. In enclosed public places, smoking is generally prohibited except in a "separate smoking lounge" that is designated for this purpose.

PROCEDURE D.A.B.E., Inc. (the plaintiffs), a group consisting of owners of bars, restaurants, and bowling alleys, filed a suit in a federal district court, claiming that the ordinance constituted a taking of their property in violation of the Fifth Amendment to the U.S. Constitution. The plaintiffs also argued that the ordinance was preempted by a state statute that regulated smoking "in places of public assembly," excluding restaurants, bowling alleys, and bars. The court ruled in favor of the city. The plaintiffs appealed to the U.S. Court of Appeals for the Sixth Circuit.

ISSUES (1) Does the ordinance deny the plaintiffs "economically viable use of their property," as required to prove a taking? (2) Does the state indoor smoking statute preempt the city ordinance?

DECISION (1) No. (2) No. The U.S. Court of Appeals for the Sixth Circuit affirmed the lower court's ruling, denying the injunction and holding in favor of the defendants.

REASONING The Fifth Amendment provides that private property shall not "be taken for public use, without just compensation." A taking occurs when an ordinance denies an owner economically viable use of his or her property. In this case, the plaintiffs alleged that they had lost customers because of the ordinance. The court reasoned that the ordinance's only effect on the plaintiffs' businesses was to restrict the areas in which customers could smoke and the conditions under which smoking was permitted. This might "require some financial investment, but an ordinance does not effect a taking merely because compliance with it requires the expenditure of money." Besides, the owners could elect to make other uses of their property. As for the preemption issue, a state statute takes precedence over a local ordinance when they conflict. In this case, a statute prohibits smoking in certain locations, but "it does not contain the slightest hint that the legislature intended to create a positive right to smoke in all public places where it did not expressly forbid smoking. Nothing in the [statute] is inconsistent with a local jurisdiction's decision to impose greater limits on public smoking."

HOLDING The ordinance did not prevent the plaintiffs from using their property in an economically productive way, because it did not categorically prohibit smoking but only regulated it. The state indoor smoking statute did not cover the excluded businesses, and the legislature did not indicate an intent to bar a city from restricting smoking in those places.

Evidence, and various other rules, including the Rules of Civil Procedure and the Rules of Criminal Procedure. This useful set of approximately two hundred volumes includes historical notes relating to the text of each statute, along with any amendments to the act. Annotations offer additional research assistance by listing cases that have analyzed, discussed, or interpreted the particular statute. The other unofficial version of the code is the *United States Code Service* (U.S.C.S.), also published by West Group. The U.S.C.S. and

EXHIBIT 17.12
Titles in the *United States Code*

TITLES OF UNITED STATES CODE

*1. General Provisions.	27. Intoxicating Liquors.
2. The Congress.	*28. Judiciary and Judicial Procedure; and Appendix.
*3. The President.	
*4. Flag and Seal, Seat of Government, and the States.	29. Labor.
	30. Mineral Lands and Mining.
*5. Government Organization and Employees; and Appendix.	*31. Money and Finance.
†6. [Surety Bonds.]	*32. National Guard.
7. Agriculture.	33. Navigation and Navigable Waters.
8. Aliens and Nationality.	‡34. [Navy.]
*9. Arbitration.	*35. Patents.
*10. Armed Forces; and Appendix.	36. Patriotic Societies and Observances.
*11. Bankruptcy; and Appendix.	*37. Pay and Allowances of the Uniformed Services.
12. Banks and Banking.	
*13. Census.	*38. Veterans' Benefits.
*14. Coast Guard.	*39. Postal Service.
15. Commerce and Trade.	40. Public Buildings, Property, and Works.
16. Conservation.	41. Public Contracts.
*17. Copyrights.	42. The Public Health and Welfare.
*18. Crimes and Criminal Procedure; and Appendix.	43. Public Lands.
	*44. Public Printing and Documents.
19. Customs Duties.	45. Railroads.
20. Education.	*46. Shipping; and Appendix.
21. Food and Drugs.	47. Telegraphs, Telephones, and Radiotelegraphs.
22. Foreign Relations and Intercourse.	
*23. Highways.	48. Territories and Insular Possessions.
24. Hospitals and Asylums.	*49. Transportation; and Appendix.
25. Indians.	50. War and National Defense; and Appendix.
26. Internal Revenue Code.	

*This title has been enacted as law. However, any Appendix to this title has not been enacted as law.
†This title was enacted as law and has been repealed by the enactment of Title 31.
‡This title has been eliminated by the enactment of Title 10.

Page III

the U.S.C.A. are distinguishable by the research tools they provide. For example, the U.S.C.S. contains references and citations to some sources, such as legal periodicals and the legal encyclopedia *American Jurisprudence,* that are not included in the U.S.C.A.

State Statutes

State codes follow the U.S.C. pattern of arranging statutes by subject. They may be called codes, revisions, compilations, consolidations, general statutes, or statutes, depending on the preference of the states. In some codes, subjects are designated by number. In others, they are designated by name. For example, "13 Pennsylvania Consolidated Statutes Section 1101" means that the statute can be found in Section 1101 of Title 13 of the Pennsylvania code. "California Commercial Code Section 1101" means that the statute can be found in Section 1101 under the heading "Commercial" in the California Code. Abbreviations may

Developing Paralegal Skills

RESEARCHING THE U.S.C.A.

Natalie Martin has completed her factual analysis of the case involving David Berriman (see the *Developing Paralegal Skills* feature entitled "Defining the Issues to Be Researched" on page 631) and begins her research. The issue she is researching is whether the government, which arrested David for the transportation and distribution of cocaine, had the authority to confiscate David's car and cell phone. Natalie's supervising attorney has told her to start her research by going to the *United States Code Annotated* (U.S.C.A.) to find the relevant federal statutes.

CHECKLIST FOR RESEARCHING THE U.S.C.A.

* Start with general index volumes unless you know the U.S.C.A. title (topic) number or a popular name.
* If you know the specific title number, begin in the title index. If you know the popular name of a statute, begin in the *Popular Name* Table.
* Look up topics, either by factual categories or legal categories, in the index. Here, the topic could be "drugs."
* Look up subtopics within topics. Here, "forfeiture" and "property" could be subtopics under "drugs."
* Write down the citations to the U.S.C.A. volumes containing the topics.
* Look up the citations in those volumes.
* Read the relevant sections of the statute to determine if they apply to the research.
* Check to see if there are any amendments to the statute and determine if they apply to the research.
* Check the annotations following the statute sections for case law in which the statute has been applied and interpreted.
* Review any cases that appear relevant.
* Use an online citator, such as Westlaw's KeyCite, to check both statutes and cases to make sure that they are still "good law." (Online citators will be discussed briefly at the end of this chapter and in more detail in Chapter 18.)

be used. For example, "13 Pennsylvania Consolidated Statutes Section 1101" may be abbreviated to "13 Pa.C.S. § 1101," and "California Commercial Code Section 1101" may be abbreviated to "Cal. Com. Code § 1101."

In many states, official codes are supplemented by annotated codes published by private publishers. Annotated codes follow the numbering scheme set forth in the official state code but provide outlines and indexes to assist in locating information. These codes also provide references to case law, legislative history sources, and other documents in which the statute has been considered or discussed.

ANALYZING STATUTORY LAW

Because of the tremendous growth in statutory and regulatory law in the last century, the legal issues dealt with by attorneys are frequently governed by statutes and administrative agency regulations. Paralegals must understand how to interpret and analyze this body of law. Although we use the terms *statute* and *statutory law* in this section, the following discussion applies equally well to the regulations issued by administrative agencies.

Developing Paralegal Skills

READING STATUTORY LAW

Karen Wickson, a paralegal, has been asked to research a statute for an attorney in her firm. The attorney's client was fired from her job as a receptionist in a small medical practice because she suffered from carpal tunnel syndrome. Because of this syndrome, she could not use the computer for extended time periods without incurring severe wrist pain. The client asked the employer to accommodate her disability by letting her work as a nursing assistant in the office, a job that did not require much work at the computer. The employer refused her request. The attorney wants Karen to research the Americans with Disabilities Act (ADA) of 1990 to find out if the client's injury is covered under that act. Under the ADA, an employer may not fire an employee with disabilities if the employer can "reasonably accommodate" the employee's needs.

Karen knows that her research will eventually involve not only a careful scrutiny of the statute but also some research into case law to learn how the courts have interpreted and applied the statute. Today, though, she focuses solely on the statute's provisions. First, she locates the statute and scans through it, identifying the various sections and subsections of the act. She knows that statutes frequently contain several levels of subsections, and at times she finds it helpful to diagram the structure of the statute to discern the interrelationship of the various sections.

Next, Karen carefully reads the definitions section in the statute to learn how the ADA defines the terms *disability* and *reasonable accommodation*. These definitions are important to the decision of whether the client will have a cause of action under the act. Then she reads the section indicating who is covered by the act. Karen learns that the ADA extends its protections to employees in all private-sector workplaces with fifteen or more workers. She makes a note to find out from the client how many employees there are in the client's workplace.

Finally, Karen checks the date on which the statute went into effect. This is important because the effective date of a statute may be a year or two later than the date on which the statute was enacted into law. The ADA of 1990, for example, did not take effect until 1992.

TIPS FOR READING STATUTORY LAW

- Scan through the statute to identify the basic sections and subsections of the law, diagramming the relationships between these parts if necessary.

- Read carefully the statute's definitions of terms and phrases that are important to the application of the statute.

- Determine the coverage of the statute—that is, who is protected or what actions are regulated by the act.

- Make a note of the act's effective date.

If a statute applies to the legal issues in your case, you must understand the statute thoroughly before evaluating how it does or does not apply to the issue that you are researching. The first step in statutory analysis is therefore to read the language of the statute very carefully.

As with court cases, some statutes are more difficult to read than others. Some are extremely wordy or lengthy or difficult to understand for some other reason. By carefully reading and rereading a statute, however, you can usually determine the reasons for the statute's enactment, the date on which the statute became effective, the class of people to which the statute applies, the kind of conduct being regulated by the statute, and the circumstances in which that conduct is prohibited, required, or permitted. You can also learn whether the statute allows for any exceptions and, if so, in what circumstances.

The second step in statutory analysis is to interpret the meaning of the statute. Generally, when trying to understand the meaning of statutes, you should do as the courts do. We therefore now look at some of the typical techniques used by courts when they are faced with the task of interpreting the meaning of a given statute or statutory provision.

Rules of Construction

Certain statutory rules of interpretation, called **rules of construction**, may prove helpful in your analysis of the statute's language and intent. Examples of statutory rules of interpretation used in many jurisdictions are the following:

- Specific provisions are given greater weight than general provisions when there is a conflict between the two.
- Recent provisions are given greater weight than earlier provisions when there is a conflict between the two.
- Masculine pronouns refer to both males and females.
- Singular nouns also include the plural forms of the nouns.

rules of construction
The rules that control the judicial interpretation of statutes.

The Plain Meaning Rule

In interpreting statutory language, courts also apply the **plain meaning rule**. Under this rule, the words chosen by the legislature must be understood according to their common meanings. If the statute is clear and unambiguous *on its face* (in its apparent and obvious meaning), and therefore capable of only one interpretation, that interpretation must be given to it. No additional inquiries, such as inquiries into legislative intent or history, are permitted when the meaning of the statute is clear on its face.

The plain meaning rule, although seemingly simple, is usually not so simple to apply. For one thing, the plain meaning of a statute is rarely totally clear, because legal language, especially in statutes, is difficult to understand and often inherently ambiguous. Also, each word or phrase in a statute takes on meaning only in context—as it relates to the surrounding text. Thus, the interpretation of the meaning of a statutory word, phrase, or provision remains ultimately subjective.

Furthermore, laws, by their very nature, cannot be too specific. When enacting a statute, the legislators often state a broad principle of law and then leave it up to the courts to apply this principle to specific circumstances—which vary from case to case. In interpreting a particular provision, you may therefore need to research case law to see how the courts have interpreted the provision or study the legislative history of the act to understand the legislators' intent in wording the provision in a particular way.

plain meaning rule
A rule of statutory interpretation. If the meaning of a statute is clear on its face, then that is the interpretation the court will give to it; inquiry into the legislative history of the statute will not be undertaken.

Previous Judicial Interpretation

Paralegals often find that researching statutory law also involves researching case law—to see how the courts have interpreted and applied statutory provisions. As discussed, courts are obligated to follow the precedents set by higher courts in their jurisdictions. A statutory interpretation made by a higher court therefore must be accepted as binding by lower courts in the same jurisdiction. You can find citations to court cases relating to specific statutes by referring to annotated versions of state or federal statutory codes.

Legislative Intent

Another common technique employed in statutory interpretation is learning the intent of the legislature. A court relying on this method determines the meaning of the statute by attempting to find out why the legislators chose to phrase the statute in the particular language they used or, more generally, what the legislators sought to accomplish by enacting the statute. To discern the intent of the legislators who drafted a particular law, it is often necessary to investigate the legislative history of the statute. This can be done by researching such sources as committee reports and records of congressional hearings and other proceedings.

Before you can study these sources, of course, you need to know how to find them. The easiest way to locate them is to refer to the unofficial, annotated versions of the federal code, such as the U.S.C.A. and the U.S.C.S. These codes often contain information regarding the legislative history of a statute. For example, the statute's date of passage is included in these annotated codes, as are cross-references to sources that will provide you with more detailed information on a statute's legislative history. Each source that you discover will likely lead you to other useful sources.

Committee Reports

Committee reports provide the most important source of legislative history. Congressional committees produce reports for each bill, and these reports often contain the full text of the bill, a description of its purpose, and the committee's recommendations. Several tables are also included to set out dates for certain actions. The dates can help the researcher locate floor debates and committee testimony in the *Congressional Record* (described below) and various other publications. Committee reports are published according to a numerical series and are available through the U.S. Government Printing Office.

The Congressional Record

The *Congressional Record*, which is published daily while Congress is in session, contains *verbatim* (word-for-word) transcripts of congressional debates and proceedings. The transcripts include remarks made by various members of Congress, proposed amendments, votes, and occasionally the text of the bill under discussion.

Legislative hearings, another important source of legislative research, can be found in the transcripts of testimony before the House and Senate committees considering the proposed legislation. The purpose of conducting hearings is to determine if such legislation is needed. As a result, many types of testimony are presented. The researcher may find some helpful testimony in these sources, yet it is important to remember that much of it may be biased because of the interested positions of the parties presenting the information. Hearings may be informative but are not as authoritative as committee reports in determining legislative intent.

Other Sources of Legislative History

The two tools most frequently used in conducting research on legislative history are the *United States Code Congressional and Administrative News* (U.S.C.C.A.N.) and the *Congressional Information Service* (C.I.S.). The U.S.C.C.A.N., a West publication, contains reprints of statutes and sections describing the statutes' legislative history, including committee reports. Statutes in the U.S.C.A. are followed by notations directing the researcher to the corresponding legislative history in the U.S.C.C.A.N. The C.I.S., a U.S. government publication, contains information from committee reports, hearing reports, documents from both houses, and special publications. Both the C.I.S. and the U.S.C.C.A.N. provide a system of indexing and abstracting that allows quick access to information.

RESEARCHING ADMINISTRATIVE LAW

Administrative rules and regulations constitute a growing source of American law. As discussed in Chapter 5, Congress frequently delegates authority to administrative agencies through enabling legislation. For example, in 1914 Congress passed the Federal Trade

Commission Act, which established the Federal Trade Commission, or FTC. The act gave the FTC the authority to issue and enforce rules and regulations relating to unfair trade practices in the United States. Other federal administrative agencies include the Occupational Safety and Health Administration, the Consumer Product Safety Commission, and the Securities and Exchange Commission. The orders, regulations, and decisions of such agencies are legally binding and, as such, are primary sources of law.

The *Code of Federal Regulations*

The *Code of Federal Regulations* (C.F.R.) is a government publication containing all federal administrative agency regulations (see Exhibit 17.13). The regulations are compiled from the *Federal Register,* a daily government publication consisting of executive orders and administrative regulations, in which administrative regulations are first published. (See Chapter 5 for a discussion of administrative rulemaking procedure.)

The C.F.R. uses the same titles as the *United States Code* (shown previously in Exhibit 17.12 on page 662). This subject-matter organization allows the researcher to determine the section in the C.F.R. in which a regulation will appear. Each title of the C.F.R. is divided into chapters, subchapters, parts, and sections.

The C.F.R. is revised and republished four times a year. Recent regulations appear in the *Federal Register* until they are incorporated into the C.F.R. If, as a paralegal, you are searching for administrative regulations in the C.F.R., you should begin with the index section of the *Index and Finding Aids* volume. This index will allow you to locate the relevant title and the section of the C.F.R. that pertains to the problem. The next step is locating the regulation in the most recent volume of that title in the C.F.R. You should also review the *List of C.F.R. Sections Affected,* issued in monthly pamphlets, to determine if any changes have been made to the section since the last revision.

Finding Tools for Administrative Law

The *Congressional Information Service* (C.I.S.) also provides an index to the C.F.R. The C.I.S. index is helpful in locating C.F.R. regulations by subject matter and also in determining the geographical areas affected by the regulation. The *American Digest System,* one of West's multivolume digests, can be of additional help to the paralegal, because it provides coverage of court cases dealing with administrative questions. The digests, however, do not contain any agency rulings. Additionally, certain loose-leaf services provide administrative decisions for particular specialty fields, such as taxation. If available, they are a useful research tool.

Whenever you need to research administrative law, remember that the most efficient way to find what you are looking for may be simply to call the agency and ask agency personnel how to access information relevant to your research topic.

FINDING CONSTITUTIONAL LAW

The federal government and all fifty states have their own constitutions describing the powers, responsibilities, and limitations of the various branches of government. Constitutions can be replaced or amended, and it is important that researchers have access to both current versions and older ones.

The text of the U.S. Constitution can be found in a number of publications. A useful source of federal constitutional law is *The Constitution of the United States of America,* published under the authority of the U.S. Senate and available through the Library of Congress. It includes the full text of the U.S. Constitution, corresponding annotations concerning United States Supreme Court decisions interpreting the Constitution, and a discussion of each provision, including

EXHIBIT 17.13
Code of Federal Regulations

Reprinted with permission of Thomson/West.

background information on its history and interpretation. Additional constitutional sources are found in the U.S.C.A. and the U.S.C.S., both of which contain the entire text of the Constitution and its amendments as well as citations to cases discussing particular constitutional provisions. Annotated state codes provide a similar service for their state constitutions. Constitutional annotations are updated through supplementary pocket parts. State constitutions are usually included in the publications containing state statutes.

UPDATING THE LAW— LEARNING TO USE CITATORS

Almost every day, new court decisions are made, new regulations are issued, and new statutes are enacted or existing statutes amended. Because the law is ever changing, a critical factor to consider when researching a topic or point of law is whether a given court opinion, statute, or regulation is still valid. A case decided six months ago, for example, may prove to be "bad law" today if it has been reversed or significantly modified on appeal. The careful researcher will avoid assuming that the case law or statutory law on a specific issue is the same today as it was last month or last year. This section will show you how to make sure that a law or court interpretation of the law is up to date and still "good law"—that is, currently valid law.

Case Law

Shepard's Citations, which is published by Shepard's, is a research tool with which all paralegals should become familiar. *Shepard's* contains the most comprehensive system of case citators in the United States. A **citator** provides a list of legal references that have cited or interpreted a case or law. A *case citator* provides, in addition, a history of the particular case. *Shepard's* lists every case published in an official or unofficial reporter by its citation.

  Shepard's citators are available for nearly every jurisdiction. *Shepard's United States Citations* covers the decisions of the United States Supreme Court as reported in *United States Reports, Supreme Court Reporter,* and *Lawyers' Edition of the Supreme Court Reports.* *Shepard's Federal Reporter Citations* provides coverage of the various federal courts of appeals and district courts. Shepard's citators also exist for the reports of every state, the District of Columbia, and Puerto Rico. Every region of the National Reporter System is covered by *Shepard's.* Exhibit 17.14 shows a *Shepard's* case citator.

  One of the most valuable functions of *Shepard's* is that it provides the researcher with a means to verify the history of a case. For example, if a paralegal wants to know whether a certain court decision has been reversed by a higher court, *Shepard's* provides that information. Note, though, that it takes some time before the hardcover printed versions of *Shepard's* citators are updated. In conducting research in *Shepard's,* you will therefore need to check the softcover supplements that accompany and update the most recent hardbound volumes. The supplements are color coded (red, blue, or yellow) and placed next to the *Shepard's* volumes on the library shelf. In addition, to make absolutely sure that your research is truly up to date, you will want to use one of the online citators provided by computerized legal research services and discussed later in this section and in Chapter 18.

The Organization of Shepard's Citations

At first glance, the unique organizational structure and language of *Shepard's* can appear confusing. The researcher begins by finding the appropriate citator, the one that corresponds with the researched case's citation. For example, if the citation for the main case indi-

---

citator

A book or online service that provides the history and interpretation of a statute, regulation, or court decision and a list of the cases, statutes, and regulations that have interpreted, applied, or modified a statute or regulation.

EXHIBIT 17.14
Shepard's Citations

Reprinted with the permission of LexisNexis, a division of Reed Elsevier, Inc. Further reproduction is strictly prohibited without the permission of LexisNexis.

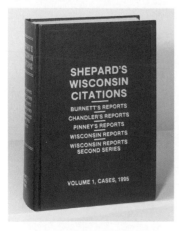

cates that it is from the *Atlantic Reporter,* the citator to locate is *Shepard's Atlantic Citations.* Then, to locate the case in this publication, the researcher finds the pages covering the relevant volume of the *Atlantic Reporter.* The volume numbers are printed in the upper left-hand corner of each page for easy reference. Once the correct pages are found, the researcher reviews the listings to locate the page on which the case begins. Parallel citations to other reporters are listed in parentheses with the case. Following this is a listing of citations identifying any higher courts that have reviewed the case. Then comes a listing of cases that have cited the main case.

Types of Information Provided by Shepard's Citations

Paralegals can use *Shepard's* citators to accomplish several research objectives:

- Parallel citations—*Shepard's* provides parallel citations for the cited cases, allowing the paralegal to locate the case in other official or unofficial reporters.

- Other cases—*Shepard's* lists other cases ("citing cases") that have cited the main case ("the cited case"). For example, suppose that in researching a matter you have found a case on point. You can check *Shepard's Citations* to find out what other cases have dealt with one or more issues in your case (the cited case). Also, *Shepard's* listing of citing cases may include other cases on point that you will want to check.

- References to periodicals—If you are researching a case on point, *Shepard's* provides further research tips by referring to helpful periodical articles and annotations in the *American Law Reports.*

- Case history—As mentioned, *Shepard's* provides a history of the cited case. If the decision in your case on point has been overturned on appeal (or if any further action has been taken), *Shepard's* will indicate this.

Note that *Shepard's* has an elaborate abbreviation system to provide information on how the cited case has been used in the citing case. For example, if the ruling in the cited case has been followed by a citing case, the symbol *f* (for "followed") will appear after the name of the citing case. Exhibit 17.15 on page 670 explains other symbols used in *Shepard's.*

Constitutional Law

Shepard's citators for constitutions are similar to the case citators. The cited constitutional sources are listed by section number on each page and appear in boldfaced print for quick reference. *Shepard's* can serve as a valuable tool in constitutional research by identifying other sources that have discussed the researched provision and by providing information on the status of the provision.

Administrative Regulations

Shepard's Code of Federal Regulations Citations provides citations to decisions of federal and state courts relating to administrative law, articles in legal periodicals discussing sections of the C.F.R., and other reference sources. The citation lists in *Shepard's* C.F.R. are organized by title and C.F.R. section. To acknowledge the frequent republication of the C.F.R., each citation is followed by either the date of the publication of the C.F.R. edition cited or the date of the citing reference. *Shepard's* uses a system of abbreviations, including those listed below, to indicate the impact that a court decision has had on the cited regulation.

- **C** (constitutional).
- **U** (unconstitutional).
- **Up** (unconstitutional in part).

EXHIBIT 17.15

Abbreviations Used in *Shepard's*

Reprinted with the permission of LexisNexis, a division of Reed Elsevier, Inc. Further reproduction is strictly prohibited without the permission of LexisNexis.

	ABBREVIATIONS—ANALYSIS	
History of Case		
a	(affirmed)	Same case affirmed on rehearing.
cc	(connected case)	Different case from case cited but arising out of same subject matter or intimately connected therewith.
m	(modified)	Same case modified on rehearing.
r	(reversed)	Same case reversed on rehearing.
s	(same case)	Same case as case cited.
S	(superseded)	Substitution for former opinion.
v	(vacated)	Same case vacated.
US	cert den	*Certiorari* denied by U.S. Supreme Court.
US	cert dis	*Certiorari* dismissed by U.S. Supreme Court.
US	reh den	Rehearing denied by U.S. Supreme Court.
US	reh dis	Rehearing dismissed by U.S. Supreme Court.
Treatment of Case		
c	(criticized)	Soundness of decision or reasoning in cited case criticized for reasons given.
d	(distinguished)	Case at bar different either in law or fact from case cited for reasons given.
e	(explained)	Statement of import of decision in cited case. Not merely a restatement of the facts.
f	(followed)	Cited as controlling.
h	(harmonized)	Apparent inconsistency explained and shown not to exist.
j	(dissenting opinion)	Citation in dissenting option.
L	(limited)	Refusal to extend decision of cited case beyond precise issues involved.
o	(overruled)	Ruling in cited case expressly overruled.
p	(parallel)	Citing case substantially alike or on all fours with cited case in its law or facts.
q	(questioned)	Soundness of decision or reasoning in cited case questioned.

- **V** (void).
- **Va** (valid).

Shepard's also publishes a variety of topical citators covering the regulations of federal agencies in specific areas. Examples include *Occupational Safety and Health Citations, Federal Energy Law Citations,* and *Bankruptcy Citations.*

Legal Periodicals

Shepard's Law Review Citations includes citations to approximately two hundred legal periodicals and law reviews. Researchers can use it to locate references to law review articles mentioned in court decisions and other legal services. The researcher finds the cited source by looking for the name of the legal periodical and then locating the volume and page number. Once the specific article has been found, the researcher reviews the list of citing sources that have referred to the article. *Shepard's* provides coverage of local law reviews and twenty national law reviews in each of its state citators. At the federal level, *Shepard's* publishes

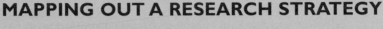

Today's Professional Paralegal

MAPPING OUT A RESEARCH STRATEGY

Bill Cather is a paralegal in a criminal defense firm located in a major metropolitan area. Bill has been assigned a research project on a case involving one of the firm's clients, who was arrested for drug dealing. The police had seen the client making phone calls from a public telephone booth and suspected that he was engaged in drug trafficking. The police placed an electronic device in the phone booth—without a warrant—and learned that what they suspected was true. Bill is now going to map out his research strategy before he undertakes the project.

STEP ONE: IDENTIFYING THE ISSUE

Bill's first step is to analyze the facts and identify the issue involved. He knows that the police may search certain areas without a warrant. The courts determine which areas are entitled to the protection of a warrant by considering whether a person has a reasonable expectation of privacy in the area. Bill wonders whether a person has a reasonable expectation of privacy in a public phone booth. Do people customarily expect others to hear what they are saying on the phone when they are in a phone booth with the door closed? Bill will have to research the issue. If a person using a phone booth is entitled to a reasonable expectation of privacy, then probably the police would have to obtain a search warrant before using an electronic device to listen to—and record—any telephone conversation taking place in a public phone booth.

STEP TWO: IDENTIFYING SECONDARY SOURCES

Because he is not familiar with the topic that he is going to research, Bill will begin by doing some background research. He can choose from a variety of secondary sources, such as legal encyclopedias and treatises. He prefers legal encyclopedias because they are easy to read and understand. He particularly prefers the *Corpus Juris Secundum (C.J.S.)* because it provides numerous citations to cases. He writes "C.J.S." on his list as the first source to consult. Because Bill knows that organization is the key to research, he always tries to make his checklist complete so that he does not have return to the same source later. He therefore writes "pocket part" on his list under *C.J.S.* so that he will remember to check the supplement to get the citations to the most recent cases on the issue.

STEP THREE: IDENTIFYING PRIMARY SOURCES

Next, he will want to consult the various primary sources of law. He will want to look at the Fourth Amendment to the U.S. Constitution to find the exact wording of the amendment in regard to freedom from unreasonable searches and seizures and the warrant requirement. He can find the Constitution in the U.S.C.A. He writes "U.S.C.A.—Constitution" on his list of primary sources to check, and "pocket part" beneath it. Once he has found the most recent case annotations citing the Fourth Amendment in the pocket part, he will put a check next to that item in his list. Bill also includes a notation to check a West federal digest for other relevant cases.

Bill will also want to consult state and federal statutory codes to find out whether a wiretapping statute exists and, if so, whether the police's action violated it. He therefore writes "U.S.C.A.—Wiretapping" to check for a federal statute and "State Annotated Code—Wiretapping" to check for a state statute, including the notation "pocket part" below each so that he remembers to check for updates.

STEP FOUR: UPDATING AND VERIFYING RESEARCH RESULTS

After Bill finds and reads relevant cases, he will have to verify in *Shepard's* that they are still good law. *Shepard's* will also provide an additional source of case law because it includes every subsequent case that cited the case being "Shepardized." He writes "*Shepard's*" on his list.

As a final measure, Bill will use an online citator to verify that his research results are as up to date as possible. Bill adds "online citator" to his list. Once Bill completes his research, he will prepare a memorandum of law to inform his supervisor of his findings.

Federal Law Citations in Selected Law Reviews, which provides indexes of law-review citations to federal court cases and other statutory information.

Online Citators

Several computerized legal-research services provide online citators. Online citators are extremely useful to legal researchers because they are more up to date than the printed citators just discussed. You can access Westlaw or Lexis online to update the law within seconds. You can also learn the history of a particular case, find out what other cases have cited it, and so on. You will read about online citators in further detail in Chapter 18.

KEY TERMS AND CONCEPTS

annotation 635	*dicta* 659	plain meaning rule 665
briefing a case 659	digest 635	pocket part 633
business invitee 631	headnote 635	reporter 635
case on "all fours" 632	holding 659	rules of construction 665
case on point 632	hornbook 640	slip opinion 650
citation 643	key number 635	syllabus 650
citator 668	parallel citation 643	treatise 640
code 660	persuasive authority 632	

chapter summary Legal Research and Analysis

Researching Case Law— The Preliminary Steps

1. *Defining the issue*—The first step in the research process is to identify the legal question, or issue, to be researched (often, more than one issue will be involved).

2. *Determining your research goals*—The next step is to determine the goal of the research project. In researching case law, the researcher's goal is to find cases that are on point (ideally, cases on "all fours") and that are binding authorities.

   a. Binding authorities are all legal authorities (statutes, regulations, constitutions, and cases) that courts must follow in making their decisions.

   b. Courts are not bound to follow persuasive authorities (such as cases decided in other jurisdictions), although courts often consider such authorities, particularly when deciding cases of first impression.

Primary and Secondary Sources

Primary sources of law consist of all documents that establish the law, including court decisions, statutes, regulations, constitutions, and presidential orders. *Secondary sources of law* are publications written about the law, such as legal encyclopedias, digests, treatises, and periodicals.

Finding Relevant Cases

1. *Legal encyclopedias*—Legal encyclopedias provide detailed summaries of legal rules and concepts and are useful for researchers who want to find background information on the issue being researched. These books arrange topics alphabetically and contain citations to cases and statutes relating to the topic.

   a. Two popular legal encyclopedias are *American Jurisprudence,* Second Edition, and *Corpus Juris Secundum.*

   b. A third encyclopedia, *Words and Phrases,* covers legal terms and phrases and cites cases in which the terms or phrases appear.

2. *Case digests*—West's case digests are major secondary sources of law and helpful finding tools. These digests, which use the West system of topic classification and key numbers, provide cross-references to topics contained in other West publications. Digests arrange topics alphabetically with annotations to cases on each topic but are not as detailed as encyclopedias.

3. *American Law Reports*—The *American Law Reports* are multivolume sets that present leading cases, each followed by an annotation that discusses the key issues in the case and that refers the researcher to other sources on the issues.

4. *Other secondary sources*—Other secondary sources of law include the following:

   a. Treatises—Treatises are scholarly publications that discuss specific legal topics or areas of law. They summarize, evaluate, or interpret the law either in a single volume or in multivolume sets. Hornbooks are single-volume treatises.

   b. *Restatements of the Law*—The *Restatements of the Law* are highly respected scholarly compilations of the common law and legal periodicals, such as law reviews. They present particular cases as examples and also discuss variations.

   c. Legal periodicals—Legal periodicals, such as law reviews, contain thoroughly researched articles on specific areas of law.

The Case Reporting System

The primary sources of case law are the cases themselves. You will find the cases in various case reporters.

1. *State court decisions*—

   a. Most state trial court decisions are not published in printed volumes. State appellate court opinions, including those of state supreme courts, are normally published in official state reporters. Many states have now eliminated their own reporters in favor of West's National Reporter System, which reports state cases in its regional reporters.

   b. To locate a case in a reporter, you use the case citation. There are five parts to a standard case citation: the case name, the volume number, the abbreviated name of the book, the page number on which the decision begins, and the year the case was decided. A parallel citation may appear after the first citation when the case is reported in more than one book.

2. *Federal court decisions*—Federal trial court opinions are published unofficially in West's *Federal Supplement,* and opinions from the federal circuit courts of appeals are

(Continued)

published unofficially in West's *Federal Reporter*. United States Supreme Court opinions are published officially in the *United States Reports*, published by the federal government, and unofficially in West's *Supreme Court Reporter* and the *Lawyers' Edition of the Supreme Court Reports*.

Analyzing Case Law

1. *Case format*—Reported cases contain more information than just the court's decision. Typically, case formats include the following components:

   a. The title (case name, usually plaintiff versus defendant).

   b. The name of the court that decided the case.

   c. The case citation.

   d. The docket number assigned by the court.

   e. The date on which the case was decided.

   f. The syllabus (a brief synopsis of the facts, issues, and ruling).

   g. The headnotes (short paragraphs that summarize the rules of law discussed in the case; in West's reporters, headnotes correlate with the key-number system).

   h. The names of counsel.

   i. The name of the judge who authored the opinion.

   j. The opinion (the court's own words on the matter).

   k. The conclusion (holding, ruling).

2. *Briefing cases*—Legal professionals often brief, or summarize, the cases they research. Knowing how to read, analyze, and summarize cases makes it easier to compare and synthesize research results accurately and efficiently. Although the format of briefs varies, the following headings are typical: citation, facts, procedure, issue, decision, reasoning, and holding.

Researching Statutory Law

Bills and ordinances that are passed by legislative bodies (federal, state, and local) become statutory law, a primary source of American law. Statutes that are enacted are eventually published in codes, which are updated by supplemental pocket parts and loose-leaf services.

1. *Federal statutes*—Federal laws are published officially in the *United States Code* (U.S.C.). The U.S.C. organizes statutes into fifty subjects, or titles, and further subdivides each title into chapters (sections) and subchapters. The *United States Code Annotated* and the *United States Code Service* are unofficial publications of federal statutes. Both of these sources are useful to researchers because they provide annotations and citations to other resources.

2. *State statutes*—State codes follow the U.S.C. pattern of arranging statutes by subject. They may be called codes, revisions, compilations, general statutes, or statutes, depending on the state. In many states, official codes are supplemented by annotated codes published by private publishers.

Analyzing Statutory Law

1. *Reading statutory law*—Reading and analyzing statutory law is often difficult, so careful reading and rereading are often required.

2. *Interpreting statutes*—In interpreting statutory law, the paralegal can turn to several helpful guidelines: the statutory rules of construction; the plain meaning rule; previous judicial interpretations of the statute, if any exist; and the legislative history of the statute.

3. *Legislative intent*—The legislative history of a statute can reveal the intent of the legislature and thus help to establish the relevance of the statute to the issue being researched. Important sources for researching legislative history include transcripts of committee reports and hearings, transcripts of congressional proceedings, and the wording of statutes as first published. Helpful resources in this area include the *Congressional Record,* the *United States Code Congressional and Administrative News,* and the *Congressional Information Service.*

Researching Administrative Law

Regulations issued by federal administrative agencies are primary sources of law. Agency regulations are published in the *Code of Federal Regulations* (C.F.R.). The C.F.R. follows a format similar to that of the *United States Code* (U.S.C.), and the subject classifications (titles) of the C.F.R. correspond to the titles in the U.S.C. To locate recently published regulations, the researcher should refer to the *Federal Register*'s cumulative *List of C.F.R. Sections Affected,* which reflects changes made during the current month.

Finding Constitutional Law

Constitutions are also primary sources of law. The U.S. Constitution can be found in a number of publications, including *The Constitution of the United States of America* (available through the Library of Congress), the U.S.C.A., and the U.S.C.S. Annotated versions of state constitutions are also available.

Updating the Law—Learning to Use Citators

Crucial in legal research is using citators to make sure that the research results are still valid.

1. *Shepard's Citations*—The various volumes of *Shepard's Citations* allow the researcher to verify the current status of a law—for example, whether a case has been overruled or reversed.

2. *Online citators*—Online citators, including those provided by Lexis and Westlaw, enable the researcher to access cases, statutes, or regulations (or amendments or modifications to existing statutes or regulations) that have not yet been included in printed citators and thus ensure that research results are as up to date as possible.

QUESTIONS FOR REVIEW

1. What is a case on point? What is a case on "all fours"? Why is finding such a case important when researching case law? What is the difference between a binding authority and a persuasive authority?

2. What are the differences between primary and secondary sources of law? How is each of these types of sources used in legal research?

3. How are legal encyclopedias, case digests, and other secondary sources used to find case law relevant to a research topic? What is the West key-number system, and how does it simplify the legal research process?

4. Describe how court decisions are published, from their initial publication to their final published form.

5. Identify the various parts of a case citation. How do case citations help you locate a case? List and briefly describe the components of a reported case. Which part should you focus on when analyzing a case?

6. How do you brief a case? What is the purpose of briefing a case? What should be included in a case brief?

7. Describe how statutes are published. How are regulations published? What government bodies create statutes and regulations?

8. What are some points to consider when reading and interpreting statutory law? What guidelines do the courts traditionally use to interpret a statute?

9. What is meant by the term *legislative history*? What resources are available for researching the legislative history of a statute?

10. Why is it important to find the most current law? How can you verify that your research results are up to date?

ETHICAL QUESTIONS

1. Kristine Connolly, a paralegal in a litigation firm, has finished reading a brief that the opposing side submitted to the court in support of a motion for summary judgment. In the brief, she notices a citation to a state supreme court case of which she is unaware. She is experienced in the field and keeps current with new cases as they are decided. She wants to look at the case because it gives the other side a winning edge. She checks in case digests and state encyclopedias, as well as on Westlaw. She finally calls the state supreme court clerk's office and asks about the case. The office has no record of such a case. She asks the legal assistant for the opposing counsel to give her a copy of the case. When she does not receive it, she decides that the case is probably fictional. What should Kristine do?

2. Barbara Coltiers is a legal assistant in a very busy litigation practice. She gets a call from a nervous attorney in her firm thirty minutes before the attorney is to appear in court. He wants her to do some research before he goes to court. He has just heard about a case decided two years ago that might help him win and gives her the citation. Because he is in a hurry, he gives her the wrong volume number. She has a hard time finding the case, but after about fifteen minutes of searching, she locates the citation. She quickly copies the case and runs to his office with it so that he can hurry across the street to the court for his appearance. She is in such a hurry that she forgets to check the subsequent history of the case.

It turns out that the case has been overruled by the state supreme court and is therefore no longer controlling in the jurisdiction. The attorney is chastised by the judge for citing it. In fact, the judge is so annoyed with the attorney for making an argument that is not based on existing law that he denies the attorney's motion and makes the attorney pay the other side's court costs. When the client finds out why the motion was denied, she is irate. Does the client have any remedy against the attorney? Against Barbara?

PRACTICE QUESTIONS AND ASSIGNMENTS

1. Identify the case name, volume number, reporter abbreviation, page number, and year of decision for each of the following case citations, including the parallel citations:

   a. *Smith v. James*, 400 Mich. 19, 630 N.W.2d 98 (1999).

   b. *Johnson v. Fassler Wrecking, Inc.*, 10 Cal.4th 539, 27 Cal.Rptr.2d 201 (1999).

   c. *Barnes v. Barnes*, 95 N.Y.2d 101, 637 N.E.2d 23, 654 N.Y.S. 13 (1999).

    d. *Miranda v. Arizona,* 384 U.S. 436, 86 S.Ct. 1602, 16 L.Ed.2d 694 (1966).

2. Identify the title number, code abbreviation, and section number for the following statutory citations:

    a. 42 U.S.C. Section 1161(a).

    b. 20 C.F.R. 404.101(a).

3. Indicate whether the following sources are primary or secondary sources:

    a. A case digest.

    b. A case in a case reporter.

    c. A legal encyclopedia.

    d. A statute.

    e. A regulation in the *Code of Federal Regulations.*

4. Sleeping Beauty is awakened by a kiss from Prince Charming. She can think of nothing more repulsive than to be kissed by him. Sleeping Beauty suffers from nightmares and depression as a result of this incident and contacts a law firm regarding filing a lawsuit against the prince for the damages, which include medical expenses, that she has suffered as a result of the kiss. The paralegal is assigned the task of researching Sleeping Beauty's case to determine whether she can sue. What are the issue(s) to be researched? What would the paralegal's research goals be?

5. Mr. John D. Consumer bought a new car eight months ago. The car frequently stalls. The problem began the first week after he purchased the vehicle. It stalled late at night on an expressway while he was returning home from a business trip. It has stalled at least monthly since then, often in potentially dangerous areas. Not only has he taken the car to the dealer, who has repeatedly attempted to repair the problem without success, but he has also notified the manufacturer in writing of the problem.

    Most states have a lemon law that requires manufacturers to replace vehicles that cannot be repaired, even if the warranty has expired. Does your state have a lemon law? If so, would the lemon law help Mr. Consumer?

    Research this question and try to find the answer to Mr. Consumer's problem. Begin by analyzing the facts. Then make a list of relevant legal terms to look up in an index. Select a legal resource—such as, *American Jurisprudence* or *Corpus Juris Secundum*—to use in your research. Write down the name of the source. Consult the general index volumes.

    a. Write down the index topics under which you found relevant information. (If you have difficulty locating relevant information, try checking the topic indexes in the individual volumes.)

    b. Write down the citations to sections containing relevant information.

    c. Look up these citations in the appropriate volumes of the legal resource to find an answer to Mr. Consumer's problem. Be sure to check the pocket part for more current citations. According to the resource, what is the answer to John D. Consumer's problem?

6. After analyzing the facts of Mr. Consumer's problem and making a list of legally and factually relevant terms, as described in Practice Question 5, do the following:

    a. Locate the index to the annotated version of your state statutes. Using your list of terms, look in the index for citations to relevant statute sections. Write down the citations.

    b. Refer back to Practice Question 5 above. Compare how you found the citations in the index to your state statutes with how you found them in the legal resource you selected. Under what topics did you look in each situation?

    c. Now that you have found relevant citations, go to the volume of the statute containing the cited sections and read those sections. (Be sure to check the pocket part of the volume.) What answer does the statute in your state give to Mr. Consumer's problem? Is the answer given in the resource you selected the same as the answer for Question 5 above? If not, how do the answers differ?

7. Using the annotated version of your state statutes, look for relevant case law on Mr. Consumer's problem. If no annotated version of your state statute exists or if no cases appear in the annotated version—or if you want to learn to use another source—locate a state digest. Find the relevant section(s) and locate case law that interprets the statute and that is as similar to Mr. Consumer's problem as possible.

    a. Write down the citations to no more than three relevant cases. Now look up those cases in the case reporters.

    b. Read through the summary and headnotes of each case. Do the cases still appear to be relevant? If not, go back to the annotated statute or digest and look for more relevant cases.

    c. What did you find? Did the courts' application of the statute change in any way your answer to the problem facing Mr. Consumer?

8. The hypothetical case discussed in the chapter involving a lawsuit brought by Trent Hoffman against Better Homes Store for negligence is based on an actual case: *Ward v. K-Mart Corp.,* 136 Ill.2d 132, 554 N.E.2d 223 (1990). Obtain a copy of the case. Using the materials presented in the chapter, answer the following questions about the case:

a. What is the docket number?

b. What court rendered the decision in the case?

c. What are the names of the attorneys who were involved in the case?

d. What does headnote number 4 say?

e. What does the synopsis of the case say?

9. Read through the court's opinion in the case *Ward v. K-Mart Corp.,* 136 Ill.2d 132, 554 N.E.2d 223 (1990), and then do the following:

a. Find at least one statement made by the court that constitutes *dicta.*

b. Brief the case.

10. Obtain a copy of the case *Kelo v. City of New London, Connecticut,* ___ U.S. ___, 125 S.Ct. 2655, 162 L.Ed.2d 439 (2005). Read through the case, and then answer the following questions:

a. Why did Suzette Kelo and others bring this lawsuit against the city of New London, Connecticut? What constitutional clause provided the basis for their claim?

b. What was the procedural background to this case? What did the lower courts decide?

c. Why did the United States Supreme Court grant *certiorari* (agree to review) in this case?

d. How did the Court interpret the phrase *public use* in the constitutional clause at issue? Why was the Court's interpretation of that phrase important to the outcome of the case?

e. What was the Court's holding in this case, and on what legal reasoning was the holding based?

11. Using the material presented in Exhibit 17.15 on page 670, *Abbreviations Used in* Shepard's, answer the following questions:

a. Under the section entitled "History of Case," what does the abbreviation "a" stand for? The abbreviation "r"? Why are these abbreviations significant?

b. Under the section entitled "Treatment of Case," what does the abbreviation "d" stand for? The abbreviation "o"? Why are these significant?

QUESTIONS FOR CRITICAL ANALYSIS

1. Sources of law are divided into two broad categories, primary and secondary sources. What is the difference between these two types? Why do attorneys generally cite only primary sources in documents filed with the courts?

2. What is the difference between a binding and a persuasive authority? Why is this distinction important for the courts? Which source is preferable to find when doing legal research? Why?

3. What is the difference between a case on point and a case on "all fours"? Which is it preferable to locate? How do these cases fit into the research goals? How likely is it that you might find a case on point or on "all fours"?

4. Legal encyclopedias, legal digests, and *American Law Reports* are secondary sources. For what is each source used? How are these sources different? How are they similar? Which source is preferable to use, and why?

5. What is an annotation? How is it used in a digest?

6. Explain the West key-number system. What is its purpose? Is its use limited to digests? How can the key-number system be of assistance to a researcher?

7. What is a parallel citation? Why are parallel citations used?

8. The written opinions of judges sitting on state and federal appellate courts are usually published in reporters. Why is it that trial court decisions are not routinely published in reporters?

9. What is West's National Reporter System? What geographical units does it include? Is it widely used? Why or why not? How might the West key-number system tie into it?

10. *The Bluebook* provides rules for citation. Why are these rules needed? What would happen without these rules? Can you think of a better system?

11. What is the difference between case law and statutory law? Why is the difference significant? In what forms are statutes published? What is the name of the official code containing the statutes of the U.S. government?

12. Why is statutory language often difficult to understand? What factors must legislators consider when drafting statutes? How is statutory law interpreted?

13. What role do case law and legislative history play in the interpretation of statutory law?

14. What is the purpose of *Shepard's Citations?* What might result if *Shepard's* citators were not used? Are there other methods of accomplishing the same objective?

PROJECTS

1. Using a state bar directory or other type of legal directory, find out which law libraries in your area are open to the public. Make arrangements to visit a law library. If tours of the library are offered, try to be present for a tour.

2. Make arrangements through your professor, a local bar association, or your personal contacts to visit the law library of a law firm or the legal department of a corporation or government office. If you also participated in Project 1 above, compare the materials available in the libraries of firms or government agencies with those available in law libraries. Why is it necessary for legal professionals to use law libraries other than those located in their offices?

3. Find out if your state has an official reporter for its appellate courts. If it does, find out where the reporter is printed.

4. Obtain a copy of *The Bluebook: A Uniform System of Citation* or the *ALWD Citation Manual* and look up the citation formats for your state court reporters and statutes.

5. Using information from Chapter 6, make a diagram of the federal court system. List the reporters for each court in the system, using the information given in this chapter.

USING INTERNET RESOURCES

1. Go to the U.S. government's official Web site at **http://firstgov.gov**. Browse through the page that opens, and then answer the following questions:

   a. Under "Reference Center," select "Laws and Regulations." What types of primary sources can you access through this site?

   b. Now click on "Code of Federal Regulations— Electronic" from the list. On the page that opens, select one of the titles of the *Code of Federal Regulations* (C.F.R.) from the drop-down menu and click "Go." How are the sections and subsections of the C.F.R. title organized on this page? Is this a user-friendly site for the researcher?

2. The *United States Code,* which contains the statutes passed by Congress, can be accessed through Cornell Law School's Legal Information Institute at **http://www. cornell.edu/uscode**. Access this Web site.

   a. How many ways are there to access the *United States Code* within the Web site? What are they?

   b. Scroll down to the title listing. How many titles are there? Click on Title 42. What does it cover? How many chapters are in Title 42? In the "Search Title 42" box, enter "Superfund Act." Describe the results you obtain.

   c. Go back to the *United States Code* home page. Using the section entitled "Find U.S. Code Materials by Title and Section," enter "42" in the title box and "9601" in the section box; then click on "Go to title and section." Describe what you find. In what chapter is this act located? In addition to the statutory section, what else is available?

3.  For additional resources, visit our Web site at **http://www.paralegal.delmar. cengage.com**.

END NOTES

1. Sarah K. Cron and Darrell Patton, eds., "*LAT*'s 5th Annual Technology Survey Results," *Legal Assistant Today,* May/June 2006, pp. 53–61.

2. Some scholars maintain that this phrase originated from the Latin adage that "nothing similar is identical unless it runs on all four feet."

COMPUTER-ASSISTED LEGAL RESEARCH

CHAPTER 18

CHAPTER OUTLINE

AFTER COMPLETING THIS CHAPTER, YOU WILL KNOW:

▶ What the Internet is and how it can be navigated.

▶ Some strategies for planning and conducting research on the Internet.

▶ How you can find people and investigate companies using Internet search tools and databases.

▶ How to find some of the best legal resources available on the Internet.

▶ How CD-ROMs and legal research services provided by Westlaw and Lexis help legal professionals in computer-assisted legal research (CALR).

INTRODUCTION

Computers and online databases have greatly simplified the tasks of paralegals in all areas of legal work. This is particularly true in the area of legal research. One of the great benefits of computer technology for legal practitioners is **computer-assisted legal research (CALR)**. As you learned in Chapter 17, thorough and up-to-date legal research requires access to voluminous source materials, including state and federal court decisions and statutory law. Today, attorneys and paralegals can access many of these materials online—either through the use of proprietary software and a modem connection or via the Internet. In fact, a survey of two thousand subscribers to *Legal Assistant Today* taken in 2006 indicated that 90.8 percent of the respondents now use the Internet for most of their legal research, and only 5.5 percent use printed sources (books).[1]

An obvious advantage of CALR is that you can locate and print out court cases, statutory provisions, and other legal documents within a matter of minutes without leaving your work station. Another key advantage of CALR is that new case decisions and changes in statutory law are entered almost immediately into certain online legal databases, including those of Westlaw and Lexis. This means that you can find out easily and quickly whether a case decided three months ago is still "good law" today.

In this chapter we first look at the Internet—what it is and how it can be used to conduct online research efficiently. We explain how to evaluate whether the Internet is the best tool for particular research projects and also describe some of the best resources available on the Internet. Then, after a brief discussion of the use of CD-ROMs in legal research, we describe in some detail the two leading computerized legal research services—Westlaw and Lexis.

By the time you read this chapter, some of what we say will have changed, particularly with respect to Internet resources. Some of these resources may have improved, others may have been removed, and still others may have been added. (See this chapter's *Featured Guest* article on pages 682 and 683 for information on how to keep abreast of computer technology.) The general approach to conducting research online will not have altered, however. If you master the basic principles of online research discussed in this chapter, you will be able to conduct research on the Internet no matter how much its content changes.

computer-assisted legal research (CALR)
Any legal research conducted with the assistance of computers. CALR includes the use of CD-ROMs, fee-based providers such as Westlaw and Lexis, and the Internet.

Over the last decade, expanded online access to legal resources has changed the nature of legal research. Today, paralegals and attorneys conduct most of their legal research online, without leaving their desks.

(Courtesy of ©Purestock/Alamy)

Brent Roper

FEATURED **Guest**

KEEPING CURRENT ON COMPUTER TECHNOLOGY

BIOGRAPHICAL NOTE

Brent Roper received his degree in law and his master's degree in business administration from Washburn University in Topeka, Kansas. He has published a number of textbooks and articles on law office computing and law office management.

Aside from ethics, competency, and meeting client needs, keeping up to date on changing computer technology in the law office is one of the most important tasks of any legal professional.

The widespread use of computers during the last thirty to forty years has had a profound impact on how law is practiced in the twenty-first century. In the 1960s and 1970s, only the largest law firms used computers, and they were mainly used for "back-office" functions, such as accounting and billing. Today, computers are used daily by almost all law office staff members—senior partners, legal assistants, and mail clerks alike. The computer is an indispensable tool that permeates nearly every function of any law practice, regardless of whether the practice consists of a global law firm with a thousand attorneys or a small-town solo practitioner. The accompanying table shows the many ways in which computers may be used in a law firm.

WHY IT IS CRITICAL TO BE SAVVY IN COMPUTER TECHNOLOGY

The list of computer uses in the law office grows longer every day. And while it is difficult to stay abreast of the changes in computer technology, it is critical for every legal professional to do so. Keeping current on computer trends and how they affect law practices is not about "keeping up with the Joneses" or bragging about having the latest computer. Rather, it allows you to do the following:

- Provide the best-quality services to clients.
- Provide the most convenient services to clients.
- Increase productivity and efficiency.
- Meet ethical obligations to clients and courts and keep information secure.

> *"The list of computer uses in the law office grows longer every day."*

- Keep costs down.
- Maintain a competitive advantage for clients.
- Have the tools to compete and survive in a very competitive legal environment.

Computer technology and innovation directly affect these matters in almost every law office function, so it is critical to continue to learn and to increase your computer skills. In this day and age, it is almost impossible to provide legal services to clients and stay competitive in the legal marketplace without using a computer, investing regularly in technology, and constantly learning about new computer techniques and software. It is *not* enough to know just the basics; most legal professionals *need* to know advanced features of many software products to really get the most out of them. It takes time, but the payoff can be substantial.

WAYS TO STAY ABREAST OF COMPUTER TECHNOLOGY

Most legal professionals are extremely busy, juggling a variety of client cases and responsibilities and constantly meeting deadlines. Here are some ideas on how you can keep current on legal technology issues:

- **Read and study computer articles in legal publications**—Most legal professionals subscribe to legal journals and periodicals. Most of these publications have articles that cover computer and technology topics. Instead of skimming the articles quickly to get them off your desk or skipping them entirely, take the time to read, study, and apply them in your everyday activities.

- **Subscribe to a general computer magazine**—Many general computer magazines are available. Even these general magazines have a wealth of information related to word-processing programs, spreadsheets, databases, e-mail, and other software that is used every day in most law offices.

- **Subscribe to a law-specific computer magazine**—Several law-specific magazines, such as *Law Office Computing* and *Law Practice Management,* cover law office computing topics. These publications can help you keep current on law office computing trends and the most recent software created specifically for law offices.

- **Subscribe to electronic legal computing newsletters and discussion lists**—A number of resources exist on the Internet for information about legal computing, including legal computing newsletters via e-mail, discussion groups that focus on legal computing needs, and general Internet resources for legal professionals.

- **Take the time to learn from other users and take time to experiment**—Watch and learn from other legal professionals, ask questions about how others use their computers and software, and compare notes. Also, one of the best ways to learn techniques is to try new things and experiment when you have a new problem to be solved.

- **Obtain training in computing**—There are a wide variety of options for learning how to use computers and computer programs. These options may include on-site classes at your law office. Additional options are training workshops offered by vendors, computer courses or continuing education workshops on computing topics, and Web tutorials on software programs. Take advantage of these whenever possible.

- **Upgrade to new products**— Support product upgrades (some practices fail to upgrade to the latest versions of products because of the cost), and use new product features when you can.

FUNCTION/APPLICATION	DESCRIPTION
Accounting/budgeting	Tracking and managing the firm's finances
Asset management	Tracking and accounting relating to the firm's property
Calendar/docket control/case management	Tracking, controlling, and managing appointments, deadlines, and work to be done on client cases
Connectivity/network software/groupware/security	Linking and sharing information on a global basis in a secured environment
Database management	Tracking, sorting, and retrieving information
Electronic mail	Client, interoffice, court, and law practice communication, including the ability to electronically transfer documents
Factual/substantive research	Finding and discovering information via the Internet and other resources relating to client cases
Legal research	Computer-assisted legal research (Westlaw, Lexis, Internet legal resources, CD-ROM libraries, and other electronic law-related information resources)
Legal-specific software	Managing, organizing, and producing client-related work information regarding specific legal functions or fields (for example, software designed to meet the needs of a law office in specific practice areas such as real estate, criminal law, estate planning, wills, and taxes)
Litigation support	Organizing, storing, retrieving, and summarizing case-related information for litigation
Marketing	Newsletters, Web sites, and other marketing materials
Payroll	Paying employees and accounting for taxes and withholdings
Presentation generation	Preparing electronic presentations
Project management	Organizing, tracking, and sequencing a large number of items for a complex project/assignment
Record keeping	Tracking and storing client case files
Spreadsheets	Electronic number processing
Timekeeping and billing	Invoicing and collecting monies from clients for services that have been rendered
Word processing	Electronic document preparation

GOING ONLINE—AN INTERNET PRIMER

Today, paralegals and other legal professionals regularly take advantage of the vast resources on the Internet to better serve their firms' clients. The Internet is a global communication network of interconnected computers. Business computers, university and college computers, government computers, personal computers—these and many more comprise the "network of networks" that constitutes cyberspace. In the pages that follow, we discuss many ways in which you can use the Internet to conduct legal and fact-based research. We begin by looking at Internet tools and navigation methods. You may already be familiar with these tools and methods. If so, consider this section a review of the basics of Internet access and use.

Internet Tools

Two of the most widely used parts of the Internet are e-mail and the World Wide Web. Getting around on the World Wide Web requires the use of uniform resource locators (URLs).

E-Mail

One of the most common uses of the Internet is for e-mail (short for "electronic mail"). We mentioned various uses of e-mail in earlier chapters. E-mail can at times be a research tool as well. For example, e-mail is the basis for services associated with listservs and newsgroups, which are discussed later in this chapter.

World Wide Web

World Wide Web
A hypertext-based system through which specially formatted documents are accessible on the Internet.

home page
The main page of a Web site. Often, the home page serves as a table of contents to other pages at the site.

When most people think of the Internet, they think of the World Wide Web (the Web). To the user, the Web is a system of Web pages or Web sites. A home page is the main page of a Web site, which generally serves as a table of contents to other pages in the site. Technically, the Web is a hypertext-based information system that makes specially formatted documents available on the Internet through a browser (discussed shortly). *Hypertext* refers to a means of linking disparate objects (text, graphics, and so on) together. Thus, in a hypertext-based system, we can jump easily from one object to another, even if their formats are different.

Uniform Resource Locators

hypertext transfer protocol (http)
An interface program that enables computers to communicate. Hypertext is a system by which disparate objects, such as text and graphics, can be linked. A protocol is a system of formats and rules.

A uniform resource locator (URL) is an Internet "address." A paralegal might think of a URL as an electronic citation. The basic format of a URL is "service://directorypath/filename." For example, **http://www.paralegal.delmar.cengage.com** is the URL for the Delmar, Cengage Learning Paralegal Web site, a resource center for paralegal instructors, students, and professionals (shown in Exhibit 18.1). This URL indicates that you use the *http* service to reach the directory path *www.paralegal.delmar.cengage.com*. The letters **http** stand for **hypertext transfer protocol**, which is an interface that enables computers to communicate. Several protocols are used on the Internet, but "http" is the one used on the World Wide Web—which, as noted, is a hypertext-based system. Thus, all URLs for Web sites begin with "http." When you enter a URL into a browser, you normally do not need to type in "http://" or "www." The browser will enter those terms automatically.

Note also that in many cases, a specific URL may no longer function due to the quickly evolving nature of the Internet. In this situation, try renaming the URL by removing the characters following the last slash. Continue this process until you find a functional Web page on which you can look for a link to the information you are seeking. If this does not help you locate a particular Web site, use one of the search engines listed on page 686.

EXHIBIT 18.1
**The Home Page
of Delmar, Cengage Learning
Paralegal Studies**

Reprinted with permission.

Navigating the Internet

Using the Internet to conduct legal research involves navigating through vast numbers of Internet resources until you find the information you are seeking. The Internet is similar to an enormous library, but there is a key difference—the Internet has no centralized, comprehensive card catalogue. In place of a card catalogue, a researcher uses browsers, guides, directories, and search engines.

Browsers

The Web is accessed through a software program called a *browser*. The most popular browsers are Microsoft Internet Explorer (**http://www.microsoft.com/windows/ie**) and Mozilla Firefox (**http://www.mozilla.com**). Other popular browsers include Apple Safari (**http://apple.com/Safari**), Opera (**http://www.opera.com**), and Netscape Navigator (**http://browser.netscape.com**). These browsers can be used with any Internet service.

Browsers enable computers to roam the Web. They also make it possible to copy text from Web sites and paste it into a word-processing document. With a browser, you can download images, software, and documents to your computer. Finally, with a browser you can search only the document that appears in your window. This last feature is most helpful when the document is long and your time is short.

Guides and Directories

The lack of a single, comprehensive catalogue of what is available on the Internet has led to hundreds of attempts to survey and map the Web. Lists of Web sites categorized by subject are organized into guides and directories, which can be accessed at Web sites online. These

EXHIBIT 18.2
The Home Page for FindLaw

Reproduced with permission.

sites provide menus of topics that are usually subdivided into narrower subtopics, which themselves may be subdivided, until a list of URLs is reached. If you're uncertain of which menu to use, directories allow you to run a search of the directory site. Popular examples of online directories include Yahoo (**http://www.yahoo.com**) and, for legal professionals, FindLaw (**http://www.findlaw.com**). Exhibit 18.2 presents FindLaw's home page. FindLaw, now a part of West Group, offers an increasingly complete array of resources. Topic areas include cases and codes, U.S. federal resources, forms, legal subjects, software and technology, reference resources, law student resources, and many others. You should familiarize yourself with FindLaw before you undertake any legal research.

Search Engines

Next to browsers, the most important tools for conducting research on the Web are search engines. A search engine scans the Web and indexes the contents of pages into a database. Whereas people compile directories, a computer generates most of the results delivered by a search engine. This means that the results are limited by the researcher's ability to phrase a query within the constraints of the search engine's capabilities. Search engines include the following:

- Google (**http://www.google.com**).
- Yahoo (**http://www.yahoo.com**).
- Ask (**http://www.ask.com**).
- AOL Search (**http://search.aol.com**).
- AlltheWeb (**http://www.alltheweb.com**).
- MSN Search (**http://search.msn.com**).

Search Engine Variations. Some search engines search only specific categories of resources, particularly for law research. For example, FindLaw provides a tool at **http://lawcrawler.findlaw.com** that searches only legal resources on the Web. This FindLaw tool can be further limited to search specified databases, such as federal government sites only. The Internet Legal Research Group provides another legal search engine at **http://ilrg.com**.

Meta search engines run searches on more than one search engine simultaneously. They are the best tools for searching the most Web space possible. It should be noted that nothing searches the entire Web, however. Meta search engines include the following:

- Dogpile (**http://www.dogpile.com**) draws results from many leading search engines, including Google, Yahoo!, Ask, and MSN, and allows users to compare these search engines side by side.

- Vivisimo (**http://vivisimo.com**) organizes results into categories using multiple search engines, including Ask and MSN.

- Kartoo (**http://www.kartoo.com**) visually displays topics on a map according to each page's relationship to others.

- SurfWax (**http://www.surfwax.com**) searches within the relevant domain (such as news or government) and then allows users to refine the search from a list of focus words.

- Excite (**http://www.excite.com**) includes a customizable browser menu with various current-events windows.

- Ujiko (**http://www.ujiko.com**) uses Kartoo search technology with a distinct visual interface that categorizes results by color.

Kinds of Searches. Search engines conduct searches in two ways: by key word and by concept. A key-word search generates Web sources that use the exact terms that the researcher types in. A concept search adds sources that use related words. In general, the best results are obtained in a search for Web pages that contain very specific terms. Exhibit 18.3 on the following page provides a look at the results of running a search.

Search Operators. In a response to a search query, a Web search engine will likely return many irrelevant results. Sometimes, a researcher can eliminate irrelevant sites only by going to the sites and scrolling through them. The use of certain *operators* can greatly refine search results and help you to avoid this problem.

Quotation marks are one of the most useful operators available in most search engines. Placing quotation marks around words or phrases that must appear together in a specific order will effectively narrow search results. For example, a Google search using the key words "Arizona Music Educators" in quotation marks may return roughly five hundred results. A Google search using the same key words but without the quotation marks around the phrase may return over ten million results.

Other useful operators are the so-called logical operators of Boolean logic. As it is used in Internet search engines, **Boolean logic** is a system in which connecting words, primarily *and, or,* and *not,* are used to link key words and make search requests more precise. The effect of using each of these logical operators is shown in Exhibit 18.4 on page 689. As you can see, using *and* or *not* can be an effective way to narrow a search. Many search engines automatically use *and* between key words if you do not specify the connector to be used.

Some search engines also allow proximity operators, such as *near* or *n/5* (within five words). Here, a source is included in the search results only if the key words appear close together in the source.

Boolean logic
As applied to Internet search engines, a system in which connecting words (primarily *and, or,* and *not*) are used to establish a logical relationship among key words in order to make a search more precise.

EXHIBIT 18.3
Results of a Search Using Dogpile®

©2006 InfoSpace, Inc. All rights reserved. Reprinted with permission of InfoSpace, Inc.

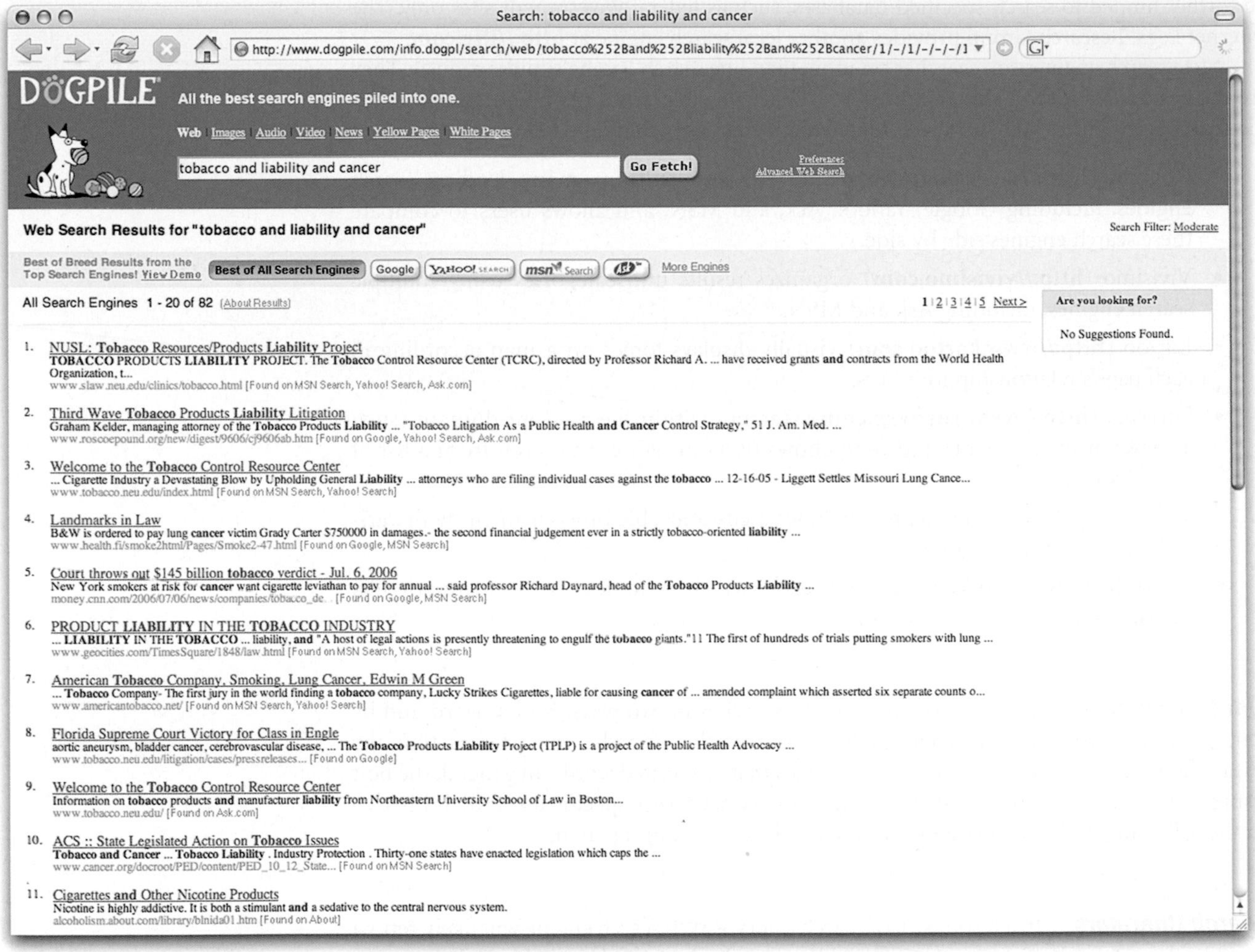

Choosing a Search Engine.   Search engines vary in the size and scope of their databases, in the flexibility of possible queries, in the search technology used, and in the presentation of results. When you search the Internet, experiment with numerous search engines and choose those that most readily deliver the results you seek in a format you like. A capable researcher will also keep abreast of developments in search engines. It is helpful to periodically review search engine descriptions and ratings such as those listed at **http://searchenginewatch.com**.

For legal research, even the best search engine cannot match the extensive database resources available from a commercial, fee-based database such as Lexis or Westlaw (discussed later in this chapter). The search tools on Lexis or Westlaw allow a researcher to pinpoint anything—such as a specific code or case law document—in the service's database.

CONDUCTING ONLINE RESEARCH

Your goal when conducting online research is to find accurate, up-to-date information on the topic you are researching in a minimum amount of time. As anyone who has used the Internet knows, it is possible to spend hours navigating through cyberspace to find specific

EXHIBIT 18.4
Examples of Boolean Searches

When you use the Boolean connector AND between key words, only pages including all of the key words will be returned. The shaded area below shows the results of a search for "Georgia AND bankruptcy AND forms."

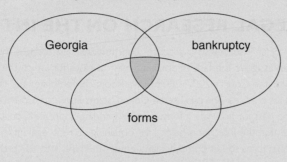

When you use the connector OR between key words, any page containing at least one of the key words will be included in the search results. The shaded area below shows the results of a search for "vehicle OR car OR automobile."

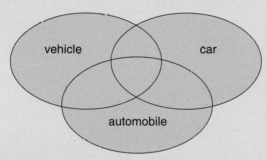

The connector NOT can be used to exclude certain key words. The shaded area below shows the results of a search for "gambling NOT online NOT Internet." These results will include only pages that contain the key word *gambling* but not either of the other two key words.

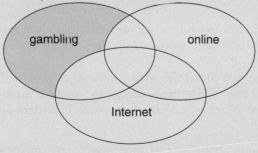

data or information. Planning your research in advance and using various research strategies, such as those discussed in this section, can help you achieve your goal of conducting online research efficiently. First, though, as a preliminary matter, you need to decide whether the Internet is the right research tool for your project.

A Threshold Question: Is the Internet the Right Research Tool for Your Project?

The Internet is only one tool for doing research. Knowing which tool to use and when to use it is the key to obtaining quick, accurate results. Ask yourself the following questions: What sources are needed? Are they on the Internet? Are they available elsewhere? Either

Developing Paralegal Skills

CONDUCTING LEGAL RESEARCH ON THE INTERNET

Robin Marks works as a paralegal for an attorney who practices constitutional law. Today is the first Monday in October 2007, and Robin has been assigned the task of obtaining a list of cases for which the United States Supreme Court granted *certiorari* for the Court's 2007–2008 term. Robin contemplates the fastest and most efficient method for obtaining this list of cases. She has used a United States Supreme Court database at **http://www.usscplus.com** in the past for accurate information on pending Supreme Court decisions. Robin also knows from experience that the Internet is helpful for obtaining current legal information, such as recently issued court opinions. Robin turns to her computer and enters the URL into her browser to obtain the list of cases to be heard during the upcoming term.

TIPS FOR DOING LEGAL RESEARCH ON THE INTERNET

- Determine your research goals.
- Determine whether the legal material to be located is current or was published prior to 1990.
- Determine whether your legal issue is broad or narrow—narrow issues are easier to locate.
- Compile a list of law-related Web sites.
- Bookmark the Web sites that are most useful.

way, what is the cost? How much time do you have to produce results? The availability (accessibility) of a source, what it costs, and the time it would take to use it are the basic considerations.

Answering the question concerning what sources are needed is, of course, only the first step. You must also be able to determine whether the source is available online and, if so, how to find the desired information within that source. Important points to keep in mind include the following:

- Discussion groups on the Internet cover nearly every conceivable topic.
- Most business firms, colleges, universities, and trade organizations have Web sites.
- Complete books are not online to the extent that fee-based periodicals are.
- Many additional resources are available online and can be subscribed to for a fee.

In terms of availability and cost, keep in mind that many sources on the Internet are free, but some are not. It may be more cost-effective to pull a book off a shelf than to pay for the same material online. It may also be faster to flip through the pages of a book, such as a dictionary, than to take the time to go online and click through a few links to find the same information.

In general, the Internet is most useful when the most up-to-date material is needed. Additionally, it is not as useful for conducting in-depth legal research as it is for conducting fact-based research.

Conducting Legal Research on the Internet

Many primary sources of law—including federal and state statutes, federal and state regulations, and the decisions of numerous courts—are accessible via the Internet. (Later in this chapter, you will learn some of the best sites to access when you are looking for online legal resources.) *Primary sources* of law available on the Internet include:

- The U.S. Constitution, U.S. treaties, and other selected important historical documents.

- United States Supreme Court decisions.

- Decisions issued by the U.S. courts of appeals over at least the last two or three years.

- The entire *United States Code* (all federal statutes). See the U.S. House of Representatives Office of the Law Revision Counsel at **http://uscode.house.gov**.

- The entire *Code of Federal Regulations* (all federal administrative agency rules). For example, the National Archives and Records Administration at **http://www.gpoaccess.gov/cfr** includes the *Code of Federal Regulations*.

- Materials focused on specific areas of the law, such as intellectual property.

- Sources related to each state's law. These sources vary in the depth of their coverage. A list of numerous and varied state resources is indexed at **http://www.llsdc.org/sourcebook/state-leg.htm**.

- Foreign law, which can be hard to find in many law libraries. An example is the "Foreign Government Information" page on the University of California at Berkeley Web site at **http://www.lib.berkeley.edu/doemoff/govinfo/foreign**.

What is available online in terms of secondary sources of law (comments or explanations by experts on particular topics) varies. Traditional secondary sources, such as the legal encyclopedias and legal treatises familiar to paralegals and lawyers in their print versions, are generally *not* available. Other sources are online, however, to help a researcher focus his or her research (see, for example, the resources provided by Nolo Press at **http://www.nolo.com**). Many law firms provide background material at their sites.

The Limited Scope of Online Legal Sources

Although numerous legal materials are available online, their scope is limited. Research into court cases to determine whether a law is constitutional should be conducted in a law library or through a commercial, fee-based Internet service, such as Westlaw or Lexis (discussed later in the chapter). Although more legal resources are constantly being added to the Web, material that predates the 1990s is generally not available. One reason for the limits to what is available online has to do with the expense of data compilation and storage. Most information providers are selective in converting their data into an electronic resource. It also takes time to compile a large historical database.

Conducting Fact-Based Research on the Internet

Lawyers and paralegals need to know more than the law. They often need to locate people, investigate companies, and conduct other practical, fact-based research into matters not directly related to legal issues. The numerous databases available online make it possible to perform such research quickly and efficiently.

Indeed, the great value of the Internet to all researchers is the wealth of sources of fact based information available. These include library catalogues, phone books, public records, company Web sites, and databases of government information. In fact, some government agencies plan to put all of their files online, making them instantly available to anyone who needs the information that they contain. (An excellent starting point for federal agency

Developing Paralegal Skills

MEDICAL RESEARCH ON THE INTERNET

Tom Shannon needs to locate information on bipolar disorder. Tom's supervising attorney is trying to prove that the defendant in a case has this mental disorder. Tom, who has worked as a paralegal for ten years, knows the Internet is an excellent source for medical information. Tom accesses the American Medical Association's Web site at **http://www.ama-assn.org**. He searches for articles describing this disorder. Tom finds several citations to articles, along with summaries of the articles, but the full text of the articles is not online. He prints out the information he has found and goes to the library at the local medical school to obtain the full text of the articles.

TIPS FOR PERFORMING MEDICAL RESEARCH ONLINE

- Become familiar with medical terminology.
- Search the appropriate medical categories on the Web site.
- Locate appropriate articles and summaries.
- If the full text of the articles is not available online, go to the nearest medical school's library to obtain them.

information is the Government Information Locator Service at **http://www.access.gpo. gov/su_docs/gils.**)

Plan Ahead—Analyze the Facts and Identify the Issues

If you have decided that the Internet is the right tool for a particular research project, you should plan your research steps before going online. The first step is to know what it is you are seeking. To avoid wasting time and money, outline your objectives clearly and be sure that you understand your goals. To narrow the scope of your research, you may need to know the reason for the research or how the results will be used.

The second step is to determine which sources are most likely to lead you to the desired results. One way to gain a sense of where you want to look is to use a guidebook (see, for example, the most recent edition of *The Internet for Dummies,* written by John R. Levine and published by Wiley). A good guide can point you in the direction of the right Web sites to visit to begin your research, to narrow its focus, or to find exactly what you need. (As you embark on your research, be aware that the unexpected may occur, as described in this chapter's *Technology and Today's Paralegal* feature on pages 694 and 695.)

Online Research Strategies

On the Internet, a researcher uses both traditional and innovative approaches to conduct research. For example, the use of a search engine is usually the first step in online research. It may not be the last resort, however, if posting to a newsgroup (an online bulletin board service) would yield a more reliable response from a primary source with less effort on your part. (Newsgroups will be discussed in more detail later in this chapter.)

Starting Points

Sometimes, a research session begins with one of the online directories or guides discussed earlier in this chapter. For example, if the object of your search is to find a law firm that practices in a specialized area of the law, you could start with Yahoo's "Law" menu at **http://dir.yahoo.com/government/law**. On this page, you will see various submenus, including one titled "Law Firms and Legal Services." Within that list is a general list of "Firms," which can be arranged alphabetically (see Exhibit 18.5 on page 696).

A search engine or a meta search engine (such as **http://www.refdesk.com**) can be used to compile a list of Web sites containing certain key words. A search engine tailored to zero in on specific topical sites may be more useful than either a general search engine or a meta search engine, depending on your research goals. Keep in mind the limitations of search engines, however. Your search may locate many irrelevant sources and may not spot every site that you would find helpful. In addition, different search engines will yield different results. For this reason, it is best to use more than one search engine in conducting a search.

From the preliminary results of a general search, you can click on the links to visit the sites and determine which are useful. Many sites include their own links to other sources you may find helpful. Some Web sites attempt to collect links to all online resources about particular topics. These sites include directories, which were discussed earlier, as well as other sites, such as FirstGov (**http://www.firstgov.gov**), which provides links to federal offices and agencies. For more experienced researchers, there is Hieros Gamos (**http://www.hg.org/index.html**), an extensive guide to legal information available online. Some sites are more eclectic in what they offer (see, for example, the 'Lectric Law Library at **http://www.lectlaw.com**).

Discovering What Resources Are Available

Despite your best intentions and attempts to focus your research, you may have to approach a project without a clear objective regarding what you need to find. Your initial research goal may be to discover the extent of resources available online, with your ultimate goal to obtain more precise results.

Similar to the popular guides and directories such as Excite (**http://www.excite.com**), less familiar Web pages contain links to important resources in particular topic areas. These pages often include directory-style menus and search utilities. For example, legal resource search engines, such as CataLaw (see **http://www.catalaw.com**), find sites related to legal topics. Remember that these sources often change and may even disappear, and new ones can develop overnight.

Many libraries provide access to their catalogues online (see, for example, the New York Public Library's Web site at **http://catnyp.nypl.org**). You can search these catalogues on the Internet in the same way that you would search them in the library. This can save the time that otherwise might be spent in a futile trip to the library. You can search the catalogues of your local libraries as well as those of more distant libraries. Often, you can arrange to have source material in a distant library delivered to a closer library, where you can more conveniently review it.

Another way to find out what resources are available is to begin with a listserv list, a newsgroup, or a blog. These can also be used to update your research.

Listservs. A listserv list (or mailing list) is basically a list of e-mail addresses of persons interested in a particular topic. By placing their names on the list, they agree to receive e-mail from others about the topic. A message sent to the list's address is automatically sent to everyone on the list. Anyone on the list can respond to whoever sent the message. As a

listserv list
A list of e-mail addresses of persons who have agreed to receive e-mail about a particular topic.

Technology and Today's Paralegal

BE PREPARED FOR THE UNEXPECTED

As noted elsewhere in this chapter, the Internet has dramatically changed the way in which legal research is conducted. Chances are, you will become familiar with Westlaw or Lexis during your paralegal studies. You will experience how easy it is to locate cases, statutes, and regulations—as well as a variety of secondary sources—using one of these services. Generally, your paralegal program will prepare you to handle most of the basic tasks that you will be expected to perform when you begin working as a paralegal. Once on the job, though, inevitably you will encounter problems that many other paralegals have faced. We look at some of those problems here.

NO ACCESS TO WESTLAW OR LEXIS

Many paralegals learn how to do legal research using Westlaw and Lexis (these fee-based computerized legal research services will be discussed later in this chapter) but then take jobs with small law firms that do not subscribe to either service. If you find yourself in this situation, you will need to decide what resources you can obtain via the Internet and which resources require a trip to the law library. Because trips to the library are time consuming, you will want to minimize such trips by trying to obtain as many documents as possible from free databases on the Web.

During your paralegal studies, it is therefore a good idea to explore Web databases, including those discussed in this chapter, to find out what types of free sources you can locate on the Internet. It is also a good idea to start keeping a file containing a list of Web sites and the resources available at each site. Eventually, when you are working as a paralegal, you might want to expand this file into a more complex, computerized Web research file in which you can also include research results on various topics. For example, suppose you spend thirty minutes searching on the Web for a specific state statutory provision. If you can foresee ever needing to refer to this provision again, you can simply download it into your research file. Then, the next time you need to access this provision, it will take you only seconds to retrieve it from your file.

DISAPPEARING WEB SITES AND PAGES

Another challenge facing paralegals (and others) who use the Internet for research purposes is the impermanence of many Web sites. As many researchers have discovered, what's there today may not be there tomorrow. Because of this, it is a good rule of thumb to download any particularly useful information on the Web for your research files.

researcher, you might post a message that asks for suggestions about online resources for your research. You can also add your name to the list to receive mass e-mailings. In some cases, you may be able to browse an archive of messages to see if another researcher has previously called attention to a resource that matches your search. For an example of a listserv list, go to **http://www.tile.net/lists.**

Newsgroups.   A newsgroup (also known as a Usenet group) is a forum that resembles a community bulletin board. A researcher can select a newsgroup by topic, post a question or problem (for example, "Does anyone know a good source for what I want to know?"), and check back hours or days later for others' responses. A researcher might also browse the newsgroup's archive, although messages are typically stored only for limited periods of time. There are perhaps tens of thousands of newsgroups (a few hundred focus on law-related topics). You can skim newsgroup directories at such sites as Usenet (**http://www.usenet.com**). You can also search newsgroups with specialized search engines, such as Newsville (**http://www.newsville.com/news/groups**).

newsgroup (Usenet group)
An online bulletin board service. A newsgroup is a forum, or discussion group, that usually focuses on a particular topic.

This rule of thumb also applies to relatively stable Web sites. Web sites are periodically redesigned, and information that you might want to access again may disappear—or, in the new layout, may be located on a page within the site that is difficult to find. News articles are especially ephemeral. For example, suppose you find information relevant to your research in an online news publication. If you return to the site in a few days, you may not be able to find the article. Some online news publications, such as the *New York Times*, place previously published articles in their online archives. Normally, though, archived articles cannot be accessed without a subscription and a password.

COMPUTER CRASHES AND INTERNET-CONNECTION FAILURES

It is hard to overemphasize how important it is to create back-up copies of your research results. If your computer crashes after you have spent hours on a research project, you may not be able to recover all of your documents. In fact, depending on what caused your system to crash, you may not be able to recover any of your work. Part of being a professional paralegal is to be prepared for such contingencies and back up your work as you go along—through a Web-based back-up system, CD-ROM, DVD, or flash drive.

When you are engaged in online research, there is nothing more frustrating than having your Internet connection fail. Virtually all Internet users face this problem at one point or another. Sometimes, you may not be able to use the Internet system for a matter of hours. At times, your system may not function for a day or more. The only thing that you can do to prepare for this contingency is to make sure that you never put off your online research until the last minute. If you have a deadline for completing your research project, start the work as soon as you feasibly can. Even if you know that the project will only require, say, two hours of online searching, do not wait until the last minute to do the searching.

TECHNOLOGY TIP

No matter how sophisticated the world of legal research becomes, you should keep in mind that things can—and do—go wrong. Legal database services such as Lexis and Westlaw are expensive and are not always available to paralegals. Crucial information on a Web site may disappear overnight. Computer systems can fail, glitches in software can make a planned task impossible to perform, and an Internet connection may not be up and running for hours or even days. There is little that you can do to prevent these problems from arising, but you *can* be prepared for them—by downloading important Web information and creating research files, by backing up your computer documents frequently, and by not putting off online research tasks until the last minute.

Blogs.   Millions of people generate blogs on a regular basis, and millions more will be doing so in the future. A *blog,* short for "Weblog," is essentially an online journal. To find blogs on legal topics, try the links regularly provided by **http://www.inter-alia.net**. If you click on "Current Issue," you can find links to up-to-date stories on legal issues, improvements and refinements in standard search engines, and more. To view more legal blogs, type "legal blogs" into any search engine.

Browsing the Links

Traveling around on the Internet to see what is available is known as "surfing the Web." Clicking on links within a site to open other Web pages is called "browsing the links." As you browse through the links that could be potentially useful for your research, two problems will become apparent. First, you will need to keep track of the Web sites you visit. Second, the speed at which your computer browses may be slow.

EXHIBIT 18.5a
**http://dir.yahoo.com/
government**

©2006 Yahoo!, Inc. YAHOO! and the
YAHOO! logo are trademarks of
Yahoo!, Inc. Reproduced with
permission.

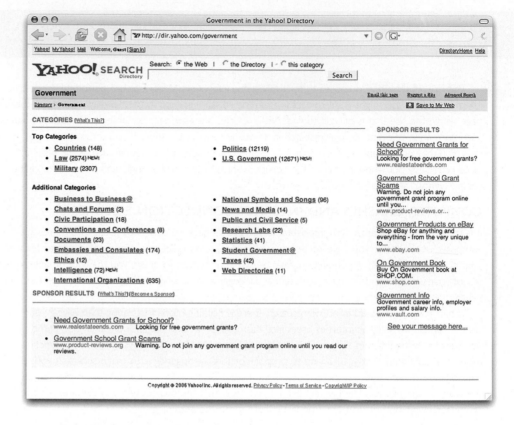

EXHIBIT 18.5b
**http://dir.yahoo.com/
government/law**

©2006 Yahoo!, Inc. YAHOO! and the
YAHOO! logo are trademarks of
Yahoo!, Inc. Reproduced with
permission.

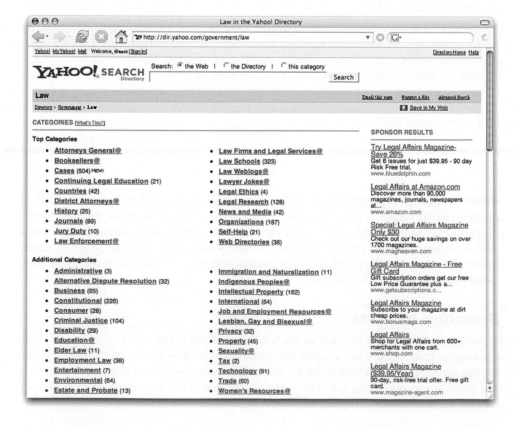

Ethics Watch!

SURFING THE WEB

A problem faced by paralegals who are novices in conducting online research is how to avoid spending hours surfing the Web for a site that contains the information being sought. You know the information is "out there" somewhere on the Web, but how can you locate it? What key terms can you use in a search that will enable you to find the information but that will also narrow the search enough to prevent you from retrieving hundreds of thousands of documents? Over time, of course, you will become familiar with the best sites for information in your area of practice. In the meantime, how can you avoid giving the impression to your employer that you are "wasting" time surfing the Web? One thing you can do is explain to your employer at the outset that surfing the Web is part of the learning process and that this "learning time" is essential if you are to become efficient in online research.

Marking a site as a "Favorite" (Explorer) or adding a "Bookmark" (Firefox or Safari) for the site is an electronic substitute for keeping a book on your desk. With one of these tools, you can create an automatic link to any point on the Web and return to it at any time. For example, you might want an automatic link to the site at which you begin your research: a directory, a search engine, or a site that has many links that relate to what you need.

Slow speed can be more of a problem. It may be the result of something that you can correct, such as an outmoded browser. It is not always so easily overcome, however. It can result from bad cable connections, your service provider's problems, the limits of equipment (yours or someone else's), quirks in the weather, and so on.

Before going online, you may want to take steps to avoid some of the causes of slow speed. For example, to avoid the difficulty of accessing a popular site during its busiest times, you might go online early in the morning or late in the day. You should be aware that if traffic is heavy at a particular site, there could be a **mirror site** with the same data. A site will note on its home page if a mirror site is available. You might also avoid downloading or uploading large files at a site's busy times. It may be possible to increase your speed by selecting the text-only option when you browse. This may be particularly helpful when you use a low-performance computer or modem to access a site that has rich graphics. With some sites, this may not be an option, however, because the graphics may be necessary to navigate the sites.

mirror site
A Web site that duplicates another site. A mirror site is used to improve the availability of access to the original site.

Narrowing Your Focus

Once you find a Web site that could be useful, you will probably need to zero in on specific data within that site. One way to do this, of course, is to use the links within the site. Some sites include internal search utilities with which you can look for specific information within the sites. Internal utilities differ, but in general, they work in the same way as search engines. (See, for example, Harvard University's internal search tool at **http://search.harvard.edu:8765**, which allows you to search an extensive database of more than nine hundred sites.)

EXHIBIT 18.6
The Securities and Exchange Commission's EDGAR Database

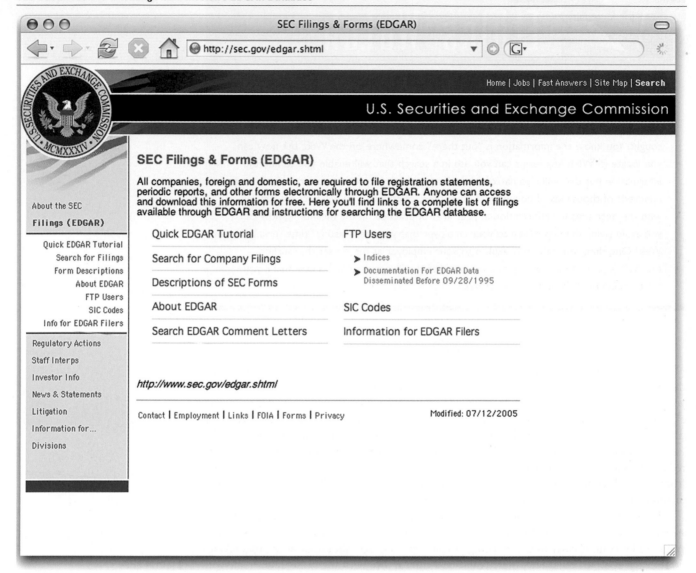

Remember that your browser also has the ability to search an individual Web page that you are viewing. This can be particularly helpful when scrolling through a document for a bit of information would be tedious and time consuming. Using your browser's "find" tool, you can search, for example, the text of a specific bill before Congress at the Library of Congress's THOMAS site (**http://thomas.loc.gov**), which contains legislative information. You might also use your find tool to search a company's document in the Electronic Data Gathering, Analysis, and Retrieval (EDGAR) database of the Securities and Exchange Commission (SEC) (**http://www.sec.gov/edgar.shtml**). EDGAR is an indexed collection of documents and forms that public companies and others are required to file with the SEC. Exhibit 18.6 presents the first page of the EDGAR online collection.

Alternatively, you can access EDGAR's private-sector competitor, Edgar Online at **http://www.edgar-online.com**.

Evaluating What You Find

After you have found what appears to be exactly what you are looking for, you need to consider its reliability. In evaluating data revealed through a search on the Internet, a researcher applies the same evaluative skills he or she would use to evaluate data found in other, more traditional ways. The researcher needs to be aware of how old the data are, for example. Furthermore, because anyone with access to a computer can put anything on the Internet, you should carefully evaluate every source of data obtained on the Internet for its credibility.

Identifying the Type of Source

In evaluating a source's credibility, you need to ask yourself whether the source of the information is a primary, a secondary, or a tertiary source. Primary sources include experts and persons with firsthand knowledge. For example, the inventor of a product would be a primary source for information about his or her invention. Publicly filed documents are also good primary sources. For example, the legal forms that some companies are required to file with the Securities and Exchange Commission are good primary sources for the information that they contain (see the discussion of company investigations later in this chapter). Secondary sources include books and periodicals (such as newspapers and magazines) and their online equivalents that contain "secondhand" information. Tertiary sources are any other sources that might be used in research (*tertiary* means "third" or "thirdhand"). It is always a good idea to find and interpret primary sources yourself before forming conclusions based on secondary or tertiary sources.

Is the Source Reputable?

A researcher also needs to be aware of whether a source is reputable. A reputable source might be an organization that has established itself as an excellent resource in a particular field. A less reputable source might be an individual's own self-serving home page. Was the information placed on the Web by a source that may be biased in a certain way? Some people providing information on the Internet may not even be who they represent themselves to be.

Several online resources are available to help you evaluate Web sites.

- Questions to use when considering the reliability and accuracy of a particular Web site are listed at a site titled "Ten Cs for Evaluating Internet Resources." The URL is **http://www.uwec.edu/Library/Guides/tencs.html**.

- Questions are also listed at "Thinking Critically about World Wide Web Resources." The URL for this site is **http://www.library.ucla.edu/libraries/college/help/critical/index.htm**.

- Ohio State University has an excellent Web site that includes an interactive tutorial and checklist for evaluating Web sites. You can access this tutorial by going to **http://gateway.lib.ohio-state.edu/tutor** and selecting "Evaluating Web Sites."

Updating Your Results

Staying current with events in the law, and in other areas that relate to your research, is important. One way to confirm whether your research results represent the most recent data available is by going online. News sites abound on the Internet. There are general, consumer-oriented sites sponsored by such well-known news organizations as CNN (see http://www.cnn.com). There are sites directed at those interested only in updates in specific subjects, such as the law (for example, FindLaw offers a free daily legal news e-mail and a free Supreme Court e-mail service at **http://www.findlaw.com**). Corporate press releases—both current and from archives—can be reviewed at PRNewswire's site (**http://www.prnewswire.com**). In addition, a computer desktop can be set to receive immediate distribution of news (see, for example, the Yahoo news ticker at **http://www.my.yahoo.com/ticker.html** and the business search engine at **http://www.business.com**). Other sources for updating research results include newsgroups (or Usenet groups) and listserv lists, both of which were discussed earlier in this chapter.

LOCATING PEOPLE AND INVESTIGATING COMPANIES

Paralegals often need to locate people or find information about specific companies. As mentioned earlier, the Internet can be an especially useful research tool in searching for this type of information.

Finding People

A paralegal may need to find particular persons to assist a lawyer in collecting debts, administering an estate, preparing a case for court, and so on. Public records are helpful in looking for people, but some of these records (including most historic records) are not on the Internet. Despite this limitation, Web searches can be useful; and they can also be cheaper and faster than going to a government office or a library. Sometimes, using a commercial locator service or database can also be less costly than a trip out of the office.

Broad Searches

On the Web, a researcher can run a broad search with a general search engine such as Yahoo (**http://www.yahoo.com**). A researcher might also narrow the focus of a search to, for example, all U.S. telephone books. There are several phone book Web sites. Each has unique features. Some provide e-mail addresses (for example, Yahoo People Search at **http://people.yahoo.com**). Some include business listings (for example, the Business Center at **http://www.superpages.com**). Some can conduct a search with a telephone number or an e-mail address to reveal a name and a street address (for example, the Internet Address Finder at **http://www.iaf.net**). Some international telephone books can also be searched (see, for example, World Pages at **http://www.worldpages.com**).

Narrow Searches

If you know something about the person you are searching for, you can use that information to narrow the search. Narrowed searches can be based on various characteristics, such as the person's profession or place of employment. For example, if you are looking for an attorney, you can link to *West's Legal Directory,* a comprehensive compilation of lawyers in the United States, from **http://www.findlaw.com**. On the home page, use "Lawyer Search" to access a search engine powered by *West's Legal Directory.*

If you are looking for a professor at a particular university or an employee at a certain company, you can check whether the staff directory of the school or business firm is available, and searchable, online. (See, for example, the directory for the faculty of Yale Law School at **http://www.law.yale.edu/outside/html/faculty**).

With the right database, a person's business license can be verified, information about a federal prison inmate can be accessed, and a military member or veteran can be found.

Michele M. Boerder, CP   PARALEGAL **profile**

LITIGATION PARALEGAL

Michele M. Boerder, CP, completed the associate's degree paralegal program at El Centro College in Dallas, Texas, in 1979 and received a bachelor of applied arts and sciences degree magna cum laude *from the University of North Texas in 2003. She has worked with the same attorneys for twenty years and has moved with those lawyers to several firms during that time. In 1998, Boerder, along with her attorneys, joined the large Dallas firm of Hughes & Luce,* LLP, *where she works in specialty litigation, including tax litigation, white-collar criminal defense, and complex commercial litigation.*

Boerder joined the Dallas Area Paralegal Association in 1982 and served as its president in 1988–1989. She has also served as president of the Paralegal Division of the State Bar of Texas and as a director of that division representing Dallas. She is on the editorial advisory board for Legal Assistant Today *magazine and has been a member of the* State Bar of Texas Paralegal Committee since 1991. Boerder has written paralegal textbooks as well as articles for various publications and helped to structure what became the Specialty Certification for Texas paralegals. In addition, Boerder worked on the first PACE (Paralegal Advanced Competency Exam) and today remains a member of the NFPA-PACE Standards Committee.

What do you like best about your work?

"Working in litigation means always learning something, not just about the case and facts in the litigation but also about various industries, technologies, products, businesses, and segments of our government and laws. Litigation also usually involves reviewing documents, talking to witnesses, and gathering information. It is particularly satisfying when I am able to use these methods to find evidence that supports the case for the client. Today, much of my work is done by using technology. Many times, I feel like an 'information miner' who chips away at the rocks of data and documents to find the small veins of gold that are valuable to the position of the client's case."

What is the greatest challenge that you face in your area of work?

"The profession of law itself is challenging with its changing rules, regulations, and deadlines. The greatest challenge for me, however,

> *"Technology has developed to provide database tools for case management and has become an area of expanded expertise for paralegals."*

is working for many different attorneys and providing them with quality paralegal support that not only meets their needs but also fits with their individual workstyles and preferences. It took me about ten years to learn that just as attorneys fit their practice to clients, I needed to provide my support to attorneys on an individualized basis."

What advice do you have for would-be paralegals in your area of work?

"Every case is unique. Even cases involving the same client and subject matter are not identical. If you use database support for your cases, it is important to structure each database carefully to ensure that it captures the needed data. Databases are only as useful as the information they contain. Technology has developed to provide database tools for case management and has become an area of expanded expertise for paralegals. However, you must manage technology—applying knowledge and administering the process are required to make the technology effective. Attorneys rely on paralegals to provide this oversight, which has created new roles for paralegals."

What are some tips for success as a paralegal in your area of work?

"In any litigation matter, organization is primary to doing your job accurately and efficiently. First, gather documents and background information and organize them so that you can identify what I call the 'players'— persons, companies or other entities, lawyers, and paralegals. Some databases, such as *Summation,* have a 'people' segment for creating this list. The list is useful later in, for example, composing a witness list. It is also helpful to create a timeline early in the case to enable the team to see the progression of events, the relationships of facts and issues integral to the case, and proof of the client's position. Begin a 'contact sheet' that includes the style of the case and contact information for the attorneys, parties, court, and other persons that you may need to contact frequently. Next, begin the case calendar and docket. Even an unfiled case can benefit from a case calendar. It may show the initial meeting, memorandum of the meeting, follow-up with the client, and later, the court dates, filing deadline dates, and ticklers for those deadlines."

Michele Boerder is also featured in the forthcoming book, Lessons from the Top Paralegal Experts, *by Carole Bruno.*

(See, for example, **http://www.gisearch.com**.) Information can also be obtained about persons who contribute to federal election campaigns (see the Web site for the Political Money Line at **http://www.politicalmoneyline.com**).

Adoptees and their birth parents can be located through databases such as **http://www.adoption.com** and **http://www.omnitrace.com**. For genealogy searches, there are databases that include all persons who have died since 1962, American marriages before 1800, graves, and so on (see, for example, **http://www.ancestry.com**).

States' driving and vehicle registration records and motor vehicle accident data may be available on the Web (see, for example, the state of Texas's list of licensed drivers at **http://www.publicdata.com**). Forwarding addresses and name changes for individuals and companies can be found at such databases as Semaphore Corporation's "Where Did They Go?" at **http://www.semaphorecorp.com**.

Locating Expert Witnesses

To find a person to serve as an expert witness, you can search the National Directory of Expert Witnesses at **http://www.claims.com** or choose a different Web source from the Expert Witness Info on the Internet list of the Northern California Association of Law Libraries (**http://www.nocall.org/experts.htm**).

Fee-Based Searches

Some commercial services provide access to their compilations of information only for a price. For example, possible aliases, home value and property ownership, bankruptcies, tax liens, and small claims civil judgments can be searched through U.S. Search at **http://www.ussearch.com**. Through a service with access to states' incorporation data and other information, people can be pinpointed based on their ownership interest in business organizations. Real property records, bankruptcy filings, and documents relating to court dockets, lawsuits, and judgments can be searched through such sites as KnowX at **http://www.knowx.com**. Social Security numbers can also be verified (see **http://www.veris-ssn.com**).

Investigating Companies

Lawyers often need to know about their clients' companies and the companies of their clients' competitors. For example, if a client has suffered an injury caused by a defectively designed product, a lawyer will need to identify the defendant manufacturer, find out whether the manufacturer is the subsidiary of a larger company, and learn the defendant's address. If a client wants to acquire or invest in a particular business firm, research into the firm's background may be vital. There are many ways to find this type of information on the Web.

It is important to remember that sites on the Web can be searched online anonymously (without the awareness of the firm about which information is sought). Because of this anonymity, clients can learn of competitive threats and opportunities without alerting their competitors.

Finding Company Names and Addresses

A researcher can run a search with a telephone number to find a company's name and address (for example, see the GTE Superpages at Verizon Superpages at **http://www.superpages.com**). Without a telephone number, a company's name and address can be found with the help of a directory that searches by industry and state (see the Switchboard.com page at **http://www.switchboard.com**, for example). A search with such a directory can also help determine whether a specific firm name is in use anywhere in the United States. You can find out who owns a domain name by using the free services of Network Solutions, now owned by VeriSign (**http://www.networksolutions.com**). At the top left of the home page, click on WHOIS.

Uncovering Detailed Information about Public Companies

To discover more than a company's name and address, an in-depth search is necessary. A guide to uncovering company information on the Web is located at **http://www. virtualchase.com/coinfo**. You can find out about small publicly held companies at Companies Online, now maintained by InfoSpace (**http://www.infospace.com/_1_106760383__categ/ bizweb.htm**). Most companies maintain their own Web sites, which may contain annual reports, press releases, and price lists. Some companies put their staff directories online.

Information may be available through the sites of government agencies. For example, the Occupational Safety and Health Administration (OSHA) site (**http://www.osha.gov**) identifies manufacturers whose products have caused injuries or deaths at any time in the last twelve years, and the Consumer Product Safety Commission (CPSC) site (**http://www.cpsc.gov**) lists products that have been recalled. The Securities and Exchange Commission (SEC) regulates public companies and requires them to file documents and forms revealing certain information. The documents include annual reports and proxies, which contain information on directors and stock issues. This material can be accessed through the SEC's EDGAR database (at **http://www.sec.gov/edgar.shtml**), as already mentioned. More up-to-date filings can be found at Edgar Online (**http://www.edgar-online. com**). Some states make their corporate records available online. For links to many states' records offices, see **http://www.internet-prospector.org/company.html**.

Other information about public companies can be found at numerous free sites, as well as fee-based sites. Some free sites provide data on the companies and links to the companies' home pages and other sources of information, such as news articles. Fee-based sites, such as the *Wall Street Journal* at **http://www.wsj.com**, often include archives of information that may span decades and may cover companies in other countries.

Learning about Privately Held Companies

Data on privately held companies is more difficult to find because these firms are not subject to the SEC's disclosure requirements. Much of the information available includes only what the companies want to reveal. There are a few sites that compile some data on private companies, associations, and nonprofit organizations. For example, Hoover's Online at **http://www.hoovers.com** provides brief profiles of many companies, with links to other sites, including search engines. For a fee, Hoover's will provide expanded profiles. Another source, which also gives information on virtually all public companies, is at **http://www. corporateinformation.com**.

SOME OF THE BEST LEGAL RESOURCE SITES ON THE INTERNET

As we have said elsewhere in this chapter, what is available on the Web changes rapidly. New sites come online. Old favorites disappear. Familiar sites move. URLs change. This section lists selected sites that a legal professional might find helpful. Many of these sites are not otherwise noted in this chapter. Included are references to valuable sites that have been on the Web for some time and have been kept up to date.

Basic Resources

Important Web resources for a legal professional include more than law-related sites. As indicated earlier, other important sites may include those of your clients' competitors. Sometimes, however, all that is needed is some basic information: the meaning of a word, the area code for a telephone number, or a local map, for example. Sites with such basic information include those listed in Exhibit 18.7 on the following page.

EXHIBIT 18.7
Some Useful Web Sites

RESOURCE	HOST	WEB SITE
Almanacs and Nonlegal Encyclopedias	Information Please	http://www.infoplease.com
Area Codes	Search.com	http://www.555-1212.com/mindex.jsp
Case Citation Guides	Legal Information Institute: *The Bluebook: A Uniform System of Citation*	http://www.law.cornell.edu/citation
	ALWD Citation Manual	http://www.alwd.org/cm
Dictionaries	Merriam-Webster Online	http://www.m-w.com
E-Mail Addresses	Address Finder	http://www.iaf.net
Information about the Internet	WhatIs?Com	http://whatis.techtarget.com
	Internet Society	http://www.isoc.org
Internet Directories	Yahoo!	http://www.yahoo.com
	E-Map	http://www.e-map.com
	Librarians' Internet Index	http://lii.org
Internet Search Tools	Google	http://www.google.com
	Ask	http://www.ask.com
Internet Service Providers	ISP Finder	http://www.ispfinder.com
	Internet Access Providers Meta-List	http://herbison.com/iap_meta_list.html
	America Online	http://www.aol.com
Legal Dictionaries	The 'Lectric Law Lexicon	http://www.lectlaw.com/def.htm
	Duhaime Law	http://www.duhaime.org/diction.htm
Legal Ethics	Internet Legal Services	http://www.legalethics.com
Library Catalogues	Yahoo's Library Collection	http://www.yahoo.com
Reference/Libraries	Library of Congress (links to other libraries' catalogues)	http://www.loc.gov/z3950/gateway.html
	Hieros Gamos	http://www.hg.org/toplibrary.html
Maps	U.S. Street Maps	http://www.mapblast.com
	MapQuest	http://www.mapquest.com
	World Maps	http://www.lib.utexas.edu/maps
	Yahoo Maps	http://maps.yahoo.com
Specialized Dictionaries	One Look (searches many specialized dictionaries)	http://www.onelook.com
Telephone Directories	Switchboard	http://www.switchboard.com
	AT&T	http://www.att.com/directory
Thesauri	Merriam-Webster Online	http://www.m-w.com
	Bartelby.com	http://www.bartleby.com/110
	Thesaurus.com	http://www.thesaurus.com
Translation Dictionaries	yourDictionary.com	http://www.yourdictionary.com
ZIP Codes	U.S. Postal Service	http://www.usps.com/zip4

FINDING ETHICAL OPINIONS ON THE WEB

Paralegals can provide a valuable service to their employers by knowing how to access online the ethical opinions issued by the American Bar Association (ABA) and state bar associations. For example, suppose that your supervising attorney is defending a client in court, and the attorney learns that the client has given testimony that the attorney knows is false. What is the attorney's ethical responsibility in this situation? Should the attorney disclose the client's perjury to the court? Would this be a violation of the attorney-client privilege? Or suppose the attorney learns that the client intends to testify falsely in court. Must the attorney inform the court of the client's intention? In these situations, the attorney may ask you to find out if the state bar association or the ABA has issued an ethical opinion on this issue. You can find this information quickly by going online and accessing **http://www.abanet.org/cpr/ethicopinions.html**, where the ABA posts summaries of its ethical opinions. To find ethical opinions issued by state bar associations, go to **http://www.legalethics.com/ethics.law**. From the drop-down menu under "State Ethics Materials," select the name of your state.

University Sites

Many universities, colleges, law schools, and other academic institutions are dedicated to making the Internet and its related technology an essential part of professional research. Their Web sites are often good points from which to start because in general they provide updated material and links to other resources. Some of these sites are discussed in the following subsections.

Law-Related Starting Points

The Legal Information Institute at Cornell Law School is a good starting place for online legal research. The URL is **http://www.law.cornell.edu**. This site includes many United States Supreme Court decisions (within hours of their release) and links to many other law-related sites and services.

Another good site is the World Wide Web Virtual Law Library maintained by the Indiana University School of Law at **http://www.law.indiana.edu/v-lib**. This is a comprehensive, up-to-date subject index of law-related topics.

Meta-Index for Legal Research at the Georgia State University College of Law (**http://gsulaw.gsu.edu/metaindex**) enables a researcher to use several Web sites' internal search tools simultaneously.

WashLaw WEB at **http://www.washlaw.edu** is hosted by Washburn University. This site includes a comprehensive collection of links to legal resources on the Web.

Digital audio of the oral arguments from many important United States Supreme Court cases can be found at the multimedia site of the Oyez Project (**http://www.oyez.org**). The Oyez Project, formerly hosted by Northwestern University and still largely supported by that university, also includes recordings of some of the announcements of the Court's opinions.

Government Resources Listings

The site of the Documents Center of the University of Michigan Library is a reference point for local, state, federal, foreign, and international law resources on the Web. The URL is **http://www.lib.umich.edu/govdocs**. This site has one of the most comprehensive lists of links to government documents on the Web, with descriptions of what is included at each link.

Government Sites

The government—the federal government, in particular—provides many excellent resources online. Every federal agency now has its own Web site. The following are some of the most useful sites for a paralegal.

Federal Law Starting Points

FirstGov (**http://firstgov.gov**), the official portal to U.S. government information, provides links to every branch of the federal government, including federal agencies. The U.S. Government Printing Office (**http://www.gpoaccess.gov**) also posts official information from each of the three branches of the federal government. Click on "A–Z Resource List" to access the *Code of Federal Regulations,* the *Congressional Record,* the *Federal Register,* all bills introduced in Congress, the *United States Code,* and other government publications. The Library of Congress's THOMAS site (**http://thomas.loc.gov**) provides a daily congressional digest, a link to the Law Library of Congress, and full text and summaries of bills. The U.S. Department of Justice (**http://www.usdoj.gov**) provides information on many areas of law, including civil rights, employment discrimination, crime, and immigration.

Federal Legislative Home Pages

The U.S. House of Representatives Web site at **http://www.house.gov** provides links to representatives' roll-call votes, the congressional schedule, current debates on the House floor, and Web sites of representatives. The Web site of the U.S. Senate at **http://www.senate.gov** hosts a Virtual Reference Desk with Senate procedures explained via Web links arranged according to topic. The Senate site also provides roll-call votes, information about recent legislative activity, and links to the Web sites of senators.

Business and Economic Information

The Web site of the U.S. Department of Commerce (**http://www.commerce.gov**) provides a wealth of business and economic statistical data and other information. Some of it is available only for a fee. The U.S. Patent and Trademark Office provides many educational resources regarding patents and trademarks on its Web site at **http://www.uspto.gov**. Information on copyrights and a searchable database of copyright records is provided by the U.S. Copyright Office at **http://www.copyright.gov**. The Equal Employment Opportunity Commission (EEOC) posts information on employment discrimination, EEOC regulations, compliance, and enforcement at **http://www.eeoc.gov**. Numerous resources to help in forming, financing, and operating small businesses are offered by the U.S. Small Business Administration at **http://www.sbaonline.sba.gov**.

Information about Public Companies

As mentioned earlier, the EDGAR database of the Securities and Exchange Commission (**http://www.sec.gov/edgar.shtml**) contains public companies' electronic filings of documents and forms required by the commission. This is one of the best resources on the Web for information about public companies.

Environmental Regulations

The Environmental Protection Agency (EPA) offers information on environmental laws, regulations, and compliance assistance. Access to state environmental regulatory agencies is available from the Environmental Professional's home page at **http://www.clay.net/statag.html** and the Small Business Environmental home page at **http://www.smallbiz-enviroweb.org**.

Sites for Associations and Organizations

Some online databases that catalogue associations, professional organizations, and non-profit organizations include the following.

Associations

Associations Online includes Web links to more than five hundred associations divided into categories. The address is **http://www.ipl.org/div/aon**. Yahoo's directory includes a list of professional associations at **http://www.yahoo.com/Business_and_Economy/Organizations/Professional**.

Professional Organizations

Professional organizations indexed according to business category (accounting, banking, law, and so on) can be found at **http://www.nvst.com/resources/pnvProAssc.asp**. (For Web sites for bar associations and paralegal organizations, see Chapters 1 and 3.)

Nonprofit Organizations

More than a million nonprofit organizations are included in a database maintained by Idealist.org at **http://www.idealist.org/it/idealist/en/FAQ/NonprofitHome/default**. This site includes links to the Web pages of many nonprofit organizations.

Free Commercial Sites

Commercial sites are Web pages that are maintained or supported by for-profit organizations (as opposed to academic institutions, the government, and nonprofit organizations). Some commercial sites are fee based. Other sites pay for themselves with on-site advertising. These are free commercial sites. Free commercial sites that may be of value to a legal professional include those discussed next.

All-Purpose Starting Points

Yahoo organizes, categorizes, and subdivides the most comprehensive list of URLs on the Web. New Web addresses are added at the rate of hundreds per day. Yahoo's address is **http://www.yahoo.com**. Another good starting point is the Google site, located at **http://www.google.com**.

Internet orientation, Internet tools, and Internet guides are the subjects of the Internet Web Text Index at **http://www.december.com/web/text**.

A collection of references to various subject guides can be found at the Internet Public Library at **http://www.ipl.org**.

EXHIBIT 18.8
The Home Page of the 'Lectric Law Library

Reprinted with permission. Contact **http://www.LectLaw.com** or **staff@LectLaw.com**.

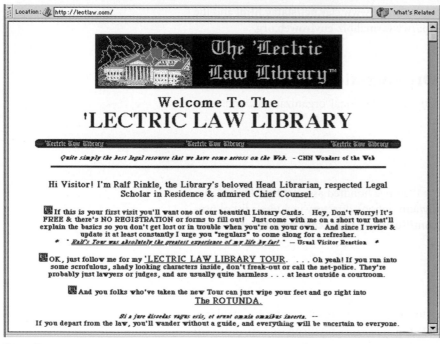

"Legal Professional's Lounge" in "The Rotunda"

Home Page

Law-Related Starting Points

The Delmar, Cengage Learning Paralegal site (**http://www.paralegal.delmar.cengage.com**) is a paralegal resource center. The site provides access to resources for professionals, students, and instructors, including links to nearly a thousand legal and paralegal information Web sites.

Other Cengage Learning resources are websites accompanying various business law texts. The site **www.academic.cengage.com/blaw** will take you to several products covering business law. Click on some to view the "Companion Site" for those books. There are hosts of helpful legal tools and resources on these sites.

The "Internet Legal Resource Group," at **http://www.ilrg.com**, offers an index of more than four thousand law-related Web sites, categorized by topic. The site also includes the "LawRunner: A Legal Research Tool," which is programmed to run your search terms in Google's more than three billion indexed Web sites. LawRunner only searches in those pages related to legal research.

The producers of the periodical *legal.online* offer links at their site at **http://www. legalonline.com** to legal resources on the Web that the producers find to be particularly useful. These resources include government sites as well as sites maintained by libraries, law schools, law firms, private companies, and others.

Law-related search engines are linked at "Legal Search Engines," a site hosted by Virtual Sites and produced by Virtual Search Engines, at **http://www.virtualfreesites.com/ search.legal.html**. This site also includes a number of basic references (dictionaries, for example) and links to search engines for other topics.

Thousands of law-related materials and products are available through the 'Lectric Law Library at **http://www.lectlaw.com**. Most of the information files are not links to other sites but are actually at this site, with plain text and simple graphics. Most of the larger items are compressed for downloading. Also included are legal forms and a law dictionary. Pages from the 'Lectric Law Library are shown in Exhibit 18.8 on the facing page.

"Law Library Resource Xchange" (LLRX), at **http://www.llrx.com**, provides links to a number of resource sites on the Web, ranging from legal research to library products and services. This site, which is maintained by Law Library Resource Xchange, L.L.C., includes timely and updated articles relating to research and library topics.

Media Directory

The American Journalism Review site, at **http://newslink.org/menu.html**, contains more than eight thousand links to the online pages of newspapers, magazines, and other media.

CD-ROMS AND LEGAL RESEARCH

Paralegals sometimes use research materials available in CD-ROM ("compact disc, read-only memory") format. CD-ROMs are accessed through a CD-ROM reader, which normally is contained within the computer, but can also be attached to the computer with a cable. A paralegal using CD-ROMs for legal research would find the CD-ROM containing the relevant reference materials—a legal encyclopedia, for example—and use the CD-ROM's index or search tool to quickly locate a given topic or subtopic.

Advantages of Using CD-ROMs

Most law firms have law libraries containing legal encyclopedias, case digests, statutory compilations, and other research materials frequently used by the firms' attorneys and paralegals. Law libraries and the physical space required to house them are expensive, particularly for small law firms. An obvious advantage of using legal reference materials on CD-ROMs is that they are far less costly to purchase and require much less space than their printed counterparts.

A CD-ROM can store approximately 300,000 pages, or more than a hundred volumes of legal reference materials. For example, the entire *United States Code Annotated* (discussed in Chapter 17) is contained on only two CD-ROMs. Many federal government publications, legal encyclopedias, West reporters, and other research sources are also available in CD-ROM format. Exhibit 18.9 shows a photograph of CD-ROM legal libraries. CD-ROMs can also be easily transported. They can be used on laptop or notebook computers while traveling or even in the courtroom. A further advantage of using CD-ROMs is that searching their contents is easier and quicker than searching printed reference sources. For example, if you are researching a state statute, you can search through the statute for certain words or section numbers using the search command, which saves valuable research time. West's CD-ROM libraries offer the advantage of the key-number system. As discussed in Chapter 17, this system simplifies legal research by allowing you to search key numbers to find relevant case law or other legal sources. You can also copy segments of the statute directly to your computer, which reduces the amount of time you spend in document preparation as well as lessening the risk of error.

EXHIBIT 18.9
West CD-ROM Libraries

Reprinted with permission of Thomson/West.

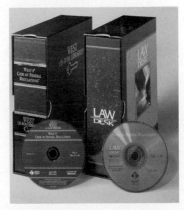

Disadvantages of Using CD-ROMs

The major disadvantage of using CD-ROMs in legal research is that, like their printed equivalents, they can become outdated. Suppose that you want to locate recent court cases interpreting a particular provision of the *United States Code*. If your CD-ROM containing the

United States Code Annotated was purchased five years ago, clearly you will be unable to find the latest annotations on that CD-ROM. In other words, just as when conducting research using printed legal reference materials, you need to keep in mind the date of the materials included on the CD-ROM. Note that even the most recently issued CD-ROM version of a legal encyclopedia or other reference work may be somewhat outdated, just as a printed text is, because of the time it takes to create and distribute the CD-ROM. The best way to ensure that your research is really up to date is to check an online legal database.

The need to have up-to-date legal resources is one of the reasons that most law firms today prefer to use online legal databases for their research. Generally, the increasing use of the Internet for legal research may help to explain why, according to the *Legal Assistant Today* survey mentioned at the beginning of this chapter, less than 1 percent of the respondents conducted most of their legal research using CD-ROMs.

WESTLAW AND LEXIS

Legal professionals also conduct online research using databases provided through commercial legal research services. Two premier legal research services often used by attorneys and paralegals are Westlaw and Lexis. To use these legal research services, a law firm or other user signs a contract with the provider of the services and becomes a subscriber. Westlaw subscribers may be charged either by the hour or by the transaction. Lexis subscribers may pay separately to review each document or may subscribe to Lexis and pay according to the amount of research needed.

The Westlaw and Lexis databases contain extensive legal and business information. Westlaw, for example, is organized into more than twenty thousand databases covering all areas of the law. It is possible to access such primary sources as federal and state statutes, court cases, and administrative regulations. Materials are also accessible through specialized databases, such as bankruptcy, insurance, and taxation. Secondary sources include legal texts and periodicals, public records, and other sources of business and financial information.

Accessing Westlaw or Lexis

A subscriber can access Westlaw and Lexis via the Internet at **http://www.westlaw.com** and **http://www.lexis.com**, respectively. To use most of the legal research tools offered by these services, you must subscribe to them and obtain a password. Once you have a password, when you sign on to the service, a welcome page is displayed. (The opening page of Westlaw is shown in Exhibit 18.10.) You can then begin your research. You can conduct a search, check citations, review documents related to a case or topic, set up alerts, and track previous research trails.

Conducting a Search

Both Westlaw and Lexis allow subscribers to locate documents using various search and browse methods. If you have the citation for a document, such as a court case or statute, you can enter the number and quickly call up the document. If you do not know the citation number, you can search according to legal topic, by case or party name, or by publication. If you do not know the best search terms to use for a particular search, both services will suggest terms to use. You can search up to ten databases on Westlaw at one time. You can also direct Lexis to search multiple sources simultaneously, and you can sort results by source type (cases, statutes and regulations, and law reviews and journals).

In addition to using the search methods just described, you can locate documents with Westlaw using two different browsing methods. Westlaw's "Table of Contents" organizes the

EXHIBIT 18.10
The Opening Page of Westlaw

Reproduced with permission
of Thomson/West.

federal, state, and municipal laws of several countries into submenus, including both primary and secondary sources of law. Westlaw also allows you to browse a directory of laws, practice areas, periodicals, public records, news, and many other topics and subtopics arranged hierarchically into menus.

Checking a Citation

Westlaw and Lexis both provide online citators. Recall from Chapter 17 that a citator, such as one of *Shepard's* citators, shows the history of a case and provides a list of legal references that have cited or interpreted the case. Online citators are extremely useful to legal researchers because they are more up to date than printed citators.

For example, suppose that you want to find out whether the holding in a particular case decided by a California appellate court is still "good law." If you are using Lexis, you can use the Auto-Cite citator to find out if the decision was appealed to the California Supreme Court (or to the United States Supreme Court) and, if so, whether the holding was affirmed, overturned, or modified on appeal. You can also "Shepardize" the case to find out how courts in other jurisdictions have dealt with the same issue.

If you are using Westlaw, you can use the KeyCite citator service. An important editorial enhancement to documents accessible through Westlaw is the KeyCite case status flag, which indicates when there is case history that should be investigated. A case status flag, depending on its color, will warn you that a case is not good law for at least one of its points, that the case has some negative history but its holding has not been reversed, or that the case has been overruled. KeyCite provides other features to make research more efficient as well. Suppose that you have found a case in the KeyCite database that cites the case you are researching. Stars added to the citation of the citing case show the extent to which your case is discussed in the citing case. For example, four stars indicate that the citing case contains an extended discussion of your case, usually more than a printed page of text. One star indicates that the reference is brief, usually no more than as part of a list of case citations.

If your search results include a statute or an agency rule, Westlaw enables you to check for any recent changes. The service displays any documents on Westlaw that amend or repeal

Auto-Cite
An aid to legal research developed by the editors of Lexis. On Lexis, Auto-Cite can be used to find the history of a case, to verify whether the case is still good law, and to perform other functions.

KeyCite
An aid to legal research developed by the editors of Westlaw. On Westlaw, KeyCite can trace case history, retrieve secondary sources, categorize legal citations by legal issue, and perform other functions.

Developing Paralegal Skills

CITE CHECKING ON WESTLAW

Katie, a paralegal, needs to quickly check a citation for a case from the court of appeals to see if it is still good law. Her supervising attorney wants to use the case in a brief that must be filed within a few hours. Katie accesses Westlaw. She enters her password and client-identifying information. Once she has gained access, she clicks on the "KeyCite this citation" box and enters the case citation. The search turns up a red flag, which means that the case has been reversed or overruled and is no longer good law. Katie clicks on the red flag, which takes her to the decision in which the case was reversed or overruled. It turns out that the case was reversed on grounds that were not related to the rule of law for which her supervising attorney wants to cite the case. Katie and her supervisor can use the case in their brief after all. For their purpose, it is still good law.

TIPS FOR USING KEYCITE

- A red flag means that a case has been reversed or overruled for at least one point of law and must be reviewed.

- A yellow flag means that the case has been questioned and should be checked.

- Never cite a case without verifying that it is still good law.

- Always read a citing case to find out why your case has a red or yellow flag and to determine what issue in your case has been questioned, reversed, or overruled.

the statute or rule you are viewing and automatically retrieves references, notes, or annotations that apply to a title, chapter, or subchapter of the statute or rule. It also displays tables that track statute numbers through amendments and other changes. The annotations are hyperlinked so that when you click on a reference, Westlaw instantly brings up the document onto the screen.

These and other tools allow you to access updated law within seconds. As emphasized in Chapter 17, a crucial part of legal research is making sure your findings are accurate and up to date. If your supervising attorney is preparing for trial, for example, the attorney will want to base his or her legal argument on current authorities. A precedential case that may have been good law yesterday may not remain so today. Making sure that your research results reflect current law is thus a crucial step in legal research.

Selecting a Database

The legal research materials available through Westlaw and Lexis draw from thousands of databases, so a search by case name or legal topic can easily return an overwhelming number of documents. As a result, paralegals often need to limit their searches to specified databases. To do this, you first select a database that you want to search. If you are using Westlaw, for example, you click on the box labeled "Search These Databases" and enter a database identifier (for example, "ca-cs" to search all California cases). If you do not know the abbreviation for the database you wish to search, you can choose "View Westlaw Directory" or "Find a Database Wizard." The directory provides a list of databases and their identifiers. The database wizard service prompts you with on-screen questions, then directs you to the appropriate database. Either way, you will find the database you want.

CUTTING THE COST OF LEGAL RESEARCH

As a paralegal, you have an ethical duty to the client to minimize costs, including the cost of computerized research—which, after all, is paid for by the client. One way you can reduce research costs is to plan your search queries carefully before accessing a service such as Lexis or Westlaw. This way, you do not have to spend online time making such decisions.

For example, suppose that your supervising attorney has asked you to research case law on the liability of tobacco products manufacturers for cancer caused by the use of those products. To do a thorough investigation, you will need to search the databases containing decisions from all state courts as well as from all federal courts. By working your way through Westlaw directories, you will be able to find the databases containing decisions from all state courts and all federal courts.

After you become familiar with the database identifiers on whatever service you are using, you can access that database more directly. For example, on the opening page of Westlaw, you can click on "Find a Database Wizard" at the bottom left-hand of the screen. From the list provided, you select the information you wish to research, such as "Case, statute, or legal text." Next you can select the specific database you want, such as "Cases–Federal" and then "ALL FEDS."

Searching a Database

Once you have chosen a specific database, such as "ALL FEDS," a search box will open on the screen. You will enter your *search query* in this box. In addition to the "terms and connectors" (Boolean) method of searching, both services allow users to draft search queries using natural language (or "plain English"). Before beginning your search, you should indicate in the search box which method you will use.

The Terms and Connectors Method

In a search employing terms and connectors, you use numerical and grammatical connectors to specify the relationships of the terms. For example, to find cases on the liability of tobacco products manufacturers for cancer caused by the use of those products, you could type the following terms and connectors in the query box:

liability /p cancer /s tobacco

This would retrieve all cases in which the term *liability* is in the same paragraph ("/p") as the term *cancer,* with the term *cancer* in the same sentence ("/s") as the term *tobacco.* To restrict the scope of your search, you can add a field restriction. For example, you might want to retrieve only court opinions rendered after 2003. If you are using Westlaw, you could add the following to your query to restrict the search results to cases decided after 2003:

& added date (after 1/1/2004)

Exhibit 18.11 on the next page illustrates the results of running a search with these terms and connectors on Westlaw.

EXHIBIT 18.11
Search Results on Westlaw

Reproduced with permission of Thomson/West.

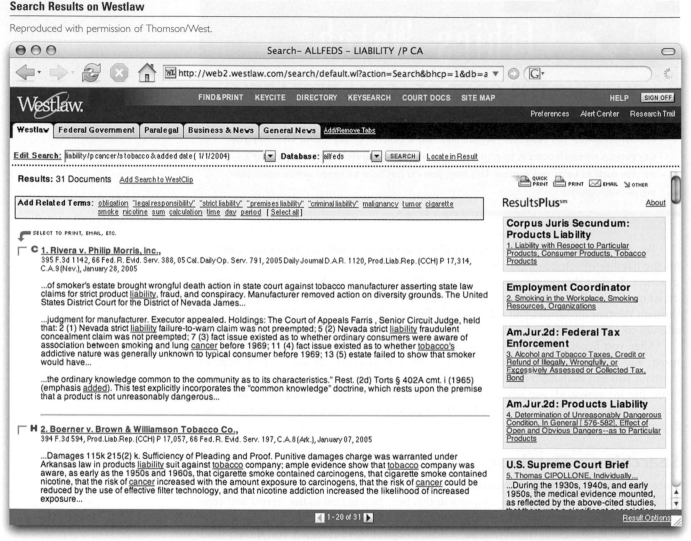

Numerous other grammatical and numerical connectors can be used to efficiently search a database. These are listed in the instructions provided to Lexis and Westlaw subscribers.

Generally, when drafting queries, you want to make sure your query is not too broad. If you entered just the term *liability,* for example, your search would be futile because so many thousands of documents contain that term. At the same time, you do not want your search to be so narrow that no cases will be retrieved.

The Natural Language Method

The natural language method allows you to type a description of an issue in plain English to retrieve the most relevant documents. In searching for cases relating to the topic in the previous example, your query might read as follows:

> Is a tobacco manufacturer liable for cancer caused by the use of its products?

This query would retrieve the documents most closely matching your description.

Today's Professional Paralegal

LOCATING GUARDIANS AND WARDS

Patrick Mitchell works as a legal assistant for a sole practitioner, Anne Urso. Anne takes probate court assignments in which the court appoints her guardian *ad litem*. (A guardian *ad litem* is a special guardian appointed by a court to protect the interests of minors or incapacitated persons in legal proceedings.) This requires Anne to determine whether someone who has previously been appointed as a legal guardian for an incapacitated person needs to continue as guardian. In order to make this determination, Anne must visit the ward and meet with the guardian.

Today, Anne has received an envelope in the mail appointing her guardian *ad litem* in five cases. The paperwork that comes from the court contains the names and addresses of both the guardian and the ward. Anne knows from experience that the court's records are often out of date and that this information needs to be updated.

Anne assigns the task of locating the guardians and wards to Patrick. He will call them first to see if the information from the court is accurate and to set up a meeting between them and either Anne or himself. The forms have to be submitted to the court within two weeks of their receipt by Anne, which is a quick turnaround time, especially in light of Anne's caseload. Patrick calls the ward and the guardian on the first sheet and finds that their telephone numbers have been disconnected. He sets this sheet aside and calls the people listed on the next sheet. He succeeds in contacting the guardian and learns that the ward, an eighty-five-year-old man, Mr. Ahern, died almost a year ago. Patrick adds this to his notes for Anne. Patrick continues calling the guardians and wards listed on the sheets. He is able to contact the next three and sets up appointments with them.

Now Patrick must locate the guardian and the ward from the first sheet. He decides that the fastest way to do this is to use a people locator on the Internet. From past experience, Patrick is familiar with a number of reliable Web sites. These sites include KnowX, Bigfoot, and MapQuest. He accesses **http://www.bigfoot.com**. He enters the name of the ward, Thomas Ford, and the address, 2335 Three Mile Drive, Detroit, Michigan, and clicks on "Search." Within a few seconds, the computer retrieves a telephone number and an address for Mr. Ford. The telephone number is different from the one that was on the court's forms. Patrick runs another search for the guardian and turns up a new telephone number and address for him as well. Patrick then calls the guardian and the ward and schedules an appointment to meet with them.

Patrick then goes online to the Web site **http://www.knowx.com** to verify the death records of the second ward, Mr. Ahern. Using Mr. Ahern's Social Security number, he is able to access these records and print out a copy to include with his report. Patrick places a copy in the file.

Next, Patrick needs to use a mapping Web site to create maps for, and driving directions to, the five different locations to which he and Anne will need to go. Patrick accesses **http://www.mapquest.com**. He enters the address of the office and then the address of the first ward. He clicks on "Search," and a map with driving directions soon appears on the screen. Patrick prints out five maps with driving directions and places them in the file. Having finished this project, he then turns to his next task.

Including synonyms in the search may sometimes be necessary to produce more comprehensive results. A thesaurus feature on Westlaw (and a "Suggest Terms for My Search" function on Lexis) can suggest additional terms for your search. After entering your natural language query on Westlaw, click on "Thesaurus." Select a term from the list and then click on "View Related Terms." If you want to add one of the terms to your description, select the term and click on "Add Term to Description." Note that Westlaw may also suggest additional terms without being asked to do so.

Searching within Results

Often, once you have retrieved your search results, you would like to quickly locate certain key information. For example, suppose that your search resulted in a list of twenty cases relevant to your topic. At this point, Westlaw's "Locate in Results" tool allows you to scan the documents in your search result for terms that were not included in your query. Assume that your original request was, in natural language, "Is a tobacco manufacturer liable for cancer caused by the use of its products?" If you want to know whether "death" is discussed in any of your search-result documents, you can use the "Locate" tool.

When browsing through your search results, remember that the time you spend using the service is costly. If you have found a case or cases that appear to be on point, you can print them out (or download them to your computer) for further study or analysis.

Additional Research Features

Both Westlaw and Lexis offer many additional features. In Westlaw, for example, a feature called *My Westlaw* allows you to customize Westlaw by selecting tabs to be displayed across the top of each page. These tabs allow you direct access to practice areas or specific jurisdictions that you use often. Westlaw and Lexis also offer features to automatically monitor the status of laws, regulations, and case histories and alert you about new changes. These notices can be delivered to an e-mail address, a fax machine, a printer, or some other destination.

Both Westlaw and Lexis allow you to search for motions, pleadings, court dockets, and testimony from expert witnesses. You can also gather information about a judge, an attorney, an arbitrator, a company, or an expert witness using the *LexisNexis Analyzer*. Both services allow you to refer back to previous research trails as well. These research trails can be very helpful when you need to replicate your search history or resume a search after an interruption.

Additionally, Westlaw and Lexis offer links to numerous other documents and databases. While reviewing documents that you have searched for, for example, you will also find lists of related analytical materials, along with active links to many of those materials. These links may lead to helpful new sources of information for your project. Westlaw has added links to people finders, company information, and many other types of information; the availability of these links normally depends on the Westlaw package that was purchased.

KEY TERMS AND CONCEPTS

chapter summary   Computer-Assisted Legal Research

Going Online—
An Internet Primer

Today's legal professionals can access a vast amount of information using the Internet, which is a global communication network of interconnected computers. Many online resources are available for free, while others charge a fee for accessing their databases.

1. *Internet tools*—Commonly used Internet tools include e-mail, which transmits messages via the Internet to specific e-mail addresses, and the World Wide Web, a data network on the Internet that is accessed through a browser.

2. *Navigating the Internet*—Getting around on the Web requires the use of uniform resource locators (URLs), which are Internet addresses. To navigate the Internet, which has no card catalogue as a library does, one uses browsers (software such as Microsoft Explorer and Mozilla Firefox that allows a computer to roam the Web), guides and directories (menus of topics at various Web sites), and search engines (such as Google and Yahoo) that scan the Web for certain key words or concepts.

Conducting Online Research

1. *Before going online*—Before beginning an online research session, you should first decide whether the Internet is the right tool for your research project. Ask yourself what sources you will need and whether they are available on the Internet. At this time, there are limited primary and secondary legal sources on the Web for conducting in-depth legal research. There are, however, an increasing number of primary sources online. For fact-based research, such as locating people and public records, the Internet offers an abundance of useful information.

2. *Plan ahead*—To avoid wasting time, define what you are seeking and determine which sources are most likely to lead you to the desired results.

3. *Research strategies*—Once online, you can use various search tools and other resources (such as listservs, newsgroups, and blogs) to locate information relevant to your topic. Often, researchers need to "browse the links" for a time before finding a site that is particularly relevant. Once you find a useful site, you can use your browser or the site's internal search tool to look for specific information within the site.

4. *Evaluating what you find*—In evaluating your research results, it is especially important to consider the reliability of any information obtained online.

5. *Updating your results*—To update results, you can access news sites online to look for articles or press releases concerning recent developments in the area you are researching.

Locating People and Investigating Companies

Paralegals often engage in online research to locate information about persons and to investigate companies. Sometimes, a person can be located through a broad search of the Web using a search engine such as Yahoo. Narrow searches can be conducted by accessing—for free or for a fee—specialized databases, such as compilations of physicians, lawyers, or expert witnesses. Searches for persons may also be conducted based on specific characteristics, such as veteran status or vehicle registration. Numerous online sites contain information about both private and public companies.

Some of the Best Legal Resource Sites on the Internet

Basic resources that you can find on the Web range from almanacs to ZIP code directories. Various university and government sites offer links to a number of primary and secondary legal sources. There are also online databases that catalogue associations, professional organizations, and nonprofit organizations, as well as several free commercial sites that serve as all-purpose starting points for online research.

(Continued)

CD-ROMS and Legal Research

Computer-assisted legal research sometimes involves using CD-ROMs. An advantage of using legal resources in CD-ROM format is that they are less costly to purchase and require less physical space than printed resources. CD-ROMs can also be easily transported, which means they can be used while traveling, in the courtroom, or anywhere outside the office. The major disadvantage of using CD-ROMs in legal research is that they, like their printed equivalents, eventually become outdated.

Westlaw and Lexis

For serious legal research, legal professionals often use online commercial legal research services, particularly Lexis and Westlaw. Subscribers to these fee-based services can access the services' databases via the Internet. Both Lexis and Westlaw provide their users with access to an extensive collection of legal, business, and other resources. Using these services, paralegals can access specific documents, check citations, update the law, and search hundreds of databases. Both Lexis and Westlaw allow users to search databases with queries using terms and connectors or natural language.

QUESTIONS FOR REVIEW

1. What is the difference between the Internet and the World Wide Web? What are uniform resource locators?

2. What is a browser? What are Internet guides and directories?

3. What should you do before going online to conduct a research session? Is the Internet a good research tool for serious legal research? Why or why not?

4. What are some starting points in doing online research? How can you discover what resources are available on the Web? Why is it important to evaluate the reliability of information found online and to update the results of an Internet research session?

5. What online search techniques could you use when trying to find information on a specific person? How would you go about finding company names and addresses in an Internet search?

6. List five basic, nonlegal resources that can be accessed via the Internet. Name four universities whose law schools or legal institutes provide extensive Internet legal libraries or links to Internet legal resources.

7. What kinds of legal resources can be accessed at various government sites? What resources or search tools can be found at sites for associations and organizations and at free commercial sites?

8. What are some of the advantages and disadvantages of using legal resources in CD-ROM format when conducting legal research?

9. What is Westlaw? What is Lexis? How do legal professionals access these services? What kinds of legal sources do these services make available to users?

10. How can these services be used to update the law? Describe two ways in which you can search databases on Lexis and Westlaw.

ETHICAL QUESTIONS

1. Janice, a paralegal in a firm specializing in labor law, joins a listserv. It is called **AWD@counterpoint.com**. It is a discussion group about the Americans with Disabilities Act (ADA) of 1990 and related laws. Another member of the group posts a question about what companies the ADA applies to and whether his company is subject to the law. Janice knows the answer and could answer it. Should Janice answer the question? Why or why not?

2. The partners in the law firm of Dewey & Howe learn about a plane crash in the morning newspaper. They instruct their legal assistant to contact all of the families of the victims via e-mail to see if they are interested in filing a class-action lawsuit against the airline. Is this type of activity allowed under the ethical rules?

3. The partners in the law firm of Smith & Varney decide that the firm needs a Web page to advertise its services over the Internet. They assign the task to paralegal Mark Hampton. Mark develops a Web site that contains a biography of each attorney, e-mail addresses for all attorneys, and Web links to helpful and related practice areas. Is this type of Web site allowable advertising under the ethical rules?

4. Samantha, a paralegal, runs a credit check on a client over the Internet without using an encryption program. The client's Visa number is intercepted, and unauthorized purchases amounting to $4,320 are charged on the client's account. What kind of ethical problems result?

5. John Hernandez is studying at a local college to be a paralegal. The college has Westlaw for its students to use. The software license specifically prohibits the faculty or students of the college from using the program for personal work. John knows that Kathy, a classmate, has a part-time job with a law firm, and he becomes aware that Kathy is using Westlaw regularly to do research for her supervising attorney in that firm. What should John do?

PRACTICE QUESTIONS AND ASSIGNMENTS

1. Explain the parts of the following URL:

    http://www.urisko.edu

2. Create your own URL, using your name to create a Web site for commercial purposes.

3. Using the material presented in the chapter, make a list of the Web sites that you would search to find the name, address, and telephone number of a particular company. Would you search the same sites for more detailed information? If not, where would you search? Does it make a difference whether the company is public or private? If so, where would you search for information on public companies? Where would you search for information on private companies?

4. Assume that the legal researchers in the situations described below all have access to an excellent law library, to Web resources, and to Westlaw or Lexis. Which of these three research sources or tools would you advise the legal professional to use for his or her particular research need? Why?

    a. Matthew, a paralegal, needs to find out if a case cited in a legal motion he is drafting is still good law.

    b. Cindy, an attorney, needs to locate a psychiatric expert witness.

    c. Robert, a paralegal, has been asked to locate a statutory provision; he needs to make sure that the result is up to date.

    d. Tom, a paralegal, needs to locate a witness to a car accident.

    e. Megan, a paralegal, needs to find an heir who is to inherit $500,000 under her uncle's will.

5. Using the material presented in the chapter on Westlaw, answer the following questions:

    a. How would you gain access to Westlaw?

    b. How would you find the case *Tasini v. New York Times Co., Inc.*, 184 F.Supp.2d 350 (2002)? How would you find out whether the holding in that case is still good law?

    c. What specific steps would you take to find the database of decisions made by courts in your state?

6. Suppose that one of your clients is suing a restaurant that served her tainted oysters. The oysters contained bacteria that caused the client to suffer serious health injuries, including permanent nerve damage. What databases would you search on Westlaw to find out whether there are any other cases involving this issue or a similar issue? How would you draft a query in natural language to retrieve these cases from the selected database(s)? What key terms would you use to draft a query using terms and connectors?

QUESTIONS FOR CRITICAL ANALYSIS

1. The Internet offers vast resources and provides these resources instantly. What are the advantages of the Internet? Are there any disadvantages? If so, what are they?

2. What impact does the Internet have on how legal professionals perform their work? What impact does it have on society as a whole? Is the impact positive or negative, or both?

3. What is a browser? How do directories and search engines differ?

4. What benefit can Boolean logic provide regarding search engines? If you wanted to find information about copyright attorneys through a search engine, what operators could you use to narrow your search?

5. Why would a paralegal who is performing factual research on the Internet need to evaluate the credibility of the Web sites located? Would this be necessary for government Web sites as well? What might the results be if a researcher does not evaluate the credibility of Web sites?

6. Why would an attorney invest in a legal encyclopedia contained on a CD-ROM instead of a printed set of encyclopedias? In conducting legal research, would you prefer to use legal sources in CD-ROM format rather than printed legal sources? Why or why not?

7. Legal professionals must pay a significant fee to access legal databases provided by commercial services such as Westlaw and Lexis. Why would it ever be preferable to use these fee-based services for research instead of the World Wide Web, which offers free access to numerous online legal and other resources?

8. What are some advantages of using Westlaw or Lexis when doing legal research rather than using the printed resources in a law library? Are there any disadvantages?

 ## PROJECTS

1. Most colleges and universities provide Internet access to students. Find out if the school you attend provides such access. If it does, find out which Web browser is used. Also, find out if it is possible for students to have an e-mail account at the school.

2. Do a research project on how and why the Internet was created. Write a two-page paper summarizing the results of your research.

3. Using a word-processing program, create a Web page for yourself, your employer, or your paralegal program. What information needs to be included?

4. Contact the West Group sales representative for your area. Request information on West's research products. Write a one-page paper describing what is available and how much Westlaw costs.

 ## USING INTERNET RESOURCES

1. Sign on to Westlaw or Lexis using your instructor-assigned password. If you do not have a Westlaw or Lexis instructor-assigned password, click on the following link to sign up for two free weeks of Westlaw: **http://www.westlaw.com/NewUser/trial.wl**. Refer back to Chapter 17 and do Practice Question and Assignment 5 on Westlaw or Lexis. Before logging on to either service, read the assignment and make a list of relevant terms. Use natural language and search in the legal encyclopedia database for an article on automobile lemon laws.

   a. To answer 5a, copy and paste the list of sources that comes up when you run the search.

   b. For 5b, copy and paste the sections that you read to find the answer to Mr. Consumer's problem.

   c. For 5c, make sure that you write down the section that gives you Mr. Consumer's remedy, along with the remedy from the encyclopedia.

   d. If your search result contains articles from two or more legal encyclopedias, write a one-paragraph description of the differences in the coverage of the topic in these sources.

2. The American Bar Association's Web site contains helpful information on legal research sources on the Internet. Access the Web site at

   http://www.abanet.org/lpm/var/research.shtml

   Answer the following questions about the research sources available online:

   a. What categories of research materials are available?

   b. Go to the "Legal Resources" category. Click on "National Conference of State Legislatures." How is the site organized?

   c. Click on the "Back" button. Select "Cornell's Legal Information Institute's U.S. Code." What are the different ways that a user can access the material here?

3.  For additional resources, visit our Web site at **http://www.paralegal.delmar.cengage.com**.

END NOTES

1. Sarah K. Cron and Darrell Patton, eds., "*LAT's* 5th Annual Technology Survey Results," *Legal Assistant Today,* May/June 2006, pp. 53–61.

LEGAL WRITING: FORM AND SUBSTANCE

CHAPTER

CHAPTER OUTLINE

AFTER COMPLETING THIS CHAPTER, YOU WILL KNOW:

- ▶ What factors you should consider before undertaking a legal-writing assignment.
- ▶ What factors you should consider when drafting a legal document.
- ▶ Some techniques for improving your writing skills.
- ▶ Some basic guidelines for structuring sentences and paragraphs.
- ▶ The purpose and format of the most common types of legal letters.
- ▶ How to prepare a legal memorandum.

INTRODUCTION

To a certain extent, legal research, analysis, and writing are all part of the same process. Once you locate the law that applies to a particular issue in dispute, you need to interpret that law and analyze how it applies to the facts of the client's case. After that, you must be able to summarize the results of your research and analysis in writing to communicate those results clearly to your supervising attorney.

Much legal writing, of course, is not directly related to the research process. As a paralegal, your day will frequently involve other types of writing responsibilities as well. You will be expected to know how to draft letters to clients and opposing counsel, internal memos, pleadings to be submitted to the court, and a variety of other documents.

Although a paralegal may be involved in drafting many kinds of legal documents, the same basic principles of writing apply to all. In this chapter, we provide some guidelines and suggestions for how to write effectively and describe some of the types and formats of legal documents commonly prepared by paralegals.

LEGAL WRITING—THE PRELIMINARIES

Much of your work as a paralegal will involve writing assignments. We will look at writing skills and the kinds of legal materials that paralegals create in subsequent sections. Here, you will read about some general requirements involved in legal writing.

Whenever you receive a writing assignment, you need to understand at the outset (1) the nature of your writing assignment, (2) when it must be completed, and (3) what type of writing approach is appropriate to the assignment. We examine each of these basic requirements here.

Understanding the Assignment

The practice of law is often hectic, and frequently paralegals are asked to research, analyze, and report their results on particular issues within a short time period. When you receive a writing assignment, you should always make sure that you understand the exact nature of the request so that you can execute your task as efficiently as possible. The writing style, format, and methodological approach used in legal writing vary, depending on the specific objectives of the document you are supposed to create. If you need to ask questions, do so. You should never equate asking questions with incompetence. As the adage states, the only "dumb question" is the one that is not asked.

Time Constraints and Flexibility

The time factor is an important consideration in legal writing. When you receive a writing assignment, you need to understand clearly when the assignment must be completed. In some situations, you will be required to submit writings to a court by a certain date, which is inflexible. Additionally, clients usually demand quick responses to questions. And frequently, during the course of litigation or other legal activities, crucial new issues arise that must be addressed immediately, often overnight or within two or three days. As a paralegal, you will need to assess such situations realistically. If little time is given for the completion of a project, you will have to use your informed judgment, deciding what information is crucial to the writing and what can be omitted.

In addition to time constraints, other circumstances may influence the way a paralegal handles an assignment. For example, external circumstances, such as newly enacted laws, may affect the legal treatment of an issue. Additionally, a client may unexpectedly demand

Much of a paralegal's work involves legal writing, whether it be a research memorandum, a letter to a client, or a pleading or motion to be filed with a court. Excellent writing skills are a must for the professional paralegal.

(Courtesy of ©Inmagine/Alamy)

a change in the course of action. These situations require flexibility. Whenever you undertake a writing task, you should be prepared for the possibility that you may have to make quick changes and go in new directions before your assignment is completed.

Writing Approaches

Another thing you should determine when you receive a writing assignment is what type of writing is required. Some documents require an *objective* (unbiased) analysis, which either focuses on the facts or presents a balanced discussion of both sides of an issue. Other documents are *persuasive* and require you to advocate by presenting the facts and issues in the light most favorable to your client.

For example, assume that your supervising attorney hands you two lease agreements and asks you to compare them and note whether the differences in the wording of the agreements lead to different obligations. Your concern will not be to point out which agreement is better but to analyze and compare the documents objectively and point out which clauses lead to what kinds of obligations. Objective analysis may also be required when an attorney seeks assistance in providing clients with information regarding a particular legal matter. Clients often seek the advice of an attorney to determine whether they have a claim that merits the filing of a lawsuit. In this situation, an attorney may request the paralegal to investigate the issues thoroughly and provide a memorandum containing an accurate and unbiased analysis of the issue.

If the writing assignment is intended to advocate a position, the style of writing will be somewhat different. For example, if your supervising attorney asks you to draft a pretrial motion asking the court to exclude certain evidence from a trial, you will need to adopt a persuasive style of writing. Your goal will be to convince the judge that the argument proposed is stronger than the opposing party's position. You will therefore need to develop supportive legal arguments and present the matter in the light most favorable to the client.

(Realize, though, that attorneys have a duty of candor toward the court. This duty requires an attorney to disclose mandatory authorities to the court even if those authorities are adverse to the client's position. The attorney can, of course, still argue that the client's case should be distinguished from the controlling authority.)

THE IMPORTANCE OF GOOD WRITING SKILLS

The legal profession is primarily a communications profession. Effective written communications are particularly crucial in the legal arena. For paralegals, good writing skills therefore go hand in hand with successful job performance. The more competent a writer you are, the more likely it is that your finished products will be satisfactory to the attorney with whom you are working. You should also keep in mind that some of your written projects, such as correspondence, represent the firm for which you work. A well-written document is a positive reflection on the firm and upholds the firm's reputation for good performance.

Each writing assignment you receive will give you an opportunity to improve and perfect your writing skills. In the following sections, we offer some guidelines you can follow as you strive to improve your writing. Paralegals seriously interested in improving their writing skills also will have close at hand a good dictionary, a thesaurus, a style manual (such as Strunk and White's *The Elements of Style* or the *Chicago Manual of Style*), and perhaps a book or two on basic English grammar.

Organize and Outline Your Presentation

Once you know what it is you want to demonstrate, discuss, or prove to your reader, you need to decide how best to organize your ideas to achieve this end. Because organization is essential to effective legal writing, you should have your organizational framework in mind before you begin writing. Most people find that an outline—whether it is a simple sketch in pencil on a scrap of paper or a detailed outline created by a specialized computer program— makes writing easier. It not only saves time but also produces a more organized result.

When creating an outline, you decide the sequence in which topics should be discussed. Often, lawyers put their strongest argument first in legal writing. Aside from that, some issues will need to be addressed before others, either for logical reasons or for purposes of clarity and readability. Similar issues should be grouped together, either in the same section or under the same topic heading. Other factors you will want to consider when organizing your presentation are format and structural devices.

Choice of Format

An important requirement in legal writing is selecting the appropriate format. The format of a document concerns such things as the width of margins, the indentation of paragraphs, and the number of line spaces between paragraphs or other sections, for example. Documents to be filed with a court must conform to the procedural rules of the particular jurisdiction. Most law firms also adopt special formats for other types of documents, such as correspondence sent to clients and opposing counsel and internal legal memoranda. When writing these types of documents, you need to know what format your firm prefers to use.

Structural Devices

If you are writing about a complex legal research project involving numerous issues, you may want to divide your presentation into several sections, with each section dealing with one issue. You can make it easier for the reader to follow the discussion by including a "road

Developing Paralegal Skills

CREATING A USER-FRIENDLY DOCUMENT

Lisa Barnes works as a paralegal for a large law firm. The managing partner of the firm asks Lisa to draft a policy on sexual harassment for a corporate client. The attorney gives Lisa several sheets of handwritten instructions and notes on what should be contained in the document. Lisa creates a draft of the policy and begins to proofread it. She realizes that although she used plain English whenever possible and followed all of the rules of good writing, the document is somewhat daunting in its appearance. She decides to add a series of headings and subheadings to the document to break up the "fine print" and make the document more inviting to readers.

TIPS FOR CREATING A USER-FRIENDLY DOCUMENT

- Use plain English whenever it is feasible to do so, especially when writing for an audience that may have little legal training.

- Use short sentences, but do not overdo it—too many short sentences in a row can make the writing choppy and interrupt the flow of the text.

- Use the active voice unless the situation calls for a passive construction.

- Be consistent in style and word usage. For example, do not hyphenate a phrase in one place in the document and not elsewhere, and use the same line spacing between paragraphs and sections in the document.

- Format the document attractively. For example, add enough margin space to frame the text appropriately.

- Divide the document into sections preceded by headings to make the progression of thought immediately clear to the reader.

- Add subheadings to further divide visually long sections of text. If you add subheadings, always add at least two.

- Make sure that the relationship between the sections and subsections is clear to the reader. Often, this can be made clear in the document's introduction. Alternatively, transitional sentences at the beginning of each section or subsection can be used to clarify the progression of thought from one section or subsection to the next.

map" to the document. For example, you might preface the writing with an introduction that highlights the points that will be discussed and the conclusion that will be reached, thus orienting the reader to the document's contents. You might also use numbered or bulleted lists as a device to let the reader know the structure of your argument or discussion. In addition, try to "walk" your reader through the analysis and discussion by including descriptive headings and subheadings in the body of the document so that the reader never gets lost.

Arranging events **chronologically**—that is, in a time sequence—can also serve as a structural device. A chronologically structured discussion is sometimes easier for the reader to follow. This is particularly true when you are describing the factual background leading to a lawsuit. Presenting the facts and events in chronological order helps to orient the reader. Even if you are discussing legal issues instead of facts, you might want to use a chronological structure for at least part of your discussion. For example, if you are writing about the historical development of a particular rule of law, you will want to structure that part of the discussion chronologically.

chronologically
In a time sequence; naming or listing events in the time order in which they occurred.

Write to Your Audience

Paralegals prepare legal documents and correspondence for a wide range of people. Whenever you draft legal correspondence or legal documents of any kind, you should keep in mind that legal documents are not ends in themselves. They are created for someone (a judge, an attorney, a client, a witness, or some other person) to read. The ultimate goal of legal writing is to *communicate* information or ideas clearly to your reader. It is therefore important to tailor the writing to the intended audience. For example, a letter directed to an attorney may include legal terms and concepts that would be inappropriate in a letter to a layperson, who probably would not understand them. Similarly, a motion written to present to a judge should not include detailed explanations of classic cases, as the judge would be familiar with the facts of such cases. You must therefore consider to whom the legal writing is directed and what legal understanding the reader possesses.

In addition to the reader's legal knowledge, paralegals should consider how well the reader understands the subject matter. You cannot presume, especially in cases dealing with technical and scientific matters, that your reader knows as much as the attorney or yourself. Indeed, you should normally assume the contrary—that the reader has had neither the time nor the background to gain a comprehensive understanding of every legal or factual matter presented. Both in consideration of your reader's needs and in the interests of effective communication, you should present your information or analysis clearly, carefully leading the reader from Point A to Point B, from Point B to Point C, and so on.

Avoid Legalese: Use Everyday English

As a paralegal, writing to your audience often requires you to minimize or eliminate legal jargon, or legalese. Legalese consists of terms that are used by legal professionals but that are unknown to most people outside the legal profession. Therefore, if you are writing a letter to a client, either avoid using legal terms the client may not understand or define such terms for your reader. For example, if you are advising a client of the date on which *voir dire* will take place, consider saying "jury selection"—or perhaps *"voir dire* (jury selection)"—instead. Although a certain amount of legal terminology in legal writing is unavoidable, you should minimize the use of language that may confuse the reader. (See this chapter's *Technology and Today's Paralegal* feature for a discussion of online sources offering instructions on and some examples of "plain English" writing.)

Lawyers have traditionally used certain terms in legal documents—words such as *hereof, therein,* and *thereto,* for example—that you should avoid whenever possible in your writing. These and similar words sound strange and excessively formal to the ordinary person. Legal documents are also often filled with redundancies. Consider, for example, the following phrase from an agreement to finance a business:

> If Borrower shall have made any representation or warranty herein . . . which shall be in any material respect false and/or erroneous and/or incorrect . . .

What is the difference between *false, erroneous,* and *incorrect?* Often, these terms are used synonymously, and it is hard to imagine that something could be erroneous and still be correct—so why should it be necessary to add *incorrect* to the clause?

Other commonly used legal phrases containing obvious redundancies include *all the rest, residue, and remainder; null and void; full and complete;* and *cease and desist.* In the first phrase, the words *rest, residue,* and *remainder* mean essentially the same thing. In the second phrase, the words *null* and *void* are synonymous, as are the coupled terms in the other phrases. Yet these types of phrases are commonplace in legal documents, largely because they have traditionally been used in the legal profession and because of the natural inclination of lawyers to want to make sure that all aspects of a given subject are covered.

Technology and Today's Paralegal

ONLINE "PLAIN ENGLISH" GUIDELINES

The ability to write clearly and effectively is a valuable asset to any paralegal, because virtually every paralegal is required to do a certain amount of writing as a part of his or her job. As mentioned elsewhere, clear and effective writing means keeping legalese—legal terminology typically understood only by legal professionals—to a minimum or even eliminating it entirely. The problem is how to convert traditional legal language into clear and understandable prose. Today's paralegals can find helpful instruction in the art of writing in plain English at many online locations.

GOVERNMENT PUBLICATIONS

The U.S. government publishes some of the best online plain English guides. *A Plain English Handbook*, put out by the Securities and Exchange Commission (SEC), is available at **http://www.sec.gov/pdf/handbook.pdf**. Although the handbook was intended to help individuals create clearer and more informative SEC disclosure documents, the guidelines given in the booklet can apply to any written communication. The U.S. Small Business Administration also publishes an online guide explaining how to write in plain language at **http://www.sba.gov/plain/whatis.html**. In addition, the Office of the Federal Register's booklet *Drafting Legal Documents* can be found at **http://www.archives.gov/federal_register/write/legal-docs**.

The U.S. government has an official Web site dedicated to the use of plain language (**http://www.plainlanguage.gov**) and publishes a guide called *Writing User-Friendly Documents*. Foreign governments also may provide useful information. For example, the Australian government publishes a booklet called *Plain English at Work* that can be accessed at **http://www.dest.gov.au/archive/publications/plain_en**.

WORLDWIDE ORGANIZATIONS

Since the 1970s, the plain English movement, which is fighting to have public information (such as laws) written in plain English, has received worldwide attention. A British organization called the Plain English Campaign is one of the most prominent groups in this movement. The Plain English Campaign has worked to promote the use of plain English in many nations, including the United States. You can find (and download) several helpful guides at its Web site (**http://www.plainenglishcampaign.com**), including *How to Write in Plain English* and *The A-Z of Alternative Words*. Another campaign, called Fight the Fog, is directed at institutions in the European Union (EU). At its Web site, **http://ec.europa.eu/comm/translation/en/ftfog**, you can read a booklet called *How to Write Clearly*, as well as other news and publications in several languages.

TECHNOLOGY TIP

Paralegals interested in improving their plain English writing skills have many Internet resources to which they can turn. The guides mentioned above provide practical information and suggest alternative wording. In addition, paralegals can take online writing courses, such as that offered by Purdue University at **http://www.web.ca/~plain/PlainTrain/Digest.html**.

As a paralegal, you should strive to minimize the use of legalese, including redundancies, in your own writing. When translating legalese into plain English, however, you need to make sure that you correctly understand the intent of the legal phrase. If you have any doubts, always ask your supervising attorney.

EXHIBIT 19.1
Using Words Efficiently

Do not write:
Ms. Carpenter never drives at night due to the fact that she has poor night vision.

Write instead:
Ms. Carpenter does not drive at night because she has poor night vision.

Do not write:
The new client who brought his business to our attention yesterday has a number of issues pertaining to his legal problems that he needs to discuss with us as soon as possible.

Write instead:
The client who hired us yesterday needs to discuss his legal problems immediately.

Do not write:
The defendant worked for one of the members of an organized crime ring for a period of seven years. During that seven-year period of time, the defendant witnessed crimes numbering in the hundreds.

Write instead:
During the seven years that the defendant worked for a member of an organized crime ring, he witnessed hundreds of crimes.

Be Brief and to the Point

Just as the use of legalese can hinder communication, so, too, can the use of too many words. Writing effectively requires efficiency in word usage. Omit surplus words. Unnecessary words can become stumbling blocks for your reader and prevent a clear understanding of the point you wish to make. Moreover, concise statements are much more powerful and persuasive. When proofreading your document, take time to make sure that your statements are brief and to the point. Exhibit 19.1 offers some examples of how efficient word usage can enhance clarity.

Generally, you should only use words essential to the point you are making; unnecessary words may distract and confuse the reader. Similarly, you should include in your writing only concepts or facts directly relevant to your topic.

Writing Basics: Sentences

A good writer uses a high proportion of short, concrete sentences because they are easier to understand. Additionally, forceful sentences include active, dynamic verbs rather than nominalizations (verbs transformed into nouns). For example, it is simpler and more effective to say "the plaintiff decided to settle the case" than "the plaintiff made a decision to settle the case." In the first example, the verb *decide* is direct and forceful. In the second example, the conversion of *decided* into *made a decision* detracts from the forcefulness of the verb.

Writing in the active voice also makes sentences easier to understand. The active voice sets up a subject-verb-object sentence structure, whereas the passive voice uses an object-verb-subject format. For example, "The defendant stole the diamond" uses the active voice. Contrast the simplicity and strength of this statement with its passive equivalent: "The diamond was stolen by the defendant." The use of the active voice puts people, actors, movers, and doers into your writing and thus makes your writing more reflective of reality. Sometimes, however, you may want to maintain the facelessness of the actor or doer. For example, if your firm is defending a plaintiff who has been accused of stealing a diamond, consider writing "the diamond that was stolen" instead of "the diamond that the plaintiff allegedly stole." In this situation, the passive voice effectively removes the plaintiff from the action.

You should also make sure you use correct grammar when writing legal documents. Grammatical and punctuation errors, such as those in the following sentences, distract your reader and may reflect poorly on your (and your firm's) professional reputation and status.

- *Incorrect:* The plaintiff should *of* consulted with the defendant.
- *Correct:* The plaintiff should *have* consulted with the defendant.
- *Incorrect:* The defendant could not possibly have *did* what the plaintiff alleged.
- *Correct:* The defendant could not possibly have *done* what the plaintiff alleged.
- *Incorrect:* The *plaintiffs* allegations were vague and ambiguous.
- *Correct:* The *plaintiff's* allegations were vague and ambiguous.

When proofreading your documents, make sure they are free of any errors involving subject-verb agreement, punctuation, spelling, the use of apostrophes, and other elements.

Writing Basics: Paragraphs and Transitions

A paragraph is a group of sentences that develops a particular idea. A paragraph should have unity and coherence. Each paragraph should begin with a *topic sentence* that indicates what the paragraph is about. Each subsequent sentence in the paragraph should contribute to the development of the topic; if it does not, consider placing the sentence elsewhere or simply deleting it. When you write, be conscious of why you begin a new paragraph—or why you do not. Keep paragraphs short, if possible. Create a new paragraph whenever you start discussing another idea. Paragraphs that are not logically constructed are often confusing and may seem pointless to the reader.

Take your reader with you as you move from one paragraph to another. Although the connection between paragraphs may be clear to you, the writer, it may not be clear to your reader. You need to show, by including transitional sentences or phrases, how a topic discussed in one paragraph relates to the subsequent paragraph. Exhibit 19.2 on the next page lists some terms and phrases writers commonly use to effect smooth transitions.

Be Alert for Sexist Language

The language of the law has traditionally used masculine pronouns inclusively—that is, to refer to both males and females. Jurists, legal scholars, and others in the legal profession are consciously moving away from this tradition. As a paralegal, you should take special care to become aware of and avoid sexist language in your own writing. For example, if you see a word with "man" or "men" in it (such as *policeman, fireman,* or *workmen's compensation*) use a gender-neutral substitute (such as *police officer, firefighter,* or *workers' compensation*). In the past few decades, writers have devised various ways to avoid using masculine pronouns when the referent's gender is unknown, including the following:

- Use *he* or *she* rather than *he.*
- Alternate between the use of masculine and feminine pronouns.
- Make the noun plural so that a gender-neutral plural pronoun (*they, their,* or *them*) can be used.
- Repeat the noun rather than using a pronoun.

Proofread and Revise Your Document

A crucial part of legal writing involves proofreading and revising your document. When you receive a writing assignment, you should always allow time to proofread and revise whatever you are writing. Virtually no writer can turn out an error-free document on the first try, and

EXHIBIT 19.2
Transitional Terms and Phrases

1. **Words that indicate a conceptual or causal sequence or relationship. Examples:**

   The *third* element required for a cause of action under negligence theory is that the plaintiff must have suffered a legally recognizable injury.

   As a result of the fall, the plaintiff was injured.

2. **Words that indicate a chronological sequence of events. Examples:**

   After the fall, the plaintiff was taken to Nita City Hospital & Clinic.

   Before the plaintiff's accident, she was in excellent health.

3. **Words that refer back to the subject discussed in the previous paragraph. Examples:**

   Courts make exceptions to *this rule* in certain situations, however.

   The act does not apply to employers who have fewer than fifteen employees, however.

   If the *above-mentioned conditions* are not met, the injured party cannot recover damages.

   In contrast to negligence actions, actions in strict liability do not require the plaintiff to prove that the defendant breached a duty of care.

   If the *plaintiff* had not been *injured in the fall*, then she would have no cause of action against the store owner.

4. **Words that introduce summaries. Examples:**

   In short, the plaintiff has a valid claim against the defendant.

   In summary, the plaintiff met all four conditions for a negligence action against the defendant.

   To conclude, the plaintiff established the element of causation by demonstrating that she would not have been injured if it had not been for the defendant's actions.

as a paralegal, you will be especially concerned with accuracy. Proofreading your document allows you to discover and correct typographical errors, to see whether your document reflects a logical progression of thought from one topic to another, and to verify whether you have covered all of the relevant facts or issues. You should use the spell checker in your computer, and perhaps the grammar checker as well, to assist you in proofreading. Don't, however, count on these tools to catch all your errors.

Writing is a process, and the best legal writing goes through many drafts before it is submitted to a court or sent to an opponent. When going over the initial drafts of a document, look for gaps in the content development or legal reasoning. Check to make sure that the argument is organized effectively and the rationale is well developed. It is often helpful to read the document out loud or have someone else who is unfamiliar with the case or topic read the draft to provide you with constructive criticism. Another technique is to take a break and work on another project, then come back to revise the document when you can look at it from a fresh perspective. Ask yourself whether the document says what you intended it to say and what you can do to improve its effectiveness (for example, use more descriptive headings, fewer words, or better transitions).

When you write your first draft, you have much to think about, and you may overlook many details. When proofreading your document, you can pay more attention to organiza-

ETHICS AND TIME MANAGEMENT

Many paralegals learn the hard way—through trial and error—that the ability to manage their time effectively is an essential part of doing a good job. One of the easiest things to overlook when engaging in research and writing is that good writing takes time—you may need to revise a document more than once before you are satisfied with its quality. Whenever you are given a writing assignment, you should make sure you allow yourself enough time to revise and polish your final document. As a paralegal, you have an ethical duty to your supervising attorney, the firm, and the client to serve their best interests. In regard to legal writing, their interests are served by the production of clear and convincing legal documents—and by your ability to manage your time so that this goal can be achieved.

tional coherence, transitions, paragraph construction, sentence formation, word choice, sexist language, and the like. You might find it helpful to develop a "writing checklist" to remind you of certain things you want to avoid or achieve in your writing—particularly if there is a required format for the particular type of document on which you are working. In short, when you are writing legal documents, realize that creating a polished document takes time, and a good portion of that time should be spent in proofreading and revising your written work product. (For some tips for making your legal writing easier, see this chapter's *Featured Guest* article on the following pages.)

PLEADINGS AND DISCOVERY

Many writing tasks undertaken by paralegals involve forms that must be submitted to the court or to opposing counsel before a trial begins or after the trial has commenced. These documents were covered in detail earlier in this text, in Chapters 13, 15, and 16. You can review those chapters for explanations and illustrations of the forms required for pretrial procedures (pleadings, discovery procedures, and pretrial motions) and for motions made during the trial. Keep in mind that virtually every document that is submitted to the court should be written persuasively.

It is especially important that such documents contain the required information and be presented in the appropriate format. Form books and computerized forms offer guidelines, but you should always become familiar with the rules of the court in which the documents are being filed to ensure that you use the proper format.

GENERAL LEGAL CORRESPONDENCE

Paralegals are often asked to draft letters to clients, witnesses, opposing counsel, and others. Even when a message has already been conveyed orally (in person or by phone) to one of these parties, the paralegal may be asked to write a letter confirming in writing what was

William Putman

FEATURED **Guest**

TIPS FOR MAKING LEGAL WRITING EASIER

BIOGRAPHICAL NOTE

William Putman received his Juris Doctor degree from the University of New Mexico School of Law and has been a member of the New Mexico Bar since 1975. He was an instructor in the Legal Assistant Studies Program at Albuquerque TVI, a community college, and the Paralegal Studies Program at Santa Fe Community College for ten years.

Putman authored the textbooks Legal Research, Legal Analysis, and Writing for Paralegals; Legal Research, Analysis, and Writing; *and the* Pocket Guide to Legal Writing, *published by Thomson Delmar Learning. He also wrote the legal-writing column in* Legal Assistant Today *for two years and published several articles on legal analysis and writing in that magazine.*

UNDERSTAND THE ASSIGNMENT

A legal-writing assignment may seem to be a daunting task. But all writing assignments are made easier if you answer some preliminary questions before you begin to conduct research or start writing.

Is the assignment clearly understood? An important step in the writing process is to be sure that you understand the task you have been assigned. If you have any questions concerning the general nature or specifics of the assignment, ask. Most attorneys welcome inquiries and prefer that a paralegal ask questions rather than proceed in a wrong direction. Misunderstanding the assignment can result in wasting a great deal of time performing the wrong task or addressing the wrong issue.

What type of legal writing (document) is required? Before you begin, determine what type of legal writing the assignment requires—a legal research memorandum, correspondence, the rough draft of a court brief, and so on. This is important because each type of legal writing has a different function, requirements, and format.

Who is the audience? When assessing the requirements of an assignment, identify the intended audience. The intended reader may be a judge, an attorney, or a client. It is necessary to ensure that the writing is crafted in a manner suited to meet the needs of that reader. A legal writing designed to inform a client or other layperson of the legal analysis of an issue is drafted differently than a writing designed to convey the same information to an attorney.

What are the constraints on the assignment? Most assignments have time and length constraints. Assignments usually have a time deadline. Most assignments have a length constraint—that is, they should not exceed a certain number of pages. These constraints govern the amount of research you will conduct and require that you allocate sufficient time for both research and writing.

What is the format for the type of document being prepared? Most law offices have rules or guidelines that govern the organization and format of most types of legal writing, such as case briefs, office memoranda, and correspondence. Courts have formal rules governing the format and style of briefs and other documents submitted for filing. Because the assignment must be drafted within the constraints of the required format, identify the format at the beginning of the process.

discussed. Lawyers are extremely conscious of the need to document communications to avoid future problems. The existence of the written document clarifies any ambiguities that might arise in connection with the oral conversation and confirms that the conversation took place.

Law firms normally have an official letterhead and stationery. The letterhead contains certain information about the firm. Most letterheads include the firm's name, address, and phone and fax numbers. More and more commonly, they also include an e-mail address. Some firms have more descriptive letterheads that include the names of partners in the firm or the various geographical locations in which the firm has offices. You should always use your firm's letterhead when writing a letter on behalf of one of the firm's attorneys or when writing as a representative of the firm. The first page of any correspondence from the firm

These preliminary questions are often overlooked or not given sufficient attention by beginning writers, resulting in headaches later. The task is made easier if you answer these questions.

SOME WRITING TIPS

Many paralegals assigned a legal-writing task find it difficult to make the transition from the research stage to the drafting stage. Here are some guidelines that help make the writing process easier.

Select the right time and place for your writing. Write during the time of day when you do your best work. For example, if you are a "morning person," write in the morning and save other tasks for later in the day. Also, make sure that the work environment is pleasant and physically comfortable. Have available and at hand all of the resources you will need, such as writing paper, a computer, research materials, and so on. Legal writing requires focus and concentration. Therefore, select a writing time and an environment that allow you to be as free from interruptions and distractions as possible.

Begin writing—do not procrastinate. Often, one of the most difficult steps in writing is starting to write. Do not put it off. The longer you put it off, the harder it will become to start your writing project. Start writing anything that has to do with the project. Do not expect what you start with to be great—just start. Once you begin writing, it will get easier.

Begin with a part of the assignment about which you feel confident. You do not have to write in the sequence of the outline.

"[A]ll writing assignments are made easier if you answer some preliminary questions . . . . "

Write the easiest material first, especially if you are having trouble starting.

Do not try to make the first draft the final draft. The goal of the first draft should be to translate the research and analysis into organized paragraphs and sentences, not to produce a finished product. Just write the information in rough form. It is much easier to polish a rough draft than to try to make the first draft a finished product.

Do not begin to write until you are prepared. Do all the research and analysis before you begin to write. It is much easier to write a rough draft if you have completed the research and if the research is thorough.

If you become stuck, move to another part of the assignment. If you are stuck on a particular section, leave it. The mind continues to work on a problem when you are unaware of it. That is why solutions to problems often seem to appear in the morning. Let the subconscious work on the problem while you move on. The solution to the difficulty may become apparent when you return to the problem.

Establish a timetable. Break the project into logical units and allocate your time accordingly. This helps you avoid spending too much time on one section of the writing and running out of time. Do not become fanatical about the time schedule, however. You created the timetable, and you can break it. It is there as a guide to keep you on track and alert you to the overall time constraints.

should be composed on letterhead paper. Any additional pages can be printed on numbered continuing sheets using plain, matching stationery.

In this section, you will read about some typical requirements relating to legal correspondence. Keep in mind, though, that the particular law firm, corporate legal department, or government agency for which you work will probably have its own specific procedures and requirements, which you will need to follow.

General Format for Legal Correspondence

Although there are many types of legal correspondence, the general format of a legal letter includes the components discussed below and illustrated in Exhibit 19.3 on page 735.

Developing Paralegal Skills

EFFECTIVE EDITING

Paralegal Dixie Guiliano is asked by her supervising attorney to draft a letter on behalf of the firm's client, Nora Ferguson, to an insurance company demanding settlement. Nora is an eighty-year-old woman who will never be able to walk again because her physician allegedly performed her hip-replacement surgery poorly. The attorney wants to settle the case out of court because of Nora's age and declining health.

Dixie creates the first draft using a settlement letter from another case as a sample. She then uses the spell-check and grammar-check features on her word-processing program to check for errors. Dixie knows, however, that using these features is only a preliminary step in proofreading the document. She also knows that careful editing will improve the quality and persuasiveness of her letter.

TIPS FOR EDITING

- Always edit from a printed copy of the document. It is much easier to proofread and revise on paper than on a computer screen.

- If you use another document as a sample, or cut and paste text from another document, double-check that you have accurately changed the names, dates, and other information.

- Allow some time to pass (preferably a day) before editing the first draft so that you can look at what you have written more critically. Review each draft in its entirety, checking for different elements.

- Edit the content first. Ensure that the document is complete and says what you intended. Look for gaps in your reasoning. Make sure you have discussed all the points (including cases or statutes) that you planned to discuss. Check the organization so there is a logical progression of ideas.

- Next, look at your style. Make sure the document is aimed at the appropriate audience and that you have omitted unnecessary words. Change passive sentences into active voice, if possible.

- Make sure that you use terms, headings, and other devices (such as numbered lists) consistently throughout the document.

- Check your grammar and spelling. Confirm that the verb agrees with the subject in every sentence and that the proper verb tense is used. Check plurals and possessives.

- Finally, check your punctuation to verify that it is correct and used consistently throughout the document.

Date

Legal correspondence must be *dated*. The date appears below the official letterhead of the firm. You should make sure that the date is correctly keyed in. Be especially careful after the turn of a year. Many people continue to use the preceding year on correspondence, checks, and other documents simply out of habit. In a legal document, however, entering the wrong year could have important legal consequences.

As explained earlier, dates serve an important function in legal matters. The date of a letter may be critical in matters involving legal notice of a particular event. Additionally, legal correspondence normally is filed chronologically. Without any indication of when the letter was written, accurate filing of the letter would be difficult, if not impossible. As a general rule, you should always place a date on every written item that you create, including telephone messages, memos to file, and personal reminders to yourself.

EXHIBIT 19.3
Components of a Legal Letter

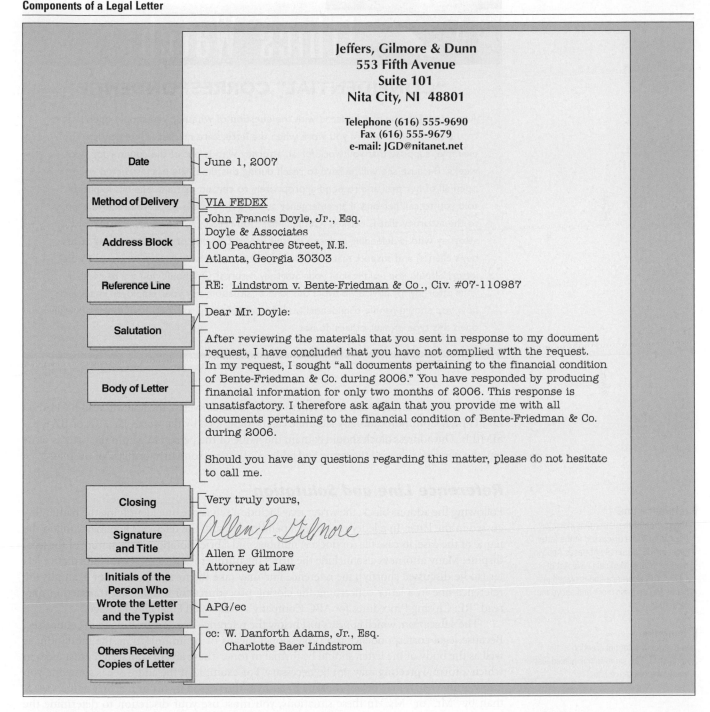

	Jeffers, Gilmore & Dunn **553 Fifth Avenue** **Suite 101** **Nita City, NI 48801** Telephone (616) 555-9690 Fax (616) 555-9679 e-mail: JGD@nitanet.net
Date	June 1, 2007
Method of Delivery	VIA FEDEX
Address Block	John Francis Doyle, Jr., Esq. Doyle & Associates 100 Peachtree Street, N.E. Atlanta, Georgia 30303
Reference Line	RE: Lindstrom v. Bente-Friedman & Co., Civ. #07-110987
Salutation	Dear Mr. Doyle:
Body of Letter	After reviewing the materials that you sent in response to my document request, I have concluded that you have not complied with the request. In my request, I sought "all documents pertaining to the financial condition of Bente-Friedman & Co. during 2006." You have responded by producing financial information for only two months of 2006. This response is unsatisfactory. I therefore ask again that you provide me with all documents pertaining to the financial condition of Bente-Friedman & Co. during 2006. Should you have any questions regarding this matter, please do not hesitate to call me.
Closing	Very truly yours,
Signature and Title	*Allen P. Gilmore* Allen P Gilmore Attorney at Law
Initials of the Person Who Wrote the Letter and the Typist	APG/ec
Others Receiving Copies of Letter	cc: W. Danforth Adams, Jr., Esq. Charlotte Baer Lindstrom

Method of Delivery and Address Block

Below the date is a line indicating the method of delivery, or how the letter is to be sent (if other than by U.S. mail), which is followed by the **address block**, which indicates to whom the letter is addressed. If the letter is to be sent by FedEx, the line before the recipient's name and

address block
The part of a letter that indicates to whom the letter is addressed. The address block is placed in the upper left-hand portion of the letter, above the salutation (or reference line, if one is included).

"CONFIDENTIAL" CORRESPONDENCE

As a paralegal, you may be faced with the question of whether you should open letters to the attorney for whom you work when the letters are marked "Confidential." For example, suppose that you work for an attorney who is out of the country for two weeks. Because she will be hard to reach during this time, she has instructed you to open all of her mail and respond appropriately to certain matters. She has explicitly told you to call her only if an emergency arises. While she is gone, you receive a letter to the attorney that is marked "Confidential." You recognize the sender's name (an attorney who is defending against a lawsuit brought by one of your supervising attorney's clients) and suspect that the letter pertains to the lawsuit. Should you open the letter? Should you hold it until your attorney returns? Or should you try to contact your attorney for advice? To avoid this kind of situation, ask your employer in advance how you should handle confidential mail. Some attorneys routinely have their paralegals open this type of mail; others do not.

address will read VIA FEDEX. If the letter is to be hand-delivered, the line will read BY HAND DELIVERY. Communication by facsimile can be described by the words BY FAX or BY FAC-SIMILE. The address block should contain the name of the person to whom the letter is written, the person's title, and the name and address of the person's firm or place of business.

Reference Line and Salutation

<div class="margin">

reference line
The portion of the letter that indicates the matter to be discussed in the letter, such as "RE: Summary of Cases Applying the Family and Medical Leave Act of 1993." The reference line is placed just below the address block and above the salutation.

salutation
In a letter, the formal greeting to the addressee. The salutation is placed just below the reference line.

</div>

Following the address block, the writer may include a **reference line** identifying the matter discussed in the letter. In a letter regarding a pending lawsuit, the reference line may contain the name of the case, its case file (or docket) number, and a brief notation of the nature of the legal dispute. Many attorneys also include the firm's file number for the case. In an informative letter (to be discussed shortly), the reference line may take the form of a title. For example, the reference line in a letter concerning the closing procedures for a financing transaction may read "RE: Closing Procedures for ABC Company's $4,000,000 Financing Package."

The **salutation**, which appears just below the reference line, is a greeting to the addressee. Because legal correspondence is a professional means of communication, the salutation, as well as the body of the letter, should be formal in tone. There are, of course, circumstances in which a formal greeting may not be necessary. For example, if the addressee is someone you know quite well, it may be appropriate to address the person by his or her first name, rather than by "Mr." or "Ms." In these situations, you must use your discretion to determine the appropriate level of formality. Generally, when in doubt, use a formal salutation.

Body and Closing

The main part of the letter is the body of the letter. The body of the letter should be formal and should effectively communicate information to the reader. As a representative of the firm, the paralegal must be careful to proofread all outgoing correspondence to ensure that the letter contains accurate information, is clearly written, and is free of any grammatical or spelling errors.

Following the body of the letter are standard concluding sentences. These final sentences are usually courteous statements such as "Thank you for your time and attention to this matter," or "Should you have any questions or comments, please call me at the above-listed number." These brief concluding statements are followed by the **closing**. The closing in legal correspondence is formal—for example, "Sincerely" or "Very truly yours."

Finally, you should always include your title in any correspondence written by you on behalf of the firm. Your title ("Paralegal" or "Legal Assistant" or other title) should immediately follow your name. This, of course, is not a concern when you prepare correspondence for an attorney who will provide a signature.

closing
In a letter, an ending word or phrase placed above the signature, such as "Sincerely" or "Very truly yours."

Types of Legal Letters

There are several types of legal correspondence, and each type serves a different purpose. Types of legal letters with which you should become familiar include the following:

- Informative letters.
- Confirmation letters.
- Opinion (advisory) letters.
- Demand letters.

Informative Letters

A letter that conveys information to another party is an **informative letter**. As a paralegal, you will write many such letters—to clients, for example. Informative letters might be written to advise a client about current developments in a case, an upcoming meeting or procedure, the general background on a legal issue, or simply a breakdown of the firm's bill. The letters you write should be tailored to the client's level of legal understanding.

Informative letters are also sent to opposing counsel and other individuals. For example, law firms often send litigation-scheduling information to opposing counsel, witnesses, and other persons who may be involved in a trial. Informative letters may also be used as transmittal (cover) letters when documents or other materials are sent to a client, a court, opposing counsel, or some other person. Exhibit 19.4 on the following page shows a sample letter written to an individual who will testify during an arbitration procedure.

informative letter
A letter that conveys certain information to a client, a witness, an adversary's counsel, or some other person regarding some legal matter (such as the date, time, place, and purpose of a meeting) or a cover letter that accompanies other documents being sent to a person or court.

Confirmation Letters

Another type of letter frequently written by paralegals is the confirmation letter. **Confirmation letters** are similar to informative letters in that they communicate certain information to the reader. Confirmation letters put into written form the contents of an oral discussion. In addition to providing attorneys with a permanent record of earlier conversations, confirmation letters also safeguard against any misinterpretation or misunderstanding of what was communicated orally. See Exhibit 19.5 on page 739 for an example of a confirmation letter.

confirmation letter
A letter that states the substance of a previously conducted verbal discussion to provide a permanent record of the oral conversation.

Opinion Letters

The function of an **opinion letter**, or **advisory letter**, is to provide not only information but also advice. In contrast to informative letters, opinion letters actually give a legal opinion about the matter discussed. Attorneys providing opinion letters are required to provide a detailed analysis of the law and to bring the analysis to a definite conclusion, setting forth the firm's opinion on the matter.

opinion (advisory) letter
A letter from an attorney to a client containing a legal opinion on an issue raised by the client's question or legal claim. The opinion is based on a detailed analysis of the law.

EXHIBIT 19.4
A Sample Informative Letter

Jeffers, Gilmore & Dunn
553 Fifth Avenue
Suite 101
Nita City, NI 48801

Telephone (616) 555-9690
Fax (616) 555-9679
e-mail: JGD@nitanet.net

June 24, 2007

Bernadette P. Williams
149 Snowflake Drive
Irving, TX 75062

RE: Kempf/Joseph Arbitration Proceedings

Dear Ms. Williams:

The arbitration will resume on Monday, August 1, 2007. Please arrive at the offices of the American Arbitration Association (the AAA) before 8:30 A.M. The offices of the AAA are located at 400 West Ferry Boulevard in Dallas. You will be called as a witness sometime before 12:00 noon.

Should you have any questions or concerns regarding your responsibilities as a witness, please do not hesitate to contact me.

Sincerely,

Elena Lopez

Elena Lopez
Paralegal

In addition to rendering the law firm's legal opinion, opinion letters may also be used to inform a client of the legal validity of a specific action. For example, a company seeking to establish operations in a foreign country may seek a lawyer's opinion on whether a certain action it plans to undertake is legally permissible. The attorney (or a paralegal) will research the issue and then draft an advisory letter to the client. Opinion letters are commonly quite long and include detailed explanations of how the law applies to the client's factual situation. Sometimes, the attorney just summarizes his or her conclusion in the opinion letter (as in the opinion letter shown in Exhibit 19.6 on page 740) and attaches a legal memorandum to the letter explaining the legal sources and reasoning used in forming that conclusion.

Opinion letters issued by a firm reflect legal expertise and advice on which a client can rely. Note that opinion letters must be signed by attorneys. Should doubts about the legal validity of an opinion letter surface at a later date, the client may bring a malpractice suit against the firm. The signature of an attorney represents the attorney's acceptance of responsibility for what is stated in the document and can serve as the basis for liability.

demand letter
A letter in which one party explains its legal position in a dispute and requests that the recipient take some action (such as paying money owed).

Demand Letters

Another basic type of letter is the demand letter. In a **demand letter**, one party explains its legal position in a dispute and requests that the recipient take some action (such as paying money owed). Typically, attorneys send a demand letter to a person or company

EXHIBIT 19.5
A Sample Confirmation Letter

Jeffers, Gilmore & Dunn
553 Fifth Avenue
Suite 101
Nita City, NI 48801

Telephone (616) 555-9690
Fax (616) 555-9679
e-mail: JGD@nitanet.net

August 3, 2007

Pauline C. Dunbar
President
Minute-Magic Corporation
7689 Industrial Boulevard
San Francisco, CA 80021

RE: Purchase of real estate from C. C. Barnes, Inc.

Dear Ms. Dunbar:

The following information describes the current status of the negotiations between C. C. Barnes, Inc., and Minute-Magic Corporation:

   Selling Price: $800,000
   Financing Agreement: Citywide Bank
   Interest Rate: 7.5%

This information confirms what I told you on the phone today, August 3, 2007. I look forward to seeing you next week. Should you have any questions or comments in the meantime, please give me a call.

Very truly yours,

Allen P. Gilmore

Allen P. Gilmore
Attorney at Law

APG/ec

before filing a lawsuit against that person or company. For example, your supervising attorney may ask you to draft a letter to a client's debtor demanding payment for an amount owed. Whatever the content of a demand letter, its purpose is to demand something of the recipient on behalf of the client. In some situations, a demand letter is actually a prerequisite to filing suit (as is the case for suits based on certain consumer protection laws).

The demand letter should adopt a serious and persuasive tone, and the client's demand must not be frivolous. Although the letter should be insistent and adversarial, it should not come across as unreasonable or harassing. After all, demand letters seek to accomplish something rather than foreclose opportunities. A common form of demand letter in litigation firms is a letter in which an attorney requests a response from an adversarial party in a lawsuit to an offer to settle the case. Exhibit 19.7 on page 741 illustrates this type of demand letter.

EXHIBIT 19.6
A Sample Opinion Letter

Jeffers, Gilmore & Dunn
553 Fifth Avenue
Suite 101
Nita City, NI 48801

Telephone (616) 555-9690
Fax (616) 555-9679
e-mail:JGD@nitanet.com

December 9, 2007

J. D. Joslyn
President and Chief Executive Officer
Joslyn Footwear, Inc.
700 Kings Avenue, Suite 4000
New City, NI 48023

Dear Ms. Joslyn:

After careful consideration of your plans to expand Joslyn Footwear, Inc., into Latin American markets, I have concluded that to implement the current plans would subject you to potentially significant liability.

The most serious flaw in the current plans concerns your construction of massive shoe-producing industrial plants. Unfortunately, the plans fail to conform to the minimum legal and industrial regulations in Mexico, Uruguay, and Argentina.

The enclosed legal memorandum explains in detail how the law applies to your situation and the reasons for my conclusion. Please call me if you have any questions.

Very truly yours,

Allen P. Gilmore
Attorney at Law

APG/ec

Enclosure

THE LEGAL MEMORANDUM

The legal memorandum is prepared for internal use within a law firm, legal department, or other organization or agency. As a paralegal, you may be asked to draft a legal memorandum for your supervising attorney. Generally, the legal memo presents a thorough summary and analysis of a particular legal problem.

The attorney for whom the document is prepared may be relying on the memo for a number of reasons. For example, the attorney may be preparing a brief on behalf of a client or an opinion letter regarding a client's claim. Thus, if you are asked to draft the memo, you will want it to be extremely thorough and clearly written. Because the legal memo is directed to attorneys who are knowledgeable in the law, there is no need to avoid sophisticated legal terminology or to define basic legal theories or procedures.

EXHIBIT 19.7
A Sample Demand Letter

Jeffers, Gilmore & Dunn
553 Fifth Avenue
Suite 101
Nita City, NI 48801

Telephone (616) 555-9690
Fax (616) 555-9679
e-mail:JGD@nitanet.com

June 15, 2007

Christopher P. Nelson, Esq.
Nelson, Johnson, Callan & Sietz
200 Way Bridge
Philadelphia, PA 40022

RE: *Furman v. Thompson*

Dear Mr. Nelson:

This morning, I met with my clients, Mark and Andrea Furman, the plaintiffs in the lawsuit against your client, Laura Thompson. Both Mark and Andrea expressed a desire to withdraw their complaint and settle with Ms. Thompson. The Furmans' settlement demand is $50,000, payable by certified check no later than July 7, 2007. Considering the strength of the plaintiffs' claims against Ms. Thompson and the possibility of a jury award exceeding $200,000, the Furmans and I think that you and your client will find this demand quite reasonable.

Please contact me by Friday, June 25, 2007, if you plan to take advantage of the Furmans' settlement demand. If we do not hear from you by that date, we will interpret your inaction as a rejection of the Furmans' settlement offer.

Very truly yours,

Allen P. Gilmore

Allen P. Gilmore
Attorney at Law

APG/cc

The purpose of the memo is to provide an attorney with all relevant information regarding the case, so the document is written objectively. It is an explanatory memo informing the attorney of all sides of the issues presented, including both the strengths and weaknesses of the client's claim or defense. You should keep in mind that your goal in drafting a legal memorandum is to inform, explain, and evaluate the client's claim or defense.

A legal memorandum is organized in a logical manner. Although there is no one way to structure the legal memo, most are divided into sections that perform distinct functions. Of course, if the law firm or the attorney for whom you are working prefers a particular format, that format should be followed. Generally, legal memos contain the following sections:

- Heading.
- Statement of the facts.
- Questions presented.

Developing Paralegal Skills

REVIEWING ATTORNEY-GENERATED DOCUMENTS

Leslie Carroll works as a paralegal for Jeremy O'Connell, a sole practitioner who owns a small general law practice. Jeremy frequently creates motions and other legal documents himself, because Leslie has her hands full with other writing tasks and general legal work associated with the practice. Typically, Jeremy will e-mail his documents to Leslie, instructing her to send them to the recipients (if they are letters) or file them with a court (if they are pleadings, motions, or similar documents). Usually, though, Leslie takes the time to quickly review Jeremy's documents. Even though Jeremy has practiced law for more than twenty years, Leslie occasionally finds errors in his documents, some of which could have serious consequences.

TIPS FOR REVIEWING AN ATTORNEY'S DOCUMENTS

- Check all names, addresses, and other client data in the documents to ensure that they are current and correct. The attorney may have forgotten that a client moved to a different address recently, for example, and may have mistakenly taken the client's address from an older document.

- Check any documents to be filed with the court against the applicable court rules regarding the form and style that should be used in those documents.

- If you have a file on specific judges' preferences, review the information on the relevant judge to confirm that the document complies with his or her preferences.

- Make sure that you have the court's most current rules, and see to it that the document is filed with the court before the required deadline. Court rules and deadlines change, and it's important to keep up to date on the current rules.

- Check with the attorney if you have any question about how a particular document should be delivered.

- Brief conclusion in response to the questions presented.
- Discussion and analysis of the facts and the applicable law.
- Conclusion.

Heading

The *heading* of a legal memorandum contains four pieces of information:

- The date on which the memo is submitted.
- The name of the person for whom the memo was prepared.
- The name of the person submitting the memo.
- A brief description of the matter, usually in the form of a reference line.

Exhibit 19.8 illustrates a sample heading for a legal memorandum.

Statement of the Facts

The *statement of the facts* introduces the legal issues by describing the factual elements of the dispute. Only the relevant facts are included in this section. Thus, a key requirement of paralegals is that they learn which facts are legally significant. In other words, as a paralegal, you

Ethics Watch!

LETTERS AND THE UNAUTHORIZED PRACTICE OF LAW

As has frequently been stressed in this text, engaging in the unauthorized practice of law is one of the most serious potential ethical and legal problems facing paralegals. To avoid liability for the unauthorized practice of law, you should never sign opinion (advisory) letters with your own name, and when you sign other types of letters, you should always indicate your status as a paralegal. Even if the person to whom you are sending the letter knows you quite well and knows you are a paralegal, you should indicate your status on the letter itself. By doing so, you will prevent potential confusion as well as potential legal liability. Even if your name and status are included in the letterhead (as is permitted under some state laws), as a precaution, you should type your title below your name at the end of the letter as well.

will need to determine which facts have a bearing on the legal issues in the case and which facts are irrelevant.

Facts presented in a legal memo must not be slanted in favor of the client. The legal memo is not an adversarial argument on the client's behalf. Rather, it is an objective presentation of both the facts and the legal issues. Therefore, you should never omit facts that are unfavorable to the client's claim or defense. The attorney for whom you work needs to know all of the facts that will influence the outcome of the case.

The statement of the facts should contain a logical and concise description of the events surrounding the conflict. Presenting events chronologically often helps to clarify the factual pattern in a case. Alternatively, facts relating to the same issue can be grouped together. The latter organizational technique is especially useful when the facts are complicated and numerous legal issues are presented.

Exhibit 19.9 on page 745 indicates what kinds of information are typically included in a statement of the facts. It also shows what writing style is generally used.

Questions Presented

The *questions presented* address the legal issues presented by the factual circumstances described in the statement of the facts. The questions should be specific and straightforward. They should refer to the parties by name, succinctly set out the legal problems, and

EXHIBIT 19.8
Legal Memorandum—Heading

MEMORANDUM

DATE: August 6, 2007

TO: Allen P. Gilmore, Partner

FROM: Elena Lopez, Paralegal

RE: Neely, Rachel: Emotional Distress—File No. 00-2146
         Neely, Rachel, and Melanie: Emotional Distress—File No. 00-2147

LITIGATION PARALEGAL

Celia C. Elwell, RP, is a paralegal with the Oklahoma City law firm of Mullins, Hirsch & Jones, P.C., where she specializes in civil litigation. Elwell began working as a paralegal in 1984 and graduated from the University of Oklahoma Department of Legal Assistant Education in 1986. She taught paralegal courses at the University of Oklahoma's ABA-approved paralegal program for fifteen years.

Elwell is a co-author of Practical Legal Writing for Legal Assistants *(Thomson West, 1996) and the PACE Study Manual (contributing author, legal-writing chapter), published by the National Federation of Paralegal Associations (NFPA). For a couple of years, she was the legal research and legal-writing columnist for* Legal Assistant Today. *Elwell has lectured at numerous paralegal seminars and workshops and assisted in drafting the minimum standards for education and experience for Oklahoma paralegals. Elwell was also the first legal assistant to work for the Oklahoma Supreme Court.*

Elwell has served as the NFPA's PACE coordinator, assistant PACE coordinator for education, and Internet communications coordinator; she has also served as the Kansas Paralegal Association's primary and secondary delegate and PACE ambassador. She has been a member of the Kansas Paralegal Association, the National Federation of Paralegal Associations, and the American Association for Paralegal Education.

What do you like best about your work?

"There are several things I like best about being a paralegal. I love litigation and the various assignments that come with it. I never know exactly what may happen next. I also love research and writing, and I have been fortunate to work with attorneys who give me challenging projects and value my skills. I get the same satisfaction from researching and analyzing a legal problem as some people get from working crossword or jigsaw puzzles. The challenge is getting all those little pieces to fit. I also enjoy working with people and helping them with their problems. Our clients depend on us and trust us to do the very best we can to resolve their situation. These are the main reasons I enjoy the paralegal profession so much—the constant challenge, the complexity of the issues, the variety, and the emphasis on doing your absolute best for the client."

What is the greatest challenge that you face in your area of work?

"The greatest challenge I face is juggling deadlines and making sure that every case gets the attention it needs. I am constantly referring to the docket, ticklers, and my 'to do' lists to make sure that nothing slips through the cracks. I use Outlook flag reminders and my lists to keep track of each assignment and deadlines. When setting deadlines and ticklers, I try to foresee what could go wrong and allow for delays, mistakes, and other last-minute emergencies that might cause me to fail."

What advice do you have for would-be paralegals in your area of work?

> *"I get the same satisfaction from researching and analyzing a legal problem as some people get from working crossword or jigsaw puzzles."*

"Start with the basics—this is true of all writing, not just legal writing. We have all read long, cumbersome sentences and paragraphs. Whenever we write something that is hard to understand, like a long sentence or paragraph, or whenever we use an unfamiliar word, the reader gets the meaning either slowly or, worse, not at all. This is why our writing must be as clear and concise as we can make it. Exemplary legal writing takes the reader systematically through all the logical points of the document. Leave nothing to chance. Do not ever assume that the reader will understand what you have written. Lead the reader point by point up to the conclusion. You want the reader to be nodding in agreement with every point you make."

What are some tips for success as a paralegal in your area of work?

"After the attorney has given you complete instructions for an assignment, take a minute and think about the assignment. (1) Did you fully understand the assignment? (2) Do you know where to find the files you will need? (3) Are there unanswered questions as to whom to contact or how to obtain certain information? Do not try to guess the attorney's meaning or intentions. If you are not sure, it is better to ask for clarification than to guess. There is no such thing as a stupid question. Do not be afraid to say, 'I don't know.' It is always better to admit that you do not know something than to flounder around trying to figure it out. Even the most qualified, experienced, and highly paid lawyers and paralegals do not know how to do everything."

Celia C. Elwell is also featured in the forthcoming book, Lessons from the Top Paralegal Experts, *by Carole Bruno.*

EXHIBIT 19.9
Legal Memorandum—
Statement of the Facts

STATEMENT OF THE FACTS

Rachel Neely ("Neely") and Melanie Neely ("Melanie"), our clients, seek advice in connection with possible emotional distress claims against Miles Thompson ("Thompson"). The claims arose as a result of (1) Neely's distress at hearing a car crash caused by Thompson and involving her eleven-year-old daughter, Melanie, and subsequently viewing Melanie's injuries; and (2) Melanie's distress related to statements made by Thompson.

In February 2005, Neely and Melanie moved to Union City from San Francisco. Neely immediately began working for an investment firm in downtown Union City. At that firm, she became acquainted with the defendant, Thompson. Thompson was Neely's boss. At first, the two had a friendly, professional relationship.

The relationship between Thompson and Neely became strained approximately six months after Neely began working with Thompson. Tension between the parties arose as a result of Thompson's expression of romantic interest in Neely.

On April 2, 2007, Thompson visited the Neely home. Melanie was not fully aware of the problem her mother was having with Thompson. Thompson came to the door and invited Melanie for a ride in his Corvette. Melanie willingly went with him. Meanwhile, Neely, who had gone to the grocery store, returned to the house to find Melanie missing. She panicked, called the neighbors, and then called the police.

Thompson, who claims that he took Melanie for a ride so that she could be informed about her mother's "bad behavior," drove around Union City with Melanie for approximately thirty minutes. During this ride, Thompson told Melanie that her mother was a "wicked, selfish, woman" who did not care about Melanie. Thompson also told Melanie that her mother was a "no-good, sex-crazed woman" who would leave Melanie "once the right man came along." Upon returning to the Neely home, Thompson made a left turn from Oak Street onto Maple Road, and his car was hit by an oncoming vehicle. According to the police report of the accident, Thompson's blood-alcohol level indicated that he was intoxicated.

The Neely home is located on the corner of the intersection of Maple Road and Oak Street. Neely heard the crash and ran outside. Seeing the accident and recognizing Thompson's car, she approached the site of the accident. There, she saw Melanie bleeding profusely from head injuries. As a result of the accident, Melanie spent two days at Union City Memorial Hospital, where she was kept under observation for possible internal injuries. Melanie continues to be severely depressed and emotionally unstable as a result of Thompson's comments. Additionally, she has frequent nightmares and finds it difficult to speak without stuttering. Since the time of the accident, she has been under psychiatric therapy for these problems. Neely, who fainted after viewing her daughter's injuries, spent one day in Union City Memorial Hospital for extreme anxiety and trauma.

specifically indicate the important and relevant events. The questions-presented section may involve just one simple issue or a number of complex issues. Regardless of the complexity of the matter, this section helps bring the main points of the conflict into focus. See Exhibit 19.10 for an example of how the questions presented might be phrased.

Brief Conclusion

The *brief conclusion* (or *short answer* or *brief answer*) sets forth succinct responses to the questions presented in the previous section. The responses may vary in length. For example, as indicated in Exhibit 19.11 on the next page, certain questions can be answered simply by

EXHIBIT 19.10
Legal Memorandum—
Questions Presented

QUESTIONS PRESENTED

1. Does Neely have a claim for the negligent infliction of emotional distress as a result of viewing the injuries sustained by her daughter in a car accident caused by Thompson's negligence?

2. Does Melanie have a claim for the intentional infliction of emotional distress arising out of Thompson's statements to her on April 2, 2007?

EXHIBIT 19.11
Legal Memorandum—
Brief Conclusion

BRIEF CONCLUSION

1. Probably not. Neely cannot recover under the rule that is currently applied in this jurisdiction. This rule requires that the plaintiff be present at the scene when the accident occurs.

2. Most likely, yes. Thompson's conduct toward Melanie appears to have been (1) reckless, (2) outrageous and extreme, and (3) the direct cause of Melanie's severe emotional distress.

"yes," "no," "probably so," or "probably not," followed by a brief sentence summarizing the reason for that answer. For complicated legal questions, a more detailed statement might be appropriate. Even so, each conclusion should be limited to a maximum of one paragraph. The discussion of the legal analysis, which is the main part of the memo, provides ample opportunity for supporting details.

Discussion and Analysis

The *discussion and analysis* section of the legal memorandum, as the phrase implies, contains a discussion and legal analysis of each issue to be resolved. If the facts of the dispute concern only one legal issue, the entire discussion will revolve around that issue. Legal memoranda usually address multiple issues, however. When multiple issues are involved, the paralegal should organize the discussion into separate parts so that each legal issue can be analyzed separately. For example, if the dispute involves two potential legal claims, the discussion should be divided into two sections with a descriptive heading for each section. The headings of the two sections might read as follows:

   I. Negligent Infliction of Emotional Distress.

  II. Intentional Infliction of Emotional Distress.

The legal analysis presented in the memo should answer the following questions:

- What is the likelihood that the client's claim or defense will be successful?
- What law supports the strongest position?
- Is it case law or statutory law?
- If the strongest argument is under case law, how are the relevant cases factually similar and factually distinct from the client's?
- What law (or case) goes against the client's claim or defense?
- What arguments could the other side make?
- How can the attorney respond to the other side's strongest arguments?
- Are there any other options available to the client for resolving the dispute?

The discussion is the core of the legal memo. This section provides an opportunity for paralegals to demonstrate good research and writing skills. After the research is completed, you must relate the legal findings to the facts of the matter. The reader expects to find a thorough analysis of the law. One method of legal reasoning and analysis commonly used by paralegals and other legal professionals is called the *IRAC method*. IRAC is an acronym consisting of the first letters of the words *issue, rule, application,* and *conclusion.* To use the IRAC

Ethics Watch!

OBJECTIVITY AND THE LEGAL MEMORANDUM

Assume that you are conducting research on behalf of a client who is bringing a lawsuit against a restaurant for negligence. The client's wife choked to death on a piece of meat, and none of the restaurant's employees offered to help. As a member of the legal team representing the client's interests, your goal is to maximize the client's chances of winning in court. During your research, you discover that although no precedential cases involving a similar fact pattern have been decided in your jurisdiction, another state's supreme court has recently held for the defendant restaurant in a very similar case. Because the courts in your state are not obligated to follow this ruling, you might be tempted to downplay the case's significance in your legal memorandum. Do not do this. In deciding whether the client should sue, the attorney needs to make an informed judgment—and he or she will be relying on you to supply objective information. It is in the best interests of the client to point out to your attorney the potential arguments of opposing counsel.

method, you first state the issue you are researching. Then you state the rule of law that applies to the issue. The rule of law may be a rule stated by the courts in previous decisions, a state or federal statute, or a state or federal administrative agency regulation. Next, you apply the rule of law to the set of facts involved in the client's case. Finally, you set forth your conclusion on the matter. If there are two or more issues involved in the client's case, you can analyze each issue using the IRAC method.

Points of law should be identified and supported with proper citations. Occasionally, legal sources will directly address a point that applies to the case at hand. In these situations, it is effective to quote directly from the text of the case, statute, or other legal source. You should not rely too heavily on quoted material, however. Although quotations from a case or other legal authority can lend extremely helpful support, the attorney for whom you are preparing the memo wants to see your analysis, not a reiteration of a court's opinion. Exhibit 19.12 on the following page presents a portion of a discussion section in a legal memorandum. We have annotated the exhibit to illustrate the basic IRAC elements.

When discussing how other cases have addressed certain issues, you need to include citations to the cases. As mentioned in Chapter 17, there are various guides to citation formats, including *The Bluebook: A Uniform System of Citation,* which is published by the Harvard Law Review Association, and the *ALWD Citation Manual,* which is published by the Association of Legal Writing Directors.

Conclusion

The *conclusion* is the culmination of the legal memo. Many issues have been analyzed, and both the strengths and weaknesses of the client's matter have been evaluated. Now you should conclude the analysis by taking a position. The conclusion is your opinion of how the issues discussed may be resolved. Exhibit 19.13 on the next page shows an example of a conclusion to a legal memorandum.

EXHIBIT 19.12

Legal Memorandum— Discussion (Excerpt)

DISCUSSION (excerpt)

I. Negligent Infliction of Emotional Distress

<u>Recovery Restriction</u>

Issue

Are there any restrictions on recovering for the negligent infliction of emotional distress?

Rule

An individual's right to emotional tranquillity is recognized by the law protecting persons against the negligent infliction of emotional distress. The method for determining whether protection should be afforded for emotional distress caused by the knowledge of a third person's injury as a result of a defendant's negligent actions is clear in this jurisdiction. *The rule adopted in this jurisdiction is the "impact rule," which requires that a plaintiff alleging emotional distress must also suffer a direct, physical impact from the same force that injured the victim. Saechao v. Matskoun,* 78 Or.App. 340, 717 P.2d 165, *rev. dismissed* 302 Or. 155, 727 P.2d 126 (1986). This "bright line" rule provides the courts with a test from which they can easily determine the relationship between compensability and the defendant's breach of duty owed to the victim. *Id.* at 169.

Application

Neely was in her house when the accident occurred. She heard the crash and ran outside. Recognizing Thompson's car, Neely approached it and found Melanie bleeding profusely from head injuries. Neely did not suffer any direct physical impact from the car accident that injured Melanie. Thus, Neely could not recover under the impact rule because she did not suffer any direct physical impact and Thompson owed her no duty.

Conclusion

The impact rule originated a century ago in some of the first cases recognizing negligent infliction of emotional distress. Although many states used to follow this rule, most jurisdictions have now abandoned it in favor of the "relative bystander" test or the "zone of danger" test. Some strong arguments can be made against the application of the impact rule. Although the rule limits a defendant's liability and offers an easy decision-making criterion for the courts, it also lends itself to arbitrary and often unjust results.

Our state, however, most closely follows the rule as set forth in the Oregon courts. The impact test applied by the Oregon courts allows emotional distress claims only when (1) the defendant's conduct was intentional or equivalently reckless of another's feelings in a responsible relationship or (2) the defendant's conduct infringed some legally protected interest apart from causing the claimed distress, even when only negligently. See, e.g., *Hammond v. Central Lane Communications Center,* 312 Or. 17, 24, 816 P.2d 593 (1991); *Sherwood v. Oregon Department of Transportation,* 11 P.3d 664, 170 Or.App. 66 (2000); *Chouinard v. Health Ventures,* 179 Or.App. 507, 39 P.3d 951 (2002).

EXHIBIT 19.13

Legal Memorandum— Conclusion

CONCLUSION

It is unlikely that Neely has a cause of action against Thompson for the emotional distress that she suffered due to Thompson's negligence.

It is likely that Melanie has a cause of action for the intentional infliction of emotional distress based on Thompson's outrageous comments to her about her mother.

Note that Neely might pursue, on her own behalf, a claim for the intentional infliction of emotional distress against Thompson for Thompson's reckless behavior in taking Melanie from her home and telling Melanie outrageous things. I recommend that we speak with Neely about the effect on her of Thompson's statements to Melanie. This, in my opinion, is a strong claim. I believe that we could argue successfully that Thompson intended to injure Neely through this egregious act.

Today's Professional Paralegal

PREPARING THE INTERNAL MEMORANDUM

Ken Lawson, a legal assistant, works for Rhonda Mulhaven. Rhonda is representing the defendant, the Gourmet House Restaurant, in a slip-and-fall case. Ken is surprised that the plaintiff filed suit, because the plaintiff admitted that she saw water on the floor but walked through it anyway, apparently so that she could get to the telephone. Ken knows that there are several defenses available, including contributory or comparative negligence and assumption of risk.

RESEARCHING AND ANALYZING CASE LAW

Ken consults an online legal encyclopedia, which defines *assumption of risk* as follows:

> The plaintiff knew that the situation was dangerous and, despite her knowledge of the danger involved, voluntarily subjected herself to the danger or risk. When a plaintiff has assumed the risk of danger, then the plaintiff cannot recover from the defendant for her injuries.

Ken often uses the IRAC method to analyze legal problems. First, he states the issue. Second, he states the rule of law. Third, he applies the rule to the client's facts. And fourth, he reaches a conclusion. Ken has found this method useful because it helps him to think through all aspects of the problem and to apply the law to the facts to reach a conclusion. He decides to apply the IRAC method to the case on which he is working to determine whether the defense of assumption of risk could be successfully applied.

APPLYING THE IRAC METHOD

First, Ken identifies the issue: Did the plaintiff assume the risk of falling when she walked across the wet floor? Next, Ken notes the applicable rule of law: a plaintiff who knows of a dangerous condition and voluntarily subjects himself or herself to it has assumed the risk and cannot hold a defendant liable. Ken then applies the rule of law to the facts: The plaintiff knew of the dangerous condition, because she knew that the floor was wet. She voluntarily subjected herself to the danger by walking across the wet floor to get to the telephone. Ken then forms a conclusion: because the plaintiff knew of the dangerous condition and voluntarily subjected herself to it, she assumed the risk involved in walking across the wet floor. She normally cannot hold the defendant liable when she assumed the risk and was injured as a result.

Ken believes that the defense of assumption of risk might be appropriate in the client's case. He decides to continue researching case law and looks through a state digest. There he finds several cases that contain a definition of assumption of risk similar to the one he read in the encyclopedia. He reviews the cases and then uses KeyCite to check each case on Westlaw to make sure that it is still current law.

CREATING THE LEGAL MEMORANDUM

Ken sits down at his computer and prepares the following outline for a memorandum to Rhonda:

I. Statement of the Facts—A chronological statement of the events that led to the injury.
II. Question Presented—Did the plaintiff assume the risk of falling when she walked across the wet floor?
III. Brief Conclusion—Yes.
IV. Discussion
    A. Did the plaintiff assume the risk of falling when she walked across the wet floor?
    B. Check the encyclopedia's definition of assumption-of-risk defense and state case law supporting this definition.
    C. Apply the rules in B above to the facts in this case.
V. Conclusion—Based on the results of C above.

Having outlined the memo, Ken writes a first draft, edits and revises it, proofreads it carefully, and delivers it to Rhonda. Rhonda says that based on his research and the memorandum, she has been able to settle the case by convincing the plaintiff's attorney that his client has a weak case.

The concluding section may acknowledge the fact that research into a particular area bore little fruit. For example, there may be no cases on point to support one of the issues. The conclusion also may instruct the attorney that more information is needed or may demonstrate that a certain issue needs to be evaluated further. Finally, this section presents you with an opportunity to make strategic suggestions. Paralegals should feel comfortable—especially after a careful legal analysis—in recommending a course of action. Not only do your recommendations reflect thorough analysis, but they also indicate that you are willing to exercise initiative and make a mature judgment, which will be helpful to your supervising attorney.

KEY TERMS AND CONCEPTS

address block 735	confirmation letter 737	opinion (advisory) letter 737
chronologically 725	demand letter 738	reference line 736
closing 737	informative letter 737	salutation 736

chapter summary   Legal Writing: Form and Substance

Legal Writing—The Preliminaries

On receiving a writing assignment, the paralegal should make sure that he or she clearly understands the nature of the assignment, when the assignment should be completed, and what type of writing approach should be used.

1. *Objective approach*—Some documents, such as legal memoranda, require an objective, or unbiased, analysis.

2. *Persuasive approach*—Other documents, such as pretrial motions, are persuasive and require the writer to advocate a particular position. Documents filed with the court must disclose mandatory authorities even if they are adverse to the client's position.

The Importance of Good Writing Skills

Good writing skills are essential for creating legal documents. The quality of your writing can improve with practice if you keep in mind the following guidelines:

1. *Organization*—The writing should be well organized and in the appropriate format. Create an outline before you begin writing. Use structural devices to help the reader follow the discussion.

2. *Audience*—Tailor your writing to the intended audience.

3. *Language*—Avoid legalese in your writing: use plain English. Be brief and to the point, omitting unnecessary words that may distract the reader.

4. *Grammar*—Present well-constructed sentences and paragraphs. Use short, concrete words and the active voice (subject-verb-object arrangement), if possible. Use effective transitions and gender-neutral pronouns.

5. *Proofread your documents*—Creating a polished document takes time, and a good portion of that time should be spent in proofreading and revising your written work product. Proofread to make sure that the document reflects a logical progression of thought from one topic to another, as well as for spelling, typographical, and other errors.

Pleadings and Discovery

Much legal writing consists of documents relating to litigation procedures, such as pleadings and discovery documents. Documents filed with the court are nearly always written persuasively. It is especially important that such documents contain all required information and be formatted correctly for the particular court.

General Legal Correspondence

Paralegals frequently are responsible for maintaining correspondence files and writing legal letters.

1. *Format*—Most firms (and other employers) have a preferred format for legal correspondence with which the paralegal should become familiar. The first page of a letter typically is printed on the firm's letterhead. Generally, letters should be formal in tone and include the following:

   a. The date.

   b. The method of delivery (mail, fax, hand delivery).

   c. The address block.

   d. The reference line (including case or file numbers when appropriate).

   e. The salutation.

   f. The body of the letter.

   g. The closing.

   h. The signature and title of the author (always include your title as a paralegal on letters you write).

   i. The initials of the person who wrote the letter and the typist.

   j. The names of any other persons who received a copy of the letter.

2. *Types of letters*—Paralegals commonly draft the following types of letters.

   a. Informative letters notify clients or others of some action or procedure or serve as transmittal documents (cover letters).

   b. Confirmation letters confirm an oral transaction, agreement, or conversation.

   c. Opinion letters convey to a client or other party a formal legal opinion or give advice on an issue. Only attorneys can sign opinion letters (not paralegals).

   d. Demand letters are letters in which one party explains its legal position in a dispute and requests the recipient to take some action (such as paying money owed).

(Continued)

The Legal Memorandum

The legal memorandum is a thoroughly researched and objectively written summation of the facts, issues, and applicable law relating to a particular legal claim. The purpose of the memo is to inform the attorney for whom the document is written of the strengths and weaknesses of the client's position.

1. *Format*—Generally, the legal memo is presented in a format that includes the following sections:

   a. Heading.

   b. Statement of facts.

   c. Questions presented.

   d. Brief conclusion in response to questions presented.

   e. Discussion and analysis of the facts and the applicable law.

   f. Conclusion.

2. *Legal analysis*—In addition to assessing the strengths and weaknesses of a client's case, a memorandum should analyze and present the legal arguments that the opponent can offer and explain how the attorney can respond to those arguments. Other options available to the client to resolve the dispute should also be analyzed.

 QUESTIONS FOR REVIEW

1. What factors should you consider before undertaking a legal-writing assignment?

2. List and describe each of the guidelines for effective writing. What is meant by the statement "You should write to your audience"?

3. What is plain English? Why should you write in plain English?

4. What is the active voice? What is the passive voice? Why is it better to use the active voice in your legal writing?

5. What are some basic guidelines for the structure of a paragraph? List three transitional phrases that can be used to connect ideas between paragraphs.

6. List the component parts of a typical legal letter.

7. What are the four types of letters discussed in this chapter? What is the function of each type?

8. How is an internal memorandum organized? List and describe its components.

9. What must you know and understand before you begin to prepare a legal memorandum?

10. What are some questions that should be answered in the legal analysis section of a legal memorandum?

 ETHICAL QUESTIONS

1. Lynette Bennett, a paralegal, works as a clerk for a judge in the county circuit court. She has just finished reviewing the plaintiff's and defendant's briefs in an auto accident case. The plaintiff's brief described the injury as follows:

   The plaintiff was struck by the defendant's car as she crossed Lincoln Avenue at the crosswalk. She sustained serious injuries to her left knee, for which she had surgery. She also experiences pain and discomfort in her back and neck.

   The defendant's brief described the injury as follows:

   The plaintiff was struck when she suddenly stepped in front of the defendant's vehicle. The defendant's vehicle was traveling at a speed of five miles per hour. In her lawsuit against the defendant, the plaintiff claims that she sustained significant injuries from this minor accident.

Lynette is disturbed by the disparity in the two descriptions of the plaintiff's injuries. It sounds to Lynette as if someone is lying. What do you think? What impact would falsifying the facts have on the writer's credibility?

2. Bill Richardson, a legal assistant, has been asked by his supervising attorney to prepare an internal memorandum analyzing a client's claim. When Bill reviews the facts, he realizes that the client has a very weak case and will probably lose. But Bill thinks that the client was taken advantage of and that she should be given a chance to try to recover at least something. He knows that his supervisor will not take a losing case to court, so he writes the memo in such a way as to favor the client's position as much as possible. He is not objective in analyzing the potential pitfalls of the case. Is what Bill has done ethical? Is it professional? How should he have handled the situation?

3. David Thomas, a paralegal, is sending out a letter to a client. It is an informative letter advising the client of the status of her case and explaining what the next step in the litigation process will be. David signs the letter without including his title. He mails the letter to the client. The client has questions, and she calls David, thinking that he is the attorney. How should David handle this situation? What should he have done to prevent it?

4. Ken Hall, a legal assistant, is handling all of his supervising attorney's mail while she is out of town on business for the week. The supervising attorney only wants to be contacted if absolutely necessary. She receives a letter marked "personal and confidential." Ken does not recognize the return address on the letter. How should Ken handle the situation?

 ## PRACTICE QUESTIONS AND ASSIGNMENTS

1. Clip an article out of the newspaper or a news journal. Then follow the instructions and answer the questions given below:

   a. Underline all of the active verbs and circle all of the passive verbs. Did the writer use more active verbs than passive verbs in writing the article?

   b. Count the number of words in each sentence. What is the average sentence length? Do short sentences predominate?

   c. Locate the topic sentence in each paragraph. Is the writer's paragraph construction effective?

   d. Notice how the author uses transitional sentences when moving from one paragraph to the next. Underline the key transitional words or phrases.

2. Analyze the construction of the following paragraphs. How could they be improved?

   The first is knowing of the danger. The second is voluntarily subjecting oneself to the danger. The defense of assumption of risk has two elements.

   She did not voluntarily subject herself to the danger when the stadium assigned seats to season-ticket holders. She knew that balls were often hit into the stands. The plaintiff knew of the danger involved in attending a baseball game.

3. Proofread the following paragraph, circling all of the mistakes. Then rewrite the paragraph.

   The defendent was aressted and chrge with drunk driving. Blood alcohol level of .15. He refused to take a breahalyzer test at first. After the police explained to him that he would loose his lisense if he did not take it, he concented. He also has ablood test to verify the results of the breathalyzer.

4. Review the *Practice Questions and Assignments* at the end of Chapter 17. If you did the research required by those questions, use the lemon law and the cases and statutes that you found to prepare a legal memorandum analyzing Mr. Consumer's problem and whether the lemon law in your state will help him. Be sure to include your opinion of the strength of his case.

5. Using the research results from Question 5 in the *Practice Questions and Assignments* at the end of Chapter 17, draft an opinion letter from your supervising attorney to Mr. Consumer, advising him as to how the state's lemon law applies to his case and what type of relief he can expect.

6. Prepare an informative letter to a client using the following facts:

   The client, Dr. Brown, is being sued for medical malpractice and is going to be deposed on January 15, 2007, at 1:00 P.M. The deposition will take place at the law offices of Callaghan & Young. The offices are located at 151 East Jefferson Avenue, Cincinnati, Ohio. The client needs to call your supervising attorney's office to set up an appointment, so that the attorney can prepare Dr. Brown for the deposition.

QUESTIONS FOR CRITICAL ANALYSIS

1. The Americans with Disabilities Act (ADA) of 1990 does not require employers to accommodate persons with disabilities if those persons pose a direct threat to the health and safety of others. Read the following case annotations and synthesize the annotations into the rule of law regarding the type of threat that is required to prevent employment under the "direct threat" provision of the ADA.

   a. Orthopedic surgeon posed a direct threat to the health of his patients as a result of his HIV-positive status, and thus, hospitals did not violate ADA by prohibiting the surgeon from performing surgery without patient consent given patients' knowledge of surgeon's HIV status; although current knowledge about HIV transmission from surgeon to patient is uncertain, because there is no known cure, the duration of risk posed by a surgeon in a surgical setting was permanent and the severity of the harm was that the disease was, at present, fatal in most cases. *Scoles v. Mercy Health Corp.,* 887 F.Supp. 765 (E.D.Pa. 1994).

   b. Employer's executive director's inability to drive did not pose significant risk of substantial harm to health and safety of director or others that could not be eliminated or reduced by reasonable accommodation, as required to support employer's direct threat defense; driving was not an essential function of executive director's position, and providing the executive director with an alternative mode of transportation was a reasonable accommodation. *Equal Employment Opportunity Commission v. AIC Security Investigation, Ltd.,* 820 F.Supp. 1060 (N.D.Ill. 1993).

   c. Even if Georgia Ports Authority police officer had timely complained of his "benign essential tremor" disability, which caused him to fail a firearms proficiency test, and had requested an accommodation, the officer failed to show how this could be done so as to prevail on his ADA claim; GPA police officer who could not shoot straight posed an unacceptable risk to others, and the officer did not show how his deficiency, and the

   direct threat to the health of others that it represented, could be reasonably accommodated. *Fussell v. Georgia Ports Authority,* 906 F.Supp. 1561 (S.D.Ga. 1995).

   d. Neurologist with attention deficit disorder (ADD) that affected his short-term memory and led to mistakes on patients' charts and in dispensing of medicine to patients posed a direct threat to the health and safety of others, and thus, the employer was not required under the ADA to accommodate his disability. *Robertson v. Neuromedical Center,* 983 F.Supp. 669 (M.D.La. 1997).

2. Why is it important to write to your audience? To what audience should legislators write when drafting legislation?

3. Analyze the following hypothetical by applying the IRAC method, and write a one-page paper reporting your results:

   Mr. Damien is a teacher at the Wabash Academy, a private boarding school. He has a twenty-one-year-old son who has bipolar affective disorder, formerly called manic-depressive psychosis, a mood disorder. While visiting Mr. Damien, his son has repeatedly threatened members of the school community. On one occasion, Mr. Damien's son abducted the headmaster's sixteen-year-old daughter and attempted to have the teenager admitted to a psychiatric hospital. Mr. Damien's son also made threatening phone calls to the headmaster. In one such call, he claimed to have drained several quarts of his own blood from his body because he was not permitted to communicate with the headmaster's sixteen-year-old daughter. Mr. and Mrs. Damien refuse to prevent their son from visiting their home on the school's campus. As a result, the school has fired Mr. Damien. Mr. Damien claims that the termination of his employment violates the Americans with Disabilities Act (ADA) of 1990.

   The case law interpreting the ADA does not require employment of an individual with disabilities if that individual, or that individual's disabled relative or associate, poses a direct threat to the health and safety of others.

PROJECTS

1. Compare Microsoft Word and Corel WordPerfect word-processing software. Write a one-page paper summarizing which you prefer, and why. Be sure to note the legal applications each software package has available.

2. If possible, find a copy of a business letter. Identify its com-

ponent parts. How does it differ from the sample legal letter presented in Exhibit 19.3 on page 735? How is it similar?

3. Contact the court of appeals in your state. Ask if the court gives tours, has any programs available for college students, or allows observation of oral arguments. If you

can, arrange to take a tour and observe an oral argument. Obtain a copy of each side's brief and read it prior to the oral argument if possible. Check with your instructor for any special directions before contacting the court. Write a one-page paper summarizing your visit to the court of appeals. Include a comparison of trial court proceedings, as described in Chapter 6, and appellate court oral arguments.

4. Review your state's court rules that apply to the preparation of documents—such as pleadings and motions—to be filed with the courts. Are there any specific instructions for the format of these documents, such as page limits or requirements for double spacing or separately numbered paragraphs or allegations? Make a list of the rules, and summarize the requirements. Your list and accompanying summary should not exceed two typewritten pages.

USING INTERNET RESOURCES

1. Access the Securities and Exchange Commission's *A Plain English Handbook* at the following site:

    http://www.sec.gov/pdf/handbook.pdf

    Scroll through the handbook to find answers to the following questions:

    a. Describe the "unoriginal but useful" writing tip given in the handbook's preface. Why did the writer of the preface find the tip useful?

    b. How does Chapter 1 of the handbook describe a plain English document?

    c. Browse through Chapter 6, titled "Writing in Plain English." Write down two "before-and-after" examples showing how the use of plain English improved the writing.

    d. What is a nominalization? Write a sentence including a nominalization (not one of those listed in Chapter 6), and then rewrite the sentence to make the nominalization the main verb of the sentence.

2. The American Bar Association's Web site contains helpful articles on legal writing, particularly in the section on law practice management.

    a. Access the search home page of the Web site at **http://www.abanet.org/lpm/home.shtml**. Enter the words "legal writing" in the "Search" box and click on "Go." How many articles did your search retrieve? Scan the articles. Do the titles of any of the articles listed refer to plain English or the plain English movement? Now search on the words "plain English." How many articles does that search retrieve? What do you conclude based on your comparison of the numbers of articles retrieved by the searches?

    b. Read one article that appeals to you, and write a one-page summary of the author's main points. Include the name of the article for your instructor's reference. Your instructor may ask you to present your summary to the class. Did anyone else in the class read that same article? If so, compare the summaries to see if you and the other student or students interpreted the author's points differently.

3.  For additional resources, visit our Web site at **http://www.paralegal.delmar. cengage.com**.

A legal assistant must adhere strictly to the accepted standards of legal ethics and to the general principles of proper conduct. The performance of the duties of the legal assistant shall be governed by specific canons as defined herein so that justice will be served and goals of the profession attained. (See Model Standards and Guidelines for Utilization of Legal Assistants, Section II.)

The canons of ethics set forth hereafter are adopted by the National Association of Legal Assistants, Inc., as a general guide intended to aid legal assistants and attorneys. The enumeration of these rules does not mean there are not others of equal importance although not specifically mentioned. Court rules, agency rules, and statutes must be taken into consideration when interpreting the canons.

DEFINITION

Legal assistants, also known as paralegals, are a distinguishable group of persons who assist attorneys in the delivery of legal services. Through formal education, training and experience, legal assistants have knowledge and expertise regarding the legal system and substantive and procedural law which qualify them to do work of a legal nature under the supervision of an attorney.

Canon 1

A legal assistant must not perform any of the duties that attorneys only may perform nor take any actions that attorneys may not take.

Canon 2

A legal assistant may perform any task which is properly delegated and supervised by an attorney, as long as the attorney is ultimately responsible to the client, maintains a direct relationship with the client, and assumes professional responsibility for the work product. (See NALA Model Standards and Guidelines, Section IV, Guideline 5.)

757

Canon 3

A legal assistant must not:

- (a) Engage in, encourage, or contribute to any act which could constitute the unauthorized practice of law; and
- (b) Establish attorney-client relationships, set fees, give legal opinions or advice, or represent a client before a court or agency unless so authorized by that court or agency; and
- (c) Engage in conduct or take any action which would assist or involve the attorney in a violation of professional ethics or give the appearance of professional impropriety.

(See NALA Model Standards and Guidelines, Section IV, Guideline 2.)

Canon 4

A legal assistant must use discretion and professional judgment commensurate with knowledge and experience but must not render independent legal judgment in place of an attorney. The services of an attorney are essential in the public interest whenever such legal judgment is required. (See NALA Model Standards and Guidelines, Section IV, Guideline 3.)

Canon 5

A legal assistant must disclose his or her status as a legal assistant at the outset of any professional relationship with a client, attorney, a court or administrative agency or personnel thereof, or a member of the general public. A legal assistant must act prudently in determining the extent to which a client may be assisted without the presence of an attorney. (See NALA Model Standards and Guidelines, Section IV, Guideline 1.)

Canon 6

A legal assistant must strive to maintain integrity and a high degree of competency through education and training with respect to professional responsibility, local rules and practice, and through continuing education in substantive areas of law to better assist the legal profession in fulfilling its duty to provide legal service.

Canon 7

A legal assistant must protect the confidences of a client and must not violate any rule or statute now in effect or hereafter enacted controlling the doctrine of privileged communications between a client and an attorney. (See NALA Model Standards and Guidelines, Section IV, Guideline 1.)

Canon 8

A legal assistant must do all other things incidental, necessary, or expedient for the attainment of the ethics and responsibilities as defined by statute or rule of court.

Canon 9

A legal assistant's conduct is guided by bar associations' codes of professional responsibility and rules of professional conduct.

First adopted on May 1, 1975. Revised in 1979, 1988, and 1995. Courtesy of the ©National Association of Legal Assistants, Inc. Reprinted with permission.

NALA'S MODEL STANDARDS AND GUIDELINES FOR UTILIZATION OF LEGAL ASSISTANTS

NALA's study of the professional responsibility and ethical considerations of legal assistants is ongoing. This research led to the development of the NALA Model Standards and Guidelines for Utilization of Legal Assistants. This guide summarizes case law, guidelines, and ethical opinions of the various states affecting legal assistants. It provides an outline of minimum qualifications and standards necessary for legal assistant professionals to assure the public and the legal profession that they are, indeed, qualified. The following is a listing of the standards and guidelines.

The annotated version of the Model was revised extensively in 1997. It is online (NALA Model Standards and Guidelines) and may be ordered through NALA headquarters.

PREAMBLE

Proper utilization of the services of legal assistants contributes to the delivery of cost-effective, high-quality legal services. Legal assistants and the legal profession should be assured that measures exist for identifying legal assistants and their role in assisting attorneys in the delivery of legal services. Therefore, the National Association of Legal Assistants, Inc., hereby adopts these Standards and Guidelines as an educational document for the benefit of legal assistants and the legal profession.

DEFINITION

The National Association of Legal Assistants adopted the following definition in 1984:

Legal assistants, also known as paralegals, are a distinguishable group of persons who assist attorneys in the delivery of legal services. Through formal education, training, and experience, legal assistants have knowledge and expertise regarding the legal system and substantive and procedural law which qualify them to do work of a legal nature under the supervision of an attorney.

In recognition of the similarity of the definitions and the need for one clear definition, in July 2001, the NALA membership approved a resolution to adopt the definition of the American Bar Association as well. The ABA definition reads as follows:

> A legal assistant or paralegal is a person qualified by education, training, or work experience who is employed or retained by a lawyer, law office, corporation, governmental agency, or other entity who performs specifically delegated substantive legal work for which a lawyer is responsible. (Adopted by the ABA in 1997.)

STANDARDS

A legal assistant should meet certain minimum qualifications. The following standards may be used to determine an individual's qualifications as legal assistant:

1. Successful completion of the Certified Legal Assistant (CLA)/Certified Paralegal (CP) certifying examination of the National Association of Legal Assistants, Inc.;

2. Graduation from an ABA-approved program of study for legal assistants;

3. Graduation from a course study for legal assistants which is institutionally accredited but not ABA approved, and which requires not less than the equivalent of 60 semester hours of classroom study;

4. Graduation from a course of study for legal assistants, other than those set forth in (2) and (3) above, plus not less than six months of in-house training as a legal assistant;

5. A baccalaureate degree in any field, plus not less than six months of in-house training as a legal assistant;

6. A minimum of three years of law-related experience under the supervision of an attorney, including at least six months of in-house training as a legal assistant; or

7. Two years of in-house training as a legal assistant.

For purposes of these Standards, "in-house training as a legal assistant" means attorney education of the employee concerning legal assistant duties and these Guidelines. In addition to review and analysis of assignments, the legal assistant should receive a reasonable amount of instruction directly related to the duties and obligations of the legal assistant.

GUIDELINES

These Guidelines relating to standards of performance and professional responsibility are intended to aid legal assistants and attorneys. The ultimate responsibility rests with an attorney who employs legal assistants to educate them with respect to the duties they are assigned and to supervise the manner in which such duties are accomplished.

Guideline 1

Legal assistants should:

1. Disclose their status as legal assistants at the outset of any professional relationship with a client, other attorneys, a court or administrative agency or personnel thereof, or members of the general public;

2. Preserve the confidences and secrets of all clients; and

3. Understand the attorney's Rules of Professional Responsibility and these Guidelines in order to avoid any action which would involve the attorney in a violation of the Rules, or give the appearance of professional impropriety.

Guideline 2

Legal assistants should not:

1. Establish attorney-client relationships; set legal fees, give legal opinions or advice; or represent a client before a court, unless authorized to do so by said court; nor

2. Engage in, encourage, or contribute to any act which could constitute the unauthorized practice of law.

Guideline 3

Legal assistants may perform services for an attorney in the representation of a client, provided:

1. The services performed by the legal assistant do not require the exercise of independent professional legal judgment;

2. The attorney maintains a direct relationship with the client and maintains control of all client matters;

3. The attorney supervises the legal assistant;

4. The attorney remains professionally responsible for all work on behalf of the client, including any actions taken or not taken by the legal assistant in connection therewith; and

5. The services performed supplement, merge with, and become the attorney's work product.

Guideline 4

In the supervision of a legal assistant, consideration should be given to:

1. Designating work assignments that correspond to the legal assistant's abilities, knowledge, training, and experience;

2. Educating and training the legal assistant with respect to professional responsibility, local rules and practices, and firm policies;

3. Monitoring the work and professional conduct of the legal assistant to ensure that the work is substantively correct and timely performed;

4. Providing continuing education for the legal assistant in substantive matters through courses, institutes, workshops, seminars, and in-house training; and

5. Encouraging and supporting membership and active participation in professional organizations.

Guideline 5

Except as otherwise provided by statute, court rule or decision, administrative rule or regulation, or the attorney's rules of professional responsibility, and within the preceding parameters and proscriptions, a legal assistant may perform any function delegated by an attorney, including but not limited to the following:

1. Conduct client interviews and maintain general contact with the client after the establishment of the attorney-client relationship, so long as the client is aware of the status and function of the legal assistant, and the client contact is under the supervision of the attorney.

2. Locate and interview witnesses, so long as the witnesses are aware of the status and function of the legal assistant.

3. Conduct investigations and statistical and documentary research for review by the attorney.

4. Conduct legal research for review by the attorney.

5. Draft legal documents for review by the attorney.

6. Draft correspondence and pleadings for review by and signature of the attorney.

7. Summarize depositions, interrogatories, and testimony for review by the attorney.

8. Attend executions of wills, real estate closings, depositions, court or administrative hearings, and trials with the attorney.

9. Author and sign letters providing the legal assistant's status is clearly indicated and the correspondence does not contain independent legal opinions or legal advice.

CONCLUSION

These Standards and Guidelines were developed from generally accepted practices. Each supervising attorney must be aware of the specific rules, decisions, and statutes applicable to legal assistants within his or her jurisdiction.

©2005; Adopted 1984; Revised 1991, 1997, 2005. Courtesy of the ©National Association of Legal Assistants, Inc. Reprinted with permission.

NFPA'S MODEL CODE OF ETHICS AND PROFESSIONAL RESPONSIBILITY AND GUIDELINES FOR ENFORCEMENT

PREAMBLE

The National Federation of Paralegal Associations, Inc. ("NFPA"), is a professional organization comprised of paralegal associations and individual paralegals throughout the United States and Canada. Members of NFPA have varying backgrounds, experiences, education, and job responsibilities that reflect the diversity of the paralegal profession. NFPA promotes the growth, development, and recognition of the paralegal profession as an integral partner in the delivery of legal services.

In May 1993, NFPA adopted its Model Code of Ethics and Professional Responsibility ("Model Code") to delineate the principles for ethics and conduct to which every paralegal should aspire.

Many paralegal associations throughout the United States have endorsed the concept and content of NFPA's Model Code through the adoption of their own ethical codes. In doing so, paralegals have confirmed the profession's commitment to increase the quality and efficiency of legal services, as well as recognized its responsibilities to the public, the legal community, and colleagues.

Paralegals have recognized, and will continue to recognize, that the profession must continue to evolve to enhance their roles in the delivery of legal services. With increased levels of responsibility comes the need to define and enforce mandatory rules of professional conduct. Enforcement of codes of paralegal conduct is a logical and necessary step to enhance and ensure the confidence of the legal community and the public in the integrity and professional responsibility of paralegals.

In April 1997, NFPA adopted the Model Disciplinary Rules ("Model Rules") to make possible the enforcement of the Canons and Ethical Considerations contained in the NFPA Model Code. A concurrent determination was made that the Model Code of Ethics and

Professional Responsibility, formerly aspirational in nature, should be recognized as setting forth the enforceable obligations of all paralegals.

The Model Code and Model Rules offer a framework for professional discipline, either voluntarily or through formal regulatory programs.

§1. NFPA MODEL DISCIPLINARY RULES AND ETHICAL CONSIDERATIONS

1.1 A Paralegal Shall Achieve and Maintain a High Level of Competence.

Ethical Considerations

EC–1.1(a) A paralegal shall achieve competency through education, training, and work experience.

EC–1.1(b) A paralegal shall aspire to participate in a minimum of twelve (12) hours of continuing legal education, to include at least one (1) hour of ethics education, every two (2) years in order to remain current on developments in the law.

EC–1.1(c) A paralegal shall perform all assignments promptly and efficiently.

1.2 A Paralegal Shall Maintain a High Level of Personal and Professional Integrity.

Ethical Considerations

EC–1.2(a) A paralegal shall not engage in any *ex parte* communications involving the courts or any other adjudicatory body in an attempt to exert undue influence or to obtain advantage or the benefit of only one party.

EC–1.2(b) A paralegal shall not communicate, or cause another to communicate, with a party the paralegal knows to be represented by a lawyer in a pending matter without the prior consent of the lawyer representing such other party.

EC–1.2(c) A paralegal shall ensure that all timekeeping and billing records prepared by the paralegal are thorough, accurate, honest, and complete.

EC–1.2(d) A paralegal shall not knowingly engage in fraudulent billing practices. Such practices may include, but are not limited to: inflation of hours billed to a client or employer; misrepresentation of the nature of tasks performed; and/or submission of fraudulent expense and disbursement documentation.

EC–1.2(e) A paralegal shall be scrupulous, thorough, and honest in the identification and maintenance of all funds, securities, and other assets of a client and shall provide accurate accounting as appropriate.

EC–1.2(f) A paralegal shall advise the proper authority of nonconfidential knowledge of any dishonest or fraudulent acts by any person pertaining to the handling of the funds, securities, or other assets of a client. The authority to whom the report is made shall depend on the nature and circumstances of the possible misconduct (for example, ethics committees of law firms, corporations and/or paralegal associations, local or state bar associations, local prosecutors, administrative agencies, etc.). Failure to report such knowledge is in itself misconduct and shall be treated as such under these rules.

1.3 A Paralegal Shall Maintain a High Standard of Professional Conduct.

Ethical Considerations

EC–1.3(a) A paralegal shall refrain from engaging in any conduct that offends the dignity and decorum of proceedings before a court or other adjudicatory body and shall be respectful of all rules and procedures.

EC–1.3(b) A paralegal shall avoid impropriety and the appearance of impropriety and shall not engage in any conduct that would adversely affect his/her fitness to practice. Such conduct may include, but is not limited to: violence, dishonesty, interference with the administration of justice, and/or abuse of a professional position or public office.

EC–1.3(c) Should a paralegal's fitness to practice be compromised by physical or mental illness, causing that paralegal to commit an act that is in direct violation of the Model Code/Model Rules and/or the rules and/or laws governing the jurisdiction in which the paralegal practices, that paralegal may be protected from sanction upon review of the nature and circumstances of that illness.

EC–1.3(d) A paralegal shall advise the proper authority of nonconfidential knowledge of any action of another legal professional that clearly demonstrates fraud, deceit, dishonesty, or misrepresentation. The authority to whom the report is made shall depend on the nature and circumstances of the possible misconduct (for example, ethics committees of law firms, corporations and/or paralegal associations, local or state bar associations, local prosecutors, administrative agencies, etc.). Failure to report such knowledge is in itself misconduct and shall be treated as such under these rules.

EC–1.3(e) A paralegal shall not knowingly assist any individual with the commission of an act that is in direct violation of the Model Code/Model Rules and/or the rules and/or laws governing the jurisdiction in which the paralegal practices.

EC–1.3(f) If a paralegal possesses knowledge of future criminal activity, that knowledge must be reported to the appropriate authority immediately.

1.4 A Paralegal Shall Serve the Public Interest by Contributing to the Improvement of the Legal System and Delivery of Quality Legal Services, Including *Pro Bono Publico* Services.

Ethical Considerations

EC–1.4(a) A paralegal shall be sensitive to the legal needs of the public and shall promote the development and implementation of programs that address those needs.

EC–1.4(b) A paralegal shall support efforts to improve the legal system and access thereto and shall assist in making changes.

EC–1.4(c) A paralegal shall support and participate in the delivery of *Pro Bono Publico* services directed toward implementing and improving access to justice, the law, the legal system, or the paralegal and legal professions.

EC–1.4(d) A paralegal should aspire annually to contribute twenty-four (24) hours of *Pro Bono Publico* services under the supervision of an attorney or as authorized by administrative, statutory, or court authority to:

1. persons of limited means; or

2. charitable, religious, civic, community, governmental, and educational organizations in matters that are designed primarily to address the legal needs of persons with limited means; or

3. individuals, groups, or organizations seeking to secure or protect civil rights, civil liberties, or public rights.

The twenty-four (24) hours of *Pro Bono Publico* services contributed annually by a paralegal may consist of such services as detailed in this EC-1.4(d), and/or administrative matters designed to develop and implement the attainment of this aspiration as detailed above in EC-1.4(a) B (c), or any combination of the two.

1.5 A Paralegal Shall Preserve All Confidential Information Provided by the Client or Acquired from Other Sources before, during, and after the Course of the Professional Relationship.

Ethical Considerations

EC–1.5(a) A paralegal shall be aware of and abide by all legal authority governing confidential information in the jurisdiction in which the paralegal practices.

EC–1.5(b) A paralegal shall not use confidential information to the disadvantage of the client.

EC–1.5(c) A paralegal shall not use confidential information to the advantage of the paralegal or of a third person.

EC–1.5(d) A paralegal may reveal confidential information only after full disclosure and with the client's written consent; or, when required by law or court order; or, when necessary to prevent the client from committing an act that could result in death or serious bodily harm.

EC–1.5(e) A paralegal shall keep those individuals responsible for the legal representation of a client fully informed of any confidential information the paralegal may have pertaining to that client.

EC–1.5(f) A paralegal shall not engage in any indiscreet communications concerning clients.

1.6 A Paralegal Shall Avoid Conflicts of Interest and Shall Disclose Any Possible Conflict to the Employer or Client, as Well as to the Prospective Employers or Clients.

Ethical Considerations

EC–1.6(a) A paralegal shall act within the bounds of the law, solely for the benefit of the client, and shall be free of compromising influences and loyalties. Neither the paralegal's personal or business interest, nor those of other clients or third persons, should compromise the paralegal's professional judgment and loyalty to the client.

EC–1.6(b) A paralegal shall avoid conflicts of interest that may arise from previous assignments, whether for a present or past employer or client.

EC–1.6(c) A paralegal shall avoid conflicts of interest that may arise from family relationships and from personal and business interests.

EC–1.6(d) In order to be able to determine whether an actual or potential conflict of interest exists a paralegal shall create and maintain an effective record-keeping system that identifies clients, matters, and parties with which the paralegal has worked.

EC–1.6(e) A paralegal shall reveal sufficient nonconfidential information about a client or former client to reasonably ascertain if an actual or potential conflict of interest exists.

EC–1.6(f) A paralegal shall not participate in or conduct work on any matter where a conflict of interest has been identified.

EC–1.6(g) In matters where a conflict of interest has been identified and the client consents to continued representation, a paralegal shall comply fully with the implementation and maintenance of an Ethical Wall.

1.7 A Paralegal's Title Shall Be Fully Disclosed.
Ethical Considerations

EC 1.7(a) A paralegal's title shall clearly indicate the individual's status and shall be disclosed in all business and professional communications to avoid misunderstandings and misconceptions about the paralegal's role and responsibilities.

EC 1.7(b) A paralegal's title shall be included if the paralegal's name appears on business cards, letterhead, brochures, directories, and advertisements.

EC–1.7(c) A paralegal shall not use letterhead, business cards, or other promotional materials to create a fraudulent impression of his/her status or ability to practice in the jurisdiction in which the paralegal practices.

EC 1.7(d) A paralegal shall not practice under color of any record, diploma, or certificate that has been illegally or fraudulently obtained or issued or which is misrepresentative in any way.

EC–1.7(e) A paralegal shall not participate in the creation, issuance, or dissemination of fraudulent records, diplomas, or certificates.

1.8 A Paralegal Shall Not Engage in the Unauthorized Practice of Law.
Ethical Considerations

EC–1.8(a) A paralegal shall comply with the applicable legal authority governing the unauthorized practice of law in the jurisdiction in which the paralegal practices.

§2. NFPA GUIDELINES FOR THE ENFORCEMENT OF THE MODEL CODE OF ETHICS AND PROFESSIONAL RESPONSIBILITY

2.1 Basis for Discipline

2.1(a) Disciplinary investigations and proceedings brought under authority of the Rules shall be conducted in accord with obligations imposed on the paralegal professional by the Model Code of Ethics and Professional Responsibility.

2.2 Structure of Disciplinary Committee

2.2(a) The Disciplinary Committee ("Committee") shall be made up of nine (9) members including the Chair.

2.2(b) Each member of the Committee, including any temporary replacement members, shall have demonstrated working knowledge of ethics/professional responsibility–related issues and activities.

2.2(c) The Committee shall represent a cross section of practice areas and work experience. The following recommendations are made regarding the members of the Committee.

1. At least one paralegal with one to three years of law-related work experience.
2. At least one paralegal with five to seven years of law-related work experience.
3. At least one paralegal with over ten years of law-related work experience.
4. One paralegal educator with five to seven years of work experience, preferably in the area of ethics/professional responsibility.
5. One paralegal manager.
6. One lawyer with five to seven years of law-related work experience.
7. One lay member.

2.2(d) The Chair of the Committee shall be appointed within thirty (30) days of its members' induction. The Chair shall have no fewer than ten (10) years of law-related work experience.

2.2(e) The terms of all members of the Committee shall be staggered. Of those members initially appointed, a simple majority plus one shall be appointed to a term of one year, and the remaining members shall be appointed to a term of two years. Thereafter, all members of the Committee shall be appointed to terms of two years.

2.2(f) If for any reason the terms of a majority of the Committee will expire at the same time, members may be appointed to terms of one year to maintain continuity of the Committee.

2.2(g) The Committee shall organize from its members a three-tiered structure to investigate, prosecute, and/or adjudicate charges of misconduct. The members shall be rotated among the tiers.

2.3 Operation of Committee

2.3(a) The Committee shall meet on an as-needed basis to discuss, investigate, and/or adjudicate alleged violations of the Model Code/Model Rules.

2.3(b) A majority of the members of the Committee present at a meeting shall constitute a quorum.

2.3(c) A Recording Secretary shall be designated to maintain complete and accurate minutes of all Committee meetings. All such minutes shall be kept confidential until a decision has been made that the matter will be set for hearing as set forth in Section 6.1 below.

2.3(d) If any member of the Committee has a conflict of interest with the Charging Party, the Responding Party, or the allegations of misconduct, that member shall not take part in any hearing or deliberations concerning those allegations. If the absence of that member creates a lack of a quorum for the Committee, then a temporary replacement for the member shall be appointed.

2.3(e) Either the Charging Party or the Responding Party may request that, for good cause shown, any member of the Committee not participate in a hearing or deliberation. All such requests shall be honored. If the absence of a Committee member under those circumstances creates a lack of a quorum for the Committee, then a temporary replacement for that member shall be appointed.

2.3(f) All discussions and correspondence of the Committee shall be kept confidential until a decision has been made that the matter will be set for hearing as set forth in Section 6.1 below.

2.3(g) All correspondence from the Committee to the Responding Party regarding any charge of misconduct and any decisions made regarding the charge shall be mailed certified mail, return receipt requested, to the Responding Party's last known address and shall be clearly marked with a "Confidential" designation.

2.4 Procedure for the Reporting of Alleged Violations of the Model Code/Disciplinary Rules

2.4(a) An individual or entity in possession of nonconfidential knowledge or information concerning possible instances of misconduct shall make a confidential written report to the Committee within thirty (30) days of obtaining same. This report shall include all details of the alleged misconduct.

2.4(b) The Committee so notified shall inform the Responding Party of the allegation(s) of misconduct no later than ten (10) business days after receiving the confidential written report from the Charging Party.

2.4(c) Notification to the Responding Party shall include the identity of the Charging Party, unless, for good cause shown, the Charging Party requests anonymity.

2.4(d) The Responding Party shall reply to the allegations within ten (10) business days of notification.

2.5 Procedure for the Investigation of a Charge of Misconduct

2.5(a) Upon receipt of a Charge of Misconduct ("Charge"), or on its own initiative, the Committee shall initiate an investigation.

2.5(b) If, upon initial or preliminary review, the Committee makes a determination that the charges are either without basis in fact or, if proven, would not constitute professional misconduct, the Committee shall dismiss the allegations of misconduct. If such determination of dismissal cannot be made, a formal investigation shall be initiated.

2.5(c) Upon the decision to conduct a formal investigation, the Committee shall:

1. mail to the Charging and Responding Parties within three (3) business days of that decision notice of the commencement of a formal investigation. That notification shall be in writing and shall contain a complete explanation of all Charge(s), as well as the reasons for a formal investigation, and shall cite the applicable codes and rules;

2. allow the Responding Party thirty (30) days to prepare and submit a confidential response to the Committee, which response shall address each charge specifically and shall be in writing; and

3. upon receipt of the response to the notification, have thirty (30) days to investigate the Charge(s). If an extension of time is deemed necessary, that extension shall not exceed ninety (90) days.

2.5(d) Upon conclusion of the investigation, the Committee may:

1. dismiss the Charge upon the finding that it has no basis in fact;

2. dismiss the Charge upon the finding that, if proven, the Charge would not constitute Misconduct;

3. refer the matter for hearing by the Tribunal; or

4. in the case of criminal activity, refer the Charge(s) and all investigation results to the appropriate authority.

2.6 Procedure for a Misconduct Hearing before a Tribunal

2.6(a) Upon the decision by the Committee that a matter should be heard, all parties shall be notified and a hearing date shall be set. The hearing shall take place no more than thirty (30) days from the conclusion of the formal investigation.

2.6(b) The Responding Party shall have the right to counsel. The parties and the Tribunal shall have the right to call any witnesses and introduce any documentation that they believe will lead to the fair and reasonable resolution of the matter.

2.6(c) Upon completion of the hearing, the Tribunal shall deliberate and present a written decision to the parties in accordance with procedures as set forth by the Tribunal.

2.6(d) Notice of the decision of the Tribunal shall be appropriately published.

2.7 Sanctions

2.7(a) Upon a finding of the Tribunal that misconduct has occurred, any of the following sanctions, or others as may be deemed appropriate, may be imposed upon the Responding Party, either singularly or in combination:

1. Letter of reprimand to the Responding Party; counseling;
2. Attendance at an ethics course approved by the Tribunal; probation;
3. Suspension of license/authority to practice; revocation of license/authority to practice;
4. Imposition of a fine; assessment of costs; or
5. In the instance of criminal activity, referral to the appropriate authority.

2.7(b) Upon the expiration of any period of probation, suspension, or revocation, the Responding Party may make application for reinstatement. With the application for reinstatement, the Responding Party must show proof of having complied with all aspects of the sanctions imposed by the Tribunal.

2.8 Appellate Procedures

2.8(a) The parties shall have the right to appeal the decision of the Tribunal in accordance with the procedure as set forth by the Tribunal.

DEFINITIONS

APPELLATE BODY means a body established to adjudicate an appeal to any decision made by a Tribunal or other decision-making body with respect to formally heard Charges of Misconduct.

CHARGE OF MISCONDUCT means a written submission by any individual or entity to an ethics committee, paralegal association, bar association, law enforcement agency, judicial body, government agency, or other appropriate body or entity, that sets forth nonconfidential information regarding any instance of alleged misconduct by an individual paralegal or paralegal entity.

CHARGING PARTY means any individual or entity who submits a Charge of Misconduct against an individual paralegal or paralegal entity.

COMPETENCY means the demonstration of: diligence, education, skill, and mental, emotional, and physical fitness reasonably necessary for the performance of paralegal services.

CONFIDENTIAL INFORMATION means information relating to a client, whatever its source, that is not public knowledge nor available to the public. ("Non-Confidential Information" would generally include the name of the client and the identity of the matter for which the paralegal provided services.)

DISCIPLINARY COMMITTEE means any committee that has been established by an entity such as a paralegal association, bar association, judicial body, or government agency to: (a) identify, define, and investigate general ethical considerations and concerns with respect to paralegal practice; (b) administer and enforce the Model Code and Model Rules and; (c) discipline any individual paralegal or paralegal entity found to be in violation of same.

DISCIPLINARY HEARING means the confidential proceeding conducted by a committee or other designated body or entity concerning any instance of alleged misconduct by an individual paralegal or paralegal entity.

DISCLOSE means communication of information reasonably sufficient to permit identification of the significance of the matter in question.

ETHICAL WALL means the screening method implemented in order to protect a client from a conflict of interest. An Ethical Wall generally includes, but is not limited to, the following elements: (1) prohibit the paralegal from having any connection with the matter; (2) ban discussions with or the transfer of documents to or from the paralegal; (3) restrict access to files; and (4) educate all members of the firm, corporation, or entity as to the separation of the paralegal (both organizationally and physically) from the pending matter. For more information regarding the Ethical Wall, see the NFPA publication entitled "The Ethical Wall—Its Application to Paralegals."

EX PARTE means actions or communications conducted at the instance and for the benefit of one party only, and without notice to, or contestation by, any person adversely interested.

INVESTIGATION means the investigation of any charge(s) of misconduct filed against an individual paralegal or paralegal entity by a Committee.

LETTER OF REPRIMAND means a written notice of formal censure or severe reproof administered to an individual paralegal or paralegal entity for unethical or improper conduct.

MISCONDUCT means the knowing or unknowing commission of an act that is in direct violation of those Canons and Ethical Considerations of any and all applicable codes and/or rules of conduct.

PARALEGAL is synonymous with "Legal Assistant" and is defined as a person qualified through education, training, or work experience to perform substantive legal work that requires knowledge of legal concepts and is customarily but not exclusively performed by a lawyer. This person may be retained or employed by a lawyer, law office, governmental agency, or other entity or may be authorized by administrative, statutory, or court authority to perform this work.

PRO BONO PUBLICO means providing or assisting to provide quality legal services in order to enhance access to justice for persons of limited means; charitable, religious, civic, community, governmental, and educational organizations in matters that are designed primarily to address the legal needs of persons with limited means; or individuals, groups, or organizations seeking to secure or protect civil rights, civil liberties, or public rights.

PROPER AUTHORITY   means the local paralegal association, the local or state bar association, committee(s) of the local paralegal or bar association(s), local prosecutor, administrative agency, or other tribunal empowered to investigate or act upon an instance of alleged misconduct.

RESPONDING PARTY   means an individual paralegal or paralegal entity against whom a Charge of Misconduct has been submitted.

REVOCATION   means the rescission of the license, certificate, or other authority to practice of an individual paralegal or paralegal entity found in violation of those Canons and Ethical Considerations of any and all applicable codes and/or rules of conduct.

SUSPENSION   means the suspension of the license, certificate, or other authority to practice of an individual paralegal or paralegal entity found in violation of those Canons and Ethical Considerations of any and all applicable codes and/or rules of conduct.

TRIBUNAL   means the body designated to adjudicate allegations of misconduct.

Courtesy of the National Federation of Paralegal Associations, Inc. Reprinted with permission.

NALS CODE OF ETHICS

INTRODUCTION

Members of NALS are bound by the objectives of this association and the standards of conduct required of the legal profession.

Every member shall:

- Encourage respect for the law and the administration of justice;
- Observe rules governing privileged communications and confidential information;
- Promote and exemplify high standards of loyalty, cooperation, and courtesy;
- Perform all duties of the profession with integrity and competence; and
- Pursue a high order of professional attainment.

Integrity and high standards of conduct are fundamental to the success of our professional association. This Code is promulgated by the NALS and accepted by its members to accomplish these ends.

Canon 1

Members of this association shall maintain a high degree of competency and integrity through continuing education to better assist the legal profession in fulfilling its duty to provide quality legal services to the public.

Canon 2

Members of this association shall maintain a high standard of ethical conduct and shall contribute to the integrity of the association and the legal profession.

Canon 3

Members of this association shall avoid a conflict of interest pertaining to a client matter.

Canon 4

Members of this association shall preserve and protect the confidences and privileged communications of a client.

Canon 5

Members of this association shall exercise care in using independent professional judgment and in determining the extent to which a client may be assisted without the presence of a lawyer and shall not act in matters involving professional legal judgment.

Canon 6

Members of this association shall not solicit legal business on behalf of a lawyer.

Canon 7

Members of this association, unless permitted by law, shall not perform paralegal functions except under the direct supervision of a lawyer and shall not advertise or contract with members of the general public for the performance of paralegal functions.

Canon 8

Members of this association, unless permitted by law, shall not perform any of the duties restricted to lawyers or do things which lawyers themselves may not do and shall assist in preventing the unauthorized practice of law.

Canon 9

Members of this association not licensed to practice law shall not engage in the practice of law as defined by statutes or court decisions.

Canon 10

Members of this association shall do all other things incidental, necessary, or expedient to enhance professional responsibility and participation in the administration of justice and public service in cooperation with the legal profession.

Courtesy of NALS ... the association for legal professionals. Reprinted with permission.

PARALEGAL ETHICS AND REGULATION: HOW TO FIND STATE-SPECIFIC INFORMATION

NALA NET FILES

Current information about the legal assistant profession helps you do your job better. Introduced in 1992, NALA Net is the first online information service for the legal assistant profession. NALA Net captures relevant information concerning such issues as ethics, bar guidelines, case law updates, legislative activities, bar activities, and significant research articles about the utilization of legal assistants.

Categories of Information

Information on NALA Net is organized into several categories, as follows:

- **Legislative Activities.** Bills considered by state legislatures concerning the legal assistant profession, such as fee award statutes and UPL [unauthorized practice of law] regulations.

- **Ethics.** Ethical opinions from among the fifty states concerning legal assistants and lay personnel in the delivery of legal services.

- **Cases.** Summaries of court decisions concerning the legal assistant profession, including awards for their time in attorney fee awards, supervision, and the unauthorized practice of law.

- **Guidelines.** Several state bar associations have adopted guidelines for the utilization of legal assistants in the delivery of legal services. State supreme courts and court decisions also serve to establish guidelines.

- **Membership.** Several state and county bar associations offer associate membership to paralegals. This area includes summaries of the membership requirements.

- **Articles.** Significant articles and discussions concerning our profession.

- **Other.** General information and announcements of paralegal activities among the states.

In many instances, we have kept older documents on file for historical background and to show trends in the development of the profession. This is particularly useful in the areas of legislation and ethics.

How to Use NALA Net

The WebFind form is your ticket to NALA Net documents. In your search, you can use "and" and "or" between your key words; and "and" applies by default. You may search by titles or text, which searches all of the 800+ files for your expression.

Sample Search Expressions

The following examples illustrate the kind of expressions that you can use to search the index(es):

- Definitions
- Fees
- Supervision
- Standards

Courtesy of the ©National Association of Legal Assistants, Inc. Reprinted with permission.

PARALEGAL ASSOCIATIONS

NFPA ASSOCIATIONS

Region I

Alaska Association of Paralegals
P.O. Box 101956
Anchorage, AK 99510-1956

Hawaii Paralegal Association
P.O. Box 674
Honolulu, HI 96809

Oregon Paralegal Association
P.O. Box 8523
Portland, OR 97207

Paralegal Association of Southern Nevada
P.O. Box 1752
Las Vegas, NV 89125-1752

Sacramento Valley Paralegal Association
P.O. Box 453
Sacramento, CA 95812-0453

San Francisco Paralegal Association
985 Darien Way
San Francisco, CA 94127

Washington State Paralegal Association
P.O. Box 58530
Seattle, WA 98138-1530

Region II

Arkansas Paralegal Association
c/o Wal-Mart Stores, Inc.
702 SW 8th St., Mailstop 0215
Bentonville, AR 72716-0215

Dallas Area Paralegal Association
P.O. Box 12533
Dallas, TX 75225-0533

Illinois Paralegal Association
P.O. Box 452
New Lenox, IL 60451-0452

Kansas Paralegal Association
P.O. Box 1675
Topeka, KS 66601

Minnesota Paralegal Association
1711 W. County Road B, #300N
Roseville, MN 55113-4036

New Orleans Paralegal Association
P.O. Box 30604
New Orleans, LA 70190

Rocky Mountain Paralegal Association
P.O. Box 481864
Denver, CO 80248-1864

Springfield Paralegal Association
1845 S. National
Springfield, MO 65804

Region III

Carolina Paralegal Association
c/o Laura Wiseman
P.O. Box 1268
Sumter, SC 29151

Cleveland Association of Paralegals
P.O. Box 14517
Cleveland, OH 44114-0517

Georgia Association of Paralegals
1199 Euclid Ave. NE
Atlanta, GA 30307

The Greater Dayton Paralegal Association, Inc.
P.O. Box 10515, Mid-City Station
Dayton, OH 45402

Greater Lexington Paralegal Association, Inc.
P.O. Box 574
Lexington, KY 40586

Indiana Paralegal Association, Inc.
P.O. Box 44518
Indianapolis, IN 46204

Memphis Paralegal Association
P.O. Box 3646
Memphis, TN 38173-0646

The Michiana Paralegal Association, Inc.
P.O. Box 11458
South Bend, IN 46634

Middle Tennessee Paralegal Association
P.O. Box 198006
Nashville, TN 37219

Northeast Indiana Paralegal Association, Inc.
P.O. Box 13646
Fort Wayne, IN 46865

Palmetto Paralegal Association
P.O. Box 11634
Columbia, SC 29211-1634

Paralegal Association of Central Ohio
P.O. Box 15182
Columbus, OH 43215-0182

Tampa Bay Paralegal Organization
P.O. Box 2840
Tampa, FL 33601

Region IV

Central Pennsylvania Paralegal Association
P.O. Box 11814
Harrisburg, PA 17108

Lycoming County Paralegal Association
P.O. Box 991
Williamsport, PA 17703

Montgomery County Paralegal Association
P.O. Box 1765
Blue Bell, PA 19422

National Capital Area Paralegal Association
P.O. Box 27607
Washington, DC 20038-7607

Navy Legalmen Association
Washington Navy Yard
Washington, DC 20374-5006

The Philadelphia Association of Paralegals
P.O. Box 59179
Philadelphia, PA 19102-9179

Pittsburgh Paralegal Association
P.O. Box 2485
Pittsburgh, PA 15230

South Jersey Paralegal Association
P.O. Box 355
Haddonfield, NJ 08033

Region V

Capital District Paralegal Association
P.O. Box 12562
Albany, NY 12212-2562

Central Connecticut Paralegal Association
P.O. Box 230594
Hartford, CT 06123-0594

Central Massachusetts Paralegal Association
P.O. Box 444
Worcester, MA 01614

Connecticut Association of Paralegals
P.O. Box 134
Bridgeport, CT 06601-0134

Long Island Paralegal Association
1877 Bly Road
East Meadow, NY 11556

Maryland Association of Paralegals
550 M Ritchie Hwy., PMB #203
Severna Park, MD 21146

Massachusetts Paralegal Association, Inc.
P.O. Box 1381
Marblehead, MA 01945

The New Haven County Association
   of Paralegals
P.O. Box 862
New Haven, CT 06504-0862

Paralegal Association of New Hampshire
P.O. Box 728
Manchester, NH 03105-0728

Paralegal Association of Rochester, Inc.
P.O. Box 40567
Rochester, NY 14604

Rhode Island Paralegals Association
P.O. Box 1003
Providence, RI 02901

Vermont Paralegal Organization
P.O. Box 5755
Burlington, VT 05402

Western Massachusetts Paralegal
   Association, Inc.
P.O. Box 30005
Springfield, MA 01103

Western New York Paralegal Association, Inc.
Niagara Square Station
P.O. Box 207
Buffalo, NY 14201

NALA STATE AND LOCAL AFFILIATES

Alabama

Alabama Association of Paralegals
http://www.aaopi.com
  President:
  Ann D. Riley, CLA
  Birmingham, AL

  Liaison:
  Stephanie A. Hunter, CLA
  Birmingham, AL

Legal Assistant Society of Virginia College
Virginia College at Birmingham
  Faculty Adviser:
  Bettie Sullivan, J.D.,
    Legal Dept.
  Birmingham, AL

NE Alabama Litigation Support Association
  President:
  Lynne M. Smith, CLA
  Gadsden, AL
  Liaison:
  Carla Moncil
  Collinsville, AL

Samford Paralegal Association
  Faculty Adviser:
  Les Ennis
  Birmingham, AL

Alaska

Fairbanks Association of Legal Assistants
  President:
  Bernice K. Hall, CLA
  Fairbanks, AK
  Liaison:
  Deana M. Waters, CLA
  Fairbanks, AK

Arizona

Arizona Paralegal Association
http://www.azparalegal.org
  President:
  Joanie L. Littrel
  Phoenix, AZ
  Liaison:
  Karen L. Trumpower, CLA
  Phoenix, AZ

Legal Assistants of Metropolitan Phoenix
http://www.geocities.com/azlamp
  President:
  Kathy A. Richardson
  Maricopa, AZ
  Liaison:
  Ruth M. Murphy, CLA
  Phoenix, AZ

Tucson Association of Legal Assistants
http://www.tucsonlegalassistants.org
  President:
  Martha Anne Lavaty, CP
  Tucson, AZ

Liaison:
Sue A. Mahon
Tucson, AZ

Arkansas

Arkansas Association of Legal Assistants
http://www.aala-legal.org
President:
Jenny L. Disney, CLA
Springdale, AR
Liaison:
Constance F. Helmich, CLA
Little Rock, AR

California

Fresno Paralegal Association
http://www.fresnoparalegal.org
President:
Donna Johnston
Fresno, CA
Liaison:
Orlene S. Malloy
Fresno, CA

Inland Counties Association of Paralegals
http://www.icaponline.org
President:
Donna F. Dupree, CLAS
Riverside, CA
Liaison:
Donna F. Dupree, CLAS
Riverside, CA

Los Angeles Paralegal Association
http://www.lapa.org
President:
Lorryn K. Abbott, CLA
Los Angeles, CA
Liaison:
Donna Reznick-Goodich, CLA
Los Angeles, CA

Orange County Paralegal Association
http://www.ocparalegal.org
President:
Gabrielle J. Roudabush, CLA
Irvine, CA
Liaison:
Carolyn Yellis, CLA
Anaheim, CA

**Paralegal Association
    of Santa Clara County**
http://www.sccparalegal.org
President:
April M. Piercey, CLA
Saratoga, CA

Liaison:
April M. Piercey, CLA
Saratoga, CA

Santa Barbara Paralegal Association
http://www.sbparalegals.org
President:
Josefina R. Martinez
Santa Barbara, CA
Liaison:
Sandra Biesinger
Santa Barbara, CA

Ventura County Paralegal Association
http://www.vcparalegal.org
President:
Laurie Orlando
Camarillo, CA
Liaison:
Cyndi Williams Hitsman, CLA
Ventura, CA

Colorado

Pikes Peak Paralegals
http://www.pikespeakparalegals.org
President:
Doris Silva
Greenwood Villa, CO

**Colorado Association of Professional
    Paralegals and Legal Assistants, Inc.**
http://www.capplaweb.org
President:
Kimberly L. Sawyer, CLA
Denver, CO
Liaison:
Jennifer D. Sutherland, CLA
Denver, CO

Legal Assistants of the Western Slope
President:
Vicki C. Warren
Grand Junction, CO
Liaison:
Cheryl Juntilla, CLAS
Clifton, CO

Florida

Central Florida Paralegal Association
http://www.cfpainc.com
President:
Cassie D. Snyder, CP
Maitland, FL
Liaison:
Anne Marie Greer, CP, CFLA
Winter Park, FL

Northeast Florida Paralegal Association
http://www.nefpa.org
President:
Donna F. Demetree, CLAS
Jacksonville, FL
Liaison:
Margaret, C. Costa, CP
Jacksonville, FL

Northwest Florida Paralegal Association
http://www.nwfpa.com
President:
Debra A. Shally, CLA
Pensacola, FL
Liaison:
Kristine M. Hill, CLA
Pensacola, FL

Paralegal Association of Florida, Inc.
http://www.pafinc.org
President:
Johnna A. Phillips, CLA
Shalimar, FL
Liaison:
Margaret J. Averill, CLAS, CFLA
Vero Beach, FL

South Florida Paralegal Association
http://www.sfpa.info
President:
Mark Workman
Miami, FL
Liaison:
Margarita Diaz, CLA
Miami, FL

Southwest Florida Paralegal Association
http://www.swfloridaparalegals.com
President:
Sally Mabrey Taylor
Sarasota, FL
Liaison:
Elise J. Duranceau, CLA
Venice, FL

Volusia Association of Paralegals
http://www.volusiaparalegals.org
President:
Linda Dill Johnson, CLA
Port Orange, FL
Liaison:
Joanne Shamy Lee, CLA
Daytona Beach, FL

Georgia

Metro Atlanta Legal Assistants Association
http://www.malaa.org/
President:
Renee Holloway, CLA
Duluth, GA

Southeastern Association of Legal
Assistants of Georgia
http://www.seala.org
President:
Eunice Bolen
Savannah, GA
Liaison:
Pamela K. Bebon, CLA
Savannah, GA

Illinois

Central Illinois Paralegal Association
http://hometown.aol.com/cipa/info/
myhomepage/club/html
President:
Ann G. Hill, CLA
Bloomington, IL
Liaison:
Lisa J. Craghead, CLA
Bloomington, IL

Iowa

Iowa Association of Legal Assistants
http://www.ialanet.org
President:
Sheri Womble
Des Moines, IA
Liaison:
Traci M. Evans
Council Bluffs, IA

Kansas

Heartland Association of Legal Assistants
http://www.accesskansas.org/hala
President:
Joan Polifka
Overland Park, KS
Liaison:
William K. Schmidt, CLA
Kansas City, MO

Kansas Association of Legal Assistants
http://www.ink.org/public/kala
President:
Kimberly R. Knowles, CLA
Witchita, KS
Liaison:
Cheryl L. Clark, CLA
Wichita, KS

Kentucky

Western Kentucky Paralegals
President:
Joan H. Hobgood, CLA
Madisonville, KY

Liaison:
Julie P. Franklin, CLA
Madisonville, KY

Louisiana

Louisiana State Paralegal Association
http://www.la-paralegals.org
President:
Rebecca Mentin Maum
Baton Rouge, LA
Liaison:
Lupe L. Acosta
Lafayette, LA

Northwest Louisiana Paralegal Association
President:
Pamela H. East, CLA, LCP
Shreveport, LA
Liaison:
Jan L. Melton, CLA, LCP
Shreveport, LA

Maryland

Baltimore City Paralegal Association
President:
Carole Walker
Baltimore, MD
Liaison:
Theodora J.F.M. Howell, CLA
Baltimore, MD

Michigan

Legal Assistants Association of Michigan
http://www.laamnet.org
President:
Renee J. Jent, CLA
Okemos, MI
Liaison:
Christine Welton
Traverse City, MI

Mississippi

Mississippi Association of Legal Assistants
http://www.msmala.com
President:
LaTricia M. Nelson, CLAS
Raymond, MS
Liaison:
Lisa D. Taylor, CLA
Jackson, MS

University of Southern Mississippi
Society for Paralegal Studies
President:
Trisha Trigg
Hattiesburg, MS

Missouri

St. Louis Association of Legal Assistants
http://www.slala.org
President:
Kristin A. Noll
St. Louis, MO
Liaison:
Mary E. Hatfield
St. Louis, MO

Montana

Montana Association of Legal Assistants
http://www.malanet.org
President:
Annette R. Brown, CLAS
Missoula, MT
Liaison:
Deborah L. Ethridge, CLAS
Missoula, MT

Nebraska

Nebraska Association of Legal Assistants
http://www.neala.org
President:
Stephanie R. Henson, CLA
Omaha, NE
Liaison:
Linda R. Hess, CP Specialist
Omaha, NE

Nevada

Nevada Paralegal Association
http://www.nevadaparalegal.org
President:
Patricia L. Altstatt, CLAS
Las Vegas, NV
Liaison:
Ellen J. Sternhill, CLA
Las Vegas, NV

Sierra Nevada Association of Paralegals
http://www.snapreno.com
President:
Anna M. Buchner
Reno, NV

Liaison:
Christine M. Saito, CLA
Reno, NV

New Jersey

**Legal Assistants Association
of New Jersey**
http://www.laanj.org
President:
Ana P. Pierro
Elizabeth, NJ
Liaison:
Kathleen Bonelli, CLA
Livingston, NJ

North Carolina

Metrolina Paralegal Association
http://www.charlotteareaparalegals.com
President:
Barbara C. Brown
Charlotte, NC
Liaison:
Cynthia T. Frye, CLA
Charlotte, NC

North Carolina Paralegal Association, Inc.
http://www.ncparalegal.org
President:
Erin N. Burris, CP
Research Triangle Park, NC
Liaison:
Darlene M. Patz, CLA
Rock Hill, SC

North Dakota

Red River Valley Paralegal Association
http://www.rrvpa.org
President:
Joshua Roaldson
West Fargo, ND
Liaison:
Jeanine L. Rodvold, CLA
Fargo, ND

**Western Dakota Association of Legal
Assistants**
http://www.wdala.org
President:
Michelle M. Erdmann, CLA
Minot, ND
Liaison:
Melissa M. Klimpel, CLA
Bismarck, ND

Ohio

Paralegal Association of Northwest Ohio
http://www.panonet.org
President:
Diane M. Hieber, CLA
Toledo, OH
Liaison:
Evelyn D. Evans-Eck, CLAS
Toledo, OH

Oklahoma

City College Legal Association
Faculty Adviser:
Jack Moore
Norman, OK

Oklahoma Paralegal Association
http://www.okparalegal.org
President:
Cynthia A. Kirby ,CLA
Stroud, OK
Liaison:
Lennis D. Ailey, CLA
Ponca City, OK

**TCC Student Association
of Legal Assistants**
Faculty Adviser:
Sherry Taylor
Tulsa, OK

Tulsa Association of Legal Assistants
http://www.tulsatala.org
President:
Barbara Blackburn, CLAS
Tulsa, OK
Liaison:
Terri Cooper, CLA
Tulsa, OK

Oregon

Pacific Northwest Paralegal Association
http://www.pnpa.org
President:
Sandra D. Hatch, CLA
Portland, OR
Liaison:
Krtistin K. Vermilyea, CLA
Lake Oswego, OR

South Carolina

Charleston Association of Legal Assistants
President:
Deneen Copeland Bell
Charleston, SC

Liaison:
Danielle M. Walker
Charleston, SC

**South Carolina Upstate
Paralegal Association**
http://www.scupa.org
President:
Dorothy L. Sizemore
Greenville, SC
Liaison:
Rebecca J. Maxson, CLAS
Greenville, SC

South Dakota

South Dakota Paralegal Association, Inc.
http://www.sdparalegals.com
President:
Michelle M. Schmidt, CLAS
Spearfish, SD
Liaison:
Dixie A. Bader, CLA
Sioux Falls, SD

Tennessee

Greater Memphis Paralegal Alliance
http://www.memphisparalegals.org
President:
Kathy Pleasants
Memphis, TN
Liaison:
Carol Kuhn
Memphis, TN

Smoky Mountain Paralegal Association
http://www.smparalegal.org
President:
Tracie L. Livesay, CLAS
Maryville, TN
Liaison:
Carolyn E.H. Sudlow, CLA
Knoxville, TN

Tennessee Paralegal Association
http://www.tnparalegal.org
President:
Susan E. Veal
Chattanooga, TN
Liaison:
Caleeta L. Beagles
Chattanooga, TN

Texas

Capital Area Paralegal Association
http://www.capatx.org

President:
Thelma Alvarado-Garza
Austin, TX
Liaison:
Michele Flowers Brooks
Austin, TX

El Paso Paralegal Association
http://www.epala.org
President:
Heidi Beginski
El Paso, TX
Liaison:
Mary K. La Rue, CP
El Paso, TX

Houston Corporate Paralegal Association
http://www.hcpa.cc
President:
Joyce Allen-Dennis
Houston, TX
Liaison:
Debbie Michelli, CLA
Houston, TX

Houston Paralegal Assocation
http://www.houstonparalegalassociation.org
President:
Gina Shannon
Houston, TX
Liaison:
Linda A. Carrette, CLA
Houston, TX

Paralegal Association/Permian Basin
http://www.paralegalspb.org
President:
Janet L. McDaniel, CLA
Midland, TX
Liaison:
Cecile N. Wiginton, CLA
Midland, TX

North Texas Paralegal Association
http://www.lantaweb.org
President:
Penny Grawunder
Dallas, TX
Liaison:
Kathryn S. Moore, CP
Dallas, TX

**Northeast Texas Association
of Legal Assistants**
http://www.ntala.net
President:
Mona H. Chandler, CLA
Longview, TX

Liaison:
Lori E. Sanders, CLA
Longview, TX

South Texas Organization of Paralegals, Inc.
http://www.southtexasparalegals.org
President:
Charlene B. Carroll, CLA
San Antonio, TX
Liaison:
Charlene B. Carroll, CLA
San Antonio, TX

**Southeast Texas Association
of Legal Assistants**
http://www.setala.org
President:
Sheila Milbrandt
Beaumont, TX
Liaison:
Michelle Stutes
Beaumont, TX

Texas Panhandle Paralegal Association
President:
Susan Grim, CLAS
Amarillo, TX
Liaison:
Charlotte R. Martin, CP
Borger, TX

**Tyler Area Association of Legal
Professionals**
President:
Rosa L. Ferguson
Tyler, TX
Liaison:
Lynda M. Barron, CLAS
Tyler, TX

West Texas Association of Legal Assistants
President:
Nabeth Crenshaw
Lubbock, TX
Liaison:
Sheila M. Veach, CLA
Lubbock, TX

Utah

Legal Assistants Association of Utah
President:
Mary H. Black, CLA
West Valley City, UT
Liaison:
Patty H. Allred, CP
Salt Lake City, UT

Virgin Islands

**Virgin Islands Association
of Legal Assistants**
President:
Jonetta Darden
St. Thomas, VI
Liaison:
Georgeann Peters
McNicholas, CLA
St. Thomas, VI

Virginia

Richmond Paralegal Association
http://www.richmondparalegals.org
President:
Michele Rundstrom
Richmond, VA
Liaison:
Cathy W. Eagles
Richmond, VA

Roanoke Valley Paralegal Association
President:
Susan L. Albert
Roanoke, VA
Liaison:
Colleen A. Doyle, CLA
Roanoke, VA

Tidewater Paralegal Association
President:
Tammy L. Grosch, CP
Norfolk, VA
Liaison:
Doreen H. Hall, CP
Norfolk, VA

Virginia Peninsula Paralegal Association
http://www.vappa.org
President:
Kathy S. Owen
Newport News, VA
Liaison:
Claire Etta Smith, CLA
Newport News, VA

NALS STATE AND CHAPTER ASSOCIATIONS

NALS . . . the association for legal professionals is a multi-level association with state and chapter associations.

Following is a list of all NALS state and chapter associations. If you would like contact information for a specific state or chapter association, please contact membership services at the NALS Resource Center at

NALS Resource Center
314 East Third Street, Suite 210
Tulsa, OK 74120
(918) 582-5188
(918) 582-5907
info@nals.org
http://www.nals.org

Region 1

Maine
Maine, NALS of
Central Maine, NALS of
Mid-Coast Maine, NALS of
Northeast Maine, NALS of
Southern Maine, NALS of

New York
New York Inc., NALS of
New York City, NALS of
Central New York, NALS of
Lower Hudson Valley, NALS of
Nassau County, NALS of
Suffolk, NALS of
SUNY-Jefferson, NALS Students of

Region 2

District of Columbia
DC LSA

New Jersey
New Jersey ALS
Hunterdon County LSA
Monmouth LSA
Morris County LSA
Somerset LSA
Union-Essex LPA

Pennsylvania
Pennsylvania, NALS of
Capital Area ALP
Lehigh-Northhampton Co.
Philadelphia LSA
Pittsburgh LSA
Schuylkill County LSA

Virginia
Virginia ALS-LSP
Charlottesville-Albermarle
Fredericksburg Area LSA

New River Valley LSA
Norfolk-Portsmouth LSA
Northern Virginia LSA
Peninsula ALS
Prince William County ALSP
Richmond LSA
Roanoke Valley LSA
Virginia Beach
Virginia Highlands LSA

Region 3

Illinois
Illinois, NALS of

Michigan
Michigan, NALS of
Berrien-Cass LSP
Calhoun County, NALS of
Detroit, NALS of
Genesee ALSP
Greater Kalamazoo, NALS of
Grand Traverse County LSP
Jackson County LSP
Lansing, NALS of
Livingston County LSA
Mid-Michigan ALSP
Northern Michigan, NALS of
Oakland County, NALS of
Washtenaw, NALS of
West Michigan, NALS of

Ohio
Ohio, NALS of
Central Ohio, NALS of
Mahoning County LSA
Medina County ALP
Muskingum County LSA
Stark County, NALS of
Trumbull County LSA

Region 4

Alabama
Alabama ALS
Baldwin County ALP
Birmingham LSA
Dallas County LSA
Mobile LSA
Montgomery ALS
Shelby County, NALS of
Tuscaloosa County LPA
Virginia College at Mobile, NALS of

Florida
Central Florida, NALS of

Georgia
Georgia, NALS of
Atlanta, NALS of
Central Savannah River Student Association
Cobb County LSA

South Carolina
South Carolina, LSP of
Greenville, LSP of
Hilton Head SP
Lowcountry, LSP of
Midlands, LSP of
Orangeburg LSP
Spartanburg County LSP

Tennessee
Tennessee, LP of
Chattanooga LP
MLSA-LP of Memphis
Nashville NALS-ALP
Rutherford/Cannon County LP
Williamson County LP
Wilson County LP

Region 5

Minnesota
Greater Minnesota, NALS of
Twin Cities, NALS of

North Dakota
Fargo-Moorhead LSA
Minot LSA

South Dakota
Black Hills LPA

Wisconsin
Wisconsin ALP
Brown County ALP
East Central LPA
Fox Valley ALP
Greater Milwaukee ALP
Lakeshore Area ALP
North Central ALP
Racine-Kenosha LP
St. Croix Valley LP
South Central Wisconsin, LP of

Region 6

Arkansas
Arkansas ALS
Garland County LSP
Greater Little Rock LSP
Jefferson County ALSP

Northeast Arkansas LSP
Saline County LSP
White County LSP

Mississippi
Mississippi, Division of NALS, Inc.
Columbus LPA
Greenwood LPA
Gulf Coast ALSP
Jackson LSA
Metro LPA
Pine Belt LP

Missouri
Missouri, NALS of
Central Ozarks LSA
Franklin County ALSP
Greater St. Louis, NALS of
Heart of America LPA
Kansas City LSA
Lakes Area LSA
St. Louis County ALP
Springfield Area LSP
Tri-County ALP

Oklahoma
Oklahoma, NALS of

Texas
Texas ALP
Amarillo, NALS of
Arlington LPA
Austin LSA, Inc.
Beaumont LSA
Corpus Christi Association of LP
Dallam-Hartley-Moore Co.
Dallas ALS
East Texas Area LPA
El Paso County LSA

Fort Worth ALP
Greater Dallas Association of LP
Houston ALP
Lubbock LPA
Midland LSA
San Antonio LSA
Texas State Tech College
    Harlingen Student Chapter
Waco LPA
Wichita County LSA

Region 7

Alaska
Anchorage, NALS of

Idaho
Idaho ALS
Boise LSA
Lewiston LSA
North Idaho ALS

Montana
Montana, NALS of

Oregon
Oregon, NALS of
Central Oregon Legal Professors
Douglas County, LP of
Lane County LSP
Mid-Willamette Valley, NALS of
Mt. Hood LP
Portland, NALS of
South Oregon Coast, NALS of

Washington
Washington, NALS of
East King County LSP
Greater Seattle, NALS of

Greater Wenatchee, NALS of
Kitsap County, NALS of
Pierce County, NALS of
Snohomish, NALS of
Spokane, NALS of
Thurston County, NALS of
Yakima, NALS of

Region 8

Arizona
Arizona, NALS of
Phoenix, NALS of
Tucson & South Arizona, NALS of
Yavapai County, NALS of

California
California, NALS of
Orange County, NALS of
Port Stockton LSA

Colorado
Colorado, NALS of

Hawaii
Hawaii LSP

Nevada
Nevada, NALS of
Douglas-Carson LP
Las Vegas, NALS of
Washoe County, NALS of

New Mexico
Albuquerque ALP

Utah
Utah Legal Professionals Association

Courtesy of NFPA, NALA, and NALS. Reprinted with permission.

THE CLA/CP PROGRAM

The Certified Legal Assistant/Certified Paralegal credential is key to respect and opportunity throughout the legal profession. Whether the preferred term is "paralegal" or "legal assistant," the CLA/CP program certifies that the person has passed a demanding examination of the skills and knowledge needed to provide paralegal services. Earning this credential is a proud achievement, and maintaining the right to use it is a career-long commitment. Certification must be maintained through continuing education relevant to the demands of the paralegal career.

Growth of the Program

When the NALA was founded in 1975, continuing paralegal education was a top priority in the fledgling association. A strong and responsive self-regulatory program offering nationwide certification for paralegals was seen as the cornerstone of career development demonstrating academic excellence while also providing measurable evidence of expertise.

The CLA/CP program was created to realize this objective. With thirty years of research and development now behind it, the program continues to evolve to meet challenging professional needs and standards. It is under constant review to be certain that academic standards are of the highest caliber, and to ensure that it remains relevant to the profession.

The CLA/CP program establishes and serves as a:

- National professional standard for paralegals;
- Means of identifying those who have reached this standard;
- Credentialing program responsive to the needs of paralegals and responsive to the fact that this form of self-regulation is necessary to strengthen and expand the career field; and

- Positive, ongoing, voluntary program to encourage the growth of the paralegal profession, attesting to and encouraging a high level of achievement.

Recognition of the Program

Firms, corporations, and agencies recognize the CLA/CP as a credible measure of paralegal competence. National surveys by NALA consistently show that Certified Paralegals are better utilized in fields where attorneys require a dependable measure of ability. The credential has been acknowledged by the American Bar Association as a mark of high professional achievement, and more than forty-seven paralegal organizations and numerous bar associations also acknowledge the CLA/CP as the definitive paralegal certification.

Some Examples

- The State Bar of Texas passed a resolution in 1982 recognizing the CLA/CP as a means of identifying qualified legal assistants/paralegals.
- The American Bar Association Standing Committee on Legal Assistants submitted a letter in 1986 recognizing the CLA/CP as a hallmark of higher achievement.

EXHIBIT G–1
Growth of CLA/CP
Program since 1975

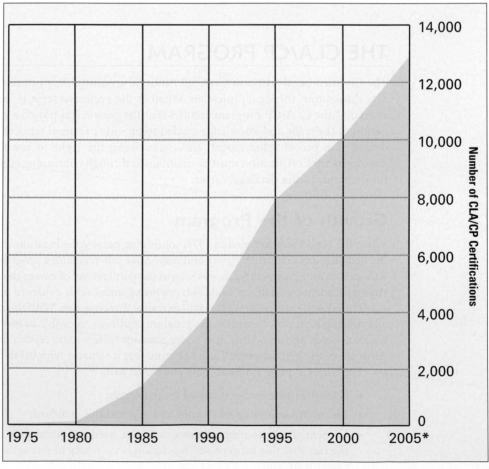

As of February 1, 2006, the CLA/CP Program reached 13,326.

- The ABA Section of Law Practice Management, in its 1993 publication *Leveraging with Legal Assistants,* states that it would be safe for hiring attorneys to assume that a "CLA can immediately bring experience and capability to the practice." The publication also pointed out the importance of distinguishing between CLA/CP professional certification and a certificate of completion from an educational institution.

- *Mississippi Bar Ethics Committee, Opinion 223,* 1995, called the CLA a reputable program, and allowed use of the credentials on law firm letterhead.

- New York Committee on Professional Ethics, *Opinion 695,* 1997, held that an "attorney may include on letterhead and other materials the identification of a nonlegal employee as a 'Certified Legal Assistant' provided that the term is accompanied by the statement that the certification is afforded" by NALA.

In 2001, participation in the CLA/CP paralegal certification program was approved by the U.S. Department of Defense as a reimbursable expense under the G.I. Bill. Veterans will be reimbursed for exam fees, including retake fees, under the licensing and certification benefit.

Administration

The Certifying Board for Legal Assistants is responsible for content, standards, and administration of the CLA/CP program. This board is composed of paralegals who have received the advanced CLA Specialist (CLAS) designation, attorneys, and paralegal educators.

In the technical areas of statistical analysis, examination construction, and reliability and validity tests, the board contracts with a professional consulting firm offering expertise in these areas as well as in occupational research. Experts in tests and measurements conduct ongoing technical analyses of the CLA/CP examination to ensure integrity of the examination. Content analyses of the test design, accuracy of questions, and topic/subject mix for each exam section are continual processes of the Certifying Board.

The board also makes use of occupational data available through surveys of paralegals and other means, including review of textbooks and research within the field of paralegal education. Through these analyses and procedures, the board ensures that the examination reflects and responds to workplace realities and demands.

The Certifying Board is also responsible for admission requirements, disciplinary procedures, and maintaining and administering the continuing education requirements for renewal of the credential.

EXAMINATION SUBJECTS

The CLA/CP examination is a comprehensive two-day assessment based on federal law and procedure. There are five sections of the examination as described below.

Communications

- Word usage, punctuation, capitalization, grammar;
- Correspondence, concise writing, vocabulary;
- Rules of composition;
- Nonverbal communications;
- Skills encompassing professional and social contacts with employer, clients, office visitors, co-workers, and the public; and
- General understanding of authorized practice, ethical rules, practice rules, delegation of authority, and consequences of delegation and confidentiality.

Interviewing questions are integrated into the communications section, including basic principles of interviewing, and the following specifics:

- Interviewing situation (courtesy, empathy, physical setting, body language);
- Initial roadblocks to interviewing—lapse of time, prejudice, etc.;
- Manner of questions;
- Use of checklists for specific matters;
- Special situations—the elderly, the very young; and
- Interviewing clients and witnesses, initial and subsequent interviews.

Ethics

- Ethical responsibilities centering on performance of delegated work including confidentiality, unauthorized practice of law, legal advice, conflict of interest, billing and client communications;
- Client/public contact including identification as a nonlawyer, advertising and initial client contact;
- Professional integrity/competence including knowledge of legal assistant codes of ethics;
- Relationships with co-workers and support staff; and
- Attorney codes/discipline.

Knowledge of the American Bar Association's *Rules of Professional Conduct* and the NALA *Code of Ethics and Professional Responsibility* is required for this examination.

Legal Research

- Sources of law, including primary authority, secondary authority, and understanding how law is recorded;
- Research skills, including citing the law, "Shepardizing," updating decisions, and procedural rules of citation; and
- Analysis of a research problem, including identification of relevant facts and legal issues.

Judgment and Analytical Ability

- Analyzing and categorizing facts and evidence;
- Reading comprehension and data interpretation;
- Paralegal's relationship with the lawyer, support staff, clients, courts, other law firms; and
- Dealing with specific situations; telephone communications.

This section contains an essay question which requires analysis of a research request, finding applicable law, and writing a responsive memo. Familiarity with the *Rules of Professional Conduct* of the American Bar Association and the *Code of Ethics and Professional Responsibility* of NALA will be helpful. Knowledge of logical reasoning techniques is valuable, as well as experience as a paralegal.

Substantive Law

The substantive law section of the exam consists of five subsections. The first section, "Substantive Law—General," covers concepts of the American legal system. All examinees are required to take this section, which includes the following subjects:

- Court system including court structure and jurisdiction;
- Branches of government, agencies, and concepts such as separation of powers;

- Legal concepts and principles including sources of law, judicial decision making, appellate process; and
- Sources and classifications of law including the constitution, statutes, common law, civil law, statutory law, and equity law.

The other four subsections are electives chosen by exam applicants from a list of nine substantive areas of the law:

- Administrative law
- Bankruptcy
- Business organizations
- Civil litigation
- Contracts
- Criminal law and procedure
- Estate planning and probate
- Family law
- Real estate

The skills required by these tests involve recall of facts and principles that form the basis of the specialty practice area. Examinees must also demonstrate an understanding of the structure of the law and procedures to be followed in each specialty practice area.

ELIGIBILITY

To be eligible for the CLA/CP examination, a paralegal must meet one of the following requirements:

1. **Graduation from a legal assistant program** that is:
   - Approved by the American Bar Association, or
   - An associate degree program, or
   - A postbaccalaureate certificate program in legal assistant studies, or
   - A bachelor's degree program in legal assistant studies, or
   - A legal assistant program which consists of a minimum of 60 semester hours (900 clock hours or 90 quarter hours) of which at least 15 semester hours (225 clock hours or 22.5 quarter hours) are substantive legal courses.

2. **A bachelor's degree** in any field plus one year of paralegal experience. Successful completion of at least 15 semester hours (or 225 clock hours or 22.5 quarter hours) of substantive legal assistant courses will be considered equivalent to one year of experience as a legal assistant.

3. **A high school diploma or equivalent** and seven years of experience as a legal assistant under the supervision of a member of the Bar, plus evidence of a minimum of twenty hours of continuing legal education credit to have been completed within a two (2)-year period prior to the examination date.

For Paralegal Students

Paralegal students who are nearing graduation may take the examination under certain conditions. For example, if a student is scheduled to graduate after the March/April exam but before May 31, the student may take the Spring CLA/CP examination in March (or April, depending on when Easter occurs).

Information on NALA, C...

EXHIBIT G–2
How Graduation Dates
Affect Examination Dates

Examination Date	Graduation Date No Later Than
March or April Exam (depending on Easter)	May 31
July Exam	August 31
December Exam	January 31

This option also requires:

- An original statement signed by the paralegal program director confirming the student's pending graduation date; and

- An original statement signed by the student acknowledging that if, for any reason, graduation requirements are not met and the student does not complete the program, the examination will not be graded and the examination fee will be forfeited.

CLA OR CP?

It has long been recognized that the terms *legal assistant* and *paralegal* are synonymous terms. This is not an opinion of NALA, but a well-documented fact throughout the United States—supported by state Supreme Court rules, statutes, ethical opinions, bar association guidelines, and other similar documents. These are the same documents that provide recognition of the paralegal profession and encourage the use of legal assistants in the delivery of legal services.

NALA is sensitive to the fact that even though the terms mean the same thing—just as "lawyer" and "attorney" are synonymous—a preference for one term or the other is emerging in different geographic areas. For this reason, the association filed for a "CP" certification mark with the U.S. Patent and Trademark Office. The certification mark CP® was officially registered on July 20, 2004.

MAINTAINING THE CLA/CP CREDENTIAL

The CLA/CP credential is valid for a period of five years. At least fifty hours of continuing education every five years is required to maintain use of the credential—lifetime certification is not available. Because the continual change in laws and procedures has a direct impact on the work performed by paralegals, continuing legal education is an essential part of the certification process—as important to the credential as taking and passing the examination.

Credit for continuing legal education is awarded on the basis of hours of actual instruction. If a four-hour program includes an hour for lunch, then credit will be awarded for three hours. There are a variety of programs and ways in which the CLA/CP may maintain certification.

Credit is granted for participation in most CLE programs offered by reputable organizations as long as the subject matter is related to work as a legal assistant.

Participation in the following types of programs may qualify:

- Conferences, seminars, etc. offered by NALA-affiliated associations, bar associations, or seminar providers;

- Teaching in a paralegal program or teaching a session at a CLE seminar;

- Participation in online educational programs;

- Completion of a class at a college or community college; or

- Achievement of an advanced paralegal certification credential such as that offered by NALA, or a NALA-recognized state credentialing program (offered in California, Florida, and Texas).

EXHIBIT G–3
CLA/CP Examination Data by State as of February 1, 2006

Alabama 168	Maine 70	Pennsylvania 86
Alaska 83	Maryland 24	Puerto Rico 2
Arizona 962	Massachusetts 19	Rhode Island 4
Arkansas 87	Michigan 159	South Carolina 123
California 738	Minnesota 32	South Dakota 137
Colorado 234	Mississippi 151	Tennessee 247
Connecticut 7	Missouri 106	Texas 2,661
Delaware 3	Montana 63	Utah 128
District of Columbia 6	Nebraska 137	Vermont 2
Florida 3,415	Nevada 248	Virginia 288
Georgia 174	New Hampshire 82	Virgin Islands 40
Hawaii 4	New Jersey 76	Washington 59
Idaho 42	New Mexico 188	West Virginia 97
Illinois 71	New York 82	Wisconsin 37
Indiana 49	North Carolina 385	Wyoming 126
Iowa 124	North Dakota 104	Canada 2
Kansas 208	Ohio 124	France 1
Kentucky............. 23	Oklahoma 555	
Louisiana 157	Oregon 126	**Total:** 13,326

Through December 1990, 3,974 legal assistants were certified throughout the country. As of the December 2005 testing session, there were 13,326 Certified Legal Assistants. This represents an increase of over 200 percent in the number of Certified Legal Assistants in the last twelve years. Since the examination was first administered in 1976, more than 25,000 legal assistants have participated in this program.

In order to pass, a legal assistant must successfully complete all five sections of the CLA/CP examination within a three-year period.

PREPARING FOR THE EXAM

To order books or learn more about NALA Campus programs, NALA exam review programs, or programs offered by NALA affiliated associations, please visit the NALA Web site. Following are some of the support options NALA offers paralegals preparing for the CLA/CP examination.

Published Material

The following books, published by NALA through Delmar, Cengage Learning Paralegal, are suitable for exam preparation:

- *CLA Review Manual, Second Edition* by Virginia Koerselman, attorney
- *NALA Manual for Legal Assistants, Fourth Edition,* authored by NALA members

- *CLA Study Guide and Mock Examination, Third Edition,* authored by NALA members
- *Real Estate Law Specialty Review Manual,* by attorney John Dunn and Karen M. Dunn, CLAS
- *Business Organizations Specialty Review Manual,* by attorney Denise Hill, edited by Virginia Koerselman, attorney

Live Seminars and Review Programs

Twice a year, NALA provides live CLA/CP exam review programs. The CLA Short Course is offered each October, and the Essential Skills Program is offered at the NALA Annual Convention in July. Both are excellent programs taught by experienced attorneys and paralegals.

Affiliated Association Review Programs

Review programs are also available through state and local paralegal associations located in the states shown in Exhibit G–4.

EXHIBIT G–4
States That Offer
Review Programs

Alabama	North Carolina
California	North Dakota
Florida	Ohio
Georgia	Oklahoma
Illinois	South Carolina
Kansas	Tennessee
Mississippi	Texas
Montana	Virginia
Nevada	West Virginia

A list of these associations and Web sites may be found in the affiliated associations area of the NALA Web site.

Web-Based Programs

For those who have difficulties with the time and travel requirements for live seminars, online programs are available through NALA Campus Self-Study and NALA Campus LIVE! programs. The self-study programs, prepared or edited by Virginia Koerselman, attorney and author, are available around the clock, allowing students to pick their own time and set their own pace. Subjects include the following:

- Written communications
- Judgment and legal analysis
- Legal research
- American legal system
- Legal ethics
- Civil litigation
- Contracts
- Real estate law

The NALA Campus LIVE! programs are live Web-based presentations. Members of the CLA/CP Short Course faculty present sessions on communications, legal analysis, and trial preparation. Attorneys and experts also present a selection of substantive law topics.

These popular programs provide opportunities for participants to discuss questions with the presenters and other students. A computer with a high-speed Internet connection and a telephone are all that is needed to take advantage of this innovative and effective program. Details about the NALA Campus Self-Study and LIVE! programs are at the NALA Campus Web site at **http://www.nalacampus.com**.

ADVANCED PARALEGAL CERTIFICATION

The purposes of the CLA/CP Advanced Certification programs are to:

- Provide first class continuing education courses for paralegals in various specialty practice areas; and

- Provide a certification process to recognize those who have achieved the CLA/CP certification and successfully complete an advanced certification program in a specific practice area.

The CLA Specialty program began in 1982 with examinations for paralegals working in the areas of civil litigation and probate and estate planning. In 1984, the corporations/business and criminal law and procedure examinations were offered. A Real Estate specialty examination was added in 1987, followed by bankruptcy in 1992, and intellectual property in 1995. As of June 1, 2005, 1,108 Certified Paralegals have received the CLAS credential.

The CLA Specialty Program is now entering a new phase to stay in step with the accelerating pace and evolving needs of the paralegal profession. A shift from the current written exam program to a curriculum-based Internet learning and assessment process is the main transformation.

The transition to curriculum-based certification is a slow and deliberate process involving dedicated individual and team effort by paralegals, subject experts, and technical experts. Recommended changes in the program were first introduced to paralegals at NALA's annual convention in July 2003. The presentation described the Paralegal Advanced Certification Board review and evaluation methodology, and explained the rationale behind the recommendations.

Why Change?

The paralegal work environment of today is entirely different than when the CLAS program was launched twenty years ago. Devising a program with curricula to meet the ever-sharpening professional focus now demanded by employers was a key element in the board's desire to retailor the specialty program. This aim is supported by consistent feedback from certified paralegals who have asked for more narrowly focused advanced certifications.

The Paralegal Advanced Certification Board also sought a program that would better serve CLA/CPs wishing to enter new areas of specialty practice areas, as well as those seeking advanced credentials in their current specialty areas. This recommendation was based on the observation that the current program is aimed at those who either have the experience to pass the exam in a certain area of law, or who are willing to undertake a grueling (and often indistinct) regimen of self-study to achieve the required knowledge.

Logistical issues surrounding location and times of examinations were also addressed. The current four-hour written exam given three times a year at locations nationwide requires the inconvenience, or hardship, of travel for many who wish to earn advanced certification. A more "user-friendly" means of qualifying for the CLAS was sought, without compromising the required level of expertise.

Program Criteria

In order to meet the recommendations for more narrowly focused specialty areas and greater service to CLA/CPs who want to change areas of specialty practice, the Paralegal Advanced Certification Board set specific criteria to be met by the advanced program. These include:

1. Participants must hold the CLA/CP credential to earn the advanced credential.

2. The program must be relevant to the workplace. Employers represented on the board emphasized that if employers were to support the new program, the current reality of narrow specialization, rather than broad areas of practice, must be reflected in the curriculum. In addition, the program description must clearly state the meaning of the advanced certification—that the individual paralegal has demonstrated specific knowledge in a specific area of law.

3. Defensible national standards must be maintained. The program must withstand evaluation by outside experts just as the CLA/CP examination and the current CLAS program have.

4. The program must be accessible and offered at a reasonable cost.

When?

The first specialty subject area in development for advanced certification is "Contracts Administration & Management." The course is complete and actual implementation is expected before the end of 2006. Because the subject of contracts touches many areas of law, this is believed to be an excellent subject with which to begin.

Other specialty areas will be developed according to the needs of CLA/CPs. While the Paralegal Advanced Certification Board is considering a wide range of possibilities, each program will be designed to reflect the work of paralegals in specific practice areas. The board will seek input from CLA/CPs and NALA members; it will review survey data and consider other information to determine specific specialty areas. Some areas under consideration are personal injury, real property/land use, discovery, business organizations, trademark law, patent law, elder law, and complex litigation management.

The current CLAS examination program will be phased out with the July 2005 examination session.

More information about this progressive specialty program is available by contacting NALA headquarters or checking the Web site.

The Marks

CLA®, CLAS®, and CP® are certification marks duly registered with the U.S. Patent and Trademark Office (No. 113199, No. 1751731, and No. 78213275, respectively). Unauthorized use of these credentials is strictly forbidden.

Courtesy of the ©National Association of Legal Assistants, Inc. Reprinted with permission.

INFORMATION ON
NFPA'S PACE EXAMINATION

INTRODUCTION

The legal service industry is facing great change. While containing costs, it is trying to respond to an increased number of pending cases, rapid changes in technology, and increased demands from consumers for a higher level of client service.

As an active and vital part of the legal service industry, the paralegal profession is facing possible regulation through certification, licensing, or other means. The National Federation of Paralegal Associations, Inc., gathered this information to describe the bold step it is undertaking—a step that may dramatically change the entire profession.

A BOLD STEP FORWARD

A grassroots organization, NFPA is directed by its membership—each member association has one vote in the future of the national organization and the profession. During NFPA's 1994 Mid-Year Meeting, the membership voted overwhelmingly to develop an exam to test the competency level of experienced paralegals.

The overwhelmingly positive vote to develop this exam is a conscientious effort by these paralegals to direct the future of the paralegal profession and acknowledges the vital role of paralegals within the legal service industry. It is also a direct response to states that are considering regulation of the paralegal profession and are seeking a method to measure job competency. While NFPA believes in the criteria the members established to take this exam, it recognizes any state may adopt the exam and modify the criteria.

The Paralegal Advanced Competency Exam (PACE) will be developed in two stages, identified as tiers. Tier I, comprising general and ethics questions, is already available; state-specific modules will be developed within particular jurisdictions as the need arises. Tier II will comprise specialty sections.

PACE = Paralegal Advanced Competency Exam

Offering experienced paralegals an option to:

- Validate your experience and job skills;
- Establish credentials; and
- Increase your value to your organizations and clients.

The only exam of its kind, PACE:

- Was developed by a professional testing firm;
- Is administered by an independent test administration company;
- Tests concepts across practice areas;
- Offers the profession a national standard of evaluation; and
- Is offered at multiple locations on numerous dates and at various times.

PACE = Personal Advancement for the Experienced Paralegal

Paralegals receive two major benefits by taking PACE. The exam:

- Provides a fair evaluation of paralegal competency across all practice areas; and
- Creates a professional level of expertise by which all paralegals can be evaluated.

EXPERIENCE AND EDUCATION

Requirements for a paralegal to take either tier of PACE include work experience and education. The paralegal cannot have been convicted of a felony nor be under suspension, termination, or revocation of a certificate, registration, or license by any entity. PACE has generated a great deal of interest since the resolution to develop it was passed. Based on this interest, and the number of paralegals who may apply to take the exam (a number reported by the U.S. Department of Labor to exceed 113,000), a need exists for global grandparenting.

Requirements for Tier I Are

- A minimum of four (4) years' experience as a paralegal obtained by December 31, 2000, **OR**
- A bachelor's degree, and completion of a paralegal program within an institutionally accredited school (which may be embodied in the bachelor's degree), and a minimum of two (2) years' experience as a paralegal.

Requirements for Tier II Are

- Successful completion of Tier I, **AND** *one of the following:*
- A minimum of six (6) years' experience as a paralegal, **OR**
- A bachelor's degree, and completion of a paralegal program within an institutionally accredited school (which may be embodied in the bachelor's degree), **and** a minimum of four (4) years' experience as a paralegal.

NFPA'S ROLE

First organized in 1974, NFPA was created to provide a communications network and develop channels to expand the role of the paralegal profession. In addition, NFPA has assisted the profession in evaluating educational standards and responding to organizations and entities that appear interested in regulating the profession.

NFPA membership has significantly increased since its inception. In 2000, it included 55 associations, located throughout the United States, with more than 17,000 members.

Independent and Fair

NFPA strongly believes PACE must produce legitimate and verifiable results and consistently pass only paralegals who demonstrate an established level of knowledge, skills, and competency. PACE was developed in cooperation with the independent test development firm, Professional Examination Service (PES).

PES was selected through an extensive proposal process and a personal interview with the NFPA Board of Directors. PES has developed professional exams for more than fifty years for groups such as the Federal Reserve System, the National Association of Securities Dealers, Inc., the Environmental Protection Agency, and the Emergency Medical Technicians and Paramedics Association. PES currently works with more than 75 professional associations and more than 300 licensing boards in 62 jurisdictions in the United States and Canada.

PES does not work alone, however. An independent task force of paralegals, paralegal educators, attorneys, and other public members who are legal advocates assist in every step, from the preparation of the job analysis for paralegals through creation of the initial exam and ongoing revisions. To ensure test results are valid, the test is administered by PES, an independent firm. All profits received from the exam program will be passed to the "Foundation for the Advancement of the Paralegal Profession," an independent foundation, and will be used to further the entire paralegal profession.

Preparing for the Future

PACE presents a bold opportunity to all paralegals to advance the profession. This exam provides hard facts about the competency of experienced paralegals. While PACE does not address all the issues of regulation, including certification and licensing, it does provide the legal service industry with an option to evaluate the competency level of experienced paralegals.

As members of a self-directed profession, all paralegals should consider the vital role the profession performs within the legal service industry. PACE is independently monitored and well structured. PACE provides test results across practice areas and, possibly, state-specific laws. While the test is offered on a voluntary basis, all experienced paralegals are encouraged to sit for the exam.

NFPA is committed to ensuring that the paralegal profession responds to the changing needs of the public and legal service industry. In voting to develop PACE, NFPA's membership took a bold step toward addressing the future issues facing the profession.

Lexis-Nexis has sponsored a twenty-minute presentation on paralegals which highlights PACE. This presentation is available on video or CD-ROM.

Credential

Those who pass PACE and maintain the continuing education requirement may use the designation "PACE—Registered Paralegal" or "RP."

To maintain the RP credential, twelve hours of continuing legal or specialty education is required every two years, with at least one hour in legal ethics.

Registered Paralegals should review the "Facts Every RP Should Know" found at **http://www.paralegals.org** to be aware of the ways the PACE credential can be used and information on registraton of CLE credits. Also included in the fact sheet is information on nonrenewal status, inactive status, suspension and revocation of the use of the RP credential, and the appeals process.

Inactive status may be granted by the PACE Standards Committee upon completion of an application. One-half of the CLE requirement is required while in inactive status.

How to Prepare and Register

To prepare for the exam, paralegals may use any of the following options:

- *A study manual*;
- *A sample exam disc,* which contains one hundred sample questions, grading of the answers, and a listing of further resources for incorrect answer;
- *Seminars* sponsored by local paralegal associations and NFPA, which can be found on the NFPA's calendar;
- *PACE Review Course,* a seven-week course provided through the Internet; or
- *Online seminars* can be found on NFPA's CLE page.

To register to take the exam, send $15 to NFPA, P.O. Box 33108, Kansas City, MO 64114-0108, for a *Candidate Handbook,* which includes an application, information on exam content, sample exam questions, and logistical information on taking the exam. The $15 fee will be applied to the overall examination fee of $225. Once the application has been approved, the exam must be taken within ninety days.

PACE is a four-hour, computer-generated test and is offered at more than two hundred Sylvan Technology Centers, also known as Prometric, throughout the country. Once approved, each applicant can schedule the date and time to take the test at his or her convenience on any day except Sundays and holidays. Please note: not all Sylvan Learning Centers are Technology Centers.

Courtesy of the National Federation of Paralegal Associations, Inc. Reprinted with permission.

INFORMATION ON
NALS CERTIFICATION

NALS offers members and nonmembers the opportunity to sit for three unique certifications dedicated to the legal services profession. The exams are of varying levels and are developed by professionals in the industry. ALS . . . the basic certification for legal professionals and PLS . . . the advanced certification for legal professionals are two certifications dedicated to legal professionals of all types. The third certification is dedicated to those professionals performing paralegal duties. The Professional Paralegal (PP) certification was developed by paralegals for paralegals. Each of the three certifications is developed by NALS and takes advantage of the more than seventy-five years of experience and dedication to the legal services industry only NALS has to offer.

As of March 2006, there are 2,393 people certified as an ALS, 5,355 certified PLSs, and 339 Professional Paralegals.

ALS . . . THE BASIC CERTIFICATION FOR LEGAL PROFESSIONALS—A CAREER GOAL

One way to demonstrate your preparedness for the demanding field of law is by becoming an ALS. This designation is awarded after passing a four-hour, three-part examination. Attaining this goal demonstrates your commitment and aptitude for succeeding in the ever-changing legal environment.

The ALS Examination

- Demonstrates ability to perform business communication tasks;
- Gauges ability to maintain office records and calendars, and prioritize multiple tasks when given real-life scenarios;

799

- Measures understanding of office equipment and related procedures;
- Denotes aptitude for understanding legal terminology, legal complexities, and supporting documents;
- Assesses recognition of accounting terms to solve accounting problems; and
- Appraises knowledge of law office protocol as prescribed by ethical codes.

ALS Examination Eligibility

To sit for the examination, you must have completed one of the following:

- An accredited business/legal course,
- The NALS Legal Training Course, or
- One year of general office experience.

Membership in NALS is not a requirement.

What the Exam Covers

The examination covers the following parts:

- PART 1: Written Communications
- PART 2: Office Procedures and Legal Knowledge
- PART 3: Ethics, Human Relations, and Judgment

Examination Guidelines

All three parts of the examination must be taken on the first attempt. If you do not pass the entire examination on the first attempt, you may retake the examination parts you did not pass. All failed parts must be retaken at the same time. Those passing the exam will receive a certificate that is valid for five years. Certification may be extended through continuing education, based on NALS guidelines, for one year.

Examination Dates and Application Deadlines

- March: First Saturday (Postmarked by January 1)
- June: First Saturday* (Postmarked by April 15)
- September: Last Saturday (Postmarked by August 1)
- December: First Saturday* (Postmarked by October 15)

  *June and December testing are for those who have completed
  the Basic or Advanced NALS Legal Training Course.

Examination Fees

- Student/LTC Participant (minimum of 9 credit hours): $50
- NALS member (not a full-time student): $75
- Nonmember (not a full-time student): $100
- Retake fees:
  Members/students/one part: $40
  Nonmembers/one part: $50
  Students/two or more parts: $50
  Members/two or more parts: $75
  Nonmembers/two or more parts: $100

PLS . . . THE ADVANCED CERTIFICATION FOR LEGAL PROFESSIONALS—A CAREER GOAL

How do your skills compare with the hallmark of a professional? PLS is the designation for lawyer's assistants who want to be identified as exceptional. Certification is received after passing a one-day, four-part examination which demonstrates not only dedication to professionalism but acceptance of the challenge to be exceptional. Personal motivation is necessary to attain such a goal.

The purpose of the examination is to certify a lawyer's assistant as a person who possesses:

- A mastery of office skills;
- The ability to interact on a professional level with attorneys, clients, and other support staff;
- The discipline to assume responsibility and exercise initiative and judgment; and
- A working knowledge of procedural law, the law library, and how to prepare legal documents.

PLS Examination Eligibility

Any person who has had three years' experience in the legal field may take the examination. Membership in NALS is not a requirement. A partial waiver of the three-year legal experience requirement may be granted for postsecondary degrees, successful completion of the ALS exam, or other certifications. The maximum waiver is one year.

The PLS Certification Exam Covers

- PART 1: Written Communications
- PART 2: Office Procedures and Technology
- PART 3: Ethics and Judgment
- PART 4: Legal Knowledge and Skills

Examination Guidelines

All four parts of the examination must be taken on the first attempt. If you do not pass the entire examination on the first attempt, but do pass one or more parts, you may retake the part (or parts) you failed. All failed parts must be retaken at the same time.

Those passing the exam will receive a certificate that is valid for five years. Recertification is required every five years and may be achieved through the accumulation of continuing legal education hours and activities.

Examination Dates Each Year and Application Deadlines

- March: First Saturday in March (Postmarked by January 1)
- September: Last Saturday in September (Postmarked by August 1)

Examination Fees

- For the initial examination: Members—$150; Nonmembers—$200
- For part retakes: Members—$40 per part; Nonmembers—$50 per part

PROFESSIONAL PARALEGAL (PP)

Are you looking for a way to establish your credentials nationwide as a Professional Paralegal? Established in 2004 at our members' request, the Certified PP designation is an attainable goal for paralegals who wish to be identified as exceptional in all areas of law. The certificate is received after passing a one-day, four-part examination.

Successful completion of the PP examination demonstrates:

- A mastery of procedural skills and communication skills;
- An advanced knowledge of procedural law, the law library, and the preparation of legal documents;
- A working knowledge of substantive law and the ability to perform specifically delegated substantive legal work under an attorney's supervision;
- The ability to interact on a professional level with attorneys, clients, and other staff; and
- The discipline to assume responsibility and exercise initiative and judgment while adhering to legal ethical standards at all times.

Working under the supervision of a practicing lawyer or a judge, the Certified PP is expected to possess:

- The same high standard of ethical conduct imposed upon members of the Bar;
- Excellent written and verbal communication skills;
- Knowledge and understanding of legal terminology and procedures, as well as procedural and substantive law; and
- The ability to assume responsibility, exercise initiative and judgment, and prepare substantive legal documents within the scope of assigned authority.

Attaining this goal demonstrates dedication to professionalism and acceptance of the challenge to be exceptional. Personal motivation is necessary to attain such a goal.

PP Examination Eligibility

Any person who has five years' experience performing paralegal/legal assistant duties (a candidate may receive a partial waiver of one year if he or she has a postsecondary degree, other certification, or a paralegal certificate; a candidate with a paralegal degree may receive a two-year partial waiver).

The Exam Covers

- PART 1: Written Communications
- PART 2: Legal Knowledge and Skills
- PART 3: Ethics and Judgment Skills
- PART 4: Substantive Law

Examination Guidelines

All four parts of the examination must be taken on the first attempt with the exception of current PLSs, for which only Part 4 in Substantive Law is needed. If you do not pass the entire examination on the first attempt, but do pass one or more parts, you may retake the part (or parts) you failed. All failed parts must be retaken at the same time.

Those passing the exam will receive a certificate that is valid for five years. Recertification is required every five years and may be achieved through the accumulation of continuing legal education hours and activities.

Examination Dates and Application Deadlines

- March: First Saturday (Postmarked by January 1)
- September: Last Saturday (Postmarked by August 1)

Examination Fees

- For current PLSs Members: $150
  For nonmembers: $200
- For non-PLSs Members: $200
  For nonmembers: $250
- Retake fees:
  For members: $50 per part
  For nonmembers: $60 per part

OTHER INFORMATION

Transfer/Refund Policy

If you are unable to sit for the examination at your chosen time, you may transfer to another examination date by paying a $25 transfer fee and by making the request no later than two weeks prior to the test date.

If you are unable to sit for the examination at any time following submission of your application, the entire fee, less a 25 percent processing fee, may be refunded if requested thirty days or more before the scheduled examination date. If you are unable to sit for the examination after transferring to another examination date, no refund will be given.

Testing Centers

There are no predetermined testing centers. You may choose two major cities as your first and second choice testing centers. About two weeks prior to the examination date, NALS will evaluate the choices selected by the applicants and determine national testing sites based on these choices. The goal is to have a testing site within one hundred miles of every applicant.

Study Materials

A complete list of required and optional study materials can be found in the Store area of the NALS Web site at **http://www.nals.org**.

Online Study Group

The Online Study Group is set up to assist those preparing to take a NALS Certification exam but is open to the public and offers wonderful information for all legal professionals.

The Online Study Group has been revamped to make it easier and more inclusive for everyone taking a NALS Certification exam. There will be less sessions with more coverage of all parts of all three exams. These sessions will include information for the ALS, PLS, and the Professional Paralegal (PP) exams and they will wrap up with reviews specific to each exam and a general session with test-taking tips.

College Credits

NALS Certifications are the only ACE Certified Exams Dedicated to the Legal Industry!

NALS PROCEDURE REGARDING COLLEGE CREDITS for the ALS and PLS EXAMINATIONS (PP APPROVAL IN PROCESS)

In April 2002, NALS successfully completed the five-year reevaluation of the PLS examination by the American Council on Education (ACE).

A team of content and technical experts selected from college faculty by ACE reviewed the PLS and ALS examinations and concur that the examinations are eligible for college-level credit recommendations. (Professional Paralegal certification accreditation is in process.)

Some colleges have determined the minimum score for awarding credit to be 65 for each part; however, other colleges may require scores up to 70. It is possible to earn up to 27 college-level credits. Although ACE makes the recommendation, it is up to the college or university you select to make the final decision on the number of credits awarded. They can accept some or all of the credits, depending on their policies and procedures, your course of study, and other transfer credits.

ALS Credit Recommendation In the lower division baccalaureate/associate degree category, 3 semester hours in Business Procedures and 3 semester hours in Business Communications. The 3 semester hours in Business Communications do not apply if the examinee has received this credit from the PLS examination.

PLS (four-part exam) Credit Recommendation At the lower division baccalaureate/associate degree category, 3 semester hours in Office Management, 3 semester hours in Computer Literacy, 3 semester hours in Ethics, 3 semester hours in Business Communications, and 3 semester hours in either Introduction to Law or Business Law. The 3 semester hours in Business Communications do not apply if the examinee has received this credit from the ALS examination.

PLS (seven-part exam) Credit Recommendation At the lower division baccalaureate/associate degree category, 3 semester hours in Business Communications, 2 semester hours in Legal/Business Ethics or Professional Responsibility, 3 semester hours in Legal Office Procedures, 1 semester hour in Computer Literacy, 3 semester hours in Office Accounting or Introductory Accounting, 3 semester hours in Legal Terminology, 3 semester hours in Legal Methods or Legal Bibliography, 3 semester hours in Legal Secretarial Capstone or Legal Secretarial Judgment, 3 semester hours in Applied Legal Office Skills, and 3 semester hours in Legal Document Formatting and Preparation.

Courtesy of NALS . . . the association for legal professionals. Reprinted with permission.

THE CONSTITUTION OF THE UNITED STATES

J

PREAMBLE

We the People of the United States, in Order to form a more perfect Union, establish Justice, insure domestic Tranquility, provide for the common defence, promote the general Welfare, and secure the Blessings of Liberty to ourselves and our Posterity, do ordain and establish this Constitution for the United States of America.

Article I

SECTION 1.   All legislative Powers herein granted shall be vested in a Congress of the United States, which shall consist of a Senate and House of Representatives.

SECTION 2.   The House of Representatives shall be composed of Members chosen every second Year by the People of the several States, and the Electors in each State shall have the Qualifications requisite for Electors of the most numerous Branch of the State Legislature.

No Person shall be a Representative who shall not have attained to the Age of twenty five Years, and been seven Years a Citizen of the United States, and who shall not, when elected, be an Inhabitant of that State in which he shall be chosen.

Representatives and direct Taxes shall be apportioned among the several States which may be included within this Union, according to their respective Numbers, which shall be determined by adding to the whole Number of free Persons, including those bound to Service for a Term of Years, and excluding Indians not taxed, three fifths of all other Persons. The actual Enumeration shall be made within three Years after the first Meeting of the Congress of the United States, and within every subsequent Term of ten Years, in such Manner as they shall by Law direct. The Number of Representatives shall not exceed one for every thirty Thousand, but each State shall have at Least one Representative; and until such enumeration shall be made, the State of New Hampshire shall be entitled to chuse three, Massachusetts eight,

Rhode Island and Providence Plantations one, Connecticut five, New York six, New Jersey four, Pennsylvania eight, Delaware one, Maryland six, Virginia ten, North Carolina five, South Carolina five, and Georgia three.

When vacancies happen in the Representation from any State, the Executive Authority thereof shall issue Writs of Election to fill such Vacancies.

The House of Representatives shall chuse their Speaker and other Officers; and shall have the sole Power of Impeachment.

SECTION 3.　The Senate of the United States shall be composed of two Senators from each State, chosen by the Legislature thereof, for six Years; and each Senator shall have one Vote.

Immediately after they shall be assembled in Consequence of the first Election, they shall be divided as equally as may be into three Classes. The Seats of the Senators of the first Class shall be vacated at the Expiration of the second Year, of the second Class at the Expiration of the fourth Year, and of the third Class at the Expiration of the sixth Year, so that one third may be chosen every second Year; and if Vacancies happen by Resignation, or otherwise, during the Recess of the Legislature of any State, the Executive thereof may make temporary Appointments until the next Meeting of the Legislature, which shall then fill such Vacancies.

No Person shall be a Senator who shall not have attained to the Age of thirty Years, and been nine Years a Citizen of the United States, and who shall not, when elected, be an Inhabitant of that State for which he shall be chosen.

The Vice President of the United States shall be President of the Senate, but shall have no Vote, unless they be equally divided.

The Senate shall chuse their other Officers, and also a President pro tempore, in the Absence of the Vice President, or when he shall exercise the Office of President of the United States.

The Senate shall have the sole Power to try all Impeachments. When sitting for that Purpose, they shall be on Oath or Affirmation. When the President of the United States is tried, the Chief Justice shall preside: And no Person shall be convicted without the Concurrence of two thirds of the Members present.

Judgment in Cases of Impeachment shall not extend further than to removal from Office, and disqualification to hold and enjoy any Office of honor, Trust, or Profit under the United States: but the Party convicted shall nevertheless be liable and subject to Indictment, Trial, Judgment, and Punishment, according to Law.

SECTION 4.　The Times, Places and Manner of holding Elections for Senators and Representatives, shall be prescribed in each State by the Legislature thereof; but the Congress may at any time by Law make or alter such Regulations, except as to the Places of chusing Senators.

The Congress shall assemble at least once in every Year, and such Meeting shall be on the first Monday in December, unless they shall by Law appoint a different Day.

SECTION 5.　Each House shall be the Judge of the Elections, Returns, and Qualifications of its own Members, and a Majority of each shall constitute a Quorum to do Business; but a smaller Number may adjourn from day to day, and may be authorized to compel the Attendance of absent Members, in such Manner, and under such Penalties as each House may provide.

Each House may determine the Rules of its Proceedings, punish its Members for disorderly Behavior, and, with the Concurrence of two thirds, expel a Member.

Each House shall keep a Journal of its Proceedings, and from time to time publish the same, excepting such Parts as may in their Judgment require Secrecy; and the Yeas and Nays of the Members of either House on any question shall, at the Desire of one fifth of those Present, be entered on the Journal.

Neither House, during the Session of Congress, shall, without the Consent of the other, adjourn for more than three days, nor to any other Place than that in which the two Houses shall be sitting.

SECTION 6. The Senators and Representatives shall receive a Compensation for their Services, to be ascertained by Law, and paid out of the Treasury of the United States. They shall in all Cases, except Treason, Felony and Breach of the Peace, be privileged from Arrest during their Attendance at the Session of their respective Houses, and in going to and returning from the same; and for any Speech or Debate in either House, they shall not be questioned in any other Place.

No Senator or Representative shall, during the Time for which he was elected, be appointed to any civil Office under the Authority of the United States, which shall have been created, or the Emoluments whereof shall have been increased during such time; and no Person holding any Office under the United States, shall be a Member of either House during his Continuance in Office.

SECTION 7. All Bills for raising Revenue shall originate in the House of Representatives; but the Senate may propose or concur with Amendments as on other Bills.

Every Bill which shall have passed the House of Representatives and the Senate, shall, before it become a Law, be presented to the President of the United States; If he approve he shall sign it, but if not he shall return it, with his Objections to the House in which it shall have originated, who shall enter the Objections at large on their Journal, and proceed to reconsider it. If after such Reconsideration two thirds of that House shall agree to pass the Bill, it shall be sent together with the Objections, to the other House, by which it shall likewise be reconsidered, and if approved by two thirds of that House, it shall become a Law. But in all such Cases the Votes of both Houses shall be determined by Yeas and Nays, and the Names of the Persons voting for and against the Bill shall be entered on the Journal of each House respectively. If any Bill shall not be returned by the President within ten Days (Sundays excepted) after it shall have been presented to him, the Same shall be a Law, in like Manner as if he had signed it, unless the Congress by their Adjournment prevent its Return in which Case it shall not be a Law.

Every Order, Resolution, or Vote, to which the Concurrence of the Senate and House of Representatives may be necessary (except on a question of Adjournment) shall be presented to the President of the United States; and before the Same shall take Effect, shall be approved by him, or being disapproved by him, shall be repassed by two thirds of the Senate and House of Representatives, according to the Rules and Limitations prescribed in the Case of a Bill.

SECTION 8. The Congress shall have Power To lay and collect Taxes, Duties, Imposts and Excises, to pay the Debts and provide for the common Defence and general Welfare of the United States; but all Duties, Imposts and Excises shall be uniform throughout the United States;

To borrow Money on the credit of the United States;

To regulate Commerce with foreign Nations, and among the several States, and with the Indian Tribes;

To establish an uniform Rule of Naturalization, and uniform Laws on the subject of Bankruptcies throughout the United States;

To coin Money, regulate the Value thereof, and of foreign Coin, and fix the Standard of Weights and Measures;

To provide for the Punishment of counterfeiting the Securities and current Coin of the United States;

To establish Post Offices and post Roads;

To promote the Progress of Science and useful Arts, by securing for limited Times to Authors and Inventors the exclusive Right to their respective Writings and Discoveries;

To constitute Tribunals inferior to the supreme Court;

To define and punish Piracies and Felonies committed on the high Seas, and Offenses against the Law of Nations;

To declare War, grant Letters of Marque and Reprisal, and make Rules concerning Captures on Land and Water;

To raise and support Armies, but no Appropriation of Money to that Use shall be for a longer Term than two Years;

To provide and maintain a Navy;

To make Rules for the Government and Regulation of the land and naval Forces;

To provide for calling forth the Militia to execute the Laws of the Union, suppress Insurrections and repel Invasions;

To provide for organizing, arming, and disciplining, the Militia, and for governing such Part of them as may be employed in the Service of the United States, reserving to the States respectively, the Appointment of the Officers, and the Authority of training the Militia according to the discipline prescribed by Congress;

To exercise exclusive Legislation in all Cases whatsoever, over such District (not exceeding ten Miles square) as may, by Cession of particular States, and the Acceptance of Congress, become the Seat of the Government of the United States, and to exercise like Authority over all Places purchased by the Consent of the Legislature of the State in which the Same shall be, for the Erection of Forts, Magazines, Arsenals, dock-Yards, and other needful Buildings;—And

To make all Laws which shall be necessary and proper for carrying into Execution the foregoing Powers, and all other Powers vested by this Constitution in the Government of the United States, or in any Department or Officer thereof.

SECTION 9.   The Migration or Importation of such Persons as any of the States now existing shall think proper to admit, shall not be prohibited by the Congress prior to the Year one thousand eight hundred and eight, but a Tax or duty may be imposed on such Importation, not exceeding ten dollars for each Person.

The privilege of the Writ of Habeas Corpus shall not be suspended, unless when in Cases of Rebellion or Invasion the public Safety may require it.

No Bill of Attainder or ex post facto Law shall be passed.

No Capitation, or other direct, Tax shall be laid, unless in Proportion to the Census or Enumeration herein before directed to be taken.

No Tax or Duty shall be laid on Articles exported from any State.

No Preference shall be given by any Regulation of Commerce or Revenue to the Ports of one State over those of another: nor shall Vessels bound to, or from, one State be obliged to enter, clear, or pay Duties in another.

No Money shall be drawn from the Treasury, but in Consequence of Appropriations made by Law; and a regular Statement and Account of the Receipts and Expenditures of all public Money shall be published from time to time.

No Title of Nobility shall be granted by the United States: And no Person holding any Office of Profit or Trust under them, shall, without the Consent of the Congress, accept of any present, Emolument, Office, or Title, of any kind whatever, from any King, Prince, or foreign State.

SECTION 10.   No State shall enter into any Treaty, Alliance, or Confederation; grant Letters of Marque and Reprisal; coin Money; emit Bills of Credit; make any Thing but gold and silver Coin a Tender in Payment of Debts; pass any Bill of Attainder, ex post facto Law, or Law impairing the Obligation of Contracts, or grant any Title of Nobility.

No State shall, without the Consent of the Congress, lay any Imposts or Duties on Imports or Exports, except what may be absolutely necessary for executing its inspection Laws: and the net Produce of all Duties and Imposts, laid by any State on Imports or Exports, shall be for the Use of the Treasury of the United States; and all such Laws shall be subject to the Revision and Controul of the Congress.

No State shall, without the Consent of Congress, lay any Duty of Tonnage, keep Troops, or Ships of War in time of Peace, enter into any Agreement or Compact with another State, or with a foreign Power, or engage in War, unless actually invaded, or in such imminent Danger as will not admit of delay.

Article II

SECTION 1.   The executive Power shall be vested in a President of the United States of America. He shall hold his Office during the Term of four Years, and, together with the Vice President, chosen for the same Term, be elected, as follows:

Each State shall appoint, in such Manner as the Legislature thereof may direct, a Number of Electors, equal to the whole Number of Senators and Representatives to which the State may be entitled in the Congress; but no Senator or Representative, or Person holding an Office of Trust or Profit under the United States, shall be appointed an Elector.

The Electors shall meet in their respective States, and vote by Ballot for two Persons, of whom one at least shall not be an Inhabitant of the same State with themselves. And they shall make a List of all the Persons voted for, and of the Number of Votes for each; which List they shall sign and certify, and transmit sealed to the Seat of the Government of the United States, directed to the President of the Senate. The President of the Senate shall, in the Presence of the Senate and House of Representatives, open all the Certificates, and the Votes shall then be counted. The Person having the greatest Number of Votes shall be the President, if such Number be a Majority of the whole Number of Electors appointed; and if there be more than one who have such Majority, and have an equal Number of Votes, then the House of Representatives shall immediately chuse by Ballot one of them for President; and if no Person have a Majority, then from the five highest on the List the said House shall in like Manner chuse the President. But in chusing the President, the Votes shall be taken by States, the Representation from each State having one Vote; A quorum for this Purpose shall consist of a Member or Members from two thirds of the States, and a Majority of all the States shall be necessary to a Choice. In every Case, after the Choice of the President, the Person having the greater Number of Votes of the Electors shall be the Vice President. But if there should remain two or more who have equal Votes, the Senate shall chuse from them by Ballot the Vice President.

The Congress may determine the Time of chusing the Electors, and the Day on which they shall give their Votes; which Day shall be the same throughout the United States.

No person except a natural born Citizen, or a Citizen of the United States, at the time of the Adoption of this Constitution, shall be eligible to the Office of President; neither shall any Person be eligible to that Office who shall not have attained to the Age of thirty five Years, and been fourteen Years a Resident within the United States.

In Case of the Removal of the President from Office, or of his Death, Resignation or Inability to discharge the Powers and Duties of the said Office, the same shall devolve on the Vice President, and the Congress may by Law provide for the Case of Removal, Death, Resignation or Inability, both of the President and Vice President, declaring what Officer shall then act as President, and such Officer shall act accordingly, until the Disability be removed, or a President shall be elected.

The President shall, at stated Times, receive for his Services, a Compensation, which shall neither be increased nor diminished during the Period for which he shall have been elected, and he shall not receive within that Period any other Emolument from the United States, or any of them.

Before he enter on the Execution of his Office, he shall take the following Oath or Affirmation: "I do solemnly swear (or affirm) that I will faithfully execute the Office of President of the United States, and will to the best of my Ability, preserve, protect and defend the Constitution of the United States."

SECTION 2. The President shall be Commander in Chief of the Army and Navy of the United States, and of the Militia of the several States, when called into the actual Service of the United States; he may require the Opinion, in writing, of the principal Officer in each of the executive Departments, upon any Subject relating to the Duties of their respective Offices, and he shall have Power to grant Reprieves and Pardons for Offenses against the United States, except in Cases of Impeachment.

He shall have Power, by and with the Advice and Consent of the Senate to make Treaties, provided two thirds of the Senators present concur; and he shall nominate, and by and with the Advice and Consent of the Senate, shall appoint Ambassadors, other public Ministers and Consuls, Judges of the supreme Court, and all other Officers of the United States, whose Appointments are not herein otherwise provided for, and which shall be established by Law; but the Congress may by Law vest the Appointment of such inferior Officers, as they think proper, in the President alone, in the Courts of Law, or in the Heads of Departments.

The President shall have Power to fill up all Vacancies that may happen during the Recess of the Senate, by granting Commissions which shall expire at the End of their next Session.

SECTION 3. He shall from time to time give to the Congress Information of the State of the Union, and recommend to their Consideration such Measures as he shall judge necessary and expedient; he may, on extraordinary Occasions, convene both Houses, or either of them, and in Case of Disagreement between them, with Respect to the Time of Adjournment, he may adjourn them to such Time as he shall think proper; he shall receive Ambassadors and other public Ministers; he shall take Care that the Laws be faithfully executed, and shall Commission all the Officers of the United States.

SECTION 4. The President, Vice President and all civil Officers of the United States, shall be removed from Office on Impeachment for, and Conviction of, Treason, Bribery, or other high Crimes and Misdemeanors.

Article III

SECTION 1. The judicial Power of the United States, shall be vested in one supreme Court, and in such inferior Courts as the Congress may from time to time ordain and establish. The Judges, both of the supreme and inferior Courts, shall hold their Offices during good Behaviour, and shall, at stated Times, receive for their Services a Compensation, which shall not be diminished during their Continuance in Office.

SECTION 2. The judicial Power shall extend to all Cases, in Law and Equity, arising under this Constitution, the Laws of the United States, and Treaties made, or which shall be made, under their Authority;—to all Cases affecting Ambassadors, other public Ministers and Consuls;—to all Cases of admiralty and maritime Jurisdiction;—to Controversies to which the United States shall be a Party;—to Controversies between two or more States;—between a State and Citizens of another State;—between Citizens of different States;—between Citizens of the same State claiming Lands under Grants of different States, and between a State, or the Citizens thereof, and foreign States, Citizens or Subjects.

In all Cases affecting Ambassadors, other public Ministers and Consuls, and those in which a State shall be a Party, the supreme Court shall have original Jurisdiction. In all the other Cases before mentioned, the supreme Court shall have appellate Jurisdiction, both as to Law and Fact, with such Exceptions, and under such Regulations as the Congress shall make.

The Trial of all Crimes, except in Cases of Impeachment, shall be by Jury; and such Trial shall be held in the State where the said Crimes shall have been committed; but when not committed within any State, the Trial shall be at such Place or Places as the Congress may by Law have directed.

SECTION 3. Treason against the United States, shall consist only in levying War against them, or, in adhering to their Enemies, giving them Aid and Comfort. No Person shall be convicted of Treason unless on the Testimony of two Witnesses to the same overt Act, or on Confession in open Court.

The Congress shall have Power to declare the Punishment of Treason, but no Attainder of Treason shall work Corruption of Blood, or Forfeiture except during the Life of the Person attainted.

Article IV

SECTION 1. Full Faith and Credit shall be given in each State to the public Acts, Records, and judicial Proceedings of every other State. And the Congress may by general Laws prescribe the Manner in which such Acts, Records and Proceedings shall be proved, and the Effect thereof.

SECTION 2. The Citizens of each State shall be entitled to all Privileges and Immunities of Citizens in the several States.

A Person charged in any State with Treason, Felony, or other Crime, who shall flee from Justice, and be found in another State, shall on Demand of the executive Authority of the State from which he fled, be delivered up, to be removed to the State having Jurisdiction of the Crime.

No Person held to Service or Labour in one State, under the Laws thereof, escaping into another, shall, in Consequence of any Law or Regulation therein, be discharged from such Service or Labour, but shall be delivered up on Claim of the Party to whom such Service or Labour may be due.

SECTION 3. New States may be admitted by the Congress into this Union; but no new State shall be formed or erected within the Jurisdiction of any other State; nor any State be formed by the Junction of two or more States, or Parts of States, without the Consent of the Legislatures of the States concerned as well as of the Congress.

The Congress shall have Power to dispose of and make all needful Rules and Regulations respecting the Territory or other Property belonging to the United States; and nothing in this Constitution shall be so construed as to Prejudice any Claims of the United States, or of any particular State.

SECTION 4. United States shall guarantee to every State in this Union a Republican Form of Government, and shall protect each of them against Invasion; and on Application of the Legislature, or of the Executive (when the Legislature cannot be convened) against domestic Violence.

Article V

The Congress, whenever two thirds of both Houses shall deem it necessary, shall propose Amendments to this Constitution, or, on the Application of the Legislatures of two thirds of the several States, shall call a Convention for proposing Amendments, which, in either Case, shall be valid to all Intents and Purposes, as part of this Constitution, when ratified by the Legislatures of three fourths of the several States, or by Conventions in three fourths thereof, as the one or the other Mode of Ratification may be proposed by the Congress; Provided that no Amendment which may be made prior to the Year One thousand eight hundred and eight shall in any Manner affect the first and fourth Clauses in the Ninth Section of the first Article; and that no State, without its Consent, shall be deprived of its equal Suffrage in the Senate.

Article VI

All Debts contracted and Engagements entered into, before the Adoption of this Constitution shall be as valid against the United States under this Constitution, as under the Confederation.

This Constitution, and the Laws of the United States which shall be made in Pursuance thereof; and all Treaties made, or which shall be made, under the Authority of the United States, shall be the supreme Law of the Land; and the Judges in every State shall be bound thereby, any Thing in the Constitution or Laws of any State to the Contrary notwithstanding.

The Senators and Representatives before mentioned, and the Members of the several State Legislatures, and all executive and judicial Officers, both of the United States and of the several States, shall be bound by Oath or Affirmation, to support this Constitution; but no religious Test shall ever be required as a Qualification to any Office or public Trust under the United States.

Article VII

The Ratification of the Conventions of nine States shall be sufficient for the Establishment of this Constitution between the States so ratifying the Same.

Amendment I [1791]

Congress shall make no law respecting an establishment of religion, or prohibiting the free exercise thereof; or abridging the freedom of speech, or of the press; or the right of the people peaceably to assembly, and to petition the Government for a redress of grievances.

Amendment II [1791]

A well regulated Militia, being necessary to the security of a free State, the right of the people to keep and bear Arms, shall not be infringed.

Amendment III [1791]

No Soldier shall, in time of peace be quartered in any house, without the consent of the Owner, nor in time of war, but in a manner to be prescribed by law.

Amendment IV [1791]

The right of the people to be secure in their persons, houses, papers, and effects, against unreasonable searches and seizures, shall not be violated, and no Warrants shall issue, but upon probable cause, supported by Oath or affirmation, and particularly describing the place to be searched, and the persons or things to be seized.

Amendment V [1791]

No person shall be held to answer for a capital, or otherwise infamous crime, unless on a presentment or indictment of a Grand Jury, except in cases arising in the land or naval forces, or in the Militia, when in actual service in time of War or public danger; nor shall any person be subject for the same offence to be twice put in jeopardy of life or limb; nor shall be compelled in any criminal case to be a witness against himself, nor be deprived of life, liberty, or property, without due process of law; nor shall private property be taken for public use, without just compensation.

Amendment VI [1791]

In all criminal prosecutions, the accused shall enjoy the right to a speedy and public trial, by an impartial jury of the State and district wherein the crime shall have been committed, which district shall have been previously ascertained by law, and to be informed of the nature and cause of the accusation; to be confronted with the witnesses against him; to have compulsory process for obtaining witnesses in his favor, and to have the Assistance of Counsel for his defence.

Amendment VII [1791]

In Suits at common law, where the value in controversy shall exceed twenty dollars, the right of trial by jury shall be preserved, and no fact tried by jury, shall be otherwise reexamined in any Court of the United States, than according to the rules of the common law.

Amendment VIII [1791]

Excessive bail shall not be required, nor excessive fines imposed, nor cruel and unusual punishments inflicted.

Amendment IX [1791]

The enumeration in the Constitution, of certain rights, shall not be construed to deny or disparage others retained by the people.

Amendment X [1791]

The powers not delegated to the United States by the Constitution, nor prohibited by it to the States, are reserved to the States respectively, or to the people.

Amendment XI [1798]

The Judicial power of the United States shall not be construed to extend to any suit in law or equity, commenced or prosecuted against one of the United States by Citizens of another State, or by Citizens or Subjects of any Foreign State.

Amendment XII [1804]

The Electors shall meet in their respective states, and vote by ballot for President and Vice-President, one of whom, at least, shall not be an inhabitant of the same state with themselves; they shall name in their ballots the person voted for as President, and in distinct ballots the person voted for as Vice-President, and they shall make distinct lists of all persons voted for as President, and of all persons voted for as Vice-President, and of the number of votes for each, which lists they shall sign and certify, and transmit sealed to the seat of the government of the United States, directed to the President of the Senate;—The President of the Senate shall, in the presence of the Senate and House of Representatives, open all the certificates and the votes shall then be counted;—The person having the greatest number of votes for President, shall be the President, if such number be a majority of the whole number of Electors appointed; and if no person have such majority, then from the persons having the highest numbers not exceeding three on the list of those voted for as President, the House of Representatives shall choose immediately, by ballot, the President. But in choosing the President, the votes shall be taken by states, the representation from each state having one vote; a quorum for this purpose shall consist of a member or members from two-thirds of the states, and a majority of all states shall be necessary to a choice. And if the House of Representatives shall not choose a President whenever the right of choice shall devolve upon them, before the fourth day of March next following, then the Vice-President shall act as President, as in the case of the death or other constitutional disability of the President.—The person having the greatest number of votes as Vice-President, shall be the Vice-President, if such number be a majority of the whole number of Electors appointed, and if no person have a majority, then from the two highest numbers on the list, the Senate shall choose the Vice-President; a quorum for the purpose shall consist of two-thirds of the whole number of Senators, and a majority of the whole number shall be necessary to a choice. But no person constitutionally ineligible to the office of President shall be eligible to that of Vice-President of the United States.

Amendment XIII [1865]

SECTION 1.   Neither slavery nor involuntary servitude, except as a punishment for crime whereof the party shall have been duly convicted, shall exist within the United States, or any place subject to their jurisdiction.

SECTION 2.   Congress shall have power to enforce this article by appropriate legislation.

Amendment XIV [1868]

SECTION 1.   All persons born or naturalized in the United States, and subject to the jurisdiction thereof, are citizens of the United States and of the State wherein they reside. No State shall make or enforce any law which shall abridge the privileges or immunities of citizens of the United States; nor shall any State deprive any person of life, liberty, or property, without due process of law; nor deny to any person within its jurisdiction the equal protection of the laws.

SECTION 2.   Representatives shall be apportioned among the several States according to their respective numbers, counting the whole number of persons in each State, excluding Indians not taxed. But when the right to vote at any election for the choice of electors for President and Vice President of the United States, Representatives in Congress, the Executive and Judicial officers of a State, or the members of the Legislature thereof, is denied to any of the male inhabitants of such State, being twenty-one years of age, and citizens of the United States, or in any way abridged, except for participation in rebellion, or other crime, the basis of representation therein shall be reduced in the proportion which the number of such male citizens shall bear to the whole number of male citizens twenty-one years of age in such State.

SECTION 3.   No person shall be a Senator or Representative in Congress, or elector of President and Vice President, or hold any office, civil or military, under the United States, or under any State, who having previously taken an oath, as a member of Congress, or as an officer of the United States, or as a member of any State legislature, or as an executive or judicial officer of any State, to support the Constitution of the United States, shall have engaged in insurrection or rebellion against the same, or given aid or comfort to the enemies thereof. But Congress may by a vote of two-thirds of each House, remove such disability.

SECTION 4.   The validity of the public debt of the United States, authorized by law, including debts incurred for payment of pensions and bounties for services in suppressing insurrection or rebellion, shall not be questioned. But neither the United States nor any State shall assume or pay any debt or obligation incurred in aid of insurrection or rebellion against the United States, or any claim for the loss or emancipation of any slave; but all such debts, obligations and claims shall be held illegal and void.

SECTION 5.   The Congress shall have power to enforce, by appropriate legislation, the provisions of this article.

Amendment XV [1870]

SECTION 1.   The right of citizens of the United States to vote shall not be denied or abridged by the United States or by any State on account of race, color, or previous condition of servitude.

SECTION 2.   The Congress shall have power to enforce this article by appropriate legislation.

Amendment XVI [1913]

The Congress shall have power to lay and collect taxes on incomes, from whatever source derived, without apportionment among the several States, and without regard to any census or enumeration.

Amendment XVII [1913]

SECTION 1.   The Senate of the United States shall be composed of two Senators from each State, elected by the people thereof, for six years; and each Senator shall have one vote. The electors in each State shall have the qualifications requisite for electors of the most numerous branch of the State legislatures.

SECTION 2.   When vacancies happen in the representation of any State in the Senate, the executive authority of such State shall issue writs of election to fill such vacancies: *Provided*, That the legislature of any State may empower the executive thereof to make temporary appointments until the people fill the vacancies by election as the legislature may direct.

SECTION 3.   This amendment shall not be so construed as to affect the election or term of any Senator chosen before it becomes valid as part of the Constitution.

Amendment XVIII [1919]

SECTION 1.   After one year from the ratification of this article the manufacture, sale, or transportation of intoxicating liquors within, the importation thereof into, or the exportation thereof from the United States and all territory subject to the jurisdiction thereof for beverage purposes is hereby prohibited.

SECTION 2.   The Congress and the several States shall have concurrent power to enforce this article by appropriate legislation.

SECTION 3.   This article shall be inoperative unless it shall have been ratified as an amendment to the Constitution by the legislatures of the several States, as provided in the Constitution, within seven years from the date of the submission hereof to the States by the Congress.

Amendment XIX [1920]

SECTION 1.   The right of citizens of the United States to vote shall not be denied or abridged by the United States or by any State on account of sex.

SECTION 2.   Congress shall have power to enforce this article by appropriate legislation.

Amendment XX [1933]

SECTION 1.   The terms of the President and Vice President shall end at noon on the 20th day of January, and the terms of Senators and Representatives at noon on the 3d day of January, of the years in which such terms would have ended if this article had not been ratified; and the terms of their successors shall then begin.

SECTION 2.   The Congress shall assemble at least once in every year, and such meeting shall begin at noon on the 3d day of January, unless they shall by law appoint a different day.

SECTION 3.   If, at the time fixed for the beginning of the term of the President, the President elect shall have died, the Vice President elect shall become President. If the President shall not have been chosen before the time fixed for the beginning of his term, or if the President elect shall have failed to qualify, then the Vice President elect shall act as President until a President shall have qualified; and the Congress may by law provide for the case wherein neither a President elect nor a Vice President elect shall have qualified, declaring who shall then act as President, or the manner in which one who is to act shall be selected, and such person shall act accordingly until a President or Vice President shall have qualified.

SECTION 4.   The Congress may by law provide for the case of the death of any of the persons from whom the House of Representatives may choose a President whenever the right of choice shall have devolved upon them, and for the case of the death of any of the persons from whom the Senate may choose a Vice President whenever the right of choice shall have devolved upon them.

SECTION 5.   Sections 1 and 2 shall take effect on the 15th day of October following the ratification of this article.

SECTION 6.   This article shall be inoperative unless it shall have been ratified as an amendment to the Constitution by the legislatures of three-fourths of the several States within seven years from the date of its submission.

Amendment XXI [1933]

SECTION 1.   The eighteenth article of amendment to the Constitution of the United States is hereby repealed.

SECTION 2.   The transportation or importation into any State, Territory, or possession of the United States for delivery or use therein of intoxicating liquors, in violation of the laws thereof, is hereby prohibited.

SECTION 3.   This article shall be inoperative unless it shall have been ratified as an amendment to the Constitution by conventions in the several States, as provided in the Constitution, within seven years from the date of the submission hereof to the States by the Congress.

Amendment XXII [1951]

SECTION 1.   No person shall be elected to the office of the President more than twice, and no person who has held the office of President, or acted as President, for more than two years of a term to which some other person was elected President shall be elected to the office of President more than once. But this Article shall not apply to any person holding the office of President when this Article was proposed by the Congress, and shall not prevent any person who may be holding the office of President, or acting as President, during the term within which this Article becomes operative from holding the office of President or acting as President during the remainder of such term.

SECTION 2.   This article shall be inoperative unless it shall have been ratified as an amendment to the Constitution by the legislatures of three-fourths of the several States within seven years from the date of its submission to the States by the Congress.

Amendment XXIII [1961]

SECTION 1.   The District constituting the seat of Government of the United States shall appoint in such manner as the Congress may direct:

A number of electors of President and Vice President equal to the whole number of Senators and Representatives in Congress to which the District would be entitled if it were a State, but in no event more than the least populous state; they shall be in addition to those appointed by the states, but they shall be considered, for the purposes of the election of President and Vice President, to be electors appointed by a state; and they shall meet in the District and perform such duties as provided by the twelfth article of amendment.

SECTION 2.   The Congress shall have power to enforce this article by appropriate legislation.

Amendment XXIV [1964]

SECTION 1.   The right of citizens of the United States to vote in any primary or other election for President or Vice President, for electors for President or Vice President, or for Senator or Representative in Congress, shall not be denied or abridged by the United States, or any State by reason of failure to pay any poll tax or other tax.

SECTION 2.   The Congress shall have power to enforce this article by appropriate legislation.

Amendment XXV [1967]

SECTION 1.   In case of the removal of the President from office or of his death or resignation, the Vice President shall become President.

SECTION 2.   Whenever there is a vacancy in the office of the Vice President, the President shall nominate a Vice President who shall take office upon confirmation by a majority vote of both Houses of Congress.

SECTION 3.   Whenever the President transmits to the President pro tempore of the Senate and the Speaker of the House of Representatives his written declaration that he is unable to discharge the powers and duties of his office, and until he transmits to them a written declaration to the contrary, such powers and duties shall be discharged by the Vice President as Acting President.

SECTION 4.   Whenever the Vice President and a majority of either the principal officers of the executive departments or of such other body as Congress may by law provide, transmit to the President pro tempore of the Senate and the Speaker of the House of Representatives their written declaration that the President is unable to discharge the powers and duties of his office, the Vice President shall immediately assume the powers and duties of the office as Acting President.

Thereafter, when the President transmits to the President pro tempore of the Senate and the Speaker of the House of Representatives his written declaration that no inability exists, he shall resume the powers and duties of his office unless the Vice President and a majority of either the principal officers of the executive department or of such other body as Congress may by law provide, transmit within four days to the President pro tempore of the Senate and the Speaker of the House of Representatives their written declaration that the President is unable to discharge the powers and duties of his office. Thereupon Congress shall decide the issue, assembling within forty-eight hours for that purpose if not in session. If the Congress, within twenty-one days after receipt of the latter written declaration, or, if Congress is not in session, within twenty-one days after Congress is required to assemble, determines by two-thirds vote of both Houses that the President is unable to discharge the powers and duties of his office, the Vice President shall continue to discharge the same as Acting President; otherwise, the President shall resume the powers and duties of his office.

Amendment XXVI [1971]

SECTION 1.   The right of citizens of the United States, who are eighteen years of age or older, to vote shall not be denied or abridged by the United States or by any State on account of age.

SECTION 2.   The Congress shall have power to enforce this article by appropriate legislation.

Amendment XXVII [1992]

No law, varying the compensation for the services of the Senators and Representatives, shall take effect, until an election of Representatives shall have intervened.

Abandoned property: bienes abandonados

Acceptance: aceptación; consentimiento; acuerdo

Acceptor: aceptante

Accession: toma de posesión; aumento; accesión

Accommodation indorser: avalista de favor

Accommodation party: firmante de favor

Accord: acuerdo; convenio; arregio

Accord and satisfaction: transacción ejecutada

Act of state doctrine: doctrina de acto de gobierno

Administrative law: derecho administrativo

Administrative process: procedimiento o metódo administrativo

Administrator: administrador (-a)

Adverse possession: posesión de hecho susceptible de proscripción adquisitiva

Affirmative action: acción afirmativa

Affirmative defense: defensa afirmativa

After-acquired property: bienes adquiridos con posterioridad a un hecho dado

Agency: mandato; agencia

Agent: mandatorio; agente; representante

Agreement: convenio; acuerdo; contrato

Alien corporation: empresa extranjera

Allonge: hojas adicionales de endosos

Answer: contestación de la demande; alegato

Anticipatory repudiation: anuncio previo de las partes de su imposibilidad de cumplir con el contrato

Appeal: apelación; recurso de apelación

Appellate jurisdiction: jurisdicción de apelaciones

Appraisal right: derecho de valuación

Arbitration: arbitraje

Arson: incendio intencional

Articles of partnership: contrato social

Artisan's lien: derecho de retención que ejerce al artesano

Assault: asalto; ataque; agresión

Assignment of rights: transmisión; transferencia; cesión

Assumption of risk: no resarcimiento por exposición voluntaria al peligro

Attachment: auto judicial que autoriza el embargo; embargo

Bailee: depositario

Bailment: depósito; constitución en depósito

Bailor: depositante

Bankruptcy trustee: síndico de la quiebra

Battery: agresión; física

Bearer: portador; tenedor

Bearer instrument: documento al portador

Bequest or legacy: legado (de bienes muebles)

Bilateral contract: contrato bilateral

Bill of lading: conocimiento de embarque; carta de porte

Bill of Rights: declaración de derechos

Binder: póliza de seguro provisoria; recibo de pago a cuenta del precio

Blank indorsement: endoso en blanco
Blue sky laws: leyes reguladoras del comercio bursátil
Bond: título de crédito; garantía; caución
Bond indenture: contrato de emisión de bonos; contrato del empréstito
Breach of contract: incumplimiento de contrato
Brief: escrito; resumen; informe
Burglary: violación de domicilio
Business judgment rule: regla de juicio comercial
Business tort: agravio comercial

Case law: ley de casos; derecho casuístico
Cashier's check: cheque de caja
Causation in fact: causalidad en realidad
Cease-and-desist order: orden para cesar y desistir
Certificate of deposit: certificado de depósito
Certified check: cheque certificado
Charitable trust: fideicomiso para fines benéficos
Chattel: bien mueble
Check: cheque
Chose in action: derecho inmaterial; derecho de acción
Civil law: derecho civil
Close corporation: sociedad de un solo accionista o de un grupo restringido de accionistas
Closed shop: taller agremiado (emplea solamente a miembros de un gremio)
Closing argument: argumento al final
Codicil: codicilo
Collateral: garantía; bien objeto de la garantía real
Comity: cortesía; cortesía entre naciones
Commercial paper: instrumentos negociables; documentos a valores commerciales
Common law: derecho consuetudinario; derecho común; ley común
Common stock: acción ordinaria
Comparative negligence: negligencia comparada
Compensatory damages: daños y perjuicios reales o compensatorios

Concurrent conditions: condiciones concurrentes
Concurrent jurisdiction: competencia concurrente de varios tribunales para entender en una misma causa
Concurring opinion: opinión concurrente
Condition: condición
Condition precedent: condición suspensiva
Condition subsequent: condición resolutoria
Confiscation: confiscación
Confusion: confusión; fusión
Conglomerate merger: fusión de firmas que operan en distintos mercados
Consent decree: acuerdo entre las partes aprobado por un tribunal
Consequential damages: daños y perjuicios indirectos
Consideration: consideración; motivo; contraprestación
Consolidation: consolidación
Constructive delivery: entrega simbólica
Constructive trust: fideicomiso creado por aplicación de la ley
Consumer protection law: ley para proteger el consumidor
Contract: contrato
Contract under seal: contrato formal o sellado
Contributory negligence: negligencia de la parte actora
Conversion: usurpación; conversión de valores
Copyright: derecho de autor
Corporation: sociedad anónima; corporación; persona juridica
Co-sureties: cogarantes
Counterclaim: reconvención; contrademanda
Counteroffer: contraoferta
Course of dealing: curso de transacciones
Course of performance: curso de cumplimiento
Covenant: pacto; garantía; contrato
Covenant not to sue: pacto or contrato a no demandar
Covenant of quiet enjoyment: garantía del uso y goce pacífico del inmueble

Creditors' composition agreement: concordato preventivo
Crime: crimen; delito; contravención
Criminal law: derecho penal
Cross-examination: contrainterrogatorio
Cure: cura; cuidado; derecho de remediar un vicio contractual
Customs receipts: recibos de derechos aduaneros

Damages: daños; indemnización por daños y perjuicios
Debit card: tarjeta de dé bito
Debtor: deudor
Debt securities: seguridades de deuda
Deceptive advertising: publicidad engañosa
Deed: escritura; título; acta translativa de domino
Defamation: difamación
Delegation of duties: delegación de obligaciones
Demand deposit: depósito a la vista
Depositions: declaración de un testigo fuera del tribunal
Devise: legado; deposición testamentaria (bienes inmuebles)
Direct examination: interrogatorio directo; primer interrogatorio
Directed verdict: veredicto según orden del juez y sin participación activa del jurado
Disaffirmance: repudiación; renuncia; anulación
Discharge: descargo; liberación; cumplimiento
Disclosed principal: mandante revelado
Discovery: descubrimiento; producción de la prueba
Dissenting opinion: opinión disidente
Dissolution: disolución; terminación
Diversity of citizenship: competencia de los tribunales federales para entender en causas cuyas partes intervinientes son cuidadanos de distintos estados
Divestiture: extinción premature de derechos reales
Dividend: dividendo
Docket: orden del día; lista de causas pendientes

Domestic corporation: sociedad local
Draft: orden de pago; letrade cambio
Drawee: girado; beneficiario
Drawer: librador
Duress: coacción; violencia

Easement: servidumbre
Embezzlement: desfalco; malversación
Eminent domain: poder de expropiación
Employment discrimination: discriminación en el empleo
Entrepreneur: empresario
Environmental law: ley ambiental
Equal dignity rule: regla de dignidad egual
Equity security: tipo de participación en una sociedad
Estate: propiedad; patrimonio; derecho
Estop: impedir; prevenir
Ethical issue: cuestión ética
Exclusive jurisdiction: competencia exclusiva
Exculpatory clause: cláusula eximente
Executed contract: contrato ejecutado
Execution: ejecución; cumplimiento
Executor: albacea
Executory contract: contrato aún no completamente consumado
Executory interest: derecho futuro
Express contract: contrato expreso
Expropriation: expropriación

Federal question: caso federal
Fee simple: pleno dominio; dominio absoluto
Fee simple absolute: dominio absoluto
Fee simple defeasible: dominio sujeta a una condición resolutoria
Felony: crimen; delito grave
Fictitlous payee: beneficiario ficticio
Fiduciary: fiduciaro
Firm offer: oferta en firme
Fixture: inmueble por destino, incorporación a anexación
Floating lien: gravamen continuado
Foreign corporation: sociedad extranjera; U.S. sociedad constituída en otro estado
Forgery: falso; falsificación
Formal contract: contrato formal
Franchise: privilegio; franquicia; concesión

Franchisee: persona que recibe una concesión
Franchisor: persona que vende una concesión
Fraud: fraude; dolo; engaño
Future interest: bien futuro

Garnishment: embargo de derechos
General partner: socio comanditario
General warranty deed: escritura translativa de domino con garantía de título
Gift: donación
Gift *causa mortis*: donación por causa de muerte
Gift *inter vivos*: donación entre vivos
Good faith: buena fe
Good faith purchaser: comprador de buena fe

Holder: tenedor por contraprestación
Holder in due course: tenedor legítimo
Holographic will: testamento ológrafico
Homestead exemption laws: leyes que exceptúan las casas de familia de ejecución por duedas generales
Horizontal merger: fusión horizontal

Identification: identificación
Implied-in-fact contract: contrato implícito en realidad
Implied warranty: guarantía implícita
Implied warranty of merchantability: garantía implícita de vendibilidad
Impossibility of performance: imposibilidad de cumplir un contrato
Imposter: imposter
Incidental beneficiary: beneficiario incidental; beneficiario secundario
Incidental damages: daños incidentales
Indictment: auto de acusación; acusación
Indorsee: endorsatario
Indorsement: endoso
Indorser: endosante
Informal contract: contrato no formal; contrato verbal
Information: acusación hecha por el ministerio público
Injunction: mandamiento; orden de no innovar
Innkeeper's lien: derecho de retención que ejerce el posadero

Installment contract: contrato de pago en cuotas
Insurable interest: interés asegurable
Intended beneficiary: beneficiario destinado
Intentional tort: agravio; cuasidelito intencrónal
International law: derecho internaciónal
Interrogatories: preguntas escritas sometidas por una parte a la otra o a un testigo
***Inter vivos* trust:** fideicomiso entre vivos
Intestacy laws: leyes de la condición de morir intestado
Intestate: intestado
Investment company: compañia de inversiones
Issue: emisión

Joint tenancy: derechos conjuntos en un bien inmueble en favor del beneficiario sobreviviente
Judgment *n.o.v.*: juicio no obstante veredicto
Judgment rate of interest: interés de juicio
Judicial process: acto de procedimiento; proceso jurídico
Judicial review: revisión judicial
Jurisdiction: jurisdicción

Larceny: robo; hurto
Law: derecho; ley; jurisprudencia
Lease: contrato de locación; contrato de alquiler
Leasehold estate: bienes forales
Legal rate of interest: interés legal
Legatee: legatario
Letter of credit: carta de crédito
Levy: embargo; comiso
Libel: libelo; difamación escrita
Life estate: usufructo
Limited partner: comanditario
Limited partnership: sociedad en comandita
Liquidation: liquidación; realización
Lost property: objetos perdidos

Majority opinion: opinión de la mayoría

Maker: persona que realiza u ordena; librador

Mechanic's lien: gravamen de constructor

Mediation: mediación; intervención

Merger: fusión

Mirror image rule: fallo de reflejo

Misdemeanor: infracción; contravención

Mislaid property: bienes extraviados

Mitigation of damages: reducción de daños

Mortgage: hypoteca

Motion to dismiss: excepción parentoria

Mutual fund: fondo mutual

Negotiable instrument: instrumento negociable

Negotiation: negociación

Nominal damages: daños y perjuicios nominales

Novation: novación

Nuncupative will: testamento nuncupativo

Objective theory of contracts: teoria objetiva de contratos

Offer: oferta

Offeree: persona que recibe una oferta

Offeror: oferente

Order instrument: instrumento o documento a la orden

Original jurisdiction: jurisdicción de primera instancia

Output contract: contrato de producción

Parol evidence rule: regla relativa a la prueba oral

Partially disclosed principal: mandante revelado en parte

Partnership: sociedad colectiva; asociación; asociación de participación

Past consideration: causa o contraprestación anterior

Patent: patente; privilegio

Pattern or practice: muestra o práctica

Payee: beneficiario de un pago

Penalty: pena; penalidad

Per capita: por cabeza

Per stirpes: por estirpe

Perfection: perfeción

Performance: cumplimiento; ejecución

Personal defenses: excepciones personales

Personal property: bienes muebles

Plea bargaining: regateo por un alegato

Pleadings: alegatos

Pledge: prenda

Police powers: poders de policia y de prevención del crimen

Policy: póliza

Positive law: derecho positivo; ley positiva

Possibility of reverter: posibilidad de reversión

Precedent: precedente

Preemptive right: derecho de prelación

Preferred stock: acciones preferidas

Premium: recompensa; prima

Presentment warranty: garantía de presentación

Price discrimination: discriminación en los precios

Principal: mandante; principal

Privity: nexo jurídico

Privity of contract: relación contractual

Probable cause: causa probable

Probate: verificación; verificación del testamento

Probate court: tribunal de sucesiones y tutelas

Proceeds: resultados; ingresos

Profit: beneficio; utilidad; lucro

Promise: promesa

Promisee: beneficiario de una promesa

Promisor: promtente

Promissory estoppel: impedimento promisorio

Promissory note: pagaré; nota de pago

Promoter: promotor; fundador

Proximate cause: causa inmediata o próxima

Proxy: apoderado; poder

Punitive, or exemplary, damages: daños y perjuicios punitivos o ejemplares

Qualified indorsement: endoso con reservas

Quasi contract: contrato tácito o implícito

Quitclaim deed: acto de transferencia de una propiedad por finiquito, pero sin ninguna garantía sobre la validez del título transferido

Ratification: ratificación

Real property: bienes inmuebles

Reasonable doubt: duda razonable

Rebuttal: refutación

Recognizance: promesa; compromiso; reconocimiento

Recording statutes: leyes estatales sobre registros oficiales

Redress: reporacíon

Reformation: rectificación; reforma; corrección

Rejoinder: dúplica; contrarréplica

Release: liberación; renuncia a un derecho

Remainder: substitución; reversión

Remedy: recurso; remedio; reparación

Replevin: acción reivindicatoria; reivindicación

Reply: réplica

Requirements contract: contrato de suministro

Res judicata: cosa juzgada; res judicata

Rescission: rescisión

Respondeat superior: responsabilidad del mandante o del maestro

Restitution: restitución

Restrictive indorsement: endoso restrictivo

Resulting trust: fideicomiso implícito

Reversion: reversión; sustitución

Revocation: revocación; derogación

Right of contribution: derecho de contribución

Right of reimbursement: derecho de reembolso

Right of subrogation: derecho de subrogación

Right-to-work law: ley de libertad de trabajo

Robbery: robo

Rule 10b-5: Regla 10b-5

Sale: venta; contrato de compreventa

Sale on approval: venta a ensayo; venta sujeta a la aprobación del comprador

Sale or return: venta con derecho de devolución

Sales contract: contrato de compraventa; boleto de compraventa

Satisfaction: satisfacción; pago

Scienter: a sabiendas

S corporation: S corporación

Secured party: acreedor garantizado

Secured transaction: transacción garantizada

Securities: volares; titulos; seguridades

Security agreement: convenio de seguridad

Security interest: interés en un bien dado en garantía que permite a quien lo detenta venderlo en caso de incumplimiento

Service mark: marca de identificación de servicios

Shareholder's derivative suit: acción judicial entablada por un accionista en nombre de la sociedad

Signature: firma; rúbrica

Slander: difamación oral; calumnia

Sovereign immunity: immunidad soberana

Special indorsement: endoso especial; endoso a la orden de una person en particular

Specific performance: ejecución precisa, según los términos del contrato

Spendthrift trust: fideicomiso para pródigos

Stale check: cheque vencido

Stare decisis: acatar las decisiones, observar los precedentes

Statutory law: derecho estatutario; derecho legislado; derecho escrito

Stock: acciones

Stock warrant: certificado para la compra de acciones

Stop-payment order: orden de suspensión del pago de un cheque dada por el librador del mismo

Strict liability: responsabilidad uncondicional

Summary judgment: fallo sumario

Tangible property: bienes corpóreos

Tenancy at will: inguilino por tiempo indeterminado (según la voluntad del propietario)

Tenancy by sufferance: posesión por tolerancia

Tenancy by the entirety: locación conyugal conjunta

Tenancy for years: inguilino por un término fijo

Tenancy in common: specie de copropiedad indivisa

Tender: oferta de pago; oferta de ejecución

Testamentary trust: fideicomiso testamentario

Testator: testador (-a)

Third party beneficiary contract: contrato para el beneficio del tercero-beneficiario

Tort: agravio; cuasidelito

Totten trust: fideicomiso creado por un depósito bancario

Trade acceptance: letra de cambio aceptada

Trade name: nombre comercial; razón social

Trademark: marca registrada

Traveler's check: cheque del viajero

Trespass to land: ingreso no authorizado a las tierras de otro

Trespass to personal property: violación de los derechos posesorios de un tercero con respecto a bienes muebles

Trust: fideicomiso; trust

Ultra vires: ultra vires; fuera de la facultad (de una sociedad anónima)

Unanimous opinion: opinión unámine

Unconscionable contract or clause: contrato leonino; cláusula leonino

Underwriter: subscriptor; asegurador

Unenforceable contract: contrato que no se puede hacer cumplir

Unilateral contract: contrato unilateral

Union shop: taller agremiado; empresa en la que todos los empleados son miembros del gremio o sindicato

Universal defenses: defensas legitimas o legales

Usage of trade: uso comercial

Usury: usura

Valid contract: contrato válido

Venue: lugar; sede del proceso

Vertical merger: fusión vertical de empresas

Void contract: contrato nulo; contrato inválido, sin fuerza legal

Voidable contract: contrato anulable

Voir dire: examen preliminar de un testigo a jurado por el tribunal para determinar su competencia

Voting trust: fideicomiso para ejercer el derecho de voto

Waiver: renuncia; abandono

Warranty of habitability: garantía de habitabilidad

Watered stock: acciones diluídos; capital inflado

White-collar crime: crimen administrativo

Writ of attachment: mandamiento de ejecución; mandamiento de embargo

Writ of *certiorari*: auto de avocación; auto de certiorari

Writ of execution: auto ejecutivo; mandamiento de ejecutión

Writ of mandamus: auto de mandamus; mandamiento; orden judicial

ABA-approved program A legal or paralegal educational program that satisfies the standards for paralegal training set forth by the American Bar Association.

acceptance In contract law, the offeree's indication to the offeror that the offeree agrees to be bound by the terms of the offeror's offer, or proposal to form a contract.

acquittal A certification or declaration following a trial that the individual accused of a crime is innocent, or free from guilt, in the eyes of the law and is thus absolved of the charges.

actionable Capable of serving as the basis of a lawsuit. An actionable claim can be pursued in a lawsuit or other court action.

active listening The act of listening attentively to the speaker's message and responding by giving appropriate feedback to show that you understand what the speaker is saying; restating the speaker's message in your own words to confirm that you accurately interpreted what was said.

actual malice Real and demonstrable evil intent. In a defamation suit, a statement made about a public figure normally must be made with actual malice (with either knowledge of its falsity or a reckless disregard of the truth) for liability to be incurred.

actus reus A guilty (prohibited) act. The commission of a prohibited act is one of the two essential elements required for criminal liability; the other element is the intent to commit a crime.

address block That part of a letter that indicates to whom the letter is addressed. The address block is placed in the upper left-hand portion of the letter, above the salutation (or reference line, if one is included).

adhesion contract A contract drafted by the dominant party and then presented to the other—adhering—party on a "take-it-or-leave-it" basis.

adjudication The act of resolving a controversy and rendering an order or decision based on a review of the evidence presented.

administrative agency A federal or state government agency established to perform a specific function. Administrative agencies are authorized by legislative acts to make and enforce rules relating to the purpose for which they were established.

administrative law A body of law created by administrative agencies in the form of rules, regulations, orders, and decisions in order to carry out their duties and responsibilities.

administrative law judge (ALJ) One who presides over an administrative agency hearing and who has the power to administer oaths, take testimony, rule on questions of evidence, and make determinations otherwise authorized by law.

administrative process The procedure used by administrative agencies in the administration of law.

administrator A person appointed by a court to serve as a personal representative for a person who died intestate (without a valid will) or if the executor named in the will cannot serve.

adoption A procedure in which persons become the legal parents of a child who is not their biological child.

Advanced Paralegal Certification (APC) A credential awarded by the National Association of Legal Assistants to a Certified Paralegal (CP) or Certified Legal Assistant (CLA) whose competency in a legal specialty has been certified following an examination of the paralegal's knowledge and skills in the specialty area.

adversarial system of justice A legal system in which the parties to a lawsuit are opponents, or adversaries, and present their cases in the light most favorable to themselves. The impartial decision maker (the judge or jury) determines who wins and who loses based on the evidence presented.

affidavit A written statement of facts, confirmed by the oath or affirmation of the party making it and made before a person having the authority to administer the oath or affirmation.

affirm To uphold the judgment of a lower court.

affirmative defense A response to a plaintiff's claim that does not deny the plaintiff's facts but attacks the plaintiff's legal right to bring an action.

agency A relationship between two persons in which one person (the agent) represents or acts in the place of another (the principal).

825

agent A person who is authorized to act for or in the place of another person (the principal).

agreement A meeting of the minds, and a requirement for a valid contract. Agreement involves two distinct events: an offer to form a contract and the acceptance of that offer by the offeree.

alimony Money paid to support a former spouse after a marriage has been terminated. The alimony may be permanent or temporary (rehabilitative).

allegation A party's statement, claim, or assertion made in a pleading to the court. The allegation sets forth the issue that the party expects to prove.

alternative dispute resolution (ADR) The resolution of disputes in ways other than those involved in the traditional judicial process. Negotiation, mediation, and arbitration are forms of ADR.

American Arbitration Association (AAA) The major organization offering arbitration services in the United States.

American Association for Paralegal Education (AAfPE) A national organization of paralegal educators; the AAfPE was established in 1981 to promote high standards for paralegal education.

American Bar Association (ABA) A voluntary national association of attorneys. The ABA plays an active role in developing educational and ethical standards for attorneys and in pursuing improvements in the administration of justice.

annotation A brief comment, an explanation of a legal point, or a case summary found in a case digest or other legal source.

annulment A court decree that invalidates (nullifies) a marriage. Although the marriage itself is deemed nonexistent, children of a marriage that is annulled are deemed legitimate.

answer A defendant's response to a plaintiff's complaint.

appeal The process of seeking a higher court's review of a lower court's decision for the purpose of correcting or changing the lower court's judgment or decision.

appellate court A court that reviews decisions made by lower courts, such as trial courts; a court of appeals.

appellate jurisdiction The power of a court to hear and decide an appeal; that is, the power and authority of a court to review cases that already have been tried in a lower court and the power to make decisions about them without actually holding a trial. This process is called appellate review.

appropriation In tort law, the use by one person of another person's name, likeness, or other identifying characteristic without permission and for the benefit of the user.

arbitration A method of settling disputes in which a dispute is submitted to a disinterested third party (other than a court), who renders a decision that may or may not be legally binding.

arbitration clause A clause in a contract that provides that, in case of a dispute, the parties will determine their rights by arbitration rather than through the judicial system.

arraignment A court proceeding in which the suspect is formally charged with the criminal offense stated in the indictment. The suspect then enters a plea (guilty, not guilty, or *nolo contendere*) in response.

arrest To take into custody a person suspected of criminal activity.

arrest warrant A written order, based on probable cause and issued by a judge or public official (magistrate), commanding that the person named on the warrant be arrested by the police.

arson The willful and malicious burning of a building (and, in some states, personal property) owned by another; arson statutes have been extended to cover the destruction of any building, regardless of ownership, by fire or explosion.

articles of incorporation The document filed with the appropriate state official, usually the secretary of state, when a business is incorporated. State statutes usually prescribe what kind of information must be contained in the articles of incorporation.

assault Any word or action intended to make another person fearful of immediate physical harm; a reasonably believable threat.

associate attorney An attorney working for a law firm who is not a partner and does not have an ownership interest in the firm. Associates are usually less experienced attorneys and may be invited to become partners after working for the firm for several years.

assumption of risk Voluntarily taking on oneself a known risk. Assumption of risk is a defense against negligence that can be used when the plaintiff has knowledge of and appreciates a danger and voluntarily exposes himself or herself to the danger.

attorney-client privilege A rule of evidence requiring that confidential communications between a client and his or her attorney (relating to their professional relationship) be kept confidential, unless the client consents to disclosure.

authentication The process of establishing the genuineness of an item that is to be introduced as evidence in a trial.

Auto-Cite An aid to legal research developed by the editors of Lexis. On Lexis, Auto-Cite can be used to find the history of a case, to verify whether the case is still good law, and to perform other functions.

automatic stay A suspension of all judicial proceedings on the occurrence of an independent event. Under the Bankruptcy Code, the moment a petition to initiate bankruptcy proceedings is filed, all litigation or other legal action by creditors against a debtor and the debtor's property is suspended.

award In the context of ADR, the decision rendered by an arbitrator.

bail The amount of money or conditions set by the court to assure that an individual accused of a crime will appear for further criminal proceedings. If the accused person provides bail, whether in cash or by means of a bail bond, then the person is released from jail.

bankruptcy court A federal court of limited jurisdiction that hears only bankruptcy proceedings.

bankruptcy law The body of federal law that governs bankruptcy proceedings. The twin goals of bankruptcy law are (1) to protect a debtor by giving him or her a fresh start, free from creditors' claims; and (2) to ensure that creditors who are competing for a debtor's assets are treated fairly.

bankruptcy trustee A person appointed by the bankruptcy court to administer the debtor's estate in the interests of both the debtor and the creditors. The basic duty of the bankruptcy trustee is to collect and reduce to money the estate in property and to close up the estate as speedily as is compatible with the best interests of the parties.

battery The intentional and offensive touching of another without lawful justification.

beyond a reasonable doubt The standard used to determine the guilt or innocence of a person charged with a crime. To be guilty of a crime, a suspect must be proved guilty "beyond and to the exclusion of every reasonable doubt."

bigamy The act of entering into marriage with one person while still legally married to another.

Bill of Rights The first ten amendments to the U.S. Constitution.

billable hours Hours or fractions of hours that attorneys and paralegals spend in work that requires legal expertise and that can be billed directly to clients.

binder A written, temporary insurance policy.

binding authority Any source of law that a court must follow when deciding a case. Binding authorities include constitutions, statutes, and regulations that govern the issue being decided, as well as court decisions that are controlling precedents within the jurisdiction.

binding mediation A form of ADR in which a mediator attempts to facilitate agreement between the parties but then issues a legally binding decision if no agreement is reached.

bonus An end-of-the-year payment to a salaried employee in appreciation for that employee's overtime work, work quality, diligence, or dedication to the firm.

booking The process of entering a suspect's name, offense, and arrival time into the police log (blotter) following his or her arrest.

Boolean logic As applied to Internet search engines, a system in which connecting words (primarily *and, or,* and *not*) are used to establish a logical relationship among search terms in order to make a search more precise.

breach To violate a legal duty by an act or a failure to act.

breach of contract The failure, without legal excuse, of a contractual party to perform the obligations assumed in a contract.

briefing a case Summarizing a case. A typical case brief will indicate the full citation for the case, the factual background and procedural history of the case, the issue or issues raised in the case, the court's decision, the court's holding, and the legal reasoning on which the court based its decision. The brief may also include conclusions or notes concerning the case made by the one briefing it.

browse-wrap terms Terms and conditions of use that are presented to an Internet user at the time the user downloads certain products, such as software, but that the user need not agree to (by clicking "I agree," for example) before being able to install or use the products.

bureaucracy In relation to government, the organizational structure, consisting of bureaus and agencies, through which the government implements and enforces the laws.

burglary Breaking and entering onto the property of another with the intent to commit a felony.

business invitee A person, such as a customer or client, who is invited onto business premises by the owner of those premises for business purposes.

business tort Wrongful interference with another's business rights.

bylaws A set of governing rules adopted by a corporation or other association.

case law Rules of law announced in court decisions.

case of first impression A case presenting a legal issue that has not yet been addressed by a court in a particular jurisdiction.

case on "all fours" A case in which all four elements of a case (the parties, the circumstances, the legal issues involved, and the remedies sought by the plaintiff) are very similar to those in the case being researched.

case on point A case involving factual circumstances and issues that are similar to those in the case being researched.

causation in fact Causation brought about by an act or omission without which an event would not have occurred.

cease-and-desist order An administrative or judicial order prohibiting a person or business firm from conducting activities that an agency or court has deemed illegal.

certificate of incorporation (corporate charter) The document issued by a state official (usually the secretary of state) granting a corporation legal existence and the right to function.

certification Formal recognition by a private group or a state agency that an individual has satisfied the group's standards of proficiency, knowledge, and competence; ordinarily accomplished through the taking of an examination.

Certified Legal Assistant (CLA) or Certified Paralegal (CP) A legal assistant or paralegal whose legal competency has been certified by the National Association of Legal Assistants (NALA) following an examination that tests the legal assistant's knowledge and skills.

Certified Legal Assistant Specialist (CLAS) A legal assistant whose competency in a legal specialty has been certified by the National Association of Legal Assistants (NALA) following an examination of the legal assistant's knowledge and skills in the specialty area.

chain of custody A series describing the movement and location of evidence from the time it is obtained to the time it is presented in court. The court requires that evidence be preserved in the condition in which it was obtained if it is to be admitted into evidence at trial.

challenge An attorney's objection, during *voir dire,* to the inclusion of a particular person on the jury.

challenge for cause A *voir dire* challenge for which an attorney states the reason why a prospective juror should not be included in the jury.

charge The judge's instruction to the jury, following the attorneys' closing arguments, setting forth the rules of law that the jury must apply in reaching its decision, or verdict.

check A draft drawn on a bank by which the drawer of the check orders the bank to pay a fixed amount of money on demand.

checks and balances A system in which each of the three branches of the national government—executive, legislative, and judicial—exercises a check on the actions of the other two branches.

child support The financial support necessary to provide for a child's needs. Commonly, when a marriage is terminated, the noncustodial spouse agrees or is required by the court to make child-support payments to the custodial spouse.

chronologically In a time sequence; naming or listing events in the time order in which they occurred.

circumstantial evidence Indirect evidence that is offered to establish, by inference, the likelihood of a fact that is in question.

citation In case law, a reference to the volume number, name, and page number of the reporter in which a case can be found. In statutory and administrative law, a reference to the title number, name, and section of the code in which a statute or regulation can be found. In criminal procedure, an order for a defendant to appear in court or indicating that a person has violated a legal rule.

citator A book or online service that provides the history and interpretation of a statute, regulation, or court decision and a list of the cases, statutes, and regulations that have interpreted, applied, or modified a statute or regulation.

civil law The branch of law dealing with the definition and enforcement of private or public rights, as opposed to criminal matters.

civil law system A system of law derived from that of the Roman Empire and based on a code rather than case law; the predominant system of law in the nations of continental Europe and the nations that were once their colonies.

click-on agreement An agreement that arises when a buyer, engaging in a transaction on a computer, indicates his or her assent to be bound by the terms of an offer by clicking on a button that says, for example, "I agree"; sometimes referred to as a *click-on license* or a *click-wrap agreement.*

close corporation A corporation owned by a small group of shareholders, often family members; also called a *closely held corporation.* Shares in close corporations cannot be publicly traded on the stock market, and often other restrictions on stock transfer apply. Some close corporations qualify for special tax status as *S corporations.*

closed-ended question A question phrased in such a way that it elicits a simple "yes" or "no" answer.

closing A final phrase in a letter that is placed above the signature, such as "Sincerely" or "Very truly yours."

closing argument An argument made by each side's attorney after the cases for the plaintiff and defendant have been presented. Closing arguments are made prior to the jury charge.

code A systematic and topically organized presentation of laws, rules, or regulations.

collective bargaining The process by which labor and management negotiate the terms and conditions of employment, including wages, benefits, working conditions, and other matters.

commerce clause The provision in Article 1, Section 8, of the U.S. Constitution that gives the national government the power to regulate interstate commerce.

common law A body of law developed from custom or judicial decisions in English and U.S. courts and not by a legislature.

common law marriage A marriage that is formed solely by mutual consent and without a marriage license or ceremony. The couple must be eligible to marry, must have a present and continuing agreement to be husband and wife, must live together as husband and wife, and must hold themselves out to the public as husband and wife. Only fourteen states recognize common law marriages.

community property Defined in ten states as all property acquired during the marriage, except for inheritances or gifts received during the marriage by either marital partner. Each spouse has a one-half ownership interest in community property.

comparative negligence A theory in tort law under which the liability for injuries resulting from negligent acts is shared by all persons who were guilty of negligence (including the injured party) on the basis of each person's proportionate carelessness.

compensatory damages A money award equivalent to the actual value of injuries or damages sustained by the aggrieved party.

complaint The pleading made by a plaintiff or a charge made by the state alleging wrongdoing on the part of the defendant.

computer-assisted legal research (CALR) Any legal research conducted with the assistance of computers. CALR includes the use of CD-ROMs, fee-based providers such as Westlaw and Lexis, and the Internet.

concurrent jurisdiction Jurisdiction that exists when two different courts have the power to hear a case. For example, some cases can be heard in either a federal or a state court.

confirmation letter A letter that states the substance of a previously conducted verbal discussion to provide a permanent record of the oral conversation.

conflict of interest A situation in which two or more duties or interests come into conflict, as when an attorney attempts to represent opposing parties in a legal dispute.

conflicts check A procedure for determining whether an agreement to represent a potential client will result in a conflict of interest.

consideration Something of value, such as money or the performance of an action not otherwise required, that motivates the formation of a contract. Each party must give consideration for the contract to be binding.

consolidation A process in which two or more corporations join to become a completely new corporation. The original corporations cease to exist.

constitutional law Law based on the U.S. Constitution and the constitutions of the various states.

constructive discharge A termination of employment that occurs when the employer causes the employee's working conditions to be so intolerable that a reasonable person in the employee's position would feel compelled to quit.

consumer An individual who purchases products and services for personal or household use.

consumer-debtor A debtor whose debts are primarily consumer debts—that is, debts for purchases that are primarily for household or personal use.

consumer law Statutes, agency rules, and judicial decisions protecting consumers of goods and services.

contempt of court The intentional obstruction or frustration of the court's attempt to administer justice. A party to a lawsuit may be held in contempt of court (punishable by a fine or jail sentence) for refusing to comply with a court's order.

contingency fee A legal fee that consists of a specified percentage (such as 30 percent) of the amount the plaintiff recovers in a civil lawsuit. The fee must be paid only if the plaintiff prevails in the lawsuit (recovers damages).

contract An agreement or bargain struck between parties in which each party assumes a legal duty to the other party. The requirements for a valid contract are agreement, consideration, contractual capacity, and legality.

contractual capacity The threshold mental capacity required by law for a party who enters into a contract to be bound by that contract.

continuing legal education (CLE) program Courses through which attorneys and other legal professionals extend their education beyond school.

contributory negligence A theory in tort law under which a complaining party's own negligence contributed to or caused his or her injuries. Contributory negligence is an absolute bar to recovery in a minority of jurisdictions.

conversion The act of wrongfully taking or retaining of a person's personal property and placing it in the service of another.

copyright The exclusive right of an author (or other creator) to publish, print, or sell an intellectual production for a statutory period of time.

corporate law Law that governs the formation, financing, merger and acquisition, and termination of corporations, as well as the rights and duties of those who own and run the corporation.

counteradvertising New advertising undertaken pursuant to a Federal Trade Commission order for the purpose of correcting earlier false claims that were made about a product.

counterclaim A claim made by a defendant in a civil lawsuit against the plaintiff; in effect, a counterclaiming defendant is suing the plaintiff.

court of equity A court that decides controversies and administers justice according to the rules, principles, and precedents of equity.

court of law A court in which the only remedies that could be granted were things of value, such as money damages. In early England, courts of law were distinct from courts of equity.

crime A broad term for violations of law that are punishable by the state and are codified by legislatures. The objective of criminal law is to protect the public.

criminal law The branch of law that governs and defines those actions that are crimes and that subjects persons convicted of crimes to punishment imposed by the government (a fine or jail time).

cross-claim A claim asserted by a defendant in a civil lawsuit against another defendant or by a plaintiff against another plaintiff.

cross-examination The questioning of an opposing witness during the trial.

cyber crime A crime that occurs online, in the virtual community of the Internet, as opposed to the physical world.

cyber tort A tort committed in cyberspace.

cybernotary A legally recognized authority that can certify the validity of digital signatures.

cyberstalker A person who commits the crime of stalking in cyberspace. The cyber stalker usually finds a victim through Internet chat rooms, newsgroups, bulletin boards, or e-mail and proceeds to harass that person or put the person in reasonable fear for his or her safety or the safety of his or her immediate family.

damages Money awarded as a remedy for a civil wrong, such as a breach of contract or a tortious act.

deceptive advertising Advertising that misleads consumers, either by unjustified claims concerning a product's performance or by the failure to disclose relevant information concerning the product's composition or performance.

deed A document by which title to property is transferred from one party to another.

defamation Anything published or publicly spoken that causes injury to another's good name, reputation, or character.

default judgment A judgment entered by a clerk or court against a party who has failed to appear in court to answer or defend against a claim that has been brought against him or her by another party.

defendant A party against whom a lawsuit is brought.

defense The reasons that a defendant offers and alleges why the plaintiff should not recover or establish what she or he seeks in a lawsuit.

defense of others The use of reasonable force to protect others from harm.

defense of property The use of reasonable force to protect one's property from the harm threatened by another. The use of deadly force in defending one's property is seldom justified.

delegation doctrine A doctrine that authorizes Congress to delegate some of its lawmaking authority to administrative agencies. The doctrine is implied by Article I of the U.S. Constitution, which grants specific powers to Congress to enact and oversee the implementation of laws.

demand letter A letter in which one party explains its legal position in a dispute and requests that the recipient take some action (such as paying money owed).

deponent A party or witness who testifies under oath during a deposition.

deposition A pretrial question-and-answer proceeding, usually conducted orally, in which a party or witness answers an attorney's questions. The answers are given under oath, and the session is recorded.

deposition transcript The official transcription of the recording taken during a deposition.

dicta A Latin term referring to nonbinding (nonprecedential) judicial statements that are not directly related to the facts or issues presented in the case and thus not essential to the holding.

digest A compilation in which brief summaries of court cases are arranged by subject and subdivided by jurisdiction and court.

direct evidence Evidence establishing the existence of a fact that is in question without relying on inferences.

direct examination The examination of a witness by the attorney who calls the witness to the stand to testify on behalf of the attorney's client.

director A person elected by the shareholders to direct corporate affairs.

disbarment A severe disciplinary sanction in which an attorney's license to practice law in the state is revoked because of unethical or illegal conduct.

discharge The termination of an obligation. A discharge in bankruptcy terminates the debtor's obligation to pay the debts discharged by the court.

discovery Formal investigation prior to trial. During discovery, opposing parties use various methods, such as interrogatories and depositions, to obtain information from each other and from witnesses to prepare for trial.

discovery plan A plan formed by the attorneys litigating a lawsuit, on behalf of their clients, that indicates the types of information that will be disclosed by each party to the other prior to trial, the testimony and evidence that each party will or may introduce at trial, and the general schedule for pretrial disclosures and events.

dissolution The formal disbanding of a partnership or a corporation.

diversion program In some jurisdictions, an alternative to prosecution that is offered to certain felony suspects to deter them from future unlawful acts.

diversity of citizenship Under Article III, Section 2 of the Constitution, a basis for federal district court jurisdiction over a lawsuit between (1) citizens of different states, (2) a foreign country and citizens of a state or different states, or (3) citizens of a state and citizens or subjects of a foreign country. The amount in controversy must be more than $75,000 before a federal court can take jurisdiction in such cases.

dividend A distribution of profits to corporate shareholders, disbursed in proportion to the number of shares held.

divorce A formal court proceeding that legally dissolves a marriage.

docket The list of cases entered on a court's calendar and thus scheduled to be heard by the court.

double billing Billing more than one client for the same billable time period.

double jeopardy To place at risk (jeopardize) a person's life or liberty twice. The Fifth Amendment to the Constitution prohibits a second prosecution for the same criminal offense in all but a few circumstances.

draft An unconditional written order by which the party creating the draft (the drawer) orders another party (the drawee) to pay money, usually to a third party (the payee).

dram shop act A state statute that imposes liability on the owners of bars and taverns, as well as those who serve alcoholic drinks to the public, for injuries resulting from accidents caused by intoxicated persons when the sellers or servers of alcoholic drinks contributed to the intoxication.

drawee The party that is ordered to pay a draft (such as a check). With a check, a bank or a financial institution is always the drawee.

drawer The party that issues a draft (such as a check), thereby ordering the drawee to pay.

due process of law Fair, reasonable, and standard procedures that must be used by the government in any legal action against a citizen. The Fifth Amendment to the U.S. Constitution prohibits the deprivation of "life, liberty, or property without due process of law."

duty of care The duty of all persons, as established by tort law, to exercise a reasonable amount of care in their dealings with others. Failure to exercise due care, which is normally determined by the reasonable person standard, constitutes the tort of negligence.

early neutral case evaluation A form of ADR in which a neutral third party evaluates the strengths and weaknesses of the disputing parties' positions; the evaluator's opinion forms the basis for negotiating a settlement.

easement The right of a person to make limited use of another person's real property without taking anything from the property.

elder law A relatively new legal specialty that involves servicing the needs of older clients, such as estate planning and making arrangements for long-term care.

emancipation The legal relinquishment by a child's parents or guardian of the legal right to exercise control over the child. Usually, a child who moves out of the parents' home and supports himself or herself is considered emancipated.

embezzlement The fraudulent appropriation of the property or money of another by a person entrusted with that property or money.

employment at will A common law doctrine under which employment is considered to be "at will"—that is, either party may terminate the employment relationship at any time and for any reason, unless a contract specifies otherwise.

employment manual A firm's handbook or written statement that specifies the policies and procedures that govern the firm's employees and employer-employee relationships.

enabling legislation A statute enacted by a legislature that authorizes the creation of an administrative agency and specifies the name, purpose, composition, and powers of the agency being created.

environmental impact statement (EIS) A statement required by the National Environmental Policy Act for any major federal action that will significantly affect the quality of the environment. The statement must analyze the action's impact on the environment and explore alternative actions that might be taken.

environmental law All state and federal laws or regulations enacted or issued to protect the environment and preserve environmental resources.

equitable principles and maxims Propositions or general statements of rules of law that are frequently involved in equity jurisdiction.

e-signature An electronic sound, symbol, or process attached to or logically associated with a record and executed or adopted by a person with the intent to sign the record, according to the Uniform Electronic Transactions Act.

estate administration The process in which a decedent's personal representative settles the affairs of the decedent's estate (collects assets, pays debts and taxes, and distributes the remaining assets to heirs); the process is usually overseen by a probate court.

estate in property In bankruptcy proceedings, all of the debtor's interests in property presently held and wherever located, as well as interests in certain property to which the debtor becomes entitled within 180 days after filing for bankruptcy.

estate planning Making arrangements, during a person's lifetime, for the transfer of that person's property or obligations to others on the person's death. Estate planning often involves executing a will, establishing a trust fund, or taking out a life insurance policy to provide for others, such as a spouse or children, on one's death.

ethical wall A term that refers to the procedures used to create a screen around a legal employee to shield him or her from information about a case in which there is a conflict of interest.

evidence Anything that is used to prove the existence or nonexistence of a fact.

exclusionary rule In criminal procedure, a rule under which any evidence that is obtained in violation of the accused's constitutional rights, as well as any evidence derived from illegally obtained evidence, will not be admissible in court.

exclusive jurisdiction Jurisdiction that exists when a case can be heard only in a particular court, such as a federal court.

executive agency A type of administrative agency that is either a cabinet department or a subagency within a cabinet department. Executive agencies fall under the authority of the president, who has the power to appoint and remove federal officers.

executor A person appointed by a testator to serve as a personal representative on the testator's death.

expense slip A slip of paper on which any expense, or cost, that is incurred on behalf of a client (such as the payment of court fees or long-distance telephone charges) is recorded.

expert witness A witness with professional training or substantial experience qualifying him or her to testify as to his or her opinion on a particular subject.

eyewitness A witness who testifies about an event that he or she observed or has experienced firsthand.

family law Law relating to family matters, such as marriage, divorce, child support, and child custody.

federal question A question that pertains to the U.S. Constitution, acts of Congress, or treaties. A federal question provides a basis for jurisdiction by the federal courts. This jurisdiction is authorized by Article III, Section 2, of the Constitution.

Federal Rules of Civil Procedure (FRCP) The rules controlling all procedural matters in civil trials brought before the federal district courts.

federal system The system of government established by the founders of the United States, in which the national government and the state governments share sovereign powers.

fee simple Ownership rights entitling the holder to use, possess, or dispose of the property however he or she chooses during his or her lifetime.

felony A crime—such as arson, murder, rape, or robbery—that carries the most severe sanctions. Sanctions range from one year in a state or federal prison to life imprisonment or (in some states) the death penalty.

fiduciary relationship A relationship involving a high degree of trust and confidence.

fixed fee A fee paid to the attorney by his or her client for having rendered a specified legal service, such as the creation of a simple will.

forgery The fraudulent making or altering of any writing in a way that changes the legal rights and liabilities of another.

forms file A reference file containing copies of the firm's commonly used legal documents and informational forms. The documents in the forms file serve as a model for drafting new documents.

foster care A temporary arrangement in which a family is paid by the state to care for a child for a limited period of time, often pending adoption.

fraudulent misrepresentation Any misrepresentation, either by misstatement or by omission of a material fact, knowingly made with the intention of deceiving another and on which a reasonable person would and does rely to his or her detriment.

freelance paralegal A paralegal who operates his or her own business and provides services to attorneys on a contractual basis. A freelance paralegal works under the supervision of an attorney, who assumes responsibility for the paralegal's work product.

friendly witness A witness who is biased against your client's adversary or sympathetic toward your client in a lawsuit or other legal proceeding.

garnishment A proceeding in which a creditor legally seizes a portion of a debtor's property (such as wages) that is in the possession of a third party (such as an employer).

general licensing A type of licensing in which all individuals within a specific profession or group (such as paralegals) must meet licensing requirements imposed by the state before they may legally practice their profession.

general partner A partner who participates in managing the business of a partnership and has all the rights and liabilities that arise under traditional partnership law.

genuineness of assent Knowing and voluntary assent to the contract terms. If a contract is formed as a result of mistake, misrepresentation, undue influence, or duress, genuineness of assent is lacking, and the contract will be voidable.

Good Samaritan statute A state statute stipulating that persons who provide emergency services to, or rescue, others in peril—unless they do so recklessly, thus causing further harm—cannot be sued for negligence.

grand jury The group of citizens called to decide whether probable cause exists to believe that a suspect committed the crime with which he or she has been charged and should stand trial.

guardian *ad litem* A person appointed by the court to represent the interests of a child or a mentally incompetent person before the court.

hacker A person who uses one computer to break into another.

headnote A note near the beginning of a reported case summarizing the court's ruling on an issue.

hearsay Testimony that is given in court by a witness who relates not what he or she knows personally but what another person said. Hearsay is generally not admissible as evidence.

holder As defined by the UCC, any person in possession of an instrument drawn, issued, or indorsed to him or her, to his or her order, to bearer, or in blank.

holder in due course (HDC) A holder of a negotiable instrument who acquired the instrument for value; in good faith; and without notice that the instrument is overdue, that it has been dishonored, that any person has a defense against it or a claim to it, or that the instrument contains unauthorized signatures, has been altered, or is so irregular or incomplete as to call into question its authenticity.

holding The binding legal principle, or precedent, that is drawn from the court's decision in a case.

home page The main page of a Web site. Often, the home page serves as a table of contents to other pages at the site.

hornbook A single-volume scholarly discussion, or treatise, on a particular legal subject (such as property law).

hostile witness A witness who is biased against your client or friendly toward your client's adversary in a lawsuit or other legal proceeding; an adverse witness.

hung jury A jury whose members are so irreconcilably divided in their opinions that they cannot reach a verdict. The judge in this situation may order a new trial.

hypertext transfer protocol (http) An interface program that enables computers to communicate. Hypertext is a database system by which distinct objects, such as text and graphics, can be linked. A protocol is a system of formats and rules.

hypothetical question A question based on hypothesis, conjecture, or fiction.

identity theft The theft of a form of identification, such as a name, date of birth, or Social Security number, which is then used to access the victim's financial resources.

impeach To call into question the credibility of a witness by challenging the truth or accuracy of his or her trial statement.

independent adoption A privately arranged adoption, as when a doctor, lawyer, or other individual puts a couple seeking to adopt a child in contact with a pregnant woman who has decided to give up her child for adoption.

independent contractor A person who is hired to perform a specific undertaking but who is free to choose how and when to perform the work. An independent contractor may or may not be an agent.

independent paralegal (or legal technician) A paralegal who offers services directly to the public, normally for a fee, without attorney supervision. Independent paralegals assist consumers by supplying them with forms and procedural knowledge relating to simple or routine legal procedures.

independent regulatory agency A type of administrative agency that is more independent of presidential control than an executive agency. Officials of independent regulatory agencies cannot be removed without cause.

indictment A charge or written accusation, issued by a grand jury, that probable cause exists to believe that a named person has committed a crime for which he or she should stand trial.

indorsement A signature, with or without additional words or statements, that is most often written on the back of an instrument.

information A formal criminal charge made by a prosecutor without a grand jury indictment.

informative letter A letter that conveys certain information to a client, a witness, an adversary's counsel, or other person regarding some legal matter (such as the date, time, place, and purpose of a meeting) or a cover letter that accompanies other documents being sent to a person or court.

injunction A court decree ordering a person to do or refrain from doing a certain act or activity.

insider trading Trading in the stock of a publicly listed corporation based on inside information about the corporation that is not available to the public. One who possesses inside information and has a duty not to disclose it to outsiders may not profit from the purchase or sale of securities based on that information until that information is available to the public.

insurable interest An interest either in a person's life or well-being or in property that is sufficiently substantial to justify insuring against injury to or death of the person or damage to the property.

insurance A contract by which an insurance company (the insurer) promises to pay a sum of money or give something of value to another (either the insured or the beneficiary) to compensate the other for a specified loss.

intellectual property Property that results from intellectual, creative processes. Copyrights, patents, and trademarks are examples of intellectual property.

intentional tort A wrongful act knowingly committed.

international law The law that governs relations among nations. International customs and treaties are generally considered to be two of the most important sources of international law.

interrogatories A series of written questions for which written answers are prepared and then signed under oath by a party to a lawsuit (the plaintiff or the defendant).

interviewee The person who is being interviewed.

inter vivos **trust** A trust created by the grantor (settlor) and effective during the grantor's lifetime—that is, a trust not established by a will.

intestacy laws State statutes that specify how property will be distributed when a person dies intestate (without a valid will).

intestate The state of having died without a valid will.

investigation plan A plan that lists each step involved in obtaining and verifying the facts and information that are relevant to the legal problem being investigated.

joint and several liability Shared and individual liability. In partnership law, joint and several liability means that a third party may sue one or more of the partners separately or all of them together. This is true even if one of the partners sued did not participate in or know about whatever gave rise to the cause of action.

joint custody Custody of a child following the termination of a marriage that is shared by the parents.

joint liability Shared liability. In partnership law, partners incur joint liability for partnership obligations and debts.

joint tenancy The joint ownership of property by two or more co-owners in which each co-owner owns an undivided portion of the property. On the death of one of the joint tenants, his or her interest automatically passes to the surviving joint tenant or tenants.

judgment The court's final decision regarding the rights and claims of the parties to a lawsuit.

judgment creditor A creditor who is legally entitled, by a court's judgment, to collect the amount of the judgment from a debtor.

jurisdiction The authority of a court to hear and decide a specific action.

justiciable controversy A controversy that is real and substantial, as opposed to hypothetical or academic.

KeyCite An aid to legal research developed by the editors of Westlaw. On Westlaw, KeyCite can trace case history, retrieve secondary sources, categorize legal citations by legal issue, and perform other functions.

key number A number (accompanied by the symbol of a key) corresponding to a specific topic within West's key-number system to facilitate legal research of case law.

larceny The wrongful or fraudulent taking and carrying away of another person's personal property with the intent to deprive the person permanently of the property.

law A body of rules of conduct established and enforced by the controlling authority (the government) of a society.

law clerk A law student working as an apprentice with a law firm, during the summer or part-time during the school year, to gain practical experience. Some law firms refer to law clerks as *summer associates.*

lay witness A witness who can truthfully and accurately testify on a fact in question without having specialized training or knowledge; an ordinary witness.

leading question A question that suggests, or "leads to," a desired answer. Interviewers may use leading questions to elicit responses from witnesses who otherwise would not be forthcoming. Generally, in court leading questions may be asked only of hostile witnesses.

lease In real property law, a contract by which the owner of real property (the landlord) grants to a person (the tenant) an exclusive right to use and possess the property, usually for a specified period of time, in return for rent or some other form of payment.

legal administrator An administrative employee of a law firm who manages the day-to-day operations of the firm. In smaller law firms, legal administrators are usually called office managers.

legal assistant (or paralegal) A person qualified by education, training, or work experience who is employed or retained by a lawyer, law office, corporation, governmental agency or other entity who performs specifically delegated substantive legal work, for which a lawyer is responsible.

legal-assistant manager An employee in a law firm who is responsible for overseeing the paralegal staff and paralegal professional development.

legal custody Custody of a child that confers on the parent the right to make major decisions about the child's life without consulting the other parent.

legal nurse consultant (LNC) A nurse who consults with legal professionals and others about medical aspects of legal claims or issues. Legal nurse consultants normally must have at least a bachelor's degree in nursing and a significant amount of nursing experience.

legal technician (or independent paralegal) A paralegal who offers services directly to the public, normally for a fee, without attorney supervision. Independent paralegals assist consumers by supplying them with forms and procedural knowledge relating to simple or routine legal procedures.

legislative rule A rule created by an administrative agency that is as legally binding as a law enacted by a legislature.

libel Defamation in writing or some other form (such as videotape) having the quality of permanence.

licensing A government's official act of granting permission to an individual, such as an attorney, to do something that would be illegal in the absence of such permission.

limited liability company (LLC) A hybrid form of business organization authorized by a state in which the owners of the business have limited liability and taxes on profits are passed through the business entity to the owners.

limited liability partnership (LLP) A business organizational form designed for professionals who normally do business as partners in a partnership. The LLP is a pass-through entity for tax purposes, like the general partnership, but limits the personal liability of partners.

limited licensing A type of licensing in which a limited number of individuals within a specific profession or group (such as legal technicians within the paralegal profession) must meet licensing requirements imposed by the state before those individuals may legally practice their profession.

limited partner One who invests in a limited partnership but does not play an active role in managing the operation of the business. Unlike general partners, limited partners are only liable for partnership debts up to the amount that they have invested.

limited partnership A partnership consisting of one or more general partners and one or more limited partners.

liquidation In regard to corporations, the process by which corporate assets are converted into cash and distributed among creditors and shareholders according to specific rules of preference. In regard to bankruptcy, a proceeding under Chapter 7 of the Bankruptcy Code (often referred to as *ordinary,* or *straight,* bankruptcy), in which a debtor states his or her debts and turns all assets over to a trustee, who sells the nonexempt assets and distributes the proceeds to creditors. With certain exceptions, the remaining debts are then discharged and the debtor is relieved of the obligation to pay the debts.

listserv list A list of e-mail addresses of persons who have agreed to receive e-mail about a particular topic.

litigation The process of working a lawsuit through the court system.

litigation paralegal A paralegal who specializes in assisting attorneys in the litigation process.

long arm statute A state statute that permits a state to obtain jurisdiction over nonresident individuals and corporations. Individuals or corporations, however, must have certain "minimum contacts" with that state for the statute to apply.

magistrate A public civil officer or official with limited judicial authority, such as the authority to issue an arrest warrant.

mailbox rule A rule providing that an acceptance of an offer takes effect at the time it is communicated via the mode expressly or impliedly authorized by the offeror, rather than at the time it is actually received by the offeror. If acceptance is to be by mail, for example, it becomes effective the moment it is placed in the mailbox.

malpractice Professional misconduct or negligence—the failure to exercise due care—on the part of a professional, such as an attorney or a physician.

managing partner The partner in a law firm who makes decisions relating to the firm's policies and procedures and who generally oversees the business operations of the firm.

marital property All property acquired during the course of a marriage, apart from inheritances and gifts made to one or the other of the spouses.

material fact A fact that is important to the subject matter of the contract.

mediation A method of settling disputes outside of court by using the services of a neutral third party, who acts as a communicating agent between the parties; a method of dispute settlement that is less formal than arbitration.

mediation arbitration (Med-Arb) A form of ADR in which an arbitrator first attempts to help the parties reach an agreement, just as a mediator would. If no agreement is reached, then formal arbitration is undertaken, and the arbitrator issues a legally binding decision.

memorandum of law A document (known as a brief in some states) that delineates the legal theories, statutes, and cases on which a motion is based.

mens rea A wrongful mental state, or intent. A wrongful mental state is a requirement for criminal liability. What constitutes a wrongful mental state varies according to the nature of the crime.

merger A process in which one corporation (the surviving corporation) acquires all of the assets and liabilities of another corporation (the merged corporation).

metadata Embedded electronic data recorded by a computer in association with a particular file, including the file's location, path, creator, date created, date last accessed, hidden notes, earlier versions, passwords, and formatting. Metadata reveal information about how, when, and by whom a document was created, accessed, modified, and transmitted.

mini-trial A private proceeding that assists disputing parties in determining whether to take their case to court. During the proceeding, each party's attorney briefly argues the party's case before the other party and (usually) a neutral third party, who acts as an adviser. If the parties fail to reach an agreement, the adviser renders an opinion as to how a court would likely decide the issue.

Miranda **rights** Certain constitutional rights of accused persons taken into custody by law enforcement officials, such as the right to remain silent and the right to counsel, as established by the United States Supreme Court's decision in *Miranda v. Arizona.*

mirror image rule A common law rule that requires that the terms of the offeree's acceptance adhere exactly to the terms of the offeror's offer for a valid contract to be formed.

mirror site A Web site that duplicates another site. A mirror site is used to improve the availability of access to the original site.

misdemeanor A less serious crime than a felony, punishable by a fine or incarceration for up to one year in jail (not a state or federal penitentiary).

money laundering Falsely reporting income that has been obtained through criminal activity, such as illegal drug transactions, as income obtained through a legitimate business enterprise to make the "dirty" money "clean."

mortgage A written instrument giving a creditor an interest in the debtor's property as security for a debt.

motion A procedural request or application presented by an attorney to the court on behalf of a client.

motion for a change of venue A motion requesting that a trial be moved to a different location to ensure a fair and impartial proceeding, for the convenience of the parties, or for some other acceptable reason.

motion for a directed verdict (motion for judgment as a matter of law) A motion requesting that the court grant a judgment in favor of the party making the motion on the ground that the other party has not produced sufficient evidence to support his or her claim.

motion for a new trial A motion asserting that the trial was so fundamentally flawed (because of error, newly discovered evidence, prejudice, or other reason) that a new trial is needed to prevent a miscarriage of justice.

motion for judgment notwithstanding the verdict A motion (also referred to as a motion for judgment as a matter of law in federal courts) requesting that the court grant judgment in favor of the party making the motion on the ground that the jury verdict against him or her was unreasonable or erroneous.

motion for judgment on the pleadings A motion that may be filed by either party in which the party asks the court to enter a judgment in his or her favor based on information contained in the pleadings. A judgment on the pleadings will only be made if there are no facts in dispute and the only question is how the law applies to a set of undisputed facts.

motion for summary judgment A motion that may be filed by either party in which the party asks the court to enter a judgment in his or her favor without a trial. Unlike a motion for judgment on the pleadings, a motion for summary judgment can be supported by evidence outside the pleadings, such as witnesses' affidavits, answers to interrogatories, and other evidence obtained prior to or during discovery.

motion *in limine* A motion requesting that certain evidence not be brought out at the trial, such as prejudicial, irrelevant, or legally inadmissible evidence.

motion to dismiss A motion filed by the defendant in which the defendant asks the court to dismiss the case for a specified reason, such as improper service, lack of personal jurisdiction, or the plaintiff's failure to state a claim for which relief can be granted.

motion to recuse A motion to remove a particular judge from a case.

motion to sever A motion to try multiple defendants separately.

motion to suppress evidence A motion requesting that certain evidence be excluded from consideration during the trial.

mutual mistake Mistake as to the same material fact on the part of both parties to a contract. In this situation, either party can cancel the contract.

National Association of Legal Assistants (NALA) One of the two largest national paralegal associations in the United States; formed in 1975. NALA is actively involved in paralegal professional development.

National Federation of Paralegal Associations (NFPA) One of the two largest national paralegal associations in the United States; formed in 1974. NFPA is actively involved in paralegal professional development.

national law Law that pertains to a particular nation (as opposed to international law).

negligence The failure to exercise the standard of care that a reasonable person would exercise in similar circumstances.

negligence *per se* An action or failure to act in violation of a statutory requirement.

negotiable instrument A signed writing (record) that contains an unconditional promise or order to pay an exact sum of money on demand or at an exact future time to a specific person or order or to bearer.

negotiation In the context of dispute settlement, a process in which parties attempt to settle their dispute informally, with or without attorneys to represent them. In the context of negotiable instruments law, the transfer of an instrument, such as a check, in such a way that the transferee (the person to whom the instrument is transferred) receives, at the very least, the rights of the previous possessor of the instrument.

networking Making personal connections and cultivating relationships with people in a certain field, profession, or area of interest.

newsgroup (Usenet group) An online bulletin board service. A newsgroup is a forum, or discussion group, that usually focuses on a particular topic.

no-fault divorce A divorce in which neither party is deemed to be at fault for the breakdown of the marriage.

nolo contendere Latin for "I will not contest it." A criminal defendant's plea in which he or she chooses not to challenge, or contest, the charges brought by the government. Although the defendant will still be convicted and sentenced, the plea neither admits nor denies guilt.

offer A promise or commitment to do or refrain from doing some specified thing in the future.

offeree The party to whom the offer is made.

offeror The party making the offer.

office manager An administrative employee who manages the day-to-day operations of a business firm. In larger law firms, office managers are usually called legal administrators.

officer A person hired by corporate directors to assist in the management of the day-to-day operations of the corporation. Corporate officers include the corporate president, vice president, secretary, treasurer, and possibly others, such as a chief financial officer and chief executive officer. Corporate officers are employees of the corporation and subject to employment contracts.

online dispute resolution (ODR) The resolution of disputes with the assistance of an organization that offers dispute-resolution services via the Internet.

open-ended question A question phrased in such a way that it elicits a relatively unguided and lengthy narrative response.

opening statement An attorney's statement to the jury at the beginning of the trial. The attorney briefly outlines the evidence that will be offered during the trial and the legal theory that will be pursued.

opinion A statement by the court setting forth the applicable law and the reasons for its decision in a case.

opinion (advisory) letter A letter from an attorney to a client containing a legal opinion on an issue raised by the client's question or legal claim. The opinion is based on a detailed analysis of the law.

order for relief A court's grant of assistance to a complainant.

ordinance An order, rule, or law enacted by a municipal or county government to govern a local matter unaddressed by state or federal legislation.

original jurisdiction The power of a court to take a case, try it, and decide it.

overtime wages Wages paid to workers who are paid an hourly wage rate to compensate them for overtime work (hours worked beyond forty hours per week). Under federal law, overtime wages are at least one and a half times the regular hourly wage rate.

paralegal (or legal assistant) A person qualified by education, training, or work experience who is employed or retained by a lawyer, law office, corporation, governmental agency, or other entity to perform specifically delegated substantive legal work, for which a lawyer is responsible.

parallel citation A second (or third) citation for a given case. When a case is published in more than one reporter, each citation is a parallel citation to the other(s).

partner A person who has undertaken to operate a business jointly with one or more other persons. Each partner is a co-owner of the business firm.

partnership An association of two or more persons to carry on, as co-owners, a business for profit.

party With respect to lawsuits, the plaintiff or the defendant. Some cases involve multiple parties (more than one plaintiff or defendant).

passive listening The act of listening attentively to the speaker's message and responding to the speaker by providing verbal or nonverbal cues that encourage the speaker to continue; in effect, saying, "I'm listening, please go on."

patent A government grant that gives an inventor the exclusive right or privilege to make, use, or sell his or her invention for a limited time period.

paternity suit A lawsuit brought by an unmarried mother to establish that a certain person is the biological father of her child. DNA testing or a comparable procedure is often use to determine paternity.

peremptory challenge A *voir dire* challenge to exclude a potential juror from serving on the jury without any supporting reason or cause. Peremptory challenges based on racial or gender criteria are illegal.

performance In contract law, the fulfillment of one's duties arising under a contract with another; the normal way of discharging one's contractual obligations.

personal liability An individual's personal responsibility for debts or obligations. The owners of sole proprietorships and partnerships are personally liable for the debts and obligations incurred by their business firms. If their firms go bankrupt or cannot meet debts as they become due, the owners will be personally responsible for paying the debts.

personal property Any property that is not real property. Generally, any property that is movable or intangible is classified as personal property.

persuasive authority Any legal authority, or source of law, that a court may look to for guidance but on which it need not rely in making its decision. Persuasive authorities include cases from other jurisdictions and secondary sources of law, such as scholarly treatises.

persuasive precedent A precedent decided in another jurisdiction that a court may either follow or reject but that is entitled to careful consideration.

petition for divorce The document filed with the court to initiate divorce proceedings. The requirements governing the form and content of a divorce petition vary from state to state.

petition in bankruptcy An application to a bankruptcy court for relief in bankruptcy; a filing for bankruptcy. The official forms required for a petition in bankruptcy must be completed accurately, sworn to under oath, and signed by the debtor.

petty offense In criminal law, the least serious kind of wrong, such as a traffic or building-code violation.

plain meaning rule A rule of statutory interpretation. If the meaning of a statute is clear on its face, then that is the interpretation the court will give to it; inquiry into the legislative history of the statute will not be undertaken.

plaintiff A party who initiates a lawsuit.

plea bargaining The process by which the accused and the prosecutor in a criminal case work out a mutually satisfactory disposition of the case, subject to court approval. Usually, plea bargaining involves the defendant's pleading guilty to a lesser offense in return for a lighter sentence.

pleadings Statements by the plaintiff and the defendant that detail the facts, charges, and defenses involved in the litigation.

pocket part A separate pamphlet containing recent cases or changes in the law that is used to update hornbooks, legal encyclopedias, and other legal authorities. It is called a "pocket part" because it slips into a sleeve, or pocket, in the front or back binder of the volume.

policy In insurance law, a contract for insurance coverage. The policy spells out the precise terms and conditions as to what will and will not be covered under the contract.

potentially responsible party (PRP) A party who may be liable under the Comprehensive Environmental Response, Compensation, and Liability Act, or Superfund. Any person who generated hazardous waste, transported hazardous waste, owned or operated a waste site at the time of disposal, or currently owns or operates a site may be responsible for some or all of the clean-up costs involved in removing the hazardous chemicals.

prayer for relief A statement at the end of the complaint requesting that the court grant relief to the plaintiff.

precedent A court decision that furnishes an example or authority for deciding subsequent cases in which identical or similar facts are presented.

predatory behavior Business behavior that is undertaken with the intention of unlawfully driving competitors out of the market.

preemption A doctrine under which a federal law preempts, or takes precedence over, conflicting state and local laws.

preference In bankruptcy proceedings, the debtor's favoring of one creditor over others by making payments or transferring property to that creditor at the expense of the rights of other creditors. The bankruptcy trustee is allowed to recover payments made to one creditor in preference over another.

preliminary hearing An initial hearing in which a magistrate decides if there is probable cause to believe that the defendant committed the crime for which he or she is charged.

premium In insurance law, the price paid by the insured for insurance protection for a specified period of time.

prenuptial agreement A contract formed between two persons who are contemplating marriage to provide for the disposition of property in the event of a divorce or the death of one of the spouses after they have married.

pretrial conference A conference prior to trial in which the judge and the attorneys litigating the suit discuss settlement possibilities, clarify the issues in dispute, and schedule forthcoming trial-related events.

primary source In legal research, a document that establishes the law on a particular issue, such as a case decision, legislative act, administrative rule, or presidential order.

principal In agency law, a person who, by agreement or otherwise, authorizes another person (the agent) to act on the principal's behalf in such a way that the acts of the agent become binding on the principal.

privilege In tort law, the ability to act contrary to another person's right without that person's having legal redress for such acts. Privilege may be raised as a defense to defamation.

privileged information Confidential communications between certain individuals, such as an attorney and his or her client, that are protected from disclosure except under court order.

probable cause Reasonable grounds to believe the existence of facts warranting certain actions, such as the search or arrest of a person.

probate The process of "proving" the validity of a will and ensuring that the instructions in a valid will are carried out, including settling matters pertaining to the administration of a decedent's estate and guardianship of a decedent's minor children.

probate court A court that handles proceedings relating to wills and the settlement of deceased persons' estates; usually a county court.

procedural law Rules that define the manner in which the rights and duties of individuals may be enforced.

product liability The legal liability of manufacturers, sellers, and lessors of goods to consumers, users, and bystanders for injuries or damages that are caused by the goods.

professional corporation (P.C.) A firm that is owned by shareholders, who purchase the corporation's stock, or shares. The liability of shareholders is often limited to the amount of their investments.

promise An assurance that one will or will not do something in the future.

promissory estoppel A doctrine under which a promise is binding if the promise is clear and definite, the promisee justifiably relies on the promise, the reliance is reasonable and substantial, and justice will be better served by enforcement of the promise.

proof of claim A document filed with the bankruptcy court by a creditor to inform a court of a claim against a debtor's property. The proof of claim lists the creditor's name and address, as well as the amount that the creditor asserts is owed to the creditor by the debtor.

property settlement The division of property between spouses on the termination of a marriage.

prospectus A document that discloses relevant facts about a company and its operations so that those who wish to purchase stock (invest) in the corporation have the basis for making an informed decision.

proximate cause Legal cause; exists when the connection between an act and an injury is strong enough to justify imposing liability.

public defender A court-appointed attorney who is paid by the state to represent a criminal defendant who is unable to hire private counsel.

public law number An identification number assigned to a statute.

public policy A governmental policy based on widely held societal values.

public prosecutor An individual, acting as a trial lawyer, who initiates and conducts criminal cases in the government's name and on behalf of the people.

publicly held corporation A corporation whose shares are publicly traded in securities markets, such as the New York Stock Exchange.

punitive damages Money damages that may be awarded to a plaintiff to punish the defendant and deter future similar conduct.

reaffirmation agreement An agreement between a debtor and a creditor in which the debtor reaffirms, or promises to pay, a debt dischargeable in bankruptcy. To be enforceable, the agreement must be made prior to the discharge of the debt by the bankruptcy court.

real estate Land and things permanently attached to the land, such as houses, buildings, and trees and foliage.

real property Immovable property consisting of land and the buildings and plant life thereon.

reasonable person standard The standard of behavior expected of a hypothetical "reasonable person"; the standard against which negligence is measured and that must be observed to avoid liability for negligence.

record on appeal The items submitted during the trial (pleadings, motions, briefs, and exhibits) and the transcript of the trial proceedings that are forwarded to the appellate court for review when a case is appealed.

recross-examination The questioning of an opposing witness following the adverse party's redirect examination.

redirect examination The questioning of a witness following the adverse party's cross-examination.

reference line The portion of the letter that indicates the matter to be discussed in the letter, such as "RE: Summary of Cases Applying the Family and Medical Leave Act of 1993." The reference line is placed just below the address block and above the salutation.

reformation An equitable remedy granted by a court to correct, or "reform," a written contract so that it reflects the true intentions of the parties.

Registered Paralegal (RP) A paralegal whose competency has been certified by the National Federation of Paralegal Associations (NFPA) after the paralegal's successful completion of the Paralegal Advanced Competency Exam (PACE).

relevant evidence Evidence tending to prove or disprove the fact in question. Only relevant evidence is admissible in court.

remand To send a case back to a lower court for further proceedings.

remedy The means by which a right is enforced or the violation of a right is prevented or compensated for.

remedy at law A remedy available in a court of law. Money damages are awarded as a remedy at law.

remedy in equity A remedy allowed by courts in situations where remedies at law are not appropriate. Remedies in equity are based on settled rules of fairness, justice, and honesty.

reporter A book in which court cases are published, or reported.

reprimand A disciplinary sanction in which an attorney is rebuked for his or her misbehavior. Although a reprimand is the mildest sanction for attorney misconduct, it is nonetheless a serious one and may significantly damage the attorney's reputation in the legal community.

rescission A remedy whereby a contract is terminated and the parties are returned to the positions they occupied before the contract was made.

respondeat superior A doctrine in agency law under which a principal-employer may be held liable for the wrongful acts committed by agents or employees while acting within the scope of their agency or employment.

responsible corporate officer doctrine A common law doctrine under which the court may impose criminal liability on a corporate officer for actions of employees under her or his supervision regardless of whether she or he participated in, directed, or even knew about those actions.

restitution An equitable remedy under which a person is restored to his or her original position prior to loss or injury, or placed in the position that he or she would have been in had the breach not occurred.

restraining order A court order that requires one person (such as an abusing spouse) to stay away from another (such as an abused spouse).

retainer An advance payment made by a client to a law firm to cover part of the legal fees and/or costs that will need to be incurred on that client's behalf.

retainer agreement A signed document stating that the attorney or the law firm has been hired by the client to provide certain legal services and that the client agrees to pay for those services in accordance with the terms set forth in the retainer agreement.

return-of-service form A document signed by a process server and submitted to the court to prove that a defendant received a summons.

reverse To overturn the judgment of a lower court.

risk A prediction concerning potential loss based on known and unknown factors.

risk management Planning that is undertaken to reduce the risk of loss from known and unknown events. In the context of insurance, risk management involves transferring certain risks from the insured to the insurance company.

robbery The taking of money, personal property, or any other article of value from a person by means of force or fear.

rule of four A rule of the United States Supreme Court under which the Court will not issue a writ of *certiorari* unless at least four justices approve of the decision to issue the writ.

rulemaking The actions undertaken by administrative agencies when formally adopting new regulations or amending old ones.

rules of construction The rules that control the judicial interpretation of statutes.

rules of evidence Rules governing the admissibility of evidence in trial courts.

sales contract A contract for the sale of goods, as opposed to a contract for the sale of services, real property, or intangible property. Sales contracts are governed by Article 2 of the Uniform Commercial Code.

salutation The formal greeting to the addressee of the letter. The salutation is placed just below the reference line.

search warrant A written order, based on probable cause and issued by a judge or public official (magistrate), commanding that police officers or criminal investigators search a specific person, place, or property to obtain evidence.

secondary source In legal research, any publication that indexes, summarizes, or interprets the law, such as a legal encyclopedia, a treatise, or an article in a law review.

secured creditor A lender, seller, or any other person in whose favor there is a security interest.

self-defense The legally recognized privilege to protect oneself or one's property against injury by another. The privilege of self-defense only protects acts that are reasonably necessary to protect oneself or one's property.

self-incrimination The act of giving testimony that implicates oneself in criminal wrongdoing. The Fifth Amendment to the Constitution states that no person "shall be compelled in any criminal case to be a witness against himself."

self-regulation The regulation of the conduct of a professional group by members of the group. Self-regulation usually involves the establishment of ethical or professional standards of behavior with which members of the group must comply.

sentence The punishment, or penalty, ordered by the court to be inflicted on a person convicted of a crime.

separate property Property that a spouse owned before the marriage, plus inheritances and gifts acquired by the spouse during the marriage.

service of process The delivery of the summons and the complaint to a defendant.

settlement agreement An out-of-court resolution to a legal dispute, which is agreed to by the parties in writing. A settlement agreement may be reached at any time prior to or during a trial.

sexual harassment In the employment context, (1) the hiring or granting of job promotions or other benefits in return for sexual favors (*quid pro quo* harassment) or (2) language or conduct that is so sexually offensive that it creates a hostile working environment (hostile-environment harassment).

share A unit of stock; a measure of ownership interest in a corporation.

shareholder One who purchases corporate stock, or shares, and who thus becomes an owner of the corporation.

shrink-wrap agreement An agreement whose terms are expressed in a document located inside the box in which the goods (usually software) are packaged.

signature As defined by the UCC, any symbol executed or adopted by a party with a present intention to authenticate a writing.

slander Defamation in oral form.

slip opinion A judicial opinion published shortly after the decision is made and not yet included in a case reporter or advance sheets.

sole proprietorship The simplest form of business organization, in which the owner is the business. Anyone who does business without creating a formal business entity has a sole proprietorship.

specific performance An equitable remedy requiring exactly the performance that was specified in a contract; usually granted only when money damages would be an inadequate remedy and the subject matter of the contract is unique (for example, real property).

staff attorney An attorney hired by a law firm as an employee. A staff attorney has no ownership rights in the firm and will not be invited to become a partner in the firm.

standing to sue A sufficient stake in a controversy to justify bringing a lawsuit. To have standing to sue, the plaintiff must demonstrate that he or she has been either injured or threatened with injury.

stare decisis The doctrine of precedent, under which a court is obligated to follow the earlier decisions of that court or a higher court within the jurisdiction if the same points arise again in litigation. This is a defining characteristic of the common law system.

state bar association An association of attorneys within a state. In most states, an attorney must be a member of the state bar association to practice law in the state.

statute A written law enacted by a legislature under its constitutional lawmaking authority.

Statute of Frauds A state statute that requires certain types of contracts to be in writing to be enforceable.

statute of limitations A statute setting the maximum time period within which certain actions can be brought or rights enforced. After the period of time has run, no legal action can be brought.

statutory law The body of written laws enacted by the legislature.

stop-payment order An order by a bank customer to his or her bank not to pay or certify a certain check.

strict liability Liability regardless of fault. In tort law, strict liability may be imposed on a merchant who introduces into commerce a good that is so defective as to be unreasonably dangerous.

submission agreement A written agreement to submit a legal dispute to an arbitrator or arbitrating panel for resolution.

subpoena A document commanding a person to appear at a certain time and place to give testimony concerning a certain matter.

substantive law Law that defines the rights and duties of individuals with respect to each other, as opposed to procedural law, which defines the manner in which these rights and duties may be enforced.

summary jury trial (SJT) A method of settling disputes (used in some federal courts) in which a trial is held but the jury's verdict is not binding. The verdict only acts as a guide to both sides in reaching an agreement during the mandatory negotiations that immediately follow the trial. If a settlement is not reached, both sides have the right to a full trial later.

summons A document served on a defendant in a lawsuit informing the defendant that a legal action has been commenced against him or her and that the defendant must appear in court or respond to the plaintiff's complaint within a specified period of time.

support personnel Employees who provide clerical, secretarial, or other support to the legal, paralegal, and administrative staff of a law firm.

supporting affidavit An affidavit accompanying a motion that is filed by an attorney on behalf of his or her client. The sworn statements in the affidavit provide a factual basis for the motion.

supremacy clause The provision in Article VI of the U.S. Constitution that declares the Constitution, laws, and treaties of the United States to be "the supreme Law of the Land."

suspension A serious disciplinary sanction in which an attorney who has violated an ethical rule or a law is prohibited from practicing law in the state for a specified or an indefinite period of time.

syllabus A brief summary of the holding and legal principles involved in a reported case, which is followed by the court's official opinion.

tenancy in common A form of co-ownership of property in which each party owns an undivided interest that passes to his or her heirs at death.

testamentary trust A trust that is created by will and that does not take effect until the death of the testator.

testate The condition of having died with a valid will.

testator One who makes a valid will.

third party A person or entity not directly involved in an agreement (such as a contract), legal proceeding (such as a lawsuit), or relationship (such as an attorney-client relationship).

time slip A record documenting, for billing purposes, the hours (or fractions of hours) that an attorney or a paralegal worked for each client, the date on which the work was done, and the type of work that was undertaken.

tort A civil wrong not arising from a breach of contract; a breach of a legal duty that proximately causes harm or injury to another.

tortfeasor One who commits a tort.

toxic tort A wrongful act (tort) that occurs when a person or business fails to properly use or clean up toxic chemicals that cause harm to a person or to society; also used to refer to an action brought against a toxic polluter.

trade journal A newsletter, magazine, or other periodical that provides a certain trade or profession with information (products, trends, or developments) relating to that trade or profession.

trade name A term that is used to indicate part or all of a business's name and that is directly related to the business's reputation and goodwill. Trade names are protected under the common law (and under trademark law, if the business's name is the same as its trademark).

trade secret Information or processes that give a business an advantage over competitors who do not know the information or processes.

trademark A distinctive mark, motto, device, or emblem that a manufacturer stamps, prints, or otherwise affixes to the goods it produces so that they can be identified on the market and their origins made known. Once a trademark is established (under the common law or through registration), the owner is entitled to its exclusive use.

treatise In legal research, a work that provides a systematic, detailed, and scholarly review of a particular legal subject.

treaty An agreement, or compact, formed between two independent nations.

trespass to land The entry onto, above, or below the surface of land owned by another without the owner's permission or legal authorization.

trespass to personal property The unlawful taking or harming of another's personal property; interference with another's right to the exclusive possession of his or her personal property.

trial court A court in which cases begin and in which questions of fact are examined.

trial notebook A binder that contains copies of all of the documents and information that an attorney will need to have at hand during the trial.

trust An arrangement in which title to property is held by one person (a trustee) for the benefit of another (a beneficiary).

trust account A bank or escrow account in which one party (the trustee, such as an attorney) holds funds belonging to another person (such as a client); a bank account into which funds advanced to a law firm by a client are deposited.

unathorized practice of law (UPL) The act of engaging in actions defined by a legal authority, such as a state legislature, as constituting the "practice of law" without legal authorization to do so.

unconscionable contract or unconscionable clause A contract or clause that is so oppressive to one of the parties that the court will refuse to enforce the contract.

underwriter In insurance law, the insurer, or the one assuming a risk in return for the payment of a premium.

Uniform Commercial Code (UCC) A uniform code of laws governing commercial transactions that has been adopted in part or in its entirety by all of the states. Article 2 of the UCC governs contracts for the sale of goods.

unilateral mistake Mistake as to a material fact on the part of only one party to a contract. In this situation, the contract is normally enforceable against the mistaken party, with some exceptions.

unreasonably dangerous product In product liability, a product that is defective to the point of threatening a consumer's health and safety. A product will be considered unreasonably dangerous if it is dangerous beyond the expectation of the ordinary consumer or if a less dangerous alternative was economically feasible for the manufacturer, but the manufacturer failed to produce it.

venue The geographical district in which an action is tried and from which the jury is selected.

verdict A formal decision made by a jury.

vicarious liability Legal responsibility placed on one person for the acts of another.

visitation rights The right of a noncustodial parent to have contact with his or her child. Grandparents and stepparents may also be given visitation rights.

voir dire A proceeding in which attorneys for the plaintiff and the defendant ask prospective jurors questions to determine whether any potential juror is biased or has any connection with a party to the action or with a prospective witness.

warranty An express or implied promise by a seller that specific goods to be sold meet certain criteria, or standards of performance, on which the buyer may rely.

white-collar crime A crime that typically occurs only in a business context; popularly used to refer to an illegal act or series of acts committed by an individual or business entity using nonviolent means.

will A document directing how and to whom the maker's property and obligations are to be transferred on his or her death.

winding up The process of winding up all business affairs (collecting and distributing the firm's assets) after a partnership or corporation has been dissolved.

witness A person who is asked to testify under oath at a trial.

witness statement The written record of the statements made by a witness during an interview, signed by the witness.

work product An attorney's mental impressions, conclusions, and legal theories regarding a case being prepared on behalf of a client. Work product normally is regarded as privileged information.

workers' compensation statutes State laws establishing an administrative procedure for compensating workers for injuries that arise in the course of their employment, regardless of fault.

World Wide Web A hypertext-based system through which specially formatted documents are accessible on the Internet.

writ of *certiorari* A writ from a higher court asking the lower court to send it the record of a case for review. The United States Supreme Court uses *certiorari* to review most of the cases it decides to hear.

writ of execution A writ that puts in force a court's decree or judgment.

wrongful discharge An employer's termination of an employee's employment in violation of the law.

INDEX